JAMES
FENIMORE
COOPER

JAMES FENIMORE COOPER

The Early Years

WAYNE FRANKLIN

YALE UNIVERSITY PRESS/NEW HAVEN & LONDON

Published with assistance from the Louis Stern Memorial Fund.
Copyright © 2007 by Wayne Franklin.

Designed by Mary Valencia.
Set in Fournier MT type by Integrated Publishing Solutions.
Printed in the United States of America.

Library of Congress Cataloging-in-Publication Data
Franklin, Wayne.
James Fenimore Cooper : the early years / Wayne Franklin.
p. cm.
"Published with assistance from the Louis Stern Memorial Fund."
Includes bibliographical references and index.
ISBN 978-0-300-10805-7 (alk. paper)
1. Cooper, James Fenimore, 1789–1851. 2. Cooper, James
Fenimore, 1789–1851—Childhood and youth. 3. Novelists,
American—19th century—Biography. I. Title.
PS1431.F73 2007
813'.2—dc22 2006031247

A catalogue record for this book is available from the British Library.

The paper in this book meets the guidelines for permanence and
durability of the Committee on Production Guidelines for
Book Longevity of the Council on Library Resources.

10 9 8 7 6 5 4 3 2 1

Contents

Illustrations follow page 314

Acknowledgments

Accounting for the debts incurred during a long-lived writing project is a pleasurable obligation. I recall mine in chronological order. For the late Frank Nash, whose skilled mentoring of pupils at the Albany Academy bolstered my boyhood reading interests, I offer tardy public thanks. I never go back to *Moby-Dick* without thinking of how well Nash introduced us to it in the fifth form. To Thomas L. Philbrick, who assigned *The Pioneers* in a class on the American novel that I happened to take while he visited at Union College in the fall of my senior year, I am particularly happy to give this new token of my appreciation and gratitude. He taught that class so well that he had to put up with me again in a Melville seminar during the spring semester—and then for another five years, since I followed him as a graduate student back to his permanent home at the University of Pittsburgh. His support and interest hardly stopped with my graduation from Pitt in 1972. On reading an essay on Cooper that I published in 1992, he suggested that I might think about undertaking this project; for better or ill, I listened to him. Since then, he has read various drafts of different chapters and shared not only his lucid and charitable comments but also the fruits of his and his wife Marianne's own unstinted labors as editors of Cooper books.

For their son Nathaniel, who provided me encouragement and some behind-the-scenes support as this book made its way to print, I am both thankful and, recalling his parents' generosities, envious.

No one working on James Fenimore Cooper can stand fully outside the shadows cast by the late scholar James Franklin Beard. His magisterial edition of Cooper's *Letters and Journals* was only the most obvious of his many accomplishments. Without his skilled negotiations with the Cooper family from the 1940s on, the archival riches still in its hands might not have made their way to the public institutions where they now reside. Beard's plan for a biography of Cooper based on those sources ran afoul of his heroic efforts as he led a team of editors (including the Philbricks) committed to bringing out fresh versions of nearly half of Cooper's books. My debt to Beard is substantial, not only for those two publishing ventures but also for materials he gathered for his own project, and for the example of his career. I hasten to add, however, that this volume incorporates nothing drafted by him for his own biography. For all I assert, I am to blame.

To the Cooper family, especially to Henry S. F. Cooper of New York City and Cooperstown, I am similarly grateful. Henry has shared not only stories but also materials. Furthermore, his detached but supportive attitude toward my venture has been ideal. While I always thought of him and his kin as among my intended readers, I have never felt the least pressure to write for them in the first instance. Similarly, although I have benefited enormously from the astute and pathbreaking work of Alan Taylor, whose book on Cooper's father makes regular appearances in my text and notes, I of course try to tell the son's story here. At times, as I was surprised to discover, it diverged in remarkable ways from that of the father as Alan powerfully re-created it.

Friends and colleagues who have critiqued parts or all of what I have written will see, I hope, that they have improved it in measurable ways. Aside from the Philbricks, the most important of these are Dan Peck and Jeff Walker, along with Lance Schachterle, Allan Axelrad, Hugh MacDougall, and Bob Madison. Such intellectual friends as Larry Buell, Richard Forman, John Hanson Mitchell, Kent Ryden, and Frances Clark ("the Wits") deserve goodly mention, along with Steve Bullock, John Seelye, Gary Williams, Rich Morgan, and Ives Goddard. And I cannot overlook the personal support and interest of the late Sherman Paul, or of Bob Sayre, Carl Klaus, Guy Rotella, Harvey Green, and Frank Blessington. Recently, I have been warmly pleased by the place my new colleagues at the University of Connecticut have made for me in their midst. In particular, I would mention Bob Tilton and Bob Gross. My editor at Yale, John Kulka, believed in this project and enacted that belief in various ways at various junctures. I am especially grateful to my copy editor for the press, Jessie Dolch, who has helped improve the book in innumerable ways.

Financial backing is critical for projects such as mine. In 1994–1995, I held a National Endowment for the Humanities fellowship at the American Antiquarian Society. It allowed me to finish a thorough study of the Cooper materials there. From 1994 to 2005, I relied on the very generous support of the Stanton W. and Elisabeth K. Davis Foundation, which provided time to conduct my research and funds to defray costs of travel and materials. The financial support of the English department at the University of Connecticut, made possible by its head, Bob Tilton, and Dean Ross MacKinnon of the College of Liberal Arts and Sciences, has helped see the project to completion. Twice, in 1993 and again in 1997, Dan Peck included me in NEH summer seminars that allowed me to try out some of the ideas in this book. For a pleasant pair of weeks in the fall of 1997, through the good efforts of Jeff Walker, I was able to air other ideas as the Fae Rawdon Norris lecturer at Oklahoma State University. In 2004–2005, I held a generous fellowship for the Simon R. Guggenheim Foundation that allowed me to finish this volume and continue my work on Cooper past its end.

Institutions sometimes imagine future scholarly projects with such foresight that a lucky writer arrives to find materials handily arranged. I have discovered that to be the case especially at the American Antiquarian Society, where Joanne Chaison, Marie Lamoureux, Tom Knoles, Dennis Laurie, Susan Anderson, Ellen Dunlap, Nancy Burkett, John Hench, Caroline Sloat, and Marcus McCorison (along with the library's pages and the steady stream of scholars who labor there) have in their various ways made my work in Antiquarian Hall so rewarding. At the New York State Historical Association in Cooperstown, similar help has come from Wayne Wright, Adele Johnson, and Susan Dear. Staff at Yale's Beinecke Library and the New York State Library in Albany have been equally helpful and efficient during my briefer visits to those institutions. Bryan Thompson of the Town of DeKalb Historical Association graciously shared documents with me as well as his own writings on the history of that northern New York town, where the Cooper family was heavily involved after 1803.

I save my last words for my wife, Suzanne, who little imagined when we met in 1998 that the little "project" I was then working on would involve so much time, paper, or energy. I wish I could say that this is it!

Introduction

Author of the famous five-part Leather-Stocking series as well as twenty-seven other novels and a box full of historical and miscellaneous works, James Fenimore Cooper (1789–1851) remains one of the most original yet most misunderstood figures in the history of American culture. Almost single-handedly in the 1820s, Cooper invented the key forms of American fiction—the Western, the sea tale, the Revolutionary romance—forms that set a suggestive agenda for subsequent writers, even for Hollywood and television. Furthermore, in producing and shrewdly marketing fully 10 percent of all American novels in the 1820s, most of them best sellers, Cooper made it possible for other aspiring authors to earn a living by their writings. That was a rare prospect at a time when "American literature" still seemed like a contradiction in terms and when, even in England, many writers received little income from their work. Owing to this combination of literary innovation and business acumen, Cooper can be said to have invented not just an assortment of literary types but the very career of the American writer. So deep and enduring has been his effect that it is impossible to map the country's cultural landscape without him. As much as the political "Founding Fathers," Cooper left a documentary imprint on the national mind.

Yet, despite his importance, he continues to be profoundly misunderstood and therefore stands in need of a major reevaluation. His fate has been complicated by his own complicity in it. Although it was becoming common for writers in the early nineteenth century to indulge public curiosity about their lives, the usually chatty Cooper turned reticent when asked for biographical details. And only rarely did he write in a directly autobiographical mode. Furthermore, whereas such contemporaries as Sir Walter Scott and Washington Irving made prior arrangements for authorized biographies and for the publication of their journals or letters, Cooper refused to follow suit. When nearing death in 1851, he insisted instead that his wife and children protect his life and his papers from outsiders.

That injunction reflected Cooper's general reserve on personal questions, but it also had a quite specific source. While abroad during the later 1820s and early 1830s, he had spoken out against reactionary forces in various European countries, especially France. Soon he was being criticized by newspaper editors back home who had allied themselves with the Whigs, a new political party sympathetic to the French rightists. Cooper, who saw himself as a staunch defender of American political principles abroad, hardly expected this betrayal (as he regarded it) of American ideals. Nor was he prepared for the personal turn the disagreement took when some Whig editors began using "reviews" of his new books to ridicule his private character as well as his political beliefs. After Cooper's return to the United States in 1833, the acrimony of the attacks sank in. He tried to answer them but at last determined that his best recourse was to sue the editors for libel. Impressively arguing most of the suits himself, he defeated paper after paper, simultaneously bolstering his own position and publicly silencing and chastising his opponents.

His victories could not undo the damage. As late as 1850, the *Literary World*, a New York weekly edited by Democrat Evert Duyckinck, lamented that for the rising generation of readers their "great American countryman" had been shadowed, perhaps fatally, by the "abuse" of the Whigs. The word *abuse* was not too strong. When *The Deerslayer* had first come out in 1841, to cite a mild instance, newspaperman Park Benjamin taunted its author by editorializing that, although he had been "desperately trying to read" the book, he so far had had little luck: "After many severe struggles against drowsiness and the endurance of a tedium, that was really distressing, we have *tugged* through the first volume. We are now meditating an attack on the second, with but very faint hope of success. Should we survive the task, out readers shall be informed in due season. Meantime we implore their sympathy." Anyone who had read the book, which was enormously popular, knew that Benjamin was playing politics with its author. But it was in the nature of such personal attacks that they remained in circulation, tainting Cooper's reputation for many years to come.

By 1851, Cooper seems to have felt that the publication of an official biography or his personal papers would give new life to the old lies, subjecting his memory—and thereby his wife and children—to new injuries. The family, proud of his accomplishments, clearly had mixed feelings about his prohibition. Mrs. Cooper believed that her husband's "earnest charge," as she described it, should be rigidly obeyed. Her own death within months of her husband's, however, left enforcement to her five children, who soon proved to have conflicting views on the subject. The oldest of them, nature writer Susan Fenimore Cooper (1813–1894), favored openness; her only brother, Paul Fenimore Cooper (1824–1895), a lawyer then practicing in Albany, New York, wished to keep things private. As early as 1854, Susan (supported by her three sisters) decided to let a would-be biographer use the novelist's papers for what promised to be an extensive treatment of his career. When Paul caught word of the impending deal, however, he interposed and quashed it.

Over the decades following, family members showed similar conflicts both individually and as a group. Susan is a case in point. She wrote largely biographical introductions to many of her father's books; she also sketched her memories of his first years as a writer; and she published several items he had left in manuscript form, including parts of his journals and an unusual autobiographical narrative ("The Eclipse") he had written in the early 1830s. All of these items, though of limited scope, retain real value for understanding the novelist's life. On the other hand, Susan's management of the archive was at times counterproductive. There is probably little truth to rumors that she either burned "a great deal" of her father's surviving manuscripts or insisted that his most revealing journals be buried with her. Even so, she did a fair amount of damage to the collection. She freely clipped the novelist's autographs from surviving documents and passed them out, donated several hundred pages from his literary manuscripts for charity auctions, and cut others into strips that she gave away for free to friends or importunate collectors. Dispersed as they were beyond easy recovery, these items might just as well have been burned or buried.

A second James Fenimore Cooper (1858–1938), Paul F. Cooper's son and like him an Albany lawyer, inherited control of the archive from his aunt. At a time when the proper treatment of documents was a subject of considerable attention in the historical community, he guarded the hoard much more carefully. Yet, wishing (like Susan) to promote a fuller understanding of the novelist's life and times, he also opened it up in a variety of ways. He wrote his own series of historical and family sketches, some of which incorporated items the novelist had written. Between 1910 and 1930, he also assisted a series of three biographers, fact-checking their narratives and allowing them controlled access to the family papers. Most importantly, in 1922 a two-volume selection he had culled from his grandfather's correspondence was brought out by Yale University Press. Although many of the included items were, naturally enough, from hands other than Cooper's, and the editor misread some passages and silently omitted others, at last there was a cache of published documents of extensive use to biographers.

Even so, in 1930 the rest of the original archive still remained out of public sight. It held not only the remainder of the novelist's papers (including substantially complete manuscripts of several of his books), but also the personal and business records of his father, his two oldest brothers, and various other relatives. The last steward, Harvard-trained physicist Paul Fenimore Cooper (1930–1988), grandson of the second J. F. Cooper, carefully placed these items in archival folders and boxes; he also created a computer inventory of a large portion of them and had that part microfilmed in the 1950s. Like his predecessors, this family archivist undertook his own projects, especially ones related to Judge William Cooper, the father of the novelist. In addition to reissuing the elder Cooper's only book, *A Guide in the Wilderness* (1810), before his untimely death Paul Cooper studied and planned to write a book about that ancestor's activities as a politician and land developer.

He also made elaborate preparations for the future of the archive. In accordance with the terms of his will, in the early 1990s the materials were divided and sent off to two predesignated institutional homes. The William Cooper papers (already being used by historian Alan Taylor for *William Cooper's Town*, his 1995 Pulitzer prize–winning study) went to the Hartwick College library, near Cooperstown. Those of the novelist that had not been given to Yale after the publication of the *Correspondence* in the early 1920s were deposited in the American Antiquarian Society, in Massachusetts, which over the past several decades had been amassing the best collection of the nearly one thousand early printings of Cooper's books. Even now, in 2007, a few items still remain in family hands, but it is clear that the transfers arranged for by Paul Cooper finally lifted one part of the novelist's prohibition.

The other part had been lifted, in a sense, some fifty years earlier when James F. Beard, an American literature scholar, was named the novelist's literary executor and therefore gained full access to the archive. Beard, intent on writing a definitive critical biography of Cooper, soon began exhaustive preparatory labors. The family papers, along with the materials at Yale, formed a necessary but hardly sufficient source for the kind of study he envisioned. Faced with the broad dispersal of Cooper's letters in private and public collections across the globe, Beard began locating, transcribing, and meticulously annotating some twelve hundred surviving documents ranging in length from a few lines to more than twenty pages. These, along with all extant journals, were published in six volumes by Harvard University Press across the 1960s.

Having completed this project, which remains a monument of modern literary scholarship, Beard might have returned full time to the biography. Instead, he undertook a second, even more demanding editorial task. As is often the case with popular writers from a period when literary publishing was still in its beginning stages, most of Cooper's widely reprinted works survive in competing and error-strewn versions. While many of the individual problems do not crucially affect a given book's meanings, some do; and the overall numbers are such that their cumulative effect is significant. As Beard kept working on the biography, he identified sufficient materials—including original manuscripts or copies, proofs, authorized printings, authorial revisions in various forms, and correspondence between Cooper and his printers and publishers—to suggest that freshly edited versions of many of Cooper's works were possible. In the 1970s, he therefore organized a large collective of scholars to work on the "Cooper Edition," which began issuing its volumes in 1980. Since then, it has brought out carefully emended versions of twenty Cooper works.

In the case of an author of such crucial importance to the rise of American literature as Cooper, reliable texts are imperative. The Cooper Edition has been of great importance for the understanding of how Cooper wrote and how he managed his career. Yet for Beard this new project exacted an awful cost. As he became absorbed in editorial work, his biography was gradually abandoned—a tragic instance of thoroughness producing incompletion. At his death in 1989, a few drafted chapters were discovered among his papers, but nothing like the rich treatment of Cooper's life and times that his colleagues, and Beard himself, had expected. Moreover, because Beard's role as Cooper's literary executor had given him exclusive access to the family papers, his contemporaries (many of them recruited to help with the edition) were not well positioned to step into the breach. As a result, Cooper remains, more than two hundred years after his birth, the last major figure in early American culture lacking a full biography.

It would be wrong to leave the impression that the long closure of the Cooper archive prevented the novelist's life from substantial treatment prior to the present. Yet the various biographical surveys that have come out from time to time have all been partial in one of two senses: either limited in coverage by the available materials, or limited in sympathy because of the continuing influence of Cooper's bad press. These two limits have tended to operate together to his disadvantage; since they continue to affect Cooper's public image, more needs to be said of them here.

Cooper's own prohibition kept most writers before Beard ignorant of major issues—or at least unfamiliar with major bodies of evidence. Although he intended just the opposite, in the absence of an early, relatively full account of his life, half-truths arising from the old controversies ironically fixed a negative image of Cooper in the public mind. Not surprisingly, given his legal successes against the newspaper editors, he was often portrayed as a possessive, litigious, irascible figure ready to sue any opponent nervy enough to trespass on his literary or other premises. That image was wildly inaccurate. During his lifetime, Cooper was recognized by his large circle of friends as an eminently sociable man, fond of good company and lively conversation. Bright, positive in outlook, with great energy and a wide curiosity about human experience, he always welcomed a frank exchange of views. Nor was he instinctively exclusive or condescending in his relations with others; not only did he rarely stand on ceremony, he had little tolerance for it.

Moreover, far from relishing the law, Cooper had grown up distrusting and avoiding it. His fiercely partisan father, who served two terms as a Federalist congressman, apparently had wanted him trained as a lawyer. But Cooper, who became a follower of New York Republican DeWitt Clinton after 1815 and then of democratic President Andrew Jackson in the 1820s, had no more taste for the law than for Judge Cooper's top-down politics. Even at the age of thirty, when faced with dire threats to his own financial welfare and to his family's sorely depleted estate, Cooper purposely shunned the courts until experience at last impressed on him that the law indeed had its uses. Later still, when he became embroiled in the newspaper fight, he had recourse to the courts precisely because by then he understood the cost of passivity.

With a few exceptions, these aspects of Cooper's character were lost to view after his death. The only significant biography produced in the nineteenth century did little to dispel the half-truths and caricatures. Indeed, it gave them new life. Written by Thomas R. Lounsbury, a famous Chaucer scholar at Yale, and published in the "American Men of Letters" series in 1882, it was hampered by the family's continued refusal to open up the novelist's papers. Furthermore, although Lounsbury diligently searched for available information in public sources, what he found was often colored by the suspicions adrift in the press. As a result, he uncovered little to answer the worst clichés. And, while he acknowledged "the essential sweetness of Cooper's nature" (a quite astute characterization), Lounsbury showed no real sympathy for Cooper or his works; he had undertaken the assignment only because the general editor of the series, Charles Dudley Warner, kept urging it on him. Predictably, Lounsbury's *James Fenimore Cooper*, which was to remain the basic biography of Cooper for another seventy years, promulgated a distorted view of the novelist as aloof, cold, and unsociable. It also failed to explore Cooper's revolutionary role in the establishment of American literature. That it was elegantly written made it more damaging.

Other major treatments of Cooper since Lounsbury have been fuller and more fair. But even the best of them have been affected by the relative inaccessibility of Cooper's papers. Robert E. Spiller, whose quasi-biographical view of Cooper as a social critic has been especially influential since the publication of *Fenimore Cooper: Critic of His Times* in 1931, apparently was not given free rein with the papers still in the hands of the Coopers after the gift to Yale. By contrast, Henry W. Boynton and Marcel Clavel, whose purposes were more fully biographical, were granted broad access to the Cooperstown archive but produced books that proved less useful and less influential than Spiller's. Boynton's *James Fenimore Cooper* tended to avoid the knotty problems of Cooper's very public career, which Spiller stressed, preferring instead to emphasize the hearty sailor and gentleman farmer who somewhat surprisingly turned writer in 1820— an image that, although it did serve to counteract the worst of the newspaper distortions, fades in the full light of the whole archive. Had more of Cooper's own letters been in the family's hands, Boynton might have gained greater insight into the novelist's interior life, his engagement with political and cultural issues, and his involvement in an array of public causes. Clavel's work, drawing on a fuller range of other sources, was more meticulous than Boynton's, especially in its tracing out of Cooper's reputation in the early years; but Clavel's inability to complete the project beyond the year 1826 (when Cooper, having published his sixth novel, relocated for several years to Paris) left *Fenimore Cooper: Sa Vie et Son Oeuvre: La Jeunesse* (1938) truncated at the point when Clavel's expertise in the history and culture of his native France might have made the effort indispensable. By necessity, the book's incompletion also kept Cooper's political coming-of-age and the subsequent fights with the press completely out of the picture. A final major treatment of Cooper, lawyer James Grossman's *James Fenimore Cooper* (1949), in the second American Men of Letters series, is the most balanced and readable (and, surprisingly, the most recent) of the modern biographies. Yet, although it was written with great judgment and enthusiasm, it was based on little new research. Since this was precisely the moment when the Cooper family, having forged its understanding with James F. Beard, was counting on him to at last tell the full story, Grossman enjoyed very little access to the novelist's papers.

The biographical difficulties in which Cooper has languished for so long were only part of his problem from a modern perspective. Almost from the start of his career, Cooper was admired, imitated, recited, memorized—not only in the United States but throughout Europe. In his day, he was reportedly the foreign author most widely translated into German, for instance, and what has been called "Coopermania" hit France especially hard as early as the 1820s. Yet from the outset he also was subjected to various criticisms that, when combined with the later politically motivated assaults, have hampered his true appreciation. In their introduction to *Fenimore Cooper: The Critical Heritage*, George Dekker and John P. McWilliams have summarized the reception of his first half-dozen books in contemporary journals. They note that, in addition to praising Cooper's narrative and descriptive powers and his handling of such "low" figures as Natty Bumppo, critics at times faulted him for his unconvincing treatment of genteel characters, his occasional bad grammar, his leisurely pacing, and his general inability to eclipse his greatest contemporary and model, Sir Walter Scott. As early as 1822, in a review of Cooper's first successful book, *The Spy*, Boston critic W. H. Gardiner sounded most of these themes. From that moment on, Gardiner's points were to have a long life, partly because they touched on real issues in Cooper's first books and partly because they gave other reviewers easy formulas for dealing with his unceasing flood of new publications. In the 1830s, even though reviewers in the monthly and quarterly journals were generally aloof from the political fray acting out in the newspapers of Park Benjamin and other Whigs, the same critical points continued to be scored against Cooper. Together, the two negatives acted as a drag on his reputation.

The critical strictures were not, as I suggested a moment ago, without their basis in fact. Yet the supposed problems in Cooper's first books need to be understood in their proper context. Beard and his colleagues in the Cooper Edition were convinced, for instance, that many of the apparent slips in Cooper's style resulted not from his own lax practices but rather from sloppy editing and typesetting. In 1977, Beard went so far as to assert that "Cooper was, for his time, an extremely careful craftsman," and one purpose of the Cooper Edition has been to demonstrate that point by using all surviving materials for any given book to judiciously correct its text. On the weaknesses in Cooper's handling of character and plot, or how he fared in a head-to-head competition with Scott, similar extenuations might be offered. It is only fair to point out that at least some of Cooper's failings were owing to the very newness of what he was attempting. As an American venturing into a field where few of his fellow citizens had had any success at all—indeed, hardly had a presence—he was undertaking something quite different from what Walter Scott had accomplished. It also was hardly clear at the time how American materials (the frontier or the Revolution, for instance) might form a basis for literary art. Cooper's priority meant that he had virtually no American books to read while growing up, a fate from which his own success spared his successors: for, after Cooper had venturesomely shown the way, other writers could more easily (and more artistically) follow his example. Robert E. Spiller summed up this point in 1931 by noting that Cooper "always suffered from the crudities of the experimenter." Cooper's first reviewers, given their own limited position and the very nature of their function, hardly were able to gauge his broader significance. They judged his accomplishments book-by-book but could not give due consideration to the way he was opening up the whole field for those who came after him.

Other factors stuck more deeply. Cooper had a remarkably fecund imagination but, especially in his early years, was dogged by a lack of self-confidence that was personal as much as cultural in origin. Although books, especially British books, had been freely available in his boyhood home, and he had read them avidly, he hardly had dreamed of literary fame or been driven to write before the quite sudden start of his career in 1820. Once he did begin writing, he naturally enough suffered relapses into his customary silence. Following a serious breakdown in his health in 1823, what is more, he was physically as well as psychologically shaky. These factors conspired to keep him from devoting as much time or energy as he should have to the production of his first books. Beard's point about Cooper's craftsmanship therefore requires, I think, some modification for his initial years. Cooper was mindful of the need to revise his manuscripts and proofs then, but he rarely managed to do so as thoroughly as he himself wished. Although he incessantly apologized for his tightly packed, hard-to-decipher manuscripts and spoke of having more legible copies made of them, before 1827 none of them in fact was copied. The result was that various errors were inadvertently introduced into the printed books, only some of which were ever caught and corrected. Moreover, Cooper's failure to sufficiently revise his first works meant that his usually strong vision in a given book—that which sustained him as he wrote—was often only partially expressed. When he later took the time to go back over his tales, as he sometimes did when early reprints were required as well as during two more concentrated efforts in the early 1830s and the later 1840s, he demonstrated that a good many of the flaws in his books were not the result of ineptitude but rather of the circumstances under which he had originally worked.

Those circumstances were, what is more, general as well as peculiar to Cooper. To trace them out in Cooper's case is therefore to write the cultural history of his post-colonial nation's precise situation. It is critical to remember how uncentralized, even disorganized, the conditions of the American book trade were when Cooper began writing. Writers in the early Republic enjoyed virtually no feedback. There were no real copy editors aside from the at-times astute but at-times impertinent typesetters, who alternately queried uncertain readings, silently changed things to suit themselves, or left untouched the errors they saw or failed to see. Cooper had cause to complain of all these varieties of inconsistent treatment. Yet, again in keeping with contemporary practice as much as his own circumstances, he himself was largely inconsistent in how he readied things for the typesetters. The fault lay on both sides.

There was another surface to this question. More than anything else, Cooper at the start of his career was driven by an imperious need for money. Like his father's other heirs after the patriarch's death in 1809, Cooper watched as the large inheritance they had been promised simply evaporated. By 1820, Cooper was so desperate for resources to pay current bills and old debts that, madly reasoning from Walter Scott's unexampled literary success with the Waverley novels, he launched his own career in the expectation that it would solve all his financial ills. That he implausibly enough succeeded is part of what made his example so important for American culture at the time. Yet the drive to succeed and the need for cash that underlay it always kept Cooper pushing production as, had there been more time and money, he probably would not have done. Not until he had written several books was he at last in a position to enjoy a reasonably good return on new projects; then he could attend to the early problems. Only at that point did the craftsmanship Beard attributed to him really begin to show itself.

The change came about through another of his innovations. Publishing, by which one means the more or less complete coordination of physical production practices with the business management of acquired literary projects, was itself a slowly emerging trade at the time both in the United States and in Europe. Before 1826, Cooper had no publishers as such. He produced his initial books completely at his own risk, employing first one and then a second New York bookseller as his agent. Those men made all the practical arrangements with paper suppliers, printers, binders, and wholesale and retail merchants, but they were not responsible for "editing" the books, reading proofs, or giving Cooper any regular form of advice—activities that would eventually form part of the "publisher's" proper function. In return for their management of his projects, the chosen booksellers received only a relatively modest commission.

Under such conditions it is remarkable that Cooper managed to see most of his projects through to completion. But as they succeeded, it became possible for him to negotiate a very lucrative arrangement with the Philadelphia firm of Carey and Lea, one of the nation's pioneering publishers, for whom he was the first and for many years most lucrative American author. From 1826 until the early 1840s, Carey and Lea would handle much of Cooper's American work. When in 1826 they paid him $5,000, a princely sum, for *The Last of the Mohicans,* no one could doubt that "American literature" had been created as a cultural and an economic reality. Cooper's own risky improvisations had established both the modes in which American books might be written and the market for their distribution and appreciation.

With Carey and Lea handling the American side of the business, Cooper soon set out for Paris, where he was intent on securing the still largely untapped proceeds from the many "pirated" editions of his works pouring from presses there and elsewhere in Europe. Again he managed to improvise methods that added an even more comfortable margin to his operations. Although the United States would not become a party to international copyright laws until forty years after Cooper's death, he ingeniously profited from the sale of prepublication proof sets to publishers in a variety of European countries. Here, too (also because of his imperative need for cash), Cooper led the way for his fellow citizens. One consequence of these economic innovations, as of Cooper's more nearly aesthetic ones, was that American writers in later periods operated in a vastly different literary marketplace from the one he had faced in 1820. As early as 1824, one American magazine humorously portrayed an unnamed New York publisher as swamped with imitations of Cooper (replete with "the backwoods, an Indian, a panther and a squatter"), for which the ambitious authors were demanding high prices and half the profits. Such a joke, unthinkable when Cooper began writing a mere four years earlier, indicated his dramatic influence on the American literary marketplace.

Cooper was not without recognition among the later writers whose careers he enabled. Herman Melville, who by the 1850s was producing prose unimaginable at the time Cooper began writing, certainly paid him generous tribute. Born just when Cooper started writing his first books, Melville quite literally had grown up on them. He especially devoured the sea tales. Later recalling the "vivid and awakening power" they had exerted on his own young mind, Melville expansively declared in 1852 that Cooper was "a great, robust-souled man"—as true an estimate as anyone has yet uttered. Like his good friend Evert Duyckinck, Melville did not overlook the denigrations of Cooper's talent and character that were perennial in the American press. But these, he concluded, had more to do with mere "fashion" than Cooper's inherent worth or historical importance. Melville trusted that time would restore Cooper to his rightful place: "a grateful posterity," as he put it, would "take the best care of Fenimore Cooper."

The gratitude has been long in coming. In the later decades of the nineteenth century, fresh editions of Cooper's collected works continued to appear, indicating his strong residual appeal among ordinary readers. At the same time, his stock in the contemporary literary world had begun a long slide that the old lies and the lack of accurate information about his career accelerated. So low did his official reputation sink by the 1880s that Thomas R. Lounsbury's tepid praise for him, itself an indication of the larger problem, was enough to push Mark Twain to commit the most famous of the resulting assassinations—a pair of essays whose success is suggested by the fact that they are better known to many readers today than any of Cooper's own books. In them, the former newspaperman attacked "Fenimore Cooper's Literary Offenses" with a comically ex post facto insistence on the universality of the laws of Realism. In many ways, his slams on Cooper were hardly new. They rehearsed criticisms dating from the first decade of Cooper's career, criticisms that Edgar Allan Poe more forcefully and cogently summarized in his lengthy review of one of Cooper's late forest tales, *Wyandotté* (1843). Their relation to the newspaper wars is also notable.

Mark Twain's contributions to this sort of buffoonery lay not in his aesthetic principles or practical analysis of Cooper but rather in the deeper deviltry of his wit. As Dekker and McWilliams have shrewdly observed, Mark Twain's method was "critically specious yet wholly unanswerable." Rewriting Cooper in such a way that his own small alterations turned quite plausible scenes into apparent absurdities, he baited would-be defenders of Cooper. If, as James F. Beard wrote, one ventures to answer his parodic outrages, one looks foolish for taking him seriously in the first place. But if one ignores him, one runs an equal risk of seeming to endorse all he said. There is much amusement in Mark Twain's tours de force. Considered as creative works in their own right, they appear ingenious; considered as critical estimates of one writer by another, however, they finally are both unfair and dishonest. They conceive of Cooper as obtuse and a failure, when in fact he was neither. Insofar as Cooper failed to be Mark Twain, which one gathers was his basic offense, he was not rejecting the obvious future but rather choosing the more obvious present: he was being true to his age, which was a romantic more than a realistic one. Had Cooper written like Mark Twain, what, after all, would one expect Mark Twain to do—write like Faulkner?

Furthermore, in being true to his own situation, Cooper enabled what Mark Twain accomplished. Here is where the deeper dishonesty of his essays comes in. Without Cooper, there could have been no Mark Twain, as Mark Twain himself admitted by the savagery of his attacks: for if Cooper had already died of aesthetic atrophy, as the "Literary Offenses" implied, it would not have been necessary to bludgeon him anew. Anyone who reads the Leather-Stocking Tales and the Mississippi River books of Mark Twain, especially *Adventures of Huckleberry Finn*, sees at once that in terms of setting, theme, and indeed characterization, the latter book owed much to Cooper's series. In fact, *Adventures of Huckleberry Finn*, a fair bit of romance on its own terms, is a prime instance of just how pervasively influential Cooper's innovations were. The spiritual father of Huck Finn was none other than Natty Bumppo—a demotic Euro-American hero who resists the confines of "sivilization" and, with a member of another race as his companion, finds his freedom in nature. No wonder that Mark Twain felt a need to hunt down and kill Natty's own progenitor.

Purposely misreading *The Deerslayer*, Mark Twain parodied Cooper as a way of destroying him. This is not to say that all the "flaws" Mark Twain pretended to discover in the Leather-Stocking Tales were imaginary. Even putting to one side the changes in taste that made his humor possible, or his own outrageous distortions, some of the miscues are certainly there, and I have no wish to make my case for Cooper's importance by ignoring them. Yet a fair number of them were, as suggested earlier, the result of factors other than the sheer incompetence of which Mark Twain accused him. With Cooper long dead and the nature of his career and accomplishments widely unappreciated, it was easy to blame Cooper for the very circumstances that Cooper in fact had fought against, overcome, and rendered obsolete.

That said, it remains to suggest why Cooper is worth reading—and reading about—today. Some of the reasons are, I think, already indicated. But there are others. We might start with his literary importance and then move to larger questions. Cooper's most innovative work as a writer probably lay in the field of sea fiction. Before *The Pilot* (1824), writers had used the sea only minimally. When it figured in novels and tales at all, it served largely as a backdrop for essentially social or moral action. Daniel Defoe's *Robinson Crusoe* (1719), probably the best-known early example, expressed the deep imaginative reaction of Europeans to the maritime expansion that had begun in the fifteenth century. Its hero, engaged in a variety of commercial adventures, is a figure who drifts morally as well as spatially; his experience copies the course of early modern Europe's history, and the sea is therefore a realistic venue for his story.

That said, Defoe's is a very pale sea indeed. When, having been delivered from his captivity in Africa, Crusoe sets sail for South America in a Portuguese vessel, the whole experience is written off in a mere sentence: "We had a very good voyage to the Brazils, and I arrived in the Bay de Todos los Santos, or All Saints' Bay, in about twenty-two days." Similarly, when he agrees to return to Guinea on a clandestine slaving voyage, the ultimate occasion of his shipwreck, the crossing is vaguely narrated until a hurricane strikes the vessel, blowing it about for twelve otherwise undescribed days. Before one knows it, a second storm hits, driving the ship aground and leading to its final abandonment and the start of Crusoe's long, nearly solitary exile.

Although in writing of Crusoe's shipboard experiences, Defoe uses such terms as "the wild sea," we are not really shown its active fury: we do not sense its heft or energy, nor do we even know its color under different skies or in different zones. And, as for the men who travel with Crusoe, we are given no memorable examples of their seamanship: they bear the storms rather than fight them. Crusoe, proud of his gentlemanly status and scornful of taking a place before the mast, is of course no sailor. Nor was Defoe, who generally was at a loss about how to deal with the sea as a complex three-dimensional environment. Instead, he used the sea as a means of isolating Crusoe from his homeland (indeed, from his poor abandoned parents), thereby inducing a long process of spiritual introspection. Hardly a setting, the sea is an engine for the book's plot. When Defoe published his third part of the tale, he appropriately enough called it *Serious Reflections . . . of Robinson Crusoe* (1720). In it, the allegory displaced geography altogether. Like the maritime paintings of his era, which tended to portray ships at rest against a relatively vague sea, Defoe could neither imagine the ocean nor fairly see it.

By the time Cooper began writing, the sea and seamanship alike had begun to figure more fully in literature and art. In the hundred years separating the two writers, Europe's maritime expansion had been exceptionally dramatic. Moreover, shifts in key cultural values had given all of the natural world an intense attraction for writers and other artists. Like such other natural zones as forests and mountains, the romantic sea was sublime, a place of vastness, power, and obscurity. One can hardly imagine a better contrast to Defoe's pale Atlantic, for instance, than the rich imagery and eerie atmospherics of Samuel Taylor Coleridge's ocean in *The Rime of the Ancient Mariner* (1798). Whether describing a ship running before the wind ("The fair breeze blew, the white foam flew, / The furrow streamed off free") or the chill beauty of towering icebergs that glow "green as emerald," Coleridge most of all caught the sea in motion, with high energy and a powerful vertical axis. If he allegorized the sea, it was not to preach about moral duty but rather to express the dark emotions lurking in the human soul. Such things Defoe's period never imagined.

The visual equivalent to Coleridge's poem was captured by his own (and indeed Cooper's) future friend Washington Allston in "Rising of a Thunderstorm at Sea," an 1804 scene the American painted while living in Europe. In a frail pilot boat that teeters on the crest of a huge, foaming swell, Allston placed several tiny figures. Galvanized into action by the dark tempest that has suddenly obscured their formerly clear sky, these men are seemingly lost. Certainly they are unseen by anyone on the serene three-masted ship that is running off from the storm in the background. Frantically, the four sailors work to control their boat's boom as the wind threatens to tear the sails or capsize the vessel altogether. The whole seascape seems meant to represent, as art historian Roger B. Stein once noted, the human predicament in a world of force. Not only does the painting present the romantic trope of "outer risk-taking," the human willingness to test the world, it portrays as well the "inner psychological response to the vastness of the sea and sky which overwhelms us."

Cooper was aware of such changes in the representation of the sea and human experience on it when he began his career. Yet he also clearly felt that the actual sea, the sea he had known as a merchant sailor and naval midshipman, had barely entered art and literature. When he discussed Walter Scott's latest book, a nautical romance called *The Pirate*, with friends in New York City in 1822, he was surprised to hear the author praised for his intimate familiarity with the sea. Cooper to the contrary thought that Scott never actually got his feet wet. Hence his own book, soon begun as a counterexample, was meant to show exactly what a sailor might do with the subject. In the process, *The Pilot* also became a singular demonstration of how the American might outdo the Scotsman. Opening with a gale off the English coast that nearly wrecks two American vessels, Cooper's book at once established him as a master of this new environment. Scott himself soon advised fellow novelist Maria Edgeworth to read the "very clever" tale, whose "sea-scenes and characters," he added, were "admirably drawn." Later, in response to another Cooper sea tale, *The Bravo* (1832), Russian critic V. G. Belinsky would call "utterly ridiculous" the common view that Cooper was an offshoot of Scott: "Cooper is a completely independent, original writer," Belinsky enthused, "a writer of genius, every bit as great as the Scottish novelist." Not every reader understood the seamanship of Cooper's sea tales, or grasped the point of using the sea as a setting for fiction. But from 1824 on, anyone who made literary use of the sea did so in Cooper's wake. His fifteen sea tales were an undeniable proof of his fecundity. Cooper did not merely repeat formulas as he returned to deep water in book after book. Not content merely to pioneer nautical fiction, he remained very much in the thick of its further development up to his death.

Without such venturesome uses of the sea on Cooper's part, Melville's exploration of the landless immensities of *Moby-Dick* (1851) hardly would have occurred. Cooper was, in this sense, the essential background of Melville's remarkable achievement, as Melville's generous tributes acknowledged. Nor was Cooper's importance on this question confined to American literature. In fact, his sea fiction made him more immediately available to writers from other cultures than, with some exceptions, his forest tales ever did. The Anglo-Polish master Joseph Conrad, for instance, was as impressed as Melville by "the true artistic intent" with which Cooper had imagined the sea, and he clearly benefited from Cooper's specific as well as general example. Not only did Conrad defend Cooper against Mark Twain ("whose dismal jargon . . . smirches whatever he touches," Conrad wrote a friend in 1908), he also rallied to Cooper's defense on a variety of fronts. "In his sea tales," Conrad impressionistically but insightfully concluded in 1898, "the sea inter-penetrates with life; it is in a subtle way the problem of existence, and, for all its greatness, it is always in touch with the men, who, bound on errands of war or gain, traverse its immense solitudes." Cooper, in other words, did not just use the sea as a setting. He understood it both as a realm of human action and as a physical system full of potential emotional meaning. His ocean was *alive* as only someone familiar with blue water could make it. As such, it became a new venue for literary experimentation in a variety of contexts far beyond the American shore.

Important as Cooper's sea tales indisputably are, he remains better known at present for his other major body of work—his wilderness novels, which are more readable and more moving today than even his best nautical tales. Reflecting back over his career a year before his death, Cooper himself concluded that the center of his achievement lay in the five Leather-Stocking Tales. That immense collective monument, a mythic chronicle stretching from the 1740s to the time of Lewis and Clark, captured the key epochs and themes of American life: it was, as historian Francis Parkman would put it in 1852, "an epitome of American history." True to his position as the first writer to work with the frontier, Cooper did not envision the whole series from the outset. He wrote *The Pioneers* (1823) as a fictional exploration of his now-lost boyhood home, Cooperstown, and introduced the figure of Natty Bumppo into it almost inadvertently—not as the intended hero but as a "low" character probably meant to provide little more than a bit of local color. Yet Leather-Stocking soon took over a good deal of the book's meaning, winning the author's regard as well as that of his readers. Ralph Waldo Emerson, barely out of Harvard, read "that national novel" with such enthusiasm that, many years later, he would write of the debt that ("in common with almost all who speak English") he owed Cooper for the "happy days" spent with that and other books. Emerson was notorious for his low opinion of fiction, but even he had been swept along during those first days of Cooper's fame.

There were those for whom the profoundly new subject matter of *The Pioneers* posed problems. They did not see how the ordinary stuff of American settlement, displayed in the rough clearings stretching even then from the Canadian border to the Gulf of Mexico, could form the theme of serious art. But, especially as Cooper extended Natty's saga in *The Last of the Mohicans* (1826) and *The Prairie* (1827), and eventually in *The Pathfinder* (1840) and *The Deerslayer* (1841), there was little doubt that he had invented the core myth of the expansive new nation. The accumulating poetry of his uncouth woodsman's life made the frontier the country's essential cultural and literary matter. When Francis Parkman, who in 1852 was poised to become the great historian of the frontier, looked back at a youth spent ranging the woods at his grandfather's farm outside Boston, he like Emerson recalled Cooper's books as "the chosen favorites" of his boyhood reading. Parkman's own first ventures into literature were stories he wrote of frontier warfare and forest wandering, and once he turned to history with the publication of *The Conspiracy of Pontiac* in 1851, his purpose was to ballast Cooper's vision with the weight of historical truth. Parkman's project—

writing a "history of the American forest"—was itself a tribute to Cooper's profound influence on shaping the imagination of the country at large.

Calling Cooper "the most original" American writer (even as he critiqued certain of his habits), Parkman saw his greatest gift as the figure of Natty. Cooper returned with seemingly inexhaustible imaginative power to Natty again and again but never simply made him the subject of a sequel—or a prequel, for that matter. It was as if the character lived outside the books, as if Cooper merely entered his life and then left it, only to enter it again at some different moment. Natty was, as Parkman had it, *real:* "The tall, gaunt form of Leather-Stocking, the weather-beaten face, the bony hand, the cap of fox-skin, and the old hunting frock, polished with long service, seem so palpable and real, that, in some moods of mind, one may easily confound them with the memories of his own experience." This tribute was echoed a century later by poet and critic Yvor Winters: Natty Bumppo, he wrote, has "a life over and above the life of the books in which he appears, a reality surpassing that even of an historical figure such as Daniel Boone." Winters went on to claim, rightly in my view, that the seventh chapter of *The Deerslayer,* in which Natty confronts, peacefully parts from, and then is forced to kill an Indian warrior out of a sort of tentative urge toward self-defense, was "probably as great an achievement of its length as one will find in American fiction outside of Melville."

To be sure, in considering Cooper merely as a writer, as a stylist, Winters saw him as great only in fragments (here, Beard's concern with reediting Cooper has its obvious purpose). That view to some extent underscored the old lingering problems in Cooper's texts, even as it also marked the recoil of a modernist from the mannerisms of a less spare age. Yet in thinking about the essential myths on which Cooper built his tales, myths that became those of a people, Winters expressed enormous respect for Cooper's core accomplishment: "the figure of the Leather-stocking emerges from the débris of the five novels in which he was created, independent, authentic, and unforgettable." D. H. Lawrence, as iconoclastic as Winters and as picky, found the same sort of "yearning myth" in the Leather-Stocking novels. He wrote of the "marvelously beautiful" scenes in *The Pioneers:* "Pictures!" he exclaimed. "Some of the loveliest, most glamorous pictures in all literature." Those pictures lacked, he thought, "the cruel iron of reality"—he was wrong about that, as it happens. But such a complaint was added after he had spent half a page listing all the lovely lies that made the book so memorable to him. Then there was *The Prairie,* "a strange, splendid book, full of [a] sense of doom," with a "shadow of violence and dark cruelty flickering in the air." Or *The Deerslayer,* a "gem of a book," with a setting, "the Glimmerglass" (Lake Otsego, where Cooper grew up), that "*could* not be more exquisite." Lawrence backed and filled somewhat, awkward about liking Cooper's works so much when, given what he probably knew of the American's character from Lounsbury's distorted biography, he did not like Cooper the man. But Lawrence was an honest reader, one who responded to the power of a book more than to its more superficial qualities. As H. Daniel Peck has argued in his study of Cooper's spatial imagery, *A World by Itself*, Lawrence was absolutely right in directing us to the power inherent in Cooper's images. The historian Parkman was hardly alone in recalling how "haunted" he was by the images in Cooper's books—by "the dark gleaming hill-embosomed lakes," the "tracery of forest against the red evening sky," even the "dark and rugged scenery" of the bloodiest of Cooper's books, *The Last of the Mohicans*. In Cooper, landscape is not a series of pretty pictures; it takes on moral value in itself. Like the sea, it is no backdrop but a fundamental fact of life, a contingent force in human experience.

In his frontier fictions especially, it is clear, Cooper set the terms of American dreaming. That he made his myths complex, full of concern for the fate of the leveled continent and the scattered native populations, meant, too, that he did not merely cheer on the wanton "progress" of Euro-American pioneers. This was part of what Lawrence did *not* see. Cooper apprehended the great energy that ordinary settlers expended in moving west, and the heroic visions that drove them. But he was never blind to the pettiness, the squalor, the wastefulness, or the injustice—all of which in fact show up precisely in those "glamorous pictures" in *The Pioneers*. The sad slaughter of the passenger pigeons by the inhabitants of Templeton is a case in point. In Cooper's youth, those birds had been legendary for the enormous flocks that darkened the sky all across the East; at his death, they were in precipitous decline because of overhunting, and in 1914 the last lonely individual was to die in the Cincinnati Zoo. D. H. Lawrence enthused about the "clouds of pigeons flying from the south, myriads of pigeons, shot in heaps"; Cooper to the contrary chose to direct his reader's attention to the pathetic eyes with which the wounded birds, lying in those "heaps," look up at Natty "as if they only wanted tongues to say their thoughts." Judge Temple, whose own enthusiasm for the hunt dies in the victims' pain, takes Natty's hint: "I see nothing but eyes, in every direction. . . . I think it is time to end the sport, if sport it be." Yet, to use a biblical formula Cooper knew and understood, even the tender mercies of the wicked are cruel: the judge thus recruits the village schoolboys to end the suffering of the birds by twisting off their heads. He will pay them, he promises, six cents per hundred on delivery of the trophies back in the village. By such means, Cooper insisted, does nature become "ours."

Here, clearly enough, was the defining moment, the beginning point, of an American environmental conscience. Thinking back on his own youth, Cooper remembered the naive destructiveness of the earlier era and endeavored to set it right. His vision of a continent ravaged in its "settlement" called his fellow citizens—and the world—to imagine a better way of being on the earth. Thoreau, who read Cooper while at Harvard in the 1830s, imbibed the core myth from his frontier novels. When Thoreau went to live at Walden Pond in 1845, his hut by the water literalized Natty's fictional home by the shores of Lake Otsego. At Walden, Thoreau was seeking what Cooper had urged Americans to imagine or discover—a relation to nature that did not destroy the wild but rather cherished and internalized it. In Natty, Cooper had shown the way.

Cooper's elegiac response to the crisis of Native American character and culture in the early nineteenth century was equally instructive. Far from complicit in the exterminations and removals that characterized his period, his tales traced native losses to the greed that caused them. The frontier as Cooper imagined it was no pageant. John Mohegan or Chingachgook in *The Pioneers* is, like the passenger pigeon, a doomed creature in response to whose fate the other characters reveal their essential values. Richard Jones, the sheriff who employs a cannon against the pigeons, mindlessly (if not also maliciously) urges drink on John Mohegan in the Bold Dragoon tavern. By contrast, Natty Bumppo again seeks to mitigate the damage. He has already narrated in folk epic fashion the achievements of the once "great warrior" who now shares his own humble hut: "Ah!," he adds, "Times is dreadfully altered since then." Empathetically, Natty knows what to do when the alcohol Jones has pushed on the Indian recalls rather than assuages his pain. Jolting Mohegan from his murderous but ludicrous fantasy of revenge, Natty urges patience, gesturing toward the time "when right will be done." More practically, he pays for a place for Mohegan to sleep off the effects of the white man's booze.

By giving prominence to the tragic fate thrust upon Native Americans in the process of frontier expansion, Cooper helped alter the sorry image of the Indian in the American mind. Tellingly, John Mohegan, retransformed into Chingachgook at the end of *The Pioneers*, dies a heroic death as a forest fire rages above the lake. His native language is on his tongue and the old vision lives again in his mind. While these restorations are symbolic more than actual, it is very clear that Cooper took pains to not leave Chingachgook in a drunken stupor at the book's end. Furthermore, unlike those who romanticized the Indian on the basis of little or no knowledge, Cooper based characters such as Chingachgook or Uncas on insights gleaned from remnant communities of Native Americans on the New York border, including actual Mohegans who had been displaced from New England in Cooper's youth. Later, eager to witness the oratorical prowess of Indian leaders for himself, he sought out midwestern chiefs when they visited the East. Long excoriated merely because they had stood in the way of Euro-American progress, Indians had enjoyed signally bad press in the colonies and the new nation. In the single interesting Western tale published before Cooper began his career, Charles Brockden Brown's *Edgar Huntly* (1800), they figured largely as targets, quite literally, of the settler's rage. What Cooper did was to give figures like Chingachgook and Uncas both voice and dignity. Their disappearance from the landscapes of his tales did not express his wish: rather, it reflected his realistic assessment of what was actually happening to Indian life in its old, precontact form as settlers pushed west. As he mourned the fate of the noble forest that fell before the woodchopper's relentless axe, he also lamented the destruction of Indian culture. For Cooper's land-developer father, the story of Cooperstown was obviously a story of possession; for his youngest son, partly because he saw it all slip from the family's hands, it became a tale of dispossession. Cooper's own losses made those of the land and its prior inhabitants emotionally intelligible to him.

The same point held for his portrayal of Euro-American pioneer Natty Bumppo, who opened the way for the very people who eventually displaced him. Hence the reason why Natty is allowed to poetically incorporate in his own life the deepest lessons of Native American culture. While in this regard he might be said (to use Philip J. Deloria's terms) to be "playing Indian," Natty's profound disgruntlement with his culture of origin lends credibility to his costuming. Besides, as Natty's self-consciously tedious declarations about his own ethnic origins in *The Last of the Mohicans* and the later novels suggest, Cooper purposely made Natty's "Indianness" a matter of values and skills rather than literal heritage. In drawing this distinction, he made it hard to reject the link the novels forge. Natty doesn't "pretend" to be a native; he is not playing at anything. Indeed, the novels won't allow him to. For one thing, they insist on showing that he does not and cannot exhibit all the capabilities and cultural traits that Cooper associated with Chingachgook, Uncas, and other Indian characters. What Natty can share with them, as a result, is all the more unanswerable.

Most of all, he shares a vision—of the continent, of nature in general, of the right bearing of human behavior on both. When he recalls in *The Pioneers* how he glimpsed "Creation! . . . all creation" from a Catskill escarpment years before, Natty is voicing that vision with immense lyrical power. When, in *The Deerslayer*, he responds (as H. Daniel Peck observes) with a kind of childlike, innocent wonder to the limpid surface of Glimmerglass, Cooper is once again locating the hunter's vision within nature. That is the sense in which Cooper allows Natty to bear forward an Indian value system salvaged from the torrent of destruction going on around him. If, as Yvor Winters wrote, the Leather-Stocking novels have "great defects," they have also "great vigor"; indeed, "as regards the portrayal of their particular place and period," Winters insisted, "they have no rivals." They are works of the first order—not perfect in finish but deep and powerful. And through their concern with issues that continue to matter profoundly today—issues such as ethnicity and the environment—they demand the sort of complex rereading that in fact they will amply reward.

On the basis of his literary accomplishments alone, James Fenimore Cooper would deserve a modern biography. Yet his life had an even broader significance than indicated above. Cooper was not just a pathbreaking figure in the history of authorship in the United States, or a potent visionary of forest and sea; he was a remarkably representative man. The two appeals were related, since the wide-ranging nature of his experience helped give his books a breadth of reference that contributed to his popularity then and his continuing interest today. Cooper was well acquainted with the most important arenas of activity among his con-temporaries. He was as much at home in the salons of New York City or the country houses of the rural Hudson valley as in the raw frontier villages where his family's life had taken its root and rise. Knowing the country's most charac-teristic landscapes in ways that few of his contemporaries did, Cooper wrote of them with unexampled authority. In a similar fashion, his experience in the mer-chant marine (1806–1807) took him to Europe at the height of the Napoleonic conflicts, a time of immense importance to American interests. In this way, his sea time gave him a firsthand sense of the nation's political context and thereby helped form his attitudes toward an array of international issues. The sea was not just to become a customary environment for his fiction: because of where he went and when he went there, it contributed to the emergence of his mature at-titudes and values. Moreover, Cooper's attachment to the U.S. Navy, in which he served from 1808 to 1810, gave him a lasting stake in a national institution of great significance in the age of James Lawrence and Stephen Decatur of the *Chesapeake* and the *Constitution*. Closely following the War of 1812, partly be-cause his friends fought in it and partly because so much hinged on its outcome, Cooper thereafter joined in the effort of his most influential contemporaries to forge a new culture for the reaffirmed nation. On the basis of such wider claims, one might go so far as to say that Cooper's story is almost incidentally a literary story. It is first and foremost a story of how, in literature and a hundred other ac-tivities, Americans during his period sought to solidify their political and cul-tural and economic independence from Great Britain and, as the Revolutionary generation died, stipulate what the maturing Republic was to become. Accord-ingly, such things form the heart of my own narrative here.

The first volume of this biography covers Cooper's life from his boyhood up to 1826, when, at the age of thirty-six, he left with his wife and five children for his extended stay in Europe. The second volume, now in preparation, will treat the last twenty-four years of his life—his sojourn overseas, his difficult homecoming in 1833, his political fights and lawsuits against the press, and the great rebirth of his literary art in the 1840s, when fully half his novels were written, including several of the best. Based on extensive archival research, both volumes try to place Cooper as fully as possible in his contemporary contexts. The mode is primarily narrative, although the stories are guided by the sorts of questions raised in this introduction. Because Cooper's example was to be of such deep and lasting effect, I have given special attention to what one might term the biography of his books: where the ideas for them came from, how Cooper managed the difficult task of writing American fiction almost de novo, how he moved the finished books from his writing desk through the printer's shop to the hands of his increasingly eager readers.

If there is a single motivating factor driving my narrative, it is economics. The choice of it was not mine, or at least not entirely. Economics was both Cooper's particular theme and, in yet another instance of his representativeness, that of his period. Given its importance in what follows, a bit more ought to be said about it here. It used to be asserted that Cooper was a comfortably situated country gentleman who merely "dabbled" in literature—that certainly was the view of Henry W. Boynton in his 1931 biography. There is no truth whatever to that quip. Up to his death in 1851, Cooper never enjoyed real financial security. Moreover, he left his family so negligible a legacy that they soon were forced to raise cash by selling off the old family mansion. Virtually from the start of his career, Cooper shared so deeply in the great economic anxieties of his age, a time when the market was poised to become the measure of most things, that he customarily viewed his literary works themselves as potential objects of trade. He lived by his wits in the most literal sense. As already suggested, the texture of his career was determined by seemingly irresistible economic forces: often enough, he could not revise one book because he already was at work on the next. At the same time, the economic necessity that drove him was the very force that allowed him to establish fiction as a paying career for others as well as himself. By such means the market triumphed. But by such means, as well, a culture with a seemingly thin veneer of distinctive forms and practices acquired in a short period—a mere decade—a defiantly independent set of literary and intellectual traditions.

For Cooper, the fight had a double significance. He became a writer while battling apparently fatal attacks on his father's estate, the executorship of which had been dumped in his lap in 1819 after years of slack handling by his older brothers. It was a struggle not just for the family at large but also for Cooper himself. Promised a large inheritance of $50,000 in Judge Cooper's will, he had received a mere fraction of that amount before the collapse of frontier land prices, added to poor management, brought down the whole edifice. For the decade following his marriage in 1811, Cooper struggled to pay his living expenses by borrowing against the rumored legacy, mortgaging and remortgaging any lands in his control, and juggling debts and demands against each other, often with a combination of ingenuity and mere positive thinking. Finally, he began indulging in increasingly frantic speculations—opening a general store with an incompetent cousin as partner, buying a ship and fitting it out for a series of whaling voyages, eventually even convincing himself that writing and self-publishing works of fiction might hold the key. He was lucky when the whaling venture and especially literature paid dividends, but even their returns were not big enough to fill the deep pits on whose edge he had long teetered. Not until 1834, a quarter-century after his father's death, did Cooper at last have enough of a margin from his literary earnings that he could settle the family estate. And it was a thin margin indeed. As book prices fell in the years following, even a near doubling of his output could not return him to a comfortable financial level. Hence the slender leavings on his death.

We owe to Cooper's deepening indebtedness in the early 1820s the venturesome quality of his first literary experiments, as well as some of their roughness. But to it we might also trace his insight, seen on page after page of his books, into the essential role of economics in motivating and directing human action. Material goods, along with debates about their worth and price, fill his novels, much as they were filling American houses and shops and minds in the period. Harvey Birch, the titular hero of *The Spy*, is a peddler who displays his wares under the gaze of George Washington in the first chapter of that second of Cooper's novels; his third book, *The Pioneers*, opens with an argument about who rightly owns the carcass of a shot deer, a fitting introduction to the novel's grand debate about claims to the landscape at large. Cooper's America is a land of broad fields and forests, but also a land where narrow-minded men and women dicker over petty things and small purposes. Even the great theme of wastefulness in *The Pioneers* owes something of its force to Cooper's personal sense that seeming wealth might easily vanish.

And here again it is worth stressing that Cooper's usefulness goes well beyond literature. As he avoided, then at last faced and struggled with, the collapse of his father's estate and his own finances, he copied a looming crisis in American society. It is not without significance that he took over the family estate precisely in the "panic" year of 1819. In the sheer quantity of surviving detail about how he dealt with his own disasters one can trace a larger, much more general story. Cooper was, in this as in so many other ways, deeply typical of the early Republic. His sense of the strengthening influence of the market in social relations, of the role of the law as itself an element of economic warfare, and of the threat of wealth to democracy, even his enduring tendency to view America's

social landscape as a collection of tattered surfaces and wishful incompletions—
as with the frontier village of Templeton in *The Pioneers*—suggest the degree to
which his social ethos and his aesthetic vision were shaped by the chaotic situation so many other men and women faced during that period. Rooted in the great
anxieties of his age, Cooper's life richly repays scrutiny a century and a half after
his death.

JAMES
FENIMORE
COOPER

CHAPTER ONE

The Vision

One day in the fall of 1785, New Jersey wheelwright and merchant William Cooper urged his horse up a steep wooded ridge in central New York, eager to inspect a tract of land he was angling to acquire. The long fight against British authority, nowhere bloodier than on the exposed New York border, had been over for only four years, and the 1783 treaty formally ending it was so recent that the countryside still showed deep scars. On his way there, Cooper had passed through a nearby village, Cherry Valley, that had been all but wiped out by raiding Loyalists and their Iroquois Indian allies in 1778. Only now, with British troops gone and such partisans in exile, were the old Scots-Irish villagers venturing back.[1] Elsewhere, but also tentatively, new settlers were starting to move out onto lands under American control at the war's end. Some of them, New England veterans mainly, recalled this area of rolling hills and fruitful river valleys well, having carried out reprisals against the Iroquois there a decade earlier. Finding land increasingly scarce in New England after the war, and willing to risk relocation westward, these Yankees would become soldiers in William Cooper's assault on the forests of what soon was known as Otsego County.

The alliance between Cooper and the Yankee settlers was an odd one. Cooper came from a Quaker background in the Delaware valley above Phila- delphia. Although no active Friend himself, he had followed the sect's pacifist principles in shunning a direct role in the Revolution. By contrast, the Yankee emigrants sprang from militant Puritan ancestors who had persecuted New En- gland's Quakers and other dissenters. And, although there were Loyalists enough in New England during the Revolution, the Yankee states had sent out hordes of fighters to wage war against Britain. Militarism was as ingrained among Puritans as pacifism was among Quakers. But in this new campaign against the American continent, the sometime Quaker William Cooper and these Puritan offspring would meet and join forces.[2]

The landscape around Cooper's ridge in 1785 was one of many places where such varied peoples would construct their new nation. It was a stunning spot. Rising to a height of some eighteen hundred feet, the ridge afforded an excel- lent prospect. Across the valley, another undulating hill moved along a parallel southwest-to-northeast axis. Mainly carpeted with a mix of hardwoods and pines, and backed in the western distance by seemingly endless waves of other green hills, the land here looked so promising that it would be hard to keep perceptions separate from dreams. On his route down the well-watered Middlefield valley earlier in the day, Cooper would have observed rich bottomland alternating with upland tracts and wooded summits. Already a practiced developer, he habitually saw future fields and pastures and villages where trees and grasses and brush grew. Now everything he saw appeared to flesh out his visions. Between his hill and the other one opposite glinted a stunning lake, blue-green from lime de- posits, narrow and slightly uneven as it ran up between the twin ridges for a full ten miles. At its foot, where the water poured through an outlet to give rise to the Susquehanna River, he knew he could found a village—and soon enough he would, naming it, of course, Cooperstown (Plate 1). But he was hardly oblivi- ous to the merely present beauty of the valley. This was not just a promising site for settlement—it was a profoundly good place in its own right. If the sunlight was strong that day, Lake Otsego no doubt glowed for Cooper's eyes as it still does for those who climb "the Vision," as his hill was christened almost four decades later. If a slight wind ruffled its surface, the water may even have glim- mered like shards of glass. How could he not be ravished by what he saw?

It was William Cooper's son James, not yet born in 1785, who named the Vision in 1823 and in 1841 called Lake Otsego "Glimmerglass." Young James Cooper's attachment to the region around his father's village made it inevitable that the novels he began writing in 1820 would circulate around this rich center. The Leather-Stocking series, his famous five-part saga of the white hunter Natty Bumppo and his Mohegan (or Mohican) companion Chingachgook, owed much to the Cooper family's development efforts in post-Revolutionary New York. The first of those novels to be published, *The Pioneers* (1823), opens on "the Vision," a hill so closely resembling William Cooper's 1785 peak that local residents soon adopted the fictional name for the as-yet-unnamed summit.[3] The last of the Leather-Stocking Tales to be written, *The Deerslayer* (1841), opens in the woods around the "Glimmerglass," a lake like the jade-green one William Cooper first glimpsed almost sixty years before. That name, too, soon was adopted for the real lake. Together, these two Otsego novels set the framework of James Fenimore Cooper's best imaginings. While the three other Leather-Stocking Tales ranged farther afield, they always recalled the geography of Fenimore Cooper's youth. Natty Bumppo is who he is in all five books because he spent his own youth—and, after many years away, much of his maturity—in this remembered landscape. So in fact did his creator, who passed most of his middle years (1817–1834) wandering elsewhere but who eventually came back to reclaim his old home.

That deeply private domain acquired public fame because Cooper's books were the first American novels to be widely read both at home and abroad. Like Walden Pond and its environs, although more immediately, Lake Otsego and the woods embowering it came to typify a crucial phase in American experience. Cooper, anticipating Henry David Thoreau, expressed his reverence for nature by treating this one microcosm of the American continent with extraordinary affection. Moreover, in going to *his* pond to live in *his* cabin, Thoreau was reenacting in ritual form the solitary life Cooper had imagined for his forest hero in the Leather-Stocking saga.[4] The light shining upward from the heavenly water of Walden was in that sense but the refracted glow of Cooper's Glimmerglass. In speaking of the Ganges, Thoreau might also have mentioned the Susquehanna.

This link to Thoreau will suggest that Fenimore Cooper understood his family's story differently from his father. William Cooper, proclaiming settlement an unmitigated good, was profoundly attached to the social values that dominated views of the frontier in his age. Settlers gave order to the disorder of mere nature, thereby justifying their usurpation of Native American rights as well as their destruction of native plants and animals. Looking back on a career spent settling 750,000 acres, William Cooper cast his activities in precisely these terms: "I laid me down to sleep in my watch-coat," he wrote of his first night alone in Otsego, "nothing but the melancholy Wilderness around me." Soon he was taking pride in helping reclaim "such large and fruitful tracts from the waste of the creation."[5] Thoreau, although he earned his keep in part by surveying nature into woodlot, field, and pasture, could not have naively uttered such a phrase as *the waste of the creation*. But neither could William Cooper's youngest son. In *The Pioneers*, as Natty Bumppo reminds the reader, it is the settlers who bring their "wasty ways" *into* nature with them (*PIO* 2:46), rending the fabric of the forest and deracinating the order previously established there by God and the children of God, meaning primarily the Indians but also Natty himself.

In that same novel, Natty Bumppo recalls for his young companion Oliver Edwards how loneliness sometimes drove him to a hilltop prospect overlooking the settled Hudson valley. When asked by Edwards what he saw from there, the old man replies with unhesitating eloquence, "Creation! . . . all creation, lad." Not the *waste* of the creation, but rather creation itself, the very fullness of life, the ripeness of "all that God had done or man could do" (*PIO* 2:108). Although Fenimore Cooper appreciated his father's accomplishments, he did not unthinkingly endorse them. Raised amid the natural beauty of Otsego, and infected with his own generation's more romantic attitudes, he knew nature as a source of order—and humanity as too often the cause of disharmony or worse.

There were other reasons for the family contrasts. When William Cooper died in 1809, he left a seemingly ample legacy for his five grown sons and one adult daughter. Across the following decade, however, circumstances would desolate his leavings. By the time his frontier accomplishments were reimagined in *The Pioneers*, his heirs were virtually penniless—and Fenimore Cooper, exiled from Cooperstown, was his father's sole surviving son, the others having died broke if not also broken. His father's mansion overlooking Lake Otsego was one casualty of the collapse when it was auctioned in 1821 to help pay off a creditor of the Cooper estate. Another consequence struck the novelist even closer to home. As he worked on *The Pioneers* in New York City, that same creditor sought to seize and sell the meager furnishings in the novelist's modest rented quarters. Cooper had not been back to Lake Otsego in five years, and another twelve would pass before he managed a return. The novel and the memories it embalmed—a mere string of words—were his only real inheritance.

These reverses had turned Cooper toward the idea of authorship in the first place, since he thought that writing might offer a chance to recoup lost revenue and lost self-esteem. Given the depth of his emotional distress, it is hardly surprising that *The Pioneers*, his third published novel, presented its frontier themes in complex, even conflicted ways. But the twists were not simply imported from the family story. The whole Leather-Stocking series evolved as a meditation on the competing historical, legal, and moral claims to the American continent. So upsetting was Cooper's personal sense of loss that it made him uncommonly sensitive to the losses others suffered not only on the frontier—the Indians first of all—but also in other zones of American experience. When he turned to the American Revolution in books such as *The Spy* (1821), for instance, he understood as few contemporaries did the conflicting claims that had moved Americans during that war. Cooper had no doubt about the justness of the Revolution as a war of liberation from British imperial control, but he was nonetheless intrigued by those Americans who had opposed the war, fought on behalf of Britain, or simply remained neutral. His enduring view of the Revolution as a civil war, not just a struggle for national liberation from a colonial empire, was unusual at the time. It drew on his own family's Quaker ties as well as the costly Loyalism of his wife's family, the once wealthy and powerful DeLanceys. It also drew on the woeful tales he had picked up from good people on all sides of the war, tales that struck home often enough because they echoed Cooper's own. Dispossession became the major theme in his works because it was the major theme of his early experience.

Small Beginnings

First, though, came possession, the theme of his father's more expansive life. William Cooper (Plate 2) had been born in 1754 in the then rural town of Byberry, a dozen miles north of Philadelphia, amid a scattering of Quaker relatives who were mostly small farmers. His parents, James and Hannah Hibbs Cooper, were by no means wealthy, but their secular outlook and generally upward economic path may have helped produce the ambitious spirit of their second son.[6] By the time he was fifteen, they thus had left tiny Byberry for Lower Dublin, a larger and more prosperous town nearer to Philadelphia that was wholly without Quaker institutions but full of economic opportunity. Eventually, James Cooper came to own a substantial Lower Dublin farm and was prosperous enough that, after Hannah's death, he employed seven servants to help him work it. By the end of the 1780s, then remarried, the restless man had moved again, this time to Chester County, a more sparsely settled region southwest of Philadelphia, where he purchased an even larger property. He was busy raising a second family there when he died in 1795.[7]

From early in life, James and Hannah Cooper's second son was equally alienated from the family's Quaker legacy and equally mobile. Before his parents left Byberry in the late 1760s, William, no more than thirteen or fourteen, seems already to have gone off into the world on his own. Persistent family stories suggest that he quarreled with his father and ran away, an entirely believable possibility. He may have gone to sea, as an older brother probably did, or simply been working in Philadelphia, with which he became intimately familiar early in life.[8] Eventually, his path led him back for a time to Byberry, where he served an apprenticeship in the wheelwright's trade, gaining a modest niche as a propertyless householder on the town's last pre-Revolutionary tax list.[9]

These marks of application, surprising given his earlier restlessness, reflected

Cooper's changing circumstances: married at nineteen and a father at twenty, he suddenly had serious responsibilities to shoulder. The marriage appears to have been a somewhat hasty affair. At some point, Cooper's wanderings had taken him across the Delaware River to the rural town of Willingboro, near the west Jersey capital of Burlington. There he met and courted Elizabeth Fenimore, a woman three years older than himself. She took to the lively Cooper, but her prosperous parents, Richard and Hannah Fenimore, were unimpressed with his apparently humble prospects. Not to be denied, the young wheelwright hurried Elizabeth off in November 1774 to the Willingboro mansion of Gov. William Franklin, who married the couple in a businesslike civil ceremony.[10] Prudently, Cooper immediately departed with his bride back across the Delaware and resumed his trade at Byberry.

Early in the Revolution, the couple appears to have moved south to Philadelphia, where Cooper's future partner in the Otsego business, Jersey-born Andrew Craig, was then living with his wife and children. Either together or separately, the two families migrated to the Burlington area around the time the brief British occupation of the Pennsylvania capital ended in 1778.[11] Thereafter, having already flattered the Fenimores by naming their first two children after them, William and Elizabeth Cooper were finally able to tap Richard Fenimore's considerable but long-withheld largesse. On a substantial property in Willingboro apparently given to him by his father-in-law, William Cooper set up a combination store and tavern in his family's house. Soon, having erected a few other buildings to sell or rent out, he named the modest cluster of structures Coopertown, thereby launching his career as a land developer.[12]

His straggling Jersey hamlet never attracted William Cooper's energies the way his bigger, bolder Otsego venture would. That was partly because, always eager for some new opportunity, he did not stay put in Willingboro. After a few years as a mere storekeeper, he relocated to the livelier precincts of Burlington proper, where he put on airs as a full-fledged "merchant." He had considerable financial and social success, counting the leading men of the city among his customers and enjoying the confidence of his neighbors, who in 1786 chose him as a member of their city council. But the needs of his relentlessly expanding family, packed into small rented quarters through these years, outran his accomplishments. By the time his eleventh child, James, was born in a narrow stucco-clad two-story dwelling on High Street (now the headquarters of the county historical society), on September 15, 1789, William Cooper already had made his New York journey and, within a year, was ready to take the infant "Jem" and his six surviving siblings north to their new home on the shores of green-tinted Lake Otsego.[13]

Merchant Cooper had snared his Otsego lands from business associates in Burlington who had claims on the tangled estate of a notorious frontier trader

named George Croghan. With the help of Sir William Johnson, British superintendent of northern Indians, Croghan had finagled his way to the control of
vast holdings in several areas, among them a tract of a hundred thousand acres
in Otsego that included the future site of Cooperstown. Habitually cash poor but
well-connected and persuasive, Croghan had mortgaged his Otsego patent in
1768 to Gov. William Franklin of New Jersey—the same man who, coincidentally enough, was to preside over the marriage of William Cooper and Elizabeth
Fenimore six years later. Franklin in turn had quickly laid off some of the debt
on a local group of investors known as the Burlington Company, in which he
eventually would become a shareholder.

When Croghan's note came due in 1771 and he failed to pay it, Franklin won
a court judgment against him, but the legal chaos that followed the start of the
Revolution and his own exile as a Loyalist wiped out that victory. Not until the
end of the war, when he was living in London, was he able to reassert his
claim—as did the current owners of remaining shares in the Burlington Company and various other Croghan creditors in New York and Pennsylvania. In
1785, Burlington arrivistes William Cooper and Andrew Craig, taking shrewd
advantage of this renewed activity on Croghan's holdings and obligations, purchased the rights of some of the remaining Burlington Company members, who
were out of patience with the whole drawn-out business. On this slender basis,
the partners sought to seize the Otsego lands and conduct a long-delayed foreclosure sale authorized under William Franklin's prewar court decree. With
Alexander Hamilton as their attorney, Cooper and Craig had that decree revived, then rushed to organize a January 1786 auction covering a portion of
Croghan's Otsego holdings. The auction was to be held in Canajoharie, a Mohawk valley village close to the lands in question but very far, especially in the
middle of the winter, from the various other parties interested in the liquidation
of Croghan's assets.[14]

It was fitting that Hamilton's opposing counsel in this new battle was Aaron
Burr, who acted as attorney for Croghan's heirs and for the executors of John
Morgan, one of Croghan's New York City creditors. Burr protested the planned
auction before New York's Chancery Court and secured an injunction, but
Cooper nonetheless pushed the sale forward. Surprisingly, Dr. John Morgan, the
deceased creditor's son, braved the winter and showed up in person in Canajoharie, where he proceeded to make the highest bid on the lands. Probably lacking
sufficient cash to meet that bid, however, he momentarily withdrew; in his absence, the sheriff reopened the auction and knocked the property down to the
original second highest bidder—William Cooper—this time for a third less than
Cooper had bid the first time. Although it seemed likely that this irregular proceeding would be protested, for the present Cooper could rush home to Burling-

ton with the good news that he had just purchased some forty thousand acres at a spectacularly low price. So far everything was going his and Craig's way.[15]

In May 1786, despite Dr. John Morgan's widely published warnings, Cooper returned to Otsego with a party of surveyors. Camped on an old Indian clearing at the foot of the lake, the site where Croghan had once erected an ambitious log mansion, he opened land sales even as the boundaries were being laid out. By July, he had disposed of much of the patent. Sales were brisk in part because he and Craig offered liberal terms. Prices were low, down payments were unnecessary, and purchasers could occupy and use their land for a term of ten years while making only annual interest payments at the legal 7 percent rate. Cooper and Craig also allowed ordinary individuals to buy and subdivide larger parcels, thereby defraying the future cost of their own farms. Finally, concerned that purchasers might hesitate because of claims urged by Morgan and others, including Croghan's heirs (chiefly his son-in-law, Augustine Prevost), the partners personally guaranteed the title to all parcels. If their opponents won in court, the two men would be ruined. But if they did not take this risk, none of the annual interest payments due from hundreds of purchasers, small though each payment might be, would start to materialize. It was all or nothing.[16]

Once actual settlers crowded the lands, it was unlikely that other claimants to Croghan's patent would succeed in their suits. But that prospect did not keep them from intermittently pushing their interests. Cooper and Craig reached accommodations with some of them, including a partial one with the Prevost family, immediately following the initial sales. From time to time thereafter, other legal action flared up. William Franklin, still exiled, at first did very little. In 1791, he and Augustine Prevost began cooperating, but very ineffectively, and on Franklin's death in 1813 his case entirely fizzled. In the meantime, Prevost's sons, George and John, had some success recovering their due from the owners of another Otsego County patent that also had been preemptively sold. Encouraged by that result, they next attacked the Coopers. But the heirs of William Cooper were hardly about to give up what he had so cannily won. They delayed the legal process so successfully that by 1821, with their personal resources exhausted, the Prevosts permanently withdrew their suit. The cessation of their action signaled the final triumph of the Cooper family over all the original claimants to the Otsego patent: the great gamble of 1785 had finally paid off.[17]

First Settlers

James Cooper grew up in Otsego amid an array of wonders. Here, for one thing, he gained his first insights into Native American life and the earliest, wildest phase of Euro-American settlement. In the case of Native Americans, those insights were tantalizingly vague. Although the recipients of British land grants were required to secure Indian deeds before the government would confirm their rights, no Native Americans had permanently lived in the Lake Otsego area for a very long time—if ever. Like its nearby twin, Lake Canadarago, Otsego was resorted to only by small hunting and fishing parties. Archaeological evidence from an island in Canadarago, for instance, shows persistent use of that site for temporary shelter but not for long-term habitation, and the same appears to have been true of Otsego.[18] Early Euro-American settlers commonly found Native American artifacts on the lakeshores as well as near streams and ponds and turned up large numbers of them each spring as they replowed their newly cleared fields. But none of those artifacts conclusively indicates continuing residence.

The archaeological evidence is nicely reinforced by the one documented Indian camp in the vicinity of Cooperstown, established at the foot of "Lake Utsague" in 1765. Set up by famished Indians forced north from the important permanent settlements near Oquaga, the camp was occupied over the summer and fall precisely where Cooperstown one day would stand.[19] But it was a refuge of the moment, and left the lightest of traces. Nowhere along the shores of Otsego have ruins like those discovered elsewhere in the region been found; there is no counterpart, for instance, for the impressive hilltop fortification known to exist in Cooper's day at Fort Plain, near Canajoharie in the Mohawk valley (*DS* HE xviii–xix).

The Otsego region nonetheless had considerable significance in Indian experience. For centuries, it had helped define the border between the Iroquois, who dominated much of New York during the colonial era, and more southerly Native American tribes. The Iroquois League was a complex social organization whose five constituent peoples stretched from the easternmost Mohawk through the Oneida, Onondaga, and Cayuga, to the Seneca, who defended the league's western flank against Great Lakes and Ohio valley tribes. The Mohawk, occupying many villages along the river named for them, had especially close ties to the Otsego highlands immediately south of their core domain. For centuries, Otsego had provided them with rich foraging grounds. And in the later part of the colonial era, its importance grew as it became useful for strategic purposes. By the early eighteenth century, weakened by wars with western tribes, the Iroquois League had begun forging mutually beneficial alliances with native groups farther south. In the most famous instance, the harried Tuscarora Indians of North Carolina moved north to seek refuge among their Iroquois kin. In addition to other sites, the Tuscarora took up lands bordering the Susquehanna south of its source in Lake Otsego, thereby extending the Iroquois frontier in that quarter. Other native bands displaced from Pennsylvania and the Chesapeake Bay region also began migrating northward in the eighteenth century. With the Tuscarora and individuals from other Iroquois groups, they helped give such Susquehanna settlements an intertribal complexity that was typical of the late colonial and early national frontier. Among the largest and best known of these new settlements was a cluster of villages called Otsiningo, in the vicinity of the present-day Binghamton. Another cluster, called Oquaga or Anaquago, was located some forty miles upriver, not far from the eventual limits of Otsego County. It was from the latter site, facing food shortages in 1765, that those temporary visitors to the foot of Lake Otsego derived.[20]

The Revolution profoundly altered upstate Indian life. Most Iroquois, loyal to the crown in part because London promised to restrain the flood of white settlers eager for Indian land, shared in Britain's defeat. Only the Oneida, staunch allies of the rebels, remained in the area in significant numbers when the Coopers arrived. But, as had been true of the Iroquois more generally before the war, the Oneida now were inviting other native peoples to join them in central New York. One such group was the Stockbridge Indians. This community was composed of Moheconnucks tracing descent from the Mahicanni or River Indians of the Hudson valley, kin of both the Mohegans and the Delaware. In more recent decades, they had lived in western Massachusetts but now agreed to take up lands offered them by the Oneidas in 1784. In New Stockbridge, located along the line dividing Madison and Oneida counties about forty miles northwest of Cooperstown, the Moheconnucks sought to retain their ethnic identity even as they continued their adoption of many elements of Euro-American life, including Christianity and the agricultural economy of the postwar frontier.

It is likely that Fenimore Cooper's father was personally acquainted with the settlers at New Stockbridge, who entered into the same general region in the same decade as his Otsego clients and who settled along the route from Cooperstown to Utica, soon a key trade center for all of central New York. It also seems clear that William Cooper had an active link to the other major group of New England migrant Indians in the region at the time, a mixture of Mohegans, Pequots, Narragansetts, Montauks, and other peoples for whom the missionary preacher and Mohegan leader Samson Occom had begun a relocation campaign during the 1770s. In this instance, as later with New Stockbridge, the Oneida generously offered land for the experiment. The founding of Occom's settlement—to be named Brotherton or Brothertown after a similar settlement established by missionary David Brainerd in Burlington County, New Jersey, in earlier decades—was delayed by the Revolution. At the war's end, just when William Cooper was initiating his own endeavors on the New York frontier, Brotherton was begun in earnest within what now is the town of Paris in Oneida County, just east of New Stockbridge and thus even closer to Cooperstown.

Here in these two communities were some of the supposedly "last" of those
doomed Mohicans/Mohegans with whom Fenimore Cooper would pair his fictional hunter. Cooper had personal ties to some members of these mixed Indian
communities that lasted throughout his life. His Indian lore was by no means
profound, but neither was it shallow. Indeed, among all Euro-American writers
of the first half of the nineteenth century, Cooper knew more at first hand about
Indian life than any others—except perhaps for Thoreau.[21]

Growing up in Otsego also gave Cooper his first glimpse of those pre-
agricultural white frontiersmen who were to be central to his imagination of
the colonial and early national past. Leather-Stocking has been traced to many
"real" sources. Cooper himself remarked in 1850 that in the physical details
of the character he drew on several individuals he knew in early life.[22] Like
Cooper's Mohicans, who display a sense of Delaware identity even though their
creator owed much of his inspiration to the recent migrants settled in New
Stockbridge and Brotherton, the lanky hunter was a composite who is to be explained by no single analog. Even in the novelist's own day, legendary New York
hunters such as Nicholas Stoner, Timothy Murphy, Nat Foster, and Green White
were widely known on the border. The last of these, at one time a resident of
the town of Worcester just southeast of Cooperstown, suggests how local to
Cooper's experience some of this lore could be.[23] So does the example of David
Shipman, an Otsego hunter whom the novelist knew and whom he described in
1838 as "the Leather Stocking of the region" (*COC* 26). Shipman, who had been
on the ground there before William Cooper's 1785 trip, later lived in a squatter's
cabin and was reportedly to supply fresh game for the Cooper household in the
early years. In appearance and habits he was a good match for Bumppo. As a
Cooperstown resident born in the 1790s recalled, Shipman "dressed in tanned
deerskin, and with his dogs roamed the forest, hunting deer, bears, and foxes."[24]

But *this* Leather-Stocking, among the more obvious of Cooper's sources for
his greatest character, merely typified traits common among white settlers on the
early frontier. Otsego in fact had been peppered with Euro-American settlements well before the Revolution. The county's gateway town in the northeast,
Cherry Valley, dated from the 1740s. Springfield, to the west of Cherry Valley
at the upper end of Lake Otsego, also predated the Revolution. Like the German
villages that lay well beyond the easternmost settlements of the Iroquois in the
Mohawk valley, such relatively isolated Euro-American enclaves contributed to
the marked complexity of the central New York frontier. Within this early frontier zone, figures such as David Shipman and Green White probably did not
stick out as Natty Bumppo does in Templeton. For this was a period when, as one
Yankee immigrant later recalled, all the fresh arrivals lived a "plain, coarse, and
primitive" life in the woods and clearings. In such outlying districts, newcomers

might be seen every day, he continued, "wending their way with knapsack on their backs, an axe lashed on the outside, and with gun on their shoulder, seeking a favorite resting place, prepared to grapple with the hardships and privations of frontier life."[25] For the younger Cooper, the sense of an earlier, heroic phase in the region's experience must have been widely in evidence.[26]

Yet it was also fleeting. With the founding of Cooperstown, the region began a period of rapid transformation. Barely populated in 1790, Otsego had become the most populous of all upstate counties, astonishingly enough, within twenty years. So overwhelming was the pace of development around Cooperstown, as Cooper would claim in the late 1830s, that his first full experience of the frontier had occurred not in Otsego but rather on Lake Ontario during his naval service there in 1808 and 1809. The county of Oswego, where he was stationed then, had only a tenth of Otsego's population in 1810. And Cooper rightly added that "several of the characters introduced into the Pioneers" derived from his Great Lakes memories (*LJ* 4:259). He most of all owed to Oswego, however, a dawning nostalgia for the world of his boyhood, which already was overwritten by subsequent changes. In the village of Oswego, as it were, he rediscovered his own roots. That small lake port in fact was older than Cooperstown and was full of historic echoes (see Chapter 4). Yet it lay at the end of a long, rough route through dense woods and was poised at the edge of an inland sea that emphasized the expanse of forest isolating it from the rest of New York and the nation.[27]

In that wooded landscape along Lake Ontario, Fenimore Cooper reclaimed the sense of nature's inexhaustible and sustaining wholeness that had first entered his young mind near Cooperstown years before. Otsego's timber had come crashing down from the outset as farmers opened their clearings and ran roads up valleys and over hills. But enough of the primordial pines, oaks, and hickories remained during his youth, towering over the green water, for him to recall it all with poignant emotion. As the first American writer to express a sense of concern for the wanton destruction of the environment, Cooper was making a social and indeed moral issue out of his own sense of loss. The loss was visual, as his emphasis on the ugliness of the frontier's stump-strewn landscape suggests. But it was more importantly psychological, for there was a behavioral correlative to the old wild landscape. In 1798, Cooper's sister Hannah visited him and his brother Samuel in New Jersey, where they had been staying for some months with their mother. What struck her most of all about the boys was how plain it was that "they had been bred in the woods."[28] Back in Otsego, the boys were used to having free access to those woods and doubtless ran out their hearts amid them as often as they could. Much later, when Cooper invented Natty Bumppo, one of the things the woodsman represented was the author's naturalization in the environment. Natty's cabin in the woods was a marker of the novelist's own fantasies about the richer possibilities of the place that his father and his father's clients were turning into dull, tame farmland with remarkable speed.

Natty was, in this sense, the permanently arrested child in his creator's heart. And Fenimore Cooper's attachment to Natty's world was indeed intense. A year after sister Hannah made her remark about him and Samuel, the boys' mother again took them away from their wild home for another stint in New Jersey. Elizabeth Cooper did *not* like the woods, or the village her husband had founded, or the rough house he had hastily built for his family at the foot of the lake. But when the trio barely had arrived in her old hometown of Burlington, the boys' hearts rose up in rebellion at the prospect of another long spell of days removed from their lake and woods. "[S]o great was the grief of my brother and myself at the idea of giving up our lake and our haunts," Cooper recalled forty-five years later, that they forced their mother to bring them almost immediately home (*LJ* 4:498). If Cooper owed his fundamental sense of the frontier to Lake Otsego rather than to Ontario, it was at this deep emotional level. The course of his imaginings in the Leather-Stocking series brought him at last, in *The Deerslayer*, to that lake of his boyhood wanderings and the "haunts" around its shore. Here, on the bosom of the green lake fringed by the green woods, was what deeply mattered to him. Here, in some complex refashioning of American possibility, Cooper himself could become Natty.

Removals and Arrivals

But that was a long time after those first uncertain years in William Cooper's second eponymous village. We need to backtrack. At the time Cooper attended the Canajoharie auction in January 1786, his wife Elizabeth was recovering from the birth of twins in the family's rented house in Burlington. When he opened sales on the New York patent in May, she again remained behind in Burlington, caring for infants Elizabeth and William and the couple's four other surviving children—Richard, Hannah, Isaac, and Ann. As yet there seems to have been no thought that the family would ever move to New York. Otsego was a speculation, nothing more. Over the succeeding summer, William Cooper accordingly returned to Otsego alone, laying out the first streets in the village ("Cooper Town" or simply "Foot of the Lake") he was planning for the open site on the lakeshore (*COC* 23–24).[29]

According to his youngest son, Cooper came and went a few times over the summer of 1786. He was back in Burlington by September, when his wife, still caring for the twins, became pregnant again—this time with a son, Samuel, who was to be born in May 1787. The infant's father probably did not wait for the birth before he rushed back to New York that second spring. He arrived in time to greet the large influx of Yankee hill farmers who, at the first sign of warmer weather, departed from western New England in search of fresh opportunities.[30] It was at this time that Cooper for the first time began imagining his own future in the place: in July, he thus wrote Jacob Morris, soon to be a neighbor in the western part of Otsego: "by the by [I] am Determined to take up my Abode at Lake Otsego."[31] By the end of 1787, having watched several log and frame structures go up in the still small village, William Cooper made arrangements for a new building to be erected for his own use the following year (*COC* 25–26). He then returned to Burlington again for the winter.

It was probably during this visit back home that William Cooper broke his plans to Elizabeth. She knew nothing of such wild country firsthand and may have shared the fear of the "backwoods" that was then widespread in the nation's more settled areas. And she was certainly attached to her home region and her family. So, in the face of her resistance, her husband in the spring of 1788 proposed she make a trial visit to Otsego. Their son James reported, obviously from his mother's dramatic accounts, that the couple "reached the head of the lake in a chaise," then rode a canoe down Otsego to the small clearing where William intended they would live. Elizabeth's reaction to the last stage of the journey was a true measure of her character. In general, she seems to have been happiest when ensconced in familiar and orderly surroundings. Certainly she was much less venturesome than her forge-ahead husband, probably in part because she had derived a sense of stability and security from her well-to-do parents that her runaway husband did not enjoy. But because, up to a point, she was inclined to give in to William's formidable will, she repeatedly found herself in situations that eventually alarmed her. Then she would panic or overreact, recovering her own will at long last and demanding that it be attended to. In the present case Elizabeth Cooper's panic was strong enough to set in place her long-lasting dislike for the forest patent her husband had acquired. Never would she be happy there, or even settled. In 1788, "Mrs. Cooper was so much alarmed with this [canoe] passage," as the novelist recalled her story, that the chaise was dragged down the lake, a makeshift bridge was thrown across the outlet from Lake Otsego, and a thin, sketchy road hacked through the forest on the east side of the water. The "road" was so uneven that the chaise could barely be driven up it, and a group of men had to accompany it, steadying it via ropes attached to the top. That was the only way Elizabeth Cooper would leave (*COC* 24–25).[32]

Her visit to the village evidently coincided with the start of work on the family's first house there. Her husband, of course assuming her agreement beforehand, already had secured partner Andrew Craig's release of any claim to the chosen site. Construction may have been under way even as Elizabeth arrived: the men who accompanied the chaise on its tipsy journey back to the relative civilization of Springfield could well have been workers on the project. In any case, the frame structure was soon built. It was made from green timber cut from the local forest, assuring that it would soon warp out of true. But for its place and time it was of an impressive size. By September of 1788, when William Cooper had Burlington surveyor Daniel Smith draw a map of the new settlement, the house was represented on it as a finished dwelling, two stories high and with a pair of low wings on the ends. It was sited directly on the village's main street, the one leading west from that rudimentary bridge, and stood opposite the head of a short lane leading down to the lake. Behind it were large but undeveloped grounds where a kitchen garden eventually would be laid out (OH 223–24).[33]

The proprietor must have come back to his village shortly after returning that chaise and his alarmed wife to Burlington, for a great deal of work remained for him to attend to over the summer of 1788. Daniel Smith's presence in the village then marked Cooper's now more ambitious vision for the place. Smith's map did not so much record the actual place as project its future look. In particular, it gridded the landscape into a collection of almost two hundred slim, deep lots crowded into a small, tightly packed area—along with several unbroken segments kept for future development. Cooper chose this plan in order to keep the settlers close to each other. Otherwise, he feared, they would sprawl out into the countryside, dabbling in things agricultural rather than concentrating on the quasi-urban economic skills he thought necessary for the "place of trade" he had envisioned from his mountain perch three years before.[34] Cooper's sociable definition of the village perhaps reflected his anxiety about the success of the whole endeavor. But the landscape as Smith platted it and as it mostly developed (the village lots tended to grow larger as actual purchasers combined them into bigger wholes) owed something as well to the tightly packed rural boroughs in Pennsylvania where Cooper had grown up. Cooperstown in its first incarnation resembled nothing so much as West Chester or Kennett Square. William Cooper himself drew a connection between "his" village and the "compactly settled"—and prosperous—"town of Lancaster, in Pennsylvania," and he almost certainly took his grid, down even to the street names, from Thomas Holmes's famous, orderly plan for Philadelphia.[35]

The laying out of the still meagerly populated village coincided with a further increase of settlers in the countryside. Their presence in turn gave William Cooper new responsibilities. He stayed in Burlington again during the winter of 1788–1789, when yet another son, the future novelist, was conceived. Then, once more leaving a pregnant wife in Jersey to fend for herself, he moved to the "Foot of the Lake" more or less permanently. He arrived in April of 1789 with workmen employed to finish his house, only to find a crisis facing the region.

The price of grain had risen so steeply in the Albany market the winter before that the demand there, as Cooper recalled in *A Guide in the Wilderness*, cleared out the "granaries of the Mohawk." The Otsego settlers, who usually relied on that source of supply, were desperate as famine threatened them. The provisions of salt meat and hardtack that Cooper had brought with him for his workmen and himself for the coming year were exhausted within a few days to alleviate the suffering. Then, as they awaited the first fruits of their spring plantings, the settlers turned to what they could forage from the landscape. The lucky had cows they could milk; for others, maple sugar mixed with water provided a syrupy substitute. A great many ate such large quantities of wild leeks that their breath "could be smelled at many paces distance, and when they came together, it was like cattle that had pastured in a garlic field." One unfortunate man mistook a poisonous plant for the wild leek and died from eating it. William Cooper (despite his somewhat condescending view of those leek-eating "cattle") was powerfully affected by the crisis. Petitioning the state for emergency aid, he went off to Albany in the summer to pick up and haul to Otsego by pack train the seventeen hundred bushels of corn that his appeal had produced. This bounty he passed out to each family according to its need. With a kind of biblical flourish, though, the best help came when "unusual shoals of fish were seen moving in the clear waters of the Susquehanna" and up into Lake Otsego. They proved to be herring, a rare visitation so far from the Chesapeake. Thousands were taken with crude nets woven of twigs, then distributed along with salt for their preservation until harvest came.[36]

Other things occupied Cooper's attention in the summer and fall of 1789. In June, he had gone down the Delaware River into northeastern Pennsylvania with hopeful settlers interested in the "Beech Woods," a tract of land for which he had just been hired to serve as settlement agent.[37] Then he apparently returned to Otsego before heading south to Burlington in time for the birth on September 15 of another son—James Cooper, named after a living pair of relatives, his paternal grandfather and uncle. William Cooper probably had come and gone over 1789 as he had in earlier years, and in fact may well have lingered in Burlington from the time of the boy's birth until around Christmas.[38] But the new house intended for the family was finished around the time the baby was born, and Cooper was eager to begin the shift there. As the year's end approached, he therefore returned to Otsego with his eldest son, fourteen-year-old Richard, who was to spend the winter in the woods with his father.

For much of that season Burlington resident and recent Princeton graduate Richard R. Smith joined the two Coopers in their house. Smith, whose family had old ties to the Otsego area, came to Cooper's settlement as a one-third partner and manager for the busy store Cooper began operating late in January

1790.[39] Although his stay in Cooperstown was to last only a few years, he continued to lodge with and became fondly attached to Cooper's family, especially the Cooper sons, with whom he long after maintained friendly relations. Fenimore Cooper, who was to spend time with Smith in Philadelphia when he ran away from home in 1806, repaid Smith's hospitality (and affection) by basing the character of Sheriff Richard Jones of *The Pioneers* on Smith. Smith indeed had become Otsego's first sheriff on the county's official erection in 1791 because of William Cooper's patronage, but there the parallel pretty much ended (*COC* 30).[40]

The opening of the Cooper-Smith store in the winter of 1789–1790 signaled William Cooper's intent to spend his first cold season in Otsego. This plan was another sign of his impatience for the family to make its final transition. Far from desiring to escape from Elizabeth or the society of Burlington and hibernate like a bear holed up in a tree, he had a social disposition and wanted nothing more than to have the other members of his family—beyond son Richard—join him as quickly as possible. Once back in Otsego, he made up for their absence by inaugurating the lavish hospitality for which the homes of the Coopers there were soon to be famous. He celebrated the first holiday season with a party that included Smith as well as Hendrik Frey of Canajoharie, a prominent local figure descended from early German settlers on the Mohawk. Riding around the frozen lake one day in a huge lumber sleigh pulled by four horses, Cooper and company encountered a mysterious Frenchman known as Ebbal, who lived by himself on the lakeshore and was rumored to be the exiled *L'Abbé* de Raffcourt—hence his odd backwards name. Over his vociferous protests, they insisted that Ebbal join them for the ride back to Cooper's house, where "plenty of game, with copious libations of Madeira" awaited. Later it turned out that the man, desperately short of linen, had no shirt to wear under his tightly buttoned coat: it was sheer embarrassment that had kept him from joining the fun when first invited, not misanthropy. Taking pity on his disheveled neighbor, William Cooper forced the Frenchman to don a shirt from his own bureau. The novelist later retold the story as he had heard it from Frey: "'Cooper was so polite,' added the mirth-loving Hendrik Frey, when he repeated the story for the hundredth time, 'that he supplied a shirt with ruffles at the wristbands, which made Ebbal very happy for the rest of the night. Mein Gott, how his hands did go, after he got the ruffles!'" (*COC* 26–28).

Frey was the real life of most parties. William Cooper no doubt had met the companionable man during his passages through Canajoharie, and perhaps already had enjoyed Frey's legendary hospitality in his house there—for Frey's homestead very soon became a regular stop on family itineraries. But Frey was also no stranger in Cooperstown. He was an attractive figure, "with his little black peepers, pipe, hearty laugh, broken English, and warm welcome," as the novelist reminisced in 1834 (*LJ* 3:41), and had many colorful stories to tell. He had vaguely sided with the crown during the Revolution and was arrested and imprisoned by the Patriots for his views, but he had not taken part in the fighting and now, back in control of his extensive lands on the south side of the Mohawk, was prospering there under the new republican dispensation. From him William Cooper and in good time his youngest son derived considerable insight into Frey's close associate, Sir William Johnson, and into the deeper history of the Mohawk valley, where the German's ancestors may have settled even before 1700. On Frey was to be based the equally colorful character of Major Fritz Hartmann in *The Pioneers*, whose Christmastime visit to the Temple mansion was derived from Frey's holiday jaunt in 1789–1790. In that visit lay the obvious source of such fictional details as the perilous mountain journey by lumber sleigh under the inept command of Richard Jones.[41]

The fondly remembered holiday frolic of 1789–1790 put a kind of flourish on family memories about what was in fact an uncertain period for Otsego. In reality, not even William Cooper's energetic presence in his village through those cold months could work magic. The map prepared in 1788 overstated by a good deal what one would have seen on the ground even in the summer of 1790 after the accretions of two more seasons. A census of the village made in the latter year indicated, as the novelist would recall, a mere handful of dwellings and occupants: "seven framed houses, three framed barns, and thirty-five inhabitants" (*COC* 29). Another two or three houses technically outside the village plat were close enough to be reasonably added to such a list, most likely including Monsieur Ebbal's. This was admittedly less progress than the founder probably imagined. And even in Cooper's own family, progress was ponderous at the outset. Although his eldest son's presence was a hopeful sign of the coming shift from Burlington, that shift did not occur once spring arrived. All through the summer following, as a result, the new dwelling overlooking the lake stood virtually empty. Cooperstown was to thrive, but not yet.

A convergence of factors caused the delay. In April, Cooper's partner Andrew Craig wrote to say he had just been at William's rented house in Burlington and could report that his family was "middling well in health"—all, that is, "Except two of [the] youngest Children." If the infant James was one of the two, as may have been the case, his condition surely acted as a brake on the planned move: Mrs. Cooper, after all, had reported to Craig that the two children in question had "something of the Hooping Coff." Though she (and Craig) hastened to add that their condition was "not bad," an infant with that affliction who was still nursing might well call for special treatment. Elizabeth Cooper already had lost at least three infants in previous years—and that in the relative security of Burlington—and surely had no wish to hasten her departure as long as her children's health was questionable. Even if James was not one of the ill children at this time, his tender age on its own would have prompted concern.[42]

Other issues also contributed to the delay. By June, William Cooper was visiting the Beech Woods again in an effort to sell even more land than the year before.[43] His preoccupation with that Pennsylvania tract, no doubt driven by his need to raise cash, put off his long-planned plunge into Otsego. In this sense, his conscious intent and his somewhat frantic business habits were at odds, a fact that reveals a deeper aspect of his character. In what one often assumes was a quieter time, William Cooper was usually in perpetual motion, always seeking to maximize his advantage, and the pattern he established this early was to last through much of his youngest son's boyhood and youth. It also was to engulf most of the Cooper children, whose orbits out of and back into Otsego at times seem to have been as various as the motions of the planets. For the children, often enough, the circulation was intended to expose them to opportunities— educational, cultural, professional—that proved hard to find in early Otsego. For William Cooper, it was driven instead by a deep thirst for wealth and conse- quence in a man who in his early years was often short of means. Ambitious but unable to draw on previously accumulated funds, he occupied a tenuous place in the radically new economic culture that was just then emerging in postwar America.

His manner of participating in the new economy involved two related but often conflicting strategies. First, he secured the necessary means indirectly. He acquired land cheap, as he had in the case of Otsego, then touted its value in face- to-face exchanges with individual purchasers and through articles strategically placed in newspapers. Then he sold land for modest prices, often on liberal terms that bespoke the softness of his own financial (and social) position as much as some sort of social vision. He counted on his charm and charisma to persuade the reluctant and on his continuing presence near them to keep them motivated and engaged. But his active involvement in Otsego also marked his own present impoverishment and his workingman's belief in the primary efficacy of actual labor—manual labor—as opposed to mere capital. Most of all, he could invest *himself* in the Otsego project. Here, his training as a wheelwright showed through. With no reluctance whatsoever he would dive bodily into any venture in which he took an interest. But his faith in the power of such involvement at times bordered on naiveté.

Cooper assumed the Beech Woods agency, and others like it, as a second and potentially more canny means of securing his rise in the world. At a time when the Otsego venture was suffering from famine and the tiny village he had founded there was still in danger of foundering, it was imprudent for Cooper to take on the enormous task of selling other men's land. He undertook the challenging Pennsylvania venture because he would be paid precious cash for his labors and because he craved the good opinion of the wealthy owners of the tract. Chief among the latter was the Philadelphia merchant and industrialist Henry Drinker, a man whose friendship and economic aid might mean more to Cooper than all his efforts in Otsego. The approving acceptance of men like Drinker provided another kind of capital at a time when credit, after all, depended to a large degree on an individual's reputation and credibility. Cooper no doubt rationalized any resulting delays in his Otsego project as contributing to the success of his larger ends. There was a limit to how much land Cooper could acquire in his own right at the time, or to the profits to be earned from his direct labor. Time spent on Drinker's behalf eventually might lead to an expansion of his credit in the relatively closed world of American finance. At a time when fortunes were made and lost because of forces over which individuals had very little control, it was always prudent to have many powerful allies from whom one could borrow money (or draw support) in a crisis. Henry Drinker's friendship would be an asset to be listed on the credit side of William Cooper's books.

All of that sounded good, but in fact Cooper optimistically exaggerated his efficacy as a developer. He ineptly managed the Beech Woods project, selling large blocks of land for no money down to petty speculators rather than small parcels directly to settlers intent on committing themselves to the region. In other words, pressed for time, he cut corners. Five years after his sales there began, a second Drinker agent reported to his employer that "none of those persons who purchased thy lands of William Cooper in the summer of 1789 are now on those lands." *None.* As William Cooper's biographer, Alan Taylor, points out, "Cooper recklessly overestimated the sheer power of his will and the magical effect of his policies." In the process, he wound up costing Henry Drinker and others great sums of money. If he reflected on the weakness of his materialist assumptions, he did not apply corrections to his activities as a developer elsewhere, meaning that his children would inherit the whirlwinds born of his breezy enthusiasm. In fact, the debts that beggared William Cooper's family a decade after his death stemmed from another such agency taken up in the mid-1790s for an Albany investor. There again, Cooper followed his old methods, fallible though they had proved, and wound up owing the investor a large sum of money. Eventually, the interest due on that unpaid debt sank his family.[44]

Not until sometime in September 1790—with the Otsego house ready, the next winter not long distant, the Beech Woods project for the time being set aside, and the infant James now past the critical one-year point—could William Cooper see to it that his family's belongings were packed for the journey north. The decision was a momentous one for Mrs. Cooper and the couple's seven children. Elizabeth never had lived far from her birthplace. She therefore had a fondness for old Burlington and her family ties there, despite (perhaps because of) her parents' deaths over the past two years. And her first harrowing trip to Otsego certainly did not encourage her to budge. Still, as the family was readied for the shift that September, she typically did not resist until it was almost too late to do so. At last, with most of the household furniture loaded on the several wagons forming the caravan, she planted herself firmly in an old Queen Anne armchair, an heirloom recently received from her father's estate, and refused to leave. According to this family legend, William reasoned with her to a point. Then, in the face of her recalcitrance, he bodily picked up chair and woman and put both aboard one of the conveyances. Thereafter, Otsego was to be her domicile, though for a long time it hardly was her home.[45]

The caravan of fifteen or sixteen people—nine family members, plus six or seven domestic servants and slaves—came north by an unrecorded Hudson valley route (*COC* 29).[46] Because of rains that already had hit the valley hard that fall, it may have taken the Coopers several days, perhaps a week or more, to reach Albany, 150 miles upstream. It was now clear that they could not press on with all their gear over what promised to be an even worse route. Hence they arranged to store a good deal of their furniture in Albany until brightening weather dried out the roads.[47] Passing through the Mohawk valley, where the marks of the bitter Revolution still were to be seen, they probably paused at Hendrik Frey's home in Canajoharie before heading up what was known as the old "Continental" route to Springfield, or via Cherry Valley to Middlefield. Another night's stay—perhaps two, given the conditions—along this part of the itinerary ought to have brought them by October 10, tired and sick of it all, to the tiny, rough, stump-strewn village where James Cooper henceforth was to grow up. His mother may have been reconciled to her fate by then. But she may also have seen in this agonizing journey new ammunition for her gathering war against her husband's projects. Over the next several years, she certainly fought hard to get herself—and as many of the children as she could—out of Otsego and back to the civilized world.

Settling In

But here she and they were at last. The house that had been prepared to receive Elizabeth and William and their children, plus the servants and slaves, was soon being called the Manor House in flattering reference to the colonial manors up and down the Hudson valley. The name was partly if not wholly in jest, for the house hardly was manorial. It rose to two stories, an uncommon feature for that time and place, but that was its sole mark of local distinction. Otherwise, as the novelist himself admitted, it was so "roughly built" that it was to be demoted to a storage building once the family's new brick mansion was finished in 1799 (OH 223; *COC* 71). In one of the small, low end wings William Cooper's extensive land dealings probably were centered. Perhaps there was a cellar or part cellar in which food was stored and prepared and the servants and slaves may have lived, but that is not clear. Some years later, according to the novelist, the need for more space was eased by the addition of a rear wing (OH 223). Even at its final size, though, the house provided very little space for all the inhabitants, not to mention lodgers such as Richard R. Smith and the family's frequent guests. At the outset, with parts of the house unfinished and much of the family's furniture waylaid in Albany by the mud, it must have struck Elizabeth Cooper as unaccommodating and spare. And, as it happened, there was scant time to get things organized before her first Otsego winter began. The roads had just dried up and the furniture been forwarded only a short time before ice closed Hudson River navigation south of Albany. The closing came on December 8, an unusually early date, meaning that intense cold had settled in a good week and a half earlier. Through the rest of December, the weather in Albany continued "very severe."[48] In Cooperstown, conditions would be measurably worse. The village stood almost thirteen hundred feet above the river's elevation at Albany, and it was closely set between steep hills that delayed dawn and hurried sunset. When Fenimore Cooper, opening *The Pioneers* on "the Vision" in the failing light of Christmas eve, chose to bury the valley below in "cold gloom," that meteorological event reflected both his emotional bearing on the story of the lost family domain and the typical effect in Otsego in the depths of December (*PIO* 1:60).

Here indeed was a rude awakening for Elizabeth Cooper to the realities of frontier life. At least during her first rough trip in 1788 it had been spring, and the landscape was coming to life. Now that she was living here, and under such conditions, not even the view from the front of the Manor House up the long lake would be very soothing. There was a theoretical beauty in the contrast of the deep green conifers with the bright snowfields from which they arose. But it remained theoretical, probably wholly unseen by Elizabeth Cooper. She no doubt stayed close to the roaring fires that were built on each of the family's hearths. Despite the seemingly endless supply of firewood in the environing forest, however, the dwelling was soon notorious for its chilly feel, on which Elizabeth was to blame her many illnesses in those first years.[49]

For his part, William Cooper remained as busy as usual with his many other undertakings. Among them was an effort to have a new county, centered on Cooperstown, created by the New York legislature. At present, most legal business had to be handled through Montgomery County's offices in Johnstown, forty miles away across the Mohawk. A new county would immensely simplify Cooper's many transactions regarding Otsego lands. It would also put a considerable amount of local patronage in his hands, attract professional men such as lawyers to the village, and make the advent of a newspaper a virtual certainty. In turn, all these developments would enhance Cooper's investments and help ensure that the settlers on his lands (unlike those in the Beech Woods or other similar areas) committed themselves to Otsego. And if the settlers succeeded, the man holding their mortgages could not fail.

Making Cooperstown the seat of the new county, though, was no easy task in the face of rival efforts from other villages such as Cherry Valley. To defeat them, Cooper drew on Federalist friends in Albany, including the "Patroon" (or lord of Van Rensselaer manor), Stephen Van Rensselaer, and prominent merchant Leonard Gansevoort, the future great-uncle of Herman Melville. He also shrewdly drew on a political opponent, the popular military hero and present governor, George Clinton, who could hope to gain Cooper's otherwise unlikely support by siding with him in this battle. Through such deft dealings, Cooper managed to have Otsego County created in the coming winter exactly as he wished. His village also became the new county seat, he became the county's first judge (a title he would wear well past the grave), and his business partner Richard R. Smith became sheriff. Having relocated his family to Otsego, William Cooper had solidified his control over his new home in short order.[50]

Providing the material signs of his institutional victory was the next critical step. Cooper donated a lot on Second (later Main) Street for a hastily finished thirty-foot-square structure to serve as the county building. Visiting lawyer James Kent in 1792 called the log jail on the building's lower level "snug."[51] Upstairs over it was the framed courtroom, which also provided the first space in the village suitable for various other purposes, including the village school Cooper's youngest children were to attend. Next door on the same lot stood a tavern occupied by the jailer, who handily provided a jury room as well. Less direct effects of the county-seat drive included an almost immediate building boom through the village. So many other structures went up in 1791 that by year's end, as the novelist later estimated, the village boasted twenty houses and stores and the population had reached about one hundred, a threefold increase over the 1790 count (*COC* 31).[52]

As expected, lawyers soon began locating in the village, eager to garner a share of the new business to be transacted in and near the courthouse. One of them, James Kent's younger brother Moss Kent, Jr., was to be of special importance to the Coopers and to James Cooper in particular. After Kent's store in nearby Springfield failed (partly, one suspects, because of stiff competition from Cooper and Smith's operation), William Cooper became the young lawyer's patron. He erected a law office for him, made him his agent, and invited him to lodge for free in the Manor House. Cooper also exerted his newly acquired political influence for Kent, who was appointed Otsego County surrogate by the state in March 1794, a position that assured his financial recovery. Grateful for this help, Kent relished his new consequence in Cooperstown and among the Coopers in particular. By 1795, he already had begun to fancy Cooper's eldest daughter, eighteen-year-old Hannah. He also had acquired the admiration of Hannah's youngest brother, whose first surviving letter, signed "James K. Cooper" in March 1800, records that admiration in its self-given middle initial, reputedly derived from Kent's family name (*LJ* 1:7).[53]

In between arriving at the Manor House and receiving that tribute from young James Cooper, to be sure, Kent had antagonized Judge Cooper by opposing him politically. But that conflict, perhaps motivated by Cooper's earlier triumph over him in business affairs, certainly did not end Kent's warm feelings for the young Coopers (nor, for that matter, did it permanently alienate Kent from the Judge). Kent's ties to the Cooper establishment were deeper than his political differences with its patriarch. Early in 1795, prior to the political troubles, Kent had written his brother that he was enormously happy at the Manor House. "I never lived more agreeably in my Life," he confessed. "Mrs. C[ooper] I think is a very fine woman & both she & the judge treat me with almost *parental* attention. . . . They have three little Boys from 5 to 9 who are as sweet & lovely little fellows as ever [were] born of a woman & they are extremely fond of me."[54]

Moss Kent's importance to one "lovely little fellow" in the Manor House, five-year-old James Cooper, points to the social changes that came with the physical expansion of Cooperstown in these earliest years. The boy's feelings at the same time underscore the rapidity with which he began gathering his own lasting impressions of the nascent village. Some of the latter surfaced in *The Pioneers*, others in *The Chronicles of Cooperstown* (1838), his little handbook of local history. Cooper's sensibility and the village seemed to be coeval. As the boy watched, something like a village center thus began to develop just a block west of his house, around what became known as the Four Corners, the intersection where the courthouse-cum-jail-cum-school and the adjoining tavern had been erected in 1791. Soon other businesses were being established in that same area. They were mostly small in scale and, as Moss Kent's experience in nearby Springfield suggests, unstable. Most shopkeepers in Cooperstown as elsewhere in the American countryside at the time had little capital, and the partnerships aimed at aggregating it were more often productive of disagreement than mutual aid.

Even Richard R. Smith, William Cooper's friend and partner, soon vacated his arrangement with the Judge and in 1794, four years after arriving to help set up and run the village's first store, moved back to the Delaware valley. As he successfully pursued the ampler opportunities of the Philadelphia market, he

often pined for his happy days in Cooperstown. But he did not permanently return there. Owing to such changes, when the novelist recalled in the 1830s the
early commercial landscape of the village, he could name very few shops or taverns or other concerns that had lasted from the first years into his adulthood.
Change, which had produced Otsego in so short a period, continued to mark its
early life. It would also be a hallmark of the founding family's life over the
decades following.[55]

CHAPTER TWO

Lessons

For Cooper the next big change was school. Otsego surrounded him with fresh sights that left deep impressions, but formal instruction there was so improvised and haphazard that most of his siblings had to be sent elsewhere for various periods, and he was to fare no better.[1] His father, to be sure, tried to improve the local situation in the mid-1790s by luring recent Yale graduate Joshua Dewey to Cooperstown. Judge Cooper's scheme was ambitious: he wished to found a local classical academy to prepare the best students, his youngest son hopefully among them, for college and the learned professions. And Dewey, a bright and witty man who had gone to Yale from Nathan Tisdale's famous academy in Lebanon, Connecticut, clearly was an excellent choice for the job. But, with William Cooper's promised "Otsego Academy" building unfunded and unbuilt, the increasingly disenchanted Dewey spent two years or so running a humble grammar school that, with young Cooper among the students, recited its ABCs above the jail in that multipurpose courthouse. Such a dose of frontier reality was enough to make the Latin scholar abandon teaching and revert to farming (his father's calling) and, eventually, politics. Only then, at last prompted to action, did Judge Cooper donate his own land for the academy and, with a sizable cash gift, launch a subscription drive to pay for its construction. But Dewey, a man of decisive habits, had had enough; not even the building's completion in 1796–1797 could convince him that Otsego was indeed ready for his talents. The next year, he successfully ran for the state legislature.[2]

Once erected, the Otsego Academy in fact served less lofty purposes. When a visiting minister delivered a sermon in it before the newly organized Cooperstown Masonic lodge in 1796, he initiated the practice of using the big neoclassical box as "a servant of all work," as the novelist put it in *Home as Found* (1838)— "for education, balls, preaching, town-meetings, and caucuses" (*HAF* 2:104). But never, as it happened, for the academy that it had been built to house. "All attempts at classical instruction" in the village failed, Cooper recalled in 1838: "Nothing superior to a common English education was ever taught in this [building]" (*COC* 41).[3]

As a mark of diminished expectations, the village grammar school soon was allowed to relocate to the new structure. Its teacher for many years would be Oliver Cory, a modest man who had enjoyed few of Dewey's advantages but who exerted a strong influence over Cooper and remained his friend for the rest of his life. Born in the farming community of Littleton, Massachusetts, Cory had moved with his parents to the New Hampshire frontier while still a boy. His one special talent, a facility in music, had revealed itself so early that by the time he turned twelve in 1776 he already had put in more than a year's service as a fifer in various frontline American military units. Following his war duty, the still very young Cory returned to New Hampshire, then moved to Otsego around 1793. He seems to have had little formal education beyond the common training available in rural New England, and he almost certainly never attended an academy, let alone a college. Even as an old man, however, he exhibited remarkably fine penmanship and could produce formal prose with real skill. An example of both survives in a letter he wrote in 1836, when he was seventy-two, to the U. S. commissioner of pensions, which begins: "In obedience to the requisition contain'd in your Letter of the 14th . . . to the Hon. S. Page, and from him to Henry Scott, Esq., wherein a more explicit explanation is required of me, I make the following statement with my own head and hands." If Joshua Dewey revealed Yale's classical polish upstairs at Cooperstown's courthouse, Oliver Cory there and elsewhere was a living example of the ordinary Yankee's sturdy self-reliance.[4]

Under his second teacher, Cooper learned the basics: "Oliver Cory . . . taught me to read," Cooper reminisced in Paris in 1831, adding in *Chronicles of Cooperstown* that Cory had done the same for nearly all the village children from the late 1790s through about 1805 (*LJ* 2:89; *COC* 39). In 1800, the boy wrote his father what is his earliest surviving letter, reporting, "I go to school to Mr. Cory where I write and cypher." The letter itself was proof of the teacher's success in the former lesson. As if to indicate the sort of computational lessons Cory gave his pupils, Cooper added a postscript: "18 Century, 1800" (*LJ* 1:6–7). This seemingly cryptic note indicates that Oliver Cory regarded the present year as the last of the old century, not the first of the new, and was enforcing his view of that much-debated truth on the schoolroom.[5]

Cory, who spent the rest of his long life in and near Cooperstown, was remembered fondly by his pupils and even his pupils' children. Among those who knew him well was Cooper's daughter Susan. She thought him especially good for the post because he was "upright, firm in discipline, yet patient and kindly by nature." While he obviously focused on basic lessons, Cory brought some variety to the classroom. His interest in music, for instance, led him to give the students a sudden recess when the new player organ installed in the nearby Cooper house in 1799 sent the patriotic strains of "Hail! Columbia" out into the village streets (*P&P* 49; *PIO* HE viii).[6] But Cory's special love was drama. He arranged annual exhibitions during which villagers thronged into the academy to watch his pupils, several dozen in number, hold forth in recitations from Shakespeare and other writers. Cooper recalled occasions when Brutus and Cassius, carrying wooden swords and wearing tricorn hats and blue coats with red lapels, murdered Julius Caesar (and no doubt Shakespeare's verse) there on the makeshift stage (*COC* 41). His daughter added an anecdote about how her father, when just eight years old, dressed up in "a faded cloak" and bent over a staff to give a "moving recitation" of what she knew as "The Beggar's Petition," a 1766 poem by British poet Thomas Moss. Cooper probably was using the slightly shorter (and less political) version of 1769, which begins:

> Pity the sorrows of a poor old man!
> Whose trembling limbs have borne him to your door,
> Whose days are dwindled to the shortest span.
> Oh! give relief—and heaven will bless your store.

This episode remained permanently fixed in Cooper's memory. When, as late as 1850, he met octogenarian Cory on the road outside Cooperstown and asked him home for what probably proved a last chat, their memories inevitably turned to Cooper's recitation of Moss's poem (*P&P* 49–50).[7]

Cory was a performer in his own right. His service during the Revolution hardly had been critical to the nation's founding but still provided him with a fund of anecdotes and an excuse for rehearsing them before his admiring young audience. He also seems to have embellished them. A tale about the Marquis de Lafayette preserved by Cooper from the late 1790s suggests as much: "I remember the deep, reverential, I might almost say awful, attention, with which a school of some sixty children, on a remote frontier, listened to the tale of

[Lafayette's] sufferings in the castle of Olmutz, as it was recounted to us by the instructor, who had been a soldier in his youth, and fought the battles of his country, under the orders of the 'young and gallant Frenchman'" (*Notions* 1:38–39).

This was stirring, but in fact Cory had cribbed his information about the Frenchman's imprisonment in the Austrian dungeon of Olmutz from the Cooperstown newspaper. More to the point, he never could have served under Lafayette: his pension application officially claimed service only in the earliest period of the war, from July 1775 to February 1777, months before Lafayette arrived in America.[8] Cory nonetheless was an impressive source on American origins. His tales of military activities around New York City in the fall of 1776, for instance, and particularly of his own unit's participation in the battle of White Plains that October, may have resurfaced years later to provide some background color for the largely extramilitary action of Cooper's *The Spy,* set in Westchester in 1780 (*Spy* 1:148, 2:137). And he had personally seen George Washington close-up and doubtless told his pupils so. Here were things that informed them about the nation's past but also helped shape their feelings as young Americans. In Cooper's Quakerish household, the Revolution was a largely silent chapter. In Oliver Cory's school, it was an episode rich in emotional and narrative possibilities.[9]

Cooper's attendance at Cory's school from 1796 to 1799 was often interrupted because, like his older siblings, he was sent away for better educational opportunities elsewhere. In his case, the removals had added urgency because Mrs. Cooper's chronic distaste for the frontier became acute as winter approached in 1796, and again in 1797 and 1798, forcing her to decamp with her two youngest sons and head off to the familiar precincts of Burlington.[10] The year before her first flight, when Judge Cooper, having been elected to Congress, overwintered in Philadelphia for its 1795–1796 session, she had been stuck in the cold and drafty Manor House and developed a lengthy, apparently serious illness. Not only was she "weakly" and "very thin"—she was also "very low-spirited," the congressman's former assistant Moss Kent wrote him on April 21. Missing her husband so much that she wanted him to come home before Congress ended its session, Mrs. Cooper forwarded an ultimatum. She was so "very unhappy" in Cooperstown that Kent conveyed her explicit orders to the congressman: "you should engage a House at Burlington before you return as it is her determination never to spend another winter in this country."[11]

William Cooper rented no such house for her. Instead, on arriving back in Cooperstown the following June, he busied himself with plans for replacing the family's rough-sided, timber-framed first house with a much more substantial brick dwelling, where he imagined Elizabeth would at last feel at home. His absorption in other matters at the time, however, meant that he could take care of only the preliminaries right then (*COC* 45; OH 224).[12] As a result, when he returned to Congress in the fall of 1796, his wife and two youngest sons went with him as far as the old Jersey capital, where he left them to settle in for the next several months. This sudden change in living arrangements, motivated largely by Mrs. Cooper's self-concern, in fact exposed the boys to promising new resources. Soon after arriving, they were placed in the apparently tutorial care of Patrick Higgins, "a well-known Irish pedagogue" (as Cooper described him many years later [*LJ* 4:498]) who trained them further in "English" subjects and perhaps devoted some time to preliminary classical studies even during that first winter as well.[13]

Barely had the boys begun their work with Higgins, however, when it was threatened with disruption. At the time the four Coopers left Otsego, the congressman was being favored to win reelection in December. If he did, he would have another two years in Philadelphia—meaning that Mrs. Cooper probably would expect to remain in (or at least regularly return to) Burlington across that whole period. In January, before the election returns were known, she gave up her temporary lodgings and moved into a long-term rental with the boys, obviously ready for a considerable stay.[14] Later that very month, however, it became clear that William Cooper had lost to his opponent. Soon after his current lame duck term was up early in March, he therefore packed up and went home to Otsego. But Mrs. Cooper, ensconced in her lodgings, stayed put, and Patrick Higgins kept on teaching her sons until as late as June or July. Then she also pulled up stakes and went back to Otsego with Samuel and James.[15]

The three of them passed the summer of 1797 there, but within three months or so left again—this time on their own, since William Cooper had no cause to return to Philadelphia.[16] In their absence, he pushed ahead with the new mansion, probably with the understanding that it would be ready for occupancy the following winter. Yet once again the work went so slowly that, when his wife returned with the boys late in June or early in July 1798, it was far behind schedule (see OH 224–25), a disappointment that stoked Elizabeth Cooper's assertiveness into open rebellion. Now determined to return to Burlington for good, in September of 1798 she therefore talked or bargained or forced her husband into purchasing—not just renting—a house for her in Burlington. Then off she went again, dragging the boys along for yet another stint, perhaps permanent this time, in her little city on the Delaware.[17]

Now it was that the boys, discovering the truth of the matter, staged their own rebellion, extorting from their relenting mother a return to the "lake" and their "haunts" along its shores (*LJ* 4:498). Within a month, Judge Cooper was rushing down to Burlington once again, not quite sure what was happening, knowing only that he was to escort the three exiles back to Otsego. From the old

Jersey capital early in October, he therefore wrote his oldest son, Richard, informing him that Mrs. Cooper had changed her mind and instructing him to ready the old Manor House for the family's sudden and unexpected return.[18] All was in turmoil, but Elizabeth Cooper was shrewd enough to use it to her own advantage. On her return to Otsego, her husband freshly promised that the new mansion would be finished with all due speed, a major concession, and he soon had carpenters living inside it across the winter in order to do the finish work. But he exacted his own price for this accommodation. In order to prevent a recurrence of the crisis, he permitted his wife to go to Burlington, as the novelist recalled, "no more" (*LJ* 4:498). Reelected to Congress in April 1798 for a term that was to run from December 1799 to March 1801, Cooper left Cooperstown for Philadelphia in the fall of 1799—and, true to his resolve, he went alone.[19] Never again did Elizabeth Cooper, as far as we can tell, leave Otsego County, let alone New York State. Rarely indeed, would she even leave the mansion that was finally ready to receive her in June 1799.

Otsego Hall

The new house had powerful effects on all members of the family, including Elizabeth Cooper's youngest son. Although he spent more time overall in the old house, the new one would provide the setting for most of his boyhood memories. When he wrote *The Pioneers*, for instance, he modeled Marmaduke Temple's mansion on his family's second house, not the first one.[20] Small wonder. To begin with, the old dwelling had been sited on a busy, noisy street, whereas the new one was set in the center of an enlarged, insulated, green park. Most lots in Cooperstown were so small that residents constantly bumped emotional elbows with each other. Not so the Coopers, whose mansion lay at the far end of an allée of exotic, newly fashionable Lombardy poplars. About the property, amidst "squares divided by straight, formal gravel walks," Judge Cooper established a vineyard, fruit trees, and flower and kitchen gardens. Everything was genteel and ample. With barns and stables hidden along a lane on the western margin of the grounds, the mansion enjoyed a focused vista down through the poplars to the shimmering surface of the lake that the boy had missed so much during his last visit to Burlington (OH 227).[21]

Indoors, the new house had its own rich delights. The novelist's 1840 reminiscence of Otsego Hall, aimed at recovering "the original distribution" of affairs there (that is, the way things were in the years 1799–1801), reveals that great care had gone into its design and construction (OH 225).[22] Compared with the old dwelling, Otsego Hall was much larger in plan, higher off the ground and higher overall, finer in detail, and substantially better in materials and finish. But it was not just the local cynosure. Judge Cooper set an exalted standard by choosing his friend Stephen Van Rensselaer's elegant 1760s Manor House in Albany as his model, and he refused to settle for a cheapened frontier version of that famous urban mansion.[23] The carpentry contract indicates that his imitation, at sixty-six by fifty feet, was roughly the same size as the core of Van Rensselaer's original. Each of the two main floors thus had in excess of three thousand square feet of finished space, enormous for mid-eighteenth-century Albany but completely unexampled in the central and western parts of the state in the 1790s.[24] More surprisingly, Cooper's interior resembled Van Rensselaer's in its elaborate plan and fine decor. In both structures, the biggest room (called "the great hall") stretched from front to back at the center of the first level, taking up one thousand square feet. And both great halls were equally well finished, boasting elaborate crown moldings, thick chair rails, and wainscot paneling. On the front and back walls of each, massive entry doors were capped with elaborate pediments and flanked by oversize windows and deep window seats.[25]

Cooper's insistence on heavy decoration extended even to the half-dozen other rooms entered off his great hall, suggesting the seriousness of his social ambitions. The carpentry contract speaks a language of thoroughness and weight, not mere show or anxious speed—one reason why, beyond his obvious foot-dragging, it took Cooper so long to see the project to completion. Yet there was an irony in all of this. Once achieved, the elevated tone he labored so hard to create did not really suit him or the rest of the family. The tension is apparent in the way the family soon came to occupy and use the house, and especially the great hall. As designed, the hall was notable for its lavish inutility. Here were to be displayed the trophies of the family's rise that the novelist would recall in *The Pioneers* or his 1840 reminiscence—things that would impress visitors, like the first piano west of Schenectady. Yet this cavernous temple to success was so cut off from the household's ordinary realities that it did not even hold the stairs leading up to the bedrooms or down to the kitchen. So mundane a thing as vertical circulation had to take place offstage, in an awkward side hallway reached via one of the five sidewall doors. How could such an elegant barn inspire domestic feeling?[26]

Oddly, however, the great hall soon became the Cooper family's favorite living space. The fancy dining room and drawing room that took up the whole west end of the first floor were, as Cooper recalled, virtually unused, their intended functions having been quickly absorbed back into the great hall (OH 225). The Quaker wheelwright himself probably shared some of his family's discomfort with the elaborate plan of the house, but it was Mrs. Cooper, somewhat surprisingly, who showed a special fondness for using the great hall for most daily purposes. In the years following her husband's death, Elizabeth

Cooper doted here over her increasingly large collection of native and exotic plants, before which in 1816 she posed for her only surviving portrait (Plate 3). The plants were not to impress visitors—they were to amuse and fulfill the matriarch herself, whose first-floor bedroom lay off to the east side of the hall.[27]

When the novelist drew on the interior of the family house for his third novel, it was the great hall that provided the richest details (see *PIO* CE 9; *LJ* 4:77, 258). Some items visible in the 1816 watercolor (the truncated settee, the barometer, the country chairs scattered amid such high-cult items) made their way into the fictional pastiche. Others did not. The biggest absences were associated with Mrs. Cooper. Appropriately enough, in fact, the novelist had last seen her here in the great hall, sitting in her chair amid her plants, when he and his small family, leaving Otsego for Westchester in the summer of 1817, went to bid her farewell.[28] The novel reimagined that physical setting, but without the greenery—and without his mother or an obvious substitute for her. When the young heroine of *The Pioneers* comes back to visit her father just before Christmas of 1793, she enters the widower's house and immediately feels the palpable absence of her dead mother.

Bereft parents are a novelistic staple, of course, because they simplify a plot's emotional outline. But the absence of a mother from Cooper's novel is in fact only apparent. The daughter who bears his own mother's name, young Elizabeth, carries several burdens in the book. She is, for one thing, the author's own proxy, since Cooper also wrote himself out of his story. But Elizabeth Temple's heaviest burden has to do with the mother who was not strictly a mother—Cooper's sister Hannah. His memories of Otsego Hall were especially bound up with Hannah, whose accidental death on September 10, 1800, five days before the boy's eleventh birthday, had put an abrupt end to the family's enjoyment of its new home (*COC* 55).[29] The effect on Hannah's youngest brother was especially severe because Hannah had come to fill the vacancy left by Elizabeth Cooper's growing remoteness after the last return from Burlington in October of 1798. Hence his seemingly conventional term for Hannah (she had been "a second mother" more than a sister) in an 1832 footnote to *The Pioneers* (*PIO* CE 233n) in fact expressed the young woman's deep emotional significance.

Hannah was more like Elizabeth Cooper's successor than her supplement. For long, relatively uninterrupted periods over the 1790s, Cooper had spent time with few other members of the family except his mother. In Burlington, especially, she was *his* (and Samuel's) mother, freed from her responsibilities in Otsego and apparently at ease in her most familiar world. Mrs. Cooper was the person always *there* as Cooper was moved about from place to place and as the other members of the family came and went their separate ways. That he and Samuel could force her hand in Burlington in 1798 suggests two things: that the boys really did feel rootless and yearned for the stability that a settled home, especially one near their woods and lake, could yield—and that Mrs. Cooper, whatever her own yearnings, indeed could put their interests first. But the boys paid for this victory. Once back in Otsego, Elizabeth Cooper began a steady withdrawal into a world of her own, a world that after June of 1799 was more and more synonymous with the great hall of the new house.

Hannah hardly was waiting to rush in as soon as the matriarch began her retreat. William Cooper's prize daughter, she had been given extraordinary opportunities that took her far away before 1799. She thus had spent much of the previous decade apart from her youngest brother and most of the rest of the family. She was studying in New York City in 1791 and 1792, passed the early winter of 1794–1795 in Albany, and went with her father to Philadelphia for his attendance at Congress in both 1795 and 1796. She was back in Philadelphia in 1798, first on her own and then once again with her father.[30] Hannah probably returned to Cooperstown in a serious way only during 1799, as the new house was readied and the family was set to begin enjoying it. Young James Cooper therefore could not have known her at all well before this time, as I think is suggested by the fictional homecoming with which *The Pioneers* opens.[31] That episode, in which the novelist abandoned his own memories and instead took up the imagined perspective of Hannah's surrogate in the tale, must have been based on the trip that brought Hannah not only home to Cooperstown but, for the first time, home to *him*. His closeness to her in 1800 was of quite recent origin.[32]

A second important aspect of Hannah's relationship with Cooper just prior to her death was its urgency. Before 1798, regardless of Hannah's whereabouts, the role as a "second mother" had not been hers or anyone else's to fill. Not until the collapse of the actual mother's will, starting with her truncated rebellion in Burlington in 1798, would it begin to be available. On that soon followed Elizabeth Cooper's immuration of herself within not just the Cooper grounds and Otsego Hall but even more within the hall of the Hall, where, as she built the artifice of that indoor garden, she could close out or ignore the world—including in some ways the rest of her family. The woman who could not be kept in Cooperstown before the fall of 1798 still was not there in any vital social sense. Or, and this amounted to the same thing, she was so intensely present in her own world that she seemed the prisoner of powerful centripetal forces. When a British emigrant came to Cooperstown in 1809 and visited Otsego Hall, he found William Cooper to be a "kindly" host but described Elizabeth as "a little outre [*sic*]" and "rather odd"—"an active, stirring little woman, rather plain in her manners and a little contradictory withal."[33]

Hannah, who turned twenty-one a couple of months before her mother's 1798 rebellion collapsed, filled the resulting void. Not that Hannah exactly fit her new role. She had been trained by her father, obviously, for other and "better" things. He intended her for art and culture, which gave her charms that various friends and acquaintances repeatedly noticed. In the fall of 1795, when Hannah was back for a brief visit in Cooperstown, she had such an effect on the visiting French aristocrat and former cleric Charles Maurice de Talleyrand that he penned an acrostic singing her virtues.[34] Talleyrand's spatial equivocation in the poem linked *Otsego* and *Paris* as an indication of how the American charmer brought civilized graces to the American borderland:

> Otsego is hardly gay—but habit is all.
> Paris, too, would much displease you at first sight.

The courtier's wit struck closer to the center of young Hannah's psyche than he could have imagined. She was a tense compound of the local and the faraway, so much so that after her return to Cooperstown in 1799 she recoiled from the rough surfaces there and, like her mother at an earlier time, wanted most of all to leave. Cooper thought the family's experience following its move to the new house decidedly happy, but in fact Hannah found the frontier village tedious. In September 1799, by which point she had been in Cooperstown for some months and her father was about to go off to Congress (without her for once), she wrote a friend in Philadelphia to lament her now seemingly permanent rustication: "I do not know when I shall again emerge from these northern forests. My sister [Ann Cooper] sets a noble example. She is willing to remain at home through the winter provided that I will."[35] It was fine for Talleyrand to suggest that Hannah Cooper could "read—think—write" *au milieu des deserts*, "in the midst of the wilds." It was quite another thing for Hannah herself to be deprived of Paris (or its nearest American equivalent, Philadelphia) all through the long Otsego winter. "These northern forests" was her term for what oppressed her, and a curiously vague and general term it was at that. Had she ever *really* come home?

But why, after all, was Hannah Cooper stranded in Otsego for what would prove her last winter on earth? It is likely that her congressman father would have welcomed her once again as an alluring hostess for the duration of this new session of Congress, for which he left Cooperstown in November 1799.[36] Presumably the situation at Otsego Hall dictated the actual arrangement: Hannah was deprived, that is, precisely because the new house needed a family resident in it—and that family required, in Judge Cooper's view, a ruling female presence to set the proper tone and manage everything entailed by life in the big new mansion. Hannah's skills are doubtless reflected in those displayed by Elizabeth Temple when, returning to find her father's household under the rule of Remarkable Pettibone in *The Pioneers*, she firmly subordinates that woman's authority to her own. Certainly Hannah, overseeing practical affairs in Otsego

Hall, reported to her absent father on how things were going.[37] But she also took emotional charge of the family. As Mrs. Cooper's presence faded, her youngest son found in Hannah, chambered next to him upstairs at the east end of the mansion, a feminine guide closer to him in age and spirit as well as space. Here was the mother he might have wished for as he came to terms with all the recent upheavals in the family's tumultuous life.

And then, with a sudden stroke, he lost her. On the morning of Wednesday, September 10, 1800, while Cooper and his parents and Ann and Samuel remained at home, Hannah mounted a spirited English mare and accompanied her oldest brother Richard on a visit to the Morris family in Butternuts, twenty-five miles away over rough, hilly roads. Hannah, an excellent horsewoman, managed very well until the last stretch of the arduous journey, when, as her youngest brother recalled many years later, "the mare suddenly jumped aside at a dog, threw its rider, and killed Miss Cooper, on the spot" (OH 227).[38] The rough frontier road was as much to blame as any other factor: Hannah came down hard against a tree root, fracturing her skull. In an instant, Talleyrand's "cheerful philosopher in the springtime of her age" lay dead on the late summer earth.

Old Jacob Morris, patriarch of the Butternuts clan, sent his son Richard to bear the tragic news through the midnight hills to Otsego Hall. Early the next morning, Judge Cooper drove a wagon back over the same route with a handful of friends, picked up the corpse, turned around, and arrived at Otsego Hall under a dim, late-rising moon. His youngest son, who would turn eleven four days later, always recalled the precise moment when the grim procession arrived and how the realization at last hit him. The date etched in his memory was not September 10, the day Hannah died, but rather September 11, the day her corpse came home.[39]

Never could that poplar-lined lane leading in from the street seem quite as precisely cut or as capable of closing out disagreeable facts as it had before this awful night. There, out front in a box resting in a wagon, was the "second mother" Cooper had only lately come to know well. He must have been in the great hall when the doors were propped open to bring the burden in, and seen everything. Certainly he always recalled what happened next. The box was carried up the stairs and inside, then across the great hall and into the southwest room overlooking the rear garden. Here, along the partition dividing that room from the great hall, was an old family piece, an heirloom table Mrs. Cooper had brought north with her from Burlington. The coffin was put on it for the night, and then family members retired for whatever rest they could get. The next day, the funeral was held in the great hall, a grim initiation of that space in its more public functions. Aside from Isaac, then in Philadelphia, and William, at Princeton, Judge Cooper's remaining children were all present, the boys sitting by his side facing the coffin. The surely distraught Mrs. Cooper and her remaining daughter, Ann, stayed out of sight in the parents' bedroom at the front of the first floor of the house (OH 228).

Thirty-seven-year-old Daniel Nash, a Massachusetts native and Yale graduate then serving as an Episcopal missionary on the Otsego frontier, conducted the service, preaching a pertinent if heart-wrenching sermon on Job 7:9–10: "As the cloud is consumed and vanisheth away: so he that goeth down to the grave shall come up no more. He shall return no more to his house, neither shall his place know him any more."[40] The funereal wit of the second verse ran through all Nash had to say that day and must have struck deep in the minds of the Coopers. No doubt it also affected many in the "very large concourse of weeping citizens" come to pay their respects and, probably, to catch a first glimpse of the magnificent interior of Otsego Hall. As family members and visitors sat or stood about the great room, Nash reminded them that no house, however grand or seemingly permanent, could protect even so "affectionate and tender" a child as Hannah Cooper from the assaults of the world.[41] For the future novelist, who remembered the details of this day with sharp definition decades later, the pain of Hannah's absence was keen. As if to drive home the feeling, Nash reiterated: "She went out from her father's house to return no more to it—neither shall this place know her any more." Nash tried to moralize the event for Hannah's siblings, to whom he addressed a separate lesson, but it wasn't morality that mattered. Morality wouldn't make up the loss. Nothing would.[42]

After the sermon, Hannah's coffin was borne out the front doors and taken around to a parcel of land across the street from the kitchen garden and vineyard, behind the southeast corner of the mansion's grounds. The semiwild lot, already scattered with makeshift tombstones, one day would be the location of the Episcopal churchyard, as Susan Fenimore Cooper noted in giving a bit of village history in *Rural Hours*.[43] As Cooper's daughter also surely knew, the churchyard itself was Hannah's greatest tangible memorial. Her burial there must have been responsible for the decision to locate Christ Church nearby a few years later, after which Hannah's grave, soon joined by that of her father, formed the center of a rapidly expanding Cooper plot. Perhaps in a similar way, Daniel Nash's role in the funeral may have helped decide William Cooper to formalize his own evolving relationship with the Episcopal faith, rooted in the long vacillation of his ancestors between the Quaker way and its Anglican source and competitor. More importantly, Hannah Cooper, dying young, helped root the family more deeply still in their rough new home on the New York frontier.[44]

Hannah Cooper was buried on September 12, 1800. For the relatives she left behind, life only slowly emerged from the shadows. Soon the wife of Rev. Thomas Ellison of St. Peter's Church in Albany, concerned that Hannah's sister

Ann would fall victim to "the gloom attending a residence at Cooperstown when deprived of an only Sister," wished her to spend the winter in the capital.[45] The gloom was more general. It probably was good that Hannah's father had to go off to Congress again that fall. He was in Washington by mid-November and could lose himself in the government's busy transition from Philadelphia to its new capital—if not in the proper business of the House. But any diversion derived from these activities would be short-lived. Well before Hannah's death, William Cooper had declined to run again for his seat, and by the time Congress adjourned the following March he would be done with affairs there for good. To be sure, the election of 1800, which resulted in the famous tie vote between Thomas Jefferson and Aaron Burr in the electoral college and the final adjudication by the House after New Year's, would give him a part to play in resolving this national crisis. But once Cooper's candidate—Aaron Burr—had lost, there was really no political future for him or other Federalists on the national scene. The defeat of the Federalist Party coming on the heels of Hannah's death made the fall of 1800 and the winter following doubly somber to William Cooper.[46]

With Mrs. Cooper in retreat, all Judge Cooper really had left now was the other children, for whom his various schemes—most already in play—began to attract more concern than usual. At the start of 1801, the lame duck congressman arranged for Samuel Cooper to receive a midshipman's warrant from the navy, although with the understanding that the fourteen-year-old would enter the service only when his studies were completed.[47] Later in 1801, Isaac, then in Philadelphia serving an apprenticeship in a commercial firm, would be stationed in Cooperstown and soon Albany so that he could attend to the partnership his father recently had set up for his benefit with Albany merchant Daniel Hale.[48]

For Isaac's older brother and eventual business partner Richard, an even more ambitious effort was under way. Owing to disruption of trade by the Napoleonic Wars, a worrisome shortage of copper had developed in the United States. Rumors of rich deposits around the Great Lakes led Congress, at Representative Cooper's insistence, to support exploration there: the administration of John Adams therefore was directed in April of 1800 to secure "all material information" relative to especially promising mines on the south shore of Lake Superior.[49] Drawing on his ties with Adams, William Cooper eventually succeeded in having his eldest son named to carry out the errand. At first, the coming winter and the impending change of administrations forced delays; then at the last minute the whole expedition was canceled. But for several months in between, the Cooper family had been astir with thoughts of the far frontier where Richard was poised to proceed. Thereafter, denied the opportunity, the frustrated explorer moved on to other things. Having been admitted as an attorney before New York's Supreme Court of Judicature (which handled both original cases and appeals) in the spring of 1797, he at least had the law to fall back on.[50]

For his third son and namesake, William Cooper continued a course of action begun before Hannah's death. Impressed by the boy's dawning skills and determined he would make a fine lawyer and politician, Cooper aimed to get the fifteen-year-old into Princeton. Through his friend and fellow Byberry native Benjamin Rush, Cooper secured young William's admission—and his acceptance as a boarder at the home of the college's president, Samuel Stanhope Smith. Early in 1800, the boy therefore left Otsego for the trip south with Isaac, just then bound for Philadelphia. Shortly after matriculating, he made such a good first impression that his father began to think of sending him abroad, to Edinburgh or London, after college.[51]

The boy, who had other things on his mind, certainly enjoyed college. By the summer of 1801, nine months after the death of his sister, he was so jovial that he wrote and sent home a verse letter summarizing his experiences and poking fun at his rusticated siblings, Ann and Samuel, who were stuck in Otsego. As for himself, he added that he was known at Princeton as "the famous hopper"—explaining in a footnote, "you must know that I can jump 28 feet in 3 hops."[52] This was not, of course, the kind of fame his father wished for him. A month later, President Smith wrote Judge Cooper, now back in Cooperstown, raising concerns that, despite his good health and "usual good conduct & application to his studies," William was running up rather large tabs around town. Perhaps on purpose, the boy had neglected to give his father some local merchants' bills, which Smith now forwarded for payment. "He dresses very genteelly," Smith commented in noting that the boy's shoemaker's bill was "higher than I was aware." When Smith attempted an explanation, it should have become a cause of some concern in the student's father: "there is no appearance of extravagance, except that I do not think he wears his clothes as long as he might do. And perhaps he hires a horse & carriage in the evening more frequently than is strictly necessary for his amusement." By such frivolous means, Judge Cooper's great plans for William eventually were to be laid low.[53]

William's fall was to become a warning for his youngest brother, for whom the story had many morals that no doubt were insistently drawn for him over the future. From late September 1801 to February of the following year, the fifteen-year-old collegian's account at one Princeton store included a good deal of alcohol—brandy, Madeira, and wine, often by the gallon—as well as such other articles as "25 Spanish Segars" among more proper expenses for books, pens, and paper.[54] The accompanying high jinks were also becoming more serious and more public. President Smith, always upbeat, still thought well of the boy's academic work, although he now began to admit to Judge Cooper that young

William's "reliance on your fortune . . . makes him less sensible of the value of money than I think he ought to be."[55] The Otsego patriarch, already concerned, had tried to control the boy's spending by having one shopkeeper enforce a blanket prohibition of certain articles, but William defied him and the merchant caved in. There was a larger problem, as the merchant wrote Judge Cooper: a "spirit of Licentiousness and Depravity of Manners which is becoming too general in this Institution. Houses [have] been erected in this place for the resort of Students where scenes of disapation intoxication and gluttony have been acted[,] in consiquence of which, many of them will be unable to pay their just debts." William no doubt was well known in those "Houses."[56]

What happened a little more than a week later was a frontal assault on the college. On Saturday afternoon, March 6, 1802, while the students were eating dinner, a suspicious fire broke out in the main college building, Nassau Hall, in which the students lived and went to classes. Soon the flames ate through the roof and from there spread down into the building proper, roaring uncontrolled until rain doused them at six o'clock that evening. By then, only "the thick stone walls" were standing.[57] Hints soon singled out young William Cooper as the ringleader of the arsonists. Although the college trustees admitted after their meeting in the middle of March that they could name no suspect, on the day following they expelled him along with five fellow students—expelled rather than suspended them—for specific "immoralities" and "disorders," as well as their general part in stirring things up at the college.[58]

William Cooper was also charged with arson by the town of Princeton, although that charge later was dropped, and no one ever was convicted of setting Nassau Hall afire or burning down a nearby tavern on March 7. William Cooper's escape from legal consequences, though, hardly left him unscathed. His reputation was sullied and his behavior while away from home now was being fully reported to his father and the rest of the family—by such close allies of the Coopers as Richard R. Smith of Philadelphia and Gov. Joseph Bloomfield of Burlington. William had little to hide behind and little ability to explain away the disaster he had made of his young life. Worse yet, he appears not even to have been sobered by all that went wrong up to March 6. He continued to squander the faith of those who, convinced of his sterling qualities, still doubted that he had any complicity in the fires. President Smith, perhaps concerned with his own failure to supervise the boy, remained his supporter. Writing Judge Cooper only two days after the fire, Smith downplayed what his young charge had been up to over recent days—indeed, the past year.[59] Even when William's name began showing up in discussions about responsibility for the events, Smith still believed in him. He paid the boy's bail on his first arrest in March and maintained that he was guilty only of having fallen among bad company. As late as May, in a letter to William's father, Smith avowed he had had "no suspicion . . . of his being capable of the crimes with which he had been charged." But even Smith's faith collapsed when he picked up a distressing anecdote from an acquaintance who had ridden in the stage with William and a number of other young men after his expulsion. As the president's new letter painfully revealed, this brightest of Judge Cooper's sons had told dirty stories about Smith's daughter, treating "her character . . . with the greatest indecency & indelicacy." If burning down Nassau Hall could not erase President Smith's "good opinion of [William's] heart & principles," this bit of "shameful" discourse could—and did. Little as he had learned while attending Princeton, William Cooper learned even less from his disgraceful manner of leaving it.[60]

Albany

In the summer of 1801, while William Cooper was still cheerfully hopping about Princeton, his youngest brother was about to leave Otsego for the next stage of his own education, designed to prepare him for college as well. The boy's destination, the "charming town" of Albany, was from this point on to occupy a key place on his personal map, and therefore deserves a brief description.[61] At the time he arrived there, Albany was a small city of about one thousand houses and six thousand residents. It had two boasts. First, it was defiantly urban, having received its city charter from the royal governor in 1686, only shortly after New York. Second, in 1797 this "ancient city of Albany," as Cooper accordingly called it (*SAT* CE 152), had upstaged Manhattan itself by being named the new capital of a state that was growing dramatically to the west and north. To be sure, it was not yet accustomed to the political role it was to play once the Albany Regency and its spoils system came to the fore starting in the 1820s. Well in the future, too, was the enormous economic influence that would be conferred on it after the opening of the Erie Canal in 1825. Even from its founding, however, Albany had occupied a strategic position in both military and economic terms.

Hence the series of abortive attempts to conquer the city, most recently during British General John Burgoyne's ill-fated push south from Canada in 1777. Hence, too, the heavy trade in fur, wheat, lumber, cattle, and other commodities that had centered there since the establishment of the original Dutch outpost in 1614. Although standing 150 miles upstream from Manhattan, Albany was a sea-level port washed by tidal flows, the head of navigation for the river's Dutch-inspired sloops, and, a few years after Cooper's schooling, the destination of the nation's first regularly scheduled steamboats. As a consequence of such advantages, the Hudson shore had long been crowded with warehouses and wharves.

Part of the city proper clustered near them on the low, narrow river "flatts"—
de vlackte, the Dutch had called them—that were overrun most years by spring
floods or ice jams. Roughly paralleling the Hudson on the flatts but some
distance from it, Court and Market streets met head-on, tracing out the route of
what in the future would be called Broadway. Where the two old streets joined,
a third (called *Jonker Straat* in colonial days, but recently renamed State Street to
mark Albany's ascendancy as capital) ran west up one of the hills that arose all
along this stretch of the river.

At the head of that rising street stood the ruins of old Fort Frederic, a British
installation that in its prime had been "a great building of stone surrounded with
high and thick walls," and that even in 1800 was a weighty memorial of the imperial warfare that had beset the Hudson-Champlain corridor. A dominant feature of the cityscape until its removal to make way for the new state capitol a few
years later, the old fort had caught Cooper's eye when he passed through Albany
with his family in earlier years, and now that he was there on his own it clearly
stirred his imagination. What it suggested about the region's deeper, pre-
Revolutionary past would be elaborated in both *The Last of the Mohicans* and especially *Satanstoe,* Cooper's tale of colonial Albany.[62]

Such symbols of English empire notwithstanding, Albany had a composite
cultural heritage. It was "Dutch," everybody said then—hence Cooper's assertion in *Satanstoe* that it was essentially "a Dutch town" at the time of the French
and Indian War, and that its "Dutch character" only gradually weakened over
the decades following (*SAT* CE 153). The story was actually more complex. Albany had been such a polyglot community from the outset that the Dutch themselves always had been a minority, lost among the "Flemings, Scandinavians,
Frenchmen, Portuguese, Croats, Irishmen, Englishmen, Scotsmen, Germans,
Spaniards, Blacks from Africa and the West Indies, Indians and persons of mixed
blood" who had dwelled together there since the early seventeenth century.
Cooper himself, when he later visited Belgium, suspected part of the truth, and
he certainly went out of his way in *Satanstoe* to develop another part of it in his
extensive and subtle portrait of the old Afro-Dutch festival of Pinkster, which
had been especially evident in the Albany of his youth.[63]

The most evident signs of the city's pre-Anglo era in 1800 were those
"Dutch" buildings that Cooper, like such other New York writers as Washington Irving and James Kirke Paulding, would use as marks of their state's exotic
past. In Albany, Cooper was especially familiar with one quirky structure that
defiantly occupied the center of State Street at the base of the big hill—the old
Dutch Reformed Church (Plate 4). The first sanctuary, built of wood, had been
erected there as early as 1656. Some fifty years later, a new and larger stone sanctuary had been erected *around* it, after which the old one was disassembled and

taken out piece by piece. (Cooper's note in *Satanstoe*, claiming that the fragments of the old church were "literally thrown out of the windows of its successor" [*SAT* CE 154], was only a slight exaggeration.) Although this second structure was no longer in use in 1801, having been supplanted by a neoclassical church designed by Philip Hooker for a plot several blocks north, it remained standing when Cooper arrived for his schooling and would not be demolished for another five years.[64]

The old building's presence in the middle of the street made it a fixture of Cooper's memories of Albany, an anchor, as it were, of the city's ancient ways. It had richer symbolic meaning because of its peculiar Gothic design. It was "square, with a high pointed roof, having a belfry and weather cock on its apex, windows with diamond panes and painted glass, and a porch" (*SAT* CE 154).[65] The latter feature, actually a raised entry chamber, followed the style of the surviving Dutch houses of the city, which in 1801 still punctuated the landscape. One such house, with a Dutch stoop out front and a "Crow-step" gable oriented toward the street and topped with a weathervane, appropriately enough shelters the half-Dutch character Harman Mordaunt and his daughter Anneke when they visit Albany in *Satanstoe* (see *SAT* CE 190–91).

During Cooper's time in Albany, such material relics already were being targeted for demolition by the city's Yankee newcomers, who took offense at their unfamiliar and seemingly inconvenient look and layout. New England migrants like canal promoter Elkanah Watson, who earned a reputation as "that infernal paving Yankee" among Albany's disgruntled Dutch residents because of his drive to remake the cityscape in Anglo terms, was the perfect representative of the type.[66] The reformers had many sore points, including even the city's Episcopal church, St. Peter's, just uphill from the Dutch church and, like it, located smack in the middle of State Street. This second inholding on the public roadway was also to be removed during Cooper's youth—indeed, right before his eyes, since he lodged immediately across the street while work on its replacement progressed in the fall of 1801 and in 1802.[67]

Such erasures marked the victory of Yankee modernism over the ancient Dutch city. From his family's experience with New England migrants in Otsego, Cooper was already beginning to understand that the new nation sat uneasily astride such broad cultural divides. Not surprisingly, Cooper's comic villain in *Satanstoe* would be an interloping Yankee named Jason Newcome, who seeks to upset any of the old New York customs that do not suit his taste or interest. That the career of this consummate newcomer in the book roughly parallels that of Cooper's first teacher, Yale graduate Joshua Dewey, suggests how much personal animus the novelist carried forward from his earliest experiences of the Yankee invasion of New York.[68]

Cooper's teacher in Albany, the Rev. Thomas Ellison, the rector of St. Peter's, was no Dutchman and no Yankee. To the contrary, he was an English native and a 1781 graduate of Queen's College, Oxford. For many years he had been a friend of the Cooper family—in fact, he had previously tutored Isaac Cooper, and he was so familiar with Otsego County that at one point he seems to have considered relocating there to take over the Episcopal church Judge Cooper contemplated establishing in his village.[69]

Ellison was a man of the cloth but wore it lightly. While on an official inspection visit to Otsego with fellow New York State regent Stephen Van Rensselaer in 1797, "Tomy Ellison" (the Patroon's term for him) proved an amusing and worldly companion more interested in food, tobacco, and brandy than in affairs of soul or mind (*COC* 51). Small wonder that Ellison was widely known and liked as a "gentleman of a sociable disposition and remarkable wit, whose society was much courted." Cooper's classmate and lifelong friend William Jay would remember Ellison fifty years later as "a genuine John Bull both in looks & feelings," hardly a pious image. Cooper's sense of the man confirmed Jay's. Ellison was "of the true English school," he recalled in a quasi-fictional letter addressed to Jay in his English travel book. After listing the ways in which Ellison outwardly conformed to the niceties of his station, Cooper nonetheless passed on the rumor that the rector had fled England with another man's wife, with whom he lived openly while officiating in Albany (*GE* CE 155).[70]

Like Cooper's first teacher, Joshua Dewey, Ellison nonetheless was a genuine intellectual. He not only took in classical pupils such as Isaac and James Cooper, but also some advanced scholars who studied divinity with him in Albany, among them Dartmouth graduate Philander Chase, future founder of Kenyon College.[71] Ellison's school at the time of Cooper's entry into it nonetheless was quite small: there were five students, Cooper recalled, "and all in his family, for he took no others" (*LJ* 2:155).[72] Among the five, it was William Jay who was to be Cooper's closest associate in Albany, as well as a friend at Yale and then in Westchester and New York City. This son of recent governor John Jay had preceded Cooper by some months at Ellison's, having stayed behind on the departure of most of his family from the state capital early in 1801. On Cooper's arrival there later, the two quickly became roommates and friends. The exact contemporaries passed virtually all their time together: "we began our Virgil and Cicero together, slept together, played together, and sometimes quarreled for"—not *with*—"each other," Cooper recalled in 1831 (*LJ* 2:155). Out of this constant contact with Jay in Albany no doubt came further entanglements, including visits to the Jay family home at Bedford either during the Yale years or while Cooper was serving in New York City in the navy. Once at Bedford, Cooper surely was introduced around the Jay circle of friends and family. So, despite other possible means, it is likely that the Jays introduced Cooper to his future wife, Susan DeLancey.

William Jay had other gifts to offer. He had been resident in Albany for several years during his father's state service from 1797 until the present year, ensconced in rented quarters only a few doors away from Ellison's house on State Street. Hence he was well prepared to serve as a guide for Cooper. But Cooper knew Albany tolerably well on his own before 1801. And he regarded it then, as he did later, with genuinely fond feelings. "The name of Albany . . . at the head of your letter," he wrote a correspondent from Paris three decades later, "gave me pleasure—To me Albany has always been a place of agreeable and friendly recollections—It was the only outlet we had, in my childhood, to the world and many a merry week have I passed there with boys of my own age, while my father has waited for the opening of the river to go south." William Jay surely was one of those "boys." Among the others were three exact contemporaries who were *not* at Ellison's: the Patroon's son, Stephen Van Rensselaer IV; James Stevenson (later mayor of the city); and Peter Gansevoort, whose sister Maria (just two years younger than the five boys) was to be the mother of Herman Melville, and who like Peter *may* have been among Ellison's pupils at some other time. No wonder that Cooper later stressed how "Albany is a name I love for a multitude of associations that are connected with my earliest years" (*LJ* 2:155).[73] A good deal of his fun there overflowed in the well-imagined frivolities of the Albany scenes of *Satanstoe,* such as the sled race down State Street and around the bend of the Dutch church—directly into the path of a big horse-drawn sleigh.[74]

As such activities suggest, Cooper was hardly an overly studious pupil. When he recalled the days with Jay in Albany on another occasion, it was their snowball fights that sprang to mind, not their bouts of translation of the classics (*LJ* 2:109). We have a fragmentary corroboration of their joint mischief in a recollection passed on from Cooper through the DeLanceys years later. During the preparation of the lot for the new church building across State Street from Ellison's house, a large quantity of sand had to be removed, leaving an immense excavation. Here "ringleader" Cooper and his friends would "play tag, leap frog, and do various stunts" until Ellison shouted at them to stop, at which they would "either scamper away or hide in some corner out of sight." Ellison, who already was adversely affected by a mysterious illness, could not chase the boys, but once his students finally came home they were greeted with stern lectures.[75]

Not everything was a fight. Cooper's daughter had heard that "Mr. Ellison took great pleasure in instructing the young lad from Otsego"—not just in correcting him (*PIO* HE xv; see also *P&P* 51). The boy's appeal rested on his basic facility with Latin, instilled in him back in Burlington by Patrick Higgins. When

William Jay reported on his progress to his father in 1801, he boasted, "Mr. Elli-son [has] put me in Virgil, and I can now say the first two eclogues by heart, and construe and parse and scan them."[76] Cooper, addressing to Jay that fictitious letter in his English travel book, confirmed this description. Ellison, he recalled for Jay, "compelled you and me to begin Virgil with the Eclogues, and Cicero with the knotty phrase that opens the oration in favour of the poet Archias" (*GE CE* 155). The opening of Cicero's *Pro Archia*, an oration delivered in defense of the poet A. Licinius Archias in 62 BC, is indeed "knotty"—composed of a string of nested clauses in which neophyte translators easily become lost.[77] It is not known whether either Jay or Cooper came through the passage (or the whole oration) without harm. But it is clear that Cooper did absorb a good deal of Vir-gil in Albany. Here, for instance, he must have encountered that pair of lines in *The Aeneid* used in his humorous account of rural mispronunciation at the short-lived "Academy" in *The Pioneers*.[78] The jest in that particular case was a tribute to Ellison's skillful training of his own pupils in the rudiments of the language. Moreover, in one regard, Ellison was indeed exceptional: as Jay indicated to his father, Ellison taught his charges to scan Latin as well as to pronounce and trans-late it correctly. This went far beyond what Cooper and Jay were to encounter even in their classes at Yale College.[79]

However advanced the instruction the two boys enjoyed under Ellison, their progress was surely vitiated by his increasingly shaky health over the fall and winter. He was so weak by spring that, when the boys left for Easter break, it may well have been apparent that there would be no return—and there wasn't, for he died in their absence on Monday, April 26, 1802.[80] A notice of his passing in-serted in the *Otsego Herald* praised the fortitude with which the forty-three-year-old Oxford graduate, familiar to many in Cooperstown, had borne the "long and severe illness" that claimed his life. His parishioners remembered him as a "truly good and benevolent Minister," pious but neither gloomy nor austere. Indeed, his life was a lesson in humane virtues such as "affability, hospitality, and gen-erosity," and even his preaching was noted for its eloquence as much as its theo-logical correctness.[81]

New Haven

With his college preparation cut short by Ellison's death and no alternate plans ready, Cooper stayed put in Otsego until it could be decided what to do with him. This was the precise moment of his brother's disgrace at Nassau Hall, so send-ing him to Princeton was out of the question. That left few other choices, among which Yale, the alma mater not only of Joshua Dewey but also of Episcopal priest Daniel Nash and of the new Presbyterian minister in Cooperstown, Isaac Lewis, soon emerged as the best.[82] For the preparatory work that remained undone, New Haven was likewise the obvious choice, and once his living arrangements there had been settled, Cooper was promptly shipped off in August, with brother Samuel in tow.[83]

Yale's academic requirements for admission were simple: applicants had to know how to read, translate, and analyze Cicero, Virgil, and the Greek Testament; be able to write Latin prose; and be familiar with the rules of common arithmetic.[84] Cooper would have had no trouble with Latin or arithmetic. His utter unfamiliarity with Greek meant, however, that he could not have passed the next admission exam, administered at the time of the fall commencement a month after his arrival—and that he therefore had no hope of joining the college's new session, which would begin six weeks afterwards. Studying under a private tutor from then until after the end of the year's second vacation period (early in February 1803), he at last was enrolled in the freshman class. Judge Cooper, college records indicate, paid the required bond to cover his son's expenses on February 5, after which point the belated freshman presumably moved into his lodgings in one of Yale's two dormitories. His preparatory tutor, whoever it was, cannot have worked him excessively hard in the brief interval— probably just enough to clear the hurdles.[85]

Once officially admitted, Cooper displayed the sort of immaturity one would expect of the youngest member of his class. His facility with Latin might have helped him shine, but instead allowed him "to play—a boy of thirteen! all the first year" (*LJ* 2:99). Completely unable to handle Greek texts without help, during his second year he usually prepped by putting Latin and English trots to extensive use. He would half-boast to Prof. Benjamin Silliman in 1831, for instance, that he had "never studied but *one* regular lesson in Homer" (*LJ* 2:99). If he was pinned down in class, he would offer recitation leader James L. Kingsley any excuse he could: he had been called away from his studies by the ringing of the college bell (which incessantly called students to prayer, to study, to meals, and so on); or he had caught a cold that had destroyed his concentration; or he had just received a letter from home that, possibly bearing important news, had to be read before his books could be opened.[86] These and other extenuations were as lame as any undergraduate's, but the charm with which he offered his "Homerick excuse" to Kingsley, who clearly liked him and whom he later remembered "with affection," probably helped carry the day. When another instructor handled the final examination that year for Kingsley, Cooper lucked out: he was called upon to translate part of that one lesson he fortuitously *had* done earlier in the term. The class members, who were in on the secret, were amused, and even Kingsley, sitting in, was happy—though for the wrong reasons, taking Cooper's performance as proof of how well *his* boys could do when put on the spot (*LJ* 2:99–100). If only he had known!

Kingsley, himself a graduate of the college, was one of six tutors from 1799 until 1805, when he was named professor of Hebrew, Greek, and Latin. Tutors supervised the academic and personal lives of the boys in half a class (a "division") from the time they arrived until they entered the senior year, when President Timothy Dwight himself took over the reunited halves. Each tutor visited the dorms to ensure good order and proper study habits among his charges, and "conducted all the recitations, declamations, compositions and disputes" in his division over the next three years.[87] Kingsley's intellectual influence over Cooper probably had less to do with the areas of his expertise, which Cooper skirted as best he could, than with other subjects. It is likely, for instance, that the English compositions Cooper had to write and the oral presentations he had to make while under Kingsley's supervision profited from his mentor's own considerable ability as a writer. And perhaps Kingsley's historical interests, especially his fascination with the Puritan "Regicides" (King Charles I's judges, who had fled to New England after his execution), roused Cooper's curiosity on the subject, which he was to touch upon in his one Puritan novel, *The Wept of Wish-ton-Wish* (1829).[88]

Tutor Kingsley's lore was suggestive, and Cooper's feelings for him were certainly warm. Yet his deepest sympathies among the Yale faculty were evoked instead by Prof. Benjamin Silliman. Born in 1779 near his family's ancestral home, Holland Hill, high above Long Island Sound at Fairfield, Connecticut, Silliman had entered the Yale of President Ezra Stiles at thirteen, as young as Cooper a decade later. He proceeded to graduate, though without brilliant success, at the end of 1796, shortly after Timothy Dwight took over the college. Anxious, emotionally fluent, something of a poet, Silliman was so uncertain of his future that after graduating he experimented with various occupations. He went home to try reviving the exhausted family farmstead, briefly taught school in Wethersfield, then began the study of law in New Haven. Even before being admitted to the Connecticut bar, however, he was invited back to his alma mater by Dwight to serve as a part-time tutor for the freshman class in 1799. The president clearly favored the young man, whose family he had come to know well while running his famous Greenfield Hill school near the Silliman home.[89] As a consequence, the new tutor probably imagined that further opportunities might be opened to him as the college expanded and Dwight's personal imprint on it deepened. But he was astonished when Dwight asked him in 1801 to become professor of chemistry: not only was that field in its infancy in American colleges—Silliman knew virtually nothing about it. When Cooper arrived in New Haven a year and a half later, Professor Silliman, just twenty-four, was so ill-prepared for his assignment that he was spending much of his time studying in Philadelphia, then the new nation's best scientific environment. Not until April 1804, more than a year after Cooper began college, did Silliman at last deliver his first lectures in chemistry to the senior class.[90]

An underclassman such as Cooper ordinarily would have had little continuing contact with any of Yale's professors. He had come to Silliman's attention soon after arriving in New Haven, however: first, apparently, at the home of Silliman's friend (and Yale's assistant treasurer), Stephen Twining, who with his wife seems to have provided lodgings for Cooper and his brother.[91] Further contact there, and then during meals in the college "commons" or at the weekly worship service once Cooper started at Yale, built on that chance encounter. Silliman's 1831 recollection of young Cooper as "a fine sparkling beautiful boy of alluring person & interesting manners" reveals the intensely positive (and personal) nature of his response to the student (Plate 5). Despite their differences in age and standing at the college, they in fact were friends virtually from the start. Part of the reason for the tie lay in the emotionality of Silliman, who beneath his controlled surface was capable of passionate attachments.[92]

For his part, Cooper would rely on Silliman as a confidant, the role into which he was cast even as late as 1831 in Cooper's long tale about his misdeeds under Kingsley. The tale brought back for the novelist the gratitude he felt for Silliman's aid during another tough episode in New Haven: "On one occasion, a tutor of the name of Fowler was scraped [that is, roughed up] in the Hall. Now I was charged with being one of his assailants by *himself*, and was arraigned before you all, in conclave. You presided, and appealed to my honor to know whether I scraped or not—I told you the truth that I did not, for I disliked the manner of assailing a man en masse. You believed me, for we understood each other, and I was dismissed without even a reproof—You told me you believed me, and I was not a boy to deceive any one who had that sort of confidence in me. This little event mad[e] a pleasant impression on me, which I remember to this day" (*LJ* 2:100).[93] Bancroft Fowler, like Silliman a 1796 Yale graduate (as well as the brother of a Cooper classmate), tutored at the college from 1800 until the 1804 commencement. The event in question thus must have taken place soon after Cooper's matriculation—between February 1803 and early the next year—and presumably in Connecticut Hall, where Cooper may have lodged and where all meals were served. The dining commons there was notoriously rowdy: "wholesale disorders," recalled Franklin B. Dexter sardonically, "were so far as possible discouraged by the presence of unhappy tutors feeding on elevated platforms, and by such devices as the exclusive use of pewter instead of glass and china."[94] Evidently Bancroft Fowler was purposely jostled in a crush of students as he entered or exited and was not one to take such insulting treatment without attempting retribution. Whenever the assault occurred, it is clear from Cooper's recollection that by then Silliman already had formed his good opinion of this one supposed assailant: "we understood each other" applied not just to this episode, but in a broader, deeper sense. Silliman stuck up for Cooper and "believed" him, in other words, because the two already were allied.

Cooper's manner in answering Silliman during that interrogation deepened the alliance. Needing an assistant for the laboratory set up for his chemistry lectures, delivered in rented quarters in the spring and summer of 1804 and then repeated that fall in Yale's new "Lyceum," Silliman somewhat unexpectedly chose Cooper. For the first batch of lectures, the new-made chemist had considerable doubts about how to proceed. He had been away from New Haven over the previous winter, studying again in Philadelphia and Princeton, acquiring necessary materials and apparatus, and preparing the lectures. Silliman came back to New Haven around the beginning of April 1804 and on the twelfth of that month, a Thursday, gave his first lecture in what was intended as a short trial run. "Chemistry is the science that treats of the changes that are affected in material bodies or substances by light, heat, and mixture," he read from his prepared text to a class that included not only John C. Calhoun but also Cooper's friend and dormitory mate John Chester, later a minister in Albany. Not all the members of the class of 1804 were there—only those who had an interest in the topic and had paid the required fee.[95]

The start of the endeavor was ambitious but halting. Cooper later joked to Silliman, "I often boast that you and I were the two first chemists of Yale; you as the dealer in experiments, and I as your bottle-washer" (*LJ* 4:314). "Dealer in experiments" was a bit of commercial cant, with a suggestion of showmanship or even prestidigitation. It hints at the satiric vein in which Cooper at times portrayed scientists in his fiction. But Cooper's term for his own part in those first lectures was no less of a deflation. There were bottles to wash, to be sure, including wicker-covered Florence flasks that had to be cleaned with sand and ashes, as well as plenty of glass tubing and vials. But the scope of his assignment may have been considerably broader. For one thing, Silliman also employed other, larger pieces of apparatus. He had multiple gun barrels specially prepared for experiments in the "volatilization of gas and combustion under pressure," and purchased a second-hand blacksmith's furnace in Philadelphia and had it shipped to New Haven. Its uses were many, but it required stoking and tending so that the instructor could use it during demonstrations.[96]

Did Cooper manage the furnace and the other apparatus? We do not know, but whatever his precise role, it probably required him to be present not just for the cleanup after the sessions, but also in the midst of the chemical demonstrations. The latter took place as part of the classes, meaning that Cooper perhaps was the only underclassman—he was a sophomore in early 1804—officially allowed to attend the lectures.[97] The sessions were held four times per week for an hour each time; they ran from April through July, when the seniors took their final examination and then left New Haven until their September commencement. First came thirty or forty minutes of lecturing, then enough experiments to fill out the remainder of the hour.[98] With the return of a new senior class following graduation, Cooper likewise may have assumed the same duties for Silliman's second set of lectures, which ran across fall and into winter. This time, if Cooper was there, he surely noted the difference produced by Silliman's move into the "laboratory" in the Lyceum, a facility specifically designed for this new venture. He also would have enjoyed yet further association with Silliman before his mentor and friend left for England late that following winter.

Because Silliman was not to return for some time, the lectures delivered over the fall and winter of 1804–1805 would have been his last contact with Cooper until they renewed their acquaintance some years later in New York City. Silliman probably had helped Cooper gain a more stable place at Yale, where patronage was as natural as breathing. By the same token, Silliman's departure may have left Cooper a bit aimless and thus may have contributed to the boy's drift toward more serious behavioral problems and, at last, expulsion. But some of what Cooper owed to Silliman probably stayed with the student long after he left New Haven. For one thing, the chance to have a glimpse inside a scientific laboratory in the early national era was rare indeed. Cooper was in on the ground floor of a movement in education (and industry) that would expand almost beyond comprehension by the time of his death in 1851. By then, scientific discourse had permeated society and the press. By then, too, steam navigation, the railroad, and the electric telegraph had radically changed the face of the land and the pace of life by the practical application of a few basic scientific propositions. That Cooper learned much in any particular sense while under Silliman's tutelage may be doubted. What he unquestionably gained was some insight into the scientific method. Socially, his later association with other scientists in New York, men such as James Renwick and James DeKay (both members of Cooper's New York circle, the Bread and Cheese Club, in the 1820s), probably came more naturally because of his friendship with Silliman and Silliman's growing stature in the country then.

Insofar as science entered into Cooper's fiction, the influence of Silliman's laboratory is harder to define. Often enough, the scientist as Cooper imagined him was someone whose tenacious grasp of limited truths proved an impediment rather than an aid. Thus, Dr. Obed Battius in *The Prairie* (1827)—"M.D. and fellow of several cis-atlantic learned societies" (*PR* CE 67)—hardly is a fair representative of science as men like Silliman were trying to establish it in America, in part through the founding of those very "learned societies." But Silliman's stumbling self-preparation in chemistry, about which his laboratory assistant surely knew something, may have been one source of Cooper's doubts about the profession as practiced in his time. Dr. Bat's opacity and folly, despite the fact that he holds degrees from *two* universities, make him a stock figure, a man satirized for "bookish l'arning and hard words," as Natty Bumppo dismissively characterizes his accomplishments (*PR* CE 100). This wandering bestower of names experiences nature as a reflection of his own half-formed ideas—indeed, as the signet of his own identity. Dr. Bat thus reads his account of a recent "discovery" to skeptical Ellen Wade from his journal in order to impress her:

> "Oct. 6, 1805 . . . mem. *Quadruped;* seen by star-light, and by the aid of a pocket lamp, in the Prairies of North America, see Journal for Latitude and Meridian. *Genus,* unknown, therefore named after the Discoverer, and from the happy coincidence of having been seen in the evening— *Vespertilio; Horribilis, Americanus. Dimensions* (by estimation). *Greatest length* eleven feet, *height,* six feet. *Head,* erect, *nostrils,* expansive, *eyes,* expressive and fierce, *teeth,* serrated and abundant. *Tail,* horizontal, waving, and slightly feline. *Feet,* large and hairy. *Talons,* long, arquated, dangerous. *Ears,* inconspicuous. *Horns,* elongated, diverging, and formidable, *colour,* plumbeous-ashy, with fiery spots. *Voice,* sonorous, martial and appalling. *Habits,* gregarious, carnivorous, fierce, and fearless. There," exclaimed Obed, when he had ended this sententious but comprehensive description, "there is an animal, which will be likely to dispute with the Lion his title to be called the King of the Beasts." (*PR* CE 71)

But the animal he actually has found, named for its benighted discoverer (the *vespertilio* is the "creature of the vespers"—that is, the bat), is none other than his own *Asinus Americanus,* the donkey on which Battius has ridden west into the great unknown, although one would never recognize the beast from its master's wildly inaccurate field notes on his encounter with it.

Bee-hunter Paul Hover, who uses his knowledge to "line" a bee to its hive, is in fact the better practical naturalist, applying a few elegant methods with stunningly fruitful results. Thereby Cooper creates a neat contrast in natural philosophies. Dr. Bat is not, of course, a portrait of Benjamin Silliman. Still, the ass-riding scientist does not reassure us that Silliman and his colleagues at New Haven early in the nineteenth century had impressed Cooper with the professionalism that eventually would underpin their own scientific ethos.

There was an area in which Silliman's effect on Cooper, however, was arguably profound. What matters more than knowledge of the natural world in Cooper's fiction—knowledge, say, as it is embodied both in Dr. Bat's abstract reasoning and in Paul Hover's concrete skill—is the proper moral attitude toward nature. This latter trait is what makes Natty Bumppo more admirable than even Hover, or the skilled woodsman Billy Kirby in *The Pioneers*. Nature as Leather-Stocking knows it is *whole*, not a Cartesian machine that can be manipulated piecemeal (for honey or timber or any other commodity) but rather an almost spiritual entity with which Natty aligns himself by his attitudes and actions. Nature in Cooper is thus filled with moral and religious meaning. It owes more to William Paley's *Natural Theology* (a book first published during the year Cooper went to New Haven) than to the older mechanical model of Descartes that was in fact to be of such importance during the nineteenth century. On this level, Benjamin Silliman's influence may have been pervasive in Cooper's life, for the would-be chemist was among those young men at Yale in 1802 who had participated in a religious revival stimulated by President Dwight, and throughout his career he sought to reconcile his faith in the Christian dispensation with his belief in the scientific principles he labored so hard to establish.[99]

In one branch of science in particular, astronomy, Silliman and his associates may have given Cooper a model of how that reconciliation might be achieved. Cooper certainly came to view celestial observation as a kind of divine contemplation, and he used astronomy for essentially religious ends in a number of books, including *The Crater* (1847) and *The Sea Lions* (1849). From this perspective, it does not matter whether Cooper studied astronomy at Yale with Silliman or with Silliman's colleague Jeremiah Day, a theologian who assumed the post of professor of mathematics at the college during the summer of 1803.[100] Yale gave him a fundamental sense of the convergence of knowledge with faith, a sense that the popular science movement later in the century merely deepened.

Beyond science, Benjamin Silliman may well have given Cooper guidance in another field for which the teacher had deep feelings, and which was to become of critical importance in Cooper's future—history, particularly American history. The chemist had a quite personal fund of Revolutionary War anecdotes centered on his father, Gen. Gold Selleck Silliman, a staunch Whig and militia officer in Fairfield whose agonizing story was well known in coastal Connecticut. General Silliman's regiment had seen service in New York, taking part, for instance, in the legendary battle of White Plains, during which they fought hard from the cover of stone walls before giving way under a furious assault of British artillery. Along with the White Plains tales of Oliver Cory and those the novelist later picked up in Westchester itself, the ones he probably heard in New Haven helped Cooper imagine the background of *The Spy*.[101]

Another, even more suggestive episode involving Benjamin Silliman's father dated from the war's end. Captured in May 1779 in a daring strike across Long Island Sound by a small Tory raiding party, General Silliman was held captive in New York until his exchange almost a year later for a Yale classmate,

Thomas Jones, a famous Tory (and in fact the uncle of the future Mrs. Cooper). Benjamin Silliman was born during his father's absence, reason enough for him to see special meaning in the episode, about which he and his mother told and retold tales for decades afterwards. But the poignancy of those tales lay in the fact that Selleck Silliman's liberation delivered him to an even worse fate at the hands of his fellow patriots.[102] When peace came, the militia officer began re-building his law practice, which had been devastated by his necessary inattention during the war. He barely had begun to recoup his losses when he was informed by the state of Connecticut—whose very existence he had helped assure—that items for which he had not submitted proper receipts during his military service were to be charged against him personally. To his already unmanageable per-sonal debt was thus added an immense obligation to the state. Connecticut's un-flagging demand for reimbursement, Mary Silliman later informed her sons, "sunk" their father's "spirits and discouraged him about settling his other debts." Thereafter, as he became absorbed with the injustice of his treatment, he was subject to deepening depression. Utterly broken, he was stricken down by apoplexy when Benjamin Silliman was ten. The patriot lingered through a series of fits and convulsions, then miserably died. Here was a narrative legacy very much of a piece with those Cooper would explore in his own complex legends of the nation's founding.[103]

"Little Trooper"

There was another, simpler, more dangerous lesson Professor Silliman may have offered his laboratory assistant. New York academic James Renwick described it among the many experiments listed in his *First Principles of Chemistry* (1840): "Mix ten grains of potassa with three grains of charcoal powder, and throw the mixture on a red-hot shovel, a loud explosion will ensue."[104] For even better re-sults, of course, it helps to add sulfur, since the latter element easily ignites and causes the carbon and saltpeter to explode with great violence, even without the "red-hot shovel." Cooper may well have known either formula before he arrived at Yale. Or, when the need arose in the spring of 1805, he could have purchased the gunpowder ready-made from some local source in New Haven. But there is a certain pleasure in imagining that he filched the ingredients from the absent Sil-liman's lab, mixed them as he had seen Silliman do the year before, and then went about his business.

He knew he was on a dangerous mission—institutionally as well as chemi-cally. The list of "Crimes and Misdemeanors" among the college rules forbade any student from keeping "fire-arms, or gun-powder" in his room—and from setting off "gun-powder in or near the College-yard."[105] But by this point, lab assistant Cooper did not care about those prohibitions. He had had a "scrape" with a classmate, presumably also a resident of Connecticut Hall, and wished to "even up matters." We know the details through an indirect means. Many years later, after he had begun his literary career and gone to Europe and come back and then at last returned to Cooperstown, Cooper employed a young man named Caleb Clark to chop wood and do general handyman jobs around Otsego Hall. Apparently they were talking one day and the novelist let down his guard long enough to relate the story. He had sneaked up to the closed dormitory door of the infuriating classmate and carefully poked most of a piece a cloth into the keyhole. Then, lifting up the loose end of the cloth and holding it open, he poured a fair amount of gunpowder into it. When the powder was twisted snugly inside the cloth, which formed both casing and fuse, Cooper "touched off the rag" with a spark or flame. As the fabric caught fire and burned up toward the lock, he backed away. The makeshift device was not only ingenious—it was mightily effective. When the explosion occurred, it was so powerful that it roused and frightened the classmate and did "considerable damage to the old door of the dormitory room."[106]

This was the most serious of Cooper's frolics at Yale, but hardly the first. His grandson reported a family tale regarding the occasion when he "shut a donkey in a recitation room"—presumably the room used by James Kingsley, although the tale does not indicate who precisely was being targeted, or where, for that matter, the boy procured the beast.[107] Cooper clearly earned himself a reputation as a hellion while at Yale. His standing among his fellow members of the Linonia Society, one of the two mildly competitive debating clubs recruited from Yale's student body, suggests as much. To the Linonians, as a poem written for the society early in 1805 by Cooper's classmate Daniel Mulford indicates, the youngest son of Otsego Hall was known as "Jemmy Cooper"—not a "hopper," like his brother at Princeton, but rather "a most sagacious little trooper." He was thought to be something of a rake, a son of Venus in whose presence, as the poem went on, "The ladies every where befidget."[108]

It was also Mulford who provided the best surviving insight into the gathering troubles that led to the "little trooper's" expulsion later in 1805. In his diary entry for May 30, when he had just returned to New Haven after term vacation, Mulford reported that he "heard that Boyle & Cooper both juniors had been fighting."[109] Because it had occurred on May 23, during Yale's break (May 8–29), the incident was very much the talk of the college on Mulford's return. Evidently neither Cooper nor classmate John P. Boyle had left town over the vacation, and their presence in New Haven without the usual duties and controls in force may have contributed to the incident. The two of them may have been out and about together and run afoul of each other or begun to quarrel over some common activity. One can only imagine what the latter may have been.

In one regard, the talk that Mulford heard on coming back to Yale was wrong. What had taken place—or at least what had brought the incident to the attention of authorities—was less a fight than a brutal one-sided attack by Boyle on Cooper. On the day after that attack, Boyle had his goods attached by order of Justice of the Peace Henry Daggett on the basis of a complaint made through Cooper's "friend and guardian Nathan Smith," with whom Cooper may have been staying for the vacation break. Boyle's attack apparently was such a serious violation of the general college prohibition against fighting that Nathan Smith on his own authority, without taking the time to contact Cooper's parents or, apparently, college officials, immediately swore out the complaint against the assailant, as indicated in the surviving records of the city court:[110]

> the [Plaintiff] complains & says that at said City on or about the 23d Day of May instant the [Defendant] with force and arms and without law or right an assault made on the body of him the said James and him the said James he the Deft. did then & there with fists & sticks beat bruise wound & cruelly [treat] and him the said James the Deft. did then & there severely wound by striking and bruising the face & head of the said James in such manner as greatly to endanger him the said James and at the time & place aforesaid on him the said James he the Deft. many other injuries & enormities did commit all which took place within the limits of the City of New Haven . . . and is against the peace & contrary to law & to the Plff's damage. . . .

So grave were Cooper's injuries that Smith asked for damages to "the sum of two thousand Dollars," plus costs. Trial was set for the second Tuesday of June (i.e., the eleventh) before the city court. In order to ensure that Boyle did not flee town before then, Smith additionally asked for a three-thousand-dollar bond. The sheriff was asked to attach his "goods or estate," or, in lieu of such security, to have Boyle taken into custody. The sheriff read the charges to Boyle in Smith's presence (the record does not indicate whether Cooper was also present) and indeed took bond from the young man to guarantee his appearance.[111]

When the case was heard, court records also indicate, John Boyle appeared on his own behalf and claimed that Cooper's declaration of the damages done to him was insufficient grounds for proceeding. Smith of course countered. The unnamed judge in the case agreed with Smith not only on this point but also with regard to the merit of the claims. He found John Boyle guilty and awarded Cooper the requested damages. However, the judge also allowed Boyle to appeal the case to the Superior Court, which was to meet in New Haven in July. David Daggett, a well-known New Haven attorney who was representing Boyle, went bail for him at this point and the defendant was released pending that appeal. We know little else of the proceeding. Daniel Mulford was interested enough in the case, probably because of his friendship with Cooper, to attend the city court, but he entered no further details in his diary. Nor did the *Connecticut Herald* or the *Connecticut Journal* report the initial fight or the court proceedings.[112]

The Superior Court was scheduled to meet in New Haven on July 28 under the direction of Chief Justice Jesse Root, who was joined on the bench by a panel of five other justices that included the famous Tapping Reeve.[113] Apparently it did meet then, even though several days earlier, on July 24, serious concern about the yellow fever outbreak then affecting New Haven had led President Dwight to tell students that they might leave, and college classes would not be held again until October.[114] Evidence on the question of the court case is somewhat confusing. There is some indication that the Superior Court indeed heard Boyle's appeal in July and issued a ruling in the matter, although Cooper and perhaps Boyle as well had left New Haven before then. A contemporary note on the back of the earlier ruling of the city court thus indicates that Chief Justice Root and his colleagues affirmed that court's July verdict but reduced Cooper's award to $250. On the other hand, there also is evidence indicating that the case, having been continued from the July session, was not fully settled until December, although with the same results. Boyle, who is said to have appeared on his own behalf at the latter time, accompanied by David Daggett, lost the appeal and once more was ordered to pay Cooper $250 in damages, plus costs. Cooper was not present on this occasion, when he was represented instead by "his guardian Nathan Smith." A final note in this last source indicates that the payment was made on execution of the ruling on January 1, 1806. Boyle, who had been dismissed from Yale in June because of the attack on Cooper, already had been allowed to return and begin the junior year over. Ultimately graduating with the class of 1807, he was, however, to die two years later.[115]

We do not know what led to Boyle's violent attack on Cooper. The assailant was, like Mulford and several others, a late addition to the class of 1806, having joined it only in the fall of 1804. Precious little is evident about his personal character or family background. He entered the college from Cambridge, on the eastern shore of Maryland, and was "considered a young man of considerable energy of mind," according to an 1874 letter cited by Franklin B. Dexter. Dexter's only additional bit about him may hint at a possible motivation for the ill will between him and Cooper: he was regarded as a source of much "political information" and was "strongly attached to Republican principles." It is possible that Cooper, still under the shadow of his father's Federalist principles (which had been reinforced by the prejudices of "Tomy" Ellison), goaded this southern adherent of Jefferson and the latter took it personally.[116] That Boyle used a stick in his attack suggests a kind of schoolboy version of the canings often carried out then between so-called gentlemen, especially political opponents, in the early Republic. Just such an assault was to lay Cooper's father low (at the hands of a Republican, to boot) two years later.[117]

It is natural to speculate that the gunpowder plot carried out by James Cooper sometime in late spring or early summer of 1805 was connected to Boyle's attack on him on May 23. That may or may not have been the case. Friction existing between Cooper and classmate Royal Fowler (and perhaps Fowler's older brother, that "scraped tutor") indicates that Cooper had other strained relations on campus, and his target could have been someone else, including the younger Fowler. That said, however, Boyle on balance does seem to have been Cooper's more plausible opponent. If he was, then it is likely that Cooper retaliated against him *after* May 23—Cooper's injuries and the pending complaint against Boyle notwithstanding. Mulford probably would have mentioned the gunpowder incident in connection to the "fight" if it already had happened by May 30, and it is even reasonable to assume that some mention of it would have been made in the court documents if it had led to Boyle's beating of Cooper.

With one possible exception, those documents are silent on the question. Mulford reported going to the city court for Boyle's trial not on June 11, the date originally set for it, but rather on June 21, when he indicated that it was put off for one more day. He went again that next day, noting then that the case was "repealed" until the county court in December.[118] It is just possible that the case was delayed because Cooper, taking matters into his own hands, had attacked Boyle's door sometime between the end of May, when Mulford returned to campus, and June 11. Such a delay would have allowed Yale to decide how it was going to handle Cooper's misbehavior intramurally before the legal cause was rejoined. Benjamin Silliman, in expressing regrets in 1831 that he had not been at Yale when the decision to expel Cooper was made, suggested that the attack by Boyle had preceded Cooper's own violence. Silliman doubted that his mere presence on the panel reviewing Cooper's case would have swung the decision to the boy's favor. Patronage could not trump outrage. But he now told Cooper, "I know not but you might have been reinstated to [Yale] by virtue of your misfortune."[119] I take this to mean that Cooper's injuries were of sufficient seriousness that Dwight and the faculty might have been open to the argument that Boyle's attack constituted a mitigating circumstance in the gunpowder episode. Cooper still might have been dismissed, but he also might have been taken back—as Boyle himself would be that fall.

Even if college officials might have been swayed by Silliman's advocacy or the simple fact of Cooper's prior suffering at Boyle's hands, other factors surely entered into the decision reached in his case. It is well to keep in mind that Connecticut Hall had been in fairly shabby condition when Dwight took over the presidency. Lyman Beecher, who entered Yale in 1793, remembered that the stairs in the building "were worn nearly through" and that the rooms were "defaced and dirty." At the time of Cooper's troubles, however, the structure had just been thoroughly and expensively restored.[120] The damage Cooper caused to the door by such violent means probably was viewed as an affront to Dwight and the dignity of the college regardless of what had led up to the attack. Then, too, Cooper's attack was not an isolated incident, and the reaction to it was therefore probably exemplary. Despite the revival of religion that had been so notable just before Cooper arrived, rowdy behavior remained a significant challenge to Dwight and the Yale faculty. Benjamin Silliman's colleague Moses Stuart thus wrote him during the would-be chemist's first extended stay in Philadelphia in 1802, the fall immediately after the revival, to fill him in on a multitude of student uproars.[121]

The troubles continued throughout Cooper's stay. Silliman himself, during the term when he was giving his first chemistry lectures, had been forced to fight off "insurgents" who expressed the "spirit of disorder and licentiousness" that had been much in evidence at Yale over the recent past. Having discussed the situation with Dwight and others, the professor had loaded a pistol with shot and then, lying in wait until the malefactors came near, fired it through a shutter at them. This sally not only sent them off "*in terrorem*," it also alerted the professor's accomplices, who were ready to catch the fugitives so they could be identified and punished. The episode, mostly involving southern students (including, one might postulate, John Boyle), may have sprung from political controversy rather than outright irreligion, although in Federalist New Haven impiety and Republicanism were, of course, thought to lie together without the benefit of marriage.[122]

Cooper's lone attack on a classmate's door the next year may have had its own political component. But even if he was defending the bastion of Federalism from a southern radical such as Boyle, he was still blowing up college property and therefore, in the uproarious atmosphere at the time, was rightly sacked. One consequence of the outcome was, understandably if regrettably, to deepen his prior dislike for Yankees. One can almost taste the acrid flavor in a condemnation that Cooper penned as late as 1836 in his German travel book: while amid the Puritan offspring of Yale, he had encountered, he wrote, "the lowest, the most degraded, and the most vulgar wickedness, both as to tone and deed, and the most disordered imaginations" that it had ever been his "evil fortune to witness, or to associate with." What was the signal fault of the "saints"? The conviction of their own superiority over the unenlightened: for nothing, as Cooper

had learned then, is "more vicious than self-righteousness, and the want of charity it engenders" (*GR* 90).

This analysis of the Yankee character rationalized what Cooper felt about
the so-called justice doled out to him in 1805 by President Dwight and the
faculty. In the simplest sense, his expulsion turned him against the college, the
state, and the region, confirming in him the anti-Yankee prejudices of his New
York youth. Twenty years later, in his preface to *Lionel Lincoln* (1825), Cooper
would jokingly admit that Yale could not be blamed for "all his blunders." But
he was not far off the mark when he added that the little formal learning he had
picked up there had "long since been forgotten" (*LL* CE 4). It was largely, one
suspects, the informal lessons that abided.

CHAPTER THREE

The Voyage of the Stirling

The second ex-collegian in the Cooper family left New Haven late in June or early in July 1805, probably with the marks of what Nathan Smith called his "barbarous & cruel" beating still evident on his body.[1] He arrived in Cooperstown soon afterwards to find the village in turmoil over a young man whose horrid crime and impending execution riveted everyone's attention—especially, given all that had happened to him of late, Cooper's. During his final days in New Haven, the *Connecticut Journal* printed the latest news in the Otsego case: "COOPERSTOWN, June 6. *The unhappy Arnold* was on Tuesday last [June 4], indicted, and convicted, at the circuit court held in this place by His Honor Chief Justice Kent, of the murder of Betsey Van Amburgh, an orphan, by whipping her, in such an unjustifiable and barbarous manner as to occasion her death."[2]

Although due to be hanged on July 19, Stephen Arnold was no hardened criminal. Born into a reasonably well-to-do Rhode Island family, he had arrived in Otsego in 1794, soon settling down as a farmer and schoolteacher of good repute in the town of Burlington. The hundred or so pupils in his crowded school, however, sensed some unseen weakness in Arnold and frequently taunted and defied him.[3] On January 10, 1805, "provoked even to madness" by them, Arnold had trudged home with his "accursed temper" boiling. There he encountered little Betsey Van Amburgh, Mrs. Arnold's niece, a lively, good-natured child who had been taken into the Arnold household after her father died.[4] Conveniently close at hand and powerless, poor Betsey also had a weak point: what Cooper in his later discussion of the case called a "natural infirmity" that "prevented [her] from clearly pronouncing certain words which her teacher required her to utter distinctly" (Eclipse 355). It was the kind of flaw that Arnold, after his rough treatment in school, no doubt perverted into a willful affront to his authority.

Betsey's trouble centered on the innocuous word "gig." When Arnold on this fateful day asked her to pronounce it, she gave the first letter a soft rather than hard sound. During supper Arnold corrected her, then afterwards asked her "whether she would spell and pronounce GIG aright." As the *Otsego Herald*'s account went on, "she immediately replied '*yes* sir,' but being terrified by the severity of his manner, or not having acquired the command of articulation or possibly, but not probably, from a perverse humor, she pronounced it JIG." Infuriated at this further instance of disrespect, Arnold grabbed a "number of green rods or switches about three feet in length" and, "declaring that he would whip her until she pronounced the word aright," hurried the terrified child out into the cold night. Standing her against a post and pulling her clothes up over her head so as to muffle her cries, he proceeded to whip her naked body "with great severity." When he took Betsey back into the house and asked her "if she would pronounce the word right, she, as before, replied in a humble and obedient manner, 'yes sir,' but could not or would not pronounce the g hard but still said *jig*." Over the next hour and a half, six more times he took her outside and beat her. And six more times the beating failed to correct her error.

Despite his inflamed passions, it was chilly work for Arnold. After Betsey's seventh failure, he kept her inside so he could warm himself by the fire, but told her she must face yet another beating. Upon this, Betsey "in a piteous and intreating tone said, '*Do uncle let me warm my feet, they are almost froze.*'" Utterly devoid of compassion, he "replied in an enraged manner, '*I'll warm your feet for you,*' and seizing her, repaired again to the bloody post, where he, in the most savage manner, exceeded his former tortures." So fierce were his blows on the child's tiny, naked, shivering body that the long sticks had been reduced to stubs when he was done. At last he stopped, leaving Betsey in such a woeful state that, enduring extreme agony for four days, she at last died. At the coroner's inquest, it was noted that her whole back was a "mass of bruised and lacerated raw flesh." No wonder, seeing that her tormentor had been heard to exclaim, with "neither pity nor compunction . . . discernable in his eyes," that he "*had as leave whip her to death as not.*"[5]

Cooper learned the details of this crime and its consequences as the story gradually emerged in the press.[6] When he retold Arnold's tale in a brief memoir titled "The Eclipse" that he wrote in Paris many years later, probably in 1831, Cooper clearly relied on his recollection of printed versions or the oral retellings he had heard long before. Yet he also knew something of the story firsthand. It is just possible that he was in Cooperstown on his winter vacation from Yale in January 1805 when word of Betsey's death first broke.[7] And he certainly was there on July 19, when, by his own account, he was among the more attentive of the twelve thousand people gathered to watch as Arnold was led through Cooperstown to the place of his execution. There, in a twist that dismayed the spectators, the news that a last-minute stay of execution had arrived from Albany that morning was announced, and, while the uneasy crowd dispersed, the prisoner was returned to his village jail cell. He was to remain confined over the next year, long enough for Cooper to personally encounter him during a much-anticipated total solar eclipse of June 16, 1806 (his nominal subject in the Paris memoir), when Arnold was allowed out of jail to witness that solemn celestial event.[8]

On both occasions, the sight of the condemned man deeply moved Cooper. On the day of the supposed execution, he watched events from an elevated perch in one of the spectator-filled buildings on Front Street. At the prearranged moment, the sheriff took his fettered prisoner out of the jail and seated him upon his coffin in an open wagon. As various local leaders drew near, the sheriff mounted his horse and took the head of the procession. Also marching was a band to play dirges at Arnold's expected funeral, as well as two militia companies, their drawn swords and fixed bayonets glinting in the sun. On his way to the gallows, Arnold passed close enough that Cooper fathomed the woeful look on the condemned man's countenance. "I have seen other offenders expiate their crimes with life," Cooper wrote, "but never have I beheld such agony, such a clinging to life, such mental horror at the nearness of death, as was betrayed by this miserable man" (Eclipse 355).

Cooper's initial impression of Arnold was enhanced by their more direct encounter the following summer. At that time, learning from a friend that Arnold had been let out of his viewless cell so he could watch the eclipse from an adjoining building, Cooper hurried there and found him the "very picture of utter misery"—worse, if that was possible, than the previous year: "I can see him now, standing at the window, pallid and emaciated by a year's confinement, stricken with grief, his cheeks furrowed with constant weeping, his whole frame attesting the deep and ravaging influences of conscious guilt and remorse. . . . [He] seemed to gaze upward at the awful spectacle, with an intentness and a distinctness of mental vision far beyond our own, and purchased by an agony scarcely less bitter than death. It seemed as if, for him, the curtain which veils the world beyond the grave, had been lifted" (Eclipse 356).

The abstract moral grandeur took on deep personal meaning for Cooper. "It was a lesson not lost on me," he wrote in "The Eclipse," probably aware even then that Arnold's distraught condition had struck him so sharply because of the turbulent events in his own recent past. This transference of Cooper's feelings to Arnold—or vice versa—was reflected in his curiously selective treatment of details in that memoir. The piece merely mentioned, for instance, the formal prayers recited at the gallows by two of the ministers who accompanied Arnold from the jail.[9] Cooper had an excellent vantage point on the proceedings, but all he really *heard* at the time was Arnold's "fervent 'Amen!'"—"hoarse, beseeching, and almost despairing"—when the prayers were done (Eclipse, 355–56). But Arnold in fact had also addressed the crowd, urging the hushed multitude to learn from his mistakes. Men and women should be on guard against their passions, he declared with poignant earnestness, for it was anger that had led him to murder. This overt moral Cooper also glossed over in 1831. He did so, in a sense, because he had not needed the verbal lesson and therefore had not heeded it. He had caught Arnold's emotional despair from that mere snatch of his voice as the prayers ended or the glimpse of his face as he passed Cooper's perch. Although the 1831 memoir is not as useful an account of the event as the records compiled by his friend, newspaperman Elihu Phinney, Cooper's empathy with the condemned man gave his portrait of Arnold greater depth. Phinney had been closer to the gallows and dutifully described the prayers and transcribed the condemned man's last words for the *Otsego Herald*. Yet it was Cooper, not Phinney, who mentioned that Arnold wrung his "fettered hands" as he approached the gallows, then turned his back on that "fearful object, as if the view were too frightful for endurance." Although Cooper probably watched the procession to the gallows with members of his family, he was so absorbed by the event that in "The Eclipse" he appears to be alone with the crowd and especially the criminal (Eclipse 355).[10]

A "Wayward Youth"

Turning sixteen two months after the aborted execution, Cooper malingered at home—so purposeless that even his father viewed both Samuel and him as "inclined to be idle and neglect their books." Judge Cooper therefore put them in the care of yet another private tutor, William Neill, a recent addition to the village.[11] Neill arrived in Cooperstown in October as a temporary replacement for Presbyterian minister Isaac Lewis, then about to depart for a new post elsewhere. The Coopers had helped recruit Neill over the summer—in fact, Judge Cooper himself wrote him the formal letter of invitation—and once he accepted and came to town, they took steps to get him happily settled. Judge Cooper's daughter Ann and her husband, George Pomeroy, active Presbyterians, lodged and boarded him for free until the following spring, an act of kindness Neill remembered to the end of his long life. At the same time, Judge Cooper's employment of Neill as tutor for his sons, which probably began as soon after his October arrival as possible, generously added to the slender income derived from the Presbyterians, just now struggling to pay for the new sanctuary being erected on the village lot William Cooper had given them.[12]

But the tutoring was no sinecure. William Neill was in many ways an ideal choice for a tough job. He was, for one thing, a serious scholar. A poor orphan who had lost both parents on the bloody frontier of Revolutionary Pennsylvania (an experience rich with potential tales for the Judge's sons), he had labored hard at his studies and eventually made his way to Princeton, where he paid his expenses by coaching wealthier but less able students. He graduated in 1803 and for the next two years served as a college tutor while completing advanced work in theology. When he came to Cooperstown in 1805, he therefore brought to the task of educating the Coopers a trained intellect and a habit of dedicated labor.[13] But he also brought more. During his youth, as he himself admitted, he had been "wandering" and "wayward." Worse, he had been "reckless—a child of nature," defiantly hostile to religion and "addicted to folly."[14] A serious illness briefly caused him to reflect on these attitudes, but his bad habits were so deeply seated that they returned when he got better. Only later, following a second period of soul-searching, did he join the church, enroll in a classical academy, and dedicate himself to pious self-improvement. When he arrived in Otsego County, he therefore might be held up as a prime example of the difference that right thinking could make in a young American's life. Stephen Arnold's opposite, Neill was the perfect moral guide for the Cooper boys.

The general sermon had an even more pertinent application. When Neill took the Coopers under his wing, he knew more about them than one might expect, for he in fact had been the Princeton classmate—and sometime associate—of their disgraced brother. Given his conflicted past, it is not surprising that Neill had been swept up in the riotous conduct then pervading the campus, or that he had pulled back just in time: only the Nassau Hall fire at last shocked him into a permanent reformation. Arriving in Cooperstown barely three years later, he could ascribe his successful completion of his studies and the commencement of his new career to the manner in which he had extricated himself from young William Cooper's disastrous influence in 1802. Neill seems not to have been glib about all of this, but when Judge Cooper placed *this* man in charge of two more sons at just this juncture, he was sending a shot across their bow.

The finally concerned father insisted that both boys have "daily lessons in the elements of an English education"—the dream of college for any of his children now being out of the question. Their first meetings with Neill showed how right Judge Cooper's view of their idle disposition was.[15] Brighter and more animated than the dour, likable Samuel, the younger boy apparently presented the tougher case. In future decades, Neill was to follow Cooper's literary career; probably his knowledge of his former pupil's phenomenal success somewhat colored the recollections he published at the end of his life. Even so, he persisted in remembering Cooper back in 1805 as a "wayward" youth, one of the terms he had used in characterizing himself during his various bouts with temptation. As a pupil, to begin with, Cooper had made it clear that he "cordially"—that is, thoroughly—"disliked hard study."[16] He had learned little from his wasted years at Yale, his disgraceful manner of leaving that institution, William's example, the fight with Boyle, or even the recent shocking case of Stephen Arnold—however sharply the last event, according to his later recollections, seems to have struck him at the time. In denial, he kept up his old public face. He was still the immature, self-indulgent boy whose "interesting manners" had charmed Benjamin Silliman but whose behavior might yet lead him into even more serious trouble.

In the face of all this, Neill actually made some progress with the ex-collegian. The breakthrough came when he realized that something vaguely intellectual interested the young man. Cooper was so "extravagantly fond" of "novels and amusing tales," Neill asserted, that he read them "incessantly." Here was something the boy cordially *liked*, as one might put it. We do not know what Cooper read under Neill's eye. Perhaps this was the time when he devoured the American Gothicist Brockden Brown, Neill's fellow Pennsylvanian and an important influence on Cooper's fiction. Like most Americans of the time, though, Cooper probably dined on British imports and only snacked on American works. That was true even at the time when he began his own literary career.[17]

Whatever Cooper read, one thing seems sure. William Neill proved more sympathetic as a guide to popular literature than any of the boy's previous mentors. Cooper hardly had found fiction off-limits in his mother's house, to be sure, and "Tomy" Ellison's love of wit may have been broad enough to admit Fielding and Smollett, not just Dryden and Pope, within the range of his taste. Then, too, while he was in New Haven Cooper had access to the book collections of the Linonia, which held drama, travel books, and fiction along with weightier fare. But Yale's official suspicion of light reading and artful fun probably was one of the reasons for Cooper's later aspersions on the Yankee character. A regular subject of formal debate in his college classes and even in the Linonia, for instance, concerned the theater. In Cooper's time and afterward, those who spoke in favor of dramatic representation always lost to those who condemned it. Small wonder that just attending a play or acting in it brought automatic fines from the college.[18] Poetry was permissible in Timothy Dwight's universe, as both the president and Silliman would allow, but fiction was subjected to the same negative scrutiny as the theater. In the recitation section Silliman ran while a tutor in 1801, for instance, those opposing fiction won over its partisans.[19] When Silliman himself the next year ventured near the precincts of fiction in *The Letters of Shahcoolen*, that book passed muster because he cast it as a moralistic series of "Oriental" essays garbed in a chaste, quasi-novelistic costume. It was nothing like English Gothic tales or Brockden Brown's American thrillers, in which violent murder is central to the plot, night and insanity reign, rape is threatened or even attempted, and the author betrays a vexing fondness for moral conundrums. Silliman's "Shahcoolen" was no Carwin or Clithero.

William Neill may have looked down on books like Brown's with a scholar's suspicion if not with a minister's, but he certainly did not dismiss young Cooper's interest in them. Even if his only reason for tolerating that interest was his happiness at finding something that Cooper would work on without threats and cajoling, that was sufficient. The results were good. As Neill later recalled the case, Cooper soon "devoted himself to study, [and] became a good scholar." Indeed, the boy's pleasure in reading fiction was so great that he even began imagining himself as an author. The vagueness with which the tutor told this foreshortened tale does not inspire utter confidence in it.[20] It remains clear, however, that Neill and his student, as close in age as Silliman and Cooper had been at Yale, got on well together. Later, they would meet each other again while attending the founding meeting of the American Bible Society in New York in 1816.[21] And the novelist, who kept track of Neill's career over the years following, was to remember his last tutor fondly in Paris in 1831 when he heard more of him from a correspondent in Albany (*LJ* 2:157).[22]

Neill's supervision of Judge Cooper's youngest son did not last long. The clergyman left Cooperstown briefly in the early spring of 1806, going to Utica to pick up his wife, who had spent the winter with relatives there. His absence, and the couple's busyness as they settled into their new home on returning to Otsego, caused yet another interruption to Cooper's intermittent education.[23] That did not matter much, however. By early July, two weeks or so after observing the solar eclipse and taking his closest look at Stephen Arnold, Cooper had reached a decision about his future. He had escaped the dangers of Arnold's path, the path of utter self-absorption. And he was studying now, or so Neill felt, as he had never studied before. But where was he headed? While stuck in his father's house, he could go nowhere. He wanted a purpose, a place, something to do. So he bolted.

Over the past winter, the Venezuelan patriot Francisco de Miranda had been in New York secretly recruiting volunteers for what would prove an ill-fated attempt to overthrow Spanish rule in his homeland. Well-connected with such Americans as Dr. Benjamin Rush and the lawyer and politician Rufus King, both close associates of Judge Cooper, this "Washington of South America" (as American newspapers were soon calling him) had stirred up the military idealism of many young Americans after his motives for setting sail for the Caribbean in February 1806 became clear. At a time when the great naval victory of British Admiral Horatio Nelson over the French and Spanish fleets off Trafalgar the previous October was setting many young men mad with thoughts of maritime adventure, Cooper warmed to Miranda's cause. He doubtless followed the newspaper tales and circulating rumors and, as spring led to summer, wished he was off on the freebooting expedition rather than sitting at home with a book—even a novel—in his hands. By then, it was too late to run to New York and enlist under Miranda, since that man's flotilla of three ships was long gone (so long gone, in fact, that one of the vessels already had been captured and its naive American "soldiers" clapped in irons). But there were alternatives. Cooper came to believe that by securing a berth on a southward-bound merchant ship he might catch up with the would-be liberator and make a splash in this new American revolution. He could not free Lafayette from the dungeon of Olmutz, as Oliver Cory's tales had urged, but here was a scene of action that just might include him.[24]

Apparently without fully informing anyone about the more desperate parts of his scheme, Cooper abruptly left Otsego Hall in July and headed off. He probably went first to New York City, arriving there by the tenth and spending about a week lucklessly scouring the wharves. This setback triggered the next part of his larger plan. Beyond the imagined escapade in Miranda's service, Cooper already had set his sights on the U.S. Navy. So the still shipless young adventurer proceeded to write war department accountant William Simmons to inquire about securing an appointment as a midshipman.[25] This further effort Cooper also kept secret from the family back home, probably even from his brother William, then studying the law under Richard Harison in New York. He seems not to have stayed with William, whom he may have visited earlier in 1806 on Judge Cooper's orders, perhaps meant to direct this last of his sons toward the law, too.[26]

Cooper's next step in July was to rush off to Philadelphia in search of a suitable merchant ship bound south from that port.[27] He was acting now on a very short lead time. His unlocated letter to the war department, apparently sent just at the end of the New York stay, gave as a return address the Philadelphia home of family friend Richard R. Smith. But Smith hardly knew Cooper was on his way there; he learned of the boy's approach only through a hasty letter of July 15 or 16 that Cooper's brother William sent from New York and that must have arrived on the eighteenth or so, just when Cooper himself did.[28] The impulsive would-be sailor's sudden presence at the merchant's house was clearly a problem. At sixteen, Cooper was still a minor, and his turn toward Smith indicated his unwillingness to *really* trust himself to the chances of the world. However big he felt, however accustomed he thought he was to fending for himself while in Albany and New Haven (and perhaps more recently in New York), in fact he rarely had been apart from other family members and never out of the control of some sort of parental figure—in Albany, brother Isaac and Rev. Thomas Ellison; in New Haven, Samuel Cooper and "guardian" Nathan Smith. Now, for the first time really on his own, he must have begun to feel the loneliness of true independence. That he headed for avuncular Richard R. Smith's home after a couple of weeks away from the family suggests the underlying conflicts. He also was broke. Cooper "intimated that his Finances were low," so Smith reported giving him eighty dollars, adding to Isaac that he had taken "his Draught on you for that amount."[29] Cooper evidently had established an arrangement allowing him to draw money against Isaac, who no doubt charged any advance against their father's books. Where was the independence in that?[30]

When he arrived on Smith's doorstep in Philadelphia, Cooper's vision of his watery future was still intact. Most of his plans he kept hidden; all he would admit at first was that he wished to sign up for a merchant voyage. Even before the young man arrived, Smith had written to Isaac Cooper, to whom he was quite close, to express his desire to serve the family's interests—as well as the runaway's. But what should he do? Clearly he wanted Isaac to confer with Judge Cooper and other members of the family and quickly send him guidance. By the time he wrote Isaac again early in August, Smith had received Isaac's own answer of July 30, with which was enclosed "the Judge's memorandum" as to how to deal with his wayward son. Neither Isaac's letter nor Judge Cooper's enclosure survives, and it is not easy to infer their contents from Smith's second letter to Isaac. But Smith already had tried to caution the would-be sailor pretty much as his father would have. Recalling his own tough times at sea, he spoke of the hardships of a sailor's life and, to buy time, offered to help place Cooper in a Philadelphia counting house. If the boy still insisted on a voyage, Smith would introduce him to "shipping Merchants" of his acquaintance who would treat him fairly.[31]

Over the three weeks he spent in Philadelphia, Cooper again found no vessel to suit him. Before leaving for New York on August 7, he divulged to Smith his ultimate ambitions for the navy. Knowing how strong Cooper's impulses were, Smith feared he might plunge into some potentially harmful, even fatal, arrangement. Why not, Smith soon was asking the family, let the boy go right into the service now? "I am not fond of giving advice, but were James my son, and he so resolutely bent on the Navy as he now appears to be," Smith wrote Isaac, "I would immediately apply for a Warrant." Failing that, shouldn't the boy's family and friends actively seek out some safe berth for him? He was "certainly too Young to be launched into the World without protection." Smith's own merchant friends could provide that "protection," as in its way could the navy; Miranda certainly could not.[32]

Smith's counsel predicted the ultimate resolution. Acting through the network of associates on whom they and Smith could draw, the Coopers would allow the boy to go to sea but only with as many guarantees of his safety as possible. He probably was recalled to Cooperstown, but probably agreed to go there only if assured in advance that his longings for the sea would be honored. In the meantime, Judge Cooper appears to have involved Philadelphia merchant Miers Fisher in resolving the conflict. Richard R. Smith carried on his own business in 1806 at Fisher's wharf, owned by Miers and his brothers, all of whom were among those "shipping Merchants" to whom Smith had offered to introduce young Cooper in July.[33] Miers Fisher was an especially good choice as go-between because he already was a close friend of Judge Cooper and the Cooper sons—and of fellow Quaker Jacob Barker, a New York merchant shipper who was part owner of the vessel in which Cooper eventually sailed. Barker also was the consignee of the freight the ship carried on the voyage in question.[34]

Neither Cooper nor Barker directly recorded the ensuing arrangements. For the most part, it was from the descendants of the ship's master on Cooper's first voyage, John Johnston, that the details first emerged. Johnston's nephew Alexander, in an 1883 article based on the master's now unlocated papers, gave the important information about Barker's part ownership of the vessel and his interest in the freight. But he also asserted, probably in error, that Barker "was a personal friend of Cooper's father."[35] William Cooper appears not to have known Barker, certainly not well, but he surely had heard of him and knew how to put his son in touch with him through the network sketched above. It was Barker himself who in the company of another "merchant" led young Cooper on board the vessel shortly before it sailed from New York in October. The other man may have been Richard R. Smith or Miers Fisher, or perhaps, like Barker, a New Yorker—an associate in that case, one would think, of Judge Cooper's (*NM* 22).[36]

In his "editor's" preface to *Ned Myers; or, a Life before the Mast*, Cooper summed up this next large segment of his experience: "In the year 1806, the editor, then a lad, fresh from Yale, and destined for the navy, made his first voyage in a merchantman, with a view to get some practical knowledge of his profession" (*NM* iv). The summary had the neatness of most recollections: "fresh from Yale" was certainly an evasion, and only in retrospect could the expelled ex-student claim that in 1806 he already was "destined for the navy" or had anything like a "profession"—which the navy never became for him in any case. By 1843, having absorbed the collective wisdom of others, he saw the converging accidents of the past as his own intentional plot. The resulting myth was correct in only one regard: the voyage under Johnston proved a critical episode of Cooper's life.

At the outset, his chosen ship, the *Stirling*, was as green as he was. It had been built on the west bank of the Sheepscot River in the town of Newcastle, Maine, only the year before Cooper signed on. The shipyard was within a few miles of Captain Johnston's family home across the river and downstream at Wiscasset. Johnston and his brother Alexander and their father, John, Sr., were listed as the sole owners of the vessel on the 1806 registration filed in New York City. John Johnston, Sr., an old shipbuilder and master, probably had built the ship himself and then christened it with the name of the shire of Stirling in Scotland, near Edinburgh, from which he had emigrated to Boston in 1770. Young John was Yankee-born in 1779. When Cooper shipped on the *Stirling*, the master was thus only twenty-seven, not as old as Cooper's brother Richard, but to the seventeen-year-old he must have seemed of a different generation altogether, especially given his position of authority on board.[37]

The captain of the *Stirling* had gone to sea so early that by 1806 he already had been a master for seven years. He had first commanded the *Stirling* at the start of 1806, sailing it from Wiscasset on New Year's day and heading to New York, where he took on a cargo for London. From London he passed to St. Petersburg, which he left early in July for a seventy-two-day passage back to New York.[38] The latter city must have been something of a base of operations for vessel and master, a not-uncommon practice at a time when New Englanders dominated the maritime economy there. The registration filled out in the city in October of 1806 showed Johnston as a resident of New York, as apparently did the city directory for 1805. The registration also showed only the three members of Johnston's family as owners of the ship, so if Jacob Barker was indeed part owner, it was on the sly. Barker, who had gone bankrupt around 1801 at the age of twenty-two, rebuilt his fortune precisely by acquiring shares in a fleet of vessels—a common way for merchants to spread their liability among several ventures. A New York paper, in its "Marine List" for October 16, 1806, confirmed "J. Barker" as the consignee of the cargo—and of the freight on two other vessels then leaving the port.[39]

Ned

Like any vessel, the *Stirling* was a stage on which various actors soon would play their assigned roles. One of them, another wayward youth by the name of Ned Myers, was to prove especially close to Cooper. Some time before Cooper signed on the *Stirling* as an "ordinary" sailor, as the crew list called him, Myers had come on board as a cabin boy personally apprenticed to Captain Johnston.[40] His past was thick with mystery. He told Cooper that he had been born to German parents around 1793 in Quebec, where, he said, his father was an officer in a British regiment. When trying to persuade John Johnston to take him on as an apprentice in 1806, however, Myers claimed that his father had been a sergeant of marines on the notorious British frigate *Leander*—and had been killed in an encounter with the French frigate *Ville de Milan* (*NM* 21). Other discrepancies emerged every time he spoke of his origins.[41]

The mystery was deepened by an apparently cordial link between Ned's father and a member of the British royal family—Edward Augustus, the fourth son of George III and father of the future Queen Victoria. Ned went so far as to claim that Prince Edward, along with Maj. Robert Walker of the prince's own regiment (in which Ned said his father also served), had acted as his godfathers. Such tales had a certain plausibility. For one thing, Ned's full name was Edward Robert Myers. For another, the prince indeed had been very active in the British military establishment in Canada at the time of Ned's birth, having come over first in 1791 from Gibraltar. He served in Quebec until 1793, the approximate date of Ned's birth there, before departing for a successful British campaign against the French in the Caribbean. After that, he was appointed commander-in-chief of British troops in Nova Scotia at about the time Ned and his family also relocated there. Raised to the peerage as duke of Kent and Strathern and earl of Dublin, and appointed commander-in-chief of all British forces in North America in 1799, he was honored the next year by having a new Canadian province—Prince Edward Island—named in his honor. Shortly thereafter he returned to England for good.[42]

Ned Myers first told Cooper about the prince in London during the summer of 1807, while the *Stirling* was taking on its homeward cargo and the crew had time to wander onshore. In 1843, through the alcoholic haze of Ned's many years afloat, that earlier occasion came back to him while the reunited shipmates worked on Ned's book at Cooperstown. One Sunday back in 1807, that version runs, the two young sailors "were drifting up around the palace"—probably Kensington Palace—and, Ned remembered, "I told Cooper that the Duke of Kent was my godfather." By this point, Cooper may already have had enough of Ned's storytelling to doubt the assertion; or perhaps he was just caught off guard by the casual manner it was conveyed on the spot. Ned remembered the incident with more naiveté, recalling that Cooper "tried to persuade me to make a call; saying I could do no less than pay this respect to the prince," but Ned had been "too shy, and too much afraid" to do so. By 1843, Ned couldn't help wondering how a renewal of his tie with the prince might have changed his subsequently gritty life for the better. Cooper, though, undercut Ned's moral reflections by suggesting in a footnote that his challenge to Ned in 1807 was actually a bit of "roguery." Perhaps because he didn't really believe the tale, he hadn't expected them to gain admission to the palace, and if they just happened to get inside, fine, since Cooper had his own motive—nothing more noble than "a latent wish to see the interior" of the royal dwelling (*NM* 34).[43]

Ned thought that his father had left Nova Scotia some years before Prince Edward. At that time, Ned and his sister Harriet were placed in the household of a clergyman whose name he recalled as "Marchinton," and Ned was sent to school. Acknowledging that he was by nature "an idler" with a "roving and changeful mind," the old sailor admitted that he'd had little tolerance for the schoolmaster's authority, or for Marchinton's. Back then, to be sure, he had no such insights into his own character, but simply acted on the impulses that would later bring him much distress. The sea was a natural destination for a youth so driven, and Halifax was a perfect place to begin his odyssey. Founded in 1749 as the British counterpart of the fortified French port of Louisbourg on Cape Breton, the city remained a major naval station in the early nineteenth century, and Marchinton lived close enough to the water for Ned to spend much time along the wharves. Between his temperament and the opportunities of the place, his future career seemed all but prescribed.

Ned knew other youths his own age or slightly older who already had been initiated into the world of the sea, and they filled him with stories and information and pointed out the sorts of chances that might be open to him. One of them, a British midshipman, had been sent in as "nominal prize-master" of a captured American brig, to which Ned soon began frequent visits. Like Cooper during just these years, Ned fancied the navy but was surrounded by resistant elders. Mr. Marchinton clearly sought to keep Ned away from the bad influences of the port. That was a hard task with even a docile youth in contemporary Halifax, and Ned was not docile—quite the opposite. And his impulses only strengthened under suppression. Spied atop the brig's masthead, he was severely flogged by his guardian but hurried back to the docks and befriended a pair of American boys on board a second prize ship. They, too, told him seductive tales of life at sea, and of America to boot, and their apparent freedom from hard work (for what had these captive boys to do with themselves in Halifax?) seemed to Ned "the summit of human happiness." For the better part of a year, he therefore seethed with a desire to secure a berth on a U.S.-bound ship. At last, in the summer of 1805 (just when Cooper was sent packing from Yale), Ned Myers seized on the means to fulfill his oceanic fantasies (*NM* 12–13).

Orphaned as he seems to have been, Ned nonetheless led something of a protected existence before that first voyage. For all he had learned about ships and the sea from the stories of other boys and from his own eager scramblings, he clearly didn't look like a sailor when he went on board a captured North Carolina schooner recently freed on a decision of the admiralty court. He was dressed far too genteelly—perhaps in one of the suits that he claimed Prince Edward had custom-made for him—to be taken seriously by the mate, who was alone on the vessel then. And the fact that Ned "had never done any work" must have been visible in his slight, even delicate, build and especially his soft hands. The mate looked the twelve-year-old boy up and down and began to laugh at him and his romantic ambition for the sea. Ned, realizing that he would have to draw on other resources, resorted to bribery. On leaving Nova Scotia some years earlier, the prince had given Ned "a beautiful little fowling piece," which he now offered to the mate if the man would help him get aboard. The bait tempted the man, who asked to see the gun, and when Ned snuck it out of Marchinton's house that night and brought it on board, the deal was sealed.

The mate, however, proved no better than a man susceptible to a boy's bribes ought to have been. Ned went back home and packed. He gathered what he could of his belongings, then stealthily went into his sister Harriet's room for some shirts she was making for him. He took all the gear out to the yard, where he hid it in an old cask. The next morning, he had "a black servant of Mr. Marchinton's" wake him at daybreak on the pretext that he was going out to pick berries, but instead he retrieved his hidden pack and went down to the wharf. He was so early that no one was stirring yet on the schooner, so he roused the mate, only to find him wavering on their deal. The man certainly wanted to keep the fowling piece, but tried to scare Ned off, figuring that he could retain the prize if the boy was too wary to return (*NM* 13–14).

Despite the inequalities between the two, Ned persisted and at last held the mate to their agreement. Not that it met all his expectations. Although he had wanted to be signed on as cabin boy, he found instead that he had been shipped as cook—pity the poor crew—and before assuming those duties he spent a tedious period secreted in a vegetable bin in the cabin, covered with a great weight of potatoes and nearly stifled with the dead air. When he came topside at noon, already a bit nauseous, the ship was at sea, with only a tower or two in Halifax still visible in the familiar backward distance. By then, the mate had obviously informed the captain about their extra hand, and to judge from the hearty laughter at Ned's expense, he probably had told of the bribe and the potato bin and perhaps something about Ned's evident naiveté. But Ned did not regard himself as ill-used on the longish voyage. Cooking in itself did not strain his resources, although the heavy seas kept extinguishing the fire of his stove and his tendency to rekindle it with new shingles from the cargo hold got him into trouble with the mate, since "it was against the rules of the craft to burn cargo," as anyone but a green hand would have known. "In other respects," Ned told Cooper, "I did tolerably well; and, at the end of about ten days, we entered Sandy Hook" (*NM* 15–16).

How much of this story Cooper knew in 1806 and 1807 is unclear. As he heard it or reheard it in 1843, however, it would have echoed, perhaps even helped him to recover, some of his own feelings from that earlier period. Ned experienced such a powerful attraction to the sea that he could not resist it, much as Cooper could not, and it may be suggestive of how much alike they were that both youths had some tie to the Miranda expedition, Ned actually having been placed on a vessel used by the Venezuelan liberator before the boy's apprenticeship to Johnston. In 1843, Ned was honest enough to admit that his first day on the schooner he boarded in Halifax back in 1805 had taught him to distrust his impulses. He regretted the impetuosity with which he threw away his past and whatever future the Marchintons and especially Prince Edward might have helped give him. Perhaps out of rationalization, he downplayed the royal tie as he reflected on this careless but consequential moment in his youth. He now suspected that the prince would gradually have broken off their connection. He recalled his sister Harriet's actual fate in later years, how she had been forgotten not only by the prince but even in a way by the Marchintons, who gradually stopped treating her "as one of the family" and came to regard her instead as "a sort of upper servant." With no one to actively reassert their old status, the two orphans inevitably slipped downward, Harriet into a kind of servitude, Ned into the horrors of his later life at sea. Back in 1805, enough of the original luster still clung to them that, as Ned later learned, Mr. Marchinton had caused "a great search" to be made for him at his first disappearance (*NM* 15). Because the runaway had told no one onshore of his plans, it naturally was feared that he had drowned, and several spots around Halifax harbor were dragged for the body. Only when word of his presence in New York City eventually reached Halifax was the truth, or part of it, revealed.

Even in New York, the old ties kept resurfacing. Ned himself sought out some of them, as with the Clarks, a family he and Harriet had known well in Halifax. Before he left, he had learned from his sister enough about their present whereabouts in New York that, once his schooner was temporarily moored near Fly Market (then New York's main market, running southeast from Pearl Street to the shore), he decided to find them. He went ashore after preparing the noon meal for the schooner's crew; fell in with a group of boys on the dock who, cat-like, were "licking molasses" from some empty hogsheads; and tarried long enough that when he got back the ship had been moved to a different dock. So carefree was he that he claimed he never had learned the vessel's name, and now he was unable to locate it—or his meager belongings—again. It didn't matter much to him, however. He had no money, no hat, coat, or even shoes, but, hav-ing the born idler's trust in circumstances, he "knew nothing, and feared noth-ing."[44] When he went back to his new companions, they offered what help they could, telling him he could sleep under a butcher's stall in the market. Ned had other plans. He asked them about the Clarks, but the migrants had arrived re-cently enough that none of the boys recognized the name. So, with his nakedness hardly covered, Ned simply set off to find the old friends himself, strolling up toward Maiden Lane, which began opposite the market's far end on Pearl Street. As luck would have it, while sauntering along he heard "a female voice suddenly exclaim: 'Lord! here is Edward Myers, without anything on him!'" It was Susan Clark, who spied him from the family's lodgings and came running out to fetch him inside (*NM* 16–17).[45]

Everyone was excited to see him, and they asked him so many questions that for once he told the "whole truth," or so he claimed. The family offered him new clothes and kept insisting that he should move right into their house. But he'd had troubles with them in the past—"old quarrels" with the boys, and a dispute with the overly stern Mr. Clark about robbing the latter's fruit trees (an infrac-tion that Ned of course denied). So, accompanying the superficial delight of stumbling on familiar people in a strange place was the letdown of finding that bad feelings were renewed along with good. Ned claimed in retrospect that his main reason for looking up the Clarks in any case was the desire to find out from them, if possible, the whereabouts of an old military doctor from Nova Scotia who also had moved to New York. The man in question, a German named Heizer, was known to the Clarks, but only after Ned repeatedly refused their in-sistent generosity would they reveal that he and his family were dwelling up Broadway at the corner of Hester Street. Ned soon was regaling the Clarks with his tales, after which they fed him and took him out and bought him "a neat suit of clothes" (*NM* 17–18).[46]

Like the Clarks, the Heizers seemed intent on reclaiming Ned for respect-ability. Within a week, he was back in school, where any proper youngster ought to be. And, although Ned's sister later told him otherwise, the boy thought Dr. Heizer probably contacted the Marchintons with news of his whereabouts and condition. The Heizers, aware of Ned's old connections in the army and with the prince, regarded him as if he were the son they had always longed to have. He stayed with them and their daughters about nine months, always kindly treated, but before long the restraints of middle-class life once more began to bother the youth. Again he grew tired of school and began to skip classes, wandering instead along the wharves and looking longingly at the ships. Like the Marchintons, the Heizers soon became aware of Ned's fascination with the sea and, probably sensing that they could not control him, tried to persuade him to return to Halifax. Ned saw floggings at the end of that passage, however, and steadfastly refused, holding out for permission to ship for the open sea from New York. At last, Dr. Heizer consented to the plan—"or affected to consent; I never knew which," Ned and his editor added philosophically.

The details were complicated. Through his acquaintance with someone on board Miranda's secret flagship, then moored out in the Hudson, Heizer secured the young adventurer a post on it. Perhaps Ned was taken on as an apprentice (as he would be on the *Stirling*) to the vessel's captain, New Yorker Thomas Lewis. Ned was told that the ship was going to Holland with a commercial cargo—a variation on the cover stories told to other impressionable recruits. In reality, this second *Leander* was to leave New York on February 2, 1806, for Santo Domingo, and from there would proceed to the South American mainland; by the end of April, the ship would be bested in an exchange with two Spanish vessels and its men thrust into prison. Fortunately but inadvertently, Ned was not among the captives. Offended at the amount of dockside work Captain Lewis required (and even more by the fact that he was put under the thumb of Lewis's wife onshore), he had quit his post in the hope of finding real sea duty elsewhere. For once, mere self-indulgence protected the young sailor (*NM* 19–20).[47]

The Heizers, understanding Ned better than he understood himself, again tried to persuade him to return to Halifax and the Marchinton household. In the meantime, they put him back into school, where he languished for several more months until, wandering the docks one day, he happened to cast his eye on that cliché of nineteenth-century maritime literature, the Handsome Sailor: in this instance, a "singularly good-looking" Nantucketer named John T. Irish, then mate of the new, recently arrived ship *Stirling* (*NM* 21).[48] Going on board, Ned liked what he saw, and, avoiding Irish's more probing questions, offered himself to the mate as a cabin boy. When Captain Johnston returned, the boy resorted to that grand lie about a dead father in the marines, a ploy convincing enough that Johnston asked him to gather his belongings and come back later. Returning to the Heizer household at Broadway and Hester Street around noon, Ned snuck his things outside and hid them in the yard, then ate his meal with everyone as if nothing was up. Pretending that he was going back to school, he retrieved his bundle and was off, never to see any of them again. He slept that night in Johnston's lodgings at the Old Coffee House near the slip where the *Stirling* lay, then went with the master to a slop-shop the next day where he was "rigged as a sailor" (*NM* 22). A few days later, true to his word, Johnston took Ned ashore to have the proper apprenticeship papers filled out, after which all was official and Ned felt at long last that he had a place in the world and that nobody could send him back to Halifax against his will. In the meantime, as they waited for the cargo to be loaded and the crew to return, Ned and the old cabin boy, Dan McKay ("McCoy" in *Ned Myers*), had the run of the ship, whose innards they fully explored. Dan, who had been on the voyage to Russia under Johnston, was ready for advancement to a sailor's berth in the forecastle, and Johnston assigned him to train Ned to take over in the cabin.

Atlantic Crossing

It seems likely that Ned Myers went on board the *Stirling* in late September or early October of 1806. His brief service in Miranda's flagship probably had taken place in January of that year, after which by his own estimate—admittedly vague—he lived with the Heizers "a few months longer" (*NM* 20). The *Stirling* itself had not arrived back in New York from its maiden voyage until Saturday, September 13, and because the ship's inward-bound cargo had been disposed of when Ned boarded it, he probably did not come on deck until two or perhaps three weeks after that.[49] He didn't say how long he spent in the vessel with Dan McKay and the mate and master before the ship was ready to sail again, although "soon" after he boarded, the barreled flour Johnston was to carry to Europe began to be loaded. That process—like the off-loading, carried out by steve-dores—took a fair amount of time, especially because the ship was to be so packed with cargo that the stateroom and cabin both were nearly inaccessible and, as Ned recalled, he had to "climb over the barrels to reach the berths." When at long last Cooper came on board with Jacob Barker and the other mer-chant, the flour had been completely stowed, though, and the "sails were bend-ing"—that is, they were being tied to the yards, a final preparation for sailing (*NM* 22). The next day the stevedores took the ship out into the East River, where it was anchored as the crew members were brought out by boat, after which the *Stirling* "dropped down abreast of Governor's Island," just off the Battery. The ship stayed there that night, moved farther down the bay the next day, and on the third day put to sea (*NM* 23–24).

When exactly was that? The crew list and registration for the vessel, filed in New York, both were dated on October 15. These papers, for obvious reasons, would have been completed while the ship and its master and crew still were in New York: indeed, on the latter document John Johnston personally swore that he and his father and brother were the vessel's sole owners, something he could not have done without being on the spot on the date in question. And the crew list, which included Cooper's name, could not have been made out, if we follow Ned's chronology, until within a day of the ship's departure from its slip. Probably it could have been compiled accurately only once the crew, almost entirely new to the ship and having come on board a day after Cooper did, was fully assembled and could be definitively named. This point is confirmed by the same document's indication, as its printed text stated, that the ship was "now about clearing out" for its initial foreign destination, Cowes, on the Isle of Wight off the southern English coast.[50]

The Myers-Cooper collaborative account of the *Stirling*'s progress from the day Cooper showed up is brief. Ned's most powerful memory of the Atlantic crossing centered on an embarrassment that took place that "very day": "The small stores came on board for the cabin, and Dan Mc[Kay] persuaded me to try the flavour of a bottle of cherry-bounce. I did not drink much, but the little I swallowed made me completely drunk. This was the first time I ever was in that miserable and disgraceful plight; would to God I could also say it was the last!" An often homemade liqueur concocted from rum or whiskey, cherry bounce could be quite strong, though its severe effect on Ned no doubt was exacerbated by his small size and his inexperience at sailor's fare. At least he escaped with scant punishment. For this "act of folly," Ned recalled, Captain Johnston only "pulled my ears a little," while the impish McKay, who perhaps was trying to haze the new cabin boy, "was rope's-ended for his pains." In the process, McKay at least brought Ned into parity with the rest of the crew, who came out by boat the next day "bearing about them the signs of the excesses of which they had been guilty while on shore," some of them "listless and stupid, others still labouring under the effects of liquor, and some in that fearful condition which seamen themselves term having the 'horrors'" (*NM* 23). This first sounding of a major theme of Ned's memoir as Cooper edited it—intemperance—added a note of realism to the narrative overall.

However uniformly under the weather that first day, otherwise the crew encompassed considerable diversity. Although the list showed the current residence of all the men as New York, they had come to this busy port from many quarters. Of the twelve men named (everyone except Ned Myers and John Johnston and a stranded English whaler who worked his way home), only four were said to be New York natives. Two others, Cooper and Thomas Cook, had been born in New Jersey, one in Massachusetts, another in "New London," one in Pennsylvania, another in Germany, one in Spain, and the last, the cabin boy McKay (called a Scot by Ned Myers), in "Thomas Town"—probably not Thomaston, Maine, but rather Thomastown in Kilkenny, Ireland. Ned Myers shed a bit more light on the background of some of these men. One of the supposed New Yorkers, second mate John Gillet, Ned called Portuguese. He also said that (in addition to that stranded whaler) there was an Englishman in the forecastle, perhaps the "New London" man, John Burgoyn, who later deserted in London proper. Another of the sailors according to Ned was a Dane, who also deserted in the English capital: this may have been David Christian, who did desert, though he also was described as a native of New York on the crew list. The "German," whose name was given as Joseph Large, Ned specified as coming from Prussia (*NM* 23).

The confusion about the crew's personal history was pretty normal. Like many crews of merchant ships at the time, the *Stirling*'s men were perpetually in transit. (In an era when American birth might protect sailors at least partially against impressment by the British Navy, the confusion about personal origins also may have had a political purpose.) Aside from McKay and perhaps the first mate, there is no indication that any of the others on board for the passage to Cowes had made the previous voyage in the vessel. Ned suggested how temporary any crew was when, regarding the *Stirling*'s return to Philadelphia in 1807, he commented, "Here our crew was broken up, of course," adding that of all the men he served with on the ship, including several replacements picked up in Europe, he only even *saw* two of them later in life: Cooper, and a boy named Jack Pugh personally apprenticed to the captain in London. Most of the others from the return voyage soon left Philadelphia, "went on to New York, and were swallowed up in the great vortex of seamen." Even the first mate, John T. Irish, did not stay with Johnston: Ned heard that he "died the next voyage he made, chief mate of an Indiaman" (*NM* 37).

When the *Stirling* left New York in October of 1806, there were sixteen people on board. In the cabin were five men: Johnston; first mate Irish, twenty-two years old; second mate John Gillet, aged nineteen; Ned Myers; and an unnamed English ship master whose vessel had wrecked and who was going home as a passenger. In the forecastle were eleven others. Five of them were fully accomplished "seamen": twenty-year-old "Spanish Joe," Joseph Albert; John Burgoyn, twenty-seven, the "New London" (or perhaps London) sailor; "Big Dan," Daniel Gibson, a twenty-six-year-old native of Massachusetts; the German or Prussian, Joseph Large (perhaps originally named *Gross*), thirty-six; and, somewhat surprisingly placed among this highly experienced group, Daniel McKay, at fifteen and just over five feet tall, younger and much smaller than Cooper.

As seamen, each of these five crew members would be expected to perform almost any task associated with managing the vessel, whereas the three crew members described as journeyman seamen in the original crew list would be of somewhat more modest accomplishments. This second group included twenty-six-year-old Isaac Gaines, a New Yorker; the "Dane" (if that is right), David

Christian, twenty-two; and the second New Jerseyite, Thomas Cook, at forty-six probably the oldest man on board. There also was Peter Skimpson of Pennsylvania (twenty-five, listed as the vessel's cook), and that wrecked English whaler, a cooper by trade, who may have been named John Wood.[51] Finally, there was the five-foot-eight-and-a-quarter-inch James Cooper, described as eighteen (though he had just turned seventeen only a month earlier) and tagged as an "ordinary" seaman. He was the only hand on board so described, but as Webster's 1828 *Dictionary* indicated, the term was a common one during the period: "An *ordinary* seaman is one not expert or fully skilled." On board, he was simply called "Cooper": neither Ned Myers nor Captain Johnston later even remembered what his first name was, although Cooper in turn must have known Ned's given names in order to get the point of the 1806–1807 stories about Prince Edward.[52]

How apt the term "ordinary seaman" was, Cooper proved the morning the vessel began moving down into the upper bay. First mate Irish ordered Cooper and Myers up the foremast to loosen the topsail. "I went on one yard-arm, and Cooper went on the other," Ned remembered. "In a few minutes the second mate came up, hallooing to us to 'avast,' and laughing." Instead of freeing the sail so that it would drop open and catch the wind, the two novices had begun to undo the rigging that held it to the yard. Cooper was busily untying the robins (or robbins, i.e., rope-bands), the short lines that passed through the eyes on the top of the sail and affixed it to the yardarm; at the same time, Ned was removing the cords wrapped around both the furled sail and the arm, called gaskets, which he planned to take "carefully down on deck, where," as he naively recalled, "it struck me they would be quite safe." Ned may have been a bit more savvy here, but only a bit, since the gaskets indeed would need to be undone (but would be left attached to the yard) in order to unfurl the topsail, whereas if Cooper had persisted, his half of the sail might well have dropped down onto the deck. Second mate Gillet humorously set them right, and the two were able to escape "much ridicule" because the other crew members were so busy down below that nobody looked up. "In a week, we both knew better," Ned commented (*NM* 24).

The passage to Cowes gave further opportunity to learn. Although a jaundiced Ned Myers in 1843 stated that "nothing extraordinary occurred" on the way over, the *Stirling* in fact encountered almost perpetually stormy weather in 1806. As a result, the ship had to run "on a bow-line most of the time" (sailing close-hauled on winds nearly ahead), a tedious business that accounted for its longish crossing of some forty days.[53] These conditions created plenty of opportunities for handling ropes and sails, work that was more likely to involve Cooper than Myers—since, as Cooper remarked in the preface to *Ned Myers*, the cabin boy "was not then compelled to face all the hardships and servitude that

fell to the lot of the writer" (*NM* v). The tough trip must have had moments of
relief, even delight: perhaps it was on this voyage that Cooper had, as he put it in
his French travel book, "the sweetest sleep I have ever had"—sleep "caught on
deck, in the middle watch, under a wet pee-jacket, and with a coil of rope for a
pillow" (*GF* CE 272). Although time "before the mast" in the forecastle would
make Cooper decidedly a sailor, it hardly was "sweet" down there. More than
thirty years later, when visiting a nephew in New York who was a crew member
of the London-bound packet boat *Mediator,* Cooper toured the boy's quarters
and recalled those in the *Stirling:* "The forecastle is a very good one, infinitely
better than that in which I was immured" (*LJ* 3:252). Even if the stormy weather
during the 1806 passage meant that no stars glimmered straight overhead at
night, the air on deck would have been fresh and the space free.

   Johnston and the crew brought the *Stirling* sometime in mid-November to
the Bill of Portland, the lighthouse-crowned tip of the Isle of Portland, near
Weymouth on the south Dorset coast. The ship came east through this part of
the English Channel in uninspiring weather. Captain Johnston took on a pilot,
and soon the *Stirling* was headed around St. Catherine's Point, the southernmost
spot on the precipitous Isle of Wight, and then up the island's east coast past the
imposing Foreland and into St. Helen's Roads. Here the ship was anchored while
Johnston went ashore in his boat, rowed by four of the men (mostly the foreign-
born ones [*NM* 24]—perhaps a safeguard against losing any Americans to press-
gangs onshore), to learn how and where he was to dispose of the cargo. From his
landing place, presumably the village of St. Helens, he proceeded overland to
Cowes, the island's principal port on the north shore. As the crew list made up
just before the vessel left New York indicated, and as *Ned Myers* insisted, the *Stirling* was bound for "Cowes and a market" (*NM* 22), meaning that the point
where it would dispose of the flour was at that time unknown. In fact, Cowes was
not the ship's destination, only a stop where Johnston was to receive last-minute
instructions.[54]

   Cooper later would claim that he knew the Isle of Wight well, having
"sailed entirely round it, more than once" (*GF* CE 26), but he did not see
Cowes or land on the island during the *Stirling*'s voyage. What he knew in November of 1806 was the south coast, not the Solent, the narrow, risky passage
running between the Isle of Wight and the Dorset coast eastward from the
Needles, the steep chalk-cliffed outliers off the isle's west point. In 1826, the
ship bearing Cooper and his family to Europe took that other more direct route
to Cowes, and he saw the striking Needles close up for the first time: they were
"awkwardly placed for vessels that come this way in thick weather, or in the
dark," he noted then (*GF* CE 15). It may have been the thick weather the *Stirling* encountered in 1806 that urged Johnston or his pilot to steer wide around

the south shore of the Isle of Wight, adding miles (and a margin of safety) to the ship's approach.[55]

Once the vessel came to rest off St. Helen's and Johnston left, the weather cleared. Around sunset, a cutter from a man-of-war lying somewhere in the Channel pulled alongside, and the lieutenant in charge of it, "tolerably bowsed up"—drunk—came on board and ordered first mate Irish to muster the crew. The English officer arrogantly went below to the cabin and seated himself behind the captain's table "while the men came down, and stood in the companionway passage, to be overhauled" by him. As always, the overhauler was on the lookout for presumed British subjects to commandeer for the royal navy, and (also as usual) he was none too careful. His eye fell on two of the *Stirling*'s "finelooking men," the New Jerseyite Thomas Cook and the New Yorker Isaac Gaines, both of them "prime seamen" according to Ned's recollection even though the crew list called them journeymen. Some things were clearly exaggerated by Ned's memory, and perhaps by Cooper's, too. Thomas Cook they described in their book as "a six-footer" who "had the air of a thorough sea-dog," while the crew list measured him at five foot nine-and-a-half inches, tied with Dan Gibson for tallest on board but barely taller than young Cooper in 1806.[56] In any event, Cook "filled the British lieutenant's eye mightily" and he was told to gather his belongings and prepare to leave. Like many American (and indeed foreign-born) sailors, this seaman carried a certificate from a New York official indicating that he was American-born, but the lieutenant breezily dismissed such papers: "Oh! these things are nothing—anybody can have one for two dollars, in New York. You are an Englishman, and the King has need of your services" (*NM* 24–25).

Cook had a trump card, however. Forty-six years old, the American had made many voyages and been through a great deal, including a long stint as an impressed sailor in the royal navy ship *Cambrian*. He had finally won his freedom by successfully proving his American birth, and at that time received a discharge signed by the British naval officer John Beresford, who had been in command of the *Cambrian* in the years just preceding. The lieutenant could not well ignore this second document, so he let Cook stay on the *Stirling*—but, as a lagniappe of condescension, he kept the man's New York certificate.[57]

Twenty-six-year-old New Yorker Isaac Gaines was not so fortunate. Cooper and Myers clearly believed that he was American-born, and he too may have had papers from some American authority. Furthermore, unlike many seamen, he had enough stability in his life that Captain Johnston was personally acquainted with his father and his friends back home in New York. But Gaines, "one of the best men in the ship," had no discharge like Cook, no British paper proving that he was an American. Hence, over the side and into the waiting cutter he and his chest were required to go. He came up from the cabin "with tears in his eyes," Ned remembered, and then was surrounded by the sad crew, everyone grieving for such a well-liked man. Nothing could be done—a sharp lesson for Cooper in the reality of ocean politics and his own nation's post-colonial position in a world dominated by British power. At least, having hooked one good fish, the lieutenant let the others swim free. As for Gaines, no one on board the *Stirling* saw him again. Ned drew the obvious (but apolitical) moral: "Such was often the fate of sailors, in that day, who were with you one day, and lost for ever the next" (*NM* 25).

Captain Johnston came back aboard with his four oarsmen the day following, under orders to proceed with the cargo to London. The wind was strong, almost gale-force, so the crew quickly lifted anchor and headed out into the Channel again. The ship sailed steadily all day and night, perhaps under the direction of another pilot, on past Selsey Bill and Beachy Head, then Hastings and Dungeness, until by the next morning it had entered the straits of Dover. The wind had lightened by then, but still favored them on their course past the anchorage of the Downs and the treacherous Goodwin Sands that protected it from the North Sea, until they could make the turn into the great bay leading to the Thames estuary. The waters of their route were exceptionally busy, and not just with commercial vessels, for all England was on alert once again for an invasion by Napoleon. The emperor was dramatically expanding his conquests and alliances in Europe throughout 1806, constructing a "Continental System" aimed at isolating the British Isles. Small wonder that, early in the morning, the *Stirling* encountered dozens of British cruisers, perhaps one hundred off Dungeness, plus another fleet of more than forty in the Downs, that had been on patrol all night "to prevent a surprise" (*NM* 26).[58] For Cooper, here was a firsthand taste of the great events transforming contemporary Europe. The scope of the struggle would have been impressive for someone fresh from America, where the entire naval fleet on active duty at the time numbered only about a dozen ships. Later, in novels such as *The Two Admirals* and *The Wing-and-Wing*, Cooper's feeling for the movement of big fleets and for the naval atmosphere of the Napoleonic years showed part of the legacy of his early days at sea.[59] Other insights lay ahead. The *Stirling* worked its way slowly toward the Thames, following the winds and then the tides in from the North Sea. As the ship moved into the narrowing passage between Shoeburyness on the north and Sheerness on the south, it would come within sight of the lightship that long had marked the Nore, a dangerous sandbank stretching most of the way across the water. Only nine years earlier, in June of 1797, Richard Parker led sailors in the British naval vessels anchored here in a wartime mutiny that gave the sandbank's name new meaning, an uprising amply reported, along with Parker's June 28 execution, at home in the *Otsego Herald* during Cooper's first summer back from Burlington.[60]

Although *Ned Myers* has little to say about the next part of the voyage, the novel *Afloat and Ashore*, written almost immediately as a fictional offshoot of Ned's book in the 1840s, offers something of an analog in the upriver passage of the *Amanda*, a brig liberated from its French captors by Cooper's hero, Miles Wallingford. Miles's passage up the Thames proceeded, like that of the *Stirling*, by a rhythm of floodtide advances and pauses on the ebb. "We had to tide it up to London," Miles (as narrator) recalls, "and had plenty of leisure to see all there was to be seen." It was not the natural scenery along the shores that filled his eyes—he hardly was peculiar in finding the Thames "neither a handsome, nor a very magnificent river"—but rather the great crowd of vessels jamming the waterway. Their sheer number was "amazing," but so was their variety, since they included almost every "sort of craft known to Christendom." Miles was especially impressed by the large fleets of colliers, so numerous that he thought London might be kept "a twelvemonth in fire-wood, by simply burning their spars" (*A&A* CE pt. 1:144–45).

All of this Cooper no doubt took in as the *Stirling* followed the same slow course upriver. Perhaps he also came to share the new insight into the sailor's calling that his novel would give to Miles: for the struggle to control a ship as it moved at the tide's mercy amid a jam of other vessels taught a mariner more than might be learned, Wallingford concluded, in a "voyage to Canton and back again." The fictional sailor elaborated: "The manner in which the pilot handled our brig . . . among the thousand ships that lay in tiers on each side of the narrow passage we had to thread was perfectly surprising to me; resembling the management of a coachman in a crowded thoroughfare more than the ordinary working of a ship." This "navigation from the Forelands to the bridges," Miles thought, was a special nursery of English seamanship (*A&A* CE pt. 1:145). "It was the only place I knew," Cooper recalled in his English travel book, "which gave one a vivid impression of what is meant by a forest of masts" (*GE* CE 190).

Then, emerging from that forest, the vessel drew near to London. Somewhere on the upriver passage, the *Stirling* was boarded by two customs officials, one of whom (a rogue named Swinburne) took a liking to Cooper.[61] *Afloat and Ashore*, in its fictional reworking of the English visit, gives some insight into the young author's first exposure to London under this man's guidance. The guide in the novel—also a rogue, called Sweeney—escorts Miles to such obvious sights as St. Paul's and the Great Fire monument, then to the more genteel "wonders of the West End." Eventually, revealing a good deal about his own low nature, Sweeney leads Miles "through Wapping, its purlieus and its scenes of atrocities," at last making him "a proposition" (presumably involving a brothel) that one assumes stemmed from Cooper's own tours under the direction of the equally seedy, promptly dismissed Swinburne (*A&A* CE pt 1:146–47). Overall, though, Swinburne showed Cooper more of London than he probably would have seen on his own. Ned Myers, recalling Cooper's shipboard tales of the experience, thought his friend "had a rum time of it, in his sailor rig, but hoisted in a wonderful deal of gibberish," and Cooper in turn shared the city with members of the crew, among them Ned (*NM* 26).

Another companion was a new hand shipped in London, recalled in *England* as a "gigantic fellow from Kennebunk, of the name of Stephen Stimpson." Impressed by the British some years before, Stimpson had just been discharged from the man-of-war *Boadicea* (*GE* CE 194). Signed on to the *Stirling* almost immediately after it arrived in London, the Yankee befriended Cooper and joined him in excursions about the capital.[62] Thomas Cook, the heretofore lucky sailor whose discharge papers signed by John Beresford of the *Cambrian* had saved him from impressment off the Isle of Wight, also went about London with Cooper—less luckily, as it happened. While serving on Beresford's ship, Cook had helped in the seizure of a vessel and, as those papers indicated, was due a portion of the prize money. He went with Cooper one day to the record offices in Somerset House, up along the Thames in the Strand, to secure an order for the payment. The clerk there, unsure of the amount due, asked Cook to come back in a day or two but to leave the discharge at the office in the meantime. Cook complied and left with Cooper to make his way back to the ship. The "six-footer," an obvious prize in the eye of any press-gang, was seized en route, however, and, bearing no proof at all of his American nativity, was taken off and never seen or heard from again (*NM* 24–25). For Cooper, clearly, here was another close encounter with the abuses of British imperial policy.

The first London visit lasted from the latter part of November or early December into January 1807, at which time the *Stirling*, its flour unloaded, moved out past the gates of London Dock to be filled with ballast—"shingle," or pebbles, were used—in preparation for a freightless passage to Spain, where Johnston had made arrangements to pick up a load of barilla, the impure alkali, similar to potash, produced from the burning of glasswort (or barilla) plants and used in the manufacture of soap, soda, and glass. Before sailing, Johnston had other adjustments to make. Sometime in December, three men (Burgoyn, Wood, and Large) deserted.[63] The original crew thus had been reduced by five men, two through impressment and three by desertion. These losses the captain partly made up by taking on four replacements: Stephen Stimpson; a man named Bill who supposedly was from Philadelphia; a "dull Irish lad," also named Bill; and, apparently, a man by the name of Jim Russel. He also had to pick up the same pilot used when the ship came upriver two months earlier. From London Dock, the ship's route lay through stretches of the river named for the bank-side communities of Limehouse and Greenwich and Blackwall, where a great curve bent around the Isle of Dogs, site of the new West India Dock, after which the stream twisted back around the edge of the Greenwich marshes. From there, a series of sinuous channels or "reaches" led down toward the estuary and the North Sea: Woolwich, Gallions, Barking, Halfway, Erith Reach and Erith Rands, then the straight run of the Long Reach before the double curve of St. Clements (or Fiddler's) Reach and, finally, Northfleet Hope, beyond which lay Gravesend and the last long stretch before the broad outer estuary opened. Throughout the distance, those "tiers" of ships again were to be avoided, and the tides and currents fought. Speed was mostly out of the question; any wind the sails might catch had to be used instead to control the vessel.

The Mediterranean

Once out on the wintry North Sea, the *Stirling* began to encounter persistent rough weather. Heading south, it therefore may have cut as close as conditions allowed to the Channel Islands and Cap de la Hague on the coast of Normandy before passing around the Île d'Ouessant (Ushant) and the long Brittany peninsula to enter the stormiest part of the passage to Gibraltar, the Bay of Biscay, which gave Cooper's ship "a touch of its qualities" (*NM* 26). In *The Pioneers*, Cooper put at the head of one of the chapters a snatch of anonymous song he may have joined in singing, or at least heard, on this part of the voyage: "As she lay, on that day, in the Bay of Biscay, O!" (*PIO* CE 169).

Given the rough weather on this passage, one can assume that the *Stirling* probably did not *lie* in the bay. Soon it passed Cabo Prior and Cabo Villano in the northwest of Spain, then Cabo Finisterre, and then the mouth of the Rio Miño, beyond which began Portugal. The wind must still have been strong but from some favorable quarter, since the *Stirling* ran down along the coast here in sight of land, a course that under worse conditions might have been dangerous.[64] Still, there were other hazards. At one point, the men caught sight of a felucca, a fast lateen-rigged vessel, that managed to gain on the *Stirling* whenever the wind lessened. Captain Johnston didn't like the looks of the strange craft, which appeared to be armed, so he fought hard to run before it, but once the felucca began to fire cannon and the shots came close, he ordered the men to heave to. Within ten minutes the ship had stopped and the felucca had come near enough to hail Johnston and tell him to send over a boat with his ship's papers. Because the weather had been so brisk, Johnston's jolly boat had been stowed inside the big launch, up on deck; it took time to attach tackle up in the rigging and hoist the smaller craft out and lower it to the sea. As the wind fell off during this process,

Ned scanned the stranger and its crew and became convinced that it was a pirate vessel intent on plundering his own ship—and perhaps worse. The Americans began what preparations they could for the seemingly inevitable encounter. Johnston grasped the ship's best spyglass and handed it to Ned, telling him to have Cooper hide it. Down into the hold the ordinary seaman went, scooping out a hollow in the shingle ballast and secreting it there. Meanwhile, up in the cabin, Ned helped hide a bag of guineas so well that after the encounter the money couldn't be found, and only weeks later, as they ate their way down through the contents of the cabin's bread locker, did the bag show itself again.[65]

As the felucca continued to wait, the *Stirling*'s jolly boat finally was lowered down over the side of the ship and into the water, and Johnston ordered four men—Big Dan and Spanish Joe, along with Little Dan McKay and Cooper—to clamber down into it. From on deck, the captain passed his portable writing desk, containing the ship's papers, over the side and was himself halfway over the rail when the weather suddenly worsened, kicking up a squall. So the four seamen went back onto the *Stirling* and up into the rigging to help clew down the topsails. The latter process consumed a quarter-hour, by which point the little squall had passed. Still the felucca waited. The four hands once more reluctantly began to go over the side and down into the boat when a second interruption stopped them. Just then an English frigate, coming off the coast, had taken aim at the corsair, whose commander waved the Americans back as "his craft fell off and filled, wing-and-wing, skimming away towards the coast, like a duck."[66] The air still was so thick with mist from the squall that the two other vessels soon were swallowed up, neither to be seen again as their guns kept echoing in the distance. The lucky *Stirling* hastily went on its way south (*NM* 26–28).

Before long, another mischance vexed the American ship as thick weather and westerly winds drove it as far as Cape Trafalgar on the southwest Spanish coast, where Lord Nelson had decisively defeated Napoleon's fleets less than a year and a half earlier. Captain Johnston came on deck in the darkness of the middle watch and, aware that the fleet of Lord Collingwood (Nelson's successor in the struggle against Napoleon) lay near the cape, hailed the forecastle and ordered the men to keep a sharp lookout. Hardly had he given the warning when Spanish Joe cried out that he saw a sail, and those on deck looked and saw a huge ship bearing down, aimed squarely between the *Stirling*'s fore and main masts. Johnston, ordering the helm turned sharp, yelled for Cooper to bring up the cabin lantern. At that, the youth with one leap flew down the ladder, grasped the gleaming light and within a moment was topside, then up into the rigging of the mizzen mast with it, where the oncoming vessel couldn't miss it. "That saved us," Ned calmly concluded. Everyone could hear the officer of the deck on the British ship call out, "port, hard a-port—*hard* a-port, and be d—d to you!," and then the two-decked warship barely scraped by the *Stirling*'s windward side. The ship came so close that as it rose on a swell the muzzles of its guns seemed about to smash up through the *Stirling*'s rails. Johnston's craft, sluggish and not responding well, appeared to go toward the warship rather than away, but at last it pulled clear. This was a second stroke of good luck (*NM* 28).

Soon they passed the Straits of Gibraltar, then turned northeast and began working up toward Cartagena, 250 miles distant in the province of Murcia. The deep, broad harbor there, surrounded by fortified hills, was the finest on Spain's east coast. The *Stirling*, forced into quarantine for several days, found four English warships at anchor in the harbor, their officers eager for news from London. Soon, the waiting period over, Johnston moved back down along the coast some forty miles to the small village of Aguilas, where part of his new cargo could be picked up. There the Americans lay offshore in the roadstead, taking in the barilla from boats during the day, making room for it by discharging the shingle ballast into the sea at night—secretively, for ballast dumping was illegal along many coasts owing to the disastrous effect it had on anchoring grounds. Although the water was so transparent beneath the *Stirling* that the English pebbles might be clearly seen lying in piles on the bottom, no one inspected; probably the ship was far enough from shore that the dumping would have no ill consequences. While the *Stirling* lay off Aguilas, receiving what would amount to half its freight, an English man-of-war, perhaps one of those seen in Cartagena or another one from Lord Collingwood's fleet beyond Gibraltar, was seen off the coast. The local populace was alarmed, but nothing came of the resulting rumors of an attack. Ever since Nelson's victory at Trafalgar, British naval power was virtually unopposed along the Spanish coast.

Ned Myers did not indicate how long the *Stirling* was off Aguilas, or whether the crew spent any time onshore there, but the men certainly did visit the next stop, Almeria. Located at the center of a broad gulf about ninety miles farther down the coast, just past Cabo de Gata, Almeria was, Ned noted, "an old Moorish town." The Romans knew it as Portus Magnus, the Moors, as *al-Mariyah*, "Mirror of the Sea"—and its bright, exotic architecture must have gleamed in the warm winter sun before the eyes of those in the American vessel, which again anchored a considerable distance off the land. Back in behind the town, they may have been able to see the green valley watered by rivers from the formidable coastal mountains and from even higher ones, the Sierra Nevada, rising farther inland. The ship lay there "several weeks," the men taking on the rest of the cargo and seeing it properly stowed and no doubt enjoying the warmth, perhaps even drawing out the work in order to tarry before heading back out through Gibraltar and driving up to the colder shores of England. "In that low latitude," as Cooper was to recall in *Mercedes of Castile*, his novel about

Columbus, the weather could be "genial and spring-like" even in early February (*MC* 1:115). And it wasn't just the weather that was soothing. Ned remembered going ashore "almost every day to market" (*NM* 29), probably to fetch fresh foods for the cabin—perhaps for the forecastle as well. (Forty-four years later, delighted to find fresh grapes from Almeria served at New York's Globe Hotel in the midst of winter, Cooper was to remember that town as "the port in Spain where I first tasted the delicious fruit" [*LJ* 6:141].) Much of Ned's day must have been spent making these frequent market runs. The ship's jolly boat had to go in through the surf—there was no wharf—and land on the shore near the quarantine station, a good half-mile from the town's water gate. The men had to walk to town along the beach, go to the market, then reverse their route while lugging back whatever they had procured. But the excitement of the shore must have been high, and the market goods brought to the ship were their own reward. Ned also seems to have enjoyed the "opportunity of seeing something of the Spaniards" (*NM* 29), a diversion probably not readily available when they were at Aguilas or Cartagena. Although Ned didn't say so, it seems likely that Joseph Albert—"Spanish Joe"—served as a go-between for some of these forays, and for other business throughout the passage to Spain.

Cooper also must have spent a fair amount of time wandering about onshore here. One of the new crew members Johnston had added in London "had taken a great liking to Cooper"—he was the man they called Philadelphia Bill, whom Ned remembered as "steady, trust-worthy, quiet, and respected by every man in the ship." Bill taught Cooper a good deal about sailing, "how to knot and splice, and other niceties of the calling," and in return Cooper "took him ashore with him, and amused him with historical anecdotes of the different places they visited" (*NM* 31). They may have wandered about in London before leaving for Spain, then resumed their touring in Almeria, where the fortress-looking Gothic cathedral would have been worth a visit, as well as the Moorish fort, the Alcazaba, which had stood since 773 on the site of an immeasurably more ancient Phoenician settlement. And above the town, commanding the harbor, stood the ruinous Castillo de San Cristobal. Cooper may have known less about such exotic structures, typical of Spain's colorful past, than about more recent events—especially the naval encounter between Lord Nelson and the fleet of Napoleon and his allies farther down the coast. But he could have picked up anecdotes enough from his reading and from odd moments of attentiveness in his formal schooling to keep the likes of Philadelphia Bill respectfully awed.[67]

While the barilla was being loaded and packed off Almeria, Ned's future editor was set to other tasks. The captain wanted to have some pitch boiled down, probably to refine it for eventual repair work, and ordered Cooper and former cabin boy Dan McKay to undertake the task in the galley. There they soon learned the hard way that hot pitch is inflammable, for "the pot was capsized, and the ship came near being burned." After that, the two were ordered to shift the procedure to shore, a change that entailed a punishing increase in labor. Ned, going on land for a market trip, accompanied them as they carried a fresh pot and the other tools and supplies to the quarantine station. The lack of a wharf there, not to mention the likely weight and bulk of the pot and the raw pitch, helped make the trip "a little adventure." Landing through the surf was always risky because the bay was protected only by an "elbow" of land that barely shielded it from the sea winds. The three young men brought the jolly boat ashore well on this trip, though they must have struggled to drag it high enough on the land to keep it put there. Ned helped the two laborers get set up, carrying the pitch for them while they handled the pot and everything else, then left on his errands as they were lighting the fire at the station and arranging things. On this occasion all went so well that by the time Ned returned, Cooper and McKay were done with the messy undertaking.

The swell was up by then, however, and the breakers striking the nearby shore looked "squally," suggesting that a tricky pull out to the *Stirling* lay ahead. Captain Johnston's standing orders called for anyone left onshore as such conditions approached to hurry back to the vessel. The three companions managed to reload the boat, drag it down the beach, and float it; then they jumped in and made a likely start through the surf. Suddenly a big breaker caught the bow and flipped the boat "keel uppermost," spilling everyone and everything into the sea. "We all came ashore, . . . heels over head," Ned remembered, "people, pot, boat, and oars." On the second attempt, they were missing the pitch and, Ned soon discovered, "a pair of new shoes of mine." On the third try, they managed to get through the surf and out to the ship, but still without the refined pitch or the boy's footwear. Miraculously, Ned survived despite the fact that he could not swim a stroke (*NM* 29–30).

When the long period of labor off Almeria at last ended, probably in late March or early April 1807, the *Stirling* weighed anchor. It was headed to London but first had to "fight fresh westerly gales" that drove it back and forth between the coasts of Europe and Africa until at last the Mediterranean's strong east wind, called the Levanter, arose and "shoved us out into the Atlantic."[68] In passing Gibraltar, the ship encountered Portuguese frigates that came out from the stronghold on such winds, eager to keep Barbary pirates from making it through to harass Atlantic shipping—though soon, embroiled in the Napoleonic conflict, the Portuguese would have other things to worry about. The frigates stayed in the straits as the *Stirling* passed into the ocean, where the heavy cargo in its hold made the ship sluggish in the lighter sea winds encountered there. The rest of the passage back to London took so long that, low on provisions, the captain

had to buy a barrel of salted beef from an American ship in the Bay of Biscay—
when indeed the *Stirling* must have lay to there long enough to make the transfer. As the *Stirling* finally crept close to the "chops" of the Channel, probably in
the vicinity of the Isles of Scilly, the south wind was so light that a seriously
damaged English warship passed at twice the American ship's speed. Although
that vessel went by close enough for Ned to observe one part of the crew at rest
on the deck from its stint with the pumps below, the warship took no more notice
of the merchant vessel "than if we had been a mile-stone." There was "something proud and stately in her manner of passing us," Ned thought, as if the warship somehow were removed from common routine (*NM* 30–31). Yet it went on
with an incongruous bit of awkwardness, carelessly letting fall a bucket that
bobbed in the water until the *Stirling*, coming along a half-mile behind, hauled it
aboard. Bearing the official "broad arrow" stamp that identified British government property, it later caught the eye of a customs official on the Thames, who
wanted to confiscate it.[69]

Before heading back upriver to London, the *Stirling* had other stops to
make. The men sighted the west of England first, glimpsing Land's End, with
fine weather and a fair wind at last. Normally, a London-bound ship would head
straight up the Channel here, as the *Stirling* had on arriving from New York the
previous November. But vessels coming from the Mediterranean had to lie under
quarantine before off-loading cargo or crew, and the west country was as good a
place as any for that. Johnston had only one question. He turned to Cooper, to
whom he had entrusted the helm, and asked him whether anyone on the vessel
had ever been into Falmouth, a port town inside a broad bay beyond the Lizard,
the second major point on the southwest coast. Cooper answered that his companion Philadelphia Bill, who was up on the forecastle even then naming the
headlands on the rocky coast as they passed, claimed long familiarity with that
port. Bill was a bit of a puzzle. He indeed must have known Philadelphia well
enough to maintain his sobriquet even to New Jersey native Cooper, but no
one had yet fathomed the evasive sailor's true origins. Events would soon make
them clear.

When, acting on Cooper's assurances, Johnston had Bill called aft, the man
uneasily admitted that he could guide the vessel into Falmouth. He proceeded to
bring it in without ado, handily skirting the rock that stood abreast of Pendennis
Castle, the Tudor fortress at the extreme east end of the town's peninsula. The
Stirling, ordered by Falmouth officials to anchor a few miles up the bay, worked
its way there, apparently still under Bill's guidance, and the next day a doctor's
boat came alongside. Johnston's crewmen were called on deck to show that they
were healthy, being told, Ned recalled, to "flourish our limbs, in order to make
it evident we were alive and kicking" (*NM* 32). Here, in the midst of this cursory

medical examination, Philadelphia Bill's cover story began to be lifted. Aside from the doctor in the boat, there were four oarsmen, each of whom recognized Bill as a Falmouth native who had run off from his wife twenty years earlier. The abandoned woman was still well known locally. Without speaking, Bill managed to signal the four oarsmen not to give away his secret, and somehow secured their connivance. At that point, the boat went off and the *Stirling* prepared to anchor for the required quarantine period.

On a Saturday two weeks later, at last free, the vessel dropped back down to Falmouth. The next day some of the crew, Bill included, were given their first liberty ashore. The visit to scenes he had not encountered in so many years led Bill, he admitted that night, to be "a little indiscreet." Back aboard the ship on Sunday night he seemed agitated, but when nothing happened he began to recover his composure. He still hoped, however, that the ship would make a speedy departure. Before long, the men began to work the *Stirling* out of the harbor's mouth under a light breeze. When the ship had just cleared the points, the wind started blowing fair up channel, and the captain ordered more canvas put on. Cooper was at the foretop braces with Philadelphia Bill, adjusting the sail, when the sound of a musket rang out nearby on the water. "I'm gone!," Bill exclaimed, his voice so full of emotion that those near him thought he had been shot. But when he pointed to the press-gang boat from which the shot had been fired, they understood him. Captain Johnston ordered the head braces belayed, stopping the ship, and waited for the English boat to arrive. When the officer in charge came on board, he commanded Johnston to muster the crew—a "humiliating order," of course—and all hands came aft. The officer went through the men, "easily satisfied" with their stories, "until he came to Bill": "'What countryman are *you?*' he asked. 'An American—a Philadelphian,' answered Bill. 'You are an Englishman.' 'No, sir; I was born—' 'Over here, across the bay,' interrupted the officer, with a cool smile, 'where your dear wife is at this moment. Your name is —— ——, and you are well known in Falmouth. Get your clothes, and be ready to go in the boat.'"

Bill knew that no resistance would save him. Captain Johnston paid him the wages due and his chest was brought up and lowered over the side into the boat. Then "the poor fellow" bid his shipmates goodbye and, following after it, prepared to take his place in the royal navy. It wasn't his long-abandoned "dear wife" that had been the object of the officer's concern—it was the insatiable appetite of the crown for ever more hands.

Bill knew that he was staring at his final fate: old as he was, he was sure that the seemingly endless war with France would outlast him, and as long as he did survive no one would trust him on land again. He had a special farewell for his closest companion, Cooper, who may have recalled his words when, fifteen years later, he invented Long Tom Coffin, his sea-bound archetypal sailor: "'My foot will never touch the land again,' he said to Cooper, as he squeezed his young friend's hand, 'and I am to live and die, with a ship for my prison'" (*NM* 32–33). In *The Pilot*, to be sure, the *Ariel* liberated rather than imprisoned Long Tom, but for all that, the man died in the ship—with the ship—in the wreck.

Homeward Bound

There was no help for Bill, whom they all missed as the *Stirling* went out into the offing, turned up the Channel, and headed once more for the port of London. Somewhere on the Thames, probably at Gravesend again, Johnston took on board the same pilot who had seen the vessel up and down the last time, and once more the heavily laden, sluggish ship worked up the twists and reaches, largely on the flood tide. This time the *Stirling* unloaded down at Limehouse, probably via the small freight vessels called lighters as it lay in a "tier of Americans" out in the river near the West India Dock gate. Once empty, it took on a small amount of ballast and went downstream a bit to Deptford, the famous ship-building area opposite the Isle of Dogs, where it was docked and cleaned. From there, the ship went back upriver and into the same wet dock where it had discharged the flour the previous fall. Here it spent "part of May, all of June, and most of July" picking up small consignments until Johnston had a full load of freight (*NM* 33).[70]

During the slow process of arranging for the cargo, receiving it, and stowing it in the ship, members of the crew had even more time to wander about London.[71] Once again, Ned recalled, Cooper "took me in tow, and many a drift I had with him and Dan Mc[Kay] up to St. Paul's, the parks, palaces, and the Abbey." It was at this time, in fact, that he and Cooper went "drifting up around [Kensington] palace" one Sunday and had their exchange about the duke of Kent (*NM* 33–34). Aside from "Little Dan," who along with Spanish Joe and "Peter Simpson" (*sic*) Cooper said he remembered "well" when he wrote to Captain Johnston in 1843 (*LJ* 4:374–75), the guide presumably took other crew members to visit such sites, either now or on the first stop in London.[72] From some of Ned's tales, we know that Cooper also went around London on his own. On one such occasion, he got back from an excursion just in time to save Ned from a terrible, if also comic, accident. It was another Sunday. Ned was alone on the deck when he "saw a little dog running about on board a vessel that lay outside of us." His eye was drawn to a sixpence with a hole in it, hanging from a ribbon around the dog's neck, and he decided that the coin could be put to much better use "purchasing some cherries" than adorning a wharfside dog. He must have jumped over to the neighboring ship and grabbed the animal; his troubles began when, trying to get back, he slipped between the two vessels and fell into the water. Of

course he still couldn't swim, so he "sang out, lustily, for help," and as luck would
have it Cooper right then came on board, heard his cry, and "sprang down between the ships" to his rescue. The cabin boy was duly impressed by his close
brush with death, realizing as his editor (and lifesaver) sat by him taking down his
words in Cooperstown in 1843 that, if Cooper had not intervened back in 1807,
"Ned Myers's yarn would have ended with this paragraph." For that matter, it
also might have ended with the next paragraph, which went on to tell how Ned
"had another escape from drowning, while we lay in the docks" (*NM* 33–34).

Other mischances also had happy resolutions. "One day Mr. Irish was in
high glee," Ned recalled, "having received a message from Captain Johnston, to
inform him that the latter was pressed!" Johnston thought he had evolved a system for avoiding press-gangs altogether. Whenever he went ashore in England,
he carefully sought to conceal his nautical character by donning a long blue
landsman's coat, the sort seamen called "a long-tog," as well as the "drab-
breeches and top-boots" associated with "a gentleman from the country." In the
past, the masquerade had worked, but this time, the first mate laughingly concluded, "them pressgang chaps smelt the tar in his very boots!" Johnston was
being held at a naval recruiter's "rendezvous," to which Cooper was soon dispatched with the captain's lap desk and papers. Although Johnston himself was
vulnerable to such attempts on his liberty, his seventeen-year-old, five-foot-
eight-inch liberator presumably was safe because, Alan Taylor has argued, he
was carrying some documentary shield of unusual strength (*NM* 34–35).[73]

Johnston could ill afford to lose anybody from his crew. Before the *Stirling*
finally left its berth in London Dock late in July (*NM* 35), he in fact had to find
and sign on five new men to make up for continuing desertions and losses. But
by early August that task had been accomplished and the ship was slowly working its way over the Nore and out into the North Sea, then back around the
North Foreland and into the Downs. Every inch of the route thither "was tide-
work," as Ned reminded Cooper in 1843: slow and tedious, requiring more patience than skill out here away from the river traffic. At the Downs, the ship lay
waiting several more days for the wind to come around fair. It had been blowing
out of the southwest for half the summer, right up the gut of the Channel, and
Johnston saw no point in starting the passage home in its teeth. After a series of
encounters with some of the many British warships at anchor there, one of
which ran afoul of the *Stirling* at night, Johnston thought better of his chances
against the adverse winds and currents and slowly headed toward Land's End.

As the *Stirling* did so, it passed a convoy of transports taking troops from
Falmouth to the East Anglian coast, where they were to join Adm. James Gam-
bier's pending attack on Copenhagen. The encounter brought fresh threats when
a boarding party from a smallish gun-brig came on board Cooper's ship and

forcibly mustered the crew. An unnamed Swede, one of the new hands taken on in London, caught the attention of the British officer in charge, who proceeded to spin out some theory about how Sweden and Britain were allies at the time, making the sailor technically liable to serve in the royal navy. Such twisted logic did not convince the Swede, who, "as obstinate as a bull," refused time after time a direct order to go over the side into the waiting boat. And he was seconded by Cooper, who confronted the boarding officer on the sailor's behalf, having "a little row" with him before Captain Johnston silenced him (*NM* 36). This most direct involvement of Cooper in resisting impressment—more evidence, perhaps, of his special immunity—brought to the surface his deeper political reaction to Britain during the whole voyage. Here lay some of the roots of his postcolonial rage.

After this encounter, Captain Johnston pulled a good distance off from the English coast as he slowly tided forth and back along it. Now it was that the *Stirling* "passed the Isle of Wight several times, losing on the flood, the distance made on the ebb" (*NM* 37), and allowing Cooper to rather spaciously claim in *Gleanings in Europe: France* that he had "sailed entirely round [the Isle of Wight], more than once" (*GF* CE 26). Perhaps the *Stirling* on this tedious return down the Channel passed and repassed the island so often that it seemed as if it were circulating around it endlessly, but Ned made it clear that the ship at this time stayed *outside* it to avoid complications with English authorities. The ship eventually "caught a slant," a light breeze, and on that pulled out into the Atlantic, where it had more wind and more room to maneuver (*NM* 37).

The ship seems to have spent more than a week working its way down the Thames and through the Channel, meaning that by now it must have been around the tenth of August. The passage from here on, even with the winds rising, also was a long one. The northwesterly breezes the ship at first encountered pushed it down so far that the crew caught a glimpse of Corvo, the smallest and outermost of the Azores—and considerably south of Johnston's intended route. After that, it caught winds that bore it on a northward line, perhaps farther north than Johnston would have wished. For a time, Ned remembered, there was "a very heavy blow that forced us to scud"—run virtually without sails before the wind. The wind at that time must have been not just fierce but from an unfavorable direction as well: Ned commented that, among its other weaknesses, the *Stirling* "was one of the wettest ships that ever floated, when heading up to the sea," suggesting that it otherwise would have held its position by lying-to (*NM* 37). This "very heavy blow" may have been the "Gulf tempest" (hurricane) that Captain Johnston's nephew Alexander reported the vessel encountered on this passage, adding that it claimed the life of the Swede whom Cooper had defended from the press-gang in the English Channel.[74]

Because of the prevailing westerlies, sailing ships heading west from Europe to North America typically took more time than eastbound ones. The *Stirling*'s longish outward passage in the fall of 1806, some forty days, was still almost two weeks shorter than its return, which was reported in the Philadelphia press in September as having lasted fifty-two days. Other vessels coming into Philadelphia from London or Liverpool just a day or two before Johnston took from forty-two to forty-five days, the difference perhaps being the result of his vessel's poor sailing qualities.[75] In any event, at last the *Stirling* was nearing home. The ship met an English brig when near the coast of the United States, first learning from it disturbing news about a recent violent encounter between naval vessels from the two countries. Soon afterwards the *Stirling* made land off the capes of the Delaware. Cooper was to remember that the ship entered the capes on his eighteenth birthday (September 15, 1807), a happy accident that marked the process of maturation the voyage came to signify for him (see *LJ* 4:374). From this point, Ned remarked, the ship experienced its "usual" luck, meaning that it had little wind once in the bay and on the river, but instead "tided it up" to Philadelphia under the guidance of a Delaware River pilot (*NM* 37). On the seventeenth, the *Stirling* was off Newcastle, Delaware, where a customs officer examined the manifest and, on the back of the old crew list, noted that five of the original sailors "was not produced to me." On September 18, the ship was reported as among many inbound vessels below Philadelphia, and on the next day it at last arrived.[76]

Cooper had viewed Philadelphia with a landsman's eyes during his brief stay at Richard R. Smith's the year before. Arriving overland through Jersey, he had rushed across the river on a brief ferry ride; once there, he had explored the unfamiliar waterfront with all the tentativeness of a green country youth and then departed as he had come. He wanted to go to sea but avoided water as if it might dissolve him. As he approached the city from the river in 1807, by contrast, the accomplished sailor occupied a decidedly maritime viewpoint. Now it must have been that, fresh from England, he first appreciated how much like the Thames the Delaware was—how the "long and intricate navigation, among shoals, and in a tide's way" that characterized the upriver approaches to London and Philadelphia had made each city produce "the best seamen" in their respective nations. The same sinuous cause was already conspiring to give more readily accessible ports such as New York or Liverpool strong advantages over their predecessors, but in 1807 the shift had not fully taken place.[77]

As the *Stirling*'s Delaware River pilot maneuvered the vessel upstream on the tide and brought it to Philadelphia's crowded wharves, the scene there reflected a long commercial history that had expanded dramatically since the Revolution. Visitors to Philadelphia, especially those knowing beforehand of its

original street grid and its ample open spaces, tended to voice their disappointment on finding that the improvised chaos of the increasingly busy port obscured the city's celebrated rational order. Moreau de St.-Méry in 1794 thus felt
"real sadness when docking at Philadelphia." From farther down the river, the
houses and public buildings in the city proper loomed up over the waterfront, so
that one had "a view of the whole town," and such things as "the steeple of the
Anglican Christ Church"—where Cooper's grandparents had been married—
helped give the place a decidedly urban appearance. But as his ship drew closer,
the Frenchman found his view "blocked by the construction of the wharves,
which clearly show that their builders, moved solely by their own greed, had no
consideration whatever for good taste, the appearance or well-being of the city,
or anything else of that nature." Moreau de St.-Méry was largely right. Views of
the Philadelphia waterfront published in the early 1800s show the clutter of
water and land transports; the presence of improvised structures and large, more
permanent buildings; and the general busyness of a zone packed with people and
cargo. About a month after Cooper's ship arrived, a local paper tallied the "Shipping in the Port" and reported that more than 250 active vessels were tied up
there then, plus another dozen new ones on the stocks. One can easily imagine
the thick web of spars and rigging such a congregation of ships would create.
Ever since the end of the Revolution, explosive growth had been overwhelming
Philadelphia's waterfront as America's foreign trade boomed. "The commerce
of America, in 1793, was already flourishing," Cooper rightly stressed in *The
Crater*, "and Philadelphia was then much the most important place in the country" (*CR* 1:13).[78]

As Captain Johnston's personal apprentice, Ned Myers had to remain on
board when the ship arrived in the bustling city in 1807. But he recalled that the
crew proper left as soon as the ship docked, most of them passing on to its original point of departure, New York (*NM* 37). Cooper, as free as the others, may
well have lingered a bit in the city, resurveying those districts with which he was
familiar and, given Richard R. Smith's long fondness for all the Cooper children
and his role in the eventual placement of the youngest of them on board the *Stirling,* passing along Water Street to visit Smith's counting house at Fisher's wharf
or his home a few blocks inland at the corner of Mulberry and Sixth streets.
When he was ready to leave the city, though, Cooper followed the general route
of his shipmates—perhaps even accompanied by one or more of them—across
New Jersey to New York. In *Afloat and Ashore*, the young hero Miles Wallingford comes up the Delaware in 1804 to "the wharves of what was then the largest
town in America," and then with two shipmates—his slave, Ned Clawbonny,
and the Kennebunkman, Moses Marble—travels "the South Amboy road"
across Jersey, passing in the process "through a part of the world called Feather-

bed Lane, that causes my bones to ache, even now, in recollection" (*A&A* CE pt. 2:347–48). The road in question, in all likelihood a favored Cooper family route of passage from the Delaware valley to the waters of greater New York, began at the old West Jersey capital of Burlington and passed northeast through Cross-wicks and Allentown to Cranbury, eventually reaching the terminal for the Amboy ferry on the south bank of the Raritan.[79]

Once Wallingford arrives at South Amboy during his fictional journey home, he boards a packet boat that takes him to "the Bay of New-York, by the passage of the Kills" (*A&A* CE pt. 2:348)—Arthur Kill and Kill Van Kull, the protected Jersey-side channels around Staten Island. As Cooper was to note in his late, fragmentary history of greater New York, at this time that route offered "a narrow, crooked, but practicable communication between Staten Island and the coast of New Jersey"—"rarely used by vessels going to sea, though crowded with craft plying between the neighboring rivers and . . . towns" (TM 131). On his return passage in 1804, Wallingford followed this route into upper New York Bay, then landed at White Hall slip, the facility near the Battery at Manhattan's tip where the ferry from Staten Island also docked at that time. Although we of course cannot be certain, it is plausible that the route of Wallingford's creator had been roughly similar, if not exactly the same, in 1807. It is clear that he knew the route well enough to base Wallingford's experience on it.[80]

If young Cooper followed this route toward the end of September 1807, two days at most would have seen him back in New York. Here was another familiar town bustling with activity, its landings crowded with ships and it streets full of horses and carts and pedestrians. It seems reasonable to assume that the returning sailor at least stopped to see (if not spend some time with) his brother William. More intent than ever on securing his midshipman's warrant, Cooper could empathize with this other black sheep of the family, who, just about to finish his law studies, also seemed headed toward the comparative redemption of a career. Cooper himself, having escaped the law, may have flaunted his sailor's garb and look before William and the general populace. One suspects a touch of exaggerated memory in his description of Miles Wallingford's salt-sea appearance as that returning sailor went about the streets of New York: "I would not have the reader suppose I made a mean, or a disagreeable appearance. On the contrary, standing as I did six feet one, in my shoes, attired in a neat blue round-about of mate's cloth, with a pair of quarter-deck trowsers, a clean white shirt, a black silk handkerchief, and a vest of a pretty but modest pattern, I was not at all ashamed to be seen. I had come from England, a country in which clothes are both good and cheap, and a trimmer-looking tar than I then was seldom showed himself in the lower part of town" (*A&A* CE pt. 2:353).

Like Wallingford, Cooper had good reason to parade his altered identity in his altered garb. But before too long he must have passed north to Albany, probably by water, climbing aboard the stage in the capital for the ride out the turnpike to Cherry Valley and home. He ought to have been in Cooperstown by the middle of October at the latest, almost exactly a year after he had left America under the care of Captain Johnston. No longer was he the boyish rebel uncertain of himself or the world (Plate 6). He had turned eighteen. He had converted his nautical impulse into the foundation for his future. To judge from the pages of the *Otsego Herald,* the village little noted his return or his stay there through the year's end. But inside the young man, where it mattered, a great deal was taking place. And much more soon would follow.

CHAPTER FOUR

Midshipman James Cooper

The young sailor home from the sea began the new year with a new title
—*midshipman*—conferred on him via a printed warrant signed by
President Thomas Jefferson. The document, with its grandiloquent
phrases and formal script, marked the public realization of a private dream to
which Cooper had remained staunchly committed, partly out of his love of the
sea and partly because it defined his future on his own terms rather than his family's.[1] He moved forward now, though, with the blessing and aid of his father.
Familiar with how such things were managed, Judge Cooper asked one of his
longtime political acquaintances, Democratic-Republican congressman Philip
Van Cortlandt, to lend support to his son's application to join the navy. Van
Cortlandt had never met "young Mr. Cooper," but happily complied with the request and expressed a willingness to assist in other ways in the future.[2]

Father and son left Cooperstown sometime around Christmas or New
Year's on a trip that would lead them through Albany and ultimately to New
York City. There they trusted that word of Cooper's appointment would reach
him; there as well they expected he would be told to report for duty. That is basically what happened, although the route the travelers followed was so cir-

cuitous that the warrant, mailed by Navy Secretary Robert Smith to Cooperstown early in January, and perhaps misforwarded from there, took almost seven
weeks to catch up with them. Not until February 19, as a result, did the young
man finally look over Secretary Smith's cover letter and enclosures, which included a copy of naval rules and regulations, a description of the required uniform, and a mariner's dictionary, along with a blank oath Cooper was to sign,
have witnessed, and return with his letter of acceptance. The next day he accordingly went to the dockside office of New York attorney and notary William
Williams, Jr., whom he may have remembered from Captain Johnston's employment of him to certify the *Stirling*'s crew list sixteen months before. Once
Williams had attested to Cooper's signature and Cooper in turn had sent the document back to Washington, he was officially in the navy, thus fulfilling the one
long-range intent of his youth that did not falter (*LJ* 1:9–10).[3]

Happenstance seconded Cooper's commitment. For a young man who
wished to continue at sea in the winter of 1807–1808, the navy offered the only
plausible recourse: the sweeping Embargo Act of 1807, which Congress passed
at Jefferson's request that December, virtually closed most American ports,
leaving merchants without trade and seamen without berths. Ships such as the
Stirling, for instance, now had few cargoes in sight. When Johnston's vessel had
sailed in 1806, even the stateroom and cabin were jammed with flour barrels for
the hungry British market. In 1808, however, when the tonnage of American
wheat shipped to Britain plunged to only 5 percent of recent levels, Johnston's
ship was stuck at the dock in Philadelphia, where it remained until he was at last
able to go to sea again in June 1809.[4] Nor was it only maritime enterprise that suffered. Soon after the embargo's enactment, domestic prices fell and inland districts became short of cash as commerce stagnated. By the fall of 1808, things
were so tight in Cooperstown that a local store, hiding a concern for its own
business behind an upbeat slogan, reassured customers that they should "Never
Mind the Embargo!" Until the law's repeal in March of 1809, newspapers everywhere continued to devote much space to the embargo, debating its justice and
effectiveness.[5]

It was shrewd to join the navy just as the embargo was approved. Not only
was it evident that the merchant marine would soon be devastated; it also seemed
likely, as indeed proved true, that the shorthanded navy would be expanding for
its role in enforcing the ban on trade. Yet there were other, deeper motivations
to which Cooper was sensitive. Among them was a widespread militaristic anxiety in the country, traceable to the long-simmering hostilities with Britain, the
ferment of events in Europe, and the reduction of the American naval establishment under Jefferson in 1801. The continuing presence of British naval vessels
all along the coast reified a widespread apprehension that the unprepared nation

was facing dire risk. Those vessels maintained an effective blockade of many American ports, ostensibly to frustrate the activity of French privateers, but in the process harassing neutral American ships as well. The situation took a dramatic turn in the spring of 1806, just when Cooper, poring over the news about Francisco de Miranda that filled the papers, was first letting his thoughts drift toward the sea. Late in April, the New York *Daily Advertiser* reported that British ships off Sandy Hook, at the outer entrance to New York bay, were stopping American vessels and impressing U.S. citizens into the royal navy. It predicted that outright violence would follow.[6]

It did. In the next issue, the same newspaper reported that the British naval vessel *Leander* had opened fire as the American merchant sloop *Richard*, mastered by Jesse Pierce, ran in for Sandy Hook. Pierce's brother John was instantly killed as he stood at the *Richard*'s helm. As soon as the news reached town, it inflamed public opinion. The reduced navy, vastly outpowered by the British, could undertake no credible reprisals, ensuring domestic political repercussions. As far away as Cooperstown, the *Otsego Herald* inserted many items about the episode lifted from the *Daily Advertiser*, seconding that paper's view that John Pierce's death represented "wanton and unprovoked MURDER!" In among the items attacking Britain, however, were others that showed the domestic recoil of such incidents. Another New York item reprinted from the *Daily Advertiser* thus reported on a meeting of "Federal Republicans" that placed the blame for the defenseless state of the harbor squarely on President Jefferson, declaring that his administration "consents to pay money to avoid foreign insolence, or to prevent the violation of national rights, while it sells and dismantles its Naval Force, instead of increasing and preserving it for the defense of our ports and commerce." The paper concluded that Jefferson thereby "prostrates the national honor, endangers the public safety, and invites both injustice and insult."

Amid this partisan uproar, John Pierce was laid to rest in an elaborate ceremony conducted at New York City's expense. Churches tolled their bells and American ships in the harbor lowered their flags to half-mast for the victim of British tyranny who also was fast becoming an effigy of mistaken national policy. The mounting pressure on Jefferson led him to order the arrest of the *Leander*'s captain for what even he was soon calling the "murder . . . of John Pierce, a citizen of the United States." But Jefferson's penchant for verbal warfare, soon to be pilloried by Washington Irving in *A History of New-York*, was taken as a sign of military weakness. Not surprisingly, the memory of the outrage against Pierce proved durable. When the Irish radical exile William Sampson fortuitously landed in New York on the fourth of July 1806, he found the ordinary citizens "commemorating their Independence, carousing, singing republican songs, drinking revolutionary toasts, . . . and HUZZAING FOR LIBERTY!!!" as bonfires blazed and cannon echoed across the harbor. But he also found Americans, two months after the British attack on the *Richard*, still "making an outcry about a Yankee sailor called PEARCE."[7]

The Leopard *and the* Chesapeake

As that outcry subsided during the forepart of the *Stirling*'s 1806–1807 voyage, relations between Britain and America were notably quiet. Disputes such as the one that had led to Pierce's death were now being handled through seemingly peaceable diplomatic channels. Early in 1807, for instance, the British minister relayed a royal navy request for the surrender of three deserters who were believed to be on an American warship, the *Chesapeake*, then undergoing repairs at the Washington navy yard. Although no international law required the commander of the American ship to investigate the claim, he willingly did so, only to become convinced that two of the so-called deserters, and perhaps all three, actually were of American birth. He did not dispute that the men had served on HMS *Melampus*, but, believing they had been the victims of impressment, he thought they had not deserted but rightfully escaped from (as Cooper himself later termed it) an "illegal and unjust detention" (*HN* 2:96). The American captain therefore would not surrender the men. Instead, through American naval channels, he forwarded a report to the British minister, who seemed fully satisfied with this explanation of the matter. No more discussion took place between the governments, and in due course the *Chesapeake* was moved from the navy yard on the Potomac down to Norfolk, where hasty preparations for its pending Mediterranean cruise were to be made.

In late June of 1807, the warship lay at anchor off Norfolk. It was hardly shipshape, being still cluttered with stores and supplies; worse yet, its crew was green. But since the United States was at peace, it was assumed that the decks could be cleared at sea and that the men would have time to gain familiarity with their vessel during the long Atlantic crossing. On June 22, in a light wind, the *Chesapeake* therefore headed out for the Virginia capes. Some miles ahead was a British ship, the *Leopard*, which that morning had left a small royal navy squadron resting in the American waters of Lynnhaven Bay, just east of Hampton Roads. The three other British ships in the squadron (which included the *Melampus*, from which the impressed American sailors had fled) had been anchored there for some time, ostensibly keeping an eye on a group of French frigates lying up the Chesapeake at Annapolis. The *Leopard*, however, had come in from the sea only the night before, then had promptly lifted its anchor in the morning just as the *Chesapeake* did. Closer to the strait, the ship rushed back out and disappeared behind Cape Henry before the *Chesapeake* could emerge into the open sea, but once that happened it gradually let the American vessel catch up. At that point the *Leopard* closed with the *Chesapeake*, immediately hailing its captain to indicate that it had a dispatch for him. This statement aroused no suspicion, as the British presence in the area was well known—indeed, openly tolerated— and the relaying of such dispatches was so common that one of the other ships in the British squadron at Lynnhaven had delivered a batch of them to the U. S. naval vessel *Wasp* in just this manner only days before.

The *Chesapeake* was technically commanded by Capt. James Gordon, but also on board was his superior, James Barron, the new head of the American Mediterranean squadron. Commodore Barron was handling the vessel when the encounter with the *Leopard* began. In response to the hail, he backed sails to stop the ship in anticipation of receiving a boat from the *Leopard*, which at some distance also came to. Barron saw no danger, although it was later learned that some junior American officers believed the lower ports on the British ship were open and its guns unplugged—a state of affairs the royal navy captain would not have allowed under normal sailing conditions. Much of what followed bore out this mixed appearance of diplomatic nicety and military threat. When the *Leopard*'s boat arrived, its officer in charge came aboard and was properly ushered into Commodore Barron's cabin. When he handed the so-called dispatch to Barron, it proved to be nothing more than a royal navy order issued by the vice admiral in command of the Lynnhaven squadron and other naval vessels off the Atlantic coast. Addressed not to Barron but to the vice admiral's own subordinates, it instructed all captains under his command to watch for the *Chesapeake* and, falling in with the ship outside American waters, to present the order in question and require that its American commander allow a search for royal navy deserters. To present such an order to an American commander at sea of course was an extraordinary proceeding; but no *or else* was plainly spelled out, and in fact the order called for the business to be conducted so as to preserve "the harmony subsisting between the two countries," such as that was (*HN* 2:99). Commodore Barron, having digested the document, denied having any knowledge of royal navy deserters. He also asserted that of course he could not allow the *Chesapeake*'s men to be mustered by any officers other than their own. No existing treaty between the two countries created an obligation for either to give up the other's deserters. Even so, firm as he was, Commodore Barron seems not to have refused all cooperation with the *Leopard*.

The British officer stayed long enough for his own vessel to raise a signal flag calling him back. After he left, Barron told Captain Gordon to resume clearing the still cluttered gun deck, a task that had been begun some time earlier that day. At first the order was routine, but when Barron went on deck and glanced from the gangway over toward the boat heading to the *Leopard*, he now sensed an ominous preparedness on the British ship and urged haste. The American officers who had earlier puzzled over the *Leopard*'s open ports already had seen to it that the *Chesapeake*'s guns were loaded, but things were so chaotic that the matches used to fire them could not be found. Meanwhile, Barron remained at his position in the gangway, peering over toward the *Leopard*. The British officer reboarded his vessel, which again hailed the American warship. When Barron answered that he had not understood the message, almost immediately the British captain fired a shot across the bow of the *Chesapeake*. Then, with barely a pause, he let fly a broadside, hitting the *Chesapeake* with several shots and wounding Commodore Barron and his aide. The American vessel, virtually unarmed, had a row of loaded cannon trained on the *Leopard* but remained powerless to return fire as, for the next quarter-hour, the British vessel deliberately kept reloading and pouring its full fire upon its victim. Commodore Barron retained command despite his wounds, desperately hoping that at least one of his own guns might fire back, but at last he was forced to give up. Just as he ordered the colors lowered, one of the lieutenants, holding in his bare fingers a coal brought up from the galley, finally managed to light a single gun, which sent its charge directly into the hull of the aggressor.

Such belated heroics were too much like an allegory of American impotence. Soon a boat went over to the *Leopard* to place the *Chesapeake* at its disposal, the crew of the latter were mustered by the British officers, and the three old "deserters" from the *Melampus*, as well as one from a vessel nominally listed in the vice admiral's orders, were culled and carried off. That evening, the *Chesapeake* limped back to Hampton Roads, with twenty-one casualties: three men had been killed outright and eighteen wounded, eight of them seriously. The hull had taken more than twenty hits; the lower sails had been riddled with grapeshot, much of the rigging cut to pieces, and all three of the lower masts seriously damaged.

The other injuries cannot be so easily tallied. Britain disavowed the actions of its officers, eventually made reparations, and was said never to have employed the captain of the *Leopard* on active duty again. In the United States, the political context made for unfortunate if understandable outcomes. A court martial was held for Barron, Gordon, and the marine captain on board, as well as the ship's gunner, the man perhaps most immediately responsible for the mess on the gun deck. Of the four, however, Barron suffered most, possibly because at the time he generously avoided blaming the others. The court martial trial was not primarily about the immediate causes of the disaster, in any case, but rather about the larger political crisis in the country. Because the attack was unprovoked and occurred between an American naval vessel and one belonging to a nation with which the United States was nominally at peace, in another context it might have become an easy rallying point for the whole country. Even Washington Irving and his accomplices in the humorous periodical *Salmagundi,* which had begun to appear the past January, laced their jollity in August with worries about "some new outrage at Norfolk."[8] As time passed, however, the nature of that outrage was less and less clear.

In his naval history, published in 1839, Cooper would devote some twenty pages to the *Chesapeake* story because of the crucial insight it offered into national politics, but also because of its special significance for his own life. That significance was owing in part to how he first learned of the *Leopard*'s attack. In June, when it occurred, he was on his London walkabout, mostly absorbed by the sights of the British capital. He hardly was oblivious to international affairs, however: Captain Johnston's brief encounter with the press-gang in London was but the freshest reminder of the larger situation. For part of his London tour, what is more, Cooper went around with Stephen Stimpson, the American tar who actually had been impressed into the royal navy but was now free, and who therefore had a habit of picking the glitter from the surface of English life. Cooper himself, young as he was, already was sloughing off his own naive infatuation with English culture. In part, the coldness with which many of the British regarded their transatlantic cousins drove home to him the social consequences of political history, a point that his *Gleanings in Europe: England* stressed as a lesson acquired during his boyhood visit. It also was during this early period that Cooper first began reflecting on "the broad distinction that exists between political *franchises* and political *liberty*," a mark of difference between the hemispheres that was to become a key part of his credo (*GE* CE 195).

At that time, word of the *Chesapeake*'s fate had not yet reached English waters, and the *Stirling* was to pass another five weeks in ignorance. Finally, Ned recalled, "when near the American coast, we spoke an English brig that gave us an account of the affair." Even then, the news had little impact—or rather a reverse impact—since the British tale was a lie, the officer in question claiming that "his own countrymen [had] come out second-best." His mendacity, revealed when the Delaware pilot came aboard, doubled the inevitable anger of Johnston's crew, especially first mate John Irish, who was "bitter" at the news (*NM* 37). Suddenly, all the recent examples of British arrogance that the *Stirling* and its crew had witnessed were given new meaning. This voyage itself exemplified the international crisis so well that Captain Johnston, now understanding the experience of his own vessel in new terms, is said to have turned over the *Stirling*'s logbook to the port collector of Philadelphia because of "the numerous searches, detentions, or impressments from her deck"—presumably as evidence of British wrongs.[9] For Cooper, the news had several effects. It cemented the shift of attitude toward England that he was to describe in his English *Gleanings:*

never again was he to view the land of his family's origins, imagined in earlier years with a soft focus, as a kind of second home. Once in Europe again in the 1820s, he largely avoided England, establishing his family in France and allowing his emotions to indulge themselves in Switzerland and especially in Italy but regarding England and the English with perpetual suspicion. Moreover, the naval crisis that grew across the fall of 1807, resulting in the passage of Jefferson's embargo that December, merely confirmed Cooper's sense that national policy was mistaken, even more mistaken given such recent outrages. He thought the embargo yet another instance of bad logic and cowardice, but he did not merely dislike it: it accelerated his movement toward a naval career. When the *Leopard* fired on the *Chesapeake*, it fired indirectly on James Cooper, and he now prepared himself to fire back. He took the long nonwar leading up to 1812 very personally.[10]

This point is evident even in his fiction. In his late autobiographical tale, the four-volume *Afloat and Ashore*, Cooper threw his surrogate runaway Miles Wallingford into the impressment controversy early in the century. In the novel, Cooper probably steered clear of the *Chesapeake* episode because it might prove difficult to weave fresh inventions around the long-infamous encounter. Instead, he set Miles directly on a collision course with the *Leander*, the very ship, as Miles explains in his narrative, that "afterwards became notorious on the American coast, in consequence of a man killed in a coaster by one of her shot, within twenty miles of the spot where I now saw her; an event that had its share in awakening the feeling that produced the war of 1812" (*A&A* CE pt. 2:162). Cooper's fictional anticipation of the violent historical episode between the *Leander* and the *Richard* features a shot across the bow of Miles's vessel, but in this case both ship and helmsman escape intact. Outrunning and outsmarting the English vessel, Miles offers an anachronistic object lesson for Jefferson's America about the costs incurred when, as the hero earlier remarks, the navy was "reduced to a few vessels" and "the lists of officers . . . curtailed of two thirds of their names" (*A&A* CE pt. 1:393). Had a sufficient navy existed, these affronts to American liberty never would have been tolerated. Moreover, the American navy could wish for no better role model than the savvy master of the *Dawn*, Miles Wallingford: enticing the *Leander* into difficult waters near Block Island, he uses local knowledge to baffle English presumption.[11] Adumbrating the past in the manner Cooper did here, though, had its own perils. In this murky sea stretching between history and fiction, Miles's escape might be read as the key reason why the captain of the actual *Leander*, frustrated by such merchant seamen, determined not to let the next one go so easily: poor John Pierce's real murder was thus caused, as it were, by young Wallingford's fictional evasions.[12]

Duty

In 1808, with the *Chesapeake* attack still smarting and the embargo just imposed, the navy's prospects looked momentarily promising. But that was an illusion. A few days after Cooper sent his acceptance to Washington, he was ordered to report to the navy yard just recently established in Wallabout Bay north of the village of Brooklyn, where Cmdre. John Rodgers of Maryland was presently in charge. Here, very little was happening, at least to the eyes of the young firebrand from Otsego.[13]

The navy's strategy at the time was to scale back and avoid confrontation with Britain and other potential adversaries. This was its "gunboat" phase, during which it built and deployed many small defensive vessels instead of focusing on the big ships that naval historian Cooper—and, presumably, his younger self in 1808—thought wise. In 1839, Cooper would admit that the gunboats had opened up more opportunities for younger officers to take command. This was a lesson he had learned himself, informally at least, when he was left in command of a small lake vessel during 1809. Cooper would also acknowledge that morale in the service had been higher during the gunboat period than might have been predicted. But he insisted that the gunboats considered in themselves were impractical—and expensive (see *HN* 2:114–17). Furthermore, their very puniness must have seemed like an affront to him. He spoke of Oliver Hazard Perry's involvement in gunboat construction at this time as constituting "disagreeable service." And he described the gunboats as being built by the "batch," explaining that "these useless craft were literally put into the water in flotillas, in 1808" (*LDANO* 2:157–58). The belittlement of American dignity implicit in such vessels almost struck Cooper personally. It was as if the country, instead of preparing to confront British hauteur, was in retreat from it.

The gunboat campaign, which began with passage of the navy-funding law in February 1803, was speeding up just when Cooper joined the navy. Secretary Smith wrote Sen. Samuel L. Mitchill in November of 1807 with the following figures: 69 gunboats had been built or acquired by that point, but 188 more were needed, 50 to defend New York harbor alone.[14] So many were required because the vessels were not patrol boats but rather floating adjuncts to fixed shore defenses. They were, indeed, little more than single sizable guns placed on costly nautical platforms, with perhaps two other small pieces of armament added elsewhere on the vessel. Nor were the gunboats very seaworthy. When some were dispatched for Mediterranean duty, they required significant alterations, such as the addition of large false keels to provide stability. Furthermore, although the single large gun in theory was versatile, being mounted on a swivel at the center of the gunboat's deck, it actually could be fired only over the bows (to either side of the forward mast, at that), since the gunboat was not large or stable enough to absorb sidewise recoil. Despite these many drawbacks, in this period gunboats consumed most of the navy's constructive energy.

A fair amount of it was displayed right under Cooper's eye in New York. Of the new vessels Secretary Smith mentioned in his 1807 letter to Senator Mitchill, which were funded by year's end, several were to be built there, and with the active contribution of Isaac Chauncey. One of the more notable designs, drawn up by New York shipbuilder Christian Bergh at Chauncey's request, surely would have been familiar to Cooper. This called for a double-masted vessel almost fifty feet in length, carrying a single long gun on a swivel (either a twenty-four or thirty-two pounder) and a twelve-pound short-barreled carronade on each side. Some twelve gunboats were produced in New York from this Bergh-Chauncey design from contracts let in 1806, intended largely for defending the immediate harbor.[15]

Another group of twenty-three similar vessels, begun about the time Cooper's warrant was issued, must have been under way when he reported for duty. Some of them were built by Henry Eckford, who (along with Bergh) would become well known to Cooper during his later service at Oswego on the banks of Lake Ontario. Yet here, too, as with regard to the other gunboats, Cooper's naval history was relatively silent, saying virtually nothing of Eckford's boat work during the midshipman's first tour in New York (see *HN* 2:449–50n). That the gunboats were built in private yards meant that none of the projects were carried forward at the navy yard itself. But the naval establishment under Rodgers and Chauncey actively supervised the work, not officials at Washington, so there certainly was much to see and recall for those so inclined. One feels again that Cooper's disdain for the puny craft enforced a silence on him in 1839.[16]

Cooper apparently had nothing directly to do with the gunboat projects in 1808. His first specific assignment in New York, which Chauncey gave him in March, placed him on the bomb ketch *Vesuvius*.[17] Despite its explosive name, the *Vesuvius* also exemplified the navy's commitment to smallish vessels at the time. Bomb ketches, of which only a few were in service then, mounted several guns of modest size, and in particular a mortar to be used in bombardments. Cooper's vessel, built only two years earlier in Newbury, Massachusetts, measured about eighty-two by twenty-five feet and carried twelve guns in addition to its thirteen-inch mortar. The *Vesuvius*, unlike the gunboats, apparently was thought capable of long voyages without substantial modification, since shortly after its completion in 1806 it was assigned, along with the similar ship *Etna*, to duty in New Orleans. Both vessels gained reputations as awkward sailers because of problems with their balance, however, and when the *Vesuvius* encountered a severe Bahamian gale on its way south, all the guns had to be jettisoned in order to save the ship. By the date Cooper was officially assigned to the *Vesuvius* in New York harbor (March 21, 1808), the ship had returned there; but now, barely two years old, it was in need of repairs to the hull. As a result, the vessel actually sat at its mooring during many if not all the weeks of Cooper's assignment to it. Here was the first big disappointment of his so-called career.[18]

Soon Cooper's feelings were to be lifted—temporarily—by a promising new assignment. On July 2, 1808, the navy ordered a young officer then present in Washington, Lieut. Melancthon Taylor Woolsey, to undertake a new venture on Lake Ontario. At the time, "relations between this country and England very seriously menaced war" (MTW 16), and if war came the Great Lakes frontier would assume great military importance. Hence Woolsey's venture; hence, too, the otherwise unexplained note in the muster roll of the *Vesuvius* next to Cooper's name on July 4: "To the Lakes."[19] Woolsey was to proceed first to New York City, where he would be provided with assistants (midshipmen Cooper and Thomas Gamble were among those chosen) and receive guidance from Rodgers and Chauncey about the construction of the nation's first armed vessel on the Great Lakes, to be built under his direction at the small New York settlement of Oswego.

The vessel in its "legal character" was regarded as a gunboat by the navy (*HN* 2:326) and in fact was to carry a thirty-two-pound long gun of the sort mounted on the vessels more properly deserving that designation. When finished, however, the *Oneida* was the size of the *Vesuvius* rather than the small craft being built elsewhere at the time (eighty-five feet long instead of fifty or so)—and, unlike the gunboats, it was to be named, not numbered, denoting a considerable increase in dignity. Cooper's naval history therefore correctly distinguished the *Oneida* from the "merely ordinary gun-boats" Woolsey also was instructed to build on Lake Champlain in 1808–1809: carrying sixteen guns, the ship was "a regular brig of war" (*HN* 2:117; MTW 17).[20]

Oswego, where the vessel was to be built and launched, probably was familiar to Cooper before 1808 from his family's involvement in New York's north country, a fact that may have led to his inclusion in Woolsey's party. Local knowledge would be important to the project, and at the time no naval personnel were stationed on Lake Ontario. On the other hand, the destination to which Woolsey was bound hardly was an unknown quantity. In the later colonial era and even during Cooper's residence there, the village of Oswego might have looked to casual visitors like little more than a tiny collection of buildings lost on the lakeshore at the mouth of the short but powerful Oswego River. Yet such appearances were deceiving. The site had long served as a fur trading depot where Anglo-Dutch merchants tapped the resources of the upper Great Lakes, diverting trade from Montreal to the settlements of the Mohawk and Hudson valleys by a mostly waterborne route. The same easy access from Oswego to the core of English settlement in New York had led to the building of several fortifications in the area beginning in the 1720s, first on the west bank of the river, and soon on the higher eastern side. Critical for military control of the lakes, Oswego had been conquered by the French commander Montcalm in 1756 but soon reverted to the control of the British, who held it throughout the Revolution and even up to 1796, when it was ceded to the United States under Jay's Treaty. At the time of Cooper's service there, the ruins of the largest and most recent fort, dating from the later 1750s, stood on that higher ground east of the river.

The withdrawal of the English from Oswego only twelve years before Cooper's arrival had resulted in a temporary collapse of the village's population and economic life. In 1808, as a result, it may have had as slight a presence on the land as *The Pathfinder* accorded its fictional counterpart in the 1750s. In the novel, Cooper chose to bring his heroine along the river in the night and then the next day have her survey her surroundings from a bastion in the English fort. Mabel Dunham later will prove a close observer of her world, but in this case her eyes skip over the barely visible settlement below her and dwell on the natural landscape engulfing it: "It was a scene, on one side, of apparently endless forests, while a waste of seemingly interminable water spread itself on the other. Nature had appeared to delight in producing grand effects, by setting two of her principal agents in bold relief to each other, neglecting details; the eye turning from the broad carpet of leaves, to the still broader field of fluid, from the endless but gentle heavings of the lake, to the holy calm and poetical solitude of the forest, with wonder and delight" (*PF* CE 109).

Only after reflecting on this striking pattern is Dunham able to turn to "the fore-ground of the remarkable picture," which seems barely there at all: "The Oswego threw its dark waters into the lake, between banks of some height; that on its eastern side, being bolder and projecting farther north than that on its western. The fort was on the latter, and immediately beneath it, were a few huts of logs. . . . There were two low, curved gravelly points, that had been formed with surprising regularity by the counteracting forces of the northerly winds and the swift current, and which, inclining from the storms of the lake, formed two coves within the river" (*PF* CE 112). Allowing for slight but not insignificant differences, this was pretty much what Cooper would have perceived when, like his young heroine, he climbed the heights and saw open blue water meet dense green woods, with very few human signs intervening. The village landscape in 1808 was perhaps a bit more densely written on the land, but only a bit; this young veteran of the Cooperstown frontier therefore found the Oswego scene wilder than any back home, even as he recognized that, in Euro-American terms, Oswego was also older. It was, of course, a border ground not just in the Amer-

ican sense but also the European one, a boundary between competing though related nations.[21]

Oswego as an actual human place struggled to bear such large meanings.
Cooper's brief biography of Woolsey, published in 1845, recalled the scene almost four decades before: "In 1808 Oswego was a mere hamlet of some twenty,
or five-and-twenty houses, that stood on a very irregular sort of a line, near the
water. . . . On the eastern bank of the river, and opposite to the village, . . . there
was but a solitary log house, and the ruins of the last English fort" (MTW 16).
The traveler Christian Schulz in 1807 described the village as containing "about
thirty dwellings and stores" and went on to say it had "a very contemptible appearance, from the irregular and confused manner in which the inhabitants are
permitted to build." Schulz's opinion was based on a point perhaps not known to
Cooper—namely, that the state had ordered the west bank of the river surveyed
and laid out in regular blocks some years before, although so far the survey had
been virtually ignored. Structures, Schulz commented, were "placed as suits the
convenience or whim of the owners, in the streets or elsewhere, without any regard to the original plan."[22]

If this last observation suggests a frontier settlement that at least was lively,
rather like Templeton in *The Pioneers,* Oswego was so tiny that when Woolsey
and his two midshipmen showed up in August, followed soon after by Henry
Eckford and his "strong gang of ship-carpenters, riggers, blacksmiths, &c.," the
new arrivals "produced a great commotion in that retired hamlet" (MTW 16).
Among other things, the invaders brought money with them, a signal innovation, since the primary medium of exchange beforehand was salt—from the already very active saltworks on Onondaga Lake to the south. That commodity
symbolized the economy of the place, but in Cooper's view it pretty much en-
grossed it as well. The eight or ten schooners and sloops operating from Oswego
mostly carried salt, and the male population in the village consisted of the vessels' owners and hands, the boatmen who brought salt downstream from Salina,
a few mechanics, and a "quarter-educated personage who called himself doctor"
(MTW 16).[23]

The shifting fortunes of Oswego were much noted by visitors in these
years. It had been very important to the fur trade, already a subject of romantic
interest among Americans, and had played a strategic role in the struggle of two
European powers for dominance in North America. But in the past few years it
had become engaged in the commonplace business of transporting salt and other
earthy commodities, including potash (potassium carbonate), that by-product of
forest clearing that was quite familiar to Cooper from his days in Otsego and
that, like the barilla hauled by the *Stirling* from Spain to England, was used for
such things as the manufacture of glass. One traveler passing through in 1804,

poet-ornithologist Alexander Wilson, later sang the glories of the local woods and waters in "The Foresters," published in the *Port-Folio* in 1809–1810. In the process, he experimented with images and scenes that had scant place in American writing at the time but that Cooper was to make his own in *The Pioneers* and his later forest tales. Indeed, Wilson's poem in some ways anticipated Cooper's own story of this inland sea. In descending the Oswego River, Wilson's traveler thus comes upon a scene very similar to one near the start of *The Pathfinder:*

> On yonder island, opening by degrees,
> Behold the blue smoke mounting through the trees!
> There, by his fire, 'mid sheltering brush obscured,
> His bark canoe along the margin moored,
> With lank jet locks that half his face conceal,
> The Indian hunter eats his morning meal.

When the traveler enters Oswego, on the other hand, the incipient romance of this island scene dissipates:

> Those straggling huts that on the left appear,
> Where boats and ships their crowded masts uprear,
> Where fence, or field, or cultured garden green,
> Or blessed plough, or spade were never seen,
> Is old Oswego; once renowned in trade,
> Where numerous tribes their annual visits paid . . .
> But time and war have banished all their trains,
> And nought but potash, salt, and rum remains. . . .
> From morn to night here noise and riot reign;
> From night to morn 'tis noise and roar again.

Cooper was of the opinion that the village was sleepy until his cohort arrived, but the newcomers may have only amplified the boisterous tones audible to Wilson on Ontario's shore four years earlier.[24]

The shift to Oswego required substantial preparations from Woolsey's party, some more obvious than others. Cooper himself may have had personal or family business to attend to at this time, business to which his anticipated absence on Ontario would give added urgency. In New York City even before Woolsey's appearance, he had taken a twenty-day furlough from the *Vesuvius* to visit Cooperstown, returning to his post around June 10, a sizable (but unexplained) break for someone who had been in the navy only a few months. On July 28, after being chosen for the venture, Cooper once more went to Otsego under orders from Woolsey, who stayed in New York awaiting the navy's approval of the contracts he had made with Eckford and Bergh. Once en route,

Woolsey wrote Cooper twice again, ordering him to Utica and, if he should fail
to meet the rest of the party there, on to Oswego on his own—as Cooper did,
arriving at the lake on August 22 (see *LJ* 1:14n1).[25] Although, unlike his characters at the opening of *The Pathfinder*, he did not make his way down the Oswego
in a birchbark canoe, on drawing near the village at its mouth he surely reflected
(as he was to have Mabel Dunham reflect in the novel) on "that dense, interminable forest," through which he passed on the last part of the trip, "with its
hidden, glassy lakes" and "its dark, rolling streams" (*PF* CE 108).

Some of Cooper's liveliest recollections of the Oswego period concerned
the members of his party as much as nature. The *Oneida* was built by Eckford's
men, so the naval personnel had little to do beyond supervising the project.
Hence they spent much time socializing together. Officers with "no Vessel or
public place" provided for them, as Woolsey put it (*LJ* 1:14n1), they had hired a
former tavern on the west side of the river, next door to the residence of that
"quarter-educated" doctor (MTW 16). The place proved eminently cozy.[26] As
winter began, they converted the building's old enclosed bar into a larder that
they loaded with foodstuffs provided by Woolsey, whom Cooper recalled as a
"notable caterer" (MTW 17). Their daily fare included salmon, bass, wild duck
and goose, venison, and small game such as rabbit and squirrel, often with the
men's favorite local fruit, cranberries. The mess became even livelier early in
the fall, when the three navy men were reinforced by a small detachment of
troops from the Sixth U.S. Infantry under the command of Lieut. John Chrystie.
Chrystie's men camped in the ruinous fort, while he and fellow officer Charles
Kitchel Gardner joined the naval crew in the old tavern (*LJ* 1:11; MTW 16–17).
Cooper long remembered Chrystie because he was to die only five years later in
the American campaign on Canada—a casualty of the war that Cooper himself
missed, much as Woolsey was to be one of its heroes (MTW 17). But it was Gardner, a sometime medical student under Dr. David Hosack of New York City,
who proved to be Cooper's special "messmate" at Oswego, and the two were to
remain associates up to Cooper's death.[27]

Melancthon Woolsey also proved a close friend. When his party arrived,
there was considerable local apprehension that he was there to enforce the embargo. At the time, the village was still echoing with the tumult of a summer uprising against customs collector Joel Burt, who had to request state troops to
back up his official actions. However, although President Jefferson in April of
1808 had instructed the navy to assist the revenue cutter service and customs
agents in enforcing the embargo, which hit port towns like Oswego hard, Woolsey was not charged with imposing the restrictions. That fact, and his considerable charm, soon won the confidence of the populace.[28] His men also experienced his charm—and his jovial wit: "At the fireside," the future storyteller

Cooper recalled, "Woolsey was the life of the mess in conversation, anecdote, and amusement" (MTW 17).

The stories Woolsey poured into Cooper's ear gave the midshipman his first living sense of naval history. But Woolsey, seaborne as his spirit seemed, was more than a nautical character. His parents had long lived in the northern town of Plattsburgh, which had been founded by his mother's family, and young Woolsey's intimate acquaintance with the border showed through his later naval polish. Cooper knew the border from Otsego and was learning more of it here on Ontario, so his estimate of this aspect of Woolsey's character came from deep knowledge of the subject. He thought Woolsey so fine an embodiment of the frontier spirit that he was too democratic in his instincts to rise as high in naval hierarchy as Cooper otherwise thought he deserved to. It was his "familiar association with all the classes that mingle so freely together in border life" (MTW 21), on the other hand, that made his success at Oswego so memorable. It also may have been the combination of nautical and frontier themes in Woolsey's character that suggested Oswego as the scene for Cooper's "nautico-lake-savage romance" (LJ 3:393), as he called The Pathfinder while at work on it in 1839. Woolsey as Cooper recalled him was like that abstract scene viewed by Mabel Dunham: a meeting line where different realms were both joined and separated. Cooper's memories lingered long over Woolsey and "his" inland sea.[29]

"The Handsomest Vessel in the Navy"

While socializing continued among the officers and men, so did Henry Eckford's work on the brig at his temporary shipyard, located on the east extremity, called Garrison Point or Gravelly Beach, at the river's mouth. Cooper recalled Eckford actively directing the work there that fall. A man of considerable dispatch, he went out into the forest himself, located suitable trees for the project, marked them, and had them cut, trimmed, and transported down to the water, where in a few days the frame of the vessel began to take shape. The ship was to be eighty-five-and-a-half feet long, twenty-two-and-a-half in the beam, and of 262 tons capacity, large enough in Secretary Smith's view to cope with any armed vessel then afloat on the Great Lakes. In fact, the Oneida was almost equal to the Stirling in size, the big difference being the merchant ship's greater depth of hold. The Oneida, the construction of which cost the navy just over $20,000 (plus 110 gallons of liquor for the workmen), carried a full complement of square sails fore and aft, unlike the smaller gunboats then under construction. In addition to the thirty-two pounder on a swivel atop the forecastle, the ship mounted sixteen twenty-four-pound carronades on the main deck.[30]

Familiar as Cooper was with ships before now, his observation of the brig's construction was his first opportunity to watch one built from the keel up. In writing *The Crater* near the end of his life, he drew on this experience in closely describing the construction of several vessels by shipwrecked colonist Mark Woolston and his fellows in their remote Pacific refuge. In the case of some of these fictional vessels, including two whaleships (a pair of "little brigs" each somewhat smaller than the *Oneida*), he inserted detailed descriptions of the construction process that must have derived from memories of the enterprise on Lake Ontario. As with Eckford's crew, the shipwrights in one section of *The Crater* thus work from scratch, felling timber in the woods and dragging it to the cove where they have set up a temporary shipyard. Cooper's paean in the novel to the "expert American axemen" employing "that glorious implement of American civilization, the American axe" (*CR* 1:232) recalls the rudimentary labors at Oswego in 1808: in both cases, the shipbuilders are prototypical frontiersmen, felling the forest in a "new land" to construct their craft. In no novel other than *The Crater* did Cooper devote so much attention to the shipbuilder's art, and throughout the book it was the memory of Woolsey's project—which he had codified in his biographical sketch only about a year before beginning the novel—that surely guided his pen. Here again, as in Woolsey's case, the mixture of modes and places must have struck a resonant chord in Cooper's imagination.

In the case of the *Oneida*, though, felling timber was the easy part. Not until the middle of January 1809, after many interruptions and complications, could Woolsey report to Washington that the brig was "partly caulked" and had its inside planking mostly in place. Although other problems arose, by the end of February he could add that the brig was "completely furnished outside." Woolsey named and launched the ship on March 31. Yet by May, he still had no crew because of Washington's inability to decide how to man a vessel so far from the navy's usual stations. Woolsey was proud of his accomplishments: the brig seemed to him, he wrote Smith, "the handsomest vessel in the Navy." But having it in the water meant little without a crew, so for the time being the ship lay at the wharf he had rented from customs collector Burt. Seeking to jog his superiors, Woolsey wrote that the rented berth would cost four times as much once the salt-hauling season began. He also added that the brig would be holed up in the river for good in 1809 if it was not manned and able to sail by July 1, since after that it would be "extremely difficult" to get the *Oneida* over the bar at the harbor mouth.[31]

The lack of crewmen and the fall of water levels were not the only problems. It is evident from Woolsey's letters of this time that he feared losing junior officers Cooper and Gamble if sailors were not forthcoming and the vessel remained landlocked. Cooper already had gone off for a time in midwinter, evidently taking Gamble and Gardner with him to Cooperstown in late December. He came back a month or so later with enduring excitement for the project, which was one of the most important undertakings then in progress for the navy, and he still looked forward to serving on the yet-unnamed vessel. How long his enthusiasm would last, however, was uncertain.[32]

By early April, Woolsey suspected that both his midshipmen might well ask to be transferred to "some of the Frigates now fitting out"—indeed, he believed that they were even then about to make "application to the Department for that purpose." He was right, at least in regard to Cooper, who wrote to the new navy secretary, Paul Hamilton, on the same day as Woolsey "to request (If that request should not be improper) a removal from this station, to one of actual service." The trouble with Oswego was not so much its remoteness from the sea as the navy's uncertain plans for the vessel just finished there. Cooper would happily stay at that station under his "present respected and esteem'd Commander" if "actual service" were possible. Otherwise, he trusted it would be clear that relocation would be very important to a budding officer eager about "acquiring experience" and thereby "improving in my profession" (*LJ* 1:13). That this letter to Hamilton had been coordinated with Woolsey's is made quite clear by the fact that Woolsey's included a staunch recommendation for Cooper. In the service barely fourteen months, Cooper garnered higher praise from Woolsey than the two other midshipmen on whose behalf Woolsey also spoke in the same letter: "as far as I am capable of judging (though his term of service perhaps does not entitle him to it)," Woolsey wrote of Cooper, "I think him well qualified for Promotion."[33]

Secretary Hamilton did not act on Cooper's April request for reassignment, nor on Woolsey's tentative recommendation. This left the midshipman hanging on at his present station, still largely inactive. Yet it also left Cooper available to assume a somewhat more direct role in the *Oneida*'s management when Woolsey left for Lake Champlain in June to check on the progress of the gunboat project there. As Woolsey informed the navy on June 10, his first intention was to place local pilot Augustus Ford in charge of the *Oneida*, leaving Cooper at Oswego awaiting orders from Washington. Less than two weeks later, however, the Oswego customs collector, seeking help in handling a smuggler, wrote to "James Cooper now commanding the brig Oneida," and when Woolsey, back from Champlain, was about to pass across the lake to Kingston, Ontario, in July, he formally designated Cooper as his substitute: "The U.S. Brig Oneida with all her Tackle &c I leave in your charge—You will pay particular attention to her Hull and see that she is properly wet [down] every night and morning, that her cables receive no damage by chafing and that her sails and whatever part of her rigging is left on board her are not damaged by damps or vermin etc." Even so, fighting vermin and damp air was not the sort of naval action warm-spirited Cooper had in mind. He was a ship-sitter, little more.[34]

In between the Champlain and Canadian trips, there had come, fortunately, a pleasure cruise with Woolsey along the Ontario shore west to Niagara. Recruiting four local sailors, Woolsey loaded the *Oneida*'s thirty-two-foot launch, also built by Eckford, with provisions and headed out in good weather for what promised to be a quick passage. Heavy waves, shifty winds, and an insufficient crew to man the oars, however, extended the envisioned two-day passage into a comical ordeal. The men spent four nights rocking on the open lake, plus two camped on the beach and another in a hut on the banks of the Genesee. Accustomed to the abundant larder back at Oswego, they ate so heartily that their provisions failed on the fourth day. Fortunately, Cooper, having (in a manner of speaking) stumbled across a porcupine in the brush, ran it through with his sword cane, providing a careful, picky meal. In the morning, four of the party pressed inland until they found a vacant cabin where bread and milk and even "a fresh baking of dried whortleberry pies" were there for the taking. They ate well, sent the surplus back to the other two men at the launch, left two silver dollars as pay, then fruitlessly foraged further.

Later, putting into sizable Irondequoit Bay, the sailors encountered a London Cockney and his wife who, implausibly enough, had long been settled there; the sailors bargained hard to buy a neutered ram (or "wether") from their flock of sheep. The scene struck Cooper well enough that he vividly re-created it almost forty years later: "The woman remonstrated, on a high key, and the Cockney vacillated. At one moment he was about to yield; at the next, the clamor of the woman prevailed. The scene lasted near a quarter of an hour, when Woolsey commenced an attack on the lady, by paying compliments to her fine children, three as foul little Christians as one could find on the frontier. This threw the mother off her guard, and she wavered." Taking advantage of "this unguarded moment," Woolsey slipped the Cockney a five-dollar gold coin, far more than the wether was worth. The man, Cooper went on, "uttered a faint, 'Well, captain, since you wish it—' and a signal from Woolsey caused the animal's throat to be cut incontinently. At the next instant the woman changed her mind; but it was too late, the wether was bleeding to death. Notwithstanding all this, the woman refused to be pacified until Woolsey made her a present of the skin and fleece, when the carcass was borne off in triumph."

After their mutton feast, the adventurers put out again, but a squally wind blowing across the mouth of the Genesee sent them back into the river. They finally found a haven five miles upstream, at the site where Rochester would stand by the time Cooper penned his memoir of Woolsey. The voyagers spent the night in a small log cabin, swapping some of their leftover ram and milk for bread, then in the morning went out into the squall once more. They crept along the shore, making three attempts on a headland called Devil's Nose before a shift in the wind let them pass. At last the weather became favorable, allowing them to cover the rest of their passage, another fifty miles, without incident (MTW 17–19).[35]

It was this tough progress up the lake that formed the ultimate basis of the long run of Jasper Western's cutter, the *Scud*, back along the "outline of unbroken forest" fringing the Ontario shore in *The Pathfinder:* "Various head-lands presented themselves, and the cutter, in running from one to another, stretched across bays so deep, as almost to deserve the names of gulphs, but nowhere did the eye meet with the evidences of civilization. Rivers occasionally poured their tribute into the great reservoir of the lake, but their banks could be traced inland for miles, by the same outlines of trees; and even large bays, that lay embosomed in woods, communicating with Ontario, only by narrow outlets, appeared and disappeared, without bringing with them a single trace of a human habitation" (*PF* CE 287). Such vistas come at a cost to Cooper's characters, as they had to the crew of the *Oneida's* launch. Blown mercilessly up the lake from the Thousand Islands to beyond Niagara in a three-day gale, the *Scud* fights poor visibility and lee shores and deluging rain, and what little of the land is seen from the vessel bespeaks imminent peril. In treating that fictional gale, Cooper nicely managed to evoke the wind's fury—"whistling the thousand notes of a ship" (*PF* CE 242) as he put it in the novel—as he had known it in his own supperless haul out to Niagara. And on the return trip of the *Scud*, as the above passage suggests, he was able to recover the silent beauty he had glimpsed where water and woods met as he and Woolsey and the others struggled along the Ontario shore in the summer of 1809.[36]

But not all was wild. When Woolsey's launch entered the mouth of the Niagara River just as July 4 dawned, it ushered Cooper into a scene rich with new insights about the American frontier. Niagara was as far west as he had ever been, well past the sparsely peopled country where he and Woolsey had almost "starved," yet the region from the lakeshore upriver to the falls seemed long-settled and stable. The first mark of the difference was the lighthouse at the mouth of the river, which sent its comforting beacon out into the failing night as the launch arrived. Another sign of the difference, rising on the headland east of the river, was old Fort Niagara, the French part of it dating from 1726 (this was the "château-looking house" of *The Pathfinder* [CE 283]). Now in American hands and heavily armed, it stared down its impressive British counterpart, Fort George, a mile away on the Canadian shore. Cooper had seen the remains of the British forts in Albany and in Oswego, and of course knew that the New York border had always been a complexly international ground. But Niagara drove the lesson home with special force. Nearby, over the river in Newark, had been located the original capital of Upper Canada, a reminder of the British victory over the French in the 1760s and then of the American triumph in the Revolution.

The strategic importance of the Niagara corridor had other consequences as well. Everywhere Cooper looked, the highly cultivated state of the landscape gave him a sense of how *old* the American frontier might be. Cooperstown had made him think of the border as rough and new, full of energy and awkward improvisation. Here, to the contrary, Cooper could explore the slowly evolved commercial and military frontier characteristic of the Great Lakes, an area long occupied by the European powers and Native American peoples, where a considerable finish and complexity were still apparent. He thus noted in his memoir of Woolsey that "the region around Niagara had been settled as long as that on the banks of the Hudson," and he found remarkable the transition from the wild Ontario shore to the suave landscape of the Niagara River: it was like "suddenly quitting the forest, to be placed in the midst of the labors of man" (MTW 19). The closeness of those supposed opposites would become evident in all of Cooper's frontier novels, a sign that the lesson of the Niagara trip struck deep.[37]

Before returning to Oswego, Woolsey and Cooper visited Niagara Falls (see MTW 19), which Cooper had never seen before. The spectacle impressed him less then than it would when, years later, he returned to Niagara with a heightened sense of landscape aesthetics that he owed to his European sojourn (see *LJ* 5:239, 6:207). Still, the 1809 visit resurfaced in 1821 when the novelist decided to end his first Hudson valley tale, *The Spy*, by projecting the Westchester peddler-spy Harvey Birch onto the Niagara frontier battlegrounds of the second war with Britain. It is in the gorge of the Niagara River that the now ancient Harvey makes his desperate way in a small skiff right beneath the pounding cataract, crossing to the Canadian side just as the battle of Lundy's Lane begins. Observed and greeted by two American officers perched on Table Rock above the Canadian falls, Birch recognizes one as the son of a couple he had known well during his time on Westchester's "Neutral Ground." Wounded in this successful attack of his countrymen, Birch ends his life on properly classic soil, a site of power that in 1821 Cooper knew only from his Ontario service under Woolsey (*Spy* 2:285–86).[38]

Probably the most important consequence of the Niagara voyage was a deepening personal attachment between Cooper and Woolsey. The midshipman's comment to Secretary Hamilton about his "esteemed" commander in the spring already showed that something more than mere formality obtained between them, as did Woolsey's warm recommendation of Cooper to the navy then. But the few items of correspondence that survive from the summer reveal that it was the Niagara experience that truly cemented the bond. Four days after leaving Cooper in charge of the brig in July to go over to Kingston, Woolsey sent him his orders, enclosing them in a personal letter. The orders were obviously businesslike, but not the letter itself. It began "My dear Cooper," was signed "Your Friend," and in between told of Woolsey's passage over the lake in a lively tone completely lacking in naval decorum. Late in August, after he had passed downstream to Montreal and from there to Plattsburgh, Woolsey likewise sent a formal order regarding the brig, of which Cooper was still in charge, but enclosed it in another chatty letter ("Dear Cooper," the letter began; the orders proper carried the expectable "Sir"). In his second personal letter, Woolsey wrote that he was "happy to hear you and your good neighbors are well" (Cooper had written him on July 30 and August 4, but those letters are unlocated), and he instructed Cooper to "Give my love to all around you." For Cooper personally, he added "assurances of my sincere friendship & esteem."[39] Partners in the comic adversity of their run up the lake, the two young naval officers had become close friends, a fact to which Cooper's memoir of 1845 was to give eloquent testimony.

"Brave, Brave Jim"

Even so, the two were soon to part and never again were to enjoy such companionship. Woolsey would stay on the lake into, through, and indeed beyond the war, whereas by the time he wrote those warm letters to Cooper in the summer of 1809 the midshipman already was about to depart. On September 21, Woolsey, absent again, sent Cooper what were to prove his final instructions, largely concerned with settling accounts. Perhaps he already knew that Cooper, out of patience with the passivity of naval life, had written Secretary Hamilton a week earlier, on September 13, to "request a Furlough for the purpose of making an European voyage" on a merchant ship. The midshipman summed up the past nineteen months of his life by explaining his request in the following terms: "I trust Sir, you will the more readily excuse this liberty, when I inform you, that I have never been attached to any vessel in commission since I have had the Honor of belonging to the Service." Whether he intended it or not, the "Honor" he so named had a hollow sound. On September 27, naval clerk Charles W. Goldsborough wrote on Hamilton's behalf to approve the request, ordering Cooper not to wear his uniform while on furlough and, when the merchant voyage was over, to report his return to the department (*LJ* 1:15).[40]

The furlough seemed like a reasonable alternative to what the navy offered. Although a civilian voyage would temporarily strip Cooper of his naval berth, it would put him at sea again, a powerful inducement for a young officer who had spent his first year and a half in the navy virtually shipless.[41] Moreover, the time seemed right for such a venture. By the early fall of 1809, prospects for merchant shipping were brightening. The Embargo Act had been replaced by the Non-Intercourse Act, a short-lived law that, although still technically prohibiting trade with Britain or France and their dependencies, was harder to enforce than the old one. Cooper surely expected to find the merchant marine recovering when he arrived in New York, and he was eager to take advantage of the change.

He left Oswego as soon as Goldsborough's letter arrived there early in October, detouring through Cooperstown to drop off his gear and uniform and visit the family, and arriving on Manhattan before the month was out. As soon as he hit the wharves there, he found it surprisingly difficult to locate a berth on a Europe-bound vessel; the resulting doubts sent him across the East River to the navy yard in search of advice from fellow officers. Their largely negative response, which by now he may well have hoped for, determined him to abandon the furlough as suddenly as he had asked for it. By November 8, the dream of another salt-sea venture was over (see *LJ* 1:15). That day, he also went to a tailor's shop on Wall Street and purchased a pile of items indicating his recommitment to the service, including an "undress uniform coat" and "blue cloth pantaloons." With his old gear in Cooperstown, he would need to dress himself anew for the part that he once more was ready to assume.[42]

Among the naval men Cooper consulted at the navy yard was Lieut. James Lawrence (Plate 7), current commander of the *Wasp*. Lawrence seems to have been known to Cooper from the latter's 1808 stint in New York, but the links between the two were multiple. For one thing, Lawrence also had been born in Burlington, New Jersey, where his family was known to the Coopers.[43] Lawrence's father, whom the novelist described as "a respectable lawyer" (*HN* 2: 252), had been a member of Jersey's provincial council and was mayor of Burlington at the start of the Revolution, but because of his Loyalist sympathies he suffered a precipitous decline after the start of hostilities with Britain. Going into exile in Upper Canada, he left his son in New Jersey with the hope that he, too, would become a lawyer.[44] But "Brave, Brave Jim" (as his half-sister, poet Elizabeth Lawrence Kearney, later called him) instead set his young eyes toward the navy. He received his midshipman's warrant in 1798 and was advanced to acting lieutenant during a West Indies cruise two years later. So quickly did he make a name for himself that he was retained in the face of the 1801 naval reduction. In April of 1802, still shy of twenty-one, Lawrence received regular promotion to lieutenant.[45]

This important advancement came to him in the thick of the Tripolitan War, during which he served under such celebrated Mediterranean commanders as Isaac Hull and Stephen Decatur. When the latter led the desperate but successful attempt to burn the captured American vessel *Philadelphia* (thereby preventing the Tripolitans from refitting it and sending it out against the American squadron), Lawrence was his valiant subordinate. Decatur's strategic brilliance in this affair won him the admiration of no less a naval master than Horatio Nelson, then in the Mediterranean blockading Toulon. Decatur in turn lavished strong praise on Lawrence.[46]

This heroism in battle did not protect "Brave Jim," however, from the doldrums of the gunboat era. Ordered back to New York, he was assigned to run one of the new craft over the Atlantic for use by the Mediterranean squadron. Lawrence so distrusted gunboat *No. 6* that he "had not the faintest idea that he would ever reach the Mediterranean, 'or indeed, anywhere else.'" The ocean passage in fact proved so bad that *No. 6*, when glimpsed off the Azores by a British warship, was mistaken for a raft with a few "wrecked mariners" on board (*HN* 2:84).[47] Lawrence survived the ordeal, only to find himself stranded in command of that craft for almost a year in the Mediterranean. Worse yet, having arrived too late to take part in the last engagements of the Tripolitan conflict, he saw no action whatsoever on this European tour.[48] Following his return to the United States in 1806, Lawrence was put under the command of Capt. Charles Stewart, then supervising the construction of yet more gunboats in New York, some by Bergh and Eckford. He helped recruit men for the *Chesapeake* before the deadly attack by the *Leopard* and later served (with Decatur and others) on the court martial of Commodore Barron for his conduct in that affair. About those events, and probably about the Mediterranean conflicts in which he and his friend Melancthon Woolsey had both participated at the start of the century, Lawrence doubtless shared details with Cooper in New York. Later, when Lawrence took the ill-fated *Chesapeake* into action against the British off Boston and lost both his life and the vessel, Cooper, having a good grasp of the character of the American commander, understood that event with special insight.[49]

Cooper's naval history, written two decades and more after Lawrence's death, cast a generally positive, even glowing light back on Lawrence's character, calling him "a man of noble stature, and fine personal appearance." More suave than Woolsey, without the liabilities (and benefits) of the frontier baptism Cooper thought Woolsey had undergone, "Lawrence had the air and manners of a gentleman-like sailor," and, the naval history went on, "was much beloved by his friends." Cooper, while admitting that Lawrence could be "quick and impetuous" at times, found him remarkably cool in critical situations and especially praised his talents as a saltwater sailor: "He was a perfect man-of-war's man, and an excellent quarter-deck seaman, handling his vessel not only skilfully, but with all the style of the profession." Perhaps the best measure of Lawrence's fitness as a commander was the staunch loyalty he attracted in those under him. "All his younger officers became singularly attached to him"—especially the midshipmen, in whom (as one of them recalled) he took extraordinary interest (*HN* 2: 253). In 1821, from a perspective closer to his own navy years and Lawrence's death, Cooper remembered his tragic commander's "kind and liberal friendship" but then choked up and could say little more about him (*ECE* 13).

Despite his substantial virtues, as Cooper would suggest, James Lawrence had countervailing weaknesses. In the fall of 1807, when American feelings over the *Chesapeake* were still very hot, he engaged in a battle with the New York press that centered on the supposed inability of American naval officers to guard the nation and its honor against British aggression. The editor of the *Public Advertiser* expressed public frustration when he asked, rather too pointedly for Lawrence, "Why have we gun-boats? Why are the commanders of these gun-boats suffered to be *swaggering* through our streets while they should be whetting their sabres?" Lawrence answered: "In regard to the commanders of the gun-boats, whom you term *swaggerers*, I assure you that their 'sabres' are sufficiently keen to cut off your ears, and will be inevitably employed in that service, if any future remarks injurious to their reputation should be inserted in your paper."[50] Lawrence meant what he wrote. The night after sending off his letter, he went to the offices of the *Public Advertiser* and, when repeatedly told that the editor was not there, spilled forth threats and oaths in front of the man's wife. Eventually he punched one of the newspaper's clerks in the mouth so forcefully that the victim fell backwards off his chair, blood pouring from his mouth, after which Lawrence left in high dudgeon.[51]

Both envious and suspicious of the dominant example of the British navy, American officers such as Lawrence found it hard to reconcile their personal ambitions for glory with the avowedly republican context within which they served. With the memory of the *Chesapeake-Leopard* affair still gallingly fresh, and blame for it not yet resolved (the court martial of Commodore Barron was still several months off), they felt a need to assert their honor and courage even as the Jefferson administration gave them few opportunities to do so. The proliferating gunboats that so many of the officers loathed but were forced to accept and command reified—for them as for Midshipman Cooper—the lurking suspicion that the American navy lacked not just the strength but perhaps the courage to stand up to British vessels. The successful completion of the campaign against the powers of the Barbary Coast notwithstanding, naval officers, perhaps especially the younger ones whose rise in the service was frustrated by the standdown in the later years of the Jefferson administration, were acting on mixed and contradictory signals.

James Lawrence's frustration, evident in his visit to the office of the *Public Advertiser*, was widely shared. In this era immediately following the 1804 duel between Alexander Hamilton and Aaron Burr at Weehawken, dueling and its metaphoric substitutes provided a regular recourse in contests over personal honor. Within the navy from 1799 to 1849, more than one hundred duels were fought among members of the officer corps. Just the month before the fracas at the *Public Advertiser,* for instance, two midshipmen at the Brooklyn navy yard fought a duel "said to have originated in a slight misunderstanding."[52] Stephen Decatur, who followed up at the newspaper office for Lawrence with his own swaggering aggression, had been sent home from the Mediterranean a few years earlier because of his involvement in a duel between an American midshipman and the secretary of the British governor of Malta. Perhaps more to the point, given the language both Decatur and Lawrence used in the New York newspaper office, Decatur himself had challenged a Spanish naval officer off Barcelona by leaving the following message when he paid a call on the latter's vessel: "tell him that Lieutenant Decatur of the frigate *Essex* pronounces him a cowardly scoundrel, and that, when they meet on shore, he will cut his ears off." Only by the intervention of another American officer was Decatur prevented from meeting the Spaniard; in time that same American officer, William Bainbridge, would serve as Decatur's second in the duel that ended the latter's life.[53]

On another, more famous occasion in the Mediterranean, Decatur had jokingly called his close friend Richard Somers a "fool." Somers understood the joke completely, but several young officers, thinking Somers craven for not taking offense, refused to drink wine with him. Following this slight, Somers spoke with Decatur, who offered to entertain the whole group with a dinner so as to clear up the silly misunderstanding. But Somers would have none of it. He challenged all of the young men to duels and asked Decatur to be his second. In the first duel, Somers took a pistol ball in his right arm; in the second, having refused Decatur's offer to substitute for him, he took another one in the thigh. As the third young officer approached, Somers, bloodied but undeterred, again insisted on carrying out the exchange himself, although to do so he had to shoot from a sitting position, with Decatur to his left bolstering his body and arm, since Somers could barely hold the pistol. This time, Somers wounded his opponent, after which the two or three young men who still remained in line to fight him acknowledged his courage and refused to proceed. In an oddly appropriate finale in 1804, Somers was blown to bits with his crew when the *Intrepid,* which he was taking into the harbor at Tripoli as a fireship, prematurely exploded. Some officers in the squadron thought the raiders had deliberately set off the explosion rather than surrender to the enemy when something went wrong, a rumor that built not only on the reputation of Somers but also on the general recognition of the defiant violence of the whole officer corps.[54]

The civil broils at the newspaper office in September 1807 were of a piece, rhetorically at least, with these more bloody encounters within the navy proper. So were two other episodes soon narrated in the *Public Advertiser*. On September 13, two men sailing a small pleasure craft down the East River at flood tide detoured into Wallabout Bay, where they thought they could make headway on the back eddies. As they passed near the gunboats moored there, a sentinel warned them off. The two boaters hauled out their oars and hastened away as they were told to, only to veer close to another gunboat and again be warned off. Before they could move away this time, a shot was fired at them by a midshipman onshore, and the ball crashed into the side of their sailboat perilously close to one of the men. Once off the water, the boaters complained to Commodore Rodgers, who received them "politely," promised to investigate, and soon placed the responsible midshipman under arrest. That the latter felt completely justified in shooting at civilians on his own authority suggests, though, that Rodgers was hardly on top of things at the navy yard.

The second contemporary case points to the same conclusion, although the guilty party was not just a green gun-happy midshipman. In this instance, a civilian carpenter at the navy yard gave offense when he happened to pass between a company of marines and their officers. Immediately grabbed by one of the officers, the carpenter protested his innocence and apologized. But the officer, the workman's deposition later explained, "inhumanely struck me ten or twelve blows on my face and body." As it happens, Lieut. James Lawrence intervened at this point, but hardly to reprimand his comrade-in-arms. Instead, he ordered the carpenter taken out onto gunboat *No. 57*, where the victim "was put in Irons and detained nearly two hours." When he protested, the gunboat's commander replied curtly that he was being held "agreeably to orders." He was freed from the irons only after the new orders were issued, when he was taken toward shore in a smaller boat and then was forced to jump overboard and make his way through water and mud as the boatmen kept shouting "the most bitter exclamations" at him. It evidently was Lawrence who had issued the new orders, perhaps because on reflection he realized that he had no authority to confine a civilian— indeed, a man lawfully employed at the navy yard. But the animosity of the commander of *No. 57*, and of his boat crew, obviously continued to smolder. The carpenter's ignorant disrespect for military custom garnered a rich harvest of abuse.[55]

These anecdotes paint a clear image of the impotent but embattled navy at the time of Cooper's return to the country and his pending entry into it. On their own, though, the tales cannot explain why the navy's reputation should have deteriorated so soon after the successful conclusion of the Tripolitan War. Surely

a large part of the problem with the behavior of officers such as Decatur or Lawrence (or that midshipman at the navy yard with the quick trigger finger) had to
do with the frustrations incident to the government's undigested policy direc-
tives. Exposed not only to British insults and attacks but also to the imputation
of cowardice at home, officers and men alike had been put in a classic double
bind. If they overreacted to British impertinence, they ran the risk of criticism
or worse from the government, whereas if they behaved too pliantly, they would
be publicly condemned for lack of fortitude. Those in the navy, shut out from
what they thought their rightful arena, swallowed hard and sought to do their
best. But the perhaps inevitable sarcasm they endured induced them to overreact
toward outspoken civilians.

   Such an explanation, however, will go only so far. While one might claim
that the penchant for dueling in the navy in the early Republic was likewise a
deflection of frustrated military energies toward improper targets, duels often
happened even in situations where active warfare was in progress. The code to
which men such as Stephen Decatur or Richard Somers clung had an internal
energy that, while external conditions might intensify it, did not depend on those
conditions for its continuing force. James Lawrence is a good case in point, since
he persistently betrayed a duelist's temperament almost regardless of context.
Quick to take offense when he thought his honor involved, he on more than one
occasion wrote rather sharply to his superiors in the navy when he thought himself slighted by some new order. When he was removed from the *Wasp* in 1810
to make way for another commander and placed instead on the *Argus,* he thus addressed complaints to the navy. He hoped that what he had to say would not be
thought "impertinent," but of course it was just that. He praised his own "un-
remitted care and anxiety" as commander of the *Wasp* and added, "I must confess my feelings would be wounded by a causeless removal from a command
which I had considered such an honor, and as incitive [*sic*] to the most active exertions." He ended the letter by stating that he would "leave the subject entirely
to [Navy Secretary Hamilton's] discretion," but Paul Hamilton of course already had exercised his discretion on the matter: the reassignment went forward.[56] It is suggestive of young Cooper's engagement with the same ethos that
he carried with him to Oswego in 1808 not only the sword cane with which he
defeated that porcupine but also a brace of dueling pistols purchased with money
his brother Richard had given him for that purpose. Apparently in jest, he wrote
Richard from his new posting in November of that year: "There is no prospect
of my having occasion to use them in this quarter of the world." But then he
added with a more serious twist, "I shall remember your injunctions—whenever
I may have occasion of that kind" (*LJ* 1:10).

The Wasp

Lawrence's ship in the fall of 1809, the *Wasp,* had, like Lawrence himself, a flashy appeal—and some difficulties. About twenty feet longer than the *Oneida,* it also was of twice the tonnage and, being more heavily armed, was a real warship. In the naval history, Cooper described the *Wasp* and the *Hornet,* as "efficient sloops" designed on "the most approved models," and he singled out the *Wasp* as "a beautiful and fast cruiser." Intended to carry a crew of sixty able seamen and as many ordinary seamen, plus a contingent of marines, the ship boasted an array of officers including three lieutenants and eight midshipmen. The total ideal number on board would be almost two hundred, although the usual complement "varied from 130 to 160, according to circumstances" (*HN* 2:90, 181).[57]

When Cooper came aboard in November 1809, Lawrence had been in command of the *Wasp* for only a few months. He had taken over in July and immediately gone to Europe with diplomatic dispatches, returning to the navy yard as recently as November 5, shortly after Cooper's arrival in New York City.[58] If Lawrence had not known so already, the Atlantic voyage convinced him that the ship, although commissioned only two years earlier, needed major repairs. During most of Cooper's presence on the *Wasp,* as a consequence, the crew and workers from the navy yard directed their attention to repairing its sails and spars and generally refitting the ship. Since such work was visibly under way even on November 8, the day Cooper wrote Washington with word of Lawrence's offer of a berth, he hardly went on board ignorant of the ship's condition, although he cannot have anticipated what that would mean for himself.[59]

Across the next three or four weeks, as the weather went from "clear & pleasant" to downright wintry, Cooper must have had some hand in the ongoing work, but on his role the ship's log is silent. Barely had he been taken on, in any event, when a family crisis called him away. On November 22, Cooper's father, who had left Cooperstown on one of his interminable trips two days earlier, stopped at the inn of Stewart Lewis on State Street in Albany, across from St. Peter's Church. Judge Cooper had been in reasonably good health across the past year, well enough to travel four times to his holdings along the St. Lawrence since January. Yet all was not right. Two days after checking in at the Albany inn, he was sufficiently out of sorts that he began to be seen by a local doctor. Then, on December 3, the day after his fifty-fifth birthday, a second doctor began to attend him as well. On the day following, he was ill enough that his children started arriving for visits of varying length. No document specifies what ailed him, but it obviously was serious and getting worse.[60]

Not yet a month on the *Wasp*, Cooper asked Lieutenant Lawrence for a ten-day furlough on December 7, a rainy Thursday, and rushed up the Hudson. He got there soon enough that he was able to spend a full seven days at Lewis's inn, along with several other family members, before hurrying back to resume his duties.[61] He had left his father's side a few days too soon. On December 22, with Isaac and Ann attending him, the wheelwright turned speculator and developer, and then judge and congressman, died. Apparently Elizabeth Fenimore Cooper, by then long resigned to her cloistered existence amid her greenery in Otsego Hall, did not make an effort to visit her husband of thirty-five years before he succumbed.[62]

Judge William Cooper's passing was comparatively tranquil, even anticli-mactic. An old family legend holding that his end was far more dramatic, a leg-end much distorted through various retellings, has been thoroughly discredited by historian Alan Taylor. It asserted that William Cooper had been in Albany for a political meeting, on leaving which he had been attacked from behind by an opponent who bashed him over the head. Either from the resulting injury or from pneumonia that set in as he lay bedridden, William Cooper was portrayed as having been martyred to the rough-and-tumble energies that he previously had ridden to power and success. It was a neat story that could point to any num-ber of morals—and float any number of seemingly buoyant critical interpreta-tions about the role of fathers, violence, and social upheaval in the works of his son. But it was only a story, and morals and interpretations alike have been broadsided and sunk by Taylor.[63]

Although the harbor log of the *Wasp* does not date young Cooper's return to duty, his furlough expired on December 18, and it is clear that on Christmas Day, the Monday after Judge Cooper's death, he was *not* in Cooperstown among the other members of the family and "a large concourse of citizens" who joined in the "obsequies" honoring his father's memory, as the *Otsego Her-ald* described the memorial.[64] Nor was he present there three days later when William Cooper's will, dated May 13, 1808, was probated under the direction of Otsego County surrogate Ambrose Clark. He presumably had word of its terms shortly thereafter, however, and the implications for his future must have been sinking in as he puttered about the waylaid *Wasp*.[65]

Soon he was given a new duty, recruitment, that distracted him from the an-chored vessel and his father's sudden end. Like most naval vessels when in port, the *Wasp* was chronically shorthanded even when it might appear crowded. Men were always running off, reaching the end of their enlistments, or shifting around among naval vessels. Much like a ship, as a result, a crew required peri-odic rebuilding.[66] Lacking a military draft or the habit of impressment, the gov-ernment had to make good such losses solely through recruitment, which across this period was conducted on a ship-by-ship basis, often at a temporary recruiting station or "rendezvous" onshore. The generally unsavory nature of such efforts is revealed by an 1811 case involving an English shipwright named William Bowman. Having been wrecked in Cuba, Bowman eventually found a berth on a merchant vessel bound for New York; on arriving there, he got "in liquor," only to awake in "an American rendezvous," where he learned he had been enlisted in the navy. At such places, civilian agents were commonly employed to supply the navy recruiting officer with live, or nearly live, bodies, usually for a cut of the officer's per capita premium. The civilian agent also might receive money for supplying the physical site of the rendezvous, typically his own tavern or inn. William Bowman seems to have been swept up at just such a site. One historian concluded that Bowman, after landing in New York, "undoubtedly made his headquarters at one of the crimp boarding houses and taverns combined, and commenced a spree in search of oblivion." After his wages had been drunk up, he began selling his gear and clothes and then inevitably became indebted to the place. Once the rum finally was cut off, he sobered up to find that the tavern keeper, hitherto accommodating, apparently had enlisted him to insure his own "reimbursement." Morally, it was hard to distinguish such proceedings from impressment.[67]

Perhaps partly as a result, Cooper "earnestly objected" to Lawrence's assignment of him to recruiting duty, though to no avail (*LJ* 1:76). He further expressed his objection by vowing that he would operate on the up-and-up, or so he recalled years later: "My pride and the necessities of the ship induced me to use great exertions to obtain the men *honestly*—I discountenanced entirely the base proceedings of the common crimps, and had to resort to the simple, but expensive means of music, flags, &c" (*LJ* 1:76). Because a recruiting rendezvous shifted about in the less seemly wharf districts, and was rarely advertised, a bit of music and bright colors helped attract attention. Such extra effort was especially important in 1810, when, Cooper claimed, "men were exceedingly scarce" (*LJ* 1:72). The work was frustrating as well as morally objectionable. And, especially if done honestly, it was also expensive. Each month, Cooper earned his midshipman's pay of $19 and was due ration credits of from $6 to $12. But while onshore, where he said he operated "for months," he had to rent costly lodgings part of that time and provide his own food with no adjustment to his income. Furthermore, he could not cover the band and the rendezvous, as well as many incidentals, out of the meager $2 premium paid him for each recruit. The more than $1,500 advanced him in 1810 by the navy could not be touched for such purposes: in theory, it was to be used only for the three-month pay advances due most recruits (varying by rank) and a bounty of $20 that Lieutenant Lawrence authorized Cooper to offer the better ones. When the navy in the 1820s began trying to recover what it viewed as Cooper's recruiting debt of nearly $200, its records showed that he had expended almost four-fifths of his advance in securing the thirty-five men he was credited with recruiting (*LJ* 1:73). What happened to the rest occasioned a long, ultimately unresolved disagreement between Cooper, then beginning his literary career, and the government.[68]

Hard-pressed for cash in the 1820s, Cooper would quibble then over the navy's claims. He would question when, exactly, his resignation from the service had been accepted, since if he was owed uncollected pay he thought it might defray his old debts. Going further, he would argue that he was in fact the government's creditor, because he had expended personal resources in support of his official activities in 1810 (see *LJ* 1:73). This line of response was not entirely disingenuous. The midshipman clearly had spent more money on recruiting than the $70 in premiums he received. He paid John Arnod, the keeper of the tavern where he ran his rendezvous, almost half that amount for fifteen recruits whom that man had supplied (honestly or not) and for incidental expenses such as food, drink, and boat transportation from Manhattan to the *Wasp*. At this rate, Cooper could not have hoped to break even: who, after all, was to pay the piper and the other musicians?[69]

In his later negotiations with the navy, Cooper exculpated himself in part by claiming he had been a mere "boy," a "Minor," at the time he ran the rendezvous (*LJ* 1:90, 76). Partly for that reason, he kept track of navy funds as slackly as he did of his own money—or his father's. For one thing, he mixed personal with government resources. He was able to carry out his duties only because the "well known death" of his father put money in his pocket, money that kept things going at Arnod's tavern and elsewhere (*LJ* 1:77, 91). Probably the modest funds paid him against the estate by his brothers that winter and spring floated him above the surface—otherwise, on $19 per month, he would have sunk. He also was careless in his paperwork. He apparently failed to submit receipts for the bounties he paid out, for instance, and as a result estimated that some $200 actually disbursed pursuant to Lawrence's instructions was never reflected in navy accounts. But he also may have neglected to receive, or at least did not keep, receipts covering all those bounty payments. In the 1820s, he blamed "the length of time, and the consequent loss of my papers"—"the papers of a boy of twenty"—for his inability to find more than two such receipts (*LJ* 1:72, 76, 106).

Moreover, in 1810 Lawrence gave Cooper special assignments that further vexed his operations. Although he didn't want an assistant, he was given one, Midshipman Samuel Armour, who entered the navy a week after Cooper went on board the *Wasp*. Armour's assistance was costly, especially on one occasion when Cooper was ordered off into New Jersey in pursuit of a navy deserter. Cooper drew money for that purpose from ship's purser Herman Thorn, obviously assuming that it wouldn't be charged against him personally, although apparently it was. Worse yet, while conducting this search, Cooper entrusted the collection of the security deposit for an absconded new recruit to Armour—who got the money, then went off and lost it gambling. Cooper, unjustly he thought, was held liable for the funds in question (*LJ* 1:89).[70] In another instance, Cooper on Lawrence's direct orders retroactively paid bounties to the destitute families of two recent recruits, and then backdated receipts for the funds. The purser's records for this period, insufficiently cross-fertilized with Lawrence's, shed no light on these disbursements. Having accommodated his commander, and for the most humane of reasons, Cooper was therefore left in another tough spot, as he later complained to the navy: "I am the actual dispenser of the Charity! for I am charged with the money" (*LJ* 1:90). Between the defalcations of midshipman Armour and the fuzzily documented impulses of Lawrence, Cooper was out more than another hundred dollars. So much, yet again, for naval glory.

Boston

Such developments must have made Cooper's spell as a recruiter seem longer than it was. The logbook of the *Wasp* states that he went onshore as late as March 9 to open his rendezvous. If Cooper indeed spent "months" recruiting, as he recalled, then the logbook took only sporadic, and late, note of the process. Probably his earlier recruiting activities, partly documented in other sources, involved short stints along the wharves, from which he returned repeatedly to the ship.[71]

In any case, an end came to the unpleasant duty just after the beginning of spring. Cooper's reason for taking up Lawrence's offer of a berth in November was his desire to get back to sea. At the time, Lawrence seems to have underestimated the work needed to ready the *Wasp*. Just after Christmas, the logbook mentioned preparations for a brief voyage, but those stopped when a need for further repairs was discovered. Not until three months later, on Monday, March 26, was work on the vessel finally done. Then, with twenty-eight new men taken on board in recent days owing largely to Cooper's rendezvous, the ship pulled away from the navy yard and anchored out in the river, ready for a run to Boston. The *Wasp* received two more men there, probably brought out from Manhattan in a quick trip by Cooper, who was credited with one of them.[72]

At last he was to have his way: from the groggeries near which he had been hanging out the past several weeks, he was given the sea, and a grand sea it was. The weather had been clear, with fresh southerly breezes, of late. As the *Wasp* started moving, the wind kicked up, "howling to the Eastward," and the ebb tide slackened, so the vessel anchored and stayed put in the upper bay until Tuesday morning. Through the night, at a distance of about ten miles, the lighthouse at

Sandy Hook was visible. At daybreak, those lingering on the north shore of Staten Island might have seen the *Wasp*'s distinctive shape out on the water as the men hauled in the bright green-painted cutter hanging from the stern to stow it amidships. Other preparatory tasks followed. Then at ten o'clock, under a moderate northwestward breeze, Lieutenant Lawrence ordered the men beat to quarters. They were mustered, assigned their stations, and the officers "saw all clear for action." The ship was bound only up the coast a short distance, but in these days of tense international relations the memory of the *Chesapeake* hung over every naval departure. We can be sure that the *Wasp*'s decks were *not* cluttered, and that a challenge by any British warship prowling off Sandy Hook would have called forth an aggressive response.

But no such challenge materialized. That afternoon, under clear skies and with a low west wind, the pilot was discharged, the men hoisted and secured the boats, and with its foresails and the topgallants set, the ship turned east and finally passed out onto the open sea between the Hook and Rockaway Point. Finally, all the tedious effort of the past months was beginning to pay off. At four in the afternoon on Tuesday, the entrance to New York's lower bay was already twenty miles to the ship's stern, and so steady was its progress along a course just south of east that by sunset on Wednesday sailing master John R. Grayson "went aloft but saw no land or breakers." Fully aware of coastal hazards, Grayson and Lawrence took the vessel on a prudent route well clear of Long Island's south shore and the difficult waters surrounding Martha's Vineyard and Nantucket. Then they scribed a wide turn up the Atlantic along the backside of Cape Cod. No venturesome sailing this time, only a safe passage, but a fast one at that: by six at night on Thursday, March 29, barely forty-eight hours after leaving New York behind, those on the *Wasp* could make out the lighthouse on the tip of the cape, bearing southwest by south some twenty-five miles. Eight hours later, Cape Ann light came in view to the northwest and "Monument" (Manomet) Point to the southwest.

Then things slowed. It took another twenty-four hours before they could see Boston light, located on Little Brewster Island at the entrance of the outer harbor. The main problem was a gusty westerly wind, which was hardly favorable for the pull in through Boston's many tricky features. Rain and snow fell off and on as well. In response, Lawrence seems to have taken the vessel farther north than strictly necessary, then angled in on a southerly course, all the time keeping the crew busy making and taking in sail "as the Wind & Weather [permitted]." The *Wasp* anchored at ten Friday night inside the light and, when a stronger northwest breeze arose around three the next morning, began moving in. Apparently, after passing Point Allerton and Hull, Lawrence went in through the Narrows, a deep passage leading between Georges and Lovells islands. From there the usual channel turned straight toward Castle Island, deep inside the outer harbor, where Fort Independence or Castle William dominated approaches to Boston. First built in the seventeenth century and rebuilt at several points thereafter, the fort had gone through its most recent refurbishing in the years leading up to the *Wasp*'s visit. From here British cannon had fired on the American position on nearby Dorchester Heights in March of 1776, before Britain abandoned Boston for good, the historical event with which Cooper chose to end his only Boston novel, *Lionel Lincoln*.

Lawrence gave him a good close view of the site. In fact, the *Wasp*'s coastal pilot brought the vessel to an anchorage off the fort at ten in the morning on Saturday, March 31. Around noon, the *Wasp* fired a gun to call out a harbor pilot; by four, under his direction, the ship was moored near Long Wharf, the most prominent feature in the inner harbor.[73] Almost immediately, the officers began busying themselves about one of the voyage's key purposes: taking on more men. Seventeen were shifted over from the *Chesapeake* that very day, including six recruited from the latter vessel by Cooper's closest associate on the ship, William B. Shubrick, and four by two other officers, lieutenants William Laughton and Benedic J. Neale. To begin the business so soon, the three young officers must have taken a boat over to the other warship while the *Wasp* lay off the fort, perhaps even earlier. All of the new men seem to have been recent recruits to the *Chesapeake*'s own crew, a point that helps explain the quickness of their transfer—as well as Lawrence's willingness to extend the sizable advances to them that the payroll book records.

Cooper may have assisted Shubrick and the two lieutenants in this business, although the payroll attributed no recruits directly to him. His deep unhappiness with the same task in New York had to be well known to his commander. Moreover, Lawrence understood that Cooper's disaffection ran deeper. The midshipman had complained of the "blasted prospects of the service" to his brother Richard during the latter's visit to New York City the previous winter, adding at the time that if nothing was "done for the navy" before the end of the present session of Congress early in March—just when he was sent ashore to set up his rendezvous!—he intended to resign (*LJ* 1:17). Although Lawrence may not have known of this resolve until several weeks later, he clearly thought well of Cooper and wanted him to stay on the ship, reason enough to accommodate him by keeping him clear of the recruiting business in Boston. But it may be that Cooper was simply assigned other pressing duties.

Whatever Cooper was about over the next few days, he could reflect with some satisfaction on the passage up to Boston. The *Wasp* sailed well under Lawrence's expert command. In his naval history, Cooper's observation that the vessel was "a beautiful and fast cruiser" (*HN* 2:181) must have derived from his experience on the run up the coast in 1810, when it had indeed *cruised*. William Shubrick easily could have seconded the opinion. Shubrick also may have seconded—or even helped to shape—Cooper's view of Lawrence as "a perfect man-of-war's man, and an excellent quarter-deck seaman, handling his vessel not only skilfully, but with all the style of the profession" (*HN* 2:253). The Boston voyage would have given Cooper a glimpse of such characteristics, but Shubrick's service under Lawrence on an ocean crossing the previous year surely had provided greater opportunity to gauge the commander. And Shubrick knew the vessel even better than he knew Lawrence. On enlisting in 1806, Shubrick had been ordered to the *Chesapeake* but then was shifted to the *Wasp*, which departed for the Mediterranean twelve days before the attack of the *Leopard* off Cape Henry that June. He had stayed on the *Wasp* through its Mediterranean duty, its return to America, its courier work under Lawrence, and right up to the time of Cooper's arrival in November 1809. He also stayed on the ship beyond Cooper's departure the following May, briefly becoming its sailing master in June of 1810.[74]

For most of that first week of April the *Wasp* remained at its mooring in Boston harbor. Those on board probably had a good view, over the obstructions on busy Long Wharf, up to the venerable State House. Farther still stood the soon-to-be-cut-down Beacon Hill and its twin adjuncts, Mount Pemberton and already diminished Mount Vernon. At the time of the *Wasp*'s visit, Boston was a city of 33,787 inhabitants, as the U.S. Census was to establish later in 1810—perhaps twice the size it had been in 1775 but still compact enough to give Cooper a good sense of its condition in the Revolutionary era. Still functioning under town government in 1810, by the time Cooper came back in 1824 Boston had received a city charter, had nearly 60,000 inhabitants, and had begun in earnest its aggressive campaign of filling in the surrounding waters so that it already had expanded physically far beyond its 1775 footprint. Faneuil Hall market, rightly portrayed by Cooper in his Revolutionary War novel as having at that time its original modest dimensions, had been expanded by Charles Bulfinch just before the *Wasp*'s visit. By 1824, however, its magnificent replacement as the city's marketplace (eventually to be named after the city's first mayor, Josiah Quincy) was being planned and soon would be erected, the centerpiece of an impressive reclamation of land in the vicinity of the old Town Dock. Boston as Cooper would see it in 1824 was significantly removed from its Revolutionary origins. Fifteen years earlier, he had been able to catch a glimpse of the older city and its hills, a glimpse he still could recall years afterwards when his art had use for it.[75]

The *Wasp* took in more recruits day by day until twenty-five new men had been named in the log. But the ship still must have been somewhat below its ideal complement. Perhaps partly for that reason, and out of concern that some other men might run off, the crew did not receive shore liberty during the brief Boston stay. Rather, "all hands [were kept] employed in the various Necessary duties of the Ship," as the logbook's version of the oft-repeated formula phrase ran on April 3. There would be some things to tend to that were routine, other special ones that had been discovered during the shake-down cruise from New York. Even if Cooper went onshore to aid in recruiting or for some other reason, a midshipman's usual job at such junctures was to stay on deck during the day to keep the men at their tasks.

The April weather was changeable: as Cooper put it in *Lionel Lincoln,* perhaps recalling his own experience, one day's "genial sun" was forgotten when "torrents of cold rain . . . drove before the easterly gales" (*LL* CE 66). It was clear the day the ship arrived, then on Sunday the northwest breezes shifted to the southeast and snow and rain began falling. The small coastal depression apparently responsible for this change passed north overnight, leaving clear skies and "hard gales" blowing out of the northeast that allowed the soaked sails to be loosed and dried. By that night and into Tuesday morning, the winds lessened— "fresh gales" were now blowing from the west. On Wednesday, April 4, another minor coastal system passed, clouding the sky as a strong northeast breeze blew snow into the harbor. That afternoon, though, the winds were from the north and the skies were clear again, as they remained on Thursday. On Friday, conditions were so positive that the captain's clerk called the weather "clear & pleasant," always a gift for Boston as early as April 6. It was especially welcome because this was the date when the vessel was scheduled to leave the port.

Early that morning, the harbor pilot came on board and the *Wasp* was unmoored and its anchor lifted. Little progress was made that day, but on Saturday, April 7, under "pleasant weather," north-northwest breezes pushed the ship back through the islands and out into Massachusetts Bay. There the southerly winds were strong enough that by seven that night Boston light was some twenty miles directly astern; by noon the next day, Cape Cod light was almost due south. The men were busy stowing gear, then hauling up the anchor cables to air out the cable locker below deck as, under clear skies and with variable light winds that afternoon, the vessel made south into the open sea. At seven that night, ever cautious, the officers mustered the men at their stations by "the great guns," where they would hasten in the event of a real alarm. Fifteen other vessels were in sight at sunset, none of them threatening, but a reminder nonetheless of what might lie in store for the *Wasp* as it made its way back to New York. "Great guns" or no, it was a small warship, no match for the vessels with which the royal navy still patrolled the coast in those days. Understandably, the men were exercised at their battle stations again the next day.

Over Sunday night, as the vessel rounded the backside of the cape and began making its wide southwest arc, the weather remained moderate although the sky was clouded. By nine Monday night, it was squally, ominous enough in these tricky waters that the sails were significantly reduced. As an added precaution, several times over that night and into Tuesday morning the vessel sounded, gauging the depth of water beneath its keel and pulling up samples from the bottom—black and white sand, coarse brown sand, and the like—that might help determine where it was. Rain began to fall and the westerly winds increased to "brisk gales," perhaps forty miles per hour or more, and the seas must have been high, with spindrift tumbling off the crests. By Tuesday morning, the *Wasp* had passed the worst dangers, although it may have been a mixed blessing that it actually caught a glimpse of Martha's Vineyard lying some fifteen miles north by east—perhaps too close for comfort in such weather, especially when the overcast sky allowed no observation of the ship's position at noon.[76]

The weather moderated across Tuesday afternoon, although the winds were coming now from the southwest, the direction the *Wasp* ought to have been heading. Even under the hand of a Rhode Island sound pilot, the ship therefore made little progress. Around six that night, after the men had set and taken in and endlessly adjusted the ship's sails all day, it was backed and hove to—stopped in its course—just in time to glimpse Gay Head, the Vineyard's easternmost point, visible now only about twelve miles to the northeast. Later that night, the winds came around to the northwest, allowing more sail to be set. By midnight, as a result, Montauk Point could be seen to the northwest, and by eight Wednesday morning the vessel made the Wells Hills, uplands along the south-central shore of Long Island. Now it was homeward bound in earnest. At 11:30, as the skies began to clear, the anchors were hung off the bow and enough cable readied for the ship's arrival. Lawrence ordered the main-topsail hauled up to call for a New York pilot as, under a heavy load of canvas, the vessel plunged on through high seas, driven by fresh northwesterly gales. Finally at noon, the lighthouse on Sandy Hook could be seen, and two hours later the ship came to anchor, no doubt to await the change of tide. At six that night, under light breezes and clear skies, it got under way again. With "all the working sails" set, by two on Thursday morning the ship had come to anchor "in North River, abreast the Battery." Later its anchorage was adjusted and both pilots were discharged. The bright green cutter was hauled out, and all but one of a group of men who had been borrowed from the *Enterprise* on March 24 were sent back.[77]

On April 12, with its shrinking crew, the *Wasp* was at the Brooklyn navy yard once again. On the thirteenth, the first new recruit signed up "by the recruiting officer at New York," a boy named Thomas Chester and credited to Cooper, came on board. If Lawrence had given Cooper a break from the recruiting business while the vessel was in Boston, now his vacation decidedly was over. During the next two weeks, Cooper would continue to supply men for the *Wasp*, more men, in fact, than the other two recruiters then active, Shubrick and Laughton. The logbook entry regarding young Chester clearly indicated that Cooper was still *at* New York, suggesting that he had been restationed there on the ship's return to port and that, if he came to the *Wasp* at all it was only on brief visits. A similar formula was used on Monday, April 16, for recruits not otherwise ascribed to Cooper or any other recruiter. On the twentieth a single man (also "shiped by the Recruiting Officer at New York") came aboard, and two other recruits taken aboard the *Wasp* on April 25, one of them a cook, both were recorded as having received their advances from Cooper. But these were the last men overtly credited to him. Either his sources had dried up or he had been brought back on the *Wasp*. In either case, he was surely relieved to be out of the man-hiring business.

CHAPTER FIVE

Love and War

With the return of the *Wasp* to New York in April 1810, Cooper's active days in the navy were numbered. His resumption of recruiting, for one thing, was a further reminder that this was not the service as he had imagined it. When, on May 1, one of his earlier recruits stumbled on board drunk, then careened overboard and drowned in Wallabout Bay, the futility of it all was brought home.[1] Then or soon after, Cooper composed a letter of resignation and, in keeping with naval custom, "offer'd it to Capt[.] Lawrence, for his inspection." Hardly ignorant of Cooper's simmering unhappiness, James Lawrence nonetheless seems to have been taken completely by surprise. He rejected the resignation, "very warmly" recommending that Cooper take another furlough and then reassess his views. Moved by his commander's sympathy and concern, Cooper "thought it wisest to accept this proposition," as he soon was confessing to his brother Richard. Yet he was certain that he would resign at the end of a year unless the navy had a real place for him (*LJ* 1:17).

His naval disappointments were outbalanced by a sudden rush of positive feelings elsewhere in his life. He supplied Richard with these details as well. During his time ashore, he had met a "fair damsel of eighteen" by the name of

Susan Augusta DeLancey: "I loved her like a man," he boasted, "and told her of it like a sailor" (*LJ* 1:17). Not yet twenty-one, and thus not legally a *man*, he already had asked for and tentatively won the young woman's hand and now was eager to have the Coopers line up behind him. Their connivance was critical because Susan's father wanted her to proceed with caution. John Peter DeLancey was insisting, to begin with, that Cooper secure his widowed mother's formal assent to the marriage. The young man tried to hide his anxiety from Richard by a jaunty show of sudden authority. His oldest brother was almost thirty-five now, fifteen years his senior, but Cooper addressed him like a juvenile: "you will take your Hat and go to mother, the boys, girls," Cooper instructed, "and say to them have you any objection that James Cooper shall marry at a future date, Susan De Lancey[?]" Apparently Richard complied, leaving his house, Apple Hill, to trudge up to the "the Castle," as the future novelist sometimes called Otsego Hall (*LJ* 1:26), where Mrs. Cooper had immured herself since her husband's death six months earlier. The matriarch either said nothing, a likely outcome, or at least did not object. Apparently none of the "boys" and "girls" objected, either. Perhaps they were mindful of Cooper's pseudo-threats in his letter: "If any of them forbids the bans may the Lord . . . forgive them—for I never will." Cooper clearly enjoyed the sense of his own emergent maturity that was implicit in this news. Still humorously insistent, he lined out Richard's next step: "Then take your pen and write to Mr. De Lancey, stating the *happiness* and *pleasure* it will give all the family to have this connection completed—all this I wish you to do *immediately*, as I am deprived of the pleasure of visiting my flame, [u]ntil this be done, by that confounded *bore*, delicacy" (*LJ* 1:18). "Delicacy" no doubt had been seconded by Susan's prudent father. Cooper waited impatiently in New York for Richard to send him the required note, which he then delivered in person at the DeLancey home in Westchester County. Probably by the beginning of June, the two families had agreed to the couple's plans to wed on New Year's Day, 1811.

Formally engaged now, Cooper had other things to concern him as the year advanced. With small sums of money sent him by Richard and charged against his share of Judge Cooper's estate, he paid off his account with purser Herman Thorn on the *Wasp* and began a series of modest purchases in New York City. He also ran up to Cooperstown, probably in July and August, no doubt to put things in order there and pick up items he would need once he and Susan set up housekeeping in the countryside near her family's Westchester home, as they were planning to do. By year's end, he went back to Otsego for a last visit with members of the family, whom he probably filled in on plans for the wedding even as he picked up more belongings and conferred once more with Richard and Isaac about the estate, an issue of increasing importance to him as he faced an independent life with Susan.[2]

The emotional economy of a large family is a curious alloy of gold and lead. In Cooperstown, Cooper discovered that his marriage to Susan was to take place just as his brother William's was teetering on the edge of collapse. William Cooper and Eliza Clason, the daughter of a prominent New York City merchant, apparently had been ill-suited from the start. In May or June of 1810, shortly after the birth of their first child, William and his wife had separated. This was just the moment when Midshipman Cooper was negotiating with the DeLanceys and his own family about his engagement to Susan. Cooper's residence in the city at the time may have prepared him for the break, even provided him with gory details to share once he arrived in Otsego later in the summer. But it was the family's oldest brothers, Richard and Isaac, who had to deal with the mess, and how they did so illuminates the clan's emotional habits. Richard, whose wife Ann was carrying on more-or-less openly at this time with the man she would marry right after her husband's death in 1813, took a rather jaundiced view of marriage; he was especially concerned to limit the financial consequences of William's dispute. At the time of the split from Eliza, William promised to support her but made no arrangements to reimburse Isaac Clason for his daughter's living expenses. The oversight probably expressed William's underlying resentments, but it also showed how dependent the basically unemployed lawyer was on family resources controlled by Richard and Isaac. During his visit to Otsego in June, William apparently broached the topic with them and once back in New York told Eliza's father that they would handle repayments. When Clason wrote Richard and Isaac asking what procedure he was to follow, though, he received a runaround. The duo commonly handled business together, but Richard pleaded ignorance: "I cannot tell of my Brother William's determinations respecting his Wife—when he left this place he gave my Brother Isaac a Power of Attorney to act for him as he informed me, in all cases. . . . Isaac has seen your letter perhaps he may give you more information." On the dispute's more personal surfaces, Richard hardly was more tactful. He mouthed a conventional piety about "sincerely regret[ting] the unhappy dispute" but would not agree that William was to blame for anything. To the contrary, he laid everything at Eliza's feet. Her father had been more conciliatory, acknowledging that Eliza was naive—a mere child deficient "in the information of the World." Richard crudely added, "And Sir, *I must be sincere* a Spoiled Child too."[3] Perhaps Richard saw in his sister-in-law some trace of what he was seeing in his own wife. Or perhaps on these matters in general the Coopers, aware of the discord in the marriage of their parents (and of Richard's as well), took a strictly unsentimental view of family affairs. No one in any case rushed to cover William's crisis in 1810 with vaguely optimistic wishes.

As it happened, Richard and Isaac's behavior further eroded William's prospects. Stung by his daughter's failing marriage and the intransigence of her husband's family, Isaac Clason soon drew up a will intended to invalidate any claims his errant son-in-law might someday make on his estate. The merchant had helped the couple set up their household by loaning them money in 1808. Now, with Eliza back at his home and the Coopers dodging inquiries about her means of support, Clason decided to radically cut his losses. If she and William were still separated at the time of his own death, that 1808 debt would be forgiven. She also would continue to receive the $1,000 per year in support that Clason now was giving her. But she would get nothing more; the rest of the sizable estate would pass into the hands of her siblings. Furthermore, Clason clearly intended that Eliza's annuity would end if and when she reconciled with William, as in fact she did in 1811. When Clason died in 1815, this was all news to Eliza and William. Forthwith, they embarked on a series of desperate court cases aimed at recovering what they thought their rightful share of Clason's fortune. In an effort to make the facts of their marriage meet the terms of his will, they even separated again in the hope that doing so would reactivate the long-suspended annuity.[4]

The earlier stages of this messy relationship could hardly have reinforced Cooper's expectant mood as his own wedding date drew near across 1810. The breakup may even help explain why Cooper did not insist that anyone from "home" attend his ceremony. Ironically, on the groom's side only William Cooper (without Eliza) was to attend, probably because he was still living nearby in New York City. Richard, with his rather cynical perspective on such things, either was not invited or did not come; Isaac, more of an optimist and certainly closer to Cooper, also did not make the trip from Cooperstown in the dead of winter. The first important step Cooper would take in his new life on land, it was taken without the oversight of a substantial cohort of kin.[5]

The wedding was not, as it turned out, an elaborate affair. In keeping with older customs, the ceremony was held at the bride's home in the presence of few guests. The last of Cooper's novels, *The Ways of the Hour* (1850), offers a long glance back at it in a comment on the elaborately shallow weddings becoming common in urban America at mid-century: "Extravagance and parade have taken such deep root among us that young people scarce consider themselves legally united unless there are six bride's maids, one, in particular, to 'pull off the glove;' as many attendants of the other sex, and some three or four hundred friends in the evening, to bow and curtsy before the young couple, utter a few words of nonsense, and go their way to bow and curtsy somewhere else" (*WH* Darley 498).[6] Not so on New Year's Day of 1811 at Heathcote Hill, the De-Lancey home in Mamaroneck. Samuel Haskell, rector of Christ Church in nearby Rye, officiated in a brief exchange of vows (SFM 27).

Heathcote Hill

Heathcote Hill was a large comfortable structure in a vernacular Federal style built by Susan's parents around 1791. It replaced the original dwelling of an ancestor, judge and politician Caleb Heathcote, which had burned down just before the Revolution. The new house stood (the novelist's daughter recalled) on "the brow of a low hill, immediately above the highway to Boston, and facing a broad bay of [Long Island] Sound." A lane circled down the hill out front to join the Boston road, which led to John Peter's farm on "the Neck" and, farther on, New Rochelle. A second lane, heading north from the back porch, ran off toward the village of Mamaroneck. Surrounding the house were lilacs and a scattering of fruit trees. To the rear, near the extensive gardens, stood a cluster of barns; farther back still arose a second low hill, where the cider mill and peach and apple orchards had been established. Then came, Susan recalled, "a beautiful wood, the remains of the ancient forest," amidst which stood the small family graveyard (SFM 24–25).[7] For Cooper's second daughter, Heathcote Hill was to leave long afterimages. It did the same for Cooper himself, who borrowed the De-Lanceys' location, and many details of their life there, for his portrait of Corny Littlepage's youth in the opening chapters of *Satanstoe*. The fictional neck of land that gave that novel its title was modeled on DeLancey's Neck, the location of John Peter's farm, and countless other local facts had their own deflections in the landscape of that book.

Cooper came to know the DeLancey estate well during the first months of his marriage, which the newlyweds passed there. That stay also made him intimately acquainted with Susan's parents and siblings and the other members of the family's sizable establishment—and with the many stories that animated the place. Much like other tales he had heard in his youth, these new ones had much to do with the young nation's past. Susan DeLancey's father, a former British army officer born in New York City in 1753, was close to sixty in 1811. His wife, Long Island native Elizabeth Floyd, was about five years younger. We have no surviving image of Elizabeth, although Cooper called her "lovely" (see *LJ* 5: 310).[8] As to John Peter, the "admirable likeness" by John Wesley Jarvis that Cooper commissioned for Susan in this period reveals a sharp eye set in a long, broad-browed face (Plate 8). Dressed in a fashionably high collar and a large-buttoned waistcoat that give him a hint of strength in reserve, DeLancey looks like the active man he had always been—polished and savvy, probably not overly reflective or intellectual, and, if he thought the situation demanded it, fully capable of violence. He could have been Cooper's model when, denying a common mistake, he insisted in a late novel that a gentleman was not *necessarily* a Christian: "The first is ready to lay down his life in order to wipe away an imaginary dishonor, or take the life of another; the last is taught to turn the other cheek, when smitten" (*OO* 225). DeLancey certainly was a churchman; yet, whatever his religious values, his life bore out Cooper's distinction in just these terms, as his son-in-law was to learn some years later.

No boaster, DeLancey nonetheless regaled Cooper with tales from his active past. They concerned war and sports for the most part, a gentleman's narrow repertoire, but they escaped being the clichés of his class through their pervasive sense of loss. All of them kept coming back to the personal and familial costs the DeLanceys had endured in the founding scenes of the Republic. John Peter, holding field commands in the British Army and in Loyalist units throughout the Revolution, had fled the country of his birth—the country he, too, had fought for—for exile in England. He managed to effect a return only after several years had passed. Cooper's sense of the nation's birth, already complicated by the memory of Quaker oppression at the hands of the Patriots and tales he may have heard from Benjamin Silliman in New Haven, among other places, was ready for this accession of Loyalist lore.[9]

The Revolutionary installment of the DeLancey narrative was the painful end of a long and colorful story. Parts of it Cooper already knew; parts of it he was to pick up over the years and indeed decades following. Susan's family had been at the center of New York's political affairs for much of the previous century. Like the family of Cooper's schoolmate, William Jay, with which they had been intimate from the seventeenth century and with which they had intermarried, the DeLanceys were of Huguenot extraction.[10] Both families had fled France at the revocation of the Edict of Nantes in 1685 and, like many in their tragic situation, made their way to the tolerant colony of New York. In such villages as New Rochelle and New Paltz, the French émigrés erected new houses, built Protestant churches in which to worship, and set about establishing a foothold for themselves and their children among the Dutch and English settlers.

Susan's great-grandfather, Etienne deLancy (as the name was then spelled), eventually made his home in New York City. A young member of the nobility, descendant of the Viscount de la Val et du Nouvion, at the time of the edict's revocation he had been living at his family's seat in Caen. Proud of his origins yet pragmatic, once in New York he (like his descendents after him) identified closely with English culture, even shifting allegiance from the French Protestant church there to the Anglican. Much like the Coopers themselves, although more quickly and decisively, the DeLanceys thus retrenched from radical Protestant terrain to settle into the ritualized territory of the Church of England. They also married well. Etienne deLancy had become such a rich and successful merchant by 1700 that he wed "the most eligible girl in New York of his day," Anne, the third child of Gertruy Schuyler and Stephanus Van Cortlandt, New York's chief justice. This alliance began the consolidation of fortunes and pedigrees that was to place his DeLancey descendants among the leaders of society in New York— and indeed, in the English Atlantic world. The Van Cortlandts were arguably the most important family in the colony at the time, controlling substantial holdings in New York City as well as the vast Van Cortlandt Manor in northern Westchester County.[11]

Susan DeLancey Cooper's grandfather, James DeLancey (1703–1760), the oldest son of Etienne and Anne, improved on these advantages. He was educated at Corpus Christi College, Cambridge, and studied law at the Inner Temple in London. When he returned to New York in the early 1720s as a polished lawyer, he already had become well connected in the English ruling class, thus easing his assumption of political power in New York. When barely twenty-five, James DeLancey was named by New York's governor, James Montgomerie, to his small advisory council and then three years later to the colony's very powerful supreme court, for which he was to serve as chief justice from 1744. DeLancey also became lieutenant governor of New York in 1747, more or less continuously holding that position up to his death in 1760. Recently called "the most gifted and remarkable politician of New York's colonial period," James DeLancey had skill, money, connections, and charm.[12] In addition to the alliances he had forged during his law studies in London and at Cambridge (his tutor there, Robert Herring, later became archbishop of Canterbury, for instance), he could rely on the many ties his father had built up with prominent London merchants. He also gained further superb connections through his bride, Anne Heathcote. She was the daughter and co-heir of the lord of Scarsdale Manor, Caleb Heathcote, a Derbyshire native who had arrived in New York in 1691 and served on the governor's council almost continuously from that point to his death in 1721. Combined with his own network, that of the Heathcotes made James DeLancey *the* man to reckon with in mid-eighteenth-century New York. His granddaughter, Cooper's bride, grew up knowing that she came from a renowned—if now discredited—background.[13]

John Peter DeLancey (1753–1828), Mrs. Cooper's father, was a younger, less distinguished son of this powerful figure. Sent abroad at the age of eight to be raised by an English aunt, Susannah, Lady Warren, he eventually was educated at Harrow and at Woolwich Military College near London. Entering the British Army, he eventually rose through the officer corps of the Eighteenth Regiment, known as the Royal Irish, to become a lieutenant in 1775 and a captain five years later. According to a sketch Cooper wrote of his father-in-law in 1831, DeLancey returned to America with the Royal Irish Regiment in 1774 and was posted then at Philadelphia (see *LJ* 2:50).

By that point, various members of the DeLancey family had devoted themselves to the Imperial service. But, like many other residents of New York, where opposition to the Stamp Act was fierce, the DeLanceys nonetheless vociferously resisted England's revenue policies in the 1760s and early 1770s. Indeed, for all their English affiliations, the DeLanceys operated very much in the foreground of New York protest. At the end of 1766, John Peter's elder brother, James DeLancey, Jr., was the "hero of the Sons of Liberty and the most popular man in the colony," and he and his uncle, Oliver DeLancey, may well have fomented the New York riots of 1765 against the Stamp Act.[14] From a post-Revolutionary perspective, the DeLancey family was an almost archetypal instance of unrepentant and thoroughgoing Loyalism. One historian observes, however, that, while they "were not basically hostile to the empire, to English institutions, or to those entrusted to exercise English power in the American colonies," they were "certainly whiggish in their attitude to[ward] the questions of taxation and American political autonomy." In short, they were "Whig-Loyalists."[15] They were not temperamentally attached to authority for its own sake or unwavering in their obedience to it. To the contrary, the family felt real conflict between the two increasingly opposed aspects of their identity.

And when at last most of them threw their fortunes together with the crown's, it cost them a great deal. James DeLancey, Jr., the family's head, went north through New York to Canada as early as April of 1775, right after news of Lexington and Concord reached New York City. From there he embarked for England, where he resettled and after the Revolution served as an agent, and eventually vice president, of the Loyalist claims commission. Attainted of treason by New York's rebel authorities in 1779, he eventually lost to confiscation what his brother-in-law Thomas Jones called "an amazing real estate" on Manhattan, besides "large tracts of land in almost every county in the province," including even the infant Otsego. A later inventory of the lost property estimated its value at £50,000—and that did not count large quantities sold off before the war's end. He eventually received some £26,000 in compensation from the crown, among the highest amounts paid to any Loyalist exile.[16]

Susan Cooper's father might well have copied his brother's course. His military position, however, sent him in a quite different direction. He observed the proceedings of the Continental Congress in Philadelphia shortly after his arrival back in the country, and, with other officers from the Eighteenth Regiment, dined on several occasions there with George Washington. Once hostilities broke out, however, he fought Washington at Brandywine and Germantown, then with General Howe entered and took over Philadelphia. On the British evacuation from that city in 1778, he accompanied Sir Henry Clinton on his move across Jersey to New York. Eventually DeLancey passed to the South, as much of the British force did in the next phase of the conflict, serving as a major with the Pennsylvania Loyalists in East Florida in 1780. Having lasted out the war and lost both his cause and his country, in 1783 he left in the great Loyalist exodus, heading to England.[17]

England provided him a semblance of home. There, associating with other Loyalist families, he married Elizabeth Floyd, an uprooted American with whom he already was acquainted.[18] The couple had two children in England, a fair start on a new life, but DeLancey's involvement in a serious dispute within the army in 1790 forced them to hastily uproot themselves and risk an uncertain homecoming in America. Cooper's daughter claimed with some sentimental exaggeration that her "grandfather considered himself an American, not an Englishman, and now that the war was over decided to cast in his lot with his native country." Be that as it may, she also well knew that the immediate cause of the homecoming (as Cooper himself recorded it on blank pages in her own commonplace book) was "an affair of honor with his commanding officer."[19] The DeLanceys' recovery of America thus began on a desperate professional impulse rather than in personal or political longing.[20] And at first it set in motion other losses. The couple carried their infant son Thomas James with them on the ship they boarded at Greenwich. Four-year-old daughter Anne Charlotte they were forced to leave behind with Loyalist historian Thomas Jones and his wife, John Peter's sister Anne. The girl grew up there amid considerable difficulties and was not reunited with her American kin until many years later, a permanent sign of the wrenching dislocations that the war and its aftermath had caused.[21]

The seemingly placid household at Heathcote Hill as Cooper came to see it after his engagement in 1810 was decidedly a construction, an illusion of sorts erected over the void of the past. But it was at the same time the only home Susan Augusta, born there on January 28, 1792, had yet known. A silhouette of young Susan, no doubt executed at Heathcote Hill in the early years of the nineteenth century, reveals only her dainty, small-featured head, the fine hair held back except for a wisp draping her high brow.[22] When Cooper wrote his brother Richard to secure the family's blessing, he described his "damsel" as "amiable, sweet-tempered and happy in her disposition." If he had thought otherwise, of course, one presumes he would not have pursued her. Yet all we know of her suggests the accuracy of the estimate. She had been "educated in the country," unlike Cooper's sister Hannah, but had been to "the City" often enough to "rub off the rust," the young groom-to-be went on. Cooper, who surely could have continued listing her virtues, interrupted his letter to Richard in mock defensiveness— "but hold a moment, it is enough she pleases *me* in the qualities of her *person* and *mind*" (*LJ* 1:17).

Two drawings probably made by her eldest daughter in Paris almost twenty years after the wedding (Plate 9) show the persistence of most of the physical features visible in the early profile. They portray a feminine, oval-faced woman not quite in her middle age (she would turn forty in 1832), her slender nose still showing the slight upturn revealed in the schoolgirl silhouette. The hair is all ringlets now, spilling out of the upright pleated caps Susan Cooper wears in both her daughter's portraits. It is her eyes, though, that attract the viewer's attention. They almost avoid a direct glance but exude a sense of peaceful attention, as if the sitter will listen—yet is not herself to be rushed. Below the somewhat weak chin and the soft flesh cushioning it, Susan's layered clothes are drawn tight around the waist in both of the images executed by her daughter, suggesting the womanly form Cooper meant to emphasize when in 1810 he spoke of her *person.* It was also the sort of figure that Cooper often was to give the heroines of his fiction, who are substantial and grounded rather than wispy. In *The Pioneers,* Elizabeth Temple (winter-shrouded by "cloaks, coats, shawls, and socks") thus is revealed to possess "a form of exquisite proportions, rather full and rounded for her years" when she sheds those exterior layers on her arrival at her father's mansion (*PIO* CE 66).[23] Yet if Susan DeLancey Cooper was shapely in her own regard, she was not overly tall, probably a few inches at most over five feet. Her complexion one presumes was the source of the narrator's comment in *The Spy* about the rosy cheeks that are "so eminently the property of the West-Chester fair." Her eyes may have been like those of young Frances Wharton's in the same novel: "deep blue . . . with that lustre which gives so much pleasure to the beholder, and which indicates so much internal innocence and peace." Susan certainly possessed the "feminine delicacy" that is attributed to Frances Wharton, who was modeled in general on Cooper's young wife (*Spy* CE 26–27). Susan's delicacy, though, also extended to her health: she was subject to hereditary asthma (see *LJ* 3:372).[24]

Susan was the third DeLancey child overall and the first of a half dozen native to the new place (a girl, two boys, then two more girls were to follow by 1803). Except for Anne Charlotte, whom Cooper was to meet in England much later, he had varied dealings with each of Susan's siblings from the outset. By far the most important of them in these early years was English-born Thomas James DeLancey, Susan's older brother and Cooper's nearly exact contemporary. During these years, Thomas was a student of the law in New York City, where Cooper had come to know him very well even before the wedding. An alert and witty young man well suited to Cooper's temperament, the would-be lawyer toured the city by the furloughed sailor's side, exchanging confidences with him and paying visits to mutual friends. Seriously weakened by consumption, DeLancey shared even the intimate details of his health with Cooper: he spent the first months of 1811 recuperating at Heathcote Hill while the newlyweds lingered there, then on returning to the city in June he almost immediately wrote Cooper (*not* his sister) to report on how he was faring. Thomas freely confessed that he felt worse than the year before, adding that he was undertaking new cures from a physician the young men both jokingly knew as "the Brooklyn Empiric." But he went further. Lonely without Cooper by his side in the summer of 1811, Thomas longed for the status quo ante: "you well know that there were few except yourself that I had either an opportunity or an inclination to associate with." These were rare words for Cooper to receive from a man his own age, rare certainly in the archive of his own family's correspondence, which seems more fruitful of banter and warning shots than intimacy. Yet, as Thomas finished his studies, began a law practice, married, and started a family, the intimacy with his new brother-in-law lessened. Then in the summer or early fall of 1822, the previously cordial relations abruptly ceased when DeLancey (and his father) had a falling out with Cooper (see Chapter 11), who was pressed hard for cash at that time, over two pieces of real estate the family was holding in trust for Susan. That breach remained unclosed when, a few months later, the sorely weakened thirty-two-year-old Thomas died from tuberculosis.[25]

Cooper developed important relations with other residents at Heathcote Hill at the time of his marriage. One was John Peter's unwed sister, Susannah, with whom Cooper's bride was such "a great favorite" that she designated Susan to inherit property she owned in her own right in Westchester.[26] There was also a small contingent of white domestic workers at the DeLancey compound with whom the Coopers had close contact, including one, Ann Disbrow, who had come from England with Susan's parents when very young and who in the future would work for the Coopers as a nurse, bringing along her daughter Susan as a cook.[27] Even more importantly, Heathcote Hill was home to a large group of African Americans: they had been listed as slaves in the 1800 census but, under the influence of New York's emancipation law of 1799, had been manumitted by John Peter DeLancey by 1810, when they were listed as freed workers. Performing both agricultural and domestic labor, these members of the DeLancey establishment offered Cooper his first extensive experience with African Americans. Here he no doubt observed some of the changes in civil condition and attitude that this period of enormous transformation for black New Yorkers produced: when Cooper introduced black characters in his early books, he certainly would replicate the demographic and cultural shifts he had observed at his wife's home. Like other whites of his time, he hardly understood black experience from the inside, or could claim to speak with authority on it. However, unlike most American writers in the 1820s, he positively if haltingly included black characters (and, more successfully, Native Americans) in his works, thereby complicating white claims on the nation. He was to do much more with Native Americans but did manage to create for his black characters a political viewpoint consistent with the alterations that were gradually turning enslaved New York-ers free.[28]

A case in point may be cited. When introducing the figure of the house slave into the American novel in the person of Caesar Thompson, in *The Spy*, Cooper gave him an assertive manner derived from those recent alterations. Caesar thus objects to the use of a racial epithet by the spy Harvey Birch, condemning that paragon of patriotic virtue for his blind bigotry. Although Caesar and especially his wife Dinah are introduced in Cooper's narrative as objects rather than sub-jects (we are told, for instance, how many yards of fabric it will take to make a new dress for the sizable Dinah), Caesar's "tart" retort to Birch—"No more niggar than be yourself, Mister Birch" (*Spy* CE 50)—allows him to articulate his subjective view of America's civil (and uncivil) terminology. It is of course Cooper who gives him not only his indignity, but also his indignation, revealing through the latter trait the ways in which New York's black workers, aware of coming changes and determined to define themselves, might be difficult for whites to "manage." In the 1840s, when Cooper began to include African Amer-icans in larger, semi-independent groups in his fiction, the memory of Heath-cote Hill was even more telling. Nowhere else in his fiction did he include blacks so complexly as he did in *Satanstoe*, the book that drew most heavily on his long-lingering recollections of Heathcote Hill and its varied occupants. Here one sees the degree to which the DeLancey establishment had provided Cooper's first substantial contact with the legacy of slavery as an institution and given him his first in-depth contact with African Americans. In a century when race relations were to matter more and more as time passed, this was an important gift from the world of the future novelist's new bride.[29]

Tandem Gig

Of course Cooper only began to notice such things in 1811. He and Susan lived with her parents at Heathcote Hill until early that spring, after which they rented a farm in New Rochelle, complete with a cottage where they were to set up housekeeping. When Cooper pointed out the cottage to their daughter Susan as they drove by it years later, it impressed the girl as "neat, but very small" (SFM 29). In fact the place, standing just over the Sheldrake River, was so tiny that Cooper came to call it Closet Hall, and the couple was to stay there only briefly.[30] Yet they devoted a good deal of effort, and money as well, to Closet Hall. They arranged for a carpenter to work on it that first summer, installing partitions and a pantry and doing "all the repairs that at *present* appear necessary," as a July 6 progress report from Cooper's brother-in-law Thomas informed him. Thomas (and his father) had assumed charge of the cottage then because the Coopers, houseless as long as repairs were under way, took a long-delayed honeymoon trip out of Westchester in May and June.[31]

The young couple's absence from their new home was above all leisurely. It apparently took them almost two weeks, from the time they left Mamaroneck on April 9 or 10, to get away from the lower Hudson and head on a planned trip upstate. They went first to the old Huguenot refuge of New Rochelle. Cooper's fictional travelogue of 1828, *Notions of the Americans,* portrayed this area from the perspective of a supposed European traveler sensitive to the cultural remnants of the original emigrants, whose names ("Guion, Renaud, Bonnet, Florence, Flandreau, Coutant") he found displayed on the shop signs there (*Notions* 1:86–87). Cooper even now began to learn that this, with much of the rest of the region, was Susan's domain. But New Rochelle in April of 1811 was not simply a place of vaguely exotic difference for Cooper. Susan's family used it as something of a market village, and here from April 10 to 16 the couple took care of some practical errands—among other things, buying cheap furniture for the behind-the-scenes precincts at Closet Hall. While extensive repairs were being performed on the gig they would use for their impending trip, they next went to New York City. There, near the wharf district on Manhattan that the midshipman had frequented a good deal over the past two years, they did more buying for Closet Hall. Among other things, they visited Quaker furniture maker William Burling, from whom they already had ordered custom pieces some time before, including a sideboard, dining tables, and "pillar & claw tea tables." Having paid for those pieces and seen to their storage, on April 21 the couple returned to New Rochelle, went back briefly to Mamaroneck, and then headed north.[32]

Snugly ensconced in the gig, which was harnessed to two horses tandem (one before the other), the couple left Heathcote Hill around the twenty-second of April, a Monday. Now at last they could head toward their ultimate goal— Cooperstown. This was to be Susan's first visit there, and thus her first opportunity to meet her Cooper in-laws aside from William and probably Richard, who seems to have been known to the DeLanceys. Cooper no doubt had filled her in on the village and the lake and the family until she could almost imagine it all, and as they moved on he could rehearse once more the essential family tales. Before Cooperstown, however, came the long, leisurely Hudson valley, and here Susan again had her own lore—and sense of attachment—to share. We do not know for sure their itinerary or the stops they made along the way, but later hints suggest that they explored her terrain closely, shunning the old King's Highway or Highland Road, then the valley's main route and the one with which Cooper before now was likely familiar. Instead, they seem to have followed an inland road twisting north from White Plains and crossing the Wiccopee pass near Fishkill.[33] This less frequented mountain route was the prototype for the obscure road the Wharton family follows in its flight from the Four Corners to Fishkill in Chapter 25 of *The Spy*. It also was the model for Corny Littlepage's passage by sleigh "through the centre of [Westchester] county" and on up to Albany in *Satanstoe* (*SAT* CE 144). And it was a route that in 1811 Cooper almost certainly had not yet encountered on his own.[34]

Talk during the wedding trip was not confined to the splendid vistas of the Wiccopee road, of which *The Spy* would make considerable use. Already by late April, Susan was four months pregnant and was due to deliver the couple's first child in September. The shift from Heathcote Hill had been planned in light of this fact. It also had imposed a number of other decisions on the couple across this busy spring. There was the question, first, of who would perform the work necessary to keep the new home running smoothly. Susan had been raised in a household with such ample domestic help that one assumes she was insulated from hard work, certainly from most manual labor. Whatever her own capacities or predilections, she surely expected to have a goodly amount of aid once separate married life at Closet Hall commenced. The size of the dwelling notwithstanding, the five cheap bedsteads that were among the items purchased at New Rochelle before the Coopers headed upstate most likely were for the "help." But who were they? Before leaving, Cooper and his wife may well have made arrangements for Ann (or "Nanny") Disbrow and her daughter Susan to join them in the fall. Another worker would be the young African American named Frederic, who in April of 1811 was laboring, under an indenture, for Cooper's brother Richard in Otsego. Cooper probably had decided in advance to purchase that indenture (the purchase came within a week of his arrival in Otsego) and bring Frederic back to Closet Hall. A second indentured worker was an eight-year-old white girl named Catherine or "Caty" Conklin, for whom Cooper completed arrangements just before the start of the Cooperstown trip. Perhaps the final bedstead was intended for Sam Brimmer, Cooper's "coachman," whom his daughter remembered as in the family's employ some time later in Cooperstown (SFM 10).[35]

As they journeyed to Cooperstown in late April, the Coopers also contemplated other pressing questions, among them the ex-midshipman's lingering connection to the navy. Here emotions may have run high. Susan had made it clear that her husband's naval career must end. Her opposition was not based on pacifist principles. The DeLancey men had seen such long and distinguished military service that she had grown up surrounded by the artifacts and tales and probably attitudes of soldiers and sailors. Yet she also knew that military service had cost the DeLanceys a great deal. Twice her father had fled across the Atlantic because of his standing in the army, and he and those close to him had lost much in the process. In addition, most of Susan's closest relatives had been so scattered

over the English-speaking parts of the map during the past thirty years that for
her the institution of the family was a frail thing constantly threatened by history. That perception helps explain why she clung so tightly to her parents and
siblings and why she wrote them such long letters back home from Otsego once
the Coopers relocated there, and then from Europe in the 1820s and 1830s. It
probably also helps explain why she wished her husband to amalgamate as much
as possible with the DeLanceys following their marriage. The pledge she exacted
from him to quit the navy was of a piece with all of this. A husband at sea might
prove no husband at all, especially when his armed ship sailed off on the troubled waters of the Napoleonic era. Susan DeLancey wanted nothing more or less
than Cooper's full presence in her life, a marriage that kept them together—as
their combined means would allow—without the world's intrusions. Later,
when his family's fortunes failed and Cooper cast about to find a means to support his wife and children, literature was appealing in part because it would leave
him largely at home even as it paid the bills.

    As long ago as Cooper's marriage proposal, Susan DeLancey must have de-
manded that he arrange to quit the navy. And he had made at least an effort to resign right then. Lieutenant Lawrence's resistance had deflected him toward the
longish furlough. Why, though, had Cooper listened to Lawrence? His promise
to Susan notwithstanding, he probably could not fully give up his youthful vision of himself as a naval officer. His language in the May 1810 letter to Richard
suggests a conflicted will: "At the end of a year," he wrote, "I have it [in] my
power to resign should the situation of the Country warrant it" (*LJ* 1:17). Probably he sincerely wished to please Susan but secretly longed for some other factor to mandate that he stay in the service. Taking the furlough rather than resigning outright in 1810 allowed Cooper to keep options open as long as possible.
Although he later claimed that "the consummation of the resignation is its acceptance," and added that Lawrence would not accept his own in 1810, thus forcing him on furlough (*LJ* 1:107), resigning in fact was something he had the clear
right to do at any time. Instead, Cooper used Lawrence's initial resistance as a
means of ensuring that he would have a chance to see real action if the expected
war with Britain materialized in the next year or two. In the meantime, at least
technically, he was all Susan's.

    By April of 1811, however, his official one year's furlough was about to ex-
pire. War with Britain seemed no closer now, perhaps more distant. And whatever naval dreams the young husband might have had, the expectant father now
had other obligations. Perhaps his own perception of this truth was enough. Perhaps he needed Susan to remind him that he had made her that solemn "pledge
to resign" (*LJ* 1:90). Of her role at this juncture we have no direct evidence. As
the couple passed north on the road to Cooperstown in late April 1811, however,

they were all alone together as they rarely had been since January. She must have spoken forcefully for herself but also for their unborn child. As a consequence, virtually on their arrival in Cooperstown, her husband drafted and mailed his letter to the navy under her watchful gaze. He would have to settle his recruiting accounts before all his business with the navy was closed, so he now resigned his warrant but asked that the settlement be put off until he could visit Washington in October—after, that is, the expected baby arrived (see *LJ* 1:25). Within sight of Lake Otsego, he bid the sea a regretful farewell.[36]

The couple had left New Rochelle by the twenty-second of April and the navy letter was dated at Cooperstown on Sunday the twenty-eighth, so they must have arrived there that day or perhaps on the twenty-seventh. They were to linger through most of July. There was a great deal to distract them. Since the travelers probably stayed with some of Cooper's family, either in Otsego Hall with Cooper's mother or at the homes of his brother Richard or his sister Ann Pomeroy, Susan had many opportunities to get to know the family. That was no small task. Between Richard's household at Apple Hill and Ann's at Pomeroy Place, there was a growing cadre of nieces and nephews, now nine in number, for her (and even her husband) to sort out. And there were countless family acquaintances for Susan to meet, arrayed in a series of circles that increased in size but lost definition the farther out from Otsego Hall one went. She almost certainly went to meet the Morrises at Butternuts and perhaps the Hyde Clarkes up at the north end of the lake, although the rumored dalliance of Richard Cooper's wife with the master of Hyde Clarke Hall may have placed it off-limits. We know that Susan visited old Hendrik Frey at Canajoharie, perhaps on the way into and out of Otsego: the following April that stalwart ally of the family "made kind inquiries," Cooper reported to Susan from Cooperstown then, "after your fair self" (*LJ* 1:26).

Nor was the social world in which Susan's husband had grown up the only appeal. It was spring and then early summer, the loveliest of Otsego seasons, and rides up and down the lake were mandatory pleasures as long as Susan's condition allowed it. No doubt the newlyweds first scanned in 1811 the land along the west shore of the lake that they were to christen Fenimore Farm when they moved to it in 1813. And surely Cooper, as eager to show Susan *his* country as she had been to show him hers, brought her up over the rise of what he would later call "the Vision." There she could see those wondrous transformations he had spoken of, the magical changes that already had formed the core myth of his family. Ever after, coming into Otsego or leaving it, the couple would pause here.[37]

Not all the reminders of Cooper family history in the area were sentimental. While in Otsego, Cooper continued to work out with his older brothers the complex details of their father's estate. Richard and Isaac were in the thick of their business as executors, as their youngest brother well knew. Even in his May 1810 letter about Susan and her father, urgent as the personal business then was, he had assured Richard, "I wish not to interrupt you in your attempt to clear the estate" (*LJ* 1:18). The "clearing" hardly was over by that December, when Richard (and to a lesser extent Isaac) continued to be addressed by an insistent array of correspondents about their father's affairs. A request from Philadelphia Quaker William Fisher for information about his late brother Thomas's accounts with William Cooper, for instance, was sent on December 20; a plea from a landowner in Skaneateles complaining that a lot he had purchased from William Cooper also was being claimed by three other men was inscribed a week later. How the brothers found all the necessary papers to resolve such issues, and how well they interpreted the evidence, is uncertain. They had been tending to the Judge's affairs for the past several years and were known to most if not all of their correspondents. But at a time when financial health depended on the security of personal notes—or even their perceived security—the death of a seemingly wealthy man always brought an increase in nervous inquiries.

And more may have been at issue even this early. Did Cooper's language in 1810 about Richard's "attempt to clear" the estate express his apprehension of coming problems? Perhaps not, although documents in the family archive do suggest that the executors were confronted with difficulties from the outset. Miers Fisher, brother of William and Thomas, had written Isaac in June of 1810 to lay before the Coopers a number of persistent problems regarding several thousand acres of land in Pennsylvania and New York that his family and Judge Cooper had owned together. Fisher had learned from Cooper family friend Jacob Morris that the June letter and its accompanying documents had been received in a timely fashion in Cooperstown. Six months later, however, nothing had been heard from the Cooper brothers about the complex questions, not even an acknowledgment. Fisher thus had to write another three-page letter restating his concerns and asking that his "Esteemed Friends" would "pay an early attention to all these matters."

He had brought the issues up with Judge Cooper himself during a visit to Cooperstown in July of 1808 but had found the Judge's memory faulty then. Fisher hardly sent the brothers good news when he recalled their father's forgetful management style. Asked in 1808 whether he had paid quit rents due on one tract, as Fisher recalled, Judge Cooper "could not inform me whether he had done it." The story was the same regarding four years of back taxes on another large tract: "he could not inform me with certainty." Nor, apparently, could William Cooper put his hands on papers clarifying the matters. On both questions he referred Fisher to the public records in Albany, which Fisher accordingly checked, without avail, while returning to Philadelphia in 1808. The

Judge's legacy of inattention and faulty record-keeping could not have made the job of his executors any easier, even if they had been able to exhibit more systematic exactness on their own. What is more, since every claim they settled might reduce the inheritance due them, Richard and Isaac had motive enough to be sloppy and behind hand.

So the indeterminacy continued into 1811. New Yorker Robert Troup set the darkening tone of the brothers' business archive when he wrote them in February demanding that a sizable amount due him and lawyer Richard Harison from the estate be paid forthwith. Troup placed responsibility squarely on the executors' shoulders, reminding them, as he put it, "how deeply your honor is concerned in the payment of the debt." The "good deal of trouble" Troup had been put to since the Judge's death resulted from the executors' efforts to keep "a knowledge of the facts" from him, thereby obstructing rather than facilitating a settlement. Out of patience with them, he insisted on a satisfaction date in April, only a few weeks hence. Finally, before ending with a threat of legal action, he called to mind the most astounding aspect of the brothers' resistance. One of them had engaged in a presumably volatile, perhaps even violent, exchange over this very question with Richard Harison the previous summer or fall. As time passed, the disarray in which Judge Cooper had left his affairs mattered less to those with claims on the estate than the truculent inattention of his older sons.[38]

Susan DeLancey's husband was insulated from culpability for such things, but not from his brothers' inattention and perhaps manipulation as he asserted his own demands and needs. He was not always treated with greater dispatch or more honesty than the Fisher brothers or Troup and Harison. Over the course of the year before his marriage, he had managed to elicit several small payments that were debited against his share in his father's estate. During his most recent visit home, the year-end trip in 1810 just before the wedding, he likewise drew cash to help with the newlyweds' initial living costs, and after the ceremony he arranged other small transfers to pay for the preparation of the couple's quarters at Closet Hall. But things clearly could not go on in this piecemeal fashion. Once he and Susan arrived in Cooperstown late in April, Cooper therefore sought to pry a sufficient quantity of funds from his brothers' hands to allow him to carry on for the next year or so. In June, Richard and Isaac gave in, paying him the cash yield (just over $1,400) of a large quantity of pickled pork that probably had come to them as rental payments on estate properties.[39]

Also in June, another arrangement promised more help. Richard and Isaac, in the first substantial distribution of estate assets, transferred to Cooper and his siblings full control over the leases included in the schedule of properties designated for each heir in the Judge's will. Not only did all of them receive their due allotments on the same day; each share was valued on the estate books at about the same amount—around $8,500, roughly $800 less than the nominal figure used in the Judge's original calculations. All but two of Cooper's twenty-four properties had been let out by his father on perpetual leases. They included a total of more than eighteen hundred acres of land, plus four lots and two houses in Cooperstown. The rents on most of the properties were due in commodities—wheat, corn, butter, and pork—with only the small cash sum of around $450 payable annually, most of it from the Cooperstown leases. Using contemporary prices, one can estimate the value of the in-kind rent as around $2,400, meaning that Cooper in theory could count on an income of almost $3,000 per year for the indefinite future from this source. This was far more than the average laborer or even skilled worker of 1815 could count on over a year, but at the same time it would not fund lavish living.[40]

Richard and Isaac were far more able at handling such business than their youngest brother. Still, on paper and in pocket, they at last were making significant parts of his legacy available to the twenty-one-year-old husband. Part of his reason for proposing to Susan as soon as he did in 1810 may have been the leverage his new obligations would create, leverage useful in pressing Richard and Isaac to disburse larger amounts than they had shown themselves willing (or able) to in the first months after their father's death. In the five months before Cooper's announcement of the engagement, he received less than $300 against his legacy. In the seven months thereafter, he received more than $1,400, at a time when his older brothers William and Samuel each received less than a third and a quarter of that amount, respectively. In 1811, including the stated value of transferred leases, Cooper was to receive about $13,000, also more than either of these other heirs.

For all their difficulties, the transferred leases set Cooper on the way to managing his own portion of the family fortune. In fact, the transfer allowed Cooper to embark that same week on a trip to nearby Utica, where he appears to have used his share in his father's estate—made tangible by those leases—as the basis for establishing a line of credit with banker and merchant James Platt. Over the next several years, Cooper would draw funds from Platt, turning his expected legacy into a source of present support. He would continue to receive modest amounts of cash from the estate, but the Otsego farms and the Utica line of credit meant that he no longer would have to wheedle small amounts from Richard and Isaac to meet his current living expenses.[41]

The time the newlyweds passed in Cooperstown in 1811 thus had long-range consequences. It also had an end. Toward the close of July, they must have packed their belongings in the tandem gig and headed once more toward the Hudson. They probably were gone from Otsego by July 29, when Cooper's five-month-old nephew William Cooper Pomeroy, his sister Ann's son, died there.[42]

We know that they were back in New York City by August 3, when they began to purchase a large number of items obviously intended for Closet Hall. Bankrolled by the proceeds he had received from Richard and Isaac and his line of credit, and no doubt secure in the expectation of future income from his leasehold properties, the young husband was not frugal. He and Susan picked up such genteel furnishings as Venetian carpet, a pair of expensive mirrors, and yards and yards of costly fabric. They also made final arrangements for William Burling's custom furniture to be delivered. The present was bright, the future seemed full of hope, and the new quarters awaiting them in Westchester needed so many things. About their baby, due within a month or two, they could do little but wait—wait, and finish readying Closet Hall. They had been absent four months, and as much as possible, they directed their attention now to what was soon to follow.[43]

The arrangements at the couple's rented home progressed well enough that their first baby might well have been born there. But daughter Elizabeth (named for both her grandmothers) instead came into the world at Heathcote Hill on September 27, doubtless under the supervision of Mrs. DeLancey and her corps of household servants. She was christened soon afterwards, also there, by the Episcopal minister who had married the Coopers at the start of the year. Susan may have had a rough delivery, but by late October she apparently was well enough to accompany her husband to New York City, where they purchased an extensive supply of household items. By late December, or a bit earlier, the couple clearly were on their own in earnest at Closet Hall, where they were to stay until around January 1813, when, with another child expected, they shifted again to Heathcote Hill.[44]

The Coopers spent a great deal of their time, wherever they lived, socializing with the DeLanceys. Cooper relished the closeness in part because the sort of genteel country life pursued at Heathcote Hill was quite appealing to him. If one looked past the disruptions of their actual experience since 1775, about which Cooper already had begun to learn, the DeLanceys might seem to represent the ideal of long-settled prosperity that all the Coopers aimed at but had not yet achieved. John Peter DeLancey himself, who came into Cooper's life just as William Cooper died, was probably something of a *father-in-wish* as well as father-in-law for the young husband: DeLancey had no signs of his own clumsy rise about him, as William Cooper did, only the easy occupancy of an inherited social peak so high that not even his Loyalist service during the war had permanently tumbled him off it. Furthermore, Heathcote Hill was the tangible emblem of what Cooper and his siblings now coveted. Richard Fenimore Cooper had set himself up at Apple Hill in 1800; Ann had been installed at the more modest Pomeroy Place in 1804; even then, Isaac was erecting the impressive Edgewater (see *COC* 58–59, 66). Closet Hall hardly could compete with such substantial markers of the family's solidification of its position, but Closet Hall stood near the DeLancey holdings, and at Heathcote Hill the Cooper family ideal was already richly realized. Cooper may well have had the best chance at assuming the next stage of the life the patriarch had imagined for all his children. Certainly he had made the best match. And in Westchester, where he and Susan clearly were rooting themselves at this point, John Peter could provide him the entrée he needed to local "society."[45]

Opening Shots

Amid their dalliances in rural Westchester, the sometime midshipman kept a wary ear tuned to the noise of the coming war. As far as he knew, he remained even now in the navy, inactive but at least theoretically susceptible to being called back, for he still had not received the apparently misdirected acknowledgement of his letter of resignation. Ever since that document had left his hand in Cooperstown the previous April, furthermore, there had been ample reminders of what he seemingly had foresworn. Almost immediately, even while the newlyweds still lingered in Cooperstown, more skirmishing took place off the coast. Cooper's old commander at New York, Cmdre. John Rodgers, was at home in Havre de Grace, Maryland, when word reached him that an American merchant seaman had been impressed from the brig *Spitfire* off Sandy Hook by a British frigate, reportedly the *Guerriere*. On May 10, Rodgers set sail from Annapolis on his flagship, the *President,* to inquire into this serious provocation. Before the week was out, he encountered and decisively defeated a small British vessel, the *Little Belt,* under command of Capt. Arthur B. Bingham. The mismatch between Rodgers's frigate and Bingham's sloop, as well as a dispute about how exactly the engagement began, long embroiled public opinion in the two countries, especially in America, where partisan bickering meant that the Republicans "as blindly defended" Rodgers as the Federalists "blindly condemned" him (*HN* 2:123).[46]

Cooper had not learned of such coastal events as quickly in Otsego as he might have in Westchester. Even so, the *Otsego Herald* devoted much attention to naval matters. Amid its Fourth of July coverage that summer, it reprinted a brief story about musket shot ripping the sails of an American pilot boat that ventured too near the British frigate *Melampus* off Sandy Hook. More interestingly, it copied a spirited song, just published in Boston and then making the rounds, called "Rodgers & Victory: Tit for Tat: or, the Chesapeake Paid for in British Blood." Set to the tune of "Yankee Doodle," the ballad showed in its title and many of its verses how saturated present news was with memories of the

British attack on the *Chesapeake* four years earlier. Lamenting America's weak response to such assaults and reciting the other abuses invited by national inaction in Jefferson's administration, "Rodgers & Victory" was a song so close in spirit to Cooper's views that he easily could have written it himself. Indeed, he may well have soon joined the verbal battle by contributing a letter to the *Herald* on his return from Utica. Signed "An American," the substantial piece detailed the arguments used to discredit Rodgers in his own country, tracing them to Federalist stalwart Timothy Pickering, whose role as the father of the revitalized U.S. Navy did not prevent him from vehemently opposing the impending war with England. In his sixteenth installment of "The Politician," a series reprinted in the *Cooperstown Federalist*, Pickering attacked what he called Rodgers's "hostile act" because it was "pregnant with serious consequences." Pickering held that neutral ships had no right whatsoever to detain, let alone attack, vessels of a belligerent nation. He went so far as to call the chasing of the *Little Belt* "unlawful" and concluded that "the killing of her crew, as a consequence of that unlawful act, is murder." The government would not yet confirm that Rodgers was acting on explicit orders, as in fact he was. Pickering argued that the existence of such orders could not change the nature of the acts themselves, only shift the blame for them—to the navy and, ultimately, President James Madison. These points, especially those concerning the customary rights of neutrals, were the very ones Cooper was to take special care to answer in his naval history, where he reviewed the episode at length. And the answers to them in the 1811 letter and the 1839 history were in essential agreement.[47]

It is not hard to imagine that the quasi-resigned midshipman, rusticated in Cooperstown in 1811, desired to have some influence over public opinion. Having missed the *Chesapeake* affair while absent on the *Stirling*, he was in a sense missing these new battles as well. The midshipman who wrote in the letter of April 28 of the "country's situation" and its possible need for his services was utterly in agreement with the *Herald*'s "American." Did Cooper hope, there on Otsego's shores, that the nation really *would* need him? Certainly he did not keep his keen interest in the episode secret, and for him in particular some of its implications were profound. The Anglophile Federalist press, typified by Pickering's "Politician" essays of 1811, helped solidify the process by which the son of Judge William Cooper eventually would disown his father's party and its successors and turn instead toward the Jeffersonians and, at last, toward Democrat Andrew Jackson. One legacy of his all-too-brief naval career was Cooper's political maturation.

If the *Chesapeake* affair hardened the outrage developed during Cooper's voyage on the *Stirling*, that of the *Little Belt* taught him two things. The navy itself was maturing, and the public, although restive and as yet indecisive, was un-

dergoing its own slow transformation—for the long shadow of "colonial dependence" was gradually lifting. On his return to Westchester late in the summer, Cooper found himself closer to the naval world where such skirmishing between Britain and the United States was being prosecuted. It was increasingly
clear that, should open war come, the navy would be sorely tested. Early in April
1812, Cooper was to pass an evening in New York City with the officers of two
American frigates—almost certainly the *President* (commanded by John Rodgers)
and the *Essex* (under David Porter), both vessels that, under their current commanders, had been in the thick of recent encounters. The question of "what
would be the probable result of a conflict between American and English ships,
was seriously and temperately discussed." Although the public remained uncertain of the nation's naval chances against Britain, the view of the officer corps
was beginning to shift. Rodgers, mindful of his victory the previous year over
the *Little Belt*, no doubt was hopeful that other American vessels could triumph
in more evenly matched confrontations as well. Indeed, the conclusion of all the
officers with whom Cooper spoke was sanguine: "their own chances of victory
were at least equal to those of the enemy" (*HN* 2:170n).

But such private audacity among the officers was not yet widely shared.
While in the city at the same time, Cooper, in the company of the exiled French
general Jean Victor Moreau, had observed the maneuvers of several American
vessels off Manhattan. The ships looked admirable, Moreau commented to
Cooper, but he insisted it was "impossible [that] men so inexperienced should
prevail over English vessels" (*HN* 2:171n).[48] It is likely that Cooper and Moreau
witnessed the mock attack on Castle Williams that the *President* and the *Essex*
carried out as they departed the North River on April 14. The practical purpose
of the exercise was to test with live ammunition the recently constructed fortification on Governor's Island, but there was a touch of bravado about it, too.
Thundering American cannon fired so near the city conveyed a distinct reassur-
ance. Both the New York *Mercantile Advertiser* and the *Gazette* happily reported
that Castle Williams, merely nicked by the cannonballs, promised to withstand
any hostile attack.[49] The issue was not just the strength of stone and mortar. It was
the courage and resolve of the nation, and of the navy. Witnessing this display
with the French visitor, Cooper knew how to read it. It bore out the secret opti-
mism of his comrades in the service, not the vocal doubts of General Moreau.

Even so, no one in April of 1812 knew whether war would come—or
whether, should it come, it really would involve heavy naval action. Britain, after
all, had a long, fortified frontier with the northern states, running from Maine all
the way to Lake Michigan. Its many ships off the East Coast might effectively
blockade the country's main ports before significant naval action could begin.
Cooper therefore left the city after his visits with Rodgers and Porter, and with

Moreau, hopeful about America's prospects but in the dark about what the future really held. Clarification would soon come. After a brief trip upstate, he came back through New York and was in Westchester by May 19.[50] The family's first summer at Closet Hall was about to begin when the long-expected war with Britain at last materialized in June. Putting aside everything else, Cooper rushed back to the city to survey further military preparations.

His naval history would express regret that the American navy did not launch a concerted preemptive campaign against English vessels patrolling offshore, the masters of which could not yet have known of the declaration of war. But in 1812 there was a flurry of American activity that Cooper hardly missed (*HN* 2:148–49). If he was in New York City early enough, he may have crossed paths with James Lawrence, now in command of the *Hornet,* part of a squadron then forming under Commodore Rodgers (see *ECE* 7). A midshipman in Lawrence's vessel recorded in his diary what took place on June 21 when the *Hornet* and the *President* left the harbor. Once the declaration of war was read on board and the vessels were under way, "Capt. Lawrence had the crew called to their quarters, and told them if there were any amongst them who were disaffected, or . . . had not rather sink than surrender to the enemy, with gun for gun, that he should be immediately and uninjured landed and sent back in the pilot boat." Such a procedure was not uncommon at a time when British tars, and those of other nations as well, were serving aboard American naval vessels. It also was not unheard of for men to take their captain up on such offers. In the case of the *Hornet,* however, the diarist added that "the reply was[,] fore and aft, 'Not one.'"[51] Even if Cooper did not see or know then of such stirring gestures, he surely sent his heart after the vessels as Rodgers and his "squadron passed Sandy Hook on the afternoon of the 21st of June, and ran off south-east"—language in the naval history that may suggest the eye of a spectator left behind on the bay (*HN* 2:150).[52]

To the surprise of many observers on both sides, the conflict indeed began as an all-out naval fight. The United States clearly ran risks in challenging English superiority at sea. Cooper was to emphasize in the naval history that at this point in the Napoleonic Wars Britain had more than a thousand ships, three-quarters of them ready for the fight—and it had virtually no need for any of them in European waters. By contrast, the American navy of 1812 consisted of an official total of a mere twenty vessels, if one cheated and counted the modest *Oneida* (seemingly *hors de combat* on Lake Ontario) plus two large but unseaworthy ships, the *New York* and the *Boston.* And almost half of the remaining vessels mounted fewer than two dozen guns apiece. The United States, "possessing herself but seventeen cruising vessels on the ocean, of which nine were of a class less than frigates," was about to engage in a war "with much the greatest maritime power that the world ever saw" (*HN* 2:143).

Light tonnage and small armaments were only part of the problem. The nation in 1812 was in a sense armed against itself. Still exhibiting the old colonial deference, Americans shared the almost universal superstition, amply bolstered during the Napoleonic conflicts, that *any* British naval vessel was unbeatable (see *HN* 2:145). For Americans, the general superstition had been starkly confirmed by the still smarting humiliation of the *Chesapeake*. Even in 1812, five years after that debacle, no American naval vessel left port without being in a state of perfect readiness for battle. With the declaration of hostilities, however, the nervous edginess of the Americans at last began to pay substantial dividends. Even a vessel like the previously undistinguished *Constitution*, which would owe its fame to this war, soon proved that the navy and its slender means could be put to astonishing use. Captain Isaac Hull had returned that ship to Hampton Roads early in 1812, just as the Coopers were settling in at Closet Hall. It was repaired and refitted at the Washington navy yard by Nathaniel "Jumping Billy" Haraden, a legendary Yankee who once had briefly mastered the ship himself. Haraden succeeded to such an extent that when he was finished, as Cooper later put it, the "old officers, when they came to try her, scarce knew the ship."(OI 487).[53] The *Constitution* returned to service just as war was declared in June, with Hull as captain and Cooper's friend Charles Morris ("one of the very ablest men the American marine ever possessed" [*LDANO* 1:157]) as first lieutenant. Also on board were several other young officers Cooper knew well, including New Yorker Beekman Verplanck Hoffman and William B. Shubrick's brother John. The *Constitution* became important for Cooper because of these ties as well as for the more public significance it soon acquired.

The ship put to sea in early July and sailed north along the coast. Not quite two weeks later, Hull spotted a five-ship British squadron under Sir Philip Bowes Vere Broke. Although obviously outgunned, Hull did not run off. Instead, he singled out and began to pursue the nearest enemy vessel, the *Guerriere*, a French vessel that had been captured off Norway in 1806. As the other enemy ships drew near and the wind died, Hull, deploying his boats, attempted to escape by towing the *Constitution*. Soon the main British ship, the *Shannon*, followed suit and, able to draw on the boats of the whole British squadron, threatened to pull within cannon range of the *Constitution*. Hull ran a kedge anchor out front, snagging it in the shallow seabed so that the men could warp the ship— drag it forward by means of ropes, a procedure often used in harbor or coastal waters but rarely at sea. As soon as a light breeze came up, Hull deployed all his canvas, outrunning his British opponents, who were duly impressed by his "very superiour sailing."[54]

Hull's cagey escape meant so much to Cooper and other Americans because the old ghost of the *Chesapeake* haunted their imaginations this early in the war.

The *Constitution* in this instance fought no battle and won no victory. Hull had, after all, merely escaped certain defeat. However ingenious his means, the escape would have seemed far less accomplished had the ship's long peril not recalled the other ship's doom five years earlier. The same lingering apprehensions lay behind the nation's exuberant reaction, shared by Cooper, to Hull's next accomplishment. After slipping away from the British squadron, he had taken the *Constitution* into Boston. This was at the end of July. The ship put back to sea on August 2, running east along the New England coast and into the Bay of Fundy in a fruitless search for British cruisers. It sailed on around Halifax to the Gulf of St. Lawrence, but there snagged only two small prizes. Then on August 19, as Cooper later told the story based on Hull's official report and other sources, "a sail was made from the mast heads, bearing E. S. E., and to leeward, though the distance prevented her character from being discovered." Hull put on sail and pursued the ship, which proved to be an enemy frigate—in fact, once more the *Guerriere*. Soon the latter's commander, Capt. James Richard Dacres, "laid his main-top-sail aback, in waiting for the *Constitution* to come down, with every thing ready to engage." Hull obliged Dacres, taking in sail before beating to quarters and clearing the vessel for action. He took the first shots from the *Guerriere* as he drew nearer, for he intended to get as close as he could and then pour everything he had on the enemy. Eventually, as the vessels joined in "a fair yard-arm-and-yard-arm fight," the American began to gain the upper hand. It was a narrative Cooper told with real relish even after almost thirty years because the event had enacted his own anxious wishes at the time:

> In about ten minutes, or just as the ships were fairly side by side, the mizzen-mast of the Englishman was shot away, when the American passed slowly ahead, keeping up a tremendous fire, and luffed short round his bows, to prevent being raked. In executing this manœuvre, the ship shot into the wind, got stern-way, and fell foul of her antagonist. While in this situation, the cabin of the *Constitution* took fire, from the close explosion of the forward guns of the enemy, who obtained a small, but momentary advantage from his position. The good conduct of Mr. Hoffman, who commanded in the cabin, soon repaired this accident, and a gun of the enemy's, that threatened further injury, was disabled.
>
> As the vessels touched, both parties prepared to board. The English turned all hands up from below, and mustered forward, with that object, while Mr. Morris, the first lieutenant, Mr. Alwyn, the [sailing] master, and Mr. Bush, the lieutenant of marines, sprang upon the taffrail of the *Constitution*, with a similar intention. Both sides now suffered by the closeness of the musketry; the English much the most, however. Mr. Morris was shot

through the body, but maintained his post, the bullet fortunately missing his vitals. Mr. Alwyn was wounded in the shoulder, and Mr. Bush fell dead, by a bullet through the head. It being found impossible for either party to board, in the face of such a fire, and with the heavy sea that was on, the sails were filled, and just as the *Constitution* shot ahead, the fore-mast of the enemy fell, carrying down with it his main-mast, and leaving him wallowing in the trough of the sea, a helpless wreck.

Once the rigging was tightened, Hull's vessel was repositioned in order to rake the enemy frigate. The latter soon lowered the Union Jack that somehow still was flapping from "the stump of the mizzen-mast" and sent over the third lieutenant to surrender. A prize crew passed back to the *Guerriere* with plans to take it into an American port, but the next day the capture was shipping so much water that captors and prisoners alike had to be removed to the *Constitution*. The *Guerriere* soon sank. By August 30, full of wounded prisoners, the victor was back in Boston (*HN* 2:167–70).

In the late 1830s, Cooper constructed his narrative of these first two cruises of the *Constitution* from the ship's official logbook, available in excerpts very early (for instance, in the first chapter of Abel Bowen's 1816 compilation, the *Naval Monument*). He also made use of Capt. Isaac Hull's official letter to Navy Secretary Paul Hamilton, as well as other accounts by officers, and perhaps even the report by an American prisoner who had chanced to observe the ship's July escape from the *Shannon*. All of these other sources Bowen either reprinted or summarized.[55] Some of the accounts Cooper surely encountered in the newspapers during the war, while some came to his hand later. The same is true of the private anecdotes on which he drew, those provided by Hull, Hoffman, John Shubrick, and Morris, among others.[56] But in 1839 Cooper was doing more than pasting together a collage of old texts and tales. He also was drawing on the personal feelings aroused when he first learned of what had taken place off the coast that summer. These feelings, linked to all he had felt as the struggle between America and Britain evolved over the years since 1807, were the private meaning of the public narrative—the autobiographical burden of the historical record. He ended his narrative of the defeat of the *Guerriere* by writing, "It is not easy, at this distant day, to convey to the reader the full force of the moral impression created in America by this victory of one frigate over another." The "moral impression" he was most interested in conveying to his readers in 1839 was not a disembodied public emotion: it was instead the forceful impression created in Cooper himself by the first word he had heard—probably in New York City—of the event. He went on to write at greater length of the public's views, but he anchored his prose in the opinion of the naval officer corps, among

whom he had counted himself until recently—if his resignation had indeed
been accepted yet:

> So deep had been the effect produced on the public mind by the constant
> accounts of the successes of the English over their enemies at sea, that the
> opinion, already mentioned, of their invincibility on that element, gener-
> ally prevailed; and it had been publicly predicted, that, before the contest
> had continued six months, British sloops of war would lie alongside of
> American frigates with comparative impunity. Perhaps the only portion of
> even the American population that expected different results, was that
> which composed the little body of officers on whom the trial would fall,
> and they looked forward to the struggle with a manly resolution, rather
> than with a very confident hope. But the termination of the combat just re-
> lated, far exceeded the expectations of even the most sanguine. After mak-
> ing all proper allowance for the difference of force, which certainly existed
> in favour of the Constitution, as well as for the excuses that the defeated
> party freely offered to the world, men on both sides of the Atlantic, who
> were competent to form intelligent opinions on such subjects, saw the
> promise of many future successes in this. The style in which the Constitu-
> tion had been handled; the deliberate and yet earnest manner in which she
> had been carried into battle; the extraordinary execution that had been
> made in so short a time by her fire; the readiness and gallantry with which
> she had cleared for action, so soon after destroying one British frigate, in
> which was manifested a disposition to meet another, united to produce a
> deep conviction of self-reliance, coolness and skill, that was of infinitely
> more weight than the transient feeling which might result from any acci-
> dental triumph. (*HN* 2:170–71)

This was not only an intellectual history of the era of which Cooper wrote:
it was a sketch of his own doubts, wishes, and sudden sense of vindication in
the summer of 1812. "Self-reliance," as Ralph Waldo Emerson soon would de-
clare in an essay of that title which he published two years after Cooper's first
use of the term, was the second chapter of the moral history of American independence.[57]

War in Earnest

Back in 1812, there were lesser themes that punctuated the grander ones. Late in
the summer, New York City was taking positive military steps, steps that had implications for Cooper. On August 19—the very day of the *Constitution*'s victory—Gov. Daniel D. Tompkins had ordered selected upstate militia units to

prepare for three months' service aiding local troops in the city's defense. Under Tompkins's personal leadership, "13 fine uniformed companies of artillery and infantry" therefore were assembled in New York City by September 1. Within two weeks, several others also were directed to rendezvous there.[58]

Cooper soon found himself torn between local obligations and a sense—probably a wish—that he might be called up again by the navy. He had properly enrolled in the Thirty-third Regiment of the New York militia after relocating to Westchester County in 1811. As a result, he was expected to take part in his battalion and regimental parades on September 18 and 23, 1812, respectively.[59] Believing, however, that he would soon be called back to active duty by the navy, and hence would be exempted from any further militia service, he did not show up. At the same time, he obeyed the "General Orders" published in the New York papers by Capt. Isaac Chauncey, the commanding naval officer in the city, on September 9: "All officers of the Navy now in New-York, or its vicinity, (whether under orders for other stations or not) are hereby directed to report themselves immediately to me at the Navy Yard."[60] Going to the navy yard and speaking directly with Chauncey, Cooper explained the situation of his furlough and quasi-resignation. When he asked Chauncey, however, whether he was covered by the September 9 orders, the commander was at a loss and advised him to seek clarification from Navy Secretary Hamilton. Cooper therefore wrote Hamilton a fresh letter from New Rochelle on September 15, his twenty-third birthday, stating that the silence of the navy since the previous April, and the failure to settle his accounts in October, presumably meant that he still was in the service (see *LJ* 1:27–28). To this letter Hamilton made no reply. Doubtless a check of naval records showed that he had accepted Cooper's resignation in May of 1811, instructing him to transmit his warrant to the navy. Hamilton, having no way of knowing that his letter at that time had been misdirected to another James Cooper, saw no reason to write again. As a result of the navy's silence now, as Cooper was to put it in 1822, he was kept "in great suspense, for near two years." He kept his warrant but did not know whether or not it was still valid (*LJ* 1:78).[61]

Cooper's personal suspension between the militia and the navy hardly kept the war from continuing, although it clearly colored how he viewed subsequent episodes. Off the Azores late in October, the *United States*, under Cmdr. Stephen Decatur, met, chased, defeated—and took possession of—HMS *Macedonian*, under Capt. John S. Carden. Although neither officer knew the identity of his opponent or even the name of the enemy ship until after Carden's surrender, the two men in fact already were well acquainted, as Cooper was to point out in an unsigned book review in 1821. During one of the lulls in Anglo-American contentions earlier in 1812, they had anchored their ships next to each other in Hampton Roads, Virginia, and while there (as Cooper wrote) "were in the habit of daily intercourse" (*ECE* 10). Stephen Decatur, living then at Norfolk with his wife Susan, went so far as to entertain Carden in his home.

At that time, Carden appears to have regarded the *United States*—known to be a lumbering vessel—as markedly inferior to the *Macedonian*, "then considered the finest and most powerful frigate in the British navy."[62] The contrasts were not entirely just. The British vessel certainly was the better sailer, but Decatur's ship had bigger guns, as was often the case with the muscular American frigates of the era. And Decatur's people used their ordnance with exceptional accuracy. A sailor who survived the slaughter on the *Macedonian* painted a grim picture of what it felt like to be on the receiving end of the Americans' long-endured resentment: "Grape and canister shot were pouring through our portholes like leaden rain. The large shot came against the ship's side like iron hail, shaking her to the very keel, or passing through her timbers, and scattering terrific splinters, which did a more appalling work than even their own death-giving blows." The observer was Samuel Leech, then a boy in the royal navy but later, having deserted while a prisoner in New York, an American tar. He recalled that the attack "was like some awfully tremendous thunder-storm, whose deafening roar is attended by incessant streaks of lightning, carrying death in every flash, and strewing the ground with the victims of its wrath; only, in our case, the scene was rendered more horrible than that, by the presence of torrents of blood which dyed our decks."[63]

This American victory was important partly because the ships, despite their differences, were more evenly matched than the *President* and the *Little Belt* or even the *Constitution* and the *Guerriere*. But more telling for the public and the officer corps was the fact that Decatur succeeded in bringing his prize back home. Defeated while the two nations were technically at peace, the *Little Belt* was not treated as an American prize—as the *Chesapeake* had not become a British prize five years before. The *Guerriere* would have been brought into port had it not been so badly damaged in its encounter with the *Constitution*. The *Macedonian* also suffered severe damage, but its hull was sound enough that prize master William H. Allen, a Tripolitan hero, managed to bring it across the Atlantic. He put into Newport harbor early in December, then rejoined the *United States* off New London and by the middle of that month anchored by its side at Hell Gate in the East River. The feat was singular at the time and has remained distinctive ever since: the *Macedonian* is the only British warship ever brought as a prize into an American port. Moreover, once repaired, the ship was to become a substantial addition to the small American fleet. Victory, much delayed, was indeed proving exceptionally sweet (Plate 10).[64]

As with so much else in the naval war at this time, Cooper knew something of the *Macedonian*'s arrival firsthand. In that unsigned 1821 book review, he agreed that the British frigate was indeed a fast vessel, adding, "of the fact of [her] superior sailing, we were ourselves eyewitnesses, although the prize was under jury masts at the time" (*ECE* 10). The naval history indicates that "the United States arrived off New London on the 4th of December, and about the same time the Macedonian got into Newport. Shortly after, both ships reached New York by the Hell Gate passage" (*HN* 2:180). If Cooper indeed saw the *Macedonian* sailing under jury masts, he must have watched from the shore at Mamaroneck as it passed in December—or been among those who visited the capture as it lingered in Hell Gate and eventually moved downriver. Cooper was familiar enough with the naval men in town at the time that he may well have been party to some or all of the celebrations with which Stephen Decatur, Isaac Hull, and Jacob Jones (who in Cooper's old sloop, the *Wasp*, bested yet another British vessel in the middle of October) were feted in New York City from Christmas on past New Year's.

Whether he attended some or all of them, or only learned of them through the press and his navy contacts, the public fetes made very real for Cooper both what his old friends were accomplishing and how much he himself was missing. The city was ecstatic about the victory of the *United States* over the *Macedonian* even before anyone there had beheld either ship. William Dunlap noted in his diary on December 7 that "the glorious acc[oun]t of another Naval Victory" had arrived in the city that day, adding on December 9, "We look for Decaturs Prize the frigate Macedonian to day." But it was not until three weeks later that he could note, "The wind[,] long at West[,] changed yesterday & this morning the United States and her prize the Macedonian [came] through *Helle Gat* & safe into Harbour."[65] Dunlap was right about the length and cause of the delay, which Cooper's 1821 review truncated by that phrase *shortly after*. A few days before Christmas, the New York *Columbian* was able to report, "The frigates are still at their anchors beyond Hell-Gate, the wind being too far to the westward for their passage through."[66]

But adverse winds did not keep the victorious Decatur from New York—or New York from the *United States* and its prize. The same paper, commenting on the headwinds two days earlier, had noted that "the frigates remain [anchored] in the narrows of the sound, or east river, near Harlem, and have made the village a place of great resort and liveliness by the company they attract."[67] The young tar Samuel Leech, now a prisoner on his own ship, long remembered the details. As the prize passed up Long Island Sound, it was swarmed by the sloops that were always crisscrossing the water there, from most of which Leech could hear patriotic "three cheers" being shouted forth. This greeting evoked joyous answers from the American prize crew that still controlled the *Macedonian* but gave cold comfort to the British sailors, who, prisoners in hostile waters, knew most of all that they had lost a third of their own in the bloody fray. Even more insistent instances of American exultation were still to come. Once down into Hell Gate, the *Macedonian* was thronged with "abundant visitors, curious to see the captive frigate," a sight Cooper hardly would have missed (although we do not know for sure whether he visited the ship there or at the Brooklyn navy yard later on). It was a festive experience for the Americans who boarded the vessel, which everyone knew was more than adequate compensation for the psychic costs of the *Chesapeake* disaster. By Christmas, the British captain had capitulated to the new assaults of the public, using an old hogshead to rig a chair for hauling female American visitors aboard. The exultant Americans visited with a souvenir-seeking intent.[68] The father of Knickerbocker writer Henry Brevoort, one of Cooper's friends, was "highly tickled with the success of our Navy," as Washington Irving reported to young Henry, then in Edinburgh. Irving added that "the old gentleman" was "so powerfully excited by the capture of the Macedonian, that he actually performed a journey to the Brothers"—a pair of islands near Hell Gate—"where the frigates lay, wind-bound; and he brought away a piece of the Macedonian, which he seemed to treasure up with as much devotion as a pious Catholic does a piece of the True Cross."[69]

The vessels at last came down the East River and, as the "bells rang a merry peal, and salutes were fired," sailed into New York harbor on New Year's Day.[70] In anticipation, a banquet honoring Hull and Decatur (and the absent Jones) had been held at the City Hotel on December 29, presided over by Mayor DeWitt Clinton. Irving, just back from lobbying Congress on the subject of merchants' losses due to the war, wrote of the affair to his brother Peter in Europe. It was, he said, "the most splendid entertainment of the kind I ever witnessed." He added, as Cooper might have, "I never in my life before felt the national feeling so strongly aroused, for I never before saw in this country so true a cause for national triumph." On a banner at the rear of the hall, added Samuel Woodworth's bellicose new paper, *The War*, was hung a mainsail of a ship across which an eagle had been painted, "holding a scroll in his beak on which was inscribed these words, '*Our children are the property of our Country.*'"[71]

Washington Irving also attended the "grand ball" on New Year's Eve at the City Hotel, where (as he revealed in his letter to Brevoort) "there was a vast display of great & little people"—from the naval heroes and members of clans like the Livingstons on down to scribblers such as himself.[72] But the real "little people"—the "*Brave American Tars*" of the *United States*—also were to be honored by the city. Early on the afternoon of Thursday, January 7, the men arrived by boat in the New Slip, at the foot of James Street, from which they marched two-by-two along Pearl to Wall Street and then to Broadway and the City Hotel. The *Evening Post* remarked on the bearing of the smartly uniformed sailors, and on their exceptionally fine musical accompaniment. The latter was provided by a professional European band Decatur had taken over in conquering Carden's ship. The musicians, a collection of German, French, and Italian nationals previously captured from a French vessel by the Portuguese, had been hired away from their first captors by Carden. The personal expense was not insignificant, but Carden had made great use of the musicians: they added flourishes to his ship's dockings and departures and played for him each day as he dined in his cabin. When the *United States* drew near, Carden ordered the instrumentalists to the guns, but—reminded that their original contract defined them as strict noncombatants—he let them remain mute and safe belowdecks. After Decatur's victory, it presumably took them some time to learn the new tunes that went with the new flag. By the time Herman Melville heard the remnants of Carden's band on the *United States* in the Pacific thirty years later and then introduced them into *White-Jacket*, though, he had them play "Hail Columbia" like troupers.[73]

Forcing their way through the streets packed with New Yorkers eager to see the four hundred ordinary heroes of Decatur's victory, the sailors went to the hotel for their noisy celebration, then to the Park Theatre (through another jam of cheering citizens) for a performance of William Dunlap's comedy *Fraternal Discord*, which was interspersed with songs and skits more suited to the men's mood. The house was brought down by a very heavy singer named M'Farland, dressed as a clown, when he came out to perform "Yankey Frolics." It began:

> No more of your blathering nonsense,
> 'Bout the Nelsons of old Johnny Bull
> I'll sing you a song, 'pon my conscience,
> 'Bout Jones, Decatur, and Hull.

"I leave the reader to guess the effect" of the clown's song, wrote the reporter for the *Evening Post*. "Cries of encore! were incessant; nothing else could be heard, no farther proceedings permitted, until [M'Farland] returned, to repeat the Song"—this time in sailor's garb. M'Farland ended by dancing "a sailor's hornpipe"—a feat that his great "bulk and weight" made so remarkable that he brought down the house. Despite the farcical conclusion, the night had joined the deep patriotic passion of the ordinary sailors with that of their citizen supporters.[74]

Like a vexing anticlimax to the public celebrations of the Christmas season of 1812–1813, the very next month William Hammond ("president") and Ames Worden ("sergt") addressed to militiaman Cooper the following notice: "Sir you are Heerby warned to appear at the hous of Peter Cornels White Plains on Friday the 15th inst at nine oclock in the morning to attend a Cort marshel for being absent at a battalion perrade Sept 18th and Rejimental perrade Sept 23 1812."[75]

Cooper did *not* attend the hearing. Instead, he sent an unlocated note on Friday morning offering an excuse for his failure to appear for the militia functions the previous fall. Capt. William Hammond of Greenburgh, in Westchester County, commanded a company of light infantry that entered state service in the summer of 1812 but that, as of September 10, was being held among the reserves for the defense of New York City. This evidently was the company in which Cooper was enrolled. Hammond not only served as Cooper's captain but also presided at the "Board of Officers composing the Court Martial of the 33d Regmt." As such, he acknowledged receipt of Cooper's note and reported that the board rejected his explanation, fining him ten dollars for the infractions. Hammond also pointed out that if Cooper had some other excuse he might have recourse to the commander of the Thirty-third Regiment, who could remit the fine if he saw fit.[76] There is no record that Cooper protested the fine—or paid it, for that matter. That his reluctance to show up for the militia events the previous fall was related to his confusion about his standing in the navy is suggested by the fact that he again wrote Washington about his status (see *LJ* 1:29) just a week after the White Plains court martial met.

A decade later, Cooper would recall that the uncertainty about that question in the first months of the war had left his "family unsettled" (*LJ* 1:90).[77] He may have meant that even this early the Coopers were contemplating a move to Cooperstown but had lingered in Westchester until the navy department clarified his duties. It is entirely possible that Susan, despite her desire to remain near her family after the wedding, had been sufficiently charmed by Otsego that even during the visit there in the spring of 1811 the couple indeed did scout out the land along the lake where Fenimore Farm eventually would be developed. It is clear that in the summer of 1812, while the family was staying at Closet Hall and Cooper was awaiting decisive word from the navy, he was proceeding with plans for a contemplated shift to Otsego County. He had a workman cut hay on his lakeside land, then scrape out a new cellar there, haul and lay stone, make a fence, and clean a well—and, most importantly, help to erect an unspecified new building. It is likely that the latter was a new frame house on the property, located where the New York State Historical Association headquarters now stands, although the Coopers would need new outbuildings for their agricultural activities there as well.[78]

Not until the late winter and spring of 1813 did the family manage to take advantage of these improvements. Already in early February, having finally received positive word from the navy that his resignation was accepted, Cooper was preparing for the shift. He and his family, expecting their second child in April, had moved to the DeLancey enclave at Mamaroneck within the past few weeks. But, knowing that Heathcote Hill would provide only temporary shelter, they must have left the bulk of their furnishings and farm equipment at their New Rochelle lodgings.[79] Within two weeks, Cooper was off by himself to visit the family's intended home at Fenimore Farm, then buried in the snowy upstate winter. His brother Isaac, who recorded the Cooperstown weather four times a day in his diary (much as Richard Jones and Ben Pump were to do in *The Pioneers*), noted Cooper's arrival in the village on February 26, when the temperature rose from thirteen degrees at nine in the morning to a high of twenty degrees at noon, but plunged to zero by nine that night. Isaac was expecting him: on that very day he had paid for the stone that local resident Asa Luce was supplying for the Fenimore projects.[80]

Cooper was once more between houses—and between assumptions. More than nine busy months had passed since he last visited the village, and he had much to catch up on. Among other things, his sojourn gave him a chance to learn more about the blunder-plagued land war against Britain, a subject to which Otsego's residents were especially attuned. He already knew from reports and conversations in New York that things were not going well there. The American government was set on conquering the remaining British colonies in North America. It thereby hoped to remove the perpetual worry that imperial forces, striking from just over the northern and western borders, might reverse the gains of the Revolution. But disappointments had stymied the ambitious effort almost from the start. The three-pronged invasion had been aimed at Montreal, the Niagara frontier, and the English positions opposite Detroit. In the west, Michigan territorial governor William Hull, a Revolutionary War veteran, had been appointed to take command. Having gathered his forces in Ohio early in the summer of 1812, he marched into Michigan in July. By the middle of August, a series of errors and his own pusillanimity resulted in the precipitous surrender of Fort Detroit. The prior collapse of the Americans on Mackinac Island and the loss of Fort Dearborn in Chicago (which Hull ordered evacuated, thus allowing a massacre) meant that the national cause on the far border was in a shambles within two months of the declaration of war.[81]

Because the move against Montreal, which was to be the main effort along the northern border, was delayed until late in the fall, attention next turned to the midsection of the international boundary—along the Niagara River and the Ontario shore, a region Cooper knew very well from his service at Oswego. This part of the campaign was of pressing concern to Cooperstown residents. Otsego regularly sent men to sea, like Cooper himself, and had its representatives in the far West. It also was tied closely to the Quebec frontier: William Cooper, after all, had staked a claim a decade earlier in the St. Lawrence River valley, and agents of his such as storekeeper Thomas B. Benedict were to bear their part in the military effort in the War of 1812.[82] The frontier with Upper Canada, however, was always more immediately present to the Otsego imagination. The British and Indian forces along this border, for one thing, most sharply threatened Otsego and New York's other western and central counties. And it was here, too, that Otsego's men most notably served. Village lawyer Farrand Stranahan thus was lieutenant colonel in command of a regiment that saw early service on the Niagara frontier.[83] This regiment, drawn in part from an old Otsego militia unit, recruited new members there during its muster in the summer of 1812 and soon marched off to Buffalo. When the overall commander of New York's militia, Maj. Gen. Stephen Van Rensselaer—the Patroon, and William Cooper's old political ally—ordered the abortive attack on Queenston Heights that October, Stranahan and other regimental officers and some of their men were among those taken prisoner by the British.[84]

The Otsego militiamen who came home from the disaster carried many tales with them that still must have been circulating there during Cooper's visit only a few weeks later. Surely he heard (perhaps not for the first time) how infantry lieutenant John Chrystie, his close friend at Oswego, had been wounded in the attack on Queenston. But the most vocal tale-bearer among the Otsego veterans of the battle must have been the venerable "Plough-Jogger," Judge Jedediah Peck, one of the county's most active Republicans. A sixty-four-year-old Revolutionary War veteran, Peck had volunteered for fresh service in the summer of 1812 to encourage the enlistment of young men "that was altogether ignorent of war"—young men whom "so many others [were] discouraging from turning out." That was the way Peck told the story in July of 1813, when he sought to untangle for the paymaster general of the U.S. Army the records of his service handling disbursements to the men of "the 16th Regt of detached Infantry of the state of New York commanded by Farrand Stranahan." Peck hadn't sought out such a post, having enlisted simply as a private; once Gov. Daniel D. Tompkins heard of the celebrated veteran's enlistment, however, he named him to the post. As it happened, Peck knew nothing of his appointment until just before he saddled his horse and started west "for the Niagary fruntier" in August.

From its camp there, the Sixteenth Regiment advanced to join Van Rensselaer's force, arriving the night before the attack. Fierce fighting followed, but a small group of Americans managed to take Queenston Heights. On the death of Gen. Isaac Brock, commander of British forces in Upper Canada (and victor over Gen. William Hull at Detroit), they might have carried the day if properly reinforced. Stranahan's men, still largely—if not "altogether"—"ignorent of war," were shocked by the number of dead and wounded soldiers ferried back over the Niagara River. Like many militiamen during the conflict, they also were opposed on principle to leaving U.S. soil: Van Rensselaer later complained that the militiamen in general, most of them "violent democrats," simply refused to

enter Canadian territory. "To my utter astonishment," he wrote Henry Dearborn, "I found that at the very moment when complete victory was in our hands,
the Ardor of the unengaged Troops had entirely subsided. . . . I rode in all directions—urged men by every Consideration to pass over, but in vain." Some
of them at last did volunteer to go over. According to paymaster Peck, as many
as half of the men in his regiment went across, joined by Peck himself, who, as
Van Rensselaer also noted, was running about on Canadian soil "exhorting the
companies to proceed—but all in vain." With many officers in enemy hands,
those companies fell into chaos.

This collapse made Peck's official job, already hampered by unclear proto-
cols and the lack of adequate record-keeping materials, even more difficult. His
troubles lasted for weeks afterwards. Through the winter of Cooper's visit and
into the spring and summer of 1813, when Cooper was to come back, Peck was
riding around Otsego and adjacent areas to find the returned soldiers and clarify the records of their service and settle with them. Cooper may have heard of
some of this at the time. Indeed, he may have used it when he decided to end his
first novel of the Revolution, *The Spy*, on the Niagara frontier of 1814. Although
Harvey Birch's final service to his country takes place during a later (and more
successful) American operation in that area, there could well be some trace of
perennial patriot Jedediah Peck's experience in this second enlistment of Cooper's durable and by 1814 aged Revolutionary hero in the service of the country
he, too, had helped to create.[85]

While attending to such tales of distant battlefields during his midwinter
visit to Otsego in 1813, Cooper was not immune to bad news from other quarters. On March 8, Cooperstown storekeeper Jesse H. Starr returned from Albany
with word that Cooper's oldest brother, Richard, just thirty-seven years old, had
succumbed to an unspecified illness a few days before—barely a week, in fact,
after Cooper had passed through Albany on his way west.[86] Isaac, hearing of the
event from young Starr, went off to Albany right away, and on March 9 came
back with "the corpse of RFC," which was immediately "committed to its kin-
dred dust." The timing of the trip and return may have been telescoped in Isaac's
diary, perhaps registering the distress caused by this second death of a head of
the Cooper family within a bit more than three years. Isaac's youngest brother,
staying on in Cooperstown only long enough to attend the interment and read
Richard's death notice in the *Otsego Herald* on March 13, left the next day. His
mind may well have been on mortal things as he turned home toward Susan,
who, eight months into her second pregnancy, was facing her own trials.[87]

At Heathcote Hill on April 17, a second daughter, Susan Augusta, was born.
This delivery seems not to have gone more easily than the first. Another three
weeks and the mother had not yet come downstairs (partly owing, however, to

the effects of a bad storm), and infant Susan was not to be promptly christened in Westchester, as Elizabeth had been in 1811, but rather in Cooperstown a full three months later. Shortly after the birth, in any case, the father was absent once more, having rushed back upstate to Otsego to oversee the ongoing projects at Fenimore Farm. His attention there was directed toward providing a permanent place for the growing family, but it nonetheless took him away from Susan when probably he—certainly she—wished that he could tarry. He left a few days earlier than had been planned, before her "returning strength" (Susan lamented in a letter she sent him in Cooperstown) had enabled her to "chat with [him] like old times."[88]

Isaac's diary recorded the arrival of his youngest brother in Cooperstown by stage on May 6. Cooper had traveled from Albany in the company of Jesse Starr, the young shopkeeper and family friend who had brought word of Richard's death to town in March. Almost from his arrival in the village, he was busy supervising work on the barn being erected at Fenimore (he endorsed the back of a timber receipt, "Bill for stuff for barn" on May 8) and scouting out temporary quarters for Susan and the girls, who would be joining him soon.[89] The new farmhouse apparently was not quite ready yet. In a letter written the day her husband arrived in Cooperstown, Susan, still confined to the second floor at Heathcote Hill, reminded him to let her know as soon as he had "made any arrangement for our establishment for the Summer." Apparently Isaac, waiting for his own new house to be finished along the lakefront, was occupying Richard's old house, Apple Hill, on the river: if Isaac and his family were able to move into Edgewater soon enough, Apple Hill might be available while the Fenimore house was being finished. Susan knew that they could count on the hospitality of Ann and George Pomeroy, but worried about the consequences. The Pomeroys had two children and probably some domestic help, while the Coopers would bring Elizabeth and Susan and probably their young servant Caty Conklin as well as Mrs. Disbrow—their English nanny, who had just agreed to stay on with the family, at least for the summer. Aware of the headcount here, Susan continued, "I fear so many of us will incommode Mrs. Pomeroy." So Apple Hill would be better on that front, and would give the Coopers more privacy as well.

Susan also worried about other things. She regretted that her husband had had to leave Mamaroneck three days earlier than he had planned to. But she was also reflecting on his destination and what it meant for the family. Their next meeting on his return, she wrote, would be "imbittered with the certainty of its being so immediately followed by a separation from so many dear friends and such deservedly dear friends as I"—not *we*, though the difference may not have been significant—"shall leave in Westchester." She was committed to the relocation, at least in the abstract, but she knew its costs to herself and clearly wanted her husband to remember them. She could only hope that, as her health improved, her "fortitude [would] become more equal to the trial." Her concern with where the family was to live must have expressed deeper worries as well. But at least she could add for Cooper that both their children were well: "your youngest Daughter grows nicely and continues very good, though she does cry sometimes to the great distress of Elizabeth who is very fond of her Sister Susy." Back on old family ground but full of uncertainties about where home was to be for his young family, the girls' father would have been heartened by such news as well as reminded of how his responsibilities were growing. And he probably looked out over Lake Otsego and dreamed of the ocean, now so busy and soon, with the move, to be so far away from him.[90]

Then came a sea tale that must have helped reconcile Cooper to the coming change. He probably was still busy with the farm in Otsego as late as June 8 when the first alarms about the loss of his old commander James Lawrence off Boston in the ill-fated *Chesapeake* arrived in the village: "They say the Cheaspeak is taken," wrote Isaac in his diary, adding, "I hope not!"[91] But wherever Cooper learned of this "costliest single slaughter of officers in the navy's pre-1815 history" (seven of them were killed, notes historian Christopher McKee), it provided him with a devastating finale to Lawrence's personal story and to the narrative of the ship's unlucky career.[92] It also put an end to the eleven months of splendid naval news that had uplifted America and especially Cooper as the little country entered its second, doubtful war against the assembled powers of the British Empire. Many years later, looking back at this critical juncture in America's post-colonial epoch, the naval historian drew the proper conclusion: "Perhaps the capture of no single ship ever produced so much exultation on the side of the victors, or so much depression on that of the beaten party, as that of the Chesapeake. The American nation had fallen into the error of their enemy, and had begun to imagine themselves invincible on the ocean, and this without any better reason than having been successful in a few detached combats, and its mortification was in proportion to the magnitude of its delusion; while England hailed the success of the Shannon as a proof that its ancient renown was about to be regained" (*HN* 2:253–54). Cooper may have been so moralistic in 1839 because he himself shared the "delusion" in 1813, and with special depth. The accumulating victories had intoxicated the nation, and not just because of the long toasts with which each hero was greeted at the interminable celebrations in New York. The bad news from the frontiers in 1812 and 1813 and the lingering sense of national inferiority combined to give America's success at sea uncanny force.

The fact that his old commander and friend had joined the list of certified American heroes as recently as May 4, when his victory over the British sloop of war *Peacock* was celebrated in New York, gave Cooper a very personal stake in the fantasy.[93] This was the officer whom Cooper would later call "a perfect man-of-war's man," a "chivalrous, generous, and just" American (*HN* 2:253n). In Lawrence, Cooper had invested his sense of what he too might have been had he stayed in the service. Now, in June of 1813, what exactly was that? Not only dead, Cooper would have to say, but cast for a time under a cloud that only gradually was lifted from his reputation. The "mortification" Americans felt because of the *Chesapeake*'s (and their own) drubbing by the *Shannon* probably was shared briefly by Cooper. He used it, in all likelihood, to help break his ties to the sea, to turn back inland and settle himself once more—with his own family this time—in the green inland world where he had grown up. Lawrence's tragedy made it an oddly auspicious time for Cooper to make that move.

CHAPTER SIX

Fenimore Farm

I t was a season of mortality. James Lawrence, severely wounded in the encounter with the *Shannon*, lingered several days before he died in Halifax,
where the *Chesapeake* was taken after its capture. An initial funeral was held
there on June 7, but later in the summer his body was exhumed and returned to
the United States—to Salem and Boston and then eventually New York, where,
on September 16, a crowd of up to fifty thousand mourners turned out to honor
him at his interment in Trinity churchyard.[1] Cooper surely would have joined
that crowd had he been near the city at the time. But by then, having made the
move to Otsego, he implausibly enough was in mourning there for his own
daughter Elizabeth. At the start of July, he and Susan, with the two girls and
probably young Caty Conklin, had been on their way through Cherry Valley
when Elizabeth ate some spoiled fruit that made her seriously ill. She weakened
further over the following week at the house of Cooper's sister Ann, then on the
morning of July 13 she died. Among other obituaries, the *Otsego Herald* found
room for this little one the Saturday following: "ELIZABETH COOPER, eldest
daughter of James Cooper, of this village, aged 1 year and 10 months" (SFM 10–
11, 17).[2]

From a Cooperstown merchant who had sold Cooper a secretary desk during his May visit to the village, the family now bought a child's coffin with a silver nameplate on it. In a touching ritual on July 14, Cooper had Elizabeth buried within a "pretty grove of young trees" on Fenimore Farm. His second daughter later thought it "singular" for him to separate this one grave from all the others in the village churchyard (SFM 17). Maybe it was because the girl's loss tied him to the farm with extraordinary swiftness, making it a home as few other events could. He had a rough rock wall thrown up around the spot, and soon, as if envisioning it as the future graveyard of his entire family, he ordered fancy quarried stones to enclose it. But events overtook his plans. Within a few short years the Coopers would be uprooted from Otsego, and those neatly cut stones, never installed, were to be abandoned with the farm itself. Eventually Elizabeth's lonely burial plot was swallowed back into the woods.[3]

Cooper took the girl's loss hard. "I was passionately fond of the child," he confessed to William Jay once he finally felt he could answer the latter's letter of condolence (*LJ* 1:29–30).[4] But, out of what seems like a forced but ultimately frustrated search for normalcy, life went on. On the day of Elizabeth's funeral, Rev. Daniel Nash of Christ Church in Cooperstown reminded those gathered over her grave that "man hath but a short time to live, and is full of misery." Then, four days later, he was standing before the Coopers once again in the village as he baptized their infant Susan: "Almighty and everlasting God," he prayed, ". . . Give thy Holy Spirit to this infant, that she may be born again." The loss of one daughter sped up this much-delayed ceremony for the second.[5] That was just one of several ways the living jostled the dead. On the day Cooper bought Elizabeth's tiny coffin, he also purchased more furniture for the family's new home. Then or soon afterwards, perhaps when he stopped by the carpenter's shop a day after little Susan's baptism to make a payment on his account, he dropped off other pieces that had been damaged (probably in the move hither) for the same craftsman to mend. The couple seemed set on making the best of the new situation, burying grief in the little domestications necessary to fix them in Otsego. The Coopers would never be truly settled there, but they expended great quantities of energy and money attempting to make the move work.[6]

Their efforts were centered on their sixty-five-acre farm, assembled in 1811 and 1812 from three separate parcels situated between the road and the west shore of the lake. Across the road, on the side of a hill some six hundred feet high, lay other parcels Cooper would purchase in 1813 and 1814: here he would establish his sheep farm, Mt. Ovis.[7] There probably were no existing buildings, certainly not habitable ones, on any of Fenimore parcels when Cooper bought them. Since the ambitious stone mansion he already imagined for the largest of those lots would require some time to plan and complete, the modest dwelling whose frame had been erected the past spring—just north of the proposed mansion site—would temporarily house the family (Plate 11). Although not finished yet, it had been sufficiently enclosed by the third week of August that, on a fine day toward the end of the month, the family hosted a dinner party there for Isaac and Mary Ann Cooper, with "fine watermelons from Albany" as a special housewarming treat.[8] That event was followed by a series of others. There was a "very pleasant fishing party consisting of 23 Gentlemen and Ladies" on September 1, for instance, then a tea party three weeks later, and across the fall and into winter, Fenimore Farm (the name, spelled "Fenemore," was first recorded by Isaac on January 2, when he walked there) was to be the site of several more gatherings.[9]

The snow came early and lasted the winter that year, so that by late January Isaac could report "fine sleighing" all over Otsego. Among the more contemplative rewards of living at the farmhouse must have been the "beautiful moonlight nights" he also took note of then. During the day, one could look out its windows and down toward the bright surface of Lake Otsego, admiring what Cooper in *The Pioneers*, would call "the animated brilliancy of winter" (*PIO* CE 218). The old Cooper mansion, stuck back at the end of its tree-lined lane several hundred feet from the water, afforded no such immediate view of the ice-bound lake or the events taking place on it.[10] If Cooper ever saw a pair of bald eagles take undisputed possession of the last bit of ice on Otsego and, for a week, scare off the migratory birds pouring into the valley (see *PIO* CE 242–43), it must have been from the vantage of Fenimore Farm rather than Otsego Hall. And the winter of 1813–1814, his first in Otsego in many years, may have been the very one: spring came as early and as suddenly that year as it would in the novel, rushing the wintry valley into premature life. Already by early April, Isaac was recording a famous mark of the season's change: "an immense number of Pigeons flying." He took his hand at the resultant slaughter, much as Richard Jones would in *The Pioneers*. But then, by April 13, the enormous flocks were gone and the ice was suddenly off the green lake and the trees and bushes began leafing out. The weather was pleasant enough that Isaac took a "walk to the top of [the] hill"—Mt. Ovis—and then went on down to his brother's farmhouse for yet another visit.[11]

Spring brought a multitude of plans to Fenimore for the coming year. For one thing, Cooper was beginning to establish his sheep flock; one notable merino buck named Sinbad had been relocated from Westchester already, and Sinbad's owner was in the market for more. A relatively new introduction to the United States, the merino breed was in great demand just then owing to an expansion of the American woolen industry caused by the Embargo Act's exclusion of European supplies. Here was a means for turning a bit of profit on the farm. Cooper understood well that, whereas common wool rarely brought fifty cents per pound even during dramatic production increases at the height of the War of 1812, merino fleeces could bring four to eight times that amount. So hot was the market that individual merino rams were known to sell for hundreds of dollars as farmers developed their flocks and speculators exploited the craze.[12] But Cooper was a wool-raiser, not a speculator. According to an inventory prepared on June 1, 1814, not even a year after moving to Otsego, he already had 145 sheep of various kinds at Fenimore and Mt. Ovis, and most of the animals were crosses: the two rams were full-blooded merinos, but all the ewes, half-blooded at best, were valuable primarily for their fleeces.[13]

Sheep flocks were merely one part of Cooper's business in early 1814. Work on the stone mansion got under way by March, when local carpenter Cyrus Clark began a three-month stint making window frames for it, and apparently the foundation was to be laid up that summer.[14] In the interim, Cooper had other things to supervise. He went to New York City for a ten-day visit on May 9, apparently sent off by Isaac, now sole executor of their father's estate, to tend to some related affairs.[15] When he returned, Susan, already feeling homesick, was preparing to head downstate for a visit to Heathcote Hill with their daughter, now just over a year old. In their absence, Cooper threw himself into fresh work at Fenimore. There were new apple trees and raspberry canes to put in, and a hayfield sown just that spring needed its first cutting; furthermore, Cooper's corn and other crops, "suffering greatly" because of a droughty spell that began around mid-June, had to be carefully tended so that they would pull through and mature. He obviously enjoyed such things, but in this arena too he may have been counting on the potential income. Further work was also being done at this time on the wooden farmhouse and on the grounds, where Cooper, personally engaged in "clearing the Lawn burning stumps &c.," wrote Susan that he was introducing "great alterations" (*LJ* 1:31–32). Soon, though, as Susan's visit to her family's home neared its end, Cooper headed downstate to pick her up.[16]

"Peace"

Across the fall of 1814, the Coopers remained exceptionally busy with their personal affairs.[17] But the would-be master of Fenimore Farm surely gave much attention to the two momentous public events that dominated the national and local press for weeks: the American rout at Bladensburg, Maryland, followed by the disastrous burning of Washington, both in August. The gloom traceable to these dire occurrences was only slightly relieved by accounts from western and northern New York, where American forces held Fort Erie and retook control of Lake Champlain.[18] What really set Cooper in motion, though, was the reported lack of progress in the peace negotiations, begun in Belgium in August. In October, news stories about those negotiations that derived from a recent presidential message to Congress had sent Americans scurrying to their ideological corners. The British negotiators were bluntly insisting on five points that seemed to ignore or deny most key American principles. The *Otsego Herald* printed the list as soon as this "IMPORTANT NEWS" came to hand:

> 1st. A new boundary line is to be established, giving them the whole dominion of the lakes, and part of the Province of Maine.
>
> 2d. The independence of the Indians [is] to be guaranteed, and both parties prohibited from purchasing lands within their territory.
>
> 3d. We are not to erect any fortifications on the frontier, and to abandon those already erected.
>
> 4th. The right of search [is] to be permanently settled in their favor.
>
> 5th. They will permit us to fish, but not cure our fish, on the banks of Newfoundland.[19]

The very day the paper carried this news, October 20, "a numerous and respectable meeting of citizens" gathered at the Cooperstown courthouse to discuss the impasse. Cooper, who was known for his outspoken anti-British take on the subject and apparently had helped arrange the meeting, was quickly chosen its secretary. Seizing the opportunity, he sought to push his view that the five British points constituted fresh outrages against American liberty. Probably he argued for an end to the peace talks and a return to battle in order to force Britain back to the table in a more serious manner. But the citizens of Otsego, war-weary and less bothered than the former midshipman by the British assertion of a perpetual "right of search" (that is, the right to stop and search American vessels for supposed deserters, always the opening wedge of impressment abuses), were reluctant to go that far at the moment.

Cooper's failure to carry the meeting left him in a difficult position. As secretary, he had agreed to publish the group's resolutions. He would not do so, however, without adding a personal postscript stating that in his view the original object of the meeting had been "perverted."[20] His naval sympathies and his interpretation of the war as a new test of American independence urged him to these extremes. In a sense, however, the issues debated by the citizens of Otsego were already moot. It was being rightly rumored in the fall, even before their meeting, that the American government had yielded ground on impressment, removing it as a formal subject of peace discussions, and when the Treaty of Ghent was at last finalized on Christmas Eve, 1814, in fact that document would make no concession to America on the question. Only in Great Britain's future refusal to resume the practice, exhibited first during the last flare-up of the Napoleonic Wars in 1815, was there evidence that the Republic's naval heroism had won it respect in the British Empire and, indeed, across Europe. Cooper and his naval colleagues thus far were to win the larger battle. Britain would not overtly concede, but in effect it acknowledged the truth over the decades following.[21]

That triumph was a long time in coming and lacked the drama of the war's early naval victories. When the novelist–turned–naval historian dealt with the war's end, he perhaps therefore gave inordinate attention to Andrew Jackson's lopsided (and post-treaty) defeat of the British in Louisiana. The battle of New Orleans, giving the inglorious war a fittingly dramatic end, was also a proxy for the late naval victories that mostly didn't come. Cooper was not writing a history of the *army*, he admitted in 1839, but he nonetheless had to say what he felt: "It would be difficult to find another instance in history in which a population, deficient in arms, organization, training, and numbers, so signally defeated a powerful force of disciplined troops, accustomed to war" (*HN* 2:321–22). His own later political support for Andrew Jackson, first evident during the election of 1824, had taken root in 1815 for that very reason. It was nourished by his sense that the battle of New Orleans had driven home to Britain the point that so many of his naval colleagues had lived—and died—to make early in the war. America had come of age; independence was real and would neither be given up by the Americans nor taken back by the English.

Word of the Treaty of Ghent reached Cooperstown on February 14, 1815. Two days later, as the snow was thawing in Otsego, Fenimore Farm was the scene of yet another party, this one probably intended as a kind of victory celebration for friends and relatives. By early March, the villagers in general would turn out for a grand village-wide hurrah. Several shops and homes (including that of Cooper's sister Ann and her husband George Pomeroy) displayed handmade transparencies in their windows, illuminating "the names of our Army & Naval Heroes" for the crowds in the darkened streets. All across the preserved (if not quite victorious) country similar celebrations were being mounted: meant to signalize the end of a seemingly indecisive war, in a larger sense they at last marked the end of the colonial era.[22]

Especially on the fringes of New York State, the war had hidden costs that continued long after the Treaty of Ghent. The northern town of DeKalb, which Cooper's father had purchased in 1803 and immediately begun developing, had been spared direct attack, but the war's economic effects there proved severe. Land that had been sold in sizable chunks to petty speculators, who in turn distributed it to actual settlers, came back into the hands of the Cooper estate as farmers and then developers alike reneged on their contracts. Furthermore, merchants in settlements like Williamstown (or Cooper's Village) who had been carrying on export trade with Canada before the war saw the bulk of their business

evaporate after 1812. This, too, posed problems for the Cooper estate, which had
much capital tied up in mills, a hotel, and a retail outlet there. Moreover, the very
structure of the DeKalb business spelled trouble for the Cooper heirs. Early on,
Judge Cooper had sold undivided shares in his own interest in DeKalb to a group
of investors that included New Haven lawyer Nathaniel Smith and several
wealthy New York City residents. When times turned bad for DeKalb, the
Judge's children were left with large financial obligations to these partners even
as they struggled to manage the family's faltering endeavors throughout the
north country.

The partners remained largely quiescent until shortly after Richard Fenimore Cooper's death in March of 1813, when they demanded that Isaac divide
the common holdings, thereby giving each of them a hand in managing their
risk. Somewhat at a loss, Isaac proceeded tentatively. He commissioned an inventory of the bulk of the land in DeKalb, some 62,800 acres, excluding only the
village of Williamstown and its mill seat, along with a few other parcels that
were jointly owned by the Cooper estate and a subset of the other investors,
Nathaniel Smith among them. The resulting map, finished in the fall of 1814 by
local surveyor Potter Goff, tidily divided the township into numbered parcels.
Accompanying it was an evaluation of each parcel according to its existing improvements, if any, and its agricultural potential. Various ranked categories were
established, from "First" ("Choice Lots with handsome improvements") through
"Fourth" ("Choice wild Land as to Soil & natural situation") and finally "Sixth"
("Wild Lands of less value, either mountainous Rocky or too low for immediate
settlements").[23]

Once this survey came to Isaac Cooper's hand late in April, he could proceed with the business. On May 2, 1815, in concert with his two youngest brothers and George Pomeroy, he therefore "Divided DeKalb." Each of the partners
outside the family received his or her own particular assignment of lots. Isaac
also debited each of the six original heirs (including the deceased Richard) for a
sizable share in DeKalb lands, ranging from a high of just under 4,900 acres for
his three brothers and for Richard's heirs, to about half as much for himself and
the Pomeroys. Although the bulk of the land assigned to each heir fell into the
fourth class (i.e., "Choice Wild Land") or the third (land partly improved but
abandoned by the settlers), Isaac's calculations show that among the family these
classes were considered the most valuable, probably because vacant lands could
be sold outright to new purchasers, whereas the lots already sold were of uncertain value unless the settlers on them stayed put and then met their obligations.[24]

Although Cooper received a substantial share of his father's landed property in northern New York by these distributions, its monetary value was low.
When purchasing the DeKalb land in 1803, William Cooper had paid one dollar

an acre for it. It is highly doubtful that much of the wild land remaining in family hands in St. Lawrence County in 1815 was worth five times that amount, the figure that the dividers, following the explicit instructions in Judge Cooper's will, were obliged to use. Cooper himself certainly never realized the nearly $22,000 debited against him in the estate books for this transfer, even though his overall inheritance was substantially reduced by it. Settlers resident on any of the higher category parcels in 1815 were as few as hen's teeth. When the Goff survey was made, for instance, only four of the nine lots in the first through third classes that had fallen to Cooper's personal share had active settlers on them. Two of them were especially promising by comparison with all the others still in DeKalb. Barton Carver was reported to be "very industrious, a perfect Woodsman" and was fortunate to be in possession of a "superior Lot of Land" that many thought "the best spot in the Township." Joseph Rounds, also possessed of a "choice farm," was reputed to be "the best farmer on the state road." But even the successes of DeKalb were shaky. Philo Hurlburt, an industrious settler "doing well" on a "handsome farm," wanted "to give in his betterments for wild land," the survey noted, "and to commence anew," as in time he did, leaving De-Kalb for nearby DePeyster. In the meantime, Hurlburt told Cooper's cousin Courtland in 1817 that he could not pay the money owing on his mortgage. He begged for more time, and it was two years before he actually transferred to Courtland some notes (probably of questionable value) that another resident had given him. Even Joseph Rounds, despite his well-deserved reputation among the settlers along the state road, kept putting Courtland off, promising a little barter but no money.

The other five "improved" farms drawn by Cooper in DeKalb were more than a balance to the few shining examples the survey might name. Indeed, they were abandoned. One purchaser was "absent" in Massachusetts at the time; another was in the army; a third had chopped and cleared a quarter of his lot but had never erected a house; another had sold out to an absentee owner in Ogdensburg ("*This Mortgage* ought to be foreclosed," the survey noted); and a fifth had simply "gone off"—no one knew where—after clearing a mere 6 of his 125 acres. Nor did things brighten in the immediate future. Two years after the war's end, according to a report sent to Cooper by cousin Courtland, apparently no additional settlers had taken up any of the other lots. If Cooper was to realize anything from this part of his legacy from his father, it would have to come through other means. In the meantime, DeKalb must have taught him a good deal about the deeper truths of the supposedly hopeful process of frontier settlement.[25]

The January 1815 division of DeKalb emphasized one kind of loss. Soon after the middle of that month, Cooper experienced another. In the dark of the night, someone broke into his stable at Fenimore Farm and made off with a horse and saddle. A reward of twenty dollars was offered in a notice that first ran in the *Otsego Herald* toward the end of the month. Judging from its description of the animal and the saddle, both may not have been especially valuable:

20 *Dollars Reward,*
Will be given to any person who will return a HORSE, which was stolen from the stable of the subscriber, on the 19th inst., and marked as follows: two white hind feet—mare-headed—has been nicked, but carries a bad tail—a little lame in one of his fore feet—good trotter—lively good eye—about fifteen hands high—bright bay color—has been hogged, but his mane now half grown. There was taken at the same time a common saddle and bridle, the latter having a piece of untanned skin, with the hair out, upon the head-stall.
JAMES COOPER.
Cooperstown, January 24, 1815.[26]

A month to the day after this reward notice first appeared, another of Cooper's outbuildings was broken into, although on this occasion nothing was reported missing. Brother Isaac, whose diary took no notice of the first episode, suggested by the way he recorded the second ("James C's barn plundered last night—sharp times") that the motive of the returning malefactor was something more than unlawful gain.[27] These were acts of effrontery as much as theft pure and simple. Once public notice of the original crime was given and a reward for the horse's return was set, the perpetrator had come back to rummage through the barn, asserting that he could meddle at will with his victim's property. The man in question, an impoverished farmer from the town of Burlington named Dan Chapin, indeed had an axe to grind. Fifty years old, standing about five foot nine, and having "a dark sallow complexion," as a newspaper described him that June, Chapin recently had become "addicted to intemperance." If, as Alan Taylor asserts, Chapin indeed had "bought land from Judge William Cooper" on moving to Otsego from Massachusetts years before, but had lost it and subsequently became one of the family's tenants, resentment may have fueled his attacks.[28]

Isaac Cooper became involved in the case because, a few days before the second incident, he had dispatched his youngest brother to New York City on fresh business related to the estate. In Cooper's absence, Isaac may have discovered the assault on the barn at Fenimore, or at least been called upon to deal with it by Susan, then four months pregnant with her third child. And, since Isaac's diary does not show his brother returning "from New York" until March 6, Isaac probably kept tabs on the case in the interim. Cooper probably *was* at home and could act on his own behalf when Dan Chapin, as if tied by some fatality to Fenimore Farm, returned to the stable one last time, making off on May 26 with a second, more valuable horse. Isaac's aid also was needed, however, when Chapin was identified and tracked down after the middle of June. Just then, Cooper was bound with his brother Samuel to Heathcote Hill, where they were to pick up Susan's mother so that she could help with the delivery of Susan's baby, due sometime around the third week of that month. As the birth neared, Susan evidently found the distance separating her from her mother a worrying fact.[29]

In the meantime, Dan Chapin was giving any number of people, including Isaac Cooper, a run for their money. He was taken up near Albany early in June on suspicion that the horse he was riding had been stolen. Lacking conclusive proof, the authorities there had no recourse but to let him go after a cursory examination. When word of his apprehension and a description of the horse reached Cooperstown on June 10 or 11, however, it seemed likely to the Coopers and probably to the sheriff that Chapin was the culprit who had broken into James's stable on May 26 and that the horse he was riding was the one stolen then. As a result, harness and saddle maker Roger Haskell (having been deputized by Otsego sheriff James Hawks) was dispatched from the village with a warrant charging Chapin in the theft of Cooper's second horse. Since it was suspected that the man was heading back toward Otsego County, Haskell probably was not surprised to encounter him in Cherry Valley on Sunday evening, June 12. He promptly arrested Chapin and the two spent the night there. The *Otsego Herald* soon reported the rest of the story: "On Monday [Haskell] proceeded with him, till within about four miles of this village, when Chapin (both being on horseback, and he not being bound) gave Haskell a sudden blow with a stick across his face, dismounted immediately, took his portmanteau on his shoulder, and ran for the woods, which he made shift to gain; but owing to the close pursuit of Mr. Haskell, was forced to drop his portmanteau, after which he eluded pursuit." After Chapin escaped in Middlefield, the paper went on, "[a] number of citizens immediately rallied, and have since been in search of him," though by the time this issue of the *Herald* went to press he had not been retaken. The fugitive's abandoned "bay horse," which remained in custody, proved not to be Cooper's, although the saddle definitely was. Roger Haskell was an excellent judge of both, having sold Cooper new tack only that March and having performed many repairs for him the previous year and over the coming summer. Aided by Haskell's knowledge, the authorities concluded that the fugitive's close call in the Hudson valley had led him to change horses—no doubt feloniously—somewhere on his route back to Otsego. The animal now in custody was held so that its rightful owner could claim it. As to Chapin, on the fifteenth

Haskell prepared a reward notice for insertion into the *Herald*. It offered $150 for apprehending the thief and lodging him in the county jail.[30]

Isaac Cooper interested himself keenly in these doings, which clearly sent a small shock wave through the usually calm countryside. For one thing, he knew Chapin all too well, even though he curiously never named the "thief" in his diary. And it was Isaac rather than James who appears to have handled most of the trouble the fugitive had been causing. "Horse thief eloped—all the world after him," anticipated Isaac's diary entry for June 12, which he apparently completed on the thirteenth, when Chapin actually escaped and Isaac was among those rallying citizens who went to "Burlington after Horse Thief." Chapin eluded pursuit then, causing Isaac to come home two days later—the day when Roger Haskell's reward notice was written. Three days later still, Isaac noted that the "Horse Thief [was] heard from," but not until four more days had passed could he at last report, "Horse Thief taken." By the end of August, the *Otsego Herald* could finish the story: "*Dan Chapin*, the horse thief, was tried yesterday, by the Court of General Sessions of the Peace of this county, and convicted on two separate indictments. For stealing Mr. Cooper's horse he was sentenced to 7 years imprisonment in the state-prison; and for the other _ years. He had made an attempt to break jail, by taking up a plank in the floor of his prison, and digging underneath, which was discovered by the sheriff yesterday morning. In one or two hours more he would, but for the discovery, have effected his purpose." When Roger Haskell billed Cooper for purchases and repairs at his shop running from December of 1814 up to the month of Chapin's conviction, he added a courteous note at the bottom: "Chasing Dan Chapin: Expenses Ten Dollars Exclusive of time. I wish you to allow what you please." Haskell receipted the bill as paid on November 24, but failed to note the exact consideration Cooper offered.[31]

There the episode presumably ended. Whether Dan Chapin came back in seven years to visit the Cooper family and other members of the local elite with the fires that consumed many structures in the summer of 1823 (see Chapter 12) will probably never be known. But those unsolved cases, as Alan Taylor has argued, do appear to have had a social motive similar to the one traceable in Chapin's thefts eight years earlier. Certainly the 1815 troubles, with their roots in what Isaac Cooper called the "sharp times" on the New York frontier, foreshadowed many changes that were soon to assail most of the family's property. And they may have left a deeper trace on Cooper the artist. "[S]pring had come, like a thief in the night," says his narrator in *Satanstoe* when trapped on the uncertain Hudson River ice by a sudden thaw. The Bible, of course, likens *death* to such a nocturnal visitation—not the return of life on vernal winds. It is tempting to read Cooper's uncanny comparison as a lingering memory from that "plundering" spring of 1815, when on three separate occasions his own peace had been threatened by literal thieves in the night. The point is not weakened by the fact that two "bay horses" belonging to one of the characters in *Satanstoe* are lost to the wild river—nor by the fact that anxiety about social leveling and property is the key thematic motif in the novel (*SAT* CE 242).[32]

Scuffles

Other tensions in Cooperstown at the time of Dan Chapin's thefts, and possibly related to them, were more overtly political. The deeper background in this instance was less murky. In 1807, sometime Federalist turned Republican Farrand Stranahan had had a partisan and very public fight with Judge Cooper in the streets of Cooperstown, a clash so violent that it could well have been a source of the myth about Judge Cooper's "murder" on the steps of the State Capitol in Albany in 1809. In June of 1815, Stranahan's current law partner and fellow Republican Ambrose L. Jordan deprecated Judge Cooper's memory in Cooperstown's new Republican paper, *The Watch-Tower*. Perhaps his verbal attack, of which no copy is known to survive, touched on the old street battle. It certainly stung the Judge's youngest son so sharply that he came to the village looking to whip the offender. Cooper's friend Elihu Phinney, Jr., wrote to his fiancée on June 22, the very day Dan Chapin finally was captured, about the result: "We have had a little Square fighting here in consequence of some pieces published in the Watch Tower & [reprinted in the] C[ooperstown] Federalist, which cast some reflection on the memory of Judge Cooper; this offended James Cooper so much, that notwithstanding his Republicanism, he thought proper to give the Author a genteel Cow-Hiding. This affray happened so near Jordan's House that Mrs. Jordan was very much alarmed &, it is Said Cried Murder. Jordan gave Cooper a pretty clever thump over the head with a loaded Cane & I believe they parted So, So. But I do not like to communicate this kind of news, & had almost resolved not to do it."[33]

Jordan, the novelist's exact contemporary, had arrived in Otsego in 1812, too late to have tangled personally with Judge Cooper. Perhaps he had run afoul of Richard or Isaac in some legal squabble since then, but there is no known record of any such conflict, and in 1815 or soon thereafter he actually was serving as the legal guardian of Richard's children. Nor was Jordan the sort of person who went around looking for trouble; although he was tall and imposing, his personal manner was soft-spoken and unabrasive. Why, therefore, would Jordan have set about, as he clearly did, taunting the youngest of the Cooper children? When his law partner Stranahan and William Cooper had come to blows in 1807, the cause was a fierce partisan competition. Partisanship of that obvious sort was not involved in the 1815 battle. Indeed, Elihu Phinney, himself a staunch Republican, clearly was surprised that two men who shared his own party affiliation should fight at all, let alone as seriously and publicly as they did.

It appears instead that the fight arose from emergent party splits rather than established party labels—and, most immediately, from the notoriously feisty patronage system in New York. Jordan was an ambitious young lawyer who would be appointed county attorney in 1818, serve as a delegate to the state constitutional convention three years later, be sent to the state Senate by a downstate district a decade later, and win election as state attorney general in 1847, years after he had moved his thriving practice to New York City. More to the point, in March 1815, a few weeks before his street fight with the youngest Cooper, Jordan had won appointment to his first office, that of Otsego surrogate. Herein lay the immediate occasion of his argument with Cooper.

The youthful lawyer had snagged that first political prize owing to the influence of his law partner Stranahan in the highly partisan New York Council of Appointment, a body usually presided over but not necessarily controlled by the governor. Stranahan had taken over the council in February with three political allies from the state Senate, where he was then serving. At its initial meeting on March 6, the council on Stranahan's urging abruptly removed DeWitt Clinton from his appointive office as mayor of New York City. This was a controversial move that had repercussions in the state and within the council over the months following. The pro-Clinton press certainly howled about its unfairness. Even Gov. Daniel D. Tompkins, Clinton's sometime ally and future foe, differed with Stranahan when the man first chosen to replace Clinton withdrew from the position in July. Tompkins favored Clinton ally William Paulding over Jacob Radcliff, the brother of one of Stranahan's Senate colleagues and Stranahan's personal favorite for the post. For some days there was a deadlock on the issue. Another council member sided with Tompkins, and a third, relenting the hasty removal of Clinton, "rigidly" held to the view that Clinton should be restored to the mayoralty. Clinton let it be known, however, that he would not accept such an offer, and eventually (although mysteriously) Stranahan had his way—Jacob Radcliff was named.

Radcliff was not an entire unknown. He also had been appointed mayor in 1810 when an earlier council, equally inimical to Clinton, stripped the latter of the post. Radcliff in turn was removed the next year when the resurgent Clinton finessed his own reappointment. These jockeyings make it clear that Radcliff had a history in this particular partisan fight; surely his elevation by the council in 1815 was intended not only to replace Clinton (or his short-term successor) but also to remind Clinton of previously unpleasant fights in Albany. The naming of William Paulding would have been less of a slap, but Stranahan's game was punishment rather than reconciliation. Following the present episode, Clinton had only one remaining grasp on the public business, a seat on the relatively minor canal commission, but he would famously remake himself—and the state—by his dogged pursuit of the old, largely stalled idea of a canal linking New York City with the Great Lakes. He was out, but hardly down. He would become governor in 1817 and thereafter rewrite the state's history.

The protracted fight over Clinton's replacement in 1815 seems to have been the culmination of internal struggles in the council that began almost as soon as he was dismissed in March. In April, Surrogate Ambrose Jordan was under consideration for a commission in the Otsego County militia, but this time came in second to fellow resident James Cooper. Perhaps Cooper's military experience (Jordan had none) made it hard for the council to overlook his superior qualifications. In any case, Cooper was named captain of a company in the Second Regiment of Otsego light infantry, with Jordan as his lieutenant. This pairing was not a happy one because of previous antagonisms between the two or the rivalry that was then playing itself out in the council, or both. Apparently Jordan and his superior soon clashed, after which the lawyer issued his fulminations against Cooper's father. Then came the street battle. The upshot was that Cooper, obviously unwilling to command a unit in which his subordinate already had dishonored him, resigned his position, after which the council promptly promoted Jordan in his place.

Unless copies of the offending publications turn up, we probably will never know exactly what the insults were. Perhaps Jordan taunted Cooper with the old victory of Stranahan over his father as a means of debunking Cooper's little victory in the militia business. But, given the exact coincidence in the timing of horse thief Chapin's arrest and Elihu Phinney's letter, one may also suspect that the recent humiliation of Judge Cooper's son by Chapin's bold misdeeds somehow figured in the newspaper attacks and therefore in the fight. Did Jordan suggest that Chapin, owing to rumored mistreatment at the hands of Cooper's father, had some motive for his attacks at Fenimore Farm? If so, that probably would have been enough to send Cooper out into the street in search of the lawyer. As to the shared Republicanism noted by Phinney, it may also be significant of how things already stood in 1815 that five years later Cooper would work for Clinton in the gubernatorial race while Jordan led Clinton's opponents, the "Bucktail" Republicans, to victory in Otsego County.[34]

Whatever the cause, Cooper apparently was not seriously injured by the "thumping" received at Jordan's hands. In this year of unfortunate tumults, that was at least something. The same could not be said for Isaac, Cooper's usually lucky brother. Always outgoing and sociable, Isaac had taken part in a July 4 party on the lake, then picnicked at Myrtle Grove on July 20 and August 2, perhaps with the inhabitants of Fenimore Farm. He certainly saw the Coopers on August 12, when he dined at their place, a couple of days before heading off with his wife Mary Ann and their children (and, surprisingly, his usually immovable mother) to visit Mary Ann's family in Butternuts. While there, Isaac engaged in a playful wrestling match—one of many over the years—with brother-in-law Richard Morris. Accidentally thrown against a railing on the piazza at the Morris house, he hurt his spine seriously enough that he began a long though not steady decline.[35]

The severity of Isaac's injury is indicated by his virtually complete absence from Fenimore thereafter. Isaac had been a frequent visitor at the farm since 1813, but from this point to his death on January 1, 1818, he would visit there only once or twice.[36] Isaac was "very warm-hearted and affectionate, and very benevolent," the novelist's daughter Susan recalled, drawing partly on her own observation but partly on stories her parents told her in later years. Isaac in fact was the only one of her three surviving Cooper uncles of whom Susan retained any personal recollection, even though Samuel was also in Cooperstown throughout this same period. Her warm memory almost certainly derived from early in the summer of 1815, when she was just old enough to begin retaining such things and her uncle had not yet been injured. "I remember him distinctly on one occasion," she wrote, "when he was dining at the farm-house; he took me up in his arms and wanted me to kiss him; but I was shy about it." The girl's father, obviously amused, remarked, "This young lady does not kiss gentlemen!" Mrs. Cooper, her daughter also recalled, "was much attached" to Isaac (SFM 13). Given William's unreliability and Samuel's oddity, Isaac was the last of the Cooper uncles who could help stabilize—and briefly, before his own demise, lighten—the world at Fenimore. That he owed his decline to a friendly scuffle in the summer of 1815, while his youngest brother escaped a serious affray that same season with no long-term effects, was one of the year's ironies.

Isaac Cooper's spirits hardly plummeted after his injury. Toward the end of September, he was well enough that he and his wife Mary Ann accompanied "James & Co." to Cherry Valley, tarrying overnight and then returning. The younger couple apparently went on from there to Westchester for an extended visit with Susan's family that would give them a break from the tumults of the past few months, as well as soothe Susan's deepening sense of separation from her family downstate.[37] Thanks to the anxieties raised by the depredations of Dan Chapin, Isaac was to keep an eye on things at Fenimore during their absence, at least if his condition permitted him to. In a mock-heroic vein that bespoke his still jaunty outlook, Isaac wrote the farm's master in October 1815 to narrate a tragedy that had befallen yet another animal at the place. This was Sinbad, the merino buck that Cooper had brought up from Closet Hall two years earlier. Ever mindful of his brother's love of the sea, Isaac converted the agricultural tale into a marine misadventure by means of a witty pun: "*Sinbad* the Marino," he announced, "is no more. He made a leap of sixty feet, but then lunging up, snap[p]ed the cable of his life. He run upon the rocks and beat to pieces. In other words he tumble[d] in your deep well, where he was found a few days since—perhaps you may want another therefore I communicate this to you."[38]

Sinbad's owner did not rush back to Otsego on receiving this animal fable from Isaac around the middle of October. But in November Cooper—almost certainly by himself—did briefly return to Cooperstown. Apparently staying at Fenimore, he visited Isaac and Mary Ann at Edgewater on November 22, handled some business arrangements with Uncle James's son Courtland (on which more in a moment), and then by December 11 had gone back to Westchester.[39] Obviously wishing to make the most of his agricultural operations in Otsego, he stopped in Albany on the way to leave instructions there about a shipment of wool recently shorn from his flocks and soon bound to market. Then he went on downstate, pausing at Heathcote Hill but soon shifting to New York City, where he and Susan, perhaps eager for a break from the many challenges upstate, had taken up rented quarters at 10 Cedar Street by the middle of January. The couple planned on staying there for much of the winter, while their children remained with the DeLanceys at Heathcote Hill, which the couple probably visited frequently.[40]

The concern with maximizing the proceeds from his sheep operation was matched by Cooper's rising interest in other possible sources of income during this challenging period after the division of DeKalb. His brother-in-law Thomas DeLancey, who had been charged with overseeing cordwood production at the Hickory Grove (also called "the Hickories"—the farm Susan had inherited from her aunt Susannah the previous year), sent word to Cedar Street about the project.[41] The couple even expected that Fenimore Farm would contribute something to their mounting expenses during their absence, largely through the efforts of its resident manager at the time—Cooper's slightly younger first cousin, Courtland Comly Cooper (1793–1857). Cooper knew Courtland well from the years that his Uncle James's family had spent in Otsego early in the century, and from 1815 on he came to rely on Courtland much as Judge Cooper and the older sons had relied on Courtland's father. Most recently, Courtland had lived with his parents in DeKalb, where Uncle James was running the mills built by Judge Cooper on the Oswegatchie River and seeing to other occasional matters for William's sons—as well as managing his own 150-acre farm a mile from the mills.[42] Probably at his cousin's request, Courtland had arrived in Cooperstown sometime in the fall to take on a variety of increasingly important chores. After New Year's, he traveled to DeKalb and the more distant town of Bangor in Franklin County, partly to visit his family, partly on business for Cooper, a mix that was typical of the cousins' initial dealings. When he returned to Otsego on January 26 to find a now-unlocated letter from Cooper waiting for him at Isaac's house, Courtland thus replied with family and village gossip before he got around to reporting on his northern errand.[43]

Mostly he had gone to the St. Lawrence district to collect rent ("chiefly in pork") from some of his cousin's tenants in Bangor. On his return to Otsego, he turned his attention to Fenimore Farm, where nothing fell below his notice. The "sheep and cattle," he reported, were looking good; although one horse was lame and another was still recovering from an old wound, Cooper's "large mare" was strong enough that Courtland had taken the liberty of riding it all the way to Bangor on his recent trip, probably without his cousin's prior knowledge. Courtland's report on such things may have reflected his desire to impress his cousin, as he put it in this letter, that everything at Fenimore would be "thoroughly attended to" while its owner remained absent. The relations between the two having only recently taken on a markedly economic character, Courtland was understandably eager to demonstrate that he was equal to the responsibilities vested in him. But we probably should also assume that such detailed reportage reflected Cooper's own interest in these matters. Surely he would have kept checking on things had he been in Otsego for the winter; he may even have given Courtland detailed instructions about the kinds of things he should report on. Wouldn't he want to know that construction of the stone mansion was on-going—that even in January the workmen had been hauling "brick stone and Boards"? Courtland promised more news about Otsego affairs, although only this one letter survives from his supervisory work during the winter of 1815–1816. Others may have gone astray.[44]

Cooper paid a brief visit to Cooperstown in the early spring of 1816 (Isaac's diary recorded his arrival on April 6 and departure on April 13), then returned to Heathcote Hill, where he and Susan and the girls were happily reunited again. His location downstate made it difficult to tend to some Otsego matters without such hurried returns. On the other hand, the winter in New York also had made it easier for him to handle other matters. Probably during his recent Otsego visit, Cooper thus had learned that the local Bible society was preparing to pick representatives for a national meeting of local Bible societies scheduled for New York in May. The Otsego organization, founded in the village schoolhouse on March 7, 1813 (as it happened, the night before news of Richard Fenimore Cooper's death reached Cooperstown), had seen Otsego's Presbyterians and Episcopalians join forces to promote the free distribution of Bibles among the county's poor. Its original members had included Gen. Jacob Morris, Rev. John Smith, printer and publisher John H. Prentiss, and Isaac Cooper and George

Pomeroy. Although the master of Fenimore Farm had been in Cooperstown at the time, he was not listed as among the founders. By 1816, however, he had become such an active member that Smith in a letter of April 26 called him "the parent" of the organization. Smith may have been buttering Cooper up a bit at that time, since the Otsego Bible Society had just met and named Cooper—along with two local Presbyterian ministers, both long active in the society—as its representatives for the national gathering the following month. Smith, pleading the poverty of the Otsego organization, urged Cooper to make the short trip from Mamaroneck to New York City on its behalf. Cooper's absence from Otsego thus could provide a chance to demonstrate his attachment to the society.[45]

The New York meeting, held on May 8 in City Hall, attracted an array of delegates from several states, including such celebrated New Yorkers as DeWitt Clinton and the philanthropist Henry Rutgers. By July the Otsego society had become an auxiliary of the new national organization, the American Bible Society, or ABS, which began to issue the first of its Bibles later in the year. The elite founding rosters of both organizations suggest the truth in Alan Taylor's assertion that such bodies were "private associations of wealthy men out to reshape public thought and behavior." But it is also worth noting that the American Bible Society's insistence on distributing plain text Bibles evinced a trust in the ability of common readers to navigate the sometimes rough waters of sacred text on their own. The first article of the national society's constitution as drafted in May of 1816 by Cooper and the forty-seven other delegates proclaimed its key goal to be encouraging "the wider circulation of the Holy Scriptures without note or comment." This was a profoundly democratic principle. If social control of the masses in the new market culture of the postwar years was one of the unstated motives, it was a motive implemented through innovatively open means.[46]

The growing involvement of Cooper in religious matters in Otsego had begun to show itself when he was elected a vestryman of Christ Church in 1814, the year after his first daughter's death. The following year he was named the parish delegate to the diocesan convention, held in New York City each October. As with the county Bible society, however, at that time he was able to serve another Otsego institution only because he was then far away from Cooperstown.[47] The same was true when, some time after his attendance at the 1816 ABS convention, he was delegated to order a bell for Christ Church. He forthwith contacted a pair of Albany merchants with whom he then was conducting considerable business, and in turn a bell (and cannon) maker operating near the federal arsenal north of Albany. That man had no suitable bells on hand, but promised to "cast a bell of the size Mr. Cooper may direct, warrant[ing] it not to break in one year with common good usage." Apparently the absent agent followed through for the church, although by the time the bell arrived sometime in 1817

Cooper seems to have left the area for what would prove an even longer absence. It tolled for him—tolled his farewell.[48]

Last Stand in Otsego

Susan Cooper's discontent with Otsego had been in evidence ever since the family arrived there: her 1814 visit to Heathcote Hill, her relish for the frequent visits of her relatives and friends at Fenimore Farm, not to mention the recent months she and her husband had spent in Westchester and nearby New York City, grew in part from that source. Still, when the couple returned to Cooperstown in the summer of 1816 they apparently intended to finish their stone mansion and settle down for good.[49] The new house, on which Courtland had sent his brief report in January, had been proceeding only slowly since its start in 1814. Now, with a good deal of material on hand, the walls went up to their full height across the spring and into summer. The workmen progressed rapidly enough that joists and floorboards could be put in place on the first story by June, on the second story by July, and in the garret the following month. In November, the roof was raised and shingled. After that, however, work on the building virtually ceased. With the stone walls and partitions up and the building enclosed, weather should not have been a factor in the suspension. It may instead be one of the first indications that the Coopers were considering a radical change of plans—or that the increasingly evident shortage of funds had become severe.[50] By the end of 1816, the house, most of its windows probably installed, must have looked substantially done on the outside. Closer inspection, however, would have shown that many of the finish items, although on-site, still were being stored inside the shell, where they yet remained when fire gutted the building six-and-a-half years later.[51]

Across that summer and into the fall, to be sure, the Coopers had carried on a lively social life at the farm. There were positively frivolous events, like the "tea party of young Ladys at Fenemore" on July 27. Presumably the "young Ladys" in attendance were Sue, who was three-and-a-half, her year-old sister Caroline, and Isaac and Mary Ann Cooper's five older daughters: Mary, Elizabeth, Sarah, Ann, and Catherine (as well as, perhaps, Ann Pomeroy's daughters Georgiana and Hannah). There was to be another such event at Fenimore in November. And Mary Ann Cooper, perhaps with her stair-step daughters in tow, visited the farm three more times for tea before the year was out.[52] Early on, her husband Isaac apparently was not well enough to travel even the short distance from Edgewater up to Fenimore. Come fall, however, and then winter, he at last was able to stir. By New Year's of 1817 he was mobile enough to attend a ball at a village hotel, perhaps with his brother and sister-in-law. Soon after that, prob-

ably while at Fenimore, Isaac likewise enjoyed the "fine skating" on Lake Otsego, completely frozen over ("except for an air O"—that is, *air hole*—"5 miles
up") as the temperature sunk to zero and below.[53]

The cheerful surface of things across the end of 1816 and the beginning of
1817 was to prove as fleeting as that icy surface of the lake. The breakup came as
problems continued to emerge with Judge Cooper's estate and his youngest son
was called on to help deal with them in addition to his own difficulties. His new
responsibilities were reflected in the more active role Cooper's cousin Courtland
began to play in helping manage his (and the family's) financial affairs. The two
had interacted frequently and directly on a variety of things going back to the
winter of 1815–1816, when Cooper and his wife were staying downstate. From
the time of Cooper's brief visit to Cooperstown the following April, Courtland
had kept busy with his cousin's affairs there, spending and receiving small
amounts of cash until early August, when the Coopers took up residence at Fenimore Farm again and the cousins settled their accounts.[54]

At that point, Courtland began to take on more demanding tasks related to
the Cooper estate. While Cooper was inquiring in Albany about the bell for
Christ Church, for instance, his cousin undertook a brief errand for him to
Broome County. There, on the south side of the Susquehanna River opposite the
village of Binghamton (or Chenango Point), William Cooper had once attempted
to develop his grandiloquent "Manor of Feronia." On August 31, 1816, the
Broome County sheriff turned over to Courtland $1,200 in Philadelphia bank-
notes, apparently the proceeds from a sale of lands on which one of the original
purchasers in Feronia had long since defaulted.[55] In all likelihood, the sheriff's
sale had been arranged by another Cooper family agent, Binghamton lawyer
Mason Whiting, who recently had been going after delinquent tenants, as well as
selling wild land or defaulted properties and "standing centinel" (as he named the
task) so that timber thieves did not level the estate's woodlands and send them
floating downriver to market, then a common problem on borderlands.[56]

Feronia was thinly populated and unpromising even in the more prosperous
years after the end of hostilities in 1815. Andrew Sherburne, a Revolutionary
War veteran and Baptist preacher who served as a missionary in the Chenango
Point area during the summer of 1817, reported that he often passed "five, ten
and sometimes fifteen miles or more, without seeing a single human dwelling, in
a dark woods and muddy road."[57] The accounts of Feronia that Mason Whiting
sent to the Coopers bore little but bad news. He reported, for instance, that a surveyor sent out by Isaac Cooper in 1815 had discovered that the original survey
commissioned by Judge Cooper was seriously defective, being too generous in
some areas and too skimpy elsewhere. Barely three months later, a landowner
wrote Isaac Cooper complaining that his tract had been reduced from one thou-

sand to a mere six hundred acres because of the resurvey. The man had paid or was paying for four hundred more acres than Judge Cooper's original deed conveyed. Who would reimburse him for the money paid out for suddenly nonexistent real estate?[58]

That was an ironic outcome, because the apparent purpose of the 1815 resurvey was to ready foreclosed properties and wild lands for hopefully lucrative sale. The Coopers first turned toward Feronia right after dividing DeKalb in May of the same year. This was hardly a mere coincidence, since sorting out the DeKalb mess had made the family liable for reimbursing the New York partners (as the latter thought) for all sums ever paid into the Cooper coffers on St. Lawrence County lots only now assigned to the partners individually. Where had all that money gone? Such a question had no real answer at present. But with the war's end, the Cooper brothers probably dreamed that frontier land sales would again heat up and that Feronia might become a source of cash to tide them over this very rough spot. Over the next two years, foreclosure sales such as those for which the sheriff paid Courtland that $1,200 in August of 1816 therefore were pushed forward as the family sought to entice new, cash-paying buyers into the inactive market there.[59]

Cooper became involved in the Chenango properties in his own person as well as by sending Courtland downriver on behalf of the estate. In January of 1817, he traveled to Binghamton with an English friend, James Aitchison. The two went there via an indirect route through Butternuts, at least in part for pleasure, and during the trip no doubt deepened the personal ties to which Cooper would pay tribute in dedicating his second book, *The Spy*, to Aitchison. Whatever diversions occupied the travelers, though, the main purpose of the trip was linked to Mason Whiting and his effort to pick some profit from the bones of Feronia.[60] Cooper returned to Binghamton four months later. He waited until Susan, pregnant with their fourth child, gave birth to Anne Charlotte (named for Susan's English sister) on May 14, 1817.[61] In preparation for this second trip, he conferred with Isaac, although in the sequel it was clear that the two did not see eye-to-eye about the business in hand, in which the different heirs by now may have developed distinct interests. Then he went off by himself, probably on horseback. He made good enough progress that by May 19 he was at Chenango Point, where he wrote out instructions for Mason Whiting, apparently absent at the moment. The lawyer, now appointed the brothers' official agent in their loosely coordinated efforts, was told he could offer exceptionally lenient terms to new purchasers of family holdings in Feronia: "You are requested to assume the Agency of the Lands of my Family in this vicinity and as the present situation of the Estate will not admit of a general Power of Attorney we beg you will consider this a letter of instructions for your government in the management of this property—You are authorized to sell any of the Lots at such prices as you can obtain[,] taking care however to make them average four Dollars a piece per acre[.] [Y]ou can give any credit not exceeding Ten years and you are permitted to allow the three first years to go on without Interest." The terms as Cooper articulated them were perhaps more liberal than the brothers had agreed. Isaac, when he received a copy of the letter, wrote on the back, "I do not agree to the delay of interest."[62]

Whiting himself wrote inquiringly to Isaac as late as November, "I assume these directions were intended to apply only to the unimproved lots, but that as to the improved lots, interest would be expected from the time of taking possession." In fact, however, not even these terms, whatever construction one might put on the intent Cooper had in penning them, were effective. Whiting's inquiry that fall came in his most disheartening letter to the family: "The Manor of Feronia yields no money," he wrote. "The settlers have principally left it." To be sure, once he had supervised the next round of foreclosure sales scheduled for early in December in Binghamton, he said he would work toward getting new settlers to take the place of old ones. He hoped that the effort to persuade the state legislature "to revive & amend the act for making the road from [Binghamton] thro the patent to [the] Pennsylvania line" would solve access problems preacher Andrew Sherburne encountered this very year. The Cooper family, which already had pledged $1,200 toward opening the road, obviously shared Whiting's hopes. But the real need was for settlers willing to put their signatures on mortgages—and their hands and bodies to work on the land. Neither Cooper's theoretical generosity with family property nor Mason Whiting's diligence in pursuing defaulters would salvage the venture, or the family, from the collapse that loomed.[63]

Nor would the behavior of young William Cooper. Ironically, as the one surviving member of the family trained in the law, William might have been of great use to his siblings and in-laws and nieces and nephews as the collapse of the Judge's fortune accelerated. But William had more severe troubles of his own that dated in part from an ill-fated venture on Lake Ontario during the war. Having relocated temporarily to Oswego as a merchant, in 1813 William agreed with the navy to undertake the construction of an enormous "ark," a raftlike vessel vaguely resembling the barges commonly used on the Susquehanna River in the early years. The craft is hard to even imagine: it was a rough-hewn octagon some fifty or sixty feet across and rising four or five feet above the water; one description portrayed it as "looking like a big, low, half-submerged log house" (it was thus like a hybrid between Tom Hutter's two homes in *The Deerslayer:* "Muskrat Castle," the log fortress built over the sunken island on Glimmerglass, and the floating "Ark"). William's expenditure on his project was huge, more than $5,000. The navy had promised to purchase "Cooper's Ark" for more than three times that amount once it had been floated from Oswego to Sacketts Harbor for use as a gun platform. It left Oswego around the beginning of July 1813 with a crew of fifteen but soon broke up on the lake, resulting in deaths and serious injuries among the crew. Word of the disaster arrived in Cooperstown just after William Cooper's youngest brother relocated his family there, when the *Otsego Herald* ran a terse report.[64]

The estate accounts do not show any sizable disbursement to cover William's Oswego debt. Apparently he took it upon himself to settle the matter in 1816, when his situation may have been worsened by new "Embarrassments." The latter term was used in a letter sent to Isaac in February 1817 by the young Massachusetts-born lawyer Luther Bradish. Because of the bleak situation in which William found himself in 1816, he had conveyed to Bradish an array of property in exchange for several thousand dollars in much-needed cash. The transfer included "His Tyler Bond & Mrtge., His Bangor[,] and Three fourths of his De Kalb Estates," Bradish's letter stated. The first of these items had been valued at almost $4,000 when it was assigned to William in 1815, while the latter two together were estimated at almost $23,000. Although the value of the St. Lawrence properties reflected the inflated figures insisted on by Judge Cooper's will, the overall size of the transfer suggests that William's difficulties had multiplied since his ark's sinking. Bradish seems to have provided the first word that Isaac and the other heirs heard of the transfer. Although William had indeed received a large share of DeKalb properties in 1815, later lists of holdings in that region were to omit any mention of the Judge's namesake.[65]

William's precipitate arrangement with Bradish, meant to stave off his own disaster, threw the family at large into a new crisis. He had transferred to Bradish not only his title to the lands in question, but, crucially, all monies ever received on them. Bradish therefore now owned a claim for considerable cash against the Cooper estate. Presumably William knew that Isaac did not have sufficient means to cover this claim, but he clearly did not care how much pressure he was placing on the rest of the family as he scrambled to save himself. Bradish at least was accommodating. He offered to reconvey William's property to the family in exchange for his purchase price: $7,100 for the DeKalb and Bangor properties combined, as the conveyances indicate, plus interest. Bradish wanted a speedy answer, however, and if his offer was refused, he asked that the bearer of his letter be given all papers relating to the transferred lands. More ominous still, he asked for an accounting of all monies that had been received to date on those properties, along with an indication of where those monies were.[66] Because the New York partners were asking for the same kind of accounting at the same time, and cash just then was especially scarce in the country, this new demand added to the grim difficulties besetting Isaac.

Isaac found Bradish's proposition "very friendly" in March but sought a delay with a contingent promise: "Brother James will be with you as soon as the river opens and communicate with you on the subject."[67] Then he stalled. Not until June, when Isaac was similarly trying to buy time from one of the New York partners, Frederick DePeyster, who was demanding a payment, did Cooper make the New York trip. Isaac promised DePeyster that his brother would carry the required money, but Cooper was very busy with his own purposes by then and there is no indication that he did so. Nor, despite the fact that by then the ice had long been out of the Hudson, is there any evidence that the business with Bradish was resolved or even moved forward at the time.[68]

Improvements

It is doubtless ironic that, even as the Judge's estate started a collapse that before long would leave Cooper without Fenimore Farm and Mt. Ovis, he joined with neighboring landholders and public figures to organize the Otsego County Agricultural Society (OCAS). Their inspiration was the movement begun in the Northeast by Elkanah Watson, the Albany "improver" and successful merchant who had established a model farm in western Massachusetts in the summer of 1807. Having introduced the first pair of merino sheep into the Berkshires that fall, Watson called together local farmers to view his animals. The turnout was so large that in 1810 he arranged for an exhibition of other livestock, and the next year, under a state charter, the "fair" became a permanent celebration of agricultural advances. While the roots of agricultural improvement in the United States were multiple, the influence of the Berkshire association spread rapidly, in part because of Watson's links to the merino craze.[69] Even before Cooper moved his family to Cooperstown in 1813, he had been experimenting with merinos. He also had transported a good part of his livestock operation with him to Otsego, choosing to live on the sizable acreage of Fenimore Farm rather than—like the Judge's other children—in the village proper. Hence he was well positioned by experience and temperament to take a leading role in the establishment of an agricultural society in Otsego County.

Discussion about organizing such a body began late in 1816. A doubtless small group signing itself "MANY" ran an announcement in the *Otsego Herald* shortly before Christmas: "A meeting of the Farmers, and others, friendly to the establishment of an *Agricultural Society* in the County of Otsego, is requested at the [Hotel] of Col. Francis Henry in Cooperstown on Wednesday the first day of January next, at one o'clock, P.M."[70] New Year's Day suited new efforts, but that was also when the Court of Common Pleas would be sitting in the village. The future author of *The Pioneers* knew well that on such occasions "the highways and wood-paths" would be "thronged with equestrians and footmen, bound to the haven of justice" (*PIO* 2:196). "Most" of the "large number of respectable freeholders" who showed up at the Cooperstown meeting in 1817 "were favorably inclined to the organization and many of them [became] members."[71] So wrote the corresponding secretary chosen at the official meeting of the society held on February 18—Cooper himself. Along with his friend, Rev. John Smith, he had been one of the committee members who arranged for that meeting. The other officers chosen then were men Cooper also knew well: Jacob Morris of Butternuts (president); former sheriff and state assemblyman Arunah Metcalf (first vice president); Matthew Darbyshire, Cooper's tenant at Springhill Farm in Hartwick (second vice president); Elisha Foote, a prominent local Republican official (treasurer); publisher John H. Prentiss (recording secretary); and, among the chairs of standing committees, the well-known French immigrant Judge Stanislas Pascal Franchot, Morris's neighbor in Butternuts.[72]

James Cooper's message "TO THE FREEHOLDERS OF THE COUNTY OF OTSEGO" on behalf of the membership and officers of the new organization, printed in the *Otsego Herald*, explained its purposes and solicited further support. Drawing on his family's ties, he already had distributed circulars to prominent men throughout the county, urging them to enlist new members. These men included Gen. Erastus Crafts of Laurens—supervisor, militia officer, and state assemblyman—whose reply applauded an effort that would stimulate "rivalship and enterprise among the farmers." Because the endorsements of such notables might always backfire for reasons of politics or class, the newspaper address to the "Freeholders" allowed a broader appeal. To judge by Cooper's prose in this earliest of his signed publications, he took his "official duty" seriously. Rightfully assuming that agricultural improvement was an emergent idea, not a dominant one even in the progressive society of the early Republic, he held forth on the positive effect such organizations were having elsewhere. The well-known Pennsylvania Agricultural Society, he pointed out, had "wrought a surprisingly advantageous change in the mode of farming in the elder counties of that state, and opened the most enviable of all mines to the possession of its inhabitants— a certain and ample return for the labor of the husbandman." Cooper thus stressed not only the movement's technical improvements but also its social consequences: "Hundreds of farmers in [Pennsylvania] as well as other states are in the successful practice of modes of husbandry, in the use of labor saving implements, or in the possession of improved breed[s] of cattle, who are ignorant from what source it is, that, under God, they derive those blessings."[73]

It might be argued that such organizations were used by elites as implements of social control and therefore were sorely resented by ordinary farmers. But, as with the American Bible Society's desire to place sacred knowledge directly in the hands of everyday Americans, the movement empowered those who had the savvy to appropriate the new methods to their own ends. Besides, the impetus here was materialistic and altruistic rather than partisan. A farm owner such as Cooper, had he wished only to secure his personal benefit, thereby ensuring that he would remain on the top of local society, might have kept any advanced practices to himself. But Cooper was not interested primarily in his personal benefit. Or, if he was interested in getting ahead, he also realized, as his "Freeholders" address put it, that "unity of action can alone give vigor or extension to experiments in husbandry." A single progressive farmer might run a very impressive operation, but isolated individual exertion hardly could improve general markets within a given geographical area. Local societies could push such economic improvements—and, rooted as they were in specific landscapes that were subject to peculiar conditions of soil and climate, they could help steer individual farmers toward prudent choices of crops, animals, and methods. Historical facts mattered as much as natural ones in understanding a region's potential. Otsego in 1817 was no longer a frontier. It had "passed its infancy," and as the original fertility of its soil declined, more careful efforts must replace the quick and sloppy methods of the first farmers. These guidelines were more fully articulated in an anonymous address to the "Inhabitants of Otsego County" printed in the *Otsego Herald* with the January 9 report of the agricultural society's initial meeting. If such guidelines were kept in mind, its author opined, real benefits might accrue for individual producers. From his family's experience distributing lands to would-be farmers across New York, Cooper knew that a tenant farmer with one hundred ordinary sheep did not have smaller payments to make on his land than one who gradually built up a flock of purebred or mixed merinos, which in the right market might bring far more profit. To be sure, the developer who sold the land to such a progressive farmer might be saved the cost of an ejectment suit and a forced sale if the tenant throve, since that man's success would also indemnify his creditors. But, as someone fully aware of how hard it was for dirt farmers to raise themselves out of debt, Cooper knew that improved methods, crops, and breeds were first of all in the individual farmer's interest. The democratization of knowledge was in itself a profound social good.[74]

If, as some historians argue, leaders of such organizations preached social retreat along with agricultural advance, preferring homespun to store goods, their sermon on that subject may be traced to the very real dangers of the current market revolution threatening so many in the country, poor and rich alike. The newly expansive market enticed petty producers with showy goods, draining away what little cash they had. True to its materialistic focus, the agricultural improvement effort aimed at curing America's economic ills in these difficult years leading up to the Panic of 1819. Many observers shared the view of Cooper and the other leaders of the OCAS that independence from foreign imports and luxury goods was an essential part of economic health. In the words of Elkanah Watson, they felt that "we must buy less—make more—holding CREDIT as the bane and curse of this community—thus, also, holding the lawyers and sheriffs *at defiance.*"[75]

Cooper's role in the founding of the OCAS may well have drawn on his own growing financial woes: sensing the ground suddenly tremble under his feet no doubt gave him sympathy with those for whom its perpetual motions were a continuing worry. The irony in all of this was sharp, as it also was in another aspect of Cooper's involvement in such efforts, namely, the way his activism helped root him in Otsego society precisely at a time when his economic worries were threatening to uproot him from Fenimore Farm. The OCAS, like the Otsego County Bible Society or Christ Church, helped him forge new alliances with people from all over his home region. Through his father and brothers, to be sure, he already knew many of the men who became officers and members of the OCAS. But in 1817 he was putting himself forward on his own terms—as the master of Fenimore Farm and Mt. Ovis, however temporary his tenure there might prove, not just as Judge William Cooper's son. For the first time, he also was standing forth in local events without an older brother or two leading the way. That was in part because the OCAS highlighted issues of rural life and industry that the youngest Cooper cared about personally as his Otsego kin (including his village-dwelling father during the county's formative years) did not. Later, after leaving Otsego and returning to Westchester, Cooper was to remain equally involved in agriculture and agricultural improvement. Moreover, the skills he had honed in the OCAS were to prove of more general use as well. In Westchester and then in New York City, he was to show himself an adept organizer of other similar associations that had no direct tie to rural issues.

Cooper's activity on behalf of the OCAS went beyond what one can track in the public press. Although we cannot be sure that the dinner party the Coopers held at Fenimore on December 5, 1816, was a gathering where the "MANY" could tentatively articulate the call they were to issue in public only a week later, that does seem like a plausible reading of the event. And the entertainment of Jacob Morris (and Isaac Cooper) for dinner at the farm five weeks later, on January 9, surely had to do with the organizing committee's desire to interest Morris in serving as the society's first president. Either to confirm Morris's willingness or to counter his opposition, Cooper purposefully passed through Butternuts on that journey to Binghamton with James Aitchison eleven days later, whatever other functions the trip may have served.[76] When, in February, Cooper wrote Morris with news of the board's official choice of him, the general replied as if he knew the decision was coming. Cooper wrote him again on March 13 to announce the next meeting of the officers of the society, set for Saturday, March 22, at Colonel Henry's. In his reply to this message, Morris told Cooper he was coming and would bring Pascal Franchot with him.[77] That added information is pretty good evidence that Cooper had informed the Butternuts duo that Franchot was being spoken of, probably indeed by Cooper himself, as a likely candidate for chair of one of the standing committees. Cooper busily traveled around on other OCAS business at this time as well. When Morris and Franchot showed up for the March 22 meeting, they thus heard "Mr. Cooper [make] a report of an interview had by Mr. Arunah Metcalf and himself with the Officers of the Springfield Agricultural Society." Seeking to found their own rival organization at the north end of the lake, those "Officers" had assured Metcalf and Cooper that they "were favorably inclined to a union" with the Otsego body. It certainly was an issue on which the two Otsego representatives had lobbied them at the time.[78]

A great deal of overserious fanfare was involved in the effort. In responding to Cooper's March 13 letter, Jacob Morris thus addressed the Judge's youngest son as "James Cooper Esquire / Correspond[in]g Secretary of / the O. C. Agricultural Society / Fenimore / Cooperstown." This sounded impressive enough to the village postmaster, Lawrence McNamee, that he added his own supererogatory message to the envelope before sending it off forthwith to Cooper's "Seat" (as Morris had called it on the address flap of his previous letter): "Mr. McNamee / is pleased to cause / this to be del[ivere]d / without delay"—an unusual step at a time when mail typically was held at local post offices until called for.[79] All of the to-do reflected Cooper's temporary success in knitting himself into the life of the place. To people beyond the immediate area, to be sure, the society and Cooper's involvement in it seemed quaintly provincial. Cooper's brother-in-law Thomas DeLancey chided him in April, suggesting that he appoint a deputy to do the actual secretarial work of his august position. Not only would such an appointment ease Cooper's no doubt burdensome work, it also might make life easier for those to whom the secretary wrote, since Cooper's handwriting, as Thomas suggested, was a downright puzzle. If Cooper did *not* want to take on an assistant, Thomas further advised that he give up the Roman alphabet, which he could so effortlessly mangle, and instead "write in hyerglyphics [*sic*] & employ hogs sheep cows &c &c as your symbols[,] which may by your agricultural brethren be more easily decyphered than your present scroll." The last misspelling probably was part of the joke, since *scroll* was just the sort of misconstruction into which Cooper's *scrawl* often betrayed those who tried to decode his writings, as Thomas knew all too well and as many a future typesetter would discover. The accurate slam on Cooper's handwriting was also, however, something of a satire on the whole "improvement" venture. Hence

Thomas suggested as well that Cooper, who had been deputed by the society board to "procure a seal and badges" for the group, also invent a proper coat of arms for his own new position. He himself imagined several components: "A cow rampant on the side of a hay stack with a sow & pigs couchant on the opposite side[—]Motto[,] Pecus et Porcus [i.e., "Cattle and Swine"] or if you prefer it[,] A milk maid volant [i.e., flying] through a cow yard and a boy passant with a pair of swill pails. At least however I must insist upon a Latin motto—if it is not possible to procure a Greek or Hebrew one."[80]

Cooper may have shared this quizzical viewpoint even as he threw himself into trying to make the OCAS a success. The group's proponents, probably chief among them Cooper himself, must have seen to it that the *Otsego Herald* soon reprinted from the *Albany Argus*, for instance, Elkanah Watson's address to the Berkshire Agricultural Society the previous fall, the one in which he railed against "CREDIT."[81] And Cooper's interest, as his brother-in-law sensed, had become a seriously assumed responsibility once he was elected to his post on February 18, with a charge to "conduct the correspondence of the society" with individuals and other organizations, and keep an archive of all letters received and sent.[82] When the former Otsego resident began *The Pioneers* with a maplike description of the county, he was seeing it with the inner eye of the onetime Corresponding Secretary who was peculiarly aware of the county's geographical presence and extent, its "mountains . . . generally arable to the tops," and its "vales, . . . narrow, rich, and cultivated." His novel likewise repeated the society's official view that the "expedients of the pioneers who first broke ground in the settlement of this country" eventually had to yield before "the permanent improvements of the yeoman" (*PIO* 1:1–2). Here, too, was part of his education for his future career.

Cooper took to OCAS business with considerable relish, all the more so perhaps because it allowed him to occupy an ideal agricultural landscape where foreclosure and bad surveys rarely were noticed. Although these were busy months for him, he went out of his way to attend board meetings or oversee other matters. When scheduling his second trip to Binghamton in May 1817, he thus worked around the date of the board's June 3 meeting, ensuring his availability. Furthermore, even though Susan was still recovering from childbirth during the latter month, he recruited Isaac to help him entertain several visitors, at least some of whom probably were in town for the June 3 meeting. The latter included Col. Volckert P. Van Rensselaer of Butternuts, friend and former business partner of Pascal Franchot and a society member; a Mr. Wilkins of New York or Westchester (perhaps young Gouverneur Morris Wilkins, with whom Cooper would socialize overseas in the later 1820s); and an otherwise unidentified "Col. Perry."[83]

Placed in charge of generating recognition for the society among prominent individuals beyond the county's boundaries, Cooper invested much energy in doing so. In this capacity, the board instructed him at its September meeting to inform four well-known figures of their election to honorary membership: Elkanah Watson; Gov. DeWitt Clinton; Thomas Gold (current head of the Berkshire Agricultural Society); and the "Connecticut Wit" David Humphreys, a merino fancier who had shipped a flock from Spain to the United States as early as 1802. We know from the surviving responses of Watson and Gold (printed in the *Herald* in October) that Cooper handled this task expeditiously, writing to both men on the very day that the board met. Both Gold and Watson promptly answered Cooper's "polite" letters to them, accepting the honorary membership. In addition, Watson accepted the invitation Cooper extended on behalf of the board to attend the fair in October and personally distribute the premiums. In the same issue of the paper, Watson's role in the fair was announced to the public, clearly part of a last-minute effort to boost attendance. It is remarkable that Watson chose to aid the OCAS, especially on such short notice, rather than attend his favorite Berkshire organization. He had received Cooper's invitation and the Berkshire one on the same day and had decided to lend a hand to the newer, less stable group. Securing his attendance and his good will was a real coup.[84]

Debts

With all this energy poured into the OCAS effort, Cooper had many reasons to be in attendance on Tuesday, October 14, when the first fair at last took place: "The day was fine," reported the local Republican newspaper, adding that "the occasion was honored by the attendance of a very numerous and respectable body of citizens, from all parts of the county."[85] In fact, however, Cooper was not among them. He had left the village for good over the past summer and had been able to join in final preparations for the fair only by undertaking the long journey back to Otsego when his presence was required in September. Isaac's diary notes the last departure of Cooper for New York on the twenty-fifth of that month. He still owned Fenimore Farm and Mt. Ovis and other properties in Otsego. And his infant daughter Elizabeth's grave still rested in its lonely enclosure by the brook along the lake. His own roots here, however, had been torn up by circumstances that would soon destroy a great deal more that had seemed permanent in his life. A member of the Otsego society, he no longer was a part of the society of Otsego.

The Coopers had left Cooperstown on July 7 following much hurried preparation. Cooper himself, having gone off to Binghamton in May and then come back in time for the meeting of the OCAS board on June 3, was in New York City by June 10, staying at the City Hotel.[86] By then, Susan, only three weeks after the difficult birth of Anne Charlotte, was just beginning to feel better. Before his departure, she had been about the farmhouse a bit, but not yet outside. On June 11 she therefore wrote him in a burst of premature enthusiasm, "I ran away from my sick room for the first time since you left us—wrapt myself up a la mode de winter, and promenaded the Piazza." Within a week, however, things suddenly worsened again. "Our present situation is a sad comfortless one," she wrote then, "and very dirty. My nurse left me the day her four weeks were up—She half promised to remain a fortnight more—but when she got home and saw her Mother she changed her mind." The departing young woman, forcing more hard work on Susan, left her sounding peevish: "you may think of me as weak and feeble," she went on, ". . . sitting up alone by the fire until [late] at night."[87]

The peevishness was probably strategic. Susan knew that her husband would contemplate that pathetic image of her in his own well-tended lodgings on Broadway, where the service was notably good. She wanted to be there herself. Better yet, she wanted to be in Westchester, as she surely had indicated many times since the couple's seemingly permanent return to Otsego after their long stay downstate the year before. Cooper was trying to make life as good as possible for Susan at Fenimore. He had hurried about tending to various carpentry projects at the farm before he left, things she happily took note of in her second letter, and some of his errands in New York City and then in Albany on his way home were meant to ease matters for her. Buried in domestic work, for one thing, she asked to have more servants brought up. She wanted three— a cook and two general aides, and all of them needed to be reliable and well trained so they could take over from the excellent Nanny Disbrow, who had left the family's employ within the past year to marry a farmer in the nearby town of Burlington and had taken her daughter Susan, the present cook, with her. Cooper probably planned to rely on the DeLanceys to help him fill these needs, since he was to visit Heathcote Hill during his stay in New York.[88]

In the meantime, he had other things to take care of as well. Some were routine, like a visit on Thursday, June 12, to his tailor's shop for the first of several new purchases extending over the next year. Others, like opening an account a week later at the Bank of New York, next to the tailor's shop on Wall Street, were more complex, and indeed urgent. Cooper expected that payment would soon be demanded on a $3,000 personal note, and he clearly did not have the means to meet it. Susan's father, with whom he already had conferred on the question, had written on his behalf to the bank's cashier, Charles Wilkes, about possible solutions. He also sketched them, though a bit hazily, in a brief letter he sent to Cooper at the City Hotel. DeLancey was willing to endorse the note him-self with an unnamed co-endorser in New York and leave Cooper to sort out the details with Wilkes. Or he was willing to help in some other way. Expecting Cooper at Heathcote Hill over the weekend, before a written answer from Wilkes to his own letter would reach Mamaroneck, DeLancey instructed his son-in-law to get that answer directly from Wilkes so he could bring it with him. In the ab-sence of other documentation regarding this case, it is hard to tell exactly what the situation was or even how it was resolved. Cooper and DeLancey apparently reached an agreement that weekend whereby Susan's father backed up Cooper's credit. Cooper in turn opened the account at the Bank of New York by deposit-ing a $3,000 note signed or endorsed by DeLancey on June 19, against which he drew a draft to a third party. Thus Cooper shifted the obligation from that un-named person or persons to his father-in-law. DeLancey did not seem overly concerned about the affair. He was far from insistent about terms, and with no-table (though perhaps forced) nonchalance, he added a postscript to his letter that chattily asked Cooper to pick up two packs of cards for him and bring them along to Mamaroneck.[89]

The situation nonetheless was unusual and probably worrying. Money fre-quently had changed hands between Cooper and his in-laws during the earlier years of his marriage, but usually as a matter of small convenience rather than pressing need. As Judge Cooper's estate became unstable, Cooper apparently began turning to Susan's family for substantial help. He must have used funds from them to cover living expenses and the mounting costs at Fenimore, as well as to pay off other loans. Perhaps he even used DeLancey money to bolster the estate or insulate himself from its impending collapse. By the fall of 1816, sev-eral months before the crisis about the $3,000 note, he thus was already in his father-in-law's debt for at least two-thirds of that amount. That November, Thomas DeLancey had asked whether Cooper could repay this amount by Christmas, since his absent parents (who may have been in England on an other-wise undocumented visit at the time) needed ready cash, and "bills on England" that Thomas otherwise might forward to his father were, he told James, "on the decline." It is not clear whether Cooper was able to make the desired payment at that moment, but the request that he do so if possible indicates how complicated his financial affairs were becoming.[90]

John Peter DeLancey seems to have been quite willing to help Cooper, and thereby Susan, in this way. But more was involved than just money. The new note Cooper accepted in June and those that followed over the rest of 1817 were part of an arrangement that saw him bring his family back to Westchester. This was a development that must have pleased the DeLanceys and his own wife equally. When Cooper left Cooperstown earlier in June, he and Susan were still

planning to remain there through the summer. Why else had he been personally
seeing to improvements on the farm just before leaving? Why else would he be
searching for the new servants she demanded?[91] Why else had he and Susan had
gone over all the things they needed at Fenimore so that he could purchase them
downstate and bring them back? Why else, before his visit at Heathcote Hill, had
Susan received a letter from her mother hinting that she just might come back
with him so that she could help out at Fenimore Farm? All these activities and
arrangements would make no sense if the Coopers had already decided to relocate to Westchester.[92]

And yet as soon as Cooper returned home at the very end of June, he and
Susan began packing and set about closing up their Otsego farmhouse. He
brought no servants back with him, and few if any household supplies. Instead,
he brought word of a new plan that had been worked out, clearly enough, while
he tarried at Heathcote Hill. John Peter and his wife were eager to have their
daughter and grandchildren nearby again. One imagines that DeLancey cajoled
Cooper (and with his newly won leverage, pressured him) to bring them there.
In order to sweeten the prospect, he offered to give the couple another piece of
land, a parcel on a hill to the north of the Hickory Grove that he also owned.
Here, late in 1817 and early in 1818, the Coopers accordingly were to erect the
third new home of their marriage, a structure named Angevine in memory of its
old Huguenot tenants. DeLancey's price for extending his personal credit to
James, and linking him with Charles Wilkes and the Bank of New York, was the
sudden change of living arrangements that this new house would represent. Already by the first week in July, as already noted, the family had precipitously left
Fenimore Farm.[93]

Cooper's eldest daughter, who had turned four in April, recalled some of the
details of the relocation. She remembered the hastily arranged christening of her
sister Anne Charlotte by Rev. Daniel Nash, an event Isaac's diary dates to July 6,
the day before the family left Cooperstown.[94] Susan also remembered three
farewells. The first took place as the family readied itself to leave the farmhouse.
Taking Sue by the hand, her father led her "through the grounds, across the
brook, into the inclosure where lay the grave of my little sister Elizabeth." She
continued: "He stood there in silence a few moments, and then led me back again.
I cannot remember him speaking a word at the time." As it happens, Sue recalled
little that was spoken by anyone that whole day; mostly her recollections were visual. The family piled into the old cut-down carriage they had ridden from
Westchester four years before and went out to the Pierstown road and turned left
toward the village, bound first to Otsego Hall. Here they went inside. Sue dimly
remembered "Grandmother Cooper" sitting "in the hall, with a little table near
her." But she conjured up no hugs, no words of comfort or farewell, only the

"dim recollection of her appearance" as she sat there, much as George Freeman
had pictured her the year before in that one surviving image of a woman Sue
never was to see in the flesh again (see Plate 3). Next, leaving the grounds of Otsego Hall by the north drive and heading down toward blue-green Otsego, the
family turned right on Front Street and pulled up to the door at Edgewater. Here
the scene was more animated. Isaac, who was feeling well enough then that he and
his wife would take a trip to DeKalb before summer was over, must have been his
typical vocal self as he and Mary Ann and "a group of cousins" were arrayed out
front, bidding the travelers goodbye. Again Sue's image is silent, however, like an
old movie from the preverbal depths of her young mind in a country she hardly
recalled when she returned there as a young woman in the 1830s. The dimness of
her recollections may have had as much to do with the multiple losses that had removed most of these kin from Otsego before her return as it did with the barely
formed consciousness that had received the original impressions (SFM 21).

Sue next remembered "the long climb up the Vision road." At the top there
was a touching scene, another farewell of sorts at this heart of the heart of
Cooper country. Some wild roses caught the girl's eye, and her father stopped
the carriage and, gathering "a large handful of the flowers," gave them to Sue
and Caroline. Then they were off. The baby Anne Charlotte lay on a pillow in a
basket on the floor at her mother's feet during most of the trip that July. For the
three days it took the carriage to get to Albany, Cooper sat up front, driving the
same gray horses that had pulled it from Westchester four years before. Where
they stopped Sue did not say: perhaps in Canajoharie at Frey's again, then at an
inn in Schenectady. Once they had arrived in Albany, in any event, the carriage
was abandoned for the steamboat, on which it probably was stowed for the river
trip south. Sue thought that this was her mother's first trip on such a vessel. She
remembered, aside from "a sort of faint perception of a feeling of subdued excitement among the party on the steamboat," the fact that her father rode out on
the open deck while Mrs. Cooper and the girls were inside. He kept coming into
the cabin, Sue further recalled, "to point out to my Mother the villages and country houses on the banks." Moving at a rate that made the banks slip by like the
panorama images already becoming so popular, the steamboat wed technology
to aesthetics. Here was the river landscape as few could have seen it only a
decade earlier, a landscape made coherent by speed and almost dreamlike because of the seemingly effortless transport of Robert Fulton's invention. No
sails blocked the view, no booms swung about to threaten the traveler's head.
Out on the open deck with Cooper was another man so astonished by all he saw
that he kept coming to the window and exclaiming to his wife, similarly immured
in the ladies' cabin, "I say," "I say." He repeated it so many times that little Sue,
in her child's way, thought that "I say" was the wife's name (SFM 23).

For Sue's father, who had been up and down the valley so many times that he knew those villages and country seats well, the exclamation was more internal. If this was Mrs. Cooper's first experience of the valley in this way, with the water and sky surrounding its human and natural objects, for Cooper the feeling was not just familiar. It was as fresh as his recent return from New York City that June could have made it. And there may well have been special stories for him to share in the leisure of this family passage. While in the city in June, amid everything else that was then absorbing his attention, he had been planning an excursion with a college friend, Hudson valley native Jacob Sutherland. Cooper had told his wife all about his "projected Tour" in writing her from the city, and in reply she had answered that it would be "pleasant" for him because of "all the fine things" he would see and because he would have such a good traveling companion. The hastily laid plans for relocating the family may have cut short the journey, although a surviving inn receipt for June 21, 1817, probably from somewhere in the Hudson valley, hints that Cooper indeed had fit in the adventure after all. It seems just possible that Sutherland took Cooper to the celebrated vista point, Pine Orchard, which could be reached from the turnpike that ran from Catskill toward Sutherland's home in Delaware County. If that surmise is correct, one can only reflect how right it was that in his dedication of the one novel in which a memory of that place was to figure, *The Pioneers,* Cooper should portray Sutherland as intimately familiar with the real landscapes reflected in the novel's imaginary ones (*PIO* 1:v). Sutherland of course knew Otsego and Delaware counties, but that fact alone seems insufficient for Cooper's praise. Had he unlocked to Cooper's gaze Natty's remembered retreat above the Hudson as well? Perhaps the conjoining of Cooper's first glimpse of Pine Orchard with his farewell to Lake Otsego so soon afterwards helps explain why Natty Bumppo was to recall the former from the bosom of the latter in the initial Leather-Stocking Tale.[95]

The steamboat passage in July took the family all the way to New York. There they transferred to an overland vehicle, perhaps sent down by the DeLanceys, for the "half day's journey to Mamaroneck." Young Susan was to recall little of the transfer aside from her sense of "the great city" bustling around the travelers. But her memories came to life once the door to Heathcote Hill was thrown open. She discovered there, in that already familiar place, "Grandparents, uncles and Aunts, and servants all making us welcome after the formidable journey from the wilds of Otsego to the shore of the Sound" (SFM 23–24). If the geographical connectedness of this memory seems like a later interpolation, the emotion of welcome seems right. It had been a year and a half since Sue had been there last, and although she had seen some of the DeLanceys in Otsego since then, it all must have felt fresh, a place kept alive to this point as much through her mother's longing stories as through her own embedded images. So all of it struck her mind and feelings anew and remained strong years afterward.

For the summer and on into the fall the Coopers stayed at Heathcote Hill, where those aunts and servants Sue recalled were already in place to see to her mother's (and her little sisters') needs. Aunt Caroline, sixteen now, had entered the world of New York society that last winter, spending a fortnight attending parties and even meeting "Mrs. Van Rensselaer," as her brother Thomas had reported to Cooper in January.[96] Martha, who had been in Cooperstown as late as April, was now going on fourteen. The sisters "petted" the Cooper girls, Sue recalled, and their grandfather took the children "out very often to drive with him, over his farms or about the country." Sue, big enough to sit in a high chair now, was stationed near John Peter at the table in the living room where the family ate all its meals, and at breakfast he would break open the fresh oysters and feed her the meat. Amid all this, Fenimore Farm already was fast retreating into the little girl's past (SFM 24).

CHAPTER SEVEN

Gains and Losses

The family barely had settled in with the DeLanceys at Heathcote Hill before Cooper was off again. This time he was bound to the village of Williamstown or Cooper's Falls in St. Lawrence County, where, in the latest and most complex of their joint operations, he and his cousin Courtland recently had established a general store. Courtland handled the retail operation and related undertakings (a small potash facility, for one) and spent some time hounding the settlers who owed Cooper money on lands in DeKalb and nearby Bangor. For his part, Cooper provided the store's major financial backing, probably using borrowed funds for the purpose. But he also took a hand in managing the venture. The load of goods Courtland had taken up the previous March had been picked out by both partners, for instance, and Cooper's summer trip was aimed at refreshing the inventory. Late in the spring, Courtland had sent Cooper a list of items he needed, which Cooper probably left at the Cook Brothers' store in Albany on his way downstate with Susan and the girls in July. Then he came back upriver almost immediately, picking up the shipment and personally running it through Utica to DeKalb. That accomplished, he must have been back in Westchester by early August.[1]

Once again he did not stay put there. On September 2, he was in Coopers-town for the OCAS's board meeting, but then returned to Utica, where he and Courtland were due to meet in a few days. While awaiting his cousin's arrival, Cooper attended to a knotty problem that the DeKalb store was partly intended to untangle. Scattered records suggest that for several years Cooper had been re-lying on both Utica's newly founded Ontario Branch Bank and one of its direc-tors, merchant James Platt, for sizable loans.[2] He probably had established a line of credit with Platt during his quick visit to Utica at the time of the 1811 honey-moon trip to Otsego. Right before that visit, Cooper had been given direct con-trol over the leasehold properties assigned to him in his father's will. Valuable as those properties were, they promised to provide him only slender means to cover mounting expenses at Closet Hall, and especially at Fenimore Farm. Loans from Platt and the bank appear to have funded the comfortable but costly life he and Susan led during the first half-dozen years of their marriage.[3]

When this arrangement was established, Cooper surely expected that he would be able to repay the loans once distribution of the major holdings in his father's estate began in 1815. But the dramatic fall in land values during the war, followed by the resultant difficulties with the estate and his own financial wor-ries, conspired to leave him scrambling for new funds to cover yearly interest de-mands and, if possible, reduce the sizable principal. His need to enter into the re-financing negotiations concluded with John Peter DeLancey and the Bank of New York in June suggests how dicey things were for him. And refinancing alone could not solve his problems; only substantial new sources of income could do that. Establishing the store with Courtland was the first of many expe-dients, soon to include the whaleship *Union*, a series of complicated deals in-volving real estate Cooper or his wife owned, and finally the even riskier attempt at self-published authorship, which were all aimed at generating that income. While waiting for such undertakings to pay off, Cooper needed to delay various creditors. During the September visit to Utica, he thus seems to have extended and enlarged an old note payable to Platt personally. At the same time, aiming to discharge the whole liability, Cooper set up a demanding schedule of payments that Courtland would have to make to Platt from DeKalb proceeds. Courtland probably knew something about this plan already, but he would learn the chal-lenging details only when the cousins conferred in Utica.[4]

"Rarrangements"

Cooper's hopes for the DeKalb store were grossly unrealistic, not least because the partners were inexperienced and underfunded. Although Courtland tried to pay close attention to the business, he was plagued by uncertainty. He thus confessed to Cooper, "I want your directions in everything of consequence and I will if possable [*sic*] do accordingly." This wasn't just flattery for the Judge's son. Courtland continued, with a typical display of his ingenuity as a speller, "You may rely on my faithful preformance of my duty as fare as I know how. I am perfectly sensable that I am not qualified for the business you have trusted with me but hope that I shal be able to account to you to your satisfaction for all that has been or may be put under my care."[5] He was, however, well out of his depth. Managing a retail outlet in a frontier area (where cash was short, demand was unpredictable, and goods were hard to come by) was far more complex than running errands of the sort Courtland had undertaken for Cooper in 1816. To be sure, Courtland, partly raised in the north country, had the advantage of knowing DeKalb and its people. As a merchant, however, he was woefully inexperienced. Most of all, he lacked the judgment required for handling the tough questions of character and credit that his new business inevitably raised.

Indeed, those questions proved his special undoing. At the very start, having hauled the store's initial inventory one hundred miles through late winter mud, Courtland was happy just to arrive in DeKalb and open shop. After the first three weeks of business, he enthusiastically reported selling $430 worth of goods, an impressive amount. But he took in only $50 cash then, and the following month that figure dropped to a dismal $10.[6] At a time when Cooper's New York City issues were coming to a head, he stressed to Courtland that as much cash as possible had to be forthcoming, since he had imperative need for it. At the least, he expected that new stock for the store would be paid for out of proceeds, not through further use of his already overextended credit. Courtland's indulgent manner with customers, however, meant that there never was much money to send. Only a few months into the business, he made a startling admission to his cousin: "I find it more difficult to collect debts than to make them."[7]

Had the DeKalb operation been isolated from Cooper's other financial entanglements, Courtland might have managed. Once his demanding new obligations were spelled out in Utica, however, failure was inevitable. The scheduled payments to James Platt required that he focus on accumulating large quantities of cash from new sales, settlement of customer accounts, collections from Cooper's tenants and mortgagors, and sidelines like the potash factory and a timber operation. He justifiably became concerned about whether he could make the payments on time. When he wrote Cooper a nervous letter from the St. Lawrence valley on October 1, 1817, just after his return from their Utica meeting, he explained that he had been trying frantically (as his prose showed) "to make rarrangements [to] ensure me the money I have to pay their next month."[8]

Miraculously, Courtland managed to meet that first deadline. As he began gathering funds for the second payment, however, it became clear that he could not put money aside for that purpose and also pay for the fresh inventory he soon would need. When both cousins paid visits to the Cook Brothers' store in Albany that winter, the goods they picked up accordingly had to be charged to Cooper's account there. The resulting balance was to linger unpaid for many years, a persistent reminder of the soured personal relationship that was one consequence of the DeKalb partnership.[9] By April 7, 1818, Cooper was concerned enough with the store's heavy debt burden and the shortage of cash that in a now-lost letter he agreed to acquire more medicine for the store only if he could swap land for it. Courtland (sleeping in the store by then in order to save his own cash) assented to that plan as long as it did not delay the shipment. Then he sent back a list of other expensive items he would need if he was to increase sales enough to make the next Utica payments. They were borrowing money to make money in order to pay interest (and some principal) on old debts—hardly a sound manner of proceeding.[10]

During the spring of 1818 dealings between the partners accordingly began to go bad. Cooper had not heard from Courtland since his midwinter visit to DeKalb. Mail service out of the St. Lawrence district was not particularly reliable, but in fact Courtland had not written Cooper at all in those many intervening weeks. Cooper, concerned about Platt's May payment, rightly inferred that no news was bad news. His unlocated letter of April 7 appears to have expressed considerable doubts about Courtland's overall handling of the business. Now it was that Courtland replied, self-deprecatingly, with the confession that he indeed was "not qualified for the business" that Cooper had entrusted to him. Before Cooper received this reply, he anxiously took up his pen again on April 16 to shoot off a second letter to Courtland. In this one, also unlocated, he must have criticized his cousin for failing to send timely and detailed information. As he had in the first instance, Courtland promptly replied, promising to write more frequently in the future. Probably before this second answer arrived (with its news that, again miraculously, Courtland *had* made the May payment), Cooper wrote an even more accusatory third letter to which Courtland, who received it more than a month after it was sent, replied at length on June 24. "I am very sorry that you are so much dissatisfied with the account I have given you of what I am doing and [with] my letters generally," he began. He then gave an unusually detailed report of all he had been up to. But the gist of it was that there was little cash, largely because, as he saw it, he had not been provided with sufficient inventory. He had no tea or tobacco, for instance, and the yard goods that were so much in demand were in very short supply. So who was responsible for the state in which the store stood?[11]

It hardly could have been a surprise to Cooper when Courtland wrote again a month later to indicate that he would not be able to make the third Utica payment in August. Even with his many expedients, including a trip to Montreal with barrels of potash, the storekeeper would have only a third or at most half of the funds he needed. Sales recently had been the lowest in his experience, probably not more than $150 for the past month. His competitors in the village were doing far more business than he, probably because (again) they had more ample supplies of groceries and dry goods. Still, Courtland did not feel that he could ask Cooper to send more stock right then. The complaints Cooper had made about the venture in his three most recent letters struck home. Not until Courtland had paid for what he already had sold out would he trouble his cousin to buy more.[12]

The archive of correspondence between the cousins falls silent from this point until March 1819, some eight months later. At that time, Cooper raised serious questions not about Courtland's competence or skill but rather about his honesty in handling money. In some ways these questions were rendered more pressing by the overflow of worries from other areas of Cooper's life. At this moment, he was concerned about how he would pay for the whaleship that he had just begun seeking out in New York City. The last thing he needed was to be disappointed in his expectation that Courtland's operations would yield enough money to at least keep his Utica creditors out of his hair while he tended to such other cash-generating ventures. Hence the March accusations about Courtland's mismanagement and perhaps misappropriation may well have been overstated. "You sensure [sic] me of not being honest in my accounts," Courtland replied on April 1. What was he to say? "I never have in the course of my business done any thing but what I should have been willing that you or any other person should have known." Then he gave a long recital of his dealings with more than a half dozen individuals in St. Lawrence and Otsego counties, obviously intended to convince by its sheer detail. Narrative was Courtland's substitute for exculpation.[13]

Whether the story persuaded his cousin or not we cannot tell. Cooper in any case was more interested in solutions to the financial problems they both were facing. To his suggestion that Courtland cease the operation altogether, the shopkeeper replied that auctioning off the inventory would increase the losses. So he blundered on. Still in business on June 1, by then he had very little money to forward but, as always, more extenuating verbiage: he had "a true knowledge of the Injunction that I am under to doo [sic] everything in my power to forward you money even to the last farthing that comes into my hands which you may be assured I shall do." At the same time, he confessed that Cooper's painful charges against him were well deserved: they were "no more than I mite expect from the manner in which I have failed in my payments to you but consider that I have a hard set to deal with who are very pooor [sic] and am doing all in my power to collect my debts."[14]

Although the payments to Platt were a perpetual source of friction between Cooper and Courtland, more critical was their joint debt to the Cook brothers. Those merchants, who had once operated in Cooperstown and thus knew the cousins but also were familiar with the problems facing all the Coopers at the time, did not gleefully extend credit for the 1818 restocking. To cover themselves, they insisted that Cooper sign formal articles of agreement requiring him to repay the total amount at the end of three years (February 2, 1821), with annual interest added. The Cooks also wanted him to give them a secured bond for the debt and demanded that the value of the property backing up the bond be certified by Cooperstown lawyer Robert Campbell, who was also well known to both parties. At the expiration of the first year, Cooper dutifully paid the interest, as he apparently did in 1820 as well. But thereafter the debt lay unaddressed, growing larger, until from somewhat more than $1,500, the total had edged close to $2,100.[15]

Cooper assumed legal responsibility for the whole debt but fully expected his partner to help pay it off. Courtland failed to make the store profitable enough to defray such costs; he also failed to come up with cash of his own from other sources.[16] It is instructive to note that Cooper's attack on his cousin in the March 1819 letter that broke the silence between them followed shortly after Cooper's first interest payment to the Cooks. While small enough, that payment provided a new reminder of Courtland's unreliability. Collecting money in DeKalb, either from store debtors or Cooper's tenants and mortgagors, Courtland explained at the end of 1819, was "uterrly imposable except in small sums and that [by] almost forever collecting." He added, slackly, "I shall pay some money soon but cannot tell the exact time or amount." The end of the partnership as far as Cooper was concerned came in May of 1822, when the Cooks forced a settlement of their debt. Their legal costs added a further amount to the ever-growing total. By 1824, Cooper was so pessimistic about the likelihood of repayment from his cousin that he assigned Courtland's debt to a creditor of his own. He would let those two fight it out.[17]

Transitions

Cooper's departure from Otsego in the summer of 1817 ushered in a series of other important transitions. The first came during his September trip to Utica. On Saturday the thirteenth, shortly before Courtland was due at the meeting about the Platt arrangement, an express rider from Cooperstown arrived at Cooper's lodgings with the unexpected news that his mother suddenly had died. Knowing that his brother Isaac and sister-in-law Mary Ann were not in Otsego then, but rather in DeKalb, Cooper had extra reason to hurry back. He left that night or early the next morning and by four Sunday afternoon was in Coopers-town. Courtland, finding a message from his cousin on arriving in Utica, reached Otsego on the fifteenth.[18]

Something of a cipher in the family archive through much of her life, all the more so because her husband left such a broad trail of paper from the 1780s until 1809, Elizabeth Fenimore Cooper remained only dimly seen even in death. We know that she had been sound enough the past winter to leave Otsego Hall on what was an unexampled little trip. On February 10, Isaac's astonished diary noted that "*Mrs. Cooper, that is, Mother* went to Butternuts"—along with ac-companists of uncertain species whom the diarist named "*Billy, Cod Fish, Pomp, and all!*" She returned (with "William") from her visit on February 13, appar-ently none the worse for wear. Later in the year, however, she seems to have been confined to Isaac's "invalid chair," if the passage about an afflicted female in Susan Cooper's torn June 17 letter to her husband really concerns his mother, the most plausible candidate in the family. Although we have seen that Elizabeth Cooper was well enough on July 7 to be remembered sitting next to the table downstairs in the hall when her youngest son and his family called on their way to Westchester, her seat at that time may still have been that same "invalid chair." The diarist keeping track of events in the absence of Isaac and Mary Ann Cooper in September did not seem surprised by her passing two months later: "Mrs. Eliz-abeth Cooper departed this life" is all the entry on the thirteenth of that month says. And the obituary notices in the local papers were no more stunned: "DIED—In this village, on Saturday the 13th inst.," ran one, "Mrs. ELIZABETH COOPER, aged 66, relict of William Cooper, Esq., deceased."[19]

Whether Cooper had had time to visit his mother during his most recent re-turn to Cooperstown from September 2 to 5 is uncertain. If she indeed had been ailing, it seems plausible that he would have made the time to see her—although he knew he would be back soon and may well have had his hands full at Feni-more Farm for those three days. We know that the last time he looked on her face was at her funeral. He and Courtland, along with Ann and George Pomeroy and brother Samuel and his wife Eliza and the various resident grandchildren were the only relatives in attendance. Rev. Daniel Nash, who preached in Christ Church on the fourteenth (and who had officiated at the funerals of Hannah and William Cooper), may still have been at hand when Elizabeth was placed in a coffin that bore an engraved silver plate and was buried on September 15 next to her husband in the family plot. The weather that day, Cooper's twentieth-eighth birthday, was suitably wet and "unpleasant."[20]

Cooper had little time to linger in Otsego and indulge in melancholy reflec-tions. Courtland had brought money from the store for him, and the cousins' unfinished business called them back to Utica, where they went the very next morning. When they finished there, Cooper returned by himself to Cooperstown on Saturday, September 20, went to another OCAS board meeting on the following Monday, and met with his lawyer and the local carpenter Robert R. Ward on Tuesday with regard to plans for a new house in Westchester. He lingered another day or so in the village before climbing into the stage on Thursday, September 25, and leaving for New York. As far as we know, this hasty visit was to be his last to the village for seventeen years. He left bearing grim emotions indeed.[21]

A December letter Cooper received from Isaac provided a somber postscript to the fall. In precarious health, Isaac had been forced to dictate the bulk of it to Mary Ann. He avoided that issue, however, focusing instead on the family's tangled financial affairs. The letter opened with a plea that Cooper try his best to make a New York City lawyer accept land rather than cash as satisfaction for a sizable claim against the estate. And in the postscript, the only passage in Isaac's own hand, Cooper was urged to "attend to the DeKalb affairs," which were still a mess, as Courtland's partner well knew. Sandwiched between these alarms came a long sad tale touching on the family of their long-dead brother Richard. Richard's daughter Hannah, his oldest child and the namesake of the tragic sister of them all, had taken ill late in November and, after lingering for two weeks, had died on December 10 at the age of fifteen. Now she, too, was at rest in the rapidly expanding family plot near Christ Church. Nor was that all. In an eerie foretaste of the multiplying woes soon to overwhelm the Coopers, Hannah's funeral itself had triggered another loss. It turned out that a drunken relative of Ann Cooper Clarke, the dead girl's mother, had driven his wagon home so furiously that his equally drunk sister was jostled to death on the ride home, although he never realized it.[22]

That was a grim ending to a tough year, and the next year hardly began in a more promising manner. As Cooper may have sensed from the fact that Mary Ann had to pen most of her husband's letter, Isaac was in another decline at the end of 1817. From this one there was to be no recovery. Abscesses had formed in his spine and, on New Year's Day, only thirty-six years old, he died of "exhaustion." The loss left a decided hole in Cooper's sense of the family. Isaac, in the words of the novelist's daughter Susan, had been a particularly "warm-hearted" brother. Virtually alone among the five sons of Judge Cooper, he had followed a steady path and always seemed to exhibit a kind of moral calm. With young William's troubles deepening, and Samuel left to his eccentric ways in Cooperstown, Cooper increasingly would find himself on his own in the world (SFM 13–14).

His isolation from the rest of the clan had accelerated after the hasty decision to relocate his own growing family to Westchester. At first, he and Susan and the girls lived among her kin at Heathcote Hill. Young Susan remembered spending "some months"—"a pleasant summer"—at her grandparents' home.

She and her sister Caroline, or Cally, and the baby Charlotte were the center of attention for their mother's sisters. Such attention was comfortably reassuring, but there were new things about this period at Heathcote Hill, too, things that began impressing the young girl with the difference between her mother's world and the recently abandoned "wilds of Otsego" (SFM 23–24). If the latter region was new, rough, a jumble of people from New England and the older parts of New York as well as Jersey and Pennsylvania, Westchester could evince an old—and an Old World—feel. The nurse the family found there for the children, Katie Arnault, gave a hint of this difference. She was one of the local Huguenot girls, still ensconced in the culture the DeLanceys in most ways had left behind. In Katie, Sue first heard the distinctive echoes of an ancestral culture far from that of the Coopers, a culture evoked by the names she recalled (such as Flandreau and Bonnet) and the tales of old customs that stuck in her mind. One of the latter was the Sunday morning ritual of the Huguenots of New Rochelle, who would go down to the shore of Long Island Sound, turn their faces eastward, and "waft their prayers across the Atlantic toward the coast of France, whence Louis XIV had driven them by his 'Dragonnades.'" So strong was the Huguenots' pious nostalgia that, before they had their own church at New Rochelle, on some Sundays the devout would rise in the dark and walk in groups to the French church in New York. Sue was to learn more of this part of her heritage later in France, but the lesson started in Westchester (SFM 28, 32).

There were other discoveries to make at Heathcote Hill in the summer of 1817. One was Sue's grandfather. The former British officer, comfortably Americanized, didn't seem the least bit French: he knew the French language, of course, but was an Anglican with one pew in the "parish" church at Rye and another in that at New Rochelle (although the Coopers often took their young family to the old Huguenot church at New Rochelle on Sundays, a habit Mrs. Cooper may have inherited from DeLancey practices in her childhood).[23] John Peter DeLancey's greatest passion, his love of horses, was English through and through. What impressed Sue most was his affection—as great as that of the women at Heathcote Hill, if not greater—for these first of the DeLancey grandchildren. In this transition period for the girls, DeLancey's companionship provided stability during their father's frequent absences. With their grandfather the girls spent hour on hour "driving and riding" around the landscape, Sue serving as his assistant—jumping down to open and shut gates, for instance (SFM 25, 32–33)—whereas their father seems to have been only vaguely in the Mamaroneck picture at first. There were few concrete memories of anything Cooper did with Sue or Cally then.

Sue thought her father had "returned to Fenimore after a while to look after his affairs there" (SFM 24), but this was only part of the story. The uncertain condition of Judge Cooper's estate and Cooper's own worsening finances, the demands on his time due to his newly arranged partnership with Courtland in DeKalb, the lingering ties to Otsego due to the OCAS and the Bible society as well as his farms, and at last the death of his mother (unmentioned by Sue in this part of "Small Family Memories") all took him away or kept him away through much of the summer. By the start of fall, with Courtland back at his grind in DeKalb, Cooper at last had returned to Westchester more or less for good. Thereafter, he was able to involve himself more in the concerns of the De-Lancey household and its neighborhood.

By year's end the Coopers were once more putting down roots there. The Hickory Grove farm straddled what was then called the Mamaroneck and White Plains road (now simply Mamaroneck Road) in Scarsdale. It had long been occupied by a tenant family of Huguenot background, the Secors; these were the people Cooper had recently removed in favor of his own agent. Another pair of farms lay north of it, both similarly divided by the road. On the west half of one of these had long stood the home and cemetery of another Huguenot family, the Angevines, who had occupied the place as tenants ever since John Peter's grandfather Caleb Heathcote was granted the Manor of Scarsdale in 1702. Cooper apparently was given his choice of either the forty-two-acre Angevine homestead or the fifty-seven-acre parcel east of the road, where only "a small, weather-beaten cottage of two stories and steep, pitched roof"—later used by Cooper as a studio, according to one report—then was standing.[24] John Peter merely awaited the decision, which was made sometime in the fall of 1817, and then on January 3, 1818, he formally conveyed the unoccupied part of the farm in trust to the couple, with his two oldest sons, Thomas and Edward, serving as trustees so as to protect the new farm from being "encumbered or alienated by the said James Cooper or subjected to any charge whatever on account of his debts" (quoted in *LJ* 1:87). Those "debts" obviously had become, since the June negotiations if not before, common knowledge at Heathcote Hill.[25]

The agreement Cooper reached with Otsego carpenter Robert R. Ward toward the end of his September visit to Otsego indicates how definite the family's plans for relocation were. Ward, who had labored on Fenimore, was to temporarily move to Westchester and finish the dwelling there as well as a pair of barns and other outbuildings within eight months of signing the contract—that is, by May 1818.[26] Since Ward's contract promised that the owner would furnish all materials, Cooper began scrambling to gather them almost as soon as he returned from his Utica trip. In October, he commissioned a trio of men to begin cutting timber in nearby Rye. They labored up to early December before their work was done, and the frame was erected two days later, December 10.[27] Local stories about "Cooper's Folly," as the dwelling came to be called, suggest that it was hastily built of unseasoned wood, a not-implausible observation given the speed with which the timber was cut and delivered.[28]

Whatever its soundness as a structure, the new house was not without its pretensions. In the language of Ward's contract, the place was to be erected "according to the draught or scheme furnished by the said James Cooper," and Cooper seems to have expended considerable ingenuity on it. The layout and appearance of the house are revealed in three images, including a front elevation and a first-floor plan made on the spot by Cooper's first printer, Andrew Thompson Goodrich, probably in early June of 1820, and a woodcut first published in 1853 (Plate 12) that captured the original look of the place, which survived some years beyond Cooper's death. The dwelling was a five-part house, composed of a two-story central mass three bays wide that was connected by narrow enclosed walkways to two identical single-story wings. In front of the central mass, which was set back some distance from the wings, was a covered porch or portico, the foremost edge of which was in line with the front line of the wings. Overall, the house had a decided Regency look. In fact, it shared several elements with the contemporary work of Albany architect Philip Hooker, particularly the latter's design for George and Ann Cooper Clarke's property at the north end of Otsego Lake, which, however (like Fenimore), was built of stone.[29]

The house was supposed to be ready by spring, but not until September 23, 1818—a year to the day after he signed the contract with Ward—did Cooper inform a correspondent, "I have just moved into my new house." Even then, he added that he was very much "occupied with workmen and business," a clear sign that much still remained undone on the place.[30] By then, Ward, who appears to have been responsible mostly for the rough carpentry work, had long since left; indeed, he already was inquiring about when he would be paid. The agreement called for him to receive payment once the exact amount due him had been determined by Ward's colleague (and Cooper's sometime contractor) Cyrus Clark, or someone else agreed to by both parties. It also stipulated that he would be compensated not in cash but through the transfer of as much "wild land . . . in the town of DeKalb, or in the township of Bangor, or in the Manor of Feronia in Broome County—at four dollars and fifty cents per acre," as would meet the obligation. Here is another indication of how cash-poor Cooper was as he undertook the move to Westchester.[31]

The Whaleship Union

Money was clearly becoming a critical issue in the second Westchester period. As noted earlier, even while the business arrangement with cousin Courtland was coming to its inglorious end, Cooper was embarked on yet another partnership intended to extricate him from his financial woes. It involved the potentially lu-crative whaling trade, in which the state of New York at the time played a major role. Cooper's new partner was to be Charles T. Dering, whose grandmother's family, the Sylvesters, had been associated for generations with the busy Long Island port of Sag Harbor and nearby Shelter Island. Despite his salt-sea back-ground, Dering had been living upstate for a number of years before his arrangement with Cooper: first as a businessman in Utica, then as a merchant and collector of internal revenue for the federal government in the village of Hamilton, located just west of Cooperstown in Madison County. Because Der-ing and his wife Eliza planned to move back to Long Island in 1819, however, he soon would be ideally placed to act on the partners' plans.[32]

Cooper's acquaintance with Charles Dering and their subsequent whaling partnership were among the gifts he owed to his wife. Eliza Nicoll Dering, like her husband a Shelter Islander, was Susan Cooper's cousin, and the two women seem to have been close since girlhood. Certainly Eliza's helpful visit from Ham-ilton to Fenimore Farm in the spring of 1817, when the Coopers' fourth child was born, suggests a long-standing intimacy.[33] The Coopers and the Derings began socializing not only via such neighborly calls between Hamilton and Coopers-town from 1813 to 1817, but also during the summer and autumn visits that, ac-cording to the novelist's daughter, her parents paid in their early married life to "a relative of Mrs. Cooper" on Shelter Island. At the home of Eliza Dering's fa-ther, Samuel B. Nicoll, and perhaps at Sylvester Manor, the mansion of Charles Dering's parents, the two couples spent relaxing spells together when they could get away from New York City, Westchester, or their respective upstate homes.[34] Hence the Sag Harbor tale that it was during visits to the Nicolls "in company with Charles T. Dering" that Cooper's attention first was "drawn to the whale fishery."[35]

Cooper's daughter also portrayed him as hanging about Sag Harbor during his island visits, listening to local whaling tales and thus slowly forming his plans. That seems an exaggeration, probably an anachronistic one at that. Coop-er's single biggest debt was to Charles Dering and his kin and acquaintances, who together saw to most of the local arrangements in 1819; indeed, Cooper ap-pears not to have visited Sag Harbor in person on whaling business until after his vessel returned from its first whaling voyage the following summer. Compared with Courtland, Cooper's new partner certainly was a resourceful ally. For al-most thirty years, Dering's uncle, Henry P. Dering, had served as collector of customs at Sag Harbor.[36] Henry's son Thomas in turn was to be appointed to succeed his father in 1822, while another of the sons, Nicoll R. Dering, was him-self a whaling captain. When Charles Dering was corresponding with Cooper on the details of the impending voyage, he regularly drew on such kin, as well as on other relatives and friends in New York City or on Long Island who were intimately acquainted with the trade. Although not personally involved in whaling heretofore, Dering clearly knew much about it, and in fact his partnership with Cooper led him to found a successful whaling company of his own. He purchased and outfitted many whalers from the 1820s through the 1840s.[37]

The two men had begun planning their initial venture some time before the Derings' return home. If they did not discuss the issue on their island visits or while upstate, certainly they did so during a trip to New York City that Dering made in the fall of 1818, which *may* have included a quick run out to Shelter Island. Once back in Hamilton in mid-December, Dering wrote a chatty letter about the impending partnership, expressing the hope that Cooper would visit him over the coming winter.[38] There is no indication that Cooper ever made it to Madison County then. But he was not ignoring the question. After New Year's, he went to New York City on several occasions, partly to seek out a suitable vessel and negotiate for its purchase.[39] Toward the end of March, he wrote to inform Dering that he had agreed to buy a ship; three weeks later, on April 14, the bill of sale for the 260-plus-ton ship *Union* was signed by owner Gurdon S. Mumford. Built at New Bedford in 1804, the vessel had two decks and three masts, measured ninety-two feet long by twenty-six-and-a-half feet in the beam, and drew twelve feet nine inches. It was, the registration filed by Mumford that February declared, "a square sterned ship" with no side or stern galleries. Its bow was adorned with "a Billet" (or billet head, a simple carved ornament) rather than a figurehead.[40] How Cooper settled on this vessel is not known. An advertisement for the *Union* in New York papers may have caught his eye. He would have found the ship especially appealing, perhaps, because of its relatively modest size and ordinariness, as well as its apparently good state of repair (although Cooper and Dering were to be disillusioned on this front once they took it over).[41]

However Mumford's ship came to Cooper's attention, Dering's letters clearly indicate that Cooper indeed made the choice of the vessel. Because the vessel was to be entirely his, that was only right. Only in sharing the cost for outfitting the *Union* for a whaling voyage were Cooper and Dering to be partners, and at a seventy-thirty split at that. However, once Cooper had purchased the ship, Dering was all activity—at a distance. His April 1 letter, based on sketchy information supplied by Cooper, directed the latter's attention to key issues needing consideration and supplied the name of an experienced agent—"Mr. [Rensselaer] Havens"—to guide the fitting out that was to follow. The Havenses, an old Shelter Island family with whom the Derings were intermarried, had a long-standing presence in the commercial life of New York City. Rensselaer Havens was a partner in the firm of Jenkins and Havens, shipping merchants, a firm to which Dering again directed Cooper when he wrote at the end

of April that "Mr. Fred. Jenkins," who represented various New York shipown-
ers, would be a good agent for the *Union* as well.[42]

Dering also wanted to know more details about the vessel. From the size as
Cooper had stated it to him, he concluded that the *Union* would hold fourteen
hundred barrels and would thus support two—but *not* three—boat crews.
Cooper held out for three. The issue had many ramifications. Adding a third
boat crew would not increase the amount of oil stowed in each barrel or the number of barrels the ship was able to hold. It might conceivably reduce the amount
of time required for the vessel to reach capacity. But even if that happened, the
partners would find that time indeed was money. Good men would sign on a
three-boat ship of the *Union*'s modest size only if they were guaranteed a larger
share of the ship's take—a "lower lay," in the terms familiar to every reader of
Moby-Dick—than they would be willing to accept if only two boat crews were
employed. Or, and this might prove even more costly, the partners would have
to settle for "the poorest officers and crew." Green hand that he was in this business, Cooper apparently had argued that another boat would add a third to the
ship's catch—a mistake in mathematics and logic alike. Dering tried to set him
straight on the second point: "As to the . . . difference of proceeds being $\frac{1}{3}$[,]
that cannot be the case [once the crew] fill the ship unless the ship will carry $\frac{1}{3}$
more cargo"—which of course it could not, for a full ship was a full ship. But,
with the same capacity and 5o (not 33) percent more men to attract to the *Union*
and pay off once it returned home, the partners would have less to show for all
their risk and work. Even if one assumed that the first two boat crews would compromise and agree to work a three-boat ship for the same lays as they would work
if the ship had only two, then the shares of the third boat crew must obviously
come from somewhere else—the partners' pockets. So would the money for the
additional equipment and supplies, not to mention food and drink.[43] Even though
Dering was wholly in the right on this question, he appears to have yielded to the
ship's owner on it. When the vessel left Sag Harbor in August, it had a captain
and two mates and twenty-one men, organized into three boat crews.[44]

The partners debated the question of boats and crews just when Cooper was
completing his complicated arrangements with shipowner Mumford. On April
15, he gave the merchant his binder for the deal, a secured note for $1,ooo that
was payable in sixty days. The security consisted of four of the leasehold farms
that had been transferred from Judge Cooper's estate in 1811, which Cooper now
signed over to Mumford for a token payment of one dollar. If Cooper discharged his obligation under the note by June 15, Mumford agreed to reconvey
the leaseholds to Cooper—which in fact he did on June 17, doubtless because
this temporary agreement was superseded by the final one (discussed below).[45]
But Mumford never really took possession of the leaseholds. In the separate pur-

chase-and-sale agreement he and Cooper also completed on April 15, Cooper agreed to convey or cause to be conveyed to the owner of the *Union* within the same sixty-day period four other parcels of land (totaling around 450 acres) in Otsego County, the value of which was placed at $5,000. The four properties included Mt. Ovis, Cooper's sheep farm adjoining Fenimore, which Cooper's lawyer, Robert Campbell, had told him the previous November probably would be hard to sell outright. The inclusion of Mt. Ovis in the deal with Mumford marked Cooper's seriousness about the whaling venture and, at the same time, his tight financial situation. Once Mt. Ovis was transferred, he could not easily return to the status quo ante at Fenimore.[46]

The bill of sale was in Cooper's hands once it had been filled out and signed and witnessed, but until Cooper actually conveyed to Mumford those four Otsego parcels, the vessel was not really his. He had possession of the ship and was responsible for its well-being and its care, but he could not sell it. Nor could he move it from port, as Dering rightly assumed when he advised Cooper to have necessary repairs and the outfitting begun in New York rather than waiting for the vessel's transfer to Sag Harbor. That was an efficient though potentially risky course. Not until the conveyance for the ship was completed on June 10 would the partners' expenses be fully justified. The uncertainty particularly affected Cooper, since at this point the expenses were mostly his. Dering was having difficulty liquidating his upstate assets or finding other ready resources; in May he finally reached the decision that his share of the outfit would have to be paid for with borrowed money.[47]

It was the end of June before Dering finally wrapped up his northern affairs and arrived at Shelter Island. Although the ship now legally was Cooper's, it still remained in New York, where repairs were progressing. In May, Dering had advised Cooper to have a competent carpenter do the work, suggesting Henry Eckford, whom Cooper of course knew from Oswego and whom he apparently did hire.[48] Whoever undertook the work in New York, though, it did not go quickly. The partners had discussed the use of "shifting boards," temporary bulkheads put in place to keep the potentially tricky cargo from moving about in heavy seas, but Dering investigated the issue at Sag Harbor and found that they would have to bolt bulkheads in place permanently. That took extra time and money. More of each was required for preparing the hull. The vessel evidently was careened (turned on its side) so that the hull could be cleaned, caulked, and strengthened. Given the fact that the *Union* was headed through the tropics to the Brazilian whaling grounds, steps would also have to be taken to guard against worms that might bore through its hull. Copper sheathing was a good but too costly solution. Instead, following Dering's advice, Cooper apparently directed that additional boards be tightly nailed over the hull up to the waterline. At the same time, the rudder probably was sheathed, and the sternpost (the aftermost vertical timber) as well as the rudder where it joined the sternpost required leading, also as a protection against worms.[49]

Not surprisingly, the *Union* probably lingered in New York until Dering came up island around the middle of July to sail the vessel to Sag Harbor, where he arrived sometime before August 4. During this long New York stay, the ship had been more or less under Cooper's continuing personal supervision. Dering's letters through April were addressed to Cooper at Mamaroneck; from May 6 until August, he sent them directly to the City Hotel, from which they were not forwarded, a sure sign that Cooper mostly remained in the city over this period of weeks. He often ate at the hotel, although he apparently had a room there only for a five-day period in July. Becoming owner of a whaleship, even though Cooper had no intention of sailing on it, kept him away from Susan and the girls and affairs at Angevine for a good deal of time.[50] The new investment also strained Cooper's financial resources at a time when other demands put him in a tight position. Up to the end of July, Cooper put a total of some $2,000 into the ship, and as late as the twenty-ninth he assumed a new loan for $300 from the Bank of New York "on acct. of Ship," for unstated purposes. Later, shortly after the vessel sailed, Dering estimated that the "outfits" for it when all the expenses were totaled would "exceed $5000," and he asked whether Cooper would be able to find someone else willing to become a partial backer so as to lessen the cost to the partners, especially Dering.[51]

Despite all that had been done on the ship at New York, yet more work was required at Sag Harbor. During his passage out from the city, an alarmed Dering found the ship's rigging "poor beyond description." It was so bad that he suspected the *Union* had been stripped of its good rope and bad rigging substituted for it after it arrived in New York the previous fall. Had Mumford practiced to deceive? Had Cooper, who failed to mention the issue to Dering before the latter sailed the *Union* down island, not examined the vessel as closely as a seasoned sailor could and should have?[52] Two other sources of delay slowed the ship's eventual departure even more, and one could be laid at least in part to Dering's own failures. It proved exceptionally difficult for him to sign officers and crew despite his familiarity with the business and its personnel in the area. Before the ship arrived, he claimed that the local sailors were suspicious of any ship they could not inspect with their own eyes. That the vessel was from New York made it worse, he added, because Sag Harbor officers were fearful of New York vessels—even more so of late because a New York ship had just been reported lost. Moreover, there was a good deal of competition from other local ships just coming in from successful voyages that had some openings for officers and men. All in all, he seems to have run out of local options.[53]

He therefore contemplated hiring a Nantucket captain for the *Union,* certainly a reasonable alternative given that island's heavy involvement in whaling and the difficulties facing him in ports clustered on the end of Long Island. Yet as Dering knew all too well, such a captain might actually chase away potential crewmen from Sag Harbor. As he had bluntly informed Cooper at the start of July, Long Island sailors did not like Nantucket captains (perhaps this was one source for Cooper's later use of Nantucket's nearer neighbor, the Vineyard, as the home of Jason Daggett, Long Islander Roswell Gardiner's mysterious competitor in *The Sea Lions*). All of this made the Suffolk sailors sound like a picky, skittish lot. Hence Dering's willingness to contemplate taking on as skipper a man of mixed reputation who had lost his last vessel—because of leaks, he claimed, although the owners accused him of intemperance.[54]

A full month later, on August 4, Dering at last could report that he had signed a much better captain, Jonathan Osborne, a resident of the small village of Wainscott on the south shore of Easthampton. Osborne was well known as an accomplished whaler. One story concerning his exploits was recalled many years later by a local judge, Henry P. Hedges, who when a boy had watched from land as Osborne led two boats in a long, bloody offshore pursuit of a whale. When the successful boat crews came in, the boy was impressed by "the tall and stalwart form of the Captain clad in his red flannel shirt, his face and hands almost equally red"—from the gore of the chase. Here, said Judge Hedges, could have been the model for Cooper's own whaleman, Long Tom Coffin, in *The Pilot*. Whatever his literary uses for Cooper in that novel, Jonathan Osborne seems to have been a good catch for Dering in 1819. Even with such a captain signed and an unnamed man taken on as first mate, Dering nonetheless had considerable difficulty finding a second mate. Not until August 10 could he write to inform Cooper that all hands had been shipped and the vessel was ready to depart.[55]

That was an optimistic message. Provisions and gear Cooper was to have provided before Dering took over the vessel still had not been sent, as Dering had reminded his partner on August 4. He encouraged Cooper to see to the items immediately and gave him the names of two islanders then in New York who could carry them out when they came home. Three days later, when the first of those two men arrived but had nothing for the *Union,* Dering wrote that he was "much disappointed" at Cooper's failure to take care of the issue, reminding him that "every [day] we wait is $100 to us." Unless they hurried, the *Union* would bring up the rear of that year's whaling fleet. That would be humiliating, but it also had economic implications. If the other vessels swept the whaling grounds before the *Union* managed to arrive, pickings might be slim. And if the ship were delayed too long in the South Atlantic on this voyage, it would come back too late to make a timely departure next year. Dering's urgency notwithstanding, this second letter also reached the city before Cooper had taken care of the last-minute items. On the tenth, Dering therefore sent a third letter by "Capt. Brown," who (the letter informed Cooper) was ready to bring back the items forthwith. Again Dering stressed how much it was costing the partners to keep the crew in provisions while the vessel was idle at the wharf and the men had no real work to do. Only on Saturday the fourteenth, a full ten days after sending the first letter, could Dering at last acknowledge receipt of the provisions and gear. He was eager to get everything on board quickly in order to ensure that the ship could leave the following Monday "if nothing uncommon should prevent."[56] Of course something "uncommon"—though we don't know what—*did* intervene. It was not until Thursday, August 19, that, with its twenty-one men aboard, "the Union sailed from this port . . . for the coast of Brazil & Patagonia" (as Dering wrote Cooper from Sag Harbor on the twenty-first).[57]

Debits and Credits

Thoughts of the *Union*'s course as it coasted south toward the Caribbean and the equator no doubt called up memories of Cooper's own days at sea a decade and more ago. His excitement about the venture, though, concealed deeper worries. The *Union* in fact was afloat on a sea of debt. The heavy burden Cooper was bearing at the time was of course a large part of his reason for becoming involved in the whaling business in the first place. That business in turn increased the demands on his resources even as it seemingly promised some distant relief from the overall problem. While he had managed to pay Gurdon Mumford for the vessel by signing over the four Otsego properties, outfitting the vessel had been very expensive, forcing Cooper to sell more real estate and borrow new sums in order to proceed.

As his need for money grew, his relations with his creditors turned increasingly difficult. This was especially true with regard to New York City lawyer Robert Sedgwick. The unpleasantness in this case was compounded by the fact that the two men had personal ties that long predated and to some extent appear to have survived their financial entanglements. Sedgwick's father, Theodore Sedgwick, Sr., a signer of the Declaration of Independence and a famous Massachusetts Federalist, had sat in the House of Representatives with Judge Cooper at the outset of the latter's first term, then moved briefly to the Senate (1796–1799) before returning to the House as speaker in 1799, while the elder Cooper was still there. This fundamental political link was solidified by the overlapping geographical territories of the Coopers and the Sedgwicks. Members of the latter family, long resident in the Berkshires, naturally gravitated over the New

York border into Cooper country. Robert Sedgwick's older brother Theodore
thus moved to Albany early in the nineteenth century and set up his law practice
there in partnership with Harmanus Bleecker, a long-time associate and friend of
Cooper; their sister Catharine was schooled in Albany while Cooper himself
was there at Ellison's (see *LJ* 4:31–33).[58] Among the law students of the firm of
Bleecker and Sedgwick were such other Cooper friends as Yale graduate Jacob
Sutherland and perhaps Peter Gansevoort, as well as Robert Sedgwick himself.[59]

These earlier ties between the two families probably led Cooper to socialize
with Robert Sedgwick and his brother (and law partner) Henry in New York
City in the years following the shift away from Fenimore Farm. The social con-
nection was so strong that as late as the mid-1820s, long after their financial dealings had soured (but before the final crisis), Cooper still could be found at
Robert Sedgwick's house. It was there in 1824, for instance, that William Cullen
Bryant, fresh from the Berkshires and reliant on the financial backing of the
Sedgwick brothers for his soon-to-be-launched *New York Review and Atheneum
Magazine*, first met the novelist.[60] As chronically short of cash as he was at the
time he returned to Westchester, Cooper initially drew on Robert Sedgwick's resources in the fall of 1817, right after he had set up Courtland's demanding
schedule of payments in Utica. At that time, the exchange was fairly straightforward and benign. It was less an outright loan than a real estate deal by which
Cooper probably hoped he could convert a piece of property received from his
father's estate into ready cash. Cooper thus assigned Sedgwick a judgment he
had won in the New York Supreme Court on an unpaid real estate bond from
a St. Lawrence County lawyer. In return for this assignment, Sedgwick paid
Cooper the judgment amount less an unspecified discount to cushion his risk and
provide a margin of profit once he recovered the judgment himself.[61]

This tentative deal between the two friends, which in fact was to have a
rather long and complicated future, laid the groundwork for other deals that
proved deeply vexing for Cooper.[62] For what was intended to be a short time
only, in May of 1818 Cooper borrowed somewhat less than $2,000 from Sedg-
wick, perhaps in order to finance the DeKalb operation with Courtland Cooper.[63]
As he recalled in an 1826 supreme court deposition, Cooper had "accidentally
mentioned" to Sedgwick while in New York City that he "stood in need of the
sum." Sedgwick volunteered to lend Cooper that amount for ninety days, in turn
saying that he would derive the funds from a sale of stock he owned but wished
to sell anyway. When the stock was sold, it yielded less than Sedgwick had expected; knowing that Cooper was in need of the funds, he therefore insisted that
Cooper make up the difference, presumably as a discount out of the loaned funds
themselves. Secured by Cooper's personal note, this initial debt became the basis
for others. When the note came due in August 1818, it was extended for an addi-

tional term of about three months and the debt was secured by an assignment of
real estate. Then, as the new due date approached in November, Cooper again
found himself in no position to make good on his promises. In fact, being just
then in need of yet more money, perhaps also for the DeKalb store, he not only
extended the old note but also took out a new loan for an additional $1,000 or so,
thereby increasing the total due Sedgwick to just over $3,000. At the same time,
he bolstered his security for the debt by assigning to Sedgwick a trio of Otsego
leasehold farms that had come to him from his father's estate in 1811. These
farms were to be transferred outright to Sedgwick should Cooper fail to repay
both loans by the new due date, May 1, 1819.[64]

In both cases, Cooper was liable for "legal interest" (under the 1787 New
York usury statute, not more than 7 percent per year) on each loan for its respective period. As the next payoff date approached, Cooper—now busily concerned
with the *Union* in New York City and deeply disappointed by Courtland's inability to meet his expectations for cash remittances from DeKalb—found himself unable to settle with Sedgwick yet again.[65] At the same time, he desperately
needed to recover his control over those three leasehold farms to use them
(along with a fourth from his father's legacy) as security for his initial note to
Gurdon S. Mumford for the whaleship. He therefore secured a release of the
Sedgwick assignment on March 30, 1819, two weeks before he in turn signed
the farms over to Mumford. This arrangement allowed Cooper to proceed with
the Mumford deal and thus move ahead with his whaling plans.

For releasing the properties in question, however, Robert Sedgwick had exacted a terrible cost. First, Cooper had to secure the existing loan by giving Sedgwick an assignment on a parcel of land in Cooperstown, along with the three
separate parcels composing Fenimore Farm, including all improvements—the
unfinished mansion, the barn, other outbuildings, and the wooden farmhouse. In
addition, Sedgwick insisted on an extraordinary payment in the event that Cooper
should miss his due dates on the total amount of the renewed loans, which remained at just over $3,000. On March 12, 1819, Cooper thus agreed that he would
pay Sedgwick a heavy (but at the time not uncommon) "penalty" if he failed to
make his payoffs at the scheduled six-month and twelve-month deadlines. The
penalty, if enforced, would add almost another $2,000 to Cooper's debt.[66]

Cooper probably assumed that he would be able to pay off Sedgwick and recover the newly assigned properties with the expected profits from the whaling
venture. He certainly did not think of Fenimore Farm as lost, and he still viewed
his overall financial situation as basically sound. In early 1819, as he recalled several years later, he thought he was "perfectly solvent and able to pay . . . all his
debts." At the same time, he knew very well that his lands "then lying in the interior of the State" had little immediate value "in the money market of the City

of New York," which was Robert Sedgwick's home turf. Sedgwick appreciated the quandary and, once he saw Cooper's willingness to grant the new security for the loan, pushed him harder. Cooper, eager to buy time and appease his creditor, volunteered to pay interest calculated at 1.5 percent per month. This rate was more than two-and-a-half times the legal limit. At first, as Cooper later recalled the negotiations with pointed sarcasm, Sedgwick refused Cooper's offer "on the plea of liberality, *and seeing it was me* sort of friendship" (*LJ* 1:121–22).[67] Apparently on March 12, 1819, however, the two settled on *merely* 1 percent per month and planned to meet again once Sedgwick had prepared the necessary papers for them to sign.

When Cooper returned to Sedgwick's office at the end of March, he was surprised to find that Sedgwick had extended the new interest rate back over the whole sequence of loans, thereby increasing the effective yield to 15 if not 18 percent, and putting Cooper in arrears at the outset for some $150.[68] Since Sedgwick had taken so long to draw up the agreement, Cooper was in an even tighter spot. The national economic crisis that had begun the previous fall showed no sign of easing, and land values in New York were continuing their downward slide.[69] If Cooper objected to Sedgwick's new demands and Sedgwick therefore refused at the last minute to extend the repayment date of the debt, it would be due soon and Cooper would have no ready means of repaying it. A "forced sale of his property" would follow, inflicting "loss and inconvenience" on him. Yet mixed with Cooper's feeling of vulnerability were other emotions. He felt "greatly disgusted" by Sedgwick's underhanded maneuvers. Although Cooper had first suggested the usurious rate, he had done so because of Sedgwick's feigned reluctance to extend the old debt. He could not defy Sedgwick for financial reasons alone. Yet Cooper also felt an "unwillingness to break with" Sedgwick—for financial reasons, to be sure, but also because the two were friends in a city where, the "money market" to one side, personal ties still meant a great deal. On balance, as Cooper told the tale early in 1826, he was offended by the whole exchange but trapped by his needs. He therefore retreated into a kind of noble passivity, his habit in times of moral repugnance (see *LJ* 1:122).[70]

There was another edge to the affair that Cooper later tried to use as a weapon. Sedgwick wanted to keep the appearance of legality in what was, because of the usurious interest rate, technically an illegal agreement. The judge in the first of two supreme court trials (held on Sedgwick's complaint that Cooper had not made full payment on his bond) instructed the jury, "If when the bond was made it was agreed to pay more than 7 pr ct the bond is void & the Jury must find for the Deft."[71] At the time the bond was drawn up and signed, Sedgwick reasoned that stating the true interest rate on the bond was not necessary as long as Cooper paid up and the debt was properly discharged. However, in the event that Cooper could not meet his obligations and the old friends wound up in court, as they did, Sedgwick knew that usury might become a problem. He therefore wanted "to exclude all of the usurious interest from the bond for his security," as he told Cooper when they executed the agreement, meaning that Cooper "must pay all the back usury, in some other manner."[72] That "other manner" involved most importantly the falsification of payments Cooper made on his debt. Each time a payment was made, Sedgwick receipted it in an ambiguous manner, as in the following instance: "NYork Feb 20 [18]21 Rec'd 2 yrs interest on this bond plus $281.67 in principal." Cooper made a payment of $1,000 on that date, as he would assert for the Chancery Court in 1826. Sedgwick did not state either the amount of the whole payment or the amount of the "2 yrs interest" ($725.12) because anyone would be able to figure the actual interest rate from it. To all appearances, Cooper was meeting his legal obligations on a legal debt (two years of legal interest would have been $423) and was paying down the amount of the debt as well. But the payment in question, although apparently late, in fact *did* constitute full payment of the interest at the usurious rate. That the figures do not tally exactly may well be because (as Cooper pointed out for his attorney and friend Peter A. Jay in 1825) Sedgwick tended to make his calculations in his head, muttering "in a half whisper" as he went (*LJ* 1:122). Cooper admitted that he had not paid close attention partly because of his own carelessness at the time, but mostly because he felt "a strong disgust to enter into calculations of this nature with an individual with whom he was accustomed to associate as a Gentleman." Sedgwick was a friend; when exactly he became an adversary is not a simple question. We shall return to it in Chapters 14 and 15.[73]

Cooper's profound distress at Robert Sedgwick's turpitude was balanced by his great good fortune in another set of financial dealings carried out at the same time. As he decided to divest himself of real estate in Otsego in order to finance his new activities elsewhere, he began to cultivate a lucrative relationship with wealthy lawyer Thomas Ward. Ward had held the offices of sheriff and judge in Essex County, New Jersey, before serving as a Republican congressman from Newark from 1813 to 1817. Although he was of Judge Cooper's generation, Ward seems never to have been acquainted with him or his older sons (their papers contain no references to him), so his tie to the youngest of the Coopers may have been completely of the latter's own making. Perhaps Cooper met "Colonel Ward" (as the Cooper documents refer to him) through their common involvement in Republican politics or militia affairs in the late 1810s. It also is possible that they became acquainted through Cooper's links to at least two of Ward's sons, especially Isaac Ward, Cooper's exact contemporary (see *LJ* 1:39). However the connection originated, it had become sufficiently close by 1819 that the elder Ward began paying handsomely for several parcels he acquired from

Cooper and his wife across that year. These included thirteen of the leasehold farms that had come into Cooper's hands from his father's estate in 1811. Whereas Cooper had used three of the leasehold farms as temporary security for both the Sedgwick loan in 1818 and the transfer of the *Union* the following year, in Colonel Ward's case the transfer was to prove more nearly permanent. For Cooper's interest in all thirteen properties, Ward gave him $5,000 early in September 1819, right after the whaleship had sailed for the Brazilian whaling grounds. Henceforth Cooper's income from these farms ceased, although several of the other leaseholds derived from his father's estate still remained in his possession.[74]

By the time this deal was consummated, what is more, Ward already had paid an equal sum for the bulk of the forty-two lots Cooper owned in St. Lawrence County. By smaller conveyances completed in November and the following year, Ward similarly purchased a few other DeKalb lots. Overall, the lawyer paid Cooper $6,190 for the properties there, less than a third of the inflated cash equivalency ($21,928.80) under the calculations carried out when the estate's interests there were divided among the heirs in 1815.[75] While that reduction in value was precipitous, Cooper still gained $1.25 per acre for land that might not have brought a fraction of that amount, if it brought anything, on the open market in the panic year of 1819. All told, Thomas Ward paid Cooper a total of nearly $12,000 for the Otsego and St. Lawrence county transfers. In addition, for the quite good price of $5,300 (more than $5.00 per acre), Ward purchased 916 ¼ acres of Cooper's holdings in the town of Bangor in Franklin County, a transaction agreed to in September of 1819 and finalized when the Coopers signed the conveyance on December 2. Ward also purchased Springhill Farm in Hartwick from Cooper in November for $1,800.[76] This last transaction brought the grand total of his payments to Cooper to nearly $19,000. That Ward was able to promise or actually pay this much money under the conditions prevailing in 1819 suggests the scope of his wealth. It also suggests Cooper's extraordinary luck in having found a buyer for so much of his otherwise largely unsaleable property.[77]

What Cooper did with the windfall is nowhere stated. If some or all of it came to him as cash at the time of the transfers, or as personal bonds that could be discounted for cash through a third party, he probably used some of it for the cost of outfitting the *Union*. He may well have applied much of it, however, to liquidate the old debt owed James Platt in Utica, which may have been for as much as $10,000 or more and of which in future years there appears to be no further mention.[78] It is of course possible that Cooper carefully concealed the proceeds of his deals with Ward as a way of protecting his own assets from creditors; but in his known financial dealings during this period he never acted like a man with thousands of dollars in cash squirreled away somewhere. This point is most apparent in his dealings with Robert Sedgwick at the very time when he was selling so much land for so much money to Thomas Ward. If Cooper could have paid Sedgwick in full before that man began extorting promises of high interest rates—let alone before Sedgwick brought suit against him—it is clear that he would have done so without a moment's hesitation. It probably is best, as a result, to conclude that Cooper used his proceeds from the sales to Ward to pay off his old debts even as new ones piled up. The recent gains thus covered—only partly at that—the accumulating losses of the vertiginous past decade.

CHAPTER EIGHT

A Better Book

Aﬀter the Coopers moved into Angevine in the fall of 1818, Susan, pregnant again, began spending much of her time there. This development
and Cooper's growing absorption with financial matters and with finding and preparing a whaleship across the following spring meant that the
couple's paths often diverged. (When the girl, Maria Frances, was born on Tuesday, June 15, 1819, the very day the deal for the *Union* was to be finalized, Cooper
was busy with the ship in New York City rather than by his wife's side.)[1] This
whole period was full of serious changes. Cooper's brother Samuel, just thirty-
two, had died in Cooperstown on Monday, February 15, when Cooper had been
scouting out his whaleship. A Cooperstown paper printed a modest obituary,
noting that this latest Otsego Hall funeral was "numerously attended"—though
not by many members of the family. So few of them were left in the Judge's village then that Cooper received the news not from kin but from his attorney,
Robert Campbell, who wrote him immediately, adding (as if Cooper somehow
did not already know it) that Samuel had been in decline for some time.[2]

Sam's passing meant that Cooper was one step closer to managing the estate. William, the current executor, was making such a mess of things that by

summer his sole surviving brother had become everyone's favorite substitute for him. On returning to New York from a brief trip to Angevine on June 21, Cooper thus found a letter awaiting him in which Isaac and Sam's widows expressed concern about William's poor performance and its implications for their ten "Fatherless Children."[3] Cooper had been much involved in affairs of the estate under Isaac's executorship, partly because of Isaac's chronic disability, but he was not about to visit Cooperstown again and take matters into his own hands, as the two women wished. Even though he had no legal basis for intervening, lawyer Campbell soon pressured him to do so by filling him in on William's defalcations. Not only would he "do nothing" toward settling the estate, Campbell wrote in June—he also was wasting resources: "Whatever goes into his hands is so much sunk & you and the other heirs will have to pay the debts." Among other things, William had ceased paying interest on some estate obligations, running the risk of foreclosures that might strip away valuable property. Other family members then in Cooperstown, Campbell went on, were eager to obtain an injunction against William and have the estate cut up before he had squandered or endangered everything. Cooper might have stepped in but again refused to act. Perhaps he already suspected the truth Campbell would convey about William in August: he "is in very bad health and I think he will not live long."[4]

William evinced a pointless show of concern about the estate as his health collapsed. On October 11, he printed a "Caution to Trespassers" in a village newspaper, warning the "many persons [who] have been in the habit of committing trespasses on the estate of the late WILLIAM COOPER" to cease and desist. As an incentive to informers, he offered handsome rewards. But it was a bootless gesture: he died on October 19, 1819, a little more than a week after the notice first ran. The news of his passing reached Westchester slowly and indirectly, via a letter from Albany lawyer Thomas Bridgen, one of the estate's creditors. With the estate in disarray, the sometime master of Fenimore Farm was literally the last of the Coopers. The collapse had come with frightening speed, accelerating over the past year and a half. But it was to continue until virtually everything left by Judge Cooper at his death a decade earlier had been swept away. Disaster seemed to have targeted all of the family, but for some time yet Cooper would succeed in keeping it away from his own premises.[5]

For one thing, Westchester insulated Cooper from upstate news. Almost from the moment his family returned there, he had been involving himself a good deal in local affairs. He transferred his interest in the Otsego Bible Society to the similar body in Westchester, of which John Jay had been named president on its organization in 1815 and in which several of the Jays as well as Cooper's father-in-law were serving as officers during 1817–1818.[6] He also transplanted his passion for agricultural improvement, again in association with both Jays and his father-in-law. Not only did he attend the agricultural gathering of "sundry inhabitants" at the White Plains courthouse on May 26, 1818, he also helped draft a constitution for the society founded then and assisted in organizing its fall fair.[7]

Participation in such bodies sharpened Cooper's emerging political profile. This was especially true in the case of the Westchester Agricultural Society. While not usually partisan, such organizations hardly were apolitical. Elected officials often attended agricultural fairs in particular, seeking a chance to support progressive causes even as they informally stumped for votes. When Cooper served as co-marshal of the Westchester fair in the fall of 1818 along with county sheriff Lyman Cook, the two did such expectable things as leading the members' procession from the livestock competition to the courthouse, in the process holding high the banner that Cooper and his wife had designed and made for the society (SFM 37). But the marshals also had to nimbly accommodate two surprise guests at the event—U.S. vice president Daniel D. Tompkins and New York governor DeWitt Clinton. Clinton was there as the champion of scientific agriculture, Tompkins as a local son (he had been born and raised within a mile or so of Angevine) who was now prominent on the national stage. But the real reason they attended was their ongoing battle as the heads of the state's two Republican factions—the Clintonians and the Bucktails (or Tammany wing). Former allies and now bitter foes, Tompkins and Clinton must have made for some tricky handling. Cooper, who recently had become the neighbor of Tompkins and was seeking to plant his roots anew in Susan's home district, would have something to gain by courting the vice president. Yet he never really liked Tompkins, and in any case he already had forged an alliance with Clinton that would soon deepen.[8]

Cooper probably had become acquainted with the governor in New York City during the latter's second and third terms as mayor (1808–1810, 1811–1815). The tie between the two certainly was not among the benefits the young man owed to his father or his father-in-law or their old Federalist allies such as John Jay. A staunch Jeffersonian, DeWitt Clinton had been the political enemy of Judge Cooper, who had helped Jay in his effort to defeat Clinton's uncle, George Clinton, in the bitter 1792 governor's race. William Cooper, much punished for his high-handed dealings in that instance, unrepentantly opposed the Clintonian candidate in 1801 as well.[9] In the years since the elder Cooper's death, the state's political boundaries had been radically redrawn, particularly through Clinton's efforts. Especially during his nearly successful run for the presidency in 1812, Clinton had welcomed Federalist support, a gamble that temporarily diminished his standing but that ultimately bolstered what became known as Clintonian Republicanism.[10] The success of that hybrid movement owed a good deal to Clinton's program of ambitious reform and his support for internal improvements such as the Erie Canal in later years. Although Clinton never was warmly popular, his image as a dynamic leader and his somewhat inflated reputation as an intellectual in the mold of Jefferson appealed to many New Yorkers. John Jay himself, surprisingly enough, became a Clintonian. So did young Cooper, whose disillusionment with his father's old party and uncertainty about his own future may have conspired to give Clinton's decisive public character especially strong appeal. In 1828, Cooper was to praise Clinton for the boldness of his vision and his courage in championing discredited but ultimately successful causes (see *Notions* 1:126–27).

Cooper's alliance with DeWitt Clinton was not just sentimental. Following his election to the governorship in 1817, Clinton used his increasing power over the state's Council of Appointment, at the hands of which he (and, in lesser ways, Cooper) had suffered various political embarrassments in earlier years, to secure for Cooper a series of militia appointments that helped to solidify the young man's position in Westchester society. In March of 1819, Cooper thus became paymaster of the Fourth Division of infantry, a Westchester and Rockland county unit that included some ten or twelve regiments, as well as special bodies similar to that "light infantry" company to which Cooper had belonged in Otsego in 1816.[11] That appointment probably had come at the urging of Pierre Van Cortlandt, a lifelong militia officer then approaching sixty years of age who had been named divisional major general in 1817.[12] Cooper, sure of the process as well as his own standing, had actively solicited Van Cortlandt's aid. The DeLancey kinsman and old Cooper family friend—he was the younger brother of the congressman who had written in support of Cooper's application for a naval warrant a decade earlier—sent word of his happy compliance in September 1818. Probably the general offered Cooper a temporary or brevet position on his own staff while an official appointment was forthcoming from Albany. On receiving Van Cortlandt's letter, Cooper surely knew that he had played the game well: he thus accepted Van Cortlandt's positive act "with pleasure."[13]

Cooper's assignment to the official paymaster's position the following March was a prelude to further advancements. By July 1819, just when he was seeing to some of the last details for the *Union*, he was elevated to divisional quartermaster. He probably named his own replacement in the paymaster's position, for Edward H. DeLancey, Susan's brother, was approved by the council in due order. In his second position, Cooper was one of three men on Van Cortlandt's staff—paymaster DeLancey and judge advocate Frederick J. Coffin being the others.[14] As a member of this select group, with far more prestige than the position that had been offered to him in Otsego in 1816, Cooper was a member of a county elite, hobnobbing with the brother of the lord of Van Cortlandt Manor and some 100 or 150 officers not only from Westchester but also from across the Hudson in Rockland County. So much for Bucktail Ambrose Jordan's little victory four years earlier in Otsego.[15]

Cooper had ample opportunity to strut about in his fancy uniform. A picturesque description of him in full regalia was penned by his daughter Susan, who recalled seeing her father, in his "uniform, blue and buff, cocked hat and sword, mounted on Bull-head"—his favorite but apparently none-too-disciplined (or showy) horse during this period—"before proceeding to some review." Susan was probably wrong in her assertion that Governor Clinton made her father "his aide-de-camp, with the rank of Colonel" (SFM 37). Her colorful image of him almost certainly derived from an occasion on which her father went off to join Van Cortlandt and the Fourth Division, perhaps in the fall of 1819.[16]

The two militia positions Cooper held as a result of Clinton's patronage were marks of political favor, justified in some sense by prior military experience but testifying most of all to the governor's confidence in the young man's right thinking and allegiance. Clinton knew that the sons of once-prominent Federalists were a good target as he set about building his own party in New York. But Cooper, as *Otsego Herald* publisher Elihu Phinney's description of him in his letter about the affray with Ambrose Jordan in 1815 underscores, already was known as a Republican well before he became the recipient of Clinton's largesse. Cooper had embarked on a political course that led him steadily away from his father's Federalism and toward the Jacksonian future. His attachment to Clinton, who has rightly been described as "an early and strong backer of Andrew Jackson," pointed him precisely in that direction.[17] And once he had made that initial alliance, he never faltered.

Butchering Bucktails

The military glory of Cooper's favors from Clinton was to pass quickly. When the tide again turned in the Council of Appointment early in 1821, depriving the governor of his recent power there, Cooper was superseded as quartermaster, much as even Pierre Van Cortlandt was forced to stand down as major general.[18] By then, however, Cooper already had taken on new and more important responsibilities for Clinton. As the governor faced reelection in 1820, Cooper emerged as secretary of the Clintonian Republicans in Westchester. Though he had "never worked at an election before" (as he wrote his old friend, Albany lawyer and avid Clintonian Peter Gansevoort on April 19), for six weeks he took charge of Clinton's fortunes across the county (*LJ* 1:141). By the time the polls closed on April 27, Clinton had built up a small statewide majority over the Bucktail candidate—Daniel D. Tompkins. Vice President Tompkins was reportedly tired of his life in Washington and wanted to return to New York, much as Clinton had resigned from the U.S. Senate in 1803 to accept his first appointment as mayor of New York City. The Bucktail candidate's national prominence and his previous experience in the state office made him a tough competitor for Clinton, although lingering questions about his handling of New York's finances during the war with Britain generally put him on the defensive. In several parts of the state, including the lower Hudson valley (and Otsego County), Tompkins did better than Clinton. In fact, he took his native Westchester by a narrow margin.[19]

Perhaps the closeness of the outcome redounded to Cooper's credit. Certainly he had worked hard for Clinton, in the process discovering some liking for political combat. When a Bucktail paper in New York City reported that the Westchester Clintonians had tried to bribe an inspector of elections, Walter Marshall of West Farms, Cooper scurried off to White Plains in an effort to track down the supposed target of the attempt. Off the top of his head, he knew of no such man living in West Farms, an area where the DeLanceys had interests, so he asked around the county seat and double-checked the list of jurors in the clerk's office there. Sure enough, as Cooper already suspected, it turned out that the man in question was instead a Mamaroneck resident. Cooper thereupon went to Marshall to hear his side of the story. The elector denied the whole tale. He *had* ventured the opinion a few days earlier in the city, he confessed to Cooper, that he thought "a great deal of bribery would be practised by both parties." This was the slender peg on which the Bucktail editor had hung his weighty accusations (*LJ* 1:40−41).[20]

As county secretary for Clinton, Cooper wanted not only to smoke out the real story but also to limit any damage the paper may have done to his cause. Hence he virtually insisted that Walter Marshall sign his name to a corrective statement that Cooper no doubt dictated for him and that he inserted into a pro-Clinton paper a few days later: "I observed in the National Advocate . . . that attempts have been made to bribe a person of the name of Walter Marshall, at West Farms, one of the Inspectors of Election. It has been represented as alluding to me—I therefore beg leave to state that my residence is in the town of Mamaroneck, county of Westchester, and that I am an Inspector of Elections, and that no attempt has been made to bribe me whatever."[21] Cooper went further. He thought that the *National Advocate* probably had not invented the slander or elaborated it from Marshall's offhand comment. Instead, he traced it to Mamaroneck, where it had been fabricated and set adrift in "the expectation that no one would take the trouble to contradict it." Cooper not only contradicted it—he tracked it to "a small Butcher" in that town, adding (in his April letter to fellow Clintonian Gansevoort) that he thought the real source was that man's biggest customer, "a notorious trimmer and Office seeker." So much, Cooper concluded for his upstate friend, for this "Butchering Bucktail" and his ilk (*LJ* 1:140).

Cooper was up against a good deal of opposition in Westchester even without such underhanded maneuvers. Not only was the county predicted, on the day Marshall's notice appeared, to go for Tompkins; it is likely that Mrs. Cooper's family, or at least some members of it, were staunch supporters of Tompkins as well.[22] Edward DeLancey perhaps had been weaned away by Cooper's success in having him named to take over the paymaster's position in the Fourth Division. But Thomas DeLancey had been decidedly "anti-Clinton" a number of years before, and probably remained so at present.[23] Cooper surely knew the election would be an uphill battle, but that hardly disheartened him or kept him away from predictably hostile public gatherings. Just the reverse is suggested by Cooper's canvassing activities during a visit he made to the homes of Clinton supporters John Jay and Philip Van Cortlandt, Pierre's elder brother, during a rainy stretch in the spring of 1820. The unidentified friend who accompanied Cooper kept an amused journal of the party secretary's political progress through Tompkins country. When the two men, heading north along the road from White Plains to Bedford, came into the small center of North Castle, they found the residents meeting to hold an election for town officials. The occasion seemed to offer Cooper a ready-made opportunity, but he and his fellow traveler quickly discovered that the locals were solidly Bucktail. Undeterred by the "hopeless task of converting them all to Clintonism," Cooper soon was proving to his friend that his "enthusiasm counterbalance[d] his prudence." Zeroing in on one particular resident who "appeared to be the decentest man among them," Cooper unleashed a long, forceful argument meant to demonstrate that the many financial sins of Tompkins during the War of 1812 disqualified him from filling the state's highest office. Cooper's friend sardonically summarized the outcome: "That the Bucktail, in his attempt to prove the immaculate purity of the man of his party, was foiled by the superior address and ingenuity of his antagonist, is not saying that he was convinced."

The two travelers passed on through the crowd. Finally they were approaching an individual who piqued the curiosity of Cooper's friend. "'Who is this?' whispered I. 'Dr. [Lyman] C[ook], the sheriff of the county,' replied my companion, 'and a warm Clintonian.'" Although Cook, co-marshal of the 1818 county fair with Cooper, had held the office of sheriff in 1812 and 1818 as well as at present, he most recently had assumed it as a result of the action of the then pro-Clinton Council of Appointment on February 4. As the two friends approached this welcome partisan, Cooper immediately engaged him in a long, intense conversation on the fortune of the campaign across Westchester. Cooper's fellow traveler was amused as the "two mad politicians kept up their jabber a full half-hour, cold, wind, and rain notwithstanding." In time, he and Cooper left North Castle and Bedford and went on to Van Cortlandt Manor. Once there, it was the same old story. Cooper's friend wanted to hear anecdotes of Philip Van Cortlandt's old military accomplishments, but instead the general's "attention was wholly occupied by Cooper and his plans for bringing in De Witt Clinton." In this one moment, we can clearly see how Cooper was embedding himself with increasing complexity in the social fabric of Westchester. No longer Judge Cooper's youngest son, he had become his own man. He was also giving full public expression to the political interests that had developed during and since the second war with England.[24]

Cooper's avidity outlasted the election that April. By no means defensive about the results in Westchester, Cooper capitalized on his energetic devotion to Clinton by helping to secure appointment as the county's head judge for his old school chum William Jay, who wrote him in June to thank him for his efforts. The commission from Clinton was clearly part of a partisan campaign aimed at solidifying the governor's new victory. Jay, who had first been named to the bench as one of the county's lesser judges two years earlier, kept the new, higher position until 1823, at which point he was turned out when all such appointments were terminated under the terms of the new state constitution. Obviously recalling his own expulsion from the Fourth Division in 1821, Cooper sent Jay his consolations: "I see you have been unhorsed with other clever fellows." That indeed had been Cooper's fate, almost literally, two years before, when he stopped riding his horse Bullhead to militia reviews. But Jay, unlike Cooper, who by 1823 was gone from Westchester and busy with new things elsewhere, in fact was soon reappointed to his old position and was to retain it from then on, under a variety of chief executives, for another two decades. His tenure in office thus may be regarded as the longest shadow cast by Cooper's brief but intense political career.[25]

Low Spirits and High

Electioneering kept Cooper away from New York City for much of March and April 1820, closer to home than he usually had been across the past year.[26] With the election decided in Clinton's favor, he probably expected that a variety of affairs would once more call him to the city for extended periods. During or soon after the campaign, however, tragedy struck near to home: Susan's mother, Elizabeth DeLancey, took seriously ill with typhoid fever and, after being bled by her doctor, fell into a decline that ended with her death on May 7, 1820 (SFM 45). This event plunged Susan into such "low spirits" (*LJ* 1:42) that he felt obliged to remain by her side in the country (*LJ* 1:42).

Among the few diversions that could brighten her mood was an old family habit—listening as her husband read aloud from a recent book. On one such occasion around the middle of May, she picked out a recently imported British novel and lay on the sitting-room sofa as Cooper began to read to her. From the outset, as their daughter told the story in 1861, Cooper was a bit restive because the "title and look of the book were not to his taste" (*P&P* 17). Soon, dissatisfied with the story as well, he threw the volume aside, "exclaiming, *'I could write you a better book than that myself!'*" (SFM 38).[27]

What happened next is the subject of one of the more famous anecdotes in American literary history. Jolted from her lethargy by Cooper's disgust and his jaunty boast, Susan laughingly insisted that he indeed *should* write that better book. Although such an undertaking was absurd for Cooper, "who disliked writing even a letter," he almost immediately began a brief "English" tale (SFM 38). That effort soon got out of hand and was destroyed, but Cooper unhesitatingly began a second project—a full-fledged "novel," to be called *Precaution*. By May 31, when he divulged to New York City bookseller Andrew Thompson Goodrich what he was up to, Cooper had been busy with the two manuscripts for a total of perhaps three weeks. He had *not* been dabbling: already he was at work on the eighth chapter of the novel's second volume, and he confidently predicted that he would finish the remaining sixteen chapters in an additional two weeks (*LJ* 1:42). Aside from inevitable farm chores, which at times pushed his writing off to the evening, Cooper had little else to distract him (see *LJ* 1:45, 48, 50). Accordingly, on June 12 he punctually informed Goodrich (who already had agreed to serve as Cooper's agent in the matter), "I have finished my labors this day" (*LJ* 1:43).

His speed was the result of several factors. Cooper rushed the last ten or twelve chapters, he admitted to Goodrich; but he hardly had tarried over the preceding two dozen. Indeed, he later said that "*no plot* was fixed upon until the first Vol. was half done" (*LJ* 1:66). Given Cooper's almost complete lack of preparation for authorship, something this last admission underscores, it is remarkable that he in fact fixed upon *any* plot, let alone brought it to a plausible end with such dispatch. He hardly walled himself off from family and friends in the process. In what was probably an exaggeration for effect in a letter to Goodrich that fall, he claimed that he wrote "from 14 to 28 pages of the book . . . between 9 o clock in the Morning and 9 at night" each day. Despite this grueling pace, he also took time to share the story with his wife almost daily. And he read parts of it to various friends as well, in some cases while the project was still under way (*LJ* 1: 66; SFM 38).

He was energized by a combination of naiveté and calculation. Basing his sense of proportion on Walter Scott's *Ivanhoe* (1819)—in "the Philadelphia edition" that had appeared in 1820—Cooper had done word counts on his closely written manuscript pages before first writing Goodrich. Estimating that the typical page contained eight hundred words, he knew when the end of the first volume was drawing near and therefore contrived a suitably dramatic episode for it: it is in the last chapter of that volume that the young Jane Moseley (whose lack of caution is probably the strongest exemplum in Cooper's moral plot) learns of the falsity of her lover, Colonel Egerton. Here was a milepost, in all likelihood the very chapter Cooper was sharing with his wife when their daughter, secreted beneath his worktable with her doll, overheard him and suddenly burst into tears, as she later recalled (*LJ* 1:42; SFM 38–39).

The neophyte author regarded his wife, as he told Goodrich in the June 12 letter, as his "tribunal of appeals" in the new parlor game, similar in some regards to the regular matches of chess that began in their courtship and were to continue through their married life (*LJ* 1:43; SFM 27). Although she probably did not unthinkingly support him, Susan's judgments of what he was producing seem to have been mostly positive. Despite the increasing pace with which he finished the second volume, the author thus wrote Goodrich on June 12, "Mrs. Cooper . . . says the book is better at the end than the beginning" (*LJ* 1:43). In addition to offering him direct encouragement, Susan probably suggested that he share the project with other readers whose judgment she knew they could trust. According to their daughter, the group included two English natives, James Aitchison and the banker Charles Wilkes, both of whom could scrutinize Cooper's representation of English life (*P&P* 19).[28]

Charles Wilkes's literary judgment and connections were to prove invaluable to Cooper at later points in his writing career. We know that at the time *Precaution* was being written and published, the banker (a nephew of English radical John Wilkes who had migrated to the United States with his brother John after the Revolution) served as a go-between for some of the financial arrangements. In addition, Wilkes appears to have helped Cooper imagine authorship as a career. He perhaps even broached the topic as the two discussed Cooper's dire financial straits from 1817 on. Moreover, he probably suggested, on the basis of his knowledge of publishing finances and the peculiar case of "the author of *Waverley*," that popular fiction *might* provide the cash-strapped Cooper (as it had the still-unidentified Scott) with an influx of badly needed funds. But Wilkes did not read *Precaution* or have it read to him before the book was published for the simple reason that Cooper was holed up in Westchester at that time; no surviving correspondence indicates that Wilkes had any direct knowledge of what Cooper was then writing—even that he *was* writing.[29]

What the banker did know, however, was quite pertinent to Cooper's new venture. Wilkes, probably first introduced to Cooper by John Peter DeLancey at the time of Cooper's financial crisis in the spring of 1817, was very well informed about overseas banking, especially in his native England, where he had begun his career. Through the marriage of his daughter Charlotte to Scottish lawyer and literary figure Francis Jeffrey (who edited Archibald Constable's *Edinburgh Review* from 1803 to 1829), Wilkes also had important connections to literary life in Scotland. Walter Scott and Francis Jeffrey were close friends before political differences came between them, and in the person of Constable they shared a publisher for many years. Through Jeffrey or on his own, Charles Wilkes had become well enough acquainted with Scott before 1826—probably long before 1826—that in that year Cooper was to name Wilkes as the perfect agent in his own effort to deflect earnings from pirated American editions of Scott's novels to the then nearly bankrupt Scottish author (*LJ* 1:171, 1:227). By that time, Wilkes probably knew a good deal about Scott's financial motivation for undertaking prose fiction in 1814 (when his own printing and publishing firm, Ballantyne and Company, was in a very tight situation), as well as about the ingenious methods Scott employed in order to derive as much money as possible from each of his books. Even before Scott was conclusively identified as the author of the Waverley novels, however, Wilkes already understood a good deal about the financial underpinnings of the Waverley phenomenon. Basically, Scott practiced vertical integration by seeking to control as many parts of the production process as he could. In the case of many titles, he made profits not only from sales to the public but also by insisting that Constable employ the Ballantyne press as printers. Since Constable came to learn a good deal about the secretive and convoluted financial arrangements Scott undertook during this period, he no doubt shared intriguing tidbits of it with Jeffrey, who in turn may have passed some of them on to his father-in-law.[30]

Many of the details of Scott's operations were not public knowledge. What Cooper would have known on his own in the early years of Scott's career as a novelist was the dominant story the American press disseminated about "the author of Waverley"—namely, that he was earning enormous sums from the sale of his hugely popular books. Here Cooper may have found a hint for his own literary career. Not only did Cooper follow Scott (whom he quite early identified as the author of the Waverley novels) into a career in popular fiction; as we shall see, he set up the arrangements for himself as if he were modeling his career—not just his books—on Scott's. If that was the case, then Charles Wilkes almost certainly was the source for his knowledge about the means by which the "author of Waverley" sought to maintain control of his literary property and thereby milk it for all it was worth. That Scott's motivation for writing and for this particular strategy was his own often precarious financial situation only made Cooper's imitation of Scott's example all the more apt. What Cooper thus owed to Wilkes was not so much a literary debt as a strategic one for the advice and guidance the banker gave him as he sought to straighten out his personal finances by turning to literature, of all things.[31]

With regard to James Aitchison, Cooper's other English friend, the obligation was more nearly literary. Aitchison did indeed listen as the author read *Precaution* aloud, and he gave feedback on both style and substance. Aside from the American's voracious reading, his perceptions of English scenery and society dated largely from his two visits to London on the *Stirling* in 1806–1807. This was a shallow basis for the imitation of British country-life fiction that he was attempting in *Precaution*. Aitchison could help soften the rougher edges, provide fresh details, and catch egregious blunders. Moreover, the well-educated, well-spoken gentleman had a sense of literary style to which Cooper clearly deferred. When Goodrich queried him on some passages as the sheets emerged from the printer that summer, Cooper not only pointed out the misreadings of the type-setters—he also defended his prose in general by indicating that it had been shared with "as good an English or classical scholar as the country affords," that is, James Aitchison (*LJ* 1:47, 1:66). Yet, although Aitchison clearly liked Cooper personally and spent much time in his company, he appears not to have complimented Cooper on *Precaution* or on his next two books. Only when he read the first volume of *The Pilot* in proof in 1823 did he respond warmly to what Cooper was about.[32]

Cooper read *Precaution* aloud to other close friends, including his old schoolmate William Jay. At the time, Jay was living with his wife Augusta in Bedford, where, his eyesight having proved too weak to allow him to practice law (or probably to read Cooper's close-written manuscript), he ran his father's eight-hundred-acre estate.[33] Also living there since 1818 was William's older sister, the widowed Maria Banyer, of whom Cooper was very fond and who was to prove a particularly useful critic of his early writings (*LJ* 4:366n). Sometime in May, before sending his first letter to Goodrich, Cooper had gone to Bedford with Susan and their oldest daughter to secure the advice of both these old friends before proceeding with the project (SFM 39). Along with the others who heard Cooper read installments from the first volume each night during the extended visit, Jay and Banyer urged Cooper to finish and publish it.

The return from Bedford, apparently sometime toward the end of May, must have brought Cooper back to his desk with renewed energy and clearer purpose. Soon he had finished the first eight chapters of the second volume, then written Goodrich to begin the process of seeing the manuscript into print. In turning to bookseller and publisher Goodrich, Cooper made a reasonable choice. The man's store operated at 124 Broadway, across from Cooper's usual lodgings at the City Hotel. For some time, Cooper had been patronizing Goodrich during his stays in New York. He subscribed to Goodrich's circulating library for a year starting in late 1818, while he was involved in finding and purchasing and then seeing to the repair of the *Union*. Apparently he kept some sort of link to Goodrich's library even later. In June 1820, he thus wrote the bookseller regarding a book (John G. Lockhart's *Peter's Letters to His Kinsfolk*) that he had borrowed but seemingly lost track of (see *LJ* 1:46). Cooper probably also bought various books from Goodrich. He asked Goodrich to bring Walter Scott's *The Monastery* (just published in March) with him if he visited Westchester in the near future, and Goodrich apparently did bring that Philadelphia-printed work to Angevine sometime in early June (see *LJ* 1:43–44).[34]

As this last request suggests, Goodrich was not just a business associate for Cooper. It is evident from the novelist's first surviving letter to Goodrich that he felt close to the bookseller—close enough to entrust his secret to him (insisting at the start that the whole thing was *"Most-Strictly confidential"* [*LJ* 1:41]) and close enough, perhaps more importantly, to invite him to Angevine. "I should be happy to see you," he added, a clear indication that even before *Precaution* became a business link between them, the two were friends (*LJ* 1:42). In 1823, long after he and Goodrich had parted company as business associates, Cooper paid the bookseller the compliment of a mention in *Tales for Fifteen*. A character in "Imagination" thus instructs her cousin: "Tell aunt to send by the servant a list of such books as she wants from Goodrich's, and I will get them for her" (*Tales* 49).

Andrew Thompson Goodrich was an active though minor figure in New York literary circles. He probably was never more active, in fact, than when Cooper began his short business association with him. His store had been operating since 1813, the year that the first surviving catalog of his circulating library was issued. At his Broadway location and later on Barclay Street, he was to remain active for three decades.[35] By the time Cooper brought *Precaution* to him, Goodrich also was reasonably well established as a literary publisher. Between 1817 and 1819, for instance, he had issued James Hogg's *The Queen's Wake* and a trio of texts by Byron, as well as two English novels—Anne R. Harding's *Decision* and Mary Brunton's *Emmeline*. In 1819, he also had begun the *Belles-Lettres Repository*, a monthly journal that would continue (under new ownership and title) into early 1821.[36]

Goodrich's helpfulness for Cooper stemmed from his familiarity with printing and his experience selling and distributing books. Cooper's initial letter to him posed a series of questions. The first concerned the scope of his project: "Would two Hundred and twenty four pages of manuscript, of eight Hundred words each, and a fair proportion of conversation make two common sized volumes?" (*LJ* 1:42). Cooper's tendency to speak of books in terms of their outward size, as he did here, might make him seem a literary ingénue—which he was—but it also reveals how astutely he recognized the commercial realities of the emergent literary marketplace in the United States. Besides, even in his first book Cooper paid pertinent attention to intrinsic features. His sense of how to finish what he thought would be the first volume some days before he wrote Goodrich was reasonably well developed, as suggested earlier. The end of that putative volume was approaching not merely because the requisite number of pages of eight hundred words each had almost been completed, but even more because a crisis in the action was approaching. Or, to put the issue in the light in which it probably appeared to Cooper at the time, the accumulating length of the story and the coming crisis were interdependent. Neither one determined the other or was wholly separate from it. This combined sense of mere length and the pace of the book's action in fact argues for a relatively sophisticated attitude. It is more a reader's attitude than a writer's, but it shows the degree to which the supposedly inexperienced author of *Precaution* possessed a rather well-developed literary sensibility, at least in some matters, before 1820.

Cooper's canniness also revealed itself in the no-nonsense estimate of his craft that he already displayed in 1820 and that was to deepen across his career. Brought up as he had been within a family deeply involved in the commercial revolution of the post-Revolutionary era, the author was inclined to treat literature as a business akin to those with which he already was familiar: real estate management and development, retailing, and, most recently, whaling. His other questions of Goodrich in fact showed his pragmatism. Cooper wanted to know what it would cost to print the novel in an edition of one thousand copies that copied "the style of the Philadelphia edition of Ivanhoe." Money clearly mattered. Yet something else shows through here as well. For one thing, the choice of Scott's recent book as his particular model revealed Cooper's "secret" emulation of Scott's success—monetary as much as literary. It also showed his familiarity with the book trade. That edition of Scott's novel being at hand, Cooper examined it and approved it as a reasonable example of the bookmaker's craft. He had known something of the printing business from his boyhood days, when he had spent considerable time with the young sons of newspaper editor and printer Elihu Phinney in the office of the *Otsego Herald*, as he later was to inform Goodrich (see *LJ* 1:47). He had set type and operated the press and hence understood how printed artifacts were produced.[37]

Cooper's sensitivity to book design even this early in his career is suggested by his daughter's statement that he did not like "the title and the *look* of the book" his wife had asked him to read on that fateful day in May 1820 (*P&P* 17; italics added). By "look," Susan apparently wished to indicate her father's strong sense of what was physically attractive or awkward in a given book. At the outset in the case of *Precaution*, he had insisted on having "a good paper— a full clear type," adding that the "book [h]as to[o] many imperfections in its matter to disregard the manner" (*LJ* 1:43 – 44). The very way he phrased that last concern suggests his instinctual recognition of the double identity of books as symbolic constructs and material artifacts. He was so engaged with such issues that he sent Goodrich three chapters to have them set in varying ways so that he could pick out the sample he liked best and give the go-ahead for the rest of the book. Cost was important, but so was the overall impression his book might make (see *LJ* 1:44 – 46).

Cooper also came to Goodrich from the start with decided ideas about how to handle the business end of things. He wanted to know the cost of printing because, as he told Goodrich in May and reminded him forcefully when a dispute later arose between them, he wished Goodrich to serve only as his agent in having the book printed and distributed (perhaps for that reason, although the title page of *Precaution* named Goodrich as having published the book, Cooper addressed his letters to "Mr. A. T. Goodrich, Bookseller," never *publisher*). Cooper would pay the printer's bill himself, thereby ensuring that all proceeds would remain his. Having just worked out with Charles Dering the shifting terms by which their joint venture on the *Union* was financed, and having suffered disappointments due to his unremunerative and perhaps confused dealings with his cousin Courtland, he was especially particular about such issues in this new enterprise. He did not treat the arrangements for *Precaution* as somehow above the commercial world of whaleships and frontier stores. Although he made it sound as if he did not "desire to saddle" Goodrich with the "risk" of publishing a first novel, Cooper must have figured that keeping control of his work was in his own best monetary interest (*LJ* 1:43).

At the same time, Cooper clearly recognized that Goodrich's services, including the answers he could give to a neophyte author's questions, were worth something and he intended to pay for them. In his May 31 letter, Cooper left the details of the arrangement as he envisioned it unspecified: the two would proceed, as Cooper put it, "under such terms as we may agree upon" (*LJ* 1:42 – 43). It seems likely that they came to terms during Goodrich's visit to Angevine early in June. No copy of any agreement from their meeting survives, but Cooper restated the key points in a letter he wrote once the dispute with Goodrich arose: "On the subject of funds there could be no misunderstanding—the Book is mine and you [are] an agent—I was to pay the engagements [i.e., the obligations or "bills"] and to receive the proceeds of the sale—you were to be amply compensated for your trouble &c—this was the agreement" (*LJ* 1:58).

"This Affair"

The funds for this costly experiment, Cooper reminded Goodrich at the same time, were to come from the profits of his first whaling voyage. By June 12, when he wrote with word that *Precaution* had been finished, he had heard from Dering and now assumed the *Union* would be back by month's end. The coincidence was reassuring but at the same time worrisome. Once the ship was back, Cooper would have to drop his literary business and run off to Sag Harbor. Hence he began wishing that "this affair"—seeing his book into Goodrich's hands (and the printer's)—could be finished as quickly as possible (*LJ* 1:58, 1:43). He also nervously asked Goodrich whether he had announced the book yet, something his "agent" did not get around to until early the following month. Cooper wanted to accelerate the book's commercial career. And, even though he very much wished to publish the thing without divulging his identity (one reason for using Goodrich as nominal "publisher"), he was also keen to assert his property in the venture by insisting that "Copy right" be properly attended to (*LJ* 1:44). The pending return of the vessel, which in fact was not to be in port until mid-July, no doubt turned his mind toward costs and profits.

Perhaps it also intensified Cooper's concern with the physical details of the emerging artifact. He dropped *Ivanhoe* as prototype and instead settled on Scott's *Monastery*, which he found he liked better after Goodrich had brought him that copy some weeks earlier. The preference apparently was acceded to, as *Precaution* would be printed in a typeface and size (ten-point versus eight-point modern-face roman) very similar to that used in the Philadelphia edition of the second Scott book. The choice of the larger type for *Precaution* perhaps reflected Cooper's growing concern that the book might not come out long enough. The same concern dictated his desire to have "the beginnings and ends of chapters on pages by themselves," a preference that in fact prevailed in the printed book (*LJ* 1:44–45).

The shortness of the text was the least of the problems with the manuscript. In fact, Cooper now began to recognize that its bad state might make typesetting the book challenging if not, at points anyway, next to impossible. His concern lay with penmanship and formatting more than with style per se. His handwriting was so bad, so careless at times, he admitted, that he feared the book might be "badly gotten up" unless the typesetters were scrupulous. He was especially anxious about what he called the "business of paragraphs." He had not set them off as he went, but rather needed to work back over the manuscript and insert asterisks to mark the breaks. In his effort to save paper, he similarly had not bothered to set most speeches by themselves (*LJ* 1:44–45).

When Cooper received the sample proof a week later and saw what the typesetters employed by Goodrich's printer (Cornelius S. Van Winkle) had done with his scrawl, his apprehension was confirmed. On the fourth page of the book he read about Sir Edward Moseley's wish to "relax"—not "release"—"himself from all embarrassments" (*PRE* 1:4; *LJ* 1:47).[38] This absurdity, traceable to the ambiguity of Cooper's handwriting, meant just one thing: he would have to go over all proofs himself, something he had hoped to avoid. It hardly mattered for him to talk now about his conversational model as a writer ("I have written freely—the same as I would talk—have aim'd at nothing but simplicity and clearness") or parry Goodrich's comments about the "peculiarity" of his style by admitting, lamely, that "the same thing looks differently in print and manuscript" (*LJ* 1:48). What he needed to do was rigorously revise the manuscript pages still in his hands, thus minimizing typesetting errors. Doing so also would reduce his charges and make his proofreading less onerous.

Going over the sample proof reinforced this realization. When he sent it back on July 12, he remarked that the new manuscript pages included with it (enough to cover about half of the first volume) had received especially close attention. Having discovered that the manuscript sometimes had confused characters' names, he also enclosed a list of them—probably on the now torn away blank space at the end of his letter. He had a taste for this process now, so he urged Goodrich to send more proofs as soon as possible (*LJ* 1:48–49). Haste was not, however, to be his ally. When the first substantial batch of actual proofs arrived at the farmhouse the following Monday, July 17, Cooper was astounded to find, as he took it, that the printer had "*omitted the first page of the manuscript* in the second Chapter entirely" (*LJ* 1:50). The fire was a false alarm or at least proved easy for Goodrich to put out. But it pointed to a general problem. Despite Cooper's request that Goodrich return the relevant manuscript with each set of proofs (see *LJ* 1:48), the bookseller neglected to do so. A good many of the problems Cooper found or thought he found could have been more easily resolved through the comparison of proofs with copy text. Moreover, the lack of the copy text encouraged Cooper to think worse of the printers and better of himself than probably was warranted. Convinced that he found expressions in the proofs that he was sure he had not used, he concluded that the typesetters did not make "*very many* but such as they are[,] *tremendous mistakes.*" In some instances, he discovered downright "bad gram-mar [*sic*]." Some examples of the latter may have been due to his own "inadvertence," owing to "haste," but without the manuscript in hand how could he really tell (*LJ* 1:50)?

Goodrich probably withheld the manuscript from the first two proof shipments because he and Cooper had originally agreed that the author would simply sample the printers' work, be reassured that it looked right, and then let the project proceed without close supervision. As Cooper became convinced that this laissez-faire procedure would not work, he evolved a new one without, apparently, formally revising the agreement with Goodrich. And even as he changed his assumptions, Cooper did not uniformly act on them. He had promised to go over the rest of the manuscript and ensure that it presented as few problems as possible. However, certain mechanical aspects of the manuscript remained woefully inadequate. Dialogue was so indifferently corrected that Cooper on July 17 sought to let himself off with a befuddled excuse: "I do not wish the printers to be at all guided by my arrangements in the dialogues &c— as my object was to write closely—I think if one or two of the speeches in the accompanying proof were set up by *themselves* the page would look better" (*LJ* 1:50). In fact, the book as printed did not always follow this a posteriori principle, not only in the earlier chapters where the proofs first had raised the concern for him, but also much later in the text.[39] This despite the fact that a second letter sent to Goodrich later the same day reiterated Cooper's point.

Other odd writing habits that probably made the job of the typesetters harder also came in for comment from Cooper in his two July 17 letters. He frankly stated, "I like the frequent use of the dash—and believe they have omitted [*sic*] it in one or two cases where I was at pains to insert it." Presumably Cooper took further pains to mark those places in the proofs. The following passage in the penultimate chapter of the first volume probably provides a fair sample of Cooper's impulsive habit: "The evening passed off as such evenings generally do—in gayety—listlessness—dancing—gaping, and heart-burnings, according to the dispositions and good or ill fortune of the several individuals who compose the assembly" (*PRE* 1:273). There ought to have been no misunderstanding of his intent in such a passage, although the switch from dashes to commas at the end of his catalog of diversions may well have resulted from a misreading of his hand. The issue was by no means always a simple one: in July, he added that the typesetters ought to understand that he never used periods but closed most of his sentences "with the dash." He did not mean for *these* dashes to be printed as such, but expected the tactful compositors to change them all to periods (*LJ* 1:50).[40]

With that observation, Cooper himself was about to *dash* off to Sag Harbor. He had informed Goodrich in a letter of July 2 that he expected his whaler in port any minute and would have to leave home as soon as it arrived (*LJ* 1:46). Dering was in Sag Harbor already, keeping his ears and eyes open, but not until July 17 did the *Union* show up. He immediately wrote Cooper, who got word on July 19 and hastily informed Goodrich of his plans. He wouldn't be able to leave Angevine immediately, in fact, because he had urgent business to attend to in northern Westchester the next day. *Precaution* was urgent, too—but when

Cooper begged Goodrich to come up to Angevine right away so they could confer before his Long Island trip, one expects the inevitable ulterior motive: Cooper asked the bookseller to go across the street to the City Hotel and pick up a "bundle of papers marked 'Ship Union—1819'" on his way or, if he could not come, to see that the papers were shipped to Cooper without delay (*LJ* 1:52). In fact, Dering had asked Cooper to forward those papers in February and just now reminded him that the partners would need them in order to settle with the captain and crew.[41]

Cooper told Goodrich he would leave Angevine on Monday, July 24, and we may assume he did so. Apparently he avoided New York City (otherwise he could have picked up the bundle of papers himself and dropped by Goodrich's), perhaps crossing instead from Mamaroneck to Hempstead, that "deep bay" of which a late novel, *Jack Tier* (1848), provides a tantalizing glimpse (*JT* 1:62). From there three down-island roads led toward Peconic Bay, Shelter Island, and Sag Harbor—as, of course, did the waters of Long Island Sound, which Cooper knew well. As he traveled, the novelist could review what he already knew of the ship's cruise. Capt. Jonathan Osborne had made Pernambuco, on Brazil's north-central coast, in just sixty-one days, sending a report back from there that the vessel was "tight staunch & strong." In February of 1820, a letter home from a crew member indicated that the men liked the ship very well—"no Better Sea Boat never floated" was the way he put it in his second letter, received in April and forwarded to Dering, who passed it on to Cooper. The ship took enough whales off Brazil's north coast to fill one-third of the casks. Things quieted down when the *Union* got to the main whaling grounds farther south, but only because the whales there were hard to catch— "as wild as the devil"—because of the multitude of ships. As the ship neared Sag Harbor in July, Dering gathered the local impression that the rest of its cruise had been lackluster. But in fact the hold was as full as he and Cooper might hope.[42]

Dering looked after the ship on its arrival, seeing to necessary repairs and fitting it out for the second cruise that the partners at last had decided to undertake.[43] For his part, Cooper intended to take charge of the cargo, send or bring it to market, and then pay the officers and crew according to their lays. Everything depended on the total amount and kind of oil in the casks. On July 8, before the vessel arrived, Dering estimated the total haul as about 1,300 barrels of oil— 1,100 of regular whale oil and 65 or so of sperm oil, which brought three times as much as the former and therefore was counted three-to-one in such calculations. Since the vessel's capacity was 1,400 barrels, the cargo at this point must have seemed a bit disappointing. At least prices were holding high, particularly in Boston, where ordinary oil was bringing thirty-five cents per gallon as opposed to twenty-eight in New York. Better yet, the haul proved higher once a careful barrel count could be made. On July 17, Dering thus was able to confirm that the ship held 1,000 barrels of whale oil—but as many as 220 of sperm. This revision meant not only that the ship was near its capacity but also that the cargo was worth the equivalent of 1,600 barrels of ordinary oil. More sperm whales would have boosted the value of the catch, but this had been a good first cruise.

Cooper used Dering's last figure as the basis for calculating how much oil to credit to each officer and crewman as well as Dering and himself. His reckoning was written on the address flap of Dering's July 17 letter, probably after Cooper arrived at Sag Harbor. Since, as Deacon Pratt in *The Sea Lions* instructs his niece, the barrels used in this trade would "a little overrun . . . 30 gallons" (*SL* 1:164)—Cooper used the figure of 31 gallons in his own calculations in 1820— the *Union*'s yield was on the order of 50,000 gallons. In carrying out his calculations, Cooper revealed something about the larger social economics of the voyage. Captain Osborne had agreed to ship in return for an eighteenth lay, giving him about 90 barrels of oil. The rest of the officers and the crew were due a total of just over 400 barrels. To cover their joint costs and Cooper's investment as well as provide profit, the partners therefore had fewer than 1,110 barrels to divide. In a somewhat later calculation, Cooper apparently indicated the split between the partners: not quite one-third to Dering, and the rest (850 barrels) to himself as owner and major investor in the outfit.[44]

Cooper was absent on his Sag Harbor trip for nearly a month, returning to Angevine on or around August 22 (see *LJ* 1:53). He thus had enough time to help ready the ship for a return to the ocean, as well as dispose of all or part of its first cargo. Selling it locally might have been possible, but since Sag Harbor usually had a glut of whale oil, it made sense to ship it to a major port. Dering's information indicated that Boston, though harder to reach, would be more profitable than New York. Cooper therefore off-loaded part of the cargo from the *Union*, shifted it aboard two sloops, and personally oversaw its transfer to Boston, where he sold it on August 3 (see *LJ* 1:59). The rest must have gone there later or been disposed of by other means. On the basis of the yet-rising Boston price for oil (thirty-seven-and-a-half cents per gallon), Cooper's personal share of the gross receipts of the voyage would come out near $10,000. It would cost him some portion of that to refit the vessel—perhaps $2,000 or 3,000, depending on Dering's ability to take a larger share of this voyage, as he said he wanted to.[45] This was a good return on an investment represented by the ship, its initial repairs, and the first outfit. Cooper still needed to go back to Sag Harbor to finish up, and apparently to pick up some or all of his personal yield from the voyage, but for now he could head home with the knowledge that a sizable sum was finally at his disposal.

"I Know My Rights . . ."

It is unlikely that Andrew T. Goodrich had managed to rush up to Angevine—
as Cooper hoped—before the novel-writing shipowner left for Sag Harbor in
July.[46] He therefore may have been left mostly in the dark about shifts in how
Cooper was now handling *Precaution*. Much of what was taking place at this time
is sketchy. Here, however, is what *appears* to have happened. As early as July 4,
Cooper had decided that he would have to proof the whole book, or much of it,
himself in order to eliminate absurdities (see *LJ* 1:47). Once this previously un-
planned step had been introduced, it began to change other aspects of the book's
production. For instance, on July 8, with Angevine's hay crop keeping him in his
fields from sunrise to sunset, Cooper had time to only hastily review the next
chapters he sent to New York in manuscript. He was not overly concerned with
this development; he offhandedly commented to Goodrich, "the proof sheets
will enable me to correct [those chapters] more thoroughly" (*LJ* 1:48).

Employing proof sheets for extensive authorial corrections surely was not
part of Cooper's agreement with Goodrich; nor was it a usual practice during
this period. Goodrich probably did not catch the significance of the July 8 comment because Cooper had not uniformly or extensively used earlier proofs this
way. His hay harvest over, in fact, he appears to have had more time to sit down
and correct the remaining manuscript for the first volume more circumspectly.
With his trip to Sag Harbor hanging over him after the middle of July, however,
he suddenly changed his practice and in one very brief period of spotty labor
rushed through the manuscript of the second volume. He seems to have devoted
so little time to this process that he interrupted the very letter in which he described his intent to accomplish it, then returned to the letter with a report on
what he had just done. "I intend running over the second volume immediately,
and will forward i[t] entir[e]," he announced; then, shifting tenses as if in fact he
had gone off and done it, he reported, "I *may have overlook'd* grammatical errors,
and some words may be omitted as I *read* it over very rapidly from necessity."
Cooper then empowered Goodrich to make any corrections he hadn't, adding,
"and I can see the proof afterwards" (*LJ* 1:51; italics added). He apparently enclosed his letter with the manuscript pages for the second volume and sent the
bundle off forthwith.

By July 24 or so, when he went off to Sag Harbor, Cooper probably had not
received or gone over any new proofs. Realizing that his absence, now that he
had inserted himself so centrally into the typesetting process, might cause the
book to be "greatly delayed" (*LJ* 1:51), he hastily delegated his own role to his
wife. Again he does not seem to have informed Goodrich of the change. Soon
after her husband left, Susan received and went over proof sheets for pages

eighty-four to ninety-six of the first volume, which she sent back to Goodrich on July 28 with a brief note. Several more times the same process played itself out, until by August 10 she had returned the next sixty pages of proofs. Thereafter Goodrich stopped his shipments even though the printer was forging ahead with the rest of volume one, the remaining 130 pages of which were completed by the third week of August (see *LJ* 1:53–55).

Why did Goodrich leave Susan out of the loop? One excuse he apparently offered was that she had not promptly returned one batch (owing to a change of stage drivers, as Cooper explained; see *LJ* 1:53). Another was that the bookseller did not think Susan invested with sufficient authority for the kinds of changes she was introducing (see *LJ* 1:57). But the real reason must have been more strategic. Goodrich probably objected to Cooper's view (shared by Susan) that the proofs could and should be used for making further authorial changes. And he thought it best to exploit Cooper's absence so as to make sure that the couple did not bring the typesetting process to an expensive halt. Did Cooper understand that he was costing the printers extra time and therefore money? Would he accept his liability for the changes and other costs?

On returning from Sag Harbor at the end of August, Cooper was surprised to discover that work on the book appeared to have been suspended. Not knowing that Goodrich in fact was hurrying volume one through the press, he decided that money (of which the *Union* had given him a fresh supply) would bring a return of proof shipments to Angevine: "I must stimulate you—on the completion of the 1st vol—I will remit you $200." Evidently happy at the promise of payment, Goodrich endorsed the address flap of the letter, "James Cooper to pay $200. on the 1st vol complete" (*LJ* 1:53). But the bookseller did not forward the proofs that Cooper expected. Instead, he took Cooper's offer as a further reason (not implausibly) to finish the volume as quickly as the printer could.

Once more back at work after a month's absence, Cooper was ready to resume his interrupted labors. Until fresh proofs arrived from New York, all he had before him was an earlier shipment containing the corrected proofs of the book's first chapters. On first glance, these seemed "well done" (*LJ* 1:54), but a closer inspection revealed that the printer frequently had overlooked crucial revisions. Cooper was *positive* he had corrected a host of inelegant or ungrammatical passages, as well as the printer's misreadings. In a passage describing the legacy "left *to* the disposal of the General's widow" (*PRE* 1:7), he had fine-tuned the idiom—the money was "left *at*" her disposal instead. Cooper admitted that leaving this error in the text did no real harm to his meaning. Elsewhere, however, "gross mistakes" introduced into the text by the compositors had been left standing despite his clear recollection that he had corrected them as well. The neophyte author was quickly learning that mistakes are endemic to printing, especially when the copy text is handwritten. What annoyed him in these errors was the fact that he and Susan had caught them once and carefully entered the correct readings, only to discover that their changes were mostly ignored (*LJ* 1:54).

Worse discoveries followed. When a package arrived at Angevine almost a week after his return, Cooper was stunned to find that it contained the "completed" first volume—not in proof but rather in sewn and bound pages, to all intents "*ready for the public eye.*" He opened the volume with dread; it was, he soon determined, "no better than a very imperfect proof."[47] This was a genuine disaster, and a seemingly inexplicable one at that. Cooper had made it very clear on a variety of occasions that no part of the book was to go forward unless he or Susan had thoroughly checked and approved it. Not only were the corrections they made in the proofs of the first fifteen chapters indifferently attended to, but the final ten chapters of the volume had been set and printed wholly without their intervention. As a consequence, there were "ten errors after the 15th chapter to one before it" (*LJ* 1:55). It was as if the whole process had been corrupted by the knowledge that the proofs after the latter chapter were not to be scrutinized at Angevine. Goodrich had proceeded, in other words, by subterfuge.

The bookseller enclosed some sort of explanation about his need to bring the much-delayed project to its end. But he knew how poorly the work had been done. Already he was talking about a list of errata, an expedient that sent Cooper into a paroxysm: a proper list would fill "a dozen pages," itself an embarrassment. As if to drive home his point, Cooper clinically divided the mistakes into types and exhaustively discussed them to indicate how extensive the problem was (see *LJ* 1:55–56). Perhaps at this moment he still hoped that they might be corrected in the text proper. Soon, though, it was obvious that most of them would remain glaringly visible there—many would not even be set right on the single errata page Goodrich finally planned for volume one. Bowing to the inevitable, Cooper made out the list, paring it down repeatedly until it contained only about fifty of the most outrageous errors. The rest of the gaffes would have to be covered by "the general apology" that the bookseller now was intending to put at the head of the errata (*LJ* 1:57–60). There, whether with Cooper's approval or not, Goodrich blamed the problems on the "great distance" between himself and the author.[48]

Goodrich was referring to the geographical distance between the city and Angevine, as well as the even greater problems caused by Cooper's two trips to Sag Harbor.[49] Other kinds of separation may also have been hinted at; certainly they contributed to the book's rough surface. One source of difficulty was an argument about money that arose while they were working out how to deal with the errors in volume one. Although Cooper, back from Sag Harbor with substantial funds, had informed Goodrich earlier that *Precaution* would be paid for from this source (see *LJ* 1:58), the manner in which volume one had been "finished" caused Cooper to delay payment. The delay in turn seems to have caused Goodrich considerable worry about Cooper's final intentions. Things came to a head when a letter from Goodrich arrived at Angevine around September 7 or 8 that set Cooper's blood boiling and nearly consumed their relationship as well as the adventure in authorship on which Cooper had embarked. We do not have Goodrich's letter, so we must reconstruct the falling-out from Cooper's response. It began with an ominous prediction: "Things between us, are coming to a crisis that I regret extremely on more accounts than one" (*LJ* 1:58). Cooper obviously had turned to Goodrich in May because he valued him as a friend and respected his professional judgment, and Goodrich's early dealings over *Precaution* had been satisfactory. But the misunderstanding that developed during Cooper's first Long Island trip strained their relationship, and Goodrich's September letter nearly broke it.

The bookseller, fearing that Cooper's disappointment with volume one might lead him to renege on their whole deal, must have threatened legal action to recover his due. Cooper was unyielding in his initial response. He first of all disowned Goodrich's actions. How could he be responsible for the deeds of an agent who deviated from, indeed acted counter to, his instructions? He certainly was not obligated to pay for that agent's blunders. And he would not sit idly by if Goodrich, as he also seems to have threatened, sought to recover his costs by issuing the book on his own authority. Whether the mangled physical copies of the book were paid for or not, the book itself—the literary artifact—remained inalienably the property of James Cooper. Goodrich might doubt that point, but Cooper would hold firm to it through thick and thin—unless, he added, "Chancellor Kent refuses me the justice he so freely awards to others" (*LJ* 1:58).[50]

Even as Cooper forcefully hurled warnings at Goodrich ("my resolution is taken—I know my rights, and will never yield them"), he hoped for a peaceful resolution. Hence he sent his own gig to the city in the expectation that Goodrich would break away from work and run up to Westchester for a hospitable face-to-face meeting (*LJ* 1:58–59). Goodrich apparently took him up on the offer; within a few days, the two had reached some sort of agreement that averted lawsuits, set *Precaution* back on its track to publication, and established an understanding for further work on the printing of the book. Goodrich conceded that Cooper needed to be involved in correcting (and revising) all new proofs. Some sheets for the second volume arrived within a few days, and Cooper, reenergized by the apparent clarification, urged the bookseller to send others quickly (see *LJ* 1:59–60). Further problems arose, most of them due to the same causes as earlier ones, but things never again descended into the murky depths where they had once or twice tarried earlier in the year.

By late September, when Cooper calculated that only about half of the second volume remained unchecked (see *LJ* 1:61–62), the pace of the whole endeavor was picking up. Van Winkle, probably under pressure from Goodrich and perhaps Cooper, had increased the number of compositors at work on the project. The resulting improvements in the proofs very much pleased Cooper. He especially praised the labors of printer John Forbes and artist Hannah Fowler, a woman in the shop who evidently supplemented the income from her recently founded drawing school by setting type.[51] So good was their output that Cooper urged Goodrich to use them as much as possible, promising full reimbursement for any added expenses (see *LJ* 1:62, 1:64).

As the end approached, Cooper became absorbed with marketing plans for the book. He expected to sell copies at the usual trade discounts of 25 or 33 percent. He also wanted Goodrich to insist on cash payment (*LJ* 1:63–65). As to price, he wanted to maximize the return per book, but not if he pushed himself out of the market. Walter Scott's *The Abbot* (1820), just issued in Philadelphia by Mathew Carey, was being advertised at $1.75 per set. Pirated American editions of Scott's novels of course benefited its author not at all. Yet they nonetheless set a firm upper limit for native competitors. Although Cooper understood this point, his desire for gain from the risky speculation of authorship fought against his more realistic concerns. He doubted that he should exceed Carey's price for *The Abbot* but at last decided to ask $2.00 for *Precaution*—"as much as it is worth" (*LJ* 1:67).[52]

He may have been concerned about the book's yield because its cost remained very unclear to him. It appears that he had paid Goodrich nothing at all as of the end of October. For the first time he therefore asked his agent for a full accounting. The subject was awkward. For one thing, by then Cooper had used his whaling proceeds for other purposes: "owing to your delay," he disingenuously wrote Goodrich on October 19 or 20, "I have appropriated the money I *brought* with me to give *you*" (*LJ* 1:66). More money from the *Union*'s first voyage, however, remained in Charles Dering's hands. Realizing with fresh urgency the crucial role Goodrich would play in distributing his book, Cooper therefore instructed Dering (delayed on Long Island by the sudden death of his father early in October) to forward $1,000 to banker Charles Wilkes. Wilkes in turn would be told to turn over half of that amount to Goodrich (see *LJ* 1:66–67). Once this double transfer took place, Goodrich could pay—or begin to pay—his own costs.

A key element in promoting sales was an effort to see the book well noticed in periodicals. Cooper's wish to have Goodrich promote *Precaution* conflicted, however, with his desire to dissociate himself from the project. The bookseller sought to satisfy both aims: he had received "the manuscript copy of an original and highly interesting work," ran a July announcement in a New York paper, which promised imminent publication.[53] Later, Cooper wanted to deepen such evasions. Further notices, he instructed Goodrich, should avoid any suggestion that *Precaution* was an "*original*" American work (*LJ* 1:61). While that strategy was ill-advised on one level, in other ways it was shrewd. Scott's burgeoning success in America showed how dependent on literary imports American readers (and publishers) still were. Letting on that Goodrich was republishing a British work protected Cooper's secret even as it played to the Anglophile tendencies of the native marketplace. The ruse was reasonable. Set in England and imitative of English models, *Precaution* actually could pass for an import. Various rumors connected Cooper's name with the work as fall came on, and people even seem to have gone to Goodrich's shop and asked for the book, mentioning Cooper by name (see *LJ* 1:65). But the pretense basically held.[54]

Part of Cooper's uneasiness about his association with *Precaution* was that he had begun a second book, *The Spy*, while still at work on it and soon thought the new effort vastly superior to the old one. Work on *The Spy* went on unevenly partly because Cooper recognized its greater potential and wished to realize it. When it came time to send out copies of *Precaution* for review, he told Goodrich that he did not "wish to puff" that book. He thought it "respectable" but not "great"—it could not possibly be great, given the fact that "no book was ever written with less thought and more rapidity." Such conclusions rested in large measure on what he was discovering about the art of fiction and the craft of writing from his work on *The Spy*. Hence he asserted to Goodrich, "I can make a much better one—am making a much better one." He had persisted with *Precaution* despite all the problems and disappointments because it could serve as "a pilot baloon [*sic*]" for the new book (*LJ* 1:66).

There was more to the story than that. Cooper probably enjoyed the deceptions involved in making the book seem "English" in order, as he put it, "to impose on the public," to trick his readers. There also was a certain satisfaction in seeing himself "in print." He was not completely disappointed in the results: he could "honestly own" that he was pleased with his "appearance." The pun there was revealing. By the time he wrote Goodrich this letter on October 20, he had received final copies of *Precaution* and may well have had one before him on the table. His "appearance" entailed both the look and heft of the volumes and the very fact of the translation of his difficult scrawl into public print. He was about to make an appearance, masked though it was. While he certainly hoped that it might herald the more important appearance of *The Spy*, the accomplishment signified by *Precaution* was satisfying in its own right (*LJ* 1:66). When, on Friday, November 10, 1820, a press notice announced Cooper's first literary accomplishment ("This day, published, by A. T. Goodrich & Co., No. 124 Broadway, opposite the City Hotel, Precaution, a novel, 2 vols. Price $2."), his identity was carefully concealed but his pride in the fact was substantial.[55]

"The Name of 'Edward Jones'"

Seeing his first book into the public eye in New York City initiated new worries for Cooper. Even before November 10, he had begun to consider how to prevent the pirating of *Precaution* by English publishers; now the issue became critical. His immediate motive, aside from pride of ownership, was a wish to derive as much revenue as possible from the venture. In the absence of international copyright agreements, British publishers were free to reprint American titles at will—much as Mathew Carey freely reprinted Scott, or Goodrich himself reprinted Byron. An American writer might publish in Britain first, thereby ensuring copyright under British law, but for a neophyte such as Cooper that was out of the question. At present, the only inducement he could offer British publishers was timeliness. Usually, they pirated early copies of American books rushed off to London by their own agents or American allies. If American authors or publishers made prior arrangements with London publishers, however, they might anticipate such shipments with manuscript copy or proof sheets dispatched before the date of publication in the United States. Since the first British publisher to issue a non-copyrighted foreign work acquired de facto right to it, timeliness might have real cash value. Accordingly, Cooper pushed Goodrich to identify a likely London partner who could be persuaded to pay something for permission to republish the work there (see *LJ* 1:61–62).

Cooper and Goodrich began discussions about a possible English arrangement relatively early in their dealings. Shortly after returning from Sag Harbor late in August, the author inquired of the bookseller, "What do you mean to do about England?" This query clearly suggested that the two had decided on publishing the book there during one of their face-to-face meetings some weeks earlier. Apparently it had been left to Goodrich to decide which London publisher or publishers to approach, and perhaps to begin negotiations with the chosen firm while work on the American edition progressed. As problems developed with the latter, however, Cooper nervously detailed his concerns about how the English version would be handled. In that same late August letter, he pressed Goodrich to divulge what he proposed or recommended, and to do so immediately, since the errors in the early proofs and the recently received first volume convinced Cooper that he himself "must *see* and *correct*" whatever was sent to any English publisher. With the English venture, too, Cooper concluded that he could not entrust details to others. "God forbid," he winced, "there should be a second edition as bad as the first." Goodrich thought it sufficient to send the author's manuscript to London, but given his experience with its pitfalls, Cooper was dead set against the idea: "if it is to be sent in *manuscript* mine will *not* do" (*LJ* 1:57).[56]

Despite Cooper's insistence on a prompt resolution of the issue, Goodrich did nothing for some time. Cooper therefore had to devise a plan of his own. Three or four weeks later he wrote that he needed an extra set of sheets. Onto them he could enter corrections and revisions with an eye to making the English edition markedly better than the first (*LJ* 1:61). As those sheets started arriving at Angevine, Cooper dutifully readied them. If they were carefully prepared, and Cooper had every incentive to see that they were, an English edition might actually improve on the American. But Goodrich still would do "nothing as to the English plan," as Cooper bluntly stated in another undated mid-September letter. The desire to preserve his anonymity meant that Cooper could not take over that "plan" himself. As Goodrich continued to stall, Cooper hit upon an expedient worthy of his new vocation. He explained to Goodrich: "I shall write under the name of 'Edward Jones' to the English publisher and get you to make out an assignment to him of the right for Great Britain (if it can be done) as also to forward my copies and letter." The subterfuge might work, although Cooper hardly could proceed until Goodrich supplied more information. Apparently Goodrich had settled on, but not yet made any arrangements with, a specific publisher; Cooper needed to know the firm's name and address so that he could wrap up his corrected sheets and send them off (*LJ* 1:62).

The bookseller, no doubt thinking that the "Edward Jones" strategy would fail, soon wrote to suggest a more convincing one. Some personal acquaintance of the bookseller or the author—ideally, an American resident in Britain—might be able to negotiate with a London publisher directly for a new edition of the novel. Goodrich suggested that Junius Smith, one of Cooper's acquaintances from Yale and now a lawyer living in England, could serve as an excellent intermediary. "I remember Smith well," Cooper now replied, "—and have seen him since his residence in London."[57] At first he hesitated to agree with Goodrich's suggestion, preferring to employ another acquaintance then serving as American secretary of legation in London. After taking a few days to think over the choice, however, he settled on Smith (*LJ* 1:64–65).

Cooper prepared a letter to Smith around the middle of October. On about the twentieth of that month, he brought up with Goodrich a few of the remaining issues connected to the English edition. Since everything derived from the sale of the book to an English publisher would be "clear gain," he urged Goodrich to ensure that the terms arranged through Smith be as lucrative for the author as possible. By the end of October, Cooper packed up the revised proofs and his letter and forwarded them to New York. Goodrich was to add instructions for Smith to the package and send it under his own cover to London as soon as possible (*LJ* 1:67–68).

It is not clear whether Goodrich did so. An English edition was published by Henry Colburn in Hanover Square only three months after the appearance of the American, but there is no conclusive evidence that it resulted from Goodrich's efforts.[58] Certainly Colburn used the Goodrich edition in some form as copy text for his handsomely prepared three-volume version, and in 1822 he told Washington Irving that he had "been promised to have the publication" of Cooper's second book and was then expecting a copy of it.[59] Despite the effort Cooper obviously put into preparing the annotated "English copy" for Colburn, however, it is not possible to determine whether Colburn had access to it. In some instances, Colburn's edition *did* correct errors that Cooper had noted in Goodrich's edition but that Goodrich had not corrected either in the standing type or via the errata sheet. Thus, several of the unparagraphed exchanges among the characters were reset according to the quasi-dramatic standard Cooper realized was more appropriate for such passages (see *PRE* 1:14; *PRE* 1821 1:19). While one might be tempted to see these alterations as authorial, in fact other similar passages were left untouched or were inconsistently changed in the 1821 edition (see *PRE* 1821 1:18, 1:35–36, 1:286). Cooper conceivably could have overlooked the uncorrected instances. But in regard to other features of the text that he specifically singled out in his comments to Goodrich (such as the overuse of dashes), the 1821 text made little improvement over Goodrich's. One dash-filled passage was copied by Colburn exactly from the *unrevised* American text (see *PRE* 2:224; *PRE* 1821 3:145). On the other hand, a garbled passage in the first volume about which Cooper asked Goodrich "What does it mean?" (*LJ* 1:56; see *PRE* 1:214) was given a radically new shape in Colburn's edition. When Cooper himself came to rework the same passage in 1838, however, he did so as if the careful revision given to it in 1821 had never occurred or had occurred utterly without his knowledge (see *PRE* 1821 2:4–5; *PRE* 1838 1:133; *PRE* 1839 1:186). Moreover, in some instances in which the Colburn text introduced considerable improvements to the original despite the fact that Cooper had made no record of his concern about them, the 1838 revision in fact did virtually nothing to the prose (see *PRE* 1:197–98; *PRE* 1821 1:286; *PRE* 1838 1:123).

In the light of such conflicting evidence, one can reach few sweeping conclusions. It is clear that the Colburn edition of 1821 tackled some of the same issues that had concerned the author over the course of 1820. Yet the manner in which it tackled them makes it virtually impossible to determine whether Cooper was involved in the process. That Cooper gave a copy of the Colburn edition to banker Charles Wilkes in 1825 proves that he certainly had seen it by then if not before; and it may even indicate his approval of—if not his control over—the improvements Colburn made over Goodrich's edition. Without more definitive evidence, however, such questions must remain open.

Even without resolution, however, the questions are important because of what they suggest about the transatlantic literary market at the time Cooper began writing and about how Cooper came to deal with it. That market was characterized by just this lack of articulation between authors and publishers on opposing sides of the ocean. Aside from the absence of an international copyright agreement, the fact that English and American publishers operated independently even when they cooperated left authors in a boggy middle ground. Goodrich's likely suggestion that Cooper employ go-betweens from among his acquaintances rested on a shrewd estimate of how *personal* the transatlantic business was. In this regard, it was no different from other transatlantic enterprises. The very presence of Junius Smith in Britain, where he would spend most of his adult life, reflected the immense utility of personal contacts and personal investment in any business carried on across the sea.

Literature was and was not like other forms of commerce. After the end of American hostilities with Britain in 1815 and the return of peace to much of Europe, naval war and piracy on the high seas gave place to a renewal of legitimate commerce between American merchants and their European counterparts. Tangible commercial goods—textiles, pottery, cutlery, and the like—were somewhat susceptible of competitive replication ("knockoffs" are not a strictly modern problem), but wholesale substitution of the sort seen in literary commerce was relatively rare. Printing made literature intrinsically vulnerable to piracy precisely because publication was all about virtual substitution—about "copies," not the rarely seen original, even within a closed, legally protected national system. In publishing, there was no getting around the virtual. Without substitution of the sort that Cooper learned so much about while struggling with Goodrich and his printers in 1820, there would be no literary marketplace in America itself. The difficulty did not spring from the means of production or the nature of the article. The difficulty lay in controlling what happened to the reproduction once it was made available to the public. Cooper was to spend many days and nights seeking out means of control that would maximize his access to an English (and soon a European) audience while at the same time maximizing his financial returns. Within six years he would leave the United States for Europe in part so that he could carry out his own transatlantic negotiations with printers and publishers. In the process, he would show signal inventiveness and would reap sizable returns. *Precaution* taught him a great deal indeed about his suddenly adopted career.

An American Tale

Cooper's push to have his first book issued in England sprang from his secret plan to launch the literary career that, with the help of Charles Wilkes, he already had imagined for himself. He knew that this goal would require, as he wrote Andrew Thompson Goodrich in September or October of 1820, "preparing the way" for other books (*LJ* 1:64). It would also require *writing* those other books. Happily, the next one had begun to emerge very early. On June 28 of that year, when barely done with *Precaution*, Cooper informed Goodrich that he had "commenced another tale to be called the 'Spy' scene in West-Chester County, and time of the revolutionary war" (*LJ* 1:44). He knew from the outset that *The Spy* would be a tale of national origins, a subject worthy of Walter Scott. But he was not just imitating Scott's typical subject in the early Waverley novels. As his designs on the English reading public suggest, Cooper was imitating the larger outlines of Scott's career.[1]

Scott's example exhilarated but also cowed Cooper. He had dashed off some sixty crowded pages of manuscript (about half of the eventual first volume of *The Spy*) by the time he divulged the new project to Goodrich, on the basis of which he giddily predicted that he would be finished within a mere three months—that is, by October. Even in making this forecast, however, Cooper expressed a concern about the greater demands placed on him by his second book: "the task of making American manners and American scenes interesting to an American reader," he confided to the bookseller, would be "arduous" (*LJ* 1:44).[2] Moreover, the excitement caused by the second book depleted the energy needed to finish the first. As he revised *Precaution* and simultaneously worked on *The Spy*, Cooper saw that the former novel was "so—very—very—inferior—to the 'Spy'" that he confessed he had lost most of his "expectations of its success" (*LJ* 1:48). Something was about to crash as Cooper juggled the two undertakings. He referred to the new book one more time over the summer, in his letter to Goodrich on July 12, when he admitted, "The 'Spy' goes on slowly and will not be finish'd until late in the fall" (*LJ* 1:49).

Cooper's pace slowed so much over the coming months that by year's end he could turn over to his new agents, the booksellers and publishers Charles Wiley and Oliver Halsted (on whom more later), only enough manuscript to fill out the first volume of *The Spy*. And, while he obviously must have conveyed to the firm his ongoing commitment to the project, Cooper apparently could make no definite promise as to when he would be finished with it. Had they been the actual publishers of the project, with their own funds directly at risk, the new firm might well have balked at this point. But, as the author's agents, Wiley and Halsted had no choice but to move ahead. By January (just the moment when *Precaution*, with all its sins glaring on page after page, was delivered to the world), printer William Grattan in his shop at 8 Thames Street, a short distance uptown from Wiley's, had begun setting type for *The Spy*.[3]

This development did not, however, send Cooper charging home to finish the interrupted project. In 1887, his eldest daughter recalled Cooper saying that a "misgiving" had seized him when he was done with the first volume, forcing him to put the project aside "for some months": he feared, she said, that *The Spy* would do no better than *Precaution*.[4] Over the remainder of the first half of 1821, part of which Cooper spent in New York, he was writing other things, but did little or nothing on *The Spy*. A note that January in the *Literary and Scientific Repository* (published by Wiley and Halsted and edited by Cooper's old Oswego messmate, Charles K. Gardner) indicated that *The Spy* was in press. The quasi-authorized bit of gossip was both accurate and deceptive. We know, for instance, that the first volume not only was set in type but also was proofed, and a thousand copies of it printed, before Cooper even sat down to *begin* the second one. In 1843, the novelist recalled for literary journalist Rufus Griswold that he had received a bound copy of that first volume and had suffered it to lie around Angevine for "weeks" before (as he somewhat evasively put it—note the double corrections) "a line of the second volume was <written> <commenced?>

thought of" (*LJ* 4:341–42). In fact, he seems not to have put any more of the book down on paper until the anniversary of his energetic start had come and gone in June 1821.[5]

To be sure, not everything about *The Spy* could just be ignored. Cooper recalled well the lessons he learned from his running argument with Goodrich over the financial pressures caused by delays in moving *Precaution* along at the printer's. The delays in the present instance were of a different sort, although that hardly made them less worrisome. Cooper, probably ensconced at the City Hotel (on Broadway near Thames) late in February 1821, tried to reassure his present agents by putting one hundred dollars in his pocket and going the very short distance to Grattan's shop and then a bit farther to Wiley and Halsted's. He gave each of them a fifty-dollar payment toward what he owed for the printing and the paper, respectively. But these were merely down payments. Not until October 1821, when Cooper began staying in the city for extended periods to finish the book, would his bill from Wiley and Halsted be paid "in full."[6]

Of the two creditors, Wiley and Halsted clearly were more important to the author than Grattan. That was partly because the plans Cooper had for even more books would require their help. They of course would handle practical arrangements for him, meaning that he would not have to deal directly with printers. *The Spy* was also a more important project for Wiley and Halsted than for Grattan. They were expecting a commission on their sales of the book in New York, where they could peddle it themselves at their shop as well as discount it to other dealers. And they would also receive a sizable consideration for distributing it to booksellers operating well beyond the city. Here, not in the modest charges they had passed on to Cooper for printer's paper, was their margin on the venture.[7]

All of that would be foregone, though, if the project were left hanging between the certainties of the printed volume and its vaguely imagined but not yet written sequel. Apparently Wiley and Halsted were relatively patient from their receipt of that first payment in February on into the summer. News of the author's likely resumption of his work that July must have quieted them longer. Better yet, it was not just news that came their way. In his 1843 letter to Rufus Griswold, Cooper recalled that he started feeding his new chapters to Wiley and Halsted in small batches as he finished them. From that firm the packets were passed on to Grattan's crew and set in type. The process was encouraging because of the novel's emerging finality. Yet at this point new worries seem to have arisen, particularly for Charles Wiley. The second volume was threatening to outsize the first (as in fact it would) because Cooper was twisting the plot into a series of new turns, probably not all of them foreseen in 1820. The "spy," Harvey Birch, was left under arrest and facing apparent execution at the end of the first volume, but was allowed to escape in female disguise at the start of the new volume. After his escape, he began assuming a quasi-supernatural aura in the minds of several other characters. For one thing, the lowly peddler of questionable loyalty soon was becoming almost magically omnipresent in the book's landscape, a seemingly allegorical figure aimed at some final apotheosis. Much more attention was directed toward him, meaning that unfinished issues touching on the other characters—the Wharton family and their circle, in particular—might be rushed or dropped. Other changes may also have raised red flags for Wiley. The physical displacement of the book's action from the now-ruinous Wharton house, The Locusts, to the crossroads village of Four Corners and then to Fishkill introduced shifts of scene and event not really prepared for in volume one. All of this and considerably more Cooper had put into play by Chapter 9 of the second volume. How, Wiley should well have asked, would he—or could he—bring everything to a fitting end and still keep the book of a manageable size?[8]

To answer this concern (and perhaps to spur himself on as well), Cooper decided to jump ahead and actually write the book's final chapter before, as he explained to Griswold in 1843, he had even conceived "several of the preceding ones" (*LJ* 4:341). There may be some recollective exaggeration in the story, but certain details of the book as it was published bear out the anecdote. If the first half of the second volume is lavish of new incident, the second half—particularly from Chapter 16 on—seems headlong in the way it disposes of a variety of earlier issues. Chapter 17 sketchily describes new duties assigned to the Virginia Dragoons, whose role in the book Cooper now seems eager to bring to an end. That chapter, opening on the field of the Neutral Ground, narrates a battle in which Captain Lawton is killed and Major Dunwoodie wounded. Then it rushes through a terse summary of the remainder of the fall and the following winter. The next chapter picks up the pace even more, referring to the southern campaign of "Greene and Rawdon" during early 1781 in a first brief paragraph, to Washington's feints with regard to New York City in a second (even briefer) one, and in the briefest of all—a paragraph of a single fifteen-word sentence—hurries the reader forward to the fall of 1781: "At length as autumn approached, every indication was given that the final moment had arrived." If all this haste seems to indicate that the chapter in hand will narrate the climactic scene of the war, the reader is bound to be disappointed. In fact, that story is suspended: we are told instead of the final encounter between George Washington and Harvey Birch, during which the spy refuses the gold Washington offers him and affirms that he shares the commander's selfless commitment to the nation. Only then does the narrator give an account, again very brief, of the war's end.

Cooper's later tale about how he finished the book further explains that he did not just write the final chapter and give it to Wiley as a guarantee that *some* end was in sight. He had Wiley pass that final installment of the manuscript on to Grattan, who was instructed to set it and page it (that is, assign final page numbers to it) so that Cooper would have a specific target toward which he would have to aim as he proceeded.[9] The author could not easily trespass beyond the 286-page limit thereby established. The Yorktown chapter in the book as finally published, extremely sketchy, shows the main consequence of this peculiar arrangement. It has to tell its many tales so briefly because Cooper had only seven-and-a-half pages left by the time he came to its opening. It was among the very shortest chapters Cooper ever wrote precisely because he was writing up against the self-imposed limit of the already paged ending. Cooper himself admitted the result in his letter to Griswold: "the *denouement* of the story is crowded and hurried" (*LJ* 4:341).[10]

This anecdote gives a not entirely accurate suggestion that Cooper took as cavalier an attitude toward his second novel as toward his first. If his manner of ensuring his story an end was improvised and literalistic, in other regards his approach to *The Spy* was systematic. Whereas he had essentially thrown up his hands as the troubles affecting *Precaution* grew after his Sag Harbor trip in July and August of 1820, his renewal of work on *The Spy* the following summer showed an increase of active concern. In particular, as fall approached in 1821, he shifted his literary work from Angevine to New York City, thereby lessening distractions and streamlining the transfer of materials from author to printer and back. A notice of copyright for the work was filed in New York on September 7, 1821, probably an indication that the prematurely written final chapter of the second volume had been given to Wiley by then and that Wiley, on its basis, had taken the logical next step as Cooper's agent in moving toward publication. That go-ahead having been given, Cooper now was ready to shift his labors from Westchester to Manhattan.[11]

His readiness was overdetermined. However earnest he was in turning over to Wiley that token final chapter, other things about which Wiley may have known little or nothing were pushing and pulling Cooper as well. The early fall of 1821 was especially critical for him because he now knew, as Chapter 10 will make clear, that the first sale of properties from the Cooper estate due to the "Bridgen decree" was in the offing. As he considered his options, he may well have figured that letting the sale proceed might be the best course. He thus could buy time—fifteen months worth under the state's redemption law—and then he could step in toward the end of 1822 to pay off the debts and interest, thereby reclaiming the properties. The necessary funds could be raised by his own sale of other estate assets either on the open market or to handpicked investors. In the intervening months, land prices might recover some of their older value, meaning that Thomas Bridgen could be paid off by using relatively fewer assets. And there were, of course, other plausible sources of redemption funds. The *Union* was back at sea again, promising useful returns, and the ship could even be sold at the time it returned from its third voyage (as it was to be), freeing more resources just when Cooper might need them to clear the board in the Bridgen matter.

Most importantly, however, Cooper had an even newer prospect for income in the fall of 1821. His seemingly passive behavior regarding the Bridgen sale at that time in fact freed him to tend to this third option. He did not go to Cooperstown for the sale, as rumor had it he would and as attorney Robert Campbell encouraged him to. But he also did not remain at home in Westchester fretting or doing nothing. Instead, shortly after the sale of Otsego Hall and the other family properties in Cooperstown had been announced, he made up his mind that his truest future as an economic creature lay not in real estate but rather in the territories of literary art. He would not play at imitating Walter Scott's financial or literary example any longer. He would put his whole heart and mind into the effort. At the worst, assuming that he could not rescue the estate, literary success might give Cooper a viable alternative to his long—now clearly ending—dependence on his father's wealth. It would also give him some new identity, a new grasp on the world. He was, one may well imagine, eager for that.

On Tuesday morning, October 2, about two weeks after he probably received attorney Campbell's letter of September 10 (which bore him a clipping from the *Otsego Herald* containing the sheriff's notice for the Bridgen sale), Cooper therefore packed his bags and left for New York.[12] Arriving at the City Hotel just at tea time, he began the first of several extended stays in the city during which he took *The Spy* in hand and brought it to an end (Plate 13). Departing from home and holing up at the hotel was a means of making real to himself—perhaps to Susan and others as well—the new seriousness with which he regarded his "secret" plan. In all likelihood, *The Spy* was two-thirds or three-fourths done by this point. Not much labor would be required to finish it. But time would not hang on his hands in the city; new ideas were welling up in him as well. That this very moment when his family mansion was going on the block was also the time that he had his first thoughts about writing *The Pioneers* indicates how the growing crisis in his old identity emotionally funded the new one he was even then imagining for himself. Cooper appears to have begun work on this third novel, focused on the world he was beginning to think he might lose, as early as November or December 1821 while in the city attending to the last details of its predecessor. Certainly he was to mention it for the first time to Wiley at the end of 1821 or the very start of the new year.[13]

Residence in New York during Cooper's several visits there over the fall, however important symbolically, made great practical sense for the work at hand. Indeed, his decision on how and when to visit the city must have been based on two concerns related to *The Spy*. First, he needed to be close to the printer so that he could deliver fresh manuscript, as well as receive and promptly correct and return proofs. His experience with Goodrich the year before probably had convinced him that this time the pace and accuracy of his work would improve if "distance" were not an issue. At the City Hotel, he was lodged only a few doors away from the printer (and from Wiley and Halsted): any obvious problems could be attended to without delay, and materials passing either way could be hand-delivered daily or indeed hourly. And Cooper was on-site to insist that any glaring errors in typesetting uncovered at the hotel were corrected speedily and properly at William Grattan's printing shop.

Overall, Cooper spent about fifty days in New York City during the weeks leading up to Christmas. Each week in October except the one that began on the twenty-second (the week when Susan gave birth to their first son, Fenimore [SFM 47]), he arrived from the country, usually on Monday and usually just in time for "dinner"—a notation that in the 1820s still might indicate any hour from noon into the evening. He would spend two, three, or more nights at the City Hotel, most of the time apparently renting both a lodging room and one of that establishment's private adjoining "parlours"—in effect, a suite—to serve as a daytime workspace.[14] Then he would leave and head back to Scarsdale, either in the morning right after breakfast or following a presumably early dinner.[15] He thus came and went at Angevine week after week, but stayed away for increasingly longer periods as the fall progressed. In November, for instance, his absences at first were fewer and shorter, perhaps because his wife needed him at home or there was a lull in work on the book. By the end of that month, however, he began a four-week period of virtually constant presence in New York leading almost up to Christmas. For each of those weeks, he arrived at the City Hotel "at dinner" on Monday and did not leave until Saturday morning after breakfast (except on Friday, December 21, the end of this stay, when he left right after breakfast). This period of twenty-two days, broken only by three brief returns to Scarsdale, must have come at the time when Cooper was reading and correcting the bulk of the final proofs for the second volume of *The Spy*, with some odd hours devoted to preliminary work on *The Pioneers* as well. Probably he had finished writing his Revolutionary War novel sometime in October or November and now had to attend only to this last comparatively passive but crucial task. Grattan's crew had to finish setting and correcting type soon enough to ensure that one thousand copies of the second volume could be produced, bound, and labeled in time for the book's official publication on December 22—the day after Cooper finally left town for holidays in Scarsdale.[16]

To all appearances, the author's intensive participation continued right up to the very end. Doubtless his baggage on the way home on December 21 included several bound copies of the second volume. Perhaps he also had with him fresh copies of the first volume, into which his dedication (to English friend Aitchison) and original preface were inserted *after* the rest had been set and, in all likelihood, printed, since those items occupy a separately paged gathering added to the front of the first volume of the first edition, a gathering that includes the September 7 copyright notice (on the reverse of the title page) and that therefore could not have been prepared before that date. This expedient on Grattan's part probably indicates two things: that the "bound copy" Cooper had lying around Angevine early in 1821 did *not* contain those two items; and that Cooper composed these preliminary parts of the book sometime in the fall, perhaps once work on production started again in earnest, even as late as his last brief visit to the city just prior to its publication. Only a finished book, after all, would need such introductory flourishes.

Public Memory

If this is how Cooper actually wrote and produced *The Spy* in 1820 and 1821, it remains to be suggested how he had settled on its subject in the first place. The sources of the book were complex. Walter Scott's concern with the origins of the modern British state clearly offered powerful hints to Cooper, for whom the Revolution was the obvious American counterpart (however different its political meanings) for the unsuccessful Jacobite rebellion that was the foundation of Scott's political universe. But regardless of Scott's precedent, the atmosphere in the United States in 1820 was right for the first full literary exploration of the country's birth.

The immediate catalyst was the recently ended second war with Britain. With its early and spectacular naval victories, its long and largely undistinguished middle, and its post-treaty rout of the British from the outskirts of New Orleans early in 1815, the new conflict had set Americans thinking about the legacy of the Revolution. For one thing, despite the fact that the United States had declared war on Britain, not vice versa, Britain clearly had welcomed the fight as a chance to reduce the new nation to its old colonial dependency. In the United States, the recent conflict was therefore widely called the Second War of American Independence—or, as Cooper explained in 1828, "while the war of '76 is called the war of the revolution, that of '12 is emphatically termed the war of independence" (*Notions* 1:315). The first war had created the nation; the second had reaffirmed and renewed its accomplishments. This linkage ennobled the lackluster second war but at the same time stirred deepening interest in the Revolution, about which most Americans alive in 1820 had no firsthand knowledge. In this sense, *The Spy* offered readers a very useful national myth.[17]

Cooper's sense of the old war helped to shape a new consensus as much as it reflected a preexisting one. The Revolution as Americans began remembering and commemorating it in the 1810s and 1820s was not a single, simple event but a large, complex piece of unfinished business. Everything Cooper had heard over his youth and early adulthood told him so. The DeLanceys were hardly alone, for instance, in considering the war as a disruptive crisis of the status quo ante. They had made their peace with the English defeat and come "home," but like other former Loyalists they were wary of the new political and social order. Even for non-Loyalists, the political settlement of the 1780s and 1790s was at best tentative. Support for the war had been uncertain in many quarters, not just among its outright opponents; and for those who had fought it or endured its violence, it had been a wrenching ordeal punctuated with doubt. In some ways, as the second war indicated, even the final victory had been incomplete. Britain had continued to regard the United States with a mix of truculent disdain and condescension—hence the importance of the impressment issue for Cooper and others. Worse yet, Americans themselves vacillated between faith in their own experiment and fawning deference to British opinion, a perfect instance of the postcolonial mind-set. Such deference was nowhere more evident than in the new country's literary marketplace, which was dominated by imports from Britain.

Americans in 1820 were certainly reading Scott far more than they were reading homebred novelists. Indeed, there were *no* homebred novelists to speak of, and *Precaution*, as good an example of post-colonial "mimicry" as could be imagined, hardly suggested that one had just come on the scene.[18] When, however, Cooper decided not only to set his second novel in America, but also to center its plot on the very question of the nation's emergence, he challenged other Americans to read him in lieu of the royalist author of *Waverley*. In this sense, the American cultural revolution began not with the publication of Ralph Waldo Emerson's *The American Scholar* in New England in 1837, but rather with the appearance of *The Spy* in New York sixteen years before. Cooper's book, written in Scott's mode but very much against his grain, did not *call* for cultural independence, as Emerson's lecture did; it *enacted* it.

This is not to say that its view of the Revolution was tantamount to a Fourth of July oration. In American terms, not just international ones, *The Spy* was a partisan book rather than a pious effort to which unified assent could be expected. Its view of the Revolution, for one thing, derived from and in turn reinforced an emergent class-bound interpretation that itself was part of the readjustment in American values following on the end of the second war. Americans pondering the violent events that had given rise to their country did not simply recall the Revolution—they debated it. They reasked old questions and added new ones. Who had fought the war—continental soldiers or sturdy militiamen?

Had it been directed from above or waged from below? As a patriotic property, who therefore "owned" it—the ruling elite who largely had taken credit for it since 1776, using it to bolster and enhance their power; or the ordinary citizens who, as a veteran would bitterly observe in 1830, had plunged themselves into "an ocean of distress" and then, having at last carried the day, had been told, "soldiers, look to yourselves; we want no more of you"? Had the Revolution simply ended British power in the original states or begun a process of social and political change in the new nation? Whose freedom had it secured, what did that freedom entail, and how much farther might the Revolution's liberating energies go?[19]

Something of this emerging debate may be detected, for instance, in a quite pertinent discussion that took place on the floor of the House of Representatives early in 1817. It was stimulated by the presentation of a petition by a modest New York veteran named John Paulding who, aged and ailing, was in tough straits. His petition asked for an increase in the $200 annuity he had been enjoying for the past thirty-six years along with two fellow militia men, Isaac Van Wart and David Williams. The trio had been rewarded for stunning service to the nation: it was these ordinary Westchester residents who, stopping and seizing the disguised English officer John André on a fall morning in 1780, had led to the discovery of Gen. Benedict Arnold's secret plot to turn over West Point to the British and thereby collapse the American revolt from within. So important was their intervention that George Washington himself had presented them with medals, Congress had bestowed their pensions, and the state of New York had given each of them a farm.

Such rewards for ordinary men had been highly unusual in America in 1780. And the new Republic remained so famously stingy in 1817 that common soldiers who had served in the Continental army or the various militia units, the vast majority unpensioned when Paulding drafted his petition, were still "looking to themselves." At the outset of the House discussion, Paulding was shown due respect for his services to the nation. But the general lack of support for Revolutionary veterans created a drag on congressional sympathy. Enhanced generosity toward one man would, after all, highlight the disregard visited on all the other deserving veterans still eking out a living across the United States.

Sentiment rested at this awkward poise when, like a thunderbolt, a congressman from Connecticut named Benjamin Tallmadge rose to condemn Paulding's request—and Paulding himself, along with the two other captors of Major André. Tallmadge had been intimately involved in the American espionage service in the Hudson valley, and in fact knew a good deal about the André business. However, it was not knowledge that moved him to speak. Aristocratic, wealthy, a man of impeccable credentials, the Connecticut Federalist scorned the captors because, commoners that they were, they did not deserve special attention. That was particularly true of these three commoners, who, Tallmadge asserted, had acted out of greed rather than patriotism. He went on to claim that when André (whom he had befriended when guarding him before execution) was unable to offer his captors the gold they demanded, they hurried him to the nearest American post in the belief that they would be fully compensated for turning him in. The medal from Washington, the farms from New York, the federal pension all proved them (and Tallmadge) right. Moreover, Tallmadge added, the three captors had stopped André in search of plunder in the first place; morally incapable of principled behavior, they had not just succumbed to temporary weakness. The *Annals of Congress* summarized his conclusions: "These persons indeed, he said, were of that class of people who passed between both armies, as often in one camp as the other"—men of such corrupt natures that if he himself had encountered them at the time, he would have seized them as soon as he would have arrested Major André.[20]

Given the vitriol of this attack, it is not surprising that Paulding's petition was rejected. In Congress, "the André cult" won out. But "appearances deceived," writes historian Robert Cray, for the three captors were soon enshrined as "icons of the Revolution, among the very first ordinary participants to enjoy such apotheosis."[21] Particularly in Paulding's native Hudson valley, the shift began with a storm of protest. Cooper's future militia commander, Pierre Van Cortlandt, Jr., thus drafted a series of powerful and detailed responses to what he called "the calumny pronounced by Tallmadge on the floor of Congress against one of the most virtuous Patriots which this or any other country can boast of." Van Cortlandt found Tallmadge's "wanton abuse" of all three captors inexplicable unless the congressman himself had something to hide: had Tallmadge, Van Cortlandt asked, aided Benedict Arnold's escape?[22] It is hard to imagine that Van Cortlandt did not pass on this suspicion to Cooper and the rest of his staff as they carried out their militia reviews in future years. For Cooper, whose wife's cousin had married Tallmadge, the subject was doubly charged; Tallmadge was well known among the DeLanceys and Coopers alike.

More important for Cooper than Van Cortlandt's harangue was the withering public assault delivered by another of the novelist's close friends, Egbert Benson. Like Tallmadge, Benson had been a sometime spymaster in the Hudson valley during the Revolution. His *Vindication of the Captors of Major André* (1817), a collection of original documents in the case that ends with his own astute analysis, demolished Tallmadge's assumption of superiority by recalling for the present generation the ambiguities that had permeated and demoralized the Neutral Ground of Westchester during the war. Benson did not deny that Paulding and his comrades had been out for plunder; but he noted that if they were, it was because residents of the region during the war were interested above all in survival. Furthermore, for Benson, suspect motives hardly meant that the captors utterly lacked honor or principles. Susceptible to the grinding realities of the war, which were worse in Westchester than anywhere else, the trio had done the right thing in delivering André to American authorities. Tallmadge had himself admitted this latter point but had quibbled that any virtue in the deed was voided by the men's base motives. Benson thought this distinction itself vicious. Tallmadge was not interested in moral fine points; seduced by the upper-class allure of "the unfortunate André," as the briber of Benedict Arnold was long known in American patrician circles, he had little interest in protecting the reputations of the three lowly partisans. Federalist Benson, who like his Republican friend Pierre Van Cortlandt had served in Congress with Tallmadge, knew the man of whom he wrote. Choosing sides, he ended his closely reasoned analysis of the case with a devastating assertion about his former colleague: "there never was an instance of such total disregard of what others may feel and suffer, and for a purpose so utterly, utterly trivial."[23]

Partly owing to Paulding's plight and widespread outrage about it, the issue of the nation's general debt to Revolutionary veterans soon was being debated afresh in Congress. Following a summer tour of the northeastern states during which he visited old battlegrounds and reminisced with fellow survivors of the war, Republican President James Monroe proposed in December that the federal government provide pensions for all surviving Revolutionary soldiers. Early in the new year, Congress, having given extensive and at times heated consideration to the question, approved the first general pension law in American history. Paulding had already died by then, but at a symbolic level this new law righted the wrongs visited on him by Benjamin Tallmadge. Soon, in courthouses across the country, aged men were coming forward with proof of their service so that they might draw the modest annuities newly awarded them.[24]

Although it did not go as far as originally envisioned, the pension law exemplified the new prominence accorded ordinary citizens in postwar political culture. Cooper engaged with and endorsed the new values by putting just such an ordinary figure at the center of his Revolutionary novel. To be sure, the book only slowly reveals the selfless patriotism of the ill-educated peddler Harvey Birch. And it first insists not only on introducing George Washington (in disguise as "Mr. Harper") but also on situating him, during his chance visit to the upper-class Whartons, in a suitably elite social context. Furthermore, "Harper" is handsome, wise, observant—and scrupulously fair, suggesting that part of Cooper's purpose in the book was to rehabilitate Washington from the partisan bickering that had marked the last decade of his life, but also from lingering concerns that he had erred in having an officer of André's standing condemned to death, and death by hanging at that.[25] At the outset, Washington's political and personal character thus promises to be at the center of the book. In a similar fashion, one is led to suspect at first that the Wharton family, whose members sort out on different sides of the conflict—Patriot, Loyalist, neutral—will provide the main locus of the plot, as would certainly be the case if Scott had written the novel. The title of Cooper's book is even given its first application when young Henry Wharton, a genteel British captain stationed in New York City, imprudently dons a disguise so that he can visit his ailing father following the evacuation of the Whartons from Manhattan to their Westchester country house. Caught up in a sudden skirmish, Captain Wharton is arrested for espionage because his condition exactly fits the official definition: he is, after all, out of uniform in enemy territory. He thus shares the situation, though hardly the motives, of Maj. John André, whose execution for espionage, we are told, has taken place across the Hudson River shortly before the opening of the novel. Thus far in the book, Cooper seems intent on paralleling the story of André in the mischances attending his own "unfortunate" British officer.

But Cooper did not take Tallmadge's view of André, as is shown by his 1828 treatment of him as bungling rather than "unfortunate" (see *Notions* 1:208–23), and in 1821 the André story did not interest him even if it could be engaged via elite substitutes. The fact that it would have been difficult to retell so notorious a story directly in a novel was reason enough to avoid it; but that is not why Cooper placed André and his execution offstage. Putting aside that darling of nostalgic Anglophiles such as Tallmadge allowed Cooper to resituate the Revolution as the beginning of American political experience rather than the end of the colonial system. André, who marked the old post-colonial regret that had held back true independence ever since 1776, was to be mentioned in *The Spy,* but passed over.

It soon turns out that the elite start to Cooper's book has simply prepared the ground for a radical experiment in reshaping American political memory. Once the genteel refuge of the Whartons' country house is burned down in what one may call an act of authorial arson, even its usually cushioned inhabitants are forced out into the field of military action. More importantly, Henry Wharton is shown not to be the only spy in the novel—indeed, he is shown to be no spy at all. When "Harper" first enters the Wharton household one stormy October evening, the family is busy inspecting the wares of their lowly neighbor, Birch, whose nominal occupation as a peddler is in fact a cover for the risky espionage he carries out for Washington himself. As the action progresses, Birch suffers verbal and physical abuse for his supposed self-absorption and is nearly killed by Patriot forces ignorant of his actual position in the war. In the end, however, after he has risked his neck to save innocent young Wharton, his high patriotism is fully revealed to the reader. Here is a hero worthy of American fiction, a hero to liberate American readers as much as a country.

Harvey Birch came to Cooper from these contemporary debates in an even more direct way than one may imagine. John Jay, once the political ally of Cooper's father and now Cooper's neighbor and close friend, had been Egbert Benson's collaborator on New York's espionage committee; in fact it was Jay who supplied Cooper with the germ of the new novel. Sometime in the past, probably in the summer of 1817, when Cooper returned to Westchester in the wake of the Paulding controversy, Jay had passed on an anecdote about a secret agent whom he had managed early in the Revolution. When, some years later, Cooper decided to write a Revolutionary novel, that anecdote provided his moral theme as well as key episodes of his plot. He did not invent Harvey Birch on the spur of the moment: even though the specific episodes of course had to be imagined as he wrote, he knew from the start who Birch was, what he was to do, and what his actions would mean (see *Spy* CE 12–20; *P&P* 29).[26]

Although Jay never divulged the spy's identity to Cooper, there can be little doubt that he was a Hudson valley shoemaker and farmer by the name of Enoch Crosby. Crosby, born on Cape Cod in 1750, had come to New York as a child, been apprenticed to a cordwainer near his home in 1766, and at the time of Lexington and Concord was working over the state line in Danbury, Connecticut. He enlisted there immediately and was marched off to the Boston area, served later in Gen. James Montgomery's ill-fated invasion of Canada, fell sick, and by the fall of 1776 was back home in Dutchess County. There he enlisted again, this time in a militia company; but when traveling south through Westchester to join it, he chanced upon a Tory recruiter and, striking up a guarded conversation with him, managed to win the man's confidence. This contact opened up such valuable possibilities that by December, having been recruited by Jay's "Committee for Detecting Conspiracies" (then meeting in Fishkill), Crosby was a regular secret agent. On the twenty-third of that month, for instance, he was supplied with passes and false papers and ordered to proceed to a Loyalist neighborhood. Once there, he was to "use his utmost Art to discover the designs, Places of Resort, and Route, of certain disaffected Persons in that Quarter, who have form'd a Design of Joining the Enemy."

This was exceptionally dangerous work in a region where an individual's true position was often veiled or double-veiled and the cost of exposure might be death. Crosby not only had to deceive the Tories; in order to keep his credibility among them, he had to fool the Patriots as well. When, in January of 1777, a Patriot force was dispatched to arrest a body of Tories among whom Crosby was then secretly working, it was necessary for the spy himself to be arrested. But special instructions were sent to the leader of the Patriot force: "Give our friend . . . Enoch Crosbey Alias John Brown," he was told, a chance to "escape before you bring him Two miles on your way to Committee." Adept as Crosby was at keeping his own counsel under the most trying circumstances, it was lucky that he was not suspected by the Tories or shot by his own unwitting allies on this or other occasions. The effective life of such an agent even if he was unusually fortunate was short. By May 1777, Crosby therefore was cycled out of duty. Later in the war, he enlisted again, but in regular military units; in fact, he was on guard duty at Tappan the day André was put to death there.[27]

John Jay had lost track of Crosby in the years since the war. The statesman "had made enquiries after the man," Cooper told visiting Englishman Edward Stanley in 1824, "but never could discover what his end had been" and therefore had concluded "that he had probably gone to his grave stigmatized as a Tory Spy." In fact, Crosby was alive and well and farming in Putnam County in the 1820s, and later in the decade was to be publicly identified (probably by Egbert Benson) during his visit to a New York City courtroom. Soon after that chance event, he was huzzahed at the theater where Charles P. Clinch's adaptation of *The Spy* was being performed. A year later, a book "unmasking" Birch as Crosby was published, and the real-life spy became an established fixture in the New York patriotic pantheon.[28] Former New York City mayor Philip Hone, who had seen Crosby side-by-side with the prominent Seneca leader Red-Jacket in 1829, saw him again the next year, taking part in a grand two-and-a-half-mile-long procession on Broadway. In the latter instance, fittingly enough, "Enoch Crosby, the Harvey Birch of the Revolution," was accompanied by the last survivor of André's captors, David Williams. Cooper's indirect recognition of Crosby—and, through the novel, Crosby's many comrades—had helped raise such men into public attention.[29]

Cooper rejected the linkage between Birch and Crosby (see *LJ* 6:212), but there is no indication that he ever asked Jay to deny or confirm it.[30] What mattered to the novelist in any case was not the biographical specifics in themselves but rather the political and cultural lesson: that such a man, "poor, ignorant, so far as usual instruction was concerned; but cool, shrewd, and fearless by nature" (*Spy* CE 13), had risked his life and property to counter pro-British efforts— and, when offered recompense by Jay on the eve of the latter's departure for his mission to Spain, had refused gold with the surprising observation that the country needed the money more than he. Jay left the secret meeting with "a deep respect for the man who had so long hazarded his life, unrequited, for the cause they served in common" (*Spy* CE 14–15). Herein lay the source of the novel's climactic interview between Birch and "Harper."[31]

The anecdote as Cooper recalled it in his 1831 and 1849 prefaces to the novel hinged precisely on the disinterested capacity of ordinary soldiers to fight for principle, not for immediate benefit. Elite historiography had long portrayed ordinary men and women as responding only to brute physical appetites, a view

with which Tallmadge's condemnation of Paulding and his comrades was utterly consistent. Only gentlemen and officers, by contrast, were thought capable
of high-sounding abstractions.[32] Jay, elitist though he was in some regards, had
already made his name as an antislavery activist, and during these years was in
the midst of remaking himself as a Republican. Besides, he himself, as Cooper
understood, had *seen* the ideological drive in Crosby and other similar men and
did not doubt what the nation owed them. He shared his story with Cooper as a
powerful instance of the capacity of ordinary citizens to act on the noblest impulses. Like Benson, Jay answered Tallmadge—though in private rather than in
public. It was left to Cooper to carry the answer into the public arena.

When he heard Jay's story, Cooper already knew a great deal about the
other side of the war, that on which his wife's family had mostly fought. In
telling Birch's tale, he also introduced not only the "Skinners," the irregular pro-
American fighters who had roamed Westchester, but the "Cowboys," their British counterparts—"De Lancey's men" (*Spy* CE 52), as the novel openly refers
to them. Not just Mrs. Cooper's kinsmen, but the novelist's neighbors in Westchester during his two periods of residence there (1811–1813 and from 1817 on),
had passed on bits and pieces of local lore dating from the 1770s and 1780s. Behind all this were the Otsego tales, those of Oliver Cory and Cooper's own
uncle, and the stories circulating at Yale—stories of President Dwight's service
as a chaplain in the demoralized landscape of Westchester, perhaps; almost certainly, stories of Benjamin Silliman's tragic father, whose link to the DeLancey
clan through his old Yale classmate and then opponent Thomas Jones (Susan
Cooper's great-uncle, for whom Silliman's father was to be swapped out of British hands) was uncannily suggestive of the narrative and political tangle of the
war in this part of the country. But there can be little doubt that it was the political controversy surrounding John Paulding and the other captors, giving rise as
it must have to John Jay's anecdote, that crystallized this knowledge for Cooper.
As Americans lined up in the subsequent fray, Cooper's political evolution away
from the elite Federalism of his father and toward DeWitt Clinton and eventually the flawed master of American democracy, Andrew Jackson, had reached
the point at which he knew what sort of tale he had to write. *The Spy* in this sense
was not just about the Revolution—it was revolutionary in its reconfiguring of
how that critical episode of the national past was to be remembered and understood. Harvey Birch, the fearless though ignorant spy, was the first great com-
moner in American literature. More than a counter to Benjamin Tallmadge's
sniveling dismemberment of John Paulding on the floor of Congress, Harvey
Birch was a figure who suggested future possibilities as well as historical truths.
He was a new ideal, rough but noble, a man exactly suited for America's *next*
revolution.

New Friends and Old

While Cooper's work on *The Spy* lay suspended from the fall of 1820 across the first half of 1821, he turned his hand to other literary projects that came to him through Charles Wiley, his new publishing agent. Wiley, the well-educated son of a New York distiller and staunch Revolutionary patriot who was to cheer *The Spy* on its publication, had been in the book business since 1807, when he had turned twenty-five, operating first on his own and then with Cornelius S. Van Winkle, with whom he issued early American editions of Scott's novels. More recently, he had set up a partnership with a kinsman, Oliver Halsted, and in 1820 was much more in the thick of literary publishing in New York than Andrew T. Goodrich ever had been or would be. The firm of Wiley and Co. issued Fitz-Greene Halleck's wildly popular satiric poem *Fanny* in 1819. It also played a largely invisible hand in the American edition of the "parts" of Irving's *The Sketch Book* the following year, of which Wiley served as de facto publisher.[33]

Wiley was a well-read man who enjoyed lively and literate discussion, a fact that made his various shops a popular meeting ground for New York's intelligentsia. They especially gathered in the small back room of his second shop, at the corner of Wall Street and Broadway, a space Cooper is said to have nicknamed "the Den" following the start of his association with Wiley's firm.[34] Here, even before the founding of Cooper's more formal Bread and Cheese Club early in 1823, the author probably discovered an environment that nurtured his emerging literary talent.[35] James Grant Wilson's description of the meetings in the Den captures the flavor of this happy moment in the novelist's early career: "Here Cooper was in the habit of holding forth to an admiring audience, very much as Christopher North did about the same time in 'Blackwood's' back parlour in George Street, in Edinburgh."[36] Cooper's closest associate during this period was Wiley himself, who (before his business and health both failed in 1825) offered encouragement and advice and generally handled Cooper's books with skill. So intimate did the two men become that Cooper's memory of their relationship was to linger long after Wiley's untimely death in 1826. When in Europe in 1831, Cooper warmly recalled "poor Wiley"—"whom I loved, credulous and weak as he was in some respects, though at bottom an excellent fellow, and of great good sense—nay, even of talent" (*LJ* 2:150).

There was a rare openness in this thumbnail sketch of Wiley that suggests how close the two had been. Herein lay part of the reason for Cooper's central role in setting up and maintaining the little community in Wiley's back room. His visits there during his various stays in New York gave the budding novelist an immediate audience for his plans and his writings. No doubt it was here, for instance, that he divulged to Wiley his vague thoughts about writing a collection of tales. These would probably have been akin to Mrs. Opie's *Tales of the Heart*, which Wiley (in conjunction with Goodrich and another partner) published in New York in 1820. Perhaps, in James F. Beard's view, as "Cooper's hopes for *The Spy* faded" over the first half of 1821, he recurred to "the type of imitative writing he had attempted in *Precaution*" (*Tales* viii).[37] Yet if so, at this moment he could no more sustain this effort than he could his second novel. The book of tales was announced in the fall of 1821, but a letter from Wiley several months later asked Cooper, "Have you forgotten 'the American Tales,' which were commenced by a certain lady a long time ago?"[38] The "lady" was part of the mask by which Cooper hoped to hide his own agency in these *Tales for Fifteen*, which when the slim volume containing "Imagination" and "Heart" finally appeared in 1823 was ascribed on its title page to the utterly fictitious "Jane Morgan." Wiley's prodding seems to have jolted Cooper back to the project, for in May 1822 the *Literary and Scientific Repository* ran a detailed announcement that "*American Tales*, by a Lady, viz. Imagination—Heart—Matter—Manner —Matter and Manner" was in press, with Wiley and his partner Halsted listed as the publishers of the two-volume work (*Tales* ix). That was another false alarm on the question of timing—and also on the book's contents: what happened to those three other tales we do not know; probably they were never even begun.

Cooper's second diversionary undertaking in the months while *The Spy* lay beached stemmed from another literary acquaintance struck up in New York during the months after *Precaution* appeared. This was Charles Kitchel Gardner, the editor of Wiley's *Repository* and Cooper's old Oswego messmate. Two years older than Cooper, Gardner was another Jersey native who had grown up in New York State. Unlike Cooper, he had remained in the military service long enough to see real fighting in the second war with Britain. He rose to command of the Twenty-fifth Infantry at Sackets Harbor in 1813, and the following year was appointed adjutant general by Maj. Gen. Jacob J. Brown, commander of American forces on the northern border. It was in this capacity that Colonel Gardner became intimately involved in the fierce Niagara frontier battles about which he seems to have told Cooper. After the war, Gardner soured on the service, left it in 1818, and headed to the city to seek out other opportunities. His first "literary" venture, a bridge between his two worlds, was a revision of a standard infantry handbook that he issued in 1819. The following July, just when Cooper was busy with both *Precaution* and *The Spy*, Gardner began the *Repository*, an anti-British journal that served as a rallying point for the new "Americanist" cultural movement then under way in New York.[39]

A second issue of Gardner's journal came out in the fall, while Cooper's anxious work with Goodrich and his printers was drawing to a close. Both issues were sizable, but the venture was on shaky footing. In fact, Gardner pirated most

of his early content from British sources, an embarrassment given his quasi-po-
litical purpose. In the first issue, only about 12 percent of the contents, according to one count, derived from American writers. Three months later, the figure
increased threefold, and by the third issue the following January, American contributions accounted for more than half the bulk.[40] Gardner's old messmate was
one of the key reasons for this dramatic improvement. In the January 1821 issue
appeared the first of six unsigned contributions identified with varying degrees
of certainty by James F. Beard as Cooper's. From then until May 1822, when
Gardner was forced to halt publication, only one issue seems to have lacked
something from Cooper, who had supplied copy for roughly half an issue out of
the eight Gardner published.[41]

Fortuitously, Gardner's turn toward intellectual journalism coincided almost exactly with Cooper's discovery of his literary ambitions. Loyalty to an old
friend thus provided Cooper an opportunity to involve himself in New York's
public culture. That he was not overtly named as author of any reviews—all
contributions to the *Repository* were unattributed—did not prevent his being
known as a substantial presence in the quarterly. Those in New York City who
were familiar with Gardner's "associations and friendships," as Gardner himself
later put it in explaining why he refrained from reviewing either *The Spy* or *The
Pioneers*, knew that the author of those books was "a frequent contributor" to the
journal (*ECE* x). The benefits accruing to Cooper from his association with the
Repository were multiple. In the process, he solidified ties that would be essential
to his own advancement, including those with Wiley and Halsted, to whom
Cooper's connection may well have been established through Gardner. He also
learned how to write for a journalistic venue, reviewing current publications and
addressing issues of present public concern. But most importantly, the *Repository*
allowed Cooper to explore issues of interest to himself and lay his own positions
before the world. The essayistic part of his writing in future years—the preach-
ments in the novels, but also the habits of social observation and commentary
seen in a spate of nonfiction works, including many other contributions to newspapers and periodicals—had its first forthright expression in the *Repository* in
1821 and 1822.

The initial piece Cooper wrote for the *Repository* is an excellent case in
point. It was a seventeen-page essay playing off Thomas Clark's *Naval History
of the United States*, a two-volume work published by Mathew Carey in Philadelphia in 1814.[42] A review of a book published seven years earlier is no review
at all. Clark's volume most likely had been picked by Cooper, not Gardner (who
tended to focus on recent books throughout the *Repository*'s brief career), and
picked because its subject was very much on Cooper's mind. He wanted more
than anything else to construct a compact analytical account of American naval

performance in the second war with Britain. Clark, a military engineer with no naval experience, gave him the pretext of doing so: not surprisingly, Cooper's review dropped Clark's book almost immediately in favor of his own interpretation of the navy's recent past. The force of his arguments is impressive. While in no way dismissing the importance of America's political difference from Britain, Cooper put forward a material rather than ideological explanation for American naval triumphs of the war. This nation had far fewer ships than the English, but those it had were bigger, better armed, and more keenly manned. If there was a less material difference between the two sides it derived from the contempt in which the English had customarily held all other navies, not just the American: "we had been taunted and sneered at by our enemy, as a people deficient in every quality necessary to form fighting men or officers.—Contempt is a dangerous weapon, to him who uses it, and a powerful incentive to him who is hurt by it" (*ECE* 19).

The condensed narrative of a dozen engagements that precedes and justifies this realistic conclusion is a stunning accomplishment for an author writing his first historical prose. Cooper's account begins with the small squadron under John Rodgers that left New York harbor on June 18, 1812, and ends with the defeat of David Porter in the *Essex* off Valparaiso on March 28, 1814—with a coda praising Thomas ap Catesby Jones for his brilliant use of a squadron of "little gun boats" to delay the British before the battle of New Orleans at the war's end. The accounts of individual engagements can be crisp and stirring (one action of his old vessel, the *Wasp*, "was fought running, before the wind," he writes), but mere details never obscure the analytical purpose of the essay as a whole. Everywhere one finds the issues of materiality and morale given prominent place (*ECE* 19, 12, 10).

In pushing this analysis, to be sure, Cooper hardly eschews personal observations. Such things as his inspection of the *Hornet*'s undamaged hull or his glimpse of the *Macedonian* under jury masts on her ignominious way to New York help anchor his narrative in the concrete perceptions that only a naval veteran could offer. There is also a kind of muted eulogy to his own last commander, "high-souled Lawrence." "Linked as we were to the regretted Lawrence," Cooper explains, he cannot give the detailed narrative of "that ill-fated ship, the Chesapeake," that he might like to. "We have witnessed his coolness in danger—were familiar with his lofty and generous spirit—and have experienced his kind and liberal friendship, in too many instances—to speak of his services with that impartiality which the subject requires" (*ECE* 13).

For Cooper in 1821, the tribute to Lawrence was a personal gesture, but it also had public utility. Recurring to Lawrence at the end of the essay, Cooper used his famous last words ("Don't give up the ship") as a two-pronged message for Americans. With peace might return the temptation to reduce the navy again, much as it had been reduced early in the Jefferson administration. That would be a dangerous mistake. If American officers needed to mind the personal meaning in Lawrence's eloquent (if ineffectual) cry, since personal courage had been a key element in the victories over Britain, the nation at large also needed to ensure that the material instrument through which that courage had expressed itself not be neglected. "We *must* have a navy—powerful, in some measure, as our nation," Cooper urged. Don't give up the *ships,* in other words—don't give up those already built and don't neglect to build those that might be needed in the future. Previous reductions still smarted (*ECE* 19).

Economics

Cooper wrote other reviews for Gardner across 1821 and into 1822 that allowed him to explore other public issues. The composition of the different pieces, unlike his work on *The Spy* or even what became *Tales for Fifteen*, was discontinuous, for other things often interrupted him during these months. Yet it makes some sense to consider together the four essays for which evidence of Cooper's authorship is firm. The three that followed the review of Clark show, like that piece, the emergence of Cooper's critical intelligence, a capacity for engaging social, political, and cultural questions that was also to be reflected in his fiction from *The Spy* on. And they document as well his increasing involvement in the intellectual life of New York City.

The pieces resulted from the give-and-take of his relations with Gardner, to begin with, but also a variety of other New Yorkers. In reading the piece on Clark, for instance, one can easily imagine the continuing discussions with his old naval colleagues who were still in New York or who passed through there in the years following the war's end. One catches a shadowy glimpse of this aspect of Cooper's life at the beginning of the 1820s in a surviving letter written in May 1821 to his old companion William Shubrick, then stationed at the Charlestown navy yard. Cooper wrote the letter to introduce John M. O'Connor, "late of the Army," who was about to depart New York on a visit to Massachusetts. But this act of courtesy for someone who obviously was in his circle in New York also provided a chance to alert Shubrick to the essay on Clark's history. "You will see there," Cooper wrote, "that I can give you a niche in the temple of Fame with a single breath—Our friend Catesby Jones by the way of example" (*LJ* 1:68–69). The tale about the efforts of Thomas ap Catesby Jones in the waters of Louisiana at the end of the war was not, then, a matter of simple historical narration. It was a gesture of respect within the fraternity of which Cooper in 1820 still considered himself a member. While he wrote the essay in the voice of a serious citizen attempting an honest review of naval events, to other members of the old naval circle he might speak in other accents. He was mediating the navy to the nation as much as he was judging the navy in terms of national values. His introduction of John O'Connor to Shubrick and his service to Jones were similar acts.

The other essays in Gardner's quarterly evince similar entanglements in Cooper's intellectual life at this time, though not so sharply. Indeed, a lack of sharpness in other senses is the first issue to be addressed in regard to them. As indicated earlier, it is unclear which reviews—or even how many reviews— Cooper wrote for Gardner. His authorship of the piece stimulated by Thomas Clark's book is rendered certain not only by his mention of it in the letter to Shubrick, but also by the various personal references in the piece (as well as by the attribution of it to him in a file of the quarterly owned by the University of Michigan library [see *ECE* x]). Attributions in the case of the other five items Beard reprinted in 1955 are less certain. We may begin with the safer and then move to the riskier ascriptions. We know on the basis of a letter from Gardner to Cooper that he was expecting Cooper to review William Parry's *Journal of a Voyage for the Discovery of a North-West Passage* (1821) for the January 1822 issue.[43] That issue contained such an essay, which we are fully justified in ascribing to Cooper. And Beard's argument regarding an earlier review (in the July 1821 issue) of William Scoresby's *An Account of the Arctic Regions, with a History and Description of the Northern Whale Fishery* (1820) is unexceptionable. Cooper's intimate involvement in the whale fishery gave him not only a good deal of knowledge about whales and whaling but also a strong motive for reading and commenting on the book, which of course was to be a primary source for Herman Melville three decades later.

If the Scoresby review was Cooper's, then it seems likely that he also wrote a still earlier piece to which that piece refers—an essay in the April 1821 issue on America's international trade and balance of payments. The essay was occasioned by an unsigned tract, *An Examination of the New Tariff Proposed by the Hon. Henry Baldwin, a Representative in Congress* (1821), now attributed to a close associate of Cooper, Tammany congressman and free trade advocate Churchill Caldom Cambreleng. Cooper, who quoted the "general sentiments of the writer" with "unqualified approbation" (*ECE* 22), perhaps knew who wrote the piece beforehand and had found the pamphlet's ideas congenial in part because he already had found the man to be congenial. Or, and this may be the more likely situation, his strong agreement with the *Examination* in his review for Gardner caused Cambreleng to seek him out, after which the two (perhaps already acquainted) became fast friends. Cambreleng, three years older than Cooper, had moved to New York City from North Carolina as a very young man in 1801. After clerking for one of the city's most prosperous merchants, by the age of twenty-six he began the first of several partnerships that soon made him a wealthy man. If Cooper knew Cambreleng before the 1821 tariff controversy of that year, it may have been through Cambreleng's frequent presence in the dining room at the City Hotel.[44]

However and whenever the two migrants to New York met, Cambreleng in some ways made an odd ally for the Westchester secretary for the Clintonian Republicans. Tammany had favored Daniel D. Tompkins for the governor's office in 1820, and Cambreleng himself would win his first election to Congress in 1821 on a Tammany ticket—much as he would long be the ally of Martin Van Buren and the Albany Regency. Besides, there is not much in the *Repository*'s essay on economics that seems to have a natural connection with Cooper's other activities in this period. Indeed, the review's upbeat view of trade would appear to run counter to the dismal sense of commerce Cooper entertained as a result of his disastrous experiment with his cousin Courtland on the Canadian border in the recent past. How *could* he quote the passage from Cambreleng's argument about the "price of cotton shirting" (*ECE* 36) at New York for the five years ending in 1820 without recalling the letters from Courtland asking Cooper to send more of that dreary commodity to DeKalb during that very period? Nor were the echoes rumbling in the prose a matter of such depressing minutiae. Even in its grand painting of recent events in the Atlantic world, Cambreleng's pamphlet portrayed the economic effects of the end of the European wars in terms that might have eerily described Cooper's private experience:

> [I]n 1815, . . . the capital and enterprise of the world were let loose by a general peace: this circumstance was sufficient of itself; but other causes, almost as powerful, assisted in giving impetuosity to the tide of commerce. Men who had been almost for a generation idle, or occupied in the various employments of war, suddenly, and without experience, entered into a new business. . . . The years 1815 and 1816 yielded larger profits; we were all buyers, and the productions of one country were hurried to another. . . .
>
> In 1817 and 1818, we were all sellers, and prices fell. Still the debts of the world were to be paid, and property of every description, real estate, ships, manufacture and produce, were sacrificed for the payment of these debts; this sacrifice and this fall were simultaneous throughout the world, as well as the bankruptcies of 1818 and 1819; which together, relieved mankind from that mass of debt, which they had been tempted to contract by the great profits on trade in 1815 and 1816. (*ECE* 24–25)

At last, Cambreleng saw a happy reverse: "The year 1820 has brought us some relief; we may congratulate ourselves, that the storm is over, and we may once more venture abroad. We are no longer alarmed with the fear of bankruptcies; confidence has returned to give an impulse to trade, and will, through that, operate on industry of every kind in the country" (*ECE* 25). For Cooper, "the year 1820"—with all the excitement suggested by his persistence with *Precaution* and the profits realized from the *Union*—teetered on the edge of an abyss. He cannot have copied this passage from Cambreleng without at some level recognizing the dissonance.

Other parts of the argument Cambreleng put forward on behalf of "free trade" may have struck a more positive note. The pamphlet suggested that no simple balance sheet between imports and exports could really total up the gains and losses of foreign commerce. It was not a fine enough instrument for detecting the real profits and costs involved in such a complex situation. Especially difficult, to take one example, was tracking an American merchant's use of profits earned on one part of a foreign voyage to purchase overseas goods that were to be disposed of in a third country, thereby yielding profits *on the profits* even though the goods purchased abroad and sold outside the United States might well be counted—wrongly—as American imports. Cooper, his experience of the *Stirling*'s passage to Spain for a cargo destined for England still vivid in his mind, would heartily concur. Indeed, with regard to another part of the pamphlet, he did not have to go back nearly as far as his own merchant voyage to verify Cambreleng's point. Praising the "perspicuous view" of the whaling industry that the pamphlet developed, he could offer his own brief comments on a maritime activity that required "the exportation of no other cargo than professional materials and skill," while its "returns are either beneficially employed at home, or profitably invested abroad." This much anyone in the least familiar with the business might know, although in Cooper's phrasing one detects the pointed condensation of someone deeply involved in it. His proud words about the "adroit" manner in which Americans pursued the whale may even betray the pride of a whaleship owner. Likewise, when the reviewer in the *Repository* sang the praises of the American merchant marine ("decidedly superior to any in the world, in skill, in courage, as well as in the knowledge and sagacity by which its operations are guided"), one is surely right to detect again the voice of a partisan fully identified with the "profession" under discussion. American merchants pursued "every new species of traffic" with vigor and a will to master the competition. These traits would make protectionism unnecessary once they showed themselves in manufacturing as much as commerce (*ECE* 26–30).

But the "profession" with which Cooper identified in putting forward these arguments was maritime enterprise rather than commerce at large. In fact, Cooper parted company with Cambreleng when he turned to more theoretical concerns. His review of Cambreleng's pamphlet placed him solidly on the side not only of free trade, the merchant-congressman's main concern, but also of fair prices. The issue of the balance of payments could be shown to rest on shaky calculations and its pertinence to current deliberations over tariffs thereby weakened. Cooper agreed with Cambreleng on this question. But Cooper also wished to direct his own readers to an argument against protectionism that Cambreleng did not address. His concern throughout was with the final costs of protection and who was to pay them. His analysis was unflinching: "The restricting of importations gives our manufacturers a monopoly in furnishing the articles required for the home market, but for every advantage which results to them, the consumer must suffer a loss." Here Cooper left behind the obviously commercial sympathies of Cambreleng. The effect of high tariffs on necessary imports would not be to stimulate domestic manufacture and thereby lower prices. It would be to create exclusive suppliers whose "natural tendency" would be "to accumulate large profits, and thus to take from the pittance of the labourer to increase the hoard of the affluent." The act of Congress that would legalize such theft would be unconscionable, for "it is obviously impolitic"—not just unwise, but a violation of the polity itself—"to compel the consumers of this country to pay high prices for what they purchase, for the purpose of supporting any separate *class* of citizens" (*ECE* 38; italics added).

The radical tendency in Cooper's thought at this point is striking. Nonetheless, here as in his praise for Cambreleng's analysis of recent economic history one may detect a disconnect between his opinions as an essayist and his realities as a private citizen—indeed, as an author. If literature were to be regarded as an object of trade (as it was in Cooper's recent correspondence with Goodrich), then the argument might turn out a little differently. Did Cooper favor the unimpeded importation of English printed "goods" so as to ensure that American "consumers" of books—let us say novels, for the sake of argument—could purchase their entertainment at the lowest possible price? One must conclude that he did not. Nor did he look kindly on those English pirates (and their American agents) who would frustrate the export of his American printed "goods" to Britain. The analogy did not hold completely, of course, since books have an ideological element mostly absent from American grain or English calicoes. Still, one cannot help wondering why Cooper did *not* see how applicable some tendencies of his thought might be to the industriousness with which he, like those American merchants, was seeking to exploit "every new species of traffic" in literary wares (*ECE* 30). If he opposed the "restrictive system" in the case of manufacturers of calico or china, why not in the case of books?[45]

The next item reprinted in Beard's collection, the July review of Scoresby, may be ascribed to Cooper on several grounds. First, it is here that the reviewer refers back to the previous issue's treatment of Cambreleng's pamphlet: "We have already expressed (in our last number) our ideas on the subject of trade. We think it should be left very much to the interests and discernment of the merchant; the government taking care to raise just so much revenue from it, as it will be the interest of the trader to pay, in preference to running the risk of smuggling" (*ECE* 58). Although it is possible that Gardner inserted such a reference, the whole body of the Scoresby review seems consistent with this brief restatement of the antiprotectionist position developed in the April issue.[46] The second basis for attribution stems from the reviewer's enthusiasm for and knowledge of whaling. No armchair writer could have undertaken the task. Not only did the reviewer display an intimate knowledge of the proper terminology of the "profession" (*ECE* 53); more decisively, he created his own narrative of the whole process of pursuing, taking, and processing a whale, explaining that he has "had some opportunities of acquiring information on the subject" (*ECE* 59). Finally, he anticipated with considerable impatience the moment when he would have in his hands another work that we know Gardner wanted Cooper to review— William Parry's *Journal of a Voyage for the Discovery of a North-West Passage* (*ECE* 43, 57).

A narrative of the typical Brazil-grounds whaling voyage is the most impressive part of the Scoresby review. Unfortunately, Scoresby's account of the arctic fishery failed to present a succinct narration of the process of hunting, capturing, and trying out a whale. The reviewer's job in this case (much as it had been in Clark's) therefore involved supplying what the book under consideration did not—hence the Brazil-grounds account. In American prose before Melville, there are few expositions of this particular business more anchored than Cooper's in the materiality of the actual process. Utterly secure in what he knew, he made his verbal choices in an especially felicitous though by no means perfect manner. Here one first senses that fascination with physical detail that was to give Cooper's adventure tales at their best, as first Joseph Conrad and then the critic Marius Bewley noted, a sense of contingent weight and reality.[47] Rarely, if ever, had the mysteries of whale-craft been so forthrightly unveiled to the uninitiated: "The labours of the whalers by no means end with the death of the fish.[48] In a small boat, in the midst of the ocean, sometimes alone, and with seldom more than three such boats together—in a heavy sea—the prospects of a gale of wind—the ship far to lee-ward, and perhaps out of sight—the reader will not be surprised to learn that their game is often abandoned, even when dead. When, however, they proceed to secure the prize, his fins are lashed together, and the boats take him in tow, the ship at the same time plying to windward to join her fishermen. On getting to the ship, the fish is fastened to the starboard side of the vessel, and then commences the process of 'cutting-in'" (*ECE* 62).

Cooper next described how "strips of blubber, about eighteen inches or two feet in width, are cut with the 'spades,'" after which, attached to very powerful tackle, they are hauled on deck by the crew working the windlass. As it rises well into the rigging, "the blubber is torn spirally from the fish, which turns in the water" like a pared apple, until the big strip is "cut and lowered between decks, and a fresh piece fastened to the [tackle]. In this manner the whale is stript of its blubber, and the carcase is sent adrift." Cooper continued the gruesome narrative: "The operation of tearing the bone from the head is one of great labor, and can only be done to advantage in good weather. . . . If the prize should be a 'Spermaceti,' the 'head matter,' much the most valuable part of the animal, is to be secured. In some cases, where the whale is small, the whole head, weighing perhaps eight or ten tons, is hoisted inboard. The head of the Spermaceti is to be laid open, and its contents bailed out with buckets. The matter undergoes a boiling in the try-pots, however, before it is committed to the casks; and is submitted to a chemical process at home to render it fit for use" (*ECE* 62). Although Cooper never wrote a whaling novel, he was to include a whaleman among the characters in his first nautical tale (Tom Coffin in *The Pilot*), and in the late novel he called *The Sea Lions* (1849) he had his seal hunters turn aside from their regular business to chase and capture a sperm whale off the coast of Brazil. Here Cooper was drawing on what he had learned through his ownership of the *Union*. But he also drew on what he discovered in Scoresby, as Thomas L. Philbrick has observed. His journeyman work in the *Repository* thus was to have long-lived consequences for his art.[49]

Cooper's interest in Scoresby in 1820 surely owed a great deal to his current involvement in whaling. But books of travel and exploration had fascinated him long before his purchase of the *Union*. The same interest must have been evident to Cooper's friends from their conversations in Wiley's Den and elsewhere about the city at this time, since Charles K. Gardner expressly asked that Cooper would "favor" him by reviewing such books. In the letter that spoke of the Parry review, Gardner mentioned in particular two other recent titles: the just-published *Letters from Paris and Other Cities of France, Holland, &c.* (1822) by Franklin James Didier, and *Letters on the Eastern States* (1819), a book by Gardner's rival editor William Tudor of the *North American Review*. Either time did not allow Cooper to undertake those reviews or Cooper did not wish to do them. Gardner had to settle for the essay on Parry that both he and Cooper especially wanted to see in the *Repository*.

The accomplishments of William Parry (along with James Ross) were very much in the news at the time. The two explorers had been sent out by the British admiralty after the end of the Napoleonic Wars, partly because peace created a surplus of men and ships, partly because the reports of northern whalers like

Scoresby were encouraging fresh scientific and commercial interest in the Arctic. Over the next three decades, a great deal more would be revealed by English explorers such as Sir John Franklin and Americans including Elisha Kent Kane. But in 1820, the fact that Arctic exploration had only recently been resumed after a long hiatus meant that many people on both sides of the Atlantic were eager to read about the impending results. Cooper was clearly among them. As noted earlier, he digressed in the Scoresby essay to voice his eagerness: he was waiting "impatiently for the moment when an authentic relation of [Parry's] progress" would become available. So keen was his interest in what Parry might have learned about the waters above the tenth parallel that he had not just waited for the *Journal* of the expedition to appear in print. In the meantime, he had *"devoured* the gleanings of information" to be found in British magazines (*ECE* 43; italics added). While some readers no doubt found the Arctic narratives full of adventurous details, as Cooper also did, his personal interest in Parry's efforts was in large part intellectual (*ECE* 44).

So abiding was this interest that it to some extent colored Cooper's treatment of Scoresby. He thought the whaling captain "an expert and scientific seaman" (*ECE* 64) and was pleased that the first volume of the *Account of the Arctic Regions* contained information about "various experiments" that, minor as their scientific interest might be, he had carried out. Yet Cooper completely bypassed that first volume of Scoresby's book because he was certain that "the official report of Mr. Parry" would provide richer scientific results (*ECE* 44). To all appearances, he wanted to defer treating Scoresby's scientific observations until he saw Parry's, implying that the former might enter into his discussions of Parry's expedition. So rich did the results of Parry's voyage prove, however, that the review of him does not even mention Scoresby. It focuses instead almost exclusively on Parry's extension of knowledge about the Arctic regions, an effort about which Parry was far more programmatic than Scoresby.[50]

Parry delivered Cooper into a rarefied world of intellectual ambition and accomplishment. Fortunately, Parry's *Journal* was not a travel book in the ordinary sense of the term. It was a necessary consequence of the "nature of this voyage," Cooper opened the review, "that a detail of its incidents should be monotonous." There were no new peoples to write about, no "smiling scenes to portray," no open ocean to roam over in search of mere novelty (*ECE* 65–66). So narration in the ordinary sense was out of the question here. Parry was instead a hero of ideas, and as such was notably daring. He pursued a northern passageway in the very place where his superior on an earlier voyage, John Ross, had decisively declared only a dead end was to be found. This fearless dedication to his own ideas made Parry's undertaking in 1819–1820, as Cooper put it, "such a chivalric enterprise" that the reviewer had to confess his emotional investment on the explorer's behalf: "We not only wished him success, because we were anxious to penetrate into the geographical mysteries of the north, but because we felt that so much good sense, urged with such modesty, deserved it" (*ECE* 66).

Cooper's response to this aspect of Parry's book is of particular interest. The somewhat uneven impact of the new scientific learning on Cooper during his years at Yale would lead him to make the most obvious scientist among the hundreds of characters in his novels, Dr. Obed Battius in *The Prairie*, a figure of ridicule. There is neither "good sense" nor "modesty" in Bat's makeup. But Cooper's primary mentor in New Haven, Benjamin Silliman, was no benighted, self-important wanderer like Bat. Cooper's tutelage under Silliman had given him familiarity with the scientific method. But it also had given him insight into the scientific mind. Hence he saw exploration in Parry's case as an act of the mind, not just a risk of the body. Ordinary sense might well force a polar explorer to reject farther advances precisely where science would urge perseverance. "Scientific facts," Cooper wrote, "are so intimately blended, that it is impossible to predict what a flood of light may not burst upon us by the possession of a single fact." To turn back prematurely was to close the mind to the possibility of real discoveries. Hence Parry, although he had been frozen in the ice over the winter of 1819–1820, remained determined to push yet farther into the unknown Arctic. Even as Cooper was reviewing his just-published account of that effort, Parry was already at sea again. Cooper thought him bound to be disappointed in the route he apparently was following but could "heartily wish him success" because his heroic devotion was so admirable (*ECE* 95).

Giving added appeal to Parry was the fact that he was a naval officer. Reading Parry's *Journal* sent Cooper back into his memories not only of Silliman's laboratory but also of his time as a merchant seaman and a midshipman after his expulsion from Yale. He emphasized the fact that such British voyages as Parry's (or the first of the new series, under Ross in 1818) were possible only because the final defeat of Napoleon once more had opened the seas to human curiosity. This very linkage to the war and to the navy caused Cooper to digress about Parry's ships—refitted naval vessels, in fact—about which the former midshipman offered more detail than his purpose in the review required. Perhaps his lack of knowledge about the Arctic drove him into the safer harbor of his nautical experience.[51]

His enthusiasm for this subject rising, Cooper went on to suggest not only how to manage crews on such ventures, but also how to better rig their vessels. To some extent, this was simply a personal injection of his own expertise into the subject under review. But Cooper's comments on the arrangements under which Parry sailed also represented an American critique of British practice that was in line with the *Repository*'s foundational text, Robert Walsh's *Appeal from the Judg-*

ments of Great Britain. Despite his admiration for Parry, the reviewer felt utterly free in expressing his doubts about the wisdom with which the admiralty had fitted out the expedition. Here Cooper was writing not only as a former naval officer but also as the owner of a whaler. He *knew* that sailors, often poorly accommodated and subjected to such danger, responded best to fair and even thoughtful treatment: "The life of a common sailor affords at the best but few motives for extraordinary zeal, although they so often display it; and there is no class of men more sensible of being well commanded, or more alive to the presence or absence of comforts, notwithstanding their ordinary privations and hardships" (*ECE* 67). Similarly, he *knew* that Parry's vessels, instead of having only their aftermost masts rerigged with more easily controllable fore-and-aft sails (in place of their original square ones), might better have had all of the masts so arranged. "It is important to a vessel, that is to work her way through narrow and crooked channels, that she can be easily managed, and that, in the language of seaman"—here the future author of *The Pilot* already showed the verbal drift of his imagination—"she will lie near the wind. Vessels rigged with fore-and-aft sails, will frequently sail within four, and four and a half points, of the wind, and will generally, in smooth water, make good their course within five points." To be sure, there were objections to fore-and-aft rigging. But, drawing on his memories of the *Stirling*'s voyage, Cooper dismissed them: "These objections, for all the purposes of a northwest voyage, are easily obviated:—we remember to have seen, and that in the docks of London, a vessel, of between four and five hundred tons, rigged in this manner" (*ECE* 67). Here the American trump card involved an appeal *to* the working judgments of British owners and masters as Cooper could recall them from his brief tour about the docks of London in 1806–1807.

The digression reveals a good deal about Cooper's evolving sense of how to deploy his own experiential knowledge in his new business of writing. Yet he was aware here that it was his "task to write of what Mr. Parry has already done, rather than to frame theories and plans of our own" (*ECE* 68). This was not his voyage but Parry's—not a novel or a maritime history but a review. Hence he turned to a summary of events from the time of Parry's arrival at Cape Farewell, Greenland, until the vessels entered Baffin Bay some weeks later. Then he quoted Parry's account of the "laborious and dangerous passage" across that body of ice-infested water. This tedious experience led Parry to the moment when his doubts about his former commander's views at last were to be tested. After his return to England with Ross, he had asserted that open water lay beyond this point, the "bay" of Ross being nothing but an "optical illusion." Cooper explained: "If he found nothing but a bay—his modest unbelief, seconded as it was with sound reason, would be termed arrogant pretension, in the face of respectable testimony: but if there did indeed exist a passage, and he could penetrate it, he was at once placed in that niche in the temple of fame, that already contained Van Dieman, Magellan, De Gama, Cook—and a few others" (*ECE* 73).

That was, of course, Cooper's own dilemma as he ventured into the realm of art. Just when he was writing the review—in the fall or early winter of 1821–1822—he also was at last finishing *The Spy*. Due to that odd coincidence, what he saw in Parry was in some ways what he wished to see in himself. Although *The Spy* would soon be issued and meet with huge success after New Year's, just when the Parry review came out in the *Repository*, copy for the latter probably was turned in to Gardner before news of the novel's coup reached Cooper in Westchester. All his aspirations and his doubts he threw into the review. Was he as right in his own persistence as he judged Parry to have been right? Fame was Cooper's personal obsession at the time, however pertinent the issue also was to Parry (or to Catesby Jones, with regard to whom he had used that same conventional phrase in his letter to Shubrick the previous May). Cooper could bestow fame on Jones, and he could record its rightful bestowal on Parry. But could he win it, really win it, for himself? As he continued to quote passages from Parry's narrative, interspersing his own summaries and comments among them, Cooper was inching ahead on his experiment. But so was Parry, who even now was absent on his next voyage into the unknown Arctic. Science may have been the flag under which Parry sailed, but what sustained him and made him such an heroic figure was his faith in himself and the depth of his commitment to the undertaking.

At the end of his Parry review, Cooper wrote that it would be "improper to close this account of his book, without saying something of the author." Whatever the proprieties of the matter, Cooper had to admit that he knew nothing of Parry's history. Having only the man's deeds before him was nonetheless sufficient. He evoked the example of James Cook, the most famous English explorer of the past half-century, to suggest how highly he thought of Parry. Cook's eventful life (and tragic death) were familiar to anyone interested in the topic of exploration, so the comparison on that basis alone was shrewd. But in other ways it was more than shrewd—it was positively daring. In Cooper's view, Parry was not Cook's equal: he was vastly superior to Cook. For with what could Cook be credited but "a tissue of minor actions"? Some readers might balk at that dismissive characterization of a man whose own "niche in the temple of fame" was very large indeed. Cooper's point, however, had less to do with Cook's accomplishments than with his character as a man and sailor. Cook "seems always to have been afraid of the ice," Cooper condescendingly observed (*ECE* 95), and that fear kept him from penetrating as far as he might have toward the southern pole. Parry's staunch confidence and seriousness of purpose by contrast took him farther and farther into the chill unknown of the northern ocean.

In *The Sea Lions,* Cooper was to make Roswell Gardiner a mariner in Parry's mold rather than Cook's: as a lesser officer on other ships, Gardiner had several times "penetrated as far south as the Ne Plus Ultra of Cook," we learn, but on this voyage (like Parry's, it is said to have occurred in 1819–1820) Gardiner is at last in command. Now that he is captain, he fronts "the momentous and closely approaching difficulties" of the unknown polar sea with thoughtful gravity, not fear. And he pushes on. While *The Sea Lions* drew on the author's experience with the *Union* and its voyages southward from Long Island, as suggested earlier, in another sense it memorialized the inward artistic voyage on which Cooper was embarked even as the *Union* sailed. In Parry's undertaking, Cooper read an allegory of his own ambitions as a writer. The novel that extrapolated the *Union*'s venture by reference to Parry's exploits was also a bit of submerged autobiography. That Cooper knew nothing of Parry's "history, or his previous life" in 1822 made his own identification with the explorer easier to effect (*ECE* 95; *SL* Darley 218, 221).

CHAPTER TEN

Legal Troubles

A s Cooper followed William Parry on his polar cruise and simultaneously brought *The Spy* to its overdue end over the fall of 1821, certain outward events were driving him hard. Most concerned money.[1] The gravest among them was what the Coopers referred to as the "Bridgen suit." That legal challenge was not actually a single suit. Rather, it was a series of three successive New York Chancery Court "bills" filed against the Cooper heirs by Albany resident Thomas Bridgen in the years leading up to 1822. Bridgen, a lawyer and soon a master of Chancery—that is, an assistant to the chief judge or chancellor of that court—had no personal claim against the Coopers. He was acting instead in his capacity as administrator of the estate of his father, Dr. Thomas B. Bridgen of New York City, who had been Judge Cooper's partner in a failed real estate deal in the 1790s. At the time of the elder Bridgen's death in 1804, Judge Cooper still owed him several thousand dollars; on Cooper's own death five years later, the issue remained unsettled. Across this period, and in fact into the 1820s, interest on the original debt steadily accumulated.

The younger Bridgen first approached Isaac Cooper, then Judge Cooper's sole executor, in 1815 with a request that the two sons establish the current value of their fathers' accounts and arrange for a settlement. Isaac initially stalled as a way of blunting the matter, causing Bridgen to file his first chancery bill that November. This move in turn brought Isaac around. Apparently with his youngest brother's help, he worked out a voluntary arrangement and a repayment plan that was incorporated into the 1815 chancery file. Future events, including Isaac Cooper's slow decline in health, were to delay implementation of the accord. After Isaac's death in January 1818, the executorship of the Cooper estate passed to the third son, William, whose initial promptness in dealing with the matter at last promised a speedy resolution. Within a couple of months, William had settled the most important remaining questions with Bridgen and agreed to a five-year schedule for paying nearly $11,000 to cover the debt's principal and accumulated interest. The debt was to be secured by the assignment of Cooper estate properties, and repayment was to begin in March 1819. Once he had signed off on these terms, however, William did nothing to put them into effect—he failed to assign the required properties and skipped the first annual payment. On William's death in October 1819, the youngest Cooper son was left to sort out a worsening crisis. Indeed, eight months before William's death a distraught Thomas Bridgen already had implored James Cooper to step in and take action to move the stalled process along.

Cooper's involvement in the matter at that time and while aiding Isaac at least gave him some familiarity with the case. More importantly, it also had made him acquainted with young Bridgen—or perhaps reacquainted with him, since it appears that the two had enjoyed some association in Albany at the start of the century.[2] Because of their earlier acquaintance or a sympathy that emerged in these younger sons charged with straightening out their fathers' estates, a rather surprising closeness developed between the two in 1819 and 1820. Bridgen, for instance, openly shared with Cooper the painful details of his personal financial situation and the emotional burden he bore as he waited for the issue to be resolved. For his part, Cooper not only willingly met with Bridgen on neutral territory to go over the issue—he also entertained him once, and probably more than once, at his new home at Angevine. And, in a revealing letter written while Bridgen was fretting about young William Cooper's lack of action in the winter of 1818–1819, he would express his honest empathy for Bridgen's position.

That position was in fact an unfortunate one. Bridgen's father, an English native who had emigrated to New York before the Revolution, had done very well for himself—partly as a physician and apothecary, partly as a merchant and Tory privateer during the war. Thereafter, however, he saw his wealth sapped by the wasteful imprudence of his oldest son, lawyer Charles Bridgen.[3] Following the wastrel's death around 1800, his creditors moved against Dr. Bridgen. Eventually they managed to seize much of the latter's property, forcing a life of penury on him and the ten or so children he had had by his three wives. Thomas Bridgen the younger, Charles's half-brother, had to rely on his mother's family in Albany along with his sisters, Anna Maria and Catherine. On their father's death in New Jersey in 1804, the three had little hope for recovering any of his fortune or old social standing. Still, that bleak prospect could not stop Thomas from forming the high but seemingly Quixotic ambition that he described in an 1816 letter to an English kinsman: "the most ardent desire of my soul is to settle my dear Father's distracted affairs as honorably as I can and retrieve something if possible from the merciless grip of his creditors."[4]

Once the young lawyer's Albany practice began to turn a profit, he ploughed every available cent—$16,000 by his own reckoning—into buying back legal judgments against Dr. Bridgen's estate. He thereby hoped to refurbish his father's reputation and recover at least some of the family's old lands for himself and his siblings.[5] Another part of his strategy involved identifying overlooked assets listed in his father's books and papers. During that process, he discovered evidence of the long-neglected Cooper debt: an 1801 statement in his father's hand indicating that "there was at that time due to him $12,000 & upwards from Judge Cooper."[6] This figure was inflated, as we shall see, but it suggested the seriousness of the issue confronting Isaac Cooper and subsequent executors of the Cooper estate once Bridgen turned to them.

The origins of the debt were somewhat involved. Like other wealthy New Yorkers in the years immediately following the Revolution, Dr. Bridgen had invested in land. Among his properties was a half-interest, totaling seventy-two hundred acres, in twenty-five parcels spread over nearly two dozen new townships in central New York State. The other half-interest originally was held by an associate of Judge Cooper, the eminent New York City lawyer Josiah Ogden Hoffman. When Hoffman sold his share of the property outright to Cooper in May 1794, Cooper in a sense inherited the partnership with Bridgen. He acknowledged Bridgen's interest and, since he had agreed to be the managing partner of the whole property, executed a trust agreement obligating him to split the net proceeds from any sales. To make matters still more complex, Cooper at the same time divided both his own interest in the same twenty-five parcels and his undivided ownership of an additional thirty-two hundred acres in seven other nearby tracts with two other New York lawyers, Robert Troup and Richard Harison. They, too, agreed to let Cooper manage the operation.[7]

Cooper was well positioned to shoulder such responsibilities. For one thing, all of the parcels in question lay in the so-called New Military Tract, which had been set aside by New York State just west of Otsego County to provide long-promised lands for the state's Revolutionary veterans. Distributed by lottery starting in January 1791, the small lots were not immediately available to speculators. Men such as Bridgen, Hoffman, Harison, and Troup tediously aggregated larger parcels by buying up dispersed individual claims from nonmigrating veterans. Only then could such investors sell their lands to actual settlers or—as Cooper and his partners did—transfer them to small-scale developers who in turn would retail them. Since Cooper was well known by then as a developer active in central New York, his association with the New York City partners and his intimate familiarity with the region made him an ideal go-between. From June to October 1794, he sold all 17,500 acres at his disposal to a collection of seven petty speculators at an average price of $1.37 per acre and a total yield of just under $24,000.[8]

Cooper made very short work of the initial sales. That was the good news. Soon, it was being balanced and then obliterated by reports of serious difficulties with land titles in the tract. The essential problem stemmed from the chaotic manner of the lands' initial distribution. That problem was exacerbated in the case of the Cooper-Bridgen alliance by the easy credit Cooper extended to his purchasers. Because he typically allowed buyers eight years to pay off principal and interest, the actual cash yield in 1794 was quite small. And the purchasers' commitment to the tract was accordingly weak. Writing to young Charles Bridgen after having sold what he called "all our joint interest in the Military Tract" but before he had completed his final calculations, William Cooper emphasized the *value* of the contracts rather than the actual proceeds in hand. He thus reported the Bridgen share of the sales as amounting to £3,600, equivalent to some $9,000, soon revised upward to $9,700. Amid this cheering news, Cooper initially downplayed his doubts about land titles. But hints of future trouble already were emerging. Lacking clear title, he had not been able to give out actual deeds for the parcels sold, only articles of agreement or personal contracts. And to secure the lands and give force to those articles, he insisted on having possession taken of the lots: that way, if conflicts about ownership arose, actual possessors would have an edge. Furthermore, he also inserted an automatic fine into the contracts so as to make the titles "more secure." Even in the fall of 1794, Cooper nonetheless admitted to Charles Bridgen that the titles to lots in one town, Manlius, already were being "disputed."[9]

Subsequent reports told a progressively bleaker story. Interest payments totaling around $1,700 should have started a year after the sales. Probably because Cooper sent Bridgen neither his share nor an explanation of his failure, late in 1795 Bridgen requested a detailed accounting. Cooper's response the following January was sobering. He now admitted that title problems had led some purchasers to withhold their payments. More ominous was the fact that Cooper himself had turned down most of the other payments that other purchasers *did* offer. Anyone familiar with Cooper's boldly preemptive methods would have found his caution in this instance very troubling. He asserted to Charles Bridgen that "Every thing to Secure the titel [*sic*] hath been done," but his actions were not reassuring.[10]

In coming years, a tide of problems swept over the whole of the New Military Tract. But it is worth pointing out that the problems, endemic to the region, hardly were of Cooper's making. Some impoverished veterans, tired of waiting so long for their Revolutionary bounty lands, had sold their lottery rights long before the state's official drawing. Others had a devilish talent for perpetually remarketing their rights to different capitalists, a ploy that allowed them to take revenge on the speculators who sought to exploit their meager and long-postponed rewards for tough service in the War of Independence.[11] Such practices threw land titles in the region into such disarray that small farmers were wary of committing themselves to the heavy personal and financial costs of developing farms there while unencumbered parcels were available just over the horizon. The developers to whom William Cooper had sold the partners' lands either could not attract settlers or found that such purchasers did not carry through. As their own interest payments came due, the developers in turn mostly balked or bolted and nobody would repurchase their lands. As a result, the three controlling partners in the operation—Cooper, Harison, and Troup—faced inevitable failure. By 1807, the three had divided their originally common investment into individual shares, much as the Judge's sons in 1815 would divide DeKalb among his heirs and the other group of New York partners who in quite similar fashion had been taken on by William Cooper for that later venture. Richard Harison, who had bailed out William Cooper's third son and namesake in 1802 by taking the expelled collegian into his law office, confessed to Judge Cooper in 1807 that all the New Military Tract lots that had fallen to him in the division of the partners' holdings had "been claimed under better Titles." He added, "I may, therefore, consider them as gone."[12]

Agreement

Such a philosophical response, proper enough for men playing with their own money, may well have been shared by Thomas B. Bridgen and his son Charles. They, after all, knew that frontier investments often went awry. But after their deaths, Dr. Bridgen's surviving heirs came to view the Military Tract losses as a source of hope rather than regret. A great deal of money was at issue. From the start of sales in 1794 to his death a decade later, Dr. Bridgen had received only about $1,100 in payments from Judge Cooper, about 10 percent of the theoretical total.[13] By the time Bridgen's son Thomas began seeking restitution in 1815, accumulating interest on the unpaid balance would have swelled the amount due to almost $28,000. Small wonder, then, that the Coopers at first resisted the younger Bridgen's attempt at recovery. When he conferred with another of Judge Cooper's old partners in the New Military Tract business, Robert Troup, in November of 1815, Bridgen revealed that he already had made "repeated offers of Compromise & Settlement" to the Coopers. To Bridgen's chagrin, he reported that he had been "treated in such a manner as to leave no doubt of their intention to defraud me out of my dues if possible." As a result, he had every right to be upset.[14]

The rebuff steeled Bridgen's resolve. Soon after consulting with Troup, he filed his first chancery bill. It claimed that, despite the "friendly manner" in which the Bridgens had always addressed the Coopers, Judge Cooper and his executors had resisted all attempts to settle accounts. Indeed, at present, Thomas Bridgen believed that the Judge's heirs were "combining and confederating together to injure and oppress" his family.[15] Stung by these charges, Isaac Cooper began a search through his father's papers and at last found what he took to be a definitive resolution of the issue. In September 1816, he reported that an 1804 sheriff's sale held on behalf of two of Charles Bridgen's creditors had stripped away "all the interest of [Dr.] Thomas Bridgen in the property held in trust by Wm Cooper for said Bridgen." Although to Isaac's mind this discovery must have appeared to close the matter, in fact it soon was determined that those sales had eaten up only about half of Dr. Bridgen's "interest," reducing but not eliminating the Cooper debt.[16] Thomas Bridgen accepted the reduction and by the end of 1816 had entered negotiations with Isaac aimed at reaching an amicable settlement. The future novelist, involved in the process because of Isaac's lingering ill health, indicated the nature of the agreement when he wrote that December to Albany lawyer John V. Henry for Isaac. Cooper told Henry, who regularly did business with the Coopers, that the family was "ready and willing to submit to the Arbitration" proposed for resolving Bridgen's claim (*LJ* 1:35). Attorney Henry himself was to serve as a referee in the case, along with Abraham Van Vechten, the attorney who had filed Bridgen's bill in the first place.

Although never brought to a satisfactory end, this arbitration guided further discussions. Cooper appears to have had at least one face-to-face meeting with Thomas Bridgen in Albany sometime during 1817, the year when the master of Fenimore was shuttling between Otsego and Westchester as he worked out his own financial crisis with John Peter DeLancey and then relocated his family downstate. Judging from the written agreement that his brother William was to sign with Bridgen the following year, Cooper's discussions with Bridgen probably focused on several issues: determining the total amount due, identifying a suitable group of properties to assign to Bridgen as security for the debt, and setting up a schedule for paying off the full principal and interest. The second of these issues probably explains why Cooper and the younger Bridgen were corresponding in 1817 about a "tour" they were planning to undertake together. Presumably Cooper and Bridgen were to travel to Cooperstown, where they could confer with Isaac (and attorney Robert Campbell), and from there head to Broome or Onondaga county and, perhaps, the St. Lawrence region. In those places, Bridgen could view for himself not only the Military Tract lands but also those most likely to be used as security for the Cooper debt.

Initially, the two men planned to take their trip in the fall, after contractor Robert Ward had raised the posts and beams of Cooper's new Westchester house. Preliminary work on the house took so long, however, that the frame was not erected until December 10. Two days later, Cooper wrote Bridgen a chatty note asking to put the trip off for a month or so. He wanted to spend Christmas and New Year's with his family (especially New Year's, the Coopers' seventh wedding anniversary) and assumed that Bridgen would have his own holiday plans. If they took the trip in January, after winter had set in for good, Cooper suggested that they might use his own sleigh—an easier and more enjoyable means of travel.[17] The January trip, however, did not materialize. Isaac Cooper's death on New Year's Day meant that young William Cooper would become the executor of Judge Cooper's estate. And William, although he could have benefited from his youngest brother's aid even more than Isaac had, quickly dispensed with it. For a full year or more, the future novelist was left in the dark.[18]

As already noted, William Cooper's dealings with Thomas Bridgen began on a promising note. The two men entered discussions that by March of 1818 had produced a draft accord based on the principles the family already had worked out with Bridgen. Now, as before, Bridgen showed an admirable spirit of compromise. Accepting reductions in the debt for the 1804 forced sale and for several documented payments made during Judge Cooper's life, Bridgen assented to valuing the debt, as of 1794, at around $4,700. With all interest added, the total amount due in 1818 was still about $11,000, a figure both sides accepted during a March 9 meeting in Cooperstown between Bridgen and William Cooper, with lawyer Robert Campbell sitting in. In view of Bridgen's spirit of compromise, William Cooper agreed to two further points, both of them probably contemplated by his brothers the year before. The Cooper estate would give the Bridgen heirs (Thomas and his unmarried sisters, Anna Maria and Catherine, among others) a mortgage on "Sufficient Lands in the Townships of Edwards and Scriba in the County of St. Lawrence" to cover the whole debt. In addition, William Cooper as executor promised to begin making a series of five annual principal payments, to start on March 9, 1819, to fully discharge that mortgage. The Bridgens in return promised to execute a release of all their claims against the Cooper estate.[19]

The whole debt would have been amicably discharged by March of 1823 had William Cooper not backed away from the agreement almost as soon as completing it. He does not seem to have paid a single cent to Bridgen or even picked out, let alone transferred, the required lands. When Robert Campbell wrote the youngest Cooper son in November 1818, he therefore asserted, "The Bridgen business remains as it was left by the agreement made by William & Bridgen last winter."[20] By early in the new year, Bridgen himself, having lost track of William's whereabouts, despairingly turned toward Cooper. A February letter detailing his frustrations indicated that he had written William again and again but received no answers, after which he had gone to Cooperstown in person, also to no avail. It was clear to him that William was not simply distracted or busy. He refused to cooperate in the least.

Bridgen, who clearly had won Cooper's confidence during earlier dealings on the matter of the debt (if not in Albany years before), now laid out everything without reserve: "I appeal my dear Mr. Cooper," his corrected draft of the letter runs, "to your liberal and generous feelings—feelings which I know you possess to a Degree—to excuse this ~~frank~~ demand of your attention. I do not wish to draw down the sensure [sic] of your Brother upon me because I am in his power. I therefore wish this letter to be Considered Confidential." Bridgen was moved to this risky course because the executor's unresponsiveness left him in a tight spot. He spelled out to Cooper on this occasion more than he probably had to any of the Judge's sons heretofore: "I am my dear sir oppressed & have relied & made calculations upon receiving the one fifth [payment of principal] & Interest on the 9th March next—pray help." Perhaps it was self-praise when he claimed he had been "as patient as a lamb," but in fact he *had* been more long-suffering than the Coopers probably deserved. But now, encircled by "necessities" that were almost too "great" to bear, he could not forbear much longer. "I have paid $16,000 for my father's Estate in 4 years," he told his new confidant, "—& have drained myself [of] every dollar I could Command—pray let me hear from you & advise me what to do." Bridgen had no confidence that William Cooper was going to pay him the $3,000 due in March. "It is a great pitty [sic] ~~you~~ the Executor would not assign me some good Bonds & Mortgages for the Amt. of my claim—& settle the simple points in difference between us without any further unnecessary delay—Would to god he would resign his Executorship—pardon this long letter I could write three times as much."[21]

Bridgen probably had written quite enough for his own good, but his letter reached Cooper at a fortunate moment and elicited a prompt and sympathetic response. Recently absent in New York City with Susan, probably tending to the whaling business, Cooper had chanced upon his brother William in the street and actually talked with him there about the Bridgen business—and this barely twenty-four hours before he returned to Westchester and picked up Bridgen's letter from the post office there.[22] Of course, Cooper had had no advance word of William's travels, so it must have felt strange to learn from Bridgen, "Your Brother left here last Sunday [January 31] for Newyork [*sic*]. He went off & I know not when I shall see him again."[23] But the mere coincidence received no comment amidst all the other things Cooper felt urged to say in his reply.

Overall, his response exhibited a complex balancing act among the claims of friendship, family loyalty, and the truth as Cooper (whose own interest in this matter did not coincide with his correspondent's) wished to define it between himself and Bridgen at the moment. Cooper was shocked by what Bridgen divulged about William's apparent alienation of Albany lawyer John V. Henry, who had told Bridgen that he was done with the Coopers altogether.[24] Professing "profound ignorance" about the matter, Cooper nonetheless admitted that "something of an extraordinary nature must have occurred" to turn the old ally of his father into another enemy. What really concerned him, however, was the main issue between Bridgen and himself, on which he offered a complexly revealing response: "As regards your claim, I have never had but one opinion and that was if my Father or elder Brother"—Richard—"were alive[,] very much if not all of it would be met adversely to your present interest." He acknowledged his father's "negligent manner of doing business," particularly his slack accounting practices. But Cooper also knew that Judge Cooper and his oldest son had shown great skill in answering legal challenges by telling plausible, even charming tales drawn from the family's archive of last resort—that is, personal memory. Against that weapon, Bridgen's case might well have faltered in an equity court. Yet Cooper, even in this longing glimpse back on a garrulous family now all-too-silenced by loss, tried to give his friend Bridgen his due. If the Coopers in the past or by some newly revived grace might manage to outtalk Bridgen, that did not mean that Bridgen should be cowed by their diversionary narratives.[25]

"I am sensible that you are and ought only to be satisfied with legal proofs," Cooper continued. He added that he was "not in the habit" of giving such candid, and of course potentially self-damaging, advice to others. Bridgen, though, clearly deserved it. In adopting this disinterested view and urging it on Bridgen, Cooper was spinning his own little piece of oral persuasion. So far the family gift was his—as indeed it would be in the dozens of fictions he soon was to start making up and marketing as his primary escape from the disaster that even now, though he hardly recognized the fact, was encircling the remains of his family. Yet Cooper was being something other than cagily inventive here. He was letting down his guard and acknowledging that issues of principle were involved in business dealings as much as in any other human exchange. Cooper would not tell others that their case was faulty when the actual weakness lay on his own family's side. He would not lie regardless of what the truth might cost him. This would also prove an enduring feature of his later public career.

Cooper's honesty was funded in part by his optimistic impression that William indeed *was* about to live up to his obligations. The executor, he wrote Bridgen, intended to "go to Philadelphia for the purpose of endeavoring to sell a tract of Land we own in Broome County"—that is, the so-called Manor of Feronia—"which at the very low price he offers will raise $10,000 *cash.*" Already divided into six roughly equal parts but not yet legally distributed to Judge Cooper's heirs, that seven-thousand-acre property *might* yield such a total. Cooper added that he would willingly give up his own claim on Feronia if, as William promised him, all proceeds from a sale there would be paid to the estate's creditors—to Bridgen first of all. Cooper hedged when he added, "All his conversation with me tended to manifest a disposition to act decisively," but he certainly wanted to believe that the lingering business might be so easily settled.[26]

Such faith in William derived from Cooper's plan to return from Angevine to New York City the following day, when he expected to see his brother again. Eager to reassure Bridgen, he promised to bring up then the undecided question of how interest on the remaining principal would be calculated. He would, he wrote, insist that "the *Legal* was the only way"—that is, the 7 percent legal maximum, rather than the lower rate (or cheaper method) William probably had been pushing when he talked about the issue at all. Bridgen would be happy to hear that. He also would be relieved by Cooper's offer to immediately sign over his own share in Feronia as a way of securing the scheduled March payment. Cooper would go forward with this generous proposition, to be sure, only if William guaranteed him protection against all future actions on the Bridgen claim. That was smart, given William's unreliability, but it is worth pointing out that Cooper wanted to do the right thing by Bridgen and, as he went on to say, all other creditors of his father's estate, regardless of what it cost him. He thought that the assets in the estate were "ample [enough] to pay all demands and leave a large surplus." Even if such were not the case, he added, "I should feel it my duty to pay all debts of my Father's estate as far as I am able." In closing this truly remarkable letter, Cooper expressed a willingness to see Bridgen in the city, and promised to meet with him in Albany if he was called upriver first. Cooper had been planning a trip northward to meet with Charles T. Dering, then in Hamilton, about their whaling venture. He also had spoken with Robert Campbell about a joint trip to DeKalb on affairs related to Isaac Cooper's estate. No doubt Cooper figured that he could see Bridgen on the way to either destination.[27]

Although he did not head upstate in February 1819, Cooper was reasonably well informed by the mail about events in that quarter. Primed by Bridgen's concerns and his own discussion with his brother William, he probably would have written lawyer Campbell right away except for one thing—his pressing desire to find and purchase a whaling vessel, the purpose that took him back to New York on February 12. As it happens, within a week of writing Bridgen, Cooper heard from Campbell, who sent word of Samuel Cooper's death, along with the odd note that Sam's apparent failure to leave a will would "add something to the embarrassment of settling your father's estate." *Embarrassment* was not a term that Cooper had thought to use in his recent optimistic analysis of the estate's affairs for Bridgen. Still, Campbell's alarm about such things passed quickly as he focused on other issues. One of them in fact touched on the *Union:* another Otsego lawyer working for shipowner Mumford, Campbell reported, had inquired about the properties Cooper was using as collateral in buying the vessel.[28]

Campbell's letter, forwarded from Westchester to the City Hotel on February 23, must have reached Cooper there around the twenty-fifth. Although busy about the *Union* for most of the time he tarried in New York, he apparently wrote back on March 4, the day before he left the city for home again.[29] Once at Angevine, he wrote and sent a second letter on March 16. Neither survives, but Campbell's eventual answer to both, written on April 5 (and forwarded from Mamaroneck on April 14 to the City Hotel), indicates that a good part of one or both had concerned the recent correspondence with Thomas Bridgen. Evidently Cooper had asked very particular questions about what William had been up to as executor, especially with regard to the scheduled March 9 payment (now due or, by the time of his second letter, overdue). One may infer from the direct manner of Campbell's answer not only the pointedness of Cooper's questions but also a bit else: for instance, that Cooper may *not* have seen William in New York City again. That eventuality would have left him ignorant on the very subjects he had promised Bridgen he would discuss with William.

Campbell's information ought to have been eye-opening for Cooper. Although the lawyer knew that William had been disposing of estate properties, he could not enlighten Cooper on what if anything William had done or would do with regard to Bridgen. As William's health weakened over the summer, Campbell became convinced that the answer was "nothing." To be sure, by August, when another letter bore that conclusion to Cooper, the lawyer did not think that William's inaction was entirely bad: "those who are interested here"—the Pomeroys and the other heirs—"are desirous that he should not do any thing further." While William Cooper would not, as Thomas Bridgen wished in February 1819, "resign his Executorship," over the remaining months of his life, he abused and in effect vacated it.[30]

By fall, Bridgen began exploring other ways to enforce the agreement. He went yet again to Cooperstown in October to scout out new information and while there talked to the Pomeroys and other heirs as well as Campbell. All of them, he soon wrote Cooper, shared "a very anxious concern and corresponding disposition to have the matter finally disposed of." Bridgen may have spoken with Cooper's ailing brother during his visit, although it is probably significant that he reported no such conversation.[31] Other evidence suggests instead that more talk with William struck him as pointless. For instance, while in Otsego he arranged for a village lawyer, Samuel Starkweather, to spy on the Coopers there and help prepare legal action against them in the local court. He hoped that he would be able "to sue them all immediately," or at least move against the executor, about whose actions he told Starkweather to prepare a detailed memorandum. If successful, he could afford to be generous in allowing the family time to make restitution. But, he added to Starkweather in a letter specifying their arrangement, he would never show the Coopers the least consideration "if they vex or Cross me." Needless to say, he mentioned none of this to his sympathetic friend at Angevine.[32]

Attorney Starkweather provided Bridgen with useful intelligence from the start. Among other things, he kept a kind of death watch on William Cooper's quarters in Otsego Hall. On October 19, he sent a hasty note to Albany: "[William] Cooper will die in a short time—beyond doubt." When his prediction proved uncommonly accurate (William died later that day), Starkweather dutifully updated Bridgen in another communication on the twenty-first.[33] It was Bridgen who in turn informed the last of Judge Cooper's sons about this latest fatality—without stating how he learned of it: "You have no doubt by this heard of the death of your brother Wm Cooper Esqr.," began Bridgen's October 26 letter, but in fact Cooper opened his reply by admitting that Bridgen's missive "contained the first information of the death of my Brother which I received."[34]

Faced with the confusion into which William's loss might send his own affairs, Bridgen now set about convincing Cooper that he *must* step forward. Cooper would not simply become the executor on William's death; like William, he would have to voluntarily swear an oath to carry out the duties imposed by his father's will. Perhaps Cooper already had told Bridgen he was reluctant to become executor or Bridgen had heard something to that effect during his recent Otsego trip. Bridgen employed a telling combination of laments, threats, and compliments to ensure that Cooper did not pass. He knew that he did not need to itemize his personal difficulties again, only mention them. He also did not need to map the torturous legal route that had led him to the Chancery Court in 1815 before he could persuade Isaac (and the other Coopers) to take his claims seriously. But he wanted Cooper to know that legal remedies remained an option. While he was silent on Starkweather's current preparations for a new court suit in Otsego, he made vaguer threats of "proceeding by a [chancery] bill against all the heirs of Judge Cooper." Such a second bill would name Cooper, not his brother Isaac, as the key defendant. At a minimum, he would have to go to Cooperstown and take over the family archive and mount and manage a defense. Returning to court was not something Bridgen wished for—as he wrote Cooper rather disingenuously, such a course "would be attended with great expenses to all parties as well as much trouble and delay"—yet he clearly wanted to cultivate an image of himself as desperate and determined.

Bridgen combined threats with praise for Cooper's good qualities. If Cooper would take on the executorship, his "disposition to accommodate and adjust the affair" might lead to a speedy and inexpensive resolution. Bridgen remembered the good times the two men had spent together. But he recalled more clearly the stunning honesty of the letter Cooper had sent him the previous February. That letter had indeed displayed an accommodating disposition. How might Bridgen reciprocate? He had seen a great deal of mismanagement visited on Judge Cooper's estate but still believed that it contained "immense" resources—enough to pay off all obligations and, if properly managed, restore the family to its old prosperity. It would be foolish for Cooper to squander that potential by avoiding his duty, especially given his considerable talents for business.[35] And then there were, beyond the praise, more appeals for pity: "Do let me entreat you my dear sir," Bridgen added, "to give my case all the Consideration it justly deserves— I am somewhat embarrassed in consequence of the delay I have already experienced and must urge you for a speedy and favorable answer." The answer, from New York City, was prompt, brief, and to Bridgen must have seemed positive. Not until he received Bridgen's plea did Cooper "[decide] to act as Executor." Even so, this good news had fuzzy edges. "I shall act," Cooper went on, but then temporized: "my private affairs will not admit of my leaving this [place] before next month when early attention will be given to yours in common with the other business of the Estate of my Father."[36]

"A Judgment at Law"

Apparently Cooper had every intention of visiting Albany and Otsego once he could leave New York that fall, and soon wrote Bridgen a now unlocated letter to set a date. Toward the end of January 1820, with that date now past, a sorely disappointed Bridgen wrote to complain. Cooper in his reply again cited his ever-pressing "private business," which had "imperiously called" him to the city again and made it "extremely inconvenient" to head upstate at the time "first contemplated." Perhaps Cooper already was involved in preliminaries for the 1820 gubernatorial campaign, an effort that soon would take his attention and

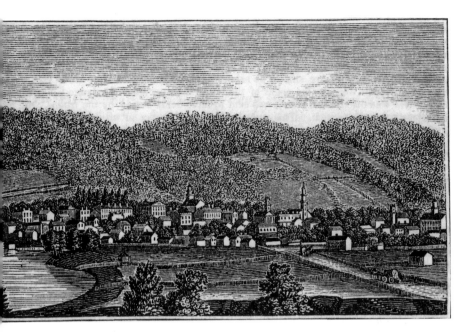

PLATE 1. *Western View of Cooperstown*, John W. Barber, woodcut, *Historical Collections of the State of New York*, 1842. By the time this orderly woodcut of Cooperstown was published, the village had long since passed its frontier period and settled into a state of rural charm. Cooper was proud of the village (it was "better built than common," he wrote in 1838), but most of all he loved its setting at the south end of blue-green Lake Otsego. (Collection of the author.)

PLATE 2. *William Cooper,* Charles Balthazar Julien Fevret de Saint-Mémin, drawing on paper, ca. 1800. In 1834, on his first visit back to Cooperstown in seventeen years, Cooper wrote his wife that the nearby landscape "recalled my noble looking, warm hearted, witty father, with his deep laugh, sweet voice and fine rich eye, as he used to lighten the way, with his anecdote and fun." This profile, made with the aid of a drawing device called a "physiognotrace," suggests with photographic exactitude a good deal about the elder Cooper's unapologetic, "noble" character. (Courtesy of the Department of College Archives and Special Collections, Olin Library, Rollins College, Winter Park, Florida.)

PLATE 3. *Elizabeth Fenimore Cooper,* George Freeman, watercolor on paper, 1816. A year before her death, Cooper's widowed mother sat for this domestic portrait in the great hall of the second Cooper mansion in Cooperstown. The portrait rightly suggests that the hall was Mrs. Cooper's peculiar space by placing her downstage center, with Joseph Stewart ("the governor," the family's free black servant) barely inside and her array of plants pushed back until they block the rear entry of the twenty-by-fifty-foot room. (Courtesy of Fenimore Art Museum, Cooperstown, New York.)

PLATE 4. *View of State Street from St. Peter's Downhill to Dutch Church*, James Eights, watercolor on paper, ca. 1850. This view of Albany, New York, looking down State Street toward the oddly sited Dutch church, captures the city as it appeared when Cooper arrived in 1801 to begin his studies there. The church was "always to be found in the middle of State street," an early resident recalled, "looking as if it had been wheeled out of line by the giants of old, and there left; or had dropped down from the clouds in a dark night, and had stuck fast where it fell." Five years after Cooper left, in 1806, it was torn down. (Courtesy of the Albany Institute of History and Art. Bequest of Ledyard Cogswell, Jr., 1954.59.70)

PLATE 5. *Silhouette of James Fenimore Cooper,* Anonymous, 1805. Then fifteen or sixteen years old, Cooper sat for this silhouette during his short career at Yale. Chemistry professor Benjamin Silliman, whose lab assistant Cooper became in 1804, remembered him almost thirty years later as "a fine sparkling beautiful boy." (Courtesy of Manuscripts and Archives, Yale University Library.)

PLATE 6. *Miniature of James Fenimore Cooper,* Anonymous, ca. 1808–1810. This painting shows the soft yet riveting gray eyes that Cooper's contemporaries noted in him. It probably dates from the time when, as a merchant seaman and then a midshipman, he was passionately devoted to the sea. (Reproduced from Henry Walcott Boynton, *James Fenimore Cooper,* 1931. Collection of the author.)

PLATE 7. *James Lawrence, Esqr.*, David Edwin, after Gilbert Stuart, stipple engraving, 1813. Midshipman Cooper served aboard Lawrence's ship, the USS *Wasp*, in 1809 and 1810. Although eight years older than Cooper, and his commander, Lawrence soon became his warm friend. Cooper followed Lawrence's subsequent career closely; on his death aboard the captured *Chesapeake* off Boston in 1813, the "high-souled" Lawrence became for Cooper a tragic symbol of American courage. (Courtesy of the American Antiquarian Society.)

PLATE 8. *John Peter DeLancey*, John Wesley Jarvis, oil on canvas, 1814. John Peter DeLancey must have looked Cooper up and down a bit when the twenty-year-old midshipman asked for his daughter Susan Augusta's hand in 1810. But DeLancey soon warmed to Susan's suitor, treating him with generous affection, and Cooper in turn viewed him as the ideal country gentleman. The novelist's daughter Susan recalled that this portrait was the "chief ornament" of the family's parlor during the time they lived at Fenimore Farm (1813–1817). (Courtesy of Fenimore Art Museum, Cooperstown, New York.)

PLATE 9. *Mrs. James Fenimore Cooper and son Paul,* Susan Fenimore Cooper (?), drawing on paper, ca. 1831. Few images of Susan DeLancey Cooper survive. This portrait was apparently executed in Paris by her oldest daughter, then about eighteen, during the family's seven years abroad. Paul, the Coopers' youngest child, would have been about seven at the time. (From Mary E. Phillips, *James Fenimore Cooper,* 1913. Collection of the author.)

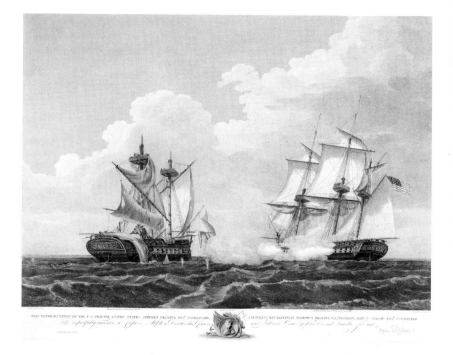

PLATE 10. *Frigate* United States *Capturing His Britannic Majesty's Macedonian,* Samuel Seymour, after Thomas Birch, engraving, 1815. One of the best American victories of the War of 1812 was Stephen Decatur's resounding defeat of HMS *Macedonian* south of the Azores in October 1812. Ex-midshipman Cooper, living in Westchester County at the time, probably saw the captured vessel as Decatur's men brought it in through Long Island Sound to the East River. In his naval history (1839), Cooper rightly pointed out that Decatur's victory was owing not just to superior sailing and fighting but also to the fact that American "super" frigates of the time were bigger, more heavily armed, and more numerously manned than their British counterparts. (Collection of the New-York Historical Society, negative number 78782d.)

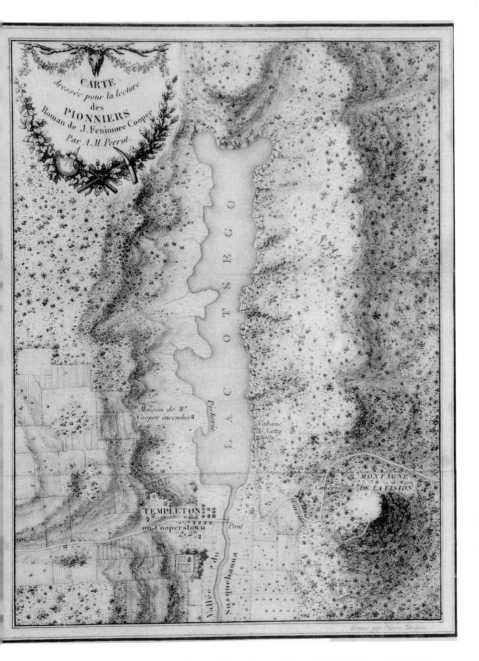

PLATE 11. *Carte dressée pour la lecture des Pionniers*, Pierre Tardieu, after A. M. Perrot, 1828. This map was made for an 1828 French translation of Cooper's third novel, *The Pioneers*. It promoted the tendency of readers to equate Cooper's fictional landscape with his biographical one, showing Lake Otsego and the village of Templeton (or Cooperstown), Natty Bumppo's cabin ("Cabane de Natty") and cave ("Caverne"), the Vision ("Montagne de la Vision"), along with the original site of Cooper's stone mansion at Fenimore Farm, which had been burned by an apparent arsonist in 1823 ("Maison de Mr. Cooper incendiée"). (Courtesy of the American Antiquarian Society.)

PLATE 12. *View of Angevine*, Richardson and Cox, after Thomas A. Richards, engraving, 1853. When the Coopers moved from Otsego to Westchester County in July 1817, they built this pretentious five-part wooden structure on the farm Susan Cooper's father gave them. The new house took its name, Angevine, from the Huguenot family that had long rented the farm from the De-Lanceys. (Collection of the author.)

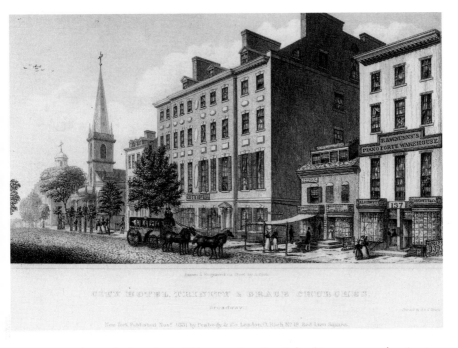

PLATE 13. *City Hotel*, Alexander L. Dick, engraving, 1831. Before his permanent relocation to Manhattan in the fall of 1822, Cooper often stayed at the City Hotel while attending to his literary business. Erected in the mid-1790s on the site of an old tavern once owned by Cooper's in-laws, it occupied the whole block on Broadway between Thames and Cedar streets. The impressive establishment was the largest and most fashionable in New York at the time. In addition to its private chambers and day parlors, it had a ballroom where countless public events were hosted— from a series of naval galas during the War of 1812 to the farewell dinner Cooper's friends gave him when he and his family left for Europe in 1826. (Collection of the author.)

Broadway-gatan och Rådhuset i Newyork.

PLATE 14. *Broadway-Street and the City Hall in New York,* Carl Fredrik Akrell, etching/aquatint, after A. L. Klinckowström, 1824. Cooper called Broadway in New York City "a noble street" and the city's "fashionable mall" and took his lodgings on it or near it once he was living in New York. This etching shows Broadway at Ann Street, just below City Hall Park. (Collection of the New-York Historical Society, negative number 76379.)

PLATE 15. *Interior of the Park Theatre, New York City,* John Searle, watercolor on paper, 1822. In the 1820s, as Manhattan solidified its claims to being the cultural capital of the United States, the new Park Theatre, just off Broadway near City Hall, made a brilliant statement of the city's ambitions. Among the plays performed here soon after the rebuilt Park opened in 1821 were several based on Cooper's novels, including *The Spy* in 1822, *The Pioneers* in 1823, and *The Pilot* in 1824. (Collection of the New-York Historical Society, accession number 1875.3.)

PLATE 16. *Bust of Cooper*, Pierre Jean David (David d'Angers), marble, 1828. Soon after the sculptor David d'Angers was introduced to Cooper by a Paris bookseller in December 1826, the two men became close friends. Cooper rightly thought him one of the best sculptors in France, "if not the very best," and David, who knew Cooper through his books before he met him, said of those novels, "they delighted my very soul." Work on this bust began in the fall of 1827. As one of the first representations of Cooper created after serious health problems began in 1823, its thinner, even gaunt face reveals his lingering weakness. (Private collection; photograph courtesy of the New York State Historical Association, Cooperstown, New York.)

PLATE 17. *Bridge at Glens Fall (on the Hudson)*, Francis W. Topham, after William H. Bartlett, engraving, 1840. In July of 1824, Cooper led the young English nobleman and future prime minister Edward Smith-Stanley into the Adirondacks, where both men were struck by the elemental power of this scene. The two men descended to a cavern hidden behind the falls, where, Smith-Stanley recalled, Cooper "exclaimed, 'I must place one of my old Indians here'—'The last of the Mohicans' was the result." (Collection of the author.)

Peter Maverick sc.

PLATE 18. *Lake George,* Peter Maverick, engraving, 1841. In *The Pioneers,* Cooper had hinted that his old hunter and guide, Natty Bumppo, once had played a key historical role on the shores of Lake George. Seeing the site for the first time in 1824, and walking through the ruins of the Fort William Henry at the south end of the lake, he knew that the heart of *The Last of the Mohicans* would be the infamous "massacre" at that English fort in 1757. (Collection of the author.)

PLATE 19. *Reception of Gen. Lafayette at the City Hall, New York, August 16, 1824,* Samuel Maverick, engraved cover for snuffbox lid, probably English, 1824–1825. Cooper witnessed the arrival of the Marquis de Lafayette at the southern tip of Manhattan, after which "the Nation's Guest" was escorted north along Broadway as throngs filling the streets and buildings threw flowers on his entourage. Once he had arrived at City Hall, Mayor (and sometime writer) William Paulding formally welcomed the "gallant Frenchman who consecrated his youth, his talents, his fortune, and his exertions" to the American cause a half-century before. In this contemporary view of the City Hall reception, the figure of George Washington hovers like an angel to the right of the dome: for Cooper's generation, the association was inescapable. (Collection of the New-York Historical Society, accession number 1931.13ab.)

PLATE 20. *Big Elk, or Great Orator: Omawhaw* (Ongpatonga), Charles Bird King, oil on canvas, 1822. The Omaha leader Ongpatonga, or Big Elk, who was part of a delegation of upper Midwest chiefs visiting New York City in December 1821, presented Cooper with a living model of the heroic Indian warriors he included among his characters. Cooper later wrote that he "knew Ongpatonga i.e. le gros cerf personally" and described him as "a chief of great dignity and . . . eloquence." (Courtesy of the Library, American Museum of Natural History.)

energy even farther afield from his father's estate. He would not specify the details, however, and his vague explanation probably suggested a familiar pattern to the long-suffering heir of Dr. Bridgen. Nor was the lawyer likely to be soothed by extenuations such as the following: "I can only say that no exertion of mine is wanting to enable me to see you as soon as possible and I am the more anxious as I have not as yet taken a single step in the affairs of the Estate nor can I until I command the papers not one of which I [have] yet seen."[37]

When Cooper added at the end of this letter that he was sure Bridgen would feel neglected, he was drawing on reservoirs of goodwill that time had drained very low. Had he been privy to Bridgen's letter to Starkweather early the next month he would have been both enlightened and alarmed. Bridgen had met with Starkweather, probably in Cooperstown, shortly before writing Cooper about the missed appointment, and now he wrote to fill in his Otsego agent and set him urgent new tasks. "Shortly after I last saw you," Bridgen reported, "I wrote to Mr. James Cooper on the subject of my claim wishing to know to a certainty when I might expect to see him &c. to which I shortly after received (what might be termed from him) rather a Condescending reply—but by no means a definite one." Unaccustomed to such treatment from Cooper, Bridgen resolved to force an end. He was bound to New York City on other business within a week or so and intended to call on Cooper unannounced and confront him with documents ready for signature so that the old settlement could at last be finalized. Bridgen spelled out the details for Starkweather. He directed the Otsego lawyer to send him the 1818 accord with William Cooper and the accompanying calculations of what was due. He also wanted Starkweather to draft and forward a "stipulation or agreement from James Cooper Exr. &c to Thomas Bridgen Admr. &c placing James Cooper in the shoes of Wm Cooper deceased." Assuming that Cooper would indeed sign this last document, Bridgen intended to endorse it on the back of the 1818 agreement, after which the latter might be immediately activated. Yet something devious was also afoot, as Bridgen further explained to Starkweather. "You will understand, I want to get James to place himself in the shoes of William, so that we can proceed against him immediately as Exr. & get a Decree—a Judgment at Law." The 1815 bill in chancery had not resulted in such a decree, and Bridgen knew very well where that outcome had left him. This time it would be different.[38]

This development was bad enough for Cooper. Worse was the fact that Bridgen, probably during his January visit to Cooperstown, had explored the possibility of forging a covert agreement with George Pomeroy, Ann's husband, that could have sweeping implications for the future of the Cooper estate and all its surviving heirs. Ann Cooper Pomeroy's somewhat protected niche in her father's will provided the basis for such an agreement. Although she had been left

$50,000, like her brothers, her situation differed from theirs in two crucial re-
gards. The Judge's sons were to divide among them all surplus estate properties,
in which Ann was not to share. But she enjoyed a singular protection against the
sons' shared liability for any debts. She would receive no bonus, but she also had
no exposure.[39]

By 1819–1820, after death had claimed all but her youngest brother, Ann
Cooper Pomeroy and her husband feared that she might never receive the last
several thousand dollars of her legacy. With depression wreaking havoc throughout the American economy and unforeseen claims now surfacing against the
Cooper estate, they also seemed to have concluded that they should pursue a
separate course of action. To their thinking, Ann's denial of a share in any surplus meant that her claim should be fully discharged before any other heirs (including the sixteen surviving children of her dead brothers) received a penny
more than their stated shares. And there was more to their efforts than this. The
couple probably felt that, if claims against the estate outran assets, their own
property might be seized along with that of the other heirs to pay off creditors
like Bridgen. Ann's supposed exemption from debt might be swept away once
the issue was taken to the courts.

To ensure that Ann would be fully paid and protected from any seizures, she
and her husband had few easy options. Over the winter of 1819–1820, they
therefore seem to have discussed with Thomas Bridgen how they might join
forces. Samuel Starkweather undoubtedly had been tilling this rocky field after
Bridgen opened it during his visit the previous fall. Bridgen himself must have
conferred with the Pomeroys again during his more recent trip. To be sure, as he
laid out for Starkweather early in 1820 the course he would follow, he was probably going beyond any clear agreement he had with them. The "Judgment at
Law" Bridgen would seek against Cooper, he told Starkweather, "I will assign
to G. Pomeroy—if [he and Ann] will pay it up or secure me satisfactorily—a
proposition I think they ought to accede [sic] to." Bridgen clearly was improvising as he wrote Starkweather: "excuse my hasty manner of writing[—]I am in
great hast[e] & hurry of business at present & have not given this letter the reflection it ought to have had." Yet it seems certain that he had discussed the issue
sufficiently with the Pomeroys to conclude that they might well "accede" to such
an arrangement. The frustrated couple would do so because his suit would serve
their ends as well as his own. All the Pomeroys would have to do would be to
give Bridgen the money required to settle his claim or sign over to him sufficient
property of their own to cover that amount. He then would transfer to them the
right to move against any and all properties of the Cooper estate and have them
sold at public auction until their payment to him, their costs, and their claim
under Judge Cooper's will were all recovered.[40]

Bridgen's plan, ultimately enacted in a modified form, was forestalled at this point in 1820 by a new arrangement he forged with Ann Pomeroy's sole surviving brother. But Ann and her husband were not out of the picture. Indeed, they almost certainly lay behind this new development. In April, the Pomeroys filed a bill of their own in chancery. Perhaps Bridgen's discussions with them had led them to entertain this step. Perhaps he had caught wind of their own inclinations and therefore sought to join forces with them, although in fact his correspondence with Starkweather says nothing of their impending bill.[41] In any event, the Pomeroys' action, to which we shall return, must have stimulated Cooper, once he was informed of it by the court, to move toward resolution in the Bridgen case. The initiative nonetheless was Bridgen's. On May 25 (just when Cooper was in the thick of writing the first parts of *Precaution*), Bridgen showed up in person at Angevine, apparently unannounced, with the draft of a new chancery bill. In drawing it up, he obviously had used the materials supplied by Starkweather some months earlier. As a chancery insider, if not through his contacts in Cooperstown, Bridgen surely had learned of the Pomeroy bill by then and was therefore eager to revive and implement the 1818 agreement before Cooper was prevented from complying with it by any decree in favor of the Pomeroys. He therefore also brought with him a draft "answer" (or defendant's statement) he thought Cooper ought to submit in response to his own second bill. What Bridgen proposed, based on his understanding of Cooper's sympathy and willingness to settle and perhaps on earlier discussions between the two friends, was an amicable bill: that is, one in which complainant and defendant joined in petitioning the court to help work out the resolution sought by both parties. It was not an uncommon recourse for both sides to ask the court's guidance in resolving complex equity issues, especially when the actions of one or both of them might be subject to strictures from other interested parties.

The 1815 bill had produced a similar, though unintended, outcome. Its amicable agreement was the basis on which Bridgen and Cooper might proceed in 1820. Cooper, however, initially balked at a second amicable filing. For one thing, Bridgen's visit caught him off guard. (One can easily imagine how the knock on the door affected Cooper at a moment when he was in the midst of his work on *Precaution*, a book premised on the end of the financial "embarrassments" that have long afflicted its main characters.) Nonetheless, Cooper hospitably received Bridgen and heard him out and eventually came to share his basic assumptions. Not that Cooper was utterly passive. He agreed with the new action only after helping Bridgen enter many revisions in the draft of the bill, some of which survive in Cooper's own hand.[42] Such a bill obviously would serve Bridgen's ends, but it could be helpful to Cooper as well. He wanted to buy time in the hope that the dismal land market might improve, and therefore insisted that Bridgen acknowledge and accommodate that concern before the two went ahead with the new bill.

But Cooper's real gain here concerned his potential liability as executor. Involving the court meant that Chancellor James Kent, long a family ally, would give his formal approval to the impending resolution of the old debt. Cooper and Bridgen could have proceeded on their own outside the court, but in that event anything Cooper did might come back to haunt—and injure—him. In a narrative summary of the 1820 Angevine meeting he produced the following year, Cooper noted that he had told Bridgen he "was willing to settle the business amicably and justly as far as he was authorized to do *without incurring personal responsibility*" (italics added).[43] Presumably Cooper already had digested the Pomeroy bill. He would know from it that part of Ann's purpose was to have the court determine whether Judge Cooper's executors had properly handled the estate's finances. In particular, she wanted a ruling on whether "any of the assets" of Judge Cooper "had been misapplied, wasted, or otherwise disposed of" by her brothers and their respective heirs.[44] Cooper's concern in reaching his accord with Bridgen in May 1820 was to guard himself against accusations that, by accepting the 1818 agreement (the claims and assertions in which he had no way of personally verifying) and transferring the properties and making the payments it called for, he would at some future point be held to have violated his trust as executor. He was obviously still very inexperienced in that role, and as far as appears from the archive had not yet either visited Cooperstown to search through or secure his father's and brothers' papers or asked Robert Campbell, who had them in hand, to forward any of them. The scope of the 1818 settlement *did* exceed his knowledge. He would proceed on its basis only if errors in it or in other estate documents were overlooked now, yet would remain subject to later revision. He wanted to be exonerated in advance for any tentative actions undertaken on the basis of incomplete present knowledge.

Under normal chancery procedures, Bridgen's second bill would represent only his own point of view as his father's administrator. Cooper would have a chance to see it after its filing and then to file his own answer, which might contest its assertions and critique or even strenuously oppose the sort of relief it sought. In the 1815 case, the eventual agreement emerged only after both sides had had their say. In the present instance, however, Bridgen hoped to rush the matter through the court by securing Cooper's prior agreement to the bill and arranging for his answer to support rather than take issue with it. The answer Bridgen also brought along to Scarsdale in May for Cooper to read and sign was part of the package necessary if things were to go forward speedily. Cooper in fact *did* sign the answer. He then handed it to Bridgen to take back to Albany along with a third document, a relatively straightforward joint petition they had both signed during Bridgen's visit. This item asked that the bill be treated as an amicable one: "It is agreed to submit this cause," it read, "upon the bill and answer to his Honor the Chancellor, who will be pleased to make such Decree therein as he shall deem agreeable to the equity of the Complainant's case."[45]

While all of this may have sounded plausible enough during Bridgen's surprise visit to Angevine, something more sinister was at work. Bridgen's secret discussions with the Pomeroys and his use of attorney Starkweather will suggest as much. It appears that the formal copy of the bill as submitted by Bridgen after his meeting with Cooper fairly represented the issues as the draft had stated them (the water-stained and faded draft, already referred to, is hard to follow at many points, but its presence in the Chancery Court file is presumptive proof that Bridgen had accurately reproduced it in the fair copy). Bridgen also submitted Cooper's answer and the joint petition in the copy both men had signed on May 25. He thereby established the amicable nature of the bill. However, in his oral representations on the matter either in formal sessions before James Kent or otherwise, Bridgen appears not to have fully or accurately conveyed Cooper's understanding of what would happen after the bill had been considered. Bridgen himself had assented to Cooper's two key points. First, he had agreed to a delay in sales that would protect estate property from the presently bad real estate market. And second, he had agreed that, if sales eventually were required, Cooper would control the list of properties to be sold as well as the manner and timing of the auctions. There would, in other words, be no "forced" sales. Having secured Cooper's prior assent to his bill by these concessions, Bridgen in fact rushed the case through the court. When, on June 7, not even two weeks after the discussions at Angevine, Chancellor Kent gave him an order mandating forced sales within sixty days if Cooper failed to make the two overdue payments, Bridgen said nothing to Kent about Cooper's concerns. Pleased that his object was at last within his penurious grasp, he violated the understanding that had allowed for an amicable bill in the first place.

In fact, Bridgen's manner of proceeding caused the very delays he wished to avoid. There were several irregularities in the case, some of which Cooper eventually pointed out to the court. In his answer to another chancery filing by Bridgen in 1822, first of all, Cooper would take exception to Bridgen's claim that the answer to the June bill had been composed and submitted entirely on Cooper's own. That Bridgen would assert this point to the court was, indeed, troubling, although Cooper offered no reflections on Bridgen's motives. He simply pointed out that at the time of Bridgen's 1820 visit he had no knowledge of the proper form to use in such a document. He also noted that he of course was unable to consult with his counsel on the matter while Bridgen stood by at Angevine. Conveniently enough, Bridgen had brought along a fair copy of the answer in seemingly proper form. Since Cooper was in essential agreement with the bill, and Bridgen expressed his understanding of Cooper's hesitations on the question of sales, Cooper had signed it. But he had not written it himself or had his attorneys draft it for him; it was Bridgen's document, and Cooper wanted the court to know that fact and interpret it as Chancellor Kent saw fit. Cooper's second later observation about Bridgen's behavior in 1820 concerned a more serious question. Before signing the answer and the joint petition on May 25, Cooper had asked for and received Bridgen's promise that a full twenty days would be allowed for him to "Consult Counsel before any Steps were taken in the Said Cause or a decree applied for." One can therefore imagine his indignant surprise when he received a letter from Bridgen, "dated at Albany on the ninth day of June," which contained "two copies of a Decree obtained in the said cause on the Seventh day of the Same month of June." Cooper was astonished by the speed with which Bridgen had acted. The bill had been filed on June 7, he noted to the court in 1821, well "within the twenty days Stipulated to be allowed this defendant for the purpose of consulting Counsel." And the court had acted on the very day it received the bill and other documents![46]

Silence

Bridgen's haste caused a breakdown in his dealings with Cooper. "This defendant," Cooper explained to the court in 1821, "perceiving that the agreement made between him and the said Complainant had been violated by the Said Complainant, and being apprehensive that the Said Complainant meditated to take some advantage of the Said Defendant, the Said Defendant determined to consider the proceedings no further as amicable, and resolved to leave the Said Complainant to pursue a Strict Course"—that is, a strictly legal course, without the benefit of Cooper's aid—"in prosecuting his rights." Having been cheated in the game, Cooper would pull back from the table.[47] On receiving Chancellor Kent's order from Bridgen very soon after its issuance on June 7, 1820, Cooper intentionally ignored the matter. He put the papers aside and turned to things over which he had more control. For the remainder of the summer, the master of Angevine alternated among three tasks: managing the production of his first book, dabbling a bit in his second, and awaiting and then dealing with the return of his whaleship to Sag Harbor. All of these activities had their good and bad moments, but in none of them would Cooper have found himself subject to deception at the hands of a supposed friend. Even at the very worst moment he had with Andrew T. Goodrich on his return from Sag Harbor early in September, the moment when he discovered the bookseller's apparent decision to rush the first volume of *Precaution* through the press without heeding the author's instructions, Cooper cannot have felt as injured as when he had uncovered Bridgen's "violation" of their agreement in June.[48]

All summer, as Bridgen would claim in September, he found Cooper maddeningly beyond his reach. Probably for good reason, the lawyer would not undertake another unannounced visit to Angevine, confining himself instead to the more formal—and safer—distance of the mails. As already indicated, he sent Cooper a letter on June 9 or 10 enclosing two copies of the court order. Although we know that Cooper received this package, he mailed back neither an acknowledgement nor a substantive response. Bridgen asserted in September that he had written Cooper again on June 24; again there was no answer. Twice more in coming weeks, Bridgen wrote and personally mailed letters to Cooper. That he recalled with convincing particularity the details of each instance suggests that he in fact had sent them. Neither of these further letters brought any reply from Angevine.[49]

There is no reason to believe that any of these items failed to reach Cooper— or at least the post office at Mamaroneck. Besides, we have Cooper's later admission that the first of Bridgen's mailings indeed arrived in due course. Cooper also spoke of having found an August dispatch from Bridgen waiting for him on his return from Sag Harbor. It seems clear that, having reached the conclusion from Bridgen's June 9–10 missive that the lawyer had violated their agreement, Cooper simply refused to pay the postage on the others or paid it and then threw them away unopened. If he had done either, he was technically correct in writing on September 4, in response to Bridgen's August letter, "In it you speak of others *I have never seen*" (italics added).[50] Cooper had no interest (psychologically or financially) in helping move things along or even in learning where things stood. His unresponsiveness across the summer, which Bridgen rightly took as an affront, chastised that man for trying to rush things to a conclusion that ignored Cooper's position. It also, of course, had the effect of slowing everything down—indeed, of stopping the action completely. Bridgen's unopened or refused and presumably ever-more-frantic letters must have called for Cooper to make the payments that Chancellor Kent's ruling required him to make on or before August 6. As that date drew near and then passed, Bridgen must have begun imploring Cooper to send him the "directions" on how to proceed with the sales—directions that, according to his understanding, Cooper was to forward within two months of the decree "at farthest."[51] The contemplated sales under an amicable bill would not need writs from the court, unless Cooper demanded them as a further guarantee that he was acting with due care as executor. But they would require advertising and other practical preparations (including coordination of Bridgen's efforts with those of the Pomeroys, if his alliance with them was still viable). Had Cooper supplied the list of the Otsego,

Broome, or St. Lawrence properties in a timely fashion, Bridgen could have made the necessary arrangements. Barring that, if Cooper had simply let Bridgen know *anything* about his plans or views at this time, Bridgen would have had a better sense of the next steps he—or they—would have to take. But Cooper wrote not a single line to Bridgen, who as a result was left in the darkness of his own greedy contriving.[52]

What Cooper really gained over the summer was a sense of moral mastery in what might otherwise have been a humiliating situation. Bridgen clearly was thrown off balance by Cooper's silence, so much so that when he wrote his fifth letter sometime toward the end of August he adopted a tone of voice for which, once he finally did hear from Cooper, he soon felt compelled to apologize. When Cooper returned from Sag Harbor on August 22, he found this latest letter awaiting him in Mamaroneck. He seems to have put it aside for some days, then opened it on or shortly before September 4, on which date he at last sat down to break his silence. Bridgen's letter, of which we have no copy, probably spelled out the meaning of the court's June order and the powers it gave him in the event of Cooper's continued refusal to cooperate. It may have threatened to use those powers vindictively or to return to the court with an aggressive new bill. Cooper's response, in view of the machinations aimed at his interest now and heretofore, was remarkably well-tempered. His moral calm was evident. Bridgen had mentioned all the unanswered letters and, probably hinting that Cooper had vacated his premises in Westchester in order to avoid the court's ruling, had melodramatically threatened to blanket all Cooper's other possible addresses (probably including Cooperstown, the City Hotel, perhaps even DeKalb) with further mailings aimed at flushing him out. Having played the scoundrel himself, Bridgen of course saw his opponent in the same light. The deadline for his receipt of the first two payments on the debt having passed at the start of the month, he also made it plain (as Cooper would summarize the issue) that he wanted money and wanted it immediately: Bridgen no longer demanded "security" for the debt, as Cooper's answer put it, he demanded "cash."[53]

Having located Bridgen in the crass precincts of the marketplace, Cooper himself took the high ground. He would be "happy to have the misunderstanding explained and that as soon as possible." He was off to Sag Harbor again in a few days but would be back at Angevine by month's end—"where," he added with controlled graciousness, "I sincerely hope nothing of the unpleasant nature you allude to will prevent my seeing you again." Probably Bridgen had warned that he was about to consult Chancellor Kent and, now that the date for making up the overdue payments had passed, secure the writs necessary to proceed unsentimentally against any and all property of the estate. Perhaps he tipped his hand with regard to his continuing conversations with the Pomeroys. Cooper was not frightened by such prospects, which represented only *unpleasant* possibilities. Of course, he even now clung to his belief in the ampleness of the estate. But this was not illusion talking. It was moral authority born of his manipulation of a process that had been hijacked by his supposed friend. He employed some of that authority in an effort to entice Bridgen back to the bargaining table by extending to him, despite all the lawyer had done and said, the hospitality of Angevine once more. At bottom, they were still friends, were they not?[54]

Cooper's strategy of cool but hospitable superiority paid off. The lawyer's answer to Cooper's September 4 letter was militant but contrite and conciliatory. As he took up the subject of his unanswered mailings over the summer, he seemed to attack, then quickly diluted his anger—only to concentrate it again: "You say 'I have never seen them.' If that be *the Case Sir*, I am sorry for the manner I wrote. It is held to be ungentlemanly in the extreme for one Gentleman not to answer another and situated and distressed as I am I expected immediate replys [*sic*], at least to one of my four several letters." Bridgen was right in this rendering of genteel protocol, even if he had not quite been acting the part of a "Gentleman" himself. It is worth stressing that Cooper had not said anything on September 4 about the way Bridgen had "violated" their agreement (that charge would come to light only in the new answer submitted to chancery in April 1821), but Bridgen's apprehension on that point probably caused some of the fluctuations in his tone. On the one hand, he tried to play for sympathy by repeating for Cooper the lament he already had delivered during their "several and repeated Conversations": that he was "distressed for money beyond all measure." Yet, riled by Cooper's renewed insistence on controlling any sales from the estate (to which Bridgen had assented in May), the supposedly penniless attorney lashed out: "You must be jesting with me[,] you certainly do not wish to insult ~~my understanding~~ me." Defiantly, he laid out his present assumptions: if the long-overdue 1819 payment was not made by August 6, the court authorized Bridgen "to sell under my decree sufficient [property] to raise that amt."

Driven as he was by powerful feelings, Bridgen still had to watch his step. He knew very well that amicable bills rested on the pretense that both sides to a dispute were actually allies. He also knew that everything that had taken place since the May meeting at Angevine showed how fragile that pretense was in this instance. Cooper, who had done nothing but withdraw from active participation in the proceedings, thereby had gained the upper hand. Despite his hunger for cash, Bridgen would have to compromise on the question of sales if only because Cooper's continued resistance would render the present court order ineffective. There had been an amicable filing not because Bridgen had the paperwork for it but rather because Cooper had exacted certain promises from him in exchange for the signed documents. Finally, therefore, Bridgen relented. He admitted that he had allowed Cooper considerable latitude in directing sales of estate property. Cooper was to pick the parcels and set the terms. He therefore might sell off lands (such as those in Feronia) entirely on his own and use the proceeds to make the mandated payments. Or he might work out some arrangement with Bridgen whereby the two cooperated to produce mutually agreeable results. Chagrined by his own outbursts but also by his sense of how vulnerable his position now was, Bridgen reiterated the concession he had made in May: "I generously told you I never wished you to sacrifice any property of the estate."

His "generosity" was grounded in policy. In view of the likelihood that Cooper might refuse to cooperate in a speedy sale of estate assets, Bridgen's attorneys already had advised him that he could *not* secure an execution on his own under their joint decree. (Hence the utter shrewdness of Cooper's strategy once Bridgen's "violation" of their understanding had occurred.) Accordingly, Bridgen now told Cooper what he was contemplating: he would have to proceed by another "Bill in Chancery against yourself as Executor & all the Heirs &c of Judge Cooper." This new bill, filed on November 13, 1820, aimed at determining the extent and nature of the estate's assets and liabilities. Accordingly, it requested that subpoenas be served on all defendants in the case, who were also ordered to appear and answer questions on these issues. Eager to expedite the matter, Bridgen had informed his attorney, William A. Duer of Albany, that he was willing to make out the paperwork for those subpoenas, and apparently he did so.[55] Bridgen also traveled to Cooperstown in the middle of November and on the sixteenth of that month personally served subpoenas on the widows of Richard, Isaac, and Samuel Cooper, and (through their attorneys and/or guardians) on all sixteen "infant defendants" named in his bill.[56] New York City attorney Henry B. Davis, acting as Bridgen's agent in the matter, was deputed to serve the two remaining defendants, Cooper and his brother William's widow, on November 30. The subpoenas required all defendants to appear before the court on December 4, although "appearing" was a legal ritual rather than a literal requirement. According to a later petition Bridgen filed in the case, Cooper complied by causing "his appearance to be entered" on December 3 at the New York City office of attorney Edmund Elmendorf, a clerk in chancery, and such compliance was completely acceptable to the court.[57] Perhaps on December 3, as well, Cooper picked up copies of the new Bridgen bill that had been forwarded to the law office of another creditor, Robert Sedgwick, for him. Sedgwick had written Bridgen the day before to report his previous lack of progress on the matter: "I have seen Cooper in Town but once & then he said he would call on me, which he did not do."[58]

On December 26, 1820, six weeks after the filing date and three after Cooper's "appearance" in the city, James Kent held a court session at his house in Albany. All defendants apparently had complied with the demand that they appear, probably through means similar to those Cooper used. Chancellor Kent thereupon directed all defendants, including Cooper, to answer Bridgen's latest bill within another six weeks of the date when notice of his order reached them. Most of them, as it happened, dragged their feet for a full ten weeks before finally filing answers on March 5, 1821. Even at that late moment, however, two defendants had not yet complied: the Pomeroys and, not surprisingly, Cooper. Another three weeks passed in silence. Then, in a court session held at the state capitol on March 26, Chancellor Kent took note of Cooper's unresponsiveness in particular and renewed his order, requiring that the executor of the Cooper estate answer the bill within a further three weeks. Already, nineteen weeks had passed since Bridgen's November filing. Surely aware of the defendants' elastic notions of time, Kent in this new order set a definite limit. If Cooper did not respond by April 17, Bridgen's bill would be accepted *pro confesso:* the court would issue a decree on the assumption that Cooper agreed to and accepted every assertion and claim the bill contained. It was this last order of the court that called forth Cooper's answer, filed at the last moment.[59]

In that 1821 "Several Answer," the executor called Bridgen to account for his erroneous statement that the 1820 "answer" had been written entirely on Cooper's own. Cooper also indicated that Bridgen's rush to present his 1820 bill to the court had broken his promise that Cooper would have twenty days to consult counsel. He also explained his subsequent refusal to cooperate in that supposedly amicable bill because of his apprehension that Bridgen might "take some advantage" of him. He furthermore indicated his view that the estate's assets were sufficient to cover all obligations, although he reiterated what Bridgen's bill asserted: "this defendant Since the Office and duty of Executor has devolved upon him has not received any personal assets." Finally, he stated for the record the reasoning behind his resistance to Bridgen and his willingness to refer the matter yet again to the court. Having no way of knowing whether the 1818 settlement was accurate, he felt that he could not make the payments it required unless the court would certify it and thereby indemnify him against any later charge that he had wrongly distributed assets of his father's estate.[60]

In a session held at Kent's house in Albany on June 28, 1821, and attended by lawyer William Hale of New York City as Cooper's counsel, the chancellor took notice of Cooper's request that the court back him up in any needed sales. He also ruled, rightly it would seem, that Cooper's answer amounted to a "consent," that is, that the present case was essentially amicable. The accompanying order therefore promised a swift resolution. Within thirty days, Bridgen was to receive the first *three* overdue annual payments (totaling around $9,000), plus updated interest on those payments and on the residue of the debt, along with his costs. This money was to come from all the defendants except for the Pomeroys, whose exemption from liability the court for the most part accepted. If the defendants did not pay the money from available cash, Bridgen was to have execution against any property remaining in Judge Cooper's estate. If that property could not meet his due, he was to have execution against any estate property now in the hands of any of the defendants, except, again, for the Pomeroys. In the event that property also did not suffice, he could move against any other property held by any of the defendants (except the Pomeroys) that had come to them from "their respective ancestors"—not just from Judge Cooper's estate. Finally, only if all those other resources were exhausted and Bridgen's claim remained unsatisfied could he move against any estate property inherited by the Pomeroys.[61]

James Cooper had no intention of giving Bridgen a cash payment before the thirty-day deadline expired. He also seems to have abandoned any assumption that he could control the sales that therefore would be necessary. At the same time, however, he made no move to provide Bridgen or the court with a list of properties eligible for sale. That list came instead from another source in the family. In the Pomeroys' eventual answer to this Bridgen bill, which they filed on July 4, 1821, they made an exhaustive accounting of Judge Cooper's estate. This document, like the one they had presented to the court in 1820 with their own bill, contained long extracts from the estate's books and indicated which properties the estate still owned. The latter list probably proved very useful to Bridgen.[62] On August 30, the court, noting that James Cooper and the other defendants had "neglected to comply with all and singular the matters and things required of them in and by the said decree" (that is, the June 28 order), authorized Bridgen to request a writ (called a *fieri facias* or *fi. fa.*—shorthand for "cause it to be done"), which a chancery clerk in Albany soon directed to the Otsego sheriff. In view of the failure of the Coopers to make any cash restitution to Bridgen, the court no longer concerned itself solely with the overdue payments under the 1818 agreement. Instead, following Kent's direction, the clerk instructed the sheriff to conduct sales of properties belonging to the estate or to any of the defendants except the Pomeroys until Bridgen had recovered *all* his dues—that is, the amount of the debt, plus the steadily accumulating interest, which boosted the total to nearly $14,000, with another 1 percent or so added for costs. The money realized through the sales was to be returned to the court by the last Monday in September 1821, a bit more than three weeks away.[63]

Needing more time to identify suitable estate properties, post sale notices, and prepare the necessary documents, the Otsego sheriff could not hold the auction that soon. On September 10, the Cooperstown *Watch-Tower* for the first time alerted the public that it would go forward on October 22. The properties to be sold included the parcel "on which the mansion house of the late William

Cooper stands" (and its "appurtenances," including of course the mansion itself, Otsego Hall), a forty-acre woodlot along the west shore of Lake Otsego just above Fenimore, and six other sizable properties scattered about Otsego County. Also on the block was a sentimental bit of the family's legacy: "all that piece or parcel of land situate on the west side of and adjoining the Otsego Lake aforesaid, commonly called 'Three-Mile Point' or 'Myrtle Grove' containing about an acre of land, more or less."[64] That pleasure ground on the lake, according to Judge Cooper's will, should have been kept in the estate until 1850, when it was to have been deeded to his youngest namesake in the family. In 1821, however, it was about to be offered for sale to anyone with ready cash. So much for the perpetuation of names and memories.

As the October 22 auction drew near, Cooper considered his options for minimizing its effects. In September, he apparently was planning a trip back to Cooperstown, presumably to deal with the issue, but instead went to New York City and devoted his energies to finishing his long-interrupted second novel.[65] Probably he had concluded that things were serious at present, but not yet critical. No such sale would be final until the fifteen-month redemption period had run out; during it, any heir could step in and personally repurchase the properties. If Cooper stood aside and waited that fall, Bridgen did not. When the sale occurred, the successful bidder on the family mansion, Cooperstown lawyer and businessman William Holt Averell, was not just a casual participant out for a chance bargain. Averell had no personal animus against Cooper: indeed, the two were unknown to each other then and for many years afterwards. But he nonetheless attended the sale with malice aforethought. Having clerked some years earlier for Samuel Starkweather, Bridgen's local agent, Averell must have learned of the impending sale from that source. Before long, he was an intimate associate of Bridgen (and, as we shall see, the Pomeroys as well) in what proved a particularly insidious cartel.[66]

Over the next year or more, these associates coordinated their actions with such care that they managed to bring many of the Cooper estate's remaining assets under their control. They were in a position to do so in large part because the prices fetched by the properties sold in the hastily arranged October sale were very modest indeed. William Cooper's will valued Otsego Hall and its lot at $15,000. While this may have been an inflated figure (it had not induced any of his heirs to act on the chance to snap it up after Elizabeth Cooper's death in 1817), Averell paid only the bargain price of $1,650 for the land and improvements. For all the properties sold then, the sheriff reported receiving a mere $2,885.24, about a fifth of what the court had required him to realize.[67] Within a month, the chancery clerk therefore issued a second execution, this time to the Broome County sheriff. The sale there proved even more disappointing. When an eager Thomas Bridgen, personally attending it, received the proceeds on January 16, 1822, the total showed that, despite Cooper's insistence on not sacrificing the lands in his father's estate, that was precisely what was happening. Almost four thousand acres of holdings in Feronia, estimated at $4.00 per acre as recently as 1817 and planned for sale by William Cooper in 1819 at the bargain price of $1.50, now netted only $1,642.[68] With this amount subtracted from the balance and with interest updated yet again, the Broome County yield left $9,778.72 still owing. The court therefore issued a third execution, this time to the St. Lawrence County sheriff, instructing him to hold a sale of estate assets there by the fourth Monday in March. He did so, but although it consumed another twenty-five thousand acres of family holdings, only about half of the required amount was realized. Turning back to Otsego County, the court then ordered a sale of assets remaining there by August 1, 1822. This time, with more than two thousand acres in the countryside and eight lots in Cooperstown on the block, the sales at last netted enough to convey the balance due, just over $5,300, to Bridgen, who was again in attendance. For close to a year, across the state, the Cooper estate had been bleeding land and money.[69]

The Pomeroy Bill

Even with Bridgen satisfied, the bloodletting hardly ceased. The Pomeroy bill, filed in the spring of 1820 but since then apparently put on hold pending progress on Bridgen's effort, now came into full play. In an order issued on April 6, 1822 (in between the sale in St. Lawrence County and the second one in Otsego), Chancellor Kent at last took note that all defendants in the Pomeroy matter had filed their answers with the court—except for James Cooper. Therefore, with regard to him, Kent ruled that "the Complainant's Bill has been duly ordered to be taken *pro confesso*."[70] By default, Cooper had assented to all the Pomeroys' assertions. Moreover, since none of the defendants had offered objections to the plaintiffs' claims, the bill was treated as an amicable one, clearing the way for a speedy resolution.

We do not know precisely what the Pomeroy bill entailed, for neither the original as submitted nor any copies made during the court's proceedings appear to survive. From Chancellor Kent's April order and subsequent documents in the case, however, its outlines are clear. The Pomeroys had two main concerns. First, they wanted to receive the full value of Ann's legacy under her father's will. In their view this ought to have been a straightforward and uncontroversial demand. Their difficulty in securing payment from previous executors suggested, however, that the estate might lack (or be represented as lacking) the necessary assets. The Pomeroys therefore also asked the court to determine whether Judge Cooper's various executors had acted in a proper and responsible manner. If there was a shortage traceable to mismanagement or malfeasance, action against the widows and heirs of the three dead brothers or against Cooper might be a possibility.

Although Cooper thus became a victim of his sister's legal maneuvers, he hardly was singled out—it certainly is not accurate to conclude that the Pomeroys, in order to "safeguard their share in the crumbling estate from James's mismanagement," had filed their bill specifically "against his executorship."[71] Cooper was in most ways incidental to the bill. The Pomeroys' willingness to discuss the estate and their concerns about it with Bridgen as early as 1819 indicates that, like the other Cooperstown heirs, they had been alarmed by young William's behavior well before the youngest son took over as executor. Perhaps more decisive action on Cooper's part the following winter could have forestalled the bill. But nothing he did or failed to do caused it; he inherited the underlying issues much as he inherited the Bridgen debt and the legal fight it occasioned. Indeed, he conceivably welcomed the Pomeroy bill because of its potential clarification of his own obligations: hence his seeming passivity vis-à-vis the court even as, once the bill had been filed, he sought to ensure that his dealings with Bridgen as executor met all possible tests. Wholly within the scope of the court's review of the estate's books was, for instance, a determination of whether or not William Cooper the younger had properly calculated the amount of the Bridgen debt in 1818. If the answer was affirmative, then the way would be cleared to reach a final settlement with Thomas Bridgen.[72]

Although Cooper in general accepted his sister's bill, he certainly did not countenance the alliance she and her husband formed with Bridgen and his associates. At the time that alliance began, he knew nothing about it. Not until its effects began to emerge in the public sphere across 1822 and 1823 were he and his associate Robert Campbell able to piece together what was happening, and by then the damage mostly had been done. Soon after purchasing Otsego Hall, Averell was exchanging intelligence about the Coopers with Thomas Bridgen, whom he had probably met during Bridgen's visits to Cooperstown in 1819–1820. In January of 1822, the two men attended the Broome County sale together, using Bridgen's map of Feronia (probably secured through the Pomeroys) as a guide to the lands up for grab there. Averell was the high bidder on all thirty-five parcels auctioned. In the coming months the tie between the two lawyers tightened. In February, returning the Feronia map to Bridgen, Averell wrote that he had "hopes of visiting Albany in a few weeks," and at that time promised to "propose an arrangement." Already Averell had asked Bridgen to keep him posted on future sales triggered by his writs, and for some years the two continued their collaboration (as late as 1826, Averell offered to buy former Cooper lands directly from Bridgen's sisters).[73]

Yet Averell's best collaborators were the Pomeroys, whom he recruited just after Christmas, 1822, by striking a deal modeled on the "arrangement" Bridgen had hoped to make with them two years earlier. This deal exploited a series of steps taken in the case over the past several months. The April 1822 order issued by James Kent had directed prominent Albany attorney and Master in Chancery James King (the personal choice of the Pomeroys for this task) to investigate the records of the Cooper estate. He was to determine the extent of all the estate's debts, explore how well the various executors had performed their duties, and prepare a "master's report" on these matters. Early in the summer, King accordingly ran notices in various New York State newspapers calling on creditors to present their claims to him in person on July 1. Meeting in King's office on that date, the assembled creditors and attorneys for the various defendants went over the details together. Cooper had been alerted to the meeting through his current attorney in New York City, but neither man chose to attend.[74] Three months later, on October 12, King held a second meeting at which he read his draft report and entertained comments and criticisms of it. On this occasion, Cooper *did* attend, but only for "a few minutes," during which he "took no part in settling the said report."[75]

What he heard then must have been sobering. James King had determined that the estate's outstanding debts (excluding Ann Pomeroy's claim) totaled more than $15,000, including interest charges. Now that Bridgen's claim had been settled, the largest debt was a sum of almost $10,500 owed to the estate of a long-dead New York City merchant from whom, almost thirty years before, William Cooper and his original partner Andrew Craig had borrowed a sizable amount. Judge Cooper, having assumed the whole debt when he subsequently bought out Craig, had managed to discharge much of it before his death. Later additions for interest, however, once more had swelled the total. And in this case, as in that of the Bridgens, a dogged administrator was determined to recover the whole. As early as 1819, that man was rumored to be contemplating immediate court action against William Cooper the younger.[76] When the Chancery Court's notice to creditors of the Cooper estate began appearing in the press, he vigorously and successfully pushed to have his claim included in King's report. In addition to this claim, King accepted two other sizable ones that added another $5,000 to the total. Finally, he found that Ann Pomeroy had received only about $45,000 of her $50,000 legacy by January 1, 1815, the great bulk of it via land transfers. Subsequent transfers of land had reduced that amount, but in October of 1822, with new interest added, she still was owed $4,486.68.

The second issue before James King concerned the management of the Cooper estate by its successive executors. Here decisive resolution was less possible. Instead of tracking all expenditures and transfers from 1809 to the present, a monumental task, King drew up a list of assets recently listed on the estate's books and noted their disposition. Not surprisingly, he found that the great bulk of these lands had been sold on the "Bridgen decree." The four sheriff's sales had swept away a total of more than twenty thousand acres in Otsego, Broome, and St. Lawrence counties, plus such prime small properties as Otsego Hall and the valuable saw and grist mills and associated parcels in DeKalb. Other not-yet-sold properties may have escaped King's attention, but the only piece he positively identified as remaining in the estate was "Nobleborough," a tract of wild land in Herkimer County, to the north of the Mohawk River. In what might have served as an epitaph for the once ample estate, King asserted that Nobleborough was "worthless and unsold."[77]

In New York City on November 26, 1822, Chancellor Kent accepted and confirmed James King's report. He then ordered Cooper and the other defendants in the case to pay Ann Pomeroy the full balance of her legacy plus costs within sixty days. Furthermore, he instructed the defendants as a group to pay off all the other debts listed in King's report by May 1, 1823, with interest updated to that moment. Where the necessary funds were to come from certainly was a question in Chancellor Kent's mind. The estate as a legal entity had just been shown to afford very slender pickings. Kent therefore ruled that if the defendants did not make the mandated payments, the Pomeroys and any of the creditors named in King's report would be issued executions against the "lands and tenements" derived from the Cooper estate that were "then in the hands of the respective defendants." This further ruling meant that no property originally held in Judge Cooper's estate was safe in the hands of any of the heirs—including the four widows of the Judge's dead sons (or any of their children, who were instructed by Kent to address the court within six months of reaching their majority with evidence, if any, arguing for their exemption from the ruling).

Although among the heirs of Judge Cooper, Ann Pomeroy and her husband were protected from the creditors named by King because they were the original plaintiffs in this bill. On paper at any rate, Cooper himself appears to have been the most visible and vulnerable of the defendants. If any creditors could not recover their due from property of the estate by the means already described, the court decreed that executions would be issued against any property in the hands of the defendants regardless of the source of that property. In fact, however, Kent exempted from this last step all the other defendants aside from Cooper. He personally was to be the source of last resort for funding Ann's legacy and settling the other long-lingering debts of his father's estate. Indeed, in a further ominous step, the chancellor added that if any other previously unknown creditors of the estate should come forward, they also would have the right to sue for recovery from James Cooper in his proper person.[78]

With the court's favorable ruling at last in their hands, Ann and George Pomeroy faced new problems. Given how little property the estate still had, they would have to rely on the sale of former estate properties now in the possession of Cooper, his brothers' widows, or the trustees overseeing the welfare of the juvenile defendants. Such sales, always subject to delays, could prove unproductive—this the Bridgen decree had shown—leaving only the slender personal resources of Cooper himself to tap. Some or all of these steps were strategically uncertain; some may also have been morally distasteful. Although the Pomeroys were not willing to forestall the necessary slaughter, at the same time they did not want to bloody themselves in the business. So, on December 28, little more than a month after Kent's ruling, they signed their sweeping "arrangement" with William H. Averell. He agreed to pay the couple the full amount of their chancery award, plus interest, by the first of May following. In return, they assigned him their decree in chancery. They also identified for Averell the estate and personal properties subject to sale.[79]

Once Averell had the Pomeroys' decree in hand in May 1823, he used the court's authority with speedy thoroughness. Robert Campbell wrote Cooper from Otsego that very month to inform him that "the sale of all the [estate] property in this county belonging to the children of R. F. Cooper, Isaac Cooper and Samuel Cooper, is advertised to take place on the first day of July next. It will strip them, it is to be feared, entirely."[80] Campbell scarcely exaggerated; the two-and-a-half-column advertisement to which he referred began with a short list of miscellaneous lands remaining in the estate proper, which James King had overlooked. The notice then went on to detail virtually all the Otsego properties once owned by Isaac, Samuel, Richard, and William Cooper as heirs of their father, properties now forming the primary legacy of their fatherless children.[81]

The newspaper notice did not name the person or persons at whose request the execution had been issued. Hence neither Cooper nor attorney Robert Campbell (who was trustee for some of those children) was yet aware that the catastrophe, predictable as its coming was, had taken the particularly bitter form it in fact had assumed. By autumn, when the truth was clear, they were scrambling to come up with countermeasures. Cooper wrote Campbell a now unlocated letter in October, a few months after the first of these latest sales had gone off, laying out a means of opposing "the course of George Pomeroy & wife" as Averell's accomplices. Cooper proposed that he assign properties to Averell as security for some of the decrees Averell had acquired—*if* Averell would agree to discharge Cooper from the rest of them. It was a desperate and unrealistic plan. What property Cooper might use as security was anybody's guess. And why would Averell let Cooper off the hook with regard to all the other judgments simply because he might provide security for a mere part of the overall

indebtedness? The only thing Cooper could offer was a perhaps speedier resolution than the sales might yield.

Besides, Averell had a more devious plan of his own currently in play, a plan
in which Cooper's sister and brother-in-law also willingly collaborated. With regard to the Pomeroys' collusion, Campbell reassured Cooper that "the whole
business has been conducted without my knowledge, consent, or approbation."
The scope of that "whole business" was beyond belief. The couple not only had
assigned their own decree to Averell; they also had managed to acquire for him
those of several other creditors of the estate listed in James King's master's report, including what was the largest obligation of all, worth almost $10,500. Pre-
sumably Averell paid these other creditors, as he had the Pomeroys, what was
due under the decree. He thereby acquired further leverage against Cooper: he
could force sales to satisfy these new demands at will. The very decrees Cooper
hoped to extinguish by his proposed deal with Averell were in Averell's hands
precisely because of Ann and George Pomeroy's treachery.[82]

In the course of such things, all proceeds from the sales forced by Averell
would go to him until each of the judgments he owned was satisfied. That process would pay off the debts of the Cooper estate and leave Averell back where
he started—that is, with no essential gain aside from interest charges added to the
debts during the time he owned them. Averell, however, did not seek mere reimbursement for his "investments." Instead, he played a more slippery game. He
wanted the sales to pay back his outlays as much as possible, but most of all he
wanted to use forced sales and the redemption process to gain control of Cooper
lands at drastically reduced prices. To accomplish this, he personally bid for some
properties put up for sale on his own executions. More importantly, he used the
right of redemption he acquired with the chancery "decrees"—or the right of
the Pomeroys as Cooper heirs—to acquire great quantities of land auctioned in
the first place to other purchasers. In the case of the sale on July 1, 1823, the first
on the Pomeroy decree, Averell spent a mere $318 to purchase only four proper-
ties, totaling around two hundred acres, in his own person. However, by making
use of the right of redemption fifteen months later, he gobbled up close to another three thousand acres, plus several village lots and buildings (including Isaac
Cooper's spectacular house, Edgewater, which sold for a pittance, $256), for a
total of less than $7,500.[83] The outlay Averell made in October 1824 in fact was
only apparently large. As the present legal holder of the decrees, he would be
given any money received during auctions or via redemptions. Redemption did
not mean, as Robert Campbell wrongly reported to James Cooper in 1823, that
Averell thereby took "the property without satisfying the debts." It meant instead
that William Holt Averell was acquiring, as Campbell rightly told Cooper, the
"exclusive right & power of speculating on the ruins of your father's estate."[84]

Neither Ann nor George Pomeroy left any explanation of what led them to cooperate with a speculator who was driven by such an insatiable hunger for her family's property. Selling court judgments was a not-uncommon recourse during the period, and the reasons for availing oneself of it were many. Usually one did so in order to have the cash in hand sooner rather than later, and without the trouble and uncertainty of going through forced sales and then the long redemption period. The Pomeroys thus received from Averell in cash the remainder of Ann's legacy under her father's will. In this case, given the fact that the dispute cut a wide swath through the dramatically thinned and weakened ranks of the Cooper family, Averell's intervention may also have insulated the Pomeroys from the pain they were causing their relatives. It is also quite possible that they did not fully grasp Averell's intent until it began to reveal itself across the period from 1823 to 1825. Indeed, Averell's purposes may have evolved as the sales began and continued. Whatever their motives, however, the Pomeroys not only had set in motion the lawsuit that would devastate Judge Cooper's estate and those of Ann's brothers; they also had lent considerable force to the machine that, driven by the outcome of that lawsuit, would deliver ruin through a particularly bruising, crushing process.

CHAPTER ELEVEN

Settlement

Shuttling between Angevine and New York City over the fall of 1821 as he sought to bring *The Spy* to its long-delayed close and see it through production, Cooper also began to imagine the outlines of a third book. The American scene was again to be his focus, but in a much more personal way. As the auctioneer's hammer fell in Otsego, knocking down Otsego Hall and Three Mile Point and other Cooper family properties to the scavengers, Cooperstown itself emerged as his new theme.

He had not been back to Otsego in more than four years. But the looming losses there probably helped him realize that there never could be another naive homecoming: no ride up and over the great hill east of town—and no glimpse of the valley below, with its blue-green lake, its lingering clusters of hemlocks and hardwoods and white pines, or its noisy, busy village straddling the outflow where the sinuous Susquehanna took its rise. That was all behind him now. And yet the actual Cooperstown, only thinly disguised, indeed could become the locus of a new book. And the auctions and uprootings that had been taking place there of late, destructive and distressing as they were in fact, could energize his art. Those painful events would not, to be sure, form his overt plot. Only in its pervasive sense of loss (and the tenderness with which it explored the scenes of his youth) would *The Pioneers,* set in the early 1790s, give expression to the more recent past.

Cooper acknowledged the book's personal intensity from the outset. He thus proclaimed with unusual candor in his 1823 preface: "The third [book] has been written, exclusively, to please myself" (*PIO* CE 3). With a wealth of pictorial detail, he described the process of frontier settlement as only someone familiar with it could. He knew the story so well that he could close his eyes and trace out the whole of Otsego—town by town, road by road, hill by hill—and catalog all the changes of the past few decades, as in fact the first chapter of the novel did through its focus on a landscape that "only forty years" before had been "a wilderness" (*PIO* CE 16). He caught with particular finesse the sense of hurried expansion that marked the post-Revolutionary years. Euro-Americans had always been "settlers." Before the 1780s, however, settlement had been an additive process that in most instances had nibbled off bits of "wild" land and slowly ingested them into the colonial domain. During the years leading up to the Revolution, pressure for bolder movements to the West had been rising, but Britain, vowing to protect Native American interests and eager to control colonial expansion, had officially discountenanced them. With the peace treaty ending the war, New York in particular, emptied of many of the Loyalist Iroquois, witnessed a sudden increase in new territory. Yankees began swarming in from New England as early as 1784 and 1785, just when William Cooper and his Jersey neighbor Andrew Craig were acquiring the old Croghan lands in Otsego and throwing that region open for development. Soon followed such an extraordinary flood that the settlement of the "new" West, even more than the war that had preceded and enabled it, was to become the first great national theme.

The establishment of that theme was owing almost completely to Cooper. In penning *The Pioneers,* he was able to produce—as he had in a different sense with *The Spy*—an extraordinarily *useful* fiction. Its utility had to do with the unsettled aspect of the theme of settlement itself. Despite the familiarity of Euro-Americans in Cooper's generation with the process of spatial expansion, very little of its lore had been codified by 1820. Yale president Timothy Dwight, who spent much time between the late 1790s and 1815 looking into the condition of American society across the Northeast, paid special attention to life on the border. Widely read and extensively connected, Dwight concluded that "the settlement of a new country" was a topic that had "not been hitherto described . . . by any writer." Dwight therefore undertook his own description, but even he left only a few pages on the topic in the four large volumes of his *Travels in New England and New York* (1821–1822).[1]

Dwight was essentially right in judging the theme to be unformed. In 1790, the year Cooper was taken to Otsego as an infant, all the cities in the United States lay on tidewater. Nowhere was there a significant settlement located more than two days' travel from the coast. Cooperstown itself, so recently founded that it had not yet assumed its eponymous name, was among the last outposts of Euro-American culture in New York. By contrast, when Cooper wrote *The Pioneers* a mere thirty years later, five of the seven most populous counties in New York were "western" ones, including Otsego, which was ranked fifth—ahead even of Albany County. Nationally, the changes were equally dramatic. In 1820, the "new" states of Ohio and Kentucky each reported populations in excess of five hundred thousand; Cincinnati, with around ten thousand inhabitants, had just been incorporated as a city; and the line of Euro-American settlement had passed so far inland that it now touched (and in the case of Louisiana and Missouri crossed) the Mississippi River. Of the total of eleven new states added to the union since 1791, only Maine (before 1820 a part of Massachusetts) lay on the Atlantic coast. Settlers, long accustomed to the woodland ecosystem of the eastern seaboard, had begun to encounter their first "prairies" in Illinois, although as yet their antiquated plows were ineffectual against the thick, tough sod and they clung to the familiar wooded margins of the flat land's winding streams.[2]

The year Cooper took up the theme of border settlement in fact marked the end of a brief period of particularly fast-paced spatial growth. Across the twenty-one years from 1791 to 1812, only five new states had been added, followed by a hiatus during the war with Britain. Then, beginning in 1816 and running up to the summer just before Cooper undertook *The Pioneers*, one new state was added each year. Once that string of additions ended in August 1821, a period of less showy growth began as settlers filled out the newest states and began moving into the farther territories; it would be another fifteen years, in fact, before a single new state joined the union.

The intensity of the period from 1816 to 1821 may have helped prepare Cooper's audience—perhaps even Cooper himself—for a literary treatment of this rapid process of spatial expansion. Although we may assume that the frontier has always been central to American experience and American writing, what is especially striking is the fact that writers before Cooper had completely ignored the topic. Brockden Brown set *Edgar Huntly* (1800) in an almost symbolic wilderness within a night's somnambulistic ramble of his hero's proto-European home. There was, as it were, no middle ground. To be sure, on Huntly's escape from the mad precincts of "Norwalk" (whose name Brown borrowed not from the farther reaches of the map of his native Pennsylvania but rather from the unique Connecticut town he must have known through his extended visit to that state in 1793), the now murderous wanderer reverses American spatial order as he moves back to settled ground. That is, he moves through an architectural series, from log hovel to farmhouse to mansion, that unwinds the progressive plot of American expansion. These dwellings are strung on lines in the landscape, "obscure paths" that eventually yield to more heavily used "tracks," then to a cart path, then a road. But the irony of this pair of backwards series is part of Brown's point here. He shuns settlement because his theme is the derangement of the wild land and the almost occult bearing it has on the human psyche. It is not without meaning that as the Euro-American habitations become more stylish and costly on Huntly's journey home, their inhabitants exhibit a moral decline. Brown glanced at the theme of settlement but did not really know what to make of it.[3]

That was partly because he and his contemporaries were at a loss for words. The theme was so new that its terminology was still emergent in the national press twenty years after the publication of *Edgar Huntly*. This surprising fact is reflected in Cooper's experience. He had chosen the title for his third book at the very outset. Charles Wiley, writing the novelist early in 1822 to congratulate him on the instantaneous success of *The Spy*, thus added, "You speak of being engaged about 'the Pioneers.'"[4] To a modern reader, this choice of title seems completely unremarkable. It was, though, far from natural at the time. Its freshness has paled because the book's very success eventually helped fix "pioneers" as the all-but-obvious term for frontier figures who had been known by a variety of handles theretofore, but only rarely by *that* one. If one glanced around the publishing scene in the early Republic, one would hardly find that term deployed in any prominent way. For instance, aside from a magazine briefly edited in Pittsburgh by David Graham in the first months of 1812, not a single American publication—book, pamphlet, magazine, or newspaper—appears to have used it yet as part of its title.[5] Nor was it widely used in early discussions of the process of border settlement. J. Hector St. Jean de Crèvecoeur employed the term only once in *Letters from an American Farmer* (1782), for instance, preferring instead to use other expressions—such as "back settlers" or "first settlers"—for the frontier inhabitants to whom he initially turned literary attention in the Revolutionary era.[6] And when he presented them as "our precursors or pioneers," he hardly was using the latter word in the heroic guise it later would acquire. Instead, fully aware of the military origin of the term (in French, *les pionniers* were an army's advance guard, its shock troops), he was emphasizing the role the first settlers played in what he also called the "march of the Europeans toward the interior parts of this continent." Wary of the tendency of Europeans to degenerate in the woods, he portrayed such initial inhabitants as "a kind of forlorn hope, preceding by ten or twelve years the most respectable army of veterans which come after them." "Forlorn hope" (*verloren hoop*, a Dutch analog of *pionniers*) was another, more fanciful term for the initial wave of troops, desperate soldiers sent on desperate missions.[7]

At the time Crèvecoeur wrote, neither the figural implications of his language nor the specific terms were the clichés they would become by the mid-nineteenth century. As Crèvecoeur demonstrated and a variety of modern scholars including Edwin Fussell and Leo Lemay have pointed out, the unsettled regions of the colonies had often been viewed as zones of declension, a view reflected in a group of often-used terms such as "backcountry" and "backwoods."[8] The largely nineteenth-century term that regularly has been counterpointed to these "back-" formations in modern discussions—"frontier"—has been taken to mark a shift in orientation and values in early national culture. As this argument has it, the *backsettlers* were moral backsliders who gave themselves up to the woods, Kurtzian figures, whereas the *frontiersman* or *frontierswoman* looked forward, fronting the future emergent in the West through their disciplined hard work. Such a change in viewpoint and meaning certainly took place in the first decades of Cooper's life, helping account for the importance Natty Bumppo would have for the novelist and his readers. But the redefinition of places and terms was more complex than Fussell or Lemay indicate.

Hugh Henry Brackenridge, who grew up in a newly settled part of central Pennsylvania in the 1750s and 1760s, and thus like Cooper knew whereof he wrote, played on the shifts when he penned the following waggish comment on the rambles of Captain Farrago and Teague O'Regan in the sixth volume of *Modern Chivalry* (1805): "The settlement in which they now were, was called the back settlement; not because it was the farthest back; but because it had been once the frontier. The name *back*, still continued to be tacked to it; now when it had become the midland country."[9] "Frontier," as the term with which the change in value is most closely associated, had been only rarely used in the colonial era. In what is surely the urtext of frontier literature in the early national period, John Filson's *Discovery, Settlement and Present State of Kentucke* (1784), Filson thus described Daniel Boone not as a "frontiersman" (or "backwoodsman," for that matter), but rather quite simply as "one of the first Settlers" of Kentucky. In Boone's autobiographical sketch, dictated to and edited by Filson, the "first settler" himself likewise shunned the former terms. Nor did he speak of Kentucky as a "frontier" region.[10]

During Filson's era, the term "frontier"—usually in the plural, with the definite article ("the frontiers")—had a rather different, more particular sense, from which the abstract significations of the nineteenth century slowly evolved. Crèvecoeur's usage usually followed this older pattern: he thus wrote at one point of a boy "taken on the frontiers of Canada by the Indians."[11] The seemingly slight difference between the word's older and newer forms was actually critical. The "frontiers" of any colony constituted the more-or-less political border area that divided it from competing social and/or cultural systems. In

New England and New York across much of the eighteenth century, for instance, the "frontiers" were not vaguely conceptual; the word denoted the specific geographical zone where, by formal or de facto means, one system was thought to yield to another: English to French, European to Native American. This state of affairs reflected that in much of Europe, where, for instance, a French traveler bound for Spain passed "the frontiers" of the two countries. The parties divided by and joined at such frontiers *fronted* each other across some real or imaginary line; the word was plural, without doubt, because it indicated the dual occupation of the zone in question.

When Brackenridge used the word in the singular in 1805, he was marking the new form it was assuming even as his own meaning remained geographically specific. And in any case he tended *not* to use the word at all, preferring (as would Cooper) such vernacular alternatives as "new settlements" or "new country."[12] These were undoubtedly the terms that the actual settlers themselves used in Otsego and in Brackenridge's boyhood district near York, Pennsylvania. "Frontier" is a term that Cooper's critics have used far more often than Cooper himself ever did. It is instructive to note that Cooper never calls Templeton a "frontier village." Even in 1840, looking back at his original intent in *The Pioneers,* he clung to the vernacular formulation, averring that the book "was intended to describe the sort of life that belongs to a 'new country'" (*LJ* 4:73). The novel itself used *that* simple phrase a half-dozen times. Only on a single page, by contrast, did it employ the term "frontier." And it did so in the old colonial sense, mentioning Edward Effingham's service against the French and Indians "on the western frontier of Pennsylvania" (*PIO* CE 34). (One notes that Cooper, like Brackenridge, here adopted the new form of the word but adhered to the old meaning.) In *The Last of the Mohicans* (1826), despite the apparent rightness of "frontiers" in the old sense for a novel set on the French borderlands of northern New York in the 1750s, Cooper again mostly shunned that word. On the first page of his first chapter, he spoke of the "the wide extent of the intermediate frontiers" separating the French and English domains—and of "the frontiers of Canada"—and used the word in singular or plural form a few other times. But his favored language for depicting the landscape emphasized the concrete details of the physical world (*forests, rapids, rugged passes, mountains,* all of which occur on the opening page before the two uses of *frontiers*) rather than the jurisdictional facts of colonial politics or the ideological abstractions of national expansion. Nor did Cooper overburden his most famous "frontiersman" with *that* term (*LOM* CE 11). In the 1820s, he used it only once—in *The Last of the Mohicans*—and in fact there Cooper put it into Natty's own mouth rather than applying it to him from the outside: Natty, arranging with Uncas for a concerted attack on their enemies, tells the young warrior, "when they come in range of our pieces, we will give them a blow, that I pledge the good name of an old frontiersman, shall make their line bend, like an ashen bow" (*LOM* CE 325).

One is apt to be surprised by the degree to which Cooper understated what to later generations of readers seems to be the utter amalgamation of his most important character with the grand language of the Westering Republic. His reticence stemmed in part, as I have suggested, from his deep familiarity with the usage of ordinary emigrants, who were not given to inflating their importance: settlers were settlers—less because they organized the supposedly unsettled land than because, their own wandering over or suspended, they at last settled down somewhere. But it also derived from Cooper's ambivalence toward the domineering presumptions of the nation. Personal experience of loss taught him to view what we call the frontier from both sides of the line, and to see Euro-America's victory as someone else's defeat.[13]

The scarcity of frontier terminology in Cooper's early books went hand in hand with his conscious attempts at innovation. His title for *The Pioneers* was a venturesome choice, as indicated earlier, for he employed a term that was by no means widely used even in 1820. Timothy Dwight, narrating a 1798 "Journey to Vergennes" in his *Travels*, published just as Cooper was writing his novel and almost certainly known to Cooper then, in fact felt that he had to defend his use of it: "A considerable portion of those, who *begin* the cultivation of the wilderness, may be denominated *foresters*, or *Pioneers*. The business of these persons is no other than to cut down trees, build log-homes, lay open forested grounds to cultivation, and prepare the way for those who come after them."[14] Dwight's explanation suggests the core thrust of Cooper's conception: in particular, it recalls the last words of *The Pioneers*, which describe Natty Bumppo (rather ironically, given the course of the novel) as "the foremost in that band of Pioneers, who are opening the way for the march of civilization across the continent" (*PIO* CE 456). Cooper first used the same term in the same sense at the outset of the book: "The expedients of the pioneers who first broke ground in the settlement of this country, are succeeded by the permanent improvements of the yeoman" (*PIO* CE 16). Even so, these two strategically placed examples are the *only* ones in the whole novel. The much preferred term is the simpler, vernacular one already noted: *settler(s)* appears about sixty times. "Pioneer" retained for Cooper its old essential meaning even after he had written and published his third novel. In his next one, *The Pilot* (1824), he thus had Captain Manual of the marines use it in its military sense, with no hint of its emergent American significance: asked for advice in planning a raid on the English coast, Manual advises sending a party of seamen ashore to "act as pioneers" for him and his men (*PIL* CE 75).

Five years after *The Pioneers* appeared, Noah Webster's *American Dictionary of the English Language* (1828) did not yet see fit to define *pioneer* in its new,

"American," sense, suggesting that it had not yet been generally accepted. In the meantime, in *The Last of the Mohicans*, Cooper eschewed the word completely; that his avoidance of it there was owing to something more than the tale's pre-Revolutionary setting is suggested by his similar avoidance of it in *The Prairie* (1827), a book in which the Westering impulse of the Bush family might have provided ample opportunities to employ it, since those "squatters" (the vernacular term the book typically uses for them) are clearly the first band of what one might call "pioneers" in the plains, and their character is in general keeping with Dwight's rather negative comments on such figures. Cooper used the word only once in this book (for Obed Battius), and in its old sense of "predecessor": Natty thus waits for some signal before following what the narrative terms that "learned Pioneer" (*PR* CE 182).[15]

The slowness with which the new word caught on may help explain why Timothy Dwight's own preferred term in *Travels* was not "pioneers" at all but rather "foresters." This word was more widely used at the time but after the publication of Cooper's novel would prove something of a linguistic dead end. In 1828, Webster defined the word only in its English senses: "FORESTER . . . In England, an officer appointed to watch a forest, preserve the game, and institute suits for trespass. Encyc. 2. An inhabitant of a forest. Shak. 3. A forest tree. Evelyn." There was a hint of Dwight's sense in Webster's second definition, but only a hint: it was not the fact of inhabiting the forest that defined Dwight's "forester," after all, but rather the much more fundamental act of making the forest itself inhabitable. For the root noun, *forest*, to be sure, Webster did manage some distinctions that were important for their inclusion of American nuance and American practice: "FOREST . . . 1. An extensive wood, or a large tract of land covered with trees. In *America*, the word is usually applied to a wood of native growth, or a tract of woodland which has never been cultivated. It differs from wood or woods chiefly in extent. We read of the Hercynian *forest*, in Germany, and the *forest* of Ardennes, in France or Gaul. 2. In *law*, in Great Britain, a certain territory of woody grounds and pastures, privileged for wild beasts and fowls of forest, chase and warren, to rest and abide in, under the protection of the king, for his pleasure. *In this sense, the word has no application in America.*"[16]

Alexander Wilson, the poet-ornithologist whose response to the Oswego area in 1804 was noted in Chapter 4, had used the term "foresters" a decade before Dwight's book was finally published. It served to describe the rustic characters encountered on his "pedestrian journey" to Niagara, and his poem about the trip was also called *The Foresters* (1809). Cooper, who probably knew Wilson's poem, had many appropriate opportunities to use the same term in *The Pioneers*, especially because he took pains to imaginatively associate Natty Bumppo and his allies with the forest from which they first visually emerge into the story. But for the most part, in a pattern that would be typical of the whole Leather-Stocking series, he tended to call Natty and Edwards "hunters"—the "old hunter" and the "young hunter," respectively—deriving his term for them from their first action in the novel (*PIO* CE 21, 82, 137, 153, 195). This stylistic habit, seen also in Cooper's sobriquet for Billy Kirby (the "wood-chopper"), suggests a certain low-key intent in the book's rhetoric. The author might call the novel *The Pioneers*, but page-by-page his tendency was more vernacular than declamatory: thematically keyed names were replaced by operative nouns derived from the usual occupations of the characters. Only twice did he offer Wilson's (and Dwight's) other term as a proper one, the second instance perhaps suggesting some tie to one or both of those recent works: "the foresters, for the three hunters, notwithstanding their difference in character, well deserved this common name" (*PIO* CE 206; see also 153). The meaning of the term here is roughly equivalent to "woodsman" or "woodman," duly noted in Webster's dictionary as either "a forest officer, appointed to take care of the king's wood" or "a sportsman, a hunter." In *The Last of the Mohicans*, Natty along with Chingachgook and Uncas are also called "foresters" some dozen times. In *The Pilot*, the British officer Borroughcliffe with similar broad intent refers to the "rude foresters" of America (*PIL* CE 373).

Exfoliation

By such borrowings from vernacular practice, Cooper managed to base his "border" tale on the things of this world. Given his later reputation as a writer not averse to indirect phrasings, it is in fact quite instructive to note these patterns. The patterns at the same time remind us of the fundamental cultural innovations underpinning them: in few things are writers more influential in a worldly sense than in their happiest coinages. This does not mean that Cooper was ignorant or dismissive of textual predecessors, which we should consider next. Brockden Brown was one writer who was very much in Cooper's thoughts just as he began *The Pioneers*. The point is clear from the late preface Cooper wrote in the fall of 1821 for *The Spy*. This preface is famous for its dismissal of Brown's misguided attempt to create a national literature in *Edgar Huntly* by assembling "an American, a savage, a wild cat, and a tomahawk, in a conjunction that never did, nor ever will occur" (*Spy* CE 2). Brown's novel hardly was the sort one might imagine Cooper singling out in an attempt to differentiate his own accomplishment in *The Spy* from the work of his predecessors. Brown, after all, hardly claimed to be producing historical fiction in that book—or any of his others. But it was not in all likelihood *The Spy* that spurred Cooper to this attack. It was instead *The Pioneers*, about which he already must have been thinking (and may have begun writing) as he penned the preface in question. Brown *was* important for attempting to get the American landscape, especially the frontier landscape, into his novel. Few writers had done that before 1800 or since.

We do not know exactly when Cooper wrote the preface to his second novel or began actually drafting his third, or to what extent he was literally at work on both books late in 1821. But some educated guesses may be of use. First, one may note the more obvious interconnections between the two novels. The clearest involves the widowed camp follower and famous drink-mixer Betty Flanagan of *The Spy,* whose improvised hotel at the "Four Corners" serves as the headquarters of the American troops in the second half of that novel. Carried over into *The Pioneers,* the Irishwoman appropriately enough runs a landmark Otsego tavern with her second husband, Captain Hollister of the Templeton militia. Hollister, also a character in *The Spy* (where he holds the rank of sergeant and serves as orderly to Capt. John Lawton of the Virginia dragoons), was the comrade-in-arms of the late lamented Michael Flanagan, Betty's first husband, before that man fell in battle. As events throw him together with Betty in the later parts of *The Spy,* Hollister emerges as her new favorite. By the time of their introduction in *The Pioneers,* the two have been married and settled long enough in Templeton that the returning Elizabeth Temple finds their tavern to be one of the few recognizable structures in the much-changed village.

When Elizabeth sees the Hollisters emerge from the tavern on their way to the Christmas Eve service in the tenth chapter, she greets them and a discussion ensues about what she calls the "dear sign" yet swinging before its door. Painted by Richard Jones, as Elizabeth recalls, the crude placard appropriately represents "the figure of a horseman, armed with sabre and pistols, and surmounted by a bear-skin cap, with the fiery animal that he bestrode 'rampant'" (*PIO* CE 114). Dragoons by definition may all be "bold," but Betty and her husband had a quite particular horseman in mind when they christened the place and made Jones paint the sign to suit their preconception. Their first conversation with Elizabeth hints at the source of the image: "Is it the bould dragoon ye mane? and what name would he have, who niver was known by any other[?]," Betty asks (*PIO* CE 115). This is a bit obscure, but when the tavern-keepers later rehash some of the memories they bear forward from *The Spy,* it becomes clear that they named their establishment in honor of the fearless Captain Lawton himself. Lawton, killed in the last battle of the Neutral Ground when, attempting to rally the retreating American infantry, he rushed boldly toward the enemy and was cut down by a fusillade, is specifically memorialized by Betty Hollister in *The Pioneers:* "gone this many a year," as Hollister puts it, he survives as a painted figure of Revolutionary valor in the less heroic, more fractious world of 1793 (*PIO* CE 148). The tavern keeper laments Lawton's "sudden ind," pointedly adding,

"But it's to be hoped, that he was justified by the cause" (*PIO* CE 115). Was he? Set at a time when one consequence of the American Revolution (the French Reign of Terror) is raging overseas, and the local community is torn by trivial and not-so-trivial disputes, the new novel lies downstream of the American war but rarely mentions it and never simply celebrates it.[17]

The reintroduction of the Hollisters and their memories of the hulking and heroic Lawton in *The Pioneers* serves to link the books thematically even as it opens a breach between them. The carryover also has biographical significance. It suggests that Cooper was writing the early chapters of *The Pioneers* even as he finished the penultimate ones of *The Spy*. Indeed, one notes that in *The Pioneers* the Bible-obsessed Captain Hollister takes up a discussion of Joshua that had been suspended, as it were, in Chapter 33 of *The Spy*, which treats Lawton's death, the second-to-last of those that Cooper had to finish as he worked toward the limit represented by the already printed final chapter in October or November (*Spy* CE 405; *PIO* CE 147). One should recall, too, that Sergeant Hollister and Betty Flanagan were among his newest inventions in *The Spy;* first mentioned in the opening chapters of the second volume, they are the last major characters brought into the book. They thus must have been particularly fresh in Cooper's mind as he labored to end the often-delayed work. That he gave them so prominent a place in the scene in which Captain Lawton, contemptuous of human imperfection, charges toward his fate, may indicate that the two low characters, like Harvey Birch himself, were rising in importance for the novelist as he finished the story. It may even be the case that he already had created a place for them in Templeton and therefore wanted to anchor them more securely in the universe of the "previous" book.

Other, more diffuse ties between *The Spy* and *The Pioneers* reinforce the impression that Cooper cowrote the two novels during his concentrated period of labor in New York City.[18] They have to do with the rising importance of physical action in the former book and of the landscape where that action occurs. From the first page of *The Spy*, when "Mr. Harper" rides across a dark and rainy scene, landscape has been given a particularly dramatic role. The site of the Wharton house in the vicinity of Angevine itself; the use of the historical Westchester crossroads known as the Four Corners as the setting for Betty Flanagan's "Hotel"; the apparent employment of the inland Wiccopee road north through Westchester as the model for the route of the Whartons toward what is directly named as Fishkill—all these geo-literary choices Cooper made as he imagined and wrote the tale demonstrate how rooted in the actual countryside the verbal landscape of the novel was to be.

Nothing in the English drawing rooms of *Precaution* presaged this aspect of Cooper's art. But the contrast did not result from the mere shift to American locales. Landscape in *Tales for Fifteen*, nominally American—indeed, Cooper set both "Imagination" and "Heart" in New York—was flat and pictorial even if it did evince more particularization. The Hudson Highlands thus are named in "Imagination" but not really used: a bromide ("The passage of the Highlands is most delightful") is the most that the letter-writing traveler Anna Miller can muster as she passes upriver by steamboat (*Tales* 43). The infamously sandy Pine Bush district between Albany and Schenectady, well known to Cooper from his boyhood travels across it, likewise is mentioned in "Imagination," but only mentioned. "Words are wanting to paint the melancholy beauties of the ride to Schenectady," Anna ventures, "through gloomy forests, where the silvery pine waves in solemn grandeur to the sighings of Eolus, while Boreas threatens in vain their firm-rooted trunks" (*Tales* 44). Cooper was writing *at* the landscape here rather than dramatically incorporating it into his tale.

In *The Spy*, by contrast, landscape developed into a complexly rendered and subtly employed adjunct of the action and meaning. Early in the first volume (finished by the end of 1820), Cooper made some attempt to particularize the immediate vicinity of "The Locusts," the Wharton country home, by reference to the actual surroundings in which he conceived and wrote the book. He sited the novel's first military clash, an invented skirmish between Major Dunwoodie's dragoons and marauding British regulars, in the flatlands surrounding the lower Bronx River in Scarsdale, within a short distance of Angevine.[19] That he had Frances Wharton and her kin observe the battle through the windows of their house is suggestive of the manner in which he himself probably peered outside as he wrote these very chapters, scanning the autumnal landscape of 1820 and thinking back to what the scene might have looked like in that same season just four decades earlier. Perhaps more instructively, although Cooper first introduced Harvey Birch within the confines of the Wharton house, a space reminiscent of the domestic settings of *Precaution*, he eventually moved him to the dark fields surrounding the house. Here Birch could begin to reveal his sharp-eyed, indefatigable adroitness. In this process, Cooper was learning how to create drama not out of the tensions spoken into being by dialogue but rather out of the physical demands of bodily action in space. This was a key lesson for his future success as a writer of forest and sea.

While some of this experimentation occurred in the first volume of *The Spy*, its pace accelerated as Cooper left the more easily confused (or more merely literary) "hills and dales" (*Spy* CE 309) of southern Westchester behind and instead shifted his scene north into the Highlands. The new setting was more distinctive physically, and thus easier to fix in language, and it was full of important specific associations dating from the Revolution.[20] While Cooper made very good use of the new ground of the tale, his decision to employ it does not seem to have been intended from the outset or carefully thought through as the tale unfolded. Indeed, the northward shift strikes a reader as both unprepared for and hastily contrived. Perhaps Cooper, stalled in his work and aesthetically weary of the historically and physiographically less differentiated landscape of lower Westchester as he had been able to construct and use it in volume one, could overcome his block only by some such radical change.[21] For these reasons, one is tempted to claim that this was the point at which Cooper recommenced the book in the summer and fall of 1821.

We cannot know that for certain, of course, but it is worthwhile probing the change in some detail for the light such scrutiny can shed on how Cooper's creative process evolved in this early stage of his career. We may first consider how the book accounts for the shift of scene. The northward redirection of the plot is first hinted at in Chapter 19 (that is, the third chapter of volume two), when Major Dunwoodie quite suddenly receives orders to send Henry Wharton for his trial "to the first [American] post above, under a body of dragoons" (*Spy* 2:33). Where precisely that "post" is, we are not then told, perhaps an indication that Cooper had not yet decided on a specific site—or that, temporarily disposing of Henry in this way, he as yet had no thought of sending the other characters north in his wake. Hence Dunwoodie soon watches "Henry Wharton, and his escort, defiling at a distance through a pass which led to the posts above" (*Spy* 2:34). The vagueness here may indicate that at this point the change had no immediate consequences for the book's overall setting. Cooper may have been intending, that is, to report on Henry Wharton's trial rather than show it.

If the decision to relocate the English "spy" caught Charles Wiley's attention as Cooper turned in that nineteenth chapter, it almost certainly did not cause him undue concern for precisely the reasons just sketched. As the following chapters arrived at Wiley's shop, however, causes for more serious concern surely began to pile up. Cooper's destruction of The Locusts in the Skinner raid (Chapter 22) erased the one stable point of reference in the first two-thirds of the story. Thereafter, the whole Wharton entourage was briefly removed to the Hotel Flanagan, an expedient offhandedly suggested by the surgeon, Archibald Sitgreaves, and accepted by Captain Lawton. The group was barely relocated there in Chapter 24 before, in a second sudden change, an order arrived from George Washington directing that the family be moved much farther north to await Henry's trial, which we now learn is to be held "above the Highlands"— although Fishkill is not yet named as its actual site (*Spy* 2:128). All of this together may well have been what triggered Charles Wiley's anxiety. Where exactly, he may have wondered by this point, was Cooper heading? How was he to finish the book if he kept, literally and figuratively, shifting its grounds?

Another consequence of the shift deserves reflection. It is rarely if ever no-

ticed that the book's loco-centric subtitle—*A Tale of the Neutral Ground*—
hardly applies to the last third of the action, which mostly takes place in the area
north of the Croton River (the point at which, Cooper himself remarks, "the
Neutral Ground ceased" [*Spy* 2:135]).[22] The novel after the northward shift, in
other words, is no longer properly a tale of the Neutral Ground. Yet one must
add with some irony that Cooper's abandonment of the book's first setting in
fact derived from—or at least profoundly served—his interest in setting itself
as a constructive element in storytelling. There is much more physical action in
the book's last eight chapters than in the previous twenty-seven combined. In
part, that disproportion may be owing to Cooper's need to wrap things up as the
end approached, a need that he also would come to recognize at about the same
point in his next novel (the epigraph for Chapter 25 of *The Pioneers* orders him:
"Come! to thy tale" [*PIO* CE 275]). Yet the action as it unfolds in the final rush
of chapters of *The Spy* marked a new level of writing for Cooper, not just a hastened sense of his obligation to Wiley or his audience.

A good instance of Cooper's accomplishment here is his nicely elaborated
account of the journey to Fishkill in Chapter 25.[23] Focusing on the experience of
Frances Wharton, who climbs the steep final stretch of road on foot in order to
gain some exercise and lighten the carriage load, Cooper brings the young
woman to the summit before the rest of the party. Below her, in a moment
Cooper probably modeled (albeit unconsciously) on Rip Van Winkle's survey of
his solitary surroundings in the Catskills, lies "a deep dell, but little altered by
cultivation, and dark with the gloom of a November sun-set" (*Spy* 2:140).[24] As
the venturesome young woman directs her eyes across the valley to a darkly
brooding, cone-shaped mountain, she experiences a kind of epiphany as a final
slant of sunlight moves up its rugged face, enabling her to enter "into the secrets
of that desert place." This, too, has its Irvingesque qualities, since what Frances
sees is a revelation—the sequestered hut of Birch and, soon, on the edge of a
rock, "a human figure, . . . of singular mould and unusual deformity" (*Spy* 2:
141). It is Birch himself, bent under the weight of the large peddler's pack on his
back—resembling, however, the old Dutch sailor who startles Rip ("a strange
figure," Irving writes, "slowly toiling up the rocks and bending under the weight
of something he carried on his back").[25] If Irving would not elaborate the moral
hints of American history as Cooper was attempting to in *The Spy*, having Rip
sleep through the Revolution, what he positively accomplished in *The Sketch
Book* was of such importance that Cooper seems to have deeply absorbed the lessons. He could reproduce them without, probably, knowing that he was doing so.

Frances Wharton's sturdy climb on her way to Fishkill is merely the prelude
to her further physical adventures. Five chapters later, after her brother's conviction and escape, Frances makes her solitary way across the darkening Fishkill

Plains and heads up that wild, brooding mountain where she previously had glimpsed Birch and his log hut. As she climbs, the moon begins lighting the scene, but she still is unable to locate the well-concealed hideout. For guidance, she looks back down on the now illuminated plains and, discovering the road her family had passed over in its northward trek, traces its line back up into the opposite hills until she recognizes her old solitary vantage point. Having secured that benchmark, she draws an imaginary line back to Birch's mountain, pinpointing what she thinks must be the exact location of his hut. Clambering toward that spot, she at first can discover nothing. Only when, acutely aware of her exposure, she inches to the edge of a shelving rock to glance down at the reassuring fields and distant village, does she catch a gleam of light immediately below her and feel a gust of warm air. She has done her imaginary triangulation with such skill that she is right above the smoke hole in the roof of Birch's hut. Soon, having clambered down and gone around to its front, she is "earnestly looking through the crevice" as "Mr. Harper" pores over documents. Frances, in effect, has become the book's functioning spy (*Spy* 2:216–20).

This exercise in spatial reconnoitering is an impressive instance of how Cooper maps the precipitous terrain of the book's last chapters and sets his characters in motion within it. That Frances no longer observes events from within the safe precincts of her family home, but rather acts in open space, marks the radical means by which Cooper reformulated his book and thus, I would argue, enabled himself to finish it. Having already (in Chapter 29) followed Harvey Birch and Henry Wharton as they make their way across the Fishkill Plains and up into the Highlands, he returns to them in Chapters 31 and 32 and traces their southward return to the Neutral Ground. In the process, Birch demonstrates that he is indeed the "dexterous pilot among these hills" that he earlier tells Wharton he is (*Spy* 2:207). What justifies and gives dimensionality to Cooper's set description of the Highlands and the lower Hudson in Chapter 32 is the fact that in the southward progress of Birch and Wharton to this point in the landscape he has made the whole valley intensely real to his readers. Cooper's style here may have drawn on the canons of the sublime and the picturesque, but the passage as a whole was generated by the action of the novel. It is well in advance of anything he produced in using the same scenes in "Imagination."[26]

These were accomplishments achieved as Cooper wrote the remainder of *The Spy* in the fall of 1821. But, as noted earlier, it seems likely that he was able to achieve them in part because of his coincidental work on *The Pioneers*. While the Hudson valley scene was well known to him and freighted with both personal and communal significance, it was the new tale whose spatial possibilities for the first time allowed him to explore real places that held profound personal meaning for him. In general, of course, his very conception of *The Pioneers* as a tale of settlement—of the conversion of the American landscape from woods to fields—suggested that his eye and mind were newly attuned to space as both locus and theme. *That* breakthrough also made him newly sensitive to the spatial potential of the other book then in hand.[27] Indeed, I would argue that he did not just imagine his general subject for *The Pioneers* and then go back to *The Spy.* He must instead have positively begun the new novel and then resumed the other one. In opening *The Pioneers* on the slopes of "the Vision" he was projecting a complex image of a real place he knew so well that he did not need to see it again in order to portray it or sense its larger significance. The Vision was not, to be sure, a certified historic landmark—as were the Highlands, cluttered with ruined forts and outworks and steeped in both lore and gore in the national imagination. The Otsego mountain to the contrary was converted by his book *into* a landmark—locally, through its very naming in the book; nationally, through its association with the visionary mood with which frontier action was being invested during this period. We know from the slender posthumous pamphlet of Cooper's father that the visual ravishment insisted on by the novel *did* take place as William Cooper made his way up that very hill and paused on its top in 1785. But it is also true, as noted in Chapter 1, that local archives yield no use of the term "the Vision" for that mountain before 1823. Far from passively recording the family story, Cooper's novel did much to codify and extend the significance of its salient details. Thereby Cooper provided the nation not only with *the* new term for the "settlers" or "foresters"—he provided a locus classicus for the inspiration that drove "pioneers" onward.

What Cooper was learning was a simple but powerful formula for the fictional manufacture of space. It wasn't just that he linked his characters to their settings by involving them in risky physical actions there. He also chose many of his settings with an eye toward tapping some powerful meaning already attached to their real-world counterparts. This was essentially a touristic approach to landscape, and it is not beside the point that *The Spy, The Pioneers,* and *The Last of the Mohicans,* his first three New York State books, made extensive use of New York sites already marked on the map of "the northern tour," as Henry Dilworth Gilpin would term that newly fashionable circuit in his 1825 guidebook. Cooper did not seek to disconnect the tourist's landscape from that explored in his novels. To the contrary, even in *The Spy* he linked his historic settings with their present-day counterparts so as to give readers a perceptual fix on the "old" scenes the plot was exploring. This was an act of temporal triangulation akin to the spatial reconnoitering of Frances Wharton in Fishkill. His sweeping description of the Hudson and the Highlands, inserted at the point when Birch and the young Wharton have at last emerged from the rugged terrain to the north and reentered the Neutral Ground, thus gestures toward the "scores of white sails and sluggish vessels" *now* seen there, marking the nearby presence of modern New York City (*Spy* 2:246). Such overlays of the present scene identify the setting in hand as real—as part of the verifiably public landscape inhabited by or at least accessible to Cooper's readers. The linkages also insist that travelers on the current "tour" should approach such scenes with a duly instructed eye, that they *imagine* the past much as Cooper did in writing the books. Small wonder that Dilworth's *Northern Tour* replayed the linkage in the opposite direction. In speaking of Pine Orchard, the site of the newly constructed Catskill Mountain House, Dilworth introduced a long quotation from "a favourite romance"—Natty Bumppo's musing description of the place and its astonishing vistas, from Chapter 26 of *The Pioneers*.[28]

Such settings acquired added density by Cooper's development of episodes suitable to them. He created place in part through the action it "allows": in the case of the Vision, the deer hunt with which the plot proper opens, and the returning Elizabeth's survey of the valley below; in the case of the Lake Otsego, the fishing scene; in the case of the forest at large, the fire that roars through it at the book's end. Such a complexly interdependent development of setting and plot could be traced back to Cooper's much simpler conception of the fences and stone walls of Westchester and their relation to military "action" and the flight-and-pursuit plot centered on Harvey Birch. Yet it was *The Pioneers* that allowed Cooper to develop this rudimentary relationship between place and action with far more power, in turn allowing his shift—of scene and method—in the remainder of *The Spy*. As he devoted so much of the opening chapters of *The Pioneers* to the careful elaboration of the book's milieu, his pleasure at the results urged him to expand the role of space in *The Spy* as well. He accomplished that expansion by shifting the scene northward toward the already famous Highlands and their inland adjunct, the lowering "Fishkill mountains," where the acclivity of the landforms allowed him to develop Birch's adroitness as a figure in landscape—especially wild landscape—and where the accumulated associations with the key events of national formation made the scene morally significant as well. One might also speculate that Elizabeth Temple's mountain trip and her visual survey of the valley spread below her at sunset either were invented in tandem with Frances Wharton's or that the latter owed a good deal of its invention to what Cooper was already achieving in the first chapters of *The Pioneers*.

Rough Passage

Suggestive as it was, work on *The Pioneers* did not proceed well. When Charles Wiley's letter mentioned the book by name in January 1822, apparently Cooper was very much in the thick of it—so much so that Wiley was anxious about the apparently interrupted, perhaps forgotten, "Tales." We do not know how much of the new novel had been composed by January. Perhaps the Christmas section (Chapters 1–18) was written as a coherent unit during the weeks leading up to and through the 1821–1822 holiday season. Then interruptions traceable to other business probably arose. Cooper's itinerary in these weeks suggests the scope of the distractions. After leaving the City Hotel on December 21 for home, with *The Spy* finished and in hand, Cooper took a holiday break of about a month. He had not spent much time at Angevine in recent months. Now, in between celebrating Christmas with Susan and their three daughters and new son, Fenimore—and, as usual, the couple's anniversary on New Year's Day—the expectant author of *The Spy* could busy himself with those first eighteen chapters of *The Pioneers*, in which the Christmas homecoming of young Elizabeth Temple was to be such a central concern.

The hiatus on the new book, if there was one, may have begun around the middle of January. By Wednesday the sixteenth, Cooper had returned to New York City for what would be a second series of stays.[29] At least during the later of these visits, he must have been working over the copy text for the completely reset second edition of *The Spy*, which would appear on March 5 with some three hundred authorial revisions (*Spy* CE 438–39). Perhaps during these stays as well, cheered on by the evident success of the book and called back to the "Tales" by Wiley's reminder, Cooper renewed his efforts on "Imagination" and "Heart" and brought them near to completion. In the May issue of Gardner's *Repository*, Wiley certainly announced that "*American Tales,* by a Lady," was then in press (*Tales* ix).

But by the time Cooper returned to the city in April, he was busy with other things.[30] Catharine Maria Sedgwick's *A New-England Tale* and Washington Irving's *Bracebridge Hall* had just appeared in print in New York, and if Cooper did in fact write the reviews of them that were inserted in the *Repository* the next month (an open question), he must have produced them right then. We may wonder whether, with the returning spring, he did not also sit down and rebegin *The Pioneers*: "From this time to the close of April," begins Chapter 22, "the weather continued to be a succession of great and rapid changes" (*PIO* CE 242), a further reminder of the book's sensitivity to seasonal rhythms. Once again, however, work on the new book would have been subject to interruptions. Demand for *The Spy* remained so strong that Wiley was planning yet a third edition, for which Cooper would make even more sweeping revisions, to appear in New York on May 4 (*Spy* CE 437–38).

Late the preceding month, when Cooper probably was done or almost done with those revisions, he probably began pressing ahead in earnest on *The Pioneers*—writing it, but also "preparing the way" for it abroad. Certainly he decided then that it was time to mount a fresh attack on the potentially lucrative English market. His friend Benjamin U. Coles, member of an extensive family of New York merchants (and another of Gardner's contributors to the *Repository*), was soon bound for London. In an April 24 letter of instructions, Cooper outlined a series of issues he hoped Coles could explore for him.[31]

Among other things, Cooper wanted Coles to determine how *The Spy* stood "among the trade" in England. What he knew so far led him to be "far from sanguine as to its reception" (*LJ* 1:74). Probably he already had learned what Washington Irving had reported from London in a March 6 letter to Charles Wiley. Wiley had sent an early copy of the book to Irving's English publisher, John Murray, then asked Irving to follow up and try to persuade Murray to bring out an authorized English edition. Confined to his lodgings by illness, Irving had been slow to carry out the errand. Eventually he learned that Murray (who, with Byron on his list, was then the lion of London booksellers) supposedly had shown the new American work to William Gifford, an author and for many years the acerbic editor of Murray's *Quarterly Review*. That choice was natural but did not bode well for Cooper, since Gifford was known for not tolerating American authors or books. It was no surprise that he had given Murray a lukewarm (perhaps chill) response or that Murray had not taken up the book (*CORR* 1:89). In a couple of months, another London publisher was reporting as fact that Murray had not even looked at Cooper's book: "the *Spy* was put into his hands & neglected."[32]

Irving was apologetic about his own tardiness, but added that Wiley (and Cooper) might have approached Henry Colburn instead of Murray in the first place: Colburn was "a fashionable publisher" who paid his authors well and was "anxious to get American works of merit, whereas Murray is precisely the worst sort of man that an American work can be sent to." Murray, who had his pick of new works, was a bit taken with his power. He also was "surrounded by literary advisers"—Gifford among them—who were, Irving confirmed, "prejudiced against any thing American" (*CORR* 1:89).[33] Besides, Colburn already was familiar with the work of this particular American. He had issued *Precaution* the year before, seemingly in a pirated edition, although he now was telling Irving that he had been promised the same author's next book and was awaiting copy for it. Promised it by whom? It is just possible that Colburn's *Precaution* indeed had been published through some arrangement with either Goodrich or American lawyer Junius Smith, the London agent Cooper and Goodrich had agreed to employ as a go-between in 1820. If such an arrangement had been made, however, the falling-out between Cooper and Goodrich must have voided it. Since Goodrich was not publishing *The Spy*, he hardly could have sent it to Colburn.

Irving learned much of this story when, having retrieved *The Spy* from

Murray, he took it to Colburn on his own hook, hoping to make some profitable arrangement for the author. Colburn was indeed interested but could not proceed because another publisher, the firm of G. and W. B. Whittaker, had already begun to pirate the Wiley edition. Their edition appeared a few days after Irving spoke with Colburn, probably toward the end of February. Irving read it and liked it, as he wrote Wiley, but he obviously could do nothing more on its behalf (*CORR* 1:89–90). The pirates had sunk Cooper's hopes for English profits.[34]

Cooper's April 24 letter to Benjamin Coles represented the next step in the larger effort. In addition to naming Colburn as a reasonable recourse, Irving had suggested that "authors in America" eager to tap the British market could send manuscript copies of their works to a London bookseller named John Miller, from whose premises on Fleet Street Sedgwick's *New-England Tale*, for instance, was just being issued. Miller had done some of Irving's publishing and recently had put out such other American titles as Henry Marie Brackenridge's *Voyage to South America* (1820). In Irving's view, he was the perfect agent for American writers—he was "in the American business" (something of an exaggeration when his whole body of work is considered), and if he did not publish titles himself would "dispose of them to the best advantage" to some other publisher (*CORR* 1:90). This was useful information that would guide Cooper and Wiley with regard to later books. But it also seems to have shaped the verbal instructions Cooper gave Coles after inscribing his written ones. The April 24 letter had simply asked Coles to check around among the "*trade*" in London about what terms he could get for Cooper's books. When Coles arrived in London around June 10, however, John Miller was the first publisher he visited. This can hardly have been coincidental.[35]

Cooper's letter had asked a series of pointed questions. Would London publishers pay royalties or buy books outright? Would they publish at Cooper's own risk, using his money to pay their expenses—as both Goodrich and Wiley had done? Finally, what could he learn on the spot about the legal or customary requirements for securing copyright in Great Britain? (*LJ* 1:74). Coles apparently gave Miller a copy of Cooper's letter as the shortest way to secure authoritative answers to these queries. On June 15, Miller (who thereby knew the name of the American author on whose behalf Coles was acting) sent a reasonably detailed written response to the merchant. He dealt first with the issue of copyright. Publication in Britain at least a day before publication in America would establish durable legal right. That method sounded simple, but in an era of uncertain transport it might be difficult to coordinate publication dates so closely. Hence the appeal for Cooper of the customarily informal procedures of London, which Miller went on to describe in greater detail. As long as an American author or publisher took pains to ensure that an English publisher could issue imported titles within a few days of their appearance in the United States, the effective possession of the English market would confer on him "an *honorary* Copy Right" just as good as a legal one.

In answer to another of Cooper's questions, Miller summarized the usual terms under which books, especially imported books, were published in England. The practice in the case of works of uncertain promise was for the publisher to meet all expenses, recover his outlays from first receipts, and then divide any profits fifty-fifty with the author. If, like Cooper, the author preferred to assume the risk himself, booksellers would expect their customary discount of 25 percent, while the publisher would be entitled to a 10 percent commission for distributing the title. Some authors could command better terms—Byron, Scott, Tom Moore—but Cooper hardly was in their class, as least not yet. Helpfully, though, Miller noted that *The Spy* was doing very well in England, and gave a useful estimate of what it might cost its author to produce English editions of future titles. Printing, paper, and advertising for a three-volume novel like *The Spy* would run to about "200 guineas for 750 copies, the retail price being *one guinea*"—that is, twenty-one shillings, or about $4.70 at that time.

Finally, perhaps hoping to put himself forward, Miller discouraged the idea that John Murray could or would publish the American's next work under either of these arrangements. Murray was certainly "the most extensive publisher of *valuable* Works," but he rarely reissued books, and, in Miller's view, had "declined every thing . . . offered from America, probably without examination." Another publisher about whom Coles may have asked Miller, Longman & Co., seemed to Miller so focused on "Country Business"—distributing its own or other publishers' titles in the English countryside—that it might not give Cooper's books the kind of attention they needed. Was it just possible that Miller had eliminated the most serious competition, leaving himself the obvious choice?[36]

A third firm that might publish *The Pioneers,* G. and W. B. Whittaker, were eager to do so but were on shaky negotiating ground because of their recent piracy of *The Spy*. Probably suspecting that Coles had legal or at least financial reasons for approaching them, this firm disingenuously told him that they had received a copy of Cooper's second book "by accident." Of course they had not *accidentally* pirated it; presumably what they meant was that, although in the "regular course" of business they did receive and pirate American books, *The Spy* had been mistakenly forwarded by their American agent. They tried to bury this lame explanation in comments about how well Cooper's novel had been doing for them. They had ordered an edition of 750 copies, and priced them at one guinea per three-volume set, thus far verifying Miller's hypotheticals. But if Miller was right in his other figure (i.e., that such an edition would cost 200 guineas, or about $940, up front), the Whittakers already had done handsomely on their plausible outlay, and none of the profits would have to be split with the author. The Whittakers assured Coles that they wanted to be chosen to publish Cooper's next book in England but did not think they could offer him much money for it. They promised to reconsider the question and get back to Coles in a week, but in the meantime they unsatisfactorily suggested that the author's share of profits ought to be left to their discretion.

Coles thought the Whittakers financially well-placed to undertake the project but understandably did not trust them. In addition, because their house tended to publish works of little literary merit, they were of such ill repute that they would not support Cooper's aspirations. John Miller was in both ways the opposite of the Whittakers. He had a reputation as "a very respectable & honorable man who deals much in American publications" and was "painstaking [and] industrious" in running his business. However, his financial resources were meager. Coles had checked into the background of both firms, perhaps relying on the networks to which banker Charles Wilkes was privy. He gave Cooper few details on Miller's plight, other than to say that he was "without much property." Nonetheless, Coles thought Miller was Cooper's best bet. Unlike the Whittakers, he at least stated his terms up front: he would publish the book at his own risk and split the profits fifty-fifty with the author. Overall, he seemed to offer "the greatest advantages."[37]

Neither Miller nor the Whittakers but rather haughty John Murray wound up publishing the English edition of *The Pioneers*. This surprising turn of events happened despite Irving's counsel in March and Miller's in June, not to mention Coles's own unease with Murray ("I dont like him altogether," he would confide to Cooper in July).[38] Coles had not been able to see Murray immediately, but called on Irving and, no doubt hearing from him some account of Murray's earlier response to Cooper's overture, asked him to go back to Murray and reopen discussions. Irving did so and reported that Murray had changed his tune. Irving probably touted the success of *The Spy*, which by now (as he assured Coles) he was hearing spoken of well "among the nobility & literary gentry"—indeed, he was being flooded with inquiries about the author's identity. Murray now proposed to Irving that he publish *The Pioneers* at his own risk, dividing the profits with the author, thus matching Miller's terms but offering far more in the way of prestige and support. Irving reported this offer to Coles, and the two planned a joint visit to the publishing lion at his den in Albemarle Street (*PIO* CE xxxix).

As luck would have it, Murray was away from town when the two New Yorkers showed up on June 28 or 29, prompting Coles to leave him a note on the offer. Murray, confirming it by a letter to Coles, added somewhat condescendingly that, since the book's most lucrative sales of course would be in Great Britain, he wanted to ensure his copyright by publishing *The Pioneers* himself before it had appeared in America. Coles, whose understanding was flawed, thought that doing so would preclude American copyright and therefore quickly informed Murray that he did not expect "Mr. Cooper" would agree to the demand. He did not pretend to have the power to negotiate for Cooper but wanted Murray to know that the success of *The Spy* in America (where it already had earned the author "near £1000," or nearly $4,500) made American copyright essential. He also pointed out to Murray that Cooper already was being offered "£600 for his expected work the Pioneers" in the United States.[39]

Coles did not mind baiting the lion as long as he could be bagged for Cooper—a genuine coup in 1822. Relying on Miller's explanation of the law, he therefore proposed that *The Pioneers* be published in New York a day or two before London. And he stipulated that, should Murray indeed publish the book at his own risk and expense, he would divide the profits equally and charge no commission. Having sent this message to Murray on July 11, two days later he forwarded a copy to Cooper, adding his strong encouragement that Cooper accept these terms. Then, not a week later, Coles wrote Cooper that Murray had "very willingly" agreed to them.[40] Cooper appears not to have hesitated or quibbled on receiving this good news but instead pressed on. In June and again in July, Coles had mentioned the desirability of preparing some sort of copy of the manuscript, which any authorized English edition would require. But Cooper, determined to see such an edition come to fruition, already had asked poet Fitz-Greene Halleck, bound to London and the Continent, to deliver to Coles the first one hundred pages of *The Pioneers* "in print" (*LJ* 1:75). By that point, Wiley's chosen printer, Edwin B. Clayton, obviously had set at least the initial seven or perhaps eight signatures of the text of the first volume and Cooper had gone over the sheets; then they had been corrected in the standing type and reprinted for shipment. Happily, they arrived with Cooper's friend Halleck in London on July 25, thus serving as a kind of earnest for Murray, to whom Coles conveyed them.[41]

Fevers

Under ordinary conditions, the workers in Clayton's shop on Pine Street could have been done with the typesetting before the summer was out, assuming that Cooper kept feeding them manuscript and that he and Wiley corrected proofs with due diligence. But this summer was hardly ordinary. New Yorkers were accustomed to cyclical returns of yellow fever, a mosquito-borne viral illness that tended to hit the wharf and slip district of lower Manhattan once the hot weather of August arrived and linger until the first frosts, usually in the latter part of October. There had been sieges of the disease on several occasions since the start of the century, including one in 1819. The 1822 outbreak, the last major one on record, reportedly resulted in more than twelve hundred deaths by November.[42] In 1828, Cooper wrote that it covered a more extensive area than the 1819 visitation, including parts of the city that were usually free from the fever. The lower parts of New York were largely deserted through voluntary evacuation and government mandate. Fences were erected to prevent access to the "infected districts," as Cooper told the story in *Notions of the Americans* in 1828, leaving all below their line eerily vacant (*Notions* 1:114–17). A traveler from Scotland, Peter Neilson, arriving during the height of the outbreak, saw "a picture of desolation" as he glimpsed the lower end of Manhattan from his ship. Not until the vessel was three miles upriver from the battery was it deemed safe to land. As had been true in other recent outbreaks, many residents and business proprietors from the tip of Manhattan shifted to Greenwich Village, the popularity of which as a residence dated from these temporary invasions of city dwellers, particularly the one in 1822. Neilson went ashore there and found what appeared to be "the whole of the business-part" of New York relocated to "a temporary city" thrown up with great haste. Evacuations had begun early in August, when the first streets were ordered closed, and continued until October 26, when a frost hit and reported cases plummeted. Daniel D. Arden, New York manager for Philadelphia bookseller Henry C. Carey, wrote his employer on August 19 that business near him on Broadway in lower Manhattan had "stopped." At August's end, he closed his own shop, left the area, and did not return for two months. By October 29, the *Evening Post* was telling its readers that Broadway was "a scene of happy confusion," packed with people eager to return to their long-abandoned homes, offices, and stores.[43]

Cooper was living mostly at Angevine at this time, so the evacuation did not directly affect him. Probably he avoided New York at the height of the visitation, although in general he was not overly concerned about yellow fever (see *Notions* 1:114) and in fact was in the city at least briefly on two occasions before the alarm was over—at the end of September (see *LJ* 1:76–78) and for that meeting on October 12 at attorney James King's office concerning the Pomeroy's chancery bill. Among the city residents who fled the fever, however, were Charles Wiley and Oliver Halsted. The latter went across the North River to Newark; perhaps Wiley took refuge there as well.[44] The errata notice bound into some copies of the second volume of *The Pioneers*, and probably drafted by Cooper, indicates that the bookseller was absent from the city during the outbreak (*PIO* CE 468–69). Presumably the work of the typesetters was also interrupted, since Clayton's address was well within the boundaries of the final evacuation zone; printing establishments were among the businesses specifically mentioned in the press as having been removed up island by the last week of August.[45] Furthermore, Cooper informed John Murray in November, when he sent with his friend Charles Wilkes, then bound for London, a fresh set of sheets covering the first American volume and half of the second, that the yellow fever had "caused a delay in the appearance of the Pioneers" (*LJ* 1:85).[46] Similarly, a notice in the *Commercial Advertiser* on September 11, when the city remained deserted, indicated that the appearance of the book would be delayed several weeks, probably until the middle of December, on account of the fever (*PIO* CE xl–xli).

But delay was not the only problem, or the main one. Because of the confusion and breakdown in communication resulting from the evacuation (the post office was among the institutions that moved to Greenwich Village in late August for the duration),[47] neither Wiley nor Cooper had a chance to adequately proof the sheets while it was still possible for Clayton to correct the standing type, which of course he would have to break up and distribute as his work progressed. The first American edition therefore was riddled with embarrassing errors that the errata notice acknowledged but did not really address. Cooper's November cover letter to Murray indicated that the sloppiness could not all be charged to the disruptions of the yellow fever. Having learned a good deal from the production of *Precaution* and having tried to ensure that *The Spy* was more carefully handled, Cooper had vowed to himself that his work on the third novel would be professional from start to finish. Alas, "in opposition to a thousand good resolutions," *The Pioneers* had been "more hastily and carelessly written than any of my books." No clear copy of the manuscript had been produced, meaning that Cooper's own packed and tricky scrawl had gone, as he put it, "from my desk to the printers." Indeed, he swore that he had not even had time to read the draft before sending it off. Any corrections he made in the manuscript (or perhaps the sheets) had resulted from Wiley's queries or from his own chance discoveries when "glancing" over the work. Hence, despite his claim that the printers and Andrew T. Goodrich had mangled *Precaution* when he suggested that they rectify obvious oversights in his manuscript, Cooper now gave Murray authority to correct any "errors in grammar or awkward sentences" that had poured through the gaping holes in the Wiley-Cooper colander, cautioning him, however, not to abuse this "liberty" (*LJ* 1:86).

In November, Cooper forecast for Murray that Wiley and the American printers would be done with their work before Christmas, enabling him to send off the rest of the sheets to Murray by December 20. American publication would follow by January 20. In fact, the story proved to have further twists. Wiley and Cooper, deciding that Clayton's press run was not large enough to meet likely market demand, arranged with a second New York printer, Jonathan Seymour, to completely reset much of the book using a corrected set of Clayton's sheets as copy text, and then to print a second run of the novel. Not until the last seven formes of the book (that is, those covering *PIO* 2:209–84) were being set by Clayton did the need for more copies become apparent. Seymour's edition, which had the look of Clayton's and virtually the same pagination, in fact printed six of its final seven signatures from Clayton's formes, although the text was corrected in Clayton's standing type before this new printing began.[48]

Once Murray received the package via Wilkes, he needed copy for only the last seventy-five pages of the second American volume. Cooper provided it, along with a fresh set of the rest of the entire Clayton version, in two nearly simultaneous shipments sent over by different means on January 15, one apparently with another friend and the other by the ship *Criterion*. Clearly concerned that the project, long delayed, not falter now that the end was so near, he wanted to ensure that copy text in some form for all of the book reach Murray in time to coordinate British publication with American. The versions sent to Murray had some discrepancies at various junctures, Cooper admitted, explaining that he had again revised on the run and had not bothered to enter all changes in both sets. (Presumably the Wilkes sheets also showed differences in those parts that Cooper had sent by Halleck in June.) Murray would notice some corrections on the new sheets, but these were the result of the author's eye lighting on errors here and there rather than on any systematic search. "I am ashamed to say," Cooper reiterated, "that I have not even read the printed book, regularily [*sic*]" (*LJ* 1:91–92). The proofs had not even been read through for sense let alone against some version of the manuscript, so Cooper necessarily was relying on Murray's proofreaders. In fact, the English edition, owing to Cooper's changes in the sheets and Murray's exercise of his "liberty," was taken by the editors of the 1980 text in the Cooper Edition as authorial in many instances in which it differs from either of the Wiley versions. But the fact is that Cooper managed the book awkwardly and inconsistently. By then, as the author of three novels, he might—no, should—have known better. Amid these troubles, *The Pioneers* finally appeared, to great acclaim, in New York on February 1, 1823.[49]

Some deeply extenuating circumstances frustrated Cooper's best intentions. This was the period when the Chancery Court began issuing its final orders in the Bridgen and Pomeroy cases, sapping his creative energy and giving added intensity to the themes of possession and dispossession.[50] But even more to the point, shortly after the yellow fever left New York, Cooper and his family abandoned the relative sanctuary of their Westchester farm and suddenly relocated to temporary quarters in Manhattan. It was there that his labors on *The Pioneers* were brought to their hasty and unsatisfying end.

The move involved distressing emotions that inevitably colored, and probably unsettled, his work. In his frenzied efforts to keep afloat financially over the past few years, Cooper had not only sold off a great deal of property. He also had encumbered other pieces of real estate that for one reason or another could not be sold outright. Among the latter items was the Hickory Grove, or the Hickories, the old DeLancey farm in Westchester. This was the property that Susan Cooper's aunt Susannah had deeded to John Peter DeLancey in trust for her years before; after Susannah's death in 1815, DeLancey in turn had conveyed it to Susan. As Cooper's financial difficulties worsened in the next year or two and the DeLanceys offered to help him out, they in turn sought to protect the Hickory Grove from his creditors. In January 1818, when John Peter transferred the Angevine farm to the Coopers under a deed naming Thomas and Edward DeLancey as its trustees, he therefore required that the Hickory Grove be covered with a similar arrangement.

Thomas and Edward were to oversee the latter property, paying any proceeds from it to Susan "or any other person she may appoint." Such "other person" might, of course, be Cooper, and in most instances probably was Cooper. But the transfer explicitly exempted Susan from the usual restrictions of coverture so that she might indeed act alone: it made *her* personal receipt "a sufficient Discharge" to the trustees and allowed *her* to direct them to lease the property to any party she might name. Most importantly, it restricted Cooper from doing with the property precisely what he (with Susan's connivance) proceeded to do over the years following: "the Premises shall not during the life of the said Susan Augusta Cooper be in any wise incumbered or aliened by the said James Cooper or subjected to any charges whatever on account of his debts." Susan's father knew enough about those debts from the help he had given Cooper the previous spring to be wary of the potentially omnivorous threat.[51]

It apparently was not his son-in-law's character but rather the uncertainties of the law that motivated John Peter DeLancey's caution. Indeed, Cooper himself seems to have actively embraced the process as a means of demonstrating his eagerness to put the family at ease about such matters: the wording in this particular version of the trust deed was Cooper's own.[52] Perhaps because he and Susan viewed the restrictions in this light—that is, as protecting the property from the hostile actions of third parties, not as limiting their own freedom— they behaved as if they were free to place obligation after obligation on the property. Although the Hickory Grove had been in Susan's family ever since her great-grandfather had been created lord of Scarsdale Manor in 1701, they nonetheless gave it over to the management of a hired farmer within a year or two of its inheritance. To make way for him, Cooper ejected the old Huguenot family that long had occupied the place. Having grown up in a developer's family on the frontier rather than among the upper classes of the long-settled lower Hudson valley, for whom land mattered as an aspect of social identity as well as property,

Cooper regarded the Hickory Grove with the same practical attitude that he showed toward wild lots in DeKalb or his own recently assembled farm at Fenimore. His effort to extract more profit from the Hickory Grove raised eyebrows among Susan Cooper's kin. To be sure, the DeLanceys did not rise up in immediate alarm. John Peter DeLancey and his oldest son, who wanted to help Susan's husband for her sake if not also his own, were civilized enough to recognize that different people might view the same issue from distinct perspectives without parting company or even disliking each other.[53]

But they probably were unprepared for other manipulations of the property that followed. On June 25, 1818, the Coopers mortgaged the Hickory Grove to Judge Samuel Jones of Oyster Bay, Long Island, for $3,500. The nephew of the Tory jurist Thomas Jones, Samuel Jones was a wealthy and well-connected kinsman of Susan Cooper, who evidently asked for help as the couple settled into their new life in Westchester. Since he was family, he represented something less than a full threat to the property. Even so, Jones had kept one eye on his own benefit, having accepted (perhaps demanded) a penalty clause in the agreement: if he was not repaid within a year, the debt would be doubled. Predictably, the Coopers failed to meet the agreed-upon terms, therefore becoming liable for the full $7,000. The consequences were complicated by the fact that Jones, eighty-three at the time of the loan, died before the due date. His son and executor, Elbert H. Jones, took legal recourse, eventually winning a judgment in New York's Supreme Court of Judicature awarding him the full amount plus costs. But the money was long in coming. In the summer or fall of 1820, Jones took the issue to the Chancery Court, securing an order there that authorized the public auction of the Hickory Grove, precisely the outcome the DeLanceys had hoped to avoid. When the sale went forward on May 25, 1821, Cooper, clearly hoping to mitigate the disaster, himself made the highest bid ($5,000), putting down a fraction but promising the balance within a month. When he failed to come up with the required funds, Chancellor Kent released Cooper's down payment to Jones. Jones subsequently asked the court to confirm that transfer of funds, destroy the deed tentatively prepared for Cooper, and order a second auction of the farm.[54]

Cooper managed to pay off 70 percent of the amount owed to Jones by October of the same year. Perhaps this was one of the uses to which the couple's proceeds from the sales to Col. Thomas Ward were put (see Chapter 7). Beyond this point, Cooper had to use other means, probably more worrying to the DeLanceys, for discharging the remainder of the obligation. Turning to a Scarsdale neighbor, George Willets or Willis, he deeded half of the Hickory Grove to him in return for his agreement to pay Jones around $2,000. In return, Willets agreed to indemnify Cooper against any claims made on the rest of the farm, which was to remain in Cooper's hands. This was a means of covering the farm against the

Jones claim by transferring part of it to a third party who was willing to pay Jones and receive title from him.[55]

The arrangement with Willets perforce took note of the obligation to the estate of Samuel Jones. In December 1819, a month after Jones's death and some time before his loan required repayment, the Coopers likewise acknowledged that obligation in using the entire Hickory Grove farm as security for a second mortgage. This one covered a debt in the amount of $1,900 owed to William Shotwell, a New York City hardware merchant. Cooper had done business of some undetermined sort with Shotwell at an earlier time; a series of payments to him in the range of $100 to $300 is recorded in Cooper's bank book from August 1818 to November 1819. It is possible that at least some of the debt to Shotwell arose from purchases for Angevine, although no documentation of them survives. The bulk of it in any case probably stemmed from small loans the merchant extended to Cooper, most of which at the outset Cooper was able to repay fairly soon.[56] As time passed, those sums began accumulating, until by March 1819 Cooper acknowledged owing Shotwell $1,770, for which amount he already had given him both a bond and two notes due a year later. These obligations may well have had something to do with the purchase of the *Union* or its refitting at this time.

Cooper paid off $770 of his debt to Shotwell early, at the very end of 1819. Yet Shotwell seems to have been nervous about the rest of his money. Only a little more than a week before that payment was receipted, he received the mortgage on the Hickories mentioned above, which secured prior debts in the amount of $1,900. Cooper agreed to repay $600 within six months (by June 20, 1820) and the remainder by the end of that year. Although the question is clouded by the fact that this mortgage was superseded by another for a lesser amount made out only three months later, it remains clear that Cooper and his wife did not really mortgage the property to Shotwell in exchange for fresh cash put to fresh uses. The new encumbrances, almost certainly arranged at Shotwell's insistence, secured preexisting loans. And they were completely candid about the earlier obligation to Samuel Jones recorded on the same property. Cooper may have been cutting corners as he sought to cover his debts, but he was scrupulous in his dealings—unlike, for instance, his sometime friend Robert Sedgwick. Even so, he must have wondered, as he continued shuffling around his assets and obligations, whether there would ever be an end to the business.[57]

Over time, the concerns of the DeLanceys about these complicated dealings must have deepened, leading to a breakdown in relations with the Coopers. A catalyst was the death in October 1820 of Susan's brother, Edward Floyd DeLancey, from a sudden attack of dysentery (SFM 45).[58] His passing did not affect the trust arrangements on either Angevine or the Hickory Grove, although it triggered a request by the Coopers to have a new second trustee of their own choice named (see *LJ* 1:87). This move, in keeping with the provisions of the original trust deeds, apparently gave rise to some confrontation between Cooper and Thomas J. DeLancey. During the set-to, DeLancey must have leveled some serious, perhaps insulting, charges at Cooper. His immediate concern probably was not the Hickory Grove, about which little could be done at present, but rather Angevine. There is no evidence that the Coopers ever mortgaged the Angevine property or otherwise encumbered it. It is not hard to imagine, however, that they were planning to do so when DeLancey caught wind of it and his bottled-up feelings about how the other farm had been treated burst out. Thereafter the Coopers halted the planned transaction and intercourse between the families ceased, at least temporarily. A subsequent deed for Angevine filed in 1826 notes that "a misunderstanding arose concerning the true intent and meaning of the parties" to the original trust arrangement on that property, the Coopers insisting that they had committed "no error" under its terms.[59]

Removal

But the damage had been done, the words said, the hurt felt. Angevine remained in the couple's hands, but under the circumstances they did not feel that they could continue living so close to Heathcote Hill. They therefore left the premises and relocated to lodgings at 554 Broadway, just above Prince Street, where they were well north of the recently infected district of the city. Young Susan Cooper, going on ten at the time, said nothing about the rupture, attributing the move to her father's need—clear enough—to be closer to his "printer and publisher." What she did recall was the apparent gentility of the new house. It was one of a pair just recently built for the Patroon, Stephen Van Rensselaer, and stood opposite the dwelling of John Jacob Astor, even then a name to be reckoned with amid New York's moneyed classes. The place was almost out of town, but there was a Gothic style Episcopal church nearby and a boarding school next door where Susan and Cally were enrolled along with two of Astor's granddaughters and a group of other well-placed girls (SFM 48–49).

That such glamour was only as thick as varnish did not strike the ten-year-old. Life had harder truths that Susan's father knew about even as he sought to keep them from her and her siblings and, to some extent, perhaps even from his wife. At one time possessed of immense acreages and several houses, he now, after all, could afford only rented quarters. Soon bad news and good overtook the family there: the alienation from the DeLanceys was patched over by a new tragedy. Susan's brother Thomas, Cooper's old friend and recent antagonist, suffered a renewed attack of consumption in the fall. He moved to New York City with his wife and young son, renting a house on lower Broadway near the Battery, a few blocks south of the Coopers, and his father and sisters took up residence with him for the season. But there was apparently no socializing with the Coopers until after December 22, 1822, when Thomas's fragile health gave out and he died. Word of the death came almost immediately to 554 Broadway, no doubt through the family, and Susan pushed her husband to mend fences. Cooper therefore sat down the next morning and drafted a letter intended not to resolve the difficulties but rather to urge that they be ignored in the interest of amity. He insisted that there be no explanations or concessions on either side, a point to which John Peter very quickly agreed. Susan's father was so interested in resuming his old relations with Susan and her family that he added his own stipulation: there would be no reference whatever to the "controversies" of the recent past (*LJ* 1:86–87).[60]

John Peter's quick response was gratifying to Cooper but did not smooth away all his concerns. He was torn between a wish to accommodate his wife and his sense that things remained iffy with her family. He thus wanted to run downtown to call on John Peter, building on the shift of mood in their relations, but at the same time he feared that his visit at this moment would be "irksome" to his father-in-law—and to the rest of the DeLanceys. Apparently Susan's younger sisters, inoculated by Thomas, had become immune to their old feelings toward Cooper and even toward Susan herself—hence Cooper's insistence in a second letter that Susan "is now and ever has been ready to return any tokens of sisterly attention and regard that the young ladies may choose to manifest." The burden, that is, lay on Caroline and Martha, then twenty-one and nineteen, respectively, and apparently with their one surviving brother, William Heathcote DeLancey. While Cooper reaffirmed his understanding with John Peter, he thus insisted that he would defend his "character from every assault" launched from other quarters of the family—meaning, presumably, William, who probably also was on Manhattan then, having recently finished his theological studies there. Cooper would attend the funeral the next day in the city, or at Heathcote Hill at some later point—how else would Susan go?—but he was unsure whether it would be as an official "mourner" or simply as his wife's escort. What did John Peter think? (*LJ* 1:88).

As far as we know, the services for Thomas DeLancey were performed, probably under his brother William's direction, with solemn if rather forced dignity. Soon Cooper called on his father-in-law, sending a note ahead of him to request a brief meeting to handle some "business affecting them both." There can be little doubt that the "business" in question concerned Angevine, the sole trustee of which, under the original arrangement, was now Thomas DeLancey's infant son and namesake. The Coopers, while still maintaining that nothing they had done violated the trust, offered to return the property to John Peter. Owing to the age of the current trustee (and probably to Cooper's own present obligations under the Pomeroy decree), they consulted the Chancery Court on the matter. With its blessing on February 23, 1823, three weeks after *The Pioneers* had appeared in New York City, Susan and her husband reconveyed Angevine to John Peter DeLancey.[61]

Thereafter, for almost three years, Angevine was fully back in his control. Only at the start of 1826, when the Coopers were thinking about an extended European trip, did the elder DeLancey in turn deed the property in trust to his son William, who at his father's "earnest request"—probably meaning that William still retained some of his earlier doubts about Cooper—was granted and accepted full control over it. The younger DeLancey could do anything he wanted with the property, spending its income to maintain or improve it as he saw fit, and even selling it. But Susan Cooper was once again made the first beneficiary of the trust and was to receive any proceeds from her brother. If she should predecease her husband, Cooper was to receive those proceeds, which then on his death would pass to their children. Yet he was never to own the farm or have control of it in his own right. *His* death would end the trust arrangement, allowing Susan once again to take ownership of the farm and do with it as she wished—but if she predeceased him, her death would have no similar consequences in his favor. Cooper was no longer persona non grata at Heathcote Hill, if he ever had been that, but even with his financial crisis somewhat alleviated by 1826 he would never be given a chance to sell, otherwise dispose of, or again encumber the old Angevine farm. That was that.[62]

CHAPTER TWELVE

Taking Manhattan

C ooper's abandonment of Angevine after his dispute with the DeLanceys
cannot have been emotionally easy. But in exchange for the farm where,
as his daughter Susan recalled, he had labored hard to produce a stylish
"landscape," he took Manhattan, and by all accounts the swap was very much
worth it (Plate 14).[1] When he had to leave the city for a brief visit to Boston in
January of 1824, he came back like a native son to what he happily called "good,
great, magnanimous New-York" (*LJ* 1:109). Small wonder. When he moved
there with his family in October 1822, he found a social and intellectual environment whose like he had never known before. Its first center lay in the back
room at Wiley's, where, as production of *The Pioneers* revived following the end
of the yellow fever outbreak, Cooper discovered a group of friends who soon
were circulating around his energetic, talkative self.[2] Within a short time, probably around the middle of April 1823, he had founded the Bread and Cheese
Club, or the "Lunch," an all-male soiree of expansive membership that soon
began regular Thursday evening meetings at the premises of African American
cook Abigail Jones at 300 Broadway.[3]

In 1824, Cooper described the "Bread-and-Cheese Lunch" as an "erudite and abstemious association" where he found himself "elbowed by lawyers, doctors, jurists, poets, painters, editors, congressmen, and authors of every shade and qualification, whether metaphysical, scientific, or imaginative" (*LL* CE 4). At one time or another during Cooper's active involvement in the Lunch, it included literary figures such as poets William Cullen Bryant, James A. Hillhouse, Fitz-Greene Halleck, and Robert Sands; playwright (and polymath) William Dunlap; Knickerbocker wits Henry Brevoort, Gulian Verplanck, James Kirke Paulding, and Anthony Bleecker; publisher Charles Wiley (in the early period of the club) and newspapermen Charles King, Nathaniel H. Carter, and, one assumes, Charles K. Gardner. The fine arts were represented not just by Dunlap but also by Asher Durand, Henry Inman, and Samuel F. B. Morse. Members of the bar included the Irish patriot Thomas Addis Emmet, Henry D. Sedgwick (before Cooper's falling out with his brother Robert in 1825), Philip Schuyler, James Campbell, Joseph Delafield, and even attorney's agent (and future attorney) Dudley Selden, the man who was to inventory Cooper's household belongings in the fall of 1824 (see Chapter 13). There were medical doctors, including John W. Francis (later Cooper's personal physician), James E. DeKay, Robert Greenhow, and William James McNeven; merchants such as John Hone (whose brothers Philip and Isaac joined after Cooper left for France), Jacob Harvey, and William Gracie; a pair of Columbia chemists, James Renwick and John Griscom; politicians and officeholders such as Tammany Congressman Churchill C. Cambreleng, U.S. district attorney Robert B. Tillotson, and port surveyor J. G. Swift; and military men, including Gen. Jacob Morton, Gen. Winfield Scott, and, after his shift to the Brooklyn navy yard from Charlestown, Cooper's old friend, M. Cmdr. William B. Shubrick. Finally, as Shubrick's presence suggests, there was a core of members with whom Cooper had enjoyed friendly relations before his 1822 move to the city or the informal gatherings at Wiley's Den. Cambreleng, Gardner, and Verplanck were certainly of this sort. Others not already named, including lawyers Jerry Van Rensselaer, Luther Bradish, and Chancellor James Kent, along with banker Charles Wilkes, were in various ways older— in some cases, much older—friends of Cooper, and surely were brought into the club by virtue of their relation to its founder.[4]

Ties among the membership, aside from such personal considerations, appear to have been nearly incidental: certainly no one trade, not even authorship, dominated the group. Instead, the Lunch was an interlocking directorate of New York's cultural life in the postwar years. Probably the single most important shared interest was the belief on the part of most of the members that the kinds of cultural efforts then being undertaken in New York City represented a serious attempt to establish cultural independence from Britain. In 1826, Cooper himself gave a suggestion of the club's typical agenda when he declared the pride he took in having been the cause of so much "free, social, unpretending, pleasurable, and I may add, profitable, communion" among members and guests (*LJ* 1:140). The point was not to lecture or educate, let alone harangue, but to build a large, loosely constructed social body that represented the aspirations of the city for a greater share in the nation's intellectual and cultural life.

The Lunch was in this sense New York's answer to the Boston club—offshoot of the older Anthology Club and the Athenaeum—that had been formed right after the end of the second war with Britain by Richard H. Dana, Sr., Edward T. Channing, William Tudor, and others, under whose auspices the *North American Review* was begun in 1815. In New York's Clintonian era, when the sometime mayor and governor was playing a leading role in the foundation and management of such Manhattan institutions as the New York Academy of Art (1802), the New-York Historical Society (1804), and the Literary and Philosophical Society (1811)—of all of which Clinton served as president—Cooper's club was itself a Clintonian adjunct. This is not to say that the Lunch was a partisan body. Indeed, we do not know that Clinton ever attended or joined, whereas one of Clinton's regular sparring partners in the New York press, Gulian Verplanck (a.k.a. Abimelech Coody) was a full-fledged member. But a great many of the officers in organizations such as those named above were also Cooper's friends and Lunch members: the highest ambition of the Lunch and similar bodies in New York and elsewhere was the establishment of a context within which the work of the most talented members of the new American generation, including writers, could play their true cultural part. The "free . . . communion" of which Cooper spoke in 1826 was the social correlative of international political fact. The work these bodies performed was post-colonial liberation.

Cooper's establishment of the Lunch was the high water mark of his early social fame as a writer in New York. There had been other such clubs in the city over recent decades, including the Friendly Club, in which William Dunlap and Charles Brockden Brown had been active, and some fed into the Lunch. And there would be other groups later, including the Sketch Club (1827), which derived from the Lunch and itself led to the Century Association, founded by Bryant and Durand in 1847 and still very much alive today. There was nothing revolutionary about Cooper's group in a social sense. For Cooper, though, the Lunch provided a vivid image of the "new" America his own works were helping to imagine and create. It also gave him, as his old life was in shambles, a lively and supportive social context within which to realize his new identity. Otsego and Westchester were both behind him now as the furiously expansive city became his home.

Wit and Wine and Whiskey Punch

Cooper's increasing involvement in the city's social and intellectual scene is suggested by a trio of outdoor activities in which he engaged in April and May of 1823. The first was a modest, one-day affair aimed at honoring an American hero with whom Cooper would come to be closely associated over the next decade: the Marquis de Lafayette. Following the end of the second war with Britain, New York and U.S. officials began to make improvements to New York City's defenses. The federal government employed Gen. Simon Bernard, the French military engineer (and himself, along with Cooper, an ally of Lafayette in France during the 1830s), to survey the coast and plan new fortifications. One of the structures he designed, Fort Hamilton, was soon to be erected on Long Island near the Narrows, the channel connecting the upper and lower bays, opposite Fort Richmond and other defensive works on Staten Island. As an adjunct to these positions, a masonry structure (at first dubbed Fort Diamond from its shape) was constructed on the underwater feature known as Hendrick's Reef close to the Long Island shore. When the latter "very superior" work was finished, it was officially designated as Fort Lafayette.[5]

Once the weather turned mild in the spring of 1823, a dedication ceremony was planned. On Monday morning, April 7, a party of military and civic leaders accordingly assembled on the revenue cutter *Active*, then commanded by Capt. Henry Cahoone of Rhode Island, at the Battery in lower Manhattan. It included Bernard, his sometime rival and former chief engineer of the army, Gen. Joseph Gardner Swift (a member of the Lunch), several companies of soldiers, and a variety of distinguished civilians such as Gulian "Coody" Verplanck and state senator John Lefferts—and Cooper. Once at the facility, as the wind roared and the waves crashed against its stone walls, the troops paraded, did exercises, and raised the flag. Then a potent salute was fired off, followed by a round of nine cheers for the Revolutionary hero. By 2:00 p.m., hungry and thirsty, the celebrants went to the upper story of the fortress to replenish their patriotic ardor with food and drink. "Wit and wine circulated freely," ran the report in the New York *American,* and as a consequence there were many expansive toasts.

Cooper gave two: "The Marquis De La Fayette: The child of two countries, and faithful to both"—then (right after an unnamed guest toasted "Lawrence and his last words: 'Don't give up the ship'"), "La Fayette: his heart opened to us in his youth—our arms open to him in his age." As other guests added other toasts, the commander of the two companies of troops broke out champagne that had been forwarded for the occasion by Gen. Jacob J. Brown, commander of the northern army. After several hours at the blustery and exposed new fortification, the guests went back on board the *Alert.* The vessel and the troops aboard fired a parting salute at Fort Lafayette, followed by another as the cutter arrived at the Battery close to six o'clock.[6]

That Cooper was included in the little affair suggests how his presence was already being felt beyond the literary circles of the city. Merely as a former naval officer, he had some claim to take part in such quasi-military affairs. But it was his intellectual stake in the city's life—and his continuing exploration of the nation's past in his fiction—that really dealt him in. He was fast becoming a representative figure in New York City culture. As such, Cooper gained ready access to the flood of foreign visitors who washed ashore in New York. Among them were the theatrical players who, like the now deceased George Frederick Cooke, came over to entertain American audiences. The novelist may well have witnessed the famously alcoholic Cooke himself on the New York stage in the months after he began his furlough from the navy in May 1810. He certainly knew about Cooke, whose colorful exploits and theatrical talents were legendary. The pert young Maria Osgood, one of Cooper's New York characters in his 1823 tale "Heart," thus mocks the attention given to Seymour Delafield ("the pattern for all the beaux—the magnet for all the belles") by a bit of mimicry: "girls beckon him about so—and it's Mr. Delafield, have you read Salmagundi?—and Mr. Delafield, have you seen Cooke?—and Mr. Delafield, do you think we shall have war?" (*Tales* 136, 138).[7]

Many years later, Dr. John W. Francis linked Cooper with another pair of British actors busy on the old New York stage. The first was the tragedian Edmund Kean, who arrived in 1820 to play Richard III to great applause in the Anthony Street Theatre, give his competitor Thomas Abthorpe Cooper a run for his money, and then leave—only to come back in 1825 and become the occasion for a famous riot at the Park Theatre (Plate 15). Francis went so far as to claim that it was Kean who first fully awakened the novelist's interest in the theater.[8] But that interest had other sources as well. In the spring of 1822, for instance, Cooper's friend Charles P. Clinch, an aspiring writer who served as the private secretary of shipbuilder Henry C. Eckford, was allowed to adapt *The Spy* for the stage—a first for an American novel. Clinch worked so quickly that the play was first performed at the Park Theatre on March 1, 1822 (just as the book's second edition became available), kicking off a good first run and establishing one of the century's more successful American plays.[9] Clinch's success with *The Spy* in turn urged Cooper himself (as Clinch later told William Dunlap) to attempt a dramatic adaptation of *The Pioneers*. Cooper must have been at work on that effort pretty much up to the start of its disappointing three-day run at the Park on Monday, April 21, 1823, two weeks after the affair at Fort Lafayette.[10]

Fortunately enough, Cooper was not there to witness the play's failure. Right then he was away from New York with Dr. Francis and the other English actor to whom Francis linked him—Charles Mathews, who had arrived in the city just when the Coopers took up their Broadway lodgings in the fall of 1822. Scared away from Manhattan by the yellow fever, Mathews had gone south for several weeks before returning to open at the new Park Theatre on November 7. Cooper seems not to have been at the actor's opening but over the weeks following became very close to him, probably through Dr. Francis, who had professionally attended Mathews during his scare and become his friend. Mathews did some regular acting but for a number of years had been performing his own improvised one-man shows, a combination of skits and stand-up that Charles Dickens, for one, later found immensely entertaining. He was very popular in New York over the winter after his arrival.[11]

By the following April, just when Cooper was finishing the stage adaptation of *The Pioneers,* he had become friendly enough with Mathews that he pressed the actor to accompany him on a quick tour upstate. On Saturday, April 19, the two men joined Dr. Francis and went aboard the steamboat *Chancellor Livingston* for a run up the Hudson. As luck would have it, William Dunlap was also on the boat at the time and, recognizing Francis and Cooper, struck up a conversation with them and was formally introduced to Mathews by Cooper. The quartet spent the night together as the steamboat drove north to Albany.[12]

Mathews was very much the focus of the river passage, and a curious one at that. Despite the vivacity of his performances, which were wildly successful, Mathews seemed to Dr. Francis a shy and solitary man very susceptible to emotional alarms.[13] Dunlap's first observations confirmed that view. Although traveling with Cooper and Francis, Mathews kept wandering around the deck of the *Chancellor Livingston,* returning only intermittently to his friends. The ceaseless mobility was one mark of his character. Another was his dramatic effect on a crowd—everywhere he went he was like a match thrown into a gunpowder factory. He demanded attention and relished celebrity; but with the proscenium arch removed from between him and his admirers, he felt a bit exposed, even pestered. He therefore played to and alternately mocked and fumed at the inquisitive fellow passengers who kept crowding him. Cooper probably tried to keep things from exploding by humoring Mathews even as he thoroughly enjoyed the tense spectacle. Dr. Francis many years later said that he never saw Cooper show as much "enthusiasm" as he did in conversing with Mathews when Mathews was at the top of his form, as he decidedly was on the *Chancellor Livingston.*[14]

Dunlap supplied more detail. Whenever the actor ceased his peregrinations and returned to entertain Cooper and Francis with some new bit, a swarm of eavesdroppers would press in. He would break off and move on, dispersing most of them. But one of the multitude, utterly taken with Mathews, dogged him so persistently that the actor could not escape. Cooper and Francis watched the cat-and-mouse game and amusedly pointed it out to Dunlap. Suddenly Mathews turned around, saw the man again on his trail, stopped his little act in mid-sentence, and poured out "a rhapsody of incoherent nonsense" at the top of his voice—"something like," as Dunlap improvised the memory, "Sardananpalus Heliogabalus Faustina and Kitty Fisher with their fourteen children Cecrops Moses Ariadne Robinson Crusoe Nimrod Captain Cooke Bonaparte and Jack the Giant-killer had a long confab with Nebuchadonozer Sir Walter Raleigh and the pope on the best mode of making caraway comfits." Mathews cannot have intended such tomfoolery to make him inconspicuous. It was, in fact, a perfect example of the mixed messages he sent the public. He craved attention but threw up a virtually impenetrable smoke screen.[15]

In the mild evening air, Mathews kept up his deck show until the dinner bell was rung at around 7:00 p.m. Unaccustomed to the habits of inland steamboat travel but clearly used to being at the dead center of observation, the comedian announced, apparently not in a whisper, that he was offended by "both the matter and manner" of the meal. Somewhat later, he found the collective sleeping arrangements of the vessel equally insulting. There were no private cabins; there was a separate women's cabin, but the men had to make do with bunks or, given the overcrowding on the present trip, the settees and even the floors of the various other public spaces on board. Cooper soon made special arrangements: the Mathews party, now including Dunlap, would have Capt. Samuel Wiswall's own cabin on the main deck at its disposal, with a private supper and ample whiskey punch.

Mathews paid for the compliment by becoming "the fiddle of the company," as Dunlap put it: "story, anecdote, imitation, and song poured from him." One part of the show had particular meaning for Dunlap. Mathews, as it turned out, was quite familiar with Dunlap's 1813 *Memoirs of the Life of George Frederick Cooke,* especially with an episode involving the tipsy tragedian and Mathews himself in a Dublin inn in 1795. Mathews had long included the episode in his autobiographical performance called "Youthful Days," one of a series of skits in which he single-handedly impersonated all the characters. Dunlap, who had known Cooke very well and used Cooke's journals in writing the *Memoirs,* apparently had picked up at least some of the Dublin episode from Thomas Abthorpe Cooper, who in turn must have heard the original story from Mathews. In the main, Dunlap's version was fine, Mathews conceded. Yet he ventured a single important criticism. Tom Cooper had forgotten the "termination of the story,—the real *denouement.*" With this teaser left floating in the air of the cabin, of course the playwright-painter, the doctor, and the novelist all called on Mathews to deliver that punch line. So, in the middle of the Hudson in the middle of the night, sitting in the captain's cabin on the finest of American steamboats, with whiskey punch aplenty, Mathews regaled his intimate circle with one of his regular performances.

This evening's entertainment is worth recreating for itself and as a fair sample of the lively social exchanges that vivified Cooper's New York years. Indeed, but for the whiskey punch on the *Chancellor Livingston*, one might read the excursion with Mathews as a moveable session of his normally "abstemious" (and sedentary) Bread and Cheese Club: at this moment, Francis was already a regular member of the Lunch, Dunlap soon would be, and distinguished foreign visitors such as Mathews often were invited as guests. We have few records of the actual substance of meetings of the Lunch, but those that survive bolster this reading of the river trip. At one gathering of the Lunch, for instance, the skull of the dead actor George F. Cooke, which was in the medical collection of Dr. Francis and recently had appeared as "poor Yorick" in a performance of *Hamlet* at the Park Theatre, was the subject of a postmortem phrenological analysis. New York intellectuals amused by such shenanigans would have eaten up Mathews aboard the *Chancellor Livingston*. Cooper and his companions certainly did.[16]

The Irish episode involving Cooke and Mathews had transpired at a very early moment in the latter's career. The son of a London bookseller adrift in Dublin, he was nineteen, skinny, six feet tall, and new to the stage. Improbably, one night Mathews was cast as "the Jewish beau," Mordecai, in Charles Macklin's *Love à la Mode* (1759).[17] Opposite him was the great Cooke as Sir Archy MacSarcasm, a rival suitor for the hand of young Charlotte Goodchild. The unknown Mathews naturally enough worshipped Cooke at this point. Even so, although they both had been staying at the same miserable Dublin inn, Cooke had never deigned to notice him. Small wonder that the young man, anxious about how his performance as Mordecai would be received by the master, lingered in the theater the night after his debut. But at last he was ejected from the dark building and made his way, "through mud and mist" to his "lofty but comfortless abode in Mrs. Burns's garret." As luck would have it, Cooke, already in his cups, saw the lanky young player pass on his way to the attic and called him in. The great actor ordered hot supper, poured out whiskey punch for himself and his guest, and with a show of generosity began dispensing advice on a theatrical career. Talent was the key, of course, and Cooke was generous enough to concede that Mathews had talent. But talent without prudence would get him nowhere. "Take my word for it," Cooke said, "there is nothing [that] can place a man at the head of his profession but industry and sobriety. . . . Mistress Burns! Another jug of whiskey punch, Mistress Burns."

This version of the night's events was derived almost verbatim, as Mathews admitted, from Dunlap's *Memoirs*. What he added in the present rendition was his nimble imitation of the increasingly incoherent master's features, gestures, and voice—along with a fair version of himself when young and, of course, "Mistress Burns," who complied with Cooke's first demand but became increasingly reluctant to supply fresh punch as the actor sank further into drunkenness. In his 1813 version of the episode, Dunlap rightly portrayed the innkeeper as at last refusing. It was obvious that Cooke had had far too much already, and young Mathews, having overcome his awe for the master, wanted only to leave and go to bed. Cooke was hardly willing to let him depart. Intent on giving Mathews practical instruction as well as moral advice, the late Sir Archy was screwing his face into a variety of histrionic poses, making the young actor name each passion as he aped it. On the *Chancellor Livingston,* Mathews mimicked the drunken contortions of Cooke as well as his own befuddlement as he misidentified each and every grimace: what he named as *revenge* Cooke had intended for *pity;* he saw *anger* where Cooke had sought to represent *fear;* finally, when the drunkard twisted his face until he looked like a devilish satyr, then blurted out that this was *love,* Mathews had had too much and burst into roaring laughter. The hulking Cooke, with a voice to arrest an army, was furious. Only a humorous parry by Mathews and the arrival of another jug of punch soothed him.

The fresh supply disappeared down the open drain of Cooke's throat. Against her better judgment, Mistress Burns agreed to bring him one last jug but made him promise that he would call for no more that night. He accepted her terms. As the new jug went the way of all its fellows and Mathews gratefully rose to depart, however, Cooke began to call out for the landlady, by this point in her bed downstairs, beseeching her to arise and bring yet another. "It's very late, sir," she replied. "Early, early; one jug more," was his inebriated retort. On the *Chancellor Livingston,* Mathews shifted into a very high gear as his story neared its climax, doing such a splendid job of playing all the parts that this segment particularly impressed theater manager Dunlap. Not only did the comedian imitate the farcically drunk tragedian shouting out his commands; he also, with muffled voice, mimicked Mistress Burns's defiant answers as they had arisen through the floorboards from below. Then he must have acted out Cooke's increasingly violent responses. When the actor concluded that Mistress Burns was not to be budged from her bed—or her resolve—by mere pleading, he changed tactics. Crash went the empty jug on the floor.

"Do you hear that, Mistress Burns?"

"Indeed *and I do,* and you'll be sorry for it to-morrow."

He then regularly took the chairs, one by one, and broke them on the floor immediately over Mrs. Burns's head, after every crash crying, "Do you hear that, Mistress Burns?" and she as regularly answering, "Indeed

and I do, Mister Cooke." He next opened the window, and threw the look-
ing-glass into the street.

Mathews, astonished by Cooke's behavior, edged toward the door and tried
to escape. Cooke would hear nothing of it. Everything and everyone was swept
up in his drunken passion:

> "What, sir! Desert me! I command you to remain, on your allegiance!
> Desert me in time of war! Traitor!"
> I now determined to make resistance; and feeling pot-valiant, looked
> big, and boldly answered,
> "I will *not* be commanded! I *will* go to bed!"
> "Aha!" cried the madman, in his highest key, "Aha! Do you rebel?
> Caitiff! wretch! murderer!"

The 1813 version of the anecdote in Dunlap's book stopped with Cooke's
defenestration of the looking glass, followed by a temperance lesson from Dunlap. This was not, though, the "real *denouement*," as Mathews made clear to
Cooper, Francis, and Dunlap during the steamboat trip. Although completely
inebriated, Cooke still had his wit about him. Dragging the now trembling Mathews to the selfsame window, he shouted out into the quiet night for the nearest
watchman: "Watch! watch! murder! murder!" Almost immediately, the alarms of
several watchmen could be heard as the officers converged on the inn and, looking up to the open window, cried out, "what's the matter? who's kilt?" As Cooke
called for silence, he stuck Mathews out the window and then, seemingly insane,
explained himself: "In the name of Charles Macklin, I charge this culprit, Charles
Mathews, with the most foul, cruel, deliberate and unnatural murder of the unfortunate Jew, Beau Mordecai, in the farce of *Love a la Mode.*" Like Hamlet,
Cooke was only mad north-north-west. Shutting the window and turning to
Mathews, he cried, "Now go to bed, you booby! go to bed! go to bed! go to bed!"[18]
Adding to the pleasures of the steamboat trip was the fact that the four men
did *not* go to bed—not, anyway, until "near morning" on Sunday, April 20.
Mathews held forth for some time, probably putting on other little performances.
Yet he and his improvisations hardly dominated the night. Dunlap cautioned his
readers not to misread the episode. Punch or no, the four men had not "imitated"
Cooke by drinking to excess; rather, art and ideas had stimulated "a real exchange of mind" that ranged over several other subjects.[19] For one thing, as Dr.
Francis recalled, throughout the upriver passage attention was turned toward
the landscape and its historical and moral associations. The travelers could view
the Palisades in full light and must have pondered the steep, regular face of the
basaltic cliffs, a subject that, in the words of an 1825 guidebook, attracted "the at-

tention of every traveler."[20] By the time the boat entered the rougher terrain of the Highlands (around 8:oo p.m. or so), the sun was well down beyond the precipitous western shore, plunging the river scene into evening gloom. But all was not darkness. If, as Dunlap's account suggests, the mild weather meant a clear sky, a swath of stars soon was glimmering overhead. And the moon was up and waxing: the first quarter had occurred two days earlier, meaning that two-thirds of its surface was illuminated when it passed overhead early that evening.[21] Moreover, intermittent snatches and flashes must have called the travelers' attention outward from time to time. Probably there was little light generated along shore in this forlorn, seemingly uninhabited stretch. But the glow produced by the boat itself, especially its high, spark-shooting stacks, would have helped to illuminate the narrow channel, and some of that eerie light must have found its way to the shores. How much of the show would have been visible from the captain's cabin is unclear. But Cooper's party had free access to the deck immediately outside, and the three Americans, familiar with the passage, knew exactly where they were and doubtless wanted to impress on their visitor the dramatic nature and symbolic meaning of the landscape through which the vessel, with its monotonous engine noise, was steadily passing.

In their view, this unseen territory was prime American ground. First they discussed the most recent theory of how the Hudson had been formed, the cataclysmic view circulated in particular by Col. Jonathan Williams, an engineer and the founding superintendent at West Point, who in 1810 had published a learned paper on "the Formation of Rivers" in the *American Medical and Philosophical Register*, a journal edited by Dr. Francis and his mentor, David Hosack.[22] Williams, influenced by Thomas Jefferson's views on the similar topography athwart the Potomac at Harper's Ferry, thought that some vast inland lake, long confined by the solid dam of the mountain chain reaching across the landscape here, had finally burst through, creating the modern river and the spectacular scenery through which it passed.[23]

Cooper and Dr. Francis no doubt carried this part of the conversation. Then the burden shifted almost entirely to Cooper. As the travelers continued to pass up through the dark, brooding Highlands, the talk was all about Major André and Benedict Arnold, the strategic value of the site, and, in all likelihood, the role of the three ordinary captors in helping to preserve the American cause and thus found the new nation.[24] Mathews himself brought up *The Spy,* which he had read and liked. Although the comedian knew and had used Dunlap's book about Cooke, Dr. Francis saw that Mathews recognized Cooper's literary talents as much more impressive. And Mathews's clear admiration of *The Spy* in turn prompted Cooper to drop his guard and speak of his larger intentions as a writer. He was planning, he confessed, a series of novels featuring the American landscape, the Revolutionary War, and the "red man." Already, of course, he had broached all these topics in *The Spy* and then *The Pioneers*. At present, he had in hand a second Revolutionary tale, *The Pilot*, and may have been thinking about a third, *Lionel Lincoln*, in which the landscape of Revolutionary Boston would figure prominently. Something may also have been germinating in his mind about Natty Bumppo's fictional rebirth, along with that of the Delaware warrior Chingachgook. But we should not discount the catalytic effect of this particular foray up the dark channel of the river with the witty and appreciative Mathews in 1823. As he expanded on this crucial American place, Cooper may have realized that it had been claimed for him by *The Spy*—even by one wistful moment in *The Pioneers*. Washington Irving's efforts to one side, the Hudson was Cooper's for the future as well. As Mathews played himself when young in telling the tale of drunken George Frederick Cooke in that Dublin inn, Cooper had performed his own identity by speaking of the whole of American experience—the land, the critical events of the past, the distinctive human story of the New World. He, too, carried off a complex impersonation.

Such talk continued well into the night, as Dunlap recalled. By the time the revelers turned in, the *Chancellor Livingston*, its pistons still noisily working and its side wheels churning the dark river, must have been nearing Kingston, two-thirds of the distance to Albany. If all went well, it would arrive at the capital early in the afternoon on Sunday, April 20. From there, after a brief stay, Dunlap went on his way to Utica and then to Saratoga.[25] Dr. Francis may also have gone off on business of his own as Cooper and Mathews took in the upstate sights over the next two days. Albany was a "very bustling" place at the time, and, with the Erie Canal nearing completion and a flood of other traffic always on the move, it was the gateway to "the vast western regions of the state," as Cooper's old teacher and friend, Benjamin Silliman, remarked when passing through in 1819.[26] The population had risen from the influx of Yankees over the past two decades, and the façades of the town were showing signs of many recent transformations. There were still some obviously Dutch houses about the city, but Albany more and more showed the imprint of Anglo-American taste in a spate of new buildings, many of them designed by Philip Hooker, the Connecticut-born architect whose influence had affected even Otsego during Cooper's life there. Probably on Sunday afternoon, after their arrival, the novelist and comedian went around through what remained very much a walking city, from the steamboat dock along the river to the head of State Street. Once up there, most visitors went to see one of the best sights in town, the impressive (though unfinished) Academy building, reworked by Hooker from the original design of Thomas C. Taylor.[27] Silliman, seeing the red sandstone–clad structure when he stopped on his way to Quebec, thought it "noble," and it soon acquired the reputation of being, as another visitor put it in 1829, the "handsomest edifice in the city." By position and reputation, it was hard to overlook. From there, Cooper easily could lead Mathews to the nearby state capitol, erected at the head of State Street on the old Pinkster grounds beginning in 1806. This was another of Hooker's designs and at the time a frequent topic of comment by visitors to the city because of its size, design, and materials. Silliman had much to say in praise of it: it was, he thought, "a large and handsome" structure, with commodious rooms for its various public functions, along with furnishings that showed "elegance, and even some splendor." Like most tourists, the Yale chemist went through the whole capitol, winding up at the large cupola, which was twenty feet in diameter and had a domed roof supported by eight Ionic columns and surmounted by a large statue of the Greek goddess Themis. From the cupola, Silliman gained a "rich and magnificent" view that swept from the Catskills to the south and the mountains of Vermont to the northeast, with a pastoral stretch of the Flatts along the valley forming a fine background for the city immediately below.[28]

At the capitol building, Cooper and Mathews, like Silliman, went up through its more public rooms to the attic, which was occupied by the mayor's court, the state library, and an art gallery. From here they gained access to the cupola so that Mathews could take in the sweep of the surrounding region (see *GE* CE 169). Cooper no doubt pointed out the line of the valley to the south, flanked on the right by the undulating curves of the high Catskills, which had brooded above their upriver route. And he probably directed his friend's eye north, up the valley to the point where the soon-to-be-opened Erie and Champlain canals already joined the Hudson. Those were DeWitt Clinton's projects, and Cooper was Clinton's man, but Cooper believed in the project for more than partisan reasons. In 1828, he would call it the result of a "bold and noble effort of policy," noting that many people contributed to the conception of the project but that only one, DeWitt Clinton, had had the political and personal courage to carry through with it (*Notions* 1:126–27). Clinton, a tireless reinventor of himself through a series of ups and downs in public and private life, was a hero for the son of wealth turned farmer, whaleship owner, and now novelist.

For Cooper, nearer at hand down the sloping length of State Street were less showy things he recalled very well: St. Peter's, under construction by Hooker while he, a schoolboy here, played in the sandpit on the site until the ailing Rev. Thomas Ellison yelled at him and his mates; Ellison's modest house across the way; and, a block below, the old inn of Stewart Lewis, where his father had died thirteen years ago the previous December, now a boarding house kept by the innkeeper's daughters.[29] Cooper had not been in the city in years. The tour of new ground for the celebrated English comedian was thus a homecoming of sorts for his guide—much was changed (there was a new steeple on St. Peter's, for instance, added by Hooker the year before) even as much remained recognizable.[30] If the night passage up the river had pushed Cooper to claim the Hudson valley as his own, the visit to Albany let him touch back to his early years and, as with the two canals, ally his own future longings to those of the state and nation. The panorama visible from the cupola was very much like those he had painted in the opening chapters of *The Pioneers,* in which he had tried to portray the strategic patterns shaping the modern landscape of Clintonian New York.

Clinton's canals must have been subject to even closer inspection by Cooper and Mathews when they headed out of the city on their way to another old sight that the American wanted his new friend to see. This was the impressive cataract of the Mohawk River at Cohoes, just above that river's juncture with the Hudson at Van Schaick Island, several miles north of Albany. Cooper had not told Mathews where they were going, and Mathews, suitably "intoxicated" with the sudden view of the waterfall, dutifully reported the excursion to his wife. The cataract was a quarter of a mile wide and seventy to eighty feet high, and the river, full with spring runoff, plunged straight down over a sheer rock cliff, sending up a mass of foam that looked like "smoke rising from an immense volcano."[31] Mathews turned to Cooper as they peered into the turbulent scene and remarked with suitable humor, "Now, had you told me this was Niagara, I should have gone home with all my expectations realized" (*GS* CE 237).[32]

The Cohoes trip probably ate up most of Monday, April 21, especially with adjuncts Cooper was sure to exploit on the way. The Manor House of Stephen Van Rensselaer, on which Otsego Hall had been based, stood near the banks of the Hudson just north of the built up part of the city. Next to it stood the newer house of his son, another Stephen, whom Cooper had known in Albany as a boy. This was apparently one more design by Hooker, who was very busy during these years remodeling and expanding the Manor House as well.[33] Cooper, still the tenant of the Patroon's new house on Broadway in Manhattan and in any case long familiar with the family, could have called at either house. Reminiscent of an older spatial as well as social order, the Patroon's Albany mansion was an unavoidable obstacle to a northbound traveler: Market Street, leading north from the city, abruptly terminated at his front door. When Benjamin Silliman journeyed along this route four years before, he was suitably impressed by the Patroon's mansion: it was "a palace," so "embowered" in trees and shrubs that it reminded him of the fine "villas" he had seen in Holland.[34] Mathews surely would have noticed the mansions, and it is likely that Cooper, reminded of his family's former home in Cooperstown, would have pointed them out to the comedian anyway.

Cooper and Mathews surely paused to investigate the Erie's "little basin," quite close to the Van Rensselaer houses; from it the canal proper, parallel to the river but some distance back from it, went north across the Flatts, with the road immediately alongside it.[35] Soon, in September and October of this year, formal ceremonies marking the completion of the Erie Canal to Rochester and of the Champlain Canal to its final destination at Whitehall would take place in Albany. Already in April the landscape must have shown how the canals were remaking the face and fortune of the state, and especially the cities of Albany and New York. As if to indicate the complex patterns, political and social, then emerging, the old-school Van Rensselaers in fact were staunch supporters of this "artificial river," as some contemporaries called it, that interrupted the pastoral setting of their own backyards. The Patroon had been named as one of the original canal commissioners in 1810 and in 1824 became president of the canal board.[36] In the latter year he also put his prestige and his money behind another signal innovation for the future, a technologically oriented school across the river in Troy, later Rensselaer Polytechnic Institute, that was founded in part to supply the engineering expertise needed for the immense challenges the canal projects posed. The Patroon became a patron of practical learning; old and new were teamed.[37] Even the Yankee Silliman, whose people did not look with favor on the lingering manorial institutions in the Hudson valley, had been taken aback by the Patroon's forward-looking public spirit and impressed by his taste when he passed the elegant Manor House on his way toward Canada.[38]

When Mathews and Cooper made their way back from Cohoes to Albany on Monday afternoon, the *Chancellor Livingston* still sat idle on the river. It would not depart for New York until the next morning—fortunately, since Mathews apparently was a bit under the weather and, with other plans in view for their return trip, both travelers could use a night's rest on land.[39] They left at 10:00 a.m. on Tuesday, and ten to twelve hours later disembarked at one of the steamboat's regular stops, West Point, where Cooper promised to show his companion the military academy and surrounding historic sites they had discussed on their dark way upriver. After that, the two planned to return overland to New York City, presumably by the less common route along the western shore. Because the riverfront hotels tended to stay open in expectation of steamboat guests, Cooper and Mathews must have settled in just as final inspection was being performed and lights-out was darkening the nearby cadet quarters.[40]

By the next morning it was raining steadily and Mathews was now "quite unwell," suffering from what Cooper called "a charming fit of 'the blues.'" Undaunted and eager to tour the Point, the guide left his tourist friend behind and sallied out, striking up conversations with the officers and instructors, some of whom he may already have known. Soon they were telling him about an unexpected attraction in the library. This was the full-length portrait of Thomas Jefferson that had been painted by the English-born artist Thomas Sully, another of the clubbable Dunlap's many friends. The Jefferson portrait, one of a group recently commissioned for West Point, had been begun by Sully at Monticello and finished less than a year before Cooper saw it. Dunlap in his history of American art thought the monumental canvas "fine," and indeed it is.[41] That it had become a sight worth showing to visitors soon after being hung at West Point suggests how electrifying its effect was from the start. Certainly it made a powerful impression on Cooper. He told of his reaction in a letter to his friend Gardner, then editor of the newly established *American Patriot*. Gardner in turn lifted the story from the letter and inserted it into an editorial on "The Fine Arts" that he wrote for the paper in the middle of June.

As Cooper entered the library at West Point, then regarded as "one of the finest in the United States," his eyes immediately fell on Sully's canvas.[42] He was so taken aback by it that he asked his companions to wait while he went to fetch Mathews. The comedian resisted, but Cooper knew that he was an art collector and a fair critic of paintings and insisted that he rouse himself to see this one. The Englishman was of Dunlap's opinion: he soon pronounced the portrait "one of the finest he had ever beheld," adding that he never would have forgiven Cooper had his guide allowed him to miss it. Cooper had no quarrel with the aesthetic judgment. He was no collector, but he had seen enough paintings, "hundreds of celebrated ones both here and in Europe" (*LJ* 1:95–96) to know how to evaluate and respond to such things.

The art of the piece was not the whole of it, however. Cooper had grown up in a household in which Thomas Jefferson was viewed as the devil incarnate, and he had been so poisoned by his father's vitriol that Republican Gardner often taunted him about his persistent "antipathies" ("as you please to call them," Cooper added) to the sage of Monticello. In the onetime messmates' days and nights along Lake Ontario, the recently retired Jefferson no doubt had come in for fulsome criticism for his seemingly pusillanimous naval policy. But policy was not the real issue—political ideology was. One may be sure that no grand portrait of Thomas Jefferson adorned the walls of Otsego Hall during Judge Cooper's lifetime. At best, scurrilous caricatures may have been allowed, drawn by Jefferson's virulent enemies and showing him "clad in red breeches," the garb of atheism and (worse yet) "political heresy." Indulgent or neglectful father as he sometimes was, William Cooper had done this part of his job so well that his youngest son, now a grown man, a father, a successful writer—and, indeed, a Clintonian Republican!—still felt so repulsed by the very idea of Jefferson that he "would have gone twice as far to see the picture of any other man." But as he led the queasy Mathews through the rain and into the library there stood out in front of him no caricature but "a gentleman, appearing in all republican simplicity." Cooper struggled to find the right words for what he saw and felt: "there was a dignity, a repose, I will go further, and say a loveliness, about this painting that I have never seen in any other portrait" (*LJ* 1:95–96). The new image had finally routed the old.[43]

The experience in front of Sully's canvas was extraordinary. But the groundwork for it had been long in preparation. Cooper's political evolution away from his father's assumptions had been so gradual and had had so many causes that in many ways he still defaulted to old assumptions and habits. But much was happening in these first months after his move to New York City with Susan and their children. As he came into closer contact with men like Francis and Dunlap, networked with the founders and supporters of the city's youthful cultural and scientific institutions, and found new outlets (among them Gardner's magazine and now newspaper) for the products of his own creative energy, Cooper was coming to think of himself in radically new ways. Gardner's endeavors, like those of the founders of the Historical Society, the Academy, and the Literary and Philosophical Society, were integral parts of an intellectual and political awakening, a broad effort at solidifying the nation's (and the city's) cultural independence. In making his contributions to the *Literary and Scientific Repository*, which in its intended scope and even its title surely was meant to serve as an unofficial organ for the third of those institutions, Cooper was lending his old messmate a hand. But he was also venturing his own intellectual contributions on a wide array of technical and political issues that were very much on the agenda of the city's intelligentsia. The Hudson River trip with his old friends and new had given Cooper, as suggested earlier, a renewed sense of that stretch of landscape and his own claims on its spatial and moral dimensions. It took him home to Albany, but at the same time it allowed him to achieve some integration of his new interests and newly discovered talents with his customary views. As his father's blinders fell off his eyes in the presence of Sully's artful representation of Jefferson as a Republican icon, it is not too much to claim that a new Cooper was also emerging from the chrysalis of the past.[44]

American Eclipse

Even as Cooper and Mathews returned to New York, excitement was building for a big event on Long Island that was attracting not only New Yorkers, including Cooper, but also visitors from well beyond the city. Since Cooper took part in it as a "reporter" for Gardner's newspaper, this is an even better example of how he worked his way into New York City's public culture following his permanent shift there in 1822. As with his reviews for the *Repository*, his reports for Gardner's *American Patriot* were by-products of his literary career—things written while more important projects were in suspension. But it may well be that

Cooper invested time in such activities because he was exploring what other kinds of literary work might be available to him in New York. From Irving to Bryant, Poe to Whitman, many American authors did considerable amounts of journalistic writing not only in the 1820s but for decades before and since. Such writing might provide Cooper with ready income in slack times, if not from hard-pressed Gardner then from more established quarters; and, as he no doubt knew, having experience in the field would be good preparation for such a contingency.

Besides, in the case of his reports for the *Patriot* in May 1823 the subject was one very much to his taste: horse racing. John Pintard, founder of the New-York Historical Society, mused on the subject as the big event drew near. Philadelphia might be famous for its "Ecclesiastical Assemblies and Conventions," but New York, he somewhat facetiously explained in a letter to his daughter, had an even more popular draw at the Union Race Course in Jamaica, across the East River on Long Island. Like crowds of people in the city, Pintard was quite excited by the series of races scheduled to be run there over five days (May 27–31), especially by the "great match race" to be held on Wednesday, the twenty-eighth.[45] The latter race, resulting from a challenge by Virginia breeders against their New York counterparts, was to pit the New York favorite, "American Eclipse," against an initially unnamed Virginia champion. It boasted an astounding purse that Cooper reported as "$40,000, or $20,000 per side" (*LJ* 1:99). Both of the competing states had long experience in racing. The first track in the vicinity of New York City had been laid out as long ago as 1665 on Hempstead Plain, Long Island; a course at Trinity Church Farm on Manhattan had hosted the New York Subscription Plate race from 1725 to 1753.[46] And in colonial New York, Susan Cooper's kin were very much involved in racing, as Cooper well knew. Her uncle, James DeLancey, a great importer of thoroughbreds and breeder of American horses, had his own course at his farm in lower Manhattan. But with the colonies' break from England, DeLancey had been forced to abandon that property and, apparently, his horses when he hastily went into exile in April 1775. Racing continued during the Revolution under British occupation, but the sport was banned in 1802 by the new state government, in part for its recent association with Loyalism: not for nothing has horse racing been called, after all, "the sport of kings." Not until 1820 was racing once more made legal in New York, and then only in Queens County, where the Union Course was quickly laid out.[47]

Opening the next year, the Union Course soon became famous—or infamous, depending on one's ethnic and religious viewpoints. This was one of many subjects on which the Yankee and Yorker camps in particular parted company. The amusingly opinionated Yankee emigrant Horatio Gates Spafford was so exercised by the topic that he added moralistic reflections on the evils of racing to the revised entry on Jamaica in the second edition of his *Gazetteer of the State of New-York* in 1824. During his boyhood in Vermont, Spafford lamented, cash-strapped farmers were deluded into thinking that they could "get rich by raising race-horses." In the process, many serviceable colts were run into the ground and ruined for farm work. And even if some of the colts proved to have speed, that was of much less use in rural Vermont than power. Hence, in describing Jamaica, Spafford suspended geography in order to issue his "caution to those who might otherwise be led into a like error."[48] Even John Pintard, a native New Yorker descended from Huguenot forebears, imbibed enough moralism from his associates in the American Bible Society that he viewed the 1823 races with mixed feelings. Recalling with warmth the more modest races of his boyhood before the Revolution, he very much wanted to go over to Jamaica. But he was not entirely upset that his family responsibilities now kept him in Manhattan. Otherwise, he was not sure how he would square his religious affiliations with his ordinary self and its nostalgic desires.[49]

Although Cooper had been one of the original founders of the Bible society in 1816, he took a much more secular view of such amusements. He had attended the first races at the Union Course with relish in the fall of 1821 (while at work finishing *The Spy*) and returned eagerly in 1823. Later he would describe himself as "a member of the Jockey Club of New York" (*LJ* 2:113), apparently meaning the "New York Association for the Improvement of the Breed of Horses," the organization that sponsored the races in Jamaica.[50] Cooper's interest in such things did not stem from his own active involvement in breeding or racing. He certainly was no owner of superior horse flesh. The animal stolen from Fenimore Farm in 1815 was at best an awkward beast, with its small head, "bad tail," lame forefoot, and half-grown mane. Nor did its owner lavish good tack on it: the thief fitted himself out with a "common saddle" and a bridle made from untanned, hairy cowhide that he found hanging in Cooper's stable.[51] His appreciation of fine horses was limited to that of a spectator.

In addition to enjoying the immediate spectacle of the Long Island races, Cooper supported them because they furthered that diffuse cause of "improvement" that he and many other New Yorkers supported during the Clintonian era. The ponderous name of what Cooper later shorthanded as "the Jockey Club" was hardly a smoke screen for the more carnal pleasures associated with the track: "the Improvement of the Breed of Horses" was a serious and, in the view of its supporters, even patriotic goal. As with the use of merinos to bolster the breed of "country sheep" that dominated New York farms, there was little doubt that rural inhabitants would receive direct benefits from such intensive efforts. Cooper and his allies on this issue certainly did not share Horatio Spafford's purse-centered skepticism on the topic. Furthermore, they linked even animal husbandry to the larger effort to bolster the general cultural and economic situation of the country. This was, in short, another front in the post-colonial war against English domination—as much a matter of local production and local pride as the literary efforts of Cooper's New York circle. Cooper even rationalized wagering (he himself placed "a small bet" on Eclipse) on similar grounds: it was good in that it created incentives for breeders and owners, bad only if "pecuniary speculations" became ends in themselves (*LJ* 1:102–3). This view was perhaps moralistic in its own way, but its roots lay in political and cultural causes, not religious ones.

For the most part, we may be sure that the crowds at the Union Course in May of 1823 came for the thrills—perhaps the speculations as well, but probably not the ideology. Poor Pintard, stuck on Manhattan, watched the throngs as they deserted the city for Jamaica on Wednesday, when "the great match race" was to take place. He went down to the ferry landing at six in the morning to find would-be spectators, Cooper probably among them, already filling the streets in their eagerness to get over the river. Four hours later, he went again and was astonished by what he saw: "coaches, stages, double & single horse wagons, . . . Barouches & Gigs, 4 & 8 abreast all filled with Ladies & Dandies, high life & low life, waiting their turns for 2 Steam Boats and 2 Horse Boats, incessantly plying across the Ferry, with row boats of all sorts & sizes, carrying over foot pads innumerable." At 2:00 p.m., as he was writing this very report to send off to his daughter in New Orleans, Pintard sent a messenger to learn what was happening at the ferry and across the river. "I almost palpitate," he wrote—then chastised himself, "What an old Fool!"[52]

Over in Jamaica, the weather was spectacular as Cooper surveyed the hordes. The turnout was so large that the center of the one-mile oval was completely filled with carriages, mounted spectators, and pedestrians. The open stands at the starting post held some twenty-five hundred more people, mostly men. Inside, in "the rooms" and the Club House stands, there were even more, including many women. Along the first stretch, the crowd on the ground was "immense," and the trees were all filled with men and boys eager to gain a better view. Many New Yorkers were doubtful that the southern challengers would actually show up with a horse ready to run the race, but clearly the masses (estimated at fifty to sixty thousand in some reports) were not willing to forego even a slim chance of seeing the match. Indeed, as Cooper noticed, they were so keen for the excitements of the day that they were in the betting stand laying odds on whether or not there would be any race!

By 12:30, when a Virginia animal named Sir Henry was led out onto the track, that question was settled in the affirmative. That challenger, a magnificent four-year-old, was owned by "the Napoleon of the turf," legendary breeder and trainer William Ransom Johnson. But Sir Henry's opponent, foaled in 1814 and thus more than twice his age, was himself an astonishing animal. Bred and raised by Gen. Nathaniel Coles of Dosoris, Long Island, he had been sold in 1819 to Cornelius W. Van Ranst. Although retired to stud shortly thereafter, he had been brought back to open this very track in 1821 and had raced again the following year.[53]

The 1823 match was run as the best two out of three four-mile heats—three times around the one-mile oval, then a final mile full tilt down a straightaway connected to it. It thus was an endurance trial as much as a test of speed. From his position near the betting stand, Cooper looked over the two horses as they stood near the starting post at 1:00 p.m. Both seemed to be in top form. But not everything was going according to plan. A jockey named Billy Crafts was garbed in his silks and ready to mount Eclipse in the place of the famous local rider, Sam Purdy, whom Cooper and many other spectators clearly expected would ride the horse. Purdy in fact was present: Cooper turned around to scan the crowd and found him, not three feet away. But he was in the betting stand rather than on the track; for some unstated reason he had been bypassed.

That was unfortunate. As the track was cleared of the spectators, the riders were signaled to mount and given the command to start.[54] The horses ran off "like the wind." Under the control of Billy Crafts, Eclipse led at the outset but then soon fell back and was passed by Sir Henry. Three times the horses circled the track at breakneck speed, and each time the southern challenger was thirty to sixty feet in the lead. As they entered the final straightaway, Crafts urged Eclipse on and the gap closed to a length, then half a length. But when they came to the finish line, Sir Henry held a narrow lead over his still-gaining opponent and won the heat. The time elapsed (officially 7:40—Cooper, though, timed it himself as 7:37) was astonishing. This was, Cooper reported, "the fastest running in well authenticated record."

The southerners visibly gloated while the New Yorkers looked grim, but it was not to be a grim day at the Union track. Suddenly an enormous roar went up in the crowd. The spectators were demanding that Purdy be restored to his rightful place atop Eclipse, and soon Cooper saw the man coming out from the weighing house in his crimson silks and cap, "booted and spurred," and with "a good whip" in his hand. As Eclipse jumped off the start this time, it was clear that the real race had begun. He fell behind Sir Henry for the first two laps, but then on the third Purdy pushed him into the lead. During the final mile, Sir Henry "made a desperate run" and recovered the lead, at which point Eclipse, under Purdy's whip, bolted ahead to win by thirty feet. For the final heat, Sir Henry also took a new rider and fought hard, but this time Eclipse led from the start and never faltered, crossing the finish line twenty to thirty feet ahead of the challenger. Cooper conceded that Sir Henry was "one of the finest horses that ever trod the turf," but this had been Eclipse's day. He had been among that horse's staunchest supporters and was immensely pleased that the animal ran better than ever before. After the first heat, he had been tempted to sneak back into the betting stand and hedge his bet, but happily had decided not to. His faith in the animal, the track, the New York effort, had been fully repaid (*LJ* 1:97–102).[55]

Shifting Ground

By the time he crossed the East River ferry on May 27, 1823, to attend the first of the Union Course races, Cooper had been living for some weeks in new quarters in Manhattan. At the end of April, when he and Charles Mathews came back from West Point, Mathews rushed on to his next performance as Cooper returned to Broadway to get ready for the move. Perhaps in an effort to save on rent now that their finances were so critical, on New York's traditional moving day (May 1), he and Susan shifted down island to a run-down, rat-infested house at 3 Beach Street, seven or so blocks south and farther west (near the present entrance to the Holland Tunnel), a rental property owned by Mrs. Cooper's cousin Henry Floyd Jones (SFM 53). Susan and "Harry Jones"—as Cooper called him years later (see *LJ* 3:252)—had been close since childhood. Both born in 1792, they had played during family gatherings, at least once to nearly fatal effect when Floyd Jones took a supposedly unloaded shotgun off the well-filled rack in the hall at Heathcote Hill and, pointing it melodramatically at Susan, pulled the trigger. Susan's father had a rule that hunters should discharge their guns before coming into the house, but someone had disobeyed it and the load from "Harry's" gun punched a tight pattern of holes in the wall immediately beside the young girl's head (SFM 51). By 1823, Susan's wounded feelings had healed and her fright long since had been forgotten, and her cousin's house was a useful, if objectionable, expedient in tough times. In this case, as with the loan from Harry's kinsman, Judge Samuel Jones, on the Hickory Grove four years before, Susan expended some of her family capital to help out her husband and their children.[56]

The move had little apparent effect on the Cooper household. To be sure, the novelist's daughter mistakenly thought that, during a new outbreak of yellow fever over the next few months, Beach Street lay within the infected districts, prompting her family to relocate yet again—this time well up the island. But in the main she was wrong. In 1823 there was no major outbreak, no fences, and no evacuations: her anecdotes about such things clearly derived from her father's recollections of the 1822 siege (see SFM 51). However, there was a shadow of justification for her exaggerated recollections. In fact there *was* an early alarm in

1823 about a possible visitation that proved "precipitate" (as would-be race enthusiast John Pintard recorded), but that may well have impelled Cooper to seek out safer quarters for his family for the warm months.[57] It was one thing for him to personally frequent iffy parts of the city in 1822, but with his wife and their young children by his side the case was different.

Probably in June or early July, at any event, the Coopers took up summer lodgings near Turtle Bay, a small indentation in the Manhattan shoreline along the East River at the present location of the United Nations Park. Here, several miles from the city in the midst of farmland and dispersed houses, and with easy access to the water, the hot and odorous streets of lower Manhattan, whether beset by yellow fever or not, were easily forgotten. Young Susan recalled that the "country-house" her family occupied at Turtle Bay belonged to "Mrs. Winthrop, a charming old lady" (SFM 51). If this is accurate, then the house indeed did stand on Turtle Bay Farm itself, a seventeenth-century grant controlled since 1817 by Phebe Taylor Winthrop, widow of Francis Bayard Winthrop, who had acquired it in 1792. There was a family link here as in the case of Beach Street. Mrs. Winthrop's sister was Ann Taylor, "a woman of great respectability" (LJ 5:293) who had married but then divorced one of the less reputable DeLanceys. The Coopers apparently did not know Ann Taylor intimately, but they knew who and what she was, and who her kin were—they knew enough, in other words, to turn to her sister Phebe, whom even young Susan recalled well, in search of temporary quarters for the summer. And there was a second link to Phebe Winthrop: her deceased husband's son and namesake by his first wife had married into the family of William Dunlap's wife, the Woolseys. The DeLancey tie thus may well have been seconded by one that Cooper himself could draw on because of his widening circle of friends in the city.[58]

However they came to Turtle Bay Farm in the summer of 1823, the Coopers took to it. To judge by the manuscript map of Manhattan farms drawn by surveyor John Randel in 1820, there were several houses on the farm. Mrs. Winthrop herself may have occupied the big one, called Mount Prospect Mansion House, which stood at the theoretical corner of what, under the new grid plan adopted by New York City in 1811, would be First Avenue and Forty-first Street. Although Randel showed the old Eastern Post Road still snaking its unreconstructed way through the grid, the new urban order of things was clearly emergent even this far up island in 1823: young Susan remembered driving down "the Avenue" (probably in this case Third Avenue, the nearest throughway at the time) to go shopping or to the post office while her family stayed at Turtle Bay. On the other hand, she was right in pointing out that the grand avenue was actually an "unpaved road" (SFM 51).[59]

If the site of the summer vacation was a happy one, the time the family spent there was defined by decidedly disturbing events. One was focused in Otsego County. As long ago as the previous September a "gang of villains" reportedly had been busy vandalizing private property there—indeed, even churches and graveyards. When one newspaper editor, John H. Prentiss, warned Coopers-town residents to be on the lookout for arson as well as vandalism, he was chas-tised by a rival editor for disseminating such embarrassing rumors about Otsego to the wider world. But Prentiss seems to have been premature rather than wrong.[60] The following July, a suspicious fire destroyed the leather-tanning yard of William Holt Averell's father.[61] Although Cooper probably had yet to learn of the covert alliance between the younger Averell and the Pomeroys, he cer-tainly knew that the lawyer had been snatching up Cooper properties at bargain rates. Hence he may not have wept over this news. Soon, however, came a report of a second attack that hit Cooper hard personally. Early in August, probably after one of those trips down "the Avenue" to the post office, Cooper walked into the sitting room at the Turtle Bay house with the latest *Freeman's Journal*, which he already had scanned. He walked over to his wife and pointed out to her the following alarming news story: "*Fire.*—The torch of the incendiary again caused the alarm of *fire!* among our citizens on the night of Wednesday last, at about 12 o'clock, and shortly thereafter the substantial and expensive stone build-ing owned by James Cooper, Esq. of New-York, situated near a mile northerly from the Village, was a smoking ruin." Although the mansion at Fenimore Farm was built of stone, it was crammed full of valuable combustible materials, in-cluding the unhung doors and shutters, and these and its wooden floors and roof had gone up in a quick, spectacular fire. The big place, Cooper recalled in 1838, was "destroyed to the naked walls" (*COC* 72).[62]

The fire at Fenimore Farm was even more clearly an act of arson than that at the tan yard a week or so earlier. The unoccupied building stood "quite alone, in the centre of an extensive lawn," safe from any source of accidental combus-tion (*COC* 72). In the following weeks, a rash of other fires made it clear that the destruction of Cooper's house was part of an assault on the property and peace of mind of Otsego residents during this long, fiery summer. Even into the fall and then again in 1824, several barns were torched, some in outlying areas but others in the heart of the village. On two or more occasions, flames spread to yet other structures and were put out only after great effort. As late as June 12, 1824, eleven months to the day after the arsonist or arsonists first struck, another fire occurred. Then, as suddenly as they had started, the attacks stopped.[63] Either the perpetrators had struck all their intended targets or, more likely, had left the area in search of fresh pastures and drier kindling. Cooper took note of the events in his *Chronicles of Cooperstown*. He offered no final interpretation of them; but he did add that, although those responsible had never been conclusively identified, "plausible conjectures" had been made (*COC* 72). His daughter Susan, obviously picking up on this view, similarly asserted that "one unprincipled man" had done all the damage, but she, too, did not name names (SFM 52). Nor did she mention her father's stunning discovery of a failed attempt that might have hit the family even closer to home. In the 1830s, when work on remodeling Otsego Hall was under way, a window casing was opened and arsonist's materials were found secreted in it: tinder and cotton saturated with oil, along with burnt sticks that had fizzled in an attempt, which Cooper suspected dated from the same period, to bring his father's house down (see *COC* 72).

Whether the Coopers were personally targeted is uncertain. At the time he reported the fire at Fenimore Farm, editor Prentiss of the *Freeman's Journal* surmised that its real purpose was diversionary. A nighttime conflagration of that scope on a site so plainly visible from the village would cause a rush of firefighters and spectators out of Cooperstown, leaving the hastily abandoned shops and dwellings available for easy rifling. Only quick thinking by wary citizens, Prentiss added, had frustrated the plan—if plan it was.[64] That reading of the Cooper fire is plausible but does not apply very well to any of the other attacks, which either took place in the village proper or were sited far enough away that they would not have been readily visible from there. By September 8, Prentiss had concluded that something other than thievery was afoot in these continuing acts of "infernal malice."[65] Even if malice pure and simple were the motive, however, Cooper still might have been one of a group of carefully selected targets. One wonders, to begin with, where old Dan Chapin, the horse thief of 1815, was during the summer of 1823. Yet if anyone was targeted in the series of fires, perhaps a more likely objective was the Averell family. The first fire, which was very costly, occurred at the industrial property owned by James Averell, Jr. One of the barns destroyed belonged to Horatio Averell. If Otsego Hall indeed was one of the buildings on the arson list in 1823, it could well have been because, as everyone in the village knew, it had been bought for a song at the 1821 public auction by William Holt Averell himself and thereafter had not been redeemed by any of Judge Cooper's heirs. It also was common knowledge that Fenimore Farm was up for sale (Prentiss certainly indicated as much in his story of the fire), and locally it may have been thought that Averell already had it in his clutches or soon would claim it.[66]

By the time of its destruction in the summer of 1823, the mansion hardly retained all the positive associations it once had had for the Coopers. Still, Cooper swallowed his own feelings as he shared the newspaper with Susan on that morning in early August: having handed it to her, he turned and left the room without speaking, itself an ominous irregularity in what was always a close, verbally communicative relationship. Their oldest daughter, the source of this domestic vignette, took note of the oddity but did not comprehend it at the time. She saw only that her mother looked sad.[67]

As it happens, there was another cause for that feeling. In the days or perhaps weeks leading up to this scene, the couple's youngest child, Fenimore, was in great physical distress. The supposed cause was difficulty with teething. Born in October 1821, Fenimore was about twenty months old when the problem began, so this was not his first teething experience: probably he was getting his first molars or even his canines. Painful as it may be on occasion, teething in itself is hardly fatal. But it may well mask, or be confused with, more serious conditions, including fever or influenza—a situation that can lead to unfortunate misdiagnoses. This seems to have been the case with young Fenimore, whose affliction began while the family lingered at Turtle Bay, then "became rapidly worse" after the return to Beach Street during the first week of August, leading to his death there, to the "great grief" of his parents, on August 5. Put in a mahogany coffin with a silver nameplate and pine base, "my poor little boy" (as Cooper called him in a letter a month later) was interred in the Episcopal churchyard at St. Mark's-in-the-Bouwerie, some blocks east and north of Harry Jones's house (*LJ* 1:103). Now they were two—Fenimore and Elizabeth, dead in 1813, still buried alone near the ruinous farmhouse that shared its name with the most recent victim of life's surprises.[68]

More surprises were to follow. By the time Cooper wrote that touching description of the boy, he himself had undergone a reversal in his own health. Shortly after the boy's burial, Cooper began experiencing symptoms so worrisome that they upset his already frazzled wife and, from around August 10 to the month's end, sent him scurrying off on several "short excursions to different watering places &c near the city" (*LJ* 1:104).[69] The underlying problem has never been clinically described or conclusively explained. Over the next few years, as the affliction seemed to recur and some associated symptoms became chronic, Cooper offered only a bit of sketchy guidance. It was "sketchy" in part because medical terminology at the time was imprecise. Another reason is that, in looking back at the original onset and later episodes, Cooper tended to describe his symptoms somewhat differently at different times. In 1827, he spoke of the "attack of intermittent"—that is, intermittent fever—that had, as he put it, "broke me down" in 1823 (*LJ* 1:221). In 1828, in a longer description of the original problem, he called it "the bilious attack of 1823" (*LJ* 1:241). These are not identical terms, but in the 1820s they were not mutually exclusive: at that time, an intermittent fever was characterized by an alternation of high and normal temperatures, whereas a bilious fever (whatever its temperature swings) included vomitive symptoms as well. Either term might have been appropriate for symptoms arising from a variety of conditions or diseases, ranging from influenza to more serious complaints. They might, for instance, have covered some of the symptoms of malaria, by no means uncommon in the United States then. They conceivably could have indicated even yellow fever, an especially intriguing connection given Susan Cooper's memory of the circumstances surrounding the family's shift to Turtle Bay: did she, one wonders, overhear some worried talk in her parents' parlor about her infant brother, his teething problems, and the early alarm about yellow fever in 1823? However tantalizing, that possibility is too uncertain to allow a positive answer. The simple fact is that we do not know enough to formulate a diagnosis.

We can nonetheless sharpen the picture. Cooper suffered recurrent bouts of a bundle of symptoms (fever, digestive upset, weakness, and severe headache) for some time in 1823 and 1824. Some of these symptoms also afflicted him for many years into the future. Yet, while it cannot be said that he ever recovered his customary health, neither did he fall into a progressive deterioration. He seems to have suffered a fairly debilitating attack of an unknown but serious illness in 1823. In turn, it either had chronic complications witnessed in his later bouts, or it left him in such a vulnerable condition that he was unusually susceptible to new afflictions over the years.

We also need to consider the possibility of a psychological component to his long-term problem if not to the 1823 episode. Before 1823, Cooper had been a robust person accustomed to physical exertion and rarely if ever subject to illness. So severe was the change in his health after the 1823 episode that he struggled for several years to manage his symptoms. He was weak for a considerable period after the attack and lost enough weight that representations of his appearance in the years following 1823 (Plate 16) show a very much altered countenance from, for instance, the famous, much reproduced 1822 portrait by John Wesley Jarvis. By the start of the next year, when he visited Boston for a few days, he was still wobbly enough that his old navy friend, slow-moving William B. Shubrick, for once managed to outwalk him (see *LJ* 1:109, 2:17). Cooper apparently had recurrences of "my fever," as he then proprietarily called it, in the summer of 1824 and again in the spring or early summer and fall of 1825 (*LJ* 1:120–21).[70] When, over the next winter, he began to make firm plans for a long-contemplated European visit, the hope that it might improve his health was one of its justifications (see *LJ* 1:127).

This picture of the 1823 "illness" is by no means clear. It is further clouded by the fact that two other conditions were associated with the fever. The first is relatively straightforward. In September of that year, when he wrote Shubrick (then at the Charlestown navy yard) to delay his planned visit to Boston, Cooper mentioned his August illness and the "excursions" by which he had attempted to rout it. But he focused more attention on an apparently separate attack that hit him hard at the very start of the next month. He and Susan and their oldest daughter had traveled to Westchester sometime near the end of August, when the weather was very hot. The motive for the trip, at least on Cooper's part, may have been a desire to take in a bit of country air. Susan conceivably had motives of her own. Cooper did not give many details of the visit, but he implied that while he himself had been, as he explicitly put it, at "my farm in West-Chester" (that is, the Hickory Grove), Susan and their daughter may have stayed else-where—probably at Heathcote Hill, where Cooper may not yet have felt com-fortable but where Susan, especially given her recent loss of Fenimore, surely would have wished to visit her aged father. She was knitting up loose emotional ends while her husband, glad to be out of the city for a spell, puttered about the farm, which still was rented out to tenants.

The crisis in the trip, at any rate, came on the return, by which point the three travelers were certainly together. The weather remained very hot when, on the afternoon of September 1 or 2, they went to the Mamaroneck landing and boarded the "crowded [and] disagreeable" sloop that regularly left there for the city, twenty-three miles distant. The route was tricky and subject to considerable delays. In this instance, the sloop went two-thirds of the way without incident but then was stopped in the narrow passage at Hell Gate, where the syncopated and opposing tides flowing from Long Island Sound, the Harlem River, and New York harbor could make for dangerous currents. On the present occasion, the vessel was met head-on by tidal flows that must have been coming up from the south (usually later than those in the sound), meaning that the passengers would be delayed "until midnight." Probably because of his recent illness, sit-ting on the sloop for several hours under the "broiling sun" of the afternoon and then across the hot, heavy evening did not suit Cooper. He therefore arranged for the captain to put him and Susan and their daughter ashore, either on Great Barn (later Ward's) Island, from which a relatively new bridge led over the Harlem River, or directly on Manhattan itself. From there, the three of them traveled on foot for nearly ten miles down the long, dusty road that led them to Third Avenue and the city.

Once back on Beach Street, Cooper collapsed. At best, he was seriously overheated, dehydrated, and exhausted; at worst, he had suffered full-blown heatstroke. Given his recent bouts of fever, he no doubt was more susceptible to the onslaught than he normally would have been—or than Susan (two months pregnant at the time) and their ten-year-old daughter were on this occasion. For the next week, he remained "laid up." Only on Sunday, September 7, was he at last well enough that he could write Shubrick to explain himself. He was feeling "perfectly well" on that day, well enough to think that he could plunge back into his literary labors on Monday. But in fact he did not immediately do so, or his lingering weakness kept him from being able to finish the book in hand, *The Pilot*, soon enough for it to come out the next month, as the letter to Shubrick predicted that it would. To the contrary, not until four months from the date of that letter, as we shall see, did it appear (*LJ* 1:103–4).[71]

The second complication to the attack of bilious or intermittent fever Cooper suffered in 1823 was more diffuse. The heatstroke surely intensified the symptoms he already was experiencing and probably lengthened his recovery time. But from this moment Cooper also began suffering chronic bouts of some nervous digestive disorder that persisted, apparently, over the rest of his life— it certainly plagued him for many years and may even have had some role to play in the complex of afflictions that led to his death in 1851. His daughter in 1876 called it "a form of nervous dyspepsia" (*LOM* HE xvii). In the July 1827 letter that speaks of "the intermittent," Cooper for the first time mentioned that his "stomach and spleen had got entirely out of trim" in 1823, and that his digestion was not yet back to normal four years afterwards, despite his avoidance in France of the highly seasoned American cookery that he now thought had been part of the problem before his European trip. He was convinced that "abstinence and ex-ercise" would do the trick and thus restore his "constitution" (*LJ* 1:221–23), but six months later still he admitted that he had "never quite recovered from the bil-ious attack of 1823," being subject "every now and then" to disabling sieges last-ing "three or four days" (*LJ* 1:241). Another three months later, he referred to "an old enemy (indigestion)" in begging off a dinner invitation in London (*LJ* 1:260), and at the start of 1829 he was explaining to Mary Clarkson Jay from Flo-rence that rumors about his unsociable behavior in England were dead wrong. He had to work very hard during the London visit, with the result that he had no time for some of the entertainments. But concerns about his health had also kept him in: "Late hours not only destroy my digestion, but they make sad inroads on my ability to buy any thing to digest" (*LJ* 1:354–55).

In Rome in 1830, Cooper was avoiding other English and American visitors because of "ill health, or rather prudence" (*LJ* 1:410), suggesting that he thought the condition under control but hardly cured. Only in July of that year, while in Dresden, did he feel comfortable asserting that he was at last better than he had been "in five years" (*LJ* 1:430)—or "six years," as he revised the estimate once he was back in Paris the following month. But even then he attributed the grad-ual improvement to his extensive travels over recent weeks, the more moderate climate he found on heading north from Italy for the summer, and, as he put it, his slow acquisition of "some more knowledge of my own constitution" (*LJ* 2:8). His "stomach was getting round again" was the way he expressed it in Sep-tember (*LJ* 2:14). Toward the end of 1831 he finally sent a seemingly uncondi-tional report to his publishers, Carey and Lea: "My own health, God be praised!

has not been so good in seven years, as it is now. The stomach has come round again, and I escape those nervous attacks that used to lay me up, formerly, for a week." But even then he had to add that "bad weather" still brought "severe" attacks of the old disorder—"two or three in a year" (*LJ* 2:149).

By the following April, Cooper admitted how potent those few exceptions could be. Laid up with a "fearful head-ache" (a newly emphasized but *not* new symptom) and a very bad digestive upset, he had to write the American ambassador to excuse himself from attending a reception for Martin Van Buren, then in transit through Paris to Germany (*LJ* 2:242). As much as two weeks later, on April 22, Cooper had to "seize a moment from indigestion and head-ache" to drop a line to sculptor Horatio Greenough (*LJ* 1:244). When his wife was ill enough later that year to suggest a trip to the Belgian "watering place," Spa, Cooper accompanied her; he tried the waters and did the other things expected of visitors to such a spot, but aside from a slight indisposition as a result of the mineral waters, he was feeling "perfectly well" (*LJ* 2:293, 331). Yet when he and the family returned to New York in 1833, the old problems resurfaced and continued to afflict him across that decade and through the next. Europe had not cured him, and whatever changes in behavior and diet he experimented with then were not sufficient in themselves to keep the old problems from returning.

Not all the symptoms Cooper experienced over these years can be reasonably explained as the consequence of his sudden physical affliction early in August 1823 or of the heatstroke he suffered then and, perhaps, later. Recurrent bouts of fever, to be sure, may suggest that some underlying physical infirmity or disease was responsible for that part of his health troubles. But the "nervous dyspepsia" mentioned by his daughter in 1876 and much noted in less clinical terms by Cooper himself over the years does not appear to have had ties to any definable medical condition, at least not to any that caused his problems in 1823. He may, of course, have had some disease unknown or unnamed at the time.[72] But the more one reflects on the onset of these symptoms in 1823, the more one senses audible psychological overtones in his condition. It is, in this regard, not so very odd that Cooper's own collapse came so close to the death of that "poor little boy" Fenimore. Cooper had been hit repeatedly in the previous five or six years by a series of reversals that he appeared to shrug off even as he increased his at times frantic, not to mention implausible, efforts to counter them. But those reversals were taking their covert toll in Cooper's health, and Fenimore's loss may have triggered a kind of psychic breakdown that brought the boy's father himself low. Cooper could not save the boy; but he could join him—or almost join him—and so in a sense he did.

Cooper's New York

The record of Cooper's first months in New York City late in 1822 and early the following year suggest a man of vigor and virtually unbounded energy. Probably few who encountered him then could have surmised what burdens he was bearing due to the problems with his father's estate, the still recent deaths of his three brothers, his own financial reversals, or the difficulties with the De-Lanceys. His success as an author to a great extent countered the visible effect of such things. Yet there was a peculiar emotional economy at work below the surface. His joie de vivre as witnessed by Dr. Francis during the Hudson River trip had about it a certain nervous assertiveness. Indeed, what some of his associates in the city mistook for "self-complacency" (Catharine Maria Sedgwick's dismissive term) was more plausibly an overcompensation in one part of his life, the new public one, for the doubts ruling more private spaces.[73]

Cooper may have tended to dominate social exchange in New York, as William Cullen Bryant once or twice confided to family members during this period: he "seems a little giddy with [the] great success his works have met with," Bryant wrote on first meeting Cooper.[74] When he wrote down that first impression, Bryant had a fair idea of what literary celebrity entailed. After all, he had published his own first work, *The Embargo; or, Sketches of the Times* (1809), a verse satire on President Jefferson's policies, when he was just thirteen. It sold very well, went into a second edition, and was hailed as "an extraordinary performance" by the *Monthly Anthology*.[75] He wrote "Thanatopsis" four years later, and with its 1817 publication in the *Monthly Anthology*'s successor, the *North American Review* (followed by his first collection of *Poems* in 1821), his career was launched. Gulian Verplanck, Susan Cooper's kinsman and her husband's friend (and, soon, fellow member of the Lunch), received a copy of Bryant's *Poems* from Richard Henry Dana and reviewed it warmly for his cousin Charles King's *New-York American*. A few days later Verplanck wrote a fan letter to Bryant.[76]

When Bryant moved permanently to New York City in May 1825, he was still viewing the world through the eyes of a village poet of quiet (even shy) and scholarly disposition, sharpened by his legal studies and aware of his powers but nonetheless reluctant to make too much of them in public. His initial response to Cooper was a reaction from that sort of nature to one that was opposite in most ways. Cooper was forthright and talkative, relishing the social tug of New York. Dr. Francis, who met Cooper for the first time in 1823, admired his "natural boldness of temper," which led him to express himself in a "frank, emphatic, and intrepid" manner. He found Cooper courteous to others, quick to adapt himself to their manner or style, and therefore an excellent master of ceremonies for club events, but he recognized that his boldness of thought and statement ("It was a task insurmountable to overcome a *fact* as stated by Mr. Cooper," he added) did not suit everyone.[77] This was certainly not Bryant's style, part of the reason, perhaps, that he viewed the law as a second-best choice for his profession, never thrived in it, and soon abandoned it for literature and journalism.[78]

Surely temperamental differences mattered. To a certain extent, however, disposition recapitulated region. Dr. Francis, referring to New York State rather than just the city, found Cooper "emphatically a New-York man."[79] The particular kind of combative conviviality that Cooper exhibited once he became a center of attention in the city was the epitome of the decidedly non-Yankee culture of what were then still called "the Middle States." The monoculture of Puritan New England had produced a social texture of seemingly uniform surface. It had its complex depths, and a competitiveness that sprang from and to some extent vitiated the conformity of the old theocratic lockstep. The open diversity of New York and the other Middle States, by contrast, had produced a society notable for open and heady public disagreements, conflict, and tolerance if not toleration. Cooper so identified with the Middle States as his own because in part the region was the macrocosm of his own nature.

Cooper's style was that of Dr. Francis as Edgar Allan Poe would describe it in 1839: "He speaks in a loud, clear, hearty tone, dogmatically, with his head thrown back and his chest out; never waits for an introduction to anybody; slaps a perfect stranger on the back and calls him 'Doctor' or 'Learned Theban.'"[80] The expressive play Cooper and Francis observed and indulged in with Charles Mathews on the *Chancellor Livingston* reflected this same racy openness, as indeed did the alacrity with which Cooper took to the idea of the literary career he was now, however haltingly, making for himself.

But Bryant's misreading of Cooper had psychological as well as geocultural facets. Cooper *was* giddy, even by New York standards. He threw himself into the social vortex like a sailor jumping from a sinking ship into the frothy sea. It was sink or swim, and he flailed around somewhat inefficiently at first. Cooper's "great success," as he knew all too well while struggling to bring first *The Spy*, then *The Pioneers*, and now (as we shall see) *The Pilot* to an end, depended on talents he almost *willed* into being—if not into being, then certainly into predictable functionality. But his success, to recast that sea figure, was like a pump operating in a ship with serious breaches in the hull; let that pump falter, and the normally buoyant sea would rush in. We have seen what ills plagued *Precaution* almost from the moment the manuscript left the author's home in the summer of 1820. Cooper's second and third books were more coherent in origin, but his writing of them was seriously delayed and then the production process of each was inconsistently managed. In 1823, his work on *The Pilot* had not progressed as he had hoped or Wiley had expected when he announced in February that it was so far along it ought to appear in March or April (*PIL* CE xxvii). Such delays, insofar as they can be charged to the author personally, were in part the result of his lack of experience. But in a deeper sense they reflected profound concerns Cooper had about his ability to sustain what he wished for not only as a public career but also as a way out of the financial ruin apparently facing him. In the case of each new book, he was afflicted with doubts about whether he could carry to completion what his imagination gave initial impulse to. Strategically and tactically, he was expecting a great deal of himself at a time when he was under enormous stress, however much he might ignore that stress. In his innermost feelings I think he imagined himself as the savior of his family name and fortune. He would redeem his father's lost estate not by speculating in lands (or whaleships) but rather by relying on those wits that, in the social scene of New York, he showed to be so considerable.

But even if he managed these extraordinary efforts well, there were some things that mere will could not accomplish. In the destruction of his Otsego home, and far more in the death of Fenimore soon afterwards, the headlong energies of Cooper's literary and social life in the first half of 1823 hit the immovable wall of the world's opposition to mere desire. Whatever the contributing medical factors, Cooper's collapse soon after Fenimore's painful death, the attack that (as he later put it) "broke me down," gave him a breather—an excuse for delaying labors he could not then reassume—even as it demonstrated his "weakness" without requiring him to utter that word or the worries that made him think it appropriate. Blaming his "nerves," those quasi-material and quasi-spiritual entities to which the nineteenth century often deferred, allowed him to both take and avoid responsibility for the breakdown. He could objectify the inner causation of his ills and thereby, at least to appearances, figure out ways to manage them. But his lingering, recurrent symptoms represented the sense of being out of control that was Cooper's main psychological legacy from this period of intense trial, loss, and self-doubt—as well as astounding literary and commercial success.

CHAPTER THIRTEEN

Old Tales and New

W eaving through the rich, tumultuous, painful experiences that marked Cooper's first year in New York City was the often severed thread of another novel, a sea tale set during the American Revolution. The idea for it had come to him after the American publication of a nautical romance, *The Pirate* (1821), by the still mysterious "author of *Waverley*." Few people accepted the not-yet-vindicated view, shared by Cooper (and indeed by British actor Charles Mathews), that the responsible party was none other than the acclaimed poet Walter Scott.[1] Banker Charles Wilkes, for instance, appears to have known a good deal about the financial situation of the unnamed Scottish novelist, and he enjoyed close business and personal ties to Scott's circle. It is also likely that he counseled Cooper to imitate the Waverley novels as a means of making literature into a paying career. Yet not even Wilkes was convinced by Cooper's arguments that it was Scott who had authored the Waverley novels.

Cooper began *The Pilot* in an indirect effort to prove himself correct on the issue; the book was undertaken, in this sense, as a logical exercise. Over the fall of 1822, while Cooper was visiting at Wilkes's home, the banker used *The Pirate* as a fresh proof of his own doubts.[2] The Waverley novels were remarkable, he thought, for the array of miscellaneous knowledge they displayed. He therefore concluded that their author must be a person of wide experience. The nautical details of *The Pirate* were a case in point. Wilkes held that only a person with direct and extensive maritime exposure could have managed the sea-borne scenes in that novel so successfully. He thought that Scott, a bookish lawyer of confined habits owing to his childhood bout with polio, could not have written *The Pirate* and the other Waverley novels. Cooper rejected both the general point and the use of *The Pirate* as a specific instance of it. He thought that "the author of *Waverley*" was very good at creating detailed impressions while never overwhelming his readers with mere information. It was not a matter of knowledge so much as of strategic illusion—of "*vraisemblance,*" as Cooper termed it when, almost three decades later, he recalled that night's conversation at Wilkes's. Any good novelist had to anchor a work of fiction in the real world, Cooper agreed, but depicting the real world in detail was not the usual task of fiction. As to *The Pirate*, Cooper concluded, its author had very little "seamanship" (*PIL* CE 5, 6).[3]

For ex-midshipman and navy partisan Cooper, it became a matter of pride to show how a real sailor might manage the sea. His daughter thought he had "vaguely sketched" the main outlines of *The Pilot* even as he returned up Manhattan from Wilkes's that night and on arriving home blurted out to his wife, "I must write one more book,—a sea tale,—to show what can be done in that way by a sailor" (*PIL* HE xv). In 1849, Cooper himself concurred with this story in part: his plan to write the book had been a "sudden determination," a completely "unpremeditated decision, purely an impulse" (*PIL* CE 6). Cooper's finances surely dictated that he write *some* other book at this juncture, and, among other vaguely defined options, he may have pondered writing a maritime romance. But there is scant reason to believe that exiled Briton John Paul Jones had been lurking in the back of his mind as the natural hero of some future tale—indeed, in 1822 Jones was an unlikely subject for any American book. Although his place in the Revolutionary pantheon now seems secure, when Cooper began *The Pilot* negative British propaganda portraying Jones as a traitor and a pirate still dominated even the common American view. David Ramsay's nationalistic history of the American Revolution, published in 1789, gave little attention to naval matters and did not even mention Jones. In her 1805 history, Mercy Otis Warren proved more attentive to naval engagements but still gave Jones only a single page. And, although Jones himself showed due care in preserving his papers and produced an extensive *Memoir* of his services, he died in Paris in 1792 before he had a chance to see that work into print. Then when the *Memoir* did appear in 1798, it was in a French translation; the original thereafter was lost and a retranslation of it did not appear in America until 1812, and then only in a Baltimore newspaper (see *PIL* CE xx). Even the best-known exception to the general early dearth of information about Jones, the American sailor Nathaniel Fanning's racy *Narrative of the Adventures of an American Navy Officer* (1806), larded its account of the famous 1779 encounter between the *Bonhomme Richard* and the British warship *Serapis* with broad criticism of Jones's personal character and martial conduct. As a result, Samuel Eliot Morison declared Fanning's book a "source of unpleasant and untrue stories about Paul Jones."[4]

Sea Lore

It has been claimed that Fanning's book, which was designed to appeal to fiery young American sailors like Cooper, may well have been a key source for the novel.[5] Cooper did not mention the *Narrative* in *The Pilot* (or in his naval history or his biographical sketch of Jones), but it is hard to imagine that he had not encountered it while on the *Stirling* or in the navy. In it he would have found an adventure tale penned by someone who definitely understood the sea—and war. Connecticut native Fanning, who died as a fifty-year-old naval lieutenant in 1805, had been serving as a Revolutionary privateersman when he and a number of comrades were taken prisoner during a 1778 encounter with an English frigate. Paraded on deck and roundly denounced as "a set of rebels" destined for the gallows, the captives were stripped of their belongings and thrown into the ship's hold. On reaching Portsmouth, they were confined in the infamous Forton Prison for "piracy and high treason," but a year or so later Fanning was among more than one hundred American prisoners exchanged and sent off to France.[6]

There the privateersman first met Jones, a Scottish sailor of murky past (the deaths of two of his underlings had been charged to him, for instance) who had been taken into the American service at the very start of the war. Ambitious and ruthless, but also skillful and brave, Jones did so well in various American commands that by early 1779, then in France, he was widely regarded as a great naval hero. At the time of Fanning's arrival, Jones had just been given command of a small fleet being readied by the Americans and their French allies. Offered a berth as a midshipman on the flagship, the *Bonhomme Richard*, Fanning very soon afterward served in the maintop in the bloody encounter between that vessel and the *Serapis*.

Fanning was a firsthand witness of that battle, but on much of Jones's varied career he would have offered Cooper little or no insight. Having had a falling out with Jones, he consciously distorted some episodes about which he had direct knowledge and gave fresh circulation to some of the old British lore. As for other relatively recent printed sources, probably the most relevant was Thomas Clark's *Naval History of the United States* (1814), the book Cooper had reviewed for Gardner's *Repository* at the start of 1821. In keeping with the usual terseness visited on Jones at the time, the much briefer first edition of Clark's work, published in 1813, had said very little about him. By the time he prepared the new edition, Clark had come across many more sources, including the Baltimore newspaper version of Jones's own *Memoir*, his main authority for his relatively detailed account of the encounter with the *Serapis*. When he reviewed Clark's book, however, Cooper was so wrapped up in the more recent naval encounters of the War of 1812 that he largely ignored the whole of the Revolutionary era— and Jones with it. We know Cooper read Clark (more than we can say with regard to Fanning), but that is all.[7]

In any event, it was not writings that informed Cooper on Jones but rather oral sources similar to those on which he had relied in writing *The Spy*.[8] The most likely one was retired Cmdre. Richard Dale, who, like Fanning, had served under Jones on the *Bonhomme Richard*. A southerner, Dale had joined the Continental navy just after the Declaration of Independence, only to be taken captive in 1777 and conveyed to Mill Prison in Plymouth, England. Eventually, having somehow secured a British uniform, Dale walked past the sentinels in broad daylight and out the prison gate. Making his way to London, he managed to procure a passport and openly crossed over to L'Orient at just the moment when Jones was readying the *Bonhomme Richard* and his other ships in that French port. Dale was taken on as a master's mate and, soon promoted to lieutenant, was given a key role in Jones's operations. He remained with Jones until Jones returned to the United States in 1781 (*LDANO* 2:244).

Dale, who died in 1825, shared many anecdotes of the early navy with Cooper over the years. He was, in fact, one of the key sources for Cooper's later biographical sketch of Jones—and, of course, for the sketch of Dale himself— as well as for the naval history.[9] Exactly how or when Cooper and he became personally acquainted is unclear. Dale, out of the navy for good in 1802, retired to Philadelphia and therefore was not on the scene in New York, at least not regularly, during any of Cooper's periods there (*LDANO* 2:261–62). Cooper may have met him through an otherwise unnamed officer who had served under Dale in the Mediterranean in 1801 and who "often recounted" to Cooper the story of how Dale's cool habit of command saved the *President* from sinking when that vessel ran aground on leaving Port Mahon (*LDANO* 2:261).[10] Dale certainly was not a reticent man. Even in Fanning's eyes this "good natured sea officer" was a ready conversationalist with all on board ship, a "polite," all-around "good companion."[11]

Cooper found Dale congenial but also incisive in his naval anecdotes. Dismissive of the exaggerated accounts of Jones's naval engagements still in circulation in the 1840s, Cooper asserted in his sketch of Dale that the only ones worth anything were those that "rigidly" conformed to Dale's unassuming, pragmatic vision. Dale's narrative of the "bloody and murderous fight" against the *Serapis* was especially truthful: stripped of "all its romance," the tale emerged with "clear, simple, and intelligible" force (*LDANO* 2:252). It had been an exceptionally close and very bloody fight, even for its age, and that was how Dale narrated it. If Cooper even knew Fanning's narrative, he clearly did not prefer it to Dale's.

That particular incident, to be sure, was not to figure directly in *The Pilot*. Cooper referred to it in his original preface as a topic so well known that it needed no more than a reference, even as he listed several others about which the public knew very little: Jones's "actions with the Milford, and the Solebay; . . . his captures of the Drake and Triumph; and . . . his repeated and desperate projects to carry the war into the 'island home' of our powerful enemy." It was those last-mentioned "projects" that were to provide the main thrust of Cooper's story in *The Pilot*. Steering clear of the victory over the *Serapis* allowed him to write fiction rather than history. He admired Dale's understated, truth-bound manner of narrating naval events, but he still maintained that "the privileges of the Historian and of the writer of Romances are very different, and it behooves them equally to respect each other's rights." If the novelist too closely followed Dale, he might lose his creative headway (*PIL* CE 3–4).

So the novel's debts to Dale were indirect. The wreck of the fictional *Ariel* in *The Pilot* was thus based on the near wreck of Jones's *Ariel* in a storm so fierce that it taught Jones, as the captain admitted, something new about "the awful Majesty" of the sea.[12] Cooper clearly knew about this episode through Dale, who was on the *Ariel* during its first attempt to cross the Atlantic in 1780 as well as on its second, successful attempt the following year. But, the novelist's "privileges" being distinct from those of the historian, Cooper did not simply import Dale's recollections wholesale. Some of the most telling points he actually transferred to other parts of the novel.[13] Others he used to deepen his portrait of Jones in the novel—and in his later biographical sketch. The Atlantic episode was especially rich. Of all his experiences at sea, Dale had told Cooper, the first attempt in the *Ariel* had been the most dire, but it had revealed to him as no other event could "the coolness and seamanship of Jones." On this basis, Cooper concluded in 1843 that Dale's commander "was a quick, ready seaman, never hesitating with doubts or ignorance." In a storm so fierce that the nearby French coast was strewn with wrecks and bodies and the *Ariel* itself was dismasted, Jones put down anchors with such decisive skill that they held the ship for almost sixty hours in "her crazy berth" (Cooper's 1843 phrase) between the Penmarch rocks and the granite of the Breton shore (*LDANO* 2:92–93). When the weather gave way, Jones as decisively jury-rigged the vessel, brought it back to port, saw to its repairs, and, two months later, took it back to sea and crossed to Philadelphia.[14]

Something of this extraordinary seamanship of John Paul Jones is revealed in the dramatic opening episode of the novel, when the fictional *Ariel* and the *Alacrity* encounter a sudden gale after their first arrival on the Northumberland coast. Under the recently picked up "Pilot's" cool direction, the American masters manage to avoid the shoals, clear the "Devil's-Grip," and make the open sea. Here Cooper combined some aspects of the Penmarch tale with another of Dale's stories, a narrative of the abortive 1779 raid on Leith, the port of Edinburgh, just before Jones took the *Serapis*. Fanning's version of the Leith episode emphasized the means by which Jones eventually persuaded the other captains in the flotilla, a pair of uncooperative Frenchmen, to undertake the risky raid. In order to come before the port, where Jones intended to demand a large ransom from the wealthy merchants, his ships would have to pass and repass heavily armed Edinburgh Castle. The skeptics objected so strongly to this danger that he had a tough time convincing them of the strategic value of the whole endeavor. In order to mislead British defenses and buy time, he dressed his officers in nicely counterfeited British naval uniforms. Then, supplying each of his vessels with a pilot seized off local shipping—a dim parallel to the role given Jones himself in Cooper's novel—he took the fleet into the Firth of Forth toward Leith. With northeast winds blowing fair up the passage, according to Fanning, they made good progress until the tide fell, forcing them to await its return. Before then, Fanning continued, the wind came around strong from the southwest, blowing "down the river very fresh." Still short of Leith, Jones was forced to come about and run his squadron out to sea.[15]

Thus far Fanning. Richard Dale, who had been much more actively involved in Jones's extensive preparations for the raid, told Cooper a different, more detailed story, on which both the naval history and the sketches of Jones and of Dale were to rely. The main difference between the two versions has to do with the critical fact of the weather. As Cooper rightly pointed out in his 1840s sketches, Jones had come down the northeast coast of England with the weather "thick, and the wind foul." Then when he eventually went in toward Leith, he did so "with the tide"—but "against a head wind." As the squadron made its slow way up the Firth, Richard Dale, named by Jones to command the boats that would land a party of soldiers and deliver his ultimatum to the Scots merchants, was about to go over the side of the *Bonhomme Richard* when a sudden squall turned the weather even worse and the men were brought back on board to help secure the ship against it. Jones tried to hold on against the wind in hopes of saving the operation, but at last the squall worsened to a severe gale and he was forced to run down the Firth and out into the "German Ocean" (*LDANO* 2:56–58, 245–46).

While neither of these versions of the Leith episode was taken over whole-sale by Cooper for *The Pilot,* there can be little doubt that not only the opening gale but the whole general outline of the novel's action stemmed from this attempted raid by Jones on the British coast. The aborted raid was "safe" for use because it was little known, especially by comparison with Jones's spectacular (although also technically unsuccessful) raids on the west coast of Britain the year before. In 1778, Jones had chosen as his target the stretch of coast between the modest port of Whitehaven on the Cumberland shore, where he had gone aboard his first ship in 1761, and the peninsula known as St. Mary's Isle, which juts into Kirkcudbright Bay some distance west of the spot where he had been born in 1747.[16] The first of these raids, aimed at burning merchant shipping, had only "inconsequential" results among the many vessels there at the time. The second, aimed at forcing an exchange of a high-ranking Briton for American prisoners, fizzled because the intended victim, the earl of Selkirk, was away from his house on the "Isle." There were, though, less tangible results that made both raids resounding coups. Jones's attacks on Great Britain brought him great attention on both sides of the Atlantic then and later because they demonstrated like a sudden revelation that the mother country was not immune to the kinds of assaults the British had visited on America. Jones himself, issuing his call for £50,000 in ransom money from the town of Leith in 1779, had boldly spoken of his contemplated raid as just repayment for the similar attacks already launched on American civilian targets during the Revolution.[17]

This aspect of Jones's raids on Great Britain was of special interest to Cooper. While it is true in a sense that the surface action of *The Pilot* appears to reduce the noble Revolutionary cause to a kind of love plot, as James Grossman long ago claimed, Cooper specifically wanted to draw on the lingering American memories of the coastal devastations caused by British raids during the first—and probably the second—war.[18] This aspect of the plot of Cooper's new Revolutionary romance is hardly different from the basic premise of *The Spy,* in which the Wharton household is the domestic microcosm of the broader political and military world. St. Ruth's Abbey in Northumberland, where the self-exiled American Loyalist George Howard has taken refuge from the war, thus resembles The Locusts. The raid on the abbey by Edward Griffith and Richard Barnstable does bring the military adventure of the book—the male plot, one might say—home to roost in the domestic sphere. But beyond this gendering, or perhaps regendering, of aesthetics, the invasion of the domestic spaces in both books by warfare is true to the Revolution as Americans in Westchester, or Kingston, or Fairfield, or New York City, had experienced it. Loyalist Howard's identification of his Northumbrian domain with the crown, a perpetual theme in *The Pilot,* is the counterpart of this American impression. Cooper strove to portray ideology as inevitably bolstering ordinary affairs and ordinary spaces with the support of externally connected political abstractions.[19]

If in general Cooper was recovering John Paul Jones for his audience in *The Pilot*, he was also responding to ideas already in circulation. In March 1820, the niece of Jones, Janette Taylor of Edinburgh, had written to a friend in New York asking for help in publishing a collection of her uncle's materials. The friend in turn consulted with John Pintard, current recording secretary and treasurer of the New-York Historical Society, who brought the subject up at the monthly meeting of the society in May or June. The issue sparked sufficient interest that a subcommittee was appointed to explore it further. Pintard was joined in the task by two of Cooper's acquaintances. The first was William Leete Stone, a rising star of New York journalism (presently editor of the New York *Commercial Advertiser,* he would buy that paper in 1821) who had lived in Otsego County as a youth and been an apprentice at a newspaper there. The other, more importantly, was Dr. John W. Francis. Stone was well known to Cooper already, and it is entirely plausible that the two old Otsego residents discussed Janette Taylor's project during some encounter in New York. Dr. Francis, not yet Cooper's friend, may well have reinforced the memory when, some years later, they began their frequent association.[20]

The specific channel of Cooper's knowledge about the Taylor archive does not matter. What does matter is that Taylor's initiative suggested the timeliness of Jones as a neglected hero. As Stone indicated in his paper on July 1, 1820, her holdings (and the memoir of her uncle that she had written herself and also wished to publish) promised a much-needed revision of the naval hero's public reputation. As a boy in Otsego, Stone had "read a little six-penny account"— Fanning's?—of the adventures of Jones. He also had listened with rapt attention to the lingering oral tales of the "superior prowess and desperate courage" Jones had displayed "while scouring the coasts of England and Scotland" with his tiny fleet during the Revolution. Stone obviously had become so fascinated by the incomplete presentation of Jones that, years later, he publicized Taylor's efforts at commemorating him in the *Commercial Advertiser* as well as assisting Pintard and Francis in mustering support for her project in New York. Jones was still very much in the shadows, but his niece's treasures might well help spread, in Stone's words, "an accurate and authentic account of the life and exploits of this eccentric and chivalrous officer," a man whom Stone was among the first to call "the father of our naval glory."[21]

When Cooper decided on writing a sea story in 1823, Jones did not just pop into his mind as a likely candidate for its hero. As with so much else in his fiction, the theme came out of contemporary conversations and concerns. While in a sense inventing the genre of the sea novel, in other ways Cooper was writing to order—producing a kind of tale for which there was a ready audience. Even so, once he began the book he did not rush it into print. He had begun to talk about *The Pilot* early enough for Wiley to predict in the middle of February 1823 that it would be published "in March or April."[22] Perhaps he also started writing it right away, but, as usual, things soon slowed down. Sometime toward the end of February, Cooper apparently included news of his plans for the new book (and its title) in an unlocated letter to his sometime whaling partner, Charles T. Dering. Around the middle of March, Dering replied, "I hope in the Pilot you will give a particular account of the naval action and a gale of wind at sea which I should much like to read an accurate description of."[23] Whether Dering was responding to some hints Cooper had given of his intentions for the book is unclear here. The definiteness of the first of Dering's suggestions—"*the* naval action"— may suggest that Cooper had mentioned a plan to include some naval battle in the book, a plan that he carried out in the fifteenth chapter of the second volume. But the bit about "a gale of wind at sea" implies no such divulgence from Cooper. Since the book's "gale," as we have seen, comes quite early in volume one, it is entirely possible that even this late the book was little more than a plan in Cooper's mind. Dering conceivably suggested the very notion of that episode.

From March to around July 1, Cooper busied himself with writing the whole of the first volume. This was set in type, corrected, and deposited for copyright purposes on August 1, just before the death of Cooper's son and his own collapse. According to a fall report in the New York *Spectator*, Cooper had also managed to produce about the first one hundred pages of the second volume at the same time.[24] Then his labors ceased. Cooper himself stated the fact in his September letter to Shubrick: "I have not look'd at it in near two months"— for much of the time, in other words, that he and his family had been at Turtle Bay (*LJ* 1:104). What began this delay is not obvious. Cooper's busyness with the Fort Lafayette dedication, the Hudson trip with Mathews, and then the race at the Union track, certainly cut into any time he had for writing—and probably interrupted his concentration as well. The two moves, from Broadway to Beach Street and then to Turtle Bay, also cannot have helped. Then, too, as he recalled in 1849, almost everyone to whom he mentioned the project once it was under way inveighed against it. The sea "could not be made interesting," one male friend told him: "it was tame, monotonous, and without any other movement than unpleasant storms." His female acquaintances suspected that reading such a book, reeking with "the odour of bilge-water," would make them seasick. Everyone, Cooper felt, was foreseeing "a signal failure." Hence he staggered as he wrote. He even thought, as he put it in 1849, of throwing the thing aside and starting something else. Perhaps he *did* put it aside as he rushed to finish "Imagination" and "Heart" for Wiley (*PIL* CE 6).

But he did not discard *The Pilot* and at better moments kept returning to it. At last, once he had finished the first volume and had the sheets back from the printer—probably before the shift to Turtle Bay—his interest in the project was rallied by encouragement from an unexpected quarter, "an Englishman" of learning and taste who was, however, generally prejudiced against American literature: not only did he steadfastly resist Bryant's "To a Waterfowl"—he tempered his literary approval of "Thanatopsis" with the suspicion that it was probably a plagiarism (doubtless from some English source). This picky reader appears not to have been Charles Wilkes, but rather James Aitchison, Cooper's old friend from Otsego, at this point living in Westchester.[25] Aitchison had happily vetted *Precaution* on stylistic grounds, but neither in that case nor those of *The Spy* and *The Pioneers* had he expressed any enthusiasm for what Cooper had wrought. Cooper therefore submitted the proofs of his fourth novel to the "tender mercies of this one-sided critic" with little expectation that he would have anything good to say about it. He may even have hoped that a forthcoming negative judgment would sink the project once and for all. But Aitchison liked the novel extraordinarily well and "predicted a success for the book," as Cooper modestly put it in 1849, "which it probably never attained" (*PIL* CE 6).

Aitchison certainly was encouraging. So was another trusted friend to whom Cooper turned, probably at an even earlier point in his work on the book, for a more technical response to what he was attempting to do. This was a distant cousin of the novelist then in the navy, Benjamin Cooper, who had briefly served on the *Wasp* after receiving his midshipman's warrant in January 1809.[26] The two kinsmen probably had not known each other well, if at all, before 1810, but thereafter kept in touch. Concerned about how lubbers would react to a tale with so much action on and about ships, Cooper was no less concerned that sailors respect and approve his general effort and his nautical details. As he put it in 1837, he was trying to "avoid technicalities, in order to be poetic," at the same time that his "subject imperiously required a minuteness of detail to render it intelligible." He therefore read to Benjamin Cooper, probably somewhere in New York City, the fifth chapter of the book, the one in which the *Alacrity*, under the guidance of "the Pilot" Jones, worked "off-shore, in a gale." This was the part of the book that would make or break Cooper's claim that he would show the "author of *Waverley*" (and the rest of the world) how a *real* sailor would write about the sea. Ben sat still for the opening but soon jumped up and "paced the room furiously" until Cooper was done. He was rapt by the scene and applauded its technical mastery—with one exception. Cooper had let his "jib stand too long." Ben Cooper meant two things: the novelist's words were a bit windy, but his seamanship was also at fault—the jib on the fictional ship should have been taken in sooner. At the crisis of the action in Chapter 5, as the battered ship seems headed for destruction, the Pilot calls for more sail, and the jib and mainsail are set. The latter proves crucial as the vessel manages to "keep . . . up to the wind." But soon, with a report like a cannon, the jib, "blown from the bolt-ropes," rushes off like a white cloud driven into the leeward gloom. This was a revision caused by Ben Cooper's criticism. The novelist, as he reported in his English travel book, took Ben's advice about the *Alacrity*'s jib and "blew it out of the bolt-rope, in pure spite" (*GE* CE 10).[27]

It was good to have such approval from a member of the family, but family ties did not universally bolster Cooper's will in 1823, an ominous moment in the collapse of Judge Cooper's estate. The machinery of the Chancery Court, set in motion by Ann and George Pomeroy the previous year, was just now inching very close to the remaining assets. On May 1, William H. Averell was due to pay the Pomeroys the amount of their claim against the estate, in exchange for which he would be free to proceed under their decree against any property remaining in the hands of the other heirs. Averell was indeed busy. He also purchased with the aid of the Pomeroys the even larger claim of Rufus King against the estate. Far from trying to cushion the impact of Averell's relentless progress against the other members of Ann's family, the Pomeroys actually helped accelerate the forced sales by identifying Cooper properties suitable for confiscation.[28] On May 12, as a result, much of the property belonging to the heirs of the four dead Cooper brothers was listed for sale early in the summer. At the start of the previous month, attorney Robert Campbell had revealed that rumors once again had led him to expect Cooper to show up in Otsego once the ice went out of the Hudson. Perhaps some such trip had seemed useful to the executor of the Cooper estate months before, but now that the ice was indeed gone he did not undertake it. His strategy again seems to have been to ignore the inevitable sales and apply himself to his new business in order to put his hands on the funds necessary for redeeming any properties he wished to secure.[29]

Neither Cooper nor Campbell knew what was about to come crashing down. Now it was, toward the end of May, that the lawyer wrote again to alert Cooper of the pending sale of the Otsego properties of his brothers' children, adding that they would be stripped of every last acre.[30] Cooper could have rushed north to witness the public spectacle, but to what avail? Besides, the real tragedy wasn't the fact of the sale. It was its manner. Sometime in September, perhaps earlier, Cooper began to pick up troubling hints about the collusion between the Pomeroys and Averell. By October, having decided to seek some accommodation with Averell, he wrote to ask Campbell's advice. The lawyer, pleading complete ignorance of the underhanded behavior of the Pomeroys, thought no such accommodation could be arranged. Although one might have expected Campbell to have gleaned something about the extraordinary agreement between Cooper's sister and Averell, or at least to have jumped into the fray once Cooper informed him of it, he merely replied that Cooper had no bargaining power and that he himself, owing to an old disagreement with Averell, was the last man who could work out any deal on Cooper's behalf. In an effort to excuse his passivity, Campbell assured Cooper that, had he known anything about the Pomeroy-Averell collusion before now he would have appealed the chancery decree of the previous November.[31]

Not all of this hit Cooper at one instant that summer, but whatever he learned then hardly was cheering. And once news of the deal between Averell and the Pomeroys did reach him as fall approached, the astonishing truth of his sister and brother-in-law's behavior hardly speeded his recovery from his recent collapse or increased his literary energy. Indeed, although Cooper's initial delay seems to have begun, as the September letter to Shubrick indicates, in June or July, the bad news that filtered in *after* he wrote Shubrick probably extended it. The New York *Spectator* reported early in October that young Fenimore's sickness and eventual death had interrupted Cooper's literary work in "the early part of the summer," after which the author's own illness confined him to his "room . . . for several weeks." Cooper had been able to think of taking up the book again toward the end of September but had suffered a relapse that sent him back to his bed. Only now, about the time that the news of the Pomeroy-Averell deal was reaching him and forcing him to come up with a possible counter, was Cooper able to resume work on the book, no doubt fitfully. By November 17, another New York paper reported that the convalescent author ("seriously ill for the great part of the last season") at last had resumed his work and that the book now was in press in New York and London.[32]

More distractions arose even as Cooper got back to his writing in earnest. Averell, with much invested in the various claims under the Pomeroy decree but with insufficient returns in hand, was scouring the landscape for anything owned by any of Judge Cooper's heirs. In November, one of his agents, New Yorker Dudley Selden, reported on a recent sheriff's inventory, undertaken at Averell's insistence, of the household goods in the Coopers' lodgings on Beach Street. Selden also had checked on the Westchester real estate owned by the couple. Since Angevine had been reconveyed to Susan's father with the approval of the Chancery Court, and the Hickory Grove was held in trust for Susan (but nonetheless was still heavily mortgaged), the Coopers' real property downstate had little harvestable value for Averell.[33] Nor were their household goods in New York promising. The Coopers had left the bulk of their furnishings at Fenimore when they vacated the property in 1817. Most of these had been forwarded by contractor Robert R. Ward in August or September 1818, just when the couple was finally able to move into the house Ward had erected at Angevine.[34] With the abandonment of Angevine and its legal return to the control of the De-Lanceys, the Coopers probably took some of their essentials with them to New York, but their better pieces may well have been sold off or stored out of the reach of prying hands. For some years, Cooper had been trying to realize returns anywhere he could. Not only had he sold off or otherwise disposed of large real estate holdings; in 1819, he had leased out the farmland at Fenimore, put Mt. Ovis out on shares, sold his "old gig" and various other "small articles about the house at Fenimore," and repeatedly held to an unreasonably high price for a pair of mirrors from Otsego whose gilt frames, as lawyer Robert Campbell observed when asked to sell them, had been "very much soiled by fly stains."[35] Since he had not bought any of his parents' fine furnishings from Otsego Hall on his mother's death in 1817, it is small wonder that the belongings in the Beach Street house failed to impress Selden.[36]

None of this could have made it easier for Cooper to concentrate on the efforts by which he was trying to secure his own fame and his family's fortune. Heroically, he nonetheless managed to recommence *The Pilot* in the fall of 1823 and bring it to an end. The second volume was partly set already. Finally on December 29, with the rest put into type and corrected, Wiley was able to deposit the whole of it for copyright. Shortly later, on January 7, 1824, the book—both of whose volumes bore the previous year's date on their title pages—at last was presented to the world.

Boston

Perhaps the key moment in the reenergizing of Cooper's work on *The Pilot* had been his probably hasty decision to kill off Long Tom Coffin, the demotic character who in this novel inherits the mantle of Harvey Birch and Natty Bumppo. Cooper later expressed some hesitation about the truncation of Long Tom's career. He wished that he had been able to develop his "sketch" of Coffin into a "finished picture" of the sort that he had been able to create for Bumppo (*P&P* 77). In the rush to finish, instead, Coffin had been utterly sunk, lost beyond recovery in the North Sea. Yet his creator went on. With his health still shaky, Cooper no sooner had finished work on his fourth novel in New York sometime in December than he turned to other things. Some were holdovers. Around the eleventh of the month, he addressed the latest of his series of letters to the navy department in his lingering attempt to settle his fourteen-year-old recruiting accounts. The new secretary, Samuel L. Southard, had just taken over the department, giving Cooper one reason for reviving the issue. But there were others. In November, in addition to his other expenses, he at last paid Caty Conklin, whose ten-year indenture had run out three years before, the small sum he owed her as of the expiration of her period of service.[37] That was one practical reminder that what went out of his pocket first had to come in, a principle he had not always honored in the past but one that now, grimly understood, spurred him to resume his attempts to quash the navy's due bill. If he could do that, he would be so much the gainer for his efforts. Uncle Sam would balance out necessarily patient Caty.

Another motive for reviving the navy business was more nearly emotional. Cooper's preface to *The Pilot* had made it clear that the author viewed this book as a contribution to keeping the navy's accomplishments before the public mind. *The Pilot* glorified not just the character of John Paul Jones but the navy at large, and in some illogical way Cooper may have been hoping that the claim against him might therefore be dismissed. That would make his new book pay a dividend, and a handsome one at that. Soon, in a late January 1824 letter to his old shipmate and friend Shubrick, Cooper was sharing news of navy men in New York and issuing grand directions for how the navy would be better handled— "If," he added whimsically, "I were Secratary [*sic*]." Then he conceded, "but I am not Secratary, alas!" (*LJ* 1:111). The negative answer Southard had promptly sent Cooper with regard to his old account already had made that clear.[38]

The letter to Shubrick was brimful of navy talk for two reasons. In the wake of his failure with Southard, Cooper clearly was trying to bolster his status as a navy man in all but the literal sense. He therefore passed on news about comings and goings at the Brooklyn navy yard, as well as a convoluted tale about a recent tiff involving his cousin Benjamin, "John Decatur" (evidently some kinsman of the late Stephen Decatur, perhaps his brother, John Pine Decatur), and a marine second lieutenant named M. M. Little—along with Shubrick's brother Irvine. Decatur had "bullied Ben, who taunted him with very plain language," Cooper reported, with the result that another of the navy's endless duels had seemed in the offing. It had been averted, Cooper concluded, partly by his own intervention with Ben. But the tale was an instance of the novelist's own saber rattling: he could not bend the navy department to his wishes, but his narrative power was able to dispose of such affairs readily (*LJ* 1:109–11).[39]

The unusually thick naval chatter in Cooper's January letter to Shubrick was also spillover from his long-delayed but now just finished visit to his old shipmate in Boston. The trip must have been rich in naval allusions. "Mast[er] Com[mandant]" Shubrick, as the dedication page of *The Pilot* designated him (*PIL* 1:iii), was stationed at this moment at the Charlestown navy yard, where he served as assistant to the commandant, Cmdre. William Bainbridge (see *LJ* 1:69). In that position, Shubrick had virtual run of the place and doubtless toured Cooper around the yard and perhaps, in some small vessel from the yard, about the harbor as well. But, however eager Cooper was to indulge his memories (and probably collect further anecdotes for the future naval history), navy gossip was not the real object of his journey. This was instead a working visit, and—since Cooper was now busy with a new Revolutionary War novel that was to be set in Boston, *Lionel Lincoln*—it had quite other purposes. It also had a fast pace, as Cooper's schedule indicates. Probably he did not leave Susan and the children in New York until some days afte. New Year's, as an earlier departure would have meant missing the couple's wedding anniversary. That would have been an unlikely oversight in any year; in 1824 it was especially so given Cooper's recent ill health and the fact that Susan, pregnant since June, was due to deliver the couple's seventh child early in February. Furthermore, even if Cooper had wanted to leave earlier, he may well have decided to wait until he could pick up a copy of the just-issued *Pilot* for his friend. Shubrick deserved the gift not only for old times' sake (the reason why his "old messmate" had dedicated the book to him [*PIL* CE 1]) but also because Cooper imagined that the two friends would go over the book and scout out further technical revisions for later editions. As with Ben Cooper the year before, this consultation did take place, and it, too, resulted in some refinements.[40]

The Boston visit was timely in that sense, but otherwise had been sorely delayed. Its original purpose was dead now. Shubrick had expected his friend early the previous year, while *The Pilot* was still under way. As early as April 14, 1823, in a letter to Boston writer Richard H. Dana, Sr., Cooper mentioned his plan to visit Shubrick "in the course of the summer" (see *LJ* 1:94). And he wrote Shubrick of the plan shortly thereafter, suggesting that they might commandeer the navy yard schooner and run to Nantucket in search of local color for *The Pilot*. Shubrick was enthusiastic about the trip ("I will go with you to Nantucket with great pleasure," he replied) but was skeptical that he could take "our schooner . . . for *so long* a cruise" without permission from Navy Secretary Smith Thompson, with whom Cooper's also unproductive dialogue about the recruiting business had ended in silence three months earlier. Besides, he added, "the most pleasant way to get on the island will be by way of Falmouth & Martha's Vineyard—I am sure you would be able to collect some interesting matter for the Pilot there & at Cape Cod." In that event, he hoped Cooper would go easier on "the Yankees this time" than he had in *The Pioneers:* "if they have their Doolittles & their Tods [*sic*]," he reminded Cooper, "recollect they have also had a Franklin & a Hancock." Already in Boston for several years, Shubrick had warmed to his new neighbors as Cooper never did.

As it happened, delays piled on delays to make moot Shubrick's hope that the trip might inform (and reform) Cooper. It was put off in part owing to other demands on Shubrick's time. These had little to do with the ordinary business of the yard ("for the Master Commandant of a yard is a sort of spare top mast & has nothing to do except in case of the absence or inactivity of his superior,"

Shubrick explained) than with special circumstances in 1823. The present commander, Capt. Isaac Hull, was expecting to leave his post at the beginning of July so that he could assume command of the *United States*. Because his replacement, who at this point was expected to be Capt. Charles Stewart rather than Bainbridge, probably would not arrive in time to take over then, Shubrick would be very busy for much of the summer. Furthermore, in expectation of being tied up then, Shubrick and his wife were about to leave Boston for a seven-week-long tour to the West. "Spare top mast" as he might usually be, Shubrick therefore would not be able to go anywhere with Cooper for several months. He did not name a time for the visit because he did not know what Cooper's own plans were. All he could do for now, anyway, was indicate that once the new commander came on board he himself would again "be a man of leisure" and could go where Cooper wished whenever he chose to show up.[41]

Shubrick ought to have been free by August or September, but by then other causes of delay—Fenimore's death and Cooper's illness were the chief—put the trip on hold. Besides, although Cooper had dragged his feet on the novel, by early fall he had passed the point where any Nantucket or Cape Cod observations could help him. Mindful of Shubrick's brief on behalf of New Englanders (a brief shared by Dana as well), Cooper defaulted to what he knew of them from Yale and Otsego—and, now, New York City, full of migrating New Englanders like Bryant. And he certainly succeeded in making the two key Yankees in the new book (Coffin and his commander, Richard Barnstable) more positive local types. Their names suggested Nantucket and Cape Cod, respectively, but that was as close to the landscape as Cooper got. Likewise, the whaling episode in Chapter 17 of *The Pilot* owed nothing to Nantucket. It came instead from the tales that Cooper had heard while tending to the *Union*, tales from "East Enders" on Long Island or from the seamen with whom he fraternized while running whale oil to Boston and Newport in earlier years (see *GE* CE 242–43). It also came from Cooper's reading, especially as reflected in his 1821 review of Scoresby.

Only when the awful year of 1823 was at last over, the new book was out, another one was in the works, Cooper's health had moderated, and Shubrick had settled into his new routine, could the novelist at last head east. All those factors were part of the reason why the Boston visit, which would have lasted longer the summer before, was cut short. The previous May, Shubrick had invited Susan to come with her husband so that she could socialize with his own wife (they were not yet personally acquainted) while the two old navy friends were off to Falmouth and the islands. But now a family visit was out of the question. Susan was close to full term in her pregnancy, necessitating both that she remain in New York and that Cooper not tarry in New England. Traveling alone, Cooper evidently went by land (as we know he was to return). The Yankee shipmaster in

Homeward Bound (1838), Capt. John Truck, avers that the overland route through Rhode Island would be the best means of making the trip unless a traveler preferred to "run over Nantucket shoals" and in the process add one hundred miles to the tally (*HB* 1:106). Cooper had done *that* in the *Wasp* under James Lawrence in the spring of 1810, as well as when he took those oil-laden schooners to Boston. Now, perhaps especially because of his still shaky physical condition, he probably went up the post road, through Westchester and then across Connecticut to Massachusetts. We know that he was in Boston by Monday, January 12, when a newspaper there reported that "Mr. Cooper, the author of the '*Spy*,' '*Pioneers*,' &c. is now on a visit to this city."[42]

Shubrick apparently was as free in January as he had hoped to be the previous fall. He willingly extended to Cooper the hospitality of his household, where the novelist must have stayed—for he had "unmercifully" imposed, Cooper later wrote, on Mrs. Shubrick.[43] And Shubrick spent enough time not only at the yard but also in the streets with Cooper for the novelist to make his claim that for once his "lazy" friend had outwalked him (*LJ* 2:17). From Shubrick's lodgings in Charlestown's third parish, it was not far to Breed's Hill or Bunker Hill, key sites for Cooper's new book, which was to center on a young American in the British army, Maj. Lionel Lincoln, who returns to his native Boston just at the time of the skirmishes at Lexington and Concord and then the great Charlestown battle.[44] But the two also went across the Charles River bridge to Boston proper. One afternoon, they were joined by a trio of local residents for a warmly remembered beefsteak, with drinks, at Frederic Rouillard's well-known restaurant in Milk Street.[45] One of the guests was a navy man who must have tagged along with Shubrick. Another was sometime Harvard tutor Willard Phillips, a lawyer then active among the *North American Review* group but soon to be the owner and editor of his own journal. That Phillips was to review *The Pilot* for the April issue of the *North American* suggests that he may have wanted to meet its author and somehow got himself included in the outing. But if Phillips wished to size up Cooper, he apparently did so without letting on about his motives: only in February, via a new letter from Shubrick, did Cooper receive news of the impending review.[46]

The motives of the final member of the party at Rouillard's, the painter and poet Washington Allston, were entirely aboveboard. He and Cooper had never met but were great admirers of each other's work. It was Allston, for instance, who had encouraged his own Boston friend (and, soon, brother-in-law), Richard H. Dana, Sr., to write Cooper a fan letter out of the blue the year before. Dana shared the story with mutual friend Gulian Verplanck: "I was telling Mr. Allston not long ago, how very highly I tho't of the Pioneers. 'Why don't you write Mr. Cooper?' asked he; & said he thought of doing so himself when he read the Spy but was too busy at the time." Dana took the advice, admitting to Cooper the role Allston had played in breaking the ice. In replying to Dana at that time, Cooper in turn sent back his own best wishes for Allston, promising that once he did make it to Boston he would certainly look the painter up (see *LJ* 1:94).[47] So indeed he did. Two years later, still warmly recalling the pleasure of his face-to-face meeting with Allston, Cooper successfully urged the Lunch to elect him an honorary member (see *LJ* 1:141).

The widely traveled Allston must have been a particularly good dinner guest. He had graduated from Harvard in 1800, then spent two fruitful periods in England and on the Continent before returning to Boston for good in 1818. While abroad, he had studied with the great American expatriate Benjamin West and become an intimate not only of Washington Irving, but more importantly of Samuel Taylor Coleridge, of whom he produced a magnificent portrait in 1814 and about whom he must have said something to Cooper in Boston. The two also may have talked of their mutual friend in New York, Gulian Verplanck, who was Allston's indefatigable champion: as late as 1830, then in Congress, Verplanck secured the painter a commission for two of the new monumental canvases meant to join John Trumbull's in the Capitol rotunda.[48] Like many people who met the eccentric but very sociable Allston, Cooper liked the man even more than he liked his art. That was saying something: in 1833, nine years after Allston's dark, romantic painting *Elijah in the Desert* had been bought by a visiting Englishman and sent home, Cooper searched out its owner in Britain and tried to buy it and bring it back to New York with him (see *LJ* 2:397).[49]

Reading the Past

That was one long after-shadow of the Boston trip. In the meantime, its more immediate purposes were also well served. Cooper's prior visits to Boston had acquainted him with the lay of the land. But he was not a free man while there with Lawrence in 1810, and even while taking the whale oil schooners there a decade later he had no programmatic designs on the city. In 1824, by contrast, as he planned his third Revolutionary novel, he was very interested in three things. The first, to which we shall return in greater depth, had to do with the printed and manuscript sources about the first stirrings of the Revolution in the Yankee town. Most of these Cooper could consult in New York after his return; others he could pore over more easily in Boston, perhaps exclusively there, especially at the Athenaeum (founded in 1807 and located in 1823 just off Milk Street) and the Historical Society (1791; then in Charles Bulfinch's Tontine Crescent on Franklin Street, a block to the Athenaeum's south). Among the materials not available elsewhere was the otherwise unidentified "journal of the state of the

weather" that in his 1832 preface of *Lionel Lincoln* Cooper claimed he had consulted and "rigidly respected" in writing the book (*LL* CE 7, 36). While Cooper's preface went on to defend the seeming omnipresence of moonlight in the
book, an effect one early critic had attacked, his source on "weather" cannot
have been simply a contemporary almanac giving phases of the moon in 1775,
although the latter *were* correctly used in the book (that the moon was full during Cooper's 1824 visit was a happy coincidence). The novel carefully re-creates
meteorological conditions from the period: "The winter of 1774–5 had been as
remarkable for its mildness," Cooper wrote in Chapter 6, "as the spring was cold
and lingering." That chapter ends in "driving rain"; the next speaks of the "three
days of fine, balmy, spring weather [that succeeded] to the storm" (*LL* CE 66,
76–77), and so on. Presumably Cooper's source for such minute details was a
manuscript "weather book" of the sort commonly kept during the period. If that
was the case, then it is likely Cooper sought out and found some such source
while on the ground in Boston—perhaps at or through the navy yard (from, for
instance, the harbor master or pilots). Everything else he could have located in
New York, and probably did.

But there were other kinds of things to which Cooper definitely could attend only while in New England. He needed to refresh and deepen his visual
sense of Boston—its topography, its prominent buildings, and its maritime surroundings, all of which were to figure in the carefully detailed narrative of the
British occupation. Scholar Betty Elaine Nichols provided a plausible list of
buildings Cooper must have seen if not toured during his visit. Reviewing them
and their uses in the novel will help reveal both Cooper's itinerary while in Boston and the manner in which he used its topography in imagining the complex
historical action of his new book, in some ways his most ambitious to date.[50]

First were two mansions located side by side off Clark's Square in the city's
North End. The first of these was the Clark-Frankland house (ca. 1711), which
has long been identified in local Boston sources as the basis for the Tremont
Street mansion of young Lincoln's great-aunt, Priscilla Lechmere, with whom
he lodges while in Boston.[51] The second North End structure, the somewhat
older mansion of royal governor Thomas Hutchinson, Cooper used largely as a
sign of the opulent abuses of the old order. Hence the lunatic-rebel Job Pray
(eventually revealed as Lionel's half-brother in Cooper's Gothic plot) mock-
ingly comments on the pretensions of the unpopular Hutchinson's dwelling:
"there's palaces for you! stingy Tommy lived in the one with the pile-axters, and
the flowers hanging to their tops; and . . . crowns on them too!" (*LL* CE 20–21).
Although neither of the local sources mentioning Cooper's visit to the first of
these buildings cites evidence for the assertion, his description of Mrs. Lechmere's house (*LL* CE 30) indeed draws on specific details consistent with the

Clark-Frankland mansion (for instance, the odd fact that the outermost windows on the top two stories of the front were half as wide as the five others in the center of the façade). In the case of the Hutchinson mansion, explicitly referred to by name in the novel, there likewise are the peculiar features more-or-less accurately described by Job Pray: four pilasters running from the foundation to the eaves, with crowns and festoons (Job's "flowers") atop them.[52]

In addition to this pair of famous houses, Betty Elaine Nichols named several public or semipublic buildings that Cooper also likely saw in Boston in 1824 and incorporated in *Lionel Lincoln*. These include the so-called Triangular Warehouse, a commercial structure dating from around 1680 and occupying a three-sided plot of land near the old town dock. Razed in August of 1824 as part of the improvements associated with nearby Faneuil Hall and the new project eventually known as Quincy Market, this decrepit baroque building remained on-site just long enough for Cooper to see it in January and decide to use it as the dwelling for Job Pray's impoverished mother, Abigail, once the mistress of Lionel Lincoln's father. A second, more important public structure incorporated into Cooper's Boston setting was the seventeenth-century Province House, built as a private home but converted after 1716 into the official residence of the colonial governors of Massachusetts. A tall brick structure surmounted by a cupola, the Province House originally stood in a large, tree-covered, gated lot set back from Marlborough (now Washington) Street nearly at the head of Milk Street. In the novel, as Nichols pointed out, Cooper used the building quite properly as a center of British power in 1770s Boston, setting a series of events there to establish his own political stance: a secret nighttime conference among the military leaders just before the march to Lexington and Concord (Chapter 8); the hurried meeting with General Gage when Lincoln seeks permission to take part in what becomes the battle of Bunker Hill (Chapter 15); and especially a banquet, conducted in the midst of the chaos besetting Boston's streets, at which Gage entertains the richly dressed but doomed minions of the king (Chapter 28).

Just *seeing* the old Province House in 1824 cannot have given Cooper all the hints he followed in using the building in his novel. At that time, the structure suffered from two kinds of obscurity. First, although it had been taken over by the Massachusetts government in 1776 and used for various public purposes until the new state house went up on Beacon Hill under Charles Bulfinch's direction in 1796, thereafter the place was a kind of orphan to progress. Initially it was sold to a private citizen, but his default on the contract a few years later sent it back into government hands for another fifteen years. In 1811, having no further use for the Province House, the state turned it over to the newly founded Massachusetts General Hospital as its contribution to a fund-raising drive. For the next six years, the building appears to have sat vacant or been rented out by the hospital, which did not begin active operations until 1817. At that time, the hospital's trustees leased the whole Province House property, including its spacious lot, for ninety-nine years to David Greenough (father of Harvard student and future sculptor Horatio Greenough, later a close Cooper friend). Greenough very soon cut down the trees that had shaded the front lot and proceeded to fill most of the property with houses and shops, leaving the old mansion hidden in their midst. Cut off from Marlborough Street by a row of new structures put up immediately before it, the Province House in 1824 was a fitting emblem of how the rapidly developing present was obscuring the local and indeed national past. In order to even see the old building then, one had to creep through a narrow archway between two of the new buildings in its front. Nathaniel Hawthorne a decade or so later would make this gateway a kind of portal to romance in his "Legends of the Province-House," transporting his narrator by a few steps "from the busy heart of modern Boston, into a small and secluded court-yard" where anecdotes of the Revolutionary and colonial worlds were easily collected.[53] If Cooper saw it in 1824, he doubtless found the same contrasts richly suggestive of how his art might revive and reuse the place.

This is one place where Cooper's previous experience gave some help. His 1810 visit to Boston probably had provided glimpses of various features of the old Boston landscape—for instance, the "swing bridge" over the town dock, which he was to employ in the novel but which, since it had been removed in the intervening years, he could not have seen in 1824.[54] By the same token, the old Province House of 1810 stood forth in something like its "ancient" (but no doubt distressed) presence, surrounded by open space and trees and commanding the entire neighborhood. Cooper's ability to reimagine its role in late colonial Boston in *Lionel Lincoln* may well have derived from that earlier glimpse. Otherwise, unless he looked hard in 1824, he might not even have seen the structure.

Part of Cooper's pleasure in writing the book came from the process of thinking himself backward through the present scene to some older version of the town—and of the country. He did not invent the past out of whole cloth; instead, he used his imagination as a means of carefully reenvisioning its now-obscured features. As he employed the imagination, it was a critical faculty as well as a generative one. Cooper had made similar efforts in *The Spy* and would repeat the exercise in his next book, *The Last of the Mohicans*. But those two novels were set in rural or semiwild areas, where the most important features of the past landscape endured more substantially into the 1820s. In *Lionel Lincoln*, Cooper for the first time chose an urban setting and therefore had to work harder at reimagining its former condition. Much of the book's action involved parallel efforts. In *The Spy* and *The Pilot*, Cooper had introduced "real" characters but had placed them in invented circumstances. In *Lionel Lincoln*, to the contrary, he frontally addressed the most important early episodes of the Revolutionary War. Historian George Bancroft would compliment Cooper—rightly—for his spectacular handling of the battle of Bunker Hill.[55] Cooper's accomplishment in that regard was no mere accident; he labored intensively to master both the scene and the action. One may easily conclude that his mistake in the book did not come from his decision to include such risky actualities—it came, instead, from his failure to give the rest of the story the same compelling historicity as its core, and from the implausible manner in which he resolved the tangled family relations among his characters. Or so critic George Dekker once suggested.[56] But one may also wonder whether the conservative nature of Boston memory during the period, as historian Alfred F. Young has recently described it, did not play some part in the book's lack of success in the town that it seemed especially designed to conquer. The violence of the old Revolutionary mobs had been a difficult subject for the Whig leaders in the 1770s, Young writes, and the revival of Revolutionary memory starting in the 1820s renewed the old concerns. Cooper's fascination with the staunch patriotism of the half-witted Job Pray, and that of old Ralph (who seems utterly rational in his critique of British power but later is revealed to be an escapee from an insane asylum), emphasized too clearly the link between merely personal will and political action. It was, for the Bostonians, too wild—not too tame—a tale.[57]

Be that as it may, in *The Last of the Mohicans* Cooper was to manage things much better. The madness of the action and the narrative voice there have no plausible connection to any present concern that remembering the origins of the nation might stir up old, repressed class antagonisms. The French war, after all, had little political meaning for the present nation. Furthermore, while the Revolution was indeed just being recovered (and fought over) at this time, much less was generally known about the colonial conflict that had preceded it. As a result, not only did Cooper give the massacre of Fort William Henry in 1757 so enduring a literary expression that in the culture at large his novel has *become* the historical episode; he also shaped the whole narrative around that episode, saturating the book with parallel events, themes, and images and subordinating even the family story of the Munro half-sisters and their attempt to be reunited with their father, commander at the fort, to his historical theme.

Understood as part of Cooper's experiment in creating the American historical novel, a key effort of his first decade, *Lionel Lincoln* was therefore critical despite its overall failure. And Cooper's explorations of Boston, which constituted the first deliberate "fieldwork" of his career, were quite important for this larger effort. He traveled methodically. For one thing, although he visited a good many discrete sites, as Nichols indicated, he did not just aggregate them as points on a linear itinerary. He more importantly began to think about how groups of

sites—actual or invented—might be given a complex dimensionality. His tour
of Boston was creative rather than passive, and once back in New York Cooper
began to artfully incorporate into the emerging story what he had seen there.

During his visit, for instance, he probably took in a handful of surviving
public structures, especially Old South Meeting House, King's Chapel, and Faneuil Hall. Particularly interesting was the manner in which, having picked up
the well-known tale about the conversion of Old South into a riding arena for
royal dragoons, Cooper dramatically incorporated it into the book as a potent
symbol of British abuse. Lionel Lincoln is rushing to King's Chapel in Chapter
21 to ready it for his wedding when, with his head shielded from the biting wind
by his cloak, he is mistakenly led by Job Pray to Old South, a block or so away
on Marlborough Street—as Cooper knew from his 1824 visit. Once Lincoln uncovers his head and looks up, the evident contrast in architectural styles between
the two buildings (a nice mark of Cooper's visual grasp of the two structures)
makes the error obvious.[58] As he sets about upbraiding the apologetic simpleton
for this worrisome delay, however, Lincoln is struck by Job's offhand remark that
"what the people built for a temple, the king has turned into a stable!" The British
major is immediately greeted by the "strong smell of horses," and then, throwing open the door to Old South and scanning the devastated interior, he feels
outrage not only at the "abominations of the place" but also at the fact, evident
when he rushes out into Marlborough Street and sees the Province House in its
"silent dignity," that the violation of the sanctuary had occurred "directly under
the windows of the governor." In this triangulation of the three nearby sites—
King's Chapel, Old South, and the Province House—Cooper very creatively
used the town's landscape for his historical and thematic ends (*LL* CE 235–36).[59]

Cooper's use of all these structures in *Lionel Lincoln* prompts a few general
conclusions. First, despite the brevity of his 1824 visit to Boston, it seems likely
that he already had a clear sense of the subject of the novel, whose quasi-archaic
subtitle (*The Leaguer of Boston*) refers to the *beleaguering* or *siege* of the town in
1775. For that purpose, he would need to have a relatively good grasp of the core
of Boston as it existed at that earlier time. As it happens, the seven structures
mentioned above essentially mapped that core area. Indeed, it is reasonable to
conclude that on the day when Cooper was to dine at Rouillard's, he explored
with Shubrick the part of the city that contained the Province House, Old South,
and King's Chapel. The day's explorations probably covered even more ground.
The other four key structures all were clustered around the old town dock and
Clark's Square, not far from Copp's Hill, from whose graveyard-crowned summit Lincoln was to observe the battle of Bunker Hill. It is therefore likely that the
old friends had toured them right after crossing the Charles River Bridge before
passing on to Rouillard's and then the sites near there. When Cooper recalled

how Shubrick outwalked him, he may have been thinking of their probable exploration of Breed's Hill and Bunker Hill in Charlestown at some other time—or of this longer itinerary, with a detour up Copp's Hill to boot (see *LJ* 2:17).[60]

The afternoon excursion from Charlestown through the North End of Boston and then to Milk Street and back supplied Cooper with a clear sense of the itinerary that was to be followed time and time again by the characters in his new novel. His own significant alteration in the town's map—his "transporting" of the Clark-Frankland house from the North End to Tremont Street—made sense, in fact, precisely because it elongated that itinerary and thereby clarified the urban scene imagined in the book. Had Cooper left that mansion in its actual position, the scenes in which Lionel Lincoln and other characters move through the center of the town—past the Province House and the "Funnel," Old South and King's Chapel—on their way from the vicinity of the Triangular Warehouse all the way to Mrs. Lechmere's distant mansion, for instance, would have been many fewer. Placing Lincoln in his great-aunt's relocated house was a strategic move intended to enable and organize a whole series of subordinate events. What Cooper had intuited about the use of space in *The Spy* (or by creating a dialectic between the woods and village in *The Pioneers*) became somewhat more programmatic as, during his research trip to Boston, he grasped the key spatial points that would make this tale very much an urban one. As much as he wished to reimagine the past landscape of the city, he also wanted to put it to plausible use in the invented elements of his plot.

In addition to touring Boston with Cooper, Shubrick arranged for a substitute when his naval responsibilities intervened—his own nephew, South Carolinian Paul Trapier, presently a student at Harvard and soon to be an Episcopal clergyman. Cooper and Trapier got on so well that the novelist apparently borrowed the young guide's name for his own second son, born just days after his return to New York.[61] Although Trapier's studies at Harvard may have helped Cooper gain additional insight into the local historical scene in Boston (on which more in a moment), his personal usefulness for the novelist probably had as much to do with the Revolution at large as with its Boston venues. For one thing, Trapier's grandfather had served under the legendary Gen. Francis Marion, about whom wildly inaccurate stories were rife by the 1820s. Anything Trapier could share on that subject would have been eagerly snatched up by the novelist. More pertinent still may have been the Harvard student's close personal connection to another Revolutionary figure, Maj. Alexander Garden, who had been aide-de-camp for the great Quaker general, Nathanael Greene, during the final months of the war in the South.[62] Trapier had grown up next door to Major Garden, who took such paternal interest in the expectant Harvard freshman that he chaperoned him all the way to New York in 1822. Garden's own usefulness as a source on the Revolution was literary more than personal. He had achieved no great fame as a fighter, but ever since then he had been gathering stories about the war and in 1822 had issued the first of two collections of *Anecdotes of the Revolutionary War in America.* More to the point, Garden's history reiterated a pattern Cooper knew well, a pattern his present project would explore further. The son of a prominent southern Loyalist, Garden had been educated in England but had come back to fight for the American cause. While there is no easy fit between the Garden saga and that of the Lincoln family in *Lionel Lincoln,* Cooper's gloomy tale of family strife and political doubt laid over the turmoil of the Revolution may have owed something to Trapier's Carolina lore. It is even possible that Cooper's sketch of the eccentric southerner Charles Lee in Chapter 30 of the novel derived from anecdotes passed through Trapier from Garden, who knew Lee and described him in similar fashion in his *Anecdotes.*[63]

The riches Trapier offered were important, but the young collegian also guided Cooper *somewhere* during the Boston visit—although where, exactly, is unclear. In 1845, Trapier simply recalled that they had gone "together over the fields, which the 'leaguer of Boston' was soon to invest with fresh interest."[64] The term "fields" may well point toward the wider landscapes beyond Boston, on which Cooper also drew in the novel—specifically, the route of the British sortie in April 1775 from the Cambridge shore out to Lexington and Concord. Perhaps, if the roads permitted, the two tourists used Shubrick's "horse and *chay,*" which Cooper had promised to put to "pretty severe" use when he was making his initial plans for the Boston trip (*LJ* 1:104).

But any visit to Lexington and Concord must have been hasty. Certainly the novel is much less exacting in its deployment of village and countryside than of the city. Here is its description of the British approach to Lexington: "The road now led into a vale, and at some distance a small hamlet of houses was dimly seen through the morning haze, clustered around one of the humble, but decent temples, so common in Massachusetts" (*LL* CE 103). This is generic rather than particular. As in Cooper's later treatment of the British advance on Concord, various things are lacking that one might expect had Cooper carefully traced the route himself in 1824. There is little sense of actual topography ("a vale" and "at some distance" do not suggest an eye recently attentive to the actual nuances of the land), and the distances between stopping points in the narrative are not well defined.[65]

The same impression is conveyed by the generality of the book's description of Concord and the country through which the British moved in retreating from it. Here is a sample of how Lionel Lincoln sees that country: "On either side of the highway, along the skirts of every wood or orchard, in the open

fields, and from every house, barn, or cover in sight, the flash of fire-arms was
to be seen, while the shouts of the English grew, at each instant, feebler and less
inspiriting. Heavy clouds of smoke rose above the valley, into which he looked,
and mingled with the dust of the march, drawing an impenetrable veil before the
view; but as the wind, at moments, shoved it aside, he caught glimpses of the
worried and faltering platoons of the party" (*LL* CE 115). As with the Lexington passage, things are disposed about the scene to verbal rather than genuinely
tactical effect: "either side," "every wood or orchard," "every house, barn, or
cover," "each instant," all suggest a mind at work stipulating a reality rather than
recalling it. Indeed, this passage might have been derived exclusively from the
well-known contemporary report sent to the earl of Dartmouth by Gen.
Thomas Gage (who had not been present), which describes the retreat of the
British forces through "a continual Skirmish for the Space of Fifteen Miles,"
during which they received "Fire from every Hill, Fence, House, Barn, &ca."[66]
Furthermore, there seem to be outright errors: for the "vale" of the earlier passage, there is here a "valley," although the road followed by the British forces,
while indeed enclosed on either side by hills, was relatively flat through much of
this distance.

Perhaps the most telling effect in both scenes, however, is the way in which
Cooper's descriptive anxiety is itself veiled by the "morning haze" and the
"clouds of smoke": his failure to see or imagine things clearly and crisply is, in
other words, deflected onto the landscape. When one contrasts the vagueness
of the Lexington and Concord section of the novel with the particularity with
which the Boston locales of the book are presented, it becomes evident that the
recent and close investigations on which Cooper drew with regard to the latter
had scant parallel in the case of the former. Just before he is whisked off to
Cambridge at the start of the April expedition, Lionel Lincoln thus climbs to
the top of Beacon Hill, where he stands "on the margin of the little platform of
earth that had been formed by leveling the apex of the natural cone" (*LL* CE
96). In an earlier ascent of the hill, Lincoln encounters the old "Beacon" that
gave it its name, a "tall post" supporting a "grate" in which combustible materials could be set afire to alarm the populace (*LL* CE 43). In the former instance, the landscape is enveloped in mist, but Cooper nonetheless orients the
scene by using landmarks true to the period: "nothing but fog—nay, I see *there*
is a steeple, and *yonder* is the smoking sea, and *here* are the chimneys of Hancock's house beneath us, smoking too, as if their rebellious master were at
home, and preparing his feed" (*LL* CE 47). *There* was the evidence that *Lionel Lincoln* had benefited from its author's investigations of the new book's
"scenery."[67]

Return

However extensive Cooper might have wished his explorations of Boston to be, he had to leave and return to New York within a few days. Around January 16 or so, he headed off overland to Providence, where he spent part of three days (one of them a Sunday, probably January 18) visiting with two old friends, navy lieutenant Henry Stearns Newcomb and lawyer John Whipple. Newcomb, who was to drown the next year and whom Cooper later remembered as "a very excellent young officer" (*NH* 2:309), had received his midshipman's warrant at the start of 1809 and must have been in New York during the time Cooper and Shubrick served there on the *Wasp*. He was promoted to lieutenant during the second war with Britain, serving under Cmdre. John Rodgers on the *President*. Later, in 1814, he was one of Rodgers's aides (along with Cooper's old friend from Oswego, Thomas Gamble), as the commodore awkwardly scurried about on land in a desperate effort to protect Baltimore from the British invasion force in 1814.[68] Landsman Whipple, born in 1784 and educated at Brown, made his living representing New England cotton manufacturers, hardly a core maritime business, but he had his own nautical connections. He was the descendent of two Yankee skippers, both known as Capt. John Whipple, and had an even more famous kinsman—Cmdre. Abraham Whipple, the leader of the attack on the British schooner *Gaspee* in 1772 and "one of the most able captains to serve in the Continental navy."[69]

The three men therefore had salt-sea things to say as they gathered at Whipple's house Sunday night. A "*good time* we had of it," Cooper confided to Shubrick on his return to Manhattan, partly because of some "old *Blaze-Castle*" Madeira they shared, partly because of "certain legends of captures in the Revolution, and perils by land and perils by water" that Whipple and Newcomb dispensed as the three gathered about the bottle. Newcomb, with his "man-of-war noodle," was skeptical about the quality of Whipple's wine for a time, but once he saw Cooper down six glasses in succession he joined in with gusto. It was all like a scene in *The Pilot* between the American marine, Lieutenant Manual, and the British veteran, Captain Burroughcliffe, who incessantly banter about "southside Madeira." Whipple's stuff was so good that the sherry Cooper had imbibed at Shubrick's "was dish-water to it"—"Ay, I repeat it to your face," Cooper taunted his Boston friend, "*cold* dish-water to it!" Cooper felt he could write "two volumes duodecimo" on the theme of sherry, but—fortunately for *Lionel Lincoln* (and Charles Wiley)—he left it at that (*LJ* 1:109, 112; 3:29–30). Perhaps this drinking bout and the one at Rouillard's in Boston with Shubrick gave rise to the Yankee rumor voiced by Eliza Lee Cabot in a letter to her close friend Catharine Maria Sedgwick the following March: "I hear Cooper gets tipsey is it true?"[70]

Cooper dined again the next day with Newcomb and Newcomb's "very sensible, clever" wife (*LJ* 1:109), then had to leave, probably by stagecoach: presumably it was his own experience that supplied the character of Captain Truck, in *Homeward Bound*, with an anecdote about the time he ran down from Providence to New London in a four-horse stage that tore up the newly opened road on part of the route.[71] In Cooper's case, smooth roads and tolerable weather made his return to "good, great, magnanimous" New York relatively uneventful. Presumably he passed through New London and New Haven, with memories welling up from his carefree days at Yale—carefree till that final spring now nineteen years before. But he could not stop, however much his thoughts lingered. He passed on into Westchester, where Heathcote Hill was as visible now as Caleb Heathcote's original house there had been to Madam Sarah Kemble Knight when, bound for New York in 1704 along this route, she commented on its "very fine" location and look.[72] He probably was home by January 21, a Wednesday, feeling "hearty and hungry"—though soon enough he found himself, as he explained to Shubrick, "*stuff'd up* with a cold." Apparently this illness had nothing to do with his breakdown the summer before or its recurrence in the fall, but it was enough to put him off his regular diet of writing for a time. It was almost a week before he was able to pen his chatty letter to Shubrick, and as for taking up his new book, the means by which he was now paying for trips to Boston and bottles of Madeira and everything else, his own epithet for professional writing ("that dirty employment") suggests something about his recent cold, but probably more about his general outlook at this time. He had had his fling and now, back in the traces, he had much heavy pulling to do. Perhaps it was made a bit more onerous by the knowledge that Susan, like Mrs. Shubrick (so Cooper's "old messmate" informed him only half-jokingly in February), did not "approve of 'tavern dinners' or any such *old bachelor habits*."[73] Thirteen years out of his bachelorhood now, with an attentive but reasonably demanding (and very pregnant) wife, and four daughters ranging in age from ten to four, Cooper had other things to attend to without delay (*LJ* 1:109).

Legends

O n his return to Beach Street late in January 1824, Cooper encountered
two pressing demands on his attention. Both were good. Sales of *The
Pilot* had been so brisk, he learned shortly after his homecoming, that
Wiley already had a team of five printers rushing a second edition, which was to
appear on February 11. Presumably Cooper had worked through the book during his absence in order to finish his revisions, relying in part on Shubrick's expert nautical advice.[1] Once his marked-up copy or list of changes had been
handed to Wiley and parceled out to the printers, Cooper could settle down at
home. There he nursed his head cold, began but abandoned a long letter to his
Boston host, and, with Susan now near the end of her pregnancy, most of all
awaited the birth of their "fine boy"—the second bit of good news—on the
night of February 4. Once he was sure that mother and baby were both doing
well, Cooper remembered the still unfinished letter to Shubrick and, eager to
share word of the event, added a brief postscript to it, then on the following
Monday at last mailed it off (*LJ* 1:109–13).[2]

Although, with that done, Cooper could turn his attention to *Lionel Lincoln*,
he probably did not begin writing right away. His time in Boston had helped him

establish the spatial axis of the new novel's urban action and settle some details, but its complex historical plot still called for more background reading. So did Cooper's larger plans. From very early on, he had envisioned *Lionel Lincoln* as the first of a series of "Legends of the Thirteen Republics."[3] Since each of the books in this ambitious series presumably would deal with a single critical event, running through the war from Concord and Lexington to Yorktown, Cooper would need to have a fresh, expansive sense of the whole Revolution as he pressed ahead. His reading for *Lionel Lincoln* thus would be of strategic as well as tactical use. While he depended on particular Bunker Hill sources such as participant Henry Dearborn's *Account of the Battle of Bunker Hill* and historian Samuel Swett's *Historical and Topographical Sketch of Bunker Hill Battle*, both published in 1818, he also derived details from more general publications. Among the latter, the most important appears to have been James Thacher's *A Military Journal during the American Revolutionary War, from 1775 to 1783* (1823).[4]

The use of these and other sources for *Lionel Lincoln* has been discussed in some detail both by Betty Elaine Nichols and the editors of the Cooper Edition text. It is clear, as Nichols stressed, that Swett's *Sketch* provided Cooper not only with general guidance as to the sequence of events and the participants on both sides but also with telling details. Thus Cooper follows the precise order of Swett's list of the chief British officers in Boston in his own catalog of those "proud and boasted names" (*LL* CE 157). Even more conclusive is a footnote in which Cooper, copying a similar note in Swett, explains the origin of the mascot of the Welsh Fusiliers, a goat with gilded horns (see *LL* CE 200).[5] In his narrative of the battle proper, however, Cooper abandoned Swett's, which was based on American sources, for that of a British participant. The use of Copp's Hill as a vantage point in the novel conclusively marks his debt to the brief letter sent by Gen. John Burgoyne to his nephew, Lord Stanley, shortly after the battle and soon published.[6]

It is likely that Cooper began writing as he continued to work over such sources. As early as March, the press in Boston and Philadelphia was indicating that *Lionel Lincoln* had been "lately commenced," and the New York *Statesman and Evening Advocate* even described it as "in a state of considerable forwardness." In May, word that the book would appear sometime in the summer was widely circulating (see *LL* CE xxi).[7] At this time, Cooper was forging ahead with his arrangements for it. On April 29, 1824, he thus signed an initial contract with Wiley for *Lionel Lincoln*, providing for a first edition of six thousand copies that Wiley was "now printing"—in this case as in earlier ones, type was set as Cooper wrote (see *LL* CE 7). The publication was to be "solely for the benefit and at the risque of the said James Cooper." Wiley was again to be his agent, arranging for the printing (by Daniel Fanshaw, Edwin B. Clayton's former partner and a specialist in devotional works), wholesaling bundles of copies to dealers in New York or elsewhere for a 5 percent commission and retailing the book through his own shop for a reduced margin of 30 as opposed to 33⅓ percent. After deducting the expenses of "printing—paper—& the binding of said work" (and any other "legal charges") from the "notes and securities" received from dealers for their supplies of *Lionel Lincoln,* Wiley was required by the contract to convey the balance to Cooper.[8] The day after he and Wiley signed this agreement, April 30, Cooper wrote English publisher John Miller that he expected the new novel to be finished by the middle of September. Miller accordingly advertised the book in July (see *LL* CE xxi–xxii).

Within a day or two of signing the Wiley contract and writing Miller, Cooper and his family, having had their fill of kinsman Henry Floyd Jones's ratty house on Beach Street, shifted to their third New York rental. Located at 345 Greenwich Street, on the lower West Side between Jay and Harrison, this was to be their final address in the city before the European trip (SFM 54). Such a shift need not have caused serious slowdowns in Cooper's work. Soon, though, with the arrival of summer (and potentially the yellow fever), the family again sought cooler and safer quarters on the city's outskirts. This time they went even farther away, up the East River past Hell Gate to Bayside, along Little Neck Bay on the far east side of the town of Flushing, Queens.[9] How the Coopers found the farmhouse they rented is not known. The brother of Eliza Dering, Susan's cousin, had a place in Flushing, but Cooper himself knew at least one Bayside resident, a boardinghouse owner named John L. Franklin, well enough to loan him books and agree to sell him a wagon early in his family's stay there, suggesting another possible link.[10]

Once established at Bayside, Cooper was again free to write. His distance from the city, however, must have made it difficult to deal with Wiley or even supply him with fresh copy for the printers, unless some reliable go-between was found. That may have been part of the reason why, by the third week of July, Cooper took a break and left Flushing for a time. That Wiley was to order more paper in August suggests that a new batch of manuscript arrived in his shop during Cooper's visit, and was soon dispatched to Fanshaw.[11] Probably Cooper stayed for a time in the City Hotel to make focused progress on his book, away from his family and the diversions of Bayside. Yet he hardly was a hermit while in the city. In quick succession, a series of fresh demands arose. On July 24, he received and promptly accepted an invitation for a naval dinner to be given in his honor at the City Hotel five days later. The organizing committee included two good friends, lieutenants Mathew C. Perry and William Laughton, the latter of whom had served on the *Wasp* with Cooper and Shubrick. Their invitation offered tribute not only to Cooper's time in the service but also to his literary fame, and it conveyed far-from-formulaic "best wishes" for Cooper's health. His shaky condition was also the subject of a toast during the dinner proper. In acknowledging the latter, Cooper, still looking thin and wan enough to surprise anyone who had not seen him in a year, made what one newspaper called "a neat and feeling address." To Perry and Laughton he had already written that "in attachment to the service," he would "yield to no man in the nation." On the twenty-ninth his toast reiterated his feelings: "*The Navy.*—May it prevail over the mistaken prejudices of its domestic, as triumphantly as it has humbled it foreign enemies."[12]

The naval dinner was one sign of the success of *The Pilot.* Another, less formal one emerged at about the same time. At some earlier point in the summer, New York auctioneer and broker George A. Ward, who had read and enjoyed Cooper's latest book, was walking down a Manhattan street when his eye was snagged by the signature of John Paul Jones written across an old document stuffed with other waste paper in a bakeshop window. Attuned to the significance of the much-slandered Jones by *The Pilot,* Ward went inside and made inquiries. It turned out that some seven hundred Revolutionary War manuscripts by Jones and others, including John Hancock, Benjamin Franklin, John Adams, and Lafayette, had wound up there following the death of lawyer Robert Hyslop, who had served as Jones's American executor. The bakeshop, which at one time had belonged to Hyslop's cousin, had since changed hands, and the present owner was using the unexamined treasure trove for wrapping paper: if it were not for Ward (and, indirectly, Cooper), items such as Jones's seventeen-page letter to Benjamin Franklin detailing the defeat of the *Serapis,* one of the things in Hyslop's collection, might have gone out of the obscure shop enfolding a clutch of penny loaves (see *PIL* CE xli–xlii).[13]

The sharp-eyed auctioneer soon contacted Cooper, whom he may already have known, and arranged a meeting. As enthusiastic about the find as Ward, who probably showed him samples right then, Cooper nonetheless had understandable doubts about the archive's authenticity. These were allayed when Ward, contacting him again just before the naval dinner, happily reported that he had traced the chain of possession back to Jones himself. Having counted and organized the hundreds of items, Ward sent Cooper all of those in Jones's hand, along with the most important private and official letters addressed to him. Who better than Cooper to read them? Surely he would share Ward's conclusion that the documents revealed "purer principles of action" than those usually attributed to the naval patriot. Now all that was necessary was to give the doubting public full access to the documents, a goal for which Ward sought Cooper's aid: "I trust, Dear Sir, that these papers will satisfy you that the fame of a hero and patriot needs but the sanction of your name to be rescued from calumny." Soon the New York *Evening Post,* in a detailed and generally accurate story, indicated that Cooper was expected to encourage Charles Wiley to publish them.[14]

Another news account from early August confirms Wiley's role in the effort, but Wiley, burdened with financial ills, probably could not have undertaken the venture himself even if he wanted to.[15] Cooper, well aware of Wiley's embarrassments, appears to have sent the project in a more promising direction almost immediately. The new target was John H. Sherburne, recently appointed as the U.S. Navy's "register"—that is, registrar—a man very well suited to the task. Son of a New Hampshire politician and judge (who had lost a leg during Revolutionary service), the thirty-one-year-old Sherburne had various naval ties, including a brother in the service before 1813, as well as a son who would become a midshipman in 1829 and die as a lieutenant two decades later. He also had strong literary ambitions.[16] Even before auctioneer Ward's chance discovery, moreover, Sherburne had exhibited considerable interest in Jones. According to poet Robert Sands in his 1830 biography of the naval hero, Sherburne had caught wind of Janette Taylor's archive in 1820 and had attempted to tap it for a book about her uncle. His negotiations with Taylor failed, but they evidently left a trace in the memory of some of Cooper's New York colleagues, who probably directed the novelist to Sherburne in 1824.[17] Within months, the navy's registrar published his *Life and Character of the Chevalier John Paul Jones,* printing in it many items from the bakeshop archive.

"Glenn's" and "The Horican"

Even before Cooper had a chance to closely examine the Jones materials in July of 1824, a new distraction arose. On the twenty-first, a quartet of young Englishmen had arrived from Liverpool who very much wanted to meet the author of *The Spy* and *The Pioneers.* Edward Smith-Stanley, the most prominent member of the group (he later became the fourteenth earl of Derby and would serve three terms as British prime minister), was an avid reader quite familiar with American books, especially those of Cooper and his fellow New Yorker Washington Irving.[18] In all likelihood, Irving, who during his long English sojourn became an acquaintance and great favorite of Smith-Stanley's grandfather, had furnished the travelers with a letter of introduction to Cooper. By luck, both the Britons and Cooper must have arrived at the City Hotel at almost the same moment, met and exchanged pleasantries, and soon began discussing the possibility of a tour.[19]

Within a week, shunning their hot quarters at the hotel, Smith-Stanley and his friends boarded the steamboat *James Kent* and headed up the Hudson on their own. But Cooper (and Irving) were with them in spirit. They thus got off at

Catskill and scrambled up into the mist-shrouded mountains behind the village in search of the scene of Van Winkle's "adventures." No sooner had they returned to the newly opened Catskill Mountain House at Pine Orchard than they went off on another literary jaunt—this time through the woods "about three miles to the falls, which are described by Leather stockings [*sic*] in the Pioneers."[20] Irving's effect on the Britons was the product of the immense vogue of *The Sketch Book,* which had helped initiate fashionable touring in the Catskills. The first of their two pilgrimages in the mountains was therefore rather predictable in 1824. The second of them, however, was a remarkably early instance of the touristic influence of Cooper's third book. It will be recalled that *The Pioneers* merely glimpsed "back" at the Pine Orchard site from the depths of Otsego. That Smith-Stanley knew enough to make the link and search out the "Leap" suggests how informed his reading of Cooper had been.

Informed—but also, in all probability, coached. That naval dinner would keep Cooper in New York through the morning of July 30, by which point Smith-Stanley and company were already at the Mountain House, but in addition to arranging to catch up with them in several days he seems to have outlined the early stages of their Hudson voyage.[21] Certainly, aside from the Catskills, the travelers saw precisely the sites Cooper had shown Charles Mathews the year before. Duly schooled on the importance of West Point ("the scene among many other interesting events, of the communications between the Traitor Arnold, and the lamented & accomplished Major André," as Smith-Stanley put it, with an American twist, in his journal), they tarried two days there before heading upriver.[22] With their Catskill pilgrimages behind them, they went on to Albany, where, three of them already being members of the House of Commons, they took in the flurry of the current legislative session—and, one assumes, climbed to the top of the capitol to indulge in the classic view Cooper doubtless had mentioned to them. Even more to the point was their side trip to the Cohoes Falls under the guidance of one of Cooper's boyhood friends, Steven Van Rensselaer IV, son of the Patroon, who must have been Cooper's official substitute on this leg of the trip.[23] When Cooper at last caught up with them, probably at Saratoga Springs around the second or third of August, he could easily compare notes on the various sites the Britons had been urged to visit.

Thereafter he also could serve as their guide. This role was, however, a bit odd; in 1824 Cooper personally knew very little of the landscape that lay ahead. So far, for instance, his illness had not taken him to Saratoga or nearby Ballston Spa. And the sites farther north—Glens Falls, Lake George, Lake Champlain— were, despite his frequent trips to the St. Lawrence region, completely out of his ken. The itinerary took the shape it did, in large part, precisely because these were parts of his home state that Cooper himself wished to see. Saratoga he seems to have intended visiting even before Smith-Stanley's party arrived at the City Hotel: thus his friend Shubrick had heard some time earlier that the novelist was going to be "absent on a tour to the Springs" over the summer, doubtless in another effort to bolster his health.[24] Similarly, the other sites seem to have been earmarked because Cooper's researches for *Lionel Lincoln* had inadvertently piqued his curiosity about the deeper history of the region beyond Saratoga, setting the preliminary groundwork for yet another novel.

The first stop as the group headed north was a bustling industrial village named Glens Falls athwart a precipitous bend of the Hudson in the town of Queensbury. The Hudson at this point dropped close to forty feet over rocky shelves that, jagged at their downstream edges, split its flow and set the water ceaselessly churning. Below the drop, a towering rocky island, much worn by the roiling waters, dramatically rose up and cut the stream in two. The terrain at "Glenn's" (as Cooper's sixth novel would call the place) was treacherous—so difficult that one early Indian name for the spot reportedly was *Che-pon-tuc*, signifying "a difficult place to climb or get around." But the difficulty had distinct economic value. Although most travelers in Cooper's day were intrigued by the display of natural force along this stretch of the river, even the most romantic of them (such as historian Francis Parkman, who in 1842 lamented "the way in which the New Yorkers have be-devilled Glens") hardly could avoid seeing and commenting on the many dams and mills clustered along the river here. Some had been erected in pre-Revolutionary days, but development of the site dated in particular from its acquisition in 1788 by Col. John Glen of Schenectady. Soon the whole landscape was encumbered with tottering structures, including a mill located in the midst of the stream atop the big island. In his mid-1830s view of the "Bridge at Glens Fall," English topographical artist William H. Bartlett caught the frozen energy of the whole scene: with the mill seemingly stranded on a towering flood of water, a pair of tiny, contemplative tourists stand awestruck under the jury-rigged bridge leading across the chasm directly over the falls, its piers anchored on the rock (Plate 17).[25]

The falls at "Glenn's" were hardly the equal of Niagara in height or overall effect, but, as tour guide author Henry D. Gilpin would write the year after Cooper's visit, they were "so diversified, and so rudely wild, as to occasion the most awful and sublime sensations." Largely concealed by the roadway and the bridge until a traveler was partway over, the falls were also a refreshing sight after the "dreary barren" of the route thither.[26] Smith-Stanley reported on the singular character of the scene. The dark bare rock of the river bed, "worn & broken into different channels," forced the water "down a number of very deep & narrow clefts," tumbling it into an array of broken, mist-shrouded strands that rejoined only in the flatter, calmer area below the falls, where the narrowed

Hudson snaked off in a series of quick turns. For Smith-Stanley as for other observers, it was as if the river, thrown into complete confusion by the fractured rock cliffs, lost its identity for a time. Only if one looked downstream, past the immediate chaos over which one hovered on the bridge, could one begin to recover the image of the unified Hudson again running off to the sea.[27]

The Britons' guide, who surely had heard of the spot long before visiting it with them, was equally impressed by this glimpse down into the fierce energies of nature. According to Smith-Stanley, Cooper was so struck with the scenery that he exclaimed, "I must place one of my old Indians here."[28] As any reader of *The Last of the Mohicans* recalls, it was not just some distant view of the riverscape that captured Cooper's interest. Concern for his still precarious health might well have kept him in the carriage the five men shared or on the deck of the bridge, but with Smith-Stanley and the other young travelers Cooper insisted on scurrying down off the bridge where it crossed the mill-capped island to explore the massive fragment of black rock in the water's midst, much like the tiny figures in Bartlett's drawing. Such a descent placed the travelers in the midst of the roaring waters, with spray swirling over them. It also gave them a chance to examine the pocked and fluted rock and allowed access to the caverns on the island—Cooper's Cave, the smaller one would be called before long—worn into the rock by the ever-active Hudson. In 1826, Cooper asked publisher John Miller to have a set of the English edition of *The Last of the Mohicans* "neatly bound" and sent to Smith-Stanley, adding that he and the nobleman had been together "in the caverns at Glens falls [*sic*], and it was there that I determined to write the book, promising him a Copy" (*LJ* 1:128).[29]

Cooper and Smith-Stanley hardly discovered those caverns, which were well enough known to the local inhabitants and tourists that even the guidebooks of the period described the many inscriptions scratched into the soft rock by those who explored them.[30] But their imaginative response to the site clearly was powerful enough that *The Last of the Mohicans* transformed the physical site into a cultural icon. According to Cooper's daughter, the transformation began even as he lingered on the spot: he examined the falls closely, she asserted, "with a view to accurate description at a later hour." The particularity of the setting as the novel employs it, along with the fact that this was Cooper's first and only visit to the falls before writing the book (unless he and the Britons tarried again on their way back south in a few days), makes it quite likely that he indeed did take the time to impress the scene very deeply on his mind during his 1824 visit. And Susan's further assertion—that her father already envisioned specific details of the new book's action while at the falls—may also be plausible. However, his daughter was wrong in asserting that Cooper rushed into the writing of the book as soon as he got home again. Work on his sixth tale still lay almost a year in the future. Whatever he saw or imagined in 1824 remained lodged in his mind until he was free to turn to it in earnest. That in itself is probably better proof of how much the spot had affected him (*P&P* 126).

From Glens Falls the travelers passed to the southern tip of Lake George, some nine miles farther north. This "beautiful sheet of clear water," as Spafford's 1824 *Gazetteer* described it, was already widely celebrated as yet another stopping point on the emergent "Northern tour."[31] Although for Cooper its long narrow shape and precipitous surroundings doubtless recalled Otsego, Lake George was bigger and more impressive than his boyhood lake in every way (Plate 18). In place of the Vision and the other rounded hills shouldering Otsego, on either side of Lake George, high, rough mountain ridges sprang up. And the "Lac du Saint Sacrement" (as the French Jesuit missionary Isaac Jogues had called it after his first visit there on Corpus Christi eve in 1646)—or "Horican," as Cooper was to christen it in his sixth novel (see *LOM* CE 8; *LJ* 4:482–83)—was of a scale suitable to its site: two miles broad, it snaked northeastward for more than thirty miles amid a rich collection of bright green isles, at last pouring itself through a steep narrow defile into the even grander body of Lake Champlain.[32]

Otsego was home for Cooper, domestic rather than sublime. Although he would be able to think his way back to the nearly pristine condition of its pre-1785 era in *The Deerslayer*, Lake George and its embowering woods (like the area around the naval post at Fort Oswego in 1809) gave him a glimpse of the real thing. In *Satanstoe*, written near the end of his career, he would imagine—perhaps recall—the view from one of the high mountains overlooking Lake George as a glimpse of American space in its primeval vastness: the "limpid and placid water," with the "green mantle of its interminable woods," outdid many of the grandest sites he had seen in Switzerland or on the Mediterranean during the intervening years (*SAT* CE 319).[33] In conjunction with the fierce waters at Glens Falls, Lake George thus helped suggest to Cooper the proper environment for Natty Bumppo in his prime.

To be sure, like Glens Falls, parts of Lake George already had been "bedevilled." At its south end was sited the bustling village of Caldwell (now Lake George Village), where amid an array of some fifty dwellings Cooper and Smith-Stanley and the other travelers put up at a "large unfinished wooden house, immediately upon the borders of the Lake, & very beautifully situated." The "commodious and well furnished" state of this inn (commented on by an 1825 guidebook) suggests the vital state of inbound travel at the lake even in 1824.[34] And its very existence pointed to the peculiar social and economic structure of such rapidly developing frontier communities, which had been one of Cooper's themes in *The Pioneers*. Like much else along the southern end of the lake, the inn owed its existence to local landlord and booster James Caldwell, a merchant and manufacturer from Albany. Nearby were a post office and a church, plus an assortment of stores, a printing establishment, and the county offices, for the village had been the seat of Warren County since the latter's formation in 1813. All in all, the place must have struck Cooper as a duplicate of his father's nearly coeval, also eponymous, village back in Otsego.[35]

If anything, Caldwell was even more on the make than Cooperstown. Not until after the Civil War did Otsego have its first steamboat, a smallish one at that. Caldwell, by contrast, had just received its second such vessel, the *Mountaineer*, shortly before Cooper and Smith-Stanley arrived. The Englishmen and their American guide climbed aboard it at the dock early one morning and passed up between the mountains (which Cooper long remembered, as *Satanstoe* suggests) to the portage at the lake's north end. The vessel tarried there long enough for the connecting stages to complete an exchange of passengers with the Champlain steamer, perhaps allowing Cooper and his friends time to run over for a glimpse of the larger lake and the impressive ruins of Fort Ticonderoga on the shore near the outlet of the linking creek, La Chute. Many years later, drafting a talk on the battle of Plattsburgh, Cooper would speak of the "bloody" passageway tying New York to Canada through the Hudson–Lake George–Champlain corridor. Although Melancthon Woolsey's supervision of gunboat construction on the latter lake in 1808–1809 was familiar to Cooper, he had not personally visited Champlain at that time. Not until the 1824 trip, if his daughter's narrative (*LOM* HE xiii) was accurate, was he exposed to it.[36]

Still, the 1824 voyage of the *Mountaineer* was no grand event. Although the steamboat was brand new, it was curious indeed. Of modest size (one hundred feet long and sixteen in the beam, with a capacity of 150 tons), it had various unorthodox structural features, including a very thin hull and heavy four-ply decking. Not surprisingly, it was hard to handle in rough weather. It also was captained by a man, L. C. Larabee, known for his own eccentricities, such as a habit of steaming right past would-be passengers along the shore and making them row out and catch up with his vessel. Smith-Stanley thought the *Mountaineer* efficient in the sense that it made its twice-weekly round-trips between sunrise and sunset of a single day. But Cooper demurred. While on Lake Leman four years later, he found his passage from Vévey to Geneva so slow that he could think of only one "run, or rather *walk*" by steam that was more "deliberate"—"a passage across Lake George, in which the motion seemed expressly intended for the lovers of the picturesque" (*GR* CE 195).[37]

In that regard, the *Mountaineer* gave the travelers full exposure to the natural attractions of the long, island-studded lake. Even more impressive than its picturesque delights, however, were Lake George's historical traces, which had been drawing visitors to the region for two decades or more. Yale President Timothy Dwight thus had "two principal objects in view" when he undertook his first journey to Lake George in 1802: to "examine the scenery," but perhaps more importantly to "explore the ground on which the military events of former times had taken place."[38] English-born Henry D. Gilpin certainly gave history precedence over landscape, lovely as the latter was, in *A Northern Tour:* he clearly understood that a century of struggle between France and his homeland for the control of the North American continent had made this area into classic ground. For his part, Cooper knew the general outlines of that struggle and was familiar with its map long before he set foot in the Adirondacks. Already in *The Pioneers,* furthermore, he had linked Natty Bumppo to the region—for, among other recollections, the aged squatter of Otsego mentions his service there during the 1750s under Sir William Johnson.[39]

Having introduced the region into his fiction in this roundabout way, Cooper came to Lake George in 1824 primed to explore its historical associations. One measure of the effect produced by his first visit to the lake lies in the richer, more concrete treatment accorded to the 1755 defeat of Baron Dieskau in *The Last of the Mohicans.* Here, the hunter's earlier, rather offhanded claim ("the morning we beat Dieskau" is all he says in *The Pioneers* on the subject) is adumbrated by a longer recollection of how that officer's fallen soldiers were cast into "Bloody Pond," a landscape feature at which Natty and his fellow travelers in 1757 pause as they head to Fort William Henry in Chapter 14 of *The Last of the Mohicans* (*PIO* CE 26, 154–55; *LOM* CE 135–36).

This elaboration of Natty's memories in Cooper's sixth novel does not mean that in 1822–1823 he consciously envisioned what later was called the Leather-Stocking series. Indeed, it is by no means clear that the initial inspiration for the "Indian" story mentioned to Smith-Stanley at Glens Falls even included Natty Bumppo among its essential characters. The relationship between the two books was more indirect. For one thing, it was mediated by Cooper's exposure to James Thacher's *Military Journal* and David Humphreys's *Essay on the Life of Major General Israel Putnam* during his research for *Lionel Lincoln.* Although Cooper had turned to these books for help in clarifying the affairs of Boston in 1775, in the months leading up to his northern tour they had inadvertently sharpened his interest in the colonial warfare of the New York frontier. Israel Putnam, long before his participation at Bunker Hill, in fact had seen much service in the Lake George area, often as a "Ranger" operating alongside the equally famous Robert Rogers. And in 1757 he had been very much in the thick of events surrounding the siege of Fort William Henry. Humphreys's detailed and energetic account of Putnam's experiences as a forest partisan probably distracted Cooper's attention from the purpose that had led him to that volume in the first place. It thereby planted seeds that in time germinated in *The Last of the Mohicans.*

The *Essay on the Life of Major General Israel Putnam* may even have urged the inclusion of the Lake George region on the itinerary Cooper laid out for Smith-Stanley and the other Britons over the coming summer. Once he and his associates were there, in turn, the natural landscape and its historical adjuncts intensified his interest in the cluster of stories to which they were connected. Dormant as that interest remained until he actually could begin work on the book he spoke about to Smith-Stanley, once he did start it Humphreys's narrative provided him with many particular hints. In rendering Putnam as an archetypal frontier fighter, captive, and torture victim, Humphreys supplied details for Cooper's next plot as well as suggesting how he might introduce into it a version of Natty when young. Humphreys's account of the siege of Fort William Henry clearly was a source on which Cooper drew—not only for specific incidents but also for the general mood of bloody disaster that was to pervade *The Last of the Mohicans.*[40]

Bloody Pond, which lay by the side of the road a few miles south of Caldwell, was an historic site the travelers must have mused over in 1824. They also could have paused to examine Fort George, which had been built to replace the burned-out ruins of William Henry: from its position atop a high hill on the lakeshore, the second fort still offered a rich panorama northward.[41] But for them as for most visitors at the time, the vastly more significant ruins of William Henry were the focus of attention. Its earthen ramparts, originally encased in upright timbers, still stood out on the flats of the lakeshore about a mile from the village when Henry D. Gilpin described it. As he noted, the walls, gate, and outer works could be "distinctly traced," the thirty-foot-wide ditches still ran about the perimeter, and inside the fort the well, originally some thirty feet deep, still provided water for the thirsty tourist.[42] The ruins were hard to miss not only because of their imposing appearance or the infamous events that had occurred there some seventy years before, but also because the road, breaching the ramparts at two places, passed directly through the parade ground on its way to Caldwell.[43]

Cooper's description of the structure in *The Last of the Mohicans* makes it evident that he had inspected the ruins quite closely.[44] Smith-Stanley did not have much to say specifically about Fort William Henry or any of the other historic sites around the south end of the lake, but his comment that "buttons, bullets, tomahawks, &c. &c." were collected as relics probably indicates that his party, Cooper included, foraged for such items inside its grounds.[45] Since, as indicated above, Cooper already seems to have chosen Glens Falls as a key site for

utterly fictionalized events in his next book, it is reasonable to assume that his
visit to William Henry suggested another of that book's settings. With that possibility before him, Montcalm's siege of the fort in 1757, with its horrific outcome, was all but obvious as a central event of the novel's plot.

Cooper and the British party tarried at Lake George for perhaps three or
four days before returning to Saratoga, where they must have arrived around
Monday, August 9. Here and at nearby Ballston Spa, Smith-Stanley and his comrades lingered until the following Friday, August 13, when they left for the West.
There is no indication that the four tourists encountered Cooper on their eventual return to New York, but we know that over future years Cooper ran across
some of them or sought them out while visiting England and the Continent. And
they certainly left many memories to which the novelist and his daughter would
recur in various contexts.[46]

The Nation's Guest

On Cooper's arrival in New York City from Saratoga, two matters awaited his
attention. Now that the weather had turned much more pleasant, it was time to
begin planning the return of his family from Bayside to Greenwich Street, where
he could once again devote more of his energy to the ongoing project of *Lionel
Lincoln* (see SFM 55).[47] First, however, another, even more important European
visitor needed tending to. The Marquis de Lafayette, one of the last surviving
heroes of the Revolutionary era, was expected at any moment—in fact his ship,
the *Cadmus*, arrived off Sandy Hook on the fourteenth, probably just when
Cooper returned to the city. The novelist did not seek out a personal introduction to the iconic Frenchman (see *LJ* 1:126), perhaps because he feared that he
would be swept up in yet another, and decidedly more ambitious, tour for a foreign visitor, much to the detriment of his health and his literary income. Yet, interested as he was in America's cultural politics in the era following the War of
1812, he helped arrange for several key events in Lafayette's New York schedule
and clearly paid close attention to the man's national tour over the coming
months. At the same time, his intermittent enthusiasm for *Lionel Lincoln* must
have been heartened by the way the Frenchman's visit, stirring national memory,
helped to prepare the way for his own fictional memorial of the Revolution. On
one level, Cooper relished Lafayette's tour because it reified America's political
aspirations; on another level, it was simply good for his literary business.

His part in New York's initial welcome to Lafayette is suggested by incidental details in his quasi-fictional account of the moment in *Notions of the Americans*. He must have been in the city from August 14 on to hear the expectant cry
of "Cadmus in" echo about the streets as Lafayette's vessel slowly worked its

way up from the sea to Staten Island and then to Manhattan (*Notions* 1:20–24). He also must have been on board one of the flotilla of vessels that accompanied Lafayette to the Battery on August 16.[48] The descriptions in *Notions* of the respectful silence that greeted Lafayette as he boarded the vessel, of the slight difficulty with which he walked, of his "anxious gaze" as he scanned the assembled dignitaries, or of the shock of recognition with which he and his aged fellow warrior, Col. Marinus Willett, greeted each other, likewise argue for Cooper's having been on the spot to see it all (*Notions* 1:44–46). Nobody who witnessed the greeting between the two old veterans, asserted one of the newspaper accounts of Lafayette's arrival, would "ever forget it." That would certainly seem to have been the case with Cooper.[49]

A flurry of events swept the city over the next four days, probably absorbing much of Cooper's attention and time (Plate 19). In the break offered by Lafayette's departure from New York on Friday, August 20, for a frenzied two-week tour of New England, he probably went over to Bayside and escorted his wife and children back to Manhattan. As they settled in on Greenwich Street again, Susan had amusing news from her father. Lafayette's party had rushed past Heathcote Hill as his old opponent at Brandywine endeavored to salute: "I suppose you have seen by the papers," DeLancey wrote, "that the Marquis passed our house on Saturday last and in such a cloud of dust that I was unable to distinguish the general from the Alderman, but I hope I took off my hat to the right person."[50] Soon enough, "the Marquis" was back in New York, facing a new round of celebrations in which Susan's husband had a prominent part to play.[51]

On Wednesday, September 8, Cooper joined a crowd of army officers, New York officials, and members of the elite Society of the Cincinnati on the *Chancellor Livingston* to escort Lafayette on a tour of the city's defensive works, with a reception to follow at the diamond-shaped fort just off the Long Island shore at the Narrows that had been named for the French hero the year before—with Cooper also in attendance then. This time, the novelist may well have written the report of the event for Charles King's *American*. As the crowd approached the steamboat under a dark, threatening sky, that report stated, the West Point band welcomed everyone aboard with a "fine military piece" written in Lafayette's honor by its leader, Irishman Richard Willis. By the time the vessel had covered the short distance out to Governor's Island, just off the Battery in the entrance to the East River, rain was falling in earnest. Instead of landing, the *Livingston* therefore slowly circled the island, then lay-to off its south shore as the artillery from the island's two installations, Fort Columbus and Castle William, saluted Lafayette. From there, the vessel went down along the Brooklyn shore toward the Narrows. When it was off Fort Lafayette, the downpour temporarily ended and the sky cracked open to let a sudden burst of sunlight down on the impressive structure just as its cannon fire echoed off the distant hills of Staten Island. Lafayette was led ashore between Col. William MacRea of the Second Artillery and Col. James Bankhead of the Third Artillery (a member of Cooper's Lunch), then was greeted by the fort's commander, Maj. William Gates.[52] Once inside, he reviewed the resident company of artillerists and toured the facility. As the report in the *American* emphasized, the massive stone walls of the fort and the deep gun embrasures angled into them were very impressive. During the festivities later in the day, Cooper would offer a toast forging just this linkage of the material place with its spiritual father: "The fortress and its name; the former is durable, but the latter shall be imperishable." That coincidence, along with the newspaper writer's regret that, despite the general invitation that had gone out to naval officers, "only one or two" were present—a point Cooper would be very likely to stress—makes it plausible to ascribe the report in his friend's paper to the novelist.[53]

Army personnel dominated the feast and the toasts. The head table was packed with aged members of the Cincinnati along with Lafayette and MacRea. Opposite it was a table of mostly young current army officers, clustered around Bankhead and Lafayette's son. Along the sides were the other "guests," including Cooper and the couple of unnamed naval officers referred to in the *American* report. In this facedown, with civilians along the sidelines, the newspaper writer saw a symbolic contrast of the generations: at one end sat those to whom Americans owed the origin of their freedom, at the other, those to whom they owed its preservation. Whether Cooper inscribed that neat contrast for King's paper or not, he hardly could have missed the almost diagrammatic lesson. Between the generations himself, he was seeking in his fiction (in *Lionel Lincoln* most pertinently at the moment) to link the nation's past and future through his own meditation on America's origins. When the sergeant-at-arms of New York's Society of the Cincinnati, Bryant Rosseter, led the assembled party up to the "collation," Cooper's glimpse of that man in his "picturesque" continental garb (on which the *American*'s reporter commented) must have given him an uncanny insight into the world he was trying to reimagine in his present novel.

Late in the day, the *Chancellor Livingston* delivered the celebrants back to the city, where Cooper had much to attend to. Although the continuing rains would force several postponements on the next big event, a nighttime party at Castle Garden originally planned for Friday, September 10, Cooper was very much in the thick of preparations for it.[54] Eventually on the following Tuesday, September 14, the weather cooperated. According to Dr. John W. Francis, Cooper not only was part of the planning committee but also wrote and published what is the best surviving account of the event: although close to exhaustion after remaining at the Garden until near daybreak on September 15, his thirty-fifth birthday, the still rather frail novelist rushed off to the offices of the *American* to pen his report for that day's paper.[55] Eager to engage editor King's readers from beyond the city, he began with a description of Castle Garden. Originally called Castle Clinton, the place had been erected on subsurface rocks just off the Battery a few years before as part of the effort to bolster New York's defenses. Now in private hands, it had been opened to the public only a few weeks earlier but was already among the city's favored pleasure spots. Stripped of its armaments and with theatrical boxes installed on its lower level, along with a barroom, kitchen, and sitting rooms, it sported a fourteen-foot-wide awning-covered promenade running around its top, with benches scattered about for visitors eager to savor the uninterrupted views of the bay, all the way down to the Narrows, as well as back over the city.[56]

For this particular evening the planning committee had given the Garden an elaborate treatment. A tall framework pyramid, mounted with colored lights and capped by a "large and brilliant star," stood athwart the entry to the long bridge leading out to the Garden. The night was beautiful. The sun set at 6:00 p.m., after which the arching sky over the city slowly filled with stars until a bright moon rose over Brooklyn just after 9:00 p.m. The lingering threat of more bad weather had led the committee to cover the bridge with canvas sheeting, but even this expedient enhanced the aesthetic effects. Once past the pyramid, visitors entered a magical realm where small lanterns placed amid potted evergreens cast just enough light to guide their passage to the Garden. Moving over the bridge in this hushed darkness withdrew them from ordinary life ashore: "A stranger might have supposed himself suddenly transported from a star-light evening to an evergreen forest at twilight," as another newspaper report had it, an effect enhanced by the pungent fragrance of the trees.[57] The dim crossing also readied visitors for the surprise at the far end: as they went through the massive portal of the Garden, an expansive, light-filled reality burst on their eyes. Like the bridge, the old fort also had been domed over—in this case, with a warship's sails, borrowed from the navy yard along with the great mast that anchored them at the center. The vast interior, two hundred feet across and seventy feet high at the center, was packed with thousands of brightly burning lights. Beneath the flag-draped fabric dome, ranges of seats circled one above the next, converting the space into an amphitheater.

After a visitor's eye recovered from this sudden astonishment, details of the allegorically decorated interior emerged. A triumphal arch had been erected near the entry, the whole entwined with laurel and oak wreaths and capped by a colossal bust of George Washington, Lafayette's friend during the war. From above the bust, American and French flags flowed over the sides of the arch. Halfway down was suspended a picture of "the Genius of our Country"—that is, Lib-

erty—holding a scroll inscribed *"to the Nation's Guest."* More flags were hung
near this icon, along with shields naming the key Revolutionary battles in which
Lafayette had fought (Yorktown, Monmouth, and Brandywine), while at the
center of the space the mast supporting the canvas dome, ringed with thirteen
other columns representing the original states, stood forth as a symbol of the one
central fact of political union. This statement of the nation's founding motif—
e pluribus unum—was repeated in the thirteen chandeliers that, suspended in
a circle around the mast, merged into one "immense" source of illumination,
"shedding floods of light" on the crowds pouring over the bridge or disembark-
ing from the steamboats that docked at the Garden. Here was the artificial daylight of a national jubilee.

Cooper's active role in mounting the event is suggested by his report's insistence on naming the craftsmen responsible for much of the physical work that
had readied Castle Garden. The design was the responsibility of three men:
artist Hugh Reinagle, most recently the architect of the new Park Theatre and,
in the words of his friend William Dunlap, "for many years the principal scene
painter at the New-York theatres"; New York upholsterer Henry Ritter; and a
member of the Grinnell ship-owning clan, either Henry or Moses Grinnell,
probably recruited to help with tactical support once the designs were ready to
be implemented. Construction was overseen by Martin E. Thompson, a "carpenter" in the 1816 New York directory who had since shown considerable ambition, producing the designs for the second Bank of the United States (1822–
1824) and other city landmarks, including the ingenious, soon-to-be-erected
Merchants' Exchange (1824), both of them on Wall Street.[58] A final workman
mentioned by Cooper, a gunner at the navy yard named John Lord, conceivably
was involved because of Cooper's personal intervention. When the weather on
September 10 forced the second delay in the celebration, plans were hastily made
to cover the entire Garden. A successful appeal to Commodore Rodgers, who
sent the requisite canvas and a large work party from the navy yard, thereby
"providing new proof of the friendly feeling in the navy officers" (snubbed during the army-run harbor tour of September 8), sounds like a result of Cooper's
personal efforts to patch things up.[59]

Due to all this frenzied work, the Garden was ready by Monday evening.
Lafayette's place of honor for the evening, a pavilion between the entry gate and
the "union" mast, was flanked by a pair of the cannon he had helped take from
the English at Yorktown. By the time he arrived about 10:00 p.m., five or six
thousand celebrants had taken their places inside. Escorted by a pair of old Revolutionary companions, Gen. Nicholas Fish and Gen. Jacob Morton (a member
of the Lunch), he was met at the gateway by members of the Committee on
Arrangements, including Cooper, and led to his pavilion as the West Point band

played a march named in his honor. Once he was seated, the allegorical painting of Liberty was slowly rolled up, revealing an enormous transparency on which was portrayed La Grange, the ancestral home of Lafayette's wife east of Paris. Cooper took all this in with relish. In his newspaper report, he probably was chronicling his own experience when he noted how a spectator wandering about the Garden, having seen and "read" the "allegorical parts of the embellishments," found much more to interest the eye. Crowded, light-flooded, complexly decorated, the vast space repaid his curiosity as he scanned it again and again from different perspectives. The "succession of fanciful pictures" was precisely what the committee and the designers had hoped for. The sight from above "was magical," Cooper added, especially with the brightly dressed dancers "moving in the distance to mellowed music." Hidden in the upper level of the place with his innovative keyed or "Kent" bugle, West Point bandleader Richard Willis sounded his eerie notes, deepening the impression of otherworldly illusion.[60] The mild weather allowed the canvas walls to be drawn up into festoons, letting people onshore or in the many nearby vessels see into the bright Garden. Once the moon had risen high enough in the night sky, the "animated" celebrants could look out on "the islands, the hills, in short the whole . . . lovely bay" (*LJ* 1:115–18). In re-creating the event in *Notions of the Americans,* Cooper had his European traveler speak of the uplift he felt when surveying the "broad, placid, star-lit bay" from within the delight-filled circle of the converted fortress (*Notions* 1:186).

The night, heavily staged, paid homage to Lafayette even as it celebrated New York's present and future power. The Frenchman's tour was a complex event, a combination of opportunism and idealism for him as well as many of his local and national hosts. His itinerary was unrelenting. During the Castle Garden fete, he probably had scant time to see all that Cooper reported on. For one thing, his gaze was circumscribed by the universal demand for his attention. He circulated around the Garden tirelessly, greeting celebrants and listening patiently to their "fervent and affectionate wishes." Then he had to depart at 2:00 a.m. for his next commitment, well before the dancers at last left the floor at four o'clock. After his final circuit of the place, Lafayette, with Willis and his band and many others (but not Cooper) in tow, boarded the *James Kent* and headed up the North River on the next leg of his tour. He was received at West Point the following noon, then endured event after event up the valley until at last, on the evening of September 17, he disembarked—for yet another ball—at the state capital. At 3:00 a.m. two days later, he was back in New York, where he spent two full days before departing via Jersey City for Philadelphia on September 23.[61]

Cooper's view of Lafayette at the time of the visit was largely confined to the ceremonial level. Not until he grew close to Lafayette in France in the later

1820s and early 1830s would he gain insight into the political ironies of the Frenchman's nature and his career. An intriguer who combined ambition with republican idealism in a manner few Americans appreciated during the 1824–1825 tour, Lafayette returned to the United States partly to applaud American political and cultural progress and partly to rehabilitate his own low reputation in France, where his recent attempts to undermine the conservative government of the comte de Villèle had resulted in the loss of his seat in the chamber of deputies. Rarely were his motives unmixed; rarely were his warmest embraces without their dangers. Secretary of State Henry Clay, who had been speaker of the House of Representatives at the time when the U.S. government (after much debate) decided to invite Lafayette across the Atlantic, was especially worried by the Frenchman's unpredictable behavior and the effect his intrigues vis-à-vis France might have on American interests. During a private session in Washington during Lafayette's tour, Clay therefore urged him to spend his remaining days "in dignity and tranquility, abstaining from public affairs, and most cautiously guarding against giving the least ground for the imputation of his being concerned in any Conspiracy." To appearances he did just that while in the United States. Even as his tour progressed, however, his retinue was feeding propaganda to his supporters at home, who disseminated it in the opposition press—with the result, U.S. minister to France James Brown informed Clay in 1825, that the tour had definitely worsened American relations with the French government at a time when important negotiations between the countries were ongoing. Of such things Cooper knew little until he arrived in France himself in 1826 and was befriended by James Brown, his superior while he served as U.S. consul at Lyons. Courted by Lafayette from the outset with a combination of flattery, political pressure, and genuine hospitality, Cooper would discover depths he had not sensed back in New York in 1824–1825, when things seemed ritualized, stylized, and therefore (to a modern sensibility) both superficial and stiff.[62]

Finishing Up

At least Cooper, with the rest of New York, did not have to worry about Lafayette from late September until he ultimately returned there on July 4, 1825. In the interim, the "Nation's Guest" followed a course leading through the South to New Orleans, back north to Niagara, then to Boston for his promised participation in the laying of the cornerstone of the Bunker Hill monument in Charlestown on June 17. Cooper may have crossed paths with him once during this interval: in February 1825, both men were in Washington to observe balloting for the president and vice president in the House of Representatives (see

Chapter 15).[63] In the meantime, with the semicentennial of the Revolution that Lafayette's visit began for the United States fully under way, Cooper had little to distract him from his much-interrupted fifth book. And, given its subject, he had a good deal to prompt him to rush it to its end. The anniversary of Lexington and Concord and Bunker Hill would come in the spring, an ideal target for the publication of *Lionel Lincoln*.

Between the plan and its actualization, however, other shadows fell. In the real Republic where Cooper lived, as opposed to the ideal one conjured up during the Castle Garden fete, and his account of it, money mattered more than patriotic sentiment. Across 1824, the bitter ramifications of the deal between his sister and William H. Averell were still making themselves apparent. More critically, in the spring of that year, with *The Pilot* done and work on *Lionel Lincoln* begun, the old business with New York lawyer Robert Sedgwick had suddenly become a new matter of continuing concern. Cooper had borrowed just over $3,000 from this sometime friend between March and October of 1818, probably for the DeKalb venture (see Chapter 7). Then, with his cousin Courtland's impending failure and his own purchase of the *Union* looming in 1819, Cooper had sought to extend his note with Sedgwick. The lawyer, sensing Cooper's vulnerability, pretended to be reluctant.

Doubtless there were better things Sedgwick might do with his money: leaving funds in the hands of Cooper was not particularly prudent in the panic year of 1819. Greed, however, was a more important motive for Sedgwick than caution. His staged reluctance, almost certainly as he expected, prompted Cooper to offer to pay interest at the illegally high rate of 18 percent on the debt. At this juncture, Sedgwick, feigning concern for Cooper, rejected that offer. The two men therefore parted company on the assumption that the note would be extended, but without a clear understanding of the new terms. By the time Cooper returned to Sedgwick's office to sign the formal agreement some days later, he was surprised to find that the lawyer had decided to accept usurious interest: he demanded the seemingly lower rate of 12 percent rather than 18, but insisted that it be applied retroactively to the date of the first loan, and he also insisted on a $2,000 penalty should Cooper default on the bond. Cooper felt himself trapped. Time had almost run out on the old note and he could not pay it off; at this late moment, he had little choice but to accept Sedgwick's terms. As it happened, Sedgwick had more to exact. Instead of the three leasehold properties originally used to secure the debt, which would be relatively hard to dispose of (and which Cooper in any case wished to use for the *Union*), he wanted fee simple ones, which could be liquidated without much ado should the need arise. Cooper offered a mortgage on the Fenimore Farm property, along with a lot in Cooperstown proper. Although this substitution met Cooper's own needs, he cannot have felt comfortable with the way Sedgwick, sensing Cooper's nervousness about his larger financial situation, demanded this new, ironclad arrangement.[64]

Cooper was not just surprised by Sedgwick's behavior—he was "disgusted" by it. Still, he swallowed his feelings and tried to make the best of a bad bargain. Perhaps he already knew that the payoff terms for the mortgage—half of the amount of the bond in six months, the rest in twelve—were unreasonably optimistic. All too soon it would be clear that he could not meet those terms. His first payment on the bond did not come until the expiration of a year, when he turned over a small amount of money through his brother-in-law, George Pomeroy. At this point, the mortgage was technically in default, although Sedgwick did not pursue immediate legal remedies. Over the next twenty months, Cooper gave Sedgwick directly or through his brother and fellow lawyer Henry two other cash payments, the bulk of which was used to meet the accumulating interest charges. Less than $500 was applied to the principal; nothing went toward the penalty. The first of these payments was made on February 20, 1821, soon after *Precaution* had appeared; the second came on December 5, 1821, during the final period of Cooper's work in New York City on *The Spy*. At the latter time, Cooper also transferred to Sedgwick a mortgage he owned on the St. Lawrence County property of farmer Joseph Rounds.[65]

That seems to have been the total of his attempts to meet his obligations to the New York lawyer. There is scant record of the dealings between the two men over the course of 1822, but they evidently deteriorated to such an extent that Cooper suspended all payments and transfers. At length, as Cooper recalled two years later, he himself urged Sedgwick to proceed with a foreclosure on the Otsego mortgage (a possibility explicitly mentioned in the original conveyance) by filing a bill of complaint in the Chancery Court.[66] In March of 1824, Sedgwick did just that. Cooper's quick consent to the bill meant that it would be taken *pro confesso* (that is, as an "amicable" bill), ensuring that the foreclosure would be expedited. Within another three weeks, a public notice of a sale under the court's auspices was published in the *Freeman's Journal*. Covering the three parcels of the Fenimore property plus the Cooperstown lot, the sale was slated to be held at the tavern of H. E. Dwight on August 3, just at the moment that Cooper was leading Smith-Stanley and his companions through the Adirondacks. Soon delayed to September 1, it went forward at that time under the direction of Otsego lawyer Eben Morehouse, a master in chancery.[67]

All this promised quick resolution of the lingering debt, but that was not to be. Employing a not-uncommon strategy, Sedgwick personally attended the sale and successfully bid a total of $1,540 for the three parts of the Fenimore property. His main purpose was to gain direct control of the farm at a low price. As the complainant in the chancery bill, he received his own bid back from Morehouse along with the deed. But he had no wish to retain the farm. Using Morehouse as his local agent, he then set about marketing it. Here began a new wrangle. The 1819 arrangement between the two friends had stated unequivocally that Cooper could retain the mortgaged properties if he paid off the whole debt (with interest) within a year. He had not done so. But it also stipulated that Sedgwick was to pay any "overplus" from the public sale of the properties to Cooper.[68]

Cooper insisted that he had agreed to expedite the sale only if Sedgwick took steps to guarantee that the land brought top dollar. The best approach, unless the place could be sold intact "as a country seat," was to lay it out in parcels of such a size that they would stimulate competition among Cooperstown residents, either for building lots or for small, nearby pastures. Otherwise, in Cooper's view, the property might "be needlessly sacrificed."[69] Much was at stake. Cooper remembered having paid $5,000 for the main parcel—wildly wrong, since it had cost him a mere fraction of this, only about $1,700, when he purchased it from Elihu Phinney in 1811.[70] But Sedgwick's successful bid for that one piece ($1,250) represented a 25 percent decline from Cooper's original price despite the fact that, although the stone mansion house had burned in July of 1823, the remaining improvements Cooper had made on the property were of considerable value. Aside from this important financial consideration, Sedgwick's high-handed manner of proceeding read to Cooper like another affront.

Sedgwick had acted on a different understanding. He said that he recalled no such agreement as the one Cooper claimed they had made. The mortgage had been foreclosed and then the land was sold—such were the simple facts in his view. But he hardly wanted things to be simple. Indeed, he may well have been playing William H. Averell's game—using a forced sale as a means of scooping up as much of a debtor's property as possible without significantly diminishing his own claim on the poor man's remaining assets. Given the bargain price he had paid on the farm, Sedgwick certainly still held a considerable claim against Cooper under the original bond. He clearly was intent on recovering the balance of the principal and any remaining interest, but he also seems to have set his sights on the $2,000 penalty as well. Mindful of the Averell precedent and perhaps fearing that Averell himself had forged a new covert alliance with Sedgwick, Cooper therefore became uncooperative as summer turned to fall. Sedgwick, who had waited a long time for his money—however unjust the terms—would wait no longer. A month after the sale, he at last filed suit against Cooper in the state supreme court and then or soon afterwards had Cooper placed under a considerable bond (perhaps for the balance due him, $4,000 or so plus the steep interest from December 1821 to the present) to insure that he would show up for trial. When, by November 13, 1824, Cooper had not yet pled to Sedgwick's complaint, the court at Sedgwick's request gave him a twenty-day deadline to do so.

Cooper's attorney, Peter A. Jay, already had begun throwing legal bolts of his
own. He successfully petitioned John T. Irving, Washington Irving's brother
and first judge in the Court of Common Pleas, to require that Sedgwick appear
and establish that his action had sufficient merit for the court to proceed. This
strategy would buy more time. His second aim was to lower Cooper's bail, which
Judge Irving obligingly did on November 8.[71]

Just before Christmas, 1824, Cooper received news through Jay that on January 17 the trial on Sedgwick's suit would be held in the courtroom in City Hall.
On January 6 the schedule was reaffirmed, but four days later Cooper appeared
in person before attorney Gabriel Winter at his Pine Street office, and, swearing
that his own counsel assured him he had "a good and substantial defense" to
Sedgwick's charges—that is, that he was not simply stalling—he successfully
laid the groundwork for a delay in the proceedings. Here we must leave the issue
until the next chapter.[72]

In addition to these evolving troubles with Sedgwick, other old ones also renewed themselves in 1824. For one thing, there was a reprise of those associated
with the DeLancey family properties in Westchester that had passed into (and
out of) Cooper's hands. In particular, the heavy debt load with which the Hickory Grove was encumbered was causing new concerns. Within a little more than
a week of signing his agreement with Wiley and sending his letter off to John
Miller at the end of April, Cooper in fact had assigned his own interest in the
Lionel Lincoln contract to Westchester resident Joshua Brookes as "collateral
security" for a debt dating from at least 1821, which with accumulated interest
charges he expected would total $2,351 as of the following September. Presum-
ably Brookes was assured that, with publication set for the latter month and with
prepublication notes already accumulating through Wiley's efforts, his money
was safe and nearly in sight. The background of the obligation to Brookes is
murky. Since this "gentleman," resident in the town of Mount Pleasant in the
central part of Westchester, had somehow acquired an interest in the Hickory
Grove property, his pressure on Cooper (backed up by at least two 1823 court
rulings against the novelist) was yet another consequence of the frenzied shuf-
fling about of assets and liabilities that characterized Cooper's business life at
this period.[73] In assigning a substantial part of the proceeds of *Lionel Lincoln* to
Brookes in an effort to mollify his demands, Cooper demonstrated the manner
in which his literary labors formed part of the overall structure of his financial
life. If writing was to be the major means by which Cooper provided income to
replace the lost resources of the past, books were also quite immediately available as commodities that could be moved about to cover pressing demands of the
present. Literature was in this sense fungible.

The quickness with which Cooper reached terms with Wiley, and then assigned the Wiley contract to Brookes, suggests that the author was eager to bring his newest project to an end. Other indications also support this conclusion. In the assignment to Brookes, Cooper had appointed that creditor his own agent: Brookes was to receive all monies due from Wiley, deduct the amount required to satisfy his own claim, and then pass on the surplus to Cooper. Wiley assented to this assignment a mere two days later, again suggesting a quickening pace. Yet it remains doubtful that Cooper made much substantive progress on the novel over the months immediately following this flurry of activity, especially once he and Susan had relocated to Bayside. Wiley's June 28 promise that he soon would send John Miller the complete first volume, had it been kept, might have supported Cooper's notion of a September publication date; but Wiley sent nothing to Miller all summer. Then September came and went, and, despite Cooper's July visit to Manhattan and the second paper shipment in August, no book was to be seen. Likewise with October. At last in November, with no novel finished and apparently little fresh progress on it, Cooper was forced to pay Joshua Brookes $1,000 on the debt from other sources, as Brookes's endorsement on the Wiley contract indicated. In return, Cooper apparently exacted Brookes's assent to an extension on the deadline for paying the remainder due: a further (undated) endorsement in Brookes's hand indicates "residue extended on Last of Mohicans."[74] On its face, this note would appear to derive from the following year, although it *may* indicate that Cooper already had named his new project, vaguely conceived in the north country, as early as the fall of 1824.

These changes with regard to the obligation to Brookes were necessitated in part because Cooper, pressed on all sides for cash, also had to alter his April agreement with Wiley. On November 13, with his labors on *Lionel Lincoln* languishing, he signed a second Wiley contract that obligated him to complete "the unfinished manuscript work called *Lionel Lincoln*" with "all reasonable dispatch." The reason for this pledge to his "agent" was that Wiley was, by virtue of this second contract for *Lionel Lincoln,* no longer just *that.* Desperate to squeeze ready cash from a venture that was nowhere near being done, Cooper apparently had approached Philadelphia publisher Carey and Lea with an offer to sell them the book in exchange for a cash payment. When Carey and Lea refused (see Chapter 16), Cooper transferred ownership of the novel to Wiley for a set term. He authorized Wiley to issue a second edition of not more than four thousand additional copies once the first edition of six thousand had been released to the market. He also assigned to Wiley the exclusive right of "printing, publishing and vending or selling" those two editions in North and South America for the period of a year from the date of the book's initial release. Wiley, in exchange for this potentially—but not actually—lucrative change in the agreement (and in the manner of Cooper's publishing), agreed to shoulder all the expense of producing the first edition and to give Cooper $5,000 via personal notes payable six months after publication. Cooper thereby relieved himself of the costs of production while guaranteeing himself a quick return on the book. This arrangement may have worked to his own benefit, but it must have helped expose Wiley further to the financial problems already troubling him.[75]

The "dispatch" with which Cooper promised to finish the book was a relative term. The first American edition of *Lionel Lincoln* was not copyrighted until December 7, as the notice printed on the reverse of the title page of the first volume (but, atypically, not the second) indicates. By December, Wiley knew that the second volume, although it had been in production for long enough that its title page optimistically had been dated 1824, would not be completed in time for the book to be published before New Year's. He therefore took the as-yet-unprinted copy for the first gathering of the first volume and sent it to Fanshaw: this was made up of the half-title leaf ("Legends of the Thirteen Republics," with a blank back), the title page (with the recently filed copyright notice on the back), the dedication leaf (to "William Jay," with a blank back), and Cooper's two prefaces (one to the "Legends," filling four pages, the other to *Lionel Lincoln* per se, filling another two). That these items totaled twelve pages was not accidental. Clearly, the text of the novel proper had been printed starting the previous spring without the first gathering, since the first page of the first chapter begins precisely at the *second* gathering, and the text runs from there to the end. By December, with the year's close fast approaching, Wiley reasonably enough had Fanshaw date the first volume "1825," and the book in fact was not to be published in New York until February 5, 1825.[76]

Such problems were bad enough, but those facing Cooper's English publisher, John Miller, were even worse. In December, just before copyright was secured, Miller was becoming frantic because he had yet to see any sheets for the book. He wrote Cooper on the fifth that he had been "long & anxiously expecting a portion of 'Lionel Lincoln.'"[77] Although Wiley had seen to Miller's needs some time before this letter arrived in New York, more difficulties were to follow. On the ship *Diamond*, which left New York for Liverpool on December 12, he at last sent off two sets of sheets for the first volume, one for Miller and the other for a publisher in Paris, Charles Gosselin, who was to issue a translation of the book in 1825. Four weeks later, on January 1, that vessel sank in Cardigan Bay, off the Welsh coast. If Wiley had carried through with his promise to send a duplicate set via the *Crisis*, Miller might have recouped the lost time. But the *Crisis* brought him nothing, and then when the *Cortes* arrived in Liverpool with a package for Miller, supposedly a set of sheets for the second volume, the shipment disappeared—diverted, Miller feared, to a pirate (*LL* CE xxii). On February 5, at his wits' end, he wrote again to Cooper. Unless copy arrived in the packet ship expected on February 16, he was now sure that the pirates would beat him. Then at last, after all these troubles, he had a bit of luck. The fourth vessel indeed brought him a complete run of sheets, which he rushed through the printer's shop in time to send a set of the first English edition to Cooper on the twenty-second, only six days later. The confusions and losses through which the book had emerged to the light of day in London were not bad reminders of how, once again, the best of Cooper's intentions had been mangled.[78]

CHAPTER FIFTEEN

Hawk-eye

C ooper had conceived *Lionel Lincoln* with grand ambitions sometime in
1823, perhaps as early as the summer, and had done much more by way
of preparation for this book's narrative than he had done with any
previous one (see Chapter 13). Once it finally was published in February 1825,
however, the book fell flat. For the first time since *Precaution,* no quick second
edition was called for; indeed, Wiley still had nearly a quarter of his six-thousand-
copy first edition on hand in the later part of the year (*LL* CE xxiii). Fortunately
enough for his sensibilities, Cooper was out of New York City around publication day, February 5, for a quick trip to Washington. On the ninth, he was present in the House of Representatives (as was Lafayette) for balloting on the presidency, which was in dispute because of a lack of a majority in the electoral
college.

William Dunlap, in Washington himself at the time to settle accounts with
the treasury department dating from his service as assistant paymaster for the
New York militia during the War of 1812, paid a visit to one of the candidates,
Sen. Andrew Jackson, with fellow New Yorker Christopher Van De Venter.
When the two of them returned from Jackson's they found Cooper had arrived

in town and soon were having a bit of a party with the novelist and some of "his former naval associates." Cooper was to write a longish account of the runoff election, without reference to any such party, in 1828 (see *Notions* 2:164–84). Probably he had secured a good vantage point in the house gallery through friends in the New York delegation—either Churchill C. Cambreleng or the Patroon, Stephen Van Rensselaer, both of whom Dunlap reported seeing during his own visit to the Capitol, and the latter of whom was to play the deciding part in the runoff. Like "Cadwallader" and "the Count" in *Notions,* Cooper also went to the White House to meet President and Mrs. Monroe, members of the cabinet, and Senator Jackson. The level of detail in that section of the book suggests as much; besides, we have the assertion of his friend, Samuel F. B. Morse, that Cooper attended the last White House reception held by Monroe and his wife, also on February 9. Morse remembered that Cooper and he arrived at the president's house in a carriage along with Commodore Chauncey's brother (Cmdr. Ichabod Wolcott Chauncey) and Robert Owen, the recently arrived Scots reformer.[1]

Even before Cooper went off to Washington, Wiley would have known from his prepublication orders for *Lionel Lincoln* that the book was unlikely to make a splash. On Cooper's return to New York, however, the message would be more detailed. It did not vary much over the weeks to come. Part of what had gone awry over the eighteen months between the conception of the book and its publication probably should be traced to the exhaustion of the author's body and mind following the mysterious affliction that struck him in August of 1823. But there were two ways in which his very habits as a writer were also to blame. In *The Spy,* and to a lesser extent in *The Pilot,* Cooper had shown a fascination with Loyalism that in *Lionel Lincoln* led him into a literary dead end. Perhaps his own family's Quaker background surfaced here, with DeLancey lore and the DeLancey perspective deepening Cooper's concern with the Revolution as a civil war. Whatever the cause, however, the result was clear. *Lionel Lincoln* did a remarkable job of imagining Bunker Hill for Americans on the eve of that battle's fiftieth anniversary. But its main plot hinged on the indecisive emotions of an alienated American who could neither risk everything by coming to his native country's aid nor enthusiastically embrace the royal banner to which he was technically devoted. That Lionel Lincoln's insane pro-American father, Ralph, suggests (as countless readers have noted) the utter madness of the Patriot cause merely underscores the fundamentally flawed conception on which the book rested.

If Cooper's concern with the Loyalist position was one reason for the novel's internal self-division, another was the haphazard manner of writing and producing the book. The key problem was the serial nature of the process. In this instance as in every previous one, Cooper's wish to expedite matters allowed virtually no time for thoughtful revision. In some ways, it is true, his ambitious scheme for the "Legends" represented a creative solution to the problem. Because a large course of action was to be laid out well in advance, Cooper's conception of each individual book would ideally have more time to mature. And each of them would be more sharply defined by virtue of its place in the series. Neither of these factors was the same thing as revision, and hardly could affect the first of the thirteen books, but both showed Cooper's concern with establishing some better means of proceeding.

The four novels and one book of tales he had published by 1824 each suffered in its own way from his precipitancy, his lack of both coherent plans and steady execution. As compositions, they were as much talked into being as written, and in no instance had they been adequately revised while the manuscript or initial proofs remained in his possession. Indeed, even that way of putting it suggests a more orderly procedure than he had followed in any of those cases. A brief review of his means of authoring them will suggest the seriousness of this issue. In the case of *Precaution*, Cooper had sent the hastily finished manuscript off to Goodrich with such speed that, as he later had to admit, even the punctuation was woefully confusing. The author tried to correct errors as the proofs came to him, but did so inconsistently. Furthermore, by the time the crisis came in his dealings with Goodrich, Cooper was away tending to his other big venture of the time—the whaleship *Union*—and therefore could not adequately intervene in the accumulating disaster. At last he gave up on the book, entrusting it to Goodrich even as he blamed him for errors that were the author's own. He hoped that the printers would catch some remaining errors, that the woefully insufficient errata sheet would minimize the embarrassment caused by the more egregious ones that remained, and that the public would supply the sense where it was found lacking. Such hopes did not produce success.

With regard to *The Spy*, Cooper started out with a much more coherent sense of his subject, but as his confidence wavered he intermittently lost it. In the end, more than a year after he had plunged headlong into the story, he was forced to bootstrap an ending and then drive his sluggish pen toward it from the book's unfinished middle. Although Wiley and his printers produced a better physical book, with fewer glaring errors of sense or style, Cooper managed to do much of the revision that was necessary only with the second and third editions: had the public response to the book been less enthusiastic, those improvements never would have been possible. Even so, the awkwardly truncated ending and the mid-course shifts that preceded it (like the sudden abandonment of the "Neutral Ground" for the Highlands) lived on in the book up to and beyond Cooper's death. Those shifts were indeed important for the overall evolution of Cooper's literary art, but they came as impulses rather than conscious innovations. He learned from them almost inadvertently.

Even so, the book did exceptionally well. Its energizing success in turn drove Cooper's early work on *The Pioneers*—but in this third book he also did not manage to come to terms with the troubles that had plagued his first two. There was a richer inventive power, a surer sense of how to construct scenes (as with the many set pieces of rural description), and, more than anything, a grasp of how to "capture" character rather than write it into being page-by-page. In Natty Bumppo, Cooper for the first time had a fairly complete vision of a character from the outset. This is not to say that Leather-Stocking does not change in the course of the plot. He is ennobled by his contest with the law and is given heroic stature by the deeds he accomplishes in the later chapters of the story. But he is seen steadily and whole throughout. From the moment he steps out from behind a tree in the book's first chapter to his disappearance into the woods in the last, he is complexly present as a force whose entry into human action brings the power of nature to bear on the artifice of social constructions. His invention was a tour de force that demonstrated the author's genuine talent. There was nothing like Natty Bumppo in all American literature—or other literatures— to date.

Yet for all its beauty as a series of scenes and all the deep imagining that went into the apprehension of its main character, *The Pioneers* was in its own way an unfinished book. It was unfinished first of all because the author again faltered in his production of the manuscript. He began it in a flurry in the fall of 1821, even as he struggled to close the gap between the filled-up chapters of *The Spy* and that book's artificial "ending." The new book apparently was then abandoned for several months in 1822 while Cooper tended to other things—his *Tales*, the last of his reviews for Gardner, the lawsuits. Then, even after he returned to it that summer, *The Pioneers* was further interrupted by the yellow fever outbreak. Not until well after Christmas would the novel finally appear. And this series of delays was only one of the ways in which Cooper, hindered by circumstances, failed to adequately manage the book. He once again avoided the chance to revise the novel as he worked on it, meaning that it went to press pretty much in the form in which he first committed it to paper. If its opening owed a good deal to the lessons he had learned in the happenstance of *The Spy* (especially lessons about how to use landscape in fiction), its later movements were improvised rather than composed.[2] Perhaps the deepest impulse at work in the last third of the book was the one that imported into Templeton "the law" as Cooper had been encountering it as executor of his father's estate.

In *The Pilot*, Cooper again began with a conception of his subject that showed real promise. Here for the first time he was rewriting earlier experiments: this book was both a reprise of *Precaution* as an "English" fantasy and of *The Spy* as a Revolutionary romance. But the new book went off in too many directions for it to mark a steady advance over Cooper's earlier works. The promising figure of Long Tom Coffin, snuffed out in the wreck of *The Ariel,* might indeed have led *somewhere* had Cooper given him "sea room"—but not, one suspects, to a Revolutionary War encounter on the shores of Northumberland. The interpolated whaling scene was not so much a dead end as a marker of possibilities left undeveloped because, in the book as it positively existed, they were not capable of development. Tom Coffin in that instance suggested another story, one that might really tap the resources of the sea as an aesthetic realm. But it is a story quashed. Perhaps if Cooper had been able to get away and visit Nantucket and Cape Cod with William B. Shubrick while still at work on the book, Long Tom might have had a different, fuller development. But how, exactly, would such an enhancement of his character serve the main purposes of the book as Cooper was otherwise writing it? I have tried to suggest that the John Paul Jones story in this book in fact *is* appropriate to the Revolution as Cooper understood it. Cooper grasped Coffin whole, as he had grasped Natty Bumppo in his previous book. But Coffin's proper realm of action was not St. Ruth's Abbey or the English coast. The disjunction between Cooper's vision and his plot was stark. In this sense, killing off Coffin was an unkind but necessary cut on a sprawling, double-focused novel.

In short, as he struggled to become a writer whose productions came out with suitable regularity and thereby paid him what he needed from this untried career, Cooper did not allow himself the time that coherent aesthetic revision would have required. He wrote on the run. In the process, he had wonderful creative sallies that revealed the real power of his imagination. He invented characters (Birch, Bumppo, Coffin, Jones) who came alive then and remain alive today. And he wrote scenes that gave all three of his initial "American" tales their continuing liveliness: the flight-and-pursuit game of *The Spy,* or the ruthless hanging of the Skinner partisan there; the "pictures" of *The Pioneers* that D. H. Lawrence praised so much; the opening escape of the frigate in *The Pilot* or the wreck of the schooner and the death of Long Tom. But the shaping critical intelligence that Cooper also possessed (seen, in part, in the reviews for Gardner's *Literary and Scientific Repository,* but also in how he developed hints into plots) was not fully exercised on the products of his own pen. Had he taken the time to go back over any of his books before he felt the press of time to get them out, he could have made them measurably better.

Cooper hardly was the only American (or English) writer of the early nineteenth century to let things off his desk too soon. Craft was less highly regarded then than it would be in the era of Henry James and Joseph Conrad. But in

Cooper's case the impulse was especially urgent because of his financial straits. The sense of necessity that drove him, and in his 1823 collapse almost drove him under, was implacable. It created both the need to write and the intermittent silences. And it would not let the writer, once he managed to inscribe *The End* on the last page of any work, go back over it again in any comprehensive way. It was hard enough to get to that point, and Cooper, exhausted even when he did not seem so, did not have the wherewithal to reexpose himself to the doubts and drains of another go. Unlike Henry Thoreau, who uttered *A Week on the Concord and Merrimack* in 1849 without real second thoughts, Cooper would not have five years after the appearance of *The Spy* to write and rewrite and rewrite a second American narrative. Cooper was not content to idle away his hours as an inspector of snowstorms. His creditors would not have taken kindly to such whimsy.

Cooper's manner of proceeding was about to change, though not in the straightforward sense one might imagine. His return to the Revolution in *The Pilot*, as suggested earlier, came not only from his sense that this was a lucrative field for an American writer; it came from the apprehension of unfinished business. If his third novel began, as it were, in the midst of his second (hence the importance of the Hollisters and their "Bold Dragoon"), his fourth novel (even as it opened the new field of the sea) revised the underlying premises of *The Spy:* it was an attempt to rewrite that book and not just to reproduce it. As such, of course, it could not also be itself. In *Lionel Lincoln*, Cooper revealed a more coherent approach to the business of invention. He not only planned his field trip with Shubrick (as he had for *The Pilot*) but also undertook it. And, as has been suggested, he labored very hard both on the fieldwork for the book and on the literary study that provided him for the first time a significant part of his "inspiration." His reading for the fifth novel in one sense suggested that he had at least temporarily reached the end of those personal and oral resources on which he had drawn for the previous three novels. But it also suggested his recognition that literature was *work:* that it involved something more conscious than the self-induced creativity that, luckily enough, he had been able to muster time and again as he wrote his previous books into their flawed and discontinuous reality. Ironically, extensive as it was, the research was not sufficiently integrated for the book to work as a whole.

It would be hard to imagine a more literal expression of this principle of re-iteration than the "Legends of the Thirteen Republics" Cooper envisioned in the early winter of 1823–1824. To commit himself thereby to self-replication for a decade (or more, given his actual pace as a writer) was ludicrous. Yet the important point was that Cooper really was beginning to think in blocks bigger than chapters or volumes or even whole books. His work to date had been conducted tactically; this overreaching promise of more to come marked the start of a strategic phase in his career. And with the first of those "Legends" finished, he would cease to need that promise. In his sixth book, as we shall see, he at last found the means to redouble his art, to revise his vision, while still keeping up the pace of production. *The Last of the Mohicans* and *The Prairie* were to initiate a pattern of rearticulation that would stretch across the rest of Cooper's work. His answer to the peculiar challenges of the career as it had begun, with the financial pressures that drove it, was to make the unit of work not the book but the character—or indeed the series, of which any given book gave only an imperfect and partial glimpse. His later dissatisfaction with how incomplete his treatment of Long Tom Coffin had been stemmed from the foreclosure that the *Ariel*'s wreck visited on that character. By reviving Natty Bumppo, Cooper was able to keep working on this other, far more complex, character even as more books came from his hand and went out to the public.

In the Woods

The stories about Israel Putnam's pre-Revolutionary exploits in the New York forest were like a catalyst for the next book, but the constituent elements of the Leather-Stocking series were largely of Cooper's own invention. The continuities between the first of those books to be published and the later ones were the result of retroactive linkages that can be easily deconstructed. For instance, although Cooper probably had seen references to "Bloody Pond" before 1823 (not in Humphreys, who did not mention it, but rather in such books as Timothy Dwight's *Travels* or Benjamin Silliman's *Remarks, Made on a Short Tour, between Hartford and Quebec,* first published in 1820 and reissued in August of the year of Cooper's trip to Lake George), he did not name it in glancing at the Dieskau episode in *The Pioneers.* Probably not until he saw the pond and heard tales about it on the spot in 1824 did he take real note of it and understand its potential as a landscape feature and thematic focus for the pervasive bloodiness of *The Last of the Mohicans.*[3]

By the same token, his tour through the critical military corridor leading from Albany to Lake George and Lake Champlain, stimulated or at least seconded by his recent perusal of Humphreys, made real for Cooper his previously abstract knowledge about the episodes of that conflict. At the time he was writing *The Pioneers,* his familiarity with Sir William Johnson and that man's battles around Lake George probably was not as complete as it subsequently became.[4] It was soon to be enriched by his exposure to various other sources. Aside from his wide reading in recent travel books, including those of Dwight and Silliman, Cooper at about this time must have become acquainted or reacquainted with

Jonathan Carver's *Travels through the Interior Parts of North-America* (1778) and an array of other eighteenth-century texts, including the *Review of the Military Operations in North America from 1753 to 1756,* co-authored by William Livingston, William Smith, and John Morin Scott in 1757 and reprinted in the *Collections* of the Massachusetts Historical Society in 1801.[5]

Reading was not the half of it. In an 1831 letter to his publishers, Carey and Lea, Cooper faulted James Kirke Paulding's portrait of Sir William Johnson in *The Dutchman's Fireside,* supporting his judgment by adding that he "knew a good deal" about the legendary Indian agent and soldier "by report" (*LJ* 2:150–51). The lore came to Cooper from several personal friends and relatives: Hendrik Frey, that long-time resident of the Mohawk valley, who had been one of Johnson's "intimate friends and his executor" (*LJ* 2:150) as well as a famous friend of the Coopers; Cooper's own brother-in-law, George Pomeroy, whose celebrated grandfather Seth had fought not only at Bunker Hill but also at Lake George in 1755, where he took over command of the fallen Col. Ephraim Williams's regiment just as the final defeat of Dieskau's troops began; and the DeLancey family, which claimed kinship with Sir William Johnson (his uncle, Sir Peter Warren, was Susan Cooper's great-uncle) and counted among its members two men, Oliver DeLancey the elder and James DeLancey (Susan's great-uncle and uncle, respectively), who like Seth Pomeroy had served on the northern frontier during the last French war. Furthermore, Susan Cooper's aunt, Susannah, was old enough to have tales to tell of Johnson.[6]

This array of oral sources was impressive. Even so, while writing *The Pioneers* Cooper made only indirect reference to the world in which Sir William Johnson had been such a central figure. This was so for two reasons. First, Cooper's preliminary gestures toward the French and Indian War were intended only to give his old hunter a proper background—certainly not, again, as teasers for an already-envisioned second installment of the series. (Note, too, that Natty actually brings up the encounter with Dieskau in *The Pioneers* not to sing his own praises, but rather in an effort to rehabilitate alcoholic "Old John's" image as the heroic warrior Chingachgook.) Perhaps more important, though, was the fact that until Cooper saw the ground made classic by Johnson it lacked the actuality that his other settings, from Westchester to Otsego, the sea, and now even Boston, had for him. By the time he wrote *The Last of the Mohicans,* in that book as in the earlier ones he was writing about places he personally knew.

Cooper began work on *The Last of the Mohicans* in earnest only after *Lionel Lincoln* was published and, back from his brief Washington trip, he could clear his desk and inscribe the new book's somber, scene-setting first sentence: "It was a feature peculiar to the colonial wars of North America, that the toils and dangers of the wilderness were to be encountered, before the adverse hosts could meet" (*LOM* CE 11). Once again, as further sentences followed and then the pages piled up on his desk, it was Cooper's intent to convey them in manageable groups through Wiley to the printer so that they could be set in type piecemeal. Presumably by March he was spending substantial blocks of time on the project. But then came interruptions. Some were small-scale and private. For instance, near the end of March, Cooper had a letter from his brother Richard's widow, Ann Clarke. She wrote from Otsego to ask that Cooper indeed proceed with his often mentioned effort to secure a midshipman's warrant for her sixteen-year-old son Richard. Ann had long wavered on the plan, which Cooper had proposed for both Richard and his older brother Goldsborough some time before. Recently, however, she had endorsed it for the younger boy—as Cooper, having heard from Richard himself not too long before, already knew.[7]

Also already, Cooper had taken the time to write his good friend Mathew C. Perry, then captain of the *North Carolina* at Hampton Roads, Virginia, to try to reserve Richard a berth on that vessel, soon bound for the Mediterranean. Although times were tight in the navy, Perry thought Cooper's influence substantial: along with letters from himself, John Rodgers, and Isaac Chauncey, all of which would be forthcoming, Cooper's nomination ought to produce a warrant for the boy. The *North Carolina* was another matter. Richard was more than welcome aboard, and Perry personally promised to look out for him once he joined the other midshipmen. However, the ship was due to sail so shortly that the recruit probably would have to cross the ocean in some later vessel going out to join the squadron. All of this boded well for Cooper's nephew. Once he had all the materials gathered, Cooper sent his letter of nomination, with the enclosures from Perry and the others, to Washington. Navy Secretary Samuel L. Southard promptly responded that there indeed were no available slots at present, adding that Richard's name "shall however not be overlooked when a favorable opportunity is afforded of gratifying his and your wishes." After this reversal, Richard Cooper must have changed his plans. He never entered the navy, instead becoming a Cooperstown lawyer and, eventually, Cooper's son-in-law. The 1825 episode illustrates how much thought and time—even if he had to interrupt his literary labors—Cooper gave to his fatherless nieces and nephews.[8]

Other obligations, more public and demanding, also took time away from work on *The Last of the Mohicans*. The lingering fight with New York lawyer Robert Sedgwick, which had flared up across 1824, resumed the following spring. Cooper's success in delaying Sedgwick's action against him in the New York Supreme Court early in 1825 meant that the trial date was moved to March—just the time, as it turned out, when he was to begin *The Last of the Mohicans* in earnest. When the court at long last convened, Cooper, in the thick of his work, did not attend but left matters in the capable hands of attorney

Peter A. Jay. This was not unusual, nor did it seem unwise to Cooper at the time. He knew that the only witness Sedgwick would call was his brother Henry, who had signed the original bond as a witness (even though in fact he had not been present when it was made out and signed by Cooper). In conversations over the weeks leading up to the trial, Henry Sedgwick (like Jay, a member of the Lunch) had confided in Cooper that his brother would openly admit that "he had actually received 12 per cent for his money." If that were the case, Cooper felt confident that the illegality of the interest rate alone would spell victory for himself.[9]

The Sedgwicks jointly misled their friend and host. Under cross-examination at the March trial, Henry Sedgwick asserted that the 1819 bond covered a loan on which legal interest was to be charged. He understood that Cooper had agreed to pay a higher rate, but he did not know for a fact whether that was before or after the bond had been made. And, since he had not been present on any occasion when Cooper made interest payments on the bond, he could not state that the higher rate was actually enforced on that particular loan. On one occasion, he admitted, he had conveyed an $800 payment to his brother from Cooper, but he claimed that he did not know whether that payment was for the 1819 bond. In this atmosphere of denial and obfuscation, it is small surprise that the court found for Robert Sedgwick.[10] The reason for the strategy of the Sedgwick brothers was clear. As the presiding judge for the trial instructed the jury, if Cooper and Robert Sedgwick had agreed on a 12 percent rate at the time the 1819 bond was signed, "the bond is void & the Jury must find for Def[endan]t." Since Cooper had pled "usury"—that the bond violated the state's 1787 usury statute—proof of just this single fact would relieve Cooper of the whole remaining debt. But, as the judge also indicated in his charge to the jury, it was not sufficient for Cooper to raise a suspicion of usury: "He must *prove it*[,] for usury is not to be presumed." On the other hand, the whole onus did not lie on Cooper, since any admission by Sedgwick that he had received 12 percent on the loan would be "presumptive proof of usury." Here was the reason for Henry Sedgwick's carefully deceptive testimony on his brother's behalf.[11]

Cooper, blindsided by the duplicity of the Sedgwicks, began to employ a two-pronged strategy of his own. On April 15, 1825, he petitioned for a new trial on the basis of "surprise," a legal ground that in this instance referred to the fact that Robert Sedgwick had not produced the endorsements on the 1819 bond during the first trial, as he had been expected to, so that Cooper's payments on the original debt were not adequately acknowledged.[12] While the court considered this petition, Cooper also sought to renew his claim that Sedgwick had improperly dealt with the Fenimore Farm properties, which were still in his hands. At the same time, Jay informed Sedgwick that in Cooper's view Sedgwick had

violated their agreement on how the properties were to be sold. Sedgwick answered that he recalled no such agreement, although if Cooper could refresh his
mind on the subject he would of course abide by it. He also added that following the sale, probably in September or October 1824, he and Cooper had discussed the three Fenimore parcels. He had offered Cooper a chance to recover
them by paying off the rest of what he owed on his 1819 bond or by assigning
other acceptable properties to Sedgwick. As Sedgwick remembered their conversation, Cooper had accepted the offer and promised to follow through on it
within a week, but since then, as Sedgwick asserted, "he has never condescended
to see me on the subject or to make any explanation of his neglect."[13]

Sedgwick had hardly waited long for Cooper to turn the corner on his street
and knock at his door. Eben Morehouse, the master in chancery who had handled
the sale of Fenimore on the decree in 1824 and soon thereafter became the
lawyer's Otsego agent, was instructed to receive bids on the place and positively
seek out purchasers. In April of 1825, Morehouse wrote Sedgwick to report on
his largely luckless efforts. Most of the bids that came his way were so far below
the value of Fenimore that he had not troubled Sedgwick with them. Only two
were plausible. The first, offering $1,500 for the entire property, fell through
because of an unsatisfied contingency. The second, for $200 less, was pending as
Morehouse wrote for Sedgwick's approval. Morehouse had toyed with the idea
of dividing the property into pasture lots for the villagers but was convinced that
the scheme would fail. Unless all the lots sold, the value of the remaining property would plummet. "As a farm," he added, "the great objection to it now is
that there is not land enough." Cooper, having separated the Mt. Ovis property
from those along the lake, had inadvertently lessened the value of Fenimore
Farm. Furthermore, since the three lakefront parcels had been rented out for the
past six years, they had suffered rough use by a series of tenants. As the farm
now was, it had no usable pasturage and its fields were so exhausted that it could
not produce grain crops. A further problem was that Isaac Cooper's widow,
Mary Ann, still had dower rights to the single parcel that Cooper had bought
from her husband in 1811. Morehouse was convinced she intended to push the
issue but thought Sedgwick probably could buy her out for fifty or seventy-five
dollars. This was all ammunition for Sedgwick's dealings with Cooper. He
passed the letter on to Peter A. Jay with a message: Cooper could now "have the
land on as good terms as were offered me thro' Mr. Morehouse." But Cooper
would have to move quickly, as the second bidder was waiting for word back
from Sedgwick.[14]

As he had with Thomas Bridgen, Cooper assumed that his cooperation with
Sedgwick would have some value in the latter's eyes. Persisting in his view that
the two had an understanding about how the properties in question would be

sold, he had Jay press Sedgwick not to accept the pending offer reported by Morehouse. Its terms were not acceptable to Cooper, whose claim on the "overplus" gave him, he thought, the right to veto any such bargain. He therefore insisted, as Jay informed Sedgwick, that the farm "be sold in the manner agreed upon between him & you." Cooper was ready not only to applaud Sedgwick's compliance but to reward it. If the farm was subdivided and sold in such a manner that its true potential was realized, he would "pay the money due [Sedgwick] with Interest at the rate which he agreed to pay." However, if Sedgwick turned a deaf ear to Cooper's plea, Cooper would "continue his endeavors to obtain redress."[15]

Somewhat surprisingly, this staunch insistence on Cooper's part brought Sedgwick around, at least temporarily. He wrote Jay on April 11, 1825, that "what you term my Agreement may have reference to some understanding on the part of Mr. Cooper" that Fenimore Farm should be sold "in small lots." These were slippery words, as lawyer Sedgwick surely realized, but underneath their surface they indicated that Sedgwick indeed recalled some such discussion with Cooper as long ago as 1823 or 1824. If no "understanding" had existed, Sedgwick would not have offered "to have the Property sold in such parcels as Mr. C may choose." But there was a barb in Sedgwick's bait. He wanted Cooper to give him additional security so that any shortfall from selling the farm in that manner would be covered "within a reasonable time."[16] Jay's answer does not survive, but its message is implicated in the next letter from Sedgwick: "I have only to state that I should be very glad to sell the Land in parcels if I thought it would sell better—but as it is, I shall immediately direct Mr. Morehouse to follow his own judgment."[17] Much as he might wish to have some say in how his Otsego farm was disposed of—for emotional as well as economic reasons— Cooper evidently had no other property to substitute for it as a means of securing his debt to Robert Sedgwick. On May 1, 1825, not quite three weeks later, Sedgwick accordingly received $1,300 for the three Fenimore parcels from farmer Abraham Van Horne, the client who had been awaiting word from him.[18]

But the business between Cooper and his former friend was not over. Within four days of the time that Sedgwick's last terse letter was received at Jay's office, Cooper petitioned for a new trial. In his deposition, he complained that the endorsements on the 1819 bond had not been produced during the first trial. Ordinarily, such notations of payment on a bond were inscribed on the bond itself, often on the reverse side of the written-on area, thus ensuring that any tampering with the endorsements would damage the original record of the debt. The 1819 bond was written on the top half of a full sheet of paper whose reverse was completely blank. Whenever he made a payment on the debt, Cooper noticed that Sedgwick entered the endorsements not on the back of the bond text proper but rather on the vacant lower portion of the front. This troubled him at the time, because it would be easy for an unscrupulous person to clip the endorsements off the sheet. However, he refused to believe Sedgwick, a "gentleman" and personal friend, capable of such a crime, which he viewed as "tantamount to forgery" (*LJ* 1:123). During the first trial, Sedgwick's attorney, Elijah Paine, had produced the bond—and in fact the endorsements *had* been removed! This serious discovery at the March 1825 trial (the "surprise") was the main ground for Cooper's request for a new trial. He raised other issues, speaking at some length about the terms under which the Fenimore properties were to be sold. And, since usury would remain a vital issue for the court, he reiterated that both parties had fully intended the original 1819 bond to carry 12 percent interest but that Sedgwick had hidden that fact in drafting the document. The court was suitably moved by Cooper's request for a new trial, since on the next day, April 16, 1825, Richard Riker, New York City recorder and an ex officio Court of Common Pleas judge, issued a ruling to stay all proceedings under Sedgwick's verdict until the state supreme court's next term. On May 5, the latter court sided with Cooper, setting aside the March verdict and guaranteeing a second trial.[19]

At this last hearing, Robert Sedgwick for the first time admitted having received usurious interest on the 1819 bond. However, he denied having demanded or imposed the 12 percent rate. He also added that he had not received a penny more than that. And he went so far as to offer to apply all excess interest above the legal rate to the balance of the principal if Cooper paid off the whole debt. As to Fenimore Farm, Sedgwick denied that he had agreed, as a condition for Cooper's assenting to his Chancery Court bill, to subdivide it and sell it off in small parcels. However, he now offered to apply his proceeds from the sale of that property to the bond as well. On a final point, that concerning the clipped endorsements, Sedgwick acknowledged that the sheet of paper on which the bond originally had been written had subsequently been cut in half, separating the endorsements from the bond proper. He somewhat lamely added that if the endorsements had been produced at the March trial they would *not* have shown that he had received usurious interest payments. Within a short period, notices of a new trial set for June 20 had been sent out, but over the months following it was delayed several times—first to September, then to November, and finally to December 5, 1825, when it at last went forward, as we shall see.[20]

"Images" . . . and Indians

As spring advanced and Cooper remained simultaneously immersed in the Sedgwick troubles and in the grim forest of *The Last of the Mohicans,* which bore an odd resemblance to each other, his family again was making plans to leave New York City for more pleasant quarters. On or around April 22, having successfully weathered the usual "bustle and confusion" such shifts entailed, they crossed the East River to Queens. This time, they were not to go as far as distant Bayside, on the back side of Flushing, but instead took up residence in an old farm cottage just over the river in Sunswick (now Astoria), which belonged to a member of the Lunch, Col. George Gibbs.[21] A Rhode Island native, Gibbs was an ambitious amateur mineralogist and a close friend and advisor of Benjamin Silliman, through whom Gibbs's spectacular collection of mineral specimens, purchased in Europe, went to Yale. Cooper could have met Gibbs through that connection—or by virtue of the fact that Gibbs's late daughter, Helen Elizabeth, had been the first wife of his good friend Luther Bradish. But Gibbs, an important figure in the intellectual world of New York when the Coopers moved there, just as easily could have come to the novelist's attention through his associations in the city. In 1822, for instance, Gibbs was chosen vice president of the New York Lyceum of Natural History, in which such associates of Cooper as Jeremiah Van Rensselaer, John W. Francis, James E. DeKay, and Samuel L. Mitchill were all quite active at the time. Any one of them could have brought Gibbs to the Lunch, whereupon Cooper could easily have arranged to spend the upcoming summer season in Sunswick.[22]

Once the Coopers had moved across the river from Manhattan in mid-spring, they had the run of Gibbs's magnificent Sunswick Farm. With its own wharf on the shore below Hell Gate, the estate catered to the novelist's best pleasures. The "cool stone house" (*LJ* 1:120) where he and Susan and the children lived stood on a small wooded hill only thirty feet above the water. Sitting on the green bank out front, Cooper was delighted by the busy nautical show laboring through the narrow passage between the shore and Blackwell's Island. In the evenings, his eldest daughter recalled, he would instruct the children in the lexicon of the sea: the parts of a sailing vessel's rigging, the names of the different kinds of craft, even such exotica as how to distinguish "periaguas and chebacco boats" (*LOM* HE xv).

Among the passing vessels were Manhattan steamboats that came each day to Hallett's Cove, just north of Gibbs Point, affording quick connection to the city. But Cooper soon had a little vessel of his own tied up at the wharf, a twenty-ton, broad-bowed sloop christened the *Van Tromp* after the legendary Dutch admiral. In it, he would run over to New York almost daily, his daughter Susan remembered, often taking her with him to Wall Street, where he would conduct his business with Wiley and then wait at the bookstore for the tide to change. Unlike the year before at Bayside, ready contact with the city was always possible in the summer of 1825, giving Cooper no geographical excuse for delays in his latest project. Chapter by chapter, *The Last of the Mohicans* could be delivered to Wiley and passed on to Fanshaw, who was putting it into type and running it off.

When the water and the *Van Tromp* did not beckon, the Coopers could turn about and go inland. Behind the stone cottage at Sunswick lay the plains of Newtown, home to the famed yellow Newtown Pippin, a late-ripening native American apple for which Cooper would yearn nostalgically once in Europe. At the time, this was "a perfectly quiet, rural region, [with] nothing but open farms for miles around," as his eldest daughter recalled. Suitably, the family kept "a beautiful little cow, 'Betty,'" a decided advantage at a time when urban diary products were often objectionable. To balance the sloop, Cooper had a farm wagon with a pair of black horses, perhaps relics from Angevine or even Turtle Bay; in this plain vehicle he would drive his four daughters and little Paul, fifteen months old in May, around the estate and back amid the fields and orchards. Or he would carry all of them to the beach south of the cottage, shady and shell-strewn, where they could loiter and bathe as if nothing was wrong—as if Cooper himself was healthy and as rich as Colonel Gibbs (*LOM* HE xv; SFM 57).

It was amid these wishful diversions that, within a month of the family's move, the truth reasserted itself. Answering a chatty letter from Shubrick in June, the novelist reported that he had had a touch of his "old fever," the first of two during this busy year. By June, he was "happily convalescent," indeed, was "all the better for the attack" (*LJ* 1:120). Perhaps the novelist was better, but at the height of the attack late in May his novel certainly suffered, meaning that once he recovered he had to go back to where he had left off and once more get his bearings. Cooper had begun the new book with considerable energy and was making good progress on it first at Greenwich Street and then at Sunswick Farm. Illness stopped his pen, but so strong was the grip of the suspended book that its action kept playing over in his mind, according to his eldest daughter, throughout the siege (*LOM* HE xvi; *P&P* 128). One afternoon, no longer able to restrain himself, but in a nearly delirious state, he suddenly demanded pen and paper so that he could resume the book. His will had overshot his strength. He was so weak that he still could not even hold the pen; only with his fearful wife acting as amanuensis was he able to dictate a single page of seemingly jumbled notes that sketched out the key action of a fresh chapter, the book's twelfth. Once his fever abated in a few days, he expanded the notes, thereby renewing and moving on with his work (*LOM* HE xvi–xvii).

This episode is among the more famous that Cooper's eldest daughter recorded. As usual, she got some things wrong. Most importantly, her chronology was confused. Believing that her father had written *The Last of the Mohicans* immediately after the trip with the Smith-Stanley party, and had finished the book in a three- or four-month run up to publication (February 6, 1826), she necessarily postdated that trip by a full year. In her view, Cooper had come back from Lake George with the tale sketched out in his mind in August of 1825 and had sat down and plunged into it, only to be interrupted when, as a result of "exposure" (to the sun, apparently), he was struck down that fall and forced to break off his work.[23] She was right, I think, about the effects of the fever on his literary labors. However, she completely forgot (or did not know) that he had suffered from two attacks of fever in 1825: the one late in May, about the time that he in fact was finishing work on the first third of the book; and another that apparently followed in mid-September. Presumably this second attack also interrupted Cooper's work, but of that we have no evidence aside from Susan's mistaken anecdote.[24]

The interruption offers unusual insight into the imaginative process by which Cooper produced his most famous—and most intense—work of fiction. Susan's anecdote indicates that, over the previous month or two, her father had written the first eleven chapters of the novel. These introduce the main characters (the Munro party in Chapters 1 and 2; Natty, Chingachgook, and Uncas in Chapter 3), bring them together, temporarily disperse them, then bring them together again for the tale's first serious battle at "Glenn's," the first of the two settings suggested by Cooper's tour with Smith-Stanley. That battle, a foretaste of the massacre near Fort William Henry later in the novel, results in the capture of the Munros, Gamut, and Heyward, as well as the flight of Natty, Chingachgook, and Uncas. Thereby the rest of the action in the book is basically set in motion.[25]

Once he was able to return to work, Cooper could continue right across the break from the finished chapter into the next one: "The Hurons stood aghast at this sudden visitation of death on one of their band," the latter therefore opens (*LOM* CE 111). But it was not just a simple continuity of plot that Susan's anecdote suggests. As she put it, during the height of the fever, Cooper's "mind was filled with images" from the book (*LOM* HE xvi; *P&P* 128). Herein lies the special suggestiveness of her anecdote.[26]

While one cannot be sure exactly what Susan Cooper meant by that word "images," the term resonates with the patterns of the book itself. It is of course appropriate for the feverish, phantasmagoric state she portrayed her father as inhabiting while dictating his notes. Oddly, however, Cooper himself often used the term in quite meaningful ways in the novel. He was fascinated with the "imagery" of Native American culture, to begin with: for instance, with "those oriental images" that he, like others of his era, thought suggested a link between the Indians and the cultures of Asia (*LOM* CE 342).[27] In the novel, his Indian speakers almost as a matter of reflex employ poetic, highly expressive images that state complex, at times abstract propositions in terms of sensible facts. Cooper's narrative, introducing Natty Bumppo in the third chapter, describes his eye as "small, quick, keen, and restless"; as soon as Chingachgook begins to speak, it is *he* who introduces the famous sobriquet "Hawk-eye" (*LOM* CE 30), a formula resembling the "kennings" of ancient Anglo-Saxon practice as filtered through James McPherson's pseudo-epics of "Ossian." In his 1831 preface to the novel, Cooper overtly wrote: "The imagery of the Indian, both in his poetry and in his oratory, is Oriental. . . . He draws his metaphors from the clouds, the seasons, the birds, the beasts, and the vegetable world" (*LOM* CE 5). And in the book he was at pains to demonstrate the inherently poetic nature of Indian speech, be it Chingachgook's or Tamenund's. This was one of the ways in which he transformed the largely silent John Mohegan of *The Pioneers* into a figure of eloquence.

Furthermore, the novel is richly imaged in its own narrative voice. The natural world, the source of Indian imagery in Cooper's view, also provides much of his own. There is a neat symbolic statement of this proposition in Natty's night-shrouded description of the falls in Chapter 6. Protean in energy and form, the river is roaring down the rocky chasm on either side of the Munro party as the scout endeavors to "place" them in the invisible landscape. His main point in the metaphor-rich passage is that the water, in what he calls its "perversity," constantly mimics the things of this world. Its own motions suggest a host of moods and movers: "sometimes it leaps, sometimes it tumbles; there, it skips; here, it shoots." Moreover, the water pours forth a flood of momentary visual illusions: "in one place 'tis white as snow, and in another 'tis green as grass." All of the river's fascination for Natty and for Cooper is summed up in the exquisite *discordia concors* of Leather-Stocking's startling turn toward one of the Munros: "Ay, lady, the fine cobweb-looking cloth you wear at your throat, is coarse, and like a fish-net, [compared] to little spots I can show you, where the river fabricates all sorts of images, as if, having broke loose from order, it would try its hand at everything" (*LOM* CE 55). The wild river in some of its moods can outdo the finest product of human art, the most delicate of lace. Nature overwhelms Cooper's characters with its protean, shape-mimicking power.

Cooper's target in that passage is not the Hudson River or, in some proto-Jungian sense, *water* in general. Rather, he aims to portray the deep transformative power of the world at large, the constant cycling of matter through form. His use of Glens Falls to develop this profound theme certainly tells us something about the nature of his experience at this spot in 1824. In larger terms, however, the outer influence acting on him most profoundly here was the Indian view, as he understood it from his own sources, of the deep principles of nature and the relation of human experience to the natural world. He interested himself throughout the book in nature as power rather than nature as spectacle. It is thus an ingenious stroke of his mind to make use of the falls, the key effect of which on travelers in his period was visual, during the darkness. Lest his reader think he was merely indulging in pictorial embellishment, he had Natty mediate the falls through his flowing—*leaping, tumbling, skipping, shooting*—words. In the prose itself is the first and best demonstration of what Cooper had learned from Indian culture: that art, like all else that is human, is an effect of nature, an expression of it, rather than its externally imposed frame that shapes and contains the world.

This insight had come to Cooper in all likelihood as he meditated on the book over the months following his Adirondack trip. While at Glens Falls, if we can believe Smith-Stanley's report, Cooper envisioned the new book not as a second Leather-Stocking tale but rather as an "Indian" story. Hence his comment, as recorded by the Englishman, that he had to place one of his "old Indians" there."[28] Since by this point in his career Cooper's *only* "old Indian" was Chingachgook, Natty's companion and subordinate in *The Pioneers*, one might conclude that from the outset Natty was to be a given in the novel. I think, however, that Cooper at first was more interested in Chingachgook and Uncas and that he included Natty perforce, only later giving thought to what this *second* tale about the white hunter ought to be (see *LOM* CE xx). That Chingachgook, already described in *The Pioneers* as the last remaining "representative" of his particular band of Mohegans (as *The Pioneers* spells the name), is given a son in *The Last of the Mohicans* points to his centrality in the new book. Natty is the loner here, not only a man without a cross but almost a man without a *life* as well.

Although Natty and Chingachgook are both introduced in the third chapter of *The Last of the Mohicans*, Chingachgook significantly comes first. Furthermore, while Natty is certainly garrulous in that chapter, once Chingachgook opens up he delivers an eloquent account of his people's long history that shows up as shallow and impertinent Natty's interpolated comments about his personal past ("For myself, I conclude that all the Bumppos could shoot; for I have a natural turn with a rifle" [*LOM* CE 31], and so forth). This will be Chingachgook's story in large part, as the title of the book and the prominence of his son's role in it suggest: *The Last of the Mohicans* is the only one of the Leather-Stocking Tales, in fact, not named after some theme or place intimately associated with Natty. He is "the foremost in that band of Pioneers" leading the Europeans into America in the first book (*PIO* CE 456); the eponymous "Prairie" of the third novel is his by occupation and by last rites; he *is* the Pathfinder and the Deerslayer. But he is never a Mohican, as, despite his "savage equipments" (*LOM* CE 28)—and his at-times "Indian" speech, as in the cavern scene—this "man without a cross" takes tedious pains to remind us across the "Indian" tale in which he happens to find himself.

Cooper's knowledge of Indian life and culture was certainly limited by modern standards, and in some particulars (e.g., on the genealogy of and relations among the northeastern tribes) it was hopelessly wrong. His mistakes were not atypical of his period, however; what *was* atypical relative to his nonnative contemporaries was the fact that he strove to know as much as he could and, more importantly, to use it sensitively. The stick figures of Brockden Brown's *Edgar Huntly*, with the possible exception of Old Deb, have no cultural depth. They are functions of the warfare plot—destined to be nothing more than murdered and mangled corpses. Cooper's most immediate rival, Lydia Maria Child, has been praised of late for her ability to imagine marriage between a Euro-American woman and a New England Indian in *Hobomok, A Tale of the Early Times* (1824) as a critical intervention in the typical policies and attitudes of her period. However, her Native American hero is little more than a function of the marriage plot—not mangled or murdered, to be sure, but nonetheless stripped of his dignity. He certainly lacks a cultural core. Aside from the "long stories" he is *said* to have told the heroine, Mary Conant, about the Iroquois, picked up from a visiting chieftain years before, or his "account of the ancestors of some neighboring tribe . . . dropped to earth by an eagle," he is just the available "tawny chieftain" whom Mary exploits in a fit of pique over her father's strict authority. At the end, when Mary turns from Hobomok to her long-absent *white* lover, Charles Brown, Hobomok nobly gives her up and disappears from New England forever. He is a vanishing Indian whose specific loss, the result of Mary Conant's selfish but obscured hard-heartedness, has broad symbolic meaning. That meaning is soon made clear when Mary expresses her embarrassment over the "swarthy boy" she has had with Hobomok: "I cannot go to England. . . . My boy would disgrace me." She claims to love the child, and Charles Brown agrees to adopt him. But the only way the boy, who eventually graduates from Harvard and then goes to England, can fit in is through the gradual elision of the middle name ("Charles *Hobomok* Conant," Mary had named him) that is the sole remaining mark of his Indian parentage.[29]

Small wonder that Child almost twenty years later missed the cultural truths in viewing an Indian war dance at P. T. Barnum's American Museum in New York: "I was never before so much struck with the animalism of the Indian character, as I was in the frightful war-dance of these chiefs. Their gestures were as furious as wild-cats, they howled like wolves, screamed like prairie dogs, and tramped like buffaloes. Their faces were painted fiery red, or with cross-bars of green and red, and they were decorated with all sorts of uncouth trappings of hair, and bones, and teeth. . . . The shrill howl of old Nan-Nouce-Fush-E-To ["Buffalo King," a Sac and Fox leader] . . . clove the brain like a tomahawk, and was hot with hatred."[30] Not until the post–Civil War era would she fully mend her ways, repudiating Euro-American policy in her "Appeal for the Indians" (1868).

Cooper did not live long enough to join her in that "appeal." Already in the 1820s, however, he had an advantage over Child because he had grown up within sight of more-or-less viable native communities. And, like his father, he had enjoyed some degree of personal interaction with members of those communities, who continued to frequent Cooperstown and the Cooper house as late as the 1840s. Cooper supplemented these personal impressions with information gleaned from two other sources. His reading even before the start of his literary career seems to have been especially rich in documents of male adventure, including military adventure, on the colonial and early national frontiers. This habit, as much as his roots on New York's post-Revolutionary border, was one long inadvertent preparation for his work as a writer. It is utterly typical of such interests that Cooper would be diverted from the ostensible subject of his research for *Lionel Lincoln* in David Humphreys's *Essay on the Life of Major General Israel Putnam*—Bunker Hill—and become engaged with the longer account of pre-Revolutionary Adirondack warfare contained therein. As suggested earlier, that account seems to have renewed his interest in the Lake George region and helped him decide to visit it at the earliest opportunity.

Such background readings were considerably supplemented by more recent studies. Two books by Moravian missionary John G. E. Heckewelder were of crucial importance. Cooper seemingly had read the first of them, *An Account of the History, Manners, and Customs, of the Indian Nations, who once Inhabited Pennsylvania and the Neighboring States* (1818), by the time he began work on *The Pioneers*, since he had found the name of his first Indian character, Chingachgook, there. It has, however, been suggested that his attention was called to the book by William H. Gardiner's review of *The Spy* in the July 1822 issue of the *North American Review*. In that long piece, Gardiner urged the subject of Native American life on Cooper and other American writers, and he specifically cited "the indefatigable Heckewelder" as the Indians' "best historian."[31] Gardiner's influence on Cooper seems possible, but on balance unlikely. By July of 1822, Cooper already had introduced John Mohegan into his work-in-progress, in the seventh chapter of which he elaborated his background. There he cited the character's original name, gave its translated meaning in roughly Heckewelder's form (Heckewelder: "a large snake"; Cooper: "Great Serpent"), and listed the other names by which Chingachgook subsequently had been known among his people and the Euro-Americans.[32] Since this first portion of Cooper's novel had been put into print early enough for Fitz-Greene Halleck to depart for Liverpool on July 1 with a set of sheets of "the first hundred pages of the work in print" (see *LJ* 1:75), among which must have been at least the crucial first part of Chapter 7, Cooper would appear to have encountered Heckewelder's *History, Manners, and Customs* on his own at some earlier time.[33]

The second Heckewelder book, *A Narrative of the Missions of the United Brethren among the Delaware and Mohegan Indians* (1820), may have provided

Cooper with additional insight into Native American culture. With its rich accounts of such border figures as turncoat Simon Girty, Heckewelder's *Narrative* certainly could have added a great deal to Cooper's sense of what life on the frontier between European and Native American communities entailed. But we do not know for sure that he read it as well as *History, Manners, and Customs,* which clearly was a watershed book for his understanding.

The Last of the Mohicans itself provides indications of the other readings that contributed to Cooper's vision of Native American experience and culture. This is not a matter of overt references but rather of fundamental concepts absorbed from wilderness books and deployed to considerable aesthetic effect. For instance, the facility with which Cooper's human characters merge with natural creatures—or "totems," to use a word that in fact was central to Cooper's understanding of Indian sociopoetic organization—suggests that he was self-consciously seeking to model this first of his "Indian" tales on the mental habits of the Native Americans, not just on the outward plot of their history. It is not claiming too much to assert that his sixth novel has a totemic principle at its core. This point acquires special importance when one realizes that *The Last of the Mohicans* is the first literary text credited by the *Oxford English Dictionary* with use of the Ojibway-derived term *totem,* which before 1826 had been employed only in John Long's *Voyages and Travels of an Indian Interpreter and Trader* (1791) and Alexander Henry's *Travels and Adventures in Canada and the Indian Territories* (1809), one or both of which Cooper must have read before 1825. In the novel, he calls attention to the newness of the word for his audience by having Natty use it in interrogating Yankee psalm-master Davey Gamut about some of the people in Magua's camp (who prove to be Delawares): "Had they held their corn-feast—or can you say any thing of the totems of their tribe?" Gamut, utterly ignorant of the *cultural* context of Indian life, replies matter-of-factly that the Indians he observed ate much corn: "for the grain, being in the milk, is both sweet to the mouth and comfortable to the stomach." As to Natty's other question, he admits, "Of totem, I know not the meaning" (*LOM* CE 226). Later, as if to once again emphasize the term and concept, Cooper will have Uncas deride the Hurons as "boasters" who, although their "'totem' is a moose," yet "run like snails." By contrast, he continues, "The Delawares are children of the tortoise; and they outstrip the deer!" (*LOM* CE 272). Later still, Cooper explains that the "peculiar symbol, or 'totem'" of one of Magua's Huron allies was the beaver; he therefore stops at a pond to express his "family affection" for the creatures there—one of whom turns out to be Chingachgook implausibly but significantly concealed in a beaver skin (*LOM* CE 284–85).

Cooper's deployment of the concept of the totem in *The Last of the Mohicans* should remind us that he had been an active gatherer of Indian lore for many years. Some of it came from reading, some from personal observation. As to the latter, the evidence is unfortunately slender but worth consideration. In a famous but vague story, his daughter Susan claimed that he had encountered delegations of Indian chiefs touring the east in the 1820s, and "in several instances" had even followed them to Washington (*P&P* 130). Later she expanded on the issue:

> Delegations from the western tribes were frequently seen at that period on their way to Washington. Since his interest in the race had become especially awakened, he lost no opportunity of visiting these parties, which often lingered for several months in the great eastern cities. He followed them from New York to Philadelphia, to Baltimore, to Washington; he studied the different individuals who composed these embassies of warriors; he admired their physical appearance, he was impressed with the vein of poetry and laconic eloquence, if the expression may be used, marking their brief speeches; and their natural dignity of manner and grace of gesture, blended with their strongly marked savage mien and accoutrement, struck him forcibly. He made the personal acquaintance of the prominent chiefs. He questioned the interpreters closely. The army officers who accompanied these delegations were frequently old friends. (*PR* HE xii)

Although Susan developed this particular discussion in her introduction to *The Prairie,* she intended it to have a more general application. What I want to suggest here, through recounting a specific instance, is the sort of *learning* that such contacts represented for Cooper.

Lack of documentation in Cooper's papers makes it difficult to pin down occasions on which he encountered such Indian delegations in New York, let alone followed any of them from there to other cities. Orm Överland has suggested that the visit Cooper made to Washington in February and March of 1825, when the electoral runoff for president in the House took place and the novelist attended President and Mrs. Monroe's last White House reception on February 9, was leisurely enough that Cooper would have been able to witness "the several delegations of Indians" then at the capital "arranging for the removal of their tribes to the west of the Mississippi."[34] However, Överland cited no evidence for his assertion that Cooper stayed on through the inauguration of John Quincy Adams on March 4 (which is doubtful), and did not specify precisely which Native Americans he thought Cooper might have met on this occasion. An earlier episode that is capable of tentative reconstruction offers a bit more detail but is also not definitive. Its beginning lay in an essay that first appeared in Henry Colburn's *New Monthly Magazine* in July 1821 and soon was reprinted in an American journal, *The Literary Gazette: or, Journal of Criticism, Science, and the Arts.* The piece, titled "Fragments from the Woods," concerned itself with the theme of Indian eloquence.

The British narrator of "Fragments" calls himself Outalissa out of defer-ence to the character Outalissi, father of Chactas in Chateaubriand's *Atala* (1801). He recounts how, as he perused a volume containing the speeches of Thomas Erskine, lord chancellor of England, he came across a perhaps imagi-nary, perhaps real address "of an American chieftain, justifying his animosity to the invaders of his country, and avowing his determination to defend it."[35] Struck by the "soul-stirring energy" of this example of "nature's eloquence," the essayist was sent off in search of authentic Native American speeches. Through the kindness of an unnamed American friend, he was soon able to gather a number of Indian anecdotes and a sheaf of speeches. Among the latter was an extemporaneous address delivered on July 20, 1815, by the Fox leader Mackkatananamakee ("The Black Thunder") in answer to angry charges made by Gov. William Clark of the Missouri Territory earlier that month that the Fox and related Sauk Indians had ignored their treaty obligations with the United States. In this address at Portage des Sioux, near St. Louis, The Black Thunder asserted with firm assurance the honorable behavior of the Fox. He took a high, dispassionate tone: "My father—Restrain your feelings, and hear ca[l]mly what I shall say. I shall tell it to you plainly. I shall not speak with fear and trembling. I feel no fear. I have no cause to fear. I have never injured you, and innocence can feel no fear. I turn to all, red skins and white skins, and challenge an accusa-tion against me." While on its face this opening of his speech may seem unre-markable, a bit of probing uncovers its historic importance. First printed in a St. Louis newspaper in July 1815, and from there soon reprinted in *Niles' Weekly Register* in Baltimore, the speech provided the first example in print of the terms *red skins* and *white skins* for Indians and Europeans, respectively.[36] Since Cooper was to use both these terms in *The Pioneers*, work on which began within a few months of the time Outalissa's essay appeared, we can be virtually certain that he adopted them from "Fragments from the Woods."[37] Given the fact that he ar-rived in New York City from Westchester in early October to finish off *The Spy* and at the same time to begin *The Pioneers*, it seems reasonable to conclude that he most likely found Outalissa's piece in the September number of *The Literary Gazette*, read it, and quickly adopted not only these terms but also a number of other details and emphases.[38]

Readers are so familiar with these terms—especially the first, which soon achieved wide acceptance, largely through *The Pioneers*—that Cooper's inno-vation in picking them up and using them almost always passes unnoticed. The term "red-skin" (Cooper's version in *The Pioneers*) was an accurate translation of The Black Thunder's original. As linguist Ives Goddard has conclusively

shown, the term in various upper Midwest Indian languages and in French trans-
lations from them (i.e., *Peau-Rouge*) originated in the cultural border grounds of
the Mississippi watershed in the eighteenth century. In *The Pioneers,* Cooper
used it, in Goddard's view, with no derogatory intent: that is, "as an affectless
designation for Native Americans." The Black Thunder's speech held up a neat
binary that balanced the two peoples engaged in an historic confrontation along
the thousand-mile border that, with British withdrawal from the upper Midwest
following the end of the War of 1812, had inched perilously close to his tribal
homeland in the upper Mississippi valley. That the borrowed term "redskin"
soon became a dismissive putdown for Native Americans was owing to forces
beyond Cooper's control or forecast, forces at work in Euro-American culture at
large. To those forces he overtly contributed nothing aside from the borrowed
term. That term appealed to him not because it focused attention on skin color
but rather because it was a potent example of what he took to be Indian thought
and speech habits: reducing the enormous cultural and historical contrasts across
the middle border to a visible material difference was an excellent instance of
"natural" metaphor. "Red-skin" and "white-skin" were, like "Hawk-eye," sensible truths, truths to be perceived directly through the senses.[39]

The Black Thunder's speech was clearly of considerable importance for
Cooper's emergent conception of Native American experience and attitudes.
Moreover, it was only one of several debts Cooper contracted to the article in the
1821 *Literary Gazette.* Another arose, though less directly, from a second speech
excerpted in "Fragments from the Woods." This was a funeral oration delivered
by the Omaha leader Ongpatonga (or Big Elk, although neither name was given
in the essay) for the Sioux chief Black Buffalo, who died during another session
at Portage des Sioux later in July 1815 (Plate 20).[40] While this particular oration
apparently had no immediate effect on Cooper, its "author" was in fact one of
those Indians visiting the East with whom the novelist was to become acquainted
during the first decade of his career. While in Paris in 1827, he wrote to Alber-
tine de Staël, the countess de Broglie, that he "knew Ongpatonga i.e. le gros cerf,
personally" (*LJ* 1:199). When, at the start of Chapter 12 in *The Last of the Mohicans,* the Hurons cry out "Le Cerf Agile! le Gros Serpent!" as Uncas and then
his father rush in upon them, the sobriquets are the recombined traces of Cooper's Indian learning—borrowed from Ongpatonga's name as Cooper had understood it on meeting the chief (if not before), and from Heckewelder's explanation of the Delaware language.

Ongpatonga, who at the time he visited the East was the principal chief of
the Omaha, was among the seventeen members of a delegation from several
Missouri River tribes that was brought to Washington by federal Indian agent
Benjamin O'Fallon, Governor Clark's nephew, in the late fall of 1821. Passing

via Louisville, Wheeling, and Hagerstown, the group arrived in the federal capital in two contingents on November 29 and 30. Leaving two tribal chiefs and one
interpreter in Washington, the bulk of the party under O'Fallon's guidance soon
went to Baltimore and Philadelphia, and then on to New York, where they arrived at the City Hotel on December 11. Here they stayed for six nights before
departing once again for Philadelphia. After a brief stay there (from the seventeenth to the eighteenth or nineteenth), all of them were back in Washington by
the twenty-seventh.[41]

Cooper, it will be recalled, was in New York City finishing the last details
of *The Spy* precisely at the moment of the delegation's visit. In fact, he arrived
at the City Hotel the day before the O'Fallon party did and was still there when
it left. This must have been the time when he met Ongpatonga. We do not know
the names of the two chiefs left behind in Washington, but statistically the
Omaha leader was likely to have been among those who went on the tour to New
York. And if he was present at the City Hotel, Cooper could hardly have
avoided him even if he wished to. The hotel had private rooms, but, as Edward
Smith-Stanley noted during his stay there three years later, meals were taken in
common at set hours in a large dining hall. In December 1821, both Cooper and
the O'Fallon delegation were charged for meals; there seems virtually no chance
that the novelist did not at least *see* the chiefs then.[42] And given his avid interest
in the subject of Indian culture and experience at a time when he was already at
work on *The Pioneers,* it is inconceivable that Cooper would fail to seek out positive interaction with the visitors. Ongpatonga he described to the countess de
Broglie as "a chief of great dignity," suggesting personal interaction, and added
that he was "celebrated for his eloquence," a somewhat more slippery formulation that may or may not indicate that the novelist *heard* him hold forth (*LJ*
1:199). Perhaps he witnessed the appearance of the visiting Indians at the "Gallery of Paintings" at 253 Broadway on December 13.[43] But he may not have
needed to do so, since their stay under his nose for a week must have given him
plenty of opportunities to observe and interact with them.

This must also have been the occasion when Cooper met another member
of the delegation—Petalesharo, a Pawnee Loup (more properly Skidi or Skiri
Pawnee) who later became a chief. This second native visitor to the East was also
mentioned by Cooper in his letter to the countess de Broglie as a personal acquaintance. A man who "would have been a hero in any civilization," he was "in
form . . . an Apollo." Indeed, so impressive a figure was he that Cooper had used
him as "the model of *le Coeur dur* or Hard-Heart," who would be "the principal
Indian character" in *The Prairie,* published in Paris two months later. Cooper
also stressed for the countess that he had "in no degree exaggerated" Petalesharo's "appearance" or his "imperturbable qualities" (*LJ* 1:199), giving her the

specific page reference for a confirmatory description of the heroic Petalesharo in Edwin James's *Account of an Expedition from Pittsburgh to the Rocky Mountains under the Command of Major Stephen H. Long* (1823). This major source on the prairies he evidently had brought with him from New York, but now, done with it, he sent it on to her. When she opened the book to the appropriate page, the countess would find that the Pawnee Loup chief had struck the members of Long's expedition as "of the finest form, tall, muscular, exceedingly graceful, and of a most prepossessing countenance."[44]

There is every reason to believe that Cooper's further account of Petalesharo in *Notions of the Americans* was fairly true to the novelist's own experience. Even so, some details derived from published sources. Cooper borrowed a tale, first printed in Jedidiah Morse's *Report to the Secretary of War* (1822) from the diary of one of Stephen Long's officers, about how the Pawnee had intervened to save the life of a Comanche woman captive about to be put to death in an ancient spring ritual. Morse's version of the tale, which anticipated that of Edwin James, was widely reprinted in the press, and his volume also used an image of Petalesharo as its frontispiece, making the warrior and future chief an even more appealing figure. With the publication of Edwin James's *Account,* which contained a claim (not wholly accurate) of how Petalesharo's intervention had abolished the ritual of "sanguinary sacrifice" that had long been practiced among the Skidi Pawnee, he was well on his way to heroic apotheosis. Obviously attractive to those who took a high view of Native American character, the rescue was given a prominent place in Edward Everett's review of James's *Account,* and "a doggerel poem describing and sentimentalizing" the episode appeared, as Orm Överland discovered, in the New York *Commercial Advertiser.* When Cooper retold it in *Notions of the Americans* he therefore hardly was breaking the news. Nor was his conclusion (Petalesharo had destroyed "a baneful superstition" [*Notions* 2:288]) in the least unusual. Whether the highly valued peacock feathers that his fictional Count presents to the Pawnee in *Notions of the Americans* were based on an actual gift by the novelist, we may doubt.[45]

Cooper's acquaintance with Ongpatonga and Petalesharo in New York City may have been extended in Washington. In one of her rare detailed comments on her father's contact with western Indians, Susan Fenimore Cooper indicated that Petalesharo in particular was among those whom he met in the federal capital. According to her, the meeting took place in May 1826, when she thought her father went to Washington in an effort to finalize arrangements for his pending diplomatic appointment (SFM 59). In fact, Cooper's visit for that purpose took place two months earlier, at the beginning of March (see Chapter 16). Furthermore, no information about a delegation of Skidi Pawnee visiting the federal capital at either time has turned up. It nonetheless *is* possible that Susan was recalling, albeit with considerable distortion, some earlier trip by her father to the federal capital. For instance, Cooper may well have followed Ongpatonga and Petalesharo back to Washington in the winter of 1821–1822. Once finished with *The Spy* in December, he almost surely returned to Angevine for the holidays. But he was at the City Hotel on January 16, 1822, left there on the nineteenth, then was back from the twenty-eighth to the morning of February 1. He returned on the afternoon of the seventh, left on the morning of the ninth, was there again late on the fourteenth, and finally left on the nineteenth. During most of these visits, he probably was going through revisions for the second edition of *The Spy*, which was to appear on March 5. Among the several comings and goings, however, are two that seem oddly syncopated. His return to the hotel for tea on February 7 and his unusually quick departure after breakfast, some forty hours later, suggests, in conjunction with his absence for almost a week before this visit, that he had been away somewhere else—Washington, I will argue in a moment—during the first week of the month. Stopping briefly at the hotel on his return, he stayed overnight to catch up with work on the revisions and then hurried home to Angevine, where he remained for five days before returning to the city to put in a final burst of work on the new edition. Now it happens that the week of Cooper's absence from New York (February 1–7) was an important week in Washington. On February 4, the O'Fallon delegation attended a reception at the White House. Although this has been described as a "private" reception, that simply meant that it was not open to the general public, as a celebration on New Year's Day and another on February 9 were. Jedidiah Morse was present for the February 4 occasion, for instance, so it hardly was completely closed. It thus is quite possible that Cooper "followed" Ongpatonga and Petalesharo to Washington a few days after they left on their slow return—saw them at the White House and perhaps elsewhere, then returned to New York, where he could resume work on *The Pioneers*. It is also possible that Cooper went back to Washington on February 9 for a second visit; that he was at the City Hotel for supper on the fourteenth may suggest his arrival from the south then. While none of this is documented as fully as one might like, it does have the virtue of locating a more plausible occasion for Susan Cooper's detailed, if skewed, account of her father's Washington pilgrimage.[46]

Cooper's reading and touring in the early 1820s laid a fresh layer of impressions over the substratum of his earlier experience. Cooper's father had established early ties with nearby native communities in the vicinity of Cooperstown (see Chapter 1). Even the novelist's daughter, who left Otsego at the age of four and did not return there until she was in her twenties, had heard enough to write, apropos of the treatment of Chingachgook's background in Chapter 7 of *The Pioneers*, "The account given of the Delawares and Mohegans in this chapter is

essentially based on good historical authority." Furthermore, she added: "There
were early in this century wandering Mohegans coming to Lake Otsego, and to
be met on ground farther west, much in the condition ascribed to Chingachgook
in his old age. It is believed that this name was a real one. The Lenni Lenape
tribes gave to General [Anthony] Wayne the name of Sugach-gook, or Black
Serpent" (*PIO* HE 75–76n).[47] As noted earlier, the nearest native village to
Cooperstown surviving relatively intact from the prewar period was made up of
Oneidas, the one Iroquois tribe that had fought in large numbers on the American side in the war with Britain and that now was seeking to return to its more
peaceful pursuits. Other Iroquois, including the Mohawk, had been harried from
the area by American military action in 1779, leaving the Oneida relatively isolated. Perhaps partly for that reason, in the 1780s they welcomed to their lands
those groups of displaced native peoples from farther east, the Stockbridge Indians and those who, under the leadership of Samson Occom, became known
as the Brothertons. They, too, were "settlers," sharing a good deal with Judge
Cooper's clients in Otsego, and they were very much part of his world.

It may be that Cooper's most talked-about female figure in his forest ro-
After the further migrations that removed many of these nearby Native
American groups to the Midwest, some families and individuals of each group
lingered in New York. The latter included those whom Cooper's eldest daughter
recalled as visiting her family's home in the late 1840s, claiming what she called
"an hereditary acquaintance with the master of the house"—that is, the novelist.
The literary Mohicans Cooper invented and made famous, Chingachgook and his
doomed son Uncas, were not directly imported from the landscape surrounding
Cooperstown in his youth. Yet they were not utterly unconnected to Brotherton
or New Stockbridge, either. If Cooper envisioned Native Americans as disap-
pearing from the field of action, as indeed both Chingachgook in *The Pioneers*
and his son Uncas in *The Last of the Mohicans* do, it was because on the New York
border, as he knew very well, the remnant peoples had been forced west before
the influx of white settlers. He was not imagining or wishing for their displacement. At the same time that Cooper seemingly accepted their fate, he complicated
the plot by including the Native Americans at the center of his story—and giving them a kind of voice that no one had yet given them in American fiction.[48]

It may be that Cooper's most talked-about female figure in his forest romances, Cora Munro in *The Last of the Mohicans,* can tell us even more about
how he relied on the demographic realities of the contemporary upstate scene in
his effort to engage American society in his fiction. As a woman of both Afro-
Caribbean and Euro-American heritage who falls in love with and dies with the
Mohican warrior Uncas, Cora is often taken as little more than a piece of racist
apologetics. She is seen as representing a wish that black and red peoples might
equally exit the American scene and leave the field to white actors. That Cora is

an exceptionally strong and capable woman; that her father loves her equally with her "fair" sister Alice and bristles when he thinks Duncan Heyward holds Cora's mixed heritage against her; that Cooper conceives of her and Uncas as "high" figures fully capable of tragedy—should temper this argument. But it is, nonetheless, a fruitful and necessary argument.

With what I have offered above on the "Indian" elements in Cooper's novels, and their sources in his own experience, I am led to risk another take on how he imagined Cora and Uncas and their ill-fated love. Just as his contact with the New Stockbridge and Brotherton peoples gave him particular insight into Native American experiences and viewpoints in his place and time, I think it may well have made him aware of yet another aspect of Native American identity in the contemporary social scene—that is, the pattern of intermarriage of blacks and Indians in New England in the later eighteenth and early nineteenth centuries, a topic that historians Daniel Mandell and Thomas L. Doughton, among others, have addressed. This is something Cooper could have learned about from the Native American migrants from Connecticut and Massachusetts with whom his family developed close ties in Otsego. Like much else he picked up from that source, it conceivably directed and shaped his fictional imaginings. In particular, the issue was a divisive one among the Mohegans themselves: in 1773, forty-four male and female followers of Samson Occom, leader of the Brotherton project, signed an agreement that in effect banished any of their daughters who married "strangers," as well as severed from any tribal rights the children of those who married blacks. When Brotherton was at last founded, one of the first rules put into effect there banned all "persons of negro blood." While such exclusionary practices made the demographics of Brotherton peculiarly unrepresentative of the evolving multiracialism seen in Native American communities in New England, the very subject was widely known and discussed. Although the other major division of the Mohegan, led by Ben Uncas and remaining in Connecticut, also tightened rules about tribal membership, its changes were not as restrictive, and members of that group continued to intermarry with blacks. Here was a rich context indeed for Cooper's probing of racial boundaries in his sixth novel. Since, as Mandell postulates, the emerging interconnection between Native Americans and African Americans in southern New England from 1760 on "illuminates the fundamental flaws of a bichromatic view of racial relations in American history, and . . . offers new insight into the complexity and uncertainty of ethnic identity and assimilation," Cooper's bundling of black, white, and red in *The Last of the Mohicans* might well be seen as a daring attempt to recalibrate the working categories of current cultural discourse. In any case, he was hardly alone in his concern with this question; indeed, he might be said to have followed an Indian lead in even considering it.[49]

Endings

In June 1825, with his feverish instability once more mastered, Cooper was working on his latest book "with extra diligence." By as early as the first week of that month, many of his routines seem to have been resumed. Shubrick's letter of June 4 had sent pleasant news of the navy's reassignment of him to the Brooklyn navy yard. Cooper, well enough to cross the river by the *Van Tromp* or the loathed steamboat by then, passed the announcement on to Charles King for the New York *American*, where it appeared on June 13 (*LJ* 1:119–21). Perhaps he was able to take a new batch of manuscript to Wiley at the same time.

There were other issues that may also have called him to New York then. The trial on Sedgwick's suit, originally slated for June 20, was about to be postponed to September, presumably on petition from Cooper's attorney, Peter A. Jay, and perhaps owing to Cooper's shaky condition when notice of the trial was given on May 28. Cooper's renewed energy thereafter may have been owing to temporary relief on that question as well as the continuing gains in physical strength. But shadows still lingered. Despite everything he understood about his need for cash, the fever had hit him hard enough that in June he was thinking that his present novel probably would be his last. He had vowed to produce a naval history and would keep that vow, he now told Shubrick, but as for fiction, the "Author of *The Spy*" might well be done (*LJ* 1:120).[50] The first thing was to finish *Mohicans*, so in between viewing the passing ships and taking inland rides with the children, he kept on writing.

At times there was even room for more complicated excursions. On July 4, a Monday, he must have witnessed something of the stir caused by Lafayette's long-awaited return to New York following his extended tour of the South and the West, and his second visit to New England. The long day of celebration, which included a quick trip to Brooklyn (where Lafayette picked up and kissed the future poet, Walt Whitman), ended on Manhattan with a spectacular fireworks display at Castle Garden.[51] This the Coopers could have seen from the little green knoll in front of their Sunswick cottage if they did not have some closer prospect.[52] Later in the same week, distant views would not suffice. On Saturday the ninth, Cooper piled Susan, the children, and his nephew William Y. Cooper (perhaps even the French governess, Madame de Bruges, whom the girls liked less than Miss Mellish, her predecessor) into the *Van Tromp* and piloted the vessel down the East River to the vicinity of the Battery (SFM 56). Here more honors were due to be accorded Lafayette, soon set to pay his final farewell to New York City.

For one thing, on July 9 Lafayette was to cut the stay-rope on Belgian aeronaut Eugene Robertson's hydrogen balloon, the *American Star*, which then would ascend from the Battery as a great crowd looked on. The peripatetic Robertson, who left New York for Havana in 1826 and thereafter performed throughout Latin America, was as good at public relations as at aeronautics. He thus named his balloon after a fast New York gig or Whitehall boat that, rowed by a crew of four "Whitehallers," had defeated a British wherry, the *Dart* (nicknamed *Sudden Death*), in a race late the previous fall that Cooper had personally witnessed.[53] The *Dart* was the personal property of Capt. George Harris, of HMS *Hussar*. Harris, well-liked by New Yorkers, had sailed into the harbor earlier in the fall with tales of rescuing an American merchantman from Cuban pirates. Word of his racing boat, stored on the deck of the *Hussar*, soon spread through the city, and Harris offered a $1,000 purse for a challenge match with an American boat. In rough water and heavy winds on December 9, the *American Star* pulled out from the shore to join the *Dart*. With a cannon shot from the British warship to start the race, the two boats skimmed across the water toward a "stake" boat moored off Hoboken. The Americans led the whole way, rounding the Hoboken vessel and then speeding back across to the goal boat, the launch of the *Hussar*, off the Battery. They arrived there in a mere twenty-two minutes, a full three or four hundred yards in advance of their rival. The fifty thousand spectators who braved the weather to watch from shore were deeply gratified by the result.[54]

Cooper and his unnamed companion saw the match from the upper promenade of Castle Garden, where he had glanced out over the harbor during the grand fete for Lafayette just three months earlier. Nearby on this occasion stood a "young American Naval officer," surely known to Cooper. While the result of the race was still in doubt because of the distance, the officer explained that the differing strokes of the two boat crews were a dead giveaway. The second boat, in fact the *Dart*, was being propelled with a "man-of-war stroke": her men paused slightly with every pull so that the blades of their oars could be seen even from Castle Garden. But the other boat, then in the lead, exhibited "a dead Whitehall-pull," a cadence so swift and sure that its oars seemed completely invisible. Whitehallers, famous for their breakneck speed as the water-taxi men of their day, dominated traffic on New York waters. The British oarsmen, the pick of Harris's crew, were not boatmen in the same sense as the Americans—or as the wherrymen of the Thames at London, whom Cooper had seen in the British capital two decades before. As the American victory became obvious, generous cheers arose from the launch of the *Hussar* as the English flag was lowered in honor of the Whitehallers (*Notions* 1:166–67n).[55]

Come July 9, seven months later, the *Hussar* and Harris and his *Sudden Death* were long gone from New York, but the memory of that American win was still so strong that balloonist Robertson was eager to play off it. Besides, there was another reason why he adopted the winning boat's name for his own craft: the Whitehallers had decided to honor Lafayette by giving him their *American Star* to take home with him to La Grange. But first, on this Saturday, they pulled him across the Hudson to Paulus Hook in the gig to allow him to dine with Col. Richard Varick, an old companion-in-arms who had been Benedict Arnold's subordinate at West Point in 1780. Then they brought him back to watch Robertson send his own *American Star* aloft. Early the next week, on Bastille Day, they were to take Lafayette across the Hudson again, seeing him on his way to Philadelphia, where he was expected for another round of public celebrations before passing on to the South.[56]

The New York farewell proved so hectic that Susan and the children and young nephew William weren't able to glimpse Lafayette—at least not recognizably so—amid the crush of other vessels filling the harbor and the hordes of spectators on land. Some weeks later, Cooper wrote another European acquaintance, the Swiss native F. Alph. de Syon, an amused account of the day's miscues. "It is a wonderful feeling, that binds us all, so strongly, to that old man— I went with, my whole family, in a boat, to see him and the balloon, at the same time—We saw the latter, but Mrs. C.—and the children returned quite disappointed, because they could not get a view of Lafayette—He passed us in the race boat, but it was calm, and my boat, which is very justly named the Van Tromp, from the Dutch formation of her bows, refused to fly as swiftly, as might be wished" (*LJ* 1:126). For a man whose purpose for the past year had been to be seen, almost ad nauseam, this anticlimax made for a comical farewell.[57]

Come July 14, with Lafayette's last leave-taking from New York (he would not finally depart for France until September 9, when the naval vessel *Brandywine* cleared from the Chesapeake with him aboard), the city, insofar as it could, quieted down a bit. The Coopers went back to Sunswick, where *Mohicans* remained in process. Cooper and Wiley signed their agreement for the book at the end of July. The printing of the first volume was "nearly done" by August 31, when Cooper talked with William Cullen Bryant about it.[58] Three weeks later, Cooper could report to his Swiss friend that he had given "the first volume" of the book to Édouard Louvet, a native of Calvados who then edited a French paper, *Le Reveil, journal français, littéraire, politique, et commercial,* in New York. Louvet, who would relocate to New Orleans by the start of 1827, was something of a poet, having issued a "death song" in honor of Byron in Paris in 1824; he had expressed "a wish" to translate Cooper's novel, evidently for publication in France (*LJ* 1:125).[59] When Cooper turned over the sets of proofs to Louvet sometime in September, he obviously was forging ahead into the second volume: past the massacre (which ends the first volume) and into the pattern of flight and pursuit, rich in masquerade, that composes the second volume. This is, however, the last overt news we have on Cooper's progress on the book until, at year's end, he was hurriedly attempting to interest a new publisher in his works (see Chapter 16).

The book was not, in any case, the only thing at the center of Cooper's attention that fall. In September, as noted earlier, another bout of fever laid him low. The letter to Syon, written shortly afterward, did not mention the trouble; but another, written at the same time to attorney Peter A. Jay, did mention it—largely because Cooper thought his uncertain health might keep him from the city until (and perhaps past) the next trial of the Sedgwick case, now scheduled for September 26. Jay could again act as his substitute, but that hardly would relieve Cooper from the worries traceable to Sedgwick. In lieu of the meeting he otherwise would have had with Jay, he thus had to take time away from *Mohicans* to draw up and forward the long account of the business that Jay would clearly need (see *LJ* 1:121–25). And the question was so much on Cooper's mind that he gave Syon, a mere acquaintance, an unusually candid account of the "vexatious law-suit" that, he added with understatement, "annoys me not a little." Cooper felt that he had to plead usury against Sedgwick, who had "abused my confidence, greatly," but he felt embarrassed by that necessity. "The plea is exceedingly odious here," Cooper explained to Syon, "and in my situation I would gladly have avoided it, could I as an honest man have done it." As he went on, he sounded as if the fight between Magua and the Munros and their allies in the book he was writing all-but-consciously echoed his own situation vis-à-vis Sedgwick: "I had put myself so completely in the power of my adversary, that I had but an alternative—That of incurring the odium, or sacrificing money that belong'd, justly to creditors who reposed altogether on my good faith—My antagonist has even gone so far, as to cut the endorsements from the back of my bond! The thing will be decided next week, and if I lose, I must work the harder for it—that is all" (*LJ* 1:126).

The trial was again postponed. But across the fall and on into the new year Sedgwick continued to malinger in the forest of Cooper's imagination. Indeed, looming in his fevered dreams like Magua, Sedgwick may have helped trigger the fresh attacks of Cooper's mysterious ailment. The lawsuit was indeed "vexatious." When the New York Supreme Court again heard the case on December 5, 1825, Cooper was once more absent—but not by intent this time. Quite the contrary. That very morning he had been conferring with Jay in the latter's offices, filling him in on the finer points of the complicated circumstances surrounding the bond and his various dealings with Sedgwick. Cooper left after it became apparent, probably through a messenger, that the suit would be delayed for a week or more. However, shortly thereafter Jay got a hurried call to rush to City Hall because the trial in fact was about to begin. He made it there in time and argued the case, but before Cooper could be reached and called to the court, the trial ended and the jury was charged and sent out to deliberate. Having tried to actively participate in his defense this time, Cooper must have felt especially frustrated when a jury for a second time found for the plaintiff.[60]

He was hardly out of weapons in the long battle of attrition. Probably because the Sedgwick brothers pursued such a self-serving and prevaricating course in their dealings with him and in the court, he strengthened his moral (and physical) resolve and decided to best them at their own business. This resolve, born as it doubtless was out of Cooper's financial panic, nonetheless marked a turning point in his conception of himself as a social creature. He had kept himself from examining too closely Robert Sedgwick's attitudes and actions in the run-up to the disaster. He had refused to think ill of a "gentleman," especially one with whom he had been accustomed to associate for years. Now at last he would not let his own humane generosity sink him. For anyone familiar with the dogged determination with which Cooper pursued his enemies in later years through the courts, he seems a perfect instance of American litigiousness. That was not always so. He learned to defend himself with all available resources in the last decade or so of his career from having neglected to do so in the first. In this regard, an historical understanding of his earliest lawsuits helps temper the interpretation of his later ones. That same understanding opens up other insights as well. Cooper is a very compelling example of how the backward-looking culture of the early Republic, rooted in colonial patterns of deference and cooperation, gave way to its aggressive, market-based substitute. In his legal bouts with Robert Sedgwick, Cooper learned how to define himself apart from the social networks that he had inherited or built for himself up to 1820. If becoming a writer was one means by which he articulated a new identity for himself, another was learning how to use the law to define his own interests as separate from those of others.

There is a special irony in the legal means by which Cooper bested Sedgwick. In January 1826, he seems to have been thinking about petitioning for yet another supreme court trial. After having bogged himself down in a reconstruction of the payments he had made on the 1819 bond, however, Cooper broke off the draft of a new deposition in mid-thought. With that, he gave up the idea of having recourse to the same legal channels. But he was hardly done with the law. On February 21, he presented a bill of complaint to Chancery Court—hardly his favorite venue over the past half-decade—praying for relief from Sedgwick's many abuses. In this court of equity, the whole relationship between the two men, not just the narrow terms of the 1819 bond, would be subject to review. Cooper provided fresh, compelling detail about the ways in which he had sought to satisfy Sedgwick's demand, from agreeing to usurious interest to signing over to him various other resources never yet mentioned in the documents preserved in the office of Peter A. Jay. For instance, Cooper felt that the Conant bond, a St. Lawrence obligation sold to Sedgwick for a discount in 1817, in fact had bearing on the issues he wanted the Chancery Court to review. In assigning his share in that bond to Sedgwick, Cooper had guaranteed both the principal and the interest in the event that George Conant defaulted. In the years following, Conant had not paid the interest, so Cooper had kept it current. If Conant had defaulted, Cooper could have recovered the bond by paying off the remaining principal and interest. In fact, however, Sedgwick eventually recovered both the full principal of that bond and all back interest either from Conant himself or through a forced sale of the lands in question. At that point, he should have refunded Cooper's interest payments, but did not. Cooper now rightly asked that these be applied to the 1819 bond.[61]

Furthermore, in 1824, Cooper had assigned to Sedgwick the huge debt owed him by his cousin Courtland, estimated at more than $4,000, as collateral security for the 1819 bond. Sedgwick had never rendered Cooper an account of his dealings with Courtland. Courtland had told Sedgwick that he fully intended to pay off the debt, and may have done so, but both men kept Cooper in the dark on the question. If Sedgwick had received anything from Courtland, it would also have to be deducted from the balance due from the novelist on his own bond. Finally, Cooper understood that Sedgwick had taken out an insurance policy—at Cooper's expense—on the unfinished mansion at Fenimore. Whether Cooper had actually been charged for any such policy was probably as difficult to determine as the total Cooper had paid on the bond, or the interest that had been deducted from his payments, or even the actual interest rate that had applied to various portions of the debt at various times.[62]

With regard to the insurance policy, Cooper's point was a relatively direct one. If a policy had existed and its cost had been deducted from his payments to Sedgwick, then any payout following the building's destruction ought to have been credited to Cooper on Sedgwick's books. In 1823, in fact, Sedgwick did not yet own Fenimore Farm. Even if he had personally paid for the policy, any proceeds from it ought—in equity if not by the letter of the law—to have been credited against the mortgage on the property. Depending on the face value of any such policy (after the mansion's destruction, a Cooperstown paper estimated that the building even in its unfinished state must have cost Cooper $5,000), those proceeds would have reduced Cooper's debt by a substantial amount, perhaps even canceled it. This was in itself sufficient reason for Cooper to raise the issue in an equity proceeding.[63]

But more may well have been afoot here than hiding an insurance charge or accounting for a policy's payoff. Sedgwick had visited Cooperstown and inspected Fenimore Farm at some time before the first supreme court case in 1825.

Certainly he had had the property inspected in 1819 when Cooper first assigned it to him.[64] Anyone familiar with the unfinished house would quickly conclude that, while it added to the nominal value of the property and had considerable intrinsic value, it also placed certain restrictions on disposing of it. It certainly did not promote a quick sale, since only a person of special means and taste would be likely to buy it. When the editor of the *Freeman's Journal,* John H. Prentiss, reported on the fire at Fenimore in 1823, he lamented it the more because it might have become "the chosen residence of some gentleman."[65] But Prentiss was whistling in the wind. The chance that some such wealthy person would snap it up at a forced sale and finish it was remote.

Sedgwick, in Cooper's final judgment, was a man who worshipped money (see *LJ* 1:123). He would care nothing for the tone of rural Otsego society; he would care for the bottom line. If he insured the house it was not to protect Cooper's interest but rather his own. If he got paid for the property twice—by the insurer, then by Cooper—so much the better. Nor was this all. There are two curious things about the Chancery Court bill Cooper filed on February 22, 1826. The first is that the court, under Chancellor Samuel Jones, issued an order four days later compelling Robert Sedgwick to cease and desist in all actions at law against Cooper.[66] Jones, son and namesake of the Long Island lawyer and legislator from whom the Coopers had borrowed $3,500 in 1818, hardly was an unknown quantity in the novelist's estimation. Like his brother, Henry Floyd Jones, the Coopers' landlord at the Beech Street house in 1823–1824, he was a kinsman and an old acquaintance on whom Cooper could rely for a fair, perhaps a sympathetic, hearing in 1826. That Jones had just assumed the position of chancellor at the outset of 1826 may even have determined Cooper to drop another bout in the supreme court and try his luck in the chancery. Cooper shrewdly shifted tactics at this juncture. No longer passive, no longer merely "disgusted," he clearly had decided to use all the resources at his command in order to press his case against a former friend who now had proved himself a thoroughgoing and devious adversary. The wrestling match was now, at last, more equal.

Cooper may well have attacked Sedgwick better than he knew. Perhaps it was Cooper's newly evolved connections to the court that forced a change in Sedgwick's own strategy. Although Judge Jones's cease-and-desist order was issued merely to stop proceedings until his own court could consider Cooper's bill, a not unusual turn of events, Sedgwick abruptly and completely dropped his legal pursuit of Cooper. Two days after Jones's order, on February 28, Sedgwick thus directed his attorney to collect the costs for the supreme court suit from Cooper but thereafter to vacate "the judgment obtained therein & discontinue said suit."[67] Sedgwick just gave up. Although he was entitled to answer Cooper's chancery bill, he also did not pursue that option, meaning that the issue died.

What is to account for this retreat on the part of a relentless attorney who had cornered Cooper in 1819, forced him to pay far more than the law allowed, and then insisted on his due—more than his due—at every twist of their dealings thereafter over nearly seven years? Sedgwick was not a man to back down without good reason. To be sure, Cooper's resistance over the past year had forced him to soften his position on a number of issues already. And Cooper's newly discovered pertinacity and his willingness to play the game fully against Sedgwick—using the influence of Samuel Jones, for instance—may have signaled to Sedgwick that pursuing Cooper was no longer worth it. But I think that something else may have been at work here. Cooper's mention of the other resources he had directed toward Sedgwick in seeking to satisfy his obligation, such as the Conant bond and the transferred debt from Courtland, perhaps threatened that this game might become zero-sum for Sedgwick before it was over. Indeed, those two items, along with the third element in Cooper's litany (the insurance policy on the mansion at Fenimore, if indeed there had been one), perhaps suggested to Sedgwick that *he* might owe something to Cooper before this was all over. Cutting his losses was prudent.

So was saving his neck. The mention of the insurance policy in Cooper's bill, the only reference to it in the extensive file of his dealings with Sedgwick, introduced a new element into the fight. That Sedgwick retreated so completely and so quickly after the bill was filed and the court issued its preliminary order suggests that the Chancery Court case might open up the question of what, after all, had happened to the Fenimore Farm mansion. Still unresolved two-and-a-half years after the event, the fire had reduced an ambitious and costly dwelling, quite near completion but completely unoccupied and therefore safe from most sources of fire at the time, to a mass of ruins. But it had also, from Sedgwick's perspective, removed a white elephant from a piece of farmland that could be more flexibly and quickly marketed if he did not need to find a "gentleman" to buy it as his "seat." Cooper wanted to keep his private illusions about the place alive as much as he wanted to ensure that he not be shortchanged by Sedgwick. Sedgwick cared nothing about the illusions. If the house were gone, so much the better. Given the man's documented amorality with regard to Cooper's debt, one may be justified in wondering whether the arsonist who torched the mansion in July 1823 was something other than a random disseminator of fear and destruction in the Otsego countryside. Perhaps the target was not the Averell family: perhaps it really *was* James Cooper. The lawyer's precipitous retreat in February 1826 was certainly odd; it bespoke motives of special intensity. Was the hand that torched the mansion in his employ? It certainly appears as if the mere mention of the fire and the insurance policy was at last enough to scare him away from his Magua-like pursuit of Cooper, who at long last was free.[68]

CHAPTER SIXTEEN

Literary Business

Even as the long battle with Robert Sedgwick was entering its final, critical phase, another financial concern was arising for Cooper during the fall of 1825. This one, connected to Charles Wiley, had more serious implications because it had to do with the system through which Cooper had been publishing his literary works—and producing the income that was keeping him afloat. His response in this case was to withdraw from his business relationship with Wiley and establish a new and more profitable one with the Philadelphia firm of Carey and Lea. Several factors were involved in the decision. The most important was the fact that Wiley, Cooper's agent for his second through his fifth novels, had proved increasingly unreliable in business matters. Cooper relished the companionship of Wiley's Den, and very much liked—indeed "loved"—Wiley as a friend (*LJ* 2:150). But he had no illusion about Wiley's shortcomings as a businessman. The problems worsened over time until, with his health wrecked and his establishment awash in debt, forty-five-year-old Wiley was to die in obscure circumstances at the start of 1826.

The troubles had had a considerable rehearsal. In their most recent dealings, Cooper found Wiley's customary disorganization deepening. Right after Wiley's death, William Cullen Bryant asked Cooper about the state of their mutual friend Richard Henry Dana's account at the deceased bookseller's shop. Cooper told him that Wiley's records were "so negligently kept that there is not the least probability that they exhibit the true state of the account."[1] That can only have been bitter experience speaking: Cooper clearly had seen the records in his own case, perhaps especially the more recent ones, and despaired of ever reconciling them with the reality of his sales. Wiley cannot have been oblivious to the confusion, but his manner of dealing with it was ineffective. His concern for his own impending financial ruin appears to made him inattentive not only to his account books but to some of his day-to-day business as well. James G. Percival, whose *Poems* Wiley had published in 1823, reportedly suffered from Wiley's lack of attention to the book's sales.[2] Cooper, more popular by far, probably escaped such outright neglect. But collection of the booksellers' notes that Wiley received for his shipments, not to mention proper accounting of expenses and profits, would have remained touchy issues. And the large scale of Cooper's business put him much more at risk than Percival or most of Wiley's other authors.

"Poor Wiley"

It was not just in handling his business accounts that Wiley had difficulty. His personal finances were also a shambles. Remembering the man's end five years later, Cooper recalled him as "poor Wiley": pitiable, but also broke. Aware, though, that Wiley was no simple victim, Cooper added from sore experience that Wiley could be "credulous and weak" (*LJ* 2:150). By early 1823, only a year or so into their business relationship, Wiley was so "embarrassed" that Cooper had felt moved to intervene. He therefore had recommenced work on his long languishing *Tales for Fifteen*, which he gave Wiley outright (*LJ* 4:107; see also 4:460–61). This book, as its modest title admitted, was no *Spy*, and it conceivably cost Wiley more than it earned. Yet neither it nor the terms Cooper imposed on Wiley for all his books between the contract for the second edition of *The Spy* in February 1822 and the first contract for *Lionel Lincoln* in April 1824 were responsible for Wiley's troubles and his ultimate failure.

A review of those terms will help clarify the situation. It will be recalled that, while seeing *Precaution* into print, Cooper had been pressured by Andrew T. Goodrich to come up with the required funds to pay off the printer and the supplier of the paper. In the case of the first edition of *The Spy,* handled by Wiley, he was similarly obligated to meet those expenses while the book was in production. Cooper thus had to defray the costs of those two books out of extraliterary funds. Once his second novel succeeded, however, he reasonably enough insisted that its future editions (and all later books issued through Wiley) pay for themselves. What this meant was that Wiley underwrote those new volumes. His shaky reputation as a businessman probably necessitated giving suppliers his personal notes, perhaps with the endorsements of more creditworthy men added. Wiley also may have used the common expedient of assigning to those suppliers some of the booksellers' notes he received as payment for orders.[3]

The rapid sales of *The Spy* meant that Wiley's suppliers could be paid in due order. The survival of a complete statement of account for the book's second edition demonstrates the usual practices and yields for Cooper's books handled through Wiley. Wiley bought paper for that edition on February 18, 1822, four days after he and Cooper had signed their contract, and by March 5 the total edition of fifteen hundred copies had been set in type and run off by William Grattan. The expenses for paper and printing, combined with those for cover stock and binding (along with charges for "Packing, Postage, & Portage"), brought his total for this edition to just over $900, or about 60 cents per copy. All these expenses were properly debited against Cooper in Wiley's account, as the terms of their agreement made the author responsible for every expense associated with the venture.[4]

Wiley disposed of all but a few copies of this second edition from mid-March to the start of April, satisfying backed-up demand. Aside from forty copies retailed through his own shop, and another six delivered to Cooper, most were wholesaled to established booksellers in exchange for six-month or three-month notes. Having properly assigned the bulk of those notes to Grattan and other suppliers, Wiley turned the five remaining ones (worth about $525) over to Cooper, along with his own sixty-day note dated March 21 for an additional $281. The latter probably is an indication of Wiley's sloppy management of his business—he must, that is, have used other booksellers' notes received for shipments of *The Spy* to cover obligations *not* connected to Cooper's book, and therefore had to close the gap in Cooper's account with his personal note.[5] When the account between the two men was settled on April 2, by which point Cooper was about to sign a contract with Wiley for a third edition, Wiley showed a slight credit balance of $66.67 (in addition to his as-yet-unpaid three-month note) in Cooper's favor. At that time, the three dozen copies of the second edition of *The Spy* still on hand at Wiley's shop were likewise credited to Cooper, minus the one-third discount, meaning that the author would have another $50 or so due to him once the edition was sold out.

How had the two friends fared in this brief business arrangement? Let us use exact figures here. Each copy of the book had cost 60 cents. On average, it produced $1.34 when wholesale discounts were deducted from the retail price. Of the 74 cents per copy left over after all costs were paid, Cooper received 66 cents and Wiley received 8 cents—or $964.92 and $116.96, respectively.[6] In theory, Wiley had no personal exposure on the edition, which Cooper owned and for which he was wholly responsible, but Wiley of course had overhead for the shop and for handling the printing, binding, and shipping of Cooper's work (as well as keeping Cooper's account). His share of the gross revenues for the second edition was about 6 percent of the average wholesale price. Cooper's share was slightly less than 50 percent. Since turnaround on the second and third editions of *The Spy* was rapid, Wiley's returns were not unreasonable.

In the case of the first edition, Wiley had made considerably more. That edition probably was of one thousand copies. Wiley reported to Cooper on January 7, 1822, two weeks after publication, that he had already disposed of six hundred copies, including "a very considerable number" retailed through his shop, plus lots of one hundred each to Carey and Lea in Philadelphia and to printer/bookseller Lambert Lockwood in Bridgeport, Connecticut, and fifty copies to New York City publisher and bookseller William B. Gilley; he also reported the sale of "several" shipments of twenty-four copies each to other dealers. For an edition of this size, the cost per copy for typesetting would be half again as much as for an edition of fifteen hundred copies: about 19.5 cents as opposed to 13 cents, reducing the net yield per copy from 74 cents per copy to 67 or 68 cents.[7] It is evident from Wiley's report that Cooper had already spelled out guidelines for wholesale discounts for the first edition; Wiley reported that the Carey and Lockwood sales were on six-month notes, for instance, while that to Gilley was on a three-month note. If we assume that Wiley sold more copies of the first edition through his own shop than of the second edition (say three hundred copies out of the one thousand), then his yield on the whole edition would have been in the neighborhood of $250, or about 18 percent of the average wholesale price. He thus earned 25 cents per copy, 37 percent of the gross retail profits; Cooper by comparison made 42.5 cents per copy. If we assume that the third edition of *The Spy* was about the same size as the second, and that Wiley handled it in roughly the same way as the second, then for all three editions he must have earned perhaps $450. The fourth edition, prepared in 1824 without Cooper's direct supervision but surely under his authority, probably was covered by a similar contract and may have earned Wiley another $100 or so.

Sales for *The Pioneers* also appear to have been rapid and substantial. In the case of the book's first and second editions, which went on sale virtually together on February 1, 1823, Wiley sold (that is, wholesaled and retailed) thirty-five hundred copies on the day of publication alone.[8] Because of the long delays in the book's appearance due to the 1822 yellow fever outbreak, booksellers who had been happy with *The Spy*'s continuing salability were eager to have ample stock of the same author's third novel as soon as possible. In handling this book, as a result, Wiley again had little direct personal exposure. But he may well have experienced a boost in returns. His modest 5 percent commission on all whole-sale distributions was substantially bolstered by large retail sales through his own shop, as had been the case with the first edition of *The Spy*. At a minimum, he would have grossed $235 (assuming *all* copies were wholesaled); for every one hundred copies retailed through his shop, his gross would have increased by $66.[9] If, for instance, he withheld five hundred copies from other New York dealers such as William B. Gilley, forcing customers to come to him, he would have taken in a net of almost $500 above and beyond all production costs (but not, of course, his general overhead).

Cooper's earnings on the first thirty-five hundred copies of *The Pioneers*, if we use the figures from the account for *The Spy* as a guide, must have been in excess of $2,300. If, as the editors of *The Pioneers* for the Cooper Edition surmise, the two 1823 runs totaled more than five thousand copies, Cooper's earnings would have been substantially higher: more than $3,600 for five thousand copies, almost $4,000 for six thousand, and so on. The actual yield depended on the size of each print run.[10] Any additional earnings from that source would be credited directly to Cooper's share of the book's proceeds. In a run of three thousand copies, for instance, the savings would produce an extra $390. If the two editions of *The Pioneers* totaled six thousand copies, then his overall earnings would have been on the order of almost $5,000. At those sale levels, Wiley's total income from the first two editions of the novel might have been as high as $800 or even $1,000—depending, once again, on the split between retail and wholesale.[11]

When Cooper and Wiley signed their initial contract for *Lionel Lincoln* in April 1824, the basic arrangement that had prevailed with the various editions of the three previous books again applied. In anticipation of this new project, Wiley already had ordered 154 reams of paper from New York dealer Robert M'Dermut in March, covering the cost ($477.50) with his personal note. While that exchange reflects the typical pattern in the trade at the time, all was not completely typical here. Ordinarily, Wiley might have preferred using booksellers' notes to cover this expense, since thereby he could apply anticipated income for the new book against its costs. That he did not or could not do so in this case may indicate that Cooper's ailing condition, raising concern that he might not manage to finish the much delayed book, had softened advance orders. For his part, M'Dermut (who, as we shall see, had had many other unsatisfactory financial dealings with Cooper), may have insisted on Wiley's personal note rather than assignments of third-party instruments. Even when Cooper's delay on the new novel apparently eased in August, Wiley had to give M'Dermut a second personal note when he ordered another one hundred reams, for almost $400.[12] In December, when the final chapters of the book at last must have been in his hands, Wiley arranged for a third shipment of forty-four reams, followed by a fourth and final one of eighteen reams in January (enough for the twelve-page gathering occupied by Cooper's two last-minute prefaces). For these last two shipments he apparently gave M'Dermut a final personal note for the charge of nearly $250. The total debt for the paper was thus in excess of $1,100, for all of which Wiley's notes made him liable.[13]

His liability was in fact personal, since before those last two paper orders, Cooper and Wiley had taken the unprecedented step of renegotiating their contract for the novel. Since the second contract gave Wiley ownership of the book for a single year, he now became fully responsible for all costs (including M'Dermut's) associated with producing and distributing the first edition of six thousand copies—as well as a second edition, if he wished, totaling no more than an additional four thousand copies.[14] In turn, Wiley was to have exclusive rights to the book in the Western Hemisphere for a year from the date of first publication. He was free to set the wholesale terms, thereby gaining a new measure of control over his own profits. In return, the new contract required him to pay Cooper $5,000 by giving him "approved Endorsed notes payable in Six months" from the date of publication. The endorser may well have been New York merchant Abijah Weston, who joined Wiley in making the contract with Cooper. Weston, son-in-law of printer Jonathan Seymour, must have been well known to Wiley and probably was also acquainted with Cooper. That Cooper required a cosigner for Wiley no doubt reflects his understanding of exactly where Wiley stood financially in 1824.[15]

In exercising his rights under the terms of this agreement, Wiley sold between forty-five hundred and forty-eight hundred copies of *Lionel Lincoln* from February to the middle of October 1825. We may assume that he offered wholesale customers the same discounts that Cooper had insisted on in the first contract, since these now benefited the book's "publisher" as they would not have benefited its manager. If he wholesaled all copies at the $1.34 discount price, he would have grossed between $6,000 and $6,500. But if, as seems virtually certain, he retailed a sizable number through his own shop, his gross profit on those copies would have boosted both his personal income and the overall proceeds flowing in from the edition. Had he, for instance, sold fifteen hundred copies at his shop, he would have diverted nearly $1,000 from the retail proceeds of other dealers to his own till. Under these assumptions, his gross receipts on the edition during this eight-month period would have been between $7,000 and $7,500.

Had Wiley been operating under the old arrangements with Cooper, he would have been entitled to a mere fraction of the gross proceeds: some $325 if all six thousand copies were wholesaled (that is, 5 percent of the actual sales), with the additional net of just under $60 for every one hundred copies he retailed.[16] If, for instance, he wholesaled thirty-three hundred copies and retailed fifteen hundred, under the older terms he would have enjoyed gross income of slightly more than $1,100, all of which would have been his to keep, since all expenses (aside from his usual overhead) would have devolved on Cooper. As publisher of the book under the second contract, Wiley potentially looked forward to much higher levels of income. But he was, on the other hand, solely liable for all costs. He therefore had no right to extract any profits until all the expenses were paid. Had he shrewdly managed his retail trade, he would have put himself within striking distance of paying off Cooper and all his suppliers even out of the admittedly disappointing sales accumulated through October 1825.[17]

This conclusion emerges from estimates of Wiley's production costs for *Lionel Lincoln* that are based on his account for the second edition of *The Spy* as well as figures derived from the contemporary "cost book" of Cooper's future publishers, Carey and Lea. The first edition of six thousand copies probably cost slightly more than $1,300 for typesetting, presswork, and binding, plus the cost of the paper, for a grand total of almost $2,500.[18] Since Wiley had to pay Cooper an additional $5,000 for "copyright" (that is, to purchase the book), his total obligation was nearly $7,500. Wiley might have paid off these obligations if his gross receipts reached the levels estimated above. Besides, even if the account for *Lionel Lincoln* was in the red, as the book's publisher, Wiley had an obligation to transfer the assets needed to cover his expenses from elsewhere in his overall operations. Since his business was faltering, he may have found that impossible.[19]

The actual sales of *Lionel Lincoln* were surely below expectations. On the basis of the success of Cooper's previous three books, author and publisher had estimated that an initial print run of six thousand copies would be quickly disposed of. Had that edition been sold off within a month, Wiley would have grossed more than $8,000 (if all copies were wholesaled, but more than $9,000 if fifteen hundred were retailed), more than enough to pay all production costs as well as Cooper, leaving Wiley a tidy profit of between $600 and $1,600, a range of between 8 and 21 percent of his costs. For Wiley, furthermore, it was the possible second edition of up to four thousand copies that would provide a chance for profits previously unknown in his association with Cooper. If such a second edition had been produced and sold off within a year of the book's first publication, not implausible given Cooper's recent record, Wiley would have realized between $3,500 and $4,000 beyond all costs on that second edition alone. Under these assumptions, his profit on his overall contract with Cooper could have run to almost 60 percent ($5,600) of all costs ($9,500), a very good return indeed.[20] Furthermore, whatever the prospects for that second edition, it is important to recall that Wiley entered into the November 1824 contract with Cooper with his eyes open. He hardly would have agreed to Cooper's terms if in his (admittedly flawed) judgment as a businessman he thought that they would impoverish him, an outcome that hardly would have been in Cooper's interest as an author or as Wiley's friend. The $5,000 fee to be paid to Cooper presumably represented the best estimate the two men could make about Cooper's likely earnings on the book. As suggested above, his earnings on *The Pioneers* within a month of that book's publication came close to that figure—and may have substantially passed it if the print runs were as large as some sources indicate. With the prospect of ten thousand copies of *Lionel Lincoln* being marketed, Cooper stood to make $8,000 under the April contract; he was willing to reduce that figure in Wiley's favor in return for not having to "own" and manage this book as he had those in the past.[21]

As matters actually stood across 1825, Wiley must have been pinched between the book's sales and his own incompetence. Even so, as just suggested, the copies disposed of through October ought to have been nearly sufficient to pay all production costs. For reasons never fully explained to Cooper (or at least recorded by him), however, Wiley failed to meet his obligations. The endorsed notes Cooper had received from Wiley came due in August and apparently were duly paid off, probably because of Abijah Weston's endorsement of them. Two months later, however, Cooper was informed that Wiley had failed to make payment on several other notes, including the three the bookseller had given to Robert M'Dermut for the paper used in printing *Lionel Lincoln* across 1824. In effect, Wiley had diverted just over $1,100 from the proceeds of sales of *Lionel Lincoln*. Had he been "credulous" in accepting some unreliable booksellers' notes for shipments of the book? Had he been "weak" in handling his finances, woefully confusing funds until the picture with regard to *Lionel Lincoln* was completely out of focus? Whatever the sequence of missteps or misdeeds, Cooper was inevitably involved in trying to resolve the resulting crisis. Although the problem was technically between Wiley and M'Dermut, it had implications for the future dealings between the novelist and both of these associates.

When Wiley (or perhaps M'Dermut) informed Cooper of the issue, the novelist probably went to Wall Street to examine Wiley's books—the most likely source of his comment to Bryant on that subject only three months later. He also took immediate steps to satisfy M'Dermut (and relieve Wiley) by personally endorsing the three Wiley notes, thereby assuming the debt himself. At the same time, he endorsed a fourth note of his own that had been given to the poet Fitz-Greene Halleck, a mutual friend whose phenomenally successful poem *Fanny* had been published by Wiley in 1819 and reissued in 1820. At some point in the past, Wiley had promised to pay off the Halleck debt, presumably in return for a separate obligation to Cooper or out of the proceeds of *Lionel Lincoln* or Cooper's other in-print titles. This, too, however, he had failed to do. The Halleck note indicates that the crisis engulfing Wiley, while traceable in part to the disappointing sales of *Lionel Lincoln*, was not wholly caused by them. His whole house, personally and perhaps in a business sense, was on the edge of financial collapse.[22]

The terms of Cooper's October 1825 agreement with Wiley on these four notes, which totaled more than $1,500, were complex. How could the impecunious and disorganized bookseller possibly repay Cooper? He was so short of funds that all he could do was secure the novelist's endorsements (and payments) by assigning to him his remaining stock of four books: the twelve hundred to fifteen hundred copies of *Lionel Lincoln* he thought he still had on hand, which were still his property under the November 1824 contract and which had a wholesale value of between $1,600 and $2,000 and a retail value of some 30 percent more; the rest of the second edition of *The Pilot* and of the fourth edition of *The Spy* (released in 1824), both of which, although in Wiley's warehouse, were already Cooper's property; and the rest of the second edition of James Kirke Paulding's *John Bull in America* (1825), which Wiley had published at his own risk. The bookseller also included all his "interest, right, and title" (not just his stock on hand) with regard to a fifth work, Gulian Verplanck's *Essays on the Nature and Uses of the Various Evidences of Revealed Religion* (1824).[23] Cooper, acting as Wiley's attorney, was given full right to sell these items so as to meet the obligations covered by the agreement but was to pass on any surplus to Wiley. That Cooper soon exercised these rights is suggested by an undated statement supplied to him by Wiley's partner, Oliver Halsted, showing sales of both *Lionel Lincoln* (to Carey and Lea) and the Paulding title.[24]

A more benign interpretation of the crisis might be ventured; Cooper, certainly not ignorant of Wiley's problems as a businessman, may have desired to switch to Carey and Lea not just for future works but for the remaining stock of *Lionel Lincoln* as well. In that case, before Cooper could gain control of the book, he would have to discharge any obligations Wiley still had under the terms of their contract—specifically, the debt to M'Dermut. Some documentary evidence points in this direction. On January 9, 1826, Henry C. Carey gave Cooper a brief accounting of *Lionel Lincoln* as he understood it. Here were listed total sales (presumably to November) of $6,750; since Wiley's costs for the whole edition were stated to be $8,030, however, he would need to be reimbursed $1,280 in order to be even on the book and therefore in a position to release it to Cooper. M'Dermut's notes with interest added came remarkably close to this amount. It is possible that Cooper assumed those notes (and that to Halleck) in exchange for release from his contract with Wiley for *Lionel Lincoln*, clearing the way for his switch to Carey and Lea. Available evidence does not allow definitive resolution of the issue. But the way in which the four books came into

Cooper's hands—that is, as an assignment from Wiley to cover *his* debt to Cooper, with Cooper obligated to pay any surplus beyond that amount should he sell the books—suggests to the contrary that the crisis resulted from Wiley's mismanagement and that Cooper, while now wishing to switch to Carey and Lea, intervened on Wiley's behalf to once again help him out of a mess of his own creation.[25]

However the arrangement came about, Cooper indeed inherited Wiley's unsatisfied obligations to M'Dermut. These dealings hardly were the novelist's first with that interesting man. Robert M'Dermut, born in the mid-1760s, had been a bookseller and minor publisher in New York City since 1803. In 1809, he called himself a "Law Bookseller," and from 1813 to 1817 he had as a partner in his publishing activities Daniel D. Arden. By 1819, the date of the first clear evidence of Cooper's dealings with him, M'Dermut was back on his own. Having left the publishing business behind, he remained a bookseller and stationer.[26] But he also was something of a moneylender and a dealer in financial instruments. The Cooper family seems to have had first contact with M'Dermut on the latter basis. In 1819, the novelist's last remaining brother, William, who probably was familiar with M'Dermut from time served as a law student in early nineteenth-century New York City, assigned to the bookseller a bond from Albany merchant Daniel Hale (sometime partner of Judge Cooper), which was among the assets in his father's estate. The bond passed into yet other hands when M'Dermut in turn reassigned it; by 1820, when it was presented for payment, Hale refused to honor it, sending it back into M'Dermut's possession. At the very end of that year, M'Dermut transferred it to Cooper, by then executor of the Judge's estate, for payment of the principal amount and interest then due, $1,140.[27]

Well before then, however, Cooper had had sizable dealings with M'Dermut that had nothing to do with his father's estate. Across 1819, for instance, he made a series of payments to M'Dermut totaling $1,250, apparently to cover some prior obligation of his own.[28] Although the origins and purposes of this obligation are unknown, it clearly had nothing to do with M'Dermut's much later service as supplier of paper for some of Cooper's books.[29] The 1819 payments seem not to have fully discharged the preexisting debt. In 1820, M'Dermut therefore sued Cooper in the New York Supreme Court and won a judgment, recorded on January 5, 1821, in the amount of $1,210.55.[30] Evidently in response to a request from Cooper that execution on that judgment be delayed, two weeks later M'Dermut agreed to wait six months for payment.[31] Once this grace period expired, Cooper apparently had no ready means of paying the judgment. In the months following, he therefore assigned to M'Dermut some portion of his own interest in the whaleship *Union*, then on its second voyage. On July 7, 1821, when word of the vessel's imminent arrival reached Cooper, he personally went to

M'Dermut's shop on Pearl Street and accepted his creditor's instructions on how to proceed. M'Dermut told Cooper that he was to go to Sag Harbor immediately and, taking charge of the bookseller's interest in the ship and its cargo, sell the latter either in New York or Boston (depending on where he could get the higher price) and promptly turn over to M'Dermut his legal share.[32]

Even Cooper's faithful execution of these instructions could not erase his obligation to M'Dermut. An assignment dated May 1, 1822, indicates that on that date he gave the bookseller a "legal bond and mortgage," assigning *all* his own rights over and interests in the *Union* and its outfit and cargo to M'Dermut as security for a debt of $2,000 that he was obliged to pay back in two installments, on September 1 and November 1, of that year. The origins of this obligation also are unclear, but it seems to have arisen from a fresh attempt by Cooper to pay off debts from earlier years. Nor was this all. Even as he struggled to discharge old obligations to M'Dermut, Cooper acquired new ones. On May 11, barely a week after the assignment of the whaleship was drawn up, Cooper acknowledged borrowing another sum, $700, from M'Dermut. To cover this new short-term loan, he assigned to M'Dermut his interest in the third edition of *The Spy,* published on that very day. This transaction amounted to a cash-out of Cooper's expected earnings from this fresh issue of the book: in the event that Cooper did not otherwise pay off the new note in the stipulated thirty days, M'Dermut was to receive his due from the proceeds of the book. By June 13, probably as expected, Cooper acknowledged himself unable to pay off the new note. But at the same time he added the $700 debt to the security arrangement for his old debt. If he had not paid back the $700 loan by the time the whaleship returned to port, M'Dermut was free to recover it along with the other amount from the vessel, its cargo, and its trappings. Presumably this action freed Cooper to receive any proceeds from *The Spy* himself.

The arrangement with M'Dermut with regard to the *Union* was by no means simple. Owing to the claim of Joshua Brookes on the whaleship (see Chapter 14, note 73), which the new agreement with M'Dermut fully acknowledged, Cooper further provided on May 1, 1822, that M'Dermut would have a residual claim on any surplus left should Brookes move to sell the vessel in order to recover the amount due *him.* M'Dermut in turn would have to convey to Cooper the surplus, if any, above and beyond his due. If Cooper paid Brookes off from other resources, the vessel would come fully into M'Dermut's hands; Cooper insisted only that in that case M'Dermut would give him a ten-day notice of the intent to sell the *Union.* In the event that the ship should be lost at sea, M'Dermut would be covered by the insurance policy, although again he was obligated by this assignment to pass on any surplus proceeds from the policy to Cooper.[33]

M'Dermut's 1821 supreme court judgment can have had little if anything to do with the publishing of *Precaution* or *The Spy*. With the seemingly later debts Cooper secured via the *Union*, the issue is a bit murkier. It is possible that Wiley had failed to pay charges for paper for one or more of Cooper's early books, even though in those cases he was to withhold from Cooper sufficient proceeds from sales to discharge all such obligations. But there is no overt evidence on the question. It therefore seems more likely that Cooper, prior to endorsing Wiley's notes to the paper supplier for *Lionel Lincoln*, was separately indebted to M'Dermut for some extraliterary cause. When the novelist in April 1826 was trying to settle as many financial issues as possible in expectation of his departure for Europe, he remained indebted to M'Dermut for some $1,300. This debt was not, as James F. Beard thought, for paper used on *The Last of the Mohicans* (that bill being justly charged to Carey and Lea, who paid it out of proceeds) but rather was for the Wiley notes Cooper had endorsed in October 1825 (see *LJ* 1:133–35). Cooper at last discharged the Wiley debt by persuading M'Dermut to accept a note from Carey and Lea secured by future payments due the novelist from that firm.

Carey and Lea

Cooper's intervention on behalf of Charles Wiley in October 1825 represented his continuing affection and concern for the man, something also seen in the special meeting of the Bread and Cheese Club held at the Den, surely as a benefit for Wiley, on October 24, 1825 (*LOM* CE xxvi).[34] The novelist's most important motive at this juncture, however, was the need to bolster the reputation of his literary wares, and hence his family's main income source, in the New York market.[35] Endorsing the M'Dermut notes helped toward that end but could do little for the next literary problem looming on the horizon. Cooper's sixth novel, even now in production, still had Wiley for its publisher. In the midst of everything else, Cooper had to break with Wiley and make new arrangements for *The Last of the Mohicans*.

In drawing up a contract for that book with Wiley on July 26, 1825, Cooper had basically returned to the original arrangement between them. Perhaps Wiley had expressed his dissatisfaction with the existing second agreement on *Lionel Lincoln;* by July, he certainly knew that he had not yet broken even on it, let alone reaped the profits both he and Cooper had imagined. Cooper may have hoped to sell the new book to Wiley, keeping the new pattern in effect for it; but it is also possible that he viewed that new pattern as a one-time arrangement that would let him out of the bind he had put himself in with Joshua Brookes and would yield him some ready cash to boot. Now, in any event, the contract for *The Last of the Mohicans* reinstated the old pattern. Wiley, already printing an edition of five thousand copies (at Cooper's expense), would be entitled to a 5 percent commission on all wholesaled copies and a 30 percent discount on all copies sold at his Wall Street store. After deducting expenses for paper, printing, and binding, he once more was to assign to Cooper the remaining "notes & securities" given him by booksellers. Wiley's most important role, as before, would be to act as Cooper's agent and distributor. Copies were to be priced at two dollars per set. Wholesale discounts would be offered according to a scale of values that represented a slight tightening of the terms called for in the first contract for *Lionel Lincoln:* 30 percent for four hundred or more copies (in exchange for "approved endorsed notes payable in the City of New York," apparently at six months, although that element was omitted, probably through oversight); 25 percent for ninety-nine or more copies (for three-month notes of equal security, not the six-month notes allowed at this level in the case of *Lionel Lincoln*); and 25 percent for forty-nine or more copies and 20 percent for twelve or more copies (for cash payment in both cases; in the case of *Lionel Lincoln*, cash was required only for the final category).[36]

When circumstances dictated a change of arrangements for *The Last of the Mohicans,* Cooper took the opportunity to again experiment with a genuine publisher. The question of who would take up the new book in lieu of Wiley and himself hardly was a question by the fall of 1825. For some time, the novelist had been holding conversations with the large Philadelphia publishing and bookselling firm of Carey and Lea, which had long played a significant role in wholesaling and retailing his books not only in that city but also in the large portion of the South that it supplied. The first topic of discussion between the two parties, broached through Wiley shortly after the publication of *The Spy,* in fact concerned the terms on which Cooper insisted that his works be distributed and retailed, a subject that greatly exercised the Philadelphians. Their main objection to his scheme was that the short discount allowed them on wholesale transactions (a mere third off) did not give them enough on the books they in turn distributed through their own extensive networks of booksellers. Carey and Lea instead wanted a full 50 percent discount, allowing suitable profits for the ultimate retailers as well as their own firm. From selling Cooper's novels in Philadelphia and distributing them southward, Carey and Lea learned very early that Cooper sold well—in fact, only Sir Walter Scott, whom they regularly published in large editions, did better. They thus predicted to Wiley as early as August of 1822 that they thought they would be able to sell two thousand copies of *The Pioneers,* a very large portion of the projected first edition. Adding that their firm supplied many markets that, but for them, would never see a copy of a Cooper book, they urged Wiley to insist on more generous terms from the author-owner. When Cooper refused Wiley's plea, instead offering slightly better terms on the third edition of *The Spy*, they slashed their planned order of his next book. Having failed to convince Cooper that he was diminishing his own income, they concluded to make their prophecy come true.[37]

Wishing to demonstrate to Cooper his own inexperience in the publishing business, they argued that he would be well advised to let professionals—specifically, Carey and Lea—handle his books. As early as 1822, the Philadelphia firm had begun courting Cooper for this purpose. They may have done so first through the small bookselling and publishing branch in New York City that Henry C. Carey set up in April of that year under the management of Daniel D. Arden. Arden, a minor player in the New York trade who, as noted above, had been Robert M'Dermut's partner in a publishing firm from 1813 to 1816, probably was known to Cooper by repute if not in person. He conceivably served as Carey's go-between in preliminary explorations of a possible alliance, but if that was the case, nothing came of their discussions. Hampered by the yellow fever outbreak in 1822 and never profitable, Carey's New York shop ceased operations in April 1823, when Cooper's third book, even without Carey and Lea's wholehearted cooperation, was in the midst of its very strong initial run.[38]

There were other mutual connections through which Carey and Lea could continue gathering information on Cooper that might prove useful in their long-term effort to recruit him. One was John Miller, the London bookseller and publisher who had contracted with Cooper to publish *The Pilot* and *Lionel Lincoln* in England and who in due time would also bring out *The Last of the Mohicans*. As well connected with American firms as with American authors, Miller had been acting as the London agent for Henry Carey (and his father Mathew Carey) since 1817. As such, his job was to choose likely English titles for republication in Philadelphia and then rush copy to the Careys. After 1824, Miller could and surely did fill Carey and Lea in on Cooper's strengths in foreign markets, and may have advised them (to the extent that he could) on the terms Cooper customarily enjoyed with Wiley. Nor was his aid to the Philadelphia firm merely long distance. At the very moment that the crisis in Wiley's finances unfolded during the fall of 1825, Henry Carey fortuitously enough was on the spot in London conferring with Miller. While the two associates probably knew nothing of the details of Wiley's plight at the time, they surely discussed "the American Scott" and how he might be wooed away from the New Yorker's grip. On returning to America a month or so after Cooper endorsed the M'Dermut notes, Carey probably brought with him fresh ideas on how to go about acquiring Cooper for his list.[39]

This would be his second recent attempt to do so. Sometime in 1824, apparently in the early fall, Carey and his partner and brother-in-law Isaac Lea had made Cooper an offer with regard to *Lionel Lincoln* that he "did not accept."[40]

We do not know the terms of the offer. The Philadelphia firm certainly was interested in *publishing* Cooper's new book, not just distributing it. Not intimately familiar with Cooper's customary earnings or the terms prevailing between him and Wiley, on which they surely meant their own proposal to appear like an improvement, they must have offered a purchase price that fell considerably below Cooper's expectations, leading him to temporarily break off the discussion. Soon, however, Cooper countered with a pair of fresh proposals. This effort, which must have preceded his eventual November 1824 arrangement with Wiley to take on the book himself, involved terms somewhat different from those Wiley was to accept. Under Cooper's first proposal, Carey and Lea would have had exclusive rights to the edition of the novel currently being produced in New York. In return, they would make Cooper a cash payment of $4,300 and would pay the estimated production costs of $2,500. The second proposal called for Cooper to assign all his rights to the book for a period of four years in exchange for a slightly higher cash payment of $5,000. Carey and Lea would still pay all costs but would have the option of printing other editions that might well increase their profit. On calculating the costs of Cooper's first offer, however, the firm concluded that its net profit would be a mere fifteen dollars. Perhaps offended by Cooper's tightfistedness, of which they thought they had seen plenty of evidence while merely distributing his books in the past, they rejected both his offers unequivocally: "under no possible circumstance wd. we publish any work on such terms." Carey and Lea added, "You will readily see that no man of business could possibly accede to such a proposition."[41]

This discussion did not achieve immediate positive results for the Philadelphians. Although it in fact persuaded Cooper to change his views on how to manage his literary business, a shift that would finally play to Carey and Lea's advantage, their own stinginess and their blunt rejection of his proposals sent him first back to Wiley. Perhaps Wiley's "credulous" and "weak" nature in this instance may have been to Cooper's temporary advantage: he could be made to accept terms rejected by Carey and Lea. But Wiley remained Cooper's close friend; perhaps more importantly, Wiley was in New York, where the novelist could more easily intervene in the production process than he could if Carey and Lea took over his books.[42]

Once *Lionel Lincoln* went on sale early in 1825 and Cooper began work on his long-envisioned sixth novel, he probably assumed that Wiley would also handle it. As noted earlier, their July 1825 agreement on *The Last of the Mohicans* would default to the terms prevailing before the second contract for *Lionel Lincoln*. The July agreement, signed the month before Wiley's notes for *Lionel Lincoln* were due to be paid, appears to have been unaffected by the as-yet-undisclosed debt Wiley owed for paper used for that previous book. When the

M'Dermut crisis arose in October, sharp questions about the new book's threatened future arose. Cooper, well recalling Carey and Lea's overture of the previous year and his own rejected proposals, probably wished to reopen negotiations with that firm as soon as possible. Unfortunately, Henry Carey's continuing absence in Europe forced the novelist to spend the next month or so in what must have been considerable uncertainty.[43] At last, on November 11, 1825, probably having had word of Carey's expected arrival in Philadelphia within a day or two, Cooper wrote him to take up the conversation where it had been broken off the previous year.[44] His letter, which does not appear to survive, evidently offered to sell Carey and Lea the yet-to-be-published first edition of *The Last of the Mohicans*, then nearing the end of its production in New York City.

Completely surprised on finding Cooper's letter awaiting him when he disembarked in Philadelphia on November 13, Carey took a day to catch his breath before dashing off a quick acknowledgement. Cooper had been vague about what he wanted in return for transferring the book to his firm, so Carey, professing ignorance of Wiley's terms and probably at a loss about what to propose himself, asked Cooper to be more specific. The novelist took some days to answer, but even then would not spell things out. Carey again wrote back promptly, asking for a statement of the sales for *Lionel Lincoln* and pushing Cooper to say what he would expect in return for assigning the copyright of the new book for two years. Although Carey promised to take only twenty-four hours to respond to Cooper's next letter, nothing more survives in the record until the actual contract was signed the following January. There may—indeed *must*—have been further correspondence, or personal meetings in New York, where Carey never was a stranger. But of such exchanges we know nothing directly.[45] Cooper, having given Wiley complete control of the first edition of *Lionel Lincoln* for only a single year in return for $5,000 in six-month notes, probably proposed some such arrangement with Carey and Lea for the new book, only to be met with a skeptical reply. If he wanted *that* much, then they would have to have the book for more time—for four years. These were the key terms to which the parties eventually agreed in their January contract.

Across this period, the new book was in the hands of two New York printers, Edwin B. Clayton and James Van Norden.[46] Without apprising that firm of his intent, Cooper met with Henry Carey in New York on January 10, 1826, and signed the "sub rosa" contract (Carey's term for it) that shifted the new book to the Philadelphia publishers.[47] The secretiveness may have been prudent given the fact that it was finalized within a day or so of Wiley's death. But it inevitably raised some concern among the living members of the trade in New York City who were affected by the change. For one thing, the Philadelphia partners had no contracts with the New York stationer, printer, or binder who were actually producing *their* book—a highly irregular state of affairs. Worse yet, Carey and Lea did not even know the identity of those men. The best they could do was to get the relevant names from Cooper and quickly write letters to all of the firms to arrange the final details for publication.

These letters must have given the New Yorkers the first hint that Cooper had changed from their recently deceased colleague to Carey and Lea. Clayton and Van Norden replied to Carey and Lea on Monday, January 16, with reassurances that the book was nearly done, promising that they would be able to deliver the sheets to the binder, Jonathan Seymour, either later the present week or early the next. Checking with Seymour, Carey and Lea determined that the publication date called for in the contract ("the 7th day of February . . . unless the work should be further delayed by the author") might be slightly improved upon. On January 25, the publishers therefore told Cooper that they expected to issue the book on Saturday, February 4. Up to this point, the transition seemed to be going smoothly.[48]

The optimistic timing fell victim, however, to a financial dispute. From what they knew of *The Last of the Mohicans* and the conditions of the book trade, Carey and Lea had assumed that the edition of five thousand copies should cost no more than $2,300. But in view of their lack of input up to this point, their contract with Cooper allowed for a maximum of $2,500. When they received Clayton and Van Norden's bill on January 19, they were shocked to discover that not even this ample allowance was high enough. Work that Carey and Lea felt "every other printer in New York" could have done for $650 was priced by Clayton and Van Norden at more than $830. Their outrage at this turn of events was not unreasonable. The following year, Carey and Lea were to have *The Prairie* set, and stereotype plates produced from the formes, for just over $460. When one deducts the likely cost of those plates ($160) from this amount and adds the actual printing charges for five thousand copies (around $350), it is clear that *The Prairie* would have cost almost precisely $650 to set and print in Philadelphia in an edition of exactly the same type and size as *The Last of the Mohicans*.[49]

Carey and Lea were blindsided by the bill and concerned about who would have to pay it. The root of the problem lay in the awkward interruption of Wiley's contract and the sudden shift to a distant publisher. Perhaps worried that the confusion caused by Wiley's difficulties and death and Cooper's decision to publish in Philadelphia would shortchange them—or wary instead that someone might think they were trying to exploit that confusion by padding their bill, as may indeed have been the case—Clayton and Van Norden were not inclined to take a passive line. They insisted to Carey and Lea that their contract with Wiley for the book required payment in full "as soon as the work is finished." Furthermore, knowing that the new publishers were eager to get the book out, they refused to cooperate unless their bill was accepted and paid up front.[50]

Since the printer's work was about to be finished, this was a demand that could hardly be ignored. Carey and Lea assured Cooper that one of the firm's partners would soon be in New York and would then "arrange all matters" in relation to Clayton and Van Norden. In the meantime, clearly hoping to dispute and thereby lower the printing charges, they asked Cooper to rush them copies of "the bill for Lionel & the Pioneers"—without letting the printers know what he was up to. At this point, in the depth of winter, illness seems to have disrupted any chance for immediate resolution. Henry Carey and Isaac Lea both were laid low by the influenza in Philadelphia, as was Cooper in New York, and the month ended without either of the partners going north. Not until January 31 did they at last dispatch a substitute, one of their Philadelphia clerks, to New York. In the meantime, they neither paid the printing bill nor "arranged" the issue through the mails. In fact, their further contact with Clayton and Van Norden only worsened things. In the last week of the month, they wrote the New Yorkers to complain of the matter, adopting "such style," as Carey explained to Cooper, "as might be used to greater men" than Edwin B. Clayton or James Van Norden. Always aware of his own exalted position in the world of publishing, where he assumed that mere printers occupied a much lower level, Carey was shocked to receive the sort of reply he had "rarely had from any man." Not only did Clayton and Van Norden refuse to apologize; they reminded the publishers, as Carey soon wrote to Cooper, that they had "not contracted to do any work" for the Philadelphians. Worse yet, they snidely added that they did "not care if they never should, &c &c &c." By this point, the feeling must have been fully mutual.[51]

Verbal rancor was hardly the worst of it. Clayton and Van Norden, not yet paid, already had decided to delay the transfer of printed sheets from their establishment to Seymour's as a means of driving home their point. The bulk of the order had been delivered as early as Monday, January 23, according to promise, and three days later Carey and Lea had twenty advance copies on hand in Philadelphia. In New York, Seymour was hurriedly folding and sewing the sheets, then boarding and covering the volumes, after which the finished books were to be forwarded according to Carey and Lea's instructions. Things were still at a reasonably amicable point then. Carey, eager to publish as soon as possible, advertised the book for February 4, only to find at the last minute that the printers, true to the tone of their communications, had decided to hold on to the last one thousand copies. This was an affront to the publishers by any measure. But the printers, finding their bill disputed by an out-of-town publisher with whom they had no formal agreement, probably felt that it was the only means they had of insuring payment. Or they may just have had their hackles raised by Carey's hauteur and wished to lower him a bit.

The resulting shortage of bound copies seems to have hit Carey and Lea particularly hard. If, as seems likely, they had wholesaled most of the copies that Seymour had finished, the last one thousand would have provided the bulk of their own retail supply. Certainly they soon were complaining to Cooper that they had lost the sale of "200 copies here." Unable to blame Wiley, they turned their anger briefly toward Cooper, who probably had had nothing to do with the choice of printers: "Your printers have used us very ill indeed." In his unlocated February 11 reply to this last letter, Cooper took neither side. He did, however, express his regret that such a dispute was marring his new publishing arrangements and perhaps hindering sales of *The Last of the Mohicans.* And he had no wish to protect Carey and Lea from the criticism he felt their high-handed behavior merited. He suggested that Henry Carey's heated tone in his exchanges with the New Yorkers had made a difficult situation measurably worse. This barb was pointed enough that it sent Carey back over his copies of his correspondence with the printers. He found "nothing to warrant such treatment" as he had received, but the abundant defensiveness of his answer to Cooper on February 13 suggests a man aware of his intemperance even as he remained unwilling to admit to it. Even this late, with Cooper's chastisement as a spur, Carey does not seem to have approached the printers in a spirit of compromise. He sent Cooper the agreed upon notes to cover the $5,000 payment for his copyright, and was about to pay Seymour for his binding, but on the subject of Clayton and Van Norden nothing apparently was yet done because he still did not know whether all the sheets had been delivered. Carey hoped that he would soon hear from Clayton not only on that issue but also on possible errors in the printing, which might warrant a reduction in the printer's payment.[52]

In view of the impasse with Clayton and Van Norden, Cooper seems to have been drawn into the settlement process. The printers apparently would not budge on their bill, leaving a shortfall between the publishers' liability and their demand. Cooper, accepting the responsibility for any production costs beyond the $2,500 stated in the contract, began negotiating with the paper supplier (presumably M'Dermut, although we do not know that) and with Seymour to lessen their charges so that he might thereby apply any savings toward Clayton and Van Norden's claims. He informed Carey and Lea of these efforts on February 11— too late in the stationer's case, Carey immediately let him know, because on that very day the Philadelphia firm had paid him via a short-term note. With regard to the binding charges, Cooper apparently convinced Seymour that an immediate settlement in cash, at a discount, was preferable to the six-month note with interest to which his contract with Wiley entitled him. Carey and Lea were not

opposed to this arrangement. Nor did they object to Cooper's assumption of a
further responsibility with regard to the book. Deducting what they already had
paid for the paper, they would remit to Cooper the full amount due to Seymour
and the balance of the $2,500 total to which their contract obligated them.
Cooper then would negotiate a final settlement figure with Clayton and Van
Norden. If he was shrewd or lucky enough, he might be able to make Carey and
Lea's funds satisfy both of the outstanding demands. In that way, his own earnings on the book would remain intact.[53]

Sea Change

Many things were changing across 1825 and into 1826—including Cooper's own
name. Long before, perhaps when the eighteen-year-old sailor had just returned
from the voyage of the *Stirling* and was about to enter the navy, his mother had
planted in his mind an idea that would bear fruit soon after *The Last of the Mohicans* was published. Elizabeth Fenimore was proud of her family name but had no
brothers to carry it on: following the 1789 death of the last male of the line, her
father Richard, she longed to ensure its continuance. In the fall of 1807, she may
have had another concern. Her youngest son was about to make his way into an
uncertain world without suitable support. The voyage to Europe had been a success—he had at least survived. The naval career about which something had been
said the year before had not yet materialized, however, and even if it eventually
did, it hardly could be trusted to give him a secure future. Hadn't his brother
Samuel, intended for a similar destiny some years earlier, been disappointed when
the navy was "reduced" before he was ready to enter it? Besides, a navy career in
the best of circumstances may not have struck Cooper's mother as safe enough or
noble enough or (given her Quaker heritage) proper enough for her last child.

So far, Cooper had been left out of the arrangements made for his older siblings. He certainly had not tapped his father's resources in the way most of the
older children had. Elizabeth's daughter, Ann Pomeroy, was married and living
in a substantial stone house built by Judge Cooper; her oldest boys, Richard and
Isaac, both married and building families in Cooperstown, were already deeply
involved in William Cooper's business, whose management they were destined
to inherit. Even William, having completed his legal studies in New York City,
momentarily seemed assured of the stable future of which his parents must often
have despaired. Soon he would marry a rich merchant's daughter and move into
a New York City house purchased for him by his father. Since Samuel's ill-fated
attempt on the navy, he was destined, as both Elizabeth and her husband probably assumed, to hang about the family compound, securely unspectacular. But
what of "Jem"?

And, now that her youngest child was about to leave home, what of Elizabeth Fenimore Cooper herself? In a momentary fit of mixed self-regard and motherly concern, she therefore mounted a campaign to protect her last boy from fatherly neglect or resentment—and from the larger, crueler world of which he already had had a riskier taste than any of her offspring. Like most women in her era, Mrs. Cooper owned little property in her own right. But there apparently were some lands in New Jersey that had come into her hands through her father. Probably for the sake of convenience, these had later been swapped for "eight or ten farms" in Otsego. Taking her sailor son aside, she offered him those farms if, as Cooper himself told the story in 1847, "I would take her family name in lieu of that of Cooper" (*LJ* 5:201). From Elizabeth Cooper's perspective, it must have seemed that the farms would anchor her son in Otsego, give him an income to boot, and ensure the immortality of her family name.[54]

When Judge Cooper caught wind of the negotiations, he quickly ended them, and not until he died in 1809 was his widow once more free to raise the question. From time to time, probably especially during the residence of her youngest son and his high-born bride in Otsego from 1813 to 1817, Elizabeth Cooper again pushed her offer. When the naming of their rural property Fenimore Farm did not satisfy her longings for immortality, Cooper finally agreed to meet her halfway. He had no interest in her Otsego lands, he said, and he would not give up his father's surname and take on hers: instead, he would only promise "to add her name to my father's, and to use both as a family name." Although this compromise seems to have met with her approval, Cooper did not have time to carry it out before her death in September 1817. Thereafter, as he became entangled in his many lawsuits, he hesitated to carry through with his pledge because he thought that "change might produce confusion" (*LJ* 1:201). In the meantime, he could only signal his mindfulness of the pledge by bestowing his mother's surname on his unfortunate first-born son in 1821—a memorial act seemingly undone when the boy died, eerily enough, only days after the mansion at Fenimore Farm had been set afire in 1823.

There the matter rested for another three years. Only when Cooper thought himself "extricated from the law" in 1826 did he feel free to act on his promise. In fact, it was on or before February 20, 1826, only two days before Cooper (evidently in expectation of his speedy victory) filed his chancery bill against Robert Sedgwick, that he at last petitioned the New York State assembly for permission to change his name.[55] Although a long-lived tradition asserts that he asked the legislature for permission to change his name to "James Cooper Fenimore," there is no evidence from the 1820s for such a request.[56] The earliest official notation on the question, in New York's legislative *Journal*, indicates that "the petition of James Cooper of the city of New-York praying for permission to change his name by the addition of a middle sirname [*sic*]" was first read and then referred to a "select committee" for further consideration on February 20, 1826.[57] In 1847, Cooper himself accurately recalled this intent when he wrote to Philander B. Prindle (who had seen the original petition in the assembly files and wanted to remove it to add to his manuscript autograph collection, as he apparently did): "The application was . . . to add Fenimore to the old family name, keeping both" (*LJ* 5:201). For the precise sequence of family names in this change he had the precedent of his eldest brother, Richard Fenimore Cooper, who had been christened in honor of his maternal grandfather—not to mention two nieces who both had been named Elizabeth Fenimore Cooper. But these resemblances were only apparent. The novelist was not taking on a middle name. He fully intended that he be known henceforth as a *Fenimore* Cooper. His request, as the legislative *Journal* indicated, was to add a middle *surname*.

As it worked out, that both *was* and was *not* to be. Cooper explained in his letter to Prindle: "The legislators, who always know more than their constituents, changed this application by authorizing me to take Fenimore as a middle name, a power I did not ask" (*LJ* 5:201). The restriction, which may have been the result of a mere error, had already been inserted before the bill was reported by the select committee on March 16, and remained in place when it was approved the next day.[58] A certified manuscript copy of the approved act prepared for Cooper on May 8, 1826, thus indicated that it "shall be lawful for James Cooper, formerly of Cooperstown in the County of Otsego and at present of the City of New York to assume and take the middle name of Fenimore and [he] shall hereafter be known and distinguished as James Fenimore Cooper."[59] Fully aware of the difference between his intent and the assembly's act, Cooper nonetheless immediately began signing his name "J. Fenimore Cooper," the first surviving instance occurring in a letter of March 21, 1826, to Congressman Lewis Williams of the House of Representatives (*LJ* 6:290–91). Cooper also used the signature in a presently unlocated letter of April 1 to Carey and Lea. In a pesky foretaste of a problem the novelist would face for the rest of his life, often from friends of long standing, Carey and Lea replied to "J. *Fennimore* Cooper" on April 3. He corrected them on April 4, noting, "There are two clans of the Fenimores—One, of which your humble servant bears the name, and the other a mongrel race, at which we affect to turn up our noses—We use but one *n*, as below—Yours truly—J. Fenimore Cooper" (*LJ* 1:131). As late as 1834, William Dunlap, Cooper's friend for a dozen years, was to dedicate his *History of the American Theatre* to "James Fennimore Cooper."[60]

There was in the change of name the sense of an old obligation satisfied. But in its use as his official, legal name—the name with which his literary wares would be identified—there may also have been an equal sense of new beginnings. The name marked the public figure Cooper had become by virtue of his hard labors over the past six years. It also was a better match for Susan DeLancey Cooper's hefty gentility—if not quite equal to that of her younger brother, the Rt. Rev. William Heathcote DeLancey, whose full name tied him to both the Anglo and French elements of New York history. The simple Quaker boy "Jem Cooper" could use a bit more ballast.[61]

That was especially true given the plan for a long European visit that he and Susan had been talking about for some time. The family began taking French lessons shortly after the permanent shift from Angevine to New York. Their first teacher was John Manseca, a once-wealthy St. Domingo planter who lived in exile with his family in "a miserable little two-story house, wretchedly furnished," at 24 Liberty Street, a few blocks above the Battery, and had been making ends meet for a number of years by tutoring New Yorkers. A man of scholarly pretensions, he would publish a brief treatise on how to teach languages in 1825 (through Clayton and Van Norden, perhaps at Cooper's suggestion) and was at work on a large French-English dictionary.[62] Susan Cooper thought her father had begun taking lessons from Manseca while the family was on Greenwich Street (where they were living from May 1824 on), but he may have started even earlier. She probably recalled that association because Greenwich Street was the family's address at the time when Susan herself first came under Manseca's tutelage. Three times a week she would take the long walk down island with her father to visit Manseca, whom she recalled as "a very clever but peculiar man." He presided over the two pupils with a somewhat imperious manner, giving them written lessons and then quizzing them about how well they had mastered some assigned task. He did not want to teach "magpies" who could not think, he reasoned with Cooper; but if so, his manner with Susan was hardly effective. Terrified on one occasion when he raised his voice as he towered above her, she was on the edge of tears. In the end, however, Manseca was satisfied with father and daughter alike (SFM 54–55).

Cooper for his part thought highly of Manseca. In February 1826, he described him as a man who "has thought more, labored more, and knows more of the French language, in my poor opinion, than any man I have ever met" (LJ 6:290n). He also had succeeded well enough that Cooper, "poor" as he pretended his opinion was in such things, was quite comfortable using the language in his tale of Anglo-French rivalry, The Last of the Mohicans, or in his correspondence with Swiss native F. Alph. de Syon. In France he would not only converse in French but write in it.[63]

Instruction in French was followed by work in Spanish under a twenty-eight-year-old native speaker by the name of Galvan, a medical doctor temporarily in New York. He was, Cooper had learned, "a refugee from the power of King Ferdinand"—Ferdinand VII of Spain, an absolutist who had returned to the throne in 1823. Of "retired, studious habits," Galvan apparently had been born in Latin America but had been educated in Spain and, like his friend Manseca, was at work on a book—a "Spanish Grammar"—when Cooper knew him. Cooper first met Galvan in the fall of 1825 and began his studies then, insisting that both Susan and his nephew William study Spanish as well, and they at least learned how to read it. Cooper himself progressed far enough to feel comfortable judging Galvan's Spanish "to be very good." French was still Cooper's strongest Romance language—he could tell that Galvan spoke French "with a Spanish accent," for instance—but he evidently had learned enough, with his base in Latin as well as French, to recommend his Spanish teacher for an academic post at the University of North Carolina (*LJ* 6:289–91; SFM 56).

This language instruction was part of an educational plan for the family. But the long work in French was also part of a long-matured wish of Cooper and his wife to spend some time abroad. As early as the spring of 1823, with *The Pioneers* just out, it was being rumored in Otsego that Cooper "intended to visit 'Templeton' before sailing for England," although the purpose and expected duration of that rumored trip are not clear.[64] Two-and-a-half years later (in September 1825), writing to Syon on the eve of that man's return to France with Lafayette, Cooper at last could divulge that he and Susan were talking "very seriously of making an effort to get to France for a year or two." Concerned about the cost and his finances, he asked Syon to make inquiries "as to what a plain man, like myself, might live on [in] Paris—and also near a provincial town—say Orleans" (*LJ* 1:125). Whether "J. Fenimore Cooper" was still a "plain man" or ever really had been was a good question. But the novelist just meant that he did not want to live large, and for the most part once his family finally got to France in 1826 they were to avoid sumptuous quarters, fine fare, and high company. Their purposes in going overseas were multiple. Among the more important was Cooper's sense, on which he acted almost on arriving, that being on the spot in Europe would allow him to derive more income from his future works. For this reason, he had asked Carey and Lea for advice about a contact in Paris, and they had given him the name of Hector Bossange, a printer who specialized in English language texts. Bossange would soon become deeply involved in Cooper's plans to recoup European income from his books. Whether Cooper expected such business to take as much as a year or two is unlikely. On the other hand, some of the purposes for the trip, which included his health and the education of his children in French and Italian—plus "a little pleasure in the bottom of the Cup" (see *LJ* 1:127)—might conceivably take more time.[65]

A good deal needed attention before the family could depart. Although he had groused to Shubrick the previous year that *The Last of the Mohicans* might be the last of his books, even with the prospect that the Sedgwick suit might be resolved Cooper knew that, wherever he lived, he would need some source of continuing income. Carey and Lea were delighted with their bargain for Cooper's sixth novel. They had paid him a riskily high price, sending him a set of six notes (ranging from three months to eight months maturity) for a total of nearly $5,100, to cover principal and interest, on February 8, but at the same time admitting that the book had so far done well and looked as if it would continue doing so. Cooper expressed doubts about *The Last of the Mohicans* in a letter of February 21, but by then his publishers were even more sanguine. Robert Walsh, author of *An Appeal from the Judgments of Great Britain* (1819) and an accomplished Philadelphia editor, stopped by Carey and Lea's shop on Fourth and Chestnut streets on February 22 and reported, "every body delights in it." Within another couple of weeks, the publishers were planning an immediate reprint; indeed, so sure were they of the book's continuing strength that they were thinking of paying an extra charge for stereotyping it, thereby allowing virtually unlimited future reprintings. In fact, they decided to take that risk—happily—and soon adopted stereotyping as an integral part of publishing Cooper.[66]

For there *were* to be future titles. Cooper was already thinking about the next one, *The Prairie*, by early in 1826. In that unlocated April 1 letter that first used his new name, Cooper made Carey and Lea a complicated offer that presumably followed on some face-to-face discussion between the two parties. First, he would sell them his new novel, which he had begun writing, on the "same terms as the Mohicans precisely"—$5,000 payable in a series of notes in return for the copyright and for the right of exclusive publication in the United States, though, according to an important later refinement, for a period of fourteen rather than four years. The extra length for the "leasehold" (Cooper's term, *LJ* 1:131) on *The Prairie* derived from Carey and Lea's request that the terms being worked out with regard to Cooper's assignment of all his previous titles to them be extended to the new book as well. While in Europe, Cooper could, he figured, adequately or more than adequately manage his *new* books. But it made practical sense to assign the older titles to Carey and Lea so that they could tend to the "residuals." Indeed, it made financial sense as well. For an additional $2,500, which he desperately needed in order to fund the European trip, he therefore gave the Philadelphia house control over all his previous titles (except *Precaution* and *Tales for Fifteen*) plus *The Prairie* "until the close of the term of 14 years for wh[ich] the copyright of the several works has been secured."[67]

With $7,500 due from Carey and Lea, his health relatively stable since the previous September, the Sedgwick business resolved, his tribute to his mother at last taken care of, and his plans emerging for the European trip, Cooper had new but relatively upbeat distractions to contend with. He wanted to ensure that as much as possible of the money now due him would be in his hands as cash *before* leaving for Europe. He therefore soon assigned the contract for *The Prairie* to his friend Luther Bradish, in return for cash and Bradish's agreement to pay off certain of the novelist's remaining obligations. Bradish had Cooper's power of attorney to act on these matters, and on May 18, Cooper wrote Cooperstown lawyer Robert Campbell to explain what was in the offing. Bradish would assign Carey and Lea's notes as necessary to satisfy both Campbell (on the long-delayed contract he had purchased from carpenter Robert Ward for the construction of Angevine) and another Otsego creditor. If possible, Cooper wanted to delay payment of those claims so that cash now in his hands—or soon to be there— could be taken directly to Europe. If he used such funds to discharge his lingering obligations right now, then later payments would have to pass to Europe through intermediary agents, an annoying if not risky process (*LJ* 1:137–38).[68]

As these affairs of the pocketbook were worked out, Cooper's financial picture was becoming increasingly simplified. To be sure, the great unresolved issue of his father's estate would linger in limbo for another eight years (Robert Campbell warned him this very May, for instance, that if William H. Averell knew that a certain Cooperstown lot belonged to Cooper, he would immediately have it sold under terms of the Pomeroy decree).[69] But at least his personal financial affairs were in relative order. In Bradish, furthermore, he had a trusted ally who would see to any further questions while he was himself absent. Now two things, aside from continuing work on *The Prairie*, remained on his docket. First, he had to make arrangements for his family's Atlantic passage; second, he had to see to a hundred last-minute details before actually embarking.

As recently as February, in a letter to English publisher John Miller, Cooper portrayed himself as uncertain whether the family would go to France or Italy, and at that time portrayed the trip *as* a trip rather than a long-term relocation. If things worked out, though, he was already willing to entertain a longer stay. He had told Syon in September that he wished he had the connections to receive appointment to "a good consulate, or some such thing" (*LJ* 1:125), since he would feel much better about bringing Susan and the five children with him if he had an appointment (and its proceeds) in his pocket. By February 1826, even as he hedged his bets in writing Miller, he addressed himself to his patron, Gov. DeWitt Clinton, to ask for help in getting just such an appointment. If he could, he would consider staying abroad "three or four years," he told Clinton. He would prefer a consular appointment (preferably on or near the Mediterranean) "that would yield me a moderate sum," and wondered with suitable self-effacement whether Clinton would be in a position to recommend him "to any of the Officers of the General Government." Clinton, ill at the time, replied with apologies three weeks later, adding a reassuring "I am your Friend" in lieu of a more conventional sign-off and enclosing a letter addressed to Secretary of State Henry Clay. In it, Clinton spoke of Cooper as a "gentleman" and of Cooper's works as having "reflected honor not only on himself but our Country." Taking it as a given that Clay like himself was "disposed to encourage American talent," Clinton fully supported such an appointment.[70]

Cooper was eager for Clinton's reply and the enclosure. On February 12, he had informed Bradish, recently returned from a long unofficial diplomatic mission to Turkey and presently in Washington, that he would himself be in the federal capital "about the first of March" and might see his friend there and take care of the details of their financial deal (*LJ* 1:130). Cooper had barely received Clinton's letter before he rushed down, met with Clay (perhaps with Bradish's direct help), presented Clinton's letter, and discussed the possibilities for an appointment. He apparently stayed there some days, since he was still in Washington on March 21, almost two weeks after Henry C. Carey, calling on him in Greenwich Street, found him gone from New York.[71] By March 12, snugly settled in Washington, Cooper had become acquainted with the young but already celebrated ornithologist—and nephew of Napoleon—Charles-Lucien Bonaparte, who on arriving in town had registered at his own hotel. Spending most of their time talking about "the greatest political questions" of the day, the two got along so well that their families would later socialize extensively in Italy. By the end of their time together in the federal capital, Bonaparte was so delighted with his new friend that, writing on March 27 to the New York conchologist William Cooper (a former member of the Lunch whom the novelist incorrectly took to be his cousin), he sought to "avoid confusion" by playfully attempting to "Decooperize" the novelist, referring to him instead as "Mr. Fenimore"—another indication, by the way, that Cooper's use of his new name did not await his receipt of the legislature's formal approval.[72]

The novelist's daughter Susan later reported that Clay had offered her father the position of minister to Sweden, a post for which Cooper's interests and health, not to mention linguistic training, probably made him less than enthusiastic. The big drawback there, in any case, would have been the requirement that Ambassador Fenimore Cooper actually *do* something—live in Stockholm, for one thing, and represent American interests at the court of Carl XIV, king of both Norway and Sweden and a famous associate of Charles-Lucien Bonaparte's uncle during the days of the Empire (SFM 59). If the offer was tentatively made and refused, Clay did not waste his time or Cooper's but instead suggested that the United States might be well served by establishing a new consulate at Lyons, a textile center southwest of Geneva on the Rhone, one hundred miles or so from the Mediterranean, with which American merchants carried on considerable trade (see *LJ* 1:137n).

There things stood until early in May, when Cooper wrote Clay to inquire about the status of the issue. Within a week, Cooper's commission as U.S. consul at Lyons had been filled out, signed by Clay, and passed on for President John Quincy Adams's signature. Soon approved by the Senate, it was conveyed to Cooper with a cover letter on May 26. Clay also enclosed printed "Circular Instructions and a Blank Consular Bond," adding that the second of these needed to be executed and returned to Washington. He apparently sent along Cooper's passport as well.[73] This was pushing the deadline. On moving day, May 1, Cooper and his family had left their Greenwich Street residence. Susan and the children went to Heathcote Hill for the month of May, a final farewell visit with her sisters Caroline and Martha and her father John Peter—farewell indeed, since the elder DeLancey would die before the Coopers returned to America (SFM 59). Cooper still kept his distance from Mamaroneck, moving into the City Hotel for one last, long stay there. At the hotel, Cooper ran through a last-minute pile of books and pamphlets in between handling all the details that still needed attention—and writing more of *The Prairie*, the first eleven chapters of which he seems to have finished before leaving the country.[74]

Sometime during the last week of May, Cooper received an invitation from his friends and associates of the Lunch announcing a farewell banquet planned for May 29 at the City Hotel. He happily accepted. Chair of the committee of arrangements was the merchant William Gracie. The caterers were two long-time personal friends whose complex relationship to Cooper bespoke the tough path he had followed to this point in his life: Cooper's attorney for the Sedgwick case, Peter A. Jay; and the judge who had ruled against him with regard to the Bridgen and Pomeroy bills in chancery, James Kent. A long list of invited guests included not only such close associates of Cooper in New York as Dr. John W. Francis or such friends of his childhood and young manhood as John Cox Morris of Otsego, Jerry Van Rensselaer of Albany, and William B. Shubrick of the navy, but also his patron—Gov. DeWitt Clinton of New York—along with Gov. Ethan Allen Brown of Ohio, Cmdre. Isaac Chauncey, Gen. Winfield T. Scott, New York City Mayor Philip Hone, and New York Episcopal bishop John Henry Hobart.

After an address by Charles King, editor of the New York *American*, in honor of "the Founder" of the club, Cooper rose to express his thanks for the event, the thoughtfulness and tribute it expressed, and the many friendships extended or formed by the Lunch. Having served as the group's main instigator was one of the things in his life of which he was proudest. There were others. King had called for Cooper not to abandon his pen in leaving the country. He had given much pleasure to individual readers and had shed renown on his country: no longer could it be said, King went on, as it often had been said, that a republic must have little art, and none of it great. The Lunch itself contained many counterarguments on that point, and chief among them was Cooper. For his part, Cooper was grateful for King's kind praise of his literary works—the most recent of which was still selling very strongly—and vowed that he would indeed keep writing. But, in the presence especially of Isaac Chauncey, he made a more solemn promise as well. He might write more historical romances, but the day would come when he would expiate his sins against the domains of history by penning a true narrative of the "deeds and sufferings" of the country's naval heroes. He had often told friends that he would write a naval history. Now he publicly vowed to do so.

Cooper lightened the tone a bit by proposing a toast "to the prosperity of the Lunch; and to the health and happiness of each and all of you." Other toasts followed. DeWitt Clinton spoke of the "personal worth and literary excellence" of his "talented friend." Shubrick called to mind "the Memory of Lawrence, the early friend and shipmate of our guest"—and of himself. But all was not ponderously solemn. Liverpool-born James Renwick of Columbia, chemist and engineer, stood to capture in a phrase or two the ruling principles of the Lunch: "Irony and raillery," he had concluded, comprised the chief business of the Lunch; then he added with true Knickerbocker spirit, "May they be the serious pursuits of the nation." As if on cue, New York City's best wit, Anthony Bleecker (who already had toasted "the memory of Charles Brockden Brown, the earliest American novelist"), rose to pun the company into laughs and groans, all of them at Cooper's expense. Then, on Cooper's personal motion, two of his allies in the fight for American cultural independence and recognition, the painter Washington Allston and the writer Washington Irving, were unanimously voted into the group.[75]

And then it was over. At 11:00 a.m. the next day, Susan and the children having at some point come back to town from Mamaroneck, Cooper shepherded his family to the shore at Whitehall wharf to await the small, inevitably packed steamboat that would take the expectant passengers for the Liverpool, London, and Havre packets out to their respective ships. The Coopers had wanted to go on the Havre boat, *Don Quixote*, but it was the smallest sailing then, so they settled on the London ship, the *Hudson*, a vessel of what was known as the "Black X" packet line. In 1826, it was under the command of Capt. Henry L. Champlin, a native of Connecticut whom Cooper thought a "prudent and excellent man" (*LJ* 1:147). The *Hudson*, presently moored off Bedloe's Island, was "a stout little ship" built in 1822, when Champlin first captained it. It went on the London service two years later. In 1830, during a period of exceptionally strong winds, the ship was to set a near record for the westward passage but then in 1832 would be relegated to the whaling trade.[76]

On the morning of June 1, "a flat calm" beset the waters off the Battery. Hence Cooper's *Gleanings in Europe: France,* which starts with the voyage over in 1826, recalled that the *Hudson,* along with the other packets, could do little but drop "down the bay with the ebb." But it was a spectacular day, however slow— just the right kind of weather for the emotional farewell the travelers had not allowed enough time for, especially Cooper himself, in the hurry of the last month. The waters of New York were at the peak of their loveliness. Looking back, up past Manhattan and its almost feverishly expanding material presence, Cooper could see the Hudson—the "North River," as the Manhattanese called it, but the Hudson to Cooper, who had known it from its other end since his ear- liest days. He let his thoughts drift upriver, back up the stream of time, too. Soon the vessel that bore the river's name was off the "quarantine" ground on Staten Island, where it met the incoming tide and halted for the night. Some passengers had yet to arrive; even Captain Champlin was not aboard yet. Night fell under clear skies as the passengers adjusted to their tight and odorous quarters, brac- ing for whatever might overtake them beyond Sandy Point. With dawn, there were "puffs" of wind coming out to the *Hudson* from over Staten Island, but the ship's anchor was tight in the bottom and it took some hours for the sails, billow- ing and pulling against the iron, to pry the ship free and set it full in the stream. The "people"—the crew—were sent to get their breakfasts, and by the time they were done the anchor had come loose, so the vessel caught the fresh wind blowing through the Narrows near Fort Lafayette and went down into the lower bay. There the wind lightened, but with persistence the vessel, "well com- manded, and exceedingly comfortable," went past the "low sandy spit of land" at New York's end—Rockaway Point on Coney Island—and "fairly entered the Atlantic." The pilot was discharged, the faltering wind freshened, and by sunset the Navesink Hills near Sandy Hook, on the Jersey shore, had disappeared.

Cooper stayed on deck as the other passengers, less seaworthy, were forced below. On this second day of the voyage, but the first at sea, he had things to think about. It had been many years since he had last passed this way. In 1806, two decades before, he had been a green hand on the *Stirling,* with great dreams and much energy. The dreams were tempered now by twenty years of high life and low luck, and the energy was subdued, always held in check even when Cooper could sense it lest he overdo himself into another "attack." The ship- board smells, sights, and sounds (including the sailors' lingo) helped him recover some sense of himself when young. But he wasn't young any more, not in that literal sense—not in some ways even in spirit. He had accomplished a great deal, but all of it had been dragged up into the light like something pulled from the deep ocean waters, a strange thing before unknown. And through it all on this first dark night fully at sea, he heard the echo of those words flung at him from an Englishman bound to Cuba on another passing ship. "A good run to you, Mr. [Cooper]," the other man had cried. Then he asked, "How long do you mean to be absent?" Cooper yelled back, "Five years," and the Englishman, "raven-like," threw a parting prediction across the waves: "You will never come back!" (*GF* CE 3–6).

These were, suitably enough, the last words Cooper heard on quitting his native land. He would think of them many times as his European trip of a year or two or three or four lengthened into five, then six, then seven and more. In his account of the moment, written after his final homecoming in 1833, he would celebrate the literal untruth of the English prophet. But in less actual ways the Cuba-bound voyager had been dead right. By 1833, Cooper was not the man he had been when he left. He was healthier; he was sharper culturally, deeper polit-ically, shrewder (if not yet cynical) in moral terms. But his country, as he would find to his woe in 1834, had also not sat still during that long blank period of his absence. Man and country, once so close, would come to blows, and it would take him more time still, including several years of self-imposed silence as a novelist, before he truly came home. But all of that is another story.

Notes

ABBREVIATIONS

Individuals and Institutions

HSFC	Henry S. F. Cooper, Jr.
JFB	James Franklin Beard
JFC/JC	James Fenimore Cooper/James Cooper
JFC II	James Fenimore Cooper (1858–1938)
SDC	Susan DeLancey Cooper
SFC	Susan Fenimore Cooper
TF	Tibbits family
WC	Judge William Cooper

AAS	American Antiquarian Society, Worcester, Mass.
HCA	Paul Fenimore Cooper, Jr., Archives, Hartwick College, Oneonta, N.Y.
NARA	National Archives and Records Administration
NYHS	New-York Historical Society, New York City
NYSA	New York State Archives, Albany

NYSHA   New York State Historical Association, Cooperstown
NYSL   New York State Library Manuscripts and Special Collections, Albany
YCAL   Yale Collection of American Literature, Beinecke Library, Yale University

Writings of James Fenimore Cooper

Collected Editions

CE   "Cooper Edition." *The Writings of James Fenimore Cooper*, ed. James
        Franklin Beard et al. Albany: State University of New York Press, 1980–
        1991, 17 vols.; New York: AMS Press, 2002–present, 3 vols.

Darley "Darley Edition." *Cooper's Novels, Illustrated by [F. O. C.] Darley* (spine
        title). New York: W. A. Townsend, 1859–1861, 32 vols.

HE   "Household Edition." *J. Fenimore Cooper's Works. Household Edition*
        (cover title). Boston and New York: Houghton Mifflin Co., 1876 (5 vols.:
        the Leather-Stocking Tales, all with introductions by SFC); 1881–1884
        (27 additional vols., 10 with introductions by SFC).

Individual titles

A&A   *Afloat and Ashore; or the Adventures of Miles Wallingford.* 4 vols. Philadel-
        phia: Published by the Author, 1844.

COC   *The Chronicles of Cooperstown.* Cooperstown: H. & E. Phinney, 1838.

CR   *The Crater; or, Vulcan's Peak. A Tale of the Pacific.* 2 vols. New York:
        Burgess, Stringer & Co., 1847.

DS   *The Deerslayer; or, the First Warpath.* 2 vols. Philadelphia: Lea & Blan-
        chard, 1841.

ECE   *Early Critical Essays (1820–1822), by James Fenimore Cooper*, ed. James F.
        Beard, Jr. Gainesville: Scholars' Facsimiles & Reprints, 1955.

Eclipse JFC, "The Eclipse," *Putnam's Magazine* n.s. 4(1869): 351–59.

GE   *Gleanings in Europe: England.* 2 vols. Philadelphia: Carey, Lea, and Blan-
        chard, 1837.

GF   *Gleanings in Europe. [France].* 2 vols. Philadelphia: Carey, Lea, and Blan-
        chard, 1837.

GI   *Gleanings in Europe: Italy.* 2 vols. Philadelphia: Carey, Lea, and Blan-
        chard, 1838.

GR   *Sketches of Switzerland . . . Part Second.* 2 vols. Philadelphia: Carey, Lea,
        and Blanchard, 1836. CE title: *Gleanings in Europe: The Rhine.*

GS   *Sketches of Switzerland.* 2 vols. Philadelphia: Carey, Lea, and Blanchard,
        1836. CE title: *Gleanings in Europe: Switzerland.*

HAF   *Home as Found.* 2 vols. Philadelphia: Lea & Blanchard, 1838.

HB   *Homeward Bound: or, the Chase.* 2 vols. Philadelphia: Carey, Lea, and Blanchard, 1838.

HN   *The History of the Navy of the United States of America.* 2 vols. Philadelphia: Lea & Blanchard, 1839.

JT   *Jack Tier; or, the Florida Reef.* 2 vols. New York: Burgess, Stringer & Co., 1848.

LDANO   *Lives of Distinguished American Naval Officers.* 2 vols. Philadelphia: Carey & Hart, 1846.

LJ   *Letters and Journals of James Fenimore Cooper,* ed. James Franklin Beard, 6 vols. Cambridge: Harvard University Press, 1960–1968.

LL   *Lionel Lincoln; or, the Leaguer of Boston.* 2 vols. New York: Charles Wiley, 1825.

LL CE   *Lionel Lincoln: or the Leaguer of Boston.* Edited with historical introduction and explanatory notes by Donald A. Ringe and Lucy B. Ringe. Albany: State University of New York Press, 1984.

LOM   *The Last of the Mohicans. A Narrative of 1757.* 2 vols. Philadelphia: H. C. Carey & I. Lea, 1826.

LOM CE   *The Last of the Mohicans. A Narrative of 1757.* Historical introduction by James Franklin Beard; text established with explanatory notes by James A. Sappenfield and E. N. Feltskog. Albany: State University of New York Press, 1983.

MC   *Mercedes of Castile; or, the Voyage to Cathay.* 2 vols. Philadelphia: Lea & Blanchard, 1840.

MTW   JFC, "Sketches of Naval Men: Melancthon Taylor Woolsey." *Graham's Magazine* 26(1845): 13–21.

NM   *Ned Myers; or, a Life before the Mast.* Philadelphia: Lea & Blanchard, 1843.

Notions   *Notions of the Americans: Picked up by a Travelling Bachelor.* 2 vols. Philadelphia: Carey, Lea, & Carey, 1828.

Notions CE   *Notions of the Americans: Picked up by a Travelling Bachelor.* Text established with historical introduction and textual notes by Gary Williams. Albany: State University of New York Press, 1991.

OH   JFC, "Otsego Hall," in James Fenimore Cooper (1858–1938), *The Legends and Traditions of a Northern County.* New York: G. P. Putnam's Sons, 1921, 223–31.

OI   JFC, "Old Ironsides," *Putnam's Monthly* 1(May and June 1853): 473–87, 593–607.

OO   *The Oak Openings; or, The Bee-Hunter.* 2 vols. New York: Burgess, Stringer & Co., 1848.

PF   *The Pathfinder; or, The Inland Sea.* 2 vols. Philadelphia: Lea & Blanchard, 1840.

PF CE   *The Pathfinder; or, The Inland Sea.* Edited with historical introduction by Richard Dilworth Rush. Albany: State University of New York Press, 1981.

PIL   *The Pilot; a Tale of the Sea.* 2 vols. New York: Charles Wiley, 1824.

PIL CE   *The Pilot: A Tale of the Sea.* Edited with historical introduction and explanatory notes by Kay Seymour House. Albany: State University of New York Press, 1986.

PIO   *The Pioneers; or, the Sources of the Susquehanna.* 2 vols. New York: Charles Wiley, 1823.

PIO CE   *The Pioneers; or, the Sources of the Susquehanna.* Historical introduction and explanatory notes by James Franklin Beard; text established by Lance Schachterle and Kenneth M. Andersen, Jr. Albany: State University of New York Press, 1980.

PR   *The Prairie: A Tale.* 2 vols. Philadelphia: Carey, Lea, & Carey, 1827.

PR CE   *The Prairie: A Tale.* Edited with historical introduction by James P. Elliott. Albany: State University of New York Press, 1985.

PRE   *Precaution, a Novel.* 2 vols. New York: A. T. Goodrich, 1820.

PRE 1821 *Precaution, a Novel.* 3 vols. London: Henry Colburn, 1821.

PRE 1838 *Precaution, a Novel.* A new edition, revised by the author. London: Richard Bentley, 1838 (also 1839).

PRE 1839 *Precaution, a Novel.* A new edition, revised by the author. 2 vols. Philadelphia: Lea & Blanchard, 1839.

SAT   *Satanstoe; or, The Littlepage Manuscripts. A Tale of the Colony.* 2 vols. New York: Burgess, Stringer & Co., 1845.

SAT CE   *Satanstoe; or, The Littlepage Manuscripts: A Tale of the Colony.* Historical introduction by Kay Seymour House; text established by Kay Seymour House and Constance Ayers Denne. Albany: State University of New York Press, 1990.

SL   *The Sea Lions; or, the Lost Sealers.* 2 vols. New York: Stringer & Townsend, 1849.

Spy   *The Spy; a Tale of the Neutral Ground.* 2 vols. New York: Wiley & Halsted, 1821.

Spy CE   *The Spy: A Tale of the Neutral Ground.* Historical introduction by James P. Elliott; explanatory notes James H. Pickering; text established by James P. Elliott, Lance Schachterle, and Jeffrey Walker. New York: AMS Press, 2002.

Tales   *Tales for Fifteen.* Edited by James Franklin Beard. Delmar: Scholars' Facsimiles & Reprints, 1977.

TM   JFC, "The Towns of Manhattan," Cooper's working title; surviving fragment published as *New York.* New York: William Farquhar Payson, 1930.

WH   *The Ways of the Hour: A Tale.* New York: George P. Putnam, 1850.

Writings by Other Members of the Cooper Family

James Fenimore Cooper (1858–1938; JFC's grandson)

CORR   *Correspondence of James Fenimore-Cooper.* 2 vols. New Haven: Yale University Press, 1922.

L&T   *The Legends and Traditions of a Northern County.* New York: G. P. Putnam's Sons, 1921.

REMIN   *Reminiscences of Mid-Victorian Cooperstown and Sketch of William Cooper.* Introduction by Henry S. F. Cooper, Jr. Cooperstown: Smithy-Pioneer Gallery, 1986.

Susan Fenimore Cooper (JFC's daughter)

P&P   *Pages and Pictures from the Writings of James Fenimore Cooper, with Notes by Susan Fenimore Cooper.* New York: W. A. Townsend, 1860.

RH   *Rural Hours.* New York: George P. Putnam, 1850.

SFM   "Small Family Memories," in James Fenimore Cooper (1858–1938), ed., *Correspondence of James Fenimore-Cooper.* 2 vols. New Haven: Yale University Press, 1922, 1:9–72.

General Resources

AL   *American Literature*

DAB   *Dictionary of American Biography*

DNB   *Dictionary of National Biography*

NYH   *New York History*

S&B   Robert E. Spiller and Philip C. Blackburn, *A Descriptive Bibliography of the Writings of James Fenimore Cooper.* New York: R. R. Bowker, 1934.

CHAPTER 1. THE VISION

1. William Cooper, *A Guide in the Wilderness; or, the History of the First Settlements in the Western Counties of New York, with Useful Instructions to Future Settlers* (1810; rpt. Cooperstown: Paul F. Cooper, Jr., 1986), 13–14; *COC* 8.

2. On the Coopers and Quakerism, see Wayne Franklin, "Fathering the Son: The Cultural Origins of James Fenimore Cooper," *Resources for American Literary Study* 21(2001): 149–78. Yankee diaspora: Alan Taylor, *William Cooper's Town: Power and Persuasion on the Frontier of the Early American Republic* (New York: Knopf, 1995), 89–95.

3. See Cooper's declaration, *LJ* 4:483: "the mountain called the Vision, . . . owes its appellation entirely to the Pioneers." For confirmation, see a notice of *The Pioneers* in the Cooperstown *Freeman's Journal,* 3/3/1823, which refers cumbersomely to "the mountain-side east of this Village" as the site of the hunting episode in the book. See also *COC* 8.

4. H. Daniel Peck astutely distinguishes the two bodies of water—Cooper's Glimmerglass is "immanent," there to be seen and simply discovered, while Thoreau's Walden, with its deeper connections to the transcendent soul, must first be imagined; see *A World by Itself: The Pastoral Moment in Cooper's Fiction* (New Haven: Yale University Press, 1977), 10–12. My point is parallel: that Thoreau imaginatively reenacted in his life the underlying plot of Cooper's "real" fiction. Cooper's West was just that in 1793, whereas Thoreau had to "pretend." See also Edwin Fussell's seminal study, *Frontier: American Literature and the American West* (Princeton: Princeton University Press, 1965), esp. 175–231.

5. WC, *Guide*, 13.

6. Some older sources, such as Joseph C. Martindale, *A History of the Townships of Byberry and Moreland* (Philadelphia: n.p., n.d.), 244, wrongly portray William Cooper's parents as living an impoverished life in the backwater of Byberry.

7. Their own parents were of Quaker background, but James Cooper and Hannah Hibbs had been married in 1750 in Philadelphia's preeminent Anglican establishment, Christ Church, and their names are absent from the member lists of any Philadelphia area Quaker meeting. James Cooper was to be buried in a Quaker cemetery in Chester County, but his reconciliation with the faith, if there was one, came late. In the intervening years, his alienation from it was profound. Defying the Quaker "peace testimony," he thus enrolled in a Patriot militia unit, as required by Pennsylvania law during the Revolution (although he did not actually serve). Franklin, "Fathering the Son," 163–66.

8. JFC II, *REMIN* 43; the novelist relayed to his wife in 1837 a tale picked up from a relative in Camden regarding his father's presence in Philadelphia "as a boy." This tale *may* suggest his whereabouts after running away (see *LJ* 3:254–55). The novelist's uncle and namesake served on a Pennsylvania privateer during the Revolution, and his son later opened a successful chandlery business in Oswego, New York, suggesting the possibility that some of the Coopers had considerable nautical experience. See NARA Record Group 15, microfilm M804, roll 647; Lida S. Penfield, "Three Generations of Coopers in Oswego," *Oswego Historical Society Fifth Publication* (1941): 4–6.

9. Taylor, *William Cooper's Town*, 16.

10. The small, bustling city of Burlington, older than Philadelphia and twenty-five miles upriver from it, had coincidentally been the site where the first Cooper emigrant to America, an even earlier James Cooper (1661–1732), had settled in the early 1680s. In that Quaker stronghold, Elizabeth Fenimore's parents and only sibling all became members in the local Quaker meeting; Elizabeth, like her husband, appears never to have joined there or elsewhere. Franklin, "Fathering the Son," 167–68; Taylor, *William Cooper's Town*, 17–18.

11. Andrew Craig's whereabouts: the "List of Absentees in Capt. Peale's Compy," 5/12/1777–4/26/1779, in *Collected Papers of Charles Willson Peale and His Family*,

microform edition (Millwood: Kraus Microform, 1980), indicates "Andrew Craig's" presence at most musters in this period, along with a somewhat less punctual "William Cooper" who probably was *not* his future partner. An allied muster list in *Pennsylvania Archives*, ser. 6 (Harrisburg: State Printer, 1906), 1:290–91, also lists both names, indicating that Cooper paid a fine on 11/12/1778 and that Craig had "lived in Jersey," as Cooper's partner had. Craig shows up as a Philadelphia resident in a 1774 tax list; ibid., ser. 3 (Harrisburg: State Printer, 1897), 262, but was gone from the city after 1778.

12. Taylor, *William Cooper's Town*, 18; *LJ* 3:225. This Jersey hamlet remained modest as late as 1836, when the novelist described it as comprising "a meeting-house, tavern, two stores and twelve dwellings"; *LJ* 3:226. The third eponymous settlement was Cooper's Village, founded by Cooper in St. Lawrence County, New York, following his purchase of lands there in 1803.

13. James Cooper (he added Fenimore in 1826) was the last of nine more children the Coopers had in the decade after their 1778 return to New Jersey; a final child born in Otsego in 1792 soon died. There may have been even more children. Wayne Wright, *Cooper Genealogy* (Cooperstown: NYSHA Library, 1983), 9, lists a total of twelve, but the novelist (OH 228) says that there were three others who died young. On William Cooper's Burlington career, see Taylor, *William Cooper's Town*, 18, 21.

14. Julius Goebel, Jr., and Joseph H. Smith, eds., *The Law Practice of Alexander Hamilton: Documents and Commentary* (New York: Columbia University Press, 1964–81), 4:84–93. William Franklin, on purchasing his shares in the Burlington Company in 1768, had made the other members of the company his "attorneys," a common practice. It was on this basis that Cooper and Croghan, having purchased the company shares, pretended to be acting on Franklin's behalf. The auction was held by the sheriff of Montgomery County, New York, the jurisdiction in which the lands in question were then located.

15. Taylor, *William Cooper's Town*, 70.

16. WC, *Guide*, 12–14; Taylor, *William Cooper's Town*, 71–73.

17. Taylor, *William Cooper's Town*, 396–97. Ironically, the victory over Croghan's heirs came just at the moment when the Otsego sheriff, pursuant to a Chancery Court ruling in an unrelated case, was about to begin selling many Cooper properties in Otsego, including William Cooper's grand mansion.

18. Peter C. Mancall, *Valley of Opportunity: Economic Culture along the Upper Susquehanna, 1700–1800* (Ithaca: Cornell University Press, 1991), 43, citing William A. Ritchie's 1952 report.

19. *Letters of Eleazer Wheelock's Indians*, ed. James Dow McCallum (Hanover: Dartmouth College, 1932), 20, 79.

20. Mancall, *Valley of Opportunity*, 29–46.

21. Anthony Wonderley, "Brothertown, New York, 1785–1796," *NYH* 81(2000): 457–92; Laura J. Murray, ed., *To Do Good to My Indian Brethren: The Writings of Joseph*

Johnson (Amherst: University of Massachusetts Press, 1998), 287–89; Thomas Commuck, "Sketch of the Brothertown Indians," *Wisconsin Historical Collections* 4(1859): 291–98. See also my discussion of New Stockbridge and Brotherton in Chapter 15. On Thoreau, see Robert F. Sayre, *Thoreau and the American Indians* (Princeton: Princeton University Press, 1977).

22. "Preface to the Leather-Stocking Tales," in *The Deerslayer* (New York: Stringer & Townsend, 1854), vii.

23. Jeptha R. Simms, *The Trappers of New York* (1850; St. Johnsville: Enterprise and News, 1935), 101–2.

24. D. Hamilton Hurd, *History of Otsego County, N.Y.* (Philadelphia: Everts and Fariss, 1878), 249.

25. Levi Beardsley, *Reminiscences* (New York: Charles Vinten, 1852), 31, 34.

26. One can hardly overlook the figure of Daniel Boone, about whom Richard Slotkin wrote so probingly in *Regeneration through Violence: The Mythology of the American Frontier* (Middletown: Wesleyan University Press, 1973). Yet it seems clear that Cooper's familiarity with Boone and his adventures was indirect, general, and of uncertain origin. It would be useful to know that Cooper indeed had read John Filson's 1784 account of Boone in the Brooklyn edition issued by C. Wilder in 1823, and reprinted by Henry Trumbull in the following year, for these would have been very plausible sources for him; yet Slotkin offers no evidence to back up the following assertion: "The narratives relating to Boone's life—certainly the Filson text in Wilder's and Trumbull's editions . . . formed part of his reading and supplied incidents and images to several novels in the [Leather-Stocking] series" (485). Henry Nash Smith more carefully admitted that "Boone was not exactly the prototype of Cooper's Leatherstocking"; *Virgin Land: The American West as Myth and Symbol* (New York: Random House, 1950), 64. At the same time, Smith noted that Cooper mentioned the "adventurous and venerable patriarch" of Kentucky in *The Prairie* and that, in a later note to the passage in question, Cooper named him directly as "Colonel Boon" (perhaps significantly, the form of the name used in Wilder's version); see *PR* CE 10. Even more to the point, Smith (64–65) rightly noted that the captivity of Cora and Alice Munro in *The Last of Mohicans* echoes that of Boone's daughter Jemima and the two Callaway sisters in 1776. In particular, Cora's attempt to mark her trail by breaking twigs as she and Alice are led off by Magua derives from the Boone story (and thus is, pace Mark Twain and his denigration of "the Broken Twig Series," a *realistic* detail; see John Bakeless, *Master of the Wilderness: Daniel Boone* [New York: William Morrow, 1939], 124–40, for one modern version of the girls' captivity). Smith also pointed out that reviewers from the time of *The Pioneers* concluded that Natty Bumppo had been modeled on Boone (64), useful evidence of the culture's recognition of Cooper's "sourcing" in a general sense. In the end, however, I agree with Stephen Railton, who, after summarizing some of Smith's observations, pertinently adds: "Saying that the story of Daniel Boone provided Cooper with a source for Natty's

character does not account for Cooper's initial interest in the figure of the radically aso-cial man of the woods, an interest which eventually resulted in the five Leather-Stock-ing Tales. Natty Bumppo seems, indeed, to have supplanted Boone in the American mind as the archetypal backwoodsman"; *Fenimore Cooper: A Study of His Life and Imagination* (Princeton: Princeton University Press, 1978), 90–91. Cooper had seen such "radically asocial" men all around him in the woods of New York and, romantic as he was, valued their independence of mind and the depth of their affection for nature.

27. J. H. French, *Gazetteer of the State of New York* (Syracuse: R. P. Smith, 1860), 151.

28. Hannah Cooper to Isaac Cooper, 6/25/1798, WC paps., box 19, HCA.

29. See also Taylor, *William Cooper's Town*, 74.

30. Ibid., 89–95.

31. WC to Jacob Morris, 7/29/1787, WC paps., box 17, HCA.

32. Cooper dated this trip to 1787, but that spring Elizabeth Cooper gave birth to a new baby, son Samuel (Wright, *Cooper Genealogy*, 16), and is unlikely to have traveled.

33. Taylor, *William Cooper's Town*, reproduces the map following page 278.

34. WC, *Guide*, 15; Taylor, *William Cooper's Town*, 200–2.

35. WC, *Guide*, 29–30; Franklin, "Fathering the Son," 173–74.

36. WC, *Guide*, 15–16.

37. Taylor, *William Cooper's Town*, 118.

38. Tench Francis to WC, 9/18/1789, WC paps., box 17, HCA, indicates that Cooper was then in Jersey but was about to leave for Otsego.

39. Smith's father, also Richard Smith, was a well-known lawyer and delegate to the first and second Continental Congresses. He had headed the Burlington Company for a time, and owned a tract west of Cooperstown on which he built "Smith Hall" just before the Revolution. Taylor, *William Cooper's Town*, 107–8.

40. Ibid., 163.

41. Washington Frothingham, *History of Montgomery County* (Syracuse: D. Mason, 1892), 319; in *The Pioneers*, Major Fritz Hartmann is a Palatine German settler who often visits the Temple home.

42. Andrew Craig to WC, 4/8/1790, WC paps., box 17, HCA.

43. This time he may have passed downriver from New York without going through Burlington. See Taylor, *William Cooper's Town*, 119, 150–51.

44. Ibid., 115–16, 129 (second agent); see WC to Charles J. Evans, 7/3/1790, re-garding his return to Cooperstown in July and his strategies as developer; JFC II, *L&T* 141–42; on the "Albany investor" (Thomas Bridgen), see Taylor, *William Cooper's Town*, 396–98, and my own discussion of the case in Chapter 10.

45. On Cooper's later use of the chair at his desk in Otsego Hall, see JFC II, *REMIN* 44.

46. Ibid., JFC II, *REMIN* 44. The novelist himself in 1827 wrote, "For the nearly two centuries that my family has been in America we have never held a slave," Robert E.

Spiller, ed., "Fenimore Cooper's Defense of Slave-Owning America," *American Historical Review* 35(1930): 580. However, because the New York law setting an end to slavery in the state, and encouraging emancipation in the interim, was not approved until the end of the 1790s, the two blacks accompanying the family to Otsego in 1790 were almost certainly slaves.

47. Taylor, *William Cooper's Town*, 151.

48. Joel Munsell, *The Annals of Albany*, 10 vols. (Albany: Munsell, 1850–1859), 10:401.

49. Taylor, *William Cooper's Town*, 151–53; see also my discussion of the Manor House and Otsego Hall in Chapter 2.

50. Ibid., 161–65. Writing the following March to the famed scientist and statesman Benjamin Rush, his friend and fellow Byberry native, Cooper chortled over his victory: "In Reward for my industry in this Late wilderness Part of the state, the Legislature has, at my request, Set off a County for the most part settled by my Self, Containing about 8 or ten thousand inhabitants. The Prison and Court house [are] to be built at Cooperstown this summer"; WC to Benjamin Rush, 3/12/1791, WC paps., box 17, HCA.

51. Edward P. Alexander, ed., "James Kent's 'Jaunt' to Cooperstown, 1792," *NYH* 22(1941): 454.

52. James Kent counted twenty buildings in 1792, six of them of two stories, all but one built within the past year; ibid., 454–55.

53. Ibid., 450–56; Taylor, *William Cooper's Town*, 235–36.

54. Moss Kent, Jr., to James Kent, 2/16/1795, quoted in Taylor, *William Cooper's Town*, 236.

55. Taylor, *William Cooper's Town*, 298.

CHAPTER 2. LESSONS

1. Limited opportunities in Otsego meant that Cooper's older siblings had largely been educated elsewhere: Isaac in Burlington (where Richard already had been schooled before the emigration), Philadelphia, and Albany; Hannah in New York City, Philadelphia, and Albany; and even Ann, in New York City and perhaps Newark. See Josiah O. Hoffman to WC, 10/6/1791, and William Wade to WC, 10/2/1792 (re: Hannah), WC paps., box 17, HCA; Richard R. Smith to WC, 11/10/1794, and Hannah Cooper to Isaac Cooper, 6/25/1798 (re: Isaac), WC paps., box 18, HCA; Ann Cooper to WC 5/3/1796, in Clare Benedict, *Voices out of the Past* (London: Ellis, 1929), 18, and F. LeQuoy to WC 5/11/1794 (re: Ann), WC paps., box 18, HCA.

2. *COC* 39–42; Otsego *Herald*, 5/8/1795, 5/15/1795, 5/22/1795, 9/18/1795, 5/19/1796, 7/21/1796, 8/4/1796; Jacob Morris to WC, 1/2/1796 (for 1797), and Elihu Phinney to WC, 1/4/1796, both in WC paps., box 18, HCA; compare Alan Taylor's account in *William Cooper's Town: Power and Persuasion on the Frontier of the Early American Republic* (New York: Knopf, 1995), 249–54. Joshua Dewey (1767–1864) received a

commission from President John Adams as Otsego's collector of internal revenue in 1799 and in 1809 migrated to the Cooper-founded settlement of DeKalb, in St. Lawrence County, where he became involved in governmental and educational affairs, serving at one point as the commissioner of schools. See S. T. Livermore, *A Condensed History of Cooperstown, with a Biographical Sketch of J. Fenimore Cooper* (Albany: J. Munsell, 1862), 108; Franklin B. Dexter, *Biographical Sketches of the Graduates of Yale College with Annals of the College History*, 6 vols. (New Haven: Yale University Press, 1885–1912), 4: 538–39 (Dewey was a member of Yale's class of 1787 but received his degree in 1789; I assume his recruitment by William Cooper, who certainly acted as his patron once he arrived, but I have found no direct evidence on the question); Potter Goff and Silas Spencer, "Settlers in the Township" (1814), Town of DeKalb Historical Association Collections, DeKalb Junction, N.Y., 6. On Dewey's witty career as a Federalist legislator, see his parrying of "Ploughjogger" Jedidiah Peck, *Otsego Herald*, 7/21/1796, 8/4/1796.

3. See Rev. John Camp, *A Sermon, Delivered at the Academy in Cooperstown, on the 27 of December 1796* (Cooperstown: Elihu Phinney, 1797).

4. Oliver Cory, deposition (10/16/1832) and letter (2/20/1836), NARA, Record Group 15, microfilm M804, roll 659.

5. The debate was raging in the local press at the time; see Levi Beardsley, *Reminiscences* (New York: Charles Vinten, 1852), 68.

6. That is, "The President's March," a tune that was most familiar in 1799 because of its use for Frances Hopkinson's "Hail! Columbia." Taylor, *William Cooper's Town*, 298–99, 504n9; SFC, *P&P* 49; W. Thomas Marrocco and Harold Gleason, *Music in America: An Anthology from the Landing of the Pilgrims to the Close of the Civil War, 1620–1865* (New York: W. W. Norton, 1964), 279–80, 283–85; H. Wiley Hitchcock, *Music in the United States: A Historical Introduction* (Englewood Cliffs: Prentice Hall, 1969), 27.

7. Roger Lonsdale, ed., *New Oxford Book of Eighteenth Century Verse* (New York: Oxford University Press, 1984), 552; this is stanza 3 of the original version published in 1766 (in Thomas Moss, *Poems on Several Occasions*). That the poem was a common set piece of nineteenth-century popular culture is suggested by Charles Dickens. In *Nicholas Nickleby*, he imagines (perhaps refers to) its use to adorn calico handkerchiefs, while in *Little Dorrit* he comically describes the "immense army of shabby mendicants in uniform"—that is, customs officers—who "incessantly repeated the Beggars Petition" as the trousseau of Fanny Dorrit passed through their hands on its way from Paris to London; *Little Dorrit*, ed. John Holloway (Harmondsworth: Penguin, 1967), 667.

8. Dr. Thomas Fuller, affidavit, 4/12/1836, Oliver Cory, letter, 2/23/1833, NARA, Record Group 15, microfilm M804, roll 659 (it is possible that Cooper was in error about his teacher's service under Lafayette, or that he consciously invented this dramatic "memory," which is recalled by the loosely autobiographical character John

Cadwallader in *Notions of the Americans*); on Olmutz, see *Otsego Herald*, 3/23/1797; on Lafayette's arrival in June 1777, see J. Bennett Nolan, *Lafayette in America: Day by Day* (Baltimore: Johns Hopkins University Press, 1934), 1. In the America of the 1790s, Cooper wrote in *Notions of the Americans*, "The statesman, the yeoman, or the schoolboy [i.e., Cooper himself], the matron among her offspring; the housewife amid her avocations; and the beauty in the blaze of her triumph, forgot alike the passions or interests of the moment, . . . and drew near to listen at the name of La Fayette" (*Notions* 1:38). Cory spoke the name so feelingly, Cooper went on, that his pupils "plotted among ourselves, the means of his deliverance; wondered that the nation was not in arms to redress his wrongs, and were animated by a sort of reflection of his own youthful and generous chivalry" (ibid., 1:39). When Cooper saw Lafayette in New York in 1824–1825 and soon afterwards became his political ally in France, their complex relationship was built on the emotional foundation laid by Master Cory.

9. "This deponent still recollects the personal appeal made by Genl. Washington on horseback to the Troops, whose term of service expired about the last of December or the first of January[,] for further enlistments. He stood so near him that he observed tears to trickle down the cheeks of our Country's Saviour & its answer was scarcely a dry eye among the Soldiers. It had the effect to lengthen the term of service of many soldiers among whom this deponent was one & those who left the army for home were hooted at & covered with opprobrium." Cory, letter, 2/20/1836; see also his deposition of 10/16/1832. Cooper's other early teacher, Joshua Dewey, had also seen service in the Revolution at a very early age; after the burning of New London in 1781, he substituted for an older brother in the garrison at the infamous Fort Griswold; Dexter, *Biographical Sketches*, 4:538.

10. According to the novelist, at least once since her reluctant arrival in Otsego in 1790, Elizabeth Cooper had insisted on a return, probably of considerable length, to her native Jersey town: it was there that her last child, Henry Frey Cooper, born just after Christmas in 1792, died at the age of nine months. See OH 224; Wayne Wright, *The Cooper Genealogy* (Cooperstown: NYSHA Library, 1983), 9.

11. Moss Kent to WC, 4/7/1796, 4/21/1796, 4/29/1796, WC paps., box 18, HCA.

12. See the Otsego Hall contract, Cooper family collection (coll. 123), NYSHA, and the discussion of it in Charles R. Tichy, "Otsego Hall and Its Setting, 1786–1940" (unpublished M.A. thesis, SUNY at Oneonta, 1973).

13. Certainly Higgins instructed them in Latin during the second stay, as Hannah Cooper reported when she passed through in June 1798; Hannah Cooper to Isaac Cooper, 6/25/1798, WC paps., box 19, HCA. For additional information, see Richard R. Smith to WC, 11/10/1794, and Andrew Craig to WC, 9/23/1795 and 6/24/1798, all in WC paps., boxes 18–19, HCA. There is some disagreement about exactly which years Elizabeth Cooper and her two sons spent in Burlington. Taylor, *William Cooper's Town*, 339, gives the dates as 1796–1797, 1797–1798, and 1798–1799, but I find no evidence of

three extended stays. On the other hand, James F. Beard (*LJ* 1:4), Taylor's source on this point, omits the middle stay, while Cooper himself (*LJ* 4:498) dates his *two* stays to "1796" and "1798." I have concluded that Mrs. Cooper kept the boys in Burlington from the fall of 1796 to mid-1797 and again from the fall of 1797 to mid-1798, and that the third intended stay was aborted in the fall of 1798. Cooper mentions the "well-known pedagogue Higgins," whom Beard, without documentation, identifies as "[Patrick] Higgins" (*LJ* 4:498), but he so far remains elusive. Presumably Beard took him to be the same man as P. L. H. Higgins, who published *An Exposition of the Principles on which the Infant System of Education is Conducted . . . to which is Added an Address to His Grace the Duke of Devonshire, on the Establishment of Infant Schools in Ireland* (London: T. Godyer, 1826).

14. Andrew Craig to WC, 1/23/1797, WC paps., box 19, HCA.

15. Taylor, *William Cooper's Town*, 252–53; *Otsego Herald*, 3/23/1797; U.S. Bureau of the Census and Social Science Research Council, *The Statistical History of the United States from the Colonial Period to the Present* (Stamford: Fairfield, [1965]), 690. Although Cooper later remembered having remained in Burlington for about a year on this occasion, the actual time was more like nine months; see *LJ* 4:498.

16. William Cooper may have escorted them to New Jersey, but he remained in New York State for the winter. His wife and sons apparently were gone from Otsego as early as mid-September: Stephen Van Rensselaer, who stayed at the Cooper home then, said nothing whatever about Mrs. Cooper when he wrote thanking Cooper for his hospitality, an unlikely omission had she still been there. In turn, Van Rensselaer invited Cooper to spend the coming winter at his own mansion in Albany, and Cooper may have passed at least some time there; Stephen Van Rensselaer to WC, 11/10/1797, WC paps., box 19, HCA.

17. On the house purchase see Taylor, *William Cooper's Town*, 153 (who points out that William Cooper in fact vested the title in now twenty-one-year-old Hannah, perhaps a sign of her emerging importance for the family at large). Taylor would seem to err in placing Elizabeth Cooper and her youngest sons in Burlington through the whole of 1798. Craig's letter of 6/24/1798, WC paps., box 19, HCA, indicates that by then she had returned to Otsego. Not everything in Burlington was unappealing to Cooper. He long recalled walking about the town with his mother, who never tired of pointing out the house in which he had been born and doubtless told him stories of her own girlhood there (*LJ* 4:499–500).

18. WC to Richard F. Cooper, 10/9/1798, WC paps., box 20, HCA.

19. Taylor, *William Cooper's Town*, 255; *Statistical History of the United States*, 690; for the latter part of the 6th Congress, Cooper served in Washington, where the House began meeting late in 1800; see John W. Reps, *Washington on View: The Nation's Capital Since 1790* (Chapel Hill: University of North Carolina Press, 1991), 50–51.

20. We are told, however (*PIO* 1:38), that it was in "a tall, gaunt edifice of wood,

with its gable towards the highway" that the Temple family lived for only its first three years (not the first decade, as with the Coopers) in their frontier village. That is the only direct parallel to the situation of Cooper's family. Yet, while some of the awkwardness of the Temple mansion clearly mimicked poorly completed aspects of the second Cooper house (such as the latter's porch and its columns, which indeed hung from the roof; see SFC, "note A," *PIO* HE 479), most of it came from the resurgence of Manor House memories into an anachronistic fantasy based on Otsego Hall. Cooper hardly had forgotten the old house, which as late as 1840 he rightly described as a creditable structure for 1789: "good for the country, and the times" (OH 223). For the most part, though, it was memorable mostly for its shortcomings. (It might be added that the new dwelling's name underwent several shifts over Cooper's life. The novelist said that the name Otsego Hall was first chosen by his father but soon fell out of use, the building being generally called the Mansion House. Cooper himself took credit for reviving the original term on his return from Europe in an attempt to erase the local habit of calling it Temple Hall or even Templeton Hall [*LJ* 3:351]).

21. Transplanted to *The Pioneers*, the Lombardy poplars provided one of the details Elizabeth Temple is able to glimpse as she scans the darkening village from the mountainside (*PIO* 1:38). In 1799, Lombardy poplars were still a recent introduction into the United States. William Cooper's use of rows of them to adorn the drive at Otsego Hall is a nice sign of his engagement with current canons of taste. No sooner did the native pines, oaks, and maples come down in Otsego than William Cooper thus rushed to put exotics in their place, setting them out in straight lines to emphasize the artifice of this (expensive) second nature now supplanting the first.

22. Before his purchase of the house in the 1830s, Cooper spent his longest uninterrupted period in the new house from 1799 to 1801. From then until he bought the house, his experience of it came via a series of vacations and visits. The text of "Otsego Hall" thus especially distilled Cooper's very first years in the new house, when he was nine to eleven years old. The same period would seem to be the basis for the memorial imagination of the Temple mansion in the opening pages of *The Pioneers*, which is suggestive of a child's eye rather than a young man's.

23. William Cooper must have had working plans prepared for his own new venture, although who provided them we do not know. (Perhaps a hint in *The Pioneers* linking Marmaduke Temple to Albany architect Philip Hooker, who in the mid-1790s was just beginning his career and later was to be the chosen designer for the upstate elite, indicates Hooker's involvement in the Cooper project: when Elizabeth suggests that her father has brought a surprise for Richard Jones from Albany, Jones at first thinks his cousin has brought him "the plans of the new Dutch meeting-house" [*PIO* 1:226], one of Hooker's first big commissions, as the novelist certainly knew; see Mary Raddant Tomlan and Ruth Osgood Trovato, eds., *A Neat Plain Modern Stile: Philip Hooker and His Contemporaries* [Clinton: Hamilton College, 1993], 55–62. Judge Cooper's contract for

the house mentions that at least a partial "plan" for the structure was to be provided to the carpenters, although that point is ambiguous; see Otsego Hall contract, NYSHA.) In 1911, Cooper's grandson and namesake wrote from his home in Albany to tell biographer Mary E. Phillips that his father (Paul Fenimore Cooper) "used to call my attention to the fact that the hall in the Van Rensselaer Manor House at Albany and the adjoining rooms were exactly the same size as those of Otsego Hall. Probably Judge Cooper copied his building from the manor house here [i.e., Albany], which was much older and where he was a constant visitor"; JFC II to Mary E. Phillips, 1/5/1911, Mary E. Phillips paps., Boston Public Library.

24. Otsego Hall contract, NYSHA; JFC II to Mary E. Phillips, 1/5/1911, gives the size as 70 × 52 ft.; Charles Tichy points out that different sources vary on the dimensions of the house ("Otsego Hall and Its Setting, 1786–1940," 8–9). The drawing of the house first printed in Mary E. Phillips, *James Fenimore Cooper* (New York: John Lane, 1913), 9, and prepared for her with the advice of Cooper's grandson, shows a high building, but it is neither as wide nor as deep as the original. Additional space existed in the garret and, especially, the basement.

25. The Otsego Hall contract called for the great hall to measure 20 × 50 ft. (Otsego Hall contract, NYSHA). JFC II said it was 24 × 48 ft. (JFC II to Phillips, 1/5/1911); Van Rensselaer's measured 23 ft. 8 in. × 46 ft. 9 in. (see Mitchell Wooten's drawings, in Architects' Emergency Committee, *Great Georgian Houses of America*, 2 vols. [1933–1938; New York: Dover, 1970], 1:203).

26. This removal of the stairs to a side passage (another point of comparison with the Van Rensselaer mansion) led to a slight asymmetry in the layout and appearance of the main first-floor rooms. There were two doors opening off from the west side wall of the hall, but three from the east side, the middle of these leading into the narrow side passage holding the stairs. With the stairs removed from it, Cooper's great hall was free to remain just an enormous space. Three main rooms were entered directly from it. In the northwest corner (facing the lake) was the "drawing room," originally intended as the formal dining room; behind it in the southwest corner was the second "dining room," which evidently picked up its name once the other room was converted to its new purpose (eventually it would be the novelist's study). According to Cooper, however, neither of these rooms was actually used for dining (the family ate most of its meals in the great hall)—or for much else. Opposite the "drawing room" on the lakefront of the house was the bedroom of Elizabeth and William Cooper. To its rear on the east side were the stair hall and two subordinate spaces: a pantry (entered through the third formal doorway on that side of the great hall), and behind it, off the stair hall, a small library. The basement was divided into six rooms, all with substantial doors and three of them with wood floors; this space was used to house the servants and to accommodate much of their work—the kitchen, for instance, was probably located under the original dining room, which had a trapdoor in the floor designed to bring up meals. On the sec-

ond floor were six rooms. The two largest, located above the drawing and dining rooms at the west end, were reserved for guests; they were reached by traversing the hall that led from the staircase at the east end down the length of the house. Flanking the upstairs hall in the middle of the house were a storeroom (with an extra bed) above the garden entrance and, above the lake entrance, the room reserved for eldest sons Richard and Isaac Cooper when they were at home. By the stairway was the bedroom of Hannah and Ann, in the northeast corner, and near it at the southeast corner, that used by Cooper and his brothers William and Samuel. The third-story garret was fully floored and ran the length of the house (that is, some sixty-six feet); it was illuminated by four windows, two in each end wall (OH, passim; Otsego Hall contract, NYSHA; Tichy, "Otsego Hall and Its Setting, 1786–1940," passim).

27. In the watercolor, we are standing inside the lake or north entrance, the one at the end of the poplar allée, and are looking past Mrs. Cooper toward the opposite door, beyond which lay the flower gardens at the mansion's rear. With a blooming potted plant by her side, the matriarch is seated in a slant of light that shines in from the stair hall, just off to her right through the partly visible doorway. Obviously it is morning, and the light illuminating her and casting her shadow on the carpet is coming in through the small first-floor east window that had been provided to "light the little passage"—as Cooper called the stair hall—and through the larger window lighting the corridor on the second floor to which the open stairs led. Since the stairway took no turning but went up in a single shot (it was, Cooper thought, "straight, steep, and mean"), whatever light came into either of the windows would have flooded pretty directly through the open door-way into the great hall, as the painter in fact showed it doing. No doubt this stair hall door was left open much of the time to provide as much natural light as possible in the other-wise darkish center of the long great hall (OH 226). Charlotte M. Emans has argued that the presence of the plants indoors in this summer scene (a label on the rear of the paint-ing states that it was "Painted by Mr. Freeman in the summer of 1816"—Tichy, "Otsego Hall and Its Setting, 1786–1940," 29) was owing to the fact that 1816, the so-called year without a summer, was abnormally cold, especially in such upland terrain as Otsego; see Paul D'Ambrosio and Charlotte M. Emans, *Folk Art's Many Faces: Portraits in the New York State Historical Association* (Cooperstown: NYSHA, 1987), 84. But Mrs. Cooper had scant use for the outdoors regardless of the summer weather and kept the hall filled with plants year-round. Susan Fenimore Cooper recalled from her visits as a very young girl that "the south end of the long hall was like a greenhouse" (SFM 12); elsewhere, she reminisced, "At a later day at least one third of this hall was filled with plants; Mr. Cooper's mother being passionately fond of them, every member of the family return-ing from the civilized world at Albany, New York, or Philadelphia, was expected to bring her an offering of some choice flower, and in this way the room became a sort of green-house" (*PIO* HE 479). William Leete Stone in an 1829 reminiscence about the house similarly referred to "the long rows of green-house plants, indigenous and exotic, which

[once] rendered the noble corridor at all seasons redolent of spring"; Stone, writing as "Hiram Doolittle, Jr.," *Freeman's Journal*, 9/21/1829.

28. See Chapter 7.

29. "The summer of 1799, the following winter, and the summer of 1800 were all exceedingly gay," Cooper recalled in his 1840 reminiscence of the new house (OH 227). But most of that feeling departed with Hannah, especially for Cooper.

30. Hannah Cooper's whereabouts may be established by the following sources: *1791–1792:* Josiah O. Hoffman (New York City) to WC (Cooperstown), 10/6/1791, and William Wade (New York City) to WC (Cooperstown), 10/2/1792 (both indicate that Hannah was in the city; Wade further mentions that her studies with "Mrs. Lott" would not end until the following spring), WC paps., box 17, HCA; *1794–1795:* Richard R Smith (Philadelphia) to WC (Cooperstown), 12/16/1794 ("You mention Miss Cooper is in Albany yet") and 1/1/1795 ("I fancy Miss Cooper is in Albany yet"), WC paps., box 18, HCA; *1795–1796:* Moss Kent (Cooperstown) to WC (Philadelphia) 12/28/1795 ("My respectful Compliments to Miss Cooper"), A. Ten Broeck (Cooperstown) to WC (Philadelphia), 1/18/1796 (acknowledges receipt of news about the good health of WC and Hannah), Mrs. Powel (Philadelphia) to WC (same), 2/4/1796 (invites WC and "Miss Cooper" to dinner), Ann (Nancy) Cooper (New York City) to WC (Philadelphia), 5/3/1796 (expresses expectation that Hannah will soon leave Philadelphia for Otsego), Goldsbrow Banyar (Albany) to WC (Philadelphia), 12/12/1796 (supposes Hannah is in Philadelphia with WC), WC paps., boxes 18–19, HCA; *1798:* Anna (i.e., Hannah) Cooper (Philadelphia) to Isaac Cooper (Albany), 6/25/1798, Clement Penrose (Villa, Pa.) to WC (Cooperstown), 11/18/1798 (relaying word that Hannah expects WC in Philadelphia "in about two weeks"), WC paps., boxes 19–20, HCA.

31. The surviving documentation of Hannah's whereabouts during this period is as follows: Goldsbrow Banyar (Albany) to WC (Cooperstown), 5/27/1799 ("Miss Cooper has not yet made her appearance—I expected her long 'ere this"—although her point of origin in this case is not stated, I assume that she was just then returning to Otsego, where the family was about to move into its new home); Hannah Cooper (Cooperstown) to Isaac Cooper (Philadelphia), 1/26/1800; Hannah Cooper (Cooperstown) to WC (Philadelphia), 3/3/1800; Hannah Cooper (Cooperstown) to Isaac Cooper (Philadelphia), 4/27/1800. All in WC paps., box 20, HCA.

32. To be sure, Hannah Cooper's return probably did not occur at Christmastime, as does the one in the book. Hannah had spent the winter of 1798–1799 in Philadelphia and by December of 1799 already had been back in Cooperstown for several months. The Christmas Eve return in the novel, drawing on the sentimental significance which that holiday was just beginning to acquire in New York City in the decade when Cooper wrote the novel there, seems to have expressed the emotional depth he now found in that long-ago return of a sister who all too soon would abandon him by her death.

33. Alexander Coventry also found, however, that Elizabeth Cooper "improve[d]

upon acquaintance"; quoted by Taylor, *William Cooper's Town*, 312, from *Memoirs of an Emigrant: The Journal of Alexander Coventry, M.D.* (Albany: New York State Library, 1978), 1:1197–99. A few years after Coventry's visit, Elizabeth's son Isaac, having spent four years building a new house only two blocks from Otsego Hall, was astonished when she finally made it there for a visit six-and-a-half months after he and his family had moved in. It was, he confided to his diary, the "first time she ever saw the house." In all those years, she had not been even this far from home! Isaac Cooper diary, 6/19/1814, NYSHA.

34. *Otsego Herald,* 10/2/1795:

> A imable philosophe au printems de son age,
> N i les tems ni les lieux n'alterent son esprit.
> N e cedant qu' a ses gouts, simple et sans etalage.
> A u milieu des deserts, Elle lit—pense—ecrit.
>
> C ultivez, Belle Anna, votre gout pour l'etude;
> O n ne saurait ici mieux employer son tems.
> O tsego n'est pas gai—mais, tout est habitude;
> P aris vous deplairait fort au premier moment.
> E t qui jouit de soi dans une Solitude,
> R entrant au monde, et sur d'en faire l'ornement.

Hugh MacDougall, *Cooper's Otsego County* (Cooperstown: NYSHA, 1989), 130–31, translates this freely as follows:

> Cheerful philosopher in the springtime of her life,
> Neither time nor place changes her disposition.
> Following her own taste, simple and without affectation,
> In the midst of the desert she reads—ponders—writes.
>
> Cultivate, Beautiful Anna, your taste for study;
> You cannot here better employ your time;
> Otsego is not merry—but habit is everything:
> Even Paris would much displease you at first.
> One who can be content in a wasteland,
> On returning to the world is certain to shine.

35. Taylor, *William Cooper's Town*, 302, quoting from Hannah Cooper to Catharine Wistar Bache, 9/29/1799, Bache family paps., Firestone Library, Princeton University.

36. Richard Fenimore Cooper to WC, 11/27/1799, WC paps., box 20, HCA.

37. Elizabeth Cooper hardly was in her usual low spirits again. Quite the contrary, once her husband had left, she settled down and actually enjoyed the winter. Hendrik Frey wrote the congressman the following April with news about Mrs. Cooper passed on

from the eldest Cooper son, Richard, who reported that he "Never saw his Mother so hearty as she has been this Winter." But her remarkably "[e]ven tempered" behavior probably was the result of Hannah's already having taken things over; Hendrik Frey to WC, 4/1/1800, WC paps., box 20, HCA. As proof of Hannah's new role, see her letter to her father WC, 1/26/1800: "With respect to the arrangements here—they all proceed very well. The servants conduct themselves with propriety—we have had no squabbles since you left." Hannah did not even mention her mother in this letter, nor in another written on 3/3/1800 (both in WC paps., box 20, HCA).

38. See Taylor, *William Cooper's Town*, 308–9. Compare the account of an immigrant's trip in 1790 from Cooperstown to Butternuts over the same route in John Warner Brown, *Stanislas Pascal Franchot (1774–1855)* (n.p.: n.p., 1935), 28–29.

39. For instance, on September 11, 1835, Cooper reminded family members of the "day of sorrow" when Hannah's corpse had been brought home after that "sudden and awful" accident (*LJ* 3:165).

40. Nash, who would later be the first minister of Christ Church in Cooperstown, was on his first trip to the village, but he was no stranger to the family. Since his 1797 arrival in Otsego as a deacon of the church (he would be ordained a priest in 1801), he had been especially active in the town of Butternuts. George E. DeMille, *Christ Church, Cooperstown, New York, 1810–1960: A Parish History* (Cooperstown: Christ Church, 1960), 2–3.

41. *Otsego Herald*, 9/18/1800. Daniel Nash, funeral sermon for Hannah Cooper (9/12/1800), 25–26, WC paps., box 28, HCA.

42. Nash, funeral sermon, 27–29.

43. At the time the earliest graves were dug there, Susan wrote, "the spot was in a wild condition, upon the border of the forest, the wood having been only partially cut away. In a few years other members of the little community died, one after another, at intervals, and they were also buried here, until the spot had gradually taken its present character of a burying-ground. The rubbish was cleared away, place was made for those who must follow, and ere many years had passed, the brick walls of a little church arose within the enclosure, and were consecrated to the worship of the Almighty" (*RH* 292–93); see also Ralph Birdsall, *Fenimore Cooper's Grave and Christ Churchyard* (New York: Frederick H. Hitchcock, 1911), 19 (WC's inscription), 33–35, and *COC* 32. Hannah's burial there of course went unmentioned in Susan Cooper's always circumspect text, since mentioning it would violate her father's sense that the event belonged most of all to family memory—indeed, to his own personal memory. Yet this passage in the diary-based text of *Rural Hours* in fact is *all about* Hannah's loss: the entry is dated September 11. Cooper himself was reported to have spoken openly about Hannah's loss during an 1850 séance conducted by the Fox sisters of Rochester, New York. See Richard B. Kimball, "J. Fenimore Cooper," *Frank Leslie's Popular Monthly* 9(1881): 702.

44. On the vacillation on religious matters, see Wayne Franklin, "Fathering the

Son: The Cultural Origins of James Fenimore Cooper," *Resources for American Literary Study* 27(2001): 162–72.

45. See Goldsbrow Banyar to Richard Fenimore Cooper, 10/23/1800, WC paps., box 20, HCA.

46. Joseph Griffin to WC, 11/4/1800, WC paps., box 20, HCA; Taylor, *William Cooper's Town*, 281.

47. This tentative plan soon was abandoned for Samuel but revived for the youngest son several years later; see the fuller discussion at the beginning of Chapter 4.

48. The partnership was intended to provide Isaac with a serious start in the mercantile life his father imagined for him; see Taylor, *William Cooper's Town*, 331; also, William Cooper, Jr., to Isaac Cooper, 1/13/1802, Daniel Hale to WC, 4/29/1802, and WC to Isaac Cooper, 2/7/1804, all in WC paps., box 21, HCA.

49. Resolution, 4/16/1800, quoted in Russell M. Magnaghi, "Aborted Cooper Expedition to Lake Superior Country, 1800," *Inland Seas* 36(1980): 83–84; Taylor, *William Cooper's Town*, 279; JFC II, *REMIN* 52–53; *Otsego Herald*, 10/23/1800. See also John Marshall to Richard Fenimore Cooper, 9/24/1800; Samuel Dexter to Commanding Officer at Detroit or Michilimackinac, 11/24/1800; James Wilkinson to WC, 11/28/1800; Joseph Phelps to Richard Fenimore Cooper, 3/17/1801; Levi Lincoln to Richard Fenimore Cooper, 3/30/1801; Richard Fenimore Cooper to Levi Lincoln, 4/25/1801; James Madison to Richard Fenimore Cooper, 5/13/1801; Richard Fenimore Cooper to James Madison, 5/31/1801; all in WC paps., boxes 20–21, HCA.

50. Albany *Chronicle*, 5/1/1797. In the weeks before his expected departure, Richard had married local beauty Ann Low Carey of Springfield—"a young giddy girl" incapable of taking Hannah's place in Elizabeth Cooper's heart, one of the dead woman's friends thought; Ralph Birdsall, *The Story of Cooperstown* (Cooperstown: Arthur H. Crist, 1917), 116. Soon the newlyweds, who had stayed for a time in Otsego Hall, moved to their own new mansion, Apple Hill, on the riverbank a few blocks from Otsego Hall.

51. Samuel Stanhope Smith to WC, 2/4/1800, 3/21/1800; Hannah Cooper to WC, 3/3/1800; WC to William Cooper, Jr., 7/9/1800; Smith to WC, 12/19/1800, 8/13/1801; all in WC paps., boxes 20–21, HCA.

52. William Cooper, Jr., to Isaac Cooper, 7/13/1801, WC paps., box 21, HCA.

53. Samuel Stanhope Smith to WC, 8/13/1801, WC paps., box 21, HCA.

54. Robert Voorhees to WC, 2/26/1802, enclosing bill, WC paps., box 21, HCA.

55. Samuel Stanhope Smith to WC, 2/22/1801, WC paps., box 21, HCA.

56. Voorhees to WC, 2/26/1802.

57. William Neill, *Autobiography of William Neill, D.D., with a Selection of His Sermons* (Philadelphia: Presbyterian Board of Education, 1861), 18; Taylor, *William Cooper's Town*, 336; Samuel Stanhope Smith to WC, 3/8/1802, WC paps., box 21, HCA.

58. Statement dated 3/18/1802, in Albany *Centinel*, 4/6/1802; judgment quoted in

Taylor, *William Cooper's Town,* 336. Princeton student William Neill asserted that the fire was set ("at the instigation of a club of abandoned youth") by a "profligate servant, who applied the match to the belfry, when he rung us out to dinner"; Neill, *Autobiography,* 18, and *A Discourse Reviewing a Ministry of Fifty Years* (Philadelphia: Joseph M. Wilson, 1857), 11. In his *Autobiography,* published ten years after the last of Judge Cooper's sons had died, Neill added: "The supposed ringleader in this foul affair was from the State of New York; he left the place soon after the deed was perpetrated, lived several years encompassed by suspicion, and died a worthless man"—precisely young William's fate (18).

59. Smith to WC, 3/8/1802.

60. Samuel Stanhope Smith to WC, 5/17/1802, WC paps., box 21, HCA. Training at the law was recommended to Judge Cooper for his son as a corrective for his errors (see Joseph Bloomfield to WC, 3/21/1802, WC paps., box 21, HCA). He was placed successively in the law offices of two Cooper allies, Moss Kent in Cooperstown and Richard Harison in New York City. This effort at rehabilitation also seems to have been the result of some official directive, perhaps that of the Princeton court. On this latter issue, see William Cooper, Jr., to WC, undated but ca. 1807, WC paps., box 24, HCA: "I believe I was, by the judge's order, to serve about four years and nine months [in legal training], and if the certificate [of WC's service in Kent's office beginning in 1802] was filed in season, it [the stated period] will have expired in November."

61. The naive character Anna in Cooper's 1820s tale "Imagination" finds Albany "one of the most picturesque places in the world; situated most delightfully on the banks of the Hudson, which here meanders in sylvan beauty through meadows of ever-green and desert islands" (*Tales* 44). The more experienced heroine of the tale, Julia, is less impressed with the place, but the narrator adjudicates by calling it "this charming town" (*Tales* 90). In the summer of 1801, Cooper reached Albany by accompanying a wheat farmer who drove his wagon from Otsego to the state capital over the newly opened Great Western Turnpike, in the construction of which Judge Cooper had been very much interested; *P&P* 50–51; *PIO* HE xv (note that these accounts both misdate to 1798 Cooper's shift to Albany).

62. *The America of 1750: Peter Kalm's Travels in North America, The English Version of 1770,* rev. by Adolph B. Benson, 2 vols. (1937; New York: Dover, 1966), 1:342. Enough of the fort's debris remained in 1800 for Albany artist James Eights, a youth then, to include a sizable remnant in his circa 1850 reconstruction of the view looking uphill from the river. Joe Meany, New York State Education Department, memorandum re: Colonial Community Model, 2/1/1988, enclosure four (my collection). In *Satanstoe,* Cooper's narrator, approaching the city from the river, catches the mid-eighteenth-century prospect: "It was an interesting moment to us all, when the spires and roofs of that ancient town, Albany, first appeared in view! . . . There it lay, stretching along the low land on the margin of the stream, and on its western bank, sheltered by high hills,

up the side of which, the principal street extended, for the distance of fully a quarter of a mile. Near the head of this street stood the fort, and we saw a brigade paraded in the open ground near it, wheeling and marching about" (*SAT* CE 148).

63. Charlotte Wilcoxen, *Seventeenth Century Albany: A Dutch Profile*, rev. ed. (Albany: Albany Institute of History and Art, 1984), 6. On Cooper's perception of Belgian as opposed to Dutch elements in New York, see *GR* CE 95. Pinkster, originally a Christian festival celebrated on Whitsunday that had received significant African development in the so-called Dutch areas of the Northeast, provided Cooper an attractive opportunity for portraying the cultural innovations of New York's African Americans. His detailed description of the holiday in *Satanstoe* (*SAT* CE 64–66), published decades after the festival had been forced from the public spaces of both Albany and New York City, makes the novel a prime historical document of the event: somewhere Cooper clearly had witnessed New York blacks "collected in thousands, . . . beating banjoes, singing African songs," carrying on "the traditions and usages of their original country" as they danced to rhythms drummed out "on skins drawn over the ends of hollow logs," as hundreds of curious whites such as himself, drawn by the public jubilation, toured the festival ground (ibid., 65). But he did not observe it during his stay as a schoolboy in Albany: he arrived after Whitsunday in 1801 and left before it in 1802. Probably he had observed it there at some earlier (or later) point, supplementing his knowledge with information gleaned from the allied, but less notable, celebrations in and around Manhattan. Perhaps the African Americans at the farm of his future in-laws, the DeLanceys, also kept the holiday. See David S. Cohen, "In Search of Carolus Africanus Rex," *The Journal of the Afro-American Historical and Genealogical Society* 5(1984): 149–68. In Albany, Pinkster, formerly held on the pasture behind the old fort at the head of State Street, was suppressed by the Common Council in 1811, the latest in a series of actions reflecting the increasing influence of Yankee migrants on that body, which had been controlled until as late as 1804 by members of the old Dutch merchant families. See David G. Hackett, *The Rude Hand of Innovation: Religion and Social Order in Albany, New York, 1652–1836* (New York: Oxford University Press, 1991), 3–4, 106–7.

64. Tomlan and Trovato, eds., *Neat Plain Modern Stile*, 54–62; Joel Munsell, *The Annals of Albany*, 10 vols. (Albany: Munsell, 1850–1859), 1:90; this was the architect—and the building—mentioned in *The Pioneers* (see note 23).

65. Levi Beardsley, *Reminiscences* (New York: Charles Vinten, 1852), 76–77, recalled another distinctive feature of the Dutch church: the old woman "who sold coffee and chocolate on the south side, and sometimes 'strong beer,' as it was called." He also remembered the "Dutch witch," a figure "visited by those going there from the country, who wanted to know their fortune"—the prototype of the fortune-teller Doortje in *Satanstoe;* and "*the lion* that was kept somewhere on the hill," perhaps relocated by Cooper to New York City early in the same novel.

66. Elkanah Watson, *Men and Times of the Revolution; or Memoirs of Elkanah Wat-*

son, Including His Journals of Travels in Europe and America, ed. Winslow C. Watson, 2nd ed. (New York: Dana and Co., 1856), 328.

67. Tomlan and Trovato, eds., *Neat Plain Modern Stile,* 69–71.

68. Like Dewey, Jason Newcome is born into a Connecticut farm family, goes to Yale, then is imported into New York to serve as a teacher. Later he migrates to the northern New York lands owned by the Littlepages, much as Dewey moved to the Cooper lands in DeKalb. Newcome completely lacks Dewey's abundant wit (and intelligence), however, and there is no surviving indication that Cooper's first teacher betrayed his benefactors—as Newcome certainly does in the Littlepage series.

69. Beard (*LJ* 1:8n) adds that Ellison, born in 1759, had served as curate of the ancient Church of St. Nicholas in Newcastle before coming to New York in 1786; Anna [Hannah] Cooper to Isaac Cooper, 6/25/1798, WC paps., box 19, HCA; the future novelist's classmate William Jay in 1854 wrote Susan Fenimore Cooper that, on his and her father's arrival at Ellison's in 1801, the minister had "just consented to receive into his family a few boys to instruct" (William Jay to SFC, 4/15/1854, copy in JFB paps., box 1, AAS), but he must have been mistaken. On Ellison and Otsego, see WC, "Landbook," leaf 20; 1788 Cooperstown village map by Daniel Smith, Maps and Land Surveys; Daniel Hale to Richard Fenimore Cooper, 8/6/1802, all in WC paps. (Hale letter in box 21), HCA; also, DeMille, *Christ Church, Cooperstown,* 2.

70. Stephen Van Rensselaer to WC, 11/10/1797, WC paps., box 19, HCA; Munsell, *Annals of Albany,* 6:56; William Jay to SFC, 4/15/1854. Cooper probably borrowed from his memories of Ellison in creating the Rev. Thomas Worden, the "English divine" and "rector of St. Jude's" in *Satanstoe,* who serves as Corny Littlepage's tutor. Like Ellison, Worden is "very popular among the gentry, . . . attending all the dinners, clubs, races, balls, and other diversions that were given by them, within ten miles of his residence" (*SAT* CE 22).

71. See John Carroll Chase and George Walter Chamberlain, comp., *Seven Generations of the Descendants of Aquila and Thomas Chase* (Derry: privately published, 1928), 379.

72. Cooper listed them as follows: "There were two Rensselaers, of the Greenbush branch of the family, [only] one of whom, Dr. Jeremiah Van Rensselaer of New York, is . . . living, a Livingston of the Upper Manor, who has died quite lately, William Jay, the youngest son of the Governor, and myself" (*LJ* 2:155). Susan Fenimore Cooper's account (*PIO* HE xv) gives the wrong names for two of the five who were also at Ellison's during her father's stay there (Cooper knew both Jacob Sutherland and James Stevenson well during his boyhood years, but they were *not* pupils at Ellison's school at the time). For the record, here is what we know about his schoolmates. The Van Rensselaers "of the Greenbush line," both of them vague cousins of Cooper's wife-to-be, Susan De-Lancey, were the sons of Col. Johannes Jeremias Van Rensselaer (1762–1828), a Jeffersonian Republican and sole heir of the family's Greenbush or Claverack lands, which lay

on the east side of the Hudson opposite Albany. The one schoolmate Cooper named, Jeremiah (or more accurately Jeremias) Van Rensselaer (1793–1871), later went to Yale and took up the practice of medicine in New York City in the 1820s, where Cooper socialized with "Jerry Rensselaer" (*LJ* 6:25) and included him among the members of the Bread and Cheese Club (William Jay confirmed the identification in his 4/15/1854 letter to SFC, cited in note 69). The other member of the "Greenbush line" whom Cooper knew at Ellison's probably was Jerry Rensselaer's older brother, John J. Van Rensselaer (1790–1814); see Florence Van Rensselaer, *The Van Rensselaers in Holland and America* (New York: American Historical Co., 1956), 59, 39. The "Livingston of the Upper Manor" who was not named in Cooper's recollections remains elusive. He may have been one of the sons of John and Mary Ann LeRoy Livingston of "Oak Hill," Columbia County, among whom Henry (born in 1791) seems like a plausible candidate. Like the Van Rensselaers, Henry Livingston was related in various ways to the most important of Cooper's schoolmates, William Jay, whose mother was a Livingston: indeed, Henry Livingston's stepmother was William Jay's aunt, Catharine or Kitty Livingston. William Jay in 1854, however, remembered nothing of such a schoolmate, listing only the two Van Rensselaers, Cooper, and himself as staying at Ellison's at the time (Florence Van Rensselaer, *The Livingston Family in America and Its Scottish Origins* [New York: privately printed, 1949], 93–94, 98; William Jay to SFC, 4/15/1854).

73. Alice P. Kenney, *The Gansevoorts of Albany: Dutch Patricians in the Upper Hudson Valley* (Syracuse: Syracuse University Press, 1969), 150; *LJ* 1:39–41; *LJ* 1:41n. Whether the Gansevoorts were pupils of Ellison or not, they certainly knew Cooper well in childhood; so, at any rate, Maria Gansevoort is said to have recalled: "Melville's mother remembered Cooper as a big boy who played with her brother Peter when he stayed over at the Gansevoort house waiting for the breakup of the ice on the Hudson so he could go south," writes Hershel Parker, *Herman Melville: A Biography*, 2 vols. (Baltimore: Johns Hopkins University Press, 1996–2002), 2:37; see also *LJ* 2:155. Another Albany friend at this time appears to have been Thomas Bridgen, the son of New York obstetrician Thomas A. Bridgen, a creditor of Judge Cooper whose claims, prosecuted by his son, would bring down the Cooper family fortune years later (see Chapter 10). Since his father had remarried and had other children, young Thomas and his two sisters were living in Albany with their late mother's relatives, the Ten Eycks (incidentally, close associates—indeed, relatives—of the Gansevoorts; see Parker, *Herman Melville*, 1:380), and may have been known by that surname; as such, Thomas may have been recalled by Cooper in the figure of Guert Ten Eyck in *Satanstoe*.

74. Anne MacVickar Grant emphasized the street play; see *Memoirs of an American Lady* (1809), ed. James Grant Wilson (New York: Dodd, Mead, 1909), 1:119–25. Cooper had several other guides in Albany. His brother Samuel was intermittently there. Isaac, who earlier in 1801 had returned to Cooperstown from the Philadelphia counting house where he had been working, moved to Albany that fall to take a fuller hand in the

partnership with Albany merchant Daniel Hale recently set up by Judge Cooper; William Cooper, Jr., to Isaac Cooper, 7/13/1801, 1/13/1802, Daniel Hale to WC, 4/29/1802, all in WC paps., box 21, HCA; Isaac Cooper, "Collumbus the Wagon in Account with Wm Cooper," in WC, "Land Ledger," vol. 1., WC paps., HCA. The Albany family of Goldsbrow Banyar also provided supervision for Cooper; this was especially true in the case of Banyar's daughter-in-law (and William Jay's sister), Maria Jay, who recently had married Banyar's son (Goldsborough Banyer) and, after a honeymoon trip to visit the Coopers in Cooperstown, set up housekeeping in Albany; see John Jay, *Memorials of Peter A. Jay, Compiled for His Descendants* (n.p.: privately printed, 1929), 35; *LJ* 4:365–66n. Cooper had first met Maria Jay in Albany during his pre-Ellison trips through there (perhaps as early as 1796–1797; see *LJ* 2:108); she would remain his lifelong friend and on various occasions served as his trusted literary advisor (see *LJ* 1:8, 68; 3:18, 326; 4:133; 5:408; 6:96).

75. Joseph Hooper (author of *A History of St. Peter's Church* [1900]), undated longhand fragment, in Mary E. Phillips papers, Boston Public Library; that the ultimate source of the anecdote was Cooper himself is indicated by a note in the same hand, evidently Hooper's: "This incident was told me by the late Mr. Edward Floyd de Lancey, son of the bishop of Western New York, whose sister, Susan Augusta had married James Fenimore Cooper on January 1, 1811."

76. William Jay to John Jay, 1801, in Bayard Tuckerman, *William Jay and the Constitutional Movement for the Abolition of Slavery* (1893; New York: Burt Franklin, 1969), 2.

77. See M. Tulli Ciceronis, *Pro Archia Poeta Oratio*, ed. Steven M. Cerutti (Wauconda: Bolchazy-Carducci, 1999), 3.

78. "*Tityre, tu patulae recubans sub tegmine fagi / silvestrem tenui musam meditaris avena* (You, Tityrus, lie under the canopy of a spreading beech, / wooing the woodland muse on slender reed)"; Virgil, *Eclogues, Georgics, Aeneid I–VI*, trans. H. Rushton Fairclough, rev. by G. P. Goold (Cambridge: Harvard University Press, 2001), 25 (see *PIO* CE 102: "Titty-ree too patty-lee re-coo-bans sub teg-mi-nee faa-gy / Syl-ves-trem ten-oo-i moo-sam med-i taa-ris aa-ve-ny").

79. See William Jay to SFC, 4/15/1854.

80. Ibid.

81. *Otsego Herald*, 5/6/1802.

82. Isaac Lewis for a time taught Samuel Cooper (see Hannah Cooper to Isaac Cooper, 4/13/1800; Isaac Lewis to WC, 12/15/1800, both in WC paps., box 20, HCA). Lewis became especially close to Ann Cooper, over whose marriage to George Pomeroy he presided in 1803. His father, also a minister and Yale graduate, often tutored candidates for admission to the college; see Charles Tabb Hazelrigg, *American Literary Pioneer: A Biographical Study of James A. Hillhouse* (New York: Bookman Associates, 1953), 13–14.

83. Cooper's name began to appear on New Haven merchants' accounts that August; see William Fitch, bill, 3/2/1803 (first entry 8/10/1802), JFC paps., box 4, AAS.

So did that of his brother Samuel, who, his hopes for the navy shattered, probably was sent along to act as a guardian of sorts. Samuel was still in New Haven the following March, but between then and 1804 or early 1805 at the latest he left and went home; see Samuel Cooper to Isaac Cooper, 3/12/1803, WC paps., box 22, HCA; Nathan Smith to WC, 3/1/1805 and 12/22/1805, WC paps., box 23, HCA.

84. Hazelrigg, *American Literary Pioneer*, 16; *The Laws of Yale-College* (New Haven: Thomas Green, 1800), 9. Cooper later dismissed the academic part of these requirements as slender indeed. His fictional traveler in *Notions of the Americans* (1828) comments, "I find that boys entered [American] colleges so late as the commencement of the present century, who had read a part of the Greek Testament, and a few books of Cicero and Virgil, with perhaps a little of Horace" (*Notions* 2:96).

85. In one regard, as indicated earlier, Cooper and William Jay felt themselves ahead of their professors in New Haven—the scanning of Latin verse for its peculiar meters; see William Jay to SFC, 4/15/1854; see also *A&A* CE pt. 1:19n: "In 1803, the class to which the writer then belonged at Yale, was the first that ever attempted to scan in that institution. The quantities were in sad discredit, in this country, even years after this, though Columbia and Harvard were a little in advance of Yale. All that was ever done in the last college, during the writer's time, was to scan the ordinary hexameter of Homer and Virgil"; and, finally, G. Pomeroy Keese's anecdote regarding how Cooper in 1840 took it upon himself to correct the Latin of a number of academy students gathered at his home in Cooperstown: "*Regĭna! Regĭna!,*" he shouted, mimicking their incorrect short *i* in the word. "What kind of Latin do you call that? Scan the line!" ("Memories of Distinguished Authors: James Fenimore Cooper," *Harper's Weekly*, 7/29/1871 supplement, 708). On Cooper's matriculation, see *LJ* 1:5, and Jane W. Hill (librarian of the Yale Memorabilia Collection) to JFB, 2/11/1954, JFB paps., box 1, AAS. (Here and later it is useful to know that Yale's vacations were as follows: "The first, six weeks immediately after Commencement [held on the second Wednesday of September]: The second, three weeks . . . after [the] second Wednesday in January: The third, [three weeks, starting] on the Wednesday immediately preceding the second Thursday in May"; *Laws of Yale-College*, 19, 39).

86. Those letters from home, if Cooper received and read them, were certainly not answered: for all the many months Cooper spent in New Haven, there is only a single surviving fragmentary note sent home by him—a request that William Cooper pay his overdue bill at a New Haven merchant's store and send him some extra cash, since he had "not a copper of money" in his pocket (*LJ* 1:9).

87. Franklin B. Dexter, "Student Life at Yale under the First President Dwight (1795–1817)," AAS *Proceedings*, 27[1917]: 324–26; William Jay to William Jay (grandson), quoted in Tuckerman, *William Jay*, 7.

88. Kingsley was thought to have "a special power of elegant composition" in English as well as Latin (Dexter, *Biographical Sketches*, 5:364). He retold the "Regicide"

story in his *Life of Ezra Stiles*, in the "Library of American Biography," ed. Jared Sparks, 2nd ser., vol. 6 (Boston: Little, Brown, 1844), 66–67. Stiles, Dwight's predecessor as Yale president, himself had written a *History of Three of the Judges of King Charles I* (1794), and various sites around New Haven were associated with the trio. See *LJ* 1:218n2; Dexter, *Biographical Sketches*, 6:362–67; *DAB*, s.v. "Kingsley, James Luce"; Evert A. and George L. Duyckinck, *Cyclopedia of American Literature* (New York: Charles Scribner, 1856), 1:88–89.

89. Dwight took a "parental interest" in Silliman; see Chandos Michael Brown, *Benjamin Silliman: A Life in the Young Republic* (Princeton: Princeton University Press, 1989), 69, quoting Silliman's unpublished "Reminiscences."

90. Ibid., 54–55, 69–70, 100–3; Dexter, *Biographical Sketches*, 5:220–27.

91. Benjamin Silliman to JFC, 9/19/1831, copy in JFB paps., box 2, AAS; on Twining, see Dexter, *Biographical Sketches*, 5:173–74; Cooper in an 1831 letter to Silliman asked to be remembered to both Twining and his wife, suggesting, I think, that he had lived at their house when first in New Haven (*LJ* 2:100).

92. Silliman to JFC, 9/19/1831; see Brown, *Benjamin Silliman*, 22–24.

93. A version of this story was told by JFC II, *REMIN* 50: "Judge Cooper was asked by Yale University to withdraw Jim in the latter part of his Junior year" because of a "charge, which was false, of his joining a number of other students in beating up an unpopular tutor."

94. Dexter, *Biographical Sketches*, 5:196–99, and "Student Life at Yale," 320. Royal Fowler, the tutor's brother, associated with Cooper. Their classmate Daniel Mulford, clearly drawing on Cooper's characterization of young Fowler, joked in an 1805 satire, "Old Cooper's bulldog y'clept Jowler / Look'd very much like Mr. Fowler" ("A Satire, Read Saturday March 23, 1805," copy in JFB paps., box 1, AAS).

95. Brown, *Benjamin Silliman*, 124–47. Silliman's lectures were based on the *Elements of Chemistry, delivered in the University of Edinburgh; by the late Joseph Black*, edited and published by John Robison in 1803, and especially on Thomas Thomson's four-volume *A System of Chemistry* (1802), another recent Edinburgh product.

96. Brown, *Benjamin Silliman*, 140.

97. Beard asserts (*LJ* 1:218n) that Cooper attended the 1804 lectures.

98. Brown, *Benjamin Silliman*, 140.

99. About 50 of the approximately 230 undergraduates at Yale became new members of the college chapel in the months just before Cooper's arrival, a remarkable fact given that, in the estimate of Lyman Beecher (Yale, 1797), there were only 11 undergraduates "*known* to have been professors of religion" on Dwight's arrival in 1795; Brown, *Benjamin Silliman*, 89–99.

100. Harry Hayden Clark, "Fenimore Cooper and Science," *Transactions of the Wisconsin Academy of Sciences, Arts, and Letters*, 48(1959): 180n4, asserts that Jeremiah Day was the instructor in question but does not document the assertion; Marcel Clavel,

Fenimore Cooper: sa vie et son oeuvre, la jeunesse (1789–1826) (Aix-en-Provence: Imprimerie Universitaire de Provence, 1938), 152, asserts that Cooper studied astronomy with Silliman. One bit of evidence suggests that Clavel may have been at least partly right. In *Satanstoe,* Cooper's hero, Corny Littlepage, was sent to Princeton for college. Looking back on the experience, Corny recalls: "Moral philosophy, in particular, was closely attended to, senior year, as well as Astronomy. We had a telescope that showed us all four of Jupiter's moons" (*SAT* CE 36). Benjamin Silliman's college journal contains the following entry: "In the beginning of the evening I went with a member of my class to look at the planet Jupiter through the large telescope from the Museum, which with his four moons is very easily discovered" (Dexter, "Student Life," 331). The similarity seems more than coincidental, suggesting that Silliman had shared his discovery with Cooper as a story if not also a demonstration.

101. Brown, *Benjamin Silliman,* 12–13; for a contemporary account of the battle, see Frank Moore, *Diary of the American Revolution* (New York: Charles Scribner, 1860), 1:336, which reprints from the *Pennsylvania Evening Post* of 11/14/1776 an eyewitness narrative that includes mention of the fierce artillery assault.

102. On the capture and liberation, see "A New York Diary," ed. Carson I. A. Ritchie, in *Narratives of the Revolution in New York* (New York: NYHS, 1975), 273; on the Tory raiders, see Joy Day Buel and Richard Buel, Jr., *The Way of Duty: A Woman and Her Family in Revolutionary America* (New York: W. W. Norton, 1984), 149.

103. Brown, *Benjamin Silliman,* 4–5. Brown (24–28) argues that the burden of his father's life weighed very heavily on the "confused and troubled" Benjamin, who during his convalescence from a nervous breakdown his senior year at Yale pored over his father's wartime manuscripts, sorted them, then sewed them into gatherings and bound them as a tribute to the tragic general. As a result, he knew the stories exceptionally well, and ever afterwards was to remain a "devoted student of the Revolution." Even at the end of his life, after retiring from Yale, he dutifully set about recopying his mother's manuscript autobiography, in which Selleck Silliman's tragedy figured prominently. We do not know whether Silliman shared this knotted story with Cooper, but he certainly did not regard it as a private burden: it was from him that another manuscript account of his father's captivity penned by his mother, for instance, made its way to President Dwight, who inserted it as a long footnote in his *Travels* (Brown, 315–16). For Dwight's own version, based on Mary Silliman's retelling of ca. 1815, see Timothy Dwight, *Travels in New England and New York,* ed. Barbara Miller Solomon, 4 vols. (Cambridge: Harvard University Press, 1969), 3:357–59n; Mary Silliman's fuller account of the capture, written out in 1801, is found in Thomas Jones, *History of New York,* ed. E. F. DeLancey (New York: NYHS, 1879), 2:565–71.

104. James Renwick, *First Principles of Chemistry* (New York: Harper & Bros., 1840), 303.

105. *Laws of Yale-College,* 26.

106. James Melvin Lee, as reported in *NYU Alumnus*, 1/25/1928, longhand transcription in JFB paps., box 1, AAS.

107. JFC II, "Unpublished Letters of James Fenimore Cooper," *Yale Review* 5 (July 1916): 810. The fact that Dr. Battius in *The Prairie* rides such a beast may suggest that someone on the faculty associated with science was the target, but that is speculation on my part.

108. Daniel Mulford, "A Satire, Read Saturday, March 23, 1805," copy in JFB paps., box 1, AAS. Mulford, another Jersey native, had arrived in New Haven by unusual means. Of an impoverished background and largely self-educated, he had been trained as a shoemaker until he chanced to come to the attention of someone with Yale connections, who arranged for him to join the junior class the fall before he entertained his fellows with the "Satire" (Dexter, *Biographical Sketches*, 6:47). Mulford died of pulmonary disease in 1811.

109. Quoted in Jane W. Hill to JFB, 9/21/1953, JFB paps., box 1, AAS.

110. *Laws of Yale-College*, 24–25. The specific complaint against Boyle was that he had committed "trespass" against Cooper; one needs to recall that under common law trespass was "a form of action brought to recover damages for any injury to one's person or property or relationship with another"; Harry Campbell Black, *Black's Law Dictionary*, 6th ed. (St. Paul: West Group, 1990), 1502. Nathan Smith (1770–1835) and his brother Nathaniel (1762–1822) were business associates of Judge Cooper. The elder of them, who practiced law in Woodbury, had served with Cooper in the House of Representatives, and soon after young Cooper and his brother arrived in New Haven became one of the partners in William Cooper's development of the northern New York township of DeKalb (Smith's son-in-law, Thomas B. Benedict, soon emigrated to DeKalb, where he became the managing partner in William Cooper's store there, a position he still occupied in 1815). Nathan Smith appears to have been young Cooper's more-or-less official guardian through much if not all of the boy's stay in New Haven. He received funds from William Cooper and dispensed them to the boy or used them to pay off his accounts with local merchants; see Nathan Smith to WC, 3/1/1805, WC paps., box 23, HCA.

111. Henry Daggett, justice of the peace, New Haven City Court, 5/24/1805 order (to attach John Boyle's property to insure his appearance at city court "2d Tuesday of June next"), copy in "James Cooper v. John P. Boyle," JFB paps., box 1, AAS.

112. New Haven City Court, June 11, 1805, session, copy in "Cooper v. Boyle," ibid.

113. Frank C. Mannix (assistant clerk, Superior Court in and for New Haven County) to JFB, 3/4/1954, JFB paps., box 1, AAS, names the justices; see also Dwight, *Travels in New England and New York*, 1:192.

114. Dexter, *Biographical Sketches*, 6:733; Hazelrigg, *American Literary Pioneer*, 29.

115. Hill to JFB, 9/21/1953; "James Cooper v. John P. Boyle," New Haven County Superior Court, July term 1805, with later annotations on back; typed copy of New

Haven County Superior Court ruling, 12/6/1805, in Cooper v. Boyle, continued from July term; all in JFB paps., box 1, AAS. Dexter, *Biographical Sketches*, 6:96.

116. See *GE* CE 155, which reports that Ellison "cracked his jokes daily about Mr. Jefferson and Black Sal, never failing to place his libertinism in strong relief against the approved morals of George III, of several passages in whose history, it is charity to suppose he was ignorant."

117. Taylor, *William Cooper's Town*, 369.

118. Mulford diary, quoted in Hill to JFB, 9/21/1953.

119. Silliman to JFC, 9/19/1831.

120. *The Autobiography of Lyman Beecher*, ed. Barbara M. Cross, 2 vols. (1864; Cambridge: Harvard University Press, 1961), 1:23.

121. One student had been rusticated—a punishment less severe than suspension or dismissal—for two months because he had been caught rolling barrels down the stairs of Stuart's college lodgings. Another, who had shown a penchant for "cutting bellropes" and committing "blasphemy," continued his bad behavior despite repeated punishments from Dwight. Nor were these isolated cases. "Many others stand trembling in *'fearful looking for a fiery indignation,'*" Stuart wrote his colleague, confirming his judgment that there were "more devils in college at present than were cast out of Mary Magdalene." He had just had six panes of glass knocked out of one of his windows. And, despite the chemist's absence from New Haven, his own lodgings had suffered similar damage. George P. Fisher, *Life of Benjamin Silliman* (New York: Charles Scribner and Co., 1866), 1:114–15; see also Clavel, *Fenimore Cooper*, 141–42, and Brown, *Benjamin Silliman*, 111.

122. Brown, *Benjamin Silliman*, 143.

CHAPTER 3. THE VOYAGE OF THE *STIRLING*

1. Nathan Smith to WC, 12/22/1805, WC paps., box 23, HCA.

2. *Connecticut Journal*, 6/27/1805; since no copy of the *Otsego Herald* for 6/6/1805 is known to have survived, the reprinting from which I quote is a useful substitute for it.

3. See Louis C. Jones, "The Crime and Punishment of Stephen Arnold," *NYH* 47 (1966): 250 (based on *Otsego Herald*, 1/31/1805); Alan Taylor, "'The Unhappy Stephen Arnold': An Episode of Murder and Penitence in the Early Republic," in Ronald Hoffman, Mechal Sobel, and Fredrika J. Teute, eds., *Through a Glass Darkly: Reflections on Personal Identity in Early America* (Chapel Hill: University of North Carolina Press, 1997), 98–99.

4. Jones, "Crime and Punishment," 252; *The Trial of Stephen Arnold; For the Murder of Betsey Van Amburgh, a Child of Six Years of Age* . . . (Cooperstown: Elihu Phinney, 1805), 16–17; see also Taylor, "Unhappy Stephen Arnold," 100.

5. *Otsego Herald*, 1/31/1805; see also (presiding judge) James Kent to Gov. Morgan Lewis, 7/8/1805, in *Otsego Herald*, 2/20/1806.

6. Newspaper coverage was extensive in large part because *Otsego Herald* publisher Elihu Phinney became taken with what was the county's first murder case. Over the next year and a half, reports on it in his paper dominated all other local news. Phinney also prepared and published *The Trial of Stephen Arnold*, which he announced as "just issued" on 7/18/1805, the day before Arnold's scheduled execution. Soon available as well was Arnold's own story, as told in a twelve-page pamphlet, *Life and Confession of Arnold, Who Inhumanly Whipped to Death Betsey Van Amburgh, His Little Niece—Aged Six Years* ([Albany?]: n.p., 1806).

7. The winter vacation ran for the three weeks following "the second Wednesday" in January (1/9/1805). See *The Laws of Yale-College, in New-Haven, in Connecticut, Enacted by the President and Fellows, the Sixth Day of October, A.D. 1795* (New Haven: Thomas Green and Son, 1800), 19.

8. *Otsego Herald*, 7/25/1805, 8/1/1805.

9. Ibid., 2/20/1806. More tellingly, Cooper's memoir said nothing at all about the execution sermon delivered by family friend Isaac Lewis, who for weeks had been tirelessly counseling the prisoner.

10. Jones, "Crime and Punishment," 265; *Otsego Herald*, 7/25/1805.

11. William Neill, *A Discourse Reviewing a Ministry of Fifty Years* (Philadelphia: Joseph M. Wilson, 1857), 61, wrote that Judge Cooper's "two youngest sons, James F. and Samuel, were inclined to be idle and neglect theirs books," adding that at their father's request, he "gave them, for a time, daily lessons in the elements of an English education." The clear inference is that the idleness not only was evident to Judge Cooper beforehand, but that it motivated his employment of Neill as tutor.

12. It is possible that Neill worked off his room and board by teaching the boys, but there is no proof on this issue. Clearly he enjoyed warm relations with the family, recalling William Cooper with genuine affection: "The judge possessed charming traits of character; he was of simple, easy manners, very social, friendly, and hospitable. I shared largely in his kindness and hospitality while in his neighborhood." *Autobiography of William Neill, D. D., with a Selection from His Sermons* (Philadelphia: Presbyterian Board of Education, 1861), 24. In his slightly earlier *Discourse*, Neill likewise remembered William Cooper as "a man of noble bearing—enterprising, public-spirited, and generous to a proverb" (61).

13. From his modest start in Cooperstown, Neill was to pass to positions of considerable prominence. He had a notable ministerial career in Albany and Philadelphia before becoming president of Dickinson College and then an official with the Board of Education for the Presbyterian Church. *Autobiography*, 25–59.

14. Ibid., 6–7.

15. Neill, *Discourse*, 61.

16. Neill, *Autobiography*, 24.

17. Ibid.; Neill, *Discourse*, 61; on Brown, see *Notions* 2:111; *Spy* CE 2–3.

18. Charles Tabb Hazelrigg, *American Literary Pioneer: A Biographical Study of James A. Hillhouse* (New York: Bookman Associates, 1953), 28, 31; *Laws of Yale-College*, 27.

19. Franklin B. Dexter, "Student Life at Yale under the First President Dwight (1795–1817)," AAS *Proceedings*, 27[1917]: 325.

20. But the tutor's support may have been genuine. In later years, Neill apparently read Cooper's books and took pleasure in them—and in knowing their author. See *Discourse*, 61; *Autobiography*, 24.

21. Neill, *Autobiography*, 33.

22. It is possible that Neill's fond recollections of young Cooper resulted from the tutor's ex post facto attempt to claim a kind of originating impact on the future novelist, who had died several years before Neill wrote down his reflections. Neill might be viewed as suggesting that his encouragement of Cooper's reading during the winter of 1805–1806 helped shape his eventual vocation: "After a while he conceived the idea of making [a novel] of his own. The thought was carried into effect. He devoted himself to study, became a good scholar; and, in the course of a few years, produced the 'Pioneers,' in two volumes." Neill, *Discourse*, 61–62. Perhaps Neill saw the portent of some such transformation in the boy, and it is even possible that Cooper confided in his tutor a wish to someday write a book of the sort that so absorbed his attention. On balance, though, such possibilities seem remote.

23. Neill, *Discourse*, 13.

24. William Spence Robertson, *The Life of Miranda*, 2 vols. (Chapel Hill: University of North Carolina Press, 1929), 1:293–327.

25. Richard R. Smith to Isaac Cooper, 8/8/1806, in Alan Taylor, "James Fenimore Cooper Goes to Sea: Two Unpublished Letters by a Family Friend," *Studies in the American Renaissance: 1993:* 51–52; on the letter to Simmons, see 46.

26. Richard R. Smith to Isaac Cooper, 7/18/1806, ibid., 51. William learned some details fairly soon (such as that the youth had left Otsego "rather in an uncommon manner"), but such information may have come in whole or part from Cooperstown rather than directly from his brother. On the issue of Judge Cooper's plan to train his youngest son for the law: there is no direct evidence of such a plan or of any visit to New York City earlier in 1806, but Alan Taylor, *William Cooper's Town: Power and Persuasion on the Frontier of the Early American Republic* (New York: Knopf, 1995), 339, 343, asserts that William Cooper intended his youngest son to study law, and in *Afloat and Ashore*, a novel loosely based on the author's own early maritime experience, the hero Miles Wallingford is in fact intended for the law by his father; only following his father's premature death does he run off to New York and go to sea (*A&A* CE pt. 1:14, 21–22). Similarly, other details in that book, including some connected with a lawyer named "Richard Harrison" (*sic*), suggest the author's close familiarity with New York City in this very period. So, in another sense, does Cooper's impressively circumstantial description of Pinkster in

his Albany novel, *Satanstoe,* mentioned in the previous chapter. It appears not to be true, as various scholars have claimed, that Cooper experienced the celebration of that Dutch–African American festival in the capital while attending Ellison's school (he was not in Albany at the right time in either 1801 or 1802). A return trip to Cooperstown from New York City in the late spring of 1806 would have allowed Cooper a plausible opportunity to tarry in Albany precisely at the time of the moveable festival (which was to be outlawed in 1810), then arrive in Otsego for the eclipse. Intriguingly, in "The Eclipse" Cooper insists that he was *visiting* Cooperstown after time away from it, and he clearly imagined himself at that time as already a sailor (Eclipse 352–54, 357). I think it just possible that, instead of attending to business in Richard Harison's office during his mandated visit to the city early in 1806, Cooper strolled the nearby wharves, picking up floating details about Miranda's expedition (which would have been more accessible and more current there) and convincing himself that he *had* to go to sea. On his return to Otsego, he tried hard to convince his parents that this was the future career for him, then when they resisted he fled to undertake it on his own. Stephen Railton, *Fenimore Cooper: A Study of His Life and Imagination* (Princeton: Princeton University Press, 1978), 261–62, views with skepticism Cooper's memory of himself as already a sailor in 1806, but repeats the old tale about Judge Cooper's decision to *send* his youngest son to sea, which Taylor, "Cooper Goes to Sea," 43–44, cites and properly discredits.

27. It is possible that Cooper went straight to Philadelphia, passing through New York City but not trying his luck there. William knew, however, that his younger brother "was expected to call on [Smith]" in Philadelphia, suggesting that he had spoken with the runaway in New York.

28. Smith in his letter to Isaac of 8/8/1806, written exactly three weeks after his first one, said that Cooper had just left Philadelphia, having been there "about Three Weeks" (Taylor, "Cooper Goes to Sea," 51).

29. Smith to Isaac Cooper, 8/8/1806, in Taylor, "Cooper Goes to Sea," 51.

30. The arrangement suggests the possibility that Isaac was privy to some of Cooper's plans when he fled Cooperstown in July.

31. Cooper, Smith had gathered, apparently had "some [additional] Plan fixed in his mind that he did not like to communicate to me," a "Plan" about which Smith offered tentative guesses: "I suspect he wishes to join Miranda for the present, with some future Views to the Navy." Smith's letter is our only source of knowledge about the Miranda business. *Ned Myers,* Cooper's book about one of the shipmates on his eventual first voyage, does not mention it even though the book reveals Ned's more serious dalliance with the would-be liberator (*NM* 19). Smith to Isaac Cooper, 8/8/1806, in Taylor, "Cooper Goes to Sea," 51.

32. Smith to Isaac Cooper, 8/8/1806, in Taylor, "Cooper Goes to Sea," 51–52.

33. Ibid., 51. On Smith's business address, see his entry in *Philadelphia Directory, City and County Register* (Philadelphia: James Robinson, 1806).

34. On Miers Fisher and the Coopers, see Taylor, *William Cooper's Town*, 3–4, 113, 118, 317; on Fisher and Jacob Barker, see Jacob Barker, *Incidents in the Life of Jacob Barker of New Orleans, Louisiana* (Washington: n.p., 1855), 22–23.

35. Edith A. Sawyer, "A Year of Cooper's Youth," *New England Magazine*, n.s. 37 (1907): 499 (Sawyer's essay essentially reprints an 1883 piece by the captain's nephew, Alexander Johnston, in the *Mount Desert Herald;* see *LJ* 4:375n). Neither Alan Taylor's research nor my own has turned up proof of any relationship between Judge Cooper and Jacob Barker in the Cooper papers; see Taylor, "Cooper Goes to Sea," 49.

36. Taylor, "Cooper Goes to Sea," 49. Unstated anywhere in the nineteenth-century evidence—but likely true given several incidents in the voyage—was the point Alan Taylor shrewdly makes: namely, that Cooper must have come on board under some special protection beyond the interest taken in him by Barker or Fisher or other adults. He may well have had an official paper declaring him the son of a former U.S. congressman. Cooper certainly led a charmed life aboard the *Stirling*.

37. On the Johnstons, see Sawyer, "A Year of Cooper's Youth," 499. When Cooper discovered in 1843 that his shipmate Ned Myers still was alive, the news surprised him, but so did Ned's report that he recently had visited with Captain Johnston. Only when Cooper none too accurately recalculated the differences in their ages in a letter he sent Johnston in Wiscasset could he restore the *Stirling*'s master to the world of his own active memories. "I am fifty now"—actually, he was fifty-three—"and remember I was eighteen the day we entered the Capes of the Delaware on our return passage. I thought you then about seven and twenty, which will make you about sixty-four now" (*LJ* 4:374).

38. Sawyer, "A Year of Cooper's Youth," 499; on the length of the *Stirling*'s return passage from St. Petersburg, see New York *Evening Post*, 9/13/1806.

39. Ship *Stirling*, registration, Port of New York, 10/15/1806, copy in JFB paps., box 9; *Longworth's American Almanac, New-York Register, and City Directory* (New York: David Longworth, 1805); New York *Evening Post*, 10/16/1806. For Barker, in addition to *Incidents in the Life of Jacob Barker*, see *DAB;* it is worth noting here that no surviving document confirms Barker's alleged role in securing Cooper his berth on the ship. On joint ownership of ships, see Benjamin R. Labaree et al., *America and the Sea: A Maritime History* (Mystic: Mystic Seaport, 1998), 172.

40. *Stirling* crew list, 10/15/1806, copy in JFB paps., box 9.

41. Ned's mendacity is suggested by the fact that he had learned of this naval encounter from "sea-going lads" of his acquaintance while in Canada.

42. *DNB* (s.v. "Kent and Strathern, Edward Augustus, Duke of"), and McKenzie Porter, *Overture to Victoria* (Toronto: Longmans Green, 1961), 75, 94. Ned claimed to have clear memories of the prince from his time in Halifax, and a number of his details were indeed accurate, suggesting that he had at least seen and perhaps met Edward. But Ned was fond of embellishing his story. According to Cooper's grand nephew, G. Pomeroy Keese, the novelist "had good reason for believing, and frequently so stated in pri-

vate," presumably on Ned's authority, "that the Duke occupied a still closer relation, and that Ned was, in fact, his natural son." Keese, "Memories of Distinguished Authors: James Fenimore Cooper," *Harper's Weekly*, supplement, 7/29/1871, 708n. Edward lived at Halifax with his morganatic wife, Julie de St. Laurent (about whom Ned knew something), but his illegitimate children with her seem otherwise accounted for; see Porter, 25–33, 53–54, 64–66. On balance, there seems to be little chance that Ned Myers was anything more than the son of a lesser officer in the Seventh Royal Fusiliers, the duke's regiment; indeed, it remains possible that his tales about the duke of Kent were entirely fabricated.

43. Although the duke of Kent had an official apartment in Kensington Palace, he more typically stayed with Julie de St. Laurent at their suburban dwelling, Castle Hill Lodge, in Ealing; see Porter, *Overture to Victoria*, 116.

44. Alexander Johnston the younger stated that the ship was named the *Driver*, but in fact that was the name of the vessel that had captured the American vessel and brought it into Halifax. See Sawyer, "A Year of Cooper's Youth," 498; *NM* 13.

45. George Clarke, "hair-dresser," is listed at 120 Fly-Market in *Longworth's American Almanac* (New York: David Longworth, 1806).

46. Jacob Heiser, with no occupation, is listed at 444 Pearl Street in *Longworth's American Almanac* for 1805 and 1806.

47. Robertson, *Life of Miranda*, 1:293–307.

48. The ship's papers show John T. Irish as a native and resident of the state of New York, not Nantucket, aged twenty-two, height 5 ft. 7¼ in; see *Stirling* crew list. A Thomas Irish, "mariner," is listed in *Longworth's American Almanac* for both 1805 and 1806.

49. The ship's arrival is recorded in the two New York papers, the *Evening Post* and the *Mercantile Advertiser*, 9/13/1806.

50. Beard (*LJ* 1:5) gives October 15 or 16 as the date of sailing; for confirmation, see the New York *Evening Post*, 10/16/1806; Alan Taylor, "Cooper Goes to Sea," 45, 49, 52n6, gives an approximate date of September 1, basing his conclusion on Edith Sawyer's article. But both Sawyer and her main source, Alexander Johnston, made several errors in chronology. For instance, Johnston stated that the *Stirling* arrived at London "about October 20" and stayed there "seven weeks discharging, and taking freight for Cartagena," but immediately afterward he had the ship leaving for that Spanish port "[a]bout November 12," which of course would be only slightly more than *three* weeks after its reported arrival date (Sawyer, "A Year of Cooper's Youth," 500). *Ned Myers*, to the contrary, states that the ship sailed for Spain in January 1807 (*NM* 26).

51. *Stirling* crew list. In a report made 7/20/1807, to William Lyman, U.S. consul in London, John Johnston named John Wood as one of three men who had deserted in London sometime the previous December. Johnston wrongly added that Wood was named in the crew list. Wood must, however, have been on board for the original cross-

ing. It therefore seems plausible to identify him as the wrecked English whaleman, who according to *Ned Myers* (*NM* 26) did desert in London. William Lyman statement, misdated 7/20/1808 (for 1807), copy in JFB paps., box 9, AAS.

52. Noah Webster, *An American Dictionary of the English Language* (New York: S. Converse, 1828), s.v. "ordinary." *Ned Myers* states "Cooper . . . was never called by any other appellation [but Cooper] in the ship" (*NM* 23); but this point may have been inserted under the influence of Captain Johnston's letter to Cooper of 4/5/1843: "On Ship board we call Sailors by one name, and you was allways [*sic*] called Cooper, and I little thought when reading extracts from your writings from News Papers, that you had sailed with me" (*LJ* 4:375).

53. Bow-lines were ropes used to hold sails taut when close-hauled against the wind. A close-hauled ship would make relatively slow progress because in square-rigged vessels like the *Stirling*, only modest headway could be made on winds from forward of abeam.

54. The unsettled political situation throughout Europe, and perhaps the resulting volatility of prices, undoubtedly made such a strategy prudent. Moreover, England and France had been swapping ultimatums regarding merchant ships from neutral countries, many of which each combatant seized, and it behooved Johnston to navigate carefully through these dangerous political waters. On such difficulties for American ships at the time, see Labaree et al., *America and the Sea*, 195–96.

55. *Ned Myers* makes it clear that the *Stirling* "passed the Isle of Wight several times" (*NM* 37) during its longish farewell from the British Isles: hence Cooper's point about having "sailed all round it," though I find no indication that he sailed through the Solent until 1826—indeed, his description of the south Dorset coast in his French travel book suggests that it was entirely new to his eye (see *GF* CE 14–15). Perhaps when the *Stirling* returned from Falmouth to London in the summer of 1807 it passed through the Solent (see *NM* 31–33). When Cooper visited Cowes with his family in 1826, he remembered that "the ship I was in [in 1806], anchored off this very island, though not at this precise spot" (*GF* CE 18). *Ned Myers* placed the ship's anchorage along the northeast coast at St. Helens Roads.

56. *Stirling* crew list.

57. John Beresford (1766–1844) was made a baronet and an admiral in 1814. See *DNB*.

58. The two fleets may have been one and the same. *Ned Myers* (*NM* 25–26) speaks of the smaller one in the Downs; in his English travel book, Cooper recalled two separate fleets, including the larger one off Dungeness (see *GE* 6).

59. Cooper's naval history gives the number of larger ships (aside from gunboats and ketches) in the navy as of 1805 as a dozen (*HN* 2:83).

60. See *Otsego Herald*, 8/17/1797, 8/24/1797, 9/7/1797.

61. Cooper gave an account of this part of his experience in a retrospect inserted in *Gleanings in Europe: England* (see *GE* CE 189–98; this narrative, interspersed with

Cooper's recollections of a visit to many of the same spots early in 1828 with an unnamed English poet, results in a complex crosscutting technique).

62. On Stimpson Cooper would model not only Stephen Stimson in *The Sea-Lions*, but more pertinently the "uneducated Kennebunk man" (*A&A* CE pt. 1:129), Moses Marble, in *Afloat and Ashore*, who similarly tours the city with Wallingford. While on his London excursions, Cooper apparently visited some substantial collection or collections of paintings; in 1823, before his return to Europe with his family, he bragged that, while "no judge of paintings," he had "seen hundreds of celebrated ones both here and in Europe" (*LJ* 1:95–96; attributed to Cooper by Beard). But we have scant idea of which paintings he saw or where he saw them.

63. William Lyman, statement, 7/20/1807.

64. Hence, perhaps, Ben Pump's boastful comment in *The Pioneers*: "now, in running down the coast of Spain and Portingal, you may see a nunnery stuck out on every head-land, with more steeples and outriggers, such as dog-vanes and weather-cocks, than you'll find aboard of a three-masted schooner" (*PIO* 1:143).

65. Sawyer, "A Year of Cooper's Youth," 500, placed the encounter with the felucca "off Cape Finisterre, on the northwest coast of Spain," but *Ned Myers* clearly states that it took place while the *Stirling* was "running down the coast of Portugal" (*NM* 26) and furthermore indicates that it happened only shortly before the ship passed through the Straits of Gibraltar (*NM* 28).

66. To sail "wing and wing" is to angle two sails of a vessel out in opposite directions so as to catch maximum effect from a stern wind. Cooper had sailed a felucca in Italian waters himself in the 1830s, as we shall see in volume 2, and had published his novel *The Wing-and-Wing* just the year before his reunion with Ned Myers.

67. Alexander Johnston the younger asserted that the *Stirling* also stopped at Malaga and Gibraltar "some days," adding, "The boys saw all these places and visited each neighborhood pretty thoroughly, much to the gratification of Cooper, as well as to his friends at home, as afterward learned through Mr. Barker" (Sawyer, "A Year of Cooper's Youth," 501). The assertion concerning Jacob Barker suggests that Cooper had contact with Barker, or with mutual acquaintances, after the voyage. It also suggests that Barker later communicated to the Johnstons something of Cooper's tales to his "friends at home"—and, presumably, about Barker's own involvement in placing Cooper in the *Stirling* in the first place.

68. Alexander Johnston the younger, citing no source, stated that the ship left Spain "[s]ometime near the first of March." He also asserted that it "had a long, tedious beat of it down to Gibraltar, the wind for many weeks being from the west" (Sawyer, "A Year of Cooper's Youth," 501).

69. Alexander Johnston the younger asserted that this leaky vessel was the same frigate that had chased off the felucca on the *Stirling*'s voyage down the coast of Portugal. It is possible that Captain Johnston passed on this piece of information (he is por-

trayed as identifying a "tarred-rope stain in her starboard main to[p] gallant-stu'n sail"), but in support of the assertion Johnston's nephew "quoted" from a conversation between the captain and first mate John Irish as if it derived from *Ned Myers;* it did not. See Sawyer, "A Year of Cooper's Youth," 501.

70. A cargo manifest filled out "at sea" on 8/20/1807, indicates that the ship carried industrial products such as sheet copper, copper nails, and sixty tons of iron, as well as smaller boxes of miscellaneous goods. A press report of the ship's arrival in Philadelphia indicates that its freight consisted mostly of dry goods intended for the major consignee, the merchant house of J. Warder and Sons. Jacob Barker was nowhere listed among the consignees. "Ship Sterling's Manifest," copy in JFB paps., box 9, AAS; Philadelphia *Political and Commercial Register,* 9/19/1807. In *Afloat and Ashore,* Cooper had his hero sail home in an American ship that first "went to Spain, for a cargo of barilla, which she took up to London, where she got a freight for Philadelphia" (*A&A* CE pt. 2:346).

71. Combining the two periods of the ship's presence in London, Alexander Johnston the younger wrote that Cooper "had in all fourteen weeks' tarry in London, with as frequent liberty as he desired, rambling as he wished, [and] . . . provided with all needful means, by order of Mr. Barker" (Sawyer, "A Year of Cooper's Youth," 502). The total time is probably not far off. The interesting assertion regarding Barker's instructions to Captain Johnston about Cooper's access to "all needful means" presumably rested on the family archive or on Barker's oral reports to the Johnstons.

72. In writing "Peter Simpson," Cooper in fact made a double mistake; he was not referring to the cook, Peter Skimpson, but rather to Stephen Stimpson, as is made clear by his adding that the man in question "was shipped in London" (*LJ* 4:375).

73. Taylor, "Cooper Goes to Sea," 49. Alexander Johnston the younger asserted that Captain Johnston was seized upon for "talking pretty broad Scotch" (Sawyer, "A Year of Cooper's Youth," 500); presumably the captain's nephew detected some such accent in his uncle's speech, traceable to the example of John Johnston, Sr., a native of Scotland. Yet another instance of naval injustice accompanied the ship's departure. A young Englishman, the son of the Thames pilot Johnston used on each passage of that river, had been impressed from his father's coastal vessel into the South America–bound squadron of Cmdre. Home Riggs Popham, probably the year before. Having escaped, he dreaded the omnipresent press-gangs and was secretly brought on board one night as the *Stirling* lay in the Thames so he could go off to the United States. Perhaps he came out along with his father, who apparently again guided the *Stirling* down to the estuary (*NM* 35).

74. Sawyer, "A Year of Cooper's Youth," 502. The Philadelphia *Political and Commercial Register* for 9/16/1807 reported the arrival of the *Lovely Lass* in fifty-four days from Lisbon. The captain of this vessel reported that he had spoken the New York vessel *Mary Ann,* bound for Antwerp, on August 27; the latter already had been out sixty-

seven days, surely a sign of uncooperative weather. Moreover, the captain of the *Lovely Lass* feared that the other vessel had "suffered in the gale (2 days after) which did considerable damage to the Lovely Lass [*sic*] by carrying away her boats, bulwarks, her main stays and several of her sails." That gale, which occurred on August 29, may well have been the one that took the life of Cooper's shipmate.

75. Philadelphia *Political and Commercial Register*, 9/19/1807; Philadelphia *Aurora*, 9/19/1807.

76. Ibid.; copies of Newcastle and Philadelphia customs documents in JFB paps., box 9, AAS.

77. Cooper drew the comparison in his 1840s sketch of Cmdre. William Bainbridge, who made his first voyage from Philadelphia in the early 1790s. But the observation was Cooper's, not Bainbridge's; and, while Cooper offered it as a commonplace of the early nineteenth century, it was his own long Thames trips and the *Stirling*'s slow passage up the Delaware in 1807 that first drove it vividly home for him. See *LDANO* 1:10–11.

78. [Médéric-Louis-Elie Moreau de Saint-Méry], *Moreau de St. Méry's American Journey*, trans. Kenneth and Ann M. Roberts (Garden City: Doubleday, 1947), 89; Philadelphia *Political and Commercial Register*, 10/20/1807.

79. See Wharton J. Lane, *From Indian Trail to Iron Horse: Travel and Transportation in New Jersey, 1630–1860* (Princeton: Princeton University Press, 1939), 36, 51, 122. An amusingly Chaucerian passage along this road is recounted in Philip Freneau's *A Journey from Philadelphia to New-York* (Philadelphia: Francis Bailey, 1787). The term "Feather-bed Lane" seems to have become a generalized Jersey quip for any bad road even in 1807; for a nearly contemporary application of it to a stretch of the Trenton-to-Elizabeth Road, see the area called "Devil's Feather Bed" on map 8 of S. S. Moore and T. W. Jones, *The Traveller's Directory; or, a Pocket Companion, Shewing the Course of the Main Road from Philadelphia to New-York* (Philadelphia: M. Carey, 1804).

80. See John T. Cunningham, *New Jersey: America's Main Road* (Garden City: Doubleday, 1966), 71. A few years after Cooper's return, a later edition of *Longworth's American Almanac, New-York Register, and City Directory* (New York: David Longworth, 1811) listed two separate packet boat lines between South Amboy and Exchange Slip, right next to Whitehall (50). But in 1800, crowded Whitehall Slip was described as "the natural point of Communication with Staten Island, Elizabeth Town, and many other parts of New Jersey, and . . . the only Landing place for the Ferry Boats from those places." See I. N. Phelps Stokes, *The Iconography of Manhattan Island, 1498–1909*, 6 vols. (New York: Robert H. Dodd, 1915–1928), 5:1380.

CHAPTER 4. MIDSHIPMAN JAMES COOPER

1. The original warrant is reproduced in Robert E. Spiller, *Fenimore Cooper, Critic of His Times* (New York: Minton, Blach, 1931), facing p. 52. Although Cooper's recent

voyage made him a very likely candidate for a naval appointment, in fact he was not the first Cooper to receive one. Early in 1801, Judge Cooper, still in Congress, had sought and been given a midshipman's warrant for his next-oldest son, Samuel, not yet fourteen. Permitted to "pursue his studies" until called up to active duty, Samuel was summarily discharged later that year when Congress mandated reductions in naval ships and manpower, and he never repetitioned for his warrant. See NARA, Record Group 24, microfilm M330, roll 1.

2. Philip Van Cortlandt to WC, 1/15/1808, WC paps., box 24, HCA.

3. Williams's office is listed at 140 Water Street in *Longworth's American Almanac, New-York Register, and City Directory* (New York: David Longworth, 1808).

4. Curtis P. Nettels, *The Emergence of a National Economy, 1775–1815* (New York: Holt, Rinehart, 1962), 327–28, reports that American exports fell in value from more than $100 million to less than $25 million from 1807 to 1808. Ned Myers told a different story about the effects of the embargo on the *Stirling* (*NM* 38–42); my information comes instead from the New York *Commercial Advertiser*, 7/6/1809 and 8/9/1809 (for later information on the vessel, see also 3/8/1810 and 5/26/1810).

5. *Otsego Herald*, 10/22/1808.

6. If, as suggested in a note to Chapter 3, Cooper had been sent to New York City that spring by his father to sample the law at Richard Harison's office, but had instead spent his time along the wharves, then this British activity took place quite literally under his nose.

7. New York *Daily Advertiser*, 4/26/1806, 4/27/1806; *Otsego Herald*, 5/8/1806, 5/22/1806. Washington Irving, *History, Tales and Sketches*, ed. James W. Tuttleton (New York: Library of America, 1983), 517–24. William Sampson, *The Memoirs of William Sampson* (1807; Leesburg: Samuel B. T. Caldwell, 1817), 334. Cooper, too, long remembered the episode. As a middle-aged naval historian, he lay the blame for the blunder at Jefferson's feet: "By neglecting to place the republic in an attitude to command respect, the government had unavoidably been reduced to appeal to arguments and principles, in those cases in which an appeal to force is the only preservative of national rights" (*HN* 2:94).

8. Irving, *History, Tales and Sketches*, 235; see also the same issue's "Plans for Defending Our Harbour" (238–44), which refers to contemporary concern over New York City's vulnerability to naval attack.

9. So claimed Edith A. Sawyer, "A Year of Cooper's Youth," *New England Magazine*, n.s. 37(1907): 500.

10. See *HN* 2:113–14.

11. Cooper knew this coastal sea well from sailing the whaleship *Union* in the vicinity just when he first began his literary career, as we shall see in Chapter 7.

12. That Cooper was aware of what he was doing in inventing history is suggested by the opening of his Preface to the first two volumes of *Afloat and Ashore:* "The writer

has published so much truth which the world has insisted was fiction, and so much fiction which has been received as truth, that, in the present instance, he is resolved to say nothing on the subject" (*A&A* CE pt. 1:1).

13. Robert Smith to [JC], 2/24/1808 ("Upon receipt hereof you will report to the Commanding Naval Officer at New [York?]"); copy in JFB paps., box 9, AAS. In his naval history, Cooper would give considerable prominence to Rodgers and his subordinate at the navy yard in 1808, Capt. Isaac Chauncey of Connecticut, because both men came to play important roles during the War of 1812 (Rodgers, the ranking active officer then, led the fight against British merchant shipping; Chauncey was in command on Lake Ontario). But he would give scant attention to their service together at Wallabout Bay.

14. Robert Smith to Samuel L. Mitchill, 11/18/1807, Naval Affairs Report 64 (10th Cong., 1st Sess.), *American State Papers*, 23:168. For all the importance the American government assigned to gunboats at the time, they were a recent enthusiasm in many navies. They were much employed in the European wars then; in fact, Napoleon was gathering a huge fleet of similar vessels for his planned invasion of England in 1804–1805.

15. Howard I. Chapelle, *The History of the American Sailing Navy: The Ships and Their Development* (New York: W. W. Norton, 1949), 219–23.

16. On the new group of gunboats, see ibid., 225.

17. Capt. Isaac Chauncey to JC, 3/21/1808 ("You will immediately—report yourself to the commanding officer of the US Bomb-Ketch Vesuvius"); copy in JFB paps., box 9, AAS. Cooper may have been stationed on the *Vesuvius* from the beginning of his time in New York; in any case, the vessels' accounts show his pay beginning on the receipt of his oath (February 24) and ending on July 4. On the latter date, Cooper took an advance of $78.82 against the pay due him (at $19.00 per month, plus a credit of $26.40 for undrawn rations and minus an eighty-eight cent hospital payment, the total due was $108.42), so when he finally settled on July 9, he received the balance of just less than $30.00. JC, account with the *Vesuvius*, July 1808, copy in JFB paps., box 9, AAS.

18. On the guns carried by the *Vesuvius* and its counterpart, the *Etna*, and on the cruise of the *Vesuvius* to New Orleans, see Chapelle, *Sailing Navy*, 209–10; and Robert Smith to House of Representatives, January 3, 1807, Naval Affairs Report 59 (9th Cong., 2nd Sess.), *American State Papers*, 23:162. On Cooper's assignment to the *Vesuvius*, see Louis H. Bolander, "The Naval Career of James Fenimore Cooper," U.S. Naval Institute *Proceedings* 66(1940): 544–45.

19. Bolander, "Naval Career," 545. Early that same month, Cooper's accounts with the *Vesuvius* were settled.

20. The Champlain project was to be supervised by Woolsey's subordinate, Lieut. John M. Haswell.

21. The changes in the Oswego landscape from the late colonial era up to the time of Cooper's arrival were relatively minor. Even so, in *The Pathfinder* Cooper would

imaginatively alter the 1750s scene of the book's action. For instance, he sited the single English fort on the west shore of the river, whereas there were English forts on both sides when Montcalm attacked in 1756, both of which he destroyed. When the English returned in 1758, they likewise built new forts on each side, although they emphasized especially the eastern structure, named Fort Ontario. Cooper, aware that the latter structure (in ruins in 1808) dated from this period, apparently believed that before the English reoccupation of the area the only fort was on the west side. See J. H. French, *A Gazetteer of the State of New York* (Syracuse: R. P. Smith, 1860), 519. It is likely that his misconception on this issue had a specific source: "The South View of Oswego on Lake Ontario," an engraving first published in William Smith's *The History of the Province of New-York* (1757), in which one sees the old west fort and several small structures near it, a pair of other buildings over the way, the gravelly points with their curved coves, but no fortification on the eastern heights. For Cooper's general sense of the antiquity of Oswego, see *LJ* 4:259; *PF* CE 1–2.

22. Christian Schulz, *Travels on an Inland Voyage through the States of New-York, Pennsylvania, Virginia, Ohio, Kentucky and Tennessee* (New York: Isaac Riley, 1810), 1:38–39.

23. Cooper was to transform this "Hippocrates" from the Oswego frontier into Dr. Todd in *The Pioneers;* see *PIO* HE, 67n, signed "S.F.C."

24. Alexander Wilson, *The Foresters: A Poem, Descriptive of a Pedestrian Journey to the Falls of Niagara, in the Autumn of 1804* (Newtown: S. Siegfried and J. Wilson, 1818), 66, 68–69. Wilson indicated that Fort Oswego "was finally abandoned on the 28th of October, 1804, about a week before our visit there" (101n47). I have found no direct evidence that Cooper knew this poem, although he did use one Wilson poem ("Epistle to Mr. A— C—") as the source for the epigraph at the head of Chapter 3 of *The Spy.*

25. John Rodgers to JC (noted as "present" at the Brooklyn navy yard), 5/21/1808 (grants leave of twenty days from the present date "to go to Coopers-town" and requires him to report back to the navy yard at the end of the furlough); M. T. Woolsey to JC ("present"), 7/28/1808 ("You will proceed to Cooperstown and there wait further orders"), 8/15/1808, 8/17/1808; copies in JFB paps., box 9, AAS. It is possible that Cooper's father was ill, as he dictated his will on May 13, 1808, but in the second instance, Woolsey may have ordered Cooper to Lake Otsego on some errand related to his own venture. Cooper's father and one or perhaps two of his older brothers had owned land on the west bank of the river at the village of Oswego since 1805, and hence might provide useful guidance on that area; see Lida S. Penfield, "Three Generations of Coopers in Oswego," Oswego Historical Society *Fifth Publication* (1941): 1.

26. The tavern Woolsey hired has been identified as a two-story frame house built around 1798 by Peter Sharpe on the southeast corner of West Schuyler and Water streets in Oswego; Anthony Slosek, *Oswego: Its People and Events* (Interlaken: Heart of the Lakes, 1985), 79–81.

27. On Gardner, see *LJ* 1:96–97n. In the 1820s, as editor of the *Literary and Scientific Repository, and Critical Review* and the New York *Patriot,* Gardner drew on his old friend's budding talents.

28. See Benjamin R. Labaree et al., *America and the Sea: A Maritime History* (Mystic: Mystic Seaport, 1998), 211.

29. Woolsey's father, Melancthon Lloyd Woolsey, had served as Gen. George Clinton's aide during the Revolution and later as a major general in the New York State militia. He moved to Plattsburgh in 1787, when his son was seven; see Leon N. Brown, "Commodore Melancthon Taylor Woolsey: Lake Ontario hero of the War of 1812," Oswego County Historical Society *Fifth Publication* (1941): 141–53.

30. Anthony Slosek, "Oswego 1796–1828: Fragments of Local History," Oswego County Historical Society *Twenty-third Publication* (1960): 4. The *Oneida* was eight feet deep in the hold, the *Stirling* almost twelve and a half. Otherwise, the *Stirling* was fourteen feet longer and two-and-a-half feet broader in the beam; its capacity was 274 and 63/95 tons (*Stirling* registration of 1806, copy in JFB paps., box 9, AAS). The *Oneida,* having played an active role under Woolsey's command in the War of 1812 was sold in 1815 but later repurchased by the navy. Its final disposition is unknown. See Chapelle, *Sailing Navy,* 229–30.

31. M. T. Woolsey to Robert Smith, 1/29/1809, 2/26/1809, 3/19/1809, 3/26/1809, 4/2/1809, 4/8/1809, 5/1/1809; copies in JFB paps., box 9, AAS.

32. Cooper's letter of 12/19/1808 to his brother Richard at Otsego, which was postmarked at Rome on Christmas, ran, in part: "I shall be along your way shortly accompanied by two gentlemen, one of the navy the other of the army—both fine young men" (*LJ* 1:12). Also documenting this visit to Cooperstown is a receipt for a beaver hat Cooper purchased more than a month later (Ralph Worthington receipt, 1/28/1809, JFC paps., box 4, AAS). Cooper attributed the withholding of the *Oneida* from actual service to "Erskine's arrangement," the agreement struck in 1809 between the Madison administration and the British minister, David Erskine, moderating the commercial standoff between the countries and resulting in a temporary easing of tensions (MTW 17). On this issue, see Robert Malcomson, *Lords of the Lake: The Naval War on Lake Ontario, 1812–1814* (Annapolis: Naval Institute, 1998), 18.

33. M. T. Woolsey to Paul Hamilton, 4/8/1809; copy in JFB paps., box 9, AAS.

34. M. T. Woolsey to Paul Hamilton, 4/8/1809, 5/1/1809, 5/7/1809, 6/10/1809; Collector Adams to JC, 6/23/1809; M. T. Woolsey to JC, 7/18/1809; copies in JFB paps., box 9, AAS.

35. The federal government had established a port of entry on the Genesee in 1805 and stationed a collector of customs near where the *Oneida*'s launch was tethered in 1809, but Nathaniel Rochester and his partners did not arrive in the vicinity until 1812, and their settlement did not flourish until after the war; see John W. Barber and Henry Howe, *Historical Collections of the State of New York* (New York: S. Tuttle, 1842): 266–69.

36. The episode of the gale in *The Pathfinder* runs from Chapter 16 to Chapter 18.

37. On the relative antiquity of the Niagara frontier, see also *HN* 2:324. Cooper glanced back at this experience (and his time at Oswego under Woolsey) in the final chapter of his fourth novel; see *PIL* CE 420–23.

38. Susan Fenimore Cooper in describing the 1809 Niagara visit wrote that Cooper "felt the sublime character far more deeply at a later day" (*P&P* 309).

39. M. T. Woolsey to JC, 7/18/1809, 7/22/1809, 8/23/1809; copies in JFB paps., box 9, AAS.

40. M. T. Woolsey to JC, 9/21/1809; see also M. T. Woolsey to Paul Hamilton, 8/23/1809; copies in JFB paps., box 9, AAS.

41. Cooper hardly was improvising: his recourse had become established practice among the officer corps in these years of a slender navy. William Bainbridge had taken time off for merchant cruises just before the enactment of the embargo, while John Shaw made the long voyage to Canton while on furlough some years earlier, as Cooper well knew (*LDANO* 1:56, 140). Indeed, in the summer of 1809 the secretary of the navy apparently issued orders to at least some ship commanders to send on furlough "all Officers . . . whose services could be dispensed with"—so, at any rate, one of the officers on Isaac Hull's ship, the *Chesapeake*, then in Boston, had been told by Hull late in August (Philander Jones to Paul Hamilton, 8/26/1809, NARA, Record Group 45, records of the Department of the Navy, office of the secretary of the navy, officers' letters, June–August 1809; copy in JFB paps., microfilm roll 45, AAS). Perhaps the most pertinent model for Cooper's furlough at this time was provided by the experience of his fellow midshipman at Oswego, Thomas Gamble. Gamble had twice taken furloughs for merchant cruises in earlier years, and when he left Oswego for New York in April of 1809, he soon requested another furlough for the same purpose. See NARA, Record Group 24, microfilm M330, roll 1.

42. The new purchases make it clear that Cooper must have visited Otsego on his way south. See Oakley and Randolph, statement, 1/8/1810, WC paps., box 11, HCA.

43. Indeed, the house where Cooper was born adjoined that of Lawrence's family, although the Coopers left Burlington so soon after his birth that Cooper did not know Lawrence until much later.

44. Alfred Hoyt Bill, *The Campaign of Princeton, 1776–1777* (Princeton: Princeton University Press, 1948), 36; Lorenzo Sabine, *Biographical Sketches of Loyalists of the American Revolution* (1864; Port Washington: Kennikat, 1966), 2:3–4.

45. The West Indies cruise, lasting from November 1800 to May 1801, in fact was the first voyage made by midshipman Melancthon Taylor Woolsey, just a year or so younger than Lawrence. Lawrence's commission as lieutenant was dated to April 6, 1802, but was not confirmed by the Senate until January 8, 1807; see NARA, Record Group 24, microfilm M330, roll 2. For Elizabeth Lawrence Kearney's poem on her much

younger half-brother, whose upbringing she had overseen, see Albert Gleaves, *James Lawrence: Captain, United States Navy* (New York: G. P. Putnam's Sons, 1904), 17.

46. Alexander Slidell Mackenzie, *Life of Stephen Decatur, A Commodore in the Navy of the United States* (1844; rpt. Boston: Little, Brown, 1864), 81. Cooper reported Decatur's praise for Lawrence: "there was 'no more dodge [to] him than to the main-mast'" (*HN* 2:253).

47. Gleaves, *James Lawrence*, 57. On Lawrence's service, see NARA, Record Group 24, microfilm M330, roll 2.

48. Gleaves, *James Lawrence*, 57–61.

49. Chapelle, *Sailing Navy*, 220; Gleaves, *James Lawrence*, 62, 64–69; NARA, Record Group 24, microfilm M330, roll 2.

50. *New York Public Advertiser*, 9/7/1807, 9/10/1807.

51. *New York Public Advertiser*, 9/10/1807.

52. The navy yard duel was reported in the *Otsego Herald*, 9/10/1807. Its origin lay in a typically trivial affront involving one midshipman's refusal to take off his hat when entering the mess one day; see Charles Oscar Paullin, *Commodore John Rodgers: Captain, Commodore, and Senior Officer of the American Navy, 1773–1838: A Biography* (Cleveland: Arthur H. Clark, 1910), 203.

53. *New York Public Advertiser*, 9/10/1807; Charles Lee Lewis, *The Romantic Decatur* (Philadelphia: University of Pennsylvania Press, 1937), 192–200. Decatur was shot by James Barron, who, ever since his conviction for his role in the *Chesapeake* incident, blamed Decatur (a member of the court martial) for malicious interference in his career.

54. Lewis, *Romantic Decatur*, 197–98. Cooper described Somers in his biographical sketch as "mild, amiable, and affectionate, both in disposition and deportment, though of singularly chivalrous notions of duty and honor" (*LDANO* 1:119). Many of those involved in the rash of duels recognized the absurdity of the situation. In 1807, the year Lawrence attacked the *Public Advertiser* office, he joined Oliver Hazard Perry and others to propose that disputes among naval officers in New York be referred to a "Court of Honor" instead of being routinely settled via duels. But the proposal apparently was not enacted (Paullin, *Commodore John Rodgers*, 204).

55. *New York Public Advertiser*, 9/14/1807.

56. Gleaves, *James Lawrence*, 73. Even the battle that ended Lawrence's life in 1813, although it involved his ship and that of his British opponent, was carried out precisely like a personal duel between the two officers.

57. The *Wasp* carried sixteen thirty-two-pound carronades, plus two long twelves; see Chapelle, *Sailing Navy*, 212–16. NARA, Record Group 24, microfilm M330, roll 2. The ideal complement for the *Wasp* is derived from Robert Smith, "General View of the Navy and Marine Corps, with Estimates of the Expenses for Maintaining the Whole in

Service for One Year," December 11, 1870, Naval Affairs Report 66 (10th Cong., 1st Sess.), *American State Papers*, 23: 172–73. By way of comparison, the forty-four-gun frigate *Constitution* carried almost 450 men, excluding marines (ibid., 172).

58. NARA, Record Group 24, microfilm M330, roll 2. *DAB*, s.v. "Lawrence, James"; Gleaves, *James Lawrence*, 71; Chapelle, *Sailing Navy*, 188; Bolander, "Naval Career," 548; Records of the Department of the Navy, Bureau of Navigation: "Harbour Log. On Board the U.S. Ship Wasp, James Lawrence Esqr. Commander" (NARA, Record Group 24), copy in JFB paps., microfilm roll 45, AAS (hereafter, all details of events on the *Wasp* during Cooper's service, unless otherwise specified, derive from this logbook).

59. If Cooper visited the ship at its anchorage off the navy yard or even just looked out at it on the eighth, he would have seen the men removing the rigging and taking it onshore, where the sailmakers were starting to repair the sails. The vessel's shore work was performed at the navy yard. See "Harbour Log," 11/8–11/9/1809. For Cooper's letter, see *LJ* 1:16–17; dated Wednesday, November 8, it was not postmarked until Friday the tenth. It was accepted by the department in a reply dated September 13.

60. "Judge left home for Albany" (Isaac Cooper, 11/20/1809 entry in WC, Memorandum Book, 1793–1809, WC paps., HCA; the same manuscript documents William Cooper's four trips to DeKalb that year: 1/9–2/9; 3/1–3/11; 5/29–7/4; and 9/27–?). Gorham Worth, *Random Recollections of Albany, 1800–1808*, 3rd ed. (Albany: Joel Munsell, 1866), 114–15. Alan Taylor, *William Cooper's Town: Power and Persuasion on the Frontier of the Early American Republic* (New York: Knopf, 1995), 363–68; also, "Who Murdered William Cooper?," *NYH* 72(1991): 261–83.

61. Cooper's furlough: *Wasp* log, 12/7; Lawrence approved his ten-day leave in a document dated 12/8 (copy in JFB paps., box 9, AAS). It is possible that Cooper traveled on one of Robert Fulton's steamboats, the *North River* or the *Car of Neptune*, which had recently been placed in service, although the former had been turned back by ice downstream from Albany toward the end of November; I. N. Phelps Stokes, *The Iconography of Manhattan Island, 1498–1909*, 6 vols. (New York: Robert H. Dodd, 1915–1928), 5:1512.

62. Taylor, *William Cooper's Town*, 366.

63. Ibid., 363–71.

64. *Otsego Herald*, 12/30/1809. Cooper seems never to have learned much about the details of the funeral. Nowhere did he so much as describe it.

65. Under the will, for which Richard and Isaac Cooper were named coexecutors, Elizabeth Fenimore Cooper received a life interest in Otsego Hall and its grounds and furnishings, was given eight Otsego farms in lieu of dower right, and was guaranteed an annual cash income of $750. The bulk of Judge Cooper's wealth fell to the six children. Each was left a share worth an estimated $50,000, minus earlier advances for the four oldest ones. But there was no immediate disbursal of cash. The dollar amount of the be-

quests merely provided a means of equitably accounting for eventual distribution of the estate's real property, which was not to take place until January 1, 1815. WC, will, 5/13/1808, Registry of Wills, book B, 237, Otsego Co. Surrogate's Office. For Midshipman Cooper, the first result of his father's death was that he had a bit more cash in his pocket. He drew $100 from Richard and Isaac during what seems to have been a very quick run up to St. Lawrence County late in January, and a like amount from his brother William in New York a week earlier (see JC, receipt, 1/18/1810; and JC, receipt, 1/26/1810, both in JFC paps., box 4, AAS. The second of these receipts states unambiguously that Cooper "Rec'd [at] Coopers Village Jan 26th 1810" a sum of $100 from brothers Richard and Isaac, who, according to Thomas B. Benedict, note, 1/26/1810, WC business papers, box 11, indeed were in DeKalb on that date).

66. On a single day in March 1810, a total of twenty-eight men left the *Wasp* because "their time of service [was] expired," and smaller numbers were leaving all the time; *Wasp* log, 3/22/1810.

67. Clement Cleveland Sawtell, "The Case of William Bowman, Alias William Helby, Seaman," Essex Institute Historical *Collections,* 76(1940): 138–40; Donald R. Hickey, *The War of 1812: A Forgotten Conflict* (Urbana and Chicago: University of Illinois Press, 1989), 43–44. It is worth adding that similarly crude methods were used to man merchant vessels during the period.

68. Because no complete list of the men Cooper actually signed up has survived, it is hard to track his activities against the ship's log, which names the new recruits as they came on board. It also is difficult to check his version of the financial details against that which the navy reconstructed. The navy granted him $70 in premiums for enlisting thirty-five men, also crediting this amount against the initial advance. To a considerable extent, Cooper's contentiousness in his later negotiations with the navy sprang from the intervening collapse of the family estate and his own financial difficulties. That he first was apprised of the problem when approached in November 1821 by the U.S. attorney in New York, who apparently was about to file suit on behalf of the treasury to settle the account and recover the amount due the navy, probably added to his alarmed defensiveness. In 1821, the navy figured Cooper owed it $190.70, considerably less than the actual difference between his advance and his expenses largely because, in addition to the premiums, navy accountants had credited him with an additional $111.15. This figure represented the half-pay due to Cooper for the period from May of 1810 to May of 1811, when he remained on furlough but was liable to be called back to active duty. But for Cooper in 1821, even the sum of $190.70 was a large amount of cash; under siege as he felt himself from a number of quarters just then, he furthermore would not relish the implication that he had somehow cheated the government (see *LJ* 1:71, 73).

69. Unknown hand (for John Arnod), bill, 3/24/1810; Joseph Brotherton, receipt, 4/20/1810; JC, receipt (signed with John Arnod's mark), 4/19/1810, all in JFC paps., box 4, AAS; see also *Wasp* log, 4/19/1810; *Wasp* payroll, 7/20/1807.

70. Cooper first wrote that the money Armour gambled away was "three months pay and bounty of an able seaman" (*LJ* 1:72); he later corrected himself, writing that it was collected "from the security of a man who did not appear" (*LJ* 1:89). Note that, according to the ship's log, Armour was "arrested for neglect of duty and disobedience of orders" in Boston on April 3, and finally was dismissed from the navy in November 1812; see Thomas H. S. Hamersly, ed., *General Register of the United States Navy and Marine Corps . . . 1782–1882* (Washington: Hamersly, 1882), 32.

71. A letter of 1/20/1810 from Lawrence to the navy department mentioned Cooper as already performing the duty; Bolander, "Naval Career," 547–48. The purser's payroll book indicates that Cooper began recruiting on 1/19/1810 and kept at it until May; *Wasp* payroll (7/20/1810); *Wasp* log, 3/24, 4/13, 4/16–25/1810. A sidelight on this period is offered by *Ned Myers*. As the *Stirling* lay off the Battery on March 9, 1810, the day after its arrival from Liverpool with a cargo of salt (see New York *Commercial Advertiser*, 3/8/1810), Ned recalled that "a boat came alongside with a young man in her in naval uniform." It was Cooper, who had recognized his old ship's "mast-heads" as he rowed across the East River and came over to chat; this was the very day Cooper started his recruiting work ashore (*NM* 42; *Wasp* log, 3/9/1810).

72. Presumably Cooper stayed aboard from that point on, although contemporary records are curiously mute on his whereabouts. Because Cooper left no traces in New York City during this period, either, I assume that he went on the voyage.

73. During the *Wasp*'s movement through the outer harbor, Cooper no doubt picked up some details used in writing *Lionel Lincoln* in the 1820s. Although he hastily visited the city in January of 1824 while at work on the novel, at that time Cooper left the city then by land, not by sea, and he apparently had arrived there the same way (*LJ* 1:109–12; see Chapter 13). *Lionel Lincoln* betrays a sea-borne grasp of the area: in its opening, a British ship, the *Avon* of Bristol, approaches the "rocky entrance to the harbour" under failing early spring breezes, much as the *Wasp* had, and takes on a pilot "off the Graves," pretty much where Lawrence did (*LL* 1:3–5).

74. Susan Fenimore Cooper, "Rear-Admiral William Branford Shubrick," *Harper's New Monthly Magazine* 53(1876): 401–2. These details strengthen the conclusion that Cooper indeed made the Boston voyage. Shubrick could have told Cooper much about Lawrence and the ship but probably could not have passed on the enthusiastic tone audible in what Cooper later wrote about master and vessel. A final note on this issue is provided in Cooper's 1821 review of Thomas Clark's *Naval History*, in which Cooper wrote of Lawrence, "we have witnessed his coolness in danger" (*ECE* 13). While many situations allowed Cooper to assess Lawrence's character during the stay in New York, none of them involved real danger. Only on the voyage to Boston and back—skirting the shoals near Nantucket and Martha's Vineyard and then working into Boston harbor under adverse winds—could he have witnessed Lawrence's "coolness." .

75. Perhaps his description of the Town Dock and its old "swing bridge" in *Lionel*

Lincoln (see *LL* 1:21–22, 119) derived from what he had seen onshore while the *Wasp* was moored in the harbor. See Walter Muir Whitehill, *Boston: A Topographical History*, 2nd ed. (Cambridge: Harvard University Press, 1968), 73–74. Cooper returned briefly to Boston in August 1820 while selling the whale oil from the first voyage of his whaleship *Union;* see Chapter 8.

76. In *The Sea Lions* (1849) Cooper referred to the time he had entered Holmes' Hole (that is, Vineyard Haven) in his "youth" (*SL* 1:14). Probably that visit occurred during his ownership of the *Union*, perhaps in August 1820. It is unlikely in any event that the Wasp entered Vineyard Haven during its return to New York in April 1810.

77. I want to untangle a confusing reference in one of the letters Cooper wrote to the navy in the early 1820s, since it might be interpreted to suggest that he had *not* made the Boston voyage in 1810. The reference concerns that backdated "charity" receipt mentioned a few pages earlier in the text. Cooper attempted to clear himself of liability for the money involved by arguing that on the date named on the receipt the ship in fact was not in New York, where the document had been filled out, but rather "in New-London." I assume that the men in question had been recruited before Cooper's presence on the *Wasp*. Lawrence, on subsequently learning of the tough situation their families faced, sought to provide relief by means of retroactive bounty payments, technically not a proper procedure. He thus made out a backdated receipt, which he had Cooper sign not because Cooper had had anything to do with the case, but rather because Cooper was on the *Wasp* at the time the bounty funds were paid out and was then busy recruiting other men. I have found no evidence that the *Wasp* ever stopped in New London, though; Cooper may have heard that the ship had been there on the date in question, or the men whose families received the charity may have hailed from there—or perhaps he simply misremembered that detail in the 1820s. We do not know the actual date when the receipt was filled out or the false date entered on it. But one thing is clear. Cooper was *not* asserting that the vessel had stopped in New London during its Boston voyage. Had he done so, one might justifiably doubt whether he had been on the vessel then. See *LJ* 1:77, 89–90.

CHAPTER 5. LOVE AND WAR

1. The unlucky man was a skilled sailor named John Foster. Records of the Department of the Navy, Bureau of Navigation: "Harbour Log. On Board the U.S. Ship Wasp, James Lawrence Esqr. Commander." NARA, Record Group 24; copy in JFB paps., microfilm roll 45, AAS.

2. "Account with the Estate of William Cooper," n.d., JFC paps., box 4, AAS. See New York City receipts running from 7/21/1810 to 12/7/1810, JFC paps., box 4, and in JFB paps., box 9, AAS; two of these suggest Cooper's presence in Cooperstown in July and again in December.

3. On Ann L. Cary Cooper and her liaison with George Hyde Clarke, see *LJ* 1:

11–13, and Alan Taylor, *William Cooper's Town: Power and Persuasion on the Frontier of the Early American Republic* (New York: Knopf, 1995), 375–76, 393–94. For the troubles between William and his wife Eliza, see Richard Fenimore Cooper to Isaac Clason, 7/12/1810; Clason to Cooper, 7/21/1810, both in WC paps., box 27, HCA. William and Eliza Cooper eventually reconciled and, before his death in 1819, had two more children, one named for Eliza and the other for her father Isaac. Clason's death in 1815 threw them into a panic about their financial well-being and a second separation resulted. Out of concern for William's offspring, the novelist was to bring the oldest of them, William Yeardley Cooper, into his household when he took his own family to Europe in 1826. With Eliza and Isaac, Cooper also sought to carry on a relationship, although eventually they fell into obscurity and he lost touch with them. Scattered references to their mother suggest that Cooper had very little contact with her and may well have shared his older brothers' condescending attitude toward her. The last of the references does have a certain poignancy. In 1850, while walking in New York City with "a party of navy men," Cooper passed her near Trinity Church: "She either avoided me, or did not see me. I think the first," he wrote his wife. "She turned aside, and got into an omnibus. She looked pretty well; her dress was a rustyish black, but not very bad" (*LJ* 6:151).

4. "E. Cooper v. Remsen et al.," 8/3/1821, in William Johnson's summary of New York City chancery decisions, as reprinted in Robert Desty, ed., *Reports of Cases Adjudged and Determined in the Court of Chancery of the State of New York* (Rochester: Lawyers' Co-Operative, 1888–1889), 1:1141.

5. SFM 27.

6. In another late tale, *The Oak Openings* (1848), Cooper described the radical Protestant dispensation that had ruled before the present: "Little ceremony is generally used in an American marriage. In a vast many cases no clergyman is employed at all; and where there is, most of the sects have no ring, no giving away, nor any of those observances that were practised in the churches of old." (*OO* 2:93).

7. D. A. Story, *The deLanceys: Romance of a Great Family* (n.p.: Thomas Nelson and Sons, 1931), 37.

8. When the Coopers were living in Paris in the early 1830s, one of their neighbors informed the novelist that he had been acquainted with "*M. and Mme. De Lancé*" while staying in New York decades earlier and remembered the latter as "one of the most beautiful women he had ever seen" (SFM 41, 11).

9. Most of the DeLancey family papers do not survive. My account of the family's origins and its American history is based most generally on Story, *The deLanceys,* and Thomas Jones, *History of New York during the Revolutionary War, and of the Leading Events in the Other Colonies at that Period,* ed. Edward Floyd deLancey (New York: NYHS, 1879). Other sources on which I rely for the story of the DeLanceys' political fortunes in New York include Leopold Launitz-Schürer, Jr., *Loyal Whigs and Revolutionaries: The Making of the Revolution in New York, 1765–1776* (New York: New York

University Press, 1980); Patricia U. Bonomi, *A Factious People: Politics and Society in Colonial New York* (New York: Columbia University Press, 1971); and Dixon Ryan Fox, *Caleb Heathcote: Gentleman Colonist, The Story of a Career in the Province of New York, 1692–1721* (New York: Scribner's, 1926). I also have used Lorenzo Sabine, *Biographical Sketches of the Loyalists of the American Revolution, with an Historical Essay* (1864; rpt. Port Washington: Kennikat, 1966).

10. By the time of the Revolution, the DeLanceys may have considered themselves too good for the Jays; a rumor circulating in Susan's family reported that John Jay himself had been refused the hand of two of her kinswomen. See Daniel C. Littlefield, "Jay and Slavery," *NYH* 81 (2000):120.

11. Launitz-Schürer, 9. On the Van Cortlandts and their kin, the Van Rensselaers, see S. G. Nissenson, *The Patroon's Domain* (New York: Columbia University Press, 1937).

12. Launitz-Schürer, *Loyal Whigs*, 8; for an extensive analysis of DeLancey's career, see Bonomi, *A Factious People*, 140–78.

13. Launitz-Schürer, *Loyal Whigs*, 9–10.

14. Ibid., 48, 35.

15. Ibid., 93; for backgrounds, 63–68, 72–93. For the source of the term, see William A. Benton, *Whig-Loyalism: An Aspect of Political Ideology in the American Revolutionary Era* (Rutherford: Farleigh Dickinson University Press, 1969).

16. Jones, *History of New York*, 1:154; *DNB*, "DeLancey, James." On fleeing, DeLancey left behind an array of relations who actively fought in the coming struggle, including three of particular importance: (1) his uncle, Brig. Gen. Oliver DeLancey (1718–1785), the senior Loyalist officer in America, who soon raised three regiments of five hundred men each at his own expense for the defense of Long Island. He was a favorite object of Patriot scorn—and retribution, as when his mansion on upper Manhattan, Bloomingdale, was torched in 1777 while its occupants fled for safety to the wilds of what eventually was to become Central Park. Not surprisingly denounced under New York's Attainder Act two years later, Oliver DeLancey eventually suffered the confiscation of all his New York property, valued at £100,000. He left America in 1782 for the Yorkshire town of Beverley, near Hull, died there in 1785, and was buried in the central aisle of Beverley Minster (*DAB*, "DeLancey, Oliver"; *LJ* 5:274–75, 297). (2) James DeLancey's cousin, a second Oliver DeLancey (1749–1822), who in 1774, then a captain of dragoons, was ordered to New York to make arrangements for the eventual reception of his own corps and a unit of artillery, and who in 1776 served under General William Howe in the latter's New York campaign (*DNB*, "DeLancey, Oliver, the elder"). (3) Another James DeLancey (1746–1804), also a cousin, and a native of Westchester County, served as sheriff there (1769–1776). Once the war started, he became commander of a mounted Loyalist corps originally drawn from the old county militia and soon widely known and condemned (Cooper wrote in *The Spy*) as "De Lancey's men"—"the parti-

san corps," a later note to the novel added, "called *Cow-boys* in the parlance of the country." Connected more or less loosely with his uncle Oliver's battalions, James De-
Lancey's irregulars harried the countryside where they and their commander had grown
up, stealing cattle for the British occupation force in the city and skirmishing with their
Patriot counterparts, the "Skinners," who if anything seem to have been more ruthless
and less principled (Robert Bolton, *The History of the Several Towns, Manors, and Patents
of the County of Westchester* [New York: Chas. F. Roper, 1881], 1:xvi; *Spy* CE 236–37;
Spy 1:95; *LJ* 5:300).

17. Kenneth Silverman, *A Cultural History of the American Revolution* (New York:
Crowell, 1976), 326, 334–36; Sabine, *Loyalists*, 1:371; Mark M. Boatner III, *Encyclopedia
of the American Revolution* (Mechanicsburg: Stackpole, 1994), 721; Jones, *History of New
York*, 2:85.

18. Like other New York families, the Floyds found themselves torn apart by the po-
litical energies of the previous two decades. Elizabeth's father, Richard Floyd of Mastic,
Long Island, had been elected to the first Continental Congress in 1774 but was uncer-
tain enough of his feelings that he refused to serve and was replaced by a kinsman,
William Floyd. The latter eventually signed the Declaration of Independence; Richard
Floyd to the contrary signed the Loyalist Declaration of Dependence in the fall of 1776.
Floyd the Patriot served in the Continental Congress through the war and was elected to
the first Federal Congress. By contrast, his cousin fought on the British side under John
Peter DeLancey's uncle, Brig. Gen. Oliver DeLancey. In Elizabeth Floyd DeLancey's
memory, the legend of the Revolution as a family war thus assumed a dense reality. It is
hard to imagine that she did not share at least some of her family's tangled narrative with
Cooper. And she also had tales of her own to tell. While a guest at the Manhattan home
of Brigadier General DeLancey in 1777 she was one of three Loyalist women roughly
treated when the place was destroyed by a partisan band intent on retaliating for a recent
attack on the home of a Westchester Patriot. Cooper later told the story as he had heard
it from her (see *LJ* 5:310).

19. Cooper's grandson, in a letter no doubt based on stories he had heard from his
aunt Susan, added more details. "There is a tradition in the family," he explained to biographer Mary Phillips, "that [DeLancey] challenged his Col. for abusing the subalterns
of the regiment." The regimental officers disliked their commander so thoroughly that
they agreed to draw lots after his next insult of any of them. The man pulling the fated
number (as it turned out, John Peter) was sworn to challenge the colonel to a duel. When
DeLancey called him out, however, the colonel refused the challenge and instead reported him to the elite Royal Horse Guards. The novelist's grandson had been told that
"to challenge one[']s superior was then punishable by death." If that was so, DeLancey
hardly was cowed. He knew that his career was over, so he put his wife and infant son
and the baby's nurse Ann in a boat at Greenwich with the few belongings he could
quickly gather, then went back to London and caned the colonel *in front* of the Horse

Guards. His own horse and a mounted orderly from the regiment were waiting nearby, allowing him a fast escape down to Greenwich. There he gave his horse to the orderly, jumped in the boat, went out to a waiting vessel, and fled to America. No wonder that his great-grandson advised Mary Phillips in 1935, "I think it might be better not to mention John Peter[']s military record. It was splendid but *irregular* & might cause controversy." He understood, after all, that "the King *struck* [DeLancey's] name from the army rolls with his own hand," perhaps with dark thoughts about how the defiance of those blasted Americans hardly had ended in 1783. All that DeLancey had endured, all he had lost, for the British cause, was rendered meaningless in an impetuous instant. The novelist's grandson may have been right when, reflecting on this story, he wrote Phillips that John Peter "was a man after Cooper's own heart." He had, after all, obeyed an inner sense of justice rather than mere authority. SFM 40; JFC, DeLancey genealogy, in SFC, "Commonplace Book," Cooper family paps., collection of Dr. Henry Weil, Cooperstown (thanks to Hugh MacDougall for sharing his transcript of this interesting document). JFC II to Mary E. Phillips, 4/23, 4/28/1935, Phillips paps., Boston Public Library.

20. In 1792, the New York legislature voted to allow the repatriation of "even banished Tories, providing only that they recognized the state's title to confiscated property, including slaves"; Edwin G. Burrows and Mike Wallace, *Gotham: A History of New York City to 1898* (New York: Oxford University Press, 1999), 281. But John Peter DeLancey already had returned by then.

21. See Anne DeLancey Jones to John Peter DeLancey, 4/20/—, WC paps., box 24, HCA.

22. This silhouette is reproduced in Henry W. Boyton, *James Fenimore Cooper* (New York: Century, 1931), facing p. 34.

23. Hence the inaccuracy of James Russell Lowell's smart comment in *A Fable for Critics* (1848) about Cooper's women being "all sappy as maples and flat as a prairie"; George Dekker and John P. McWilliams, eds., *Fenimore Cooper: The Critical Heritage* (London and Boston: Routledge and Kegan Paul, 1973), 239.

24. Beard reproduces both ca. 1831 sketches (*LJ* 2: following page 246).

25. SFM 45, 50; Thomas DeLancey to JC, 6/30/1811, JFC paps., box 2, AAS. Of Susan's other brothers, Edward Floyd (1795–1820) also died young, and William Heathcote (1797–1865), absent for schooling during these early years, did not become close to the Coopers until much later. Of Susan's two younger sisters, Caroline Elizabeth (1801–1860) and Martha Arabella (1803–1860), the latter, only seven at the time of the wedding, became something of an eldest daughter for the Coopers and, during long visits with them, was a special favorite of Cooper. Neither she nor Caroline ever married. They stayed on at Heathcote Hill until after the deaths of both their parents, then moved to Philadelphia to live with their brother William and his family and eventually followed him to western New York. SFM 26, 45; W. H. W. Sabine, *Suppressed History of General Nathaniel Woodhull* (New York: Colburn & Tegg, 1954), 156; *DAB*, "DeLancey, William

Heathcote." Another sister, Maria Frances, born the year after Susan, had died in 1806; Story, *The deLanceys*, 37.

26. Reporting the likely inheritance to his brother Richard at the time of the engagement, Cooper rather crudely joked that he would not have to wait long for the inevitable succession: Susannah was seventy-two, Cooper estimated for Richard, adding, "so you see Squire, *the old woman* can't weather it long." He hastened to add in his next sentence, "I write all this for you—you know I am indifferent to any thing of this nature" (*LJ* 1:18). He may have been completely sincere in that last comment. Certainly he had quite amiable relations with Susannah, who was "very clever, and very good," according to Cooper's daughter (SFM 25), and also very talkative. Having survived the Revolution in lower New York, she could tell many tales to flesh out the background—perhaps the foreground—of *The Spy*. She probably also passed on stories about her most fascinating American kinsman, Sir William Johnson, whom Susannah (unlike the much younger John Peter) was old enough to have known personally (see *LJ* 2:150–51).

27. SFM 10, 19–20 (note that Susan Fenimore Cooper's chronology may have been a bit collapsed here); *RH* 155f; SDC to JC, 5/6/1813, copy in JFB paps., box 9, AAS.

28. Federal Population Census, 1810, Westchester County, NARA, Record Group 29, microfilm M252, roll 37, p. 220; 1820, Westchester County, microfilm M33, roll 75, p. 143; 1800, Westchester County, microfilm M32, roll 27, p. 121; SFM 24. On the ambiguities in this transitional period in New York City and its outlying region, see Shane White, *Somewhat More Independent: The End of Slavery in New York City, 1770–1810* (Athens: University of Georgia Press, 1991), 47–55. Cooper's 1832 explanatory note on the legal context of slavery in New York (*PIO* CE 57) shows his awareness of those ambiguities. The Otsego census for 1800 indicates that the Cooper family owned a single slave and also employed a free black, "Governor" Joseph Stewart, who is seen in the doorway of the pantry in the 1816 watercolor of Cooper's mother reproduced in Plate 3; Federal Population Census, 1800, Otsego County, NARA, Record Group 29, microfilm M32, roll 25, p. 19.

29. The important issue of slavery deserves extended treatment. Contrary to what one sometimes reads, Cooper himself never owned any slaves outright. The changes in New York law and in the civil status of blacks do, however, make the contemporary record on the topic difficult to read. Here is how I construe it. A receipt from May of 1811 which has been taken to indicate that "James Cooper paid $50 to buy from his brother Richard a seven-year-old 'mulatto Boy called Frederic'" (Taylor, *William Cooper's Town*, 379) actually covered the purchase of the "time and service" of that indentured worker (Richard Fenimore Cooper, receipt, 5/2/1811, WC paps., box 25, HCA). Frederic seems to have been one of the freed or indentured DeLancey blacks; his indenture had been purchased and he was taken to Cooperstown by Richard Fenimore Cooper, and in 1811 he returned with the Coopers to Westchester. While living with them, Fred was paid wages; eventually, around 1820 (before his indenture was up), he deserted them and

they made no attempt to find him and bring him back. There is confirmation of his civil status in the 1820 Westchester census entry for Cooper's family, where we find a black male aged between fourteen and twenty-six (Fred would have been about sixteen then) listed as a *free* worker among the three agricultural laborers indicated for the family's Westchester household; Federal Population Census, 1820, Westchester County, microfilm M33, roll 75, p. 191; SFM 20, 37. White, *Somewhat More Independent,* 51, Table 11, clearly demonstrates the shift from slave to free black workers in greater New York at this time, but he also cautions that the dichotomy of "free" and "slave" imposed by the federal census oversimplified the fluid and complex categories in which blacks then lived (47), a point worth keeping in mind in reading both contemporary records and later recollections. On the other hand, it should be added that when the novelist claimed in 1827 that no member of his family ever owned a single slave (see Robert E. Spiller, ed., "Fenimore Cooper's Defense of Slave-Owning America," *American Historical Review* 35 [1930]: 580), he was wrong. There were extenuations. As a young boy he hardly could have had accurate knowledge on a subject of such relative complexity, and by the time he was older the pattern was even more mixed. Some light is shed on the question of the larger family's practices and views by a request passed on by Otsego lawyer Robert Campbell to Cooper in 1819 from Isaac Cooper's widow, Mary Ann Morris Cooper: "Mrs. I. Cooper's *Lizzy* was permitted to go to Albany to find a purchaser—she went to New York without leave—If you can find a purchaser for her Mrs. Cooper would be glad to have you sell her for such a price as you can get—she could have been sold to advantage in Albany without her child (which is now near two years old & very infirm so that it cannot stand), but Mrs. Cooper would not agree to keep the child—but she is now on her hands & she will sell Lizzy for such price as can be got for her—She is a good waitress as you know & Mrs. I. Cooper says perfectly honest and trust[worth]y and can probably be sold for a pretty good price—but do what you can with her & we will send a bill of sale to the purchaser, she was a slave—& will continue such to 1827—when the general emancipation takes place." Robert Campbell to JC, 7/7/1819, JFC paps., box 2, AAS. For confirmation (though with Shane White's points in mind), see the Federal Population Census, 1810, Otsego County, NARA, Record Group 29, microfilm M252, roll 34, p. 205, which indicates that both Richard F. Cooper and his brother Isaac each had two slaves in their households, along with several free black workers—three in Richard's case, one in Isaac's. There is no indication that in 1819 Cooper took Mary Ann Cooper's task regarding Lizzy upon himself. More generally, it is clear that he viewed the present condition of African Americans even in the "free" states as profoundly affected by the institution of slavery. With a typical double-barbed intent, in 1827 he wrote, "A black face is just as much *prima facie* evidence that its possessor is vulgar and uneducated, in the U. S., as titles, stars, and ribbons in Europe are evidences that their possessors are gentlemen. [It] is however possible to be mistaken in both" (*American Historical Review* 35[1930]:580). Neither skin color nor social distinctions *produced* moral identity, in other words, although both were secondary markers of experiential differences.

30. At the end of the nineteenth century Theodore F. Wolfe reported that Closet Hall, much altered but still embowered in willows dating from Cooper's time, had later served as the home of another writer, Alice B. Havens. See *Literary Haunts and Homes: American Authors* (Philadelphia: Lippincott, 1899), 157–58.

31. Thomas James DeLancey to JC, 7/6/1811, JFC paps., box 2, AAS.

32. New Rochelle and New York City receipts, JFC paps., box 4, AAS; the Quaker furniture maker had written to his "Esteemed Friend" Thomas DeLancey on April 17 with a request: "please to inform thy Sister & her Husband that I should be very glad if [their goods] could be taken away this week"; William Burling to Thomas James DeLancey, 4/17/1811, JFC paps., box 4, AAS. Young DeLancey was left to make further arrangements for the New York items; see Thomas James DeLancey to JC, Mamaroneck, 5/9/1811, copy in JFB paps., box 9, AAS.

33. Susan Fenimore Cooper had heard that her mother's "first journey, when she was a bride, was made in a gig, my Father driving the horses tandem" (SFM 23). Called the Highland Road in Cooper's day, the King's Highway or Post Road ran close to the river as far as Peekskill, then cut up through the Highlands to Fishkill and Poughkeepsie. See Christopher Colles, *A Survey of the Roads of the United States of America 1789*, ed. Walter W. Ristow (Cambridge: Harvard University Press, 1961), 122, 128–34.

34. SFM 23–24. The characters in *The Spy* follow a route through "a retired and unfrequented pass, that to this hour is but little known." It leads from Westchester up into the hills near the westernmost notch of the Connecticut border, where it passes north, and then comes down into "the plain . . . many miles from the Hudson" (*Spy* CE 309). Especially memorable for the Whartons—as for the Coopers in the spring of 1811, one may speculate—is the view down on "the plains of Fish-kill" that "broke on their sight . . . with the effect of enchantment" as the travelers went through Wiccopee pass between East Mountain and Round Mountain (*Spy* CE 314). For the topographic details, see DeLorme's CD-ROM *Topo USA*, 1998 version (search term "Wiccopee"); the road Cooper had in mind probably was the one now called Perkins Road. The characters in *Satanstoe* also travel via White Plains into the heart of the Highlands until they emerge "onto the plains of Dutchess, . . . at Fishkill." Cooper's description of the itinerary in this book was exact enough to suggest he was tapping memories from an actual itinerary of his own, perhaps from 1811: his characters thus spend their first night in "the Manor of the Van Cortlandts"—the Van Cortlandts were relatives of Mrs. Cooper—the second at Fishkill, and the third at Rhinebeck. On the fourth day, they breakfast at Claverack, then pass through "a place called Kinderhook, a village of low Dutch origin, and of some antiquity." They make it close to Albany that night but stay just below it at "a comfortable, and exceedingly neat Dutch tavern." It takes them only an hour after leaving that tavern the next day to reach the river opposite Albany (*SAT* CE 144–48). Susan De-

Lancey Cooper's engagement with this terrain derived in part from the presence of various relatives in it. In Fishkill, for instance, these included first cousin Anne Walton Verplanck and her husband, Daniel Crommeline Verplanck, who lived in the old Gulian Verplanck house, Mt. Gulian, on the river at Beacon (so far off the track of the inland road that visiting them now would have been more likely if the Coopers followed the Highland Road). A short distance north of Fishkill in the inland hamlet of New Hackensack, on the other hand, was then living another of Mrs. Cooper's cousins, the somewhat rakish Warren DeLancey, and his family; see JFC, DeLancey genealogy, in Susan Fenimore Cooper, "Commonplace Book," Cooper family paps., collection of Dr. Henry Weil, Cooperstown; on Mt. Gulian and on Warren DeLancey, see Helen Wilkinson Reynolds, *Dutchess County Doorways* (New York: William Farquhar Payson, 1931), 262–64, 233–34.

35. Caty's initial task would be to aid Mrs. Cooper and the Disbrows in the housework, although eventually she also assumed child-rearing duties (SFM 37).

36. In his letter, Cooper informed the secretary of the navy he would "await . . . orders at Cooperstown New York," implying both that he would linger there some time before departing and that he expected a quick response. The navy in fact did respond quickly, accepting his resignation outright. But because of an error in addressing its answer, which went instead to New Jersey, as far as Cooper knew the subject lay unsettled for much longer than he imagined. We do not have the original of Cooper's resignation, only a copy made perhaps a decade later when he was once more trying to iron out the recruitment accounts. See Beard's note, *LJ* 1:25. Beard's date of 4/28 is accepted here, although the date on the manuscript of the copy (JFC paps., box 2, AAS) might also be read as 4/25. On the later suspense regarding whether his resignation had been accepted, see *LJ* 1:105–6. Regarding resignations in the naval officer corps in general, and Cooper's in particular, see Christopher McKee, *A Gentlemanly and Honorable Profession: The Creation of the U.S. Naval Officer Corps, 1794–1815* (Annapolis: Naval Institute, 1991), 421–29. On Cooper's later views of his resignation, see JC to Smith Thompson, 11/15/1821: "It is true that I tendered my resignation on my marriage in 1811" (*LJ* 1:72); and JFC to S. C. Hall, 3/1831: "On my marriage I quitted the navy" (*LJ* 2:59).

37. Their daughter Susan remembered her mother recounting how the recently wed couple had ridden "over many of the wood roads of the neighborhood, and had been on Mt. Vision repeatedly, on horseback" (SFM 16–17).

38. Miers Fisher to Richard Fenimore Cooper, 12/31/1810; Robert Troup to Richard Fenimore Cooper and Isaac Cooper, 2/12/1811, WC paps., box 27, HCA. Fisher's unacknowledged letter of June 13, 1810, *was* received; it is in the same box.

39. "James Cooper in Account with the Executors of the Late Wm Cooper Esq," 2/14/1815 (with later additions), JFC paps., box 5, AAS; Richard Fenimore and Isaac Cooper, "Account of Monies received and expended from and on account of the Estate

of William Cooper, by the Executors," Cooper family paps. microfilm, HSFC, New York City—confirmed by "Account [1810–1813] with the Estate of William Cooper, decd. Cut out of the acct. book April 23d, 1827, at Paris, by Wm [Yeardley] Cooper," JFC paps., box 4, AAS; "James Cooper Leases," JFC paps., box 5, AAS. That Cooper was alone among the heirs in receiving such a transfer of rental proceeds probably indicates how much pressure he applied to the executors.

40. The wheat and corn are entered in the lease accounts as *dollar* amounts ($697.63 and $842.63, respectively). In addition, Cooper was due 2,908 pounds of butter (at a wholesale price of ten cents per pound, worth $290.08) and 7,513 pounds of pork (which would fill thirty-seven-and-a-half barrels, for a total of $496.88). In several instances, rents were in arrears to a considerable amount, meaning that Cooper inherited outstanding credits that he would have to seek to collect. In one bad case, that of Springhill Farm in Hartwick township, nine years and five months rent was owed on a ten-year lease, a total of $713.72 including interest, on a property valued at $853.12. Cooper was debited for both the value of the property *and* the overdue rent and interest. In such cases, he would have to work hard to recover anything at all. Richard Fenimore and Isaac Cooper, "Account of Monies received and expended."

41. "James Cooper's Leases," JFC paps., box 5, AAS; JFC, "Land Accounts, ca. 1810–1851," Cooper family paps. microfilm, HSFC, New York City. The Utica trip is documented in Thomas James DeLancey to JC, 7/6/1811; JFC paps., box 2, AAS. This question is treated in greater detail in Chapter 7.

42. Ann's son had been born 2/23/1811. His name memorialized not only his recently departed grandfather, but also the Pomeroys' first child, bearing exactly the same name, who had survived his birth in 1804 by only fifteen months. See Wayne W. Wright, *The Cooper Genealogy* (Cooperstown: NYSHA Library, 1983), 16.

43. All receipts for the New York City purchases, dated 8/3–8/8/1811, are in JFC paps., box 4, AAS.

44. Genealogy in Cooper family Bible, copy in JFB paps., box 53, AAS. On Mrs. Cooper's possible illness, see JFC to Paul Hamilton, 9/15/1812; Cooper there mentions that he had been confined to home for several months the previous year by "the serious illness of a very near connection." Beard guesses that Cooper "probably" was referring to Mrs. Cooper, "though possibly Elizabeth" (*LJ* 1:28). The autumn purchases, especially those in December, may well indicate the moment when they began relocating themselves to Closet Hall from Heathcote Hill; see Richard Kingsland, receipt, 10/30/1811; J. A. Hyde, receipt, 10/30/1811; George Dummer and Co., receipt, 10/30/1811; John Slidell and Co., receipt, 12/4/1811; James Wood, receipt, 12/4/1811; William L. Watkins, receipt, 12/4/1811; all in JFC paps., box 4, AAS. Pickering, "Fenimore Cooper as Country Gentleman: A New Glimpse of Cooper's Westchester Years," *New York History* 72(1991): 302, following the vague tradition that places the Coopers' honeymoon journey immediately after their wedding, writes that the newlyweds spent

the first months of their marriage at Heathcote Hill, then briefly relocated to Closet Hall before permanently returning to Heathcote Hill before Elizabeth's birth in September. JFB (*LJ* 1:23) properly separates the wedding from the trip and notes that Closet Hall was rented prior to the trip, in April of 1811. There is some uncertainty as to just how long the Coopers lived at Closet Hall. The novelist's daughter was told that her parents had "made their first attempt at house keeping" there "the year after our little sister Elizabeth was born," and added that they left the place "and returned to Heathcote Hill a short time before I was born [4/17/1813]" (SFM 29). Her father wrote to Navy Secretary William Jones from "Mamaroneck N.Y." (*not* New Rochelle) toward the end of January 1813 (*LJ* 1:29), suggesting the latter month as the time of the shift.

45. Cooper's evolving relationship with Susan's father is suggested in his later anecdote about an episode in 1811 when the two men took a pleasant sleigh ride together in Westchester after an itinerant horse-breaker quieted a particularly vicious mare at Heathcote Hill—tellingly, it was Cooper who accompanied DeLancey, not one of DeLancey's sons (see *LJ* 2:48–49). At this same time, Cooper renewed his long relationship with William Jay and Jay's family, including his statesman father, living at this time in the town of Bedford.

46. Charles Oscar Paullin, *Commodore John Rodgers: Captain, Commodore, and Senior Officer of the American Navy, 1773–1838: A Biography* (Cleveland: Arthur H. Clark, 1910), 219–30.

47. *Otsego Herald*, 7/6/1811; *Cooperstown Federalist*, 7/20/1811. Cooper evidently had access to Pickering's widely reprinted essay before its appearance in the *Federalist*. Indeed, throughout his Cooperstown stay, he must have read out-of-town papers (available at his friend Phinney's print shop) and seems to have received now-lost letters that carried other news. On 6/16/1811, Cooper wrote an unlocated letter to Thomas J. DeLancey, whose answer suggests that Cooper had broached the topic of the *Little Belt* (not yet mentioned in DeLancey's correspondence to him earlier that summer). DeLancey thus asserted, "You have seen [Capt. Arthur B.] Binghams account, directly contrary to Rogers[.] [O]ne or the other stretches a point handsomely[.]" If Cooper had mentioned Bingham's account in his lost letter, as DeLancey implies, he knew of it via non-Cooperstown sources. The *Herald* first printed a British account of the encounter as late as June 29 and did not reprint Bingham's letter until July 13. The *Cooperstown Federalist* gave the full text of Bingham's report on July 6.

48. Cooper's note in the naval history does not state that he personally spent the evening with the officers, or that he joined Moreau for the naval review, but the implication is strong in both cases. I identify the frigates on the basis of Cooper's statement that only the *President* and the *Essex* were at New York at the time (*HN* 2:149–50). Paullin, *Commodore John Rodgers*, 246, gives April 3 as the date Rodgers returned to New York in the *President*. In the company of the *Essex*, he left the harbor on April 14 with orders to seek out British vessels along the coast.

49. New York *Mercantile Advertiser*, 4/15/1812; New York *Gazette*, quoted from the available reprinting in the New York *Evening Post*, 4/15/1812.

50. Cooper had gone to New York in April 1812 because, with the river open and spring coming, he was eager to head upriver to Albany and then proceed to Otsego, where work soon would begin on the new lakeshore property, to be called Fenimore Farm, where he would relocate his family the following year; see *LJ* 1:26–27; William Sterrett (of Cooperstown), bill, "June 1813," "for Work Done . . . last summer," JFC paps., box 4, AAS; James Oakley, statement (New York), 5/14/1814 (listing 5/7/1812 purchase), Elisha Carpenter, receipt (Mamaroneck), 5/19/1812, both in JFC paps., box 4, AAS.

51. Paullin, *Commodore John Rodgers*, 249.

52. Cooper soon went with his friend Luther Bradish to pay a call on Republican politician Joseph Bloomfield, just appointed by President Madison to command all forces in greater New York (see *LJ* 2:88). This visit placed Cooper and Bradish very close to the center of things, since in fact it was General Bloomfield who on June 20 first had informed Commodore Rodgers of the declaration; I. N. Phelps Stokes, *The Iconography of Manhattan Island, 1498–1909*, 6 vols. (New York: Robert H. Dodd, 1915–1928), 5:1545–49.

53. Hence the figure briefly mentioned in an anecdote in *The Sea Lions:* "Jumping Billy," master of a naval gunboat in the Mediterranean (*SL* 2:194).

54. Captain Broke to the Admiralty, as quoted in Linda M. Maloney, *The Captain from Connecticut: The Life and Naval Times of Isaac Hull* (Boston: Northeastern University Press, 1986), 177. Or, as Cooper would put it, "The beautiful manner in which this advantage was improved, excited admiration even in the enemy" (*HN* 2:157). Cooper knew some of this almost immediately from press reports, but also via the personal sources already mentioned, chief among them Charles Morris (see Abel Bowen, *The Naval Monument, Containing Official and Other Accounts of All the Battles Fought Between the Navies of the United States and Great Britain* [1816; rpt. Boston: George Clarke, 1830], 6). For Cooper, the war began as an intensely personal affair, and it was to remain personal throughout.

55. Bowen, *Naval Monument*, 1–14.

56. For instance, see the footnote in the naval history: "An officer of the Constitution, of experience and of great respectability, who is now dead, assured the writer that he actually weighed the shot of both ships, and found the Constitution's 24's were only 3 pounds heavier than the Guerriere's 18s, and that there was nearly the same difference in favour of the latter's 32's" (*HN* 2:173n). The source in this case may well have been Lieut. Beekman Verplanck Hoffman, who had died in 1834, five years before the history's publication.

57. See also Cooper's nearly contemporary use of the term for both Mabel Dunham and Natty Bumppo in *PF* 1:54, 95. Cooper must have heard of the defeat of the *Guerriere*

within a short time of the *Constitution*'s return to Boston at the end of August, perhaps through a personal channel: barely had the vessel dropped anchor off Boston light when Lieut. John T. Shubrick went ashore in the ship's cutter, bearing Hull's dispatches for Washington. News of the victory reached New York about the time Shubrick would have been passing through, September 2, and it is plausible that Shubrick directly or indirectly shared the buoyant report with his brother's ex-shipmate. Tyrone G. Martin, *A Most Fortunate Ship: A Narrative History of Old Ironsides*, rev. ed. (Annapolis: Naval Institute Press, 2003), 164. Soon all of New York was warm with praise for Isaac Hull, who was voted the freedom of the city on September 7. He was invited to sit for a portrait by John Wesley Jarvis, the English exile who also painted John Peter DeLancey, on a commission from Cooper, around this same time. Stokes, *Iconography*, 5:1553.

58. Stokes, *Iconography*, 5:1553–54.

59. William Hamman [Hammond] and Ames Worden to JC, 1/11/1813, JFC paps., box 2, AAS.

60. Cited by JFB, *LJ* 1:28n4.

61. Cooper noted the lack of an answer from Hamilton to his 9/13/1812 letter (see *LJ* 1:29); on the misdirection of the 5/11/1811 letter from Hamilton, see *LJ* 1:78.

62. Charles Lee Lewis, *The Romantic Decatur* (Philadelphia: University of Pennsylvania Press, 1937), 108; see also Donald R. Hickey, *The War of 1812: A Forgotten Conflict* (Urbana and Chicago: University of Illinois Press, 1989), 94.

63. Samuel Leech, *A Voice from the Main Deck*, ed. Michael J. Crawford (Annapolis: Naval Institute, 1999), 86, 82. The grim suffering of the British crew was mixed with Decatur's exceptional kindness toward his old associate Carden. Decatur received the sometime lord of the *Macedonian* on board his own vessel after the battle. Once arrived back in the United States, the victor wrote his wife that "half of the satisfaction arising from the victory is destroyed in seeing the distress of poor Carden, who deserved success as much as we did. . . . I do all I can to console him." Carden long remembered what he called Decatur's "unusual goodness" (Lewis, *Romantic Decatur*, 124, 132).

64. Stokes, *Iconography*, 5:1556; Dorothy C. Barck, ed., *Diary of William Dunlap* (New York: NYHS, 1930), 2:459; Lewis, *Romantic Decatur*, 127; Hickey, *War of 1812*, 97.

65. Barck, ed., *Diary*, 2:456–59.

66. New York *Columbian*, 12/21/1812.

67. Ibid., 12/19/1812.

68. Leech, *A Voice from the Main Deck*, 99–101.

69. Washington Irving, *The Complete Works of Washington Irving: Letters I: 1802–1823*, ed. Ralph M. Aderman, Herbert Kleinfield, and Jennifer S. Banks (Boston: Twayne, 1978), 354.

70. New York *Evening Post*, 1/2/1813.

71. Irving, *Complete Works: Letters*, 1:351; *The War, Being a Faithful Record of the Transactions of the War between the United States of America and Their Territories and the*

United Kingdom of Great Britain and Ireland, and the Dependencies Thereof, Declared on the Eighteenth Day of June, 1812, 1/4/1813.

72. Irving, *Complete Works: Letters,* 1:354; New York *Evening Post,* 1/2/1813. For an extended account of the celebration, see Lewis, *Romantic Decatur,* 127–29.

73. New York *Evening Post,* 1/8/1813; James Tertius de Kay, *Chronicles of the Frigate Macedonian 1809–1922* (New York: W. W. Norton, 1995), 51–52, 69, 211; Herman Melville, *White-Jacket or the World in a Man-of-War,* ed. Harrison Hayford, Hershel Parker, G. Thomas Tanselle (Evanston and Chicago: Northwestern University Press and Newberry Library, 1970), 92; Carden's band already had been performing in New York City before the sailors' fete—at the Park Theatre itself, for instance, a week earlier (New York *Evening Post,* 1/2/1813).

74. New York *Evening Post,* 1/8/1813; Lewis, *Romantic Decatur,* 130, names the Dunlap play; on it, see Arthur Hobson Quinn, *A History of the American Drama from the Beginning to the Civil War* (New York: Appleton-Century-Crofts, 1951), 99.

75. William Hamman [Hammond] and Ames Worden to JC, 1/11/1813, JFC paps., box 2, AAS.

76. William Hammond to JC, 1/15/1813, JFC paps., box 2, AAS. On Hammond, see Hugh Hastings, ed., *Public Papers of Daniel D. Tompkins,* 3 vols. (Albany: J. B. Lyon Co., State Printers, 1902), 3:13, 117; 1:229, 370.

77. See also Beard's comment, *LJ* 1:23.

78. William Sterrett, bill, "June 1813," covering earlier work, JFC paps., box 4, AAS. Sterrett probably worked on the "temporary frame house" Beard mentions (*LJ* 1:23), but see Hugh MacDougall, *Cooper's Otsego County* (Cooperstown: NYSHA, 1989), 77, which says Cooper bought an already existing frame farmhouse.

79. JFB, *LJ* 1:29n3, notes that Secretary of the Navy William Jones wrote Cooper on 1/27/1813 to accept his resignation (see also *LJ* 1:91n, where Beard speculates that Cooper probably heard around 2/1/1813). On February 10, Cooper bought lumber and nails from the Westchester sawpit of John Haviland and in all likelihood took the materials to Closet Hall to board up the windows against curious neighbors; John Haviland, receipt, 2/10/1813, JFC paps., box 4, AAS.

80. Asa Luce, receipt, 2/26/1813 ("on contract for stone per the hands of Isaac Cooper"), JFC paps., box 4, AAS; Isaac Cooper diary, 2/26/1813, NYSHA.

81. Hickey, *War of 1812,* 80–86, 88.

82. Franklin B. Hough, *A History of St. Lawrence and Franklin Counties, New York* (Albany: Little and Co., 1853), 584.

83. Taylor, *William Cooper's Town,* 360–61, 369–71; *Otsego Herald,* 9/12/1812.

84. *Otsego Herald,* 10/24–10/31/1812.

85. Peck's tale is included in his widow's pension application file, NARA, Record Group 15, microfilm M804, roll 1900. Van Rensselaer: *Otsego Herald,* 11/7/1812.

86. Isaac Cooper diary, 3/8/1813. Richard's wife Ann, from whom he had been

more or less separated since April 1811, also lived in Albany at the time, but apparently in separate quarters. When her estranged husband died, she was pregnant with what was to be alternately regarded as his last child or the first of several she was to have with her wealthy lover, George Clarke, whom she almost immediately wed, to the disbelief and shock of the family and the region. Cooperstown *Federalist*, 4/20/1811; Isabella Ellison to "Mr. [Richard?] Cooper" (Albany), 10/2/[1812?], WC paps., box 25, HCA (but see also *LJ* 1:26); JFB, *LJ* 3:44, cites evidence that Alfred Cooper Clarke was Richard's son; see also Taylor, *William Cooper's Town*, 393–94. Wayne Wright, *Cooper Genealogy* (Cooperstown: NYSHA Library, 1983), 9, gives Richard's death date as 3/8/1813, the date ultimately inscribed on his gravestone; JFB, *LJ* 1:13, gives 3/6/1813; the *Otsego Herald*, 3/13/1813, states that Richard died on 3/5/1813 and was interred on 3/9/1813.

87. Cooper did not wait for good weather: it was snowy all day on the fourteenth, though warmer than when he had arrived not quite three weeks earlier. Isaac's notation of Cooper's destination ("J Cooper goes to N. York") may have been simply shorthand for the general region where Cooper and his wife lived (Isaac Cooper diary, 3/14/1813). But it may have indicated that Cooper indeed went first to New York City on his way to Mamaroneck. Perhaps he tarried a bit in Albany to see to some of the loose ends Richard's death surely left there, then went down the valley. He did not travel by water—the Hudson had been frozen since December 21 and the winter had continued "severe" since then; see Joel Munsell, *The Annals of Albany*, 10 vols. (Albany: Joel Munsell, 1850–1859), 10:403. Whatever his route or stops, he was in New Rochelle at John Bonnet's store by March 24, when he bought and paid for five yards of cloth, surely on an errand for Susan; see John Bonnet, Jr., receipt, 3/24/1813, JFC paps., box 4, AAS.

88. SDC to JC, 5/6/1813, copy in JFB paps., box 18, AAS; genealogy in Cooper family Bible, copy in JFB paps., box 53, AAS.

89. Isaac Cooper, diary, 5/6/1813. Levi Kelly, bill, 5/8/1813, JFC paps., box 4, AAS. Kelly, convicted of murder and executed while Cooper was in Europe in the later 1820s, was the novelist's first cousin, son of Ann Cooper Kelly, Judge William Cooper's sister; see Wright, *Cooper Genealogy*, 10, and S. T. Livermore, *A Condensed History of Cooperstown with a Biographical Sketch of J. Fenimore Cooper* (Albany: Munsell, 1862), 140–45.

90. SDC to JC, 5/6/1813.

91. Isaac Cooper diary, 6/8/1813, 6/10/1813; *Otsego Herald*, 5/15/1813, 5/22/1813, 5/29/1813.

92. McKee, *A Gentlemanly and Honorable Profession*, 399, 571n5.

93. Cooper's early departure for Otsego after his second daughter's birth in May perhaps allowed him to see Lawrence and inspect that man's current vessel, the *Hornet*, at the New York navy yard before heading upstate. Certainly he saw the vessel during this period (see *ECE* 12, where Cooper made it clear that he had personally inspected the *Hornet* soon after the engagement). On the other hand, Cooper's arrival in Cooperstown on May

6 makes it unlikely that he attended the New York dinner honoring Lawrence and his officers two evenings earlier. On the celebration, see Stokes, *Iconography,* 5:1559, 1561.

CHAPTER 6. FENIMORE FARM

1. I. N. Phelps Stokes, *The Iconography of Manhattan Island, 1498–1909,* 6 vols. (New York: Robert H. Dodd, 1915–1928), 5:1562; *The War* [New York], 9/21/1813; New York *Commercial Advertiser,* 9/15–9/16/1813.

2. Isaac Cooper diary, 7/6/1813, NYSHA; Cooper family Bible leaves, copy in JFB paps., box 53; *Otsego Herald,* 7/17/1813.

3. Isaac Cooper diary, 7/14/1813; E. F. Benjamin, receipt, Cooperstown, 7/15/1813, JFC paps., box 4, AAS; SDC to Ann Cooper Pomeroy, 3/8/1830, Cooper family paps., NYSHA.

4. Cooper's second daughter, then just an infant, learned later that he had felt Elizabeth's death "very deeply" (SFM 17); see William Jay to JC, 8/2/1813, copy in JFB paps., box 9, AAS.

5. *The Book of Common Prayer, and Administration of the Sacraments and Other Rites and Ceremonies of the Church, According to the Use of the Protestant Episcopal Church in the United States of America* (Philadelphia: S. Potter for the Common-Prayer Book Society of Pennsylvania, 1818), 153, 129; Cooper family Bible leaves.

6. E. F. Benjamin, receipt, 10/25/1813, JFC paps., box 4, AAS.

7. The first of the Fenimore parcels, the southernmost, was a thirty-three-acre tract bought from printer and publisher Elihu Phinney for nearly $1,700 at the end of November in the earlier year. The second, acquired the same week, was a sixteen-acre parcel just to the north of Phinney's, purchased for about $750 from Joshua and Huldah Starr, storekeeper Jesse's parents. The following March, Cooper added another sixteen acres to the north of the Starrs' land, sold to him by Isaac for $555. Otsego County conveyances, County Clerk's Office, Cooperstown, book O, 103, 105, 408; book R, 32, 242 (see also book Z, 314); Hugh Cooke MacDougall, *Cooper's Otsego County* (Cooperstown: NYSHA, 1989), 81. Cooper apparently paid for at least part of the cost of each parcel by having "Bonds Transfer[red] to J. Starr" and "E. Phinney" in the amount of around $750 and $465, respectively, on 11/25/1811; interest payments on the Phinney bond were also debited against the estate on the first and second anniversaries of the transaction; see Richard Fenimore and Isaac Cooper, Account Book with William Cooper estate, Cooper family paps. microfilm, HSFC, New York City (James Cooper account pages). The master of Mt. Ovis had enough Latin from his schooling to appreciate the play on words in the farm's name, which literally meant "sheep," but which Plautus used for "simpleton"—as Cooper showed himself in turning shepherd.

8. A single outbuilding located on one of the original lots when Cooper bought it was torn down in November of 1812 and replaced in the spring of 1813, before the family arrived, by a new barn. Cyrus Clark, bill, 7/21/1814, William Warren, bill ("for

James Cooper's barn"), 5/13/1813, both JFC paps., box 4. Work on the temporary farmhouse at Fenimore Farm, which continued to June of 1814 (see *LJ* 1:31), is not well documented. The charges of Cyrus Clark for sash and cellar windows (bills, 12/20/1812 and 5/17/1813, respectively, JFC paps., box 4) probably are one trace of the project. Another no doubt is the charge by Lawrence McNamee for shingles and clapboards in August 1813 (finally settled for a year later; see McNamee's bill, 9/7/1814, JFC paps., box 4). Isaac Cooper diary, 8/21/1813.

    9. Isaac Cooper diary, 9/1/1813, 1/2/1814. Sometimes the rural festivities appear to have spilled over into the village. After what Isaac called a "Fishing Party—no fishing Party" on 9/23/1813, he and Mary Ann went back to Cooperstown for evening theatricals mounted by the visiting Albany Company. Noah Miller Ludlow, who had recently joined that troupe, maintained many years later (on the basis, however, of suspiciously anachronistic hearsay) that Cooper himself attended a performance of Prince Hoare's play, *The Prize; or, 2, 5, 3, 8,* at this time. See Noah Miller Ludlow, *Dramatic Life as I Found It* (St. Louis: G. I. Jones, 1880), 9. I have found no listing for the plays presented on the date noted by Isaac Cooper, but the *Otsego Herald* of 9/25/1813 names Hoare's farce as one of the plays to be presented a week later, along with Thomas Dibdin's *The Jew and the Doctor.*

    10. Isaac Cooper diary, 1/29/1814.

    11. This was the first winter and spring Cooper had spent in Otsego in many years, a fact that may well have made it especially important for his eventual composition of *The Pioneers* and his use of a seasonal rhythm for that book's action. Isaac Cooper diary, 4/6–4/24/1814. Early in March, Cooper had gone to a men's dinner party also attended by Rev. John Smith as well as his own brother Isaac and brother-in-law George Pomeroy; this probably was a meeting of the Otsego County Bible Society, which had been founded the year before (Isaac Cooper diary, 3/9/1814).

    12. L. G. Connor, "A Brief History of the Sheep Industry in the United States," *Annual Report of the American Historical Association for the Year 1918,* 1:101–5. In January of 1814, Susan's father reported from Mamaroneck that he had found Cooper several merino bucks "far superior to Sinbad in point of size." Later in the year, DeLancey's son Thomas wrote Cooper to ask whether he was still in the market for bucks, reporting that he had found a "full blooded & handsome" pair for $130. John P. DeLancey to JC, 1/14/1814, 8/23/1814, and Thomas J. DeLancey to JC, 5/4/1814, copies in JFB paps., box 9, AAS.

    13. John Peter wrote Cooper in August of 1814 that he had secured four more bucks at fifty dollars each. By month's end he had shipped them to Cooperstown along with three of Cooper's bucks DeLancey had been caring for at Heathcote Hill and another four half-blood bucks of his own that he wanted Cooper to dispose of for him in Otsego. John P. DeLancey to JC, 8/23/1814, copy in JFB paps., box 9, AAS.

    14. Cyrus Clark, bill, 7/21/1814, JFC paps., box 4, AAS.

15. Isaac Cooper diary, 5/9/1814, 5/11/1814, 5/20/1814. See also James Oakley and Oakley and Randolph, statements of account, 5/14/1814, JFC paps., box 4, AAS. On Cooper's return on May 20, he was accompanied by Cooperstown lawyer Robert Campbell (who had "started for N.Y.," Isaac's diary indicates, on May 11), prompting Isaac to note, "James and Campbell returned—good report." Their errand may have concerned land holdings in St. Lawrence and Franklin counties, where development was at a standstill because of the war; "almost all of the settlers who had purchased DeKalb lands in 1803–1804 from William Cooper defaulted on their contracts when they became due in 1813–1814," writes Alan Taylor, *William Cooper's Town: Power and Persuasion on the Frontier of the Early American Republic* (New York: Knopf, 1995), 389.

16. Thomas J. DeLancey to JC, 5/4/1814, copy in JFB paps., box 9, AAS; William Cook and Co., statement, 7/23/1814 (hayseed, 5/2–5/12/1814; scythes, 7/2/1814), JFC paps., box 4, AAS. When the Coopers returned to Otsego on August 19 (see Isaac Cooper diary), they brought along Susan's thirteen-year-old sister, Elizabeth Caroline, who stayed for quite a long visit, perhaps even into winter, until her father came for her; John P. DeLancey to JC, 10/20/1814, JFC paps., box 2, AAS.

17. For one thing, Susan was pregnant again; she remained home in November while Cooper went off to Philadelphia to deal with unspecified issues connected to his father's estate. Isaac Cooper diary, 11/29/1814 ("James arrived from P"); Richard Fenimore and Isaac Cooper, Account Book with William Cooper estate (crediting Cooper in November 1814 for "cash advanced [by him to] Wm & expenses to Philadelphia").

18. *Otsego Herald,* 9/1–9/29/1814.

19. Ibid., 10/20/1814.

20. Ibid., 11/3/1814. The first resolution ("the situation to which our country has been reduced in consequence of the present war, requires the active and united exertions of every American in its defence") was so unobjectionable that it had received "the undivided support" of everyone present. The third one, which required Cooper to sign the document and see to its publication as secretary, he carried out despite his objections. It was the second resolution that riled Cooper: "as we are not fully informed of the rupture of the negociation [*sic*], and it is yet uncertain whether the mission may not terminate in a settlement of our differences with the enemy, it is inexpedient at this time to express an opinion upon a subject so imperfectly understood." Alan Taylor reads the October 20 meeting as revealing little but what he terms the "arrogant and prickly" individualism of "Federalist James Cooper." But prowar Cooper was no "Federalist" by this point, if he ever had been, and the political struggle mattered more than any clash of personalities. See Taylor, *William Cooper's Town,* 380.

21. Donald R. Hickey, *The War of 1812: A Forgotten Conflict* (Urbana: University of Illinois Press, 1989), 281–89.

22. Isaac Cooper diary, 2/14–2/16/1815. Cooper was out of town when the peace celebration occurred but surely heard the details when he returned (for a lively descrip-

tion of it, see Elihu Phinney, Jr., to Nancy Whiting Tiffany, 2/14–3/5/1815, Phinney family paps., NYSHA).

23. Franklin B. Hough, *A History of St. Lawrence and Franklin Counties, New York* (Albany: Little and Co., 1853), 289; Taylor, *William Cooper's Town*, 389–90, 322; William Ogden to Isaac Cooper, 6/7/1813, WC paps., box 27, HCA; WC, indenture with William Ogden and John R. Murray, 1/17/1804, Cooper family paps., NYSHA; Isaac Cooper to William Murray and Sons, 7/26/1813, WC paps., box 27, HCA; "Classification of the Township of Dekalb," DeKalb Bound Volume Collection, item 1, St. Lawrence County Historical Society archives, Canton, N.Y.; Henry M. Fine to Isaac Cooper, 9/24/1814, 11/6/1814, 11/12/1814, WC paps., box 27, HCA.

24. Isaac Cooper diary, 3/4/1815, 4/25/1815, 4/2/1815; see Taylor, *William Cooper's Town*, 390; Frederick DePeyster to Isaac Cooper, 4/18/1815, WC paps., box 27, HCA. Cooper's share included 850.5 acres in the first and second classes, valued at $4.50 per acre; 2,755 acres in the third and fourth ($5.00 per acre); 1,035.5 acres in the fifth ($3.50 per acre); and 255 acres in the sixth ($2.50 per acre). The total cash equivalency for his share of the estate's holdings in DeKalb, the highest among the heirs, was figured by Isaac in 1815 as $21,928.80. At the same time, a similar division of the estate's holding of more than 6,500 acres in the town of Bangor, in nearby Franklin County, netted Cooper 1,299 acres, valued at just over $7,000 (also the largest share, though by a much less dramatic margin). Richard Fenimore and Isaac Cooper, Account Book with William Cooper estate (debit pages for individuals named). Although a substantial piece of land, Cooper's share of DeKalb was less than 8 percent of his father's holdings there. The lots assigned to Cooper were transferred to his ownership by a deed completed on 11/30/1815 (Isaac Cooper et al. to JC, St. Lawrence County Clerk's Office, Canton, N.Y., deeds, book 4, p. 365). The Bangor lands were similarly transferred by a deed completed on 12/2/1815 (Isaac Cooper et al. to JC, Franklin County Clerk's Office, Malone, N.Y., deeds, book 1, p. 315).

25. Taylor, *William Cooper's Town*, 321; WC, will, 5/13/1808, Register of Wills, Book B, 237, Otsego County Surrogate's Office, Cooperstown; Courtland C. Cooper to JC, 10/1/1817, WC paps., old microfilm series, roll 22, HCA; same to same, 7/13/1819, JFC paps., box 2, AAS. Potter Goff and Silas Spencer, "Settlers in the Township" (1814), Town of DeKalb Historical Association Collections (DeKalb Junction, N.Y.), 29, 31, 33, 36, 49, 50, 51, 56.

26. *Otsego Herald*, 2/9/1815 (earliest extant issue containing the ad, which first appeared on 1/26 and ran through 3/9). The horse in question may have been the colt Cooper had left behind at Heathcote Hill on leaving Westchester, where Edward F. DeLancey was to break it in for him; it remained there until the DeLanceys got around to sending it to Cooperstown along with some merino sheep in August of 1814 (see John P. DeLancey to JC, 1/14/1814, JFB paps., box 9, AAS, and 10/20/1814, JFC paps., box 2, AAS). The description of the horse in the ad may suggest both Cooper's pretentious

treatment of it and the clumsy execution of his designs ("mare-headed" means the horse had a small head; "nicked" indicates that the horse's tail was cut so as to make it stand up straight, though the ad states that it didn't; "hogged" meant that the mane was cut so close it resembled a hog's hair).

27. Isaac Cooper diary, 2/26/1815.

28. *Otsego Herald*, 6/22/1815; Taylor, *William Cooper's Town*, 380, and 523n20, which however does not cite documentary proof of Chapin's *purchase* of land from William Cooper (the only evidence of land purchased by Chapin that I find in Otsego County records before 1820 is a mortgage and bond for two parcels he bought in Croghan's Patent from Josiah O. Hoffman in 1793; see Otsego County Clerk's Office, Cooperstown, mortgages, book 4, p. 206); on the leasehold see WC, will, 5/13/1808, copy in WC paps., box 10, HCA. In 1815, Chapin's rent went to Isaac Cooper, so it might have made more sense for him to attack Edgewater than Fenimore. But Isaac's house lay close to the center of Cooperstown, whereas Fenimore Farm lay a mile north in a more vulnerable location.

29. Isaac Cooper diary, 3/6/1815; *Otsego Herald*, 6/15/1815; Taylor, *William Cooper's Town*, 380. Isaac's diary (2/20/1815) recorded that "J. Cooper went to Albany." From there he went on to New York City; see Robert Troup and Richard Harison to Isaac Cooper, 3/27/1815, WC paps., box 27, HCA. John Murray to Isaac Cooper, 3/13/1815, suggests that Cooper had been in the city recently on an errand from Isaac regarding DeKalb: "The Proprietors of DeKalb have had a meeting—your Brother does not appear to be much acquainted with the affairs relative to that Town, and the Proprietors are very desirous that you Should be here, we wish that you could come down if only for a few days" (WC paps., box 27, HCA). As to the June trip to pick up Mrs. DeLancey: Caroline Martha Cooper was born at Fenimore Farm at noon on June 26, but Cooper, along with Samuel and Mrs. DeLancey, did not arrive there until the next day; see Isaac Cooper diary, 6/26–6/27/1815.

30. *Otsego Herald*, 6/15/1815, 6/22/1815; Haskell, Walbridge and Co., bill (marked paid 11/24/1815), JFC paps., box 4, AAS; on Haskell, see his advertisement, *Otsego Herald*, 4/13/1815.

31. Isaac Cooper diary, 6/12/1815, 6/18/1815, 6/22/1815; *Otsego Herald*, 8/31/1815; Taylor, *William Cooper's Town*, 380; Haskell, Walbridge and Co., bill, 11/24/1815.

32. Taylor, *William Cooper's Town*, 424–25.

33. Elihu Phinney, Jr., to Nancy Whiting Tiffany, 6/22/1815, Phinney family paps. "Square fighting": see Mitford M. Mathews, *A Dictionary of Americanisms* (Chicago: University of Chicago Press, 1951), s.v. "square," citing an 1868 text—"a good 'square fight' is an encounter or 'muss' where the opponents were in earnest."

34. Richard H. Levet, *Ambrose L. (Aqua Fortis) Jordan, Lawyer* (New York: Vantage, 1973), 49–50, 140–42, 166; Jordan was surrogate only until July, although he later

was reappointed. His service as guardian of Richard Fenimore Cooper's children is indicated by the fact that his initials are penciled in next to several leases assigned to Richard in an 1815 account of the Cooper estate; see Richard Fenimore and Isaac Cooper, Account Book with William Cooper estate, Richard Fenimore Cooper heirs' account; and, for instance, Otsego County Clerk's Office, conveyances, book KK, p. 86. Evan Cornog, *The Birth of Empire: DeWitt Clinton and the American Experience, 1769–1828* (New York: Oxford University Press, 1998), 101–3; Hugh Hastings, ed., *Military Minutes of the Council of Appointment of the State of New York, 1783–1821* (Albany: James B. Lyon, State Printer, 1901), 2:1578, 1629; Salem, N.Y., *Northern Post*, 2/16/1815; Ballston Spa *Independent American*, 2/8/1815; *Otsego Herald*, 3/9/1815; Baltimore *Patriot*, 3/13/1815; Goshen, N.Y., *Orange County Patriot*, 7/18/1815. Cooper probably had met Clinton in New York City during some of the naval celebrations during the recent war and may already have become politically interested in his career by 1815, although the first documented encounter between them would come at the American Bible Society founding meeting in New York City in 1816, discussed later in this chapter.

35. Isaac Cooper diary, 7/4/1815, 7/20/1815, 8/2/1815, 8/18/1815. The novelist cast a long, humorous look back at the family's fondness for wrestling when, in *The Prairie*, he had Dr. Batt recover from an onslaught of Natty Bumppo's windy discourse "like a fallen wrestler who is just released from the throttling grasp of his antagonist" (*PR* CE 181).

36. Isaac Cooper diary, 2/6/1816, 5/4–5/5/1816, 1/1/1818, and passim; SFM 13. See also S. O. Runyan to Isaac Cooper (still in Butternuts), 8/25/1815, which reports receiving word in Cooperstown that Isaac was "rapidly recovering" from his "late dangerous illness" (WC paps., box 27, HCA). The injury, which kept Isaac at the Morris home until 8/28/1815, was serious enough that Cooper visited him there on August 20 and—more ominously—Rev. Daniel Nash did so on August 21 (see Isaac Cooper diary for those dates).

37. Isaac Cooper diary, 9/26/1815.

38. Isaac Cooper to JC, 10/8/1815, JFC paps., box 2, AAS.

39. Isaac Cooper diary, 11/17–11/22/1815, 12/11/1815.

40. Vinal Luce to JC, 1/17/1816, 1/31/1816, JFC paps., box 2, AAS (the first of these was forwarded to Cedar Street from Mamaroneck; the second was addressed directly to New York City); probably the children were left in Westchester as protection against a smallpox epidemic then afflicting New York; see Stokes, *Iconography*, 5:1585–86 (under 12/25/1815, 1/29/1816).

41. Thomas James DeLancey to JC, 2/4/1816, 2/8/1816, copies in JFB paps., box 9, AAS. The extra money could cover rent in the city, an added expense at the time. Unfortunately, Thomas reported, the ship Cooper had chosen to carry the cordwood to New York for sale there ran aground before it managed to take on the freight.

42. Taylor, *William Cooper's Town*, 149; Goff and Spencer, "Settlers in the Town-

ship," 61; Bryan Thompson (chair, Town of DeKalb Historical Association), "Supplemental Notes to Coopers Falls Abstracts"; extracts from Abraham Fisk, "Account Book," St. Lawrence County archives, showing work performed on the Cooper Falls Grist Mill for James Cooper, 1816 (copies in author's collection); and "The Legend of Cooper[s] Falls," *The Williamstown Gazette: An Occasional Publication of the Town of DeKalb Historical Association*, III:1:[4]. I am grateful to Mr. Thompson for his generous help during my visit to "Coopers Falls" and DeKalb village and his willingness to share these useful materials with me.

43. For instance, Courtland reported that Isaac was "unwell from his old strain which he got at the Butternuts." He also offered a mock-serious account of the sudden illness of Isaac's wife, Mary Ann, who gave birth to the couple's seventh child, daughter Hannah. Isaac Cooper's diary confirms Isaac's condition at the time (1/26/1816: "Mr. Cooper very sick"), but it places Courtland's return to the village on 1/24/1816; Wayne Wright, *The Cooper Genealogy* (Cooperstown: NYSHA Library, 1983), 15.

44. Courtland C. Cooper to JC, 1/27/1816 (also forwarded to 10 Cedar Street), WC paps., old microfilm series, roll 22, HCA. Over the months he was at Fenimore, Courtland tended the farmland and buildings, collected local rents, and supervised various of his cousin's servants—apparently including both coachman Sam Brimmer and the free African American worker, Fred. See Lorenzo Bates, statement, 5/18/1815, JFC paps., box 4, AAS; "Account of C. C. Cooper," JFC paps., box 5, AAS; John Smith to JC, 4/26/1816, copy in JFB paps., box 9, AAS; Courtland C. Cooper, "Monies paid and rec'd," 1816, JFC paps., box 4, AAS.

45. John Smith to JC, 4/26/1816.

46. "Otsego County Bible Society," in S. T. Livermore, *A Condensed History of Cooperstown, with a Biographical Sketch of J. Fenimore Cooper* (Albany: J. Munsell, 1862), 118; Edwin G. Burrows and Mike Wallace, *Gotham: A History of New York City to 1898* (New York: Oxford University Press, 1999), 496; Taylor, *William Cooper's Town*, 382–83; Paul C. Gutjahr, *An American Bible: A History of the Good Book in the United States, 1777–1880* (Stanford: Stanford University Press, 1999), 29–37.

47. Cooper was participating in a family pattern here. Isaac, who had served as clerk of the parish at its organizational meeting on January 1, 1811, and (with the exception of the single year 1812) who remained head of the vestry as long as his health permitted, preceded James as delegate for the October 1812 meeting in New York. Aside from Isaac Cooper and Daniel Nash, who chaired Christ Church's organizational meeting in 1811 and went as the delegate in 1814, the parish in fact sent no other delegates to New York before 1820 except for James Cooper in 1815. George E. DeMille, *Christ Church, Cooperstown, N.Y., 1810–1960: A Parish History* (n.p.: n.p., 1960), 59, 4–6; G. Pomeroy Keese, comp., *Historic Records of Christ Church, Cooperstown, N.Y.* (Cooperstown: S. Shaw, printer, [1899]), 5–6, 7–11, [42–43], 35–36.

48. J. Hanks to JC, 9/13/1816 (with note from William Cook), JFC paps., box 2,

AAS; Horatio G. Spafford, *Gazetteer of the State of New-York* (Albany: B. D. Packard, 1824), 552–53. It is not absolutely certain that Cooper's 1816 efforts succeeded, though I think that Isaac Cooper's 1817 diary entry—"Going to have a Bell in Meeting House"— reflected the fruition of Cooper's continuing labors. Isaac Cooper diary, 3/8/1817.

49. The family had arrived back in Otsego from Westchester by late July 1816, although Cooper had been there for the first part of June as well (see notation of cash "Received of James Cooper from the 6th to the 15 of June [1816]" in Courtland C. Cooper, "Monies paid and rec'd").

50. Cyrenus Clark, bill, 1816, JFC paps., box 4, AAS; Robert Campbell, summary of Clark's remaining charges, 2/12/1821, JFC paps., box 5, AAS. Clark's last charge was for a small quantity of bricks and three thousand feet of hemlock joists in June of 1817. On the use of brick for partitions, see the materials list for Hyde Hall, in Mary Raddant Tomlan and Ruth Osgood Trovato, eds., *A Neat Plain Modern Stile: Philip Hooker and His Contemporaries* (Clinton: Hamilton College, 1993), 170.

51. At that time, it was reported that "there was a considerable quantity of materials, such as doors, shutters, &c. within its walls, (the floors having been all laid)"; Cooperstown *Freeman's Journal*, 7/28/1823. All of those wood items of course provided ready fuel for the fire.

52. Isaac Cooper diary, 7/27/1816, 11/6–12/13/1816.

53. Isaac Cooper diary, 10/14/1816, 12/31/1816, 1/14/1817. For Isaac, the year began with his virtual imprisonment at his own new home, "sick from 18th January to April," and still unable to walk at the start of May (a reference to Isaac's "invalid Chair" in a letter written by Susan Cooper the following year suggests just how serious his condition was; Isaac Cooper diary, 2/6/1816, 5/5/1816; SDC to JC, 6/17/1817, copy in JFB paps., box 10, AAS). During the fall of 1816, the Coopers had at least one house guest to entertain—Susan's youngest sister, Martha or "Pinky," now thirteen. She was there for a vacation of sorts from Westchester, but also to help supplement the domestic crew at the farm after a local girl carelessly left the infant Cally alone on a bed and she fell, fracturing her collarbone; see SFM 19; JC and SDC to Caroline DeLancey, 9/16/1816, JFC paps., box 2, AAS.

54. Courtland C. Cooper, "Monies paid and rec'd."

55. Courtland C. Cooper, "Account of Money paid me in Owego, August 21st 1816 by the Sheriff of Broom County in Philadelphia Money," 9/16/1816, JFC paps., box 4, AAS.

56. Mason Whiting to Isaac Cooper, 12/2/1813, WC paps., box 27, HCA. "Feronia" was essentially congruent with the modern boundaries of the township (as opposed to the city) of Binghamton, running from the south side of the Susquehanna River to the Pennsylvania border. For the boundaries, compare the outline of the manor on the map titled "Feronia" in WC, Landbook, WC paps., HCA, with the borders of the township of Binghamton on any modern map of Broome County. Feronia is the name of an ob-

scure Italian goddess sometimes described as a patroness of freedmen. However, the Coopers, apparently aware that bog iron was common in the area, probably coined Feronia (from *ferrum* and *onus*) to indicate that the land there was iron-bearing. See Horatio Gates Spafford, *A Gazetteer of the State of New-York* (Albany: H. C. Southwick, 1813), 161 (s.v., "Chenango," the township that then included the lands in question).

57. Andrew Sherburne, *Memoirs of Andrew Sherburne* (Utica: William Williams, 1828), 226.

58. Mason Whiting to Isaac Cooper, 8/30/1815, and Joshua Whiting to Isaac Cooper, 11/1/1815, both in WC paps., box 27, HCA. The 1815 resurvey is recorded on a map drawn by Elijah Higbe, in WC, Landbook. Although Higbe did show corner trees (marked with the initials "WC"—for *witness corner*, not for "William Cooper") and stone piles, few of his measurements exactly coincided with such markers, which also are found on the earlier Feronia map, also in the Landbook.

59. Mason Whiting to Isaac Cooper, 1/19/1815, 8/30/1815; and Lloyd S. Daubeny to Isaac Cooper, 12/13/1815; all in WC paps., box 27, HCA; John Fine to Isaac Cooper, WC paps., old microfilm series, roll 22, HCA. Although Courtland apparently turned the $1,200 over to Cooper, it probably soon went into the estate's coffers. As late as 1819, Cooper admitted to Thomas Bridgen, son of a creditor of Judge Cooper, that the lands in Feronia had been "divided but not released"—that is, not legally deeded to the different heirs; JC to Thomas Bridgen, 2/10/1819, TF paps., box 333 (SC13256), NYSL.

60. The purpose of this trip with regard to Feronia is vague; we know only that the friends came back "from Chenango Point" on January 26, just when Isaac was at last dividing the Feronia lands among the remaining heirs; Isaac Cooper diary, 1/26/1817. Cooper wound up with a total of just more than twelve hundred acres in Feronia, slightly smaller than the shares falling to William, Isaac, and Samuel but slightly larger than those assigned to the Pomeroys and Richard's heirs. The value agreed to by the Coopers for any Feronia lands was Judge Cooper's figure of $4.00 per acre, meaning that each heir gained another $5,000 at this point, but again largely on paper. See Richard Fenimore and Isaac Cooper, Account Book with William Cooper estate, WC paps., HCA.

61. Isaac Cooper diary, 5/14/1817. He probably waited another two days, too, until Betsey Walby, a domestic at Edgewater, was "initiated in the Capacity of Nurse at Mr. J. Cooper's" (ibid., 5/16/1817).

62. JC to Mason Whiting, Binghamton, 5/19/1817 (not in *LJ*), WC paps., old microfilm series, roll 22, HCA (the phrase "the present situation of the Estate" refers to the fact that, since the division of holdings among William Cooper's heirs, no one individual could extend a power of attorney for all the heirs).

63. Mason Whiting to Isaac Cooper, 11/28/1817, WC paps., old microfilm series, roll 22, HCA. At some point during this period, Cooper and Mason Whiting went off together to "Silver Lake" (perhaps the famous salmon trout lake in Susquehanna County,

Pennsylvania, due south of Binghamton; see SFC, *RH* 377) and arrived at Whiting's house as "hungry as wolves" (see Mason Whiting to JC, 2/10/1834, JFC paps., box 2, AAS). Whiting and members of his family also had visited Isaac Cooper at Edgewater at least twice in 1816; Isaac Cooper diary, 1/24/1816, 7/22/1816.

64. Lida S. Penfield, "Three Generations of Coopers in Oswego," *Fifth Publication of the Oswego Historical Society* (1941): 1–3; *Otsego Herald*, 8/21/1813. William may have moved to Oswego as early as April 1812: while visiting Cooperstown for the purpose of supervising early work on Fenimore Farm, Cooper wrote Susan then that William had embarked on a mysterious journey about which his estranged wife Eliza was as "ignorant" as "the rest of the family." The only good news on that front was that William "drew no money from here for his journey" (*LJ* 1:26).

65. Luther Bradish to Isaac Cooper, 2/7/1817, WC paps., old microfilm series, roll 22, HCA; Courtland C. Cooper to JC, 7/3/1819, JFC paps., box 5, AAS; Seth Pomeroy to Isaac Cooper, 12/19/1817, WC paps., old microfilm series, roll 22, HCA.

66. Luther Bradish to Isaac Cooper, 2/7/1817; William and Eliza Clason Cooper to Luther Bradish, conveyances, 2/7/1816, St. Lawrence County Clerk's Office, Canton, N.Y., book 4, p. 355, and Franklin County Clerk's Office, Malone, N.Y., book 1, p. 322.

67. Isaac Cooper to Luther Bradish, 3/28/1817, Isaac Cooper Letterbook, WC paps., box 10, HCA.

68. Isaac Cooper to Frederick DePeyster, 5/31/1817, Isaac Cooper Letterbook; see Frederick DePeyster to Isaac Cooper, 5/8/1817, WC paps., old microfilm series, roll 22, HCA.

69. Elkanah Watson, *Men and Times of the Revolution*, ed. Winslow C. Watson, 2nd ed. (New York: Dana, 1856), 425–27.

70. *Otsego Herald*, 12/12/1816.

71. Ibid., 3/13/1817.

72. Ibid., 2/20/1817; Darbyshire: "James Cooper's Leases," JFC paps., box 4, AAS; JC, "Land Accounts," ca. 1810–1851, p. 24, Cooper family paps. microfilm, HSFC, New York City.

73. *Otsego Herald*, 3/13/1817; Erastus Crafts to JC, 4/17/1817, copy in JFB paps., box 10, AAS. On Crafts, see D. Hamilton Hurd, *History of Otsego County* (Philadelphia: Everts and Fariss, 1878), 168.

74. *Otsego Herald*, 3/13/1817, 1/9/1817.

75. Ibid., 3/13/1817, 1/30/1817; Taylor discusses the politics of the agricultural society movement, *Williams Cooper's Town*, 384–85. At its meeting on the day of the 1817 fair, the society board voted to insist "that no person shall be entitled to a Premium from this Society hereafter, unless he shall be clothed exclusively in American manufactures" (Otsego County Agricultural Society [OCAS] minute book, 1817–1822, NYSHA, entry for 10/14/1817).

76. Isaac Cooper diary, 12/5/1816, 1/9/1817, 1/20/1817.

77. Jacob Morris to JC, 2/25/1817, copy in JFB paps., box 10, AAS; Cooper's letters to Morris do not appear to survive.

78. OCAS minute book, 3/22/1817.

79. Endorsement on Jacob Morris to JC, 3/14/1817, copy in JFB paps., box 10, AAS

80. Thomas J. DeLancey to JC, 4/24/1817, copy in JFB paps., box 10, AAS. OCAS minute book, 6/23/1817 (the badges, priced at twenty-five cents each, were available for sale from the treasurer by late August—ibid., 8/31/1817).

81. *Otsego Herald*, 1/30/1817.

82. Ibid., 3/13/1817.

83. Isaac Cooper diary, 6/1–6/2/1817 (dinner with visitors). On Franchot, see John Warner Brown, *Stanislas Pascal Franchot (1774–1855)* (privately printed, 1935), 62–68; on Wilkins, see *LJ* 1:211n.

84. *Otsego Herald*, 9/4/1817, Isaac Cooper diary, 9/22/1817 (September meeting); on Humphreys, see Connor, "Brief History of the Sheep Industry," 101; *Otsego Herald*, 10/9/1817 (Watson and Gold responses).

85. Cooperstown *Watch-Tower*, 10/16/1817.

86. Isaac Cooper diary, 7/7/1817; address flap, John P. DeLancey to JC, 6/13/1817, copy in JFB paps., box 10, AAS.

87. SDC to JC, 6/11/1817, 6/17/1817 (torn), copies in JFB paps., box 10, AAS.

88. Ibid. During Susan's confinement and the baby's delivery in May, her cousin Eliza Floyd Nicoll had come thirty miles east from her present home in Hamilton to Cooperstown to offer Susan some assistance; SFM 20, 37; Thomas J. DeLancey to JC, 4/24/1817.

89. Mapes and Oakley, bill, 6/12/1817–4/18/1818, JFC paps., box 4, AAS; John P. DeLancey to JC, 6/13/1817, 6/19/1817, copies in JFB paps., box 10, AAS. James may have used the personal note to cover a note of Isaac at the Bank of Albany (see "James Cooper's Account with the Estate," April 1817, JFC paps., box 4, AAS); if this was the case, then the debt to DeLancey was obviously part of an attempt to aid the estate—and DeLancey presumably had been informed about the problems the Coopers were facing.

90. Thomas J. DeLancey to JC, 11/19/1816, JFC paps., box 2, AAS. The terms under which Cooper resolved the crisis surrounding the $3,000 personal note are not clear. What is clear is that DeLancey continued to provide Cooper further financial aid over the next six months, but that Cooper discharged these new obligations fairly quickly even as the original one remained unpaid. After that point, he was permitted to draw on the bank itself by depositing his own notes in the account. But here, too, he gradually paid down his overall indebtedness to the bank in what was, in essence, a series of refinancings of his original note. During this whole period, he also was making regular deposits of cash on his own or through various second parties acting on his behalf. JC,

Bank of New York bank book, 1817–1819, JFC paps., box 4, AAS. From this time on he would develop a very close friendship with the bank's cashier, the Anglo-American Charles Wilkes; see Henry W. Domet, *A History of the Bank of New York* (Boston: Houghton Mifflin, 1884), 61–62, 79–84; David Longworth, *American Almanac, and New-York Register and City Directory for the Fortieth Year of American Independence* (New York: Longworth, 1815), 86.

91. When, in April, Cooper had transferred some of his livestock from Otsego to the Hickory Grove, he had no intention of moving there himself. Rather, he was stocking the Westchester property, which had long been in the hands of Huguenot tenants, so that he could remove them and put his own hired manager in their place, thereby substantially boosting his income from the farm. This shift away from the long-standing arrangement that Susan had inherited along with the Hickory Grove, understandable in view of Cooper's tight financial situation, at first caused some tension with the De-Lanceys, who apparently looked with some disfavor on the banishment of the old tenants from the farm. Thomas J. DeLancey to JC, 1/9/1817, 4/24/1817, copies in JFB paps., box 10, AAS; Robert Bolton, *The History of the Several Towns, Manors, and Patents of the County of Westchester* (New York: Chas. F. Roper, 1881), 2:231–32.

92. SDC to JC, 6/11/1817 (includes news of Mrs. DeLancey's planned visit), 6/17/1817 (torn); on the torn remainder of the second letter, addressed to Cooper in Albany, Susan wrote that she had thought of a half-dozen other things the family needed and hoped there was still time for him to purchase them. These items hardly would be needed in Otsego if the family were about to pull up its stakes there: "candles, best and common . . . two or three teapots Egyptian . . . two or three common ones . . . a mortar and pestle—groceries of all sorts."

93. James H. Pickering, "Fenimore Cooper as Country Gentleman: A New Glimpse at Cooper's Westchester Years," *NYH* 72(1991): 306, points out that the Angevine property was transferred to the Coopers early in 1818, but work on the new house there already had begun.

94. Isaac Cooper diary, 6/6/1817; Cooper family Bible leaves. Susan served as one sponsor for her daughter at the christening, along with proxies for John P. DeLancey and the baby's namesake, sister Anne Charlotte DeLancey in England (the naming of the child may be another indication that the DeLanceys in fact *had* been to England in the fall and winter of 1816–1817 and had reestablished contact with their long unseen oldest child there).

95. SDC to JC, 6/11/1817; J. and A. F. Baird receipt, 6/21/1817, JFC paps., box 4, AAS (the receipt mentions the presence of a "friend" and two or more servants at the inn with Cooper and specifies that he boarded his horses there for two days); for Sutherland, who came from Poughkeepsie, see *Catalogue of the Officers and Students in Yale-College, November, 1804* (New Haven: Comstock, Griswold, 1804).

96. Thomas J. DeLancey to JC, 1/9/1817.

CHAPTER 7. GAINS AND LOSSES

1. The decision to open the store was made in February 1817; Isaac Cooper diary, 2/25/1817, NYSHA. Courtland's financial interest in the outlet is suggested by two surviving documents: an 1822 accounting for interest and principal due on an 1817–1818 debt to Albany suppliers William and Henry B. Cook that shows a fifty-fifty split, strongly suggesting that the liability was mutual (see "1819 Feby 7 principal . . . $1540.79," JFC paps., box 5, AAS); and a court document revealing that in 1824 Cooper assigned a large debt Courtland owed him, estimated at more than $4,000, to New York lawyer Robert Sedgwick to cover debts of his own contracted at the time the store was being set up and restocked (see JC, Chancery Court bill of complaint, 2/21/1826, copy in JFB paps., box 18, AAS). Courtland mentioned his list of goods in letters to Cooper dated 6/5 and 7/4/1817, JFC paps., box 2, AAS. On Cooper's trip to DeKalb, see his notation about a cash payment from Courtland "paid me in De Kalb in July" in JC, "Cortland C. Cooper in account with James Cooper, Sept 15, 1817," JFC papers, box 5, AAS; Cooper's assignment of five properties to Joshua Brookes on 1/28/1821 (Franklin County deeds, book 2, p. 303) mentions that Cooper had leased four of them to other men in Bangor on July 15, 1817, presumably while on his DeKalb trip. On Courtland's earlier activities on Cooper's behalf, see his "Account of Money Paid me in Owego August 31st 1816," dated "Fenimore September 6th 1816," "Monies paid & rec'd" (1816), and "Account of Rents paid me and the manner in which I paid it out," 12/27/1816, all in JFC papers, box 4, AAS. Cooper's father had established a store in DeKalb in 1803, but the 1817 partnership with Courtland was not a continuation of it. Nor did it occupy the same premises. The longtime keeper of the old store, Thomas B. Benedict, fell into financial difficulties during the War of 1812 and eventually was bailed out by his father-in-law, Nathaniel Smith of New Haven. Cooper may have seen Benedict's failure as providing a chance for his own venture. He certainly knew a good deal about Benedict's woes; he undertook a "Journey to Connecticut" for the estate in April 1817, during which he received $2,700 on its behalf from "N. Smith"; see "James Cooper's Acct. with the Estate," April 1817, JFC paps., box 4, AAS.

2. Platt, the brother of Judge Cooper's Federalist colleague Jonas Platt (and thus a relative and associate of Melancthon T. Woolsey), was more importantly the grandson of Gen. William Floyd and therefore another of Susan Cooper's kinsmen. M. M. Bagg, *The Pioneers of Utica* (Utica: Curtiss and Childs, 1877), 348; J. H. French, *Gazetteer of the State of New York* (Syracuse: R. P. Smith, 1860), 471; Pomroy Jones, *Annals and Recollections of Oneida County* (Rome: P. Jones, 1851), 605–6; references to Cooper's financial dealings with Platt occur primarily in the twelve surviving letters sent him during this period from Courtland C. Cooper (JFC paps., box 2, AAS), and three others once in the Richard and Isaac Cooper correspondence that appear to survive only on roll 22 of the microfilm of the Cooper papers produced in the 1950s for Paul F. Cooper, Jr. (a set of which is in HCA).

3. Cooper's draws from the estate between 1813 and 1817 were insufficient to cover construction costs at Fenimore Farm. Isaac largely supplied him with petty cash during this period, eventually debiting a total of nearly $5,000 against him for miscellaneous advances. Some of the latter probably covered Cooper's interest payments in Utica; in March 1815, Isaac thus sent $904.50 (nearly 2 percent of his stipulated share of Judge Cooper's leavings) "to Utica" for him. Richard Fenimore Cooper and Isaac Cooper, Account Book with William Cooper estate, Cooper family paps. microfilm, HSFC, New York City (James Cooper debit 3/15/1815; see also 12/31/1814). It is worth noting that Isaac's Utica payments for Cooper were roughly equivalent to others he sent there at the same time for William and, on 3/15/1815, for Samuel as well. Conceivably, the Utica arrangement had been set up by Richard and Isaac (or at their suggestion) as a means of supplying the younger heirs with cash until the distribution of estate assets began in earnest. No evidence has surfaced to indicate that Cooper formally assigned any of his Otsego leaseholds to James Platt as collateral for his loans. Platt was notorious for his "inability to say no" (Bagg, *Pioneers of Utica*, 348)—perhaps especially to a seemingly prosperous son of wealth recently married to his cousin.

4. It is possible that Courtland's obligation to James Platt was confined to notes Cooper had given the banker to cover the cost of setting up and restocking the DeKalb store, but Courtland's indication that the May 1818 Utica payment was for $1,500 (Courtland C. Cooper to JC, 5/12/1818, JFC paps., box 2, AAS) suggests that such was not the case.

5. Courtland C. Cooper to JC, 5/5/1818, JFC paps., box 2, AAS. Courtland had his supporters. New Yorker Henry M. Fine, who assisted Potter Goff in the DeKalb survey in 1814–1815, concluded he was "a superior fellow" whose "judgment & sagacity" in view of his lack of education were "uncommon"; see "Classification of the Township of Dekalb," 61, DeKalb Bound Volume Collection, item 1, St. Lawrence County Historical Society, Canton, N.Y.

6. Courtland C. Cooper to JC, 3/11/1817, 6/5/1817, JFC paps., box 2, AAS; same to same, 4/1/1817, old microfilm series, roll 22, HCA.

7. Courtland C. Cooper to JC, 10/1/1817, 5/5/1818, 11/20/1817, JFC paps., box 2, AAS.

8. Courtland C. Cooper to JC 10/1/1817.

9. Courtland went to Albany first, purchasing a substantial bill of goods (valued at $1,441.44) that the merchants added to Cooper's tab. When Cooper himself went there on February 7, bound for DeKalb once again, the Cooks also charged his smaller order of textiles. William and Henry B. Cook, statement, JC, 2/7/1818, JFC paps., box 5, AAS. On Cooper's presence in DeKalb shortly afterwards, see JC, witnessed signature (dated 2/18/1818) on conveyance to Barton Carver, St. Lawrence County deeds, book 5, p. 339; also, Joseph Plumb's attestation (dated 2/23/1818) on JC, conveyance to Prince Merick, Franklin County deeds, book 2, p. 169.

10. During Cooper's visit to DeKalb early in 1818, the cousins resolved to widen their store's market. Soon Courtland began running an advertisement in the Ogdensburg paper, the *St. Lawrence Gazette*, alerting "Clothiers" that he had stocked items of interest to them such as "*Dye Woods, Press Papers, Jacks, &c. &c.*" The partners promised "A considerable discount . . . for cash," of course, but were realistic enough to recognize that wholesale customers, like most retail ones, would expect "low prices and long credits." Courtland also advertised "Drugs and Medicines" for physicians "at reasonable prices and usual credit." While it was questionable whether such wholesale efforts really would enhance the store's income, for the present they certainly required more outlays. *St. Lawrence Gazette*, 3/3/1818 (dated 2/18/1818; first run 2/24/1818). Courtland C. Cooper to JC, 5/5/1818. This letter is in reply to a lost letter from Cooper of 4/7/1818.

11. Courtland C. Cooper to JC, 5/5/1818, 6/24/1818, JFC paps., box 2, AAS.

12. Courtland C. Cooper to JC, 7/22/1818, JFC paps., box 2, AAS.

13. Courtland C. Cooper to JC, 4/1/1819, JFC paps., box 2, AAS.

14. Courtland C. Cooper to JC, 6/1/1819, JFC paps., box 2, AAS.

15. JC, articles of agreement with William Cook, 2/4/1818, JFC paps., box 5, AAS, and "1819 Feby 7 principal . . . $1540.79."

16. Cooper in 1826 estimated that Courtland's total debt to him, clearly derived from the DeKalb store and therefore including the obligation to the Cooks, exceeded $4,000. Courtland can hardly have invested much cash in the operation at any time. JC, Chancery Court bill of complaint, 2/21/1826.

17. Courtland C. Cooper to JC, 12/1/1819, JFC paps., box 2, AAS; "1819 Feby 7 principal . . . $1540.79." JC, Chancery Court bill of complaint, 2/21/1826.

18. Isaac Cooper diary [kept by someone else during his absence], 9/13–9/15/1817.

19. Ibid., 2/10/1817, 9/5/1817, 9/13/1817 (Pomp was among Isaac's horses; perhaps Cod Fish was as well); SDC to JC, 6/17/1817, copy in JFB paps., box 10, AAS; *Otsego Herald*, 9/18/1817.

20. John Frederick Ernst, receipt (for silver coffin plate), 9/16/1817, Cooper family paps., NYSHA; Isaac Cooper diary, 9/15/1817.

21. Isaac Cooper diary, 9/16–9/25/1817; JC, articles of agreement with Robert R. Ward, 9/23/1817, JFC paps., box 5, AAS. Isaac Cooper's diary indicates that he and Mary Ann Cooper returned from DeKalb on September 29, just in time to inventory his mother's estate. See "A True and Perfect Inventory of all and singular the Goods, Chattels and credits of Elizabeth Cooper, Deceased," WC paps., box 28, HCA; various of Mrs. Cooper's kin and acquaintances bought or took different pieces of her few leavings, but her youngest son apparently received nothing (see "Amount of Property taken by the following persons," Cooper family paps., NYSHA).

22. Isaac and Mary Ann Cooper to JC, 12/17/1817, JFC paps., box 2, AAS. The letter also revealed that Ann Cooper Pomeroy had lost an infant about three weeks earlier.

23. SFC, "A Glance Backward," *Atlantic Monthly* 59(1887): 200.

24. J. Thomas Scharf, *History of Westchester County, New York* (Philadelphia: L. E. Preston, 1886), map of Manor of Scarsdale, following 1:140; 1:673, 681; Robert Bolton, *The History of the Several Towns, Manors, and Patents of the County of Westchester* (New York: Chas. F. Roper, 1881), 2:231–32 (Bolton's assertion, 2:231, that the Angevines occupied the part of the farm that Cooper named after them is wrong).

25. James H. Pickering, "Fenimore Cooper as Country Gentleman: A New Glimpse at Cooper's Westchester Years," *NYH* 77(1991): 306.

26. Articles of agreement with Robert R. Ward; Robert R. Ward bill (for work at Fenimore), 7/23/1816, JFC paps., box 5, AAS.

27. James Worden, bill, 12/8/1817, JFC paps., box 7, AAS; JC to Thomas Bridgen, 12/12/1817, TF paps., box 331 (SC13256), NYSL, reports the raising of the house frame.

28. See Allan M. Butler, M.D., "Scarsdale," in Scharf, *History of Westchester County*, 1:681. Other details in this anecdote are wildly inaccurate: Butler gives 1840 as the year Cooper built the house, says the place was torn down soon after it was built, and describes it as resembling "the typical Swiss chalet."

29. Articles of Agreement with Robert R. Ward; Mary Raddant Tomlan, ed., *A Neat Plain Modern Stile: Philip Hooker and His Contemporaries* (Amherst: University of Massachusetts Press, 1993), 160–74. One of the wings served as a "drawing-room," where, Cooper's daughter recalled, his literary career began (SFM 35). Beard (*LJ* 1, Plate V) reproduces Goodrich's sketches.

30. JC to Pierre Van Cortlandt, 9/23/1818, in Jacob Judd, ed., *The Van Cortlandt Family Papers*, vol. 4 (Tarrytown: Sleepy Hollow Restorations, 1981), 70.

31. Ward was to pick out the parcels, but had not done so by the time the Coopers finally moved into the new house. In fact, he balked at those far-flung (and overvalued) locations. Cooper, attempting to mollify him, offered to transfer unspecified Otsego lands, but Ward instead cashed out his contract by selling it to attorney Robert Campbell in November 1818. Campbell agreed to accept land from Cooper, but likewise preferred the nearby to the faraway. Three years later, Cooper at last gave Campbell notes to cover the debt, but they remained unpaid as late as 1826, by which point the Coopers had long since abandoned their new house at Angevine, were living in New York City, and soon would depart for France. Robert Campbell to JC, 11/2/1818, 1/4/1819, 4/29–5/11/1819, 4/5/1820, 2/12/1821, 4/22/1822, 1/21/1826, all in JFC paps., box 2, AAS.

32. Cooper's partner was the oldest son of Gen. Sylvester Dering, a militia officer and agriculturalist with large holdings on Shelter Island, just above Sag Harbor. Farming supplemented the maritime income of the Derings and their Long Island kin, which included the Nicolls of Islip and Shelter Island, the family of Charles's wife Eliza. See *LJ* 1:67, 3:383–84; Silas Wood, *A Sketch of the First Settlement of the Several Towns of Long-Island* (Brooklyn: Furman Club, 1865), 152, 196–97; Benjamin F. Thompson, *History of Long Island*, 3rd ed. (New York: Robert H. Dodd, 1918), 2:218–24, 3:333–45; Ho-

ratio Gates Spafford, *A Gazetteer of the State of New-York* (Albany: B. D. Packard, 1824), 489.

33. Cooper may have encountered Eliza's brother William at Yale in 1804–1805, when the young Nicoll was a freshman; see *Catalogue of the Officers and Students in Yale-College* (New Haven: Comstock, Griswold, 1804).

34. The elder Nicoll had taken Susan Cooper's cousin, Anne Floyd, as his first wife and had long presided over the old Nicoll estate on Shelter Island. Eliza Dering was among his many children by Anne; another was Samuel Benjamin, a lawyer in nearby Riverhead, who eventually bought the family estate from his brother Richard, who had successfully outmaneuvered his many siblings to take it over on their father's death in 1828. Eliza's father probably was the Coopers' most immediate host and companion during their Shelter Island visits earlier in the century. *P&P* 390; Benjamin F. Thompson, *The History of Long Island*, 2nd ed. (New York: Gould, Banks, 1843), 2:396. In 1839, Cooper referred historian George Bancroft to Samuel B. Nicoll for further information about the family (see *LJ* 3:384); Charles Dering's partner in his business in Utica had been Richard F. Nicoll, another of Eliza's siblings; Bagg, *Pioneers of Utica*, 287; Thompson, *Long Island*, 2nd ed., 2:396–97.

35. See Anna Mulford, *A Sketch of Dr. John Smith Sage* (Sag Harbor: J. H. Hunt, 1897), 28. Although in *The Sea Lions* Cooper was to reconstruct the region as he had known it in 1819–1821 from the perspective of the island's north end, near Sylvester Manor and Dering Harbor, Mulford's linkage of the Coopers to the Nicoll house on Sachem's Neck (on the southwestern shore of the island close to Sag Harbor) is seemingly confirmed by their daughter's 1881 version of her tale about her parents' visits there; see SFC, "Introduction," *SL* HE xii. Cooper derived a good deal more from Shelter Island ("so named from the snug berth it occupies," [*SL* 1:11]) than his next financial opportunity. The sparsely populated ten-square-mile island lay at the center of a rich ecological zone that combined elements of sea, shore, and field. Cooper loved the "semi-aquatic" life of the Derings and Nicolls, his daughter Susan recalled, and often joined them in hunting and fishing trips. The sometime mariner also was attracted to the great variety of vessels plying the waters around the island—fishing smacks, sailboats, rowboats, trading sloops, and whalers (SFC, "Introduction," *SL* HE xiii).

36. Thompson, *Long Island*, 3rd ed., 2:183.

37. George A. Finckenor, *Whales and Whaling: Port of Sag Harbor, New York* (Sag Harbor: William Ewers, 1975), passim.

38. That visit may have taken place early in November 1818, when Cooper stayed for several days at the City Hotel (see Chester Jennings, bill, 3/5/1819, JFC paps., box 4, AAS); Charles Dering to JC, 12/14/1818, YCAL (no letters from Cooper to Dering appear to have survived).

39. Cooper and his wife were in the city for several days at the beginning of Febru-

ary; shortly after they returned to Westchester, he went back to New York alone; see JC to Thomas Bridgen, 2/10/1819, TF paps., box 333, NYSL.

40. The negotiations began well before Cooper informed Dering about them; see Robert Campbell to JC, 2/15/1819, reporting that Mumford already was having inquiries made into Cooper's Otsego real estate (JFC paps., box 5, AAS); Charles T. Dering to JC, 4/1/1819, YCAL; the bill of sale and ship's registration are in JFC paps., box 5, AAS.

41. New York *Mercantile Advertiser*, 2/26/1819; the *Union* was available for "Sale, Freight, or Charter."

42. Wood, *Sketch*, 196–97; "Walter Barrett" [Joseph A. Scoville], *The Old Merchants of New York City*, 3 vols. (New York: M. Doolady, 1870), 1:359–61; Charles T. Dering to JC, 4/1/1819, 4/27/1819, YCAL.

43. Charles T. Dering to JC, 4/27/1819.

44. Charles T. Dering to JC, 8/21/1819, YCAL.

45. JC, bond, 4/15/1819, to Gurdon S. Mumford, copy in JFB paps., box 10, AAS.

46. JC, conveyance, 6/10/1819, to Gurdon S. Mumford, Otsego County conveyances, liber Z, 314; JC and Gurdon S. Mumford, Purchase Agreement for the ship *Union*, 4/15/1819, copy in JFB paps., box 10, AAS. Cooper apparently had asked Robert Campbell about selling Mt. Ovis the previous fall; using it for the *Union* was therefore an alternative to disposing of it for cash. Campbell thought no one in Cooperstown would have the means to purchase it; Robert Campbell to JC, 11/2/1818, JFC paps., box 2, AAS.

47. Charles T. Dering to JC, 4/27/1819, 5/27/1819, YCAL.

48. When it later proved difficult to insure the vessel, Dering thought that having Eckford issue a certificate of its seaworthiness would help; Charles T. Dering to JC, 5/6/1819, 9/13/1819, YCAL.

49. Charles T. Dering to JC, 6/30/1819, YCAL.

50. The hotel bill shows large "board and sundries" charges for blocks of days across May, June, and July, with a room charge added for the period from July 7 to 12; Cooper may have stayed elsewhere in the city, perhaps at his brother William's house on Pine Street or even on board the *Union*, and taken meals at the Hotel. Chester Jennings, bill, 7/31/1819, JFC paps., box 7, AAS.

51. "Cash advanced by James Cooper on acct. of Whaling out-fit," YCAL. Some of the $2,000, more than $500, was debited against Dering, indicating that Cooper advanced him money for his share of the outfit; Charles T. Dering to JC, 8/10/1819, 9/3/1819, YCAL.

52. Charles T. Dering to JC, 8/14/1819, YCAL.

53. Charles T. Dering to JC, 7/4/1819, 8/4/1819, YCAL.

54. Dering to JC, 7/4/1819.

55. Dering to JC, 8/4/1819; Mulford, *Dr. John Smith Sage*, 28–29 (Cooper certainly had time to meet Osborne, though not in 1820, when he was not present during the departure of the *Union*); Dering to JC, 8/10/1819.

56. Charles T. Dering to JC, 8/4/1819, 8/7/1819, YCAL; Dering to JC, 8/10/1819, 8/14/1819.

57. Dering to JC, 8/21/1819, YCAL; Cooper wrote a brief account of whale hunting on a Brazil voyage in his review of William Scoresby, *Account of the Arctic Regions, with a Description and History of the Northern Whale Fishery*, in 1821; see *ECE* 60–63. In *The Sea Lions* (*SL* 1:149–61), Cooper inserted a brief narrative of a whale hunt carried on by his twin two-boat sealing vessels; this drew on both Scoresby and his own experience while owner of the *Union*.

58. Mary Kelley, ed., *The Power of Her Sympathy: The Autobiography and Journal of Catharine Maria Sedgwick* (Boston: Northeastern University Press, 1993), 20, 104–6.

59. Harriet Langdon Pruyn Rice, *Harmanus Bleecker: An Albany Dutchman* (Albany: William Boyd, 1924), 12–14; Alice P. Kenney, *The Gansevoorts of Albany: Dutch Patricians in the Upper Hudson Valley* (Syracuse: Syracuse University Press, 1969), 151–53, reports that Peter Gansevoort studied under Tapping Reeve.

60. *The Letters of William Cullen Bryant*, ed. William Cullen Bryant II and Thomas G. Voss, 6 vols. (New York: Fordham University Press, 1975–92), 1:122, 154. By September, Bryant was reporting that the "very warm friendship" that had once existed between Cooper and Robert Sedgwick had ended because of their financial misunderstanding and the resultant lawsuits; ibid., 1:196, and Bryant, "Reminiscences of Miss Sedgwick," in Mary E. Dewey, ed., *The Life and Letters of Catharine M. Sedgwick* (New York: Harper and Bros., 1871), 441.

61. Sedgwick may have exacted no discount because Cooper personally backed up the full amount of the judgment and promised to pay annual interest on it until Sedgwick collected. Cooper also reserved the right to collect his interest payments in turn from the St. Lawrence lawyer George C. Conant, up to 2/7/1819, and stipulated that if he paid Sedgwick the full amount due from Conant, Sedgwick would reassign the judgment to him; that may have happened, since in an endorsement made to the assignment itself on 6/1/1826, Cooper appointed Peter A. Jay his attorney to collect the interest due him (see JC, assignment of Conant bond, 10/15/1817, JFC paps., box 5, AAS). On Courtland Cooper's dealings with the lawyer for his cousin, see Courtland C. Cooper to JC, 3/11/1817, 6/5/1817, 5/17/1818, 7/22/1818, all in JFC paps., box 2, AAS.

62. In September 1820, the St. Lawrence County sheriff urged Sedgwick to be patient with lawyer Conant because the debt was secured by a valuable property and a forced sale might ruin Conant. Sedgwick forwarded the sheriff's letter to Cooper, acknowledging Conant's tough situation but insisting that Cooper pay Sedgwick at least half the money due from Conant. Sedgwick was willing to delay execution against Conant only if it cost him nothing—only, that is, if Cooper indemnified him against losses arising from a delay; D. C. Judson to Robert Sedgwick, 9/7/1820; Robert Sedgwick to JC, 9/14/1820, both in JFC paps., box 2, AAS. Cooper indicated in 1826 that he had paid Sedgwick all the interest due on the Conant bond; however, he believed at that time that

Sedgwick eventually collected not only the principal but also duplicate interest payments from Conant. In 1824, Sedgwick in fact had credited Conant's interest payments against Cooper's bond to Sedgwick. See JC, Chancery Court bill of complaint, 2/21/1826.

63. *LJ* 1:121; JC, assignment to Robert Sedgwick, 10/31/1818, JFC paps., box 5, AAS. The May 1818 loan may have been intended to cover old debts, such as the sketchily understood ones associated with the Utica bank—or, on the other hand, new expenditures associated with the DeKalb store or the erection of Angevine.

64. It is not clear what properties had been assigned to cover the original debt when the first note was extended in August. In 1825, Cooper asserted that he gave security for the extended note and then, when he borrowed the second amount from Sedgwick, there was "a blending of the securities for both loans" (*LJ* 1:121). JC, undated draft deposition [ca. January 1826], in Sedgwick v. Cooper (New York Supreme Court), copy in JFB paps., box 18, AAS.

65. See Courtland C. Cooper to JC, 4/1/1819, 6/1/1819, JFC paps., box 2, AAS.

66. *LJ* 1:121; JC, note (for $1984.32) to Robert Sedgwick, 8/1/1818; JC, note (for $1060.50) and leasehold assignment to Robert Sedgwick, 10/31/1818 (assignment canceled 3/30/1819); JC, bond (penalty amount $5021.47; nominal amount $3024.47) to Robert Sedgwick, 3/12/1819 (see *LJ* 1:121 for explanation of discrepancies in amounts), all in JFC paps., box 5. AAS. JC and SDC, mortgage to Robert Sedgwick, 3/12/1819, Otsego County Mortgages, liber G, 474. As Bruce H. Mann points out, judges often ignored penalty clauses in bonds in the event that legal action ensued; the actual damages became the operative figure. See *Republic of Debtors: Bankruptcy in the Age of American Independence* (Cambridge: Harvard University Press, 2002), 11, 268n11.

67. JC, draft deposition [ca. January 1826]. In this document, Cooper wrote that "several weeks before the maturity of these united loans, he [Cooper] made an offer to extend the period of payment to one year, and to give 18 per cent per annum for the use of the same." Sedgwick "took time to consider of the same," then when they reached a verbal agreement "refused to take more than 12 per cent per annum" but demanded the substitution of the fee simple lands in Otsego for the leaseholds.

68. Cooper let Sedgwick draw up the written agreement; when he went to sign it, Sedgwick told him that "as he had declined to take 18 per cent for the use of his money and had agreed to accept of 12," Cooper ought "to be willing to pay for the back loan"— the original May 1818 loan—"at the same rate." JC, draft deposition [ca. January 1826].

69. George Dangerfield, *The Awakening of American Nationalism, 1815–1828* (New York: Harper and Row, 1965), 84.

70. JC, draft deposition [ca. January 1826].

71. [Peter Augustus Jay], notes on trial, 3/23/1825, copy in JFB paps., box 18, AAS. The jury, however, found for the plaintiff, Sedgwick.

72. JC, draft deposition [ca. January 1826].

73. Ibid.

74. JC and SDC, conveyance to Robert Ward, 9/8/1919, Otsego County conveyances, liber Z, 493–97.

75. JC and SDC to Thomas Ward, 7/28/1819, St. Lawrence County conveyances, liber 5, 418; 11/4/1819, liber 5, 607; 12/29/1820, liber 6, 24.

76. JC and SDC, conveyance to Thomas Ward, 9/20/1819, Franklin County conveyances, liber 1, 481; JC, conveyance to Thomas Ward, 11/4/1819, Otsego County conveyances, liber BB, 476.

77. A clipping preserved in the account book of Cooper's Otsego leasehold farms notes that by the end of 1823—perhaps in consequence of having bought so much undeveloped land from Cooper in the north country—Col. Thomas Ward was officially regarded in New York State as an "absent debtor," and the confiscation of his lands and other properties in New York, Otsego, and St. Lawrence counties was threatened within a year. Eventually, at least some of the Otsego leaseholds Ward had bought from Cooper fell into the hands of William H. Averell, the Cooperstown lawyer who also eagerly picked up other former Cooper properties at auctions resulting from a series of Chancery Court cases against the Cooper estate (and James Cooper as its surviving executor) in the early 1820s (see Chapter 10). The account book pages devoted to each of the leaseholds sold to Ward indicate the date of the respective transfers; subsequent notations of rents received for each of them, in the hand of Robert Campbell, indicate that Campbell looked after the properties for Ward following the sales (JC, land account book 1810–1851, Cooper family paps. microfilm, HSFC, New York City). Why the account book wound up back in Cooper's possession is unknown; it may be that Cooper had some hand in the suits against Ward, or Campbell may have simply turned it over to Cooper because it also contained records of rents paid on other properties Cooper still owned.

78. It is uncertain whether Ward paid Cooper cash for all his purchases, at least immediately, even though that is what the various conveyances indeed assert. I believe, however, that Cooper's main purpose with these sales was to gather the means to discharge the Utica debt, which the DeKalb store had proved unable to service, let alone pay off. For this purpose, cash or its functional equivalent (e.g., an assignable note from Ward) would have been essential. The amount of the Utica debt may be roughly calculated as $10,000 or more if one assumes that the recorded payments Isaac Cooper sent there were for annual interest at the legal rate. The $904.50 Isaac sent in March 1815 in fact would be a bit less than legal interest for a year on $13,000.

CHAPTER 8. A BETTER BOOK

1. Cooper, who had taken over the vessel a few days early, received word of the birth in a letter from John Peter DeLancey, went home a couple of days later, but soon returned to the city. John Peter DeLancey to JC, 6/15/1820, copy in JFB paps., box 9, AAS; Chester Jennings, bill, 7/31/1819, JFC paps., box 4, AAS.

2. *Otsego Herald,* 2/22/1819; Robert Campbell to JC, 2/15/1819, JFC paps., box 2, AAS. Campbell foresaw difficulties owing to the fact that Sam apparently had not made a will. His own lands would remain unproductive for a time—but the oversight also would add "to the embarrassment," as the lawyer put it, of dealing with Judge Cooper's estate.

3. Mary Ann Cooper to JC, 6/18/1819, copy in JFB paps., box 10, AAS. If Cooper sent an answer to their plea, it does not survive.

4. Robert Campbell to JFC, 6/2/1819, 8/4/1819, JFC paps., box 2, AAS.

5. *Freeman's Journal,* 10/11/1819, 10/25/1819; Thomas Bridgen to JC, 10/26/1819, draft; Samuel Starkweather to Thomas Bridgen, 10/19/1819, 10/21/1819 (conveying word of William Cooper's decline and death); and JC to Thomas Bridgen, 11/11/1819 ("Your letter was received and contained the first information of the death of my Brother which I received."), all TF paps., boxes 332, 333 (SC13256), NYSL. How desperate Cooper's brother William had become at the end of his life is suggested by the manner in which he and his intermittently estranged wife Eliza sought to bend law and morality alike in contesting the terms of her father's will; see Robert Desty, ed., *Reports of Cases Adjudged and Determined in the Court of Chancery of the State of New York* (Rochester: Lawyers' Co-operative, 1888–1889), 7 vols., 1:656–57 (6/30/1818), 703–4 (10/7/1818), 1141–42 (8/3/1821).

6. William Jay, *The Life of John Jay: With Selections from His Correspondence,* 2 vols. (New York: J. and J. Harper, 1833), 1:449, 1:454; *Westchester Herald,* 5/12/1818; Cooper renewed his membership in the national body (American Bible Society, receipt for 1818–1819 dues, 6/11/1819, JFC paps., box 4, AAS).

7. Cooper drafted the constitution with William Jay and chairman James Morris; it was presented to the second meeting on June 9, which was chaired by the elder DeLancey and during which John Jay was chosen president, William Jay was named secretary, and Cooper became one of the society's twenty-one directors; *Westchester Herald,* 7/7/1818.

8. *Westchester Herald,* 11/10/1818, 12/8/1818.

9. Alan Taylor, *William Cooper's Town: Power and Persuasion on the Frontier of the Early American Republic* (New York: Knopf, 1995), 351, 170–84.

10. Craig R. Hanyan, "DeWitt Clinton and Partisanship: The Development of Clintonianism from 1811 to 1820," NYHS *Quarterly* 56(1972): 109–31.

11. B. Thalhimer, *The Annual Register, and Military Roster* (Albany: E. and E. Hosford, 1821), 162.

12. Jacob Judd, ed., *Correspondence of the Van Cortlandt Family of Cortlandt Manor, 1815–1848* (Tarrytown: Sleepy Hollow Restorations, 1981), 50–51; *Correspondence of the Van Cortlandt Family of Cortlandt Manor, 1800–1814* (Sleepy Hollow: Sleepy Hollow Restorations, 1978), xl. Van Cortlandt had married DeWitt Clinton's first cousin (and George Clinton's daughter), Catherine, in 1801, and was very close to both politicians.

13. Judd, *Correspondence . . . 1815–1848*, 70–71. Cooper assumed his new duties almost immediately. Van Cortlandt alerted him of a militia review due to be held on October 5, 1818, at the Underhill farm, a property close to Angevine. Although Cooper was very much "occupied with workmen and business, . . . having but just moved into [his] new house," he insisted that Van Cortlandt (and his aides, at the rate of "a bed a piece") stay at his farm during the October review.

14. Hugh Hastings, ed., *Military Minutes of the Council of Appointment of the State of New York, 1783–1821*, 3 vols. (Albany: James B. Lyon, 1901), 3:2031, 2095; the Fourth Division consisted of the Fifteenth Brigade of infantry from Westchester and the Twenty-ninth Brigade of infantry from Rockland County; Thalhimer, *Annual Register*, 162–64.

15. There is a brief reference to Cooper's militia activities in an 1820 letter. "I am on the staff of the Major General," Cooper wrote New York City bookseller Andrew Thompson Goodrich (serving as the agent for Cooper's soon-to-be-released first book, *Precaution*), "and must go out in Rockland County next week." He was, he confessed with the punning reference to the world of publishing fully intended, "compelled to attend the *reviews* next week" (*LJ* 1:62). In that particular case, as Cooper soon updated Goodrich, Van Cortlandt countermanded the order, canceling the review (*LJ* 1:63).

16. The same source that confirms Cooper's place on Pierre Van Cortlandt's divisional staff lists the officer attending Clinton as commander-in-chief of the state militia, and Cooper is not included there (Thalhimer, *Annual Register*, 137).

17. Evan Cornog, *The Birth of Empire: DeWitt Clinton and the American Experience, 1769–1828* (New York: Oxford University Press, 1998), 130.

18. Hastings, *Military Minutes*, 3:2325–26.

19. Alexander C. Flick, ed., *A History of New York*, 10 vols. (New York: Columbia University Press, 1933–1937), 6:52; *Otsego Herald*, 5/1/1820; for Cooper's comments on Tompkins, see *LJ* 1:40. Tompkins did so well on Shelter Island and its vicinity that Cooper's whaling partner wrote him, "Tompkins is undoubtedly elected Baa—a—"; Charles T. Dering to JC, 4/29/1820, YCAL.

20. *National Advocate*, 4/14/1820; this paper was edited by anti-Clintonian Mordecai Noah, a playwright and diplomat whose *Travels in England, France, Spain, and the Barbary States* (1819) Cooper had just recently purchased and of whom he had a mixed opinion (see *LJ* 1:50; 68).

21. New York *Columbian*, 4/21/1820. For Cooper's exaction of Marshall's statement, see *LJ* 1:40.

22. New York *Columbian*, 4/21/1820.

23. See Thomas James DeLancey to JC, 5/9/1811, copy in JFB paps., box 9, AAS.

24. *Otsego Herald*, 2/14/1820; Thalhimer, *Annual Register*, p. 111; the journal of Cooper's unidentified political friend is excerpted in J. Thomas Scharf, *History of Westchester County, New York*, 2 vols. (Philadelphia: L. E. Preston, 1886), 1:485–86.

25. William Jay to JC, 6/20/1820, JFC paps., box 2, AAS; Scharf, *History of West-chester County*, 1:529; Bayard Tuckerman, *William Jay and the Constitutional Movement against Slavery* (1893; New York: Burt Franklin, 1969), 14; Cooper may also have helped secure the post of New York City recorder for Jay's older brother Peter in 1820. For Cooper's description of a township election in rural New York that may reflect his 1820 experiences, see *Notions* 1:257–62.

26. The *Union* had kept him in New York for much of the first half of 1819, but even once the ship left port he was often in the city. In January 1820, he explained to Albany lawyer Thomas Bridgen that personal affairs had kept him extremely busy there over the winter: he had not "been at home more than one month in the last four." JC to Thomas Bridgen, 1/24/1820, TF paps., box 333, NYSL.

27. We do not know what the book in question was. In the 1880s, Cooper's daughter Susan thought it was "one of Mrs. Opie's" novels—or, she added, a book by another member "of that school" (SFM 38). Cooper in fact had "a profound admiration" for the works of Amelia Alderson Opie, whom he met in Paris through the artist Pierre Jean David and with whom he and his wife socialized at Lafayette's and elsewhere in the latter part of 1830; see Margaret Eliot Macgregor, *Amelia Alderson Opie: Worldling and Friend* (Menasha: George Banta, 1933), xi; *LJ* 2:4–5; and a draft fragment, dated 5/13/1832, in Cooper's hand and that of two unknown individuals addressed to "Mrs. Opie," perhaps intended as a note to be left on calling at her home, JFC paps., box 2, AAS. That Opie had no major work of fiction published between 1816 and 1822 would in itself seem to rule out the possibility that a "newly imported novel" from her hand could have caused Cooper's annoyance in 1820. To the contrary, Opie's body of fiction as a whole, with its emphasis on moral issues, made her an attractive general model for him. That was especially true once he gave up the initial project of correcting the offensive author of the book that displeased him by writing "a moral tale" and instead took up the more challenging task of writing "a novel." It may well be, as various scholars have argued, that Jane Austen was even more particularly his model for this revamped purpose, especially since her last book, *Persuasion*, provides so many parallels to Cooper's plot, as well as to his title (see James Wallace, *Early Cooper and His Audience* [New York: Columbia University Press, 1986], 67–68, drawing on George E. Hastings, "How Cooper Became A Novelist," *AL* 12[1940]: 20–51). Written in 1815–1816, Austen's book was published late in 1817, a few months after the author's death. Cooper's probable reliance on it does not, it should be stressed, mean that *Persuasion* was the book he threw down as he took up the gauntlet. Quite the contrary—as with Opie, his response to Austen was a sincere form of praise.

28. Susan's comment about Charles Wilkes was anticipated in the first published account of how Cooper came to write *Precaution;* see William Cullen Bryant's "Discourse," in *Memorial of James Fenimore Cooper* (New York: G. P. Putnam, 1852), 42.

29. As late as October 1820, Cooper explicitly stated to Goodrich that he had not

contacted Wilkes to give him instructions on that financial issue, adding as well, "he knows *nothing* of the book" (*LJ* 1:65–66; italics added). There is, on the other hand, the mysterious evidence of a March 14, 1825, inscription Cooper wrote in a copy of the English first edition of *Precaution:* "To Charles Wilkes Esquire who alone knows the secret history of its authorship, this book is presented by his obliged friend, James Cooper" (*Spy* CE xiii). On Wilkes's aid in arranging for the English publication of Cooper's works in 1822, see *LJ* 1:247; on their possible discussion of Scott's financial situation, see *LJ* 1:133.

30. "Walter Barrett" [Joseph A. Scoville], *The Old Merchants of New York City* (New York: M. Doolady, 1870), 2, pt. 1:257; Eric Quayle, *The Ruin of Sir Walter Scott* (New York: Clarkson N. Potter, 1969), 56–156.

31. It is *possible* that Cooper staged his disgust with the book he was reading to Susan so that he could introduce the preposterous plan with a show of spontaneous plausibility. Probably Cooper's generous attempt to aid Scott during his last financial crisis after the collapse of Constable and Company (and Ballantyne and Company) in 1826 also marks his guarded sense of gratitude for Scott's real example, which was as much financial as literary.

32. Aitchison may have been living in Westchester at the time, as he later did, or perhaps was staying at Angevine in the spring of 1820 on one of several visits there; see James Aitchison to JC, 2/9/[1824], JFC paps., box 2, AAS; SFM 44. I discuss the case of *The Pilot* in Chapter 13.

33. Tuckerman, *William Jay*, 8–9.

34. A. T. Goodrich, bills, 12/24/1818, 3/4/1819; JC, Bank of New York check drawn to Goodrich, 4/6/1819; JFC paps., box 4, AAS.

35. Susan E. Lyman, "'I Could Write You a Better Book than That Myself': Twenty-five Unpublished Letters of JFC," NYHS *Quarterly Bulletin* 29(1945): 217.

36. That successor journal, *The New-York Journal and Belles-Lettres Repository*, would publish a positive review of *Precaution;* see 4(Nov. 1820): 38–41.

37. With young Henry Phinney, Cooper is said by his daughter to have written and set in type a romance modeled on a sixteenth-century text, Jeronimo Fernandez's *Honour of Chivalry, or the Renowned and Famous History of Don Bellianis of Greece* (1547), one of the works pilloried by Cervantes in *Don Quixote* (*P&P* 19).

38. Van Winkle was identified as the book's printer by Lyman, "'I Could Write You a Better Book,'" 219; see also *LJ* 1:61.

39. See, for example, *PRE* 1:13, ll. 8–12; 1:14, ll. 7–10; compare these instances from Chapter 2 with the way dialogue is set in Chapter 3, especially 1:20–21; but Chapter 3 itself gives other instances of the run-on practice Cooper was here critiquing—for example, 1:24–25; see also 1:197, ll. 19–29.

40. The labyrinth of interpretation into which the green author thus merrily led the printer is suggested by the manner in which various passages in the novel were altered

for the first revised editions of 1838–1839: compare, for instance, *PRE* 2:224 with *PRE* 1839 2:181.

41. Charles T. Dering to JC, 2/23/1820, 7/17/1820, YCAL.

42. William Bryan to Charles T. Dering, 10/21/1819, enclosed in Henry P. Dering to JC, 12/3/1819; Charles T. Dering to JC, 2/23/1820, 4/29/1820, enclosing Augustus C. Douglass to "father," 1/30/1820; Charles T. Dering to JC, 7/8/1820; copies of all in JFB paps., box 10, AAS.

43. Dering expressed interest in it in April; Cooper did not agree to the second voyage until the end of June, but even then remained tentative; Charles T. Dering to JC, 4/29/1820, 7/8/1820.

44. Charles T. Dering to JC, 7/8/1820, 7/17/1820, and JC, notes on address flap of latter.

45. See Charles T. Dering to JC, 7/8/1820, in which the refitting of the vessel is estimated at $3,000, half of which Dering hopes he can personally assume.

46. On July 17, Cooper had asked Goodrich to bring a copy of Mary Brunton's *Discipline* with him; although Susan acknowledged its receipt on July 28, it obviously had been sent by the bookseller rather than personally delivered (*LJ* 1:51–53).

47. The first edition was issued in light blue printed boards (*S&B* 17); the date of the copyright notice (August 25, 1820; see *PRE* 1:[iv]) confirms Cooper's impression that Goodrich indeed considered the volume ready for the public.

48. *PRE*, errata sheet, found in either volume. Surely it angered Cooper that such mistakes as the following, the most famous of them all and the second referred to in his August 27 letter, remained in the book: "To this, Sir Edward cordially assented, and the old *gentleman* separated, happy in their arrangements to advance the welfare of two beings they so sincerely loved" (*PRE* 1:245; italics added).

49. Cooper expected to return to Long Island around September 1 (see *LJ* 1:53) but delayed this trip until later in the month (see *LJ* 1:60).

50. Moss Kent's older brother and a close friend of the Coopers, James Kent, was the chief judge of New York's Chancery Court, the state's equity court at the time.

51. See Lyman, "'I Could Write You a Better Book,'" 219.

52. In other ways, the debt-ridden Scott also set limits. This had been an extraordinarily active year for Scott, *The Abbot* being the third new novel issued so far in 1820. Cooper had no illusions that *Precaution* could compete with Scott merely in a commercial sense. It hadn't, of course, been written in Scott's mode. Even so, he wanted to hold off publishing his own book until "week after next" in order to "let the Abbot blow over a little" (*LJ* 1:66–67).

53. New York *Commercial Advertiser*, 7/3/1820.

54. Although Cooper certainly intended to assert ownership rights, he had arranged for Goodrich to file for copyright in his name. Evidently the two had signed an agreement by which ownership was privately ceded to Goodrich and then returned to Cooper.

55. New York *Daily Advertiser*, 11/20/1820; Lyman, "'I Could Write You a Better Book,'" 220. At least four other booksellers, including Cooper's next partners in the literary business, the firm of Charles Wiley and Oliver Halsted, also advertised the book on the same page of the newspaper as for sale in their shops.

56. Some weeks later, Cooper also made it clear that he did not want to copy over the manuscript himself: "I would rather write from my head six such books than Copy one" (*LJ* 1:67).

57. Junius Smith, a native of Plymouth, Connecticut, had trained for the law after graduating in 1802. He went to London in 1805 to petition for the return of an American merchantman seized by British authorities, and then became affiliated with a New York merchant firm operating there. Cooper probably had seen Smith in New York City during the latter's return visit in 1810, but he was better acquainted with Smith's brother Lucius, a classmate, who became an Episcopal clergyman in western New York. See Franklin B. Dexter, *Biographical Sketches of the Graduates of Yale College with Annals of the College History*, 6 vols. (New Haven: Yale University Press, 1885–1912), 6:538–40, 6:560–61.

58. Lyman, "'I Could Write You a Better Book,'" 220.

59. Washington Irving to Charles Wiley, 3/6/1822, JFC paps., box 2, AAS.

CHAPTER 9. AN AMERICAN TALE

1. It has been asserted that Cooper owed his concept of "the Neutral Ground" to Scott. George Dekker thus wrote: "*The Spy* is subtitled 'A Tale of the Neutral Ground'; and as 'neutral ground' is a phrase that crops up frequently in the Waverley Novels, Cooper's subtitle can probably be taken as an announcement that he is following in the footsteps of Sir Walter Scott"; *James Fenimore Cooper the Novelist* (London: Routledge and Kegan Paul, 1967), 33. Bruce A. Rosenberg concurred: "Many novels, particularly novels of espionage, have a No-Man's-Land, or what Cooper called, following Scott, the Neutral Ground"; *The Neutral Ground: The André Affair and the Backgrounds of Cooper's The Spy* (Westport: Greenwood, 1994), 95. Scott certainly employed the term, which had long been in general military use, but Cooper's adoption of the phrase also seems to have formalized and made virtually universal the old sense of Westchester as "neutral ground," in evidence even during the Revolution; see, for instance, Maj. John André's admission in his 9/24/1780 letter to Gen. George Washington (in Winthrop Sargent, *The Life and Career of Major John André* [Boston: Ticknor and Fields, 1861], 325) that, when captured, he had passed outside "the American posts to neutral ground." Both Dekker and Rosenberg also go on to note important thematic distinctions between Scott's usage and Cooper's.

2. For the next couple of weeks the pace of Cooper's work on *The Spy* does not appear to have slackened even though the amount of work required by *Precaution* was just then sharply increasing. His July 2 letter to Goodrich mentioned his eagerness to have

the bookseller's "opinion of the 'Spy.'" It went on, in an obviously but not completely humorous vein, to predict that the new book would be "either vastly more popular than 'Precaution' or intolerable" (*LJ* 1:46).

3. Grattan (1792?–1827) was a relatively young but quite active printer in the 1820s. Probably his most impressive accomplishment was his work on David Longworth's *American Almanac* for the years 1821–1824. Among literary figures, he did the presswork on parts I–III of Richard Henry Dana, Sr.'s serial, *The Idle Man* (1821–1822), and the expanded second edition of Fitz-Greene Halleck's *Fanny* (1821), both imprints of Wiley and Halsted.

4. SFC, "A Glance Backward," *Atlantic Monthly* 59(1887): 205. *Precaution* was not immediately reprinted in the United States, and its only significant reviews were in New York magazines with some tie to Cooper: Gardner's *Repository* and Goodrich's old vehicle, the since renamed *New-York Literary Review*. By contrast, *The Spy* was reviewed in Baltimore, Boston, and Washington as well as New York and was reprinted twice in the first five months.

5. Not until July 1821, the modern editors of *The Spy* for the Cooper Edition conclude, does he appear to have picked up the job of writing again (*Spy* CE xxi–xxii).

6. Grattan, from whom no second receipt survives, may have waited as long or longer. The small amount paid Wiley for paper in February may suggest that Grattan had not yet printed a full run of sheets—only proofs; receipts, William Grattan to JC, 2/20/1821; Wiley and Halsted to JC, 2/20/1821, 10/31/1821 ("Fifty Dollars, in full, for printing paper, &c."), JFC paps., box 5, AAS. On Cooper's probable presence at the City Hotel in February 1821: see Robert Campbell to JC, 2/12/1821, addressed to Mamaroneck but forwarded from there to City Hotel, JFC paps, box 2, AAS; Chester Jennings to JC, statement of City Hotel account, post-2/12/1822, showing Cooper with an opening balance (as of 10/1/1821) of $306.48, probably reflecting his stay there the previous winter; and statement of account, Mapes and Oakley to JC, 1818–1821, indicating that Cooper was in the store on 2/8/1821; all in JFC paps., boxes 4, 5, AAS.

7. So one may conclude from the agreement for the second edition, dated 2/14/1822; JFC paps., box 5, AAS; Wiley confirmed that he was acting as Cooper's agent, not the book's publisher, precisely Cooper's arrangement with Goodrich. See his correspondence with distributors as quoted by William Charvat, *Literary Publishing in America, 1790–1850* (1959; rpt. Amherst: University of Massachusetts Press, 1993), 51, 88n12.

8. I assume here that Wiley read the chapters as they came to him. He certainly played some role in readying the manuscript for Grattan's typesetters. But it is also true that he was a man of great literary interests; furthermore, his evolving friendship with Cooper surely would have given him added cause to at least scan what passed through his hands on its way to Thames Street.

9. Grattan almost certainly did *not* produce the thousand copies of the final gather-

ing at this time, since the penultimate chapter was to end on the first page of that gathering.

10. On the shortness of the penultimate chapter, however, it should be noted that the first chapter of the second volume was just as short.

11. We may assume that Cooper was in New York on September 7, 1821, because a letter he had written in the city the day before was postmarked there on the seventh (see *LJ* 1:70–71). Cooper's daughter in 1887 recalled him as saying, however, that the final chapter of the book had been set in pages "several weeks before the intervening chapters were even planned"; SFC, "Glance Backward," 205.

12. Robert Campbell to JC, 9/10/1821, JFC paps., box 2, AAS. Tracking Cooper's presence in New York is possible because of his account with the keeper of the City Hotel; see note 14 below.

13. The first references to *The Pioneers* occur in Charles Wiley to JC, 1/7/1821 [for 1822], and C. K. Gardner to JC, 1/7/1822 (which refers to Wiley as a source on the subject and helps establish the date of Wiley's letter), both in JFC paps., box 2, AAS. Cooper did not avoid all fun while in the city during these weeks; it was then that he must have attended the fall horse races at the Union Course in Jamaica, Long Island; see Chapter 12.

14. "James Cooper to C. Jennings, Dr.," [2/20/1822], JFC paps., box 4, AAS. This statement of account is extraordinarily condensed. I interpret the various notations "P-1" as indicating dates on which Cooper occupied a parlor as well as sleeping quarters (which Jennings seems to have indicated in a few entries as "R-1"). Some nights between Cooper's arrival and his departure in a given week he seems not to have been charged for lodgings; I presume that this was either a slip of record-keeping or an indication that on occasion he stayed with friends elsewhere in the city, near the navy yard in Brooklyn, or in the suburbs. In the 1819 statement of account from Jennings, Cooper was charged for renting a parlor for the nights when Susan was with him; in 1821, he probably used it as a work space (see Chester Jennings, bill, 3/5/1819, JFC paps., box 4, AAS).

15. Perhaps it was these nearly weekly trips that his daughter Susan, then eight, recalled when she wrote that during the time at Angevine Cooper "went frequently to New York, sometimes by the Mamaroneck stage, sometimes in his gig, occasionally on horseback"—sometimes even on foot (SFM 48).

16. The book was published on December 22; New York *American*, 12/22/1821 (*Spy* CE 453n2).

17. See also "The Battle of Plattsburgh Bay," Cooper's 1840s piece on that episode of the War of 1812, first published in 1869: "It is not generally known that the idea of recolonization, as respects this whole country, was not altogether abandoned among English statesmen, until after the peace of 1815"; *Putnam's Magazine*, n.s., 3(1869): 52. The ending of Cooper's first Revolutionary novel on the Niagara frontier during the War of 1812 may seem ill-considered aesthetically, but it unequivocally links the two national

struggles. The specific use of that phase of the second war with Britain may have derived from hints gathered in Wiley's back room. Charles K. Gardner no doubt held forth there on his experiences on the Niagara frontier during 1814, when he had played a significant part in the battle of Lundy's Lane, a brief account of which Cooper was to insert in the final chapter of *The Spy;* see Benson J. Lossing, *The Pictorial Field-Book of the War of 1812* (New York: Harper and Brothers, 1868), 804, 817–28; John D. Morris, *Sword of the Border: Major General Jacob Jennings Brown, 1775–1828* (Kent: Kent State University Press, 2000), 84, 102–4, 113–42. Some hints of the ending may also have come from tales circulating in Cooperstown about the experience of the elderly soldier Jedidiah Peck, who, as noted in Chapter 5, fought on the Niagara frontier during the summer of 1812.

18. I take the term "mimicry" from Bill Ashcroft, Gareth Griffiths, and Helen Tiffin, *The Empire Writes Back: Theory and Practice in Post-Colonial Literatures* (London: Routledge, 1989), 88.

19. Joseph Plumb Martin, *A Narrative of Some of the Adventures, Dangers and Sufferings of a Revolutionary Solider* (1830), reprinted as *Private Yankee Doodle,* ed. George F. Scheer (Boston: Little, Brown, 1962), 9, 283.

20. Tallmadge entirely missed the point: *had* he arrested them there by the bridge before André rode into the scene, of course the war would have been lost and he and all the other officers—assuming they did not recant and seek mercy—might well have been swinging from the gallows in André's place. *Annals of Congress,* 14th Cong., 2nd Sess., columns 474–75. See Robert E. Cray, Jr., "Major John André and the Three Captors: Class Dynamics and Revolutionary Memory Wars in the Early Republic, 1780–1831," *Journal of the Early Republic* 17(1997): 371–97.

21. Cray, "Memory Wars," 386. Soon the icon of the aged veteran began showing up in American paintings and prints. In 1819, the German immigrant painter John Lewis Krimmel included in "Fourth of July Celebration in Centre Square, Philadelphia," militia men and fresh recruits, as well as naval officers representing the heroes of the second war with Britain, but also an old Continental solider who bares his chest to reveal the scars of his patriotic wounds. See Anneliese Harding, *John Lewis Krimmel: Genre Artist of the Early Republic* (Winterthur: Winterthur Museum, 1994), Figure 277. The source of that detail may well be President Monroe's well-known 1817 visit with Connecticut veterans of the infamous Fort Griswold massacre; Monroe not only inspected but touched their scars (S. Putnam Waldo, *The Tour of James Monroe, President of the United States,* 2nd. ed. [Hartford: Silas Andrus, 1820], 129, 134).

22. *Van Cortlandt Family Papers, Volume Four: Correspondence . . . 1815–1848,* ed. Jacob Judd (Tarrytown: Sleepy Hollow Restorations, 1981), 43–44. This was almost certainly an answering slander, although Arnold's attempt to persuade Tallmadge to join him after he had fled to New York, the fact that Tallmadge became "deeply attached" to André while guarding him, and his famous decision never to tell all he knew of the

André episode, do strike one as odd; see *Memoir of Colonel Benjamin Tallmadge,* ed. Henry P. Johnston (New York: Gilliss, 1904), 57, 136–40.

23. Egbert Benson, *Vindication of the Captors of Major André* (New York: J. M. Bradstreet and Son, 1865), 98.

24. Monroe's tour, very unusual for a sitting president, was widely reported in newspapers across the summer of 1817. He sought out encounters with ordinary veterans and fully indulged in nostalgic sentiments with them, signaling a shift in public culture; see Waldo, *The Tour of James Monroe.* It should be noted that Tallmadge had not run for reelection in 1816 and therefore was a lame duck when he attacked Paulding. On the pension act and its roots, see John Resch, *Suffering Soldiers: Revolutionary War Veterans, Moral Sentiment, and Political Culture in the Early Republic* (Amherst: University of Massachusetts Press, 1999). Resch points out (p. 100) that in the House, Monroe's proposal was considered by a special committee chaired by Gen. Joseph Bloomfield of New Jersey—an old Cooper family friend. While Bloomfield's bill, following Monroe's suggestion, specifically included virtually all indigent veterans who had served any length of time in any unit, Continental or not, the Senate's included only veterans (including officers) who had served at least nine months in the regular army. While the Senate bill was clearly weighted against militia and state troops, suggesting an elite bias, opposition to the very idea of a pension came from Republicans in the upper house who thought *any* such entitlements contrary to American principles. In the end, the Senate's views shaped the resulting compromise, meaning that John Paulding, had he survived, would not have been eligible under it. It should also be noted that subsequent alarms over abuse of the program by veterans who were not indigent led to the introduction of a means test in the 1820 revision. Resch, *Suffering Soldiers,* 100–46.

25. Cooper was aware that "political enmity" and "personal envy" had somewhat clouded Washington's reputation in the 1790s (*Spy* CE 418).

26. One reason the actual details of the plot had to be invented was that Jay's anecdotes concerned the very first months of the war.

27. This last detail must mean that he knew Benjamin Tallmadge, who was in charge of the guard. Dorothy Barck, ed., *The Minutes of the Committee and First Commission for Detecting Conspiracies,* NYHS *Collections,* 1924–1925, 1:47, 80, 93–94; 2:420; Enoch Crosby pension file, NARA, microfilm M804, roll 604.

28. E[dward George Geoffrey Smith] Stanley [fourteenth earl of Derby], *Journal of a Tour in America, 1824–1825* ([London]: privately printed, 1930), 36. Both Benson and Crosby testified in the 1827 New York trial, which concerned John Jacob Astor's claim to lands near Crosby's Putnam County farm; when Crosby entered the courtroom, according to H. L. Barnum's *The Spy Unmasked; or, Memoirs of Enoch Crosby, Alias Harvey Birch, the Hero of Mr. Cooper's Tale of the Neutral Ground* (New York: J. and J. Harper, 1828), he was recognized by "an old gentleman who, not having heard of him for a number of years, supposed (like Jay and Cooper) that Crosby had been, long since,

numbered with the dead" (xii)—the old gentleman being, I take it, Benson himself; see Edward V. Sparhawk, *Report of the Trial, before Judges Thompson and Betts, in the Circuit Court of the U.S. for the Southern District of New-York, in the Case of James Jackson, ex dem. Theodosius Fowler and others vs. James Carver* . . . (New York: Elam Bliss, 1827), 10, 13, 15. Jay and Benson's supervision of Crosby is made clear in Barck, ed., *Minutes of the Committee*, 1:80, 93–94, 157–60, 160–65.

29. *The Diary of Philip Hone, 1828–1851*, ed. Bayard Tuckerman (New York: Dodd, Mead, 1889), 1:9, 25.

30. Cooper also reportedly told John Holmes Prentiss, the Cooperstown newspaperman, that he had "no knowledge of Enoch Crosby," but added, "Mr. Crosby may have been a patriot, may have been the very person alluded to by the distinguished statesman from whom the first idea was in truth obtained; but if such are the facts, they are entirely unknown to him" (*Freeman's Journal*, 7/20/1835).

31. Crosby himself *was* paid both during his service ($10.00; see Barck, *Minutes of the Committee*, 1:165) and, apparently, when it was over (£200; 2:406). Barnum's first edition also indicates that Crosby received $250 (a "trifling pittance") for "all his revolutionary services" (*The Spy Unmasked*, 165). In addition to Crosby's 1832 pension application narrative and the depositions of several fellow soldiers also contained in his file, there are several depositions he provided for them, which are of some interest regarding his own service: see the files of Timothy Wood (NARA microfilm M804, roll 2631), Jabez Berry (roll 226), and Daniel Crawford (roll 686). James H. Pickering, "Enoch Crosby, Secret Agent of the Neutral Ground: His Own Story," *NYH* 47(1966): 61–73, transcribes Crosby's 1832 application narrative and in his introduction to his reprint of *The Spy Unmasked* (Harrison: Harbor Hill Books, 1975) provides much information on the generally elusive Barnum. There is no doubt in my mind whatsoever that Crosby was the man Jay referred to, although the point has been much disputed, usually by writers interested in putting forward some other "original" for Birch.

32. The attitude still had vigor in the 1820s. Soon after *The Spy* was published, his daughter recalled, one of Cooper's friends ("a prominent merchant, a man of money, very well known in Wall street") accosted him on Broadway. He praised the "admirable book," which he had sat up all night reading. Cooper replied, "My friend Harvey Birch is much obliged to you." Only one thing bothered the "man of money," and in fact it concerned Birch: "here is a man getting into all sorts of scrapes, running his neck into the noose, of his own accord, and where, pray, is his motive? Of course I thought until the last page, that he would be well paid for his services—but just as I expected to see it all made clear as day, he refuses to take the gold General Washington offers him" (*P&P* 31).

33. John Wiley, pension file, NARA microfilm 804, roll 2578; the elder Wiley passed on through his son early in 1822 his complete enthusiasm for *The Spy*—he liked it so well that he promised to meet Cooper's stage the next time he came to New York City and, unhitching the horses, pull it himself the rest of the way (Charles Wiley to JC,

1/7/1821 [for 1822]). As Charles Wiley began his business the year before Cooper was first posted in the city by the navy, it is possible that the midshipman came to know the shop (if not its owner) as early as 1808–1810. An old story that the two were to meet in "western New York" in 1820, passed on without documentation by Henry W. Boynton, seems suspect because as far as can be determined Cooper did not venture that far upstate in the period when he was beginning his literary career; see *Annals of American Bookselling, 1638–1850* (New York: John Wiley and Sons, 1932), 160. Even though the title page of *The Sketch Book* showed Van Winkle as the printer, Wiley is said to have directed the business to his old partner when Irving's friend Henry Brevoort consulted Wiley on the absent author's behalf; Henry W. Boynton, "Wiley and Putnam," in *The First One Hundred and Fifty Years: A History of John Wiley and Sons, Incorporated, 1807–1957* (New York: John Wiley and Sons, 1957), 22–25 (on Wiley), 25 (on Van Winkle and *The Sketch Book*).

34. James G. Wilson, *Bryant and His Friends: Some Reminiscences of the Knicker-bocker Writers* (New York: Fords, Howard, Hulbert, 1886), 190; *The Letters of William Cullen Bryant*, ed. William Cullen Bryant II and Thomas G. Voss (New York: Fordham University Press, 1975–1992), 1:202n2.

35. Cooper's full participation in the discussions at Wiley's began only after his family's move to the city in October 1822, but since meeting Wiley late in 1820 he clearly had spent as much time there as possible. See Albert H. Marckwardt, "The Chronology and Personnel of the Bread and Cheese Club," *AL* 6(1935): 393.

36. Wilson, *Bryant and His Friends*, 190.

37. James P. Elliott suggests that the "tales" mentioned to Wiley owed their origin to that first of Cooper's fictional experiments—the tale put aside for *Precaution* when it grew too big for Cooper's emerging vision in May 1820 (see *Spy* CE xiv), but that seems unlikely; Cooper himself said he had destroyed that early attempt.

38. Wiley to JC, 1/7/1821 [for 1822].

39. Morris, *Sword of the Border*, 190–91, 251; Charles K. Gardner, *Compend of the United States System of Infantry Exercises and Manoeuvres* (New York: Wm. A. Mercein, 1819), and *Rules and Regulations for the Field Exercises and Manoeuvres of Infantry Compiled and Adapted to the Organization of the Army of the United States* (New York: T. and W. Mercein, 1815). Donald A. Ringe, "*The Literary and Scientific Repository, and Critical Review*," in Edward E. Chielens, ed., *American Literary Magazines: The Eighteenth and Nineteenth Centuries* (Westport: Greenwood, 1986), 217.

40. Ringe, in *American Literary Magazines*, 217–18.

41. Beard and Ringe both note that the reviews of Sedgwick and Irving included in *ECE* can only be *ascribed* to Cooper (*ECE* xiii–xiv; Ringe, in *American Literary Magazines*, 219–20). I do not discuss them for this reason. It might be noted here, however, that the concern of the reviewer of Sedgwick's *A New-England Tale* (1822) with her attention to "American society and manners" (*ECE* 97), her focus on "the diversities of

passion, sentiment, and behaviour" manifested in one of "our little communities, detached, as it were, from the great world" (*ECE* 98), and especially her interest in "the characters of communities, the local peculiarities of separate regions" (*ECE* 100)—and "the simple inhabitants of our comparatively waste places" (*ECE* 109)—were consistent with the present concerns of Cooper as he contemplated how to return to and finish *The Pioneers.*

42. This was a greatly enlarged version of Clark's one-volume *Sketches of the Naval History of the United States* (Philadelphia: M. Carey, 1813).

43. "I want your article on Parry—and much thanks for it—by the 20th, or before." Charles K. Gardner to JC, 1/7/1822, JFC paps., box 2, AAS.

44. One source reports that Cambreleng's popularity was such that other guests sent bottles of wine to his table whenever he was at the hotel; "Walter Barrett" [Joseph A. Scoville], *The Old Merchants of New York City* (New York: M. Doolady, 1870), 3, pt. 1:117. In the late fall of 1819, Cambreleng had become involved in a deadly street fight between a companion and the Spanish consul's son. Cooper, who later included Cambreleng in the Lunch, must have known of this tragic event (see Barrett, ibid., 117–24). On Cooper and Cambreleng, see *LJ* 3:14, 4:474, 6:333. For the reference to the Cambreleng review in that of Scoresby, see *ECE* 58.

45. Cooper's ideas may have been drifting toward just this recognition as he came to the end of the essay. Among other praise offered to Cambreleng was the ironic description of his "great fault" as an innocent disregard of "the craft and mystery of bookmaking." The densely packed, finely printed text of the *Examination* might easily have been swelled to three times its current size "by large type, broad margins, and a formal division into books, sections, and chapters" (*ECE* 41–42). Intimately familiar with large type and broad margins (and even the separation of undivided prose manuscripts into "chapters"), the author of *Precaution* in effect was signing the anonymous review by adding this very comment.

46. See also the reviewer's definition of whaling, which expands on this terse comment about materials and skill in the Cambreleng essay: "The capital employed consists of ships, casks, and provisions. The two former we make, and the latter we grow. Their application is by our own skill and industry, and immense quantities of oil and candles are exported every year" (*ECE* 58).

47. Joseph Conrad, "Tales of the Sea" (1898), in *Fenimore Cooper: The Critical Heritage*, ed. George Dekker and John P. McWilliams (London: Routledge and Kegan Paul, 1973), 287–88; Marius Bewley, *The Eccentric Design: Form in the Classic American Novel* (New York: Columbia University Press, 1959), 91–92.

48. Mindful that he was writing in the *Literary and Scientific Repository*, Cooper inserted a note at the end of the review: "We owe it to our scientific character to say distinctly, that we do not believe 'a whale is a fish,' and we would not have presumed thus openly to disobey a late decision of the learned against the use of the word, but that we

have been obliged to adopt the 'parlance' of seamen, and can only speak of marine affairs in the language they use" (*ECE* 64).

49. Philbrick points out in *James Fenimore Cooper and the Development of American Sea Fiction* (Cambridge: Harvard University Press, 1963), 224, that the episode in *The Sea Lions* in which a rope is snagged in the whale's mouth derived from a passage quoted from Scoresby in the 1821 review. Cooper also had his Pacific colonists in *The Crater* go whaling and devoted considerable space to describing the process; see *CR* 2:127–38.

50. At one point in the earlier review, Cooper rather humorously portrayed Scoresby as stopping short of possible discoveries in an ice-free stretch of ocean because he was "afraid of vitiating his policy of insurance"—as for Parry, Cooper already asked there, "What would Parry have given for such a sea?" (*ECE* 57). The two men operated in the same waters but on vastly different assumptions.

51. We thus read that one of Parry's vessels, the *Hecla*, had been a "bomb vessel in the British navy, and was employed in that capacity at the attack on Algiers, under Lord Exmouth: as she seems to have possessed the material property of sailing well, and must, from her original character, have been strongly built, she was probably well adapted to the service on which she was ordered." His other ship, the *Griper*, however, "was a *gun brig, raised upon!*" wrote the astonished reviewer. "We know the danger of commenting upon things at a distance," he conceded, "as well as the strong probability that the English admiralty were better qualified than ourselves, who have never seen the vessel, to decide upon her qualities: But the moment we read her description, we anticipated the very faults she subsequently proved to possess, viz., that she was uncomfortable for her crew, and slow" (*ECE* 66–67). Cooper kept reiterating this judgment by a series of quasi-humorous passages: "the bad qualities of the *gun brig raised upon*, were exhibiting themselves" (74), "alas, poor Griper!" (78), "the poor unfortunate Griper" (82), and so forth.

CHAPTER 10. LEGAL TROUBLES

1. See, for instance, Robert Campbell to JC, 2/12/1821, and "JC in account with RC," 4/29/1819, JFC paps., box 5, AAS; Campbell to JC, 4/19/1821 and 6/26/1821, JFC paps., box 4; Campbell to JC, 3/21/1822, JFC paps., box 2.

2. Bridgen, born in 1786 or 1787, was living in or near Albany with the members of the Ten Eyck family, his deceased mother's kin, when Cooper was studying there with Rev. Thomas Ellison. See Thomas Bridgen to John Winwood (an English kinsman), 2/20/1816 and 10/4/1816 (drafts), TF paps., box 331 (SC13256), NYSL. There may be some trace of the boys' acquaintance in Cooper's portrait of sturdy Guert Ten Eyck, the upper-class Dutch youth in *Satanstoe* with whom visitor Corny Littlepage cavorts on the streets of Albany and on the ice-bound Hudson River before Guert at last falls victim to a Huron attack in the Adirondack forest. Whether the two youths were personally acquainted or not, the social worlds of the Bridgens and the Coopers certainly overlapped.

Bridgen's sisters (Anna Maria and Catherine) thus were to remain close throughout their lives with Albany figures such as the Sedgwicks and Harmanus Bleecker, who were acquaintances of Cooper as well. See Anna Bridgen to Bleecker, in Harriet Langdon Pruyn Rice, *Harmanus Bleecker: An Albany Dutchman* (Albany: Boyd Printing, 1924), 199–201, 212–13, 222–23, 245–48; *LJ* 4:31–33. Cooper's papers and published letters and journals reveal no ties to any other members of the extended Ten Eyck family.

3. The elder Bridgen's rather obscure story must be pieced together from a variety of sources. Apparently orphaned when quite young, he seems to have been adopted by a family named Atwood in his native Shropshire—as a result of which he was known as Thomas Bridgen Atwood during his early years in New York. He reverted to his original name (Thomas B. Bridgen) around 1790 when seeking to recover an English inheritance (and incidentally submerge his old Loyalism). As a physician, his success was enhanced by a risky and innovative foray into a world previously dominated by female caregivers: "Atwood," asserted Cooper's physician and friend John W. Francis, "was the first practitioner of medicine in this city who regularly assumed, by advertisement, the functions of a male accoucheur"—that is, an obstetrician. Francis probably did not know Atwood-Bridgen personally, but he had certainly heard the story of the man's downfall: "He at one time possessed . . . great wealth, but died poor, through the conduct of his son Charles"; *Old New York; or, Reminiscences of the Past Sixty Years*, rev. ed. (New York: W. J. Widdleton, 1858), 200 (Thomas Bridgen the younger tells the story of his half-brother Charles in his previously cited 10/4/1816 letter to John Winwood). Many other details about Atwood-Bridgen's career as a merchant, his privateering activities, his change of name, and the ills visited on him by his son Charles may be derived from copies of letters to English correspondents in his letterbook, TF paps., box 341, NYSL.

4. The elder Bridgen was buried in a small cemetery in Hope Township, Warren County, New Jersey; see "Warren County Cemeteries," *Genealogical Magazine of New Jersey* 40(1965): 100. Thomas Bridgen to John Winwood, 2/20/1816.

5. Thomas Bridgen to JC, 2/2/1819 (draft), TF paps., box 333, NYSL.

6. Thomas Bridgen to Eliza Wendell Bleecker, undated (ca. 1814–1815; draft), TF paps., box 348, NYSL.

7. Indenture, Thomas B. Bridgen and William Cooper, 5/26/1794 (copy), in Thomas Bridgen v. Isaac Cooper and others (filed 12/9/1815), file B307, Miscellaneous Files in Chancery, 1772–1847, Joo87, NYSA. WC to Richard Harison, 9/10/1795, WC paps., box 18, HCA. Although Bridgen took a hands-on approach with some of his real estate ventures (his 1792–1797 diaries, TF paps., box 342, NYSL, show him visiting other frontier properties and personally dealing with settlers there), the property entrusted to William Cooper may have been too inaccessible for a man of his advancing age to actively supervise development there. As a consequence, Bridgen probably welcomed William Cooper's willingness to serve as the active partner.

8. Alexander C. Flick, ed., *History of the State of New York*, 10 vols. (New York: Columbia University Press, 1933–1938), 5:147–48; WC to Richard Harison, 9/10/1795.

9. WC to Charles Bridgen, 10/16/1794 and 1/24/1796, TF paps., NYSL, box 328. Alan Taylor notes that the speculators to whom Cooper sold the lands never moved to the Military Tract themselves and eventually defaulted on their mortgages to the partners; *William Cooper's Town: Power and Persuasion on the Frontier of the Early American Republic* (New York: Knopf, 1995), 333.

10. WC to Charles Bridgen, 1/24/1796.

11. See Richard H. Schein, "A Historical Geography of Central New York: Patterns and Processes of Colonization on the New Military Tract, 1782–1820," Ph.D. dissertation, Syracuse University, 1989, 143–45.

12. Richard Harison to WC, 12/13/1807, WC paps., box 24, HCA.

13. See William Cooper (younger) and Thomas Bridgen (younger), agreement, 3/28/1818, WC paps., box 25, HCA.

14. Thomas Bridgen to Robert Troup, 11/15/1815 (draft), TF paps., box 331, NYSL.

15. Bridgen's chancery bill against Isaac Cooper, 12/9/1815, file B307.

16. Isaac Cooper to Thomas Bridgen, 9/21/1816, TF paps., box 331, NYSL. Deed for "moiety of Bridgen lands," WC to William Steele, 8/2/1804, WC paps., box 9, HCA.

17. JC to Thomas Bridgen, 12/12/1817, TF paps., box 331, NYSL (Bridgen answered Cooper on December 20, but his answer does not appear to survive).

18. William Cooper wasted little time in assuming his duties. He swore before Otsego County surrogate Ambrose L. Jordan on January 19 that he would see to "the true performance and execution" of his father's will; Ambrose Jordan, "Probate of WC's will," dated 12/28/1809, with subsequent note dated 1/19/1818, WC paps., box 11, HCA.

19. Except for the alteration in personnel, this may have been the meeting James Cooper and the younger Bridgen were to have had during their projected "tour" to Otsego earlier that winter. Later in 1818, a recalculation showed a slightly higher balance ($11,100.55) in favor of Bridgen. Thomas Bridgen to Robert Campbell, 10/28/1818, with memorandum of the 3/9/1818 agreement between himself and William Cooper (younger), WC paps., box 25, HCA.

20. Robert Campbell to JC, 11/2/1818, JFC paps., box 2, AAS; see also Thomas Bridgen to Robert Campbell, 10/28/1818 (copy); Robert Campbell to Thomas Bridgen, 11/13/1818, TF paps., box 332, NYSL.

21. Thomas Bridgen to JC, 2/2/1819 (draft), TF paps., box 333, NYSL.

22. The couple had been in New York from 2/5 to 2/11/1819. Cooper's reply to Bridgen was "prompt" in that he wrote it the very day they returned: dated "2/10/1810" on the endorsement flap by Bridgen, it almost certainly was written on 2/11, the morn-

ing the Coopers left the City Hotel and went home; JC to Thomas Bridgen, [2/11/1819], TF paps., box 333, NYSL; Chester Jennings, bill, 3/5/1819, JFC paps., box 4, AAS. Unless otherwise indicated, the direct quotations from Cooper in the next three paragraphs derive from the February 11 letter.

23. Thomas Bridgen to JC, 2/2/1819.

24. "Mr. Henry informed me this morning that although your Brother had spent nearly four weeks in Albany he [Henry] had never had a sight of [him] and that there [are] several very interesting questions to be settled & discussed relative to the Estate & [Henry] finally concluded by saying it was impossible for him to have any thing further to do with it." Thomas Bridgen to JC, 2/2/1819. In 1822, John V. Henry, long an attorney for the Coopers, would submit to chancery master James King a statement of what the Coopers owed him for unpaid legal bills; see the records of the chancery case of George and Ann Pomeroy against JC and others (4/22/1820), file P130, Miscellaneous Files in Chancery, 1772–1847, J0087, NYSA (henceforth P130).

25. For another version of this candid confession, see "The Several [i.e., separate] Answer of James Cooper" (4/17/1821): "the defendant [Cooper] did believe that if the said Testator [Judge Cooper] or his eldest son Richard Cooper had been living they would have reduced the amount of the said claim materially from their knowledge of facts and circumstances out of the reach of this defendant, that however this defendant was willing to settle the business amicably and justly as far as he was authorized to do without incurring personal responsibility"; see Bridgen's second chancery case against JC and others (filed 11/13/1820), file B309, Miscellaneous Files in Chancery, 1772–1847, J0087, NYSA (henceforth B309).

26. William may not have been entirely bluffing. Cooper's old friend Mason Whiting of Binghamton recalled many years later, "In May 1819 your brother William spent several weeks in this village"—in part to sell lands in Feronia. He then went, Whiting believed, to St. Lawrence County. Mason Whiting to JC, 2/10/1834, JFC paps., box 2, AAS. On the distribution of Feronia, see Isaac Cooper diary, 1/26/1817, NYSHA, and Richard Fenimore and Isaac Cooper, Account Book with William Cooper Estate, Cooper family paps. microfilm, HSFC, New York City.

27. JC to Thomas Bridgen, [2/11/1819]; Robert Campbell to JC, 1/4/1819, JFC paps., box 2, AAS.

28. Robert Campbell to JC, 2/15/1819, JFC paps., box 2, AAS; in *An American Dictionary of the English Language* (New York: S. Converse, 1828), Noah Webster defined *embarrassment* in Campbell's sense as "perplexity arising from insolvency."

29. See Chester Jennings, bill, 3/5/1819.

30. Robert Campbell to JC, 4/5/1819, 8/23/1819, JFC paps., boxes 2 and 6, AAS.

31. Thomas Bridgen to JC [endorsed "Wm Cooper" by mistake], 10/26/1819 (draft), TF paps., box 332, NYSL.

32. Thomas Bridgen to Samuel Starkweather, 10/11/1819, TF paps., box 333, NYSL.

33. Samuel Starkweather to Thomas Bridgen, 10/19/1819, 10/21/1819, TF paps., box 332, NYSL.

34. Thomas Bridgen to JC, 10/26/1819 (draft); JC to Thomas Bridgen, 11/11/1819, TF paps., box 333, NYSL.

35. On which Courtland Cooper might have offered a different take, however.

36. Thomas Bridgen to JC, 10/26/1819 (draft); JC to Thomas Bridgen, 11/11/1819, TF paps., box 333, NYSL.

37. JC to Thomas Bridgen, 1/24/1820, TF paps., box 333, NYSL; Bridgen's letter complaining of the missed appointment does not survive, but he describes it in Thomas Bridgen to Samuel Starkweather, 2/11/1820, TF paps., box 333, NYSL.

38. Thomas Bridgen to Samuel Starkweather, 2/11/1820.

39. WC will, 5/13/1808, Register of Wills, Book B, 237, Otsego County Surrogate's Office, Cooperstown, N.Y.

40. Thomas Bridgen to Samuel Starkweather, 2/11/1820. Starkweather replied that he was about to leave Cooperstown on urgent business but was forwarding all papers left with him by Bridgen; Samuel Starkweather to Thomas Bridgen, 2/18/1820, TF paps., box 333, NYSL.

41. "[Pomeroy] Case," 2/25/1825, William Holt Averell paps., box 3, NYSHA.

42. The original draft Bridgen appears to have brought to Angevine is an untitled, water-damaged document in his hand later filed with his second chancery bill (B309); there are numerous marginalia in the same hand, plus a few interlinear corrections in a darker ink that are almost certainly in Cooper's hand.

43. "The Several Answer of James Cooper." The last phrase *may* express Cooper's previously expressed wish to shield his personal property from any sale of estate assets to satisfy the Bridgen debt. That was in keeping with his February 1819 statements to Bridgen that, despite the fact that Feronia had been divided, he would allow William to use such personal assets to discharge the debt to Bridgen—but only if William thereafter released him from further responsibility.

44. James Kent, order, 4/6/1822 (re: P130), Chancery Minutes, 1781–1829, 33:503–5, NYSA, J0059.

45. As quoted in Thomas Bridgen to JC, 9/12/1820 (draft), TF paps., box 333, NYSL.

46. "The Several Answer of James Cooper." Cooper's desire to consult counsel before the amicable suit proceeded was prudent. While admitting that Bridgen's cause seemed just, he was very concerned (as he put it in a letter sent to Bridgen in the fall of 1820) that no property of the estate be sold "in the present state of the times." As long as the Panic of 1819 still shadowed the land market, he was apprehensive that any sales

to fund the 1818 settlement might force him to sacrifice properties over which, as executor, he was sworn to exercise careful stewardship. This concern may have been an unspoken reason for his foot-dragging since brother William's death the previous fall. Cooper also fully assumed that he would have full freedom to choose the properties to be sold (if any) and the time and manner of their sale. See JC to Thomas Bridgen, 9/4/1820, TF paps., box 333, NYSL. Chancellor Kent's order of June 7 spelled out the means by which sufficient lands in Edwards and Scriba townships should be assigned to Bridgen to cover the debt. Cooper could not quarrel with that part of the order. However, Chancellor Kent made no allowance whatsoever for the poor state of the land market and seemed utterly ignorant of Cooper's assumption that he would be able to control any sales of estate assets necessary to fund the payments for 1819 and 1820. Instead, Kent provided Bridgen relief by mandating that Cooper make those two overdue payments, a total of almost $6,000, within a mere sixty days. If he failed to do so, the decree further promised Bridgen proper writs for the seizure and sale of Cooper estate properties sufficient to cover the amounts due. While to appearances the two friends had submitted the cause jointly, the court's order favored Bridgen and virtually ignored Cooper's concerns, surely because Cooper had relied on Bridgen to convey them to Chancellor Kent through the bill and his oral presentation. From all the surviving evidence, one must conclude that Bridgen did not do so. See James Kent, order, 6/7/1820 (re: Bridgen's first chancery case against JC and others [filed 6/7/1820], B308), Chancery Minutes, 1784–1829, 30:473–74, NYSA, J0059.

47. "The Several Answer of James Cooper."

48. Some of the anger Cooper did not express directly to Bridgen over the summer of 1820 appears to have been deflected onto his literary associates. There can be little doubt, for instance, that the terms and tone of Cooper's accusatory letter of September 7–8 to Goodrich (*LJ* 1:58–59), with its threat of taking the matter between them to Chancellor James Kent, stemmed in large part from the Bridgen matter. The hollowness of that threat is apparent when one reads Cooper's letter of the same week to Bridgen, in which Kent figures as his nemesis; see JC to Thomas Bridgen, 9/4/1820.

49. Thomas Bridgen to JC, 9/12/1820 (draft).

50. JC to Thomas Bridgen, 9/4/1820; no drafts or copies of any of the "missing" letters survive in Bridgen's papers.

51. Thomas Bridgen to JC, 9/12/1820.

52. An amicable suit depended on both parties' willingness to accept and enact the court's decision. Unless he had clear evidence that Cooper would *not* comply, Bridgen could not even go back to Chancellor Kent and use Cooper's silence as a means of speeding things up. Under the terms of the court order, the sixty days were on Cooper's side now and he chose to use them to his full benefit. Besides, now that Bridgen had tricked Cooper, Bridgen had to be very careful not to let that fact redefine the dispute.

53. "Now you speak of raising money *immediately*—then [i.e., in May] you wanted *security*, now you want *cash*." JC to Thomas Bridgen, 9/4/1820.

54. JC to Thomas Bridgen, 9/4/1820.

55. Thomas Bridgen, memo to William A. Duer, 11/11/1820, TF paps., box 348, NYSL.

56. Thomas Bridgen, affidavit of service of subpoena, 12/23/1820, B309.

57. Henry B. Davis, affidavit of service of subpoena, 12/20/1820, and Edmund Elmendorf, certification of appearance, 3/22/1821, B309.

58. Robert Sedgwick to Thomas Bridgen, 12/2/1820, TF paps., box 333, NYSL.

59. James Kent, order, 3/26/1821 (re: B309), Chancery Minutes, 1784–1829, 31:482–83, NYSA, J0059.

60. "The Several Answer of James Cooper." This set of assertions may suggest Cooper was again trying to delay the final funding of the 1818 agreement, but the effect of the Pomeroys' chancery bill on all he did as executor should not be forgotten.

61. James Kent, order, 6/28/1821 (re: B309), Chancery Minutes, 1784–1829, 32:225–28, NYSA, J0059; interestingly, this document is in the handwriting of Cooper's boyhood hero, Moss Kent, then register of the court.

62. In May 1821, just before James Kent issued his order, Bridgen wrote attorney Robert Campbell to request a "detailed statement of all the [estate's] undivided lands." Campbell directed Bridgen to the documents in the court's Pomeroy file, which he said included such a list. As a master in chancery, Bridgen could easily put his hands on it and surely did so. Thomas Bridgen to Robert Campbell, 5/4/1821 (draft), and Robert Campbell to Thomas Bridgen, 5/21/1821, TF paps., box 333, NYSL.

63. James van Ingen, *Fi. Fa.*, 8/30/1821, to Joseph B. Walton (marked received by him 9/4/1821), B309.

64. Cooperstown *Watch-Tower*, 9/17/1821 (notice dated 9/10/1821).

65. Just then, Cooper's old friend James Aitchison (to whom *The Spy* was to be dedicated) was letting it be known that Cooper might come to Otsego; see Robert Campbell to JC, 9/10/1821, JFC paps., box 2, AAS.

66. See the "User's Guide" to the Averell family paps., NYSHA; *LJ* 2:296.

67. Joseph B. Walton, sheriff, undated note on back of Van Ingen's 8/30/1821 *Fi. Fa.*, B309. Given the time elapsed since the 1818 agreement, almost all of Walton's yield was eaten up by interest accumulated on the Bridgen debt. Such was the cost of delay.

68. Taylor, *William Cooper's Town*, 397, cites the four-thousand-acre total; on the declining valuations of Feronia lands, see Isaac Cooper diary, 1/26/1817 ($4.00) and JC to Thomas Bridgen, 2/11/1819 ($1.50).

69. Taylor, *William Cooper's Town*, 397, gives the twenty-five-thousand-acre total. My own figures generally derive from contemporary receipts (in B309) completed at the time the proceeds were forwarded by the respective sheriffs or, more usually, were

turned over to Bridgen in person. They differ in some ways from the figures Taylor derived from a variety of other, somewhat later, sources.

70. James Kent, order, 4/6/1822 (re: P130), Chancery Minutes, 1781–1829, 33:503–5, NYSA, J0059.

71. Taylor, *William Cooper's Town*, 398; Taylor reached this conclusion before the records of the Pomeroy chancery bill came to light.

72. It should be recalled that the Pomeroy bill preceded Bridgen's first bill against Cooper, and that it not only colored Cooper's dealings with Bridgen but also may have contributed to his strategy for settling that man's claims.

73. Joseph Patterson, sheriff, conveyance to William H. Averell, 1/16/1822, Averell family paps., box 3, NYSHA. Averell reportedly visited Broome County again for the purpose of scooping up other Cooper family lands there; Mason Whiting recalled that he returned in "the fall of 1823" with a chancery writ that enabled him to force the sale of other land in Feronia; Mason Whiting to JC, 2/10/1834, JFC paps., box 2, AAS. William H. Averell to Thomas Bridgen, 2/4/1822, and undated [address flap indicates "January 1826"], TF paps., box 33, NYSL.

74. Attorney Isaac A. Johnson was served with a summons to the meeting on June 12, and Cooper later admitted "said service to be [as] good as on him" (note by Edmund Wilkes on copy of summons sent to Robert Sedgwick in June 1822, P130).

75. James King, master's report, 10/15/1822 (draft), P130.

76. Thomas Bridgen to Samuel Starkweather, 10/11/1819, TF paps., box 333, NYSL.

77. James King, master's report, 10/15/1822 (draft), and schedules B, D, E, F, P130; see also Taylor, *William Cooper's Town*, 398.

78. James Kent, final order, 11/26/1822, copy, in "[Pomeroy] Case," Averell family paps., box 3, NYSHA.

79. Taylor, *William Cooper's Town*, 398–99.

80. Robert Campbell to JC, 5/26/1823, JFC paps., box 2, AAS.

81. *Freeman's Journal*, 5/12–19/1823, gives 6/24 as the original sale date, but on 5/26/1823 (the date of Campbell's letter) notes its postponement to 7/1/1823; a sale of lands belonging to Richard F. Cooper's children on 5/20/1823 had been announced in the *Watch-Tower* on 4/14/1823.

82. Robert Campbell to JC, 10/28/1823, JFC paps., box 2, AAS.

83. Joseph B. Walton, sheriff, conveyances to William H. Averell, 10/3/1824, 10/21/1824, Otsego County conveyances, Book HH, 333–44, 344–46. Taylor, *William Cooper's Town*, 438, Table 17, underreports Averell's purchases.

84. Robert Campbell to JC, 10/28/1823. It seems unlikely that the Pomeroys would enjoy redemption rights in any sales resulting from their own bill; however, they would enjoy them with regard to all the Bridgen sales and those conducted on the other judgments they helped Averell acquire.

CHAPTER 11. SETTLEMENT

1. Timothy Dwight, *Travels in New England and New York*, ed. Barbara Miller Solomon, 4 vols. (Cambridge: Harvard University Press, 1969), 2:325.

2. See John Mack Faragher, *Sugar Creek: Life on the Illinois Prairie* (New Haven: Yale University Press, 1986), 61–66.

3. Charles Brockden Brown, *Edgar Huntly, or Memoirs of a Sleep-Walker*, ed. Sydney J. Krause and S. W. Reid (Kent: Kent State University Press, 1984), 182; on the landscape details, see Norman S. Grabo, *The Coincidental Art of Charles Brockden Brown* (Chapel Hill: University of North Carolina Press, 1981), 62–64.

4. Charles Wiley to JC, 1/7/1821 [1822], JFC paps., box 2, AAS.

5. This assertion is based on a search of the AAS online catalog in December 2003.

6. J. Hector St. Jean de Crèvecoeur, *Letters from an American Farmer and Sketches of Eighteenth-Century America*, ed. Albert E. Stone, Jr. (New York: Penguin, 1983), 73; Dennis D. Moore, ed., *More Letters from the American Farmer: An Edition of the Essays in English Left Unpublished by Crèvecoeur* (Athens: University of Georgia Press, 1995), 165, 178, 183.

7. Crèvecoeur, *Letters from an American Farmer*, 72–73.

8. See Edwin Fussell, *Frontier: American Literature and the American West* (Princeton: Princeton University Press, 1965), 15; J. A. Leo Lemay, "The Frontiersman from Lout to Hero," American Antiquarian Society *Proceedings* 88:2 (1978): 187–223.

9. Hugh Henry Brackenridge, *Modern Chivalry*, ed. Claude Newlin (New York: American Book Co., 1937), 517.

10. John Filson, *The Discovery, Settlement, and Present State of Kentucke* (Wilmington: James Adams, 1784), title page.

11. Crèvecoeur, *Letters from an American Farmer*, 89.

12. See, for instance, Brackenridge, *Modern Chivalry*, 555–57.

13. In the British colonies of North America, a *frontiers-man* or *frontiers-woman* was an individual whose origins lay on the Anglo-American side of such divides but who by choice or necessity inhabited, permanently or temporarily, the border ground or the lands that lay beyond them. Such a figure was the geographical opposite of the *city-dweller*. This rooted sense of the word *frontiers* is precisely the one that operates in Crèvecoeur, although his combinative forms tend to be *frontier man* and *frontier woman* (as in the titles of the twelfth "letter" in *Letters from an American Farmer* and the tenth "sketch" of *Sketches of Eighteenth-Century America*).

14. Dwight, *Travels in New England and New York*, 2:321 (this is the first example of the term *pioneer* listed in the *Dictionary of American English*).

15. Ishmael Bush is usually referred to as a "squatter" in the novel. As late as 1846, Herman Melville used the word "pioneer" in the traditional sense in describing Toby and Tommo's tough passage through the cane patch on Nukuheva: "Twenty minutes of this violent exercise almost exhausted me, but it carried us some way into the thicket; when

Toby, who had been reaping the benefit of my labors by following close at my heels, proposed to become pioneer in turn"; *Typee: A Peep at Polynesian Life*, ed. Harrison Hayford et al. (Evanston and Chicago: Northwestern University Press and Newberry Library, 1968), 38.

16. Noah Webster, *An American Dictionary of the English Language* (New York: S. Converse, 1828), s.v. "Forester," "Forest."

17. Betty calls Lawton "a free rider and a bold" in the earlier novel (*Spy* CE 294). During the attack on Natty's cabin, Betty uses the example of "the ra'al captain" to rebuke her apparently faint-hearted husband (*PIO* CE 433). This is one means by which Cooper uses the heroic atmosphere of *The Spy* to critique the "fallen" world of the early Republic.

18. It is possible that the carryover resulted from Cooper's work on revising *The Spy* in January and February, and again in April 1822, for the second and third editions. If Cooper followed this slower course, it may have taken him until summer to finish the first six chapters of *The Pioneers*.

19. James H. Pickering, "James Fenimore Cooper and the History of New York," Ph.D. dissertation, Northwestern University, 1965, 55, identifies the Bronx River.

20. A modest example of how he managed space in the first volume may be found in the description of stone walls and rail fences in Chapter 5. Doubtless from conversations with his neighbors and his own extensive travels through the county as DeWitt Clinton's local secretary, Cooper understood that the "heavy and durable [stone] walls" then serving in Westchester as "permanent barriers in the divisions of estates"—including, of course, the DeLancey estate at Heathcote Hill, and perhaps even his own smaller one at Angevine—were a deceptively recent introduction to the area. With a cultural and perhaps a political lesson in mind, he therefore wanted to help his readers reimagine the more impermanent colonial scene. On the site of Dunwoodie's impending skirmish with the British, we therefore are directed to the "slight and tottering fences of stone" thrown up by settlers as they felled trees and cleared the stony fields. In many places, these stacked walls have fallen into ruin, largely because of the abandonment and neglect caused by the war. From the more substantial laid walls immediately around the Wharton estate, Cooper thus guides our eye down into the valley, where, although a few sturdy stretches of old farm wall remain intact, most of the wavering stacks have tumbled down, offering little hindrance to the dragoons, whose mounts can easily jump them. Elsewhere, though, Dunwoodie sees wooden rail fences that need to be pulled down in order to clear the field for battle. For this purpose, he sends out a few men accustomed to such duty. They are, although Cooper does not so name them, "pioneers" in the old sense: "a small body of mounted men, whose ordinary duties were those of guides, but who, in cases of emergency, were embodied [i.e., called together] and did duty as foot soldiers: these were dismounted, and proceeded . . . to level the few fences which might interfere with the intended movements of the cavalry" (*Spy* 1:87–88).

What is most interesting here is the degree of detail with which Cooper has sought to render the narrative's scene. He is exploring the connections between physical setting and the action he is planning to locate there. Dunwoodie in this episode thinks about that setting strategically, and Cooper's own military training doubtless is revealed in his analogous conception of it. But Cooper also seems to be recognizing here for the first time that art has its own strategic requirements. He needs to prepare the field of the impending action of his tale himself. And his strategy is more than local. His establishment of the material texture of the area in this passage sets up the later scene when Harvey Birch, hotly pursued through this landscape by Captain Lawton and his troop, first attempts to blend with the fringe of dark woods on the horizon and then takes refuge behind a "fragment of a wall that had withstood the ravages made by war in the adjoining fences of wood." Throwing himself bodily over the high wall, he falls exhausted on the other side, sure that the mounts of the fast-approaching dragoons will balk at the jump. At first they do pull up short, but then the boldest of the dragoons backs off and urges his horse to undertake a second, successful attempt. The desperate Birch throws himself at horse and rider, tumbling them to earth and buying himself the time needed to run off (*Spy* 1:138). This nicely realized scene in the ninth chapter of the novel, prepared for in the earlier description of the Westchester landscape, marks, nonetheless, the limit to which Cooper's spatial imagination stretched in the first volume.

21. There was, to be sure, some historical and legendary justification for the change. From John Jay, Cooper may have learned about Crosby's (and Jay's) upriver activity, some of it centered in Fishkill, where the New York State government moved after the battle of White Plains. And he certainly knew that the Arnold-André story, so important for the atmosphere of his own tale, was intimately associated with the Hudson Highlands, West Point, and the rough country farther back from the river on the eastern shore. Shifting the action northward was justified by his particular sources and by the general record of the war in New York in the latter part of 1780.

22. As Harvey Birch and Henry Wharton approach the Croton River in Chapter 32, the narrator notes, "At length they arrived where the mountains sunk into rough and unequal hillocks, and passed at once from the barren sterility of the precipices, to the imperfect culture of the neutral ground" (*Spy* 2:243). Birch takes Wharton back across its mouth in a skiff, thereby bringing him past the last American troops and into the area under control of a British party at this time (*Spy* 2:242); note also the narrator's comment that Frances and her aunt hope the fugitives will escape from their pursuers and "reach the Neutral Ground" (*Spy* 2:210); with Chapter 33, the action in general shifts south again and at last reenters the Neutral Ground.

23. Note that Cooper cut a good deal of this in revising the novel for London publisher Richard Bentley in 1831; see *Spy* 2:131–35; and CE emendations, 524–26.

24. In Irving's tale, Rip, on his own summit above the Hudson, "looked down into

a deep mountain glen, wild, lonely and shagged, the bottom filled with fragments from the impending cliffs and scarcely lighted by the rays of the setting sun"; Washington Irving, *History, Tales and Sketches* (New York: Library of America, 1983), 774.

25. Ibid.

26. See *Spy* 2:245–46, 2:253 (where Cooper frames the Hudson in the barn door as he narrates the hanging of the Skinner by the Cowboys).

27. Frances Wharton's passage over recently cleared but abandoned farmland on her way up the mountain in Chapter 30 (*Spy* 2:213–14) may indicate one way in which the spatial themes Cooper would address in *The Pioneers* were already emergent in the setting of *The Spy*.

28. Henry Gilpin Dilworth, *A Northern Tour: Being a Guide to Saratoga, Lake George, Niagara, Canada, Boston, &c. &c.* (Philadelphia: H. C. Carey & I. Lea, 1825), 40–43.

29. He left after breakfast on Saturday, 1/19. Slightly more than a week later, on Monday 1/28, he returned for much of the week following and came back for three more stays across February: 7–9, 14–17, and 19–20. "James Cooper to C. Jennings, Dr.," [2/20/1822], JFC paps., box 4, AAS.

30. See Robert Campbell to JC, "at the City Hotel/New York," 4/5/1822, JFC paps., box 2, AAS.

31. On Coles, see "Walter Barrett" [Joseph A. Scoville], *The Old Merchants of New York City* (New York: M. Doolady, 1870), 2, pt. 1:42–43; Cooper soon described Coles to Washington Irving as "a gentleman of acquirements, and modest, pleasing manners" (*LJ* 1:75).

32. John Miller to Benjamin Coles, 6/15/1822, *S&B* 216.

33. Irving did not need to mention that he had made his way over the ramparts and into the castle of Murray himself. He was, of course, on the spot, had a strong reputation dating back a decade, and had hit just the right post-colonial note in *The Sketch Book*.

34. There are a few mistranscriptions in the printed version of Irving's letter; see the original in JFC paps., box 2, AAS. Once Cooper became acquainted with the painter-author William Dunlap later in 1822, he must have begun swapping tales of British publishers with that man. When Dunlap's *Memoirs of the Life of George Frederick Cooke* was published in New York in 1813, Irving's brother Peter, then living in England, arranged for John Miller to publish it in London and split the profits (after expenses) with Dunlap. No sooner had Dunlap heard this good news than he had word from John Howard Payne, the American theatrical prodigy who had acted with Cooke in Dunlap's theater in New York but was then in England, that *he* had found a copy of the *Memoirs* in an American ship and, wishing to help its author, had sold it to Colburn. Both publishers having invested their capital in the book and brought it out, Dunlap added, they "agreed to make the best for themselves, and sink me"; William Dunlap, *History of the Rise and Progress of the Arts of Design in the United States* (New York: Dover, 1969), 1:273.

35. Cooper did not answer Irving until July (see *LJ* 1:75) but must have received Irving's letter between the time he drafted the April 24 instructions for Coles and that man's actual departure for London.

36. John Miller to Benjamin Coles, 6/15/1822, *S&B* 215.

37. Benjamin Coles to JC, 6/17/1822, *S&B* 216–18.

38. Benjamin Coles to JC, 7/13/1822, S&B 220.

39. John Murray to Benjamin Coles, 6/10/1822, and Coles to Henry Sedgwick, 6/26/1822, as quoted in *PIO* CE, xxxviii–xxxix; Coles to JC, 7/13/1822 (which encloses a copy of Coles to Murray, 7/11/1822), *S&B* 219–20.

40. Benjamin Coles to JC, 7/17/1822, as quoted in *PIO* CE liv.

41. Benjamin Coles to JC, 6/17/1822, *S&B* 218; Nelson Frederick Adkins, *Fitz-Greene Halleck: An Early Knickerbocker Poet and Wit* (New Haven: Yale University Press, 1930), 134–35.

42. *"Our Travels, Statistical, Geographical, Mineorological* [sic], *Geological, Historical, Political and Quizzical": A Knickerbocker Tour of New York State,* ed. Louis Leonard Tucker (Albany: State Education Department, 1968), 2.

43. [Scoville], *Old Merchants of New York,* 2, pt. 1:71; Neilson and the *Evening Post* are quoted in I. N. Phelps Stokes, *The Iconography of Manhattan Island,* 6 vols. (New York: Robert H. Dodd, 1915–1928), 5:1624–25; David Kaser, *Messrs. Carey & Lea of Philadelphia: A Study in the History of the Booktrade* (Philadelphia: University of Pennsylvania Press, 1957), 28.

44. [Scoville], *Old Merchants of New York,* 3, pt. 1:49.

45. Stokes, *Iconography,* 5:1624.

46. Wilkes arrived in the English capital on January 7 and delivered the package to Murray six days later (*PIO* CE xl).

47. [Scoville], *Old Merchants of New York,* 3, pt. 1:49; Stokes, *Iconography,* 5:1625

48. See *PIO* CE 468–75, for a discussion of differences among the various 1823 versions; also, Lance Schachterle, "The Three 1823 Editions of *The Pioneers,*" AAS *Proceedings* 84(1974): 219–32.

49. A side issue that took time and perhaps energy across the fall of 1822 and in 1823 was Cooper's attempt to settle his old recruiting accounts with the navy. For this purpose he not only carried on a letter campaign from November 1821 until December 1823 (see *LJ* 1:71–74, 76–79, 89–91, 92–93, 105–9), but also traveled to Washington in September 1822 to talk with treasury department auditors and check navy records (*LJ* 1:89). The amount of money was small, but Cooper became very worked up about it, suggesting the overall fragility of his finances at the time.

50. Much has been written about the influence of the so-called Prevost claim on *The Pioneers,* specifically on Cooper's introduction of the Effingham family into it. Such arguments have some validity but are exaggerated. For one thing, the Prevosts, grandsons of George Croghan, dropped their lawsuits against all Otsego County landowners early

in 1821, meaning that the issue was effectually resolved months before Cooper began the book. For another, the relationship of William Cooper to George Croghan did not closely resemble that imagined in the novel between Marmaduke Temple and the Effinghams—Croghan was no Loyalist, and Cooper never held lands in trust for him. If one were looking for a closer parallel in Judge Cooper's experience for the book's inventions, it would more likely emerge from the tangled records of his trust arrangement during the 1790s with Thomas B. Bridgen, which ultimately led to the disastrous "Bridgen decree" just when *The Pioneers* was being written (see Chapter 10). That Cooper appears to have known the younger Bridgen under his mother's name (Ten Eyck) from Albany adds to the suggestiveness of the parallel with the disguised, name-shifting Oliver Edwards/Edward Oliver Effingham in *The Pioneers* (indeed, the confusion of names in the case of Bridgen's father, Thomas Bridgen/Thomas Bridgen Atwood/Thomas B. Bridgen, is even more teasingly apt as a parallel). In all likelihood, Cooper combined elements from both the Prevost and Bridgen cases in imagining the Effingham plot in his novel, but the pressing nature of the latter in 1821 was very much on his mind.

51. JC and SC, conveyance (in trust) to Thomas J. DeLancey and Edward F. DeLancey, 1/3/1818, copy (4/19/1821) by Robert Sedgwick, with note attached, JFC paps., box 5, AAS.

52. So Sedgwick indicated in copying the document; see previous note.

53. See Thomas J. DeLancey to JC, 1/9/1817, copy in JFB paps., box 10, AAS.

54. James H. Pickering, "Fenimore Cooper as Country Gentleman: A New Glimpse of Cooper's Westchester Years," *NYH* 72(1991): 309; D. S. Jones (brother of and attorney for E. H. Jones), petition in re: William Shotwell, Jr., v. James Cooper et al., 7/21/1821, copy in JFC paps., box 5, AAS.

55. Pickering, "Fenimore Cooper as Country Gentleman," 309; JC, conveyance to George Willets, 5/11/1824, JFC paps., box 5, AAS.

56. [Scoville], *Old Merchants of New York*, 2, pt. 2:101; JC, Bank of New York bank book, JFC paps., box 4, AAS.

57. William Shotwell, receipts, 3/18/1819, 4/26/1819, 12/29/1819; JC and SC, mortgage, 12/20/1819 (in favor of William Shotwell), JFC paps., box 4, AAS.

58. D. A. Story, *The deLanceys: A Romance of a Great Family* (n.p.: Thomas Nelson, 1931), 37, says Edward died "of an accident."

59. John P. DeLancey and William H. DeLancey, indenture, 1/11/1826, copy, JFC paps., box 5, AAS.

60. John Peter DeLancey to JC, (undated), JFC paps., box 2, AAS.

61. Westchester Co. Registry of Deeds, liber W, 305; see Pickering, "Fenimore Cooper as Country Gentleman," 310.

62. JC and SC, conveyance, to John P. DeLancey; John P. DeLancey, conveyance to William H. DeLancey, 2/3/1823 (Westchester Co. Registry of Deeds, liber 32, 79), copy, 1/11/1826, JFC paps., box 5, AAS.

CHAPTER 12. TAKING MANHATTAN

1. SFC, "A Glance Backward," *Atlantic Monthly* 59(1887): 202.

2. There, in addition to many other friends both old and new, Cooper associated with Charles K. Gardner, whose *Literary and Scientific Repository* had failed the previous May. A year after that, Gardner was embarked on his new publishing venture, the New York *Patriot*, a daily paper for which he soon recruited Cooper as a contributor.

3. The Lunch later moved to the nearby Washington Hall; Nelson F. Adkins "James Fenimore Cooper and the Bread and Cheese Club," *Modern Language Notes* 47(1932): 73. An 1825 letter from Anthony Bleecker (then secretary of the Lunch) notifying Asher B. Durand of his election, adds that the group met every Thursday at Jones's establishment; Anthony Bleecker to Asher B. Durand, 12/10/1825, copy in JFB paps., box 4, AAS. On the date of the Lunch's founding, see *LOM* CE xxiv, which, citing no source, asserts that April 14, 1825, was observed as the third or possibly fourth anniversary of the founding. It may have been more plausible in any case that the founding *day* had been the second Thursday of April, since April 14 was a Thursday only in 1825. John W. Francis, *Old New York: or, Reminiscences of the Past Sixty Years* (New York: W. J. Widdleton, 1866), 292, says he thought it met bimonthly during the winter, but that seems to be an error. At least in 1826–1827, for which period a record book exists (copy in JFB paps., box 4, AAS), the group met every week, although by then, in Cooper's absence, it had shifted to Tuesdays. It thus met on both 12/26/1826 and 1/2/1827.

4. Many members had diverse professional interests, the most obvious example being William Dunlap. James DeKay was a medical doctor by training but was much more interested in science, the field in which he achieved his greatest fame. Other individuals remembered today primarily for their writings were often enough employed at other occupations: Paulding as an agent for the navy, Halleck as Jacob Barker's private secretary, Hillhouse as a merchant, and even Bryant as an editor. Most members of the Lunch were notable for the breadth of their experiences and sympathies: Dr. Francis, for instance, was an important patron of music and a lover of literature, and had very wide connections well beyond the medical community. It should also be noted that the club attracted a steady flow of visitors: Francis mentions Daniel Webster and the French minister, Hyde de Neuville, among others. The membership began with a core around Cooper and grew by election, pieces of bread (yes) and cheese (no) being used for ballots (Francis, *Old New York*, 292, 291). Two important documents survive from the club's early days. The first, in the hand of Anthony Bleecker, is an "Exposé" or accounting that records payments received from members (to cover the regular meals) in the period ending on Thursday, March 9, 1826, when Cooper was still quite active in the Lunch. This is the only full contemporary member list, consisting of fifty-four names, for the Lunch. The second document contains minutes for the Lunch from October 5, 1826, to October 1, 1827 (after Cooper had left New York for Paris), and gives the names of weekly attendees, including guests. On the basis of these two documents, James F.

Beard constructed a table of the membership very usefully annotated with biographical information on most of the sixty-six individuals he identified. Photocopies of both documents are in the JFB paps., box 4, AAS; neither copy carries any indication of the location of the originals.

5. Benjamin F. Thompson, *The History of Long Island; from its Discovery and Settlement to the Present Time*, 2nd ed. (New York: Gould, Banks, 1841), 2:197; Horatio G. Spafford, *A Gazetteer of the State of New-York* (Albany: B. D. Packard, 1824), 345, 495; Andrew T. Goodrich, *The Picture of New-York, and Stranger's Guide to Commercial Metropolis of the United States* (New York: A. T. Goodrich, 1828), 430–31.

6. New York *American (for the Country)*, 4/7/1823.

7. A decade later, Cooper knew enough of Dunlap's *Memoirs* of Cooke to cite it as evidence that Dunlap's present project, the forthcoming *History of the American Theatre*, would prove a promising title for English publisher Richard Bentley. Cooper argued that the new book would be rich enough in anecdotes of Cooke and other English actors to interest an English audience (see *LJ* 2:353). In the case of another visiting British actor, Thomas Abthorpe Cooper, the novelist's tie was decidedly personal. Years after T. A. Cooper's arrival in the United States, the novelist, eager for "gossip of the City" during his stay in Florence, asked his friend and fellow Lunch member, Dr. James E. DeKay, for news "of Lunch, of Dunlap, of Cooper, of the Academy, of Morse and all other strange fish, Francis included" (*LJ* 1:368). And in 1841, having seen and visited with "Tom Cooper" in Philadelphia, he passed on to his wife from there the news that the actor's daughter had married President John Tyler's son and, during the lingering illness of Tyler's wife, was therefore "the lady of the White House" (*LJ* 4:159).

8. I. N. Phelps Stokes, *Iconography of Manhattan Island*, 6 vols. (New York: Robert H. Dodd, 1915–1928), 5:1652. *Memorial of James Fenimore Cooper* (New York: G. P. Putnam, 1852), 99. Francis himself became well acquainted with Kean when Kean had a fine monument erected for Cooke in the churchyard at St. Paul's in June 1821; an engraving of the monument shows Kean and Dr. Francis admiring it (Stokes, *Iconography*, Plate 90, and 3:575).

9. *Metamora and Other Plays*, "America's Lost Plays," vol. 14, ed. Eugene R. Page (Princeton: Princeton University Press, 1940), 59.

10. *Diary of William Dunlap (1766–1839)*, ed. Dorothy C. Barck, NYHS *Collections* 1929–1931, 3:679; George C. D. Odell, *Annals of the New York Stage* (New York: Columbia University Press, 1927–1949), 3:63–64, gives names of players and indicates that the third night would have been the traditional author's night. Cooper recalled a visit to the Park when he was invited to "take a seat *with the critics*" (*GI* CE 76n).

11. The famous watercolor by John Searle (Plate 15) depicting Charles Mathews's first performance incorporates portraits of eighty-five members of the audience, including many of Cooper's New York friends. Cooper himself is not named in the accompanying key and apparently was not portrayed in the watercolor; Francis is both

named and visible. Francis, in Cooper *Memorial*, 100–1; Francis, *Old New York*, 238–43. Mathews acted in a series of plays at the Park from 11/7/1822 until 11/26/1822; he began his one-man performances the next evening with "A Trip to Paris," followed by "Travels in Air, Earth, and Water" (11/29), "Mailcoach Adventures" (12/2), "The Youthful Days of Mr. Mathews" (12/4), and so on (at times with plays added), running them through 12/16, when he left New York for engagements elsewhere. Odell, *Annals of the New York Stage*, 3:49–53. He returned for a four-day series in February (Odell, 3:57) before he began his final run in April and May. On Mathews and Dickens, see Paul Schlicke, *Dickens and Popular Entertainment* (London: Allen and Unwyn, 1985), esp. 234–41.

12. In April 1823, Dunlap and Cooper were acquainted but not yet close. They had encountered each other on various occasions over the past few months at Wiley's, as Dunlap recalled; see William Dunlap, *A History of the American Theatre* (New York: J. and J. Harper, 1832), 385. Dunlap had been working as a painter in Norfolk and elsewhere for several years, did not return to New York until June 1822, and then was absent during the yellow fever outbreak; furthermore, after leaving Cooper and Mathews in Albany in April 1823, he did not come back to New York City again until that October, so it was not until the winter following, when he painted a scene from *The Spy*, that he and Cooper became closely connected ("I had recently become acquainted with him, and acquaintance has ripened into friendship"); see *History of the Rise and Progress of the Arts of Design in the United States* (New York: Dover, 1968), 1:288–93; by the time Cooper wrote the last chapter of *The Pilot* the following fall, he would refer to "the spirited pencil of Dunlap" (*PIL* CE 419). As to the details of the river excursion: Dunlap recalled leaving New York City for Utica "early in April" (*Arts of Design*, 1:291; just plain "April" in Dunlap, *American Theatre*, 385), but Beard suggests April 19 to April 24 as bracketing dates (*LJ* 1:97n1), while Mathews's letter to his wife back in England mentioning the trip was not written until April 30; see Mrs. [Anne Jackson] Mathews, *A Continuation of the Memoirs of Charles Mathews, Comedian* (Philadelphia: Lea & Blanchard, 1839), 1:247–49. Furthermore, we know that Mathews had returned to the New York stage on April 3 and acted there through April 18; he was back once more on April 24 for his final run, which ended on May 19, after which he left the country and returned to England; see Odell, *Annals of the New York Stage*, 3:62–63. For the spring season in 1823, the *Chancellor Livingston* or its counterpart, the *Richmond*, regularly took on passengers for Albany at 4:00 p.m. on Tuesdays, Thursdays, and Saturdays, and left New York on the twenty-hour run at 5:00 p.m.; the former boat was captained that year by Samuel Wiswall of Hudson; see New York *Commercial Advertiser*, 4/1/1823; and Joel Munsell, *Annals of Albany* (Albany: Munsell, 1850–1859), 10:260.

13. Francis, *Old New York*, 240–41.

14. Francis, in Cooper *Memorial*, 101.

15. Dunlap, *American Theatre*, 387.

16. Francis, *Old New York*, 292–93. Francis added that Daniel Webster was present as a guest at that particular session and that Cooper was an amused bystander, playing the part of Albinus—the great eighteenth-century German anatomist—as his companions verbally dissected the remains of Cooke (who had, chortled Francis, "enacted a great part that night"). Probably most meetings were, though, a bit more serious—as the Hudson River trip itself would prove.

17. This was a play Cooper knew well. According to his daughter, he had mounted a production at Heathcote Hill in 1817, taking the part of Sir Callahan O'Brallaghan himself (SFM 34).

18. Dunlap, *American Theatre*, 388–92; William Dunlap, *The Memoirs of George Frederick Cooke* (New York: D. Longworth, 1813), 1:95–100; Ann Mathews retold the story with some variants (the landlady's name is given as Mrs. Byrn, for instance) and less dramatic flair in the first part of her *Memoirs of Charles Mathews* (Philadelphia: Lea & Blanchard, 1839), 1:86–90.

19. Dunlap, *American Theatre*, 392.

20. Henry Dilworth Gilpin, *A Northern Tour: Being a Guide to Saratoga, Lake George, Niagara, Canada, Boston, &c. &c.* (Philadelphia: H. C. Carey & I. Lea, 1825), 17.

21. *Longworth's American Almanac, New-York Register, and City Directory* [for 1823] (New York: Thomas Longworth, 1822), correctly lists the full moon on 4/25/1823 (unpaged front matter); confirmed via data from Astronomical Applications Department, U.S. Naval Observatory (http://aa.usno.navy.mil/data/docs/RS_OneDay.html, which takes the user to http://aa.usno.navy.mil/cgi-bin/aa_pap.pl), accessed on 9/29/2004.

22. "On the Heights of the Mountains in Virginia and New York, with Observations on the Formation of Rivers," *American Medical and Philosophical Register*, 1(1810): 336–46.

23. Cooper at this point in his life probably accepted this view, at least in part. Five years later, in *Notions of the Americans*, he would suggest that erosion had done a good deal of the work of breaking down the dam formed by these "confused and romantically beautiful mountains," thereby letting the bottled up Hudson cut through and find the sea. But even then he admitted that this slower force, important as it was, must have been aided "by some violent convulsion" (*Notions* 1:204).

24. Francis, in Cooper *Memorial*, 100.

25. *Arts of Design*, 1:291–92.

26. Benjamin Silliman, *Remarks, Made on a Short Tour, between Hartford and Quebec, in the Autumn of 1819* (New Haven: S. Converse, 1820), 70.

27. Mary Raddant Tomlan, ed., *A Neat Plain Modern Stile: Philip Hooker and His Contemporaries, 1796–1836* (Amherst: University of Massachusetts Press, 1993), 136–41.

28. Silliman, *Remarks*, 66–67; Munsell, *Annals*, 10:186; Horatio G. Spafford, *A Gazetteer of the State of New-York* (Albany: H. C. Southwick, 1813), 118–119.

29. Tomlan, ed., *Neat Plain Modern Stile*, 69–77; Munsell, *Annals*, 7:139.

30. Tomlan, ed., *Neat Plain Modern Stile*, 193−94.

31. Ann Mathews, *Continuation*, 1:248.

32. Cooper himself thought Cohoes more impressive in some ways than Niagara; see *GS* CE 80−81.

33. Tomlan, ed., *Neat Plain Modern Stile*, 304−5, 44.

34. Silliman, *Remarks*, 69.

35. See the illustration by James Eights, in Joel Munsell, *Collections on the History of Albany* (Albany: Munsell, 1867), 2, facing 448.

36. Carol Sheriff, *The Artificial River: The Erie Canal and the Paradox of Progress* (New York: Hill and Wang, 1996), 19; Rufus W. Griswold, ed., *The Biographical Annual* (New York: Linen and Pennell, 1841), 285.

37. Sheriff, *Artificial River*, 18, 36; Alexander C. Flick, ed., *History of the State of New York* (New York: Columbia University Press, 1933−1937), 5:320; Dixon Ryan Fox, *The Decline of Aristocracy in the Politics of New York, 1801−1840* (New York: 1919), 323.

38. Silliman, *Remarks*, 68−69.

39. At this time, one of the North River line steamboats departed Albany on the return run to New York at 10:00 a.m. on Tuesday, Thursday, and Saturday; New York *Commercial Advertiser*, 4/1/1823.

40. Gilpin, *Northern Tour*, 28; British visitor Henry B. Fearon left New York City on the *Livingston* at 5:00 p.m. six years earlier and found it possible to secure a room at Newburgh, some sixty miles upriver, at what must have been a very late hour; even in 1817, he reported, there were "hotels which keep open regularly for steam-boat passengers"; Roger Haydon, ed., *Upstate Travels: British Views of Nineteenth-Century New York* (Syracuse: Syracuse University Press, 1982), 34.

41. *Arts of Design*, 1:285, 2:135.

42. Gilpin, *Northern Tour*, 26.

43. H. Daniel Peck nicely reads this confrontation as revealing the primacy of images and the visual in Cooper's mind and works; see *A World by Itself: The Pastoral Moment in Cooper's Fiction* (New Haven: Yale University Press, 1977), 3−5.

44. It is tempting to speculate that Cooper and Mathews in some sense collaborated in another cultural matter. The English comedian spent considerable time visiting African American institutions in New York City, including Zion African Methodist Episcopal Church and the theater established in 1821 by William Brown. Once back in England, he added to his repertoire a skit based on the black actor James Hewlett, whom he had befriended and coached while in America. Mathews's attitude toward black cultural ambitions was so dismissive, however, that in May of 1824 Hewlett published an indignant critique of the comedian's routine as it was represented in the American press. Since, as Michael Warner has noted, the founding of New York's black theater coincided with Cooper's last period of work on *The Spy*, it is tempting to infer some knowledge on his part of that effort. In particular, Warner cites the black face disguise by which Henry

Wharton manages to escape American custody in Chapter 28 of the novel. We do not know for certain when this chapter was written, but it probably was among those that Cooper composed after his shift to New York City in October 1821. While it is true, as Warner also points out, that the young Wharton is allowed to don a black mask while the slave Caesar Thompson is *not* concealed by a white one, and the substitution of master for slave is discovered when Caesar's black ear is glimpsed by the soldiers who think they have been guarding Wharton—blackness being thus undisguisable—Caesar in fact has been given white gloves to mask his hands and a "white" wig to hide his hair and his ear. The theatricality of this whole episode is, moreover, quite consistent with themes Cooper introduced at the very start of the novel when he began it some fourteen months before the opening of Brown's theater. And Cooper's portrayal of Caesar (and of the blacks in *The Pioneers*) is considerably more nuanced than anything seen in Mathews's stage mimicry. See Michael Warner et al., "A Soliloquy 'Lately Spoken at the African Theatre': Race and the Public Sphere in New York City, 1821," in *Publics and Counterpublics* (New York: Zone, 2002), 263–68. It probably is more accurate to suggest that the general sense of assertive experimentation among New York blacks chronicled by Shane White was the key influence on Cooper's conception of blacks—both as to their transitional status and their sense of indignation at their treatment at the hands of whites. See Shane White, *Stories of Freedom in Black New York* (Cambridge: Harvard University Press, 2002), 66. On Mathews and black culture, see White, esp. 132–36; also Marvin McAllister, *White People Do Not Know How to Behave at Entertainments Designed for Ladies and Gentlemen of Colour: William Brown's African and American Theater* (Chapel Hill: University of North Carolina Press, 2003); also, [Charles Mathews], *The London Mathews; Containing an Account of This Celebrated Comedian's Trip to America* (Philadelphia: M'Carty and Davis and Morgan and Yeager, 1824), 11–12, 18–22, 27; and Ann Mathews, *Continuation*, 1:239–40.

45. *Letters from John Pintard to His Daughter, Eliza Noel Pintard Davidson*, ed. Dorothy C. Barck, NYHS *Collections*, 1937–1940, 2:135; New York *American (for the Country)*, 4/8/1823.

46. Kenneth T. Jackson, ed., *The Encyclopedia of New York City* (New Haven: Yale University Press, 1995), 557–58.

47. Pintard, *Letters*, 2:136; Jackson, *Encyclopedia*, 558; Edwin G. Burrows and Mike Wallace, *Gotham: A History of New York City to 1898* (New York: Oxford University Press, 1999), 452–53.

48. Spafford, *Gazetteer* (1824), 253.

49. Pintard, *Letters*, 2:137.

50. New York *American (for the Country)*, 4/8/1823.

51. *Otsego Herald*, 2/9/1815. Cooper had other horses in these early years, but they, too, were not especially good. The pair of "grey ponies" his daughter Susan recalled from Fenimore Farm hardly sound like fast mounts. And the horse she associated with

Westchester a few years later, Bull-head, does not seem to have been much better. Cooper hitched that beast up to the gig for daily use, but sold him after he stumbled coming down the hill from Angevine, breaking the vehicle's shafts and spilling the Coopers and their eldest daughter on their way to church one alarming Sunday morning. The only other horses we know of for sure at Angevine were two that Susan vaguely associated with the cut-down carriage her father called "the *rasée*"—a black pair, presumably matched, but given their typical use, hardly matchless. The young woman may have had more experience with carriage horses than with any finer specimens kept by her father at this time. But if he did have finer mounts, why did Cooper ride old Bull-head when, dressed in his smart uniform, he set off to serve as aide-de-camp in the militia (SFM 21, 36–37)? Cooper's father to the contrary had been something of a horse fancier: witness the "spirited imported English blooded mare" (OH 227) that threw Hannah Cooper to her death in Otsego in 1800. This was not a taste, however, that his youngest son inherited, or at least could afford to indulge.

52. Pintard, *Letters*, 2:136–37. The *Chancellor Livingston* arrived in New York with 300 people to attend the races, 160 of them from Albany; Munsell, *Annals*, 8:91 (5/15/1823 newspaper notice).

53. Details are derived from the website of the National Museum of Racing and Hall of Fame, Saratoga, New York; http://www.racingmuseum.org/hall/horse.asp?ID=12 [Eclipse]; http://www.racingmuseum.org/hall/horse.asp?ID=138 [Sir Archy, sire of Sir Henry]; http://www.racingmuseum.org/hall/trainer.asp?ID=261 [William R. Johnson]; all accessed on 5/2/2005; see also *DAB* on Johnson.

54. There is surely some memory of such moments in *The Prairie*'s description of a group of Sioux warriors forced to restrain themselves from battle like horses "at the starting-post, when expecting the signal to commence the trial of speed" (*PR* CE 56).

55. Cooper went to the first and third day races as well; he reported on the latter (*Patriot* 5/29/1823; *LJ* 1:102–3). John Eisenberg has re-created the whole episode (without making use of Cooper's report) in *The Great Match Race: When North Met South in America's First Sports Spectacle* (Boston: Houghton Mifflin, 2006).

56. Floyd Jones and Susan Cooper were grandchildren of Long Island Loyalist Richard Floyd and Arabella Jones, sister of Judge Thomas Jones. He therefore was also related to Samuel Jones and his son Edward H. Jones, from whom the Coopers had borrowed money on the security of the Hickory Grove in 1819. Floyd Jones was active in militia affairs on Long Island and, in the later 1830s, became a member of the New York State Senate. Cooper knew Susan's cousin well enough that he addressed one of his imaginary letters (this one concerned with their mutual "connexion," John Loudon McAdam) to him in *Gleanings in Europe: England;* see *GE* CE 250–59. He was also friendly with "Harry's" brother, horse-fancier Thomas Floyd Jones, to whom he addressed another chatty letter; see *GE* CE 68–79. *Longworth's American Almanac,* dated 6/25/1823, shows Cooper at this address (131).

57. Pintard, *Letters*, 2:139–40.

58. "Walter Barrett" [Joseph A. Scoville], *The Old Merchants of New York City* (New York: M. Doolady, 1870), 2, pt. 1:318.

59. Stokes, *Iconography*, 6:172–76; see Randel map of farms, 3, Plate 86.

60. Cooperstown *Freeman's Journal*, 9/9/1822; see Cooperstown *Watch-Tower*, 9/16/1822.

61. *Freeman's Journal*, 7/14/1823.

62. Ibid., 7/28/1823.

63. Ibid., 9/8/1823, 11/24/1823, 6/14/1824; *Watch-Tower*, 9/1/1823, 11/24/1823, 12/8/1823, 1/26/1824, 2/23/1824.

64. *Freeman's Journal*, 7/28/1823.

65. Ibid., 9/8/1823.

66. The three parcels constituting the farm had been mortgaged to Robert Sedgwick years before, and earlier in 1823 Cooper, at last admitting that he could not pay Sedgwick the principal and accumulated interest he owed him, had authorized his sometime friend to dispose of the property in such a manner that it brought the largest possible return. Sedgwick was in the process of trying to sell it before the fire, although a dispute had arisen between him and Cooper as to how he was doing so. I argue in Chapter 15 that Sedgwick himself *may* have had a motive for having Fenimore burned.

67. Susan does not explicitly locate this event at Turtle Bay, and in fact places it after a statement that the family moved back to Beach Street once "the city was declared safe" (SFM 51). The site of the episode does not matter; the effect does.

68. Van Nostrand and Myer, receipt, 8/19/1823, JFC paps., box 5, AAS; SFM 51 gives details of where Fenimore took sick and where he died.

69. We do not know for certain where he went. There were several plausible sites, from the sea-bathing facility known as Bath House on the Long Island shore at New Utrecht, an hour or so from New York City, to such harder-to-reach spots as the Schooley Mountain Spring, west of Morristown, New Jersey; Spafford, *Gazetteer* (1824), 345; Goodrich, *Picture of New-York*, 463.

70. Cooper himself referred in 1831 to the "violent fever" from which he had suffered in "1824" (*LJ* 2:59)—but this may have been a mistake of memory. See, however, William B. Shubrick to JC, 10/4/1824, copy in JFB paps., box 2, AAS, which reports hearing that Cooper was going to "the Springs," evidently for a cure or at least for rest.

71. It is possible, though I think unlikely, that this was one of two or perhaps three sieges of heatstroke Cooper suffered during this period. His eldest daughter, who according to Cooper's own letter to Shubrick accompanied him on his walk home and who therefore *ought* to have been quite familiar with the details just cited, told a quite different narrative of the heatstroke her father had suffered in 1823. This narrative may have been confused—but it was hardly vague: Cooper was returning (apparently alone) from a visit to the Jays at Bedford, the younger Susan asserted, when "the carriage he was

driving broke down at one of the villages on the Sound." He therefore took passage in a New York–bound sloop. When the wind failed, Cooper, "anxious to reach home, took the helm himself, steering the little craft through Hell-Gate; the day was extremely sultry, and exposure to the intense heat brought on a sudden and severe attack of fever." While these details are quite different from those in Cooper's own 1823 narrative, the result according to Susan's version was virtually the same. On arriving at the Beach Street house, Cooper appeared to be suffering from sunstroke, although as he rested its severity subsided. Susan told the same story in the same way in her introduction to *The Last of the Mohicans* in the Household Edition. She also asserted in both places that in the "autumn of 1825" another instance of exposure had brought on another attack of the same "fever," during which her father had dictated part of that novel to his wife. In this instance, as we shall see in Chapter 15, she was probably right in essence, although she postdated the episode by several months (*P&P* 128–29; *LOM* HE xvi–xvii).

72. Crohn's disease might be one possibility, irritable bowel syndrome another. Both are given some plausibility by an offhand comment in a letter from Cooper to his wife in 1834. While he was away on a solo trip to Cooperstown, his daughter Caroline apparently had a fever accompanied by diarrhea. Susan, often anxious for Caroline's health, nervously speculated that she had dysentery. Cooper replied reassuringly that dysentery was not a symptom—not mere diarrhea—but rather a separate (and of course serious) disease. He was sure that Caroline instead was suffering from "a mere lax" or repeated bouts of diarrhea. This was nothing to worry about excessively. "I am very subject to the latter, owing to a nervous temperament, but they never do me harm" (*LJ* 3:45). What his eldest daughter in 1876 called "dyspepsia" apparently was not acid indigestion or reflux or any other upper gastrointestinal condition but a more deeply seated one. Cooper himself usually blamed his "stomach," as we have seen, but at the age of forty-four, with the health of a daughter and the nerves of his wife under attack, he avoided the euphemism.

73. Mary E. Dewey, *The Life and Letters of Catharine M. Sedgwick* (New York: Harper and Bros., 1871), 172.

74. *The Letters of William Cullen Bryant*, ed. William Cullen Bryant II and Thomas G. Voss (New York: Fordham University Press, 1975–1992), 1:154; see also 1:196.

75. Parke Godwin, *A Biography of William Cullen Bryant* (New York: D. Appleton, 1883), 1:71.

76. Ibid., 1:178–79.

77. Francis, in Cooper *Memorial*, 94–98.

78. See Bryant to William Baylies, who had trained him in the law, [May] 1827, *Letters*, 1:71–72.

79. Francis, in Cooper *Memorial*, 15.

80. "The Literati of New York City" (originally published in *Godey's Magazine and*

Lady's Book), in Edgar Allan Poe, *Essays and Reviews* (New York: Library of America, 1984), 1136.

CHAPTER 13. OLD TALES AND NEW

1. John W. Francis, *Old New York: or, Reminiscences of the Past Sixty Years* (New York: W. J. Widdleton, 1866), 242: "Mathews was the first individual, I heard, who gave a pretty decisive opinion that Scott was the author of the Waverley novels." Francis dated the conversation to the time of the 1822–1823 visit. Mathews thus may have influenced Cooper's opinion.

2. Wilkes left for London late in November, arriving there on 1/7/1823 (*LJ* 1:85); the discussion must have taken place in October or early November.

3. Scott later admitted that his novel was based on a brief pleasure voyage along the Scottish coast in 1814; "Introduction" (1831), *The Pirate* (Westminster: Archibald Constable and Co., 1896), 1:iii–xi. Cooper told the story of his book's origins during the conversation with Wilkes in an 1843 letter to Rufus W. Griswold (*LJ* 4:343, where Wilkes is named) and in his 1849 preface to the novel (*PIL* CE 5–6); his daughter's two versions (*P&P* 72–73; *PIL* HE xiii–xv) place the discussion at a dinner party.

4. Samuel Eliot Morison, *John Paul Jones: A Sailor's Biography* (Boston: Little, Brown, 1959), 204.

5. See Kay S. House, "Historical Introduction," *PIL* CE xx–xxv.

6. *Fanning's Narrative: The Memoirs of Nathaniel Fanning, an Officer of the American Navy, 1778–1783*, in *Magazine of History: Extra No. 21* (New York: William Abbatt, 1913), 8.

7. Compare Thomas Clark, *Sketches of the Naval History of the United States* (Philadelphia: M. Carey, 1813), 49–51, with Clark, *Naval History of the United States* (Philadelphia: M. Carey, 1814), 1:104–10.

8. One could have been James Le Ray de Chaumont, a young French émigré whose father had had extensive dealings with Jones during the Revolution—and who himself became a business associate of Judge Cooper in New York. Cooper would mention Le Ray's father in *HN* (1:179, 182) and in his sketch of Jones (*LDANO* 2:47–49), but in neither place did he positively indicate that the younger Frenchman had given him any information about Jones; if either of the Le Rays was a source, it probably was through tales passed on through William Cooper. Morison, *John Paul Jones*, 121–24, 275; John Henry Sherburne, *Life and Character of the Chevalier John Paul Jones* (New York: Vanderpoel, printer, 1825), 152–58; Alan Taylor, *William Cooper's Town: Power and Persuasion on the Frontier of the Early American Republic* (New York: Alfred A. Knopf, 1995), 112; T. Wood Clarke, *Émigrés in the Wilderness* (New York: Macmillan, 1941), 99–100; Franklin B. Hough, *A History of Jefferson County, in the State of New York* (Albany: Joel Munsell, 1854), 441–47. John Jay mentioned the possibility of raids on the British coast

in a 1781 letter to the son of American statesman (and British prisoner) Henry Laurens. On this basis, Jack Kligerman, "Notes on Cooper's Debt to John Jay," *AL* 41(1969): 415–19, has suggested that Cooper based the raid in *The Pilot* on yet further Revolutionary War anecdotes Jay shared with him. That could well have been the case, although Kligerman says nothing about Jones's attempt on the port of Leith, which I discuss later in this chapter as the likely basis for the episode in the novel.

9. For the sketch of Dale, see *LDANO* 2:233–64; for Cooper's use of Dale as an oral source for his sketch of Jones, see ibid., 2:56–58, 2:69–70 (citing "a long personal interview"), 2:79–82, 2:88, 2:93, 2:95, 2:111 ("Com. Dale used to mention him with respect, and even with attachment; often calling him Paul, with a degree of affection that spoke well for both parties").

10. Dale was active in the Episcopal Church in his later years, and it is conceivable that Cooper met him, or at least became friendly with him, through that means (ibid., 2:262; see also *HN* 1:184–206, 374–75n).

11. *Fanning's Narrative*, 111–12.

12. Morison, *John Paul Jones*, 304.

13. And also some of the minor ones: St. Mary's Isle, so named for a ruinous old abbey, surely suggested the name of George Howard's English hideaway, St. Ruth's Abbey, in *The Pilot;* the flag system invented in the novel by Katherine Plowden as a means of communicating with her fiancée, Richard Barnstable, must have been based on the similar one gotten up by Jones to supplement the secret French system he had been allowed to use in communicating with the other vessels in his 1779 flotilla; see Morison, *John Paul Jones*, 197, 206 (on 335n, Morison describes the Chevalier de Pavillon's innovative system, which used numbers keyed, like Katherine Plowden's, to specific phrases recorded in a code book).

14. Morison, *John Paul Jones*, 304–8; even Fanning, smarting under recent discipline from Jones—who had booted him in the rear to hurry him, as ordered, below deck—had to pay him his due for his handling of the *Ariel* as it lingered off the Penmarch rocks (ibid., 303–4; *Fanning's Narrative*, 80).

15. *Fanning's Narrative*, 27–30.

16. In the case of the raid in *The Pilot*, Cooper gave the mysterious "Mr. Gray" (a.k.a. the Pilot) "the advantage of knowing the ground well"—the ground and sea— for, as "the Pilot" himself assures the American lieutenant Edward Griffith, "much of my early life was passed on this dreaded coast" (*PIL* CE 43, 52). This is historically inaccurate, as Cooper certainly knew by the time he wrote his sketch of Jones in 1843. Since Fanning called Jones a native of the county of Selkirk (rather than Kirkcudbright) and asserted that at the age of nine he had run away to "Leith (the very same place that he was on the point of laying under a heavy contribution as I have before related)," and thereafter worked the waters of that stretch of coast in English colliers (*Fanning's Narra-*

tive, 95–96), this detail in the novel *may* confirm that Cooper did indeed know Fanning's narrative or at least tales derived from it.

17. Morison, *John Paul Jones*, 142, 213–14. Cooper's fictional version of Jones exemplified a principle articulated in his later sketch of the historical figure. Jones had often been "censured" for attacking his native region, as if somehow his use of local knowledge was unfair. But in "a civil war," Cooper wrote, the combatants had every right to convert things they learned during more peaceful times into the weapons of war (*LDANO* 2:44–46). Cooper's sense of the Revolution as indeed a civil war, so clearly underpinning his exploration of "the Neutral Ground" in *The Spy*, was carried over into *The Pilot*: "By what right is my dwelling thus rudely assailed?" asks Colonel George Howard; the Pilot responds, "I might answer you, Col. Howard, by saying that it is according to the laws of arms, or rather in retaliation for the thousand evils that your English troops have inflicted, between Maine and Georgia" (*PIL* CE 337). Hence Cooper's unnecessary reminder in *The Pioneers* of one such attack: "I was on that hill when Vaughan burnt 'Sopus," Natty Bumppo tells Edwards (*PIO* CE 292).

18. James Grossman, *James Fenimore Cooper* (New York: William Sloane Associates, 1949), 37–39.

19. How touchy Americans and Britons were on such issues even as late as the 1820s is suggested by Walter Scott's reaction to *The Pilot*. He thought the book "very clever" when he first read it (CE xxxvi); but, as a Lowlander, he nonetheless well recalled the pain and embarrassment caused by Jones's contemplated raid on Leith in 1779. Perhaps that is part of the reason why, when he attended a production of Englishman Edward Fitzball's travesty version of *The Pilot* at the Adelphi Theatre in London in October 1826, Scott chortled over the way all the book's "odious and ridiculous parts"—that is, those "assigned by the original author to the British"—were turned back on the Yankees by Fitzball. Scott noted that the Americans in attendance were "so displeased, that they attempted a row—which rendered the piece doubly attractive to the seamen at Wapping, who came up and crowded the house night after night, to support the honour of the British flag." Scott was all for reconciliation between Britain and the United States, he confided in his journal, but at the same time he was hardly displeased that "the original author," not yet known to him personally, got his comeuppance (Morison, *John Paul Jones*, 218); Scott personally later told Cooper of his uneasiness in 1779: see *LDANO* 2:58n; and *The Journal of Sir Walter Scott from the Original Manuscript at Abbotsford* (New York: Harper & Brothers, 1890), 1:280. To portray a disaffected Scotsman attacking his native country as Jones had done had as much propaganda value in an 1824 novel as Jones's real raids had had during the Revolution; Walter Scott may have found this plot even more unsettling because, during his 1814 voyage with the commissioners for the Northern Light-House Service, his vessel almost ran afoul of a hostile American cruiser (*Pirate*, v–vi). But landing Jones on English soil also allowed Cooper to gesture

toward "the days of unlucky Charles Stuart" (*PIL* CE 179) and "the Culloden!" (ibid. 226)—the narrative center of Scott's fictional universe. John Paul Jones was in this sense not only the hero of Cooper's book but also the model of the author's own post-colonial defiance of British domination.

20. It is also quite possible that banker Charles Wilkes, who had served as treasurer of the Historical Society from 1805 to 1819, conveyed some or all of the tale to Cooper. According to the poet and lawyer—and Lunch member—Robert Sands, who knew Janette Taylor and in 1830 edited her archive for publication, her uncle's papers were sent to New York during her negotiations with Pintard and his colleagues. At the time, the documents were found to be of great interest, but the Historical Society had not yet established its publication program and no arrangement could be made for Taylor's project. Who had access to the trove before it was returned to Taylor and how widely its contents circulated is unknown, but it is entirely possible that Cooper derived some hints about Jones's career from this source. See [Robert Sands, comp.], *Life and Correspondence of John Paul Jones, including his Narrative of the Campaign of the Liman from Original Letters and Manuscripts in the possession of Miss Janette Taylor* (New York: A. Chandler, 1830), 3–8.

21. I quote Stone's story from its reprinting in *Niles' Weekly Register,* 7/1/1820.

22. New York *Statesman,* 2/18/1823, cited in *PIL* CE xxvii.

23. Charles T. Dering to JC, 3/16/1823, YCAL.

24. Reprinted in Cooperstown *Freeman's Journal,* 10/13/1824.

25. Wilkes is often assumed to have been the "Englishman"—see, for instance, *PIL* CE xvii–xviii. This seems to me unlikely on several grounds. Cooper's 1849 preface speaks of Wilkes (though not by name) as "a friend, a man of polished taste and extensive reading," and attributes the origins of the book to the conversation about Scott held with Wilkes. When "the Englishman" is introduced on the next page as one of the two people who advised Cooper on the work while it was in progress, there would have every reason to explain that "the Englishman" and Wilkes were one and the same—but the preface in fact does not do so. Besides, that "Englishman" clearly liked the book and did not object in the least to its nautical theme (*PIL* CE 5–6). On that basis alone, he cannot have been Wilkes. In October of 1827, Cooper wrote Wilkes from Paris a now unlocated letter in which, among other things, he mentioned his new project (*The Red Rover*) as one in which Wilkes would be likely to take no interest because of its nautical nature. Wilkes to the contrary answered, "my decided opinion is that 'your home is on the deep'" (ibid. xvii). If Wilkes had been "the Englishman," Cooper would never have made that mistake. Finally, in that same letter, Wilkes went on to reminisce about the moment in 1823 when Cooper had first announced his intentions to write a sea tale. But he said nothing about subsequently having read (and liked) the first volume in proofs, an unlikely omission given the point he was trying to make about his keen interest in Cooper as a nautical writer.

26. NARA, Record Group 24, microfilm M330, roll 3, and Thomas H. S. Hamersly, *General Register of the United States Navy and Marine Corps . . . 1782–1882* (Washington: Hamersly, 1882), 165; Ben Cooper had resigned in July 1813, then was reinstated that November, made a lieutenant in 1814, and served through the remainder of the second war with Britain, thereafter making commander (1828) and captain (1838). NARA, Record Group 45, microfilm T829, roll 136 ("Muster and Pay Roll, U.S.S. Vixen, Warren, & Wasp, 1806–1836"), indicates Ben Cooper's presence on the *Wasp* from 10/20/1809 to 7/20/1810. His father, "old James [B.] Cooper," was also in the navy and known to the novelist; see *LJ* 3:260. He had served during the Revolution and then was appointed a master in 1812 and served during and well beyond the second war as well, rising to the rank of commandant by 1841 (Hamersly, *General Register*, 166).

27. That Cooper revised the passage as noted and that he referred to reading the fifth chapter to his cousin not in proof but from a "paper" copy—one assumes this was the manuscript—makes it likely that he consulted Ben Cooper before Aitchison, who, it will be recalled, *read* the "sheets" of the first volume.

28. Taylor, *William Cooper's Town*, 398.

29. See Robert Campbell's report of an Otsego rumor: "it has been said you intended to visit 'Templeton' before sailing for England"; Robert Campbell to JC, 4/10/1823, JFC paps., box 2, AAS.

30. Campbell to JC, 5/26/1823, JFC paps., box 2, AAS.

31. Campbell to JC, 10/28/1823, JFC paps., box 2, AAS.

32. See the undated report, "The Pilot," reprinted from the New York *Spectator* in *Freeman's Journal*, 10/13/1823; the New York *Statesman* report is cited in *PIL* CE xix. Cooper also had other literary business in hand that conceivably contributed to the delay with *The Pilot*. In June, Wiley finally had published what was left of the five "American Tales" Cooper had begun so long ago that they had been noted as "in press" a full twenty months earlier: that is, "Imagination" and "Heart," which together made up the slender volume called, self-effacingly, *Tales for Fifteen* (*Tales* ix). Cooper may have finished the two survivors of the lot long before June 1823; when they finally appeared it was as a gift to Wiley, then suffering his own financial reverses (see Chapter 16).

33. John P. DeLancey and William H. DeLancey, indenture, 1/11/1826, copy (7/2/1829), JFC paps., box 5, AAS.

34. Robert Campbell to JC, 9/7/1818, JFC paps., box 2, AAS.

35. Campbell to JC, 4/29/1819, 6/2/1819, 8/23/1819, JFC paps., box 2, AAS.

36. Dudley Selden to William H. Averell, 11/27/1823, Averell family paps., NYSHA. Selden may have known Averell at Union College, where they both graduated (Averell in 1816, Selden in 1819). Selden became an attorney in New York City in 1831 and briefly served in the U.S. Congress; see *Biographical Directory of the United States Congress, 1774–2005*, House Doc. 108-222. He apparently was already one of Cooper's New York associates in 1823. Beard listed him as a member of the Lunch, based on

Anthony Bleecker's "Report" of March 1826 (see "Members of the Bread and Cheese Club," JFB paps., box 5, AAS); in 1833, Selden joined such genuinely old friends of Cooper as Peter A. Jay, C. C. Cambreleng, John W. Francis, James E. DeKay, Charles P. Clinch, "Jerry" Van Rensselaer, and Fitz-Greene Halleck in inviting the novelist to a welcome-home banquet (*CORR* 1:327; *LJ* 3:14n).

37. Catherine Conklin, receipt for $117.50 [in hand of JC], "Nov [blank] 1823," Bloomfield, N.J., JFC paps., box 5, AAS. Cooper also had to supply Conklin with a feather bed that probably cost another five to ten dollars.

38. Southard soon replied that, in the absence of new evidence, he could not reverse former secretary Thompson's decision; Samuel L. Southard to JC, 12/15/1823, JFC paps., box 2, AAS. As Beard pointed out, Cooper and Southard soon became friends (*LJ* 1:108n).

39. Shubrick replied in February: "I regret that Decatur has not been able to get a more respectable man than Little (who was sent from this station for disgraceful conduct) as his friend in the affair that you mention, it is an indication how low he himself is in the estimation of his associates—how is this business to terminate?" William B. Shubrick to JC, 2/22/1824, copy in JFB paps., box 2, AAS.

40. Cooper had sent a proof sheet of the dedication to Shubrick the previous September; in its original form, it misspelled Shubrick's middle name (there was "one superfluous letter in it—my middle name is Branford not Brandford," Shubrick soon reminded Cooper; William B. Shubrick to JC, 9/13/1823, copy in JFB paps., box 2, AAS). The mistake persisted into the first edition but was corrected in the second. On revisions, see *LJ* 1:110; Cooper told Shubrick that Wiley, needing a rapid second edition, had the book in the hands of five different printers by the time the novelist returned to New York City; he added, "so much for our *joint* labors"—strongly suggesting, as Kay S. House comments, that Cooper and his friend had discussed possible revisions during the Boston trip; see *PIL* CE 439–40, where she gives some examples of possible authorial changes due to Shubrick's influence.

41. William B. Shubrick to JC, 5/10/1823, copy in JFB paps., box 2, AAS.

42. Boston *Commercial Gazette*, 1/12/1824.

43. Shubrick's wife was the former Harriet Wethered. The household included their two children (Mary, about four, and Alice, who was to die the following September) and Mrs. Shubrick's sister, Sarah, then visiting from Maryland, who was especially remembered by Cooper: "Will you mention me to Miss S. Wethered who has quite captivated me, by her goodness and kindness," he joked in his January letter to his friend (*LJ* 1:111).

44. Shubrick's whereabouts are indicated in federal census population schedule, 1820, Charlestown, Mass., p. 391.

45. This place was located in the former premises of the old "Jullien's Restorator" on Milk Street. When that ancient structure was purchased in 1823 and slated for demolition, however, Rouillard shifted his business a block west along Milk Street to another

colonial house. Nathaniel B. Shurtleff, *Topographical and Historical Description of Boston*, 3rd ed. (Boston: Boston City Council, 1890), 659. Cooper wrote Shubrick, "I should like, exceedingly, to spend another afternoon at Rouillard's" (*LJ* 1:111).

46. In his review, *North American Review* 18(1824): 314–29, Phillips had special praise for the whaling scene and for the naval sentiments animating the book (see p. 321), but overall the review was disappointing to Cooper; two decades later, he told Rufus Griswold, "the North American 'damned [*The Pilot*] with faint praise'" (*LJ* 4:343). William B. Shubrick to JC, 2/22/1824, divulged that Phillips was doing the review for the *North American*, perhaps indicating his personal acquaintance with Phillips before Cooper's visit.

47. Richard H. Dana to Gulian Verplanck, 4/2/1823, NYHS; Dana actually sent his letter for Cooper to Verplanck and asked him to forward it after supplying Cooper's first name and address, neither of which Dana yet knew; Richard H. Dana to JC, 4/2/1823, JFC paps., box 2, AAS. Since Dana certainly knew Phillips through their association with the *North American*, it is possible that Phillips attended the dinner at Rouillard's at Dana's suggestion.

48. *DAB;* Allston demurred, confessing himself unable to paint in the historical mode, for "the living mass of one of Cooper's battles" was, he added, beyond his capacity as a painter—almost certainly a reference to *Lionel Lincoln* or *The Last of the Mohicans;* Washington Allston to Gulian Verplanck, 3/1/1830, "Some Unpublished Correspondence of Washington Allston," *Scribner's Magazine* 11(1892): 77; Robert W. July, *The Essential New Yorker: Gulian Crommelin Verplanck* (Durham: Duke University Press, 1951), 117, 134.

49. In *The Prairie*, Cooper called on Allston (and a more recent artistic friend, Horatio Greenough) to turn from "the models of antiquity" long enough to represent Native Americans (*PR* CE 185).

50. Betty Elaine Nichols, "James Fenimore Cooper's *Lionel Lincoln:* A Source and Literary Study," Ph.D. dissertation, Michigan State University, 1972, 34–51.

51. For strategic reasons, Cooper transplanted this house from the town's North End to a location near the Common, about a mile-and-a-half away.

52. For views of both houses, see *LL* CE, illustrations III and IV (following p. 62). The Hutchinson house was wrecked by a Boston mob in 1765 but was rebuilt thereafter and survived, as did the Frankland house, into the 1830s; see Walter Muir Whitehill and Lawrence W. Kennedy, *Boston: A Topographical History*, 3rd ed. (Cambridge: Harvard University Press, 2000), 27–28.

53. Nathaniel Hawthorne, *Tales and Sketches* (New York: Library of America, 1982), 626.

54. Writing in 1817, Charles Shaw, *A Topographical and Historical Description of Boston* (Boston: Oliver Spear, 1817), 123, notes that the bridge had been taken down "within a few years." It still appears in the map prepared by John G. Hales in 1814; see

Alex Krieger, David Cobb, and Amy Turner, *Mapping Boston* (Cambridge: M.I.T. Press, 1999), 191.

55. "In Lionel Lincoln he described the battle of Bunker Hill better than it is described in any other work"—including Bancroft's own *History of the United States of America*—see *Memorial of James Fenimore Cooper* (New York: G. P. Putnam, 1852), 16.

56. Dekker expresses a very positive view of the book's historical elements, asserting that the battles of Lexington and Concord were "brilliantly described" and the battle of Bunker Hill "depicted with great clarity and vividness," but then concludes, "What Cooper thought he was doing [at the end] is by no means clear; what he certainly did was to wreck the novel completely." *James Fenimore Cooper the Novelist* (London: Routledge & Kegan Paul, 1967), 38–39. James Grossman, who also liked both battles (especially the earlier one) wrote, "At the dénouement Cooper by a stroke of melodrama reverses the entire meaning of the story." The mysterious stranger Ralph, who arrives in Boston on the same vessel as Lincoln and soon embraces the colonial cause, has been set up as Lincoln's political guide; we assume that under Ralph's influence the returning American will eschew the cause of the crown and fly to the aid of his native land. But Ralph instead is revealed as Lincoln's father—as well as Job Pray's—and, more puzzlingly, as an escapee from an insane asylum "whose love of freedom is embarrassingly literal." James Grossman, *James Fenimore Cooper* (New York: William Sloane Associates, 1949), 42–43.

57. Alfred F. Young, *The Shoemaker and the Tea Party: Memory and the American Revolution* (Boston: Beacon, 1999), esp. 92–120.

58. Although Cooper picked up that contrast, he interestingly enough did very little with the interior of King's Chapel even during the wedding there (Chapter 22), suggesting that it had been closed at the time of his visit.

59. Lionel Lincoln would have no plausible reason to go directly to Old South. Cooper's visit to the town, revealing the nearness of the two houses of worship, suggested Job Pray's useful mistake. It suggested as well Lincoln's contrast between the church-turned-stable and the similarly nearby Province House. Only a writer familiar with the ground could have used this part of the town in such a manner. It might be added that Cooper's use of the third public building mentioned by Nichols, Faneuil Hall, showed a careful understanding of that building's various changes—especially its great expansion in 1805–1806. As Nichols pointed out, Cooper's description of the building in the second chapter accurately renders the shape and size of the original "long, narrow, brick edifice" of two stories (*LL* CE 22). Cooper also understood that, from the 1760s to the arrival of the British troops in Boston, Faneuil Hall was the place where (as the mad patriot Ralph tells his son, Lionel Lincoln), "liberty has found so many bold advocates" (ibid.). Cooper dramatized this function by having Job Pray recall how he climbed up onto the "cornishes" (the stone lintels above the first-floor openings) and peered into the "winders" during the last town meeting (*LL* CE 23).

60. Sixty-foot-high Copp's Hill (as Cooper's likely guidebook for the visit noted) stood above Hudson's Point and thus was "directly opposite Charlestown"; Shaw, *Description*, 67, 115–16; Shurtleff, *Topographical and Historical Description*, 161. In June of 1775 its northwest edge had been the site of a British battery that targeted the Americans on Breed's Hill and then sent incendiary projectiles over the narrow channel of the Charles River to set much of Charlestown aflame during the misnamed battle of Bunker Hill. That battery had been the vantage point from which British Gen. John Burgoyne observed the battle. Cooper, finding a reprint of Burgoyne's June 25, 1775, letter to Lord Stanley about the experience (probably in the *Analectic Magazine* in 1818), chose that same spot to anchor his own description. It is in Chapters 15 and 16 that Lionel Lincoln watches the battle with the suavely detached "General Burgoyne" at his side (*LL* CE 175–76; see 372–73). It seems likely that Cooper had decided on that vantage point before his January visit and therefore singled out Copp's Hill as a site he definitely wished to see. In this regard, Burgoyne may have been backed up by other sources, some of them oral. If, as has been claimed, Cooper had indeed met fellow Otsego resident George Robert Twelves Hewes, the venerable (and soon legendary) shoemaker-veteran who seems to have taken part in or witnessed many of the important early events of the Revolution, then he may have known that "old Father Hewes" had watched the British attack on the American troops on Breed's Hill from a "narrow neck of land, extending pretty well over to Charlestown, and only visible at low water." Although less dramatic, here was the ordinary American counterpart for Burgoyne's elevated perch; see [Benjamin B. Thatcher], *Traits of the Tea Party* (New York: Harper & Brothers, 1835), 209; Young, *The Shoemaker and the Tea Party*, 71–75; James G. Wilson, "The Last Survivor of the Boston Tea Party," *American Historical Register*, n.s. 1(1897): 5–6. Hewes, who apparently had arrived in Otsego by 1815, conceivably met Cooper through one of the institutions in which Cooper took a role in the late 1810s, such as the Agricultural Society. But I am skeptical of any direct personal connection between the two. A safer bet as a local source on the battle probably was Cooper's Otsego schoolteacher, Oliver Cory, who had arrived in Boston soon enough after the fight to pick up many anecdotes that he surely shared with his Cooperstown pupils years later—among them, the firsthand report of another eventual migrant to Otsego, John Bowen, who had fought in a Connecticut unit on Breed's Hill and, after being mustered out, signed up in a Massachusetts company in which he served alongside Cory; see Oliver Cory, deposition, 2/20/1836, NARA, Record Group 15, microfilm M804, roll 659; John Bowen, filled-in printed form, 4/6/1818; Oliver Cory, deposition (in support of Bowen), 4/24/1818; Buckingham Fitch, deposition in support of Bowen's wife Abigail, 8/18/1838, NARA, Record Group 15, microfilm M804, roll 300. It is also possible that Cooper had picked up Bunker Hill anecdotes from his brother-in-law, George Pomeroy, whose aged grandfather Seth, a brigadier general in the Massachusetts militia, had fought on the front line against the British there; see *DAB*.

61. Paul Trapier, *Incidents in My Life: The Autobiography of the Rev. Paul Trapier, S.T.D. With Some of His Letters,* ed. George W. Williams, Dalcho Historical Society of the Diocese of South Carolina, *Publications,* no. 7 (1954). The influence of Trapier's given name on the Coopers is suggested by the fact that Cooper referred to Trapier as "St-Paul" (*LJ* 1:111), the term that Shubrick in turn soon was using for Cooper's young son; Shubrick to JC, 10/4/1824, copy in JFB paps., box 2, AAS.

62. Francis B. Heitman, *Historical Register of Officers of the Continental Army* (Washington: Rare Book Shop, 1914), 242.

63. Nichols, "James Fenimore Cooper's *Lionel Lincoln,*" 71–72, credits the sketch of Lee to the influence of James Thacher, *A Military Journal during the Revolutionary War* (1823), but notes that Thacher himself quotes it from Garden. On Garden (1757–1829), who published his second series of *Anecdotes* in 1828, see Trapier, *Incidents,* 9, and *DAB;* his father and namesake, the well-known botanist for whom the gardenia had been named by Linnaeus, was a Loyalist who went into exile at the peace and died in London in 1791; see Lorenzo Sabine, *Biographical Sketches of Loyalists of the American Revolution* (Port Washington: Kennikat, 1966), 1:458–59.

64. Paul Trapier to JFC, 3/3/1845, quoted in Nichols, "James Fenimore Cooper's *Lionel Lincoln,*" 36.

65. The "humble, decent" church Cooper would have seen during an 1824 visit to Lexington was not the one standing there in 1775 (that is, the second meetinghouse of 1713), but rather was the third structure, which replaced it in 1794 and which was very different in look and layout. Tellingly, the novel's phrasing is vague enough to allow a reader to imagine either structure. Samuel Adams Drake, *Historic Mansions and Highways around Boston* (Boston: Little, Brown, 1906), 360–61.

66. *The American Revolution: Writings from the War of Independence,* ed. John Rhodehamel (New York: Library of America, 2001), 20.

67. The Hancock House stood until the 1860s; Drake, *Historic Mansions,* 342. As a sidelight on the complex situation Cooper faced in trying to reimagine Revolutionary Boston, his care in tracking down descriptions of the old "Beacon" may have been for naught. There had been a pole, with a grate on top (in which Job Pray sits suspended in one scene [*LL* CE 170]), but these apparently already had been taken down by the British and a small fortification erected on their site before the battle of Bunker Hill; Shurtleff, *Topographical and Historical Description,* 170–81; Samuel Adams Drake, *Old Landmarks and Historic Personages of Boston* (Boston: Little, Brown, 1906), 349–52. The British fort on the top of Beacon Hill may be seen in the 1775 ink and watercolor drawing reproduced in David H. Fischer, *Paul Revere's Ride* (New York: Oxford University Press, 1994), 9. The beacon was reerected in 1776 but had blown down in 1789, and the following year a brick monument to the heroes of the Revolution was erected. The latter in turn was torn down in 1811, when the process of leveling off the top of the hill, not completed until the summer of 1824, began. Cooper would have seen the 1790 monument

during his cruise to Boston with Lawrence in 1810. And from the heights of the hill during 1824, such as they then remained, he could have surveyed the town and harbor—seeing, for instance, those chimneys of the yet-standing Hancock House that he nicely used
as a benchmark in the fourth chapter of the novel. But the very desire to make his tale as
specific as possible of course exposed him to possible anachronisms and mistakes.

68. Hamersly, *General Register*, 526; Charles O. Paullin, *Commodore John Rodgers:
Captain, Commodore, and Senior Officer of the American Navy* (Cleveland: Arthur H.
Clark, 1910), 263, 268, 287–95.

69. Whipple family website, http://www.whipple.org/descendants (accessed
1/10/2005); Abraham Whipple was also a descendant of the first Captain John Whipple.
For the *Gaspee*, see William Fowler, *Rebels Under Sail: The American Navy during the
Revolution* (New York: Charles Scribner's Sons, 1976), 107.

70. E. L. Cabot Follen (1781–1860) to Catharine M. Sedgwick, 3/4/1825, copy in
JFB paps., box 2, AAS. I know of no instance in which someone reported actually seeing Cooper "tipsey," but he certainly was no teetotaler.

71. Since, unlike Truck, Cooper did not travel on a Sunday—not on his way back,
at any rate—the rest of the tale may be embroidery. It is, however, charming enough.
Truck tells his passengers how the stage, for the first time passing through the area on a
Sunday, created such a stir that it emptied a whole church as it went by—"horse and
foot, parson and idlers, sinners and hypocrites, to see the four-horse power go past" (*HB*
1:107). It is possible that Cooper was recalling instead the Boston-Providence leg of his
1824 trip, although he seems not to have traveled that on a Sunday, either.

72. Wendy Martin, ed., *Colonial American Travel Narratives* (New York: Penguin,
1994), 71.

73. William B. Shubrick to JC, 2/22/1824.

CHAPTER 14. LEGENDS

1. A total of five hundred or so largely unremarkable substantive changes showed
up. Some of these may have been Wiley's, but Cooper conceivably had begun compil-
ing the list before leaving New York City; *PIL* CE 439–41. One change was the correc-
tion of Shubrick's middle name in the dedication.

2. The baby, the couple's seventh, was soon named Paul—not, as later was rumored, after the hero of his last book, John Paul Jones, but rather because Cooper "always liked short strong names for boys." Or so his eldest daughter, forgetting poor
Fenimore, thought (SFM 53). Probably, as suggested in Chapter 13, the choice was a lingering tribute instead to Paul Trapier ("St-Paul"), Shubrick's nephew, the guide during
part of the father's recent trip; see Shubrick to JC, 10/4/1824, copy in JFB paps., box 2,
AAS.

3. Wiley announced the series as early as 12/9/1823; see *LL* CE xxi.

4. Cooper apparently had secured Dearborn's narrative, first published in the *Port*

Folio and later in pamphlet form, before his Boston trip. Swett's book he apparently looked for while in Boston but without success; Shubrick soon sent it to him, in a version that also contained a reissue of *An Essay on the Life of the Honourable Major General Israel Putnam* (1788), by Hartford Wit David Humphreys; see William B. Shubrick to JC, 2/22/1824, copy in JFB paps., box 2, AAS. The Humphreys title volume was in some sense an answer to Dearborn's narrative, which was notable for its attack on Israel Putnam, who was the nominal commander at Bunker Hill but was, in participant Dearborn's view, ineffective there. Cooper was impressed with Putnam and made the hero of *Lionel Lincoln* a fan of the Connecticut soldier; see *LL* CE 148–49, 180 (as we shall see, larger-than-life Putnam provided inspiration as well for *The Last of the Mohicans*). Some of the influences here were circular. Putnam was also a favorite of Thacher, whose book Cooper probably encountered before his Boston trip as well, but Thacher in fact got much of his Putnam lore from Humphreys; see *A Military Journal during the American Revolutionary War, from 1775 to 1783*, 2nd ed. (Boston: Cottons and Barnard, 1827), 387–97. Aside from reinforcing Cooper's interest in Putnam, Thacher's book supplied a good deal else for *Lionel Lincoln*. The beating Job Pray suffers at the end of the first chapter, as Betty Elaine Nichols pointed out, probably derived from Thacher's account of an infamous tar-and-feathering administered by a British soldier to an American civilian, an event also referred to in its literal form by Cooper; see Nichols, "James Fenimore Cooper's *Lionel Lincoln:* A Source and Literary Study," Ph.D. dissertation, Michigan State University, 1972, 67–68; *LL* CE 17, 49–50. Thacher's assertion that "tea-drinking is almost tantamount to an open avowal of toryism" (*Military Journal* 14) has its counterpart early in the novel, when a tea party at Mrs. Lechmere's engenders political disagreement: the Patriot woman Agnes Danforth scorns the brew, whereas the Loyalist Cecil Dynevor owns a weakness for it (*LL* CE 38–39). When Cooper mentions the conversion of Old South into a riding academy and the destruction of Old North for firewood, a point he could have found in his likely guidebook to Boston as well as other sources, it is perhaps significant that he links the two details in a single breath, as did Thacher; *Military Journal*, 44; *LL* CE 235–36.

5. Nichols, "James Fenimore Cooper's *Lionel Lincoln*," 56, 58; Samuel Swett, in David Humphreys, *An Essay on the Life of the Honourable Major General Israel Putnam . . . with an Appendix, Containing an Historical and Topographical Sketch of Bunker Hill Battle by S. Swett* (Boston: Samuel Avery, 1818), 198.

6. Cooper probably used the reprint of Burgoyne's letter in the March 1818 issue of the *Analectic Magazine*, a Philadelphia magazine that he no doubt scanned with some frequency in its final years, when it bore the added title of *Naval Chronicle*.

7. The last of these newspaper notices cautioned that Cooper's "precarious" health threatened a delay. There is slight confirmation of those rumors in Cooper's own 1831 recollection about the "violent fever" that had struck him "in 1824" (*LJ* 2:59)—*slight*, however, because he may simply have been misdating the 1823 bout discussed in Chap-

ter 12. But, as we shall see, there certainly was to be substantial delay in the completion of the project.

8. JC and Charles Wiley, memorandum of agreement, 4/29/1824, Cooper family paps. microfilm, HSFC, New York City. This contract apparently marked an attempt by Cooper to squeeze more profit from the book by reducing the wholesale discounts offered to booksellers from a maximum of 33⅓ to 30 percent for orders of four hundred or more copies (with six-month notes), and by dropping the lower discounts for smaller quantities even more: 25 percent for ninety-nine or more copies (six-month notes), 25 percent for forty-nine or more copies (three-month notes), and 20 percent for twelve or more copies (cash payment). The earlier contracts that survive provided for more liberal terms across the board (see Chapter 16).

9. John Manseca to JC, 7/1/1824, copy in JFB paps., box 2, AAS, addressed to Flushing, provides the first evidence of the family's relocation.

10. SDC to Caroline DeLancey, 4/25/1825, copy in JFB paps., box 2, AAS; John L. Franklin to JC, 7/21/1824, JFC paps., box 2, AAS. Part of Cooper's interest in Flushing may have come from the mineral spring, discovered in 1816, that had a brief fame among the ailing citizens of New York; see Benjamin F. Thompson, *History of Long Island, from its Discovery and Settlement to the Present Time*, 3rd ed. (New York: Robert H. Dodd, 1918), 3:31–33, 42.

11. Charles Wiley, assignment to JC, 10/—/1825, and Robert M'Dermut, statement of JC's indebtedness, 10/25/1825, copies of both in JFB paps., box 2, AAS.

12. Matthew C. Perry et al. to JC, 7/24/1824, copy in JFB paps., box 2, AAS; New York *American*, 8/4/1824. Not until 1827, in a letter to his friend and Lunch member Luther Bradish, could Cooper say that he looked "better than at any time since 1823" (*LJ* 1:221).

13. Ward (1793–1864) is identified by John Henry Sherburne, ed., *Life and Character of the Chevalier John Paul Jones, A Captain in the Navy of the United States, during their Revolutionary War* (Washington: Sherburne, 1825), viii; on his career as an auctioneer, see "Walter Barrett" [Joseph A. Scoville], *The Old Merchants of New York City* (New York: M. Doolady, 1870), 3, pt. 1:241. By the early 1840s, he was a "broker"; see Ralph A. Aderman, ed., *The Letters of James Kirke Paulding* (Madison: University of Wisconsin Press, 1962), 262n. Sherburne printed Jones's letter to Franklin, *Life and Character*, 111–25.

14. George Ward to JC, 7/28/1824, copy in JFB paps., box 2, AAS; Cooperstown papers reported on the story as it unfolded—see *Watch-Tower*, 8/9/1824, for the *Evening Post* report.

15. *Niles' Weekly Register*, 8/7/1824.

16. Christopher McKee, *A Gentlemanly and Honorable Profession: The Creation of the U.S. Naval Officer Corps, 1794–1815* (Annapolis: Naval Institute Press, 1991), 464; Thomas H. S. Hamersly, *General Register of the United States Navy and Marine Corps . . .*

1782—1882 (Washington: Hamersly, 1882), 644. Later in life, Sherburne would author such fugitive items as a volume of *Erratic Poems* (of which, appropriately, no copy seems to have survived), an unpublished and now apparently lost play on the theme of the tragic Seminole warrior Osceola, a collection of *Naval Sketches* (1845), and *The Tourist's Guide; or, Pencillings in England and on the Continent* (1847), based on his service for several years as foreign correspondent for the Philadelphia *Saturday Courier;* see *Appleton's Cyclopedia of American Biography* and title page, Sherburne, *The Life and Character of John Paul Jones, a Captain in the United States Navy, during the Revolutionary War,* 2nd ed. (New York: Adriance, Sherman, 1851).

17. [Robert C. Sands], *Life and Correspondence of John Paul Jones* (New York: A. Chandler, 1830), 4.

18. The four travelers, all educated at Oxford, were Edward Smith-Stanley (1799–1869), who became fourteenth earl of Derby in 1851 and was prime minister of England for three terms (1852, 1858–59, and 1866–68); John Evelyn Denison (1800–1873), who was elected speaker of the House of Commons in 1857 and retired from that position in 1872, at which point he was created Viscount Ossington; John Stuart-Wortley (1801–1855), who became second baron Wharncliffe in 1845; and Henry Labouchere (1798–1869), who was created baron Taunton in 1859.

19. Stanley T. Williams, *The Life of Washington Irving* (New York: Oxford University Press, 1935), 1:260.

20. E[dward George Geoffrey Smith] Stanley [fourteenth earl of Derby], *Journal of a Tour in America, 1824—1825* ([London]: privately printed, 1930), 20–22.

21. Cooper was slated to receive another tribute in New York on August 3, when an honorary master's degree was to be conferred on him during the Columbia commencement (see New York *American,* 8/3/1824); but, as Beard noted (JFB paps., box 2, AAS), "if Cooper processed, he did not receive his diploma, for it was sent to him after his return from Europe in 1833."

22. Smith-Stanley, *Journal,* 16.

23. Ibid., 14–28.

24. William B. Shubrick to JC, 10/4/1824, copy in JFB paps., box 2, AAS; this information no doubt was relayed to Shubrick through naval channels. In *The Last of the Mohicans,* Cooper went out of his way to mention the 1820s vogue of Saratoga and Ballston Spa, suggesting that his visit there with the Britons was his first (*LOM* CE 123). Cooper probably turned to the springs as a source of "natural" healing, much as he had elsewhere when his mysterious affliction struck in 1823: the waters at Saratoga were thought to be particularly effective for "bilious" and "dyspeptic" disorders at the time, precisely the nature of his own problems, and substantial quantities of Saratoga mineral water were already being bottled and shipped out to markets elsewhere; see Horatio G. Spafford, *A Gazetteer of the State of New-York* (Albany: D. Packard, 1824), 470, and James Stuart, *Three Years in North America* (Edinburgh: Robert Cadell, 1833), 1:192.

25. James A. Holden, "*The Last of the Mohicans,* Cooper's Historical Inventions, and His Cave," NYSHA *Proceedings* 16(1917): 214, 245 (Parkman). Spafford, *Gazetteer,* 431, called Glens Falls "a pleasant, busy little place." Among recent visitors to the falls whom Cooper knew well was Benjamin Silliman, whose *Remarks, Made on a Short Tour, between Hartford and Quebec, in the Autumn of 1819* (New Haven: S. Converse, 1820), 142, included a description particularly pertinent to Cooper's in *The Last of the Mohicans:* "Down these [rock] platforms, and through these channels, the Hudson, when the river is full, indignantly rushes, in one broad expanse; now, in several subordinate rivers, thundering and foaming among the black rocks, and at last dashing their conflicting waters into one tumultuous raging torrent, white as the ridge of the tempest wave, shrouded with spray, and adorned with the hues of the rainbow. Such is the view from the bridge immediately at the foot of the falls, and it is finely contrasted with the solemn grandeur of the sable ledges below, which tower to a great height above the stream."

26. Henry D. Gilpin, *A Northern Tour: Being a Guide to Saratoga, Lake George, Niagara, Canada, Boston, &c. &c.* (Philadelphia: H. C. Carey & I. Lea, 1825), 67. Some tourists even missed the falls, including such an avid fan of natural scenery as Nathaniel P. Willis, who on his first trip from Saratoga to Lake George passed obliviously over the bridge with no inkling of the busy river or the rocky shelves below; see *American Scenery,* 2:84.

27. Smith-Stanley, *Journal,* 34; Gilpin, *Northern Tour,* 67, despaired of describing the scene in any detail because of its chaotic beauty.

28. Smith-Stanley, *Journal,* 34; Cooper's eldest daughter portrayed Stanley as urging him to write *The Last of the Mohicans;* see *P&P* 126; *LOM* HE xiii.

29. On Cooper's Cave, see Francis Parkman's narrative of his visit in 1842, in Holden, "*The Last of the Mohicans,*" 244–45.

30. Ibid., 242–43, citing the 1840 edition of G. M. Davison's *Traveller's Guide through the Middle and Northern States.*

31. Spafford, *Gazetteer,* 272; Gilpin, *Northern Tour,* 67, included a section called "Excursion to Glenn's Falls, and Lake George," noting, "Few persons leave Saratoga Springs, without making an excursion to these two places."

32. Frederic Van de Water, *Lake Champlain and Lake George* (Indianapolis and New York: Bobbs-Merrill, 1946), 49–50; see *Adventure in the Wilderness: The American Journals of Louis Antoine de Bougainville, 1756–1760,* trans. and ed. Edward P. Hamilton (Norman: University of Oklahoma Press, 1964), 39–41.

33. Earlier in his career, when the stunning sights he had seen in Europe were more sharply recalled, Cooper was less decisive in his praise of Lake George. Only in its island clusters, unmatched in Switzerland, did the New York lake outdo its European counterparts; see *GS* CE 102.

34. Smith-Stanley, *Journal,* 35; Gilpin, *Northern Tour,* 73.

35. Spafford, *Gazetteer,* 72–73.

36. Ralph Birdsall, *The Story of Cooperstown* (Cooperstown: Augur's Book Store, 1948), 364–66; JFC, "The Battle of Plattsburgh Bay," *Putnam's Magazine*, n.s., 3 (1869): 50.

37. Van de Water, *Lake Champlain and Lake George*, 286–87; Smith-Stanley, *Journal*, 35.

38. Timothy Dwight, *Travels in New England and New York*, ed. Barbara M. Solomon (Cambridge: Harvard University Press, 1969), 3:252–53. This was another mark of Lake George's difference from Otsego, where the sole event of note in the pre-1785 Euro-American past was the brief passing of the Sullivan-Clinton expedition in 1779.

39. In September 1755, Johnson had defeated the French under Baron Dieskau at the south end of Lac du Saint Sacrement, upon which he renamed the lake in honor of the reigning British monarch, George II. For Gilpin, see *Northern Tour*, 67–73.

40. Humphreys, *Essay*, 37–38; Thomas Philbrick, "The Sources of Cooper's Knowledge of Fort William Henry," *AL* 36(1964): 209–14.

41. An archaeologist asserted in 1999 that even at the present Fort George "may well be the most intact British military site surviving in the northeastern United States"; David R. Starbuck, *The Great Warpath: British Military Sites from Albany to Crown Point* (Hanover: University Press of New England), 15, 120–21.

42. Starbuck, *Great Warpath*, 102–8; Ian K. Steele, *Betrayals: Fort William Henry and the "Massacre"* (New York: Oxford University Press, 1990), 57–66; Gilpin, *Northern Tour*, 69.

43. Dwight, *Travels*, 3:243; Gilpin, *Northern Tour*, 69, confirmed the observation.

44. The panorama of the lake and then of the fort in Chapter 14 (*LOM* CE 139–42) is imaginatively sited on a thousand-foot-high mountain described as an outlier of the western ridge running up the lakeshore. This would be a short distance, about a mile, from Bloody Pond (it should be noted, as Starbuck points out in *Great Warpath*, 112–13, that the present landscape feature bearing that name is not the original one).

45. Smith-Stanley, *Journal*, 35.

46. Not surprisingly, the novelist had a special regard for Smith-Stanley. In *Gleanings in Europe: England*, while expressing general skepticism about the level of talent among the English aristocracy, he made an exception for two men: Lord Grey (Charles, Earl Grey, who was to be prime minister from 1830 to 1834) and Smith-Stanley, who in Cooper's view possessed "one of the acutest" minds among the nobility (*GE* CE 142; Cooper apparently encountered Smith-Stanley later in Britain: see *GF* CE 273). When Cooper met British foreign minister George Canning at a dinner in Paris in 1826, he apparently put in a good word for another of the 1824 party, John Evelyn Denison, who was made a lord of the Admiralty by Canning (then prime minister) in May of the following year (*GF* CE 94, 283–84; *LJ* 1:200–201, as well as 1:159–61). The Coopers ran into Denison and his wife in Switzerland in August 1828 and had a conversation with them about the comparative merits of American and European scenery; see *LJ* 1:292; *GS*

CE 69. Cooper had some contact with Henry Labouchere in London in 1828, when he visited the Englishman's lodgings and saw that he had Washington Allston's *Elijah in the Desert* (1818) stored in his attic. During his visit to London in the summer of 1833, Cooper unsuccessfully tried to buy the Allston canvas (*LJ* 2:397). On John Stuart-Wortley, see *GE* CE 133, and *LJ* 5:80−81.

47. On the return of "cool and agreeable" weather to the city, see the report reprinted in Cooperstown *Freeman's Journal*, 8/23/1824; in *Notions of the Americans*, Cadwallader and his European visitor are said to be staying at the City Hotel at the same time as Lafayette (*Notions* 1:50−51); if based on Cooper's experience, it may indicate that he lodged there alone (or at least took his meals there) following his return from upstate, and brought his family back from Flushing Bay only later in August.

48. *Notions* situates Cadwallader and the Count on the *Chancellor Livingston* (*Notions* 1:42); it also mentions that Gen. Philip Van Cortlandt had traveled "forty miles that morning to welcome La Fayette" (*Notions* 1:45), a detail Cooper plausibly could have learned directly from that Clintonian ally, although it was reported in the press (see New York *Commercial Advertiser*, 8/17/1824).

49. New York *Commercial Advertiser*, 8/17/1824; J. Bennett Nolan, *Lafayette in America, Day by Day* (Baltimore: Johns Hopkins University Press, 1934), 243. *Notions* CE xvi asserts, without citing evidence, that Cooper was part of the welcoming committee; he certainly was not part of New York's official "Committee on Arrangements," composed of city Recorder Richard Riker and four aldermen; Edgar E. Brandon, *Lafayette, Guest of the Nation: A Contemporary Account of the Triumphal Tour of General Lafayette*, vol. 1 (Oxford: Oxford Historical Press, 1950), 32.

50. John P. DeLancey to SC, 8/25/1824, copy in JFB paps., box 2, AAS.

51. Cooper was not in attendance on the hero's birthday, September 6, when a showy banquet was given at Washington Hall by the exclusive Society of the Cincinnati, the once controversial organization of Revolutionary officers and their descendants, in which Lafayette had been an early member. But he nonetheless may have written the report in the New York *American*, 9/9/1824, which was evidently produced by someone *not* in attendance—for instance, it comments, "After the dinner, which is said to have been of superior preparation. . . ." Cooper had ties to several members of the Cincinnati who were in attendance and could have fed him the details in the article—including Gen. Solomon Van Rensselaer (kinsman of the Patroon), Gen. Mathew Clarkson (father-in-law of his friend Peter A. Jay), Col. Lewis Morris (kin of the Morrises of Otsego County), and the ubiquitous eighty-year-old celebrant, Gen. Philip Van Cortlandt.

52. Francis B. Heitman, *Historical Register and Dictionary of the United States Army, from its Organization . . . to . . . 1903* (Washington: Government Printing Office, 1903), 1:188, 1:449, 1:682; *The Diary of Philip Hone, 1828–1851*, ed. Bayard Tuckerman (New York: Dodd, Mead, 1889), 2:143; *LJ* 5:85n2; "Members of the Bread and Cheese Club," JFB paps., box 5, AAS.

53. New York *American*, 9/9/1824.

54. The postponements hardly left Lafayette with nothing to do. The evening after the trip out to the fort, he was the guest of honor at a Park Theatre performance of *The Siege of Yorktown*, by Tammany supporter Mordecai M. Noah, editor of the *National Advocate*. The next night came another Park Theatre performance, this time of an even more pertinent play, Samuel Woodworth's *Lafayette; or the Hero of Olmutz*. We have no indication that Cooper was present for either performance, but he may well have been. Nolan, *Lafayette in America*, 248.

55. John W. Francis, in *Memorial of James Fenimore Cooper* (New York: G. P. Putnam, 1852), 95.

56. Rodman Gilder, *The Battery* (Boston: Houghton Mifflin, 1936), 129–31, 146; I. N. Phelps Stokes, *The Iconography of Manhattan Island* (New York: Robert H. Dodd, 1915–1928), 5:1639.

57. New York *Daily Advertiser*, 9/16/1824.

58. New York *Evening Post*, 9/1/1821; William Dunlap, *A History of the Rise and Progress of the Arts of Design in the United States* (New York: Dover, 1969), 2:296; *Letters from John Pintard to his Daughter, Eliza Noel Pintard Davidson, 1816–1833*, ed. Dorothy C. Barck, NYHS *Collections*, 1937–1940, 2:283; *DAB*.

59. New York *Commercial Advertiser*, 9/11/1824.

60. Willis (ca. 1795–1830), an Irish immigrant and civilian, had been hired as the first bandleader at West Point in 1817; a composer and arranger as well as a virtuoso performer, he was responsible for introducing the Kent bugle to the United States; see George E. Ryan, *A Life of Bandsman Richard Willis* (Hanover: Christopher, 2001).

61. Nolan, *Lafayette in America*, 249; *Notions* puts the Count and Cadwallader in Lafayette's party on this part of the tour.

62. *The Papers of Henry Clay*, vol. 4, ed. James F. Hopkins and Mary W. M. Hargreaves (Lexington: University Press of Kentucky, 1972), 619; vol. 7, ed. Robert Seager II (Lexington: University Press of Kentucky, 1982), 3. On Brown's view of Cooper, see vol. 6, ed. Hargreaves and Hopkins (Lexington: University Press of Kentucky, 1981), 546. In one regard, virtually everyone in the United States had mixed views of Lafayette: he included in his retinue (at the Castle Garden fete, for instance) the young Scots reformer and writer Frances Wright, with whom the aged Frenchman's personal relationship was rumored to be very close indeed; see Sylvia Neely, *Lafayette and the Liberal Ideal, 1814–1824: Politics and Conspiracy in an Age of Reaction* (Carbondale: Southern Illinois University Press, 1991), 188–91, 257–63. Cooper's refusal to mention Wright in his account of the Castle Garden event typified the way most Americans dealt with their conflicted feelings on the subject.

63. Nolan, *Lafayette in America*, 250–95; *Notions* 2:170–78; Dunlap, *Arts of Design*, 1:295.

64. Otsego County mortgages, book G, p. 474.

65. JC bond (printed form), for Robert Sedgwick, 3/12/1819, with later endorsements, JFC paps., box 5, AAS; Joseph Rounds to Robert Sedgwick, 12/24/1821, copy in JFB paps., box 18, AAS.

66. JC, deposition, 4/5/1825, copy in JFB paps., box 18, AAS.

67. Cooperstown *Freeman's Journal*, 6/21/1824; Robert Sedgwick, deposition, 5/5/1825, copy in JFB paps., box 18, AAS.

68. Otsego County mortgages, book G, p. 474.

69. JC, bill of complaint, Chancery Court, 2/21/1826, copy in JFB paps., box 18, AAS.

70. Otsego County deeds, book O, p. 103.

71. Robert Sedgwick, "Debt on Bond" (printed form), 10/30/1824, submitted to New York State Supreme Court, in re: Sedgwick v. Cooper; Elijah Paine (Sedgwick's attorney), notice of court ruling, to Peter A. Jay (Cooper's attorney), 11/13/1824; Judge John Irving, show cause order, 11/4/1824, with 11/8/1824 notation of bail reduction; copies of all in JFB paps., box 18, AAS. These proceedings may hint at Cooper's motive in rewriting the contract for *Lionel Lincoln* in November 1824 so as to make Wiley its publisher; the $5,000 payment he expected from this change could have come in handy.

72. New York Supreme Court, "Notice of Trial," 12/16/1824, "Notice of Trial," 2/26/1825 (with copy of notation regarding JC's "good and substantial defense" on reverse), addressed by Elijah Paine to Peter A. Jay, copies of both in JFB paps., box 18, AAS.

73. The details of this debt are obscure. Brookes may have acquired a claim against Cooper from a third party. Not until 1821, in any case, did Cooper slowly begin an attempt to satisfy Brookes. In January of that year, he assigned Brookes several leases in St. Lawrence County (Franklin County deeds, book 2, p. 303). That April he bound himself to repay Brookes $1,600, half of it by that September. He did pay interest on the debt across 1822 and 1823 (JC, bond, to Joshua Brookes, 4/21/1821, JFC paps., box 4, AAS), but according to James H. Pickering, who cites a Westchester deed (book W, p. 367; *NYH* 72[1991]: 310), Brookes sued Cooper in the state supreme court and secured two judgments against him before May 1823. The assignment of Cooper's interest in the first edition of *Lionel Lincoln* to Brookes evidently represented Cooper's attempt to finally settle with Brookes on those judgments and/or the old debt. Cooper had also assigned the *Union* and its cargo to Brookes before May 1, 1822; see JC, unsigned bond, 5/1/1822, to Robert M'Dermut, JFC paps., box 5, AAS.

74. JC and Charles Wiley, memorandum of agreement, 4/29/1824 (note 8 above). After the memorandum appear several later additions: Cooper's assignment of it to Brookes (5/8/1824); Wiley's acknowledgement of the assignment (5/10/1824); Brookes's receipt for a payment of $1,000 on the original debt (11/15/1824); and an undated note signed by Brookes: "Residue extended on last of Mohicans [*sic*])."

75. Agreement, JC with Charles Wiley and Abijah Weston, 11/13/1824, Cooper

family paps. microfilm. HSFC, New York City. Note that the editors of *Lionel Lincoln* for the Cooper Edition were in error when they asserted that Cooper did not sign a contract for the book until November (*LL* CE xxii); the November contract *altered* the original one executed more than six months earlier.

76. As the editors of the novel in the Cooper Edition hypothesized (*LL* CE 380), such a sequence of events would explain why the second volume, which probably had gone into production in response to a hectic but unsustained burst of activity on Cooper's part in November, and was begun on the first page of the first gathering, is dated "1824," without the still nonexistent copyright notice inserted on the reverse of the title page.

77. John Miller to JC, 5/6/1825, copy in JFB paps., box 2, AAS.

78. *LL* CE xxii–xxiii; John Miller to JC, 12/4/1824, 2/5/1825, 2/22/1825, copies in JFB paps., box 2, AAS.

CHAPTER 15. HAWK-EYE

1. William Dunlap, *A History of the Rise and Progress of the Arts of Design in the United States* (New York: Dover, 1969), 1:274, 1:294–95; regarding the Washington party, Dunlap noted: "I think [Cooper] will remember the story of the Irish sportsman rabbit hunting, who, seeing a donkey looking over a hedge swore he had found the father of all rabbits." Edward L. Morse, ed., *Samuel F. B. Morse: His Letters and Journals* (Boston: Houghton Mifflin, 1914), 1:263–64. The importance of Jackson's presence is reflected in the fact that in *Notions of the Americans* Cooper was to give the loser of the 1825 runoff his own very warm support (*Notions* 2:184–85n).

2. I will suggest below that Cooper *may* have deepened his conception of Chingachgook in response to hints in W. H. Gardiner's review of *The Spy* in the July 1822 issue of the *North American Review*. If that was so, then he indeed did reconceive the book midway (that is, in the seventh chapter).

3. This despite the fact that his main plot in that novel is set two years later than the battle with Dieskau. On "blood" in the book, see Thomas Philbrick, "*The Last of the Mohicans* and the Sounds of Discord," *AL* 43(1971): 29–30.

4. Even in 1822–1823, however, Cooper's knowledge of Johnson's life showed considerable depth and range. Witness Natty's reference to Johnson's capture of Fort Niagara in 1759, which was effected by boating his troops from Oswego westward, over the route Cooper and Woolsey followed in 1809; see *PIO* CE 154, and Arthur Pound and Richard E. Day, *Johnson of the Mohawks* (New York: Macmillan, 1930), 270–72. Here was a detail Cooper did not absolutely need to insert for the sake of his plot.

5. On Carver, see Marcel Clavel, *Fenimore Cooper: Sa vie et son ouvrage: La jeunesse (1789–1826)* (Aix-en-Provence: Imprimerie Universitaire de Provence, 1938), 567–68, and Thomas Philbrick, "The Sources of Cooper's Knowledge of Fort William Henry," *AL* 36(1964): 211–12. Note, too, that friends of Cooper's such as Chancellor James Kent had long regarded Carver's *Travels* as offering a classic eyewitness view of the massacre

at Fort William Henry; see James Kent to Benjamin Silliman, 10/14/1820, in George P. Fisher, *Life of Benjamin Silliman* (New York: Charles Scribner and Co., 1866), 1:294. Although it is not known when Cooper encountered Carver's narrative, the book was widely available and popular. Kent's comment will suggest the degree to which it was common knowledge, and a common subject of conversation, in Cooper's circle. (It might also be added here that Kent had learned quite recently some details of the 1755 defeat of Dieskau from a participant, "old Mr. Van Skoik, of Kinderhook," details that he eagerly shared with Silliman—perhaps with Cooper as well; see Benjamin Silliman, *Remarks, Made on a Short Tour, between Hartford and Quebec, in the Autumn of 1819* [New Haven: S. Converse, 1820], 158.) Timothy Dwight used the Livingston-Smith-Scott *Review;* another likely source was William Johnson's own report *To the Governours of the Several Colonies* (1755), likewise used by Dwight; see *Travels in New England and New York,* ed. Barbara M. Solomon (Cambridge: Harvard University Press, 1969), 3:255. I assume that Cooper knew Silliman's book, which was widely read and excerpted during the period—in for instance, another book Cooper surely knew, Henry D. Gilpin's *A Northern Tour: Being a Guide to Saratoga, Lake George, Niagara, Canada, Boston, &c. &c.* (Philadelphia: H. C. Carey & I. Lea, 1825). It was not just authorial pride that led Silliman to recall: "My little book met with favor. It became a *vade mecum* for travellers to Canada, and might readily have passed to a third edition, had I moved in the matter"; G. P. Fisher, *Life of Benjamin Silliman* (New York: Charles Scribner, 1866), 1:278. The old friends from New Haven kept in contact in the 1820s; the novelist's daughter recalled one occasion (dated by her to the precise moment that Cooper's work on *The Last of the Mohicans* was stopped by a renewed attack of his malady) when Silliman visited Cooper in New York. Given Silliman's uncannily similar health problems and his search for relief from them, which included travel, the frequenting of "springs," and a simplified diet, it is tempting to conclude that he shared his insights with his former pupil and lab assistant, whose condition when he saw him in New York worried him deeply (see *P&P* 129; Fisher, *Life of Benjamin Silliman,* 1:301–8, 1:311).

6. On Frey and Johnson, see James T. Flexner, *Mohawk Baronet: The Life of Sir William Johnson* (New York: Harper and Brothers, 1959), 335. On Pomeroy, see Clare Benedict, *Voices out of the Past* (London: Ellis, 1929), 260–61, and Dwight, *Travels,* 3:255–57; as Samuel Swett's *An Historical and Topographical Sketch of Bunker Hill Battle* would remind Cooper while he worked on *Lionel Lincoln* in 1824, Pomeroy was said to have personally given Dieskau his nearly fatal wound, as a result of which he had been presented with Dieskau's watch, a memento he had passed down in his family—see David Humphreys, *An Essay on the Life of the Honourable Major General Israel Putnam . . . with an Appendix, Containing an Historical and Topographical Sketch of Bunker Hill Battle* (Boston: Samuel Avery, 1818), 189, where Swett tellingly concluded that Pomeroy might well be called "the Putnam of Connecticut River." The first of the two DeLanceys involved in the Lake George area was John P. DeLancey's uncle; the second

was his elder brother; D. A. Story, *The deLanceys: A Romance of a Great Family* (Toronto: Thomas Nelson, 1931), 18–19, 69–70. On Susannah, see Chapter 5, note 26.

7. Ann L. Cooper Clarke to JC, 3/20/1825, JFC paps., box 2, AAS (Clarke mentions that Richard had written Cooper from Albany some days or weeks before; his letter is not extant).

8. Samuel L. Southard to JC, 5/16/1825, copy in JFB paps., box 2, AAS; Mathew C. Perry to JC, 3/20/1825, JFC paps., box 2, AAS. Cooper's daughter Susan recalled a visit by Goldsborough during the winter of 1824–1825, perhaps in connection with the navy question. And William and Eliza Cooper, two of William's children, were "frequently with us," Susan also recalled. Young William himself became a member of the household in the early 1820s, perhaps as early as 1823, and was destined to go with his uncle's family to Europe in 1826 (SFM 52, 56).

9. JC, draft deposition [ca. January 1826], copy in JFB paps., box 18, AAS.

10. JC, draft depositions [ca. April 1825, ca. January 1826], copies in JFB paps., box 18, AAS.

11. [Peter A. Jay?], notes on 3/23/1824 trial, Sedgwick v. Cooper, New York State Supreme Court, copy in JFB paps., box 18, AAS.; in his ca. January 1826 draft deposition, Cooper summarized the Sedgwicks' logic in this manner: "H.D.S. testified on said trial that he did not think the said Bond was usurious because his Brother the Plaintiff had told him he had taken great pains to [keep?] it from being so. And that when called on to explain, why pains should be taken to [keep?] a Bond that was not usurious from the taint of usury, he had no sufficient answer to give. And this deponent says, that he has understood the Plaintiff in this cause to say, that he did not think a Bond usurious, in which the usurious money was not included notwithstanding an agreement to pay usury, and he has also been told, that the Plaintiff has advocated a similar principle before the court." JC, draft deposition [ca. January 1826].

12. JC, deposition, 4/15/1825, copy in JFB paps., box 18, AAS.

13. Robert Sedgwick to Peter A. Jay, 4/9/1825, copy in JFB paps., box 18, AAS.

14. Eben Morehouse to Robert Sedgwick, 4/6/1825, copy in JFB paps., box 18, AAS.

15. Peter A. Jay to Robert Sedgwick, 4/9/1825, draft, copy in JFB paps., box 18, AAS.

16. Robert Sedgwick to Peter A. Jay, 4/11/1825 (1), copy in JFB paps., box 18, AAS.

17. Robert Sedgwick to Peter A. Jay, 4/11/1825 (2), copy in JFB paps., box 18, AAS.

18. Otsego County deeds, book II, p. 219.

19. JC, deposition, 4/15/1825, with ruling entered on back; New York Supreme Court, order, 5/5/1825; copies of both in JFB paps., box 18, AAS.

20. Robert Sedgwick, deposition, 5/5/1825; New York Supreme Court, subpoena (5/14/1825) and printed notices of trial (5/28/1825, 8/13/1825, 10/27/1825), copies of all in JFB paps., box 18, AAS.

21. SDC to Caroline DeLancey, 4/21/1825, copy in JFB paps., box 2, AAS.

22. Max Meisel, *Bibliography of American Natural History* (Brooklyn: Premier Pub. Co., 1924–1929), 2:235–39; Chandos M. Brown, *Benjamin Silliman: A Life in the Young Republic* (Princeton: Princeton University Press, 1989), 211–12, 303–10; *Diary of William Dunlap, 1766–1839*, ed. Dorothy C. Barck, NYHS *Collections*, 1929–1931, 2:530n.

23. If his daughter's suggestion that the fresh attack resulted from another instance of exposure was correct, perhaps that occurred on the *Van Tromp* as Cooper returned from New York City after having delivered the latest batch of text, including the eleventh chapter, to Wiley's shop. But she may have been confused; having told of the *original* instance of sunstroke on the return from Westchester in 1823 as part of this anecdote about the writing of *The Last of the Mohicans*, she added, "exposure again brought on the same disease" (*LOM* HE xvi; *P&P* 128).

24. The sole basis for concluding that Cooper had a second attack in 1825 is found in an undated letter about the Sedgwick case that Cooper wrote to Peter A. Jay, which Beard, without citing his reasons, assigned to "September? 1825" (See *LJ* 1:121–25); I here accept his dating of this letter because it alerts Jay that if, at the upcoming trial, "any endorsements [on the bond] are produced" without a clause Cooper now recalled having insisted on inserting once the interest rate was raised, Jay should "look at them, with great distrust" (*LJ* 1:123). Since the failure to produce the endorsements during the March 1825 trial was the basis for Cooper's successful petition for a new trial, such advice would indeed be very relevant as the date of that new trial (tentatively scheduled for 9/26/1825) apparently was drawing near. On the other hand, it should be noted with some skepticism that Cooper spent most of the letter filling in Jay on the background details of a case in which Jay had been acting as his attorney for more than a year; that is indeed a bit odd at so late a date. If Beard misdated the letter, the point about SFC's mistakes on the chronology of *The Last of the Mohicans* still hold (*LOM* HE xiv–xvii; *P&P* 128).

25. Perhaps the treatment of the falls and the river in Natty's impressive nighttime monologue in Chapter 6 owed something to Cooper's present musings on the turbulent East River.

26. Critical interpretation of the feverish interruption to *The Last of the Mohicans* has probably made too much of it. If the dreamlike wrestling match between Chingachgook and Magua in the twelfth chapter had the deeper psychological meaning one reader has seen in it, that meaning surely had nothing to do with the "murder" of Cooper's father in a political brawl that, Alan Taylor has pretty conclusively demonstrated, never took place; see Stephen Railton, *Fenimore Cooper: A Study of His Life and Imagination* (Princeton: Princeton University Press, 1978), 34–36; Alan Taylor, "Who Murdered William Cooper?" *NYH* 72(1991): 261–83. If there was a psychological dimension to this scene and its echoes elsewhere in the novel, perhaps we should look for it in Cooper's more immediate ills. With its twists and turns and sudden reversals, the Sedgwick business, with which Cooper grappled across 1825, was not unlike the fight between Chin-

gachgook and Magua. Nor is it entirely beside the point that the treachery which converts Magua from a forest guide into a fierce and bloody antagonist in the novel recalls the fact that Cooper's antagonist—Robert Sedgwick—was once his close friend.

27. By the term "Oriental," Cooper was indicating the sort of sensual exoticism that the West at the time associated with the East in general.

28. E[dward George Geoffrey Smith] Stanley [fourteenth earl of Derby], *Journal of a Tour in America, 1824–1825* ([London]: privately printed, 1930), 34.

29. Lydia Maria Child, *Hobomok and Other Writings on Indians,* ed. Carolyn L. Karcher (New Brunswick: Rutgers University Press, 1986), 98, 84, 140–41, 148–50.

30. *Letters from New-York* (1843), in ibid., 189.

31. Edwin L. Stockton, Jr., "The Influence of the Moravians upon the Leather-Stocking Tales," Moravian Historical Society *Transactions* 20, pt. 1(1964): 32–33; W. H. Gardiner, review of *The Spy, North American Review* 15(1822): 258.

32. John G. E. Heckewelder, *History, Manners, and Customs of the Indian Nations who Once Inhabited Pennsylvania and the Neighbouring States,* Historical Society of Pennsylvania, *Memoirs* 12(1876): 431 (this was not, however, given by Heckewelder as a personal name).

33. As I noted in Chapter 11, it is *possible* that Cooper's work on *The Pioneers* went slower. Although the overlap between *The Spy* and Cooper's third novel suggests that he was working on both at the same time in the late fall of 1821, the overlap could have resulted from his work revising the earlier book in January and again in May of 1822; in the latter event, it is also possible that Gardiner's review sent Cooper scurrying to read Heckewelder in July, after which he began the seventh chapter (*PIO* 1:92 and following), where the effect of Heckeweler is first unmistakably felt in the novel—where, for one thing, John Mohegan first is called Chingachgook (ibid. 1:96). Cooper's "hundred pages" in the Halleck shipment might well have been a round number; indeed, it must have been, since he surely sent full sheets, and these ended at pp. 84, 96, and 108—but not at p. 100. On Gardiner, see *North American Review* 23(July 1826): 150–97. It is one of the ironies of Cooper's critical reception that Gardiner would arraign him in 1826 for too closely following "the narrations of the enthusiastic and visionary Heckeweler" in *The Last of the Mohicans.*

34. Orm Överland, *James Fenimore Cooper's* The Prairie: *The Making and Meaning of an American Classic* (Oslo: Universitetsforlaget, 1973), 173n6.

35. Probably James Ridgway, ed., *The Speeches of the Hon. Thomas Erskine (Now Lord Erskine), When at the Bar,* 4 vols. (London: Ridgway, 1813).

36. *Niles' Weekly Register,* 10/14/1815. I rely here on Ives Goddard, "'I am a Red-Skin': The Adoption of a Native American Expression (1769–1826)," *European Review of Native American Studies* 19:2(2005): 1–20, as well as on personal communications from Goddard. For Portage des Sioux, see also Landon Y. Jones, "Iron Will," *Smithsonian Magazine,* August 2002.

37. See *PIO* 1:17 (red-skin),and 2:282 (white-skin).

38. *The Literary Gazette: or, Journal of Criticism, Science, and the Arts* 1:37 (9/15/1821): 586–87.

39. The single use of "white-skin" in the novel is given to Chingachgook at the end of his life: "Hawk-eye! my fathers call me to the happy hunting-grounds. The path is clear, and the eyes of Mohegan grow young. I look—but I see no white-skins; there are none to be seen but just and brave Indians." Once Chingachgook has died, Natty takes his hand in his and, wistfully looking at his face, says, "Red skin, or white, it's all over now!" (*PIO* 2:282, 2:285). It is also worth pointing out that "happy hunting-grounds," the merest of clichés today, is first reported in the *Oxford English Dictionary on Historical Principles* from Washington Irving's *Astoria* (1836); Cooper in fact preceded Irving by thirteen years in using this other instance of "natural" metaphor.

40. Big Elk's oration had been printed in *Niles' Weekly Register* in 1815; a brief excerpt from a second, somewhat later address that was attributed to him by name and that mentioned the death of "one of our red skin chiefs . . . at Portage des Sioux" appeared under the heading "Indian Treaty" in the *Otsego Herald* (9/15/1815), where Cooper could well have seen it—and the term in question.

41. For this visit, see the largely undocumented article by Herman J. Viola, "Invitation to Washington—A Bid for Peace," *The American West* 9(1972): 18–31.

42. For the bill of the O'Fallon party, see "Major O'Fallan to C. Jenings Dr.," 12/17/1821, Records Group 217, E-525, Settled Indian Accounts, B. O'Fallon, box 14 (1821–1822), NARA II (College Park, Md.), courtesy of Ives Goddard. Smith-Stanley (*Journal*, 13) pointed out that meals were taken in common at the City Hotel.

43. New York *Evening Post*, 12/13/1821; thanks to Ives Goddard for this reference.

44. Edwin James, comp., *Account of an Expedition from Pittsburgh to the Rocky Mountains under the Command of Major Stephen H. Long* (Barre: Imprint Society, 1972), 254. Cooper spelled his name "Peterlasharoo" in his letter to the countess de Broglie and in *Notions of the Americans* (*Notions* 2:287–88). See Frederick W. Hodge, ed., *Handbook of American Indians North of Mexico*, Smithsonian Institution, Bureau of American Ethnology, Bulletin 30 (Washington: Government Printing Office, 1907–1910), 2:236.

45. James, *Account of an Expedition*, 255–57. See Susan Fenimore Cooper's version of the anecdote, based on her own extensive review of the Long expedition materials, in her introduction to the novel (*PR* HE xviii–xxv). Orm Överland, *Making and Meaning of an American Classic*, 56–58; Överland indicates that Morse derived his version of the episode from the journal of Capt. John R. Bell; formerly a tactician at West Point, Bell had joined the Long expedition early in 1820 (Howard Lamar, introduction, James, xxiii).

46. Viola, "Invitation to Washington," 22, 28; see Jedidiah Morse, *Report to the Secretary of War of the United States, on Indian Affairs* (New Haven: Davis and Force, 1822), 246. Intriguingly, as Goddard indicates in "'I Am a Red-Skin,'" both Big Elk

(Ongpatonga) and the Pawnee leader Sharitarish at this event used the expression "red skins"; see *Daily National Intelligencer*, 2/16/1822; Morse, 245.

47. Susan was correct; on *achgook, suckachgook,* and related words, see Hecke-welder, *History, Manners, Customs,* 399.

48. For the Cooper family's familiarity with the migrating New England Indians, see *RH* 178–79, which tells of the Brotherton family that claimed "an hereditary ac-quaintance with the master of the house." That family's name (spelled by Susan as "Kunkerpott") she interpreted as a laughable tag applied to them by German settlers in the Mohawk valley. They were, however, Stockbridge Indians from the Oneida lands. "Konkapot" was a common Stockbridge family name, and Jacob Konkapot was a settler in New Stockbridge, the Oneida County village where his people had relocated; see Patrick Frazier, *The Mohicans of Stockbridge* (Lincoln: University of Nebraska Press, 1992), 1–3, 21–35, and passim; W. Deloss Love, *Samson Occom and the Christian Indians of New England,* ed. Margaret Connell Szasz (Syracuse: Syracuse University Press, 2000), 256, 260, and passim. See also an early article about two prominent Stockbridge leaders by tribe member Levi Konkapot, Jr., "The Last of the Mohicans," *Wisconsin Historical Collections* 4(1859): 303–7. Natty Bumppo's scornful reference in *The Pioneers* to "them Yankee Indians, who, they say, be moving up from the sea-shore" is to the Broth-erton and Stockbridge migrants (*PIO* CE 452). The scorn, though, may be the charac-ter's rather than Cooper's—although on this, see Cooper's somewhat skeptical com-ments to President Martin Van Buren regarding a Brotherton Indian who as late as 1840, then making baskets in the woods near Cooperstown, personally reported rumors to the novelist, derived from his kin in Wisconsin, about the British stirring up midwestern Indians against the United States (*LJ* 4:25–26). In *Bryant and His Friends: Some Remi-niscences of the Knickerbocker Writers* (New York: Fords, Howard, and Hulbert, 1886), James Grant Wilson reported an anecdote derived from the English traveler Charles Au-gustus Murray, author of *The Prairie Bird* (1844), in which Cooper told Murray, apropos of the latter's experience among the Plains tribes: "You have the advantage of me, for I never was among the Indians. All that I know of them is from reading, and from hear-ing my father speak of them. He saw a great deal of them when he went to the western part of New York State, about the close of the past century" (237). Murray visited Cooper at his home in Cooperstown in 1836; see Roger Haydon, ed., *Upstate Travels: British Views of Nineteenth-Century New York* (Syracuse: Syracuse University Press, 1982), 91–93. Wilson's reliability is not the highest, but the contextual details of this anecdote make it sound plausible. Whatever his acquaintance among remnant Native Americans in Otsego, Cooper hardly could have claimed to have been "among the Indi-ans" as Murray had.

49. Daniel Mandell, "Shifting Boundaries of Race and Ethnicity: Indian-Black In-termarriage in Southern New England, 1760–1880," *Journal of American History* 85 (1998): 466, 475–77, 495; Thomas L. Doughton, "'Unseen Neighbors': Native Ameri-

cans of Central Massachusetts, a People who had 'Vanished,'" in Colin G. Calloway, ed., *After King Philip's War: Presence and Persistence in Indian New England* (Hanover: University Press of New England, 1997), 207–30. Both Doughton and Jean O'Brien, "Divorced from the Land: Resistance and Survival of Indian Women in Eighteenth-Century New England," in Calloway, 144–61, stress the demographic actualities of contemporary Native American communities.

50. Word of Cooper's plans for a naval history was circulating in the press early in 1825, as a fan reported in March; see Redmond Conyngham to JC, 3/2/1825, copy in JFB paps., box 2, AAS.

51. "Old Brooklyn Days," in Walt Whitman, *Complete Poetry and Collected Prose* (New York: Library of America, 1982), 1283.

52. New York *Evening Post*, 7/6/1825, 7/8/1825.

53. The "Whitehallers" were so called because they operated from Whitehall Pier, near the Battery on the East River. The pier derived its name from the English renaming of Peter Stuyvesant's house on the shore at that point after the conquest of New Netherland.

54. Cooper thought that they did not react exuberantly—the point in appending his footnote about the event to the Count's discussion of American "coldness" (*Notions* 1:165–67).

55. John Gardner, "American Star," *Log of Mystic Seaport* 24(1972): 74f; Rodman Gilder, *The Battery* (Boston: Houghton Mifflin Co., 1936), 151. Cooper mistakenly dated the race to "the summer of 1825" (*Notions* 1:166n).

56. Gilder, *Battery*, 151; I. N. Phelps Stokes, *The Iconography of Manhattan Island* (New York: Robert H. Dodd, 1915–1928), 5:1649; J. Bennett Nolan, *Lafayette in America, Day by Day* (Baltimore: Johns Hopkins University Press, 1934), 296–97; *DAB*, "Varick."

57. Cooper's eldest daughter had such confused memories of the day that she forgot all about Robertson's balloon but thought she recalled the 1825 boat race as happening on this occasion. Obviously, she knew about the race through her father, knew that the *American Star* somehow played a part in the July 9 celebration, and many years later conflated things (SFM 57–58). Odder was her father's similar mistake. When, in 1828, he published *Notions of the Americans* and inserted a footnote reference to the episode with the *Dart*, he too remembered it as occurring "in the summer of 1825" (*Notions* 1: 166). Perhaps the confusions (and the great heat) of the July event suggested a bit more prudence for Cooper when another big public celebration took place in New York City in the autumn: the celebration of the "meeting of the waters"—of the opening of Clinton's canal—on November 4. The Coopers watched those festivities from their house on Greenwich Street (where they had returned late in September), seeing, for instance, the members of the Lunch pass by out front with uplifted canes displaying bread and cheese as a tribute to their leader (SFM 58).

58. Bryant reported the conversation the next day to Richard Henry Dana, Sr.; *The*

Letters of William Cullen Bryant, ed. William C. Bryant II and Thomas G. Voss (New York: Fordham University Press, 1975–1992), 1:196.

59. Sidney F. and Elizabeth Stege Huttner, *A Register of Artists, Engravers, Booksellers, Bookbinders, Printers, & Publishers in New York City, 1821–42* (New York: Bibliographical Society of America, 1993), 142; Édouard Louvet, *Byron et la liberté, hymne de mort* (Paris: P. Renouard, 1824). Once in New Orleans, Louvet began the weekly journal *Le Propagateur Louisianias,* which lasted for only a few months. Cooper had some interest in supplying the foreign market directly at this time. In 1824, he apparently had translated parts of *The Pilot* himself; his French instructor, John Manseca, noted in July of that year that he had received Cooper's letter "et votre traductions du Pilote"; J. Manseca to JC, 7/1/1824, copy in JFB paps., box 2, AAS (these may have been exercises rather than part of an intended full translation). *The Pilot* in any case was issued in a French translation by A.-J.-B. Defauconpret, Cooper's unofficial but regular translator, in Paris in 1824. Syon also had expressed a willingness to help Cooper have *The Last of the Mohicans* translated (*LJ* 1:125).

60. JC, draft deposition [ca. January 1826], copy in JFB paps., box 18, AAS.

61. The total amount of the original Conant bond as determined in an 1816 court judgment won by Cooper and his brother Isaac against Conant was $3,309.94; Cooper's interest in it appears to have been one-half, meaning that he transferred a claim worth more than $1,600 to Sedgwick in 1817. In 1819, Sedgwick apparently was on the verge of reviving the 1816 judgment so that he could have an execution and proceed to a sale of Conant's lands. See Robert Campbell to JC, 8/23/1819, JFC paps., box 2, AAS.

62. Cooper recalled for Peter A. Jay in 1826 how "disgusted" he was by the manner in which Sedgwick, both in 1819 and on each occasion when he made a payment on the bond, carried out his calculations in a "half-whisper"—like a miser in a stage play—without fully disclosing all the details to Cooper or recording them straightforwardly on the bond. Indeed, the endorsements, since detached, had been written in such a manner that they might support widely differing interpretations of the dealings between the men, a further mark of the lawyer's dishonesty. Sedgwick had wanted it that way in order to conceal the reality of usury, the poison ingredient in his own potentially self-incriminating machinations. In a man capable of such scheming contortions, why would one assume that anything was straightforward (*LJ* 1:122–23)?

63. Cooperstown *Freeman's Journal,* 7/28/1823.

64. Eben Morehouse to Robert Sedgwick, 4/6/1825; JC, draft deposition [ca. January 1826].

65. *Freeman's Journal,* 7/28/1823; JC, bill of complaint, Chancery Court, 2/21/1826, copy in JFB paps., box 18, AAS.

66. Judge Samuel Jones, order, Sedgwick v. Cooper, 2/26/1826, copy in JFB paps., box 18, AAS.

67. Robert Sedgwick to Elisha Paine, 2/28/1826, copy in JFB paps., box 18, AAS.

68. JC, bill of complaint, Chancery Court, 2/22/1826, copy in JFB paps., box 18, AAS.

CHAPTER 16. LITERARY BUSINESS

1. *The Letters of William Cullen Bryant,* ed. William C. Bryant II and Thomas G. Voss (New York: Fordham University Press, 1975–1992), 1:200–1.

2. James A. Hillhouse had arranged for Wiley to take on Percival's book; see Charles T. Hazelrigg, *American Literary Pioneer: A Biographical Study of James A. Hillhouse* (New York: Bookman Associates, 1953), 106–7.

3. Cooper's contract for the second edition of *The Spy* obligated Wiley to offer 33⅓ percent discount for quantities of ninety-nine or more in exchange for notes payable in six months; the same discount for quantities of forty-nine to ninety-eight copies in exchange for notes payable in three months; the same discount for quantities of twenty-four to forty-eight, but for cash only; and a discount of 25 percent for quantities of eleven to twenty-three, also for cash; JC and Charles Wiley, memorandum of agreement, 2/14/1822, JFC paps., box 5, AAS.

4. JC, in account with Wiley and Halsted, [4/2/1822], JFC paps., box 5, AAS. This is the basis for the discussion in the next paragraph as well.

5. Wiley owed just over $100 for copies retailed through his shop but was due 5 percent on all wholesaled copies—roughly the same amount. His $281 personal note did not, therefore, cover his own sales; it represented the shortfall between his receipts on the second edition and what he owed Cooper under their contract.

6. There is some confusion about how exactly Wiley accounted for the six copies delivered to Cooper, but this hardly affects the larger picture. The thirty-eight copies left unsold on April 2 were credited to Cooper as part of his due, but as they were priced at the usual wholesale level they also did not affect the overall calculation either; JC, in account with Wiley and Halsted, [4/2/1822].

7. Charles Wiley to JC, 1/7/[1822], JFC paps., box 2, AAS. The per-unit expenses (those for printing, paper and cover stock, binding, and shipping) were constant, rising in fixed increments as the number of copies was increased.

8. This result does not indicate that retail customers gobbled up the book on that day. Already by the middle of January, according to a report in the New York *Commercial Advertiser,* Wiley had so many wholesale orders from his clients that he and Cooper decided on a hastily arranged second edition, which was intended to meet this demand (*PIO* CE 473, 490).

9. Or exactly $66.00; since he would lose his 5 percent commission on those one hundred books, or $6.70, his net total for each new increment of one hundred copies retailed through his own shop would be $59.30.

10. The per-copy cost of typesetting would decrease from about twenty cents in a run of one thousand copies to about seven cents for a run three times that size.

11. Since the first edition of *The Pioneers* was presumably larger than the second edition of *The Spy* (the press on 1/16/1823 reported that it was "large"), each copy of it would have cost a bit less than the sixty cents calculated for the second edition of *The Spy* (typesetting was the one constant expense regardless of the size of an edition). Wiley's earnings would have been unaffected; Cooper's would have been slightly higher (*PIO* CE 474, 490).

12. This second order may indicate that Cooper indeed had gone to New York City in July in order to deliver or to hurriedly finish a second large installment of the book; between the first and second orders from M'Dermut, Wiley had purchased enough paper for three-quarters or so of the finished book.

13. Charles Wiley, assignment to JC, 10/—/1825, JFC paps., box 5, AAS, and Robert M'Dermut, statement of JC's indebtedness, 10/25/1825, copy in JFB paps., box 2, AAS.

14. From the size of the paper orders, which totaled 158,000 sheets approximately 12 by 14 inches in size, one assumes that some surplus was on hand, as that number of copies of *Lionel Lincoln* would have required another 236 reams. It does seem clear from Wiley's later statements that Fanshaw did produce an edition that large.

15. JC, memorandum of agreement with Charles Wiley and Abijah Weston, 11/19/1824, Cooper family holdings, HSFC, New York City (microfilm).

16. That is, 0.66 per retail copy minus the 0.067 commission lost on each copy not wholesaled.

17. Henry Carey in January 1826 estimated the average sale price of *Lionel Lincoln* as $1.50 and stated that forty-five hundred copies had been sold (H. C. Carey to JC, 1/9/1825 [for 1826], JFC paps., box 2, AAS); Wiley told Cooper he had "about twelve hundred" copies left out of the six thousand printed, indicating he had sold about forty-eight hundred (Charles Wiley, assignment to JC, 10/—/1825).

18. Carey gave $3,000 as the cost of the edition (that is, fifty cents per copy), but that is too high; he printed *The Prairie* in an edition of five thousand and had stereotype plates made for that book in 1827 at a production cost of forty-six cents per copy; stereotyping added about five cents per copy. A more reasonable price is therefore about forty cents per copy; Carey to JC, 1/9/1825 [for 1826]; David Kaser, ed., *The Cost Book of Carey & Lea, 1825–1838* (Philadelphia: University of Pennsylvania Press, 1963), 45.

19. My conclusion is based on calculations derived from the Carey and Lea cost book entries for 1825–1827, with special attention to *The Prairie* in 1827, adjusted for the added cost in that case of stereotype plates.

20. I assume a cost for the second edition of $1,900 for four thousand copies. There of course would have been no extra payment to Cooper.

21. While the edition had not sold out by October, the twelve hundred to fifteen hundred copies Wiley still had left in stock to meet future demand over the next four months were his to sell. Once he had paid off Cooper, the great bulk of his returns on

these remaining copies would be Wiley's own profit. If the value of each of those copies were calculated at $1.34, the average price Henry Carey used in discussing *Lionel Lincoln* a few months later with Cooper, Wiley thus had another up to $2,010 in value left in his hands. The whole edition even with Cooper's high price for the copyright promised Wiley a net return of more than $2,000.

22. Robert M'Dermut, statement of JC's indebtedness, 10/25/1825.

23. *The Pioneers* was not mentioned in this agreement because Wiley had issued the most recent edition in conjunction with another bookseller, Collins and Hannay, to whom Cooper had consigned his rights for a set period; see *LJ* 1:133.

24. Charles Wiley, assignment to JC, 10/—/1825. Oliver Halsted, statement to JC, [1825], JFC paps., box 5, AAS; the endorsement on the back ("O. Halsted / Account / C. Wiley's") suggests that the account predates Wiley's death only two months or so after the assignment to Cooper.

25. Henry C. Carey to JC, 1/9/[1826], JFC paps., box 2, AAS. This arrangement was complicated by the fact that Wiley's one-year exclusive contract on *Lionel Lincoln* was about to expire. Presumably, however, Cooper would have left the remaining copies in Wiley's hands, counting on him to handle their distribution.

26. Sidney F. and Elizabeth Stege Huttner, *A Register of Artists, Engravers, Booksellers, Bookbinders, Printers & Publishers in New York City, 1821–1842* (New York: Bibliographical Society of America, 1993), 145; see title pages, Joseph Chitty, Esq., *A Practical Treatise on Pleading* (New York: R. M'Dermut, 1809), and Tobias Smollett, *Peregrine Pickle* (New York: M'Dermut and Arden, 1813).

27. Robert M'Dermut, receipt, 12/29/1820, JFC paps., box 5, AAS.

28. JC, bank book, Bank of New York, 1817–1819; checks, Bank of New York, 1819, both JFC paps., box 4, AAS.

29. We have scant evidence of exactly when M'Dermut first performed the latter role, and in any event it seems clear from the record that Cooper usually did not himself pay for supplies. In the case of *Precaution*, not only did Andrew T. Goodrich handle all financial matters for the book, repeatedly pressing Cooper to pay him so that he might discharge his obligations; we also simply do not know the source of paper. In the case of *The Spy*, Charles Wiley billed Cooper for paper used in printing (or at least proofing) the first edition, with no indication of its source. For each of the subsequent editions of that book and for all the editions of the next two that he managed as Cooper's agent, Wiley also seems to have paid his suppliers out of the proceeds from his sales. Had he lived up to his obligations as publisher of *Lionel Lincoln*, he would have paid M'Dermut and Cooper would never have had to deal with the question. The contracts between Wiley and Cooper that survive indicate that while the author was obliged to defray the cost of the paper (as for the printing) prior to *Lionel Lincoln*, Wiley was required to deduct those costs from gross receipts and turn the balance over to him. In the case of the fifth novel, the final terms freed Cooper from all obligation for the costs.

30. While this judgment may have had some connection to debts covering paper supplied for the just-finished *Precaution*, the amount much exceeded any reasonable charge for paper for so small an edition. The one thousand copies Cooper wanted for his first book would have required 106 reams of paper; at the prices M'Dermut charged in 1825 for paper for *Lionel Lincoln*, the bill for *Precaution* would have been no more than $350.

31. New York Supreme Court, judgment, M'Dermut v. Cooper, 1/5/1821, JFC paps., box 5, AAS. If the judgment amount represented an original debt of $1,000 with interest added at the legal rate, then the debt may have dated from as early as 1817.

32. Robert M'Dermut to JC ("present"), 7/7/1821, JFC paps., box 2, AAS. This document *may* indicate that the money borrowed from M'Dermut was used to outfit the vessel.

33. The single surviving copy of the May 1 assignment is unsigned, but that it is referenced in the June 13 addendum to the duly executed May 11 assignment on the $700 loan indicates that it was indeed put into force; JC to Robert M'Dermut, unsigned draft assignment, 5/1/1822, JFC paps., box 5, AAS. It seems likely that in the case of the $700 loan, Cooper was anticipating his proceeds from *The Spy*. Certainly the loan cannot have represented expected charges for the paper required for the third edition of that book, which would not have differed much from that for the second edition ($381) and which we know Wiley paid off from proceeds of that earlier edition; JC in account with Wiley and Halsted, [4/2/1822], JFC paps., box 5, AAS; JC, assignment to Robert M'Dermut, 5/11/1822, with addendum, 6/13/1822 (signatures on both canceled, indicating discharge), Cooper family paps., NYSHA. It was uncommon to use the same piece of property as security for more than one debt; creditors secured by a given piece of land or other property would be compensated in the order of their priority.

34. Not coincidentally, this was the day before M'Dermut acknowledged Cooper's assumption of Wiley's debt to him.

35. William Charvat in "Cooper as Professional Author," first published in 1954, wrote that Wiley "was financially so unstable that when he died in 1826 the novelist got back a number of his unpaid promissory notes to remember him by." *The Profession of Authorship in America, 1800–1890* (New York: Columbia University Press, 1992), 78. Since this essay is undocumented, it is not clear what Charvat's sources were on this point. If he was referring to the M'Dermut notes, his understanding of that matter was incomplete. Why Cooper would get back unpaid notes of Wiley's (as I assume Charvat meant) escapes me; the only possible meaning is that these were notes that Wiley had given Cooper but that Cooper in turn had endorsed and passed on to third parties. If Wiley died bankrupt, they might then have come back to Cooper for payment. But it is by no means clear that Charvat meant to indicate this latter scenario.

36. JC and Charles Wiley, memorandum of agreement, 7/26/1825, Cooper family paps., NYSHA; see also their memorandum of agreement, 4/29/1824, Cooper family paps. microfilm, HSFC, New York City.

37. See David Kaser, *Messrs. Carey & Lea of Philadelphia: A Study in the History of the Booktrade* (Philadelphia: University of Pennsylvania Press, 1957), 76–78.

38. Ibid., 39, 27–28.

39. Miller's terms with Cooper called for all expenses to be deducted from gross proceeds, after which the net was evenly split between author and publisher; in other words, Miller published Cooper "on shares"; see "James F. Cooper Esq. in Acct. with J. Miller," 7/1/1826, JFC paps., box 5, AAS. Kaser, *Messrs. Carey & Lea*, 19, 23, 35–37.

40. H. C. Carey and I. Lea to JC, 11/28/1825, JFC paps., box 2, AAS.

41. H. C. Carey and I. Lea to JC, 1/9/1825, JFB paps., box 21, AAS.

42. When Carey and Lea were negotiating on *The Prairie* in April 1826, Cooper expressed the wish for the production to be done in New York City because, as he wrote the firm in April, "I should like to print as I go," with the first volume to be finished before his expected departure for Europe (*LJ* 1:131; see also H. C. Carey and I. Lea to JC, 4/6/1826, JFC paps., box 2, AAS).

43. Most of Cooper's surviving letters from the firm, although signed "H.C.C. & I.L.," were personally written by Henry Carey, the partner with whom Cooper seems always to have dealt. Isaac Lea's real enthusiasm was for his scientific interests rather than his business affairs. Kaser wrote, "Isaac [Lea] was not a good bookseller, nor did he even become a good publisher" (*Messrs. Carey & Lea*, 21).

44. Carey returned 11/13/1825; hence his comment in his answer, "as you may readily suppose, I have had hardly an instant to think of business, & this letter is rather an apology for a delay of an answer, than a reply to your letter"; H. C. Carey to JC, 11/15/1825, JFC paps., box 2, AAS; Kaser, *Messrs. Carey & Lea*, 37.

45. It should be recalled that Cooper was very much in the final throes of the Sedgwick business at just this moment—the last court date was December 5, 1825, and soon thereafter came the flurry that led up to Sedgwick's sudden withdrawal of his action early in February.

46. Hardly a stranger to Wiley or Cooper, Edwin B. Clayton, of 64 Pine Street, had been doing work for the friends ever since he had been tapped to print the first edition of *The Pioneers* in 1822. On his own, he also had printed the first edition of *The Pilot* at his shop. But his operation may have been too small for the increasingly large editions of Cooper's works. Wiley bypassed him for the six-thousand-copy print run of *Lionel Lincoln*, given instead to Daniel Fanshaw. Only after Clayton teamed up with James Van Norden in 1824 did Wiley send other work to the firm's shop. In that year, the new partnership did two jobs for him: a translation of Decoudray Holstein's *Memoirs of La Fayette*, one of many books quickly run off in anticipation of the marquis's impending arrival in New York, and the fourth edition of *The Spy*, the copies of which were among those books that Wiley released to Cooper in October of 1825. Wiley must have been pleased enough with the work of Clayton and Van Norden on the latter to reach an agreement with them for *The Last of the Mohicans*, the next Cooper project he was to handle.

47. H. C. Carey and I. Lea and JC, memorandum of agreement, 1/10/1826, JFC paps., box 5, AAS; this contract said nothing of Wiley's previous relation to the book because he was merely Cooper's agent with regard to it (see Charles Wiley and JC, memorandum of agreement, 7/26/1825, Cooper family paps., NYSHA).

48. H. C. Carey and I. Lea to JC, 2/6/1826, 1/25/1826, JFC paps., box 2, AAS.

49. The paper and the binding charges would be extra. My calculation for the cost of stereotyping is derived via a comparison with Scott's *Woodstock* (a book 10 percent longer than *The Prairie*), which cost $310.94 for typesetting (Kaser, *Cost Book*, 30, 45). In the case of the second edition of *The Spy*, New York printer William Grattan had set the type and run off fifteen hundred copies for only $310.28, an even lower rate.

50. H. C. Carey and I. Lea to JC, 1/19/1826, JFC paps., box 2, AAS; Cooper apparently found the bill for *Lionel Lincoln*, which proved as high as that for *The Last of the Mohicans*. That book had been printed in a larger edition, however, so unless the match with *Mohicans* was adjusted for that fact, it was misleading (see H. C. Carey and I. Lea to JC, 2/6/1826).

51. H. C. Carey and I. Lea to JC, 1/19/1826, 1/25/1826, 1/31/1826, 2/1/1826, all in JFC paps., box 2, AAS.

52. H. C. Carey and I. Lea to JC, 2/6/1826, 2/8/1826, 2/13/1826, all in JFC paps., box 2, AAS. In the last of these letters, the Philadelphia firm reported that, as of February 10, John Wiley in New York City had orders that he had to leave unfilled because not all the sheets had yet been delivered and processed.

53. H. C. Carey and I. Lea to JC, 2/13/1826, 2/22/1826, JFC paps., box 2, AAS.

54. Such arrangements were not unheard of at the time. The American husband of English actress Fanny Kemble, baptized Butler Mease on his birth in Philadelphia in 1806, changed his name to Pierce Butler in order to inherit the Georgia plantations (and slaves) of his grandfather and namesake, who died in 1822. See Catherine Clinton, *Fanny Kemble's Civil Wars* (New York: Oxford University Press, 2001), 75, 113–16.

55. Alan Taylor, *William Cooper's Town: Power and Persuasion on the Frontier of the Early American Republic* (New York: Alfred A. Knopf, 1995), 527–28n76, is mistaken in asserting that Cooper "insisted, incorrectly, that by 1826 he had become 'extricated' from his debts."

56. See Mary E. Phillips, *James Fenimore Cooper* (New York: John Lane, 1913), 2–3; Henry Walcott Boynton, *James Fenimore Cooper* (New York: Century, 1931), 142–43; Stephen Railton, *Fenimore Cooper: A Study of His Life and Imagination* (Princeton: Princeton University Press, 1978), 64–65; Taylor, *William Cooper's Town*, 400.

57. *Journal of the Assembly of the State of New-York; at Their Forty-ninth Session* (Albany: E. Crosswell, 1826), 226.

58. Ibid., 868, 906.

59. "An Act Authorizing James Cooper to assume a middle name," copy, JFC paps., box 5, AAS.

60. H. C. Carey and I. Lea to JFC, 4/4/1826, JFC paps., box 2, AAS. William Dunlap, *A History of the American Theatre* (New York: J. and J. Harper, 1834), p. [iii]. Dunlap's act of courtesy was doubly confused, since in *writing* his new name Cooper himself did not spell out "James." The year before Dunlap's book was published, when Cooper was on the verge of returning to America after his long European sojourn, he explained to English publisher Richard Bentley that "letters simply addressed to me at New-York will reach me." He added specifics: "The name of Fenimore should be written in full, for there is no other [person] of the two names now but myself—indeed it is the only proper way of writing my name, which is not Cooper, but Fenimore-Cooper, in consequence of a law of New York [conveniently "revised" by Cooper to match his original intent], the one being as much part of the family name as the other" (*LJ* 2:412). His emphasis on "writing" his name here was significant; in conversation, he was still just "Cooper" to his friends—in 1847, he stressed that point for Prindle (see *LJ* 5:201).

61. On the pronunciation of the family name, see Ralph Birdsall, *The Story of Cooperstown* (Cooperstown: Augur's Book Store, 1948), 80.

62. John Manseca, *Examination of Mr. [N. G.] Dufief's Philosophical Notions, with a Criticism upon his System and Mode of Teaching Languages. In Four Letters* (New York: printed by Clayton and Van Norden, 1825).

63. Another source of instruction for the girls was their mother, whose family kept up French at least to a certain point. And the girls had a French governess, mentioned earlier, Madame de Bruges, at Sunswick and perhaps earlier (SFM 54, 56).

64. Given the difficulties Cooper had experienced in seeking to control English and European editions of his first books, the contemplated 1823 trip probably would have been aimed at establishing better working arrangements with overseas publishers; Robert Campbell to JC, 4/10/1823, JFC paps., box 2, AAS.

65. See postscript ("Bossange, freres / Rue de Seine, No. 12 / Paris") to Henry C. Carey and I. Lea to JC, 1/10/[1826], JFC paps., box 2, AAS. In fact, as we shall see in the second volume, Cooper would make a virtue of the necessity of finishing *The Prairie* in Paris by employing Bossange to provide him with corrected proofs of the book, which he then proceeded to distribute not only to Carey and Lea but also to John Miller in London and to publishers and translators with whom Cooper made new arrangements on the Continent (*PR* CE 397–98).

66. H. C. Carey and I. Lea to JC, 2/8/1826, 2/22/1826.

67. H. C. Carey and I. Lea to JFC, 4/6/1826; see also *LJ* 1:131–32. The original copyright period for each title had been, under current law, fourteen years; that for *The Spy* would run out in September 1835, and so forth. There was an exception in this new contract in the case of *The Pioneers* because Cooper already had licensed that book to Collins and Hannay of New York City.

68. Cooper also offered Campbell the possibility of taking up the Conant claim and Courtland C. Cooper's note to the novelist, plus $100, in exchange for the Ward contract;

both of these items had been freed up by Sedgwick's withdrawal of his judgment and all other legal claims against the novelist in February; see *LJ* 1:137–38. Cooper apparently held back some of the Carey and Lea notes in order to allow Robert M'Dermut to receive payment for the old Wiley debt through an assignment of Carey and Lea's notes to him (*LJ* 1:134–35). Campbell soon wrote to accept the proposals with regard to the other Otsego creditor (Josiah Maples) and himself (he didn't want to tangle with Courtland C. Cooper's obligation or that of Conant, but he, too, would happily accept one of Carey and Lea's notes for the amount Cooper owed him); Robert Campbell to JFC, 5/24/1826, JFC paps., box 2, AAS.

69. Robert Campbell to JFC, 5/24/1826. I question Alan Taylor's conclusions (*William Cooper's Town*, 400–1) about the actual danger that Averell's purchased decrees posed to Cooper. The April 1822 Chancery Court decree on the Pomeroy bill did indeed single out Cooper as the source of last resort, in his "proper goods and chattels, lands and tenements," in New York State, for satisfying *any* of the creditors included in the survey of the William Cooper estate by James King. Cooper owned little if any such property in New York by the spring of 1823, however—that Cooperstown lot was a rare exception, and he was indeed trying to unload it so that it would not be vulnerable to seizure. He hardly left the country in 1826 to avoid its seizure.

70. Clinton thanked Cooper for the gift of *The Last of the Mohicans;* he knew "all the localities" well, as a result of which he took considerable pleasure at the "admirable graphic description" (*CORR* 1:98). The estimate of "three or four years" was repeated in the press shortly after Cooper's departure; see, for instance, the *Rhode Island Republican*, 6/8/1826.

71. See the address leaf on H. C. Carey and I. Lea to JFC, 3/9/1826: "James Cooper/ Of New York / Washington," 3/9/1826, JFC paps., box 2, AAS. Henry Carey had just returned from New York City, where he had called on Cooper only to learn that the novelist "had left there on the previous day" (ibid.). See also *LJ* 6:290.

72. Patricia Tyson Stroud, *The Emperor of Nature: Charles-Lucien Bonaparte and His World* (Philadelphia: University of Pennsylvania Press, 2000), 78, quoting a letter of March 12 (from Washington) to Bonaparte's wife Zenaide and another of March 27 (from Point Breeze, N.J.) to William Cooper. The novelist's daughter thought that her father went to Washington with Bonaparte in May and had seen Petalesharo there at that time. As indicated in Chapter 15, that was likely a mistake based on her vague knowledge of the March trip (see SFM 59). A "William Cooper," probably the conchologist, is listed as a non-paying member of the Lunch in Anthony Bleecker's 1826 "Exposé" of the club (copy), JFB paps., box 5, AAS; this Cooper, a New Jersey native, perhaps descended from the original William Cooper of Cooper's Point (Camden), to whom the novelist mistakenly traced his own family's roots (see *LJ* 5:304).

73. Henry Clay to JFC, 5/26/1826, JFC paps., box 2, AAS; the passport is in the Honeyman Collection at the Lehigh University Library, Bethlehem, Pa. According to

his daughter, Cooper was in Washington again at the time the documents were prepared (SFM 59), but that is highly doubtful given the other evidence.

74. As to those books and pamphlets, he sent those he could not take overseas himself to the USS *Lexington,* on which his friend William B. Shubrick was about to take a cruise (*GF* CE 4). I base my conclusion about *The Prairie* on Cooper's shift to French paper at this point in the manuscript of the novel; see *PR* CE 416–17.

75. New York *American,* 5/30/1826; *Eastern Argus,* 6/6/1826.

76. Carl C. Cutler, *Queens of the Western Ocean: The Story of America's Mail and Passenger Sailing Lines* (Annapolis: U.S. Naval Institute, 1961), 155–56, 389–91, 565; *GF* CE 277.

Index

Beresford, John, 83
Bergh, Christian, 110, 114
Berkshire Agricultural Society, 203,
   208, 209
Bernard, Simon, 370
Bewley, Marius, 295
Bible society, in Otsego, 196–197, 225
Big Elk (Ongpatonga), 477–478, 480, pl.20
Bingham, Arthur B., 160
Biography: archival access and, xiii–xiv,
   xvi, xvii; Beard's uncompleted project,
   xv; Cooper's prohibition on, xii, xiii;
   distortions in, xv–xvii, xviii
Black Buffalo, 477
"Black Thunder, The," speech of, 476–477
Bleecker, Anthony, 368, 519, 634n3
Bleecker, Harmanus, 234
"Bloody Pond," 438, 439, 460
Bloomfield, Joseph, 40, 582n52
Bomb ketches, 110
Bonaparte, Charles-Lucien, 517
Bonhomme Richard, 402, 403
Book design, 253–254
Book reviews, by Cooper, 288–301
Boone, Daniel, 339, 530–531n26
Bossange, Hector, 514
Boston (Massachusetts): Charlestown
   navy yard, 413, 414–415; Cooper's
   visit to, 393, 413–417, 422, 422–423;
   expansion of, 136; setting for Lionel
   Lincoln, 418–420, 421–423, 570n73,
   570–571n75, 650n59; Wasp's voyage to,
   133–139
Bowen, Abel, 166
Bowman, William, 131
Boyle, John P., 55–59
Boynton, Henry W., xvii
Bracebridge Hall (Irving), 352
Brackenridge, Henry Marie, 354
Brackenridge, Hugh Henry, 339, 340
Bradish, Luther, 202–203, 368, 516, 582n52
Brainerd, David, 10
Bravo, The (Cooper), xxv
Bread and Cheese Club, 51, 286, 374;
   benefit for Wiley, 502; farewell dinner

for JFC, 518–519; founding of, 367–
   368, 634n3; meetings of, 634n3; membership of, 368–369, 634–635n4
Brevoort, Henry, 171, 368
Bridgen, Charles, 303, 305, 306, 307
Bridgen, Thomas, 241, 274–275, 546n73;
   administrator of father's estate, 302–
   304; Albany connections of, 620–
   621n1; Averell's collusion with, 327,
   329; Pomeroys' collusion with, 315–
   317, 321; relationship with JFC, 303,
   313–314, 315, 320–323; at sheriff's
   sale, 328. See also Bridgen suit
Bridgen, Thomas B., 302, 303–304, 621n3
Bridgen suit: agreement of 1818, 303,
   308–309, 315, 317, 318, 325; agreement
   on sale of properties, 274–275, 319,
   321–322, 323–324, 326–328; bills in
   Chancery, 302, 303, 307, 315, 317–320,
   324–325; breakdown in communications, 320–323; court order, 320, 322,
   325–326, 330, 360, 633n50; negotiations with Cooper estate, 306–315;
   origins of debt, 302–306; sheriffs'
   sales to settle, 275, 326–328; source
   for The Pioneers, 633n50
Brimmer, Sam, 153
Britain: in Chesapeake attack, 104–107,
   161, 164; Cooper's view of, 107–108,
   658n46–47; Cooper's visit to, 85–87,
   94; and Embargo Act, 102, 115; Jay's
   Treaty, 112; Jones's raids on, 405–406;
   literary commerce with, 269, 294;
   Loyalists in, 148; naval blockade of
   American ports, 102–103; and Non-
   Intercourse Act, 123; President-Little
   Belt skirmish, 160–162; in Richard
   attack, 103–104. See also English edi-
   tions; Impressment; War of 1812
Broadway, New York City: pl.14; Cooper
   family lodgings, 364–365
Brock, Isaac, 175
Brookes debt, 450–451, 661n73
Brooklyn navy yard, 109, 126, 138, 168,
   171, 413, 483